BLACK AMERICANS INFORMATION DIRECTORY

ISSN 1045-8050

BLACK AMERICANS INFORMATION DIRECTORY

1994-95

Third Edition

A Guide to Approximately 5,3000 Organizations, Agencies, Institutions, Programs, and Publications Concerned with Black American Life and Culture, Including Associations, Awards, Honors, and Prizes, Colleges and Universities, Cultural Organizations, Government Agencies and Programs, Industrial and Service Companies, Libraries, Museums, Newsletters and Directories, Newspapers and Periodicals, Publishers, Radio and Television Stations, Religious Organizations, Research Centers, Scholarships, Studies Programs, and Videos

Wendy S. Van de Sande, Editor

Ned Burels, Associate Editor

Gale Research Inc. • *DETROIT* • *WASHINGTON, D.C.* • *LONDON*

Linda Hubbard, *Senior Editor*
Wendy S. Van de Sande, *Editor*
Ned Burels, *Associate Editor*

Aided by: Catherine DiMercurio, Kimberly Burton Faulkner,
Joyce Jakubiak, Anjanelle M. Klisz, Diane Sawinski, Sara Tal Waldorf

Benita L. Spight, *Data Entry Supervisor*
Gwendolyn S. Tucker, *Data Entry Group Leader*
Fredrick L. Penn, Jr., *Data Entry Associate*

Victoria B. Cariappa, *Research Manager*
Gary Oudersluys, *Research Supervisor*
Tracie A. Wade, *Editorial Associate*
Phyllis Shepherd, Barbara Thornton, *Editorial Assistants*

Mary Beth Trimper, *Production Director*
Mary Kelley, *Production Assistant*

Cynthia Baldwin, *Art Director*
C.J. Jonik, *Desktop Publisher*

Theresa Rocklin, *Systems and Programming Supervisor*
Timothy Richardson, *Programmer*

 The paper used in this publication meets the minimum requirements of American National Standard for Information Sciences--Permanence Paper for Printed Library Materials, ANSI Z39.48-1984.

CONTENTS

HIGHLIGHTS

The *Black Americans Information Directory (BAID)* is a comprehensive guide to resources for and about African Americans. *BAID* provides, in a convenient one-volume format, descriptive and contact information on a wide range of resources, including:

- Associations
- Awards, Honors & Prizes
- Colleges & Universities
- Cultural Organizations
- Directories
- Government Agencies & Programs
- Industrial & Service Companies
- Libraries
- Newsletters
- Newspapers
- Periodicals
- Publishers
- Radio & Television Stations
- Religious Organizations
- Research Centers
- Scholarships, Fellowships & Loans
- Studies Programs
- Videos

New in This Edition

The third edition of *BAID* features:

- Approximately 5,300 entries. Listings have been completely updated, with thousands of changes to addresses, phone numbers, personnel and other important details.

- A new chapter on **Scholarships, Fellowships, and Loans** that covers educational aid available from government and private resources.

- New subject access through a single **Alphabetical Name and Subject Index**. Entries are cited by present, former, and alternate names and titles, as well as more than 70 specific subject categories.

Content and Arrangement

BAID's **descriptive listings** are arranged within 18 easy-to-use chapters by type of resource. The **Alphabetical Name and Subject Index** lists all organizations and publications, any significant keywords in their names and titles, and cites entries under subject categories, all in one alphabetical sequence.

INTRODUCTION

African Americans and other minorities represent a growing and increasingly important segment of the American population. As the largest minority group in the United States, African Americans numbered 29.986 million in 1990. According to the latest statistical information from the U.S. Bureau of the Census, this number is expected to reach 33.147 million by 1995, or 12.6% of the total population. As this segment of the population continues to grow, so does the need for information on all aspects of the Black experience in the United States. It was out of this need that *Black Americans Information Directory (BAID)* was born.

BAID, now in its third edition, meets the needs of libraries, schools, businesses, civic groups, and others interested in some aspect of the Black experience. *BAID* is a comprehensive guide to approximately 5,300 information resources for and about African Americans. It provides contact and descriptive information on a wide variety of print and "live" resources, including:

- Nonprofit Associations
- Religious and Cultural Organizations
- Library Collections
- Colleges, Universities, and Black Studies Programs
- Scholarships and Awards
- Research Centers
- Federal, State, and Local Government Agencies and Programs
- Industrial and Service Companies
- Publishers and Publications
- Broadcast Media
- Videos

Features of This Edition

With approximately 5,300 entries and an easy-to-use entry format, the third edition of *BAID* meets user needs with these enhancements:

- The **Alphabetical Name and Subject Index** provides access by topic as well as by former and alternate names. Improved subject searchability will serve a wide variety of users.

- A new chapter, **Scholarships, Fellowships, and Loans**, identifies education-related financial aid given according to need and merit. The funds are offered by associations, corporations, religious groups, private organizations, federal and state governments, and others.

- Full contact data--including FAX and toll-free numbers and the names of key individuals--appears at the top of the entry, simplifying contacting an organization and speaking with the "right" person at that organization.

Arrangement, Content, and Indexing

BAID consists of 18 chapters of **descriptive listings** of resources and the **Alphabetical Name and Subject Index**.

Each chapter covers one category of information resource, as outlined on the "Contents" page. Entries typically contain complete contact data as well as descriptive information.

The **Alphabetical Name and Subject Index** provides one-stop access to all organizations, agencies, programs, publications, and other significant details mentioned within the descriptive listings. It also classifies resources under more than 70 specific subject headings.

For more information on the content, arrangement, and indexing of *BAID*, consult the "User's Guide."

Method of Compilation

BAID is compiled from a variety of sources. Information was carefully selected from other Gale Research Inc. directories, government publications, and lists and directories supplied by numerous national and local organizations. Telephone research was used in conjunction with secondary source information to verify contact information.

Specific source information on individual *BAID* chapters is provided in the "User's Guide" following this introduction.

Acknowledgments

The editor thanks *Black Enterprise* magazine (copyright June 1993, The Earl G. Graves Publishing Co., Inc., 130 Fifth Ave., New York, NY 10011. All rights reserved.) for granting permission to use their June issue in compiling the chapter on the top 100 Black industrial/service companies. Thanks also to the editors and staffs of other Gale directories that have contributed to the usefulness of *BAID*.

Available in Electronic Form and on Mailing Labels

Diskette/Magnetic Tape. The information in *BAID* is available for licensing on magnetic tape or diskette in a fielded format. Either the complete database or a custom selection of entries may be ordered. The database is available for internal data processing and nonpublishing purposes only. For more information, call 800-877-GALE.

Mailing Labels. The information in *BAID* is available in customized mailing list arrangements. For more information, call 800-877-GALE.

Comments and Suggestions Welcome

We encourage users to bring new or unlisted organizations to our attention. Every effort will be made to provide information about them in subsequent editions of the directory. Comments and suggestions for improving the directory are also welcome. Please contact:

Black Americans Information Directory
Gale Research Inc.
835 Penobscot Bldg.
Detroit, MI 48226-4094
Telephone: (313)961-2242
Toll-Free: 800-347-GALE
FAX: (313)961-6815
Telex: 810-221-7086

USER'S GUIDE

BAID consists of:

- Descriptive entries, numbered sequentially and arranged in 18 chapters by type of information resource
- Alphabetical Name and Subject Index

The content, arrangement, and indexing of each chapter is detailed below.

1. National Organizations

- **Scope:** Approximately 500 primarily nonprofit membership organizations, including social, philanthropic, professional, and business groups concerned with Black Americans or minorities.
- **Entries include:** Organization name, address, telephone number, FAX and toll-free numbers when available, name of contact, and a brief description of the organization's purpose and activities.
- **Arrangement:** Alphabetical by organization name.
- **Source:** *Encyclopedia of Associations, Volume 1*, National Organizations of the U.S., 28th Edition (published by Gale Research Inc.).
- **Indexed by:** Organization name, significant keywords, and subject

2. Regional, State, and Local Organizations

- **Scope:** More than 1,200 regional, state, and local organizations and chapters of selected national organizations including social, philanthropic, professional, and business groups concerned with African Americans and minorities. (For further information on local chapters of national organizations contact the national office listed in Chapter 1).
- **Entries include:** Organization name, address, telephone number, FAX and toll-free numbers when available, and names of contact.
- **Arrangement:** Geographical by state with organizations listed alphabetically within states.
- **Source:** *Encyclopedia of Associations: Regional, State, and Local Organizations*, 2nd Edition (published by Gale Research Inc.), lists provided by national organizations, and original research conducted by the *BAID* editorial staff.
- **Indexed by:** Organization name and significant keywords (including geographic location when included in the name) and subject.

3. Religious Organizations

- **Scope:** Covers more than 110 religious organizations, primarily founded by and for Black Americans.
- **Entries include:** A general description of the group's development, beliefs, and leaders; addresses, educational facilities, membership, and publications are included when available.
- **Arrangement:** Alphabetical by organization name.
- **Source:** *Encyclopedia of American Religions*, 4th Edition (published by Gale Research Inc.) and original research by the *BAID* editorial staff.
- **Indexed by:** Organization name and significant keywords.

4. Library Collections

- **Scope:** Approximately 180 libraries with special collections of interest to Black Americans, including historical, literary, and cultural archives.
- **Entries include:** Library name, address, telephone number, FAX and toll-free numbers when available, name of contact, and a general description of special collections, holdings, services, and other details.
- **Arrangement:** Alphabetical by institution name.
- **Source:** *Directory of Special Libraries and Information Centers*, 17th Edition (published by Gale Research Inc.).
- **Indexed by:** Institution and library name, significant keywords, and subject.

5. Museums and Other Cultural Organizations

- **Scope:** More than 200 museums, galleries, and other organizations featuring African American culture and artists.
- **Entries include:** Organization name, address, telephone number, and FAX and toll-free numbers when available. Some entries also include a brief description.
- **Arrangement:** Geographical by state with organization names listed alphabetically within states.
- **Source:** Lists of minority arts organizations provided by the National Endowment of the Arts and original research by the *BAID* editorial staff.
- **Indexed by:** Organization name, significant keywords, and subject.

6. Historically Black Colleges and Universities

- **Scope:** 109 currently operational colleges and universities founded for the education of Black Americans at a time when many existing institutions were racially exclusive.
- **Entries include:** Institution name, address, telephone number, FAX and toll-free when available, president, founding year, number of students, cost (includes room and board if appropriate), application deadlines, required tests, and name of admissions director.
- **Arrangement:** Alphabetical by institution name.
- **Source:** Original research by the *BAID* editorial staff.
- **Indexed by:** College or university name.

7. Black Studies Programs

- **Scope:** Over 200 colleges and universities that offer Black studies programs. Universities or colleges that offer one or more courses, but that lack a formal studies program were not included.
- **Entries include:** Institution name, address, telephone number, FAX and toll-free numbers when available, sponsoring department, and name of contact.
- **Arrangement:** Alphabetical by institution name within three categories: 1) Two-Year Colleges, 2) Four-Year Colleges and Universities, and 3) Graduate Programs.
- **Source:** College catalogs and directories and original research conducted by the *BAID* editorial staff.
- **Indexed by:** Institution or program name and subject.

8. Scholarships, Fellowships, and Loans

- **Scope:** Approximately 130 scholarships, fellowships, and loans offered by associations, corporations, religious groups, fraternal organizations, foundations, and other private organizations and companies awarded on both need- and merit-based criteria.
- **Entries include:** Sponsoring organization, address, telephone number, FAX and toll-free numbers when available, name of the award, and a brief description of award and eligibility requirements.

- **Arrangement:** Alphabetical by award name.
- **Source:** *Scholarships, Fellowships, and Loans*, 9th Edition (published by Gale Research Inc.).
- **Indexed by:** Award name, sponsoring organization, and subject.

9. Research Centers

- **Scope:** Over 160 university-related and other nonprofit organization research centers covering topics of concern to Blacks such as sickle cell anemia and African American life, history, and culture.
- **Entries include:** Sponsoring institution, research center name, address, telephone number, FAX and toll-free numbers when available, name of contact, and a short description of activities, facilities, and services.
- **Arrangement:** Alphabetical by institution and/or research center name.
- **Source:** *Research Centers Directory*, 18th Edition (published by Gale Research Inc.).
- **Indexed by:** Institution and research center name, significant keywords, and subject.

10. Awards, Honors, and Prizes

- **Scope:** Over 100 awards and other distinctions bestowed by government, civic, professional, and business groups. Includes recognition in such areas as human rights, education, the arts, business, and the media.
- **Entries include:** Sponsoring organization, address, telephone number, FAX and toll-free when available, name of the award, and a brief description its nature.
- **Arrangement:** Alphabetical by award name.
- **Source:** *Awards, Honors, and Prizes*, 10th Edition (published by Gale Research Inc.).
- **Indexed by:** Sponsoring organization, award name, and subject.

11. Federal Government Agencies

- **Scope:** Covers nearly 170 units of the federal government concerned with civil rights, affirmative action, equal employment opportunity, and other areas of interest to the African American community.
- **Entries include:** Sponsoring agency and sub-units, address, telephone number, FAX and toll-free when available, and contact person.
- **Arrangement:** Alphabetical by agency name.
- **Source:** *United States Government Manual* and original research by the *BAID* editorial staff.
- **Indexed by:** Sponsoring agency, unit names, significant keywords, and subject.

12. Federal Domestic Assistance Programs

- **Scope:** Approximately 48 federally funded programs offering a wide variety of benefits and services available to the Black community in areas such as minority business assistance, civil rights, and education.
- **Entries include:** Parent agency or organization, intermediate office or agency, address, telephone number, FAX and toll-free numbers when available, name of contact person, program name, and a brief description of services. Catalog of Federal Domestic Assistance numbers are also included for easy cross-reference.
- **Arrangement:** Alphabetical by agency or organization name.
- **Source:** *Catalog of Federal Domestic Assistance*.
- **Indexed by:** Parent agency, program name, significant keywords, and subject.

13. State and Local Government Agencies

- **Scope:** 280 state and local government agencies offering programs covering equal employment, fair housing, minority business development, and other areas.

- **Entries include:** Parent and intermediate agency name, address, telephone number, FAX and toll-free numbers when available, and name of contact.
- **Arrangement:** Geographical by state with agencies and programs listed alphabetically.
- **Source:** Original research by the *BAID* editorial staff.
- **Indexed by:** Parent agency and sub-unit names, state designations, significant keywords, and subject.

14. Businesses (Top 100 Industrial and Service Companies)

- **Scope:** The top 100 Black industrial/service companies in the United States as listed in the June 1993 Black Enterprise magazine. To be eligible for the Industrial/Service 100, a company must have been fully operational in the previous calendar year and be at least 51% Black-owned. It must manufacture or own the product it sells or provide industrial or consumer services. Brokerages, real estate firms, and firms that provide professional services (accountants, lawyers, etc.) are not eligible.
- **Entries include:** Company name, address, telephone numbers, FAX and toll-free numbers when available, name of chief executive, year founded, number of employees, type of business, 1992 sales, and current and former rankings.
- **Arrangement:** By descending rank.
- **Source:** Reprinted with permission from *Black Enterprise* magazine, Copyright June, 1993 (published by Earl G. Graves Publishing Co., Inc., 130 Fifth Ave., New York, NY 10011. All rights reserved).
- **Indexed by:** Company name.

15. Publications

- **Scope:** More than 550 newspapers, periodicals, newsletters, and directories with a significant focus on Black Americans or minorities, covering a wide variety of topics, including business, lifestyle, family, health, and education.
- **Entries include:** Publication and publisher name, address, telephone number, FAX and toll-free numbers when available, and a brief description including publication scope, editor, frequency, and other details.
- **Arrangement:** Alphabetical by publication title within four subcategories: 1) Newspapers, 2) Periodicals, 3) Newsletters, and 4) Directories.
- **Source:** *Gale Directory of Publications and Broadcast Media*, 126th Edition (formerly *Ayer Directory of Publications*), *Newsletters in Print*, 7th Edition, *Directories in Print*, 11th Edition, (all published by Gale Research Inc.), and original research conducted by the *BAID* editorial staff.
- **Indexed by:** Publication title, significant keywords, and subject.

16. Publishers

- **Scope:** 145 large and small firms that publish books by and about Black Americans.
- **Entries include:** Publisher name, address, telephone number, FAX and toll-free numbers when available, and a short description of representative titles or areas of publishing activity.
- **Arrangement:** Alphabetical by publisher name.
- **Source:** *Publishers Directory*, 13th Edition (published by Gale Research Inc.).
- **Indexed by:** Publisher name and subject.

17. Broadcast Media

- **Scope:** Over 480 radio and television stations and networks with music, information, and entertainment programming aimed at the Black community. (Some may offer programming segments targeted at other audiences as well).
- **Entries include:** Station call letters or network name, address, telephone number, and FAX and toll-free numbers when available. Entries for stations also include a brief description covering frequency, programming hours, contacts, year founded, and network affiliations.

- **Arrangement:** Divided into three subsections: 1) Networks, 2) Radio Stations, and 3) Television Stations. Networks are arranged alphabetically, broadcast stations are arranged alphabetically by call letters within states.
- **Source:** *Directory of Publications and Broadcast Media*, 126th Edition (Formerly *Ayer Directory of Publications*, published by Gale Research Inc.) and original research by the *BAID* editorial staff.
- **Indexed by:** Network name or station call letters.

18. Videos

- **Scope:** Approximately 580 educational and general interest videos of interest to African American, including those covering the historic role of Blacks in American society to selected contemporary entertainment films.
- **Entries include:** Video title, distributor name, address, telephone number, FAX and Toll-Free numbers when available, program description, release date, run time, format, and acquisition availability.
- **Arrangement:** Alphabetical by video title.
- **Source:** The *Video Source Book*, 14th Edition (published by Gale Research Inc.).
- **Indexed by:** Video title, significant keywords, and subject.

Alphabetical Name and Subject Index

The **Alphabetical Name and Subject Index** provides access to all entries included in *BAID*, as well as to former or alternate names which appear within entry text. Citations also appear under specific subject headings for quick access by topics. Additionally, the index provides access to entries via inversions on all significant keywords appearing in an entry name. The term "Black" has not been used as a subject keyword in the index, since, as a general category, it covers all the entries in the book. More specific terms, however, such as "Afro-American" and "African-American" have been used as subject keywords since they appear less frequently and may help direct the user to specific index citations.

Index references are to book entry numbers rather than page numbers. Entry numbers appear in the index in **boldface** type if the reference is to the name used at the top of the entry and in lightface if the reference is to a program or former or alternate name included within the text.

If several entries have the same parent organization, as is the case with many of the government groups listed in *BAID*, related units are indexed individually by name and as a group under the name of the parent organization. The names of all federal government organizations are indexed under "U.S."

BLACK AMERICANS INFORMATION DIRECTORY

(1) National Organizations

A. Philip Randolph Educational Fund

1444 I St. NW, No. 300   Ph: (202)289-2774
Washington, DC 20005   Fax: (202)371-0168
Norman Hill, Pres.

Description: Seeks to: eliminate prejudice and discrimination from all areas of life; educate individuals and groups on their rights and responsibilities; defend human and civil rights; assist in the employment and education of the underprivileged; combat community deterioration, delinquency, and crime. **Founded:** 1964.

★2★

A. Philip Randolph Institute

1444 I St. NW, No. 300   Ph: (202)289-2774
Washington, DC 20005   Fax: (202)371-0168
Norman Hill, Pres.

Description: Promotes cooperation between the labor force and the black community. Primary interest is political action through the organization of affiliate groups and the building of coalitions for social change. Major areas of activity include voter registration, labor education, and trade union leadership training. Founded by and named after A. Philip Randolph (1889-1979), founder of the Brotherhood of Sleeping Car Porters (which was absorbed by the Brotherhood of Railway, Airline and Steamship Clerks, Freight Handlers, Express and Station Employees). Presents the A. Philip Randolph/Bayard Rustin Freedom Award, the Bayard Rustin Humanitarian Award, the A. Philip Randolph Achievement Award, and the Rosina Tucker Award. Conducts research and specialized education programs. Maintains speakers' bureau and library. **Founded:** 1964. **Local Groups:** 200. **State Groups:** 13. **Publications:** Annual Report. News and Notes, bimonthly. Working Paper, annual. Also publishes the Norman Hill column.

★3★

Ad Hoc Monitoring Group on Southern Africa

2232 Rayburn House Office Bldg.
Washington, DC 20515   Ph: (202)225-3335
Rep. Thomas J. Downey, Co-Chair

Also known as: Congressional Monitoring Group on Southern Africa. **Description:** Bipartisan group of Senate and House members that monitors human rights conditions in southern Africa. Seeks congressional support for pertinent legislation. Serves as information clearinghouse on human rights violations in southern Africa. Maintains Political Prisoner Project, through which members adopt individual political prisoners, write letters to congressmen, and make statements on prisoners' behalf for inclusion in the Congressional Record. Sponsors educational seminars; presents information briefs. **Founded:** 1978. **Members:** 48.

★4★

Africa Faith and Justice Network

3700 Oakview Ter. NE
PO Box 29378   Ph: (202)832-3412
Washington, DC 20017   Fax: (202)832-9051
Sr. Maura Browne, Exec.Dir.

Description: Religious groups with personnel working in Africa; individuals concerned with justice issues as they relate to Africa. Purpose is to examine the role the network believes Europe, America, and other northern countries play in causing injustices in Africa. Challenges national policies found to be detrimental to the interest of African peoples. Gathers information on issues and policies that adversely affect Africa, analyzes the data, and makes recommendations for advocacy or action. Consults with churches of Africa, field missionaries, and other African individuals and groups. **Founded:** 1983. **Members:** 53. **Publications:** AFJN Newsletter, bimonthly.

★5★

Africa Fund

198 Broadway
New York, NY 10038   Ph: (212)962-1210
Jennifer Davis, Exec.Sec.

Description: Established by the American Committee on Africa. Works to: defend human and civil rights of needy Africans by providing or financing legal assistance; provide medical relief to Africans, particularly refugees; render aid to indigent Africans in the U.S., Africa, or elsewhere who are suffering economic, legal, or social injustices; provide educational aid or grants to Africans, particularly refugees; inform the American public about the needs of Africans; engage in study, research, and analysis of questions relating to Africa. Encourages divestment by U.S. corporations in South Africa; seeks to increase public support for U.S. economic sanctions against South Africa; has supported legislation which prevents U.S. corporations operating in South Africa from claiming U.S. tax credits for taxes paid to the South African government. Operates Unlock Apartheid's Jails Project, which seeks to inform the U.S. public about the plight of political prisoners in South Africa; disseminates information on the activities of South African puppet forces, including those in other areas of southern Africa. Provides information on southern Africa to interested individuals, organizations, and media in the U.S. Maintains Africa Fund Research Center, library, and files. **Founded:** 1966. **Members:** 5000. **Computerized Services:** Mailing list. **Publications:** Annual Report. Southern Africa Literature List, semiannual. Southern Africa Perspectives Series, periodic. Unified List of United States Companies Doing Business in South Africa, annual. **Telecommunications Services:** Cable, AMCOMMAF. **Formerly:** (1969) Africa Legal Defense and Aid Fund.

★6★
Africa Network
PO Box 1894
Evanston, IL 60204   Ph: (708)328-9305
Y. B. Holly, Sec.

Description: Professors, students, writers, and individuals working to defend just law, freedom, and human rights. Opposes "the crime of racist, apartheid law." Provides resource materials and information on South Africa; offers educational outreach program. Sponsors programs commemorating important historical events of South Africa, including Sharpeville Memorial Day and Soweto Anniversary Commemoration. Bestows annual Kwanzaa Awards for Literature, Film, and Video. (Group was originally named for Dennis Brutus, former political prisoner, South African poet, scholar, and anti-apartheid activist. Brutus was granted political asylum in the U.S. in 1983.) **Founded:** 1981. **Budget:** Less than $25,000. **Publications:** Africa Network Directory of Resources, periodic. Newsletter, periodic. Also issues newsbriefs. **Formerly:** (1988) African National Network.

★7★
Africa News Service, Inc.
PO Box 3851   Ph: (919)286-0747
Durham, NC 27702   Fax: (919)286-2614
J. Reed Kramer, Pres.

Description: News agency whose purpose is to supply material on Africa for broadcast and print media. Covers African politics, economy and culture, and U.S. policy and international issues affecting Africa. Obtains news by monitoring African radio stations on short-wave equipment, by subscribing to African publications, and through a network of reporters based in Africa. Also produces investigative stories on U.S. policy and its implications. Provides audio news and programming for radio, articles and graphics for newspapers and magazines, and prints for libraries and institutions. Carries out research for feature articles, news programs, and individuals. Maintains 5000 volume library along with 90 file cabinets of clippings and documents related to Africa. **Founded:** 1973. **Computerized Services:** Material from Africa News available through Newsnet, Human Rights Internet, Nexisand University Microfilms. **Publications:** Africa News, biweekly. Newsletter covering current events in Africa; includes annual index.

★8★
Africa World Press
PO Box 1892   Ph: (609)771-1666
Trenton, NJ 08607   Fax: (609)771-1616
Kassahun Checole, Dir.

Description: Scholar Activists and members of the African intellectual community. Promotes and maintains the development of an independent, democratic, and critical thinking African intellectual community. Utilizes the scientific knowledge and skills of the community to give service to African peoples and social movements. Conducts seminars on subjects such as the energy crisis, human rights, political repression, and food. **Founded:** 1979. **Formerly:** (1991) Africa Research and Publications Project; (1991) Africa Press.

★9★
African-American History Association
PO Box 115268   Ph: (404)344-7405
Atlanta, GA 30310   Fax: (404)730-1995
Lavonia McIntyre, Pres.

Description: Persons interested in African-American family history and genealogy. Conducts research programs and tours; maintains speakers' bureau; sponsors seminars, lectures, and workshops. Bestows annual Alex Haley Literary Award. **Founded:** 1977. **Members:** 200. **Computerized Services:** Surname databank. **Publications:** AAFHA Newsletter, quarterly. Reports on research inquiries and information on new titles.

★10★
African-American Institute
833 United Nations Plz.   Ph: (212)949-5666
New York, NY 10017   Fax: (212)682-6175
Vivian Lowery Derryck, Pres.

Description: Works to further development in Africa, improve African-American understanding, and inform Americans about Africa. Engages in training, development assistance, and informational

activites. Sponsors African-American conferences, media and congressional workshops, and regional seminars. Maintains training and visitor program offices in Washington, DC and representatives in 21 African countries. **Founded:** 1953. **Budget:** $15,000,000.

★11★
African-American Labor Center
1400 K St. NW, Ste. 700   Ph: (202)789-1020
Washington, DC 20005   Fax: (202)842-0730
Patrick J. O'Farrell, Exec.Dir.

Description: AFL-CIO. Assists, strengthens, and encourages free and democratic trade unions in Africa. Has undertaken projects in 43 countries in partnership with African trade unions. Programs are developed upon request and advice of African unions with knowledge of host government. Projects are geared to eventual assumption of complete managerial and financial responsibility by African labor movements. Objective is to help build sound national labor organizations that will be of lasting value to workers and the community, institutions that contribute to the economic and social development of their countries and to Africa's total political and economic independence. Major areas of activity are workers' education and leadership training, vocational training, cooperatives and credit unions, union medical and social service programs, administrative support for unions, and communication and information. Sponsors study tours and visitor programs to permit African and American trade unionists to become familiar with each other's politics, economies, and trade union movements; Africans are exposed to technical training not available in their homeland. Conducts basic trade union seminars and assists in establishment of labor institutes. Policy is set by board of directors, which is composed of the president and secretary-treasurer of the AFL-CIO and the presidents of 14 major American unions. **Founded:** 1964. **Publications:** AALC Reporter, bimonthly. Newsletter reporting on AFL-CIO and center projects in Africa. **Also known as:** Centre Afro-Americain du Travail.

★12★
African American Museum
1765 Crawford Rd.
Cleveland, OH 44106   Ph: (216)791-1700
Dr. Eleanor Engram, Dir.

Description: Persons in the Cleveland, OH area who are interested in building a national Afro-American history museum in that city. Goals are: to promote genealogical research; to study the Afro-American and minority race achievements and contributions; to bring about a harmonious relationship between the races through better understanding. Publicizes contributions made by the white race for the advancement of the Afro-American. Furnishes speakers for school and civic organizations; holds history classes and workshops. Sponsors observance of Afro-American History Week (February). Maintains library of 1200 volumes and Alexander E. Pushkin exhibit. **Founded:** 1953. **Members:** 37. **Publications:** African American Museum Newsletter, bimonthly. **Formerly:** (1987) Afro-American Cultural and Historical Society Museum.

★13★
African-American Natural Foods Association
c/o Cheryl A. Simms
7058 S. Clyde Ave.
Chicago, IL 60649   Ph: (312)363-3939
Cheryl A. Simms, Pres.

Description: Natural and health food retailers, health practitioners, manufacturers, and distributors; interested individuals. Works to increase awareness of natural foods and the nutritional industry in minority communities. Sponsors seminars and workshops; offers children's services; bestows awards; maintains library and speakers' bureau. Plans to establish a natural food resource and information center. **Founded:** 1990.

★14★
African-American Women's Clergy Association
PO Box 1493
Washington, DC 20013   Ph: (202)797-7460
Rev. Imagene B. Stewart, Chairperson

Description: Lay and ordained women clergy. Seeks to promote and encourage the clergy as a profession for women. Operates shelter for homeless and battered women in Washington, DC. Provides scholarships for women interested in the clergy; bestows Social Activist of the Year Award. **Founded:** 1969. **Formerly:** (1992) American Women's Clergy Association. **Local Groups:** 20. **Members:** 167.

★15★
African Heritage Center for African Dance and Music
4018 Minnesota Ave. NE
Washington, DC 20019   Ph: (202)399-5252
Melvin Deal, Founding Dir.

Description: Serves as a multicultural center for instruction and training in traditional West African dance, music, and dramatic ritualistic forms; also serves as institution for cross-cultural workshops between ethnic groups. Receives traveling artists from abroad for workshops and exchange. Presents concerts; conducts lecture demo-performances. Teaches modern and jazz dance. Maintains art gallery and a collection of traditional African musical instruments. Provides children's services; sponsors charitable program. **Budget:** $100,000. **Founded:** 1973. **Local Groups:** 4. **Members:** 20. **Publications:** None. **Regional Groups:** 2. **State Groups:** 2.

★16★
African Heritage Federation of the Americas
PO Box 2964
Pittsburgh, PA 15230   Ph: (412)361-8425
A. Ndubisi Ezekoye, Pres.

Description: Individuals of African ancestry working to promote knowledge and understanding of African heritage. Conducts educational programs; Sponsors charitable programs; maintains speakers' bureau; compiles statistics. **Founded:** 1983. **Members:** 36. **Budget:** Less than $25,000.

★17★
African Heritage Studies Association
c/o Africana Studies and Research Inst.
Queens Coll.
Flushing, NY 11367   Ph: (718)997-5478
Dr. W. Ofuatey-Kodjoe, Pres.

Description: Persons of African descent engaged in the research and teaching of African history. Purposes are: to reconstruct and present African history and cultural studies in a manner that is relevant to African people; to encourage intellectual union and cooperation among black scholars; to act as a clearinghouse for information in the structuring of a more factual African program; to present papers at conferences, seminars, and symposia; to relate, interpret, and disseminate African materials for black education. Conducts seminars and curriculum development workshops; maintains speakers' bureau. Bestows awards. **Founded:** 1969. **Budget:** Less than $25,000. **Publications:** International Journal of Africana Studies, semiannual. Newsletter, 3/year.

★18★
African Literature Association
Cornell University
Africana Studies and Research
310 Triphammer Rd.   Ph: (607)255-0534
Ithaca, NY 14850-2599   Fax: (607)255-0784
Dr. Anne V. Adams, Contact

Description: Scholars, teachers, students, and writers of African literature. Objectives are: to assemble African literature scholars and teachers from all levels of instruction and from all parts of the world; to promote the teaching of African literature; to disseminate information about African literature. Supports freedom and dignity for all people in Africa. Maintains archives of papers and historical records. **Founded:** 1974. **Members:** 800. MD $5 for African student studying in Africa; $15 for income under $15,000; $30 for income from $15,000-$35,000; $40 for income over $35,000; $50 for institutional; $80 for sponsor; $1000 for life. **Computerized Services:** Database. **Publications:** Bulletin, quarterly. Conference Papers, annual. Directory, annual. Journal: Research in African Literatures, quarterly.

★19★
African Studies Association
c/o Dr. Edna Bay
Emory University
Credit Union Bldg.   Ph: (404)329-6410
Atlanta, GA 30322   Fax: (404)329-6433
Dr. Edna Bay, Exec.Dir.

Description: Persons specializing in teaching, writing, or research on Africa including political scientists, historians, geographers, anthropologists, economists, librarians, linguists, and government officials; persons who are studying African subjects; institutional members are universities, libraries, government agencies, and others interested in receiving information about Africa. To foster communication and to stimulate research among scholars on Africa. Sponsors placement service; conducts panels and discussion groups; presents exhibits and films. Bestows annual Distinguished Africanist Awardand Distinguished Herskovits Award. **Founded:** 1957. **Members:** 2700. **Budget:** $300,000. **Computerized Services:** Mailing list (available by rental). **Publications:** African Studies Review, 3/year. ASA News, quarterly. Directory of African and Afro-American Studies in the U.S., periodic. History in Africa, annual. Issue: A Journal of Opinion, semiannual. Also publishes scholarly and bibliographical material.

★20★
Africare
440 R St. NW   Ph: (202)462-3614
Washington, DC 20001   Fax: (202)387-1034
C. Payne Lucas, Exec.Dir.

Description: Seeks to improve the quality of life in rural Africa. Provides health and environmental protection services in rural areas of Africa; works to improve African water and agricultural resources; conducts public education programs in the U.S. on African development. Maintains 3300 volume library. Sponsors competitions and bestows awards; operates speakers' bureau. **Founded:** 1971. **Members:** 2300. **Budget:** $13,000,000. **Regional Groups:** 11. **Local Groups:** 14. **Publications:** Annual Report. Newsletter, periodic. Also publishes Development Education Series (brochures).

★21★
Afro-American Cultural Foundation
10 Fiske Place, Ste. 204-206
Mt. Vernon, NY 10550   Ph: (914)665-0784
Charles Smith, Exec.Dir.

Description: Purposes are: to improve the self-esteem of African Americans; to improve the attitude of white people toward African Americans and their talents; to raise the level of awareness of the potentials and problems of African Americans; to help create a new self-image. Sponsors lectures and seminars. Conducts annual workshop, known as the Institute of Racism. Acts as consultant on African and African American history and economics. Conducts historical and economic research programs. Maintains speakers' bureau and biographical archives. Sponsors Students Essay Oratorical Contest. Bestows awards to recognize outstanding citizens. Operates library of 500 volumes on history, literature, businesswoman Madam C. J. Walker (1867-1919) and a mobile exhibit on the African American history of Westchester County, New York. Operates Committee on Higher Education for Minorities in Westchester County, NY and Community Coalitino on Education in Greenburgh, NY. **Founded:** 1969. **Members:** 500.

★22★
Afro-American Historical and Genealogical Society
PO Box 73086
Washington, DC 20056   Ph: (202)234-5350
Sylvia Cooke Martin, Pres.

Description: Individuals, libraries, and archives. Encourages scholarly research in Afro-American history and genealogy as it relates to American history and culture. Collects, maintains, and preserves relevant material, which the society makes available for research and publication. Conducts seminars and workshops; plans to maintain a library on Afro-American family and church history, now in acquisition, and to hold competitions and award 60-day internship in archive or library. **Founded:** 1977. **Members:** 1000. **Budget:** Less than $25,000. **Publications:** Journal, quarterly. Newsletter, periodic.

★23★
Afro-American Police League
PO Box 49122
Chicago, IL 60649   Ph: (312)568-7329
Edgar Gosa, Exec. Officer

Description: Police officers of Afro-American descent. Seeks to: improve the relationship between citizens of the black community and police departments; improve the relationship between black policemen and white policemen; educate the public about police departments; aid police departments in planning successful law enforcement programs in the black community. Maintains speakers' bureau. Conducts professional training seminars; presents National Law and Social Justice Leadership Award to the individual in public service who has done most to improve the relationship between the community and police department. Has initiated referral program for matters of police brutality and legal services. Conducts research on subjects such as police malfeasance and law and order legislation. Maintains 200 volume library on police science, law enforcement, and statistics. **Founded:** 1968. **Members:** 2500. **Publications:** Bulletin on Special Events, quarterly. Grapevine, quarterly. **Formerly:** (1979) Afro-American Patrolmen's League.

★24★
Afro-Asian Center
PO Box 337
Saugerties, NY 12477   Ph: (914)246-7828
Robert Carroll, Dir.

Description: Social studies teachers throughout the U.S., Africa, and Asia. Promotes international friendship and cultural understanding between students in Africa, Asia, and the U.S., through correspondence. Operates solely through cooperating teachers worldwide; provides listing teachers with outreach organizations in Africa, Latin America, the Middle East, and Asia. Promotes student contests; makes available grant applications for teachers to study and travel in Africa and Asia; offers commercial advertisements on topics dealing with Africa and Asia; sponsors seminars and discussions. Maintains speakers' bureau; bestows awards; provides children's services. **Founded:** 1972. **Budget:** Less than $25,000. **Publications:** Makes available posters and classroom display materials.

★25★
Afro-Hispanic Institute
3306 Ross Pl. NW
Washington, DC 20008   Ph: (202)966-7783
Dr. Stanley A. Cyrus, Pres.

Description: Promotes the study of Afro-Hispanic literature and culture. **Founded:** 1981. **Publications:** Short Stories by Cubena and When the Guyacans Were in Bloom and Curfew (books).

★26★
All-African People's Revolutionary Party
1738 A St. SE
Washington, DC 20003
M. Shabaka, Admin.

Description: Africans and persons of African descent who support Pan-Africanism, "the total liberation and unification of Africa under an all-African socialist government." Conducts seminars, conferences, and symposia; compiles statistics. Maintains speakers' bureau and library on African history and politics, politics of the Western Left, and revolutionary forces. **Founded:** 1971. **Members:** 783. **Regional Groups:** 5. **State Groups:** 34. **Publications:** Political and educational brochures.

★27★
Alliance of Minority Women for Business and Political Development
c/o Brenda Alford
PO Box 13933
Silver Spring, MD 20911-3933   Ph: (301)565-0258
Brenda Alford, Pres.

Description: Organiozations in support of minority women in business and politics. Seeks to increase number of minority women business owners as elected officials. **Budget:** $50,000. **Founded:** 1982.

★28★
Alpha Kappa Alpha
5656 S. Stony Island Ave.
Chicago, IL 60637   Ph: (312)684-1282
Alison Harris Alexander, Exec.Dir.

Description: Service sorority. Provides community services; presents awards; compiles statistics. Operates Cleveland Job Corps; sponsors Domestic Travel Tour Grant for female high school juniors and seniors. **Founded:** 1908. **Members:** 121,000. **Budget:** $5,000,000. **Regional Groups:** 10. Active Chapters: 819. Alumnae Chapters: 456. Undergraduate Chapters: 363. **Publications:** Along the Ivy Line, 2-3/year. Ivy Leaf Quarterly. Magazine. Contains feature stories, membership section, and obituaries.

★29★
Alpha Pi Chi
PO Box 255
Kensington, MD 20895   Ph: (310)559-4330
Magoline Carney, Pres.

Description: Service sorority - business and professional women. Conducts fundraising activities for civil rights organizations and black charities. Sponsors Talent a Rama, a charity showcase of young amateurs. Local chapters "adopt" senior citizens' homes. Awards scholarships. **Founded:** 1963. **Members:** 1300. **Publications:** The President Speaks, quarterly. Newsletter.

★30★
Alternative Education Project
c/o Radical America Journal
1 Summer St.
Somerville, MA 02143   Ph: (617)628-6585

Description: Nonprofit publisher of a bimonthly, internationally distributed journal featuring articles on American radicalism and its history, socialism, feminism, labor, and race issues. Maintains collection of 24 bound volumes of Radical America. **Founded:** 1967. **Budget:** $50,000. **Publications:** Radical America, quarterly. Concerned with grassroot organizing issues and social and economic issues worldwide. Includes poetry.

★31★
American Academy of Medical Directors
One Urban Centre, Ste. 648
Tampa, FL 33609   Ph: (813)287-2000
Michael B. Guthrie M.D., Pres.

Description: Physicians with full- or part-time administrative, management, or leadership responsibilities. Acts as an educational forum exclusively for physicians to aid them in preparing for positions of organizational leadership. Serves as placement service for members seeking new locations or career opportunities. Sponsors continuing education programs including Physician in Management Seminars. Provides career placement and counseling service through the Physician Executive Management Center. Offers scholarship program for physicians practicing management in minority fields. Compiles statistics; abstract-literature search services; direct mail membership surveying; specialized consultations. **Founded:** 1975. **Members:** 3500. **Budget:** $2,000,000. **Telecommunications Services:** Internet, network for physician managers; PIM Network and Medical Management Information Center. **Publications:** American Academy of Medical Directors—Academy Digest, bimonthly. Membership activities newsletter. Includes calendar of events and lists new members, member promotions, and employment opportunities.

★32★
American-African Affairs Association
1001 Connecticut Ave. NW, Ste. 1135
Washington, DC 20036   Ph: (202)223-5110
Lt.Gen. Max Gallimore, Chm.

Description: Individuals, foundations, and business corporations who contribute funds to carry on the program. Educational organization designed to circulate information about African countries to the people of the U.S., especially with respect to "the cause of freedom in its struggle against world Communism and the best interests of the United States of America." Distributes literature to opinion molders, political leaders, university personnel, and business leaders, both here and in other countries. Exchanges publications and information. Sponsors conferences, seminars, and meetings. **Founded:** 1965. **Publications:** Spotlight on Africa, bimonthly. Newsletter on American-African affairs. Covers such issues as foreign involvement in Africa, famine relief, and African economic issues.

★33★
American Association for Affirmative Action
11 E. Hubbard St., Ste. 200   Ph: (312)329-2512
Chicago, IL 60611   Fax: (312)329-9131
Judith C. Burnison, Exec.Dir.

Description: Equal Opportunity/Affirmative Action officers at educational institutions and industrial firms; public administration and representatives from national, state, and local EO/AA related agencies. Purposes are: to foster the implementation of affirmative action and equal opportunity in employment and in education nationwide; to provide formal liaison with federal, state, and local agencies involved with equal opportunity compliance in employment and education. Is developing speakers' bureau and training program. **Founded:** 1974. **Members:** 1000. **Budget:** $160,000. **Regional Groups:** 10. **State Groups:** 32. **Publications:** American Association for Affirmative Action–Membership Directory, annual. American Association for Affirmative Action–Newsletter, quarterly. Includes employment listings.

★34★
American Association of Blacks in Energy
801 Pennsylvania Ave. SE, Ste. 250
Washington, DC 20003   Ph: (202)547-9378
Erskine E. Cade, Chm.

Description: Blacks in energy-related professions, including engineers, scientists, consultants, academicians, and entrepreneurs; government officials and public policymakers; interested students. Represents blacks and other minorities in matters involving energy use and research, the formulation of energy policy, the ownership of energy resources, and the development of energy technologies. Seeks to increase the knowledge, understanding, and awareness of the minority community in energy issues by serving as an energy information source for policymakers, recommending blacks and other minorities to appropriate energy officials and executives, encouraging students to pursue professional careers in the energy industry, and advocating the participation of blacks and other minorities in energy programs and policymaking activities. Updates members on key legislation and regulations being developed by the Department of Energy, the Department of Interior, the Department of Commerce, the Small Business Administration, and other federal and state agencies. Provides a scholarship program for higher education students; offers information on current job openings; maintains speakers' bureau; holds seminars for minority energy professionals. Operates archive. **Founded:** 1977. **Members:** 800. **Budget:** $170,000. **Regional Groups:** 6. Chapters: 23. **Computerized Services:** Membership database. **Publications:** Energy News, quarterly.

★35★
American Baptist Black Caucus
c/o Dr. Jacob L. Chatman
St. John Missionary Baptist Church
34 W. Pleasant St.
Springfield, OH 45506   Ph: (513)323-4401
Dr. Jacob L. Chatman, Chm.

Description: Black congregations of the American Baptist Churches, U.S.A.; represents approximately 484,200 individuals. Concerned with reforming the American Baptist Convention in terms of bridging the gap between whites and minority members. Seeks to develop convention support for: scholarship aid for disadvantaged students; resources for business and religious projects in the inner city; adequate representation of minorities in the convention structure; support for black colleges and universities; open hiring policies on local, state, and national levels. Is developing a placement service in cooperation with the convention. Operates speakers' bureau. **Founded:** 1968. **Members:** 13,000. **Regional Groups:** 5. **Computerized Services:** Information services. **Publications:** ABC TAB, monthly. Black Caucus Newsletter, semiannual. The Caucus Voice, biennial. **Formerly:** (1981) Black American Baptist Churchmen.

★36★
American Black Book Writers Association
PO Box 10548
Marina del Rey, CA 90295   Ph: (310)822-5195
Will Gibson, Pres.

Description: Writers, illustrators, publishers, booksellers, literary agents, librarians, and others who promote books that are either written by black authors or have particular relevance to the U.S. black community. Represents blacks in the U.S. publishing industry. Encourages development of black authors; works to preserve and advance black literature. Promotes and gives market support to members' works; holds mutual promotions and tours; sponsors cooperative advertising in black-oriented media. Conducts research on problems affecting black authors and their works in the U.S. Compiles statistics. **Founded:** 1980. **Members:** 4000. **Publications:** ABBWA Journal, quarterly. Trade magazine reporting on trends in the industry and featuring profiles of Blacks in the field, nonpublishing news relevant to the industry, book release listings, and annual Black book guide.

★37★
American Black Chiropractors Association
1918 E. Grand Blvd.
St. Louis, MO 63107   Ph: (314)531-0615
Dr. Bobby Westbrooks, Dir.

Description: Persons who have earned a recognized doctorate degree in chiropractic and students enrolled in a chiropractic college; associate members are institutions, organizations, and interested individuals. Objectives are to: educate the public, health care institutions, and health care providers about chiropractic and promote black chiropractic in the community; develop career orientation programs for high school and college students and sponsor scholarship funds; study history of chiropractic; sponsor publicity programs, public forums, counseling services, research, and establishment of free chiropractic clinics; provide for exchange of information, techniques, and reports of researchers and clinicians. Conducts research surveys and prepares educational programs and articles on the history of blacks in chiropractic concerning aspects such as early Jim Crow chiropractic schools, discrimination in licensing and practice, and notable achievements of blacks in the profession. **Founded:** 1980. **Budget:** Less than $25,000. **Publications:** Plans to issue newsletter, conference materials, and membership directory. **Formerly:** (1981) Association of Black Chiropractors.

★38★
American Bridge Association
c/o Gloria Christler
2798 Lakewood Ave., SW
Atlanta, GA 30315   Ph: (404)768-5517
Gloria Christler, Exec.Sec.

Description: Individuals, primarily blacks, interested in the game of bridge. Encourages the playing of duplicate bridge. Sponsors annual tournaments as benefits for charitable organizations. **Founded:** 1932. **Members:** 6000. **Regional Groups:** 7. **Local Groups:** 215. **Publications:** Bulletin, bimonthly.

★39★
American Civil Liberties Union
132 W. 43rd St.
New York, NY 10036   Ph: (212)944-9800
Ira Glasser, Exec.Dir.   Fax: (212)354-5290

Description: Champions the rights set forth in the Bill of Rights of the U.S. Constitution: freedom of speech, press, assembly, and religion; due process of law and fair trial; equality before the law regardless of race, color, sexual orientation, national origin, political opinion, or religious belief. Activities include litigation, advocacy, and public education. Maintains library of more than 3000 volumes. Sponsors litigation projects on topics such as women's rights, gay and lesbian rights, and children's rights. **Founded:** 1920. **Members:** 375,000. **Local Groups:** 200. **State Groups:** 50. **Publications:** Civil Liberties, quarterly. Civil Liberties Alert, monthly. Also publishes policy statements, handbooks, reprints, and pamphlets.

★40★
American Civil Liberties Union Foundation (ACLU)
132 W. 43rd St.
New York, NY 10036   Ph: (212)944-9800
Ira Glasser, Exec.Dir.

Description: Established as the tax-exempt arm of the American Civil Liberties Union (see separate entry). Purposes are legal defense, research, and public education on behalf of civil liberties including freedom of speech, press, and other First Amendment rights. Sponsors projects on topics such as children's rights, capital punishment, censorship, women's rights, immigration, prisoners' rights, national security, voting rights, and equal employment opportunity. Conducts research and public education projects to enable citizens to know and assert their rights. Seeks funds to protect liberty guaranteed by the Bill of Rights and the Constitution. **Founded:** 1966. **Regional Groups:** 2. **Publications:** Annual Report. Civil Liberties, quarterly. Newsletter covering the legal defense, research, and public education projects of the foundation. Includes legislative news. **Formerly:** (1969) Roger Baldwin Foundation of ACLU.

★41★
American Colonization Society - Charity and Social
    Welfare Organization
PO Box 8340
New Fairfield, CT 06812
A. McAllister, Pres.

Description: Provides assistance in relocation, repatriation, and resettling of people of African-American descent to Africa. Conducts social activities; compiles statistics. **Founded:** 1817. **Publications:** none.

★42★
American Committee on Africa (ACOA)
198 Broadway   Ph: (212)962-1210
New York, NY 10038   Fax: (212)964-8570
Jennifer Davis, Exec.Dir.

Description: Devoted to supporting African people in their struggle for freedom and independence. Focuses on southern Africa and the Western Sahara and support for African liberation movements. Works with legislators, churches, trade unions, and interested students to help stop what the group feels is U.S. collaboration with racism in South Africa. Arranges speaking tours for African leaders; publicizes conditions and developments in Africa; sponsors research, rallies, and demonstrations. Serves as a coordinating and collection agency for information and materials on southern Africa. Maintains speakers' bureau. **Founded:** 1953. **Members:** 15,000. **Computerized Services:** Mailing list. **Publications:** ACOA Action News, semiannual. Committee activities newsletter.

★43★
American Constitutional and Civil Rights Union
18055 SW Jay St.
Aloha, OR 97006   Ph: (503)649-9310
Earhl R. Schooff, Exec. Officer

Description: Provides consulting services to trustees of established trusts who believe their constitutional and/or civil rights are being violated. **Founded:** 1979.

★44★
American Coordinating Committee for Equality in
    Sport and Society
c/o Center for Study of Sport
360 Huntington Ave.
Northeastern University - 244 HN   Ph: (617)437-5815
Boston, MA 02115   Fax: (617)437-5830
Dr. Richard E. Lapchick, Chairperson

Description: Coalition of 30 national civil rights, religious, political, and sports organizations. Works for equality in sports as a reflection of society; focuses on South Africa. Has worked to end all sports contacts with South Africa until its apartheid system has been eradicated. Holds seminars; maintains speakers' bureau. Compiles statistics and conducts research programs. **Founded:** 1976.

★45★
American Foundation for Negro Affairs
117 S. 17th St., Ste. 1200
Philadelphia, PA 19103   Ph: (215)854-1470
Samuel L. Evans, Pres.

Description: Has developed a model for educational programs preparing minority students for professional careers. The model, New Access Routes to Professional Careers, which has been used to implement programs for medicine and law in Philadelphia, PA and New Orleans, LA, consists of four interlocking educational phases designed to enable students to meet the academic standards of professional schools through one-to-one preceptorships, tutorials, advanced study, and counseling, beginning at the 8th grade and continuing through the completion of professional school. Among the aims of the program are solidification of the student's career identification and self-image and improvement of basic communications and abstract reasoning skills. Bestows awards; compiles statistics. Sponsors African American Hall of Fame. Maintains small library and biographical archives. Programs carried out by American Foundation for Negro Affairs National Education and Research Fund. **Founded:** 1968. **Publications:** AFNA Projections to the Year 2000 and Beyond, biennial. Monograph.

★46★
American Health and Beauty Aids Institute
401 N. Michigan   Ph: (312)644-6610
Chicago, IL 60611   Fax: (312)321-6869
Geri Duncan Jones, Exec.Dir.

Description: Minority-owned companies engaged in manufacturing and marketing health and beauty aids for the black consumer. Represents the interests of members and the industry before local, state, and federal governmental agencies. Assists with business development and economic progress within the minority community by providing informational and educational resources. Maintains speakers' bureau. Conducts annual Proud Lady Beauty Show. **Founded:** 1981. **Publications:** American Health and Beauty Aids Institute–Membership Directory, annual.

★47★
American Institute of Islamic Studies
PO Box 100398
Denver, CO 80250   Ph: (303)936-0108
Charles L. Geddes, Dir.

Description: Academic research and educational services institution. To further knowledge and understanding about the faith, history, and culture of Islam and the contemporary Muslim world; to create a climate of mutual respect and friendship between peoples of all races, religious beliefs, nationalities, and cultures. Objectives are to provide accurate, unbiased information and educational materials on the history, culture, and faith of Islam and the Muslim world, and a means of communication among students, scholars, and research and teaching institutions. Encourages and supports the preparation and publication of scholarly materials. Conducts seminars, colloquia, and meetings; sponsors exhibitions, films, and lectures. Maintains a reference collection, the Muslim Bibliographic Center, and a library of 7500 volumes, including a special collection of bibliographic materials. **Founded:** 1965. **Budget:** Less than $25,000. **Publications:** Bibliographic Series, periodic. Also publishes A Guide to Reference Books for Islamic Studies; An Analytical Guide to the Bibliographies on the Arabian Peninsula; is currently preparing An Annotated Bibliography of Bibliographies on the Muslim Peoples and A Guide to Periodicals in Western Languages for Islamic Studies.

★48★
American League of Financial Institutions
1709 New York Ave. NW, Ste. 801   Ph: (202)628-5624
Washington, DC 20006   Fax: (202)637-8983
John W. Harshaw, Pres.

Description: Federal and state chartered minority savings and loan associations in 25 states and the District of Columbia. Undertakes programs to increase the income of and savings flow into the associations including a direct solicitation effort; provides counseling and technical assistance for member associations through a series of regional conferences and seminars; offers consultant services to assist individual associations and groups wishing to organize new associations or acquire existing associations with development potential; collects, organizes, and distributes materials that will aid member associations. Conducts research to improve investment capability, resolve common management problems, and evaluate statistical data on an industry-wide basis to develop and institute training programs for management personnel. Conducts research programs; maintains placement service. **Founded:** 1948. **Members:** 49. **Publications:** ALFI Focus Magazine, periodic. Directory of Members and Associate Members, periodic. **Formerly:** (1983) American Savings and Loan League.

★49★
Amnesty International of the U.S.A.
322 8th Ave.   Ph: (212)807-8400
New York, NY 10001   Fax: (212)627-1451
John G. Healey, Exec.Dir.

Description: Works impartially for the release of men and women detained anywhere for their conscientiously held beliefs, color, ethnic origin, sex, religion, or language, provided they have neither used nor advocated violence. Opposes torture and the death penalty without reservation and advocates fair and prompt trials for all political prisoners. Has consultative status with the United Nations and the Council of Europe (see separate entry), has cooperative relations with the Inter-American Commission on Human Rights, and has observer status with the Organization of African Unity. Was the recipient of the 1977 Nobel Prize for Peace. Volunteers participate in networks: Educators; Freedom Writers; Health Professionals; Legal Professionals; Religion; Urgent Action; Women. **Founded:** 1966. **Members:** 400,000. **Local Groups:** 3000. **Publications:** Amnesty Action, bimonthly. Newsletter.

★50★
Anti-Repression Resource Team
PO Box 122
Jackson, MS 39205
Ken Lawrence, Dir.   Ph: (601)969-2269

Description: Combats all forms of political repression including: police violence and misconduct; Ku Klux Klan and Nazi terrorism; spying and covert action by secret police and intelligence agencies. Focuses on research, writing, lecturing, organizing, and publishing. Conducts training workshops for church, labor, and community organizations. Maintains library of materials on spying, repression, covert action, terrorism, and civil liberties. Maintains speakers' bureau. **Budget:** Less than $25,000. **Founded:** 1979.

★51★
AOIP
231 W. 29th St., Ste. 1205   Ph: (212)967-4008
New York, NY 10001   Fax: (212)971-4682
Benjamin Wright, Exec.Dir.

Description: Coalition of black community development organizations. Works to combat the root causes of illiteracy as well as other social ills affecting minority communities. **Founded:** 1980. **Members:** 94. **Publications:** The Advancer, weekly. National Black Monitor, monthly. Magazine. Newsletter to Board Members, semimonthly. Also publishes Who Am I? Guide To Learning. **Formerly:** (1991) Assault on Illiteracy Program.

★52★
Artists and Athletes Against Apartheid
545 8th St. SE, Ste. 200   Ph: (202)547-2550
Washington, DC 20003   Fax: (202)547-7687

Description: Celebrities in the arts and sports who vow not to perform in South Africa because of its apartheid policy of racial segregation. Objective is to implement an international sports and cultural boycott of South Africa until apartheid is no longer imposed. Seeks to educate others in sports and the performing arts about apartheid and to dissuade them from performing. Members make television and public appearances to denounce apartheid. Operates speakers' bureau. Monitors the decline in the number of art and sports celebrities working in and traveling to South Africa; organizes symposia; compiles statistics. **Founded:** 1983. **Members:** 500. **Budget:** Less than $25,000. **Publications:** Brochures.

★53★
Artists United Against Apartheid
c/o The Africa Fund
198 Broadway   Ph: (212)962-1210
New York, NY 10038   Fax: (212)964-8570

Description: Coalition of popular musicians who seek to make the public aware of the lack of freedoms for blacks under the apartheid system in South Africa through their music. Members performed on the ''Sun City'' record album and single and music video, the profits of which are donated to the Africa Fund (see separate entry). Seeks to educate performers and the public regarding conditions in South Africa. Appeals to entertainers to forego performing at the Sun City resort complex in South Africa. (The group believes that by performing there, entertainers show tacit support for apartheid.) **Members:** 54. **Publications:** Press releases. Presently inactive.

★54★
Association for Multicultural Counseling and Development
c/o American Counseling Association   Ph: (703)823-9800
5999 Stevenson Ave.   Fax: (703)823-0252
Alexandria, VA 22304   Free: 800-347-6647
Dr. Theodore P. Remley Jr., Exec.Dir.

Description: A division of the American Counseling Association. Professionals involved in counseling careers in educational settings, social services, and community agencies; interested individuals; students. Seeks to: develop programs aimed at improving ethnic and racial empathy and understanding; foster personal growth and improve educational opportunities for all minorities in the U.S.; defend human and civil rights; provide in-service and pre-service training for members and others in the profession. Works to enhance members' ability to serve as behavioral change agents. Bestows awards; offers placement service. **Founded:** 1972. **Members:** 3452. **Publications:** Journal of Multicultural Counseling and Development, quarterly. **Formerly:** (1986) Association for Non-White Concerns in Personnel and Guidance.

★55★
Association for the Preservation and Presentation of the Arts
2011 Benning Rd. NE
Washington, DC 20002   Ph: (202)529-3244
Bernice Hammond, Pres.

Description: Individuals representing the visual and performing arts; interested others. Serves as a vehicle for the promotion of blacks in the arts. Seeks to increase public awareness and appreciation of the arts and its representation of African American culture. Works on the development of musical and dance productions. Produces children's shows; sponsors lectures. Offers scholarships to children and young people interested in the arts. Bestows awards. **Founded:** 1964. **Members:** 500. **Publications:** Cultural Magnet, semiannual. Newsletter. Also publishes pamphlets and information on artists.

★56★
Association for the Study of Afro-American Life and History
1407 14th St. NW
Washington, DC 20005   Ph: (202)667-2822
Karen A. McRae, Exec.Dir.

Description: Historians, scholars, and students interested in the research and study of black people as a contributing factor in civilization. To promote historical research and writings, collect historical manuscripts and materials relating to black people throughout the world, and bring about harmony among the races by interpreting one to the other. Encourages the study of black history and training in the social sciences, history, and other disciplines. Cooperates with governmental agencies, foundations, and peoples and nations in projects designed to advance the study of ethnic history, with emphasis on black heritage and programs for the future. Maintains Carter G. Woodson home in Washington, DC. Sponsors essay contest for undergraduate and graduate students. **Founded:** 1915. **Members:** 10,000. **Budget:** $200,000. **Local Groups:** 160. **State Groups:** 30. **Publications:** Journal of Negro History, quarterly. **Formerly:** (1973) Association for the Study of Negro Life and History.

★57★
Association for the Study of Classical African Civilizations
3624 Country Club Dr.   Ph: (213)730-1155
Los Angeles, CA 90019-2010   Fax: (213)730-1155
Nzinga Ratibisha Heru, Pres.

Description: Individuals interested in the study and promotion of African civilization and an African worldview. Promotes the preservation of the ancient African heritage. Conducts research and educational programs; operates museum; maintains library and speakers' bureau. Bestows annual Leo Hansberry Award. **Founded:** 1984. **Members:** 1000. Membership Dues: $25/year; $12.50/year students and elders. **Regional Groups:** 5. **Computerized Services:** Database; mailing list. **Publications:** Critical Commentaries, annual.

★58★
Association of African-American Women Business Owners
c/o Brenda Alford
Brasman Research
PO Box 13933
Silver Spring, MD 20911-3933   Ph: (301)565-0258
Tracy Mason, Pres.

Description: Small business owners in all industries, particularly business services. Seeks to assist in developing a greater number of successful self-employed black women through business and personal development programs, networking, and legislative action. Is conducting a 2-year project identifying black women business owners as role models and historical figures; plans to establish an archive. **Founded:** 1982. **Members:** 850. **Local Groups:** 10. **Publications:** Chronicle of Minority Business, quarterly. **Formerly:** (1990) American Association of Black Women Entrepreneurs.

★59★
Association of African Studies Programs
c/o Thomas A. Hale
Pennsylvania State University
French Dept.   Ph: (814)865-8481
University Park, PA 16802   Fax: (814)865-3641
Thomas A. Hale, Chm.

Description: African studies programs, departments, and committees at universities and colleges. Works to promote, develop, and further African studies in the U.S. and Africa. Represents the interests of African studies programs before funding agencies, universities, and state and federal authorities. **Founded:** 1972. **Members:** 50. **Publications:** AASP Newsletter, semiannual.

★60★
Association of Black Admissions and Financial Aid Officers of the Ivy League and Sister Schools
c/o Lloyd Peterson
Admissions Office
149 Elm St.
Yale University
New Haven, CT 06520   Ph: (203)432-1916
Lloyd Peterson, Co-Chair

Description: Present and former minority admissions and financial aid officers employed at Ivy League or sister schools. These schools include: Brown, Columbia, Cornell, Dartmouth, Harvard/Radcliffe, Massachusetts Institute of Technology, University of Pennsylvania, Princeton, Yale, Barnard, Bryn Mawr, Mount Holyoke, Smith, and Wellesley. Aids minority students who wish to pursue a college education. Seeks to improve methods of recruitment, admittance, and financial services that support the growth and maintenance of the minority student population at these institutions. Encourages Ivy League and sister schools to respond to the needs of minority students and admissions and financial aid officers. **Founded:** 1970. **Members:** 77. **Publications:** Unequalled Opportunities (guide to Ivy League and sister schools).

★61★
Association of Black Anthropologists
c/o American Anthropological Association
1703 New Hampshire Ave. NW   Ph: (202)232-8800
Washington, DC 20009   Fax: (202)667-5345
Faye V. Harrison, Pres.

Description: Anthropologists and others interested in the study of blacks and other peoples subjected to exploitation and oppression. Works to: formulate conceptual and methodological frameworks to advance understanding of all forms of human diversity and commonality; advance theoretical efforts to explain the conditions that produce social inequalities based on race, ethnicity, class, or gender; develop research methods that involve the peoples studied and local scholars in all stages of investigation and dissemination of findings. Bestows awards; operates placement service; maintains biographical archives. **Founded:** 1970. **Members:** 130. **Computerized Services:** Mailing list, available through rental from the American Anthropological Association. **Publications:** Transforming Anthropology, semiannual. Newsletter; includes commentaries, essays, book reviews, and refereed articles. **Formerly:** (1975) Caucus of Black Anthropologists.

★62★
Association of Black Cardiologists
3201 Del Paso Blvd., Ste. 100   Ph: (916)641-2224
Sacramento, CA 95815   Fax: (916)641-1034
B. Waine Kong Ph.D., Exec.Dir.

Description: Physicians and other health professionals interested in lowering mortality and morbidity resulting from cardiovascular diseases. Seeks to improve prevention and treatment of cardiovascular diseases. Conducts educational and research programs; bestows awards; maintains speakers' bureau. **Budget:** $500,000. **Founded:** 1974. **Members:** 500.

★63★
Association of Black Catholics Against Abortion
1011 1st Ave.   Ph: (212)371-1000
New York, NY 10022   Fax: (212)319-8265
Dr. Delores Bernadette Grier, Pres.

Description: African-American Catholics who oppose abortion. Conducts educational programs, workshops, and conferences.

★64★
Association of Black CPA Firms
1101 Connecticut Ave. NW, Ste. 700
Washington, DC 20036   Ph: (202)857-1100
Sadie M. Swyne, Exec.Dir.

Description: Black and minority certified public accounting (CPA) firms united to represent their common interests. **Founded:** 1984. **Members:** 23. **Publications:** (1) ABCPAF News (newsletter), quarterly; (2) Membership Directory, annual.

★65★
Association of Black Foundation Executives
1828 L St. NW   Ph: (202)466-6512
Washington, DC 20036   Fax: (202)466-5722
Jacqui Burton, Dir.Chair

Description: Board and staff members of corporate and foundation grantmaking organizations. Encourages increased recognition of economic, educational, and social issues facing blacks in the grantmaking field. Promotes support of blacks and their status as grantmaking professionals. Seeks an increase in the number of blacks entering the grantmaking field; helps members improve their job effectiveness. Though involved with grantmaking organizations, the ABFE itself does not award grants. **Founded:** 1971.

★66★
Association of Black Nursing Faculty
5823 Queens Cove   Ph: (708)969-3809
Lisle, IL 60532   Fax: (708)969-3895
Sallie Tucker-Allen Ph.D., Exec.Dir.

Description: Black nursing faculty teaching in nursing programs accredited by the National League for Nursing. Works to promote health-related issues and educational concerns of interest to the black community and ABNF. Serves as a forum for communication and the exchange of information among members; develops strategies for expressing concerns to other individuals, institutions, and communities. Assists members in professional development; develops and sponsors continuing education activities; fosters networking and guidance in employment and recruitment activities. Promotes health-related issues of legislation, government programs, and community activities. Supports black consumer advocacy issues. Encourages research. **Founded:** 1987. **Members:** 127. **Budget:** Less than $25,000. **State Groups:** 25. **Publications:** ABNF Journal, quarterly. **Formerly:** (1992) Association of Black Nursing Faculty in Higher Education.

★67★
Association of Black Psychologists
PO Box 55999   Ph: (202)722-0808
Washington, DC 20040-5999   Fax: (202)722-5941

Description: Professional psychologists and others in associated disciplines. Aims to: enhance the psychological well-being of black people in America; define mental health in consonance with newly established psychological concepts and standards; develop policies for local, state, and national decision-making that have impact on the mental health of the black community; support established black sister organizations and aid in the development of new, independent black institutions to enhance the psychological, educational, cultural, and economic situation. Offers training and information on AIDS. Conducts seminars, workshops, and research. Bestows awards. **Founded:** 1968. **Members:** 1200. **Budget:** $500,000. **Regional Groups:** 4. **Local Groups:** 31. **State Groups:** 29. **Publications:** Journal of Black Psychology, semiannual. Provides research results. Includes book reviews.

★68★
Association of Black Sociologists
Howard University
PO Box 302   Ph: (202)806-6853
Washington, DC 20059   Fax: (202)806-4893
Walter Allen, Pres.

Description: Purposes are to: promote the professional interests of black sociologists; promote an increase in the number of professionally trained sociologists; help stimulate and improve the quality of research and the teaching of sociology; provide perspectives regarding black experiences as well as expertise for understanding and dealing with problems confronting black people; protect professional rights and safeguard the civil rights stemming from executing the above objectives. Presents annual award to black graduate student for excellence in scholarly work; conducts research programs. **Founded:** 1968. **Members:** 400. **Budget:** Less than $25,000. **Publications:** ABS Newsletter, monthly. Includes professional and career in development information, announcements, and updates. **Formerly:** (1976) Caucus of Black Sociologists.

★69★
Association of Black Women in Higher Education
c/o Lenore R. Gall
234 hudson Ave.
Albany, NY 12210   Ph: (518)472-1791
Lenore R. Gall, Pres.

Description: Faculty members, education administrators, students, retirees, consultants, managers, and affirmative action officers. Objectives are to nurture the role of black women in higher education, and to provide support for the professional development goals of black women. Conducts workshops and seminars. **Founded:** 1979. **Members:** 350. **Computerized Services:** Mailing list. **Publications:** ABWHE Newsletter, quarterly.

★70★
Association of Caribbean Studies
PO Box 22202   Ph: (606)257-6966
Lexington, KY 40522   Fax: (606)257-1074
Dr. O. R. Dathorne, Exec.Dir.

Description: Scholars and researchers concerned with the interdisciplinary nature of Caribbean studies. Objectives are to: develop knowledge and understanding of Caribbean studies through study, research, and travel; promote academic studies and disseminate information to the public; encourage research on Caribbean politics, history, linguistics, trade, psychology, music, anthropology, sociology, folk culture, religion, art, literature, and economics; promote the Caribbean as a cultural whole and use of its

languages, which include English, French, Spanish, Portuguese, Dutch, and related Creoles. Maintains speakers' bureau; compiles statistics; bestows awards. Conducts periodic seminar. **Founded:** 1978. **Members:** 1200. **Budget:** Less than $25,000. **Computerized Services:** Database; mailing list. **Publications:** Abstracts From Annual Conference. Journal of Caribbean Studies, 3/year. Newsletter, 3/year. Also publishes Hot Ice, Songs from a New World, and monographs; produces audiocassettes and audiovisual materials.

★71★
Association of Haitian Physicians Abroad
60 Plaza St.
Brooklyn, NY 11238   Ph: (718)783-0701
Claude Manigat, Pres.

Description: Haitian doctors. Purpose is to unite Haitian doctors abroad and to organize professional activities among them. Provides charitable assistance to the Haitian community. Sponsors educational programs. **Founded:** 1972. **Members:** 900. **Budget:** $35,000. **State Groups:** 8. **Publications:** Directory of Haitian Physicians in N.Y., biennial. Journal des Medecins Haitien a l'Etranger, 6/year. Also publishes educational materials. **Formerly:** (1986) Haitian Medical Association Abroad.

★72★
Association of Minority Health Professions Schools
711 2nd St. NE, Ste. 200   Ph: (202)544-7499
Washington, DC 20002   Fax: (202)546-7105
Dale P. Dirks, Exec. Officer

Description: Predominantly black health professions schools. Seeks to: increase the number of minorities in health professions; improve the health of blacks in the U.S.; increase the federal resources available to minority schools and students. Provides information to the U.S. Congress; conducts educational programs. **Founded:** 1978. **Members:** 8. **Publications:** Study of the Health Status of Minorities in the U.S., periodic.

★73★
Association of Muslim Scientists and Engineers
PO Box 38
Plainfield, IN 46168   Ph: (317)839-8157
Iqbal J. Unus, Coordinator

Description: International organization of Muslims who are graduates of three-year, post-high school programs in engineering or in the natural, life, or mathematical sciences. Works to channel the talents of Muslim scientists and engineers into providing the Muslim community with assistance and guidance and to improve the gathering, distribution, and dissemination of technical information and Islamic knowledge through publications, meetings, and other media. Provides encouragement and guidance to members in their education and careers. Places foreign students in U.S. universities; holds competitions among graduate students for writing research articles. Sponsors seminars, symposia, and workshops. Maintains small library. **Founded:** 1969. **Members:** 640. **Budget:** $75,000. **Computerized Services:** Mailing list. **Publications:** Chronological and Subject-Wise Index, annual. Directory of Muslim Scientists and Engineers, annual. International Journal of Science and Technology, biennial. Newsletter, monthly. Proceedings of Conference, annual. Publication Index Annual. Also publishes educational guide and paper reprints.

★74★
Association of Muslim Social Scientists
PO Box 669   Ph: (703)471-1133
Herndon, VA 22070   Fax: (703)471-3922
Sayyid M. Syeed, Gen.Sec.

Description: Professors and graduate students in the social sciences and humanities. Encourages members to conduct studies and research in their areas of specialization; assists in developing Islamic positions on contemporary issues and applying them to studies and research; generates Islamic thought through critical and scientific inquiry and disseminates it through various means; aids in the professional development and introduction of placement opportunities. Places foreign students in American universities. Holds writing competition for graduate students. Sponsors research projects; maintains speakers' bureau. **Founded:** 1972. **Members:**

580. **Budget:** $80,000. **Computerized Services:** Mailing list. **Publications:** American Journal of Islamic Social Sciences, 3/year.

★75★
Audience Development Committee
PO Box 30, Manhattanville Sta.
New York, NY 10027   Ph: (212)368-6906
Vivian S. Robinson, Exec.Dir.

Description: Individuals interested in or pursuing a career in black theatre. Purposes are to develop a greater appreciation of theatrical productions among blacks and to build an audience for black theatrical and dance companies. Operates black theatre archives; maintains speakers' bureau. Bestows awards for excellence in black theatre. Offers a low-cost ticket program for senior citizens, children, and those who are unable to afford tickets at box office prices. **Founded:** 1973. **Members:** 1000. **Publications:** Black Theatre Directory, periodic. Intermission, monthly. Newsletter. Overture, semiannual. Magazine.

★76★
Auxiliary to the National Medical Association
1012 10th St. NW
Washington, DC 20001   Ph: (202)371-1674
Mrs. Ruby H. Franks, Adm.Sec.

Description: Spouses of active members of the National Medical Association; widows and widowers of former members. Purposes are to: create a greater interest in the NMA; assist and encourage the medical profession in its efforts to educate and serve the public in matters of sanitation and health; develop and promote a national program on health and education with subcategories in community needs, legislation, and human relations. Conducts workshops on teenage pregnancy, breast self-examinations, high blood pressure screening, and sickle cell anemia screening. Plans and implements an annual youth forum under the auspices of the March of Dimes Birth Defects Foundation. Provides youth with professional guidance and the opportunity for peer exchange in the areas of mental and physical health; deals with the health of newborns, health services, nutrition, and teenage pregnancy. Also conducts programs for youth on parenting, socially transmitted diseases, nutrition, birth defects, and continued education after pregnancy. Bestows annual Alma Wells Givens Scholarships to medical students and the Omega Mason Memorial Scholarship Awards to outstanding student nurses. Maintains archive. **Founded:** 1935. **Regional Groups:** 6. **Local Groups:** 40. **State Groups:** 14. **Publications:** Membership Directory, periodic. **Formerly:** (1975) Women's Auxiliary to the National Medical Association.

★77★
Bessie Smith Society
c/o Prof. Michael Roth
Franklin and Marshall College
Lancaster, PA 17604   Ph: (717)291-3915
Prof. Michael Roth, Adviser

Description: Admirers of blues singer Bessie Smith, who attained her greatest success in the 1920s and 30s.

★78★
A Better Chance
419 Boylston St.   Ph: (617)421-0950
Boston, MA 02116   Fax: (617)421-0965
Judith B. Griffin, Pres.

Description: Identifies, recruits, and places academically talented and motivated minority students into leading independent secondary schools and selected public schools. Students receive need-based financial assistance from member schools. Prepares students to attend selective colleges and universities and encourages their aspirations to assume positions of responsibility and leadership in American society. Conducts research and provides technical assistance on expanded educational opportunities for minority group students in secondary and higher education. Bestows awards; maintains statistical files and biographical archives. **Founded:** 1963. **Budget:** $1,771,000. Member Schools: 160. **Publications:** Abecedarian, 2/year. Newsletter. Annual Report. Letters to Member Schools, annual. Also publishes brochure. **Formerly:** Independent Schools Talent Search Program.

★79★
Biblical Institute for Social Change
4142 22nd St. NE
Washington, DC 20018   Ph: (202)269-4311
Dr. Cain Hope Felder, Exec.Dir.

Description: Works to increase public understanding of the critical role played by individuals of African descent in biblical history in order to promote self-esteem and social change. Offers seminars and conferences and distributes educational materials to African American churches. Encourages scholarship on biblical traditions and their historical relevance to African and African American churches. Maintains library and speakers' bureau. **Founded:** 1990. **Members:** 300. **Budget:** $35,000. **Publications:** BISC Quarterly.

★80★
Big Eight Council on Black Student Government
Minority Student Services
Hester Hall, Rm. 213
731 Elm Ave.
University of Oklahoma
Norman, OK 73019
Norris Williams, Dir.

Description: Black student unions and other groups at Big Eight Athletic Conference universities. Seeks to represent the concerns of black collegians at universities where the majority of students are white. Encourages the genesis of all black student organizations and lends support to them. Seeks to effect changes in curricula and to help legitimize and develop black studies departments as accredited degree programs. Functions as a communications medium among member schools and assists in efforts to reduce the attrition rate of black students. Promotes the placement of students and the hiring of black faculty and staff. Presents group and individual awards. Member schools conduct seminars and workshops including Internships, Working for Corporate America, **Founded:** 1978. **Members:** 5000. **Budget:** $35,000. **Publications:** Big Eight Update, annual. Directory. Harambee, semiannual. New Renaissance, semiannual. Coping with Stress and Pressure, Young Entrepreneurships, and Leadership. Presently inactive.

★81★
Black Affairs Center for Training and Organizational Development
c/o Margaret V. Wright
10918 Jarboe Ct.
Silver Spring, MD 20901   Ph: (301)681-9827
Margaret V. Wright, Pres.

Description: Multidisciplinary management research organization which promotes social change, educational improvement, organization renewal and goal achievement, systematic problem solving and multicultural skills development through custom-designed training programs and consultation services. Individuals, groups, educational systems, and governmental and community agencies use programs such as Equal Employment Opportunity Training; Employee Motivation, Productivity and Improvement Training; Career Education and Development Training. Programs are continually being developed in areas including women's concerns, single parents, youth and sex, drugs and alcoholism, the aging, daycare, sexual harassment, and stress management. **Founded:** 1970. **Members:** 100. **Publications:** BAC Update, quarterly. **Formerly:** (1976) Black Affairs Division, National Training Labora Laboratories; (1989) Black Affairs Center.

★82★
Black American Cinema Society
3617 Monclair St.
Los Angeles, CA 90018   Ph: (213)737-3292
Mayme Agnew Clayton Ph.D., Founder & Dir.

Description: Faculty members, students, senior citizens, and film and jazz enthusiasts. Works to bring about an awareness of the contributions made by blacks to the motion picture industry in silent films, early talkies, and short and feature films. Feels that by viewing these films black children can see the sacrifice and humiliation endured by black actors and actresses, directors, film writers, and producers while making films. Maintains collection of early black films owned by the Western States Black Research Center. Conducts research projects, film shows, and Black History Month seminars. Provides financial support to independent black filmmakers. Maintains 30,000 volume library on black history, literature, records, films, and art that includes museum pieces and documents. Compiles statistics; maintains biographical archives, speakers' bureau, and charitable program; sponsors competitions; bestows annual Black American Cinema Society Awards. Sponsors traveling film festival. **Founded:** 1975. **Members:** 1350. **Budget:** $32,000. **Publications:** Black Talkies Souvenir Book, annual.

★83★
Black American Response to the African Community
127 N. Madison Ave., Ste. 400
Pasadena, CA 91101 Ph: (818)584-0303
Frank E. Wilson, Exec.Dir.

Description: A grass roots organization of entertainers, journalists, clergy, and business, health, and community leaders working to assist the victims of drought and famine in Africa. Focuses on emergency efforts involving medical needs, water irrigation, housing, and food supplies. Provides relief for orphans through its Family Network Program. Disseminates current information on drought-stricken areas in Africa; assists in the development of regeneration projects in affected areas. Maintains the National Education Task Force to educate Americans on the African crisis; sponsors media updates. Raises funds through television documentaries, benefit movie premieres, art exhibits, and collection boxes. Is donating proceeds and royalties from the song Love Returns to aid the African hunger crisis. **Founded:** 1984. **Publications:** Action Update Newsletter, semiannual.

★84★
Black Americans for Life
419 7th St. NW, Ste. 500
Washington, DC 20004 Ph: (202)626-8833

Description: Individuals working to educate the black community on pro-life and pro-family issues. Promotes alternatives to abortion for women with crisis pregnancies; strives to be a visible presence defending the rights of the unborn in the black community. Asserts that black women are twice as likely as white women to have abortions; believes that abortions are counterproductive to advances made through civil rights efforts. Provides information on resources and available speakers. **Publications:** Fact sheets.

★85★
Black and Indian Catholic Indian Commission
2021 H St. NW Ph: (202)331-8542
Washington, DC 20006 Fax: (202)331-8544
Rev.Msgr. Paul A. Lenz, Exec.Dir.

Description: Coordinates the distribution of funds from the annual Black and Indian Mission Collection in Catholic churches across the U.S.; these funds go to support priests, nuns, and other religious workers at black and Indian missions and schools. Compiles statistics. **Founded:** 1884. **Publications:** Posters and other promotional materials. **Formerly:** (1991) Commission for Catholic Missions among the Colored People and The Indians.

★86★
Black Awareness in Television
13217 Livernois
Detroit, MI 48238-3162 Ph: (313)931-3427
David Rambeau, Dir.

Description: Produces black media programs for television, video, radio, film, and theatre. Trains individuals in the media and conducts research projects including surveys. Produces public affairs, cultural arts, soap opera, and exercise programs; sponsors theatre companies. Seeks television exposure for black-produced products and black performing artists; promotes September is Black Reading Month program. **Founded:** 1970. **Members:** 100. **Local Groups:** 5. **Publications:** Thedamu Arts Magazine, monthly. **Also known as:** Project BAIT.

★87★
Black Business Alliance
PO Box 26443 Ph: (410)467-7427
Baltimore, MD 21207 Fax: (410)467-1271
Willie H. Scott, CEO

Description: Act as a national and international support system for black businesses, providing assistance in organizational management and resource development. Provides children's

services; sponsors fundraising events; offers placement services. Maintains library; bestows awards and scholarships. Conducts monthly seminar and speakers' bureau. **Founded:** 1979. **Members:** 250. **Regional Groups:** 3. **Local Groups:** 14. **State Groups:** 6. **Publications:** Alliance Speaks, monthly. At Your Service, annual. Directory. **Formerly:** (1986) National Black People's Assembly.

★88★
Black Caucus of the American Library Association
c/o Dr. Alex Boyd
Newark Public Library
5 Washington St. Ph: (201)733-7780
Newark, NJ 07101 Fax: (201)733-5919
Dr. Alex Boyd, Pres.

Description: Black librarians; blacks interested in library services. To promote librarianship; to encourage active participation of blacks in library associations and boards and all levels of the profession. Monitors activities of the American Library Association with regard to its policies and programs and how they affect black librarians and library users. Reviews, analyzes, evaluates, and recommends to the ALA actions that influence the recruitment, development, advancement, and general working conditions of black librarians. Facilitates library services that meet the informational needs of black people including increased availability of materials related to social and economic concerns. Encourages development of authoritative information resources concerning black people and dissemination of this information to the public. Bestows annual Distinguished Service and Trailblazer Awards. **Founded:** 1970. **Members:** 1000. **Publications:** Black Caucus Newsletter, bimonthly. Reports news of interest about black librarians. Recurring features include notices of professional opportunities and activities of individuals within the caucus and the ALA.

★89★
Black Citizens for a Fair Media
156-20 Riverside Dr., No. 13L
New York, NY 10032 Ph: (212)568-3168
Emma L. Bowen, Pres.

Description: Community organizations concerned with employment practices in the television industry, images of black people projected by television, and how those images affect viewers. Works to improve programming, employment proctices, and training of blacks; evaluates compliance with the Federal Communication Commission's equal opportunity rules for the electronic media. Believes that the airways belong to the people and seeks to prevent any change in that ownership. Has established advisory boards with New York City television stations which meet quarterly to discuss programming and employment. **Founded:** 1971. **Members:** 250. **Publications:** Brochure.

★90★
Black Coaches Association
PO Box J Ph: (515)271-3010
Des Moines, IA 50311 Fax: (515)271-4542
Marian Washington, Pres.

Description: Blacks and other minorities in the coaching profession. Promotes the creation of a positive environment in which issues such as stereotyping, lack of significant media coverage, and discrimination can be exposed, discussed, and resolved. Provides member services. Petitions the NCAA legislative bodies to design, enact, and enforce diligent guidelines and policies to improve professional mobility for minorities. **Founded:** 1986. **Members:** 2000. **Publications:** Newsletter, annual. Includes activities and awards updates.

★91★
Black Data Processing Associates
PO Box 7466
Philadelphia, PA 19101 Ph: (215)843-9120
Vivian Wilson, Pres.

Description: Persons employed in the information processing industry, including electronic data processing, electronic word processing, and data communications; others interested in information processing. Seeks to accumulate and share information processing knowledge and business expertise in order to increase the career and business potential of minorities in the information processing field. Conducts professional seminars, workshops, tutoring services, and community introductions to data processing. Bestows honorary memberships and awards to distinguished data processing professionals; offers scholarships to qualified high school graduates and makes annual donation to the United Negro College Fund. **Founded:** 1975. **Members:** 1500. **Local Groups:** 39. **Publications:** Data News, quarterly. National Journal, quarterly.

★92★
Black Entertainment and Sports Lawyers Association
PO Box 508067   Ph: (708)386-8338
Chicago, IL 60650   Fax: (708)383-7414
Maisha Mayo, Exec.Dir.

Description: Black attorneys specializing in entertainment and sports law. Purpose is to provide more efficient and effective legal representation to African-American entertainers and athletes. Offers referral system for legal representation and a resource bank for providing information to students, groups, and nonprofit and civic organizations involved in the entertainment industry; and serves as an industry watchdog in protecting the rights of blacks within the entertainment community. Bestows annual BESLA Award and Sadye Gibson Scholarship Fund. Maintains hall of fame; conducts research programs. **Founded:** 1979. **Members:** 3000. **Regional Groups:** 2. **Publications:** BESLA Mid Year Manual, semiannual. **Formerly:** (1986) Black Entertainment Lawyers Association.

★93★
Black Filmmaker Foundation
Tribeca Film Center
375 Greenwich, Ste. 600   Ph: (212)941-3944
New York, NY 10013   Fax: (212)941-3943
Andre Robinson, Exec.Dir.

Description: Serves as media arts center. Fosters audience development by programming local, national, and international film festivals. Maintains video library. Conducts seminars and workshops. Operates skills bank for job referrals. Conducts educational programs; maintains speakers' bureau. **Founded:** 1978. **Members:** 3000. MD $40 for individual; $50 for professional; $100 for organization, production company, and sponsor; $500 for benefactor; $1000 for patron. **Budget:** $300,000. **Publications:** Annual Report. BFF News, monthly. Newsletter. Includes internship and job listings, calendar of events, and calls for entries.

★94★
Black Filmmakers Hall of Fame, Inc.
405 14th St., Ste. 515   Ph: (510)465-0804
Oakland, CA 94612   Fax: (510)839-9858
Mary Perry Smith, Pres.

Description: Seeks to study, teach, and preserve the contributions of black filmmakers to American cinema. Fosters cultural awareness through educational, research, and public service programs in the film arts. Holds film-lecture series, Black Filmworks Festival, and annual International Film Competition; presents annual awards. Maintains biographical archives and speakers' bureau. **Founded:** 1973. **Members:** 500. **Budget:** $200,000. **Publications:** Black Filmworks, annual. Also publishes catalog.

★95★
Black Health Research Foundation
14 E. 60th St., Ste. 307   Ph: (212)408-3485
New York, NY 10022   Fax: (908)241-8768
Denise Gary Robinson, Pres.

Description: Voluntary health agency devoted to reducing preventable causes of premature death among African Americans. Funds scientific research in areas including AIDS, alcoholism, infant mortality, sickle cell disease, susbstance abuse, and other diseases that have a disproportionate impact on African Americans. Seeks recognition as the foremost authority on health and science regarding African Americans. Promotes professional and community education; recruits and trains volunteers. Seeks to influence public policy on crucial issues. Bestows awards. **Founded:** 1988. **Members:** 400. **Budget:** $200,000. **Publications:** Black Health Column, monthly. Newssheet on black health issues. Spirit of the Sun, quarterly. Newsletter including volunteer activities. **Formerly:** (1988) Black Medical Research Foundation.

★96★
Black, Indian, Hispanic, and Asian Women in Action
122 W. Franklin Ave., Ste. 306
Minneapolis, MN 55404   Ph: (612)870-1193
Alice O. Lynch, Contact

Description: Strives to empower Black, Indian, Hispanic, and Asian communities through implementation of educational projects. Acts as an advocate for communities of color in the areas of family violence, chemical dependence, education, and physical and mental health. Works for social change, the health of the family and advancement of socioeconomic status. **Founded:** 1983. **Members:** 200. **Budget:** $200,000. **Publications:** Unison, quarterly. Newsletter. Covers issues of concern for people of color.

★97★
Black Methodists for Church Renewal
601 W. Riverview Ave.
Dayton, OH 45406   Ph: (513)227-9460
Erenst L. Swiggett, Bd. Chairperson

Description: Black clergy and lay members of the United Methodist church. Serves as platform from which blacks can express concerns to the general church on issues such as: revival and survival of the black church; involvement of blacks within the structure of the church; the conduct of the church as it relates to investment policies and social issues; economic support in the black community; the support of the 12 black colleges. Encourages black Methodists to work for economic and social justice. Works to expose racism in agencies and institutions of the United Methodist church. Seeks improvement of educational opportunities for blacks, the strengthening of black churches, and an increase in the number of black persons in Christian-related vocations. Advocates liberation, peace, justice, and freedom for all people. Supports programs that alleviate suffering in third world countries. **Founded:** 1968. **Members:** 2000. **Publications:** Board of Directors Directory, semiannual. NOW Newsletter, 11/year. Includes association and member news.

★98★
Black Military History Institute of America
c/o Col. William A. De Shields
PO Box 1134
Ft. Meade, MD 20755   Ph: (410)757-4250
Col. William A. De Shields, Exec. Officer

Description: Individuals interested in promoting the military achievements of black Americans and publicizing other aspects of black history. Seeks to: provide archival facilities to collect, preserve, and exhibit materials pertaining to military history; motivate and support underprivileged youths by using military role models as a source of inspiration; foster a spirit of camaraderie and goodwill among all persons sharing an interest in community involvement programs for the underprivileged. Sponsors slide lectures and photographic exhibit. Maintains speakers' bureau. **Founded:** 1987. **Members:** 60. **Budget:** $50,000. **Regional Groups:** 1. **Chapters:** 1. **Publications:** Newsletter, quarterly.

★99★
Black Music Association
c/o Louise West
1775 Broadway, 7th Fl.
New York, NY 10019   Ph: (212)307-1459
Louise West, Exec. Officer

Description: Goal is to preserve, protect, and perpetuate black music on an international level and to work with schools and universities to bring blacks into music not only as performers, but as businesspersons. Sponsors seminars. Plans to sponsor annual Black Music Awards Show for television, and other educational and research projects; also plans to open a museum and institute for black music studies. **Founded:** 1978. **Members:** 2000. **Budget:** $200,000. **Publications:** Innervisions, bimonthly. Membership Directory, annual.

★100★
Black PAC
PO Drawer 6865
Mc Lean, VA 22106
William Keyes, Exec. Officer
Ph: (703)442-7510

Description: Represents political interests of working-class and middle-class African-Americans. Does not lobby, but assists in the election of favorable candidates to Congress. Supports economic growth, traditional family values, and a strong national defense. **Founded:** 1984.

★101★
Black Psychiatrists of America
c/o Dr. Isaac Slaughter
2730 Adeline St.
Oakland, CA 94607
Dr. Isaac Slaughter, Exec.Off.
Ph: (510)465-1800

Description: Black psychiatrists, either in practice or training, united to promote black behavioral science and foster high quality psychiatric care for blacks and minority group members. Sponsors public information service. Bestows awards; maintains speakers' bureau and biographical archives; compiles statistics; conducts educational programs. **Founded:** 1968. **Members:** 550. **Regional Groups:** 10. **Publications:** BPA Quarterly. Journal.

★102★
Black Resources Information Coordinating Services
614 Howard Ave.
Tallahassee, FL 32304
Emily A. Copeland, Pres.
Ph: (904)576-7522

Description: Designed to solidify the various sources of information and research by and about minority groups in America and convert them into a coordinated information system by using bibliographic control, storage, retrieval, transfer, and dissemination. Focuses on information by and about Afro-Americans, but also includes other minorities. Acts as referral and consulting service; aids in genealogical research and archival management and organization. Offers bibliographic services and lecture demonstrations on Afro-American culture. Sponsors seminars, workshops, and institutes. Conducts national exhibit program, which serves as a source of exposure for new books, publications, and other media forms. Maintains library of over 8000 items, including cassettes, slides, microfiche, and microfilms. Provides abstracting, indexing, and advisory services to black studies programs and collections. **Founded:** 1972. **Members:** 670. **Publications:** Brics Bracs, quarterly. Journal. Media Showcase, annual. Minority Information Trade Annual. Newsletter, bimonthly. Also publishes Guide to Afro-American Resources.

★103★
Black Revolutionary War Patriots Foundation
1612 K St. NW, Ste. 1104
Washington, DC 20006
Maurice A. Barboza, Pres.
Ph: (202)452-1776
Fax: (202)728-0770

Also known as: The Patriots Foundation. **Description:** Raises private funds for the establishment of a memorial, in Washington, DC, to black patriots of the American Revolutionary War. **Budget:** $200,000 **Founded:** 1985. **Local Groups:** 1. **State Groups:** 2.

★104★
Black Rock Coalition
PO Box 1054, Cooper Sta.
New York, NY 10276
Beverly Jenkins, Exec. Officer
Ph: (212)713-5097

Description: Artists, musicians, writers, and supporters of alternative/black music. (Alternative/black music refers to popular musical styles, such as rock, that are usually not performed or recorded by black artists and musicians.) Works to foster change in the conventional operation and classification of black music and musicians within the entertainment industry. Seeks to counteract competition among musicians through networking programs and the sharing of resources. Opposes what the group terms the American "apartheid-oriented" rock circuit, which BRC feels perpetuates racism, commerical restrictions, and double standards within the music industry that may deter black artists from receiving the same musical freedom of expression and marketing privileges afforded white artists. Promotes, produces, and distributes alternative/black music and provides information, technical expertise, and performance and recording opportunities for "musically and politically progressive musicians." Also works to increase the visibility of black rock artists in music media and on college radio stations. Conducts seminars on all aspects of music, musical technology, and the entertainment industry. Offers concert promotion services. Plans to develop videotape recording opportunities for the archival documentation of cultural events. **Founded:** 1985. **Members:** 250. **Budget:** Less than $25,000. **Publications:** BRC Newsletter, monthly.

★105★
Black Silent Majority Committee of the U.S.A.
Box 5519
San Antonio, TX 78201
Clay Claiborne, Dir.
Ph: (210)340-2424
Fax: (210)340-3816

Description: Seeks to show the people of America and the world that there is a black majority in the U.S. which is patriotic and believes in saluting the flag, going to church, and paying taxes. Organizes Americans who do not want to be identified with black "radicals" and emphasizes the positive gains that blacks have made. Works throughout the U.S. and the world for better race relations. Opposes forced busing and supports prayer in public schools. **Founded:** 1970. **Members:** 70,000. **Publications:** The Crusader, quarterly. Newspaper. Newsletter, bimonthly. Also publishes booklets and brochures. **Formerly:** National Black Silent Majority Committee.

★106★
Black Stuntmen's Association
8949 W. 24th St.
Los Angeles, CA 90034
Eddie Smith, Pres.
Ph: (213)870-9020
Fax: (310)842-7182

Description: Men and women (ages 18 to 50) who are members of the Screen Actors Guild and the American Federation of Television and Radio Artists. Serves as an agency for stuntpeople in motion pictures and television. Conducts stunt performances at various local schools. Maintains library of television and motion picture films. Plans to operate school for black stuntpeople. Offers placement service. **Founded:** 1966. **Members:** 34.

★107★
Black Veterans for Social Justice
686 Fulton St.
Brooklyn, NY 11217
Job Mashariki, Pres.
Ph: (718)935-1116

Description: Black veterans of the military services. To aid black veterans in obtaining information concerning their rights, ways to upgrade a less-than-honorable discharge, and Veterans Administration benefits due them and their families. Seeks to prohibit discrimination against black veterans. Provides educational programs; facilitates veterans' sharing of skills acquired while in service. Services include counseling and community workshops on veteran issues and a program to provide services to veterans in local prisons. Assists veterans who have suffered from the effects of Agent Orange, an herbicide containing dioxin, used as a defoliant in Vietnam until 1969. Provides children's services; offers placement service; maintains speakers' bureau. **Founded:** 1979. **Formerly:** (1992) Black Veterans.

★108★
Black Women in Church and Society
c/o Interdenominational Theological Center
671 Beckwith St. SW
Atlanta, GA 30314
Jacquelyn Grant Ph.D., Dir.
Ph: (404)527-7740
Fax: (404)527-0901

Description: Women in ministry, both ordained and laity. Seeks to provide: structured activities and support systems for black women whose goals include participating in leadership roles in church and society; a platform for communication between laywomen and clergywomen. Conducts research into questions and issues pivotal to black women in church and society. Sponsors charitable programs and semiannual seminar; compiles statistics. Maintains a research/resource center and a library with subject matter pertaining to liberation and black theology, feminism, and womanist movements. **Founded:** 1982. **Computerized Services:** Mailing list. **Publications:** Black Women in Ministry, quadrennial. Directory.

★109★
Black Women in Publishing
PO Box 6275, F.D.R. Sta.
New York, NY 10150   Ph: (212)772-5951
Dolores Gordon, Pres.

Description: Designers, editors, financial analysts, freelancers, personnel directors, photographers, production managers, authors, entrepreneurs, and publicists within the print industry. A networking and support group whose purpose is to encourage minorities interested in all sectors of the print industry, including book, newspaper, and magazine publishing. Promotes the image of minorities working in all phases of the book, newspaper, and magazine industries; recognizes achievements of minorities in the media. Works for a free and responsible press. Facilitates the exchange of ideas and information among members, especially regarding career planning and job security. Keeps members informed about the publishing industry and their impact on it. Encourages and works to maintain high professional standards in publishing. Collaborates with other organizations in striving to improve the status of women and minorities. Sponsors lectures, panel discussions, seminars, workshops, radio talk shows, and other programs on topics such as computers in publishing, magazine publishing, trends in multicultural literature for children, career paths publishing, getting work published, starting a publishing firm, author readings, awards presentations, and women and stress. Organizes social events. Maintains biographical archives, placement service, and a resume bank in collaboration with major corporations. **Founded:** 1979. **Publications:** Interface, bimonthly.

★110★
Black Women Organized for Educational Development
518 17th St., Ste. 202   Ph: (510)763-9501
Oakland, CA 94612   Fax: (510)736-4327
Dezie Woods-Jones, Exec.Dir.

Description: Fosters self-sufficiency in and encourages empowerment of low-income and socially disadvantaged women by establishing and maintaining programs that improve their social and economic well-being. Sponsors mentor program for junior high-age young women in low-income urban areas; offers support groups, workshops, and seminars. Maintains Black Women's Resource Center, an information and referral service for African American women and youth. **Founded:** 1984. **Publications:** BWOED Newsletter, quarterly.

★111★
Black Women's Educational Alliance
6625 Greene St.
Philadelphia, PA 19119
Deidre Farmbey, Pres.

Description: Active and retired women in the field of education. Seeks a strong union among members in order to foster their intellectual and professional growth. Conducts public awareness programs to improve educational standards and delivery of educational services; works for equal opportunities for women. Bestows student scholarships and education and service awards; maintains speakers' bureau. Conducts instructional seminars and workshops. **Founded:** 1976. **Members:** 300. **Local Groups:** 2. **Publications:** BWEA Bulletin, periodic. BWEA Newsletter, semiannual.

★112★
Black Women's Roundtable on Voter Participation
1430 K St. NW, Ste. 401
Washington, DC 20011   Ph: (202)898-2220
Sonia R. Jarvis, Exec.Dir.

Description: A program of the National Coalition on Black Voter Participation. Black women's organizations committed to social justice and economic equity through increased participation in the political process. Organizes voter registration, education, and empowerment programs in the black community; emphasizes the importance of the women's vote. Seeks to: develop women's leadership skills through nonpartisan political participation; encourage black women's involvement in discussions concerning the influence of the women's vote in elections. Supports volunteer coalitions that work on voter registration, voter education, and get-out-the vote efforts. Conducts series of forums. **Budget:** $50,000. **Founded:** 1983.

★113★
Black World Foundation
PO Box 2869   Ph: (510)547-6633
Oakland, CA 94609   Fax: (510)547-6679
Robert Chrisman, Pres.

Description: Black persons united to develop and distribute black educational materials and to develop black cultural and political thought. Offers books in the areas of black literature, history, fiction, essays, political anaylsis, social science, poetry, and art. Maintains library. **Founded:** 1969. Subscribers: 10,000. **Publications:** The Black Scholar, bimonthly. Listing of Black Books in Print, annual. Also publishes books of poetry and on black sociology.

★114★
Blacks in Government
1820 11th St. NW
Washington, DC 20001-5015   Ph: (202)667-3280
Mr. Marion Bowden, Pres.

Description: Federal, state, or local government employees or retirees concerned with the present and future status of blacks in government. Develops training and other programs to enhance the liberty and sense of well-being of blacks in government. Offers seminars and workshops for professional and nonprofessional government employees. **Founded:** 1975. **Members:** 6000. **Local Groups:** 100. **Publications:** Blacks in Government–News, quarterly. Newsletter.

★115★
Blacks in Law Enforcement
256 E. McLemore Ave.   Ph: (901)774-1118
Memphis, TN 38106   Free: 800-533-4649
Clyde R. Venson, Dir.

Description: Blacks employed by law enforcement agencies in the U.S.; others interested in the history of blacks in U.S. law enforcement. Seeks to educate the public concerning the contributions made by blacks in the field of law enforcement. Documents the lives and achievements of the first blacks to participate in law enforcement in the U.S. Develops programs to improve the public image of law enforcement officers; has established a short-term training program for law enforcement officers. Provides children's services, including the operation of an animal farm. Operates library and hall of fame. Sponsors competitions; bestows scholarships and Distinguished Officer of the Year award. Compiles statistics; maintains speakers' bureau. **Founded:** 1986. **Members:** 500. **Budget:** $45,000. **Publications:** Blacks in Law Enforcement, annual. **Formerly:** (1988) Top Blacks in Law Enforcement.

★116★
Booker T. Washington Foundation
4324 Georgia Ave. NW
Washington, DC 20011   Ph: (202)882-7100
Charles E. Tate, Pres.

Description: Funded by federal agencies, foundations, and private corporations to provide policy research, technical assistance, and development and management expertise to minority entrepreneurs who are involved in business development. Maintains library in the areas of communications technology, media, community economic development, minority ownership, and business development. Presently inactive. **Founded:** 1967.

★117★
Campaign for Political Rights
201 Massachusetts Ave., NE, Rm. 316
Washington, DC 20002   Ph: (202)547-4705
Sue Sullivan, Exec.Dir.

Description: Serves as national network of committed people and religious, civil liberties, environmental, academic, foreign policy, disarmament, press, women's, Native American, black, and Latino organizations. Objectives are to end intelligence agency abuse at home and abroad; and to promote government accountability and access to information about government policies and actions. Provides educational materials and films, organizing assistance, press and publicity advice, and referral services for organizations. **Founded:** 1977. Board Members: 11. **Publications:** ALERT (news service), monthly. Organizing Notes (newsletter), 8/year. Also publishes Former Secrets (book on Freedom of Infomation Act), special reports, and guides. **Formerly:** Campaign to Stop Government Spying.

★118★
Caribbean Action Lobby
c/o Dr. Waldaba Stewart
391 Eastern Pky. Ph: (718)756-1300
Brooklyn, NY 11216 Fax: (718)756-8519
Dr. Waldaba Stewart, Pres.

Description: Caribbeans, Caribbean-Americans, and others interested in Caribbean issues. Seeks to educate Caribbean immigrants on subjects such as U.S. immigration laws, the U.S. government, and effective voting. Works to sensitize elected American officials to the needs of and issues affecting Caribbean immigrants. Activities include lobbing, issue education, workshops, and seminars. **Founded:** 1980. **Members:** 4000. **Publications:** Newsletter, monthly.

★119★
Caribbean American Intercultural Organization
305 Webster St. NW Ph: (202)829-7468
Washington, DC 20011 Fax: (202)842-0215
Helen Madison Kinard, Pres.

Description: Citizens of the Caribbean-American community in the Washington, DC metropolitan area. Purpose is to promote, encourage, and maintain intercultural relations between the various peoples of the Caribbean and the people of the U.S. Sponsors exhibitions, forums, and audiovisual educational programs. Conducts charitable programs. Presents awards to outstanding individuals of Caribbean ancestry who have made significant contributions to the development of the U.S., Caribbean, or Third World. Maintains speakers' bureau. **Founded:** 1958. **Members:** 170. **Publications:** Newsletter, quarterly.

★120★
Caribbean Studies Association
c/o Department of Social Sciences
Interamerican University of Puerto Rico
Call Box 5100 Ph: (809)264-1912
San German, PR 00683 Fax: (809)892-6350
Gilberto Arroyo, Sec.-Treas.

Description: Scholars and other professionals interested in Caribbean studies. Encourages, supports, and conducts professional, interdisciplinary research on the Caribbean; disseminates information about developments in the Caribbean. Presents the Annual Caribbean Review Award, in collaboration with Caribbean Review, to an individual who has made an outstanding contribution to Caribbean studies. Maintains biographical archives. **Founded:** 1974. **Members:** 850. **Budget:** $40,000. **Publications:** Caribbean Studies Newsletter, quarterly. Includes occasional Spanish texts, book notes, congress and conference news, research notes, commentaries on Caribbean current events, member news, and annual conference program. **Telecommunications Services:** Fax, (809)892-6350.

★121★
Catholic Interracial Council of New York
899 10th Ave.
New York, NY 10019 Ph: (212)237-8255
Hubert Johnson, Exec.Dir.

Description: Promotes interracial justice. Works in cooperation with local parishes and governmental and voluntary groups to combat bigotry and discrimination and to promote social justice for all racial, religious, and ethnic groups. Sponsors research, educational forums, workshops, and community action programs. Presents annual John LaFarge Memorial Award for Interracial Justice to community leaders and annual Hoey Award to community leaders who have worked to promote objectives of the council. Presents scholarship awards. Maintains speakers' bureau and library of 500 volumes. **Founded:** 1934. **Members:** 1600. **Budget:** $150,000. **Publications:** Interracial Review, quarterly. News, quarterly. Also publishes transcripts of forums, symposia, conferences, and workshops.

★122★
Catholic Negro-American Mission Board
2021 H St. NW Ph: (202)331-8544
Washington, DC 20006 Fax: (202)331-8544
Rev.Msgr. Paul A. Lenz, Exec.Dir.

Description: Supports Catholic sisters' teaching program among blacks. **Founded:** 1907. **Members:** 14,000. **Budget:** $310,000. **Publications:** Educating in Faith, quarterly. **Formerly:** (1970) Catholic Board for Mission Work Among the Colored People.

★123★
Center for Constitutional Rights
666 Broadway, 7th Fl. Ph: (212)614-6464
New York, NY 10012 Fax: (212)614-6499
Miriam Thompson, Exec.Dir.

Description: "To halt and reverse the steady erosion of civil liberties in the U.S." Works in areas such as abuse of the grand jury process, women's rights, civil rights, freedom of the press, racism, electronic surveillance, criminal trials, and affirmative action. Conducts the Ella Baker Student Program, the Movement Support Network, and in Mississippi, The Voting Rights Project. Sponsors training for law student interns. Maintains speakers' bureau. Distributes legal briefs. **Founded:** 1966. **Budget:** $1,800,000. **Publications:** Annual Report. Listing of litigation and educational programs of the center. **Formerly:** (1967) Civil Rights Legal Defense Fund; (1970) Law Center for Constitutional Rights.

★124★
Center for Democratic Renewal
PO Box 50469
Atlanta, GA 30302 Ph: (404)221-0025
Daniel Levitas, Exec.Dir.

Description: Advocates federal prosecution of the Ku Klux Klan and any groups or individuals involved in racist violence. Seeks to build public opposition to racist groups and their activities, and assist victims of bigoted violence. Works with trade unions, public officials, and religious, women's, civil rights, and grass roots organizations. Programs include education, research, victims' assistance, community organizing, leadership training, and public advocacy. Acts as a national clearinghouse for community-based response to hate group activities. Maintains network of lawyers and archive on far-right activities, individuals, and organizations; conducts seminars, specialized education programs, and research on trends in the far right; compiles data; maintains speakers' bureau. Constituencies: African Americans; Educators; Labor; Legal; Media; Minorities; Religious; Women; Youth. **Founded:** 1979. **Publications:** The Monitor, bimonthly. Reports on white supremacist efforts and activities. **Formerly:** (1985) National Anti-Klan Network.

★125★
Center for Sickle Cell Disease
2121 Georgia Ave., NW
Howard University
Washington, DC 20059 Ph: (202)636-7930
Roland B. Scott M.D., Dir.

Description: Seeks to foster education and research in sickle cell disease and to improve patient care. Holds scientific seminars and sickle cell "grand rounds." Conducts experimental research on antisickling agents and preservation through freezing of sickled blood cells. Operates the Mid-Atlantic Regional Counseling Program, in collaboration with 3 other clinics, to provide screening and counseling for couples "at risk" of having children with sickle cell disease and other hemoglobinopathies. Maintains speakers' bureau and 380 volume library. Provides children's services. Compiles statistics and bestows awards. **Founded:** 1972. **Budget:** Less than $25,000. **Publications:** Bibliography, periodic. Center for Sickle Cell Disease–Annual Report. **Formerly:** Center for Sickle Cell Anemia.

★126★
Center for the Study of Human Rights
1108 International Affairs Bldg.
Columbia University Ph: (212)854-2479
New York, NY 10027 Fax: (212)864-4847
Dr. J. Paul Martin, Exec.Dir.

Description: Academic advisers (23) and directors (11). Promotes teaching and scholarship in the field of human rights. Sponsors interdisciplinary human rights research. Offers advice, fellowships, and other assistance in conducting and financing such research; provides assistance in teaching and curriculum development. Operates library; offers consultation service, which provides information on human rights research, resources, and programs at other institutions. **Founded:** 1977. **Members:** 34. **Publications:** Annual Report. Center for the Study of Human Rights–Newsletter, quarterly. Includes bibliographies, calendar of events, course listings, and information on funding opportunities.

★127★
Center for Third World Organizing
3861 Martin Luther King Jr. Way
Oakland, CA 94609   Ph: (510)654-9601
Gary Delgado, Dir.

Description: Provides training, issue analyses, and research to low-income minority organizations including welfare, immigrant, and Native American rights groups. Monitors and reports on incidents of discrimination against people of color. Sponsors Minority Activist Apprenticeship Program, which works to develop minority organizers and leaders for minority communities. Sponsors seminars on issues affecting minorities. Maintains speakers' bureau; operates placement service. Compiles statistics. **Founded:** 1980. **Budget:** $1,000,000. **Local Groups:** 200. **Publications:** Directory of Church Funding Sources, periodic. Issue Pac, quarterly. Minority Trendsetter, quarterly. Also publishes Surviving America: What You're Entitled to and How to Get It, Images of Color: A Guide to Media from and for Asian, Black, Latino and Native American Communities, occasional papers series, guides, and manuals.

★128★
Center for Urban Black Studies
Graduate Theological Union
2465 LeConte Ave.
Berkeley, CA 94709   Ph: (510)841-8401
Rev. Dorsey O. Blake, Dir.

Description: Theological students and laypersons studying for the ministry; members of community groups. Provides seminarians and laypersons with resources "to respond to life in the urban community and to represent its oppressed minority people." Develops and offers courses, seminars, and other training programs dealing with issues of race, social justice, urban life, and the black religious experience. Initiates new ministries; develops and implements community service programs; counsels and assists black seminarians in placement and in obtaining and developing employment. Conducts workshops and seminars addressing racial justice, church and race, and urban ministry. **Founded:** 1969. **Publications:** none.

★129★
Center on Budget and Policy Priorities
777 N. Capitol St. NE, Ste. 705   Ph: (202)408-1080
Washington, DC 20002   Fax: (202)543-1915
Robert Greenstein, Dir.

Description: Promotes better public understanding of the impact of federal and state governmental spending policies and programs primarily affecting low and moderate income families and individuals; acts as resource center and information clearinghouse for the media, national and local organizations (including major church denominations), and individuals. Areas of research include national poverty trends, tax policy, housing affordability, effectiveness and funding for social programs, hunger and nutrition issues, unemployment, and minimum wage. Maintains library; compiles statistics. Conducts special studies on minorities and poverty. Organizes educational campaign concerning the Earned Income Tax Credit. **Founded:** 1981. **Budget:** $1,300,000. **Publications:** Women, Infants, and Children Newsletter, monthly. Also publishes fact sheets, articles, and reports, including: A Place to Call Home: The Crisis in Housing for the Poor, Poverty in Rural America: A National Overview, Making Work Pay: A New Agenda for Poverty Policies, Shortchanged: Recent Developments in Hispanic Poverty, Income, and Unemployment, Still Far From the Dream: Recent Developments in Black Poverty, Income, and Unemployment, Saving to Serve More: Ways to Reduce WIC Infant Formula Costs, and Holes in the Safety Net: Poverty Programs and Policies in the States.

★130★
Chi Delta Mu
c/o Henry Wineglass, R.Ph.
1012 10th St. NW
Washington, DC 20001   Ph: (202)842-1111
Henry Wineglass R.Ph., Sec.

Description: To improve relationships among physicians, dentists, and pharmacists so that they may better serve their respective communities. Maintains revolving loan funds; bestows awards. **Founded:** 1913. **Members:** 650. **Budget:** Less than $25,000. **Publications:** Dragon, annual. Newsletter, quarterly. Proceedings, annual.

★131★
Chi Eta Phi Sorority
3029 13th St. NW   Ph: (202)232-3858
Washington, DC 20009   Fax: (202)232-3858
Mary H. Morris R.N., Contact

Description: Professional sorority - registered and student nurses. Objectives are to: encourage continuing education; stimulate friendship among members; develop working relationships with other professional groups for the improvement and delivery of health care services. Sponsors leadership training seminars every two years and holds additional seminars at the local, regional, and national levels. Offers educational programs for entrance into nursing and allied health fields. Presents scholarships and other financial awards to assist students. Maintains health screening and consumer health education programs; volunteers assistance to senior citizens; sponsors recruitment and retention programs for minority students in nursing. Operates speakers' bureau on health education and biographical archives on African-American nurses. **Founded:** 1932. **Members:** 5000. **Computerized Services:** Databases; mailing lists. **Publications:** Chi Line, semiannual. Newsletter. Includes membership activities.

★132★
Children's Rights Project - ACLU
132 W. 43rd St., 6th Fl.
New York, NY 10036   Ph: (212)944-9800
Marcia R. Lowry, Dir.

Description: Is concerned with litigation, education, and public policy issues affecting families and children. **Founded:** 1973. **Formerly:** (1979) Juvenile Rights Project.

★133★
ChiME (Chemical Industry for Minorities in Engineering)
PO Box 1310   Ph: (302)886-3164
Wilmington, DE 19899-1310   Fax: (302)773-4745
Debbie Hartnett, Treas.

Description: Companies within the chemical industry. Promotes the growth of a cooperative chemical industry aimed at increasing the number of minorities within the chemical engineering profession. Goals are to: support other efforts to increase the number of minority engineers in the field; develop resources and materials specific to the needs of the chemical engineering industry; provide information to educational institutions, students, faculties, and the community on the challenges and opportunities within chemical engineering and the chemical industry; establish programs designed to attract and retain minority engineering students within the chemical engineering field; develop and maintain a working relationship with educational institutions, trade associations, engineering societies, government agencies, and others. **Founded:** 1975. **Members:** 25. **Publications:** Brochure.

★134★
Cities in Schools
401 Wythe St., Ste. 200   Ph: (703)519-8999
Alexandria, VA 22314   Fax: (703)519-7213
William E. Milliken, Pres.

Description: To promote an increase in attendance and grade improvement among underprivileged school children and thus enhance their opportunities for employment. Works to help cities and communities develop leadership cooperation among public and private sector institutions (including the school system, business community, and public and private social service agencies) in order to assist in the training and education of young people. Provides training and technical assistance through national and regional centers. Since initiated in Atlanta, GA, the CIS program has been duplicated in numerous cities throughout the U.S.. **Founded:** 1974. **Budget:** $6,100,000. **Regional Groups:** 5. **Publications:** Annual Report. Newsletter, quarterly. Also publishes technical manuals and brochure.

★135★
Citizens' Commission on Civil Rights
2000 M St. NW, Ste. 400   Ph: (202)659-5565
Washington, DC 20036   Fax: (202)293-2672
Dr. Arthur Flemming, Chm.

Description: Bipartisan former federal cabinet officials concerned with achieving the goal of equality of opportunity. Objectives are to: monitor the federal government's enforcement of laws barring discrimination on the basis of race, sex, religion, ethnic background, age, or handicap; foster public understanding of civil rights issues; formulate constructive policy recommendations. **Founded:** 1982. **Members:** 16. **Publications:** Lost Opportunities, One Nation Indivisible: The Civil Rights Challenge For the 1990s, Barriers to Registration and Voting: An Agenda for Reform, and reports on fair housing, busing and the Brown Decision, and affirmative action; provides press releases.

★136★
Citizens for a Better America
PO Box 356
Halifax, VA 24558   Ph: (804)476-7757
Cora Tucker, Pres.

Description: Churches and individuals united to create a better America by strengthening individual rights in the U.S. Serves as a public advocacy organization that lobbies for civil rights and environmental legislation. Conducts legal research in civil rights cases; provides research services to communities investigating issues such as fair housing and toxic waste disposal. Maintains placement and children's services; operates charitable program; bestows awards; compiles statistics. Sponsors annual Citizenship Day of Prayer. **Founded:** 1975. **Members:** 500. **Local Groups:** 5. **Publications:** Newsletter, monthly. Yearly Report. Also publishes special issue bulletins; has also published 10-Year Report.

★137★
Citizens for Public Action on Blood Pressure and Cholesterol
7200 Wisconsin Ave., Ste. 1002   Ph: (301)907-7790
Bethesda, MD 20814   Fax: (301)907-7792
Gerald Wilson, Dir.

Description: Public education and advocacy organization that seeks to instruct health policy officials, the medical profession, and individuals on the importance of public policy and funding efforts to lower blood pressure and cholesterol and prevent heart attacks and strokes. **Founded:** 1973. **Members:** 16,000. **Budget:** $500,000. Coalitions: 21. **Publications:** Cholesterol Blood Pressure Update, bimonthly. Newsletter covering current events, public services available, and publications. Includes research reports, legislative update, book reviews, and statistics. **Formerly:** (1989) Citizens for the Treatment of High Blood Pressure; (1991) Citizens for the Treatment of High Blood Pressure - for Public Action on Cholesterol.

★138★
City Kids Foundation
57 Leonard St.   Ph: (212)925-3320
New York, NY 10013   Fax: (212)925-0128
Laurie Elizabeth Meadoff, Pres.

Description: Designs and organizes youth initiative programs including: City Kids Coalition, which works with multiracial teenagers from schools and youth groups to organize projects and events; City Kids Speak, an annual event which provides a platform for young people to express themselves on youth issues; Developing the Manhattan Empire, a youth social and cultural center in Manhattan. Collaborates with professionals to provide social services and job training. Conducts workshops. Primary programs are currently conducted in the New York City area, but plans to expand activities internationally. **Founded:** 1984. **Budget:** $1,000,000. **Publications:** Monthly Letter. **Formerly:** (1989) Network International.

★139★
Co-Ette Club
2020 W. Chicago Blvd.
Detroit, MI 48206   Ph: (313)867-0880
Mary-Agnes Miller Davis, Founder & Chm.

Description: Teenage high school girls "outstanding in one or all of the following categories - Academic Scholarship, School and Community, Extra-Curriculars, Community Volunteer Service, and Leadership"; membership consists primarily of black girls, but is open to any girl; number of members limited to 35 per chapter. Helps members channel interests and become leaders in educational, cultural, and artistic activities on local and national levels; maintains speakers' bureau and museum. Offers placement services. Raises funds for United Negro College Fund and contributes to local charity and social service groups in each community. Founder of the Metropolitan Detroit Teen Conference Coalition. Offers John Fitzgerald Kennedy Memorial Award annually for distinguished humanitarian service or professional excellence. **Founded:** 1941. **Local Groups:** 35. **Publications:** Co-Ette Manual, annual. Co-Ette Souvenir Magazine, annual. Membership Directory, periodic. Newsletter, periodic.

★140★
Coalition of Black Trade Unionists
PO Box 73120
Washington, DC 20056-3120   Ph: (202)429-1203
William Lucy, Pres.

Description: Members of 76 labor unions united to maximize the strength and influence of black and minority workers in organized labor. Activities include voter registration and education, improvement of economic development, and employment opportunities for minority and poor workers. Sponsors regional seminars. **Founded:** 1972. **Local Groups:** 27. **Publications:** Bulletin, quarterly.

★141★
College Language Association
c/o Lucy C. Grigsby
Clark Atlanta University
James P. Brawley Dr. at Fair St. SW   Ph: (404)880-8524
Atlanta, GA 30314   Fax: (404)880-8222
Lucy C. Grigsby, Sec.

Description: Teachers of English and modern foreign languages, primarily in historically black colleges and universities. Presents CLA Award for scholarly publication; also sponsors creative writing award to students in member colleges. Maintains placement service; operates speakers' bureau. **Founded:** 1937. **Members:** 350. **Publications:** CLA Journal, quarterly. Covers English language and literature. **Formerly:** (1949) Association of Modern Language Teachers in Negro Colleges.

★142★
Commission for Racial Justice
475 Riverside Dr., Rm. 1948
New York, NY 10115   Ph: (212)870-2077
Rev.Dr. Benjamin F. Chavis Jr., Exec.Dir.

Description: A racial justice agency representing the 1.7 million members of the United Church of Christ. Promotes human rights programs and strategies to foster racial justice in black, Third World, and other minority communities. **Founded:** 1963. **Budget:** $1,200,000. **Publications:** Civil Rights Journal, weekly. Commission News, 3/year. Also publishes The Black Family: An Afro-Centric Perspective and Like A Ripple On A Pond: Crisis, Challenge, Change (a resource book on the plight of displaced homemakers).

★143★
Commission on U.S.-African Relations
c/o International Center for Development
    Policy
731 8th St. SE   Ph: (202)547-3800
Washington, DC 20003   Fax: (202)546-4784
Lindsay G. Mattison, Exec.Dir.

Description: Businessmen, church officials, former government officials, scholars, and others. Primarily a research and educational commission of the International Center for Development Policy. Provides resources and information to the president, congressional representatives, and other officials on U.S.-African issues. Members, referred to as Commissioners, pool their knowledge and expertise in the preparation of reports for Congress, the media, and other interested parties. Encourages greater participation of Americans in African issues. Maintains library consisting of current publications, congressional reports, government documents, and reports from other institutions concerning African affairs. **Founded:** 1983. **Members:** 105. **Budget:** $50,000. **Publications:** Briefings and Reports, periodic.

★144★
Committee of Concerned Africans
PO Box 1892
Trenton, NJ 08608   Ph: (609)771-1666
Kassahun Checole, Coordinator

Description: Scholars, students, and other interested volunteers. Monitors violations of human rights in Africa. Publicizes issues and developments regarding such violations; petitions states and organizations regarding the conditions of peoples or individuals whose human rights are being violated; conducts seminars and teach-ins. **Founded:** 1980. **Members:** 100. **Publications:** Working Papers, monthly.

★145★
Conference of Minority Public Administrators
1120 G St. NW, Ste. 700
Washington, DC 20005   Ph: (202)393-7878
John P. Thomas, Exec.Dir.

Description: A section within the American Society for Public Administration. Members of ASPA who belong to a minority group or are interested in the promotion of minorities within public administration. Works to improve government and advance excellence in public service. **Founded:** 1971. **Members:** 700. **Publications:** COMPA Spectrum, quarterly.

★146★
Conference of Prince Hall Grand Masters
4311 Portland Ave. S.   Ph: (612)825-2474
Minneapolis, MN 55407   Fax: (612)758-5000
Morris Miller, Steering Comm.Chm.

Description: Black fraternal order united to coordinate efforts of member groups in providing leadership in and formulating goals for the black community. Sponsors seminars and workshops to train progressive leaders. Operates charitable program; maintains biographical archives; sponsors competitions and bestows awards. **Founded:** 1919. **Members:** 300,000. **State Groups:** 44. **Publications:** The Conservators, quarterly. Prince Hall Masonic Directory, biennial. Local lodges publish newsletters and proceedings.

★147★
Congress of National Black Churches
1225 I St. NW, Ste. 750   Ph: (202)371-1091
Washington, DC 20005-3914   Fax: (202)371-0908
H. Michael Lemmons, Exec.Dir.

Description: Major black denominations in the U.S. and Africa. Seeks to find answers to problems that confront blacks in the U.S. and Africa, including economic development, family and social support, housing, unemployment, education, and foreign relations. Focus is on religious education and evangelism. Conducts theological education programs and an educational program for nondegreed ministers; also conducts banking, insurance, and purchasing programs for church administrations. Compiles statistics. Plans to sponsor research programs. **Founded:** 1978. **Members:** 8. MD $10,000/year for denomination. **Budget:** $1,500,000. **Publications:** Newsletter, quarterly.

★148★
Congress of Racial Equality
1457 Flatbush Ave.
Brooklyn, NY 11210   Ph: (718)434-3580
Roy Innis, Chm.

Description: Persons of African ancestry. Black nationalist organization whose philosophy is based on the tenets of Marcus Garvey (1887-1940), Jamaican-born black nationalist leader, and his progenitors. Looks to Africa, the fatherland, for inspiration; seeks the right of black people to govern themselves in those areas which

are demographically and geographically defined as theirs. Compiles statistics; engages in research. Maintains placement service, charitable program, and speakers' bureau; bestows awards. Sponsors CORE Community School, a private alternative school for grades one through eight in the Bronx, NY and Memphis, TN. **Founded:** 1942. **Budget:** $750,000. **Regional Groups:** 5. **Local Groups:** 116. **State Groups:** 39. **Publications:** CORE Magazine, quarterly. The Correspondent, monthly. Newsletter. Equal Opportunity Employment Journal, monthly. Also publishes Population Studies and Profiles in Black.

★149★
Congressional Black Associates
1504 Longworth
Washington, DC 20515   Ph: (202)225-5865
Samuel E. Thornton III, Pres.

Description: Black congressional staff members. Provides information on the operations of the federal government to members and the black community; fosters contacts among members and the community. Works to enhance the social, political, and economic status of all people, but concentrates on the black experience in America. Organizes political education seminars; maintains placement service. **Founded:** 1979. **Publications:** CBA Newsnotes, periodic. News from Congressional Black Associates, quarterly. **Formerly:** Pendulum.

★150★
Cooperative Assistance Fund
5335 Wisconsin Ave., Ste. 440   Ph: (202)833-8543
Washington, DC 20015   Fax: (202)833-1432
Shelley M. Metz-Galloway, Exec.VP

Description: Foundations and charitable organizations. Purpose is to use private investment capital to support the economic development of minority and low-income communities. Goal is to reduce poverty and dependence by stimulating economic development. Provides the opportunity for organizations to work together to address the unfulfilled needs of these communities. Pools funds from foundations and other investors to obtain resources for equity-type program related investments (PRI). Provides PRI services such as evaluating proposals, structuring financing, and monitoring results. Conducts research on developing means of channeling capital into low-income areas. **Founded:** 1968. **Members:** 12. **Budget:** $469,000. **Publications:** Annual Report. Also publishes 20 Years: A Report from the Cooperative Assistance Fund.

★151★
Council for a Black Economic Agenda
1367 Connecticut Ave. NW
Washington, DC 20036   Ph: (202)331-1103
Robert L. Woodson Sr., Pres.

Description: Dedicated to advancing the economic self-sufficiency of black Americans. Works to reverse the dependence of many blacks on government programs; advocates strategies based on a spirit of free enterprise and individual initiative. Encourages full use of the black community's own resources for selfhelp and development. Goals include: financial incentives for development of areas with vacant or underused property; legislation allowing tax write-offs for investments in small businesses that are in distressed areas; a program of underwriting rehabilitation, ownership, and management of public housing by residents' organizations; authorization for black churches and other neighborhood institutions to arrange adoptions of those children presently within the government's foster care system; expanded educational choice for low-income persons; an increase in work incentives for poor families. The latter goal, in the council's view, would be achieved by: providing affordable day-care for children of working parents; boosting the earned income tax credit and the income tax exemption for dependents; allowing unemployment compensation and other government payments to be used for education, job training, or self-employment. **Founded:** 1984.

★152★
Council for African American Progress
PO Box 946
Little Rock, AR 72203-0946   Ph: (501)376-7415
Wayne E.X. Burt, Chief Elder

Description: Fosters an appreciation and respect for African American culture and heritage by encouraging African Americans to participate in educational, cultural, social, political, economic, and drug education and prevention issues. Current focus is on equity in education including the concept of multi-cultural curriculums. Offers courses through the Institute of African American Studies and Programs. Promotes celebration of African holidays including Kwanzaa and African Liberation Day. Plans to maintain library. Group is currently based in Little Rock, AR but plans to develop national membership.

★153★
Council for Alternatives to Stereotyping in Entertainment
139 Corson Ave.
Staten Island, NY 10301   Ph: (718)720-5378
Michael Johnson, Sec.

Description: Individuals in the arts and entertainment industry. Seeks to educate the public on the widespread, undesirable effects inflicted upon the entertainment industry by stereotyping. Disseminates information on self-image, reality perception, and receptivity to accurate performance feedback. Maintains speakers' bureau and 1000 volume library. **Founded:** 1982. **Members:** 25. **Publications:** Case Cares, quarterly.

★154★
Council of Black Architectural Schools
Tuskegee Institute
Dept. of Architecture
Tuskegee, AL 36088   Ph: (205)727-8330
Major L. Holland, Coordinator

Description: One faculty member and one student from each of seven schools of architecture united for collective effort in advancing architectural programs and funding for predominantly black schools of architecture. **Founded:** 1969. **Local Groups:** 7. **Members:** 14.

★155★
Council of 1890 College Presidents
Langston University   Ph: (405)466-3202
Langston, OK 73050   Fax: (405)466-3461
Dr. William B. DeLauder, Chm.

Description: Presidents and chancellors of land-grant institutions attended predominantly by blacks. (Land-grant institutions were established by an act of Congress in 1890). **Founded:** 1913. **Formerly:** (1955) Conference of Presidents of Negro Land Grant Colleges; (1979) Council on Cooperative College Projects. **Members:** 18.

★156★
Council of Masajid of United States
99 Woodview Dr.   Ph: (908)679-8617
Old Bridge, NJ 08857   Fax: (908)679-1260
Dawud Assad, Pres.

Description: Mosques or clergy who lead prayers at mosques. Promotes better relations and understanding between Muslims and non-Muslims. Assists in obtaining furniture, building facilities, and annexes for mosques. Administers the Association of Muslim American Lawyers. Offers children's educational programs in history, language, and religion of Islamic countries; sponsors semiannual pilgrimage training session. Conducts charitable programs; operates speakers' bureau. **Founded:** 1978. **Members:** 206. **Budget:** $75,000. **Local Groups:** 650. **Publications:** Council of Masajid Newsletter, quarterly. Dialog-Interfaith, 10/year. Also publishes circulars and handouts; has published directory.

★157★
Council of the Great City Schools
1413 K St. NW, Ste. 400
Washington, DC 20005   Ph: (202)371-0163
Michael D. Casserly, Exec.Dir.

Description: Large city school districts. Conducts studies of problems shared by urban schools; coordinates projects designed to provide solutions to these problems; uses the findings and recommendations of studies for the improvement of education in the great cities. Provides informational support for legislative activities. Conducts seminars, workshops, and special projects to provide forum for members to share successful projects and to learn of new programs. Has studied: the educational needs of urban children exposed to the effects of discrimination; school financing; teacher preparation for urban schools; more functional approaches to outmoded urban schools; current status and needs in the areas of testing and technology. Bestows annual Richard R. Green Award to member superintendent or school board member who best represents the group's ideals and commitments. **Founded:** 1961. **Members:** 45. **Publications:** Council Directory, annual. Roster of Board of Directors, periodic. Legislative Activity Report, biweekly. Newsletter. Urban Educator, monthly. Newsletter. Also publishes special reports. **Formerly:** Research Council of the Great Cities Program for School Improvement.

★158★
Council on Career Development for Minorities
1341 W. Mockingbird Ln., Ste. 412-E   Ph: (214)631-3677
Dallas, TX 75247   Fax: (214)905-2046
Verna Green Bennett, Chair

Description: Works to heighten the awareness and employability of African American, Hispanic American, and Native American college students and to improve career counseling and referral services offered to them. Provides programs to help minority students improve test-taking and learning skills. Promotes the inclusion of career education into college curricula and the establishment of career counseling and placement services. Conducts consultative visits by teams of specialists who evaluate the needs of a given institution and make recommendations for the creation or improvement of counseling and placement services. Serves as a consultant to colleges involving government grants. Sponsors training activities such as annual institute for new personnel, semiannual career services institute, and secretarial development workshops. Also provides professional development programs that offer training in techniques and theory of career development and current labor market and employment trends. Conducts Corporate Orientation Program which provides sophomore-level minority students with the opportunity to study actual business activities and the factors that affect their employability and chances for promotion in the corporate business world. Offers workshops for college presidents from historically black colleges to improve awareness of the role and importance of career counseling and placement on the college campus. Also offers consultations to advise employers on policies, practices, and strategies involving the recruitment of college-trained minorities; provides training for recruiting personnel on minority interviewing techniques. Sends association representatives to meetings of similar organizations. Maintains Julius A. Thomas Fellowship Program to grant minority students the opportunity for graduate studies; awards one or two fellowship grants annually. **Founded:** 1964. **Budget:** $350,000. **Computerized Services:** Database on historically black colleges and universities and other educational institutions with large concentrations of minority students. **Publications:** CCDM Minority Student Recruitment Guide, biennial. Lists minority fraternities, sororities, honor societies, and professional organizations. Includes enrollment statistics. **Formerly:** (1984) College Placement Services.

★159★
Council on Interracial Books for Children, Inc.
1841 Broadway, Rm. 608
New York, NY 10023   Ph: (212)757-5339
Melba Johnson Kgositsile, Exec.Dir.

Description: Promotes children's books and other learning materials that are free of bias based on race, sex, age, or physical disability. Reviews new children's books, television programs, and films; conducts studies and seminars. Develops criteria enabling teachers to identify and counteract racism and sexism in classroom materials. Administers the Racism and Sexism Resource Center for Educators, which develops and disseminates antiracist, antisexist teaching materials, books, pamphlets, lesson plans, fact sheets, and audiovisual materials. **Founded:** 1965. Sponsors: 26. Directors: 13. **Computerized Services:** Mailing list. **Publications:** Interracial Books for Children Bulletin, 8/year. Newsletter; includes book reviews, calendar of events, and research updates.

★160★
Council on Legal Education Opportunity
1800 M St. NW, Ste. 160 South
Washington, DC 20036   Ph: (202)785-4840
Denise W. Purdie, Dir.

Description: Federally funded program that assists economically and educationally disadvantaged students gain entrance to American Bar Association approved law schools. Sponsors six-week summer institutes for selected college graduates and provides a $2200 annual living stipend to those certified summer institute graduates who continue in law school. **Budget:** $1,950,000. **Founded:** 1968.

★161★
Council on Southern Africa
Box 5150
Durango, CO 81301   Ph: (303)259-4100
Ms. Don McAlvany, Contact

Description: Investors, academics, conservatives, and professionals united to objectively assess and educate Americans on the geopolitical events in southern Africa and the rest of the continent, and its strategic and economic significance to the West. Maintains library of 2000 volumes on history, the military, gold mining, politics, warfare, and international affairs. Conducts educational tours to southern Africa; sponsors seminars. **Founded:** 1974. **Formerly:** (1984) Americans Concerned about Southern Africa. **Members:** 5000.

★162★
Delta Sigma Theta
1707 New Hampshire Ave. NW   Ph: (202)986-2400
Washington, DC 20009   Fax: (202)986-2513
Roseline McKinney, Exec.Dir.

Description: Public service sorority of Black women. Maintains Delta Research and Educational Foundation. **Founded:** 1913. **Members:** 175,000. **Budget:** $2,000,000. **Regional Groups:** 7. Active Chapters: 760. **Publications:** The Delta, semiannual. Journal.

★163★
Democratic Council on Ethnic Americans
430 S. Capitol St., SE
Washington, DC 20003   Ph: (202)863-8027
Seth Levin, Exec.Dir.

Description: Works to enhance the political participation and visibility of all ethnic Americans in the processes, projects, and decisions of the Democratic party. Promotes the full participation of ethnic American Democrats in Democratic party activities. Develops, articulates, and advocates issues that concern many ethnic American communities. Coordinates a national network of ethnic American Democrats which is neighborhood-based, that utilizes multilingual press, and other local media. Supports the election and appointment of candidates for national, state, and local offices who have demonstrated commitment to the goals of the council. **Founded:** 1983. **Publications:** Democratic Ethnic Calendar, annual. Ethnic Council Update, quarterly.

★164★
Department of Civil Rights, AFL-CIO
815 16th St. NW
Washington, DC 20006   Ph: (202)637-5270
Richard Womack, Dir.

Description: Staff arm AFL-CIO Civil Rights Committee. Serves as official liaison with women's and civil rights organizations and government agencies working in the field of equal opportunity; helps to implement state and federal laws and AFL-CIO civil rights policies; aids affiliates in the development of affirmative programs to expand opportunities for minorities and women; prepares and disseminates special materials on civil rights; speaks at union and civil rights institutes, conferences, and conventions; helps affiliates resolve complaints involving unions under Title VII of the 1964 Civil Rights

Act and Executive Order 11246. **Founded:** 1955. **Publications:** AFL-CIO and Civil Rights, biennial.

★165★
Detroit Jazz Center
2628 Webb
Detroit, MI 48206
Sam Sanders, Exec.Dir.

Description: Jazz artists, composers, educators, historians, critics, broadcasters, and supporters united to create a multipurpose clearinghouse for jazz. Components include: Professional Artists Program, which will provide management consulting services to the jazz musician; Jazz Studies Program, which consolidates existing jazz instruction and educational programs; Detroit Jazz Archive, which will provide an institutional approach to the archival, historical, research, and exhibition needs of the jazz and African-American music community; Creative and Administrative Services Program, which will provide concert production, recording, videotaping, and community arts consulting services. **Founded:** 1973. **Members:** 185. **Publications:** Detroit Jazz Center Calendar, annual. World Stage, monthly. Newsletter. Also publishes Jazz Space Detroit: Photographs of Black Music, Jazz and Dance. Jazz Hot Line, and other support services. Maintains archives of 500 original tape recordings and 200 volumes. **Formerly:** (1980) Detroit Jazz Center/Jazz Research Institute.

★166★
Duncan Black Macdonald Center for the Study of Islam and Christian/Muslim Relations
c/o Hartford Seminary
77 Sherman St.   Ph: (203)232-4451
Hartford, CT 06105   Fax: (203)236-8570
David A. Kerr, Dir.

Description: Serves as an educational center that seeks increased understanding of Islam and improved relations between Christians and Muslims. Sponsors a national outreach program that provides informational materials and faculty lecturers to churches, colleges and universities, private organizations, and other groups. Maintains biographical archives and library of 40,000 volumes of Arabic and Islamic source materials. Conducts research and conferences; operates speakers' bureau; compiles statistics. Offers masters of arts program in religious studies, with a concentration in Christian-Muslim relations. Center is named for Duncan Black Macdonald (1863-1943), a theologian and Christian missionary interested in Islamic studies. **Founded:** 1972. **Publications:** The Muslim World, quarterly. Journal. Also publishes bibliographies.

★167★
Earl Warren Legal Training Program
99 Hudson St., Ste. 1600
New York, NY 10013   Ph: (212)219-1900
G. Michael Bagley, Exec.Dir.

Description: Special project of the NAACP Legal Defense and Educational Fund. Primary goal is to increase the number of practicing black lawyers in the U.S. Provides law scholarship aid (limited by available funds) to academically qualified entering students in need for the full three years of law school. Conducts one or more Lawyers Training Institutes each year, which are attended by both experienced and young minority lawyers. Seeks to retain a close personal and professional relationship with program graduates. Offers program on public interest law. Bestows awards. **Founded:** 1972.

★168★
EDGES Group
Amerada Hess Corp.
1 Hess Plz.
Woodbridge, NJ 07095   Ph: (908)750-6408
Walter Vertreace, Pres.

Description: Entrepreneurs and management personnel. Membership and activities are concentrated in New York, New Jersey, Connecticut, and Washington, DC, but the group plans to expand nationally. Facilitates the entry of blacks into the private sector, government, and industry in management positions, and introduces black vendors and suppliers of goods and services into the mainstream of American business. Focuses on issues of affirmative action and urban and community affairs. Bestows Ruth

Allen King Excalibur Award; offers scholarships. EDGES stands for employment, dissemination of information, group development, economic awareness, and solving of problems. **Founded:** 1969. **Members:** 115. **Publications:** Voice of EDGES, quarterly. Newsletter.

★169★
Episcopal Churchpeople for a Free Southern Africa
339 Lafayette St.
New York, NY 10012   Ph: (212)477-0066
William Johnston, Pres.

Description: Episcopalian group united to help strengthen those who witness for freedom and equality. "Seeks to support and succor those who suffer from racist totalitarianism in South Africa and Namibia; to inform Americans of the violent and repressive nature of the regimes of those countries; and to help prepare and guide Americans as southern Africa moves toward drastic changes which threaten to draw the United States into standing on the wrong side of history." **Founded:** 1956. **Publications:** Newsletter, periodic. **Formerly:** (1985) Episcopal Churchmen for South Africa.

★170★
Episcopal Commission for Black Ministries
c/o Episcopal Church   Ph: (212)867-8400
815 2nd Ave.   Fax: (212)949-6781
New York, NY 10017   Free: 800-334-7626
Rev. Canon Harold Lewis, Chm.

Description: Black members of the Episcopal church representing geographically diverse dioceses, including one diocese outside of the U.S. Works to strengthen the witness of black Episcopalians in the church through programs that include parish and clergy development, scholarships and grants, and international relations. Provides financial assistance and consultations to parishes and church organizations. Compiles statistics; holds workshops. A commission of the Episcopal church. **Founded:** 1973. **Members:** 15. **Publications:** Directory of Black Clergy in the Epicopal Church, annual. Linkage, 3/year. Newsletter. Has produced Black Ministries in the Episcopal Church (film).

★171★
Equal Employment Advisory Council
1015 15th St. NW, Ste. 1220
Washington, DC 20005   Ph: (202)789-8650
Jeffrey A. Norris, Pres.

Description: Principal attorneys and personnel officers representing companies and trade associations. Promotes and presents the mutual interests of employers and the public regarding affirmative action and equal employment opportunity practices. Sponsors equal employment training courses and seminars. **Founded:** 1976.

★172★
Equal Rights Congress
4167 S. Normandy Ave.
Los Angeles, CA 90037   Ph: (213)291-1092
Nacho Gonzalez, Exec.Dir.

Description: National minority organizations united to struggle for equality of all people who have been discriminated against because of nationality, color, religion, sex, or economic status. Conducts educational program and seminars; provides training and technical assistance for organizing; maintains speakers' bureau and biographical archives; compiles statistics; sponsors competitions. **Founded:** 1976. **Budget:** Less than $25,000. **Regional Groups:** 2. **Local Groups:** 35. **Publications:** Equal Rights Advocate, bimonthly. Southern Advocate, bimonthly. Also publishes a series of pamphlets.

★173★
Eta Phi Beta
c/o Elizabeth Anderson
1724 Mohawk Blvd.
Tulsa, OK 74110   Ph: (918)425-8612
Elizabeth Anderson, Pres.

Description: Professional sorority - business. Conducts national projects concerning retarded citizens and retarded children. Presents scholarships and grants. Conducts leadership and career programs and seminars; sponsors competitions. Operates speakers' bureau; provides children's services; maintains charitable program;

bestows awards. **Founded:** 1942. **Members:** 8000. **Budget:** Less than $25,000. **Regional Groups:** 6. Active Chapters: 85. **Publications:** Beeline, semiannual. Membership Directory, biennial. News, quarterly.

★174★
Ethiopian Community Mutual Assistance Association
c/o Fetene Hailu
554 W. 114th St., Ste. 2R
New York, NY 10025   Ph: (212)627-8358
Fetene Hailu, Pres.

Description: Individuals of Ethiopian descent; members reside primarily in New York City metropolitan area. To advance the economic and social welfare of Ethiopians living in the U.S. Identifies the needs of the Ethiopian community, particularly regarding immigration and civil rights, and provides appropriate assistance. Works to strengthen communication among Ethiopians; aims to preserve Ethiopian culture as a source of historical identity; promotes understanding between Ethiopians and non-Ethiopians. Operates refugee assistance project that provides newly-arrived Ethiopians refugees or migrants with access to various educational, health, and other facilities; also offers overall orientation, guidance, and job placement assistance. Conducts a community-wide educational/information program with a view to hastening the acculturation and social adjustment efforts of members. Maintains museum. Plans to establish: cultural/educational center; emergency aid fund; job data bank; referral system. **Founded:** 1981. **Members:** 500.

★175★
Ethnic Anonymous
c/o F.J. Nubee
1631 Belmont Ave., No. 107
Seattle, WA 98122   Ph: (206)325-8091
Ms. Freedom J. Nubee, Exec.Dir.

Description: Self-help group patterned after Alcoholics Anonymous World Services programs. Applies AA's 12-step program to individuals "whose common problem is an inability to view the self and others as equals and to maintain functional lives." Conducts research and educational programs. Maintains speakers' bureau. Plans to hold periodic meetings. **Founded:** 1990. **Publications:** Ethnic Anonymous Newsletter, quarterly. Also publishes Development Guidelines (training manual).

★176★
Ethnic Cultural Preservation Council
6500 S. Pulaski Rd.
Chicago, IL 60629   Ph: (312)582-5143
Stanley Balzekas Jr., Dir.

Also known as: Association of North American Museums, Libraries, Archives, Cultural Centers, and Fraternal Organizations. **Description:** Membership includes North American ethnic museums, other museums, historical societies, libraries, archives, fraternal organizations, universities, university libraries, and cultural centers. Functions as vehicle for other ethnic and nonethnic groups to become viable art and education centers in their communities; aids in the exchange of ideas and helps to facilitate development of arts and humanities programs in other institutions. Provides information on grants; conducts cultural/artistic workshops; disseminates information on ethnic activities to other individuals and institutions. Offers referrals to information on artists, ethnic groups, and institutions. Sponsors seminars and exhibits. Operates on a national level, with primary concentration in Illinois, Indiana, Wisconsin, and Michigan. **Founded:** 1977. **Members:** 100.

★177★
Ethnic Employees of the Library of Congress
6100 Eastview St.
Bethesda, MD 20817   Ph: (301)229-6366
George E. Perry, Pres.

Description: Ethnic and racial minority employees and majority employees of the Library of Congress. Objectives are to promote and strengthen brotherhood among ethnic employees and ethnic members of society, and to ensure equal employment opportunities in the Library of Congress and elsewhere. Monitors the Library of Congress with regard to its policies and practices affecting minority and majority employees through the American Black and Ethnic

Helsinki Monitoring Group made up of leadership from EELC and Black Employees of the Library of Congress. Testifies annually before Congress; compiles statistics; provides statistical background material for court litigation; assists attorneys defending employees in racial, ethnic, and sex discrimination cases. Maintains library containing congressional correspondence, drafts, testimony, and labor management materials. Conducts research program on Library of Congress budget. **Founded:** 1973. **Publications:** Aletheia (in conjunction with the ABEHMG and BELC), periodic.

★178★
Ethnic Materials and Information Exchange Round Table
c/o American Library Association
Office for Library Outreach Services   Ph: (312)280-4295
50 E. Huron   Fax: (312)280-3256
Chicago, IL 60611   Free: 800-545-2433
Patricia F. Beilke, Chm.

Description: Former members of the Social Responsibilities Round Table of the American Library Association. To exchange information about minority materials and library services for minority groups in the U.S. Conducts educational programs with a focus on multicultural librarianship. Maintains 2000-volume library at Queens College of ethnic materials, including directories, trade books, and filmstrips. **Founded:** 1971. **Members:** 700. MD $10; $15 for institutional membership. **Budget:** Less than $25,000. **Publications:** EMIE Bulletin, quarterly. **Formerly:** (1983) Ethnic Materials Information Exchange Task Force.

★179★
Executive Leadership Council
444 N. Capitol St.
Washington, DC 20001   Ph: (202)783-6339
Mannie L. Jackson, Pres.

Description: Provides Black executives with a network and leadership forum. Encourages achievement in business, economic and public policies for the Black community and corporations. Conducts educational programs; bestows awards. **Founded:** 1986. **Publications:** Newsletter, periodic.

★180★
Federation of Islamic Associations in the U.S. and Canada
25351 Five Mile Rd.   Ph: (313)534-3295
Redford, MI 48239   Fax: (313)534-1474
Nihad Hamed, Sec.Gen.

Description: Religious, political, social, and educational organization that acts as an umbrella for Muslim groups in the U.S. and Canada. Objectives are to: defend the human rights of Muslims and all oppressed people through democratic, political means; promote the spirit, ethics, philosophy, and culture of Muslim heritage; answer questions and correct misconceptions about Islam; promote friendly relations between Muslims and non-Muslims of North America. Sponsors seminars on religious affairs; conducts charitable program, specialized education, and youth programs; bestows college scholarships; distributes literature to schools, universities, and libraries. Maintains 10,000 volume library of books on Middle East religion, politics, and arts. Offers placement **Founded:** 1951. **Members:** 300,000. **Budget:** $125,000. **Publications:** Books and press releases.

★181★
Federation of Masons of the World
1017 E. 11th St.
Austin, TX 78702   Ph: (512)477-5380
M. J. Anderson Sr., Bd.Chm.

Description: Masonic jurisdictions in 22 countries. Bestows awards. **Budget:** $105,000. **Founded:** 1958. **Members:** 300,000. **Regional Groups:** 38.

★182★
Federation of Southern Cooperatives and Land Assistance Fund
100 Edgewood Ave. NE, Ste. 814
Atlanta, GA 30303   Ph: (404)524-6882
Ralph Page, Exec.Dir.

Description: Cooperative associations chartered or doing business in the 17 southern states or the District of Columbia. Objectives are to assist people in building community-owned enterprises so they can control their own livelihood and to create housing, health care, and educational programs to complement economic development. Aids in the retention, acquisition, and development of black land holdings. Sponsors training programs in membership education, board responsibilities, management, and bookkeeping. Makes available to members full-time marketing specialists in both agricultural and handicraft production; also offers technical assistance in areas of accounting, establishing credit unions, consumer education, research in co-op expansion, market and product development, and improvement of production techniques. Provides legal, technical, and limited financial assistance to black farmers and landowners throughout the Southeast. Operates the FSC Rural Training and Research Center in Sumter County, AL. Has established the "Forty Acres and a Mule" endowment fund for educational and social programs that have the potential to be self-supporting. Provides educational materials to member cooperatives. **Founded:** 1985. **Members:** 30,000. **Budget:** $850,000. **State Groups:** 9. **Publications:** Newsletter, quarterly.

★183★
Florence Ballard Fan Club
PO Box 36A02
Los Angeles, CA 90036   Ph: (213)656-7745
Alan K. White, Pres.

Description: Music fans and collectors. Purpose is to serve as a living memorial to Florence Ballard (1943-76). (Ballard was a member of the original pop/soul trio the Supremes, which also included Diana Ross (1944-) and Mary Wilson (1944-), and who recorded a string of hits in the 1960s and early '70s. Ballard was replaced by Cindy Birdsong (1939-) in 1967 and then pursued a solo recording career.) Seeks to: keep Ballard's memory alive in a positive light; honor Ballard's musical contributions and achievements; conduct research and disseminate information concerning Ballard's life and career; collect memorabilia related to Ballard and the original Supremes. Awards the Florence Ballard Scholarship annually to needy college students pursuing degrees in performing arts in accredited 4-year colleges and universities. **Founded:** 1985. **Members:** 275. **Publications:** Florence Ballard, quarterly. Newsletter; contains photographs, clippings, essays, and book and music reviews pertaining to Ballard.

★184★
Foundation for Research in the Afro-American Creative Arts
PO Drawer I
Cambria Heights, NY 11411
Prof. Joseph Southern, Pres.

Description: Promotes research into the Afro-American creative arts including music, theatre, and dance. Maintains small library on black music and history, including 15 taped oral histories of black musicians. **Founded:** 1971. **Members:** 1000. **Budget:** $45,000. **Publications:** Has published The Black Perspective in Music, annual. Journal. Back copies available for years 1973-1990.

★185★
Frederick Douglass Memorial and Historical Association
c/o Mary E.C. Gregory
10594 Twin Rivers Rd., Apt. E-1
Columbia, MD 21044   Ph: (410)854-2938
Mary E. C. Gregory, Pres. Emeritus

Description: Chartered by Congress and administered by the National Park Service, U. S. Department of the Interior. Gives daily guided tours of the Frederick Douglass Memorial Home to inform visitors of how Douglass (1817-95) lived and of his contributions to the struggle for liberty, brotherhood, and citizenship. Maintains Douglass's personal library. Sponsors competitions; bestows awards; operates speakers' bureau. **Founded:** 1900. **Budget:** Less than $25,000. **Publications:** Brochure.

★186★
Free South Africa Movement
c/o TransAfrica
545 Eighth St. SE, Ste, 200   Ph: (202)547-2550
Washington, DC 20003   Fax: (202)547-7687
Randall Robinson, Exec.Dir.

Description: A project of TransAfrica supported nationally by black leadership and created to organize protests at South African consulates, American banks providing loans to South Africa, and corporations doing business in South Africa. Supporters, whose involvement in demonstrations was solicited by FSAM, have submitted to arrest in order to call attention to demands that the apartheid system in South Africa be abolished immediately. Seeks to bring about what the group sees as a more sensitive U.S. policy toward South Africa, in accordance with the goals of the South African majority supporting democratic rule. Encourages adoption and passage of divestment legislation at all government levels. **Founded:** 1984.

★187★
Freedom Information Service
PO Box 3568
Jackson, MS 39207   Ph: (601)352-3398
Jan Hillegas, Treas.

Description: Researches activities of workers, blacks, and grass roots organizations through the FIS Deep South People's History Project. Maintains extensive Mississippi-centered library and archives. Distributes press releases on current southern news; reprints items on women's liberation and political education. **Founded:** 1965. **Budget:** Less than $25,000. **Publications:** FIS Mississippi Newsletter, periodic. Has also issued political and economic publications relevant to the civil rights movement and black candidates. **Formerly:** (1965) Freedom Information Center.

★188★
Friends of Haiti
1398 Flatbush Ave.
Brooklyn, NY 11210   Ph: (718)434-8100
Mauge Leblanc, Coordinator

Description: Volunteers interested in generating political and material support in the U.S. for the Haitian national liberation struggle, particularly the Mouvement Haitien de Liberation, an anti-imperialist, national liberation movement based in Haiti. To disseminate information on the Haitian social structure and the liberation process, with an emphasis on U.S. economic, political, and military involvement. Activities include conducting research and fundraising. Maintains data center on Haiti and the Caribbean and library of 3000 volumes. **Founded:** 1971. **Publications:** Produces slide show and film programs; contributes articles to publications.

★189★
Friends of Johnny Mathis
2700 Jasper St. SE, No. 248
Washington, DC 20020   Ph: (202)678-6731
Alice T. Williams, Pres.

Description: Admirers of Johnny Mathis (1935-), singer of love ballads, including Misty and Chances Are. Promotes interest in Mathis' career and attendance at his concerts. **Founded:** 1983. **Members:** 30. **Budget:** Less than $25,000. **Publications:** Newsletter, quarterly. Includes news and reviews. **Formerly:** Mathis Magic Fan Club.

★190★
Fund for an Open Society
311 S. Juniper St., Ste. 400
Philadelphia, PA 19107   Ph: (215)735-6915
D. Richard Wenner, Exec.Dir.

Description: Mortgage fund established to provide an economic incentive in the form of financially advantageous loans to persons making housing moves that decrease segregation, that is, moves by a minority family to a white neighborhood or by a white family to a predominantly minority or well-integrated neighborhood. Purposes are to: help neighborhoods become interracial; help existing interracial neighborhoods maintain stability; help prevent displacement in gentrifying neighborhoods; strengthen neighborhoods by facilitating the purchase and rehabilitation of abandoned homes; help solve the problem of segregated schools by breaking down walls of residential segregation. Actively seeks the support of local institutions, businesses, and community groups. Provides mortgages below the prevailing rates. **Founded:** 1975. **Members:** 10,000. **Budget:** $549,000. **Publications:** Newsletter, periodic. Also publishes pamphlets.

★191★
Funders Committee for Citizenship Participation
c/o New World Foundation
100 E. 85th St.
New York, NY 10028   Ph: (212)249-1023
Colin Greer, Co-Chair

Description: Individuals representing 25 community, corporate, and private foundations. Purpose is to broaden the base of support for nonpartisan voter education and registration, particularly among underrepresented groups such as blacks, Hispanics, women, and young people. Encourages funding organizations to support programs encouraging full political participation. Collects and disseminates information. Sponsors briefings and consultations on issues related to citizen participation in the U.S. Compiles statistics. **Founded:** 1983. **Members:** 35. **Publications:** Funding Citizenship Participation, semiannual. Newsletter. **Formerly:** (1985) Ad Hoc Funders Committee for Voter Registration and Education; (1991) Funders Committee for Voter Registration and Education.

★192★
Girl Friends
c/o Rachel Norcom Smith
2228 Lansing Ave.
Portsmouth, VA 23704   Ph: (804)397-1339
Rachel Norcom Smith, Exec. Officer

Description: Black women "who have been friends over the years." Primary aim is to "keep the fires of friendship burning." Conducts charitable projects and contributes annually to a selected charity. Bestows awards. **Founded:** 1927. **Members:** 1200. **Budget:** $120,000. **Local Groups:** 40. **Publications:** The Chatterbox, annual. Chatterletter, biennial. Directory, quinquennial. President's News and Friendship Letter, annual.

★193★
Global Women of African Heritage
PO Box 1033, Cooper Station
New York, NY 10003   Ph: (212)547-5696
Thelma Dailey-Stout, Founder & Pres.

Description: Women of African heritage worldwide. Purpose is to bring together women of African heritage to share common experiences and knowledge. Also seeks to share this knowledge with women who are not of African heritage. **Founded:** 1982.

★194★
Gospel Music Association
PO Box 23201   Ph: (615)242-0303
Nashville, TN 37202   Fax: (615)254-9755
Bruce Koblish, Exec.Dir.

Description: Music industry personnel and fans united to promote gospel music worldwide. Presents annual Dove Award for excellence in gospel music. Maintains speakers' bureau, museum, archive, library, and hall of fame; conducts educational and research programs; compiles statistics. **Founded:** 1964. **Members:** 2500. **Publications:** Gospel Music Resource Guide, periodic. Newsletter, quarterly.

★195★
Gospel Music Workshop of America
3908 W. Warren St.   Ph: (313)898-2340
Detroit, MI 48208   Fax: (313)898-4520
Edward M. Smith, Dir.

Description: Individuals interested in gospel music. Promotes the enjoyment and performance of gospel and spiritual music. Offers musical instruction in performance and composition. **Founded:** 1966. **Members:** 18,000. **Publications:** Bulletin, annual.

★196★
Grand United Order of Odd Fellows
262 S. 12th St.
Philadelphia, PA 19107   Ph: (215)735-8774
Joseph Boulware, Grand Sec.

Description: Individuals united for social and charitable purposes. Conducts seminars and professional training. Sponsors charitable and educational programs; provides children's services; maintains library. **Founded:** 1843. **Members:** 108,000. **Regional Groups:** 8. **Publications:** Bulletin, quarterly. National Directory, biennial.

★197★
Haitian and Co-Arts Association
165 Park Row, Ste. 8-D
New York, NY 10038   Ph: (212)732-9735
Andre Letellier, Pres. & Exec.Dir.

Description: Professionals, business executives, clergy, artists, and others both in the U.S. and Haiti. Serves as a charitable educational assistance program to voluntarily contribute to the elimination of hunger, eradication of disease, and promotion of literacy of deprived children of the peasants in rural areas of Haiti. Establishes rural and mobile free clinics to provide community-wide vaccination against polio, diphtheria, whooping cough, tuberculosis, yaws, malaria, and tetanus to needy children in remote villages. Provides villagers with advice on common tropical diseases, prenatal care, hygiene, and birth control. Promotes the self-sufficiency of small peasant farmers by encouraging cooperative rural agroforestry and aquaculture programs and new irrigation and farming techniques. Promotes literacy, with primary emphasis on modern industrial technology and advanced vocational trade schools. Provides medical and dental care, food, and shelter to needy schoolchildren enrolled in the five geographic departments of Haiti's rural areas. U.S. corporations and individuals donate funds, medical and dental supplies, drugs, seeds, and educational materials for distribution by the association. Also attempts to develop public interest in Haiti by sponsoring cultural endeavors in such fields as folklore, dance, music, history, literature, art, theater, photography, and wood sculpture; sponsors sports events and trade exhibits. **Founded:** 1956. **Formerly:** (1973) Haiti Voluntary Central Committee. **Members:** 450.

★198★
Haitian Coalition on AIDS
50 Court St., Ste. 605   Ph: (718)855-0972
Brooklyn, NY 11201   Fax: (718)852-5377
Yvon Rosemond, Exec.Dir.

Description: Community centers; professional groups of doctors, journalists, lawyers, nurses, social workers, and civil rights and media representatives. Purpose is to educate the public concerning what the coalition feels is the discriminatory classification of Haitians as an ethnonational group that runs a high risk of contracting AIDS. Seeks to heighten AIDS awareness within the Haitian community. Offers social services and placement for victims of AIDS; provides counseling to their families. Sponsors conferences and seminars at churches and universities. Compiles statistics; maintains database and speakers' bureau. Bestows awards; operates library. **Founded:** 1983. **Members:** 70. **Budget:** $300,000. **Regional Groups:** 8. **Local Groups:** 6. **State Groups:** 7. **Publications:** AIDS education materials for Creole-speaking individuals.

★199★
Haitian Patriotic Union
3900 Yuma St. NW
Washington, DC 20016   Ph: (202)362-4743
Paul Louis Casagnol, Pres.

Description: Exiled Haitians united to fight oppression and to promote social and economic programs that will aid in restoring the Haitian governmental structure to normalcy. Seeks to: organize a Haitian democratic opposition front and elect a democratic and constitutional government. Strongly opposes countries that support Haitian oppression and which condone the enslavement of the Haitian workers in the Dominican sugar fields. Works to restore human rights to Haiti. Promotes an integrated agricultural, industrial, and social development plan. Testifies before congressional committees and other government groups. Supports Amnesty International, Inter-American Commission on Human Rights, the United Nations, and the Human Rights Office of the State Department which have condemned the violations of human rights in

Haiti. **Founded:** 1977. **Members:** 49. **Publications:** Bulletin, periodic. Haiti Patriote, monthly. Has also published Foreign Aid: Its Promises, Its Deceptions. **Also known as:** Union Patriotique Haitienne.

★200★
Haitian Refugee Center
119 N.E. 54th St.   Ph: (305)757-8538
Miami, FL 33137   Fax: (305)758-2444
                                          Free: 800-749-8538
Rolande Dorancy, Exec.Dir.

Description: Provides free legal support and educational services to indigent Haitian aliens in their political asylum proceedings and in federal court litigation designed to protect and establish the basic constitutional and international legal rights of asylum seekers. Works to impede deportations and to publicize the plight of Haitian refugees. Documents U.S. Immigration and Naturalization Service abuses. Represents Haitian refugees in class action lawsuits resulting from violations involving political asylum. During the rule of the Duvalier family more than 1.5 million people have fled Haiti, according to the center. **Founded:** 1974. Directors: 21. **Publications:** Press releases, legal documents, and briefs.

★201★
Hola Kumba Ya!
PO Box 50173   Ph: (215)848-5118
Philadelphia, PA 19132   Fax: (215)849-6985
Imani Lumumba, Exec.Dir.

Description: Participants are folk artists including storytellers, craftsmen and women, ethnic dancers, and musicians. Works to preserve, promote, and perpetuate the work of traditional folk artists. Seeks to demonstrate how traditional arts can be used as a positive educational tool. Provides resource information to schools, museums, festivals,and communities. Sponsors folk art programs in conjunction with the Artist Network Program. Conducts workshops, showcases, storytelling performances, charitable programs, and annual Unknown Ancestors program. Maintains library, museum, and speakers' bureau. **Founded:** 1986. **Budget:** $50,000. **Publications:** Newsletter, quarterly.

★202★
Homowa Foundation for African Arts and Culture
2915 NE 15 Ave.
Portland, OR 97212   Ph: (503)288-3025
Susan Addy, Exec.Dir.

Description: Promotes African culture through performing arts. Serves as a clearinghouse for information on African performing arts. Sponsors lectures, forums, and concerts. **Budget:** $75,000. **Founded:** 1986. **Publications:** none.

★203★
Horace Mann Bond Center for Equal Education
University of Massachusetts
Library Tower
Amherst, MA 01003   Ph: (413)545-0327
Meyer Weinberg, Dir.

Description: School boards, lawyers, and teachers. To perpetuate the memory and contributions of Dr. Horace Mann Bond (1904-73), distinguished black educator and scholar. Serves as national clearinghouse of research and information on racism, desegregation, anti-Semitism, and other social issues, aimed at contributing to the achievement of a superior education for all children. Collects clippings, articles, books, dissertations, government publications, and other documents. Maintains extensive library including papers, reports, and court decisions. **Founded:** 1963. **Formerly:** (1965) Teachers for Integrated Schools.

★204★
Improved Benevolent Protective Order of Elks of the World
PO Box 159
Winton, NC 27986   Ph: (919)358-7661
Donald P. Wilson, Grand Exalted Ruler

Description: International fraternal organization of primarily black membership. Concerned with civil liberties and equal opportunity.

Provides scholarships for youth of all races. **Founded:** 1898. **Members:** 450,000. **Publications:** Elks News, bimonthly.

★205★
Inroads
1221 Locust St., Ste. 800
St. Louis, MO 63103
Reginald D. Dickson, CEO & Pres.
Ph: (314)241-7488
Fax: (314)241-9325

Description: Participants are U.S. corporations that sponsor internships for minority students and pledge to develop career opportunities for the interns. Prepares black, Hispanic, and Native American high school and college students for leadership positions within major American business corporations in their own communities. Screens and places over 4000 individuals for internships with more than 1000 American business corporations per year. Offers professional training seminars on time management, business presentation skills, team building, and decision making. Provides personal and professional guidance to pre-college and college interns. **Founded:** 1970. **Regional Groups:** 5. **Local Groups:** 37. **Computerized Services:** Database. **Publications:** Annual Report. INROADS Newsletter, quarterly.

★206★
Institute for the Advanced Study of Black Family Life and Culture
175 Filbert St., Ste. 202
Oakland, CA 94607
Wade Nobles Ph.D., Exec.Dir.
Ph: (510)836-3245

Description: Seeks to reunify African American families and to revitalize the black community. Advocates the reclamation of what the group considers traditional African American culture. Conducts research on issues impacting the black community such as teenage pregnancy, child-rearing practices, mental health support systems, and the effects of alcohol and drugs. Maintains HAWK Federation (High Achievement, Wisdom, and Knowledge Federation), a training program employed in school systems to aid in the character development of young black males. Sponsors in-service training for agencies, school systems, and the juvenile justice system. Develops training curricula for teen parents. Maintains speakers' bureau. **Publications:** African American Families - Issues, Insights, and Direction and African Psychology (books).

★207★
Institute of Black Studies
6376 Delmar Blvd.
St. Louis, MO 63130
Dr. Robert C. Johnson, Dir.
Ph: (314)889-5690

Description: Functions as a clearinghouse and serves as a base for action research, program evaluation, development of innovative cultural programs, educational, and training models and other activities appropriate to needs of the black community that are not normally provided by traditional institutions. Goals include: to bridge the gap between the community and educational institutions; to discover and develop new models for the solution of the many issues facing the black community. Supports development of psychological tests for minority groups. Conducts research and activities in areas of children, family, intelligence, language, parenting, personality, psychological testing, and juvenile deliquency. Has designed several training modules including the Black Family Cultural Heritage P roject from which developed a training model, materials, and techniques for use in teaching trainers of black parenting. Publishes A Manual of Black Parenting Education, Telecommunications and the Socialization of Black Americans, bibliographies, brochures, conference papers, and other materials. Presently inactive. **Founded:** 1970.

★208★
Institute of the Black World
87 Chestnut St., SW
Atlanta, GA 30314
Dr. Vincent Harding, Bd.Chm.
Ph: (404)523-7805

Description: An independent institution of research and political analysis and advocacy, placing special emphasis on the need to shape all elements of black education into effective instruments which may be used to advance the black movement for equality and social change. Based on "an abiding faith" in black people's collective abilities to control their destinies, the institute aims to provide blacks and other interested persons with "a clear understanding of the nature of the struggle that is being waged to shape America's future." Specific tasks have been: definition and refining of the field loosely called black studies; encouragement of basic academic research in the experiences of the peoples of African descent; encouragement of black artists; development of new materials and methods for the teaching of black children; development of a Black Policy Studies Center to create tools for social analysis of the black community; establishment of creative links with counterparts in other areas of the black world; preparation of a "new cadre" of men and women precisely trained in the scholarship of the black experience and fully committed to the struggles of the black world. Sponsors conferences, seminars, lectures, workshops, and symposia. Conducts research. The Institute is located in a house where the late Dr. W.E.B. DuBois (1868-1983), American editor, educator, writer, and black rights activist is said to have lived. Conducts summer research symposium. **Founded:** 1969. **Publications:** Monthly Report, 8/year. Newsletter, monthly. Also publishes books, pamphlets, monographs, editorials, and a series of taped lectures, radio programs and other audio and audiovisual materials.

★209★
Institute of Urban Life
1 E. Superior, No. 311
Chicago, IL 60611
Ed Marciniak, Pres.
Ph: (312)787-7525
Fax: (312)915-6433

Description: Not an association. Performs contract studies on a nonprofit basis on economic, social, and political problems of urban areas. Provides technical assistance to nonprofit inner-city institutions and groups on their urban-related concerns. **Founded:** 1962. **Publications:** Directory of Community Organizations in Chicago, annual. Has also published Reclaiming the Inner City, Chicago's Near North Revitalization Confronts Cabrini-Green, Reversing Urban Decline, Reviving an Inner City Community: The Drama of Urban Change in Chicago's East Humboldt Park, Non-Profits with Hard Hats: Building Affordable Housing, and Chicago's Private Elementary and Secondary Schools: Enrollment Trends, Is There A Better Way - Housing Options in Chicago and Its Suburbs, and Mainstreaming the Urban Poor: Enabling Non-Public Schools to Survive in Inner-City Neighborhoods (reports).

★210★
Inter-American Commission on Human Rights
1889 F St., NW, Ste. LL2, 8th Fl.
Washington, DC 20006
Dr. Edith Marquez-Rodriguez, Exec.Sec.
Ph: (202)458-6002
Fax: (202)458-3992

Description: Citizens of member nations of the Organization of American States. Promotes and protects human rights in the Caribbean, and North, Central, and South America. Maintains 5000 volume library specializing in human rights law. **Founded:** 1960. **Members:** 7. **Budget:** $1,120,400. **Publications:** Annual Report. Also publishes reports on Latin American countries.

★211★
Inter-American Travel Agents Society
c/o Almeda Travel
1020 Holcombe Blvd., Ste. 1306
Houston, TX 77030
Jackye Alton, Pres.
Ph: (713)799-1001
Fax: (713)799-8022

Description: Black owned and operated travel agencies; other travel related businesses and interested individuals. Works to unify black travel agents and increase members' market share and business contacts. Offers travel opportunities geared toward black travelers. Assists members in developing new businesses; maintains standard of ethics among member agencies. **Founded:** 1955. **Members:** 300. **Publications:** Inter-American Travel Agents Society Newsletter, quarterly. Membership List, periodic. Includes updates. Also publishes brochure.

★212★
International Association of African and American Black Business People
18900 Schoolcraft
Detroit, MI 48223
William Bert Johnson, Pres.

Description: African and African-American businesspersons. Establishes, operates, and fosters business education and related activities among African-American and African members of the business community worldwide. Conducts seminars; bestows awards; compiles statistics. **Founded:** 1965. **Members:** 84,000. **Regional Groups:** 170. **Publications:** Bulletin, bimonthly. Journal, quarterly.

★213★
International Association of Black Business Educators
3810 Palmira Ln.
Silver Spring, MD 20906
Paul A. Young, Project Dir.

Description: Institutions of higher education (55) and individuals (100) interested in promoting development of business related academic programs and educational activities designed to enhance participation of minorities in business. Purposes are to: develop channels of communication and opportunities for interfacing with constituencies; generate constructive relationships between the U.S. and other nations concerning development of business education and related fields; study and propose minority business programs; promote cooperation within and between institutions and individuals in the business community; identify and evaluate business opportunities; promote the IABBE's involvement in academic affairs. Operates Strategic Business Development Network, which designs and produces a business development educational video series. **Founded:** 1978. **Members:** 155. **Publications:** IABBE Newsletter, quarterly. Also produces videotape series on how to start, own, and operate a business.

★214★
International Association of Black Professional Fire Fighters
1025 Connecticut Ave. NW, Ste. 610   Ph: (202)296-0157
Washington, DC 20036   Fax: (202)296-0158
Romeo O. Spaulding, Pres.

Description: Fire fighters, dispatchers, and individuals in related professions. Strives to: promote interracial communication and understanding; recruit blacks for the fire services; improve working conditions for blacks in the fire services; assist blacks in career advancement; promote professionalism; represent black fire fighters before the community. **Founded:** 1970. **Members:** 8500. **Budget:** $160,000. **Regional Groups:** 6. **Local Groups:** 125. **Computerized Services:** Mailing list. **Publications:** National Express, monthly. Bulletin. Smoke, semiannual. Newsletter.

★215★
International Association of Official Human Rights Agencies
444 N. Capitol St., Ste. 634   Ph: (202)624-5410
Washington, DC 20001   Fax: (202)624-8588

Description: Governmental human rights agencies with legal enforcement powers. Objectives are to foster better human relations and to enhance human rights procedures under the law. Conducts training services that include: administration and management training; technical assistance in civil rights compliance and curriculum development for colleges and universities, business, industry, and other organizations; training for administrators and commissioners to promote awareness and capability in current literature, theory, and philosophy relative to equal opportunity. Maintains ongoing liaison with federal agencies involved with civil rights enforcement in order to coordinate development of state legislation. Has developed and conducted training and technical assistance workshops for regional planning units and state planning agencies. Plans to establish a human rights training institute. Sponsors workshops; bestows awards; compiles statistics. **Founded:** 1949. **Members:** 187. **Budget:** $100,000. **Regional Groups:** 5. **Publications:** IAOHRA Newsletter, quarterly.

★216★
International Black Peoples' Foundation
158 Clairmount
Detroit, MI 48202   Ph: (313)871-0597
Claudia Peek Corbin, Founding Dir.

Description: Works to: eradicate world hunger, especially in Africa and among persons of African descent; promote black humanitarianism. Conducts fundraising programs that supply money, food, or services to afflicted populations; works with United Nations agencies. Provides educational seminars, conferences, and workshops for selected audiences and the public. Presently inactive. **Founded:** 1981. **Budget:** $110,000. **Publications:** Newsletter, periodic.

★217★
International Black Toy Manufacturers Association
PO Box 348
Springfield Gardens, NY 11413
Yvonne Rubie, Pres.

Description: Companies designing or manufacturing toys. Works to provide shelf space and distribution opportunities commensurate with the spending power of the black community. Promotes black toy manufacturers. Conducts research on black consumers. **Founded:** 1987. **Members:** 14. **Publications:** none.

★218★
International Black Women's Congress
1081 Bergen St.   Ph: (201)926-0570
Newark, NJ 07112   Fax: (201)926-0818
Dr. La Francis Rodgers-Rose, Pres.

Description: Women of African descent; interested individuals. Objective is to unite members for mutual support and socioeconomic development through: annual networking tours to Africa; establishing support groups; assisting women in starting their own businesses; assisting members in developing resumes and other educational needs; offering to answer or discuss individual questions and concerns. Conducts workshops and charitable program; compiles statistics. Bestows Oni Award annually to the person identified as "someone who protects, defends and enhances the general well being of African people." Operates speakers' bureau. Maintains 100 volume library. **Founded:** 1983. **Members:** 5800. MD $750 for life; $100 for organizational; $35 for regular, $10 for student/senior. **Budget:** $125,000. **State Groups:** 9. Undergraduate Chapters: 3. **Publications:** International Black Women's Directory, periodic. Oni Newsletter, quarterly.

★219★
International Black Writers
PO Box 1030
Chicago, IL 60690   Ph: (312)924-3818
Mable J. Terrell, Exec.Dir. & Pres.

Description: To discover and support new black writers. Conducts research and monthly seminars in poetry, fiction, nonfiction, music, and jazz. Operates library of 500 volumes on black history. Sponsors monthly workshop and panel discussion. Provides writing services and children's services. Presents Alice Browning Award for Excellence in Writing and bestows awards in journalism and poetry. Maintains library and speakers' bureau. Sponsors competitions; offers referral service. Plans to establish hall of fame, biographical archives, and museum. **Founded:** 1970. **Members:** 1,000. **Budget:** $40,000. **Regional Groups:** 5. **Local Groups:** 1. **State Groups:** 4. **Publications:** The Black Writer, quarterly. Magazine. Bulletin, periodic. Directory of Afro-American Writers, periodic. In Touch Newsletter, monthly. Poetry Contest, annual. Urban Voices Poetry, annual. **Formerly:** (1982) International Black Writers Conference.

★220★
International Black Writers and Artists
PO Box 43576
Los Angeles, CA 90043   Ph: (213)964-3721
Linda A. Hughes, Exec. Officer

Description: Black writers and artists in the United States and West Indies. Provides encouragement and support to members. Conducts workshops annually and sponsors social gatherings. Plans to publish anthology. **Founded:** 1974. **Members:** 500.

★221★

International Committee Against Racism
239 W. 29th St.
Brooklyn, NY 11202   Ph: (212)629-0003
Carol Deak, Exec.Dir.

Description: Is dedicated to fighting all forms of racism and to building a multi-racial society. Opposes racism in all its economic, social, institutional, and cultural forms. Believes racism destroys not only those minorities that are its victims, but all people. Sponsors on-the-job, community, college, and high school workshops. **Founded:** 1973. **Members:** 2800. **Regional Groups:** 4. **Local Groups:** 28. **State Groups:** 30. **Publications:** Arrow (in English and Spanish), bimonthly. Newsletter reporting on racist incidents in the United States. Includes calendar of events, committee news, and member profiles.

★222★

International Defense and Aid Fund for Southern Africa, U.S. Committee
PO Box 17
Cambridge, MA 02138   Ph: (617)491-8343
Kenneth N. Carstens, Exec.Dir.

Description: Purposes are to aid, defend, rehabilitate, and provide for the legal defense of the "victims of unjust laws and arbitrary procedures in South Africa and Namibia;" to support their families and dependents; "to keep the conscience of the world alive to the issues at stake" through the dissemination of information on apartheid and political prisoners in South Africa and Namibia. Programs and activities have developed according to changing situations in the countries of southern Africa; primary emphasis is on political prisoners and their families. Rents slide shows. Operates speakers' bureau. **Founded:** 1972. **Budget:** $160,000. **Publications:** Focus on Political Repression in Southern Africa, bimonthly. Newsletter on political repression in South Africa and Namibia.

★223★

International Institute of Islamic Thought
555 Grove St., Ste. 101
PO Box 669   Ph: (703)471-1133
Herndon, VA 22070   Fax: (703)471-3922
Dr. Taha Jabir Al Alwani, Pres.

Description: Goal is the restoration and promotion of Islamic thought and its integration into the social sciences. Promotes research in the social sciences, particularly in methodology and on the philosophy of science, in an effort to address the problems pertinent to Islam, the Muslim community, and the world through the principles, concepts, and values of the Islamic model. Maintains a library of 25,000 volumes on Islamic social sciences, history, and jurisprudence. Grants scholarships and offers guidance and supervision to graduate students.Maintains speakers' bureau. Conducts educational and research programs. **Founded:** 1981. **Publications:** Al Muslim al Muasir (in Arabic), periodic. Journal.

★224★

International Islamic Federation of Student Organizations
555 Grove St.
PO Box 17032   Ph: (703)471-1133
Washington, DC 20041   Fax: (703)471-1211
Omar H. Kasule, Exec.Dir.

Description: Islamic student and youth groups in 45 countries, who seek to create "Ummah, the global Islamic brotherhood." Works to develop Islamic awareness among students; fosters "the attainment of an Islamic personality through providing students moral, ideological, social, and behavioral training." Encourages Muslim youth to participate in the development of their home countries and to use Islamic alternatives in addressing contemporary problems; supports social services for those in need; promotes study and understanding of Islam. Coordinates activities of and provides aid to Islamic youth organizations; promotes "productive work" for members as opposed to "propaganda and publicity." **Founded:** 1969. **Regional Groups:** 5. **Publications:** IIFSO Connection, periodic. Newsletter. Also publishes This Religion of Islam, The Individual and the State, Islam the Religion of the Future, Milestones, Islam and the World, Islam Today, Islam and Christianity, The

Muslim's Character, Forty Hadiths, A Critical Look at the Theory, and other books. Presently inactive.

★225★

International League for Human Rights
432 Park Ave. S., Rm. 1103   Ph: (212)684-1221
New York, NY 10016   Fax: (212)684-1696

Description: Individuals and national affiliates promoting human rights, including political and civil rights, racial and religious freedom, and the implementation of the Universal Declaration of Human Rights. Serves as nongovernmental agency accredited by the United Nations, International Labor Organization, United Nations Educational, Scientific and Cultural Organization, and Council of Europe (see separate entries). Participates in studies and programs on human rights. Advocates effective procedures to protect human rights, including protection of minorities; deals with issues of torture, political imprisonment, due process of law, racial discrimination, genocide, apartheid, treatment of prisoners, status of women, and religious freedom; promotes ability of local human rights groups to exist and work unimpeded by government. Intervenes directly with governments concerning violations of human rights. Sends special investigators to areas where human rights violations exist and sends observers to political trials. Bestows annual Human Rights Award. **Founded:** 1942. **Publications:** Annual Review. Human Rights Bulletin, periodic. Also publishes books, booklets, pamphlets, and special reports on worldwide human rights conditions, including Human Rights Conditions in Poland, Report of a Medical Fact-Finding Mission to El Salvador, Petitions Before the UN Trusteeship Council, and Guinea's Human Rights Record. **Formerly:** (1976) International League for the Rights of Man.

★226★

International Project for Africa
PO Box 43345   Ph: (202)792-7510
Washington, DC 20010   Fax: (202)232-4577
Gbenga Adewusi, Pres.

Description: Print and broadcast journalists. Conducts research on foreign affairs, development programs, lending conditions, strategic considerations, demographic and political implications, and related issues. Examines international trends from an African perspective. Operates a news service which available to journalists in 40 African nations. Maintains a reference library which contains books, periodicals, clippings, monographs, archival material, and government contracts and documents of all types on international relations. Maintains a speaker's bureau and offers research and educational programs. **Founded:** 1990. **Publications:** Reports and working papers.

★227★

International Rhythm and Blues Association
PO Box 16215
Chicago, IL 60616   Ph: (312)326-5270
William C. Tyson, Pres.

Description: Musicians, record companies, songwriters, and individuals in 3 countries interested in preserving and promoting rhythm and blues music. Gathers information on rhythm and blues; maintains library. Is currently raising funds for scholarships for students pursuing careers in rhythm and blues music. **Founded:** 1966. **Members:** 500.

★228★

Interracial Council for Business Opportunity
51 Madison Ave., Ste. 2212
New York, NY 10010
                                     Fax: (212)779-4365
                                     Free: 800-252-4226
Lorraine Kelsey, Exec. Officer

Description: Assists minority businessmen and women in developing, owning, and managing business ventures with substantial employment and economic impact. Services include business feasibility studies, financing, market development, and other technical assistance to start or expand minority-owned companies. Offers free management training courses. **Founded:** 1963. **Publications:** Annual Report. Newsletter, monthly.

★229★
Interracial Family Alliance
PO Box 16248
Houston, TX 77222   Ph: (713)454-5018
Ron Radcliffe, Pres.

Description: Families that are interracial through marriage, adoption across racial lines, or biracial birth. Purposes are to: strengthen and support the interracial family unit; promote acceptance of interracial families by the public; focus on solutions to problems unique to interracial families such as developing self-esteem in biracial children. Maintains resource library of books, articles, videotapes, and other materials. Conducts social activities involving biracial children; sponsors educational programs. Has compiled a bibliography on interracial family experience and transracial adoption. **Founded:** 1983. **Members:** 200. MD $25/year. **Computerized Services:** National network of interracial family organizations. **Publications:** Communique: Newspaper of the Interracial Family Alliance, quarterly. Newsletter.

★230★
Interracial-Intercultural Pride
PO Box 191752
San Francisco, CA 94119-1752   Ph: (415)399-9111
Leslie Lomax, Pres.

Description: Members of interracial and intercultural families; concerned individuals. Supports and encourages the well-being and development of children and adults who are of more than one ethnic or cultural heritage. Conducts educational forums and workshops. Maintains library and speakers' bureau. Membership is currently concentrated in the San Francisco, CA area. **Founded:** 1979. **Members:** 250. **Budget:** Less than $25,000. **Publications:** I-Pride Newsletter, monthly.

★231★
Iota Phi Lambda
503 Patterson St.
Tuskegee, AL 36088   Ph: (205)727-5210
Mrs. Billie O. Glover, Exec.Dir.

Description: Business and professional civic sorority. Seeks to: develop leadership expertise among business and professional women; promote increased interest in business education among high school and college girls through planned programs and scholarships; encourage the development of personalities for all areas of leadership through provision of educational opportunities; establish and promote civic and social service activities for youth and adults. Conducts children's services and tutoring sessions. Maintains small library. Bestows Lola M. Parker Achievement Award, Mahala S. Evans Award, and Alice Pallen Scholarship. Provides educational, tutorial, senior citizen, and health programs. **Founded:** 1929. **Members:** 5000. **Regional Groups:** 5. Chapters: 100. **Publications:** biennial Convention Proceedings. Journal, annual. Let's Chat, semiannual. Membership Directory, biennial.

★232★
Islamic Medical Association
4121 Fairview, Ste. 203
Downers Grove, IL 60515   Ph: (708)852-2122
Khursheed Mallick M.D., Exec.Dir.

Description: Muslim physicians and allied health professionals. To unite Muslim physicians and allied health professionals in the U.S. and Canada for the improvement of professional and social contact; to provide assistance to Muslim communities worldwide. Charitable programs include: scholarships awarded to needy students; donation of books, journals, and educational and research materials to medical institutions; donation of medical supplies and equipment to charity medical institutions in Muslim countries. Maintains speakers' bureau to present Islamic viewpoints on medical topics; sponsors placement service; offers assistance in orientation. Organizes conferences, seminars, and workshops to be held regularly in Muslim countries. **Founded:** 1967. **Members:** 6000. **Publications:** Journal, quarterly. Newsletter, quarterly.

★233★
Islamic Mission of America
143 State St.
Brooklyn, NY 11201   Ph: (718)875-6607
Mohamed Kabbaj, Chm.

Description: Dedicated to the propagation of the Islamic faith. Prepares students for missionary work. Maintains mosque in Brooklyn, NY and an institute for teaching religion and Arabic. Operates library on all aspects of Islamic education. **Founded:** 1938. **Members:** 15,000. **Budget:** Less than $25,000. **Publications:** The Little Giant, periodic.

★234★
Islamic Society of North American
PO Box 38   Ph: (317)839-8157
Plainfield, IN 46168   Fax: (317)839-1840
Ahmad El Hattab, Acting Sec.Gen.

Description: Students, immigrants, and U.S. citizens who are of the Muslim faith or who are interested in Islam. To assist in the formation and maintenance of Muslim student organizations and to help those organizations carry out Islamic programs and projects; to make Islam better understood by Muslims and non-Muslims. Programs and activities include: Islamic centers and mosques; Sunday schools; correspondence courses; scholarships; student houses; educational programs for women, youth, children, and adults; special programs for professional groups (doctors, engineers, and social scientists); cooperative fund. Conducts seminars, regional symposia, and leadership training program. Sponsors Muslim Students' Association of the United States and Canada. Maintains 7000 volume library and speakers' bureau. **Founded:** 1963. **Members:** 6500. **Local Groups:** 200. **Publications:** Annual Report. Islamic Horizons, monthly. Also publishes books and manuals; makes available Koranic tapes.

★235★
Jack and Jill of America Foundation
c/o Violet D. Greer
PO Drawer 3689   Ph: (615)622-4476
Chattanooga, TN 37404   Fax: (615)622-8074
Violet D. Greer, Exec.Sec.

Description: Officers of Jack and Jill of America, community leaders, parents, youth representatives, and others. Seeks to improve educational, cultural, and civic opportunities for minority youth. Monitors legislative changes affecting the development of youth. Awards grants to exemplary educational community projects throughout the country. Supports college-level achievement motivation projects, preschool programs, and college preparatory programs for high school students. Maintains library of films about foundation projects. Bestows awards. Sponsors training symposia. **Founded:** 1968. **Members:** 29. **Budget:** $200,000. **Publications:** Jack and Jill of America Foundation–Intercom, semiannual. Newsletter containing grant information and foundation news.

★236★
Jackie Robinson Foundation
3 W. 35th St.   Ph: (212)290-8600
New York, NY 10001   Fax: (212)290-8081
Betty Adams, CEO

Description: Seeks to develop the leadership and achievement potential of minority and urban youth. Founded by the friends and family of Jackie Robinson (1919-72), the first black athlete to play major league baseball. Trains minority and poor youths for sports management careers. Provides counseling, support, and placement services. Awards full college scholarships to promising minority students. Maintains library and collection of Jackie Robinson memorabilia; has produced a national touring exhibit of archival materials pertaining to Robinson. Bestows Robie Award for Humanitarianism and Robie Award for Achievement in Industry annually. **Founded:** 1973. **Budget:** $800,000. **Regional Groups:** 6. **Computerized Services:** Mailing list. Programs: Education and Scholarship; JRF Alumni Association; Sports Management. **Publications:** Jackie Robinson Foundation Awards Dinner, annual. Journal describing foundation programs and services; includes profiles of award recipients and scholarship sponsors.

★237★
Jazz for Life Project
400 City Center Bldg.
Ann Arbor, MI 48104

Description: Works to raise money, through benefit jazz concerts, to improve the lives of children six years of age and under living in low-income situations. Strives to increase public awareness of the plight of poverty-stricken children. Distributes funds to nonprofit agencies that provide nutritional, educational, and healthcare services to children. Sponsors cultural programs for children. **Founded:** 1985. **Local Groups:** 2. **Publications:** Newsletter, periodic.

★238★
Joint Center for Political and Economic Studies
1090 Vermont Ave. NW, Ste. 1100   Ph: (202)789-3500
Washington, DC 20005   Fax: (202)789-6390
Eddie N. Williams, Pres.

Description: Funded in part by the Ford Foundation. Organized to provide, on a nonpartisan basis, research, public policy analysis, and information programs for black and other minority elected and appointed public officials. Collects and analyzes data on all aspects of black political participation. Monitors elections throughout the U.S. at all levels of government; collects and disseminates statistical and interpretive data on black voting patterns and political participation. Conducts analyses of public policy issues that affect black and disadvantaged Americans and pinpoints resources that can be used by socially and economically disadvantaged communities. Provides public policy forums, which bring together experts from a variety of disciplines to focus on issues and examine alternatives. Maintains library of 3000 volumes on black politics. **Formerly:** (1990) Joint Center for Political Studies. **Founded:** 1970. **Budget:** $3,000,000. **Publications:** Annual Report. CPRJ News, periodic. Newsletter. Focus, monthly. Magazine. National Roster of Black Elected Officials, annual. NPI News, periodic. Newsletter. Quarterly Alert. Newsletter. Also publishes analyses of public policy issues, statistical studies, and monographs.

★239★
Kappa Alpha Psi
2322-24 N. Broad St.   Ph: (215)228-7184
Philadelphia, PA 19132   Fax: (215)288-7181
W. Ted Smith Ph.D., Exec.Sec.

Description: Social fraternity. Sponsors charitable and educational programs and children's services. Bestows scholarships and awards; maintains library, speakers' bureau, and placement service; compiles statistics. **Founded:** 1911. **Members:** 90,000. **Regional Groups:** 12. Active Chapters: 335. Alumni Chapters: 340. **Publications:** Confidential Bulletin, quarterly. Journal, quarterly. Also publishes The Story of Kappa Alpha Psi.

★240★
Klanwatch
PO Box 548   Ph: (205)264-0286
Montgomery, AL 36104   Fax: (205)264-0629
Danny Welch, Contact

Description: Purpose is to gather and disseminate information about the Ku Klux Klan and to create a body of law to protect the rights of those the Klan is attacking. Collects information from 13,000 U.S. publications and other sources concerning the Klan. Conducts educational programs and distributes films for schoolchildren. Compiles statistics. **Founded:** 1980. **Budget:** $230,000. **Publications:** Klanwatch Intelligence Report, bimonthly. Contains updates on white supremacy activities throughout the United States.

★241★
Knights of Peter Claver
1825 Orleans Ave.
New Orleans, LA 70116   Ph: (504)821-4225
W. Charles Keyes Jr., Exec.Sec.

Description: Fraternal society of Roman Catholic men. Objectives are to: support local pastors, parishes, and the bishop of the diocese; participate in community activities and civic improvements; encourage Apostolic and Catholic action by laypersons; foster recreational assemblies and facilities; provide social and intellectual fellowship for members, as well as guidance and participation in the ever-changing structure of social and economic life; encourages youth participation. Sponsors workshops, fundraising projects, and educational and recreational activities. Presents scholarships to needy students; donates to selected charities and organizations; bestows awards. Group derives its name from Peter Claver (1581-1654), a Catholic priest who ministered to slaves in the West Indies and was declared a saint in 1884. **Also known as:** Knights and Ladies of St. Peter Claver. **Founded:** 1909. **Members:** 35,000. **Regional Groups:** 6. **Local Groups:** 410. **State Groups:** 22. **Publications:** The Claverite, bimonthly.

★242★
Lawyers' Committee for Civil Rights Under Law
1400 I St. NW, Ste. 400
Washington, DC 20005   Ph: (202)371-1212
Barbara R. Arnwine, Dir.

Description: Operates through local committees of private lawyers in eight major cities to provide legal assistance to poor and minority groups living in urban centers. National office undertakes reform efforts in such fields as employment, voting rights, and housing discrimination. Maintains library. **Founded:** 1963. **Members:** 165. **Budget:** $3,500,000. **Local Groups:** 8. **Publications:** Annual Report. Committee Report, quarterly. **Telecommunications Services:** Cable, LAWCIV.

★243★
Leadership Conference on Civil Rights
1629 K St. NW, Ste. 1010
Washington, DC 20006   Ph: (202)466-3311
Ralph G. Neas, Exec.Dir.

Description: Coalition of national organizations working to promote passage of civil rights, social and economic legislation, and enforcement of laws already on the books. Has released studies examining former President Ronald Reagan's tax and budget programs in areas including housing, elementary and secondary education, social welfare, and Indian affairs, and tax cuts. Has evaluated the enforcement of activities in civil rights by the U.S. Department of Justice; has also reviewed civil rights activities of the U.S. Department of Education. Bestows Hubert H. Humphrey Award. **Founded:** 1950. **Members:** 185. **Publications:** LCCR Memo. **Formerly:** Civil Rights Mobilization.

★244★
Library of African Cinema
149 9th St., Rm. 420   Ph: (415)621-6196
San Francisco, CA 94103   Fax: (415)621-6522
Cornelius Moore, Dir.

Description: A national project of California Newsreel, a nonprofit educational organization which produces and distributes media materials. Media specialists, educators, religious leaders, and concerned citizens. Objective is to improve the effectiveness of film/video in church, community, and education and action programs centered around southern Africa, particularly concerning human rights in South Africa. Believes that film/video screening can help form attitudes on foreign policy. Provides information on informing and involving the community on current U.S. foreign policy issues about apartheid through film/video screenings and countering lobbying and public relations efforts of the South African Information Service. Sponsors Bring South Africa Into the Classroom, an educational program combining videocassettes and curriculum guides. Maintains film library. **Founded:** 1976. **Advisory Board:** 26. **Budget:** $165,000. **Computerized Services:** Mailing lists of individuals active in South Africa awareness work. **Publications:** Southern Africa Media Center Catalog, annual. Also distributes Together/Against Apartheid (resource and action guide) and Using Films on South Africa (handbook). Makes available films including Mapantsula Generations of Resistance, Yeelen, Lumumba, Allah Tantou, Finzan, Chain of Tears, and The Cry of Reason. **Formerly:** (1990) Southern Africa Media Center.

★245★
Lincoln Institute for Research and Education
1001 Connecticut Ave. NW, Ste. 1135
Washington, DC 20036   Ph: (202)223-5112
J. A. Parker, Pres.

Description: Studies public policy issues affecting middle-class black Americans and disseminates research findings to elected officials and the public. Re-evaluates theories and programs that it feels are harmful to the long-range interests of blacks. Transmits pro-private enterprise views to public policymakers at local, state, and federal levels. Emphasizes the common national destiny of black and white Americans; supports a strong, steadily growing economy and a strong national defense. Sponsors and cosponsors conferences, seminars, and symposia on current issues. Maintains a comprehensive research and education program. **Founded:** 1978. **Publications:** Lincoln Review, quarterly. Journal containing public policy articles, essays, and reviews on issues affecting middle-class black Americans.

★246★
Links
1200 Massachusetts Ave. NW
Washington, DC 20005-4501   Ph: (202)842-8686
Mary P. Douglass, Dir.

Description: Organization of women committed to the community through educational, cultural, and civic activities. Provides enrichment experiences for those who are educationally disadvantaged and culturally deprived, and support for talented individuals. Sponsors charitable activities and a National Grant-In-Aid program. **Founded:** 1946. **Members:** 8500. **Budget:** $550,000. **Regional Groups:** 4. **Local Groups:** 241. **State Groups:** 40. **Publications:** Journal, semiannual. Link to Link, quarterly. Newsletter. Links Directory, quadrennial. Also publishes brochure.

★247★
Majestic Eagles
2029 Rhode Island Ave. NE   Ph: (202)635-0154
Washington, DC 20018   Fax: (202)635-1086
Col Jim Dicks, Pres.

Description: Business owners. Offers outreach and support services to small and minority (especially African-American) owned businesses, and provides a clearer understanding of business operations and management of resources to individiuals interested in establishing a business. Seeks to: emphasize individual development to help members become financially secure; increase business volume among the membership and the public; encourage business ownership. Sponsors Youth Entrepreneurship Program and Real Estate Development Club; also operates a credit union.

★248★
Martin Luther King, Jr. Center for Nonviolent Social Change, Inc.
449 Auburn Ave. NE   Ph: (404)524-8969
Atlanta, GA 30312   Fax: (404)522-6932
Coretta Scott King, Pres.

Description: Participants are individuals interested in the philosophy and actions of Rev. Martin Luther King, Jr. (1929-68), American clergyman, civil rights leader, and Nobel Peace Prize winner (1964). Encourages individuals, organizations, institutions, and nations to settle disputes by nonviolent means. Works to continue Dr. King's work through study, education, training, research, and constructive action. The U.S. Congress has established the 23.5 acres that accommodate the physical facilities of the center as a Martin Luther King, Jr. National Historic Site. (1980) Martin Luther King, Jr. Center for Social Change.

★249★
MCAP Group
89-50 164th St., Ste. 2B   Ph: (718)657-6444
Jamaica, NY 11432   Fax: (718)523-2063
Sherman L. Brown, Pres.

Description: Provides bonding, financial, technical, and management assistance to minority and small construction contractors in cities for the purpose of assisting the contractors to compete for a more equitable share of the construction industry. Services include: surety bonding program; financial and construction management; financial analysis; construction project management, including estimating, engineering, joint venture, and consortia arrangements; procurement referrals for several federally funded building programs. Sponsors conferences and workshops on matters of particular interest to minority contractors, such as bonding and nonprofit housing. Operates MCAP Bonding and Insurance Agency, a for-profit subsidiary. **Founded:** 1970. **Formerly:** (1989) Minority Contractors Assistance Project.

★250★
Meiklejohn Civil Liberties Institute
PO Box 673   Ph: (510)848-0599
Berkeley, CA 94701   Fax: (510)848-6008
Ann Fagan Ginger, Exec.Dir.

Description: Established to collect attorney workpapers and unreported rulings filed in courts in cases involving civil rights, due process, and civil liberties, in order to assist attorneys and legal workers confronted with similar issues. Concentrates effort on a peace law and education project, with a brief bank of legal case files and in-depth findings and reports relating to current issues about U.S. military policies and conventional and nuclear war. Maintains extensive library of over 8000 case files. Houses archives of National Lawyers Guild (see separate entry) as well as other primary source materials documenting the Cold War Period, the Civil Rights Movement, the Free Speech Movement, and the Vietnam War era. Operates speakers' bureau. **Founded:** 1965. **Budget:** $90,000. **Computerized Services:** PeaceNet. **Publications:** Event Journal, annual. Human Rights Organizations and Periodicals Directory, biennial. News from MCLI, semiannual. Peace Law Almanac, periodic. Peace Law Docket, biennial. Has also published Human Rights Docket, The Ford Hunger March, Alexander Meiklejohn: Teacher of Freedom, The Cold War Against Labor, Peace Law Basics, PL Undergrad College Reader, PL Law School Reader, materials for the public, and specialized materials for attorneys and social scientists.

★251★
Metropolitan Travel Agents
c/o Ethan C. Smythe
Calendar Travel
227 Utica Ave.
Brooklyn, NY 11213   Ph: (718)771-8400
Ethan C. Smythe, Pres.

Description: Travel agents employed by black-owned travel agencies united to promote travel among blacks. **Budget:** $75,000. **Founded:** 1969. **Members:** 35.

★252★
Minorities in Media
c/o Barbara Noble
Parkway School District
455 N. Woods Mill Rd.
Chesterfield, MO 63017   Ph: (314)469-8538
Barbara Noble Sr., Contact

Description: Minority media professionals including librarians, media specialists, and media vendors. Facilitates communication among members; conveys members' programs and ideas to the Association for Educational Communications and Technology. Maintains collection of members' publications. Plans to make available scholarships. **Founded:** 1975. **Members:** 85. **Publications:** Newsletter, semiannual.

★253★
Minority Business Enterprise Legal Defense and Education Fund
220 I St. NE, Ste. 280   Ph: (202)543-0040
Washington, DC 20002   Fax: (202)543-4135
Anthony W. Robinson, Pres.

Description: Minority businesspersons united to defend, enhance, and expand minority business. Acts as advocate and legal representative for the minority business community, offering legal representation in matters of national or regional importance. **Founded:** 1980. **Members:** 2000. **Publications:** MBE Vanguard, quarterly. Newsletter.

★254★
Minority Business Information Institute
130 5th Ave., 10th Fl.   Ph: (212)242-8000
New York, NY 10011   Fax: (212)989-8410
Earl G. Graves, Exec.Dir.

Description: Not an association. Maintains 2200 volume library of books, periodicals, and reports focusing on minority businesses. **Founded:** 1970. **Publications:** Index to Black Enterprise, periodic. Magazine.

★255★
Minority Caucus of Family Service America
34 1/2 Beacon St.   Ph: (617)523-6400
Boston, MA 02108   Fax: (617)523-3034
Mark Allen, Exec.Dir.

Description: Any member of a minority group who is involved with a family service agency in any capacity. Works to combat racism in FSA and to make FSA more relevant to the needs of minority families. Conducts negotiations with and participates in policymaking groups. Maintains Minority Resource Council and Task Force to Eradicate Institutional Racism. Presents Grady B. Murdock Award for outstanding service to minorities. **Founded:** 1969. **Publications:** Newsletter, annual. **Formerly:** (1973) Black Caucus of Family Service Association of America; (1986) Minorities Caucus of Family Service Association of America.

★256★
Minority Rights Group U.S.A.
c/o Sue Roff
35 Claremont Ave., Box 4S
New York, NY 10027   Ph: (212)864-7986
Sue Roff, Convener

Description: A branch of Minority Rights Group. Aims are to: secure justice for minority or majority groups suffering discrimination by investigating their situation and publicizing the facts internationally; help prevent violations of human rights by using publicity and to prevent such problems from developing into dangerous and destructive conflicts; foster, by its research findings, international understanding of the factors that create prejudiced treatment and group tensions; promote the growth of a world conscience regarding human rights. Sponsors seminars on minority issues; commissions multidisciplinary research into the causes of minority problems and their solutions. Granted consultative status by the United Nations. Maintains library. **Founded:** 1968. **Publications:** Newsletter, bimonthly. Also publishes reports.

★257★
Mobility Haiti
611 Broadway, Rm. 616   Ph: (212)260-8144
New York, NY 10012   Fax: (202)387-1450
Julia Philpott, Dir.

Description: Sponsored by the Institute for Transportation and Development Policy (see separate entry). Promotes integration of non-motorized transportation such as bicycles into the rural healthcare delivery system of Haiti. Provides bicycles and other transportation supplies and equipment to healthcare extension workers; conducts training programs. **Founded:** 1982. **Publications:** Information sheet. **Telecommunications Services:** Electronic mail, PEACENET, MOBILITY; telex, 155217437 MOBILITY. **Formerly:** (1989) Haitian Development Fund.

★258★
Modern Free and Accepted Masons of the World
PO Box 1072
Columbus, GA 31902   Ph: (706)322-3326
Soammes Williams, Asst.Dir.

Description: Fellowship organization dedicated to educating members so that they may become better leaders and citizens. Holds seminars and workshops on topics such as leadership and business skills. Conducts Sunday school classes for children. **Founded:** 1917. **Members:** 18,000. **Budget:** $50,000. **Publications:** Searchlight, monthly. Newspaper.

★259★
Moslem Mosque
104 Powers St.
Brooklyn, NY 11211   Ph: (718)387-0835
Al Challis, Pres.

Description: To perpetuate the religion and faith of Islam; to provide a mosque for religious services. **Founded:** 1907. **Members:** 300. **Budget:** Less than $25,000. **Publications:** none. **Formerly:** (1965) American Mohammedan Society.

★260★
Most Worshipful National Grand Lodge Free and Accepted Ancient York Masons
PO Box 2789
Orangeburg, SC 29116-2789   Ph: (803)531-1985
Hon. Oscar Mack, Pres.

Description: Organizes and installs grand and subordinate lodges for the purpose of "mutual uplifting and moral improvement." Conducts annual seminars; sponsors scholarship programs; maintains state archives. **Founded:** 1847. **Members:** 50,000. **Budget:** $50,000. **Local Groups:** 96. **State Groups:** 38. **Publications:** York Rite Bulletin, quarterly. **Also known as:** Most Worshipful National Grand Lodge Free and Accepted Ancient York Masons Prince Hall Origin National Compact U.S.A.

★261★
Multicultural Network of the American Society for Training and Development
c/o Eric King
Digital Equipment Corp.   Ph: (508)635-7127
80 Central St.   Fax: (816)421-5538
Boxborough, MA 01719   Free: 800-821-6180
Eric King, Dir.

Description: A member service of the American Society for Training and Development. Provides training and information resources to human resource development practitioners of culturally diverse backgrounds or in the business of training and development of multicultural populations. Seeks to develop products and services that address the needs of the multicultural human resource development work force. **Members:** 2000. **Publications:** Multicultural Network News, 4/year. Newsletter. Also publishes Valuing Differences in the Workplace (monograph) and makes available The Making of a Multicultural Network (videotape).

★262★
Museum of African American History
301 Frederick Douglass St.   Ph: (313)833-9800
Detroit, MI 48202   Fax: (313)832-7933
Dr. James Wayett, Deputy Dir.

Description: Persons interested in developing the national, public-sponsored Black Historical Museum. The museum is dedicated to preserving, documenting, interpreting, and exhibiting the cultural heritage of African-Americans and their ancestors. Serves as a learning and resource center; collects and documents contributions of black people. Offers permanent and traveling exhibits. Conducts workshops, seminars, and lecture series. Bestows Paul Robeson scholarship. Sponsors competitions; bestows awards; maintains children's services; offers specialized education program. Maintains reference library containing books, films, and audiotapes of African world history, art, and culture. Plans to interview and tape stories of elderly blacks. **Founded:** 1965. **Members:** 5000. **Budget:** $350,000. **Publications:** The Gallery, quarterly. Newsletter. **Formerly:** (1969) International Afro-American Museum Committee; (1978) International Afro-American Museum; (1983) Afro-American Museum of Detroit.

★263★
Museum of Afro-American History
Abiel Smith School
46 Joy St.   Ph: (617)742-1854
Boston, MA 02114   Fax: (617)742-3589
Monica Fairbairn, Pres.

Description: A charitable nonprofit institution established "to locate, collect, conserve, preserve, and secure for exhibition and research, historical material pertaining to the life, thought, material culture, and heritage of Afro-Americans in New England." (The majority of the collection pertains to 19th and 20th century history.) Conducts research in social and architectural history and in historic archaeology. Maintains library of films and filmstrips on Afro-American history. Also jointly maintains 4000 volume library of Afro-American literature with Suffolk University. Provides guided tours of a 19th century black neighborhood (the Black Heritage Trail) and a 20th century black community (Roxbury Heritage Trail). The museum owns the African Meeting House (the oldest extant black church in North America and component of the Boston African American National Historic Site), which was built by black craftsmen in 1806 and was the founding site of the New England Anti-Slavery

Society. **Formerly:** (1968) American Museum of Negro History. **Founded:** 1965. **Members:** 750. **Publications:** Acquisitions List, Collection of Afro-American History, annual. Black Heritage Trail, periodic. Museum-Smith Court News, quarterly. Newsletter. Also produces slide-tape programs.

★264★
Mutual Musicians Foundation
1823 Highland
Kansas City, MO 64108   Ph: (816)421-9297
Marion Watkins, Pres.

Description: Musicians and other interested persons. Seeks to promote, preserve, and perpetuate the Kansas City, MO jazz heritage. Performs for youth and senior citizens' organizations. Maintains Musicians Foundation Building, which was designated as a national historic landmark. The foundation's building served as headquarters for the city's black musicians' union, and NMA hopes it will serve as the symbol of Kansas City's place in the history of jazz. Sponsors educational and charitable programs. Plans to open a museum, studio, classrooms, lounge, and entertainment hall and to offer scholarships. **Founded:** 1917. **Members:** 125. **Publications:** Plans to publish newsletter. **Formerly:** (1917) Negro Musicians Association; (1930) Black Musicians Union of the American Federation of Music.

★265★
NAACP Legal Defense and Educational Fund
99 Hudson St., 16th Fl.
New York, NY 10013   Ph: (212)219-1900
Elaine R. Jones, Dir.-Counsel

Description: Legal arm of the civil rights movement, functioning independently of the National Association for the Advancement of Colored People since the mid-1950s. Works to provide and support litigation in behalf of blacks, other racial minorities, and women defending their legal and constitutional rights against discrimination in employment, education, housing, and other areas. Represents civil rights groups as well as individual citizens who have bona fide civil rights claims. Contributed funds are used to finance court actions for equality in schools, jobs, voting, housing, municipal services, land use, and delivery of health care services. Has organized litigation campaign for prison reform and the abolition of capital punishment. Hosts annual institute to develop public awareness of new problems being faced by minorities. Maintains Herbert Lehman Education Fund, through which scholarships are awarded to black students attending state universities; sponsors Earl Warren Legal Training Program, which provides scholarships to black law students. Compiles statistics on capital punishment. Maintains library of 15,000 volumes on law. Committee of 100, a voluntary cooperative group of individuals, has sponsored the appeal of the fund since 1943. **Founded:** 1940. **Budget:** $8,900,000. **Publications:** Annual Report. Equal Justice, quarterly. Newsletter. Also publishes legal materials, brochures, press releases, and occasional watchdog reports.

★266★
Nation of Ishmael
2696 Ben Hill Rd.
East Point, GA 30344   Ph: (404)349-1153
Jacob Smith, Founder

Description: Individuals and corporations. Nondenominational religious organization working to improve the economic, educational, spiritual, and social potential of black communities in the U.S. Provides administrative assistance to and facilitates procurement of loans by minority-owned small businesses. Conducts programs for youth and senior citizens. Holds quarterly seminar for business owners. **Founded:** 1975. **Members:** 300. **Publications:** Brochures.

★267★
National Action Council for Minorities in Engineering
3 W. 35th St.   Ph: (212)279-2626
New York, NY 10001   Fax: (212)629-5178
George Campbell Jr., Pres.

Description: Seeks to increase the number of African American, Hispanic, and Native American students enrolled in and graduating from engineering schools. Offers incentive grants to engineering schools to recruit and provide financial assistance to increasing numbers of minority students. Works with local, regional, and national support organizations to motivate and encourage precollege students to engage in engineering careers. Conducts educational and research programs; operates project to assist engineering schools in improving the retention and graduation rates of minority students. Maintains speakers' bureau; bestows awards; compiles statistics. **Founded:** 1980. **Budget:** $4,000,000. **Publications:** Annual Report. Directory of Pre-College and University Minority Engineering Programs, periodic. Financial Aid Unscrambled: A Guide for Minority Engineering Students, biennial. NACME News, 3/year. Newsletter for educators, counselors, and program directors who participate in minority engineering education.

★268★
National Alliance Against Racist and Political Repression
11 John St., Rm. 702   Ph: (212)406-3330
New York, NY 10038   Fax: (212)406-3542
Charlene Mitchell, Exec.Dir.

Description: Coalition of political, labor, church, civic, student, and community organizations; individuals dedicated to protecting people's right to organize. Seeks to mobilize millions of people to unite in word and action against many forms of repression of human rights in the U.S. including: persecution and jailing of political activists; attempts to suppress prisoners' rights movements and use of behavior control against prisoners and the poor; assaults on labor's right to organize, strike, and act effectively; police crimes against the people, especially nonwhites; legislation and court decisions repressing basic rights; the death penalty. Opposes: use of grand juries and the FBI, CIA, and government spying programs to persecute those working for social change; suppression of movements for democracy and against racism in the military; failure to grant full amnesty to war resisters; attacks on lawyers who fight militantly for oppressed people; attacks on educators and students who struggle against racism and for democratic rights; harassment and deportation of the foreign-born, especially "undocumented" workers who come to the U.S. as "economic victims of U.S.-dominated countries." Conducts speaking tours, sponsors petition campaigns, and organizes demonstrations. Combines legal action with mass action. Establishes task forces. **Founded:** 1973. **Members:** 5000. **Publications:** The Organizer, quarterly. Newsletter. Also publishes pamphlets and produces slide shows and films.

★269★
National Alliance of Black Organizations
3724 Airport Blvd.
Austin, TX 78722   Ph: (512)478-9802
M. J. Anderson Sr., Pres.

Description: Presidents of black organizations and associations. Coordinates and encourages voter registration efforts among member organizations. Serves as a forum for the exchange of ideas and experiences. Assists charitable organizations. **Budget:** Less than $25,000. **Founded:** 1976. **Publications:** none.

★270★
National Alliance of Black School Educators
2816 Georgia Ave. NW   Ph: (202)483-1549
Washington, DC 20001   Fax: (202)483-8323
William J. Saunders, Exec.Dir.

Description: Black educators from all levels; others indirectly involved in the education of black youth. Purpose is to promote awareness, professional expertise, and commitment among black educators. Goals are to: eliminate and rectify the results of racism in education; work with state, local, and national leaders to raise the academic achievement level of all black students; increase members' involvement in legislative activities; facilitate the introduction of a curriculum that more completely embraces black America; improve the ability of black educators to promote problem resolution; create a meaningful and effective network of strength, talent, and professional support. Sponsors workshops, commission meetings, and special projects. Encourages research, especially as it relates to blacks, and the presentation of papers during national conferences. Plans to establish a National Black Educators Data Bank and offer placement service. **Formerly:** (1973) National Alliance of Black School Superintendents. **Founded:** 1970. **Members:** 5000. **Budget:** $600,000. **Local Groups:** 42. **Publications:** Membership Roster, annual. News Briefs, periodic.

★271★
National Alliance of Postal and Federal Employees
1628 11th St. NW
Washington, DC 20001
James M. McGee, Pres.
Ph: (202)939-6325
Fax: (202)939-6389

Description: Independent. Works to eliminate employment discrimination. Bestows scholarship awards to dependent children of members. **Founded:** 1913. **Members:** 70,000. **Budget:** $2,000,000. **Regional Groups:** 10. **Locals:** 137. **Publications:** National Alliance, monthly. Labor union newsletter covering the postal and other branches of the federal service. **Formerly:** (1968) National Alliance of Postal Employees.

★272★
National Alliance of Third World Journalists
PO Box 43208
Washington, DC 20010
Gwen McKinney, Dir.
Ph: (202)462-8197

Description: Journalists, journalism students, and persons in related communications fields. Proposes to increase the quality and quantity of media coverage of the Third World. Acts as an informational bridge between minorities in the U.S. and the Third World. Provides the opportunity for minority journalists to travel to the Third World to gain first-hand knowledge of the situation in the respective countries. Provides speakers on Third World related issues and topics, including official representatives of national liberation movements, and on media coverage of the Third World. Schedules forums and seminars. **Founded:** 1981. **Members:** 330. **Budget:** $100,000. **Regional Groups:** 4. **Local Groups:** 5. **Publications:** Media Relations Handbook.

★273★
National Alumni Council of the United Negro College Fund
c/o United Negro Coll. Fund
500 E. 62nd St.
New York, NY 10021
William H. Gray III, Pres. & CEO
Ph: (212)326-1203
Fax: (212)326-1164

Description: Inter-alumni councils, national alumni associations, and students. Purposes are to: stimulate the interest of black college alumni; acquaint the public with the value of black colleges and black higher education; inform students and the public about contributions of black college alumni to civic betterment and community progress; recruit students for member colleges; raise funds for United Negro College Fund (see separate entry); encourage and provide a structure for cooperation among black college alumni groups and friends of black higher education. Bestows awards; compiles statistics. **Founded:** 1946. **Members:** 3000. **Publications:** Conference Journal, annual. Newsletter, periodic. **Also known as:** National Alumni Council of the UNCF.

★274★
National Association for Black Veterans
PO Box 11432
Milwaukee, WI 53211
Ph: (414)265-8940
Fax: (414)332-4627
Free: 800-842-4597

Thomas H. Wynn Sr., Exec. Officer

Description: Black and other minority veterans, primarily those who fought in Vietnam. Represents the interests of minority veterans before the Veterans Administration. Operates Metropolitan Veterans Service to obtain honorable discharges for minority and low-income veterans who in the organization's opinion unjustly received a less than honorable discharge. Defends incarcerated veterans through its Readjustment Counseling Program; operates job creation program; offers services to geriatric and homeless veterans. Conducts workshops to acquaint lawyers and clinicians with problems associated with Post Traumatic Stress Disorder. Sponsors geriatric seminar and training program. Operates library of military regulations; compiles statistics; bestows awards; maintains speakers' bureau. **Founded:** 1970. **Members:** 25,000. **Budget:** $350,000. **Local Groups:** 13. **Computerized Services:** Databases; mailing list. **Publications:** Eclipse, monthly. Newspaper. **Formerly:** (1970) Interested Veterans of the Central City.

★275★
National Association for Equal Educational Opportunities
2181 Brigden Rd.
Pasadena, CA 91104
Dr. Juan Francisco Lara, Pres.
Ph: (714)856-6362
Fax: (714)856-8219

Description: College and university personnel concerned with the development and operation of secondary school and collegiate programs to serve the needs of low-income and disadvantaged students. Provides speakers on issues confronting students who are the first generations in their families to go on to higher education. Conducts seminars on the relation between postsecondary and secondary education for teachers, faculty, and administrators. Compiles statistics. **Budget:** Less than $25,000. **Founded:** 1975. **Members:** 60.

★276★
National Association for Equal Opportunity in Higher Education
Lovejoy Bldg.
400 12th St. NE, 2nd Fl.
Washington, DC 20002
Dr. Samuel L. Myers, Pres.
Ph: (202)543-9111
Fax: (202)543-9113

Description: Provides a unified framework representing historically and predominantly black universities and colleges and similarly situated institutions in their attempt to continue as viable forces in American society. Seeks to build a case for securing increased support from federal agencies, philanthropic foundations, and other sources, and to increase black leadership of educational organizations and membership on federal boards and commissions relating to education. Offers placement service. Bestows Distinguished Alumni Citation of the Year, Research Achievement, and Leadership awards. Maintains biographical data on member colleges/universities and presidents/chancellors. Compiles statistics on black graduates. **Founded:** 1969. **Members:** 117. **Budget:** $750,000. **Computerized Services:** Database on programs sponsored by the U.S. Agency for International Development. **Publications:** Black Excellence, bimonthly. Magazine for college students.

★277★
National Association for Ethnic Studies
Arizona State University
Department of English
Tempe, AZ 85287
Gretchen Bataille, Treas.
Ph: (602)965-2197
Fax: (602)965-2012

Description: Individuals, libraries, and institutions. Promotes research, study, and curriculum design in the field of ethnic studies. Annually bestows Ernest M Pon Award. **Founded:** 1975. **Members:** 300. **Budget:** Less than $25,000. **Computerized Services:** Mailing list. **Publications:** The Ethnic Reporter, semiannual. Newsletter. Monitors developments in the field, discusses educational issues; and reports on activities of the association. **Formerly:** (1976) National Association of Interdisciplinary Studies for Native American, Black, Chicano, Puerto Rican, Asian Americans; (1985) National Association of Interdisciplinary Ethnic Studies.

★278★
National Association for Free Enterprise
1322 Vermont Ave. NW
Washington, DC 20005
John Edward Hurley, Pres.
Ph: (202)483-5700

Description: Individuals, single proprietorships, partnerships and corporations. Conducts legislative and educational programs to foster and promote the competitive free enterprise system. Bestows awards; provides speakers' bureau; offers placement service; compiles statistics. **Founded:** 1974. **Members:** 5000. **Publications:** FEPAC News, monthly.

★279★
National Association for Sickle Cell Disease
3345 Wilshire Blvd., Ste. 1106
Los Angeles, CA 90010-1880
Ph: (213)736-5455
Fax: (213)736-5211
Free: 800-421-8453

Lynda King Anderson, Contact

Description: Community groups involved in sickle cell anemia programs throughout the U.S. (Sickle cell anemia is an inherited blood disease that primarily affects black people and is a major health problem within the black community.) Purposes are to: provide leadership on a national level in order to create awareness in all circles of the negative impact of sickle cell anemia on the health and economic, social, and educational well-being of the individual and his/her family and to create awareness of the requirements for resolution; prepare and distribute substantive educational materials; develop and promote implementation of service program standards that will be in the best interest of the affected population; provide ongoing technical assistance to interested groups; encourage adequate support for research. Resources include: counselor training; workshops and seminars; blood banks; screening and testing; tutorial services; camps for children with sickle cell disease; vocational rehabilitation. Operates Charles F. Whitten Sickle Cell Summer Research Apprenticeships, Roland J. Nyman Research Fund, and Rick Berry Fund. Bestows awards for outstanding service. **Founded:** 1971. **Budget:** $970,000. **Local Groups:** 86. **Publications:** HELP, A Guide to Sickle Cell Disease Programs and Services, periodic. National Association for Sickle Cell Disease–Newsletter, quarterly.

★280★
National Association for the Advancement of Black Americans in Vocational Education
c/o Dr. Ethel O. Washington
5057 Woodward, Rm. 976
Detroit, MI 48202
Ph: (313)494-1660
Fax: (313)494-1535

Dr. Ethel O. Washington, Pres.

Description: Educational institutions, teachers, administrators, students, and government employees committed to the greater involvement of black Americans in all areas of vocational/technical education. Goal is to generate national leadership and increase the impact of blacks in the field of vocational/technical education by: assuring opportunities and promoting recruitment and the retention of black Americans in all areas and levels; utilizing research discoveries as a basis for influencing key funding sources at the national, state, and local levels; providing a career information exchange system. Develops training models for marketable skills; links black talent with vocational/technical employment opportunities in the public and private sectors at the federal, state, and local levels; identifies, assesses, and evaluates critical issues that affect the extent of participation of blacks and offers recommendations for improvement. Conducts regional workshops. Maintains placement service for blacks and other minorities. Sponsors competitions. Operates speakers' bureau; compiles statistics. **Founded:** 1977. **Members:** 900. **Budget:** Less than $25,000. **State Groups:** 6. **Publications:** Conference Proceedings, annual. National Association for the Advancement of Black Americans in Vocational Education–Newsletter, quarterly. Contains discussions of equity issues and successful programs in vocational education. Includes chapter news and employment listings.

★281★
National Association for the Advancement of Colored People
4805 Mt. Hope Dr.
Baltimore, MD 21215
Ph: (212)481-4100

Benjamin F. Chavis Jr., Exec.Dir.

Description: Persons "of all races and religions" who believe in the objectives and methods of the NAACP. To achieve equal rights through the democratic process and eliminate racial prejudice by removing racial discrimination in housing, employment, voting, schools, the courts, transportation, recreation, prisons, and business enterprises. Offers referral services, tutorials, job referrals, and day care. Sponsors seminars; maintains law library. Awards Spingarn Medal annually to a black American for distinguished achievement. Sponsors the NAACP National Housing Corporation to assist in the development of low and moderate income housing for families. Compiles statistics. **Founded:** 1909. **Members:** 400,000. **Local Groups:** 1802. **Publications:** Crisis, 10/year. Report, annual.

★282★
National Association for the Southern Poor
712A 3rd St. SW
Washington, DC 20024-3104
Ph: (202)554-3265

Donald Anderson, Exec.Dir.

Description: Black, low-income individuals in Virginia, North Carolina, South Carolina, and Georgia. Seeks to create local organizations, known as Assemblies, through which low-income people can become involved in local decision-making regarding community services and opportunities. Concentrates on organizing Southern blacks in an effort toward raising levels of health, education, and income. Compiles statistics; bestows awards. Assemblies hold monthly meeting. **Founded:** 1968. **Members:** 240,000. **Publications:** The Epistle Newsletter, monthly. **Formerly:** (1976) Virginia Community Development Organization.

★283★
National Association of Bench and Bar Spouses
42 LaSalle Ave.
Piedmont, CA 94611
Ph: (510)652-3256

Bonnie Wheatley, Pres.

Description: Spouses of attorneys united to conduct civic, cultural, and social activities in order "to enhance the prestige of the legal profession" and to encourage fellowship among attorneys' spouses. Sponsors conferences on the family and child advocacy programs; maintains Dorothy Atkinson Legal Scholarship Fund for worthy law students and college students interested in careers in law. **Founded:** 1951. **Members:** 400. **Budget:** Less than $25,000. **Regional Groups:** 4. Chapters: 28. **Publications:** Membership Directory, annual. Newsletter, semiannual. Also publishes historical brochure and program aids. **Formerly:** (1987) National Barristers' Wives.

★284★
National Association of Black Accountants
220 I St. NE, Ste. 150
Washington, DC 20002
Ph: (202)546-6222
Fax: (202)547-1041

Beverly Everson-Jones, Exec.Dir.

Description: CPAs, accountants, and accounting students. To unite accountants and accounting students who have similar interests and ideals, who are committed to professional and academic excellence, who possess a sense of professional and civic responsibility, and who are concerned with enhancing opportunities for minorities in the accounting profession. Programs include: free income tax preparation; student scholarships; high school and university career seminars; regional student conferences; technical seminars and lectures. Maintains speakers' bureau and placement service. Bestows awards. **Founded:** 1969. **Members:** 3000. **Budget:** $700,000. **Local Groups:** 100. **Publications:** Chapter to Chapter, quarterly. Newsletter for students. Spectrum, semiannual. Technical and educational journal addressing current and future accounting issues.

★285★
National Association of Black and White Men Together: A Gay Multiracial Organization for All People
4753 N. Broadway, No.1200
Chicago, IL 60640-4907
Ph: (312)907-0400
Fax: (312)907-0083
Free: 800-624-2968

Robert L. Williams, Co-Chair

Description: Gay men, lesbians, and other individuals. Promotes and fosters interracial fellowship and the formation of coalitions among gays and other minorities. Opposes racism within the gay community and homophobia within ethnic communities. Sponsors seminars and litigation. Compiles literature on the black and interracial gay experience. Conducts research on resisting racism. Maintains speakers' bureau; bestows awards. Offers charitable program and discussion groups. **Founded:** 1980. **Members:** 1200. **Budget:** $870,000. **Regional Groups:** 3. **Local Groups:** 28. **Computerized Services:** Mailing list. **Publications:** Annual Convention Program. Monthly Board Memos. NABWMT Journal, annual. Collection of members' writings. Newsletter, quarterly.

★286★
National Association of Black Catholic Administrators
c/o Ministry for Black Catholics
50 N. Park Ave.
Rockville Centre, NY 11570   Ph: (516)678-5800
Barbara Horsham-Brathwaite, Exec. Officer

Description: Black administrators and representatives of archdiocesan and diocesan offices concerned with the development of Black leadership within the Catholic church. Assists the church in its role of evangelization and in defining its mission to the black community. Seeks to provide an inner resource for the social and spiritual needs and concerns of Catholics of African ancestry. Addresses world issues of civil and human rights in the local, national, and international communities. **Budget:** Less than $25,000. **Founded:** 1976. **Local Groups:** 50. **Regional Groups:** 7.

★287★
National Association of Black Consulting Engineers
6406 Georgia Ave. NW
Washington, DC 20012   Ph: (202)291-3550
John W. Levermore, Pres.

Description: Engineering consulting firms and related businesses. Purpose is to gain recognition and increase professional opportunities for black consulting engineers. Lobbies the federal government. Gives presentations to high schools on career day to promote the engineering consulting field to black students. **Founded:** 1975. **Members:** 100. **Publications:** Plans to issue newsletter. **Formerly:** (1978) National Council of Minority Consulting Engineers.

★288★
National Association of Black Geologists and
  Geophysicists
PO Box 720157
Houston, TX 77272
Reginal Spiller, Pres.

Description: Black geologists and geophysicists. Assists minority geologists and geophysicists in establishing professional and business relationships. Informs minority students of career opportunities in geology and geophysics. Seeks to motivate minority students to utilize existing programs, grants, and loans. Provides annual scholarships and oversees the educational careers of scholarship recipients. Assists minority students in their pursuit for summer employment and members interested in obtaining employees for summer positions. **Founded:** 1981. **Members:** 120. MD $15/year for student; $25/year for junior; $35/year for senior. **Computerized Services:** Database. **Publications:** Platform Network, quarterly.

★289★
National Association of Black Hospitality Professionals
PO Box 5443   Ph: (908)354-5117
Plainfield, NJ 07060-5443   Fax: (908)354-5117
Mikoel Turner, Pres.

Description: Works to develop global educational and economic opportunities for the hospitality industry through the expansion and diversification of minority involvement in the industry. Encourages professional development and opportunity in the industry through the design and implementation of workshops and seminars. Seeks to increase the number, size, and capability of minority-owned businesses within the hospitality and tourism industries. Offers placement service; conducts research programs. **Founded:** 1985. **Members:** 450. **Regional Groups:** 2. **State Groups:** 3. **Computerized Services:** Database. **Publications:** Bulletin, monthly. Insights, quarterly. Newsletter.

★290★
National Association of Black Journalists
PO Box 17212   Ph: (703)648-1270
Washington, DC 20041   Fax: (703)476-6245
Elke Milton, Office Mgr.

Description: Persons employed in the production, dissemination, and distribution of news by newspapers, magazines, and radio and television stations. Aims are to: strengthen the ties between blacks in the black media and blacks in the white media; sensitize the white media to the "institutional racism in its coverage"; expand the white media's coverage and "balanced reporting" of the black community; become an exemplary group of professionals that honors excellence and outstanding achievement among black journalists. Works with high schools to identify potential journalists; awards scholarships to journalism programs that especially support minorities. Acts as a national clearinghouse for job information. Maintains biographical archives. Sponsors competitions. **Founded:** 1975. **Members:** 2400. MD $20 for student; $35 for associate; $60 for full. **Budget:** $450,000. Chapters 50. **Publications:** NABJ Journal, 10/year. Tabloid newsletter concerned with black issues and association news.

★291★
National Association of Black Owned Broadcasters
1730 M St. NW, Rm. 412
Washington, DC 20036   Ph: (202)463-8970
James L. Winston, Exec.Dir.

Description: Black broadcast station owners; black formatted stations not currently owned or controlled by blacks; organizations having an interest in the black consumer market or black broadcast industry; individuals interested in becoming owners; and communications schools, departments, and professional groups and associations. Represents the interests of existing and potential black radio and television stations. Is currently working with the Office of Federal Procurement Policy to determine which government contracting major advertisers and advertising agencies are complying with government initiatives to increase the amount of advertising dollars received by minority-owned firms. Conducts lobbying activities; provides legal representation for the protection of minority ownership policies. Participates in the reorganization of the Advisory Committee on Radio Broadcasting. Sponsors annual Communications Awards Dinner each March. Conducts workshops; compiles statistics. **Also known as:** National Black Owned Broadcasters Association. **Founded:** 1976. **Members:** 150. **Regional Groups:** 5. **Computerized Services:** Mailing list of black-owned broadcast facilities. **Publications:** Black-Owned Station Directory, quarterly. NABOB News, monthly. Newsletter.

★292★
National Association of Black Professors
PO Box 526
Crisfield, MD 21817   Ph: (410)968-2393
Dr. Sarah Miles Woods

Description: College professors of African descent. Goals are to: provide a forum for the exchange of information among college professors; enhance education for black people and enrich the educational process in general; support and promote intellectual interests of black students. Disseminates professional improvement information. Sponsors annual public lecture. Compiles statistics; bestows awards and scholarship; maintains placement service and speakers' bureau. **Budget:** Less than $25,000. **Founded:** 1974. **Members:** 135.

★293★
National Association of Black Real Estate
  Professionals
PO Box 21421
Alexandria, VA 22320   Ph: (703)920-7661
Sherman L. Ragland II, Pres.

Description: Black professionals in real estate, including the areas of design, development, law, engineering, management, and investment. Provides a forum for the discussion of information related to the industry. Offers career development and networking opportunities. Provides placement and consulting services; maintains speakers' bureau. **Founded:** 1984. **Regional Groups:** 5.

★294★
National Association of Black Social Workers
1969 Madison Ave.
New York, NY 10035   Ph: (212)348-0035
Robert Knox, Contact

Description: Social workers and other concerned individuals. Seeks to support, develop, and sponsor community welfare projects and programs which will serve the interest of the black community and aid it in controlling its social institutions. Assists with adoption referrals. Bestows education awards; maintains library. **Founded:** 1968. **Members:** 10,000. **Publications:** Black Caucus, annual.

Proceedings, annual. Also publishes Preserving Black Families: Research and Action Beyond the Rhetoric.

★295★
National Association of Black Storytellers
PO Box 67722
Baltimore, MD 21215
Eleanora Tate, Pres.
Description: Black storytellers and enthusiasts. Seeks to establish a forum to promote the black oral tradition and to attract an audience. Works for the reissue of out-of-print story collections. Bestows Zora Neale Hurston Award to pioneers in black storytelling. **Founded:** 1984. **Members:** 350. MD $10 for senior and student; $20 for individual; $50 for contributing; $100 for organizational; $500 for life. **Publications:** NABS Newsletter, 3/year. **Formerly:** (1990) Association of Black Storytellers.

★296★
National Association of Black Women Attorneys
3711 Macomb St. NW, 2nd Fl.   Ph: (202)966-9693
Washington, DC 20016   Fax: (202)244-6648
Mabel D. Haden, Pres.
Description: Black women who are members of the bar of any U.S. state or territory; associate members include law school graduates, paralegals, and law students. Seeks to: advance jurisprudence and the administration of justice by increasing the opportunities of black and non-black women at all levels; aid in protecting the civil and human rights of all citizens and residents of the U.S.; expand opportunities for women lawyers through education; promote fellowship among women lawyers. Provides pre-law and student counseling; serves as job placement resource for firms, companies, and others interested in the field. Holds regional seminars; sponsors scholarship awards competition and brief-writing contest. Maintains hall of fame; offers charitable program. **Founded:** 1972. **Members:** 500. **Budget:** $30,000. **Regional Groups:** 8. **Local Groups:** 2. **State Groups:** 10. **Computerized Services:** Data base; mailing list. **Publications:** Convention Bulletin, annual. NABWA News, quarterly. Also publishes job announcements. **Telecommunications Services:** Telephone referral service.

★297★
National Association of Black Women Entrepreneurs
PO Box 1375   Ph: (313)341-7400
Detroit, MI 48231   Fax: (313)342-3433
Marilyn French-Hubbard, Founder
Description: Black women who own and operate their own businesses; black women interested in starting businesses; organizations and companies desiring mailing lists. Acts as a national support system for black businesswomen in the U.S. and focuses on the unique problems they face. Objective is to enhance business, professional, and technical development of both present and future black businesswomen. Maintains speakers' bureau and national networking program. Offers symposia, workshops, and forums aimed at increasing the business awareness of black women. Shares resources, lobbies, and provides placement service. Bestows annual Black Woman Entrepreneur of the Year Award. **Founded:** 1979. **Members:** 3000. **Budget:** $230,000. **Regional Groups:** 4. **State Groups:** 28. **Publications:** Making Success Happen Newsletter, bimonthly. Membership Directory, annual.

★298★
National Association of Blacks in Criminal Justice
PO Box 9499
Washington, DC 20016   Ph: (301)681-2365
Levan Gordon, Chm.
Description: Criminal justice professionals concerned with the impact of criminal justice policies and practices on the minority community. Advocates with local, state, and federal criminal justice agencies for the improvement of minority recruitment practices and for the advancement of minority career mobility within those agencies. Sponsors regional conferences, career development seminars, and annual training institutes; maintains speakers' bureau. Provides financial and in-kind services to community groups. Bestows annual awards; compiles statistics on minority involvement in the criminal justice field. **Founded:** 1972. **Members:** 5000. **Budget:** $50,000. **State Groups:** 27. **Publications:** Local Criminal Justice Issues Newsletter, bimonthly. NABCJ Annual Report.

NABCJ Minority Criminal Justice Personnel Directory, annual. NABCJ Newsletter, quarterly. Proceedings of Annual Conference..

★299★
National Association of Blacks Within Government
1820 11th St. NW
Washington, DC 20001-5015   Ph: (202)667-3280
Marion A. Bowden, Pres.
Description: Purpose is to enhance and increase the employability of black officials within government and to prepare black youths for government and private sector careers. Sponsors yearly seminar to help young people develop management, learning, interpersonal, and specialized skills. Bestows annual Black Humanitarian Award; compiles statistics. **Founded:** 1982. **Regional Groups:** 1. **Publications:** Newsletter, semiannual.

★300★
National Association of College and University Business Officers
1 Dupont Cir. NW, Ste. 500   Ph: (202)861-2500
Washington, DC 20036   Fax: (202)861-2583
Caspa L. Harris, Pres.
Description: Colleges, universities, and companies that are members of a regional association. To develop and maintain interest on a nationwide basis in improving the principles and practices of business and financial administration in higher education. Sponsors workshops in fields such as cash management, grant and contract maintenance, accounting, investment, student loan administration, and costing. Maintains library of 2000 volumes. Conducts research and information exchange programs between college and university personnel; maintains databases; compiles statistics. Bestows Cost Reduction Incentive Awards and Distinguished Business Officer Awards annually. **Founded:** 1950. **Members:** 2100. **Regional Groups:** 4. **Publications:** Business Officer, monthly. Magazine covering business and financial news affecting college and university management; includes association news, meetings schedule, and information on new publications. **Formerly:** (1962) National Federation of College and University Business Officers Associations.

★301★
National Association of College Deans, Registrars and Admissions Officers
917 Dorsett Ave.
Albany, GA 31701   Ph: (912)435-4945
Helen Mayes, Exec.Sec.
Description: Deans, registrars, and admissions officers of collegiate institutions with predominantly black student bodies. **Founded:** 1925. **Members:** 325. **Budget:** Less than $25,000. **Publications:** NACDRAO Directory, annual. Newsletter, quarterly. Proceedings, annual. **Formerly:** (1949) National Association of Collegiate Deans and Registrars in Negro Schools; (1970) National Association of College Deans and Registrars.

★302★
National Association of Colored Women's Clubs
5808 16th St. NW
Washington, DC 20011   Ph: (202)726-2044
Carole A. Early, Hdqtrs.Sec.
Description: Federation of black women's clubs. Carries on program of civic service, education, social service, and philanthropy. Sponsors National Association of Girls Clubs. **Founded:** 1896. **Members:** 45,000. **Local Groups:** 1000. **State Groups:** 38. **Publications:** National Notes, quarterly.

★303★
National Association of Educational Office Professionals
PO Box 12619   Ph: (316)942-4822
Wichita, KS 67277   Fax: (316)942-7100
Kay Blair, Contact
Description: Secretaries, stenographers, administrative assistants, bookkeepers, receptionists, and other office workers employed by schools, colleges and universities, educational associations, and county and state departments of education. Conducts professional standards program to measure the services of office personnel in education and awards certificates for achievements on five levels of

education, experience, and professional activity. Sponsors competitions; maintains speakers' bureau; annually bestows National Educational Administrator of the Year and National Educational Office Employee of the Year awards. Also annually bestows Marion T. Wood Scholarship and other awards. **Founded:** 1934. **Members:** 6500. MD $5/year for retired; $30/year for active. **Regional Groups:** 250. **Publications:** Beam, quarterly. Newsletter for retirees. **Formerly:** (1952) Maintains 7000 volume library and speakers' bureau. National Association of School Secretaries; (1980) National Association of Educational Secretaries; (1992) National Association of Educational Office Personnel.

★304★
National Association of Extension Home Economists
3611B Chain Bridge Rd.
Fairfax, VA 22030   Ph: (703)385-3801
Kathy Huggins, Exec.Dir.

Description: Conducts out-of-school educational programs. Helps individuals and families find solutions to problems concerning family life such as child care and development, nutrition, energy conservation, budgeting, and family recreation. Sponsors conferences and trains volunteer leaders to work with individuals and groups. Conducts public policy forum; bestows awards. **Founded:** 1931. **Members:** 3200. **Budget:** $350,000. **State Groups:** 52. **Publications:** The Communique, quarterly. Newsletter. The Reporter, quarterly. **Formerly:** National Association of Negro Home Demonstration Agents; National Home Demonstration Agents' Association.

★305★
National Association of Fashion and Accessory Designers
2180 E. 93rd St.
Cleveland, OH 44106   Ph: (216)231-0375
Beatrice Spencer, Pres.

Description: Persons engaged in the field of fashion design or other allied fields. Fosters the development of the black fashion designer; encourages integration of members in all phases of the fashion industry through the extension of educational and economic opportunities. Disseminates information; awards local and national scholarships. Holds workshops and fashion seminars; maintains library and Black Historical Museum of Fashion Dolls. Presented biographical archives to the Mary McLeod Bethune Historical Development Project. **Founded:** 1949. **Members:** 240. **Budget:** Less than $25,000. **Regional Groups:** 2. **Local Groups:** 12. **State Groups:** 2. **Publications:** Membership Roster, annual. Newsletter, semiannual.

★306★
National Association of Girls Clubs
5808 16th St. NW
Washington, DC 20011   Ph: (202)726-2044
Carole A. Early, Hdqtrs.Sec.

Description: Sponsored by National Association of Colored Women's Clubs. Black girls, ages 6-18. Promotes the moral, mental, and material development of members; fosters positive attitudes toward health, beauty, love, home, and service among members. **Founded:** 1930. **Formerly:** (1976) National Association of Colored Girls Clubs.

★307★
National Association of Health Services Executives
10320 Little Patuxent Pkwy., Ste. 1106   Ph: (202)628-3953
Columbia, MD 21044   Fax: (202)628-3958
Ozzie Jenkins, Dir.

Description: Black health care executive managers, planners, educators, advocates, providers, organizers, researchers, and consumers participating in academic ventures, educational forums, seminars, workshops, systems design, legislation, and other activities. Conducts National Work-Study Program and sponsors educational programs. Bestows annual Humanitarian Award for outstanding service in the field of human services. **Founded:** 1968. **Members:** 500. **Budget:** $35,000. **Local Groups:** 7. **Publications:** NAHSE Notes, quarterly. Newsletter.

★308★
National Association of Human Rights Workers
c/o Ronald McElreath
Florida Commission on Human Relations
Bldg. F., Ste. 240
325 John Knox Rd.
Tallahassee, FL 32303   Ph: (904)488-7082
Ronald McElreath, Pres.

Description: Professional association of governmental or private organization employees working in the areas of civil rights, civil liberties, interracial and interethnic relations, and religious understanding. Maintains speakers' bureau; conducts research programs; compiles statistics. **Founded:** 1947. **Members:** 350. **Budget:** Less than $25,000. **Regional Groups:** 4. **Local Groups:** 16. **Publications:** Journal of Intergroup Relations, quarterly. NAHRW Newsletter, bimonthly. **Formerly:** National Association of Intergroup Relations Officials.

★309★
National Association of Investment Companies
1111 14th St. NW, Ste. 700
Washington, DC 20005   Ph: (202)289-4336
JoAnn H. Price, Pres.

Description: Aims to: represent the minority small business investment company industry in the public sector; provide industry education; develop research material on the activities of the industry; promote the growth of minority-owned small businesses by informing the public of their contribution to the vitality of the nation's economy; collect and disseminate relevant business and trade information to members; facilitate the exchange of new ideas and financing strategies; assist organizing groups attempting to form or acquire minority enterprise small business investment companies; provide management and technical assistance to members; monitor regulatory agency actions. Conducts three professional seminars; sponsors research; compiles statistics. **Founded:** 1971. **Members:** 150. **Publications:** NAIC Membership Directory, annual. **Formerly:** (1987) American Association of Minority Enterprise Small Business Investment Companies.

★310★
National Association of Management Consultants
4200 Wisconsin NW, Ste. 106   Ph: (202)466-1601
Washington, DC 20016   Fax: (202)363-0958
Hosiah Huggins Jr., Pres.

Description: Minority management consultants. Seeks to increase minority participation in the industry. Provides for the sharing of information, collaboration on projects, and improvement of professionalism in the field. **Founded:** 1985. **Members:** 50.

★311★
National Association of Market Developers
1422 W. Peachtree NW, Ste. 500   Ph: (404)892-0244
Atlanta, GA 30309   Fax: (404)874-7100
Bunnie Jackson Ransom, Exec.Dir.

Description: Professionals engaged in marketing, sales, sales promotion, advertising, or public relations who are concerned with the delivery of goods and services to the minority consumer market. **Founded:** 1953. **Members:** 700. **Local Groups:** 18. **Publications:** Briefcase, bimonthly. Contains articles about the social position of African-Americans, convention reports, and job opportunity listings. EMPHASIS, annual. Magazine; includes chapter news, convention reports, and articles about minority markets in the U.S. President's Report, bimonthly.

★312★
National Association of Minority Automobile Dealers
23300 Greenfield, Ste. 227   Ph: (313)967-1900
Oak Park, MI 48237   Fax: (313)967-1913
                                    Free: 800-247-0293
Robert Hills, Dir.

Description: Automobile dealers. Acts as liaison between membership, the government, the community, and industry representatives; seeks to better the business conditions of its members on an ongoing basis. Acts as confidential spokesperson for dealers. Offers business analysis, financial counseling, and short- and long-term management planning. Conducts research programs;

compiles statistics. **Founded:** 1980. **Members:** 690. **Publications:** Newsletter, bimonthly.

★313★
National Association of Minority Contractors
1333 F St. NW, Ste. 500   Ph: (202)347-8259
Washington, DC 20004   Fax: (202)628-1876
Samual A. Carradine, Exec.Dir.

Description: Minority construction contractors and major corporations wishing to do business with minority contractors. Identifies procurement opportunities; provides specialized training; acts as national advocate for minority construction contractors. Holds workshops and seminars; compiles statistics; bestows awards. **Founded:** 1969. **Members:** 3500. **Local Groups:** 50. **Publications:** Building Concerns, bimonthly. Newsletter. Legislative Bulletin, periodic. Procurement Bulletin, periodic.

★314★
National Association of Minority Women in Business
906 Grand Ave., Ste. 200   Ph: (816)421-3335
Kansas City, MO 64106   Fax: (816)421-3336
Inez Kaiser, Pres.

Description: Minority women in business ownership and management positions; college students. Serves as a network for the exchange of ideas and information on business opportunities for minority women in the public and private sectors. Conducts research; sponsors workshops, conferences, seminars, and luncheons. Maintains speakers' bureau, hall of fame, and placement service; compiles statistics; bestows awards to women who have made significant contributions to the field. **Founded:** 1972. **Members:** 5000. **Publications:** Today, bimonthly. Newsletter.

★315★
National Association of Negro Business and Professional Women's Clubs
1806 New Hampshire Ave. NW   Ph: (202)483-4206
Washington, DC 20009   Fax: (202)462-7253
Ellen A. Graves, Exec. Officer

Description: Women actively engaged in a business or a profession who are committed to rendering service through club programs and activities. Seeks to direct the interest of business and professional women toward united action for improved social and civic conditions, and to provide enriching and ennobling experiences that will encourage freedom, dignity, self-respect, and self-reliance. Offers information and help regarding education, employment, health, housing, legislation, and problems of the aged and the disabled. Presents honors and awards for national and community service. Sponsors educational assistance program, which includes local and national scholarships. Conducts consumer education and prison reform programs. Maintains youth department clubs. Provides placement services; operates speakers' bureau; compiles statistics. **Founded:** 1935. **Members:** 10,000. **Budget:** $500,000 **Regional Groups:** 6. **Local Groups:** 350. **Publications:** Convention Proceedings, annual. Directory, annual. President's Newsletter, monthly. Program Idea Exchange, bimonthly. Responsibility, quarterly. Also publishes handbooks and manuals.

★316★
National Association of Negro Musicians
PO Box S-011
237 E. 115th St.   Ph: (312)779-1325
Chicago, IL 60628   Fax: (312)779-1325
Ona B. Campbell, Exec.Sec.

Description: Amateur, professional, and retired musicians; interested individuals. Promotes the advancement of all types of music, especially among young black musicians. Sponsors annual competitions in which regional winners compete for scholarships; also sponsors concerts by recognized musicians. **Founded:** 1919. **Members:** 2500. **Budget:** $150,000. **Regional Groups:** 5. **Local Groups:** 39. **Publications:** NANM Newsletter, quarterly. Post-Convention Newsletter, annual.

★317★
National Association of Securities Professionals
1360 Peachtree St. NE, Ste. 880   Ph: (404)875-2161
Atlanta, GA 30309   Fax: (404)875-1565
Raymond J. McClendon, Chm.

Description: Individuals and organizations engaging in a job function dealing with taxable or tax-exempt debt or equity instruments. Seeks to represent the interests of minorities and women in the securities industry. Maintains business records. Bestows annual Joyce Johnson and Travis Bell Awards; Maintains Joyce Johnson Scholarship Fund. **Founded:** 1985. **Members:** 300. MD $250 for individual; $5000 for corporate. **Computerized Services:** Membership directory. **Publications:** Newsletter, periodic. Also publishes brochure.

★318★
National Association of University Women
1553 Pine Forest Dr.
Tallahassee, FL 32301   Ph: (904)878-4660
Ruth R. Corbin, Pres.

Description: Women college or university graduates. Works to promote constructive work in education, civic activities, and human relations; studies educational conditions with emphasis on problems affecting women; encourages high educational standards and stimulate intellectual attainment among women generally. Theme is Women of Action: Reaching, Risking, Responding. Offers tutoring and sponsors After High School-What? youth development program. Maintains placement service. Awards annual national fellowship; four sectional groups also award scholarships annually. **Founded:** 1923. **Members:** 4000. **Regional Groups:** 5. **Local Groups:** 92. **Publications:** Bulletin, biennial. Directory of Branch Presidents and Members, annual. Journal of the National Association of University Women, biennial. **Formerly:** (1974) National Association of College Women.

★319★
National Association of Urban Bankers
1010 Wayne Ave., Ste. 1210   Ph: (301)589-2141
Silver Spring, MD 20910   Fax: (301)495-2914
Adele D. Jackson, Exec.Dir.

Description: Minority professionals in the financial services industry; financial services institutions and banks. Supports minority professionals in the banking services industry. Communicates information and sponsors programs to further careers for minority bankers. Utilizes member resources to solve problems of minority entrepreneurs. Awards scholarships to minority banking students. **Founded:** 1975. **Members:** 2000. **Budget:** $150,000. **Regional Groups:** 5. **Publications:** Conference Journal, annual. Urban Banker, quarterly. Newsletter.

★320★
National Athletic Steering Committee
Fort Valley State College
PO Box 5319   Ph: (912)825-6208
Ft. Valley, GA 31030   Fax: (912)825-6394
Douglas T. Porter, Pres.

Description: Objective is to study problems of segregation and discrimination in intercollegiate athletics on a national level. Provides recommendations for action to conference and nonconference schools whose programs are involved in "undemocratic practices." **Founded:** 1951. **Members:** 125. **Budget:** $25,000. **Publications:** none.

★321★
National Bankers Association
1802 T St. NW   Ph: (202)588-5432
Washington, DC 20009   Fax: (202)588-5443
Bruce Gamble, Exec.Dir.

Description: Minority banking institutions owned by minority individuals and institutions. To serve as an advocate for the minority banking industry. Organizes banking services, government relations, marketing, scholarship, and technical assistance programs. Sponsors conferences; offers placement services; compiles statistics; bestows awards. **Founded:** 1927. **Members:** 64. **Budget:** $360,000. **Regional Groups:** 5. **Computerized Services:** Database. **Publications:** NBA Today, semiannual. Magazine. **Formerly:** (1951) National Negro Bankers Association.

★322★
National Baptist Convention, U.S.A.
1700 Baptist World Center Dr.   Ph: (615)228-6292
Nashville, TN 37207   Fax: (615)226-5935
Dr. T. J. Jemison, Pres.

Description: Seeks to: promote home and foreign missions; encourage and support Christian education; publish and distribute Sunday School and other religious literature. Awards annual scholarships. Operates youth camps, student centers, and the American Baptist Theological Seminary. Boards: Congress of Christian Education; Foreign Mission; Home Mission; Sunday School Publishing; Women's Auxiliary. **Founded:** 1880. **Members:** 7,800,000. **Publications:** National Baptist Voice, monthly. Record of Annual Sessions.

★323★
National Bar Association
1225 11th St. NW   Ph: (202)842-3900
Washington, DC 20001   Fax: (202)289-6170
John Crump, Exec.Dir.

Description: Minority (predominantly black) attorneys, members of the judiciary, law students, and law faculty. Programs and involvements represent the interests of members and the communities they serve. Offers specialized education and research programs. Maintains hall of fame. Presents annual C. Francis Stradford Award, Gertrude E. Rush Award, and Equal Justice Award. **Founded:** 1925. **Members:** 12,500. **Budget:** $1,000,000. **Regional Groups:** 12. **Local Groups:** 76. **Publications:** NBA Bulletin, quarterly. NBA Journal, biennial. NBA Magazine, monthly. Legal information for minority legal professionals. Includes legal briefs and industry outlook.

★324★
National Bar Association - Women Lawyers Division
c/o Brenda Girton
1211 Connecticut Ave. NW, Ste. 702   Ph: (202)291-1979
Washington, DC 20036   Fax: (202)374-7127
Brenda Girton, Pres.

Description: Women lawyers, law students, and other individuals. Purposes are to: provide a forum to discuss and address issues unique to women in the legal profession; promote professional growth and honor achievements of minority attorneys; promote admission to practice at all levels of the judicial system; foster interactions between minority and other bar associations; encourage participation in community service. Awards scholarhsips; holds seminars. **Founded:** 1972. **Members:** 300. **Publications:** Newsletter, periodic.

★325★
National Beauty Culturists' League
25 Logan Cir. NW
Washington, DC 20005   Ph: (202)332-2695
Mrs. Cleolif Richardson, Pres.

Description: Beauticians, cosmetologists, and beauty products manufacturers. Encourages standardized, scientific, and approved methods of hair, scalp, and skin treatments. Offers scholarships and plans to establish a research center. Sponsors: National Institute of Cosmetology, a training course in operating and designing and business techniques; National Beauty Week. Maintains hall of fame; conducts research programs; compiles statistics. **Founded:** 1919. **Formerly:** (1920) National Hair System Culture League. **Local Groups:** 250. **Members:** 10,000. **State Groups:** 39.

★326★
National Black Alcoholism Council
1629 K St. NW, Ste. 802   Ph: (202)296-2696
Washington, DC 20006   Fax: (202)296-2707
Dr. Celia Willis, Exec.Dir.

Description: Individuals concerned about alcoholism among black Americans. Works to support and initiate activities that will improve alcoholism treatment services and lead to the prevention of alcoholism in the black community. Provides training on how to treat black alcoholics from a cultural perspective. Bestows political and service awards. Maintains biographical archives. Compiles statistics concerning alcoholism among blacks. **Founded:** 1978. **Members:** 1050. **Budget:** $85,000. Chapters: 20. **Publications:** National News and Views, semiannual. Also publishes Treatment of Black Alcoholics (book) and Model for Working With Children of Alcoholic and Drug Addicted Parents, (booklet).

★327★
National Black Alliance for Graduate Level Education
c/o Dr. John W. Wilson
University College
Spicer Hall
University of Akron
Akron, OH 44325   Ph: (216)972-7066
Dr. John W. Wilson, Pres.

Description: Black educators, administrators, students, and individuals interested in the recruitment, financial assistance, retention, and placement of black graduate students. Advocates on behalf of black students, faculty, and administrators. Provides the opportunity to discuss and resolve problems and issues affecting blacks in graduate and professional schools. Seeks to increase educational opportunities for black students. **Founded:** 1970. **Publications:** Newsletter, periodic.

★328★
National Black Association for Speech, Language and Hearing
PO Box 50605   Ph: (202)727-2608
Washington, DC 20004-0605   Fax: (301)890-0545
M. Eugene Wiggins, Exec.Dir.

Description: Professionals and other individuals concerned with communicatively handicapped blacks. Strongly encourages the recruitment and training of black professionals to work with individuals suffering from speech, language, and hearing problems; maintains that conditions such as race, socioeconomic class, and cultural differences must be taken into account in order to understand and sensitively study the communicative process, and to treat communicative disorders. Supports related research; solicits, and provides, financial support for the training of black students in speech, hearing, and language fields. Disseminates information. **Founded:** 1978. **Members:** 300. **Publications:** Echo - Newsletter.

★329★
National Black Catholic Clergy Caucus
343 N. Walnut St.
PO Box 1088
Opelousas, LA 70571   Ph: (318)942-2392
Bro. Roy Smith, Contact

Description: Black priests, brothers, seminarians, and deacons. Purpose is to support the spiritual, theological, educational, and ministerial growth of the black Catholic community within the church. Serves as a vehicle to bring contributions of the black community to the church. Advances the fight against racism within the Catholic church and society. Offers computerized service. **Founded:** 1968. **Members:** 650. **Regional Groups:** 4. **Publications:** Directory, annual. Newsletter, 6-8/year.

★330★
National Black Catholic Seminarians Association
780 Porter St.
Beaumont, TX 77701
Freddy Washington, Pres.

Description: Black Catholic seminarians united for the growth and development of each member as a person, Christian, and potential priest or religious brother. "Attempts to reflect both the heritage of the church and black people in terms of the richness of their spirituality." Stresses the importance of individual contribution and total involvement of each black seminarian to the organization. Maintains speakers' bureau and charitable programs; bestows awards; compiles statistics. **Founded:** 1969. **Members:** 330. **Budget:** Less than $25,000. **Regional Groups:** 10. **Publications:** National Black Catholic Seminarians Association–Newsletter, quarterly. Includes articles on the history, theology, and education of black seminaries in the Catholic church.

★331★
National Black Caucus of Local Elected Officials
1301 Pennsylvania Ave. NW, Ste. 600
Washington, DC 20004　　　　　　Ph: (202)626-3000
Thom McCloud, Exec.Dir.

Description: Elected black municipal and county officials united to recognize and deal with problems of members. Attempts to provide the organizational structure required to better present and respond to issues affecting constituents. Seeks to influence the National League of Cities in the development of policies affecting black Americans; promotes legislative and economic development initiatives directed toward the needs of the black community. Presents annual Liberty Award. **Founded:** 1970.

★332★
National Black Caucus of State Legislators
Hall of States
444 N. Capitol St. NW, Ste. 622　　Ph: (202)624-5457
Washington, DC 20001　　　　　　Fax: (202)508-3826
Regis F. Groft, Pres.

Description: Black state legislators. Organized to provide more political networking to black legislators from the federal and state levels. Goals are to: provide a network through which state legislators can exchange information and ideas on state and national legislation; provide a unified front or platform; serve as a focal point for involvement of black legislators in the "new federalism." Activities include arranging meetings between all governmental groups representing black elected officials and analyzing and forming a position on the "new federalism." Conducts seminars. Maintains speakers' bureau and biographical archives; compiles statistics. Bestows awards. **Founded:** 1977. **Members:** 450. **Regional Groups:** 12. **State Groups:** 47. **Publications:** Directory of Black State Legislators, biennial. Newsletter, quarterly. Also publishes Issues in State.

★333★
National Black Chamber of Commerce
5741 Telegraph Ave.
Oakland, CA 94609-1709
　　　　　　　　　　　　Fax: (510)444-5741
Oscar J. Coffey Jr., CEO & Pres.

Description: Black chambers of commerce organized to create a strategy for members of local chambers to share in the collective buying power of black minority communities. Primary focus is on the tourism industry, because, according to the association, blacks spend approximately $25 billion in the tourism market each year, but black-owned businesses net very little from this industry. Conducts training sessions to acquaint black businesspeople with the tourism market and marketing strategies. Manages Advocacy Program which researches and analyzes issues given priority by local chambers. **Founded:** 1983. **Members:** 10,451. **Budget:** $300,000. **State Groups:** 72. **Publications:** Black Business News, quarterly. **Formerly:** (1990) National Association of Black and Minority Chambers of Commerce.

★334★
National Black Child Development Institute
1023 15th St. NW, Ste. 600　　　　Ph: (202)387-1281
Washington, DC 20005　　　　　　Fax: (202)234-1738
Evelyn K. Moore, Exec.Dir.

Description: Individuals dedicated to improving the quality of life for black children and youth. Conducts direct services and advocacy campaigns aimed at both national and local public policies focusing on issues of health, child welfare, education, and child care. Organizes and trains network of members in a volunteer grassroots affiliate system to voice concerns regarding policies that affect black children and their families. Stimulates communication between black community groups, through conferences and seminars, to discuss and make recommendations that will be advantageous to the development of black children. Analyzes selected policy decisions and legislative and administrative regulations to determine their impact on black children and youth. Informs national policymakers of issues critical to black children. **Founded:** 1970. **Members:** 3250. **Regional Groups:** 42. **Publications:** Black Child Advocate, quarterly. Newsletter providing public policy and legislative updates and information on local service programs. **Formerly:** (1979) Black Child Development Institute.

★335★
National Black Coalition of Federal Aviation Employees
Washington Headquarters
PO Box 44392
Washington, DC 20026-4392　　　Ph: (202)267-9941
Alfredia Brooks, Pres.

Description: Federal Aviation Administration employees. Purposes are to: promote professionalism and equal opportunity in the workplace; locate and train qualified minorities for FAA positions; help the FAA meet its affirmative action goals; monitor black, female, and minority trainees; educate members and the public about their rights and FAA personnel and promotion qualifications; develop a voice for black, female, and minority FAA employees. Recruits minorities from community and schools who qualify for employment; sponsors seminars for members and for those who wish to be employed by the FAA. Awards scholarships; maintains speakers' bureau; sponsors competitions. **Founded:** 1976. **Members:** 1000. **Regional Groups:** 6. **Computerized Services:** Database. **Publications:** The Networker, quarterly.

★336★
National Black Evangelical Association
5736 N. Albina Ave.
Portland, OR 97217　　　　　　　Ph: (503)289-5754
Aaron M. Hamlin, Exec.Dir.

Description: Individuals of all backgrounds, churches, and religions. Conducts seminars; sponsors educational programs on drug abuse, church education, evangelism, black theology mission, and social action. Provides children's services and placement service. Bestows awards; compiles statistics. **Founded:** 1963. **Members:** 600. **Regional Groups:** 3. **Local Groups:** 13. **Publications:** Journal, annual. Outreach, quarterly. Also publishes history of NBEA. **Formerly:** National Negro Evangelical Association.

★337★
National/Black Law Student Association
1225 11th St. NW
Washington, DC 20001
Brian Roberts, Chairperson

Description: Black law students united to meet the needs of black people within the legal profession and to work for the benefit of the black community. Objectives are to: articulate and promote professional competence, needs, and goals of black law students; focus on the relationship between black students and attorneys and the American legal system; instill in black law students and attorneys a greater commitment to the black community; encourage the legal community to bring about change to meet the needs of the black community. Supports black law students at Harvard University who recently called for a boycott of a course on racial discrimination to protest the law school's faculty-hiring practices. Sponsors the Frederick Douglass Moot Court Competition; bestows awards; sponsors scholarship program; offers placement service. **Founded:** 1967. **Members:** 8000. **Regional Groups:** 6. **Local Groups:** 200. **Publications:** Reports, quarterly. **Formerly:** (1983) Black American Law Students Association.

★338★
National Black Leadership Roundtable
2135 Rayburn House Bldg.
Washington, DC 20515
Rep. Walter E. Fauntroy, Pres.

Description: Chief executive officers of national black organizations. Goals are to: provide a forum for leaders of national black organizations to discuss and exchange ideas on issues critical to black Americans; aid in the development of political, economic, and networking strategies that are advantageous to the needs of the black community; ensure that elected and appointed officials represent and are accountable to the black community. Bestows annual Youth Award to an individual who has demonstrated excellence in the fields of art, entertainment, education, and science. **Founded:** 1983. **Members:** 300. **Publications:** Roundtable Record, quarterly. Newsletter.

★339★
National Black MBA Association
180 N. Michigan Ave., Ste. 1820   Ph: (312)236-2622
Chicago, IL 60601   Fax: (312)236-4131
Derryl L. Reed, Pres.

Description: Business professionals, lawyers, accountants, and engineers concerned with the role of blacks who hold Master of Business Administration degrees. Encourages blacks to pursue continuing business education; assists students preparing to enter the business world. Provides programs for minority youths, students, and professionals, including workshops, panel discussions, and Destination MBA seminar. Sponsors student mini-conference and job fair; holds competitions. Works with graduate schools; grants scholarships to graduate business students. Presents Outstanding Educator, MBA of the Year, Silver Touch, H. Naylor Fitzhugh, and Outstanding Educational Institution awards. **Founded:** 1971. **Members:** 2000. **State Groups:** 23. **Publications:** National Black MBA Association–Newsletter, quarterly. Covers membership activities; includes business news and chapter profiles.

★340★
National Black McDonald's Operators Association
c/o Mrs. Fran Jones
6363 W. Sunset Blvd., Ste. 809
Hollywood, CA 90028-7330   Ph: (213)962-2806
Mrs. Fran Jones, Pres.

Description: Black owners of McDonald's restaurants. Provides a forum for the exchange of ideas on the improvement of community relations and on the operation and management of restaurants. Seeks to build and improve the McDonald's restaurant image throughout the community. Sponsors training seminars on marketing, better sales practices, labor relations, and profit sharing. Bestows awards; conducts charitable programs. **Founded:** 1972. **Members:** 169. **Regional Groups:** 5. **Local Groups:** 1. **Publications:** Newsletter, quarterly. Also publishes Historical Highlights (book).

★341★
National Black Media Coalition
38 New York Ave. NE
Washington, DC 20002   Ph: (202)387-8155
Carmen Marshall, Exec.Dir.

Description: Black media advocacy group seeking to maximize media access for blacks and other minorities in the communications industry through employment, ownership, and programming. Has been recognized by the FCC, Congress, and trade organizations concerned with blacks and other minorities in the media. Past activities include participating in FCC rulemaking proceedings, speaking before university and professional audiences, conducting classes, and negotiating affirmative action plans with large media corporations. Maintains resource center; offers job referral service; compiles statistics. **Founded:** 1973. **Members:** 500. **Budget:** $100,000. **Regional Groups:** 80. **Publications:** Action Bulletin, periodic. For the Record, semiannual. Media Line, monthly. Newsletter; includes information on employment opportunities.

★342★
National Black Music Caucus
Music Educators National Conference
c/o Dr. Willis Patterson
University of Michigan
Ann Arbor, MI 48109   Ph: (313)764-0586
Dr. Willis Patterson, Exec.Sec.

Description: Purpose is to foster the creation, study, and promotion of black-derived music in education. Seeks to heighten public awareness of the problems faced by black music educators and students and to increase public understanding of those problems. Provides a forum for the discussion of concerns. Coordinates and disseminates materials concerning black-derived music in order to assist music teachers in teaching black music and students. Encourages blacks to aspire to leadership positions and to demand inclusion in the development and presentation of Music Educators National Conference (see separate entry) activities, including participation in MENC's regional conferences. Sponsors collegiate and high school gospel choir competitions. Bestows annual national achievement awards to educators successful in demonstrating values inherent in music education. Compiles list of music, books, and related music materials by blacks. **Founded:** 1972. **Computerized Services:** Database of black musicians and educators. **Publications:** Con Brio, quarterly. Newsletter; reports on regional conferences, collegiate and high school gospel choir competitions, and activities of members.

★343★
National Black Nurses Association
1012 10th St. NW   Ph: (202)393-6870
Washington, DC 20001-4492   Fax: (202)347-3808
Sadako S. Holmes, Exec. Officer

Description: Registered nurses, licensed practical nurses, licensed vocational nurses, and student nurses. Functions as a professional support group and as an advocacy group for the black community and their health care. Recruits and assists blacks interested in pursuing nursing as a career. Presents scholarships to student nurses, including the Dr. Lauranne Sams and Ambi scholarships. Compiles statistics; maintains biographical archives and charitable program. **Founded:** 1971. **Members:** 5000. **Publications:** Annual Report. Journal of Black Nurses Association, semiannual.

★344★
National Black on Black Love Campaign
401 N Michigan Ave., 24th fl.   Ph: (312)644-6610
Chicago, IL 60611-4267   Fax: (312)565-4658
Geri Duncan Jones, Exec.Dir.

Description: Individuals and businesses united to promote the motto, "Replace Black on Black crime with Black on Black love" and foster love and respect in all communities where people are, the group believes, inordinately affected by crime. Organizes No Crime Day in various communities and Adopt A Building Program for businesses. Sponsors youth organizations and seminars in schools and communities to educate the public in ways of dealing with crime. Operates charitable program; bestows awards. Maintains speakers' bureau; compiles statistics. **Founded:** 1983. **State Groups:** 6.

★345★
National Black Police Association
3251 Mt. Pleasant St. NW   Ph: (202)986-2070
Washington, DC 20010-2103   Fax: (202)986-0410
Ronald E. Hampton, Exec.Dir.

Description: Male and female black police officers. Seeks to: improve relationships between police departments and the black community; recruit minority police officers on a national scale; eliminate police corruption, brutality, and racial discrimination. Bestows awards; maintains speakers' bureau. Operates charitable program. Offers scholarship. **Founded:** 1972. **Members:** 35,000. **Budget:** $125,000. **Regional Groups:** 5. **Local Groups:** 105. **Publications:** Black Police Membership Directory, annual.

★346★
National Black Programming Consortium
929 Harrison Ave., Ste. 101   Ph: (614)299-5355
Columbus, OH 43215   Fax: (614)299-4761
Mable J. Haddock, Exec.Dir.

Description: Public telecommunications systems and television stations, academic institutions, and interested individuals. Objectives are to: assist the public broadcasting system in supplying programming that serves the needs of all population segments of the U.S.; serve as a collection, distribution, and archival center for black-oriented television programming; coproduce black programming; serve as a liaison between the black community and telecommunications systems with regard to black programming; provide funds for and encourage more and better black productions. Participates in the acquisition and distribution of programs for the cable and international markets. Sponsors children's programs. Operates clearinghouse; maintains archives and library of over 2,500 films and videos. Bestows Award of Distinction and Prized Pieces Award. **Founded:** 1979. **Members:** 65. **Budget:** $450,000. **Publications:** Take One, quarterly. Newsletter. Also publishes catalog, press releases, and pamphlet.

★347★
National Black Republican Council
375 South End Ave., Plz. 400-84
New York, NY 10280   Ph: (202)662-1335
Fred Brown, Chm.

Description: Black Republicans in the U.S. Works to elect more black Republicans to national, state, and local offices. Maintains speakers' bureau. **Budget:** $100,000. **Founded:** 1972. **Members:** 25,000. **Publications:** none. **Regional Groups:** 4. **State Groups:** 44.

★348★
National Black Sisters' Conference
1001 Lawrence St. NE, Ste. 102
Washington, DC 20017   Ph: (202)529-9250
Sr. Gwynette Proctor, Exec.Dir.

Description: Black religious women. Seeks to develop the personal resources of black women; challenges society, especially the church, to address issues of racism in the U.S. Activities include: retreats; consulting, leadership, and cultural understanding; formation workshops for personnel. Maintains educational programs for facilitating change and community involvement in inner-city parochial schools and parishes. Operates Sojourner House to provide spiritual affirmation for black religious and laywomen. Bestows awards; maintains speakers' bureau. **Founded:** 1968. **Members:** 150. **Budget:** $40,000. **Publications:** Signs of Soul, 4/year. Newsletter reporting on black members of the Catholic church. Includes employment opportunities and obituaries of members.

★349★
National Black Survival Fund
PO Box 3885
Lafayette, LA 70502-3885   Ph: (318)232-7672
Rev. A. J. McKnight CS, Chm.

Description: A project of the Southern Development Foundation. Objective is to improve the ability of black and other minority poor to achieve economic progress through their own effort and initiative. Believes that the economic, cultural, and physical survival of the nation's black community is endangered due to the recession, discrimination, and the Reagan administration's cutbacks in social assistance programs. Seeks to maintain and increase support for programs that can avert the economic and human catastrophe the fund says will result if the opportunities offered to blacks are undermined by current assistance cutbacks. Maintains: Food for Survival Program in which landowners and sharecroppers in Mississippi volunteer land, equipment, and labor to provide food and employment for needy families; Health Care for Survival Program, a cooperative low-cost health center in Mississippi; Jobs for Survival Program, which has assisted in providing jobs for black workers in Alabama in construction, farming, and community service. **Founded:** 1982. **Publications:** Brochures and flyers. **Formerly:** Emergency Black Survival Fund.

★350★
National Black United Fund
50 Park Pl., Ste. 1538   Ph: (201)643-5122
Newark, NJ 07102   Fax: (201)648-8350
                                     Free: 800-223-0866
William T. Merritt, Pres. & CEO

Description: Provides financial and technical support to projects serving the critical needs of black communities nationwide. Local affiliates solicits funds through payroll deduction to support projects in the areas of education, health and human services, economic development, social justice, arts and culture, and emergency needs. Programs supported by NBUF emphasize self-help, volunteerism, and mutual aid. Maintains Walter Bremond Memorial Fund campaign. Provides charitable program. **Founded:** 1972. **Members:** 30. **Local Groups:** 15. **Publications:** Newsletter, quarterly.

★351★
National Black Women's Consciousness Raising Association
1906 N. Charles St.
Baltimore, MD 21218   Ph: (410)727-8900
Dr. Elaine Simon, Exec.Dir.

Description: Black women interested in women's rights and women's issues. Acts as a support group for women. Provides educational and informational workshops and seminars on subjects of concern to black women and women in general. Annually recognizes individuals, especially for academic achievement. **Founded:** 1975. **Members:** 750. **Budget:** Less than $25,000. **Publications:** BWCR, semiannual. Newsletter.

★352★
National Black Women's Health Project
1237 Ralph David Albernathy Blvd. SW   Ph: (404)758-9590
Atlanta, GA 30310   Fax: (404)752-6756
                                        Free: 800-ASK-
                                             BWHP
Cynthia Newbille-Marsh, Dir.

Description: Encourages mutual and selfhelp advocacy among women to bring about a reduction in health care problems prevalent among black women. Urges women to communicate with health care providers, seek out available health care resources, become aware of selfhelp approaches, and communicate with other black women to minimize feelings of powerlessness and isolation, and thus realize they have some control over their physical and mental health. Points out the higher incidence of high blood pressure, obesity, breast and cervical cancers, diabetes, kidney disease, arteriosclerosis, and teenage pregnancy among black women than among other racial or socioeconomic groups. Also notes that black infant mortality is twice that of whites and that black women are often victims of family violence. Offers seminars outlining demographic information, chronic conditions, the need for health information and access to services, and possible methods of improving the health status of black women. Sponsors Center for Black Women's Wellness. Maintains library, database, and speakers' bureau. Conducts gender and race specific health research programs. Plans to: establish black women's wellness centers; develop Empowerment Though Wellness curriculum. **Founded:** 1981. **Members:** 2000. **Budget:** $1,600,000. **Regional Groups:** 5. **Local Groups:** 150. **State Groups:** 26. **Computerized Services:** Mailing list. **Publications:** Annual Report. Vital Signs, quarterly. Newsletter. **Formerly:** (1984) Black Women's Health Project.

★353★
National Black Women's Political Leadership Caucus
3005 Bladensburg Rd. NE, No. 217
Washington, DC 20018   Ph: (202)529-2806
Juanita Kennedy Morgan, Dir.

Description: Women interested in understanding their political role and the need for females to work toward equality; auxiliary membership includes men, senior citizens, and youths. Works to educate and incorporate all black women and youth in the political and economic process through participation. Encourages women to familiarize themselves with the role of city, state, and federal governments. Presents awards for humanitarianism; trains speakers and conducts research on the black family and on topics concerning politics and economics; compiles statistics. Holds legislative, federal, state, and local workshops. Provides placement service; offers children's services; operates charitable program. **Founded:** 1971. **Regional Groups:** 3. **State Groups:** 33. **Publications:** Newsletter, semiannual. Has published election tabloids.

★354★
National Black Youth Leadership Council
250 W. 54th St., Ste. 800
New York, NY 10019   Ph: (212)541-7600
Dennis Rahiim Watson, Exec.Dir.

Description: Outreach training and motivation organization. Conducts workshops for groups involved with black youth and minority student academic and leadership development; works to reduce the number of minority students that do not finish high school. Provides resources, information, skills, and strategies for fostering such development. Advises educators and parents on their role and responsibility to display leadership and success skills to youths they come in contact with; makes available to educational institutions training and expertise on cultural diversity, multiculturalism, and problems of bigotry and racism. Sponsors drug abuse awareness programs. Maintains speakers' bureau and children's services. **Founded:** 1983.

★355★
National Bowling Association
377 Park Ave. S., 7th Fl.
New York, NY 10016   Ph: (212)689-8308
Margaret S. Lee, Exec.Sec.-Treas.

Description: Seeks to: foster good sportsmanship, fellowship, and friendship; increase the interests, talents, and skills of adult and youth bowlers; create national awareness and interest in civic and community programs. Participates in and promotes bowling tournaments and other activities. Sponsors fundraising programs for sickle cell anemia and the United Negro College Fund. Bestows bowling awards, annual special bowling and service awards, and annual national and local scholarship awards. Maintains hall of fame; compiles statistics. **Founded:** 1939. **Members:** 26,000. **Local Groups:** 80. **Publications:** Bowler, quarterly. News magazine/paper. Newsletter/Bulletin, monthly. Souvenir Yearbook. Journal. Is preparing the NBA History Book. **Formerly:** (1944) Negro National Bowling Association.

★356★
National Brotherhood of Skiers
1525 E. 53rd St., Ste. 408
Chicago, IL 60615   Ph: (312)955-4100
Samuel E. Lawler, Pres.

Description: Minority ski clubs. Promotes winter sports among minorities, with emphasis on youth. Seeks to locate and develop talented ski racers through local, regional, and national competitions. Promotes the development of Olympic-quality minority skiers. Offers two-year athletic scholarships for qualified youth to attend Ski Academies. Encourages participation in United States Ski Association competitions. Supports Building Skills and Talents programs and community-based youth motivational improvement programs. **Founded:** 1973. **Members:** 12,000. **Budget:** $125,000. **Regional Groups:** 4. **Local Groups:** 67. **Publications:** NBS Bienniel Report. NBS Directory, annual. NBS Ski Club Guide, biennial (odd years). Skiers Edge, quarterly.

★357★
National Business League
1629 K St. NW, Ste. 605   Ph: (202)466-5487
Washington, DC 20006   Fax: (202)466-5487
Sherman Copilin, Pres.

Description: Organizational vehicle for minority businesspeople. Promotes the economic development of minorities. Encourages minority ownership and management of small businesses and supports full minority participation within the free enterprise system. Maintains file of minority vendors and corporate procurement and purchasing agents. Presents awards; conducts special projects. **Founded:** 1900. **Members:** 10,000. **Budget:** $500,000. **Local Groups:** 127. **Publications:** Corporate Guide for Minority Vendors, annual. National Memo, monthly. Membership newsletter. President's Briefs, monthly. Bulletin. **Formerly:** National Negro Business League.

★358★
National Catholic Conference for Interracial Justice
3033 4th St. NE
Washington, DC 20017-1102   Ph: (202)529-6480
Jerome B. Ernst, Exec.Dir.

Description: Catholic organization working for interracial justice and social concerns in America. Initiates programs within and outside the Catholic church to end discrimination in community development, education, and employment. **Founded:** 1959. **Members:** 1151. **Publications:** Commitment, quarterly. Newsletter. Also publishes LASER: Creating Unity in Diversity (book), Workshops on Racism (manual), Pentecost: A Feast for all Peoples, Martin Luther King Jr. Holiday Celebration Packet, and pamphlets.

★359★
National Caucus and Center on Black Aged, Inc.
1424 K St. NW, Ste. 500   Ph: (202)637-8400
Washington, DC 20005   Fax: (202)347-0895
Samuel J. Simmons, Pres.

Description: Seeks to improve living conditions for low-income elderly Americans, particularly blacks. Advocates changes in federal and state laws in improving the economic, health, and social status of low-income senior citizens. Promotes community awareness of problems and issues effecting low-income aging population. Operates an employment program involving 2000 older persons in 14 states. Sponsors, owns, and manages rental housing for the elderly. Conducts training and intern programs in nursing home administration, long-term care, housing management, and commercial property maintenance. Bestows scholarships and awards. **Founded:** 1970. **Members:** 3000. **Budget:** $9,000,000. **Local Groups:** 45. **Publications:** Golden Page, quarterly. Newsletter reporting developments concerning elderly blacks; includes association news and legislative update.

★360★
National Center for Neighborhood Enterprise
1367 Connecticut Ave. NW
Washington, DC 20036   Ph: (202)331-1103
Robert L. Woodson Sr., Pres.

Description: Promotes community self-sufficiency through support of effective neighborhood mediating structures in low-income communities. Provides support and technical assistance to enable grass roots organizations to expand their role in the revitalization of urban communities. Objectives are to: recognize, promote, and explain alternative approaches to community development; identify and analyze successful program principles, strategies, and techniques that may be transferable; identify needs for developing neighborhood groups and small business leaders; simplify information technology and encourage grass roots organizations to make greater use of technological gains in solving problems; encourage financial support for programs; educate the public and private sectors; formulate policy recommendations to assist neighborhood revitalization. Conducts Resident Management for Public Housing Seminars; sponsors programs in youth entrepreneurship. **Founded:** 1981. **Budget:** $3,000,000. **Publications:** In the News, periodic. Policy Dispatch, periodic. Also publishes On the Road to Economic Freedom: An Agenda for Black Progress.

★361★
National Center for the Advancement of Blacks in the Health Professions
PO Box 21121   Ph: (313)345-4480
Detroit, MI 48221   Free: 800-NCA-BHP6

Della McGraw Goodwin, Pres.

Description: Participants belong to organizations including the American Public Health Association, National Urban League, National Black Nurses Association, and the American Hospital Association. Promotes the advancement of blacks in the health professions. Publicizes the disparity between the health of black and white Americans and its relationship to the underrepresentation of blacks in the health professions. (According to the National Center for Health Statistics, blacks have a higher death rate from cancer, heart disease, stroke, and diabetes than whites; blacks also have a higher infant mortality rate.) Acts as clearinghouse. Conducts skills development seminars for college recruiters and employers and empowerment seminars for new graduates. Demonstrates recruitment projects. Bestows Pathfinder Award. **Founded:** 1988. **Computerized Services:** Database that matches applicants with colleges and universities and graduates with employers. **Publications:** Improving the Health Status of Black Americans, annual. Lists priorities and agenda for the coming year.

★362★
National Center for Urban Ethnic Affairs
PO Box 20, Cardinal Sta.
Washington, DC 20064   Ph: (202)319-5129
Dr. John A. Kromkowski, Pres.

Description: Develops neighborhood programs and policies that are grounded in an appreciation of ethnic cultural diversity. Encourages and enables urban communities, parishes, and congregations to clarify important policy issues. Aids organized networks of neighbors and neighborhood organizations in achieving their goals and objectives. Creates partnerships among neighborhood organizations, government agencies, and the private sector for neighborhood revitalization, selfhelp development, and cultural programs. Works to improve education, human services, economic opportunities, housing, and culture and heritage for immigrants and in the ethnic and multi-ethnic neighborhoods. Provides technical assistance, advisement training, and workshops. Develops research proposals; assists neighborhood and ethnic organizations seeking financial support; makes available summer internships; sponsors speakers' bureau; compiles statistics. **Founded:** 1970. **Publications:** Buildingblocks, periodic. Newsletter. Also publishes Urban Ethnic Policy Series, Neighborhood Strategy Series, and Neighborhood Revitalization Series, Non-Profits with Hard Hats, Reclaiming the Inner City, Race and Ethnic Relations, Annual Editions, Why 435? (books, videos, and pamphlets).

★363★
National Center of Afro-American Artists
300 Walnut Ave.
Boston, MA 02119   Ph: (617)442-8614
Charles Desmond, Pres.

Description: African American artists; institutions; and interested others. Goals are to: promote cultural activites in African American history and culture; encourage the development of artistic and cultural expression within black communities; increase awareness and appreciation of the achievements of black artists. Organizes and conducts cultural events, theatrical productions, and concerts. Sponsors workshops on topics such as 19th Century Black America, Introduction to Africa, and the Caribbean. **Founded:** 1968. **Publications:** none.

★364★
National Coalition for Haitian Refugees
16 E. 42nd St., 3rd Fl.   Ph: (212)867-0020
New York, NY 10017   Fax: (212)867-1668
Jocelyn McCalla, Exec.Dir.

Description: Haitian, labor, civil rights, human rights, trade union, and religious organizations united to secure humane treatment, due process of law, and legal status for Haitians seeking asylum in the U.S. Goals are to: ensure that Haitians receive fair treatment in their quest for asylum; convince the public of the need for legal status for the refugees; end U.S. Coast Guard interdiction of Haitian boats on the high seas; deepen the public's understanding of the social, economic, and political causes of Haitian flight from Haiti. Sponsors forums on Haiti. **Founded:** 1982. **Members:** 47. **Budget:** $150,000. **Publications:** Haiti Insight, monthly. Newsletter disseminating information and analysis on current events in Haiti. **Formerly:** (1983) National Emergency Coalition for Haitian Refugees.

★365★
National Coalition for Quality Integrated Education
1201 16th St. NW   Ph: (202)822-7708
Washington, DC 20036   Fax: (202)822-7292
Dr. Arthur Flemming, Dir.

Description: National organizations committed to desegregating and improving the quality of elementary and secondary schools in the U.S. Serves as a forum for issues and developments pertaining to quality integrated education; encourages and coordinates citizen involvement in legislative developments. Sponsors educational meetings. **Founded:** 1975. **Formerly:** (1982) National Center for Quality Integrated Education. **Members:** 25.

★366★
National Coalition of Black Meeting Planners
10320 Little Patuxent Pkwy., Ste. 1106   Ph: (202)628-3952
Columbia, MD 21044   Fax: (202)628-3958
Howard Mills, Pres.

Description: Black meeting planners. Purposes are to: act as liaison with hotels, airlines, convention centers, and bureaus in an effort to assess the impact of minorities in these fields; assess the needs of the convention industry and how best to meet these needs; enhance members' sophistication in planning meetings; maximize employment of minorities in the convention industry. Maintains speakers' bureau. Conducts educational and research programs and compiles statistics on demographic employment of minorities in the convention industry. Maintains library and placement service. Bestows 6 scholarship awards annually. **Founded:** 1983. **Members:** 500. MD $100 for meeting planner; $200 for associate. **Budget:** $120,000,000. **Publications:** Directory, annual. **Formerly:** (1984) National Black Meeting Planners Coalition.

★367★
National Coalition of 100 Black Women
300 Park Ave., 2nd Fl.   Ph: (212)974-6140
New York, NY 10022   Fax: (212)838-0542
Jewell Jackson-McCabe, Chm.

Description: African-American women actively involved with issues such as economic development, health, employment, education, voting, housing, criminal justice, the status of black families, and the arts. Seeks to provide networking and career opportunities for African-American women in the process of establishing links between the organization and the corporate and political arenas. Encourages leadership development; sponsors role-model and mentor programs to provide guidance to teenage mothers and young women in high school or who have graduated from college and are striving for career advancement. Bestows Candace Awards honoring outstanding African-American women and men. **Founded:** 1981. **Members:** 6000. Chapters: 59. **Publications:** National Coalition of 100 Black Women–Statement, semiannual. Newsletter reporting on the activities and achievements of black women.

★368★
National Coalition on Black Voter Participation
1430 K St. NW, Ste. 401
Washington, DC 20005   Ph: (202)898-2220
Sonia R. Jarvis, Exec.Dir.

Description: Religious organizations, sororities, fraternities, labor groups, black caucuses, and government and political groups. Seeks to: increase black voter registration and participation in electoral voting; develop and fund local independent coalitions that will conduct campaigns to increase nonpartisan voter participation and citizenship empowerment programs. Conducts training programs. Collects and analyzes data; disseminates information on voter education including data on the black voting age population. Sponsors Operation Big Vote and Black Women's Roundtable on Voter Participation. **Founded:** 1976. **Members:** 86. **Budget:** $700,000. **Publications:** Operation Big Vote Newsletter, bimonthly. Also publishes How to Organize and Implement a Successful Nonpartisan Voter Participation Campaign (manual).

★369★
National Coalition to End Racism in America's Child Care System
22075 Koths
Taylor, MI 48180   Ph: (313)295-0257
Carol Coccia, Pres.

Description: Adoption support groups, child care agencies, state offices of the U.S. Department of Social Services, politicians, members of the news media, and interested individuals. Purpose is to assure that all children requiring placement outside the home, whether through foster care or adoption, are placed in the earliest available home most qualified to meet the child's needs. Believes that in foster care situations, the child should not be moved after initial placement to match the child's race or culture. Encourages recruitment of foster and adoptive homes of all races and cultures; feels that while race and culture should be considered in placements, no child should be denied services on the basis of race. Seeks to educate the public, members of the media, and representatives of the political and legal sectors. Coordinates efforts of individuals and groups and utilizes the media and various legal procedures to accomplish goals of the coalition. Conducts workshops; maintains speakers' bureau. **Founded:** 1984. **Members:** 1000. **Budget:** Less than $25,000. **Publications:** The Children's Voice, quarterly. Newsletter discussing member activites, court decisions and laws, and civil rights information as it pertains to racism in adoption practices.

★370★
National Committee for Independent Political Action
PO Box 170610
Brooklyn, NY 11217   Ph: (718)643-9603
Ted Glick, Coordinator

Description: Individuals who are members of community organizations, civil rights groups, women's organizations, peace groups, and other progressive political groups. Purpose is to bring together grass roots progressive movements into one organized framework in order to represent the political interests of groups not represented by either major political party and to allow independent activists to share strategy and ideas. Goal is to develop independent political and electoral activity aimed at changing society to bring about economic and political democracy. Concerns addressed include labor movement issues, racism, apartheid, women's issues, farm issues, and U.S. intervention in Central America. Maintains speakers' bureau. **Founded:** 1984. **Members:** 10,000. **Publications:** Bulletin, 4/year.

★371★
National Conference of Black Lawyers
2 W. 125th St.
New York, NY 10027   Ph: (212)864-4000
Adjoa Ayetero, Dir.

Description: Attorneys throughout the U.S. and Canada united to use legal skills in the service of black and poor communities. Maintains projects in legal services to community organizations, voting rights, and international affairs; provides public education on legal issues affecting blacks and poor people. Researches racism in law schools and bar admissions. Conducts programs of continuing legal education for member attorneys. Maintains general law library. Compiles statistics; maintains lawyer referral and placement services. Provides speakers' bureau on criminal justice issues, international human rights law, and civil rights practice. Presents awards. **Founded:** 1968. **Members:** 1000. **Local Groups:** 15. **Publications:** Notes, quarterly.

★372★
National Conference of Black Mayors
1422 W. Peachtree St. NW, Ste. 800   Ph: (404)892-0127
Atlanta, GA 30309   Fax: (404)876-4597
Michelle D. Kourouma, Exec.Dir.

Description: Nonpartisan organization dedicated to promoting the development of municipalities managed by black mayors. Objectives are to: improve the executive management capacity and efficiency of member municipalities in the delivery of municipal services; create viable communities within which normal government functions can be performed efficiently; provide the basis upon which new social overhead investments in the infrastructure of municipalities can utilize federal, state, local, and private resources to encourage new industry and increase employment; assist municipalities in stabilizing their population through improvements of the quality of life for residents and, concurrently, create alternatives to outward migration. Facilitates small town growth and development through energy conservation. Bestows awards, including Tribute to a Black American. Offers workshops; compiles demographic statistics. **Founded:** 1974. **Members:** 327. **Budget:** $125,000. **State Groups:** 17. **Publications:** Mayors Roster, annual. Directory. Municipal Watch, quarterly. Press Releases, periodic. Also publishes NCBM Fact Sheet. **Formerly:** (1977) Southern Conference of Black Mayors.

★373★
National Conference of Black Political Scientists
c/o Franklin D. Jones
Dept. of Public Affairs
Texas Southern University
Houston, TX 77045   Ph: (404)656-0763
Joseph H. Silver, Pres.

Description: Political and social science faculty, lawyers, and related professionals interested in black politics and related fields. Seeks to encourage research, publication, and scholarship by black Americans in political science; and to improve the political life of black Americans. Maintains graduate assistantship program; compiles statistics on blacks in politics and political science. Sponsors competitions; bestows awards for service and research; awards scholarship. **Founded:** 1969. **Members:** 400. **Computerized Services:** Mailing list. **Publications:** National Political Science Review, annual. Contains research articles, symposia proceedings, and book reviews.

★374★
National Conference of Editorial Writers
6223 Executive Blvd.
Rockville, MD 20852   Ph: (301)984-3015
Cora B. Everett, Exec.Sec.

Description: Editorial writers for radio and television stations, and newspapers of general circulation in the U.S. and Canada; journalism educators. "To stimulate the conscience and the quality of editorials." In cooperation with the National Association of Black Journalists (see separate entry), bestows Wells Award for Leadership to provide employment for minorities in the field of journalism. Sponsors professional seminars. **Founded:** 1947. **Members:** 560. **Budget:** $100,000. **Publications:** The Masthead, quarterly. Journal covering all aspects of the work of a professional editorial writer in any medium. Includes conference news and broadcast editorial coverage.

★375★
National Congress of Neighborhood Women
249 Manhattan Ave.
Brooklyn, NY 11211   Ph: (718)388-6666
Dr. Sandy Shieln, Exec. Officer

Description: Low-and moderate-income women from diverse ethnic and racial backgrounds united to: bring about neighborhood stabilization and revitalization; raise awareness of women's roles in neighborhood activities and organizations as well as on issues affecting low-income women; provide a voice for a new women's movement that reflects family and neighborhood values while promoting women's empowerment. Current projects include: Neighborhood Women College Program, which offers associate arts degree programs; Project Prepare, which seeks to prepare individuals to get a job through adult education classes, work experience, resume writing, child care, and counseling support. Maintains local advisory board and support groups. Offers speakers' bureau and placement **Founded:** 1975. **Budget:** $550,000. **Regional Groups:** 26. **Local Groups:** 26. **Computerized Services:** Mailing list. **Publications:** Neighborhood Women Network News, bimonthly. Also publishes Leadership Training Manual, Neighborhood Women: Putting It Together, articles, and conference reports. service. Bestows awards. Compiles statistics on women, poverty, and neighborhood development. Maintains library of articles, papers, reports, oral histories, newspapers, letters, and audiovisual materials.

★376★
National Consortium for Black Professional Development
PO Box 18308
Louisville, KY 40218-0308   Ph: (502)896-2838
Hanford D. Stafford Ph.D., Exec.Dir.

Description: Industrial corporations and business firms (32); universities, including schools of business, science, and math, and public school systems (20); affiliates (5). Goal is to increase substantially, by the year 2000, the number of black professionals in business administration, communications, applied and natural sciences, engineering, and law. Sponsors a science and engineering competition for black students and Ph.D. programs in the agricultural sciences and business administration. Maintains clearinghouse and placement bureau for black professionals seeking employment. Provides recruitment service for universities seeking qualified black faculty and students. Services several federal contracts. **Founded:** 1974. **Members:** 57. **Publications:** Journal of Minority Employment, monthly. Reports employment information concerning Hispanics, Blacks, Native Americans, and Asians.

★377★
National Consortium for Graduate Degrees for Minorities in Science and Engineering
PO Box 537   Ph: (219)287-1097
Notre Dame, IN 46556   Fax: (219)287-1486
Dr. Howard G. Adams, Exec.Dir.

Description: A graduate fellowship program operated by corporate and university representatives involved in increasing the number of minorities with master's degrees in engineering. Formed to provide opportunities for minority students to obtain a master's degree in engineering through a program of paid summer engineering experience and financial aid. Graduate fellowships are awarded to each fellow, which provide for tuition, fees, and a stipend of $6000 per academic year. Sponsors competitions. **Founded:** 1976. **Members:** 157. **Publications:** Brochure, annual. Report, semiannual. Newsletter. Also publishes Successfully Negotiating the Graduate School Process: A Guide for Minority Students. **Formerly:** (1990) National Consortium for Graduate Degrees for Minorities in Engineering.

★378★
National Consortium of Arts and Letters for Historically Black Colleges and Universities
c/o Dr. Walter Anderson
The Westbridge, Ste. 818
2555 Pennsylvania Ave. NW
Washington, DC 20037   Ph: (202)833-1327
Dr. Walter F. Anderson, Exec.Dir.

Description: Historically and/or predominantly black colleges and universities; other institutions of higher learning are associate members. Encourages academic excellence with an emphasis on cultural growth. Promotes study of African-American history and culture in the context of the scholarly study of world cultures. Offers no grants, but helps sponsor programs through fundraising efforts. **Founded:** 1984. **Members:** 38. **Publications:** Brochure; also plans to publish quarterly newsletter.

★379★
National Council for Culture and Art
1600 Broadway, Ste. 611C
New York, NY 10019   Ph: (212)757-7933
Robert H. LaPrince Ph.D., Exec.Dir. & Pres.

Description: Artists, civic and business leaders, professional performers, and visual arts organizations. Purpose is to provide exposure and employment opportunities for rural Americans, disabled Americans, and other minorities including blacks, Hispanics, American Indians, and European-Americans. Sponsors arts programs and spring and fall concert series. Operates Opening Night, a cable television show. Bestows annual Monarch Award and President's Award, and sponsors annual Monarch Scholarship Program. Offers children's and placement services; conducts charitable program; maintains hall of fame. Plans to conduct Minority Playwrights Forum, Dance Festival U.S.A., Vocal and Instrumental Competition, Film and Video Festival, and Concerts U.S.A.. **Founded:** 1980. **Members:** 1500. **Budget:** $350,000. **Publications:** Monarch Herald, quarterly. Newsletter.

★380★
National Council of Negro Women, Inc.
1167 K St. NW
Washington, DC 20006   Ph: (202)659-0006
Dorothy I. Height, Pres.

Description: A coalition of 31 national organizations and concerned individuals. Assists in the development and utilization of the leadership of women in community, national, and international life. Provides a center of information for and about women in the black community; stimulates cooperation among women in diverse economic and social interests; acts as a catalyst for constructive advocacy on a number of women's issues. Maintains Women's Center for Education and Career Advancement in New York City, which offers programs designed to aid minority women pursuing nontraditional careers; also maintains the Bethune Museum and Archives for Black Women's History. Operates offices in west and southern Africa, which serve NCNW's international projects and which were designed to improve the social and economic status of rural women in Third World countries. Founded by Mary McLeod Bethune (1875-1955), black American educator and presidential advisor. **Founded:** 1935. **Members:** 40,000. **Budget:** $1,500,000. **Local Groups:** 240. **Publications:** Black Woman's Voice, periodic. Sisters Magazine, quarterly.

★381★
National Council on Black Aging
Box 51275
Durham, NC 27717   Ph: (919)493-4858
Dr. Jacquelyne J. Jackson, Dir.

Description: Persons interested in research and policies affecting older blacks and other minorities and in the dissemination of research findings. Maintains speakers' bureau. Conducts lectures on minority aging. **Founded:** 1975. **Publications:** Research findings in Journal of Minority Aging.

★382★
National Council on Family Relations
3989 Central Ave. NE, Ste. 550   Ph: (612)781-9331
Minneapolis, MN 55421   Fax: (612)781-9348
Mary Jo Czaplewski Ph.D., Exec.Dir.

Description: Multidisciplinary group of family life professionals, including clergymen, counselors, educators, home economists, lawyers, nurses, librarians, physicians, psychologists, social workers, sociologists, and researchers. Seeks to provide opportunities for members to plan and act together to advance marriage and family life through consultation, conferences, and the dissemination of information and research. Offers awards for research, teaching, publication, service to families, videotapes, and films and filmstrips. **Founded:** 1938. **Members:** 3900. **Budget:** $900,000. **Regional Groups:** 3. **Local Groups:** 11. **State Groups:** 41. **Computerized Services:** Inventory of Marriage and Family Literature, a national online bibliographic database representing the family field. **Publications:** Directory, periodic. Family Relations: Journal of Applied Family and Child Studies, quarterly. **Formerly:** (1948) National Conference of Family Relations.

★383★
National Dental Assistants Association
c/o Elizabeth Brezill
5506 Connecticut Ave. NW, Ste. 24   Ph: (202)244-7555
Washington, DC 20015   Fax: (202)244-5992
Elizabeth Brezill, Pres.

Description: An auxiliary of the National Dental Association. Works to encourage education and certification among dental assistants. Conducts clinics and workshops to further the education of members. Bestows annual Humanitarian Award; offers scholarships. **Members:** 500. **Publications:** NDAA Journal, annual.

★384★
National Dental Association
5506 Connecticut Ave. NW, Ste. 24   Ph: (202)244-7555
Washington, DC 20015   Fax: (202)244-5992
Robert S. Johns, Exec.Dir.

Description: Professional society for dentists. Aims to provide quality dental care to the unserved and underserved public and promote knowledge of the art and science of dentistry. Advocates the inclusion of dental care services in health care programs on local, state, and national levels. Fosters the integration of minority dental health care providers in the profession, and promotes dentistry as a viable career for minorities through scholarship and support programs. Bestows awards; conducts research programs. Sponsors National Dental Health Poster Contest and working group on high blood pressure. Group is distinct from the former name of the American Dental Association. **Founded:** 1913. **Members:** 2500. **Budget:** $294,050. **Regional Groups:** 6. **Local Groups:** 31. **State Groups:** 15. **Publications:** Flossline, quarterly. Contains educational news. **Formerly:** (1932) Interstate Dental Association.

★385★
National Dental Hygienists' Association
5506 Connecticut Ave. NW, Ste. 24-25   Ph: (202)244-7555
Washington, DC 20015   Fax: (202)244-5992
Dr. Carolyn Roundtree, Pres.

Description: Minority dental hygienists. To cultivate and promote the art and science of dental hygiene and to enhance the professional image of dental hygienists. Attempts to meet the needs of society through educational, political, and social activities while giving the minority dental hygienist a voice in shaping the profession. Encourages cooperation and mutual support among minority professionals. Seeks to increase opportunities for continuing education and employment in the field of dental hygiene. Works to improve individual and community dental health. Sponsors annual seminar, fundraising events, and scholarship programs; participates in career orientation programs; counsels and assists students applying for or enrolled in dental hygiene programs. Maintains liaison with American Dental Hygienists' Association. **Founded:** 1932. **Members:** 50. **Budget:** $50,000. **State Groups:** 10. **Publications:** Newsletter, quarterly.

★386★
National Economic Association

c/o Alfred L. Edwards
University of Michigan
School of Business   Ph: (313)763-0121
Ann Arbor, MI 48109-1234   Fax: (313)763-5688
Alfred L. Edwards, Sec.-Treas.

Description: Purposes are to: promote the professional life of blacks within the economics profession; advance the study and understanding of the economic problems confronting the black community; increase the number of black economists. Bestows Samuel Z. Westerfield Award to distinguished black economists. **Founded:** 1969. **Budget:** Less than $25,000. **Publications:** Directory of Black Economists, biennial. Job Placement Bulletin, periodic. Review of Black Political Economy, quarterly. Includes book reviews, annual indexes, manuscripts, and editorial correspondence. **Formerly:** (1975) Caucus of Black Economists.

★387★
National Emergency Civil Liberties Committee

175 5th Ave., Rm. 814   Ph: (212)673-2040
New York, NY 10010   Fax: (212)460-8359
Edith Tiger, Dir.

Description: To reestablish in full the traditional freedoms guaranteed under the Constitution and Bill of Rights. Committee "stands uncompromisingly for civil liberties for everyone and every variety of dissent." Legal staff handles test cases in the courts, without charge to the clients. Also functions as information service. **Founded:** 1951. **Publications:** Bill of Rights Journal, annual. Rights, 3/year. Newsletter. **Formerly:** (1968) Emergency Civil Liberties Committee.

★388★
National Florist Association

PO Box 90776
Washington, DC 20013   Ph: (716)235-3370
Martin Hall, Pres.

Description: Black retail florists. Works to: create better relationships with florists and allied trades throughout the U.S.; guide black florists in the improvement and upgrading of their businesses and to promote among them the wire communication of flower service; create better relationships with funeral directors throughout the country. Awards annual plaques and trophies for the best original flower displays. **Founded:** 1953. **Formerly:** (1963) International Flower Association; (1988) International Florists Association. **Members:** 500.

★389★
National Forum for Black Public Administrators

777 N. Capitol St. NE, Ste. 807   Ph: (202)408-9300
Washington, DC 20002   Fax: (202)408-8558
Beverly Scott, Exec.Dir.

Description: Black city and county managers and assistant managers; chief administrative officers; agency directors; bureau and division heads; corporate executives; students. Works to promote, strengthen, and expand the role of blacks in public administration. Seeks to focus the influence of black administrators toward building and maintaining viable communities. Develops specialized training programs for managers and executives. Provides national public administrative leadership resource and skills bank. Works to further communication among black public, private, and academic institutions. Addresses issues that affect the administrative capacity of black managers. Maintains Executive Leadership Institute which grooms mid-level executives for higher positions in government, the Mentor Program which matches aspiring black managers with seasoned executives over an 8-month period, and the Leadership Institute for Small Municipalities, which provides intensive training for elected and appointed officials from small communities. Offers training programs for black South Africans intent on achieving public administrative positions in the post-apartheid era. Sponsors the National Minority Business Development Forum to increase the participation of small and minority businesses in local government procurement and contracting programs. Bestows awards; maintains hall of fame. **Founded:** 1983. **Members:** 3000. **Budget:** $1,200,000. **Local Groups:** 49. **Telecommunications Services:** Jobs hot line, (800)55-FORUM (outside Washington, DC) and (202)39-FORUM

(Washington, DC). **Publications:** The Forum, quarterly. Newsletter. Includes articles on management and professional development; provides conference, chapter, and member information.

★390★
National Funeral Directors and Morticians Association

1800 E. Linwood Blvd.   Ph: (816)921-1800
Kansas City, MO 64109   Fax: (816)924-2113
Lawrence A. Jones Jr., Exec.Dir.

Description: State, district, and local funeral directing and embalming associations and their members. Promotes ethical practices; encourages just and uniform laws pertaining to funeral directing and embalming. **Budget:** $150,000. **Founded:** 1938. **Formerly:** (1957) National Negro Funeral Directors and Morticians Association. **Members:** 2000. **State Groups:** 26.

★391★
National Hook-Up of Black Women

c/o Wynetta Frazier
5117 S. University Ave.
Chicago, IL 60615   Ph: (312)643-5866
Wynetta Frazier, Pres.

Description: Black women from business, professional, and community-oriented disciplines representing all economic, educational, and social levels. Purpose is to provide a communications network in support of black women who serve in organizational leadership positions, especially those elected or appointed to office and those wishing to elevate their status through educational and career ventures. Works to form and implement a Black Women's Agenda that would provide representation for women, families, and communities and that would help surmount economic, educational, and social barriers. Supports efforts of the Congressional Black Caucus in utilizing the legislative process to work toward total equality of opportunity in society. Seeks to highlight the achievements and contributions of black women. Sponsors workshops. Bestows Distinguished Community Service, Distinguished Family Service, Outstanding Leadership, and Hook-Up Member of the Year awards. Operates speakers' bureau. Awards over $12,000 in scholarships annually. **Founded:** 1975. **Members:** 500. **Regional Groups:** 8. **Local Groups:** 9. **Publications:** Hook-Up News and Views, quarterly. Newsletter.

★392★
National Housewives' League of America for Economic Security

3240 Gilbert
Cincinnati, OH 45207   Ph: (513)281-8822
Magnolia R. Silmond, Pres.

Description: Black women seeking to strengthen the economic base of their communities through a program of positive support for businesses and professions owned and operated by or employing blacks. Aids stores through increased purchasing; conducts tours of businesses; sponsors high school essay contest on business and economics. Maintains library of newspaper articles, bulletins, and minutes of meetings. Sponsors competitions; conducts research programs. **Founded:** 1933. **Members:** 250. **Budget:** Less than $25,000. **Local Groups:** 7. **Publications:** Souvenir conference program. **Formerly:** (1986) National Housewives' League of America.

★393★
National Hypertension Association

324 E. 30th St.   Ph: (212)889-3557
New York, NY 10016   Fax: (212)447-7032
William M. Manger M.D., Chm.

Description: Physicians, medical researchers, and business professionals dedicated to the prevention of the complications of hypertension. Seeks to combat hypertension by developing, directing, and implementing effective programs to educate physicians and the public about the severe, life-threatening dangers of this health disorder. Conducts research on the cause of hypertension through basic laboratory studies. Sponsors seminars and symposia to keep the medical profession abreast of advances in the diagnosis and treatment of hypertension; provides school children with basic information on hypertension; conducts hypertension and hypercholesterol detection programs. Offers medical consulting to those found to have high blood pressure or hypercholesterolemia. Develops **Founded:** 1977. Mailing List: 1700. Advisory Committee: 400. **Publications:** News Report, annual. Newsletter. Also publishes medical journal periodicals, books, and monographs.

★394★
National Institute Against Prejudice and Violence
31 S. Greene St.   Ph: (410)328-5170
Baltimore, MD 21201   Fax: (410)328-7551
Description: Purpose is to study and respond to the problem of violence and intimidation motivated by racial, religious, ethnic, or anti-gay prejudice. Collects, analyzes, produces, and disseminates information and materials on programs of prevention and response. Conducts research on the causes and prevalence of prejudice and violence and their effects on victims and society; provides technical assistance to public agencies, voluntary organizations, schools, and communities in conflict; analyzes and drafts model legislation; conducts educational and training programs; sponsors conferences, symposia, and other forums for information exchange among experts. Maintains reference library. Bestows annual Stanley Sollins Memorial Award of recognition for outstanding contributions to human rights and intergroup relations by individuals and business. **Founded:** 1984. **Budget:** $587,900. **Publications:** Forum, quarterly. Newsletter. **Formerly:** (1986) Institute for Prevention and Control of Violence and Extremism.

★395★
National Institute for Women of Color
1301 20th St. NW Ste. 702
Washington, DC 20036   Ph: (202)298-1118
Sharon Parker, Bd.Chm.
Description: Aims to: enhance the strengths of diversity; promote educational and economic equity for black, Hispanic, Asian-American, Pacific-Islander, American Indian, and Alaskan Native women. Focuses on mutual concerns and needs, bringing together women who have traditionally been isolated. (NIWC uses the phrase "women of color" to convey unity, self-esteem, and political status and to avoid using the term "minority," which the institute feels has a negative psychological and social impact.) Serves as a networking vehicle to: link women of color on various issues or programs; promote women of color for positions on boards and commissions; ensure that women of color are visible as speakers or presenters at major women's conferences, as well as planners or program developers; support and initiate programs; educate women and the public about the status and culture of the various racial/ethnic groups they represent; promote cooperative efforts between general women's organizations and women of color, while raising awareness about issues and principles of feminism. Sponsors seminars and workshops. Provides technical assistance; conducts internship and leadership development programs; compiles statistics. **Founded:** 1981. **Budget:** $100,000. **Publications:** Has published Brown Papers, NIWC Network News, bibliographies, bulletins, fact sheets, and other related resources.

★396★
National Institute of Hypertension Studies - Institute of Hypertension School of Research
295 Mt. Vernon   Ph: (313)872-0505
Detroit, MI 48202   Fax: (313)872-0505
Dr. H.R. Lockett, Exec.Dir.
Description: Purposes are: to help find causes of and to help prevent essential hypertension; to educate people concerning essential hypertension; to diagnose, counsel, and refer afflicted individuals for treatment and follow-up activities; to conduct research on hypertension and to extend that research into the areas of crime and drug addiction and psychosocial and occupational stress. Sponsors public seminars and hypertension detection clinics. Offers youth leadership courses. Maintains library. Compiles statistics and disseminates educational materials. Conducts research programs on psychosocial and occupational stress which offer diplomas to those completing the programs; also conducts research on drugs and hypertension. Bestows awards. **Founded:** 1975. **Publications:** IHS 1992 Report, annual. Research report on causes of essential hypertension. Magazine, periodic. OHRST Assessment Report Series, annual. **Formerly:** (1977) Institute of Hypertension Studies; (1981) Institute of Hypertension Studies - Institute of Hypertension School of Research.

★397★
National Insurance Association
PO Box 53230   Ph: (312)924-3308
Chicago, IL 60653-0230   Fax: (312)285-0064
Josephine King, Pres.
Description: Conducts annual Institute in Agency Management and Institute in Home Office Operations. Sponsors National Insurance Week. **Founded:** 1921. **Members:** 20. **Local Groups:** 8. **Publications:** Member Roster, periodic. **Formerly:** (1954) National Negro Insurance Association.

★398★
National Medical Association
1012 10th St. NW   Ph: (202)347-1895
Washington, DC 20001   Fax: (202)842-3293
William C. Garrett, Exec.VP
Description: Professional society of black physicians. Bestows awards. Maintains 19 sections representing major specialties of medicine. Plans to establish library and physician placement service. Conducts symposia and workshops. **Founded:** 1895. **Members:** 14,500. **Regional Groups:** 6. **Local Groups:** 62. **State Groups:** 32. **Computerized Services:** Mailing list (for NMA regions and affiliates only). **Publications:** Journal of the National Medical Association, monthly. National Medical Association Newsletter, quarterly.

★399★
National Minority AIDS Council
300 I St. NE, Ste. 400   Ph: (202)544-1076
Washington, DC 20002   Fax: (202)544-0378
                         Free: 800-544-0586
Paul A. Kawata, Exec.Dir.
Description: Public health departments and AIDS service organizations. Serves as a clearinghouse of information on AIDS as it affects minority communities in the U.S. Facilitates discussion among national minority organizations about AIDS. Maintains Project Health, Education, and AIDS Leadership, which provides computer usage, strategic planning, financial management, and volunteer program development assistance to AIDS service organizations, and Project Volunteer Information, Technical Assistance, and Leadership, which provides technical assistance in volunteer program development and maintenance. Conducts training conferences. Offers educational and research programs; compiles statistics. Bestows awards; maintains speakers' bureau, biographical archives, and library. **Founded:** 1986. **Members:** 200. **Budget:** $550,000. **Regional Groups:** 1. **Local Groups:** 160. **State Groups:** 20. **Publications:** Leadership Reprint Series, quarterly. Includes information on strategies for addressing HIV/AIDS and scientific updates.

★400★
National Minority Business Council
235 E. 42nd St.   Ph: (212)573-2385
New York, NY 10017   Fax: (212)573-4462
John F. Robinson, CEO & Pres.
Description: Minority businesses in all areas of industry and commerce. Seeks to increase profitability by developing marketing, sales, and management skills in minority businesses. Acts as an informational source for the national minority business community. Programs include: a legal services plan that provides free legal services to members in such areas as sales contracts, copyrights, estate planning, and investment agreement; a business referral service that develops potential customer leads; an international trade assistance program that provides technical assistance in developing foreign markets; an executive banking program that teaches members how to package a business loan for bank approval; a procurement outreach program for minority and women business owners. Conducts continuing management education and provides assistance in teaching youth the free enterprise system. Bestows awards. **Founded:** 1972. **Members:** 400. **Budget:** $350,000. **Publications:** Corporate Minority Vendor Directory, annual. Corporate Purchasing Directory, annual. NMBC Business Report, bimonthly. NMBC Corporate Purchasing Directory, periodic.

★401★
National Minority Health Association
PO Box 11876
Harrisburg, PA 17108   Ph: (717)234-3254
Leroy Robinson, Exec.Dir.

Description: Health care providers and associations, consumers, executives and administrators, educators, pharmaceutical and health insurance companies, and other corporations with an interest in health care. Seeks to identify and focus attention on the health needs of minorities. Promotes: more effective research in minority health issues; better training of health care practitioners; development of programs that encourage minorities to pursue careers in the health care industry and educate minority communities on the importance of good health. Initiates discussions with professional health organizations, academic institutions, state and federal governments, and health departments to develop strategies to improve the quality and availability of health care, health delivery systems, and health professionals to minority communities. Bestows National Health Achievement Award annually to individual or group that has made significant contributions in the area of minority health. Maintains speakers' bureau, library, and placement services; conducts research and educational programs; sponsors children's programs; complies statistics. **Founded:** 1987. **Members:** 30,000. **State Groups:** 1. **Computerized Services:** Database; mailing list. **Publications:** The National Minority Health Association News, quarterly.

★402★
National Minority Supplier Development Council
15 W. 39th St., 9th Fl.   Ph: (212)944-2430
New York, NY 10018   Fax: (212)719-9611
Harriet Michel, Pres.

Description: Minority businesspersons, corporations, government agencies, and other organizations who are members of regional purchasing councils or who have agreed to participate in the program. Regional councils certify and match minority-owned businesses with member corporations which want to purchase goods and services. Conducts sales training programs for minority entrepreneurs, and buyer training program for corporate minority purchasing programs. Bestows awards; compiles statistics. **Founded:** 1972. **Members:** 170. **Budget:** $4,500,000. **Regional Groups:** 45. **Computerized Services:** MBISYS, Minority Business Information System, an online database of certified minority-owned businesses and qualified vendors to business and industry. **Publications:** Minority Supplier News, 3/year. **Formerly:** (1980) National Minority Purchasing Council.

★403★
National Naval Officers Association
PO Box 46256   Fax: (216)261-2828
Washington, DC 20050   Free: 800-772-6662
Capt. J. Roger Bailey, Pres.

Description: Active, reserve, and retired Naval, Marine, and Coast Guard officers and students in college and military sea service programs. Promotes and assists recruitment, retention, and retirement of minorities in naval service. Conducts specialized education; maintains counseling , referral, and children's services. Makes available non-ROTC grants-in-aid. Sponsors competitions; bestows awards; operates charitable program. **Founded:** 1971. **Members:** 1245. **Budget:** $150,000. **Regional Groups:** 4. **Local Groups:** 30. **Computerized Services:** Membership database. Electronic bulletin board. **Publications:** NNOA Annual Conference Program. NNOA Meridian, quarterly. Tabloid covering sea service news and events; includes chapter news, news from other military services, statistics, and information about other organizations.

★404★
National Network of Minority Women in Science
c/o American Association for the
  Advancement of Science
Directorate for Educ. and Human
  Resources Programs
1333 H St. NW
Washington, DC 20005   Ph: (202)326-6670
Audrey B. Daniel, Coordinator

Description: Asian, Black, Mexican American, Native American, and Puerto Rican women involved in science related professions; other interested persons. Promotes the advancement of minority women in science fields and the improvement of the science and mathematics education and career awareness of minorities. Supports public policies and programs in science and technology that benefit minorities. Compiles statistics; serves as clearinghouse for identifying minority women scientists. Offers writing and conference presentations, seminars, and workshops on minority women in science and local career conferences for students. Local chapters maintain speakers' bureaus and placement services, offer children's services, sponsor competitions, and bestows awards. **Founded:** 1978. **Members:** 400. **Budget:** Less than $25,000. **Regional Groups:** 1. **Local Groups:** 3. **State Groups:** 2. **Publications:** MWIS. annual report.

★405★
National Newspaper Publishers Association
3200 13th St. NW   Ph: (202)588-8764
Washington, DC 20010   Fax: (202)588-5029
Steve G. Davis, Exec.Dir.

Description: Publishers of daily and weekly newspapers. Presents Distinguished Service Award annually to the black leader who has made the most significant contribution to black advancement during the previous year. Maintains hall of fame. Sponsors annual workshop. **Founded:** 1940. **Members:** 178. **Budget:** $215,000. **Computerized Services:** Mailing lists. **Publications:** Convention Journal, annual. **Formerly:** (1956) National Negro Newspaper Publishers Association.

★406★
National Office for Black Catholics
3025 4th St. NE
Washington, DC 20017   Ph: (202)635-1778
Walter Hubbard, Dir.

Description: Black priests, sisters, brothers, and laypersons of the Catholic church. Participating organizations: National Black Sisters' Conference; National Black Catholic Clergy Caucus. Serves as a "foundation for the renewal of the credibility of the church in the black community." Works to coordinate actions designed "to liberate black people and to serve as a unifying strength." Plans to: have specialists and technicians working within the black community to coordinate community organization and development; provide leadership training for youth; attack problems of poverty and deprivation; sensitize blacks to their heritage through historical, cultural, and liturgical experience. Seeks cooperation with groups working toward black liberation. Concerns include: training black and white clergy and religious, Catholic, and non-Catholic laity; influencing decisions involving race and the church; monitoring, in order to prevent, manifestations of racism. Sponsors Pastoral Ministry Institute and Afro-American Culture and Worship Workshop; provides evangelization workshops and leadership training for parish councils and parochial schools; maintains 400 volume library. **Founded:** 1970. **Members:** 1,000,000. **Publications:** Freeing the Spirit, quarterly. Impact, 6/year. Newsletter. Also publishes booklets.

★407★
National Optometric Association
1489 E. Livingston Ave.
Columbus, OH 43205   Ph: (614)253-5593
Dr. Clayton Hicks, Exec.Dir.

Description: Optometrists dedicated to increasing minority optometric manpower. Conducts research programs and national recruiting program. Bestows awards; maintains speakers' bureau. Offers specialized education program. **Founded:** 1969. **Members:** 350. **Budget:** Less than $25,000. **Regional Groups:** 5. **Publications:** Newsletter, quarterly.

★408★

National Organization for the Professional Advancement of Black Chemists and Chemical Engineers

525 College St. NW
Washington, DC 20059

Ph: (202)667-1699
Fax: (202)667-1705
Free: 800-776-1419

Damon Larry, Dir.

Description: Black professionals in science and chemistry. Seeks to aid black scientists and chemists in reaching their full professional potential; encourages black students to pursue scientific studies and employment; promotes participation of blacks in scientific research. Provides volunteers to teach science courses in selected elementary schools; sponsors scientific field trips for students; maintains speakers' bureau for schools; provides summer school for students of the U.S. Naval Academy. Conducts technical seminars in Africa; operates exchange program of scientific and chemical professionals with the People's Republic of China. Sponsors competitions; presents awards for significant achievements to individuals in the field. Maintains library of materials pertaining to chemistry, science, and black hisotry; keeps archive of organization's books and records. Maintains placement service; compiles statistics. **Founded:** 1972. **Members:** 2000. **Budget:** $280,000. **Regional Groups:** 5. **Local Groups:** 30. **Computerized Services:** Records file. **Publications:** Newsmagazine, quarterly. Newsletter. **Formerly:** (1989) National Organization of Black Chemists and Chemical Engineers.

★409★

National Organization of Black College Alumni

Four Washington Square Village, No. 15E
New York, NY 10012

Ph: (212)982-7726

Dr. Jean Gilbert, Coordinator

Description: Graduates, friends, and supporters of the 114 historically black colleges. Works to ensure the survival of black colleges by addressing their concerns and needs and providing resources to meet these needs. Coordinates and focuses alumni support for black colleges; strengthens existing alumni associations; urges black youth to obtain a college education. Facilitates the exchange of information. Provides consultants; holds workshops and seminars. **Founded:** 1982. **State Groups:** 50. **Publications:** NOBCA Newsletter, semiannual.

★410★

National Organization of Black County Officials

440 1st St. NW, Ste. 500
Washington, DC 20001

Ph: (202)347-6953
Fax: (202)393-6596

Crandall O. Jones, Exec.Dir.

Description: Black county officials organized to provide program planning and management assistance to selected counties in the U.S. Acts as a technical information exchange to develop resolutions to problems on the local and national levels. Promotes the sharing of knowledge and methods of improving resource utilization and government operations. Conducts seminars and training sessions. Plans to maintain resource file on the achievements and history of black county officials. **Founded:** 1982. **Members:** 2000. **Publications:** County Compass, quarterly. Newsletter; includes calendar of events and member profiles.

★411★

National Organization of Black Law Enforcement Executives

908 Pennsylvania Ave. SE
Washington, DC 20003

Ph: (202)546-8811
Fax: (202)544-8351

Dr. Cassandra E. Johnson J.D., Exec.Dir.

Description: Law enforcement executives above the rank of lieutenant; police educators; academy directors; interested individuals and organizations. Goals are: to provide a platform from which the concerns and opinions of minority law enforcement executives and command-level officers can be expressed; to facilitate the exchange of programmatic information among minority law enforcement executives; to increase minority participation at all levels of law enforcement; to eliminate racism in the field of criminal justice; to secure increased cooperation from criminal justice agencies; to reduce urban crime and violence. Seeks to develop and maintain channels of communication between law enforcement agencies and the community; encourages coordi nated community

efforts to prevent and abate crime and its causes. Offers on-site technical assistance and training to police departments; develops model policies, practices, and procedures designed to decrease racial and religious violence and harassment. Provides job referral services to organizations seeking minority executives. Conducts research and training and offers technical assistance in crime victim assistance, community oriented policing, domestic violence, use of deadly force, reduction of fear of crime, airport security assessment, and minority recruitment. Awards scholarships and offers internships and fellowships to students preparing for careers in law enforcement. Operates speakers' bureau and 300 volume library. **Founded:** 1976. **Members:** 2900. MD $30 for supporting; $45 for associate; $75 for individual; $500 for sustaining. **Budget:** $800,000. **Regional Groups:** 6. **Local Groups:** 20. **Computerized Services:** Database on domestic violence resources. **Publications:** NOBLE ACTIONS, quarterly. Newsletter reporting on current law enforcement issues and activities. Contains employment opportunities, calendar of events, and legislative information.

★412★

National Organization of Minority Architects

NOMA Office and Archives
Howard University
School of Architecture and Planning
2366 6th St.
Washington, DC 20059

Ph: (804)788-0338
Fax: (804)649-8502

Robert L. Easter, Pres.

Description: Seeks to increase the number and influence of minority architects by encouraging minority youth and taking an active role in the education of new architects. Works in cooperation with other associations, professionals, and architectural firms to promote the professional advancement of members. Bestows annual Design Excellence awards to professionals and students. Sponsors competitions; offers children's services, educational programs, and charitable programs; maintains speakers' bureau; compiles statistics. **Founded:** 1971. **Members:** 250. **Budget:** $25,000. **Publications:** NOMA News, quarterly. **Formerly:** (1973) National Organization of Black Architects.

★413★

National Podiatric Medical Association

c/o Raymond E. Lee, D.P.M.
1638 E. 87th St.
Chicago, IL 60617

Ph: (312)374-1616

Raymond E. Lee D.P.M., Contact

Description: Minority podiatrists, predominantly black. Promotes the science and art of podiatry. Seeks to: improve public health; raise the standards of the podiatric profession and education; stimulate a favorable relationship between all podiatrists; nurture growth and diffusion of podiatric information; stimulate public education concerning public health and features of podiatric medicine. Sponsors proposal of podiatric laws; works to eliminate religious and racial discrimination and segregation in American medical institutions. **Founded:** 1971. **Members:** 200. **Budget:** Less than $25,000. **Publications:** Annual Seminar Ad Book. National Podiatric Medical Association–Newsletter, annual. Includes calendar of events and news from student-affiliated associations. **Formerly:** (1987) National Podiatry Association.

★414★

National Rainbow Coalition

1700 K St. NW, Ste. 800
Washington, DC 20006

Ph: (202)728-1192
Fax: (202)728-1192

Rev. Jesse L. Jackson Sr., Pres.

Also known as: The Rainbow. **Description:** Promotes the creation of a better nation and world by lifting the hope of all Americans and assuring economic justice, peace, human rights, and dignity for all. Works to build a consensus in the areas of civil rights, government, politics, labor, education, religion, business, academia, the environment, health care, and other issues; provides a platform for debate at the national, state, and local levels. Encourages the development of a new political leadership committed to progressive domestic and international policies and programs, leading to a more humane society. Named during the 1984 presidential campaign of the Rev. Jesse L. Jackson, Sr. (1942-), prominent black civil rights leader and politician. **Founded:** 1984. **Formerly:** (1986) Rainbow Coalition. **Members:** 13,000. **State Groups:** 50.

★415★
National Society of Black Engineers
1454 Duke St.
PO Box 25588   Ph: (703)549-2207
Alexandria, VA 22313-5588   Fax: (703)683-5312
Florida Morehead, Exec.Dir.

Description: Engineering and science students. Seeks to increase the number of minority graduates in engineering and technology. Bestows awards; sponsors seminars and workshops geared toward preparing students for careers, the industry, and leadership roles. **Founded:** 1975. **Members:** 7500. **Budget:** $1,200,000. **Regional Groups:** 6. **Local Groups:** 180. **Publications:** National Conference Proceedings, annual. Newsletter, bimonthly. Also publishes pamphlet. **Telecommunications Services:** Electronic mail.

★416★
National Sorority of Phi Delta Kappa
8233 S. Martin Luther King Dr.
Chicago, IL 60619   Ph: (312)783-7379
Edna Murray, Exec.Sec.

Description: Women who teach or who hold administrative positions in education. Five-point program includes educational conferences (Teach-A-Rama), reading and study centers for youth, youth guidance, scholarship awards, and maintenance of a children's library in Liberia. Awards three lifetime memberships annually to members of the National Association for the Advancement of Colored People; offers tutorial programs. **Founded:** 1923. **Members:** 5000. **Regional Groups:** 5. **Chapters:** 113. **Computerized Services:** Mailing list. **Publications:** Bulletin, quarterly. Directory, annual. Krinon, annual.

★417★
National Technical Association
PO Box 7045   Ph: (202)829-6100
Washington, DC 20032-0145   Fax: (703)684-3952
Carrington Stewart, Pres.

Description: Persons who have attained proficiency in engineering, architecture, mathematics, and natural sciences. Seeks to: develop and integrate the minority technical input into the total scientific process; give minorities an awareness of their technical contribution to the establishment of the world's societies; provide for technical interchange among minorities; disseminate career opportunity information to minorities; motivate minority youth to consider technical careers; remove barriers against minorities entering into and advancing in technical professions. Compiles statistics; presents awards; maintains speakers' bureau. Conducts national junior and senior high school scientific and technical career awareness programs, and student technical symposia. **Founded:** 1926. **Members:** 1500. **Professional Chapters:** 40. **Student Chapters:** 30. **Publications:** Journal, quarterly. Newsletter, quarterly.

★418★
National United Affiliated Beverage Association
PO Box 9308
Philadelphia, PA 19139   Ph: (215)748-5670
Joseph T. Finn, Pres.

Description: Black and minority beverage distributors (42,000); auxiliary members (5000) are interested in the beverage industry. Seeks to broaden opportunities for minorities in the beverage industry. Monitors state and federal liquor laws and informs members of developments. Cooperates with the National Conference of Black Mayors in an effort to stimulate economic growth in U.S. cities; conducts fundraising activities for the United Negro College Fund. Supports literacy programs; regional groups offer scholarships. **Founded:** 1979. **Members:** 47,000. **Regional Groups:** 22. **Publications:** Corkscrew, monthly. Newspaper. Also publishes souvenir book.

★419★
National United Law Enforcement Officers Association
256 E. McLemore Ave.   Ph: (901)774-1118
Memphis, TN 38106   Free: 800-533-4649
Clyde R. Venson, Exec.Dir.

Description: Law enforcement officers from all departments; interested persons from the community. Develops community-based programs designed to improve the relationship between law enforcement officers and the community, with emphasis on the black community. Provides educational seminars on law enforcement that promote professionalism and improvement of performance standards; emphasizes past contributions by black officers and encourages potential leadership. Compiles data regarding the history of blacks in law enforcement. Promotes equal employment and promotional practices for black officers. Makes available scholarship program for college students. Operates hall of fame; maintains library and biographical archives; provides speakers' bureau; offers children's services. Compiles statistics. Sponsors competitions; bestows awards. **Founded:** 1969. **Members:** 5000. **Budget:** $75,000. **State Groups:** 250. **Computerized Services:** Database. **Publications:** Law Enforcement Association News, quarterly. **Telecommunications Services:** Search for Answers (information hot line).

★420★
National United Licensees Beverage Association
7141 Frankstown Ave.
Pittsburgh, PA 15208   Ph: (412)241-9344
Vivian Lane, Exec. Officer

Description: Holders of alcoholic beverage licenses. Purposes are to promote fellowship; develop, strengthen, and improve methods; promote integrity, good faith, and just and equitable principles in business and professional activity; seek uniformity in commercial usages; acquire, preserve, and distribute educational, civic, social, commercial, and economic statistics, and information. Conducts seminars. Awards annual scholarship to a needy high school honor student seeking a business education. **Founded:** 1964. **Members:** 1200. **Publications:** Newsletter, quarterly.

★421★
National Urban Coalition
8601 Georgia Ave., Ste. 500   Ph: (301)495-4999
Silver Spring, MD 20910   Fax: (301)587-0868
Ramona H. Edelin Ph.D., CEO

Description: Seeks to improve the quality of life and opportunity for the disadvantaged in urban areas through the combined efforts of leaders among minorities, business, labor, local government, women, youth, and religion. Operates Say Yes to a Youngster's Future program, which works to increase the participation of African Americans, Hispanics, Native Americans, and females in science, math, and computer education. Provides programs for urban children of color in the areas of science and mathematics; operates AIDS education and information demonstration program for teenagers in Washington, DC. Conducts advocacy on behalf of cities and the least advantaged residents of urban areas. Bestows awards to individuals who form outstanding service for urban communities. **Founded:** 1967. **Budget:** $1,800,000. **Local Groups:** 40. **Computerized Services:** National Education Information Exchange database.

★422★
National Urban League
500 E. 62nd St.   Ph: (212)310-9000
New York, NY 10021   Fax: (212)593-8250
John E. Jacob, CEO & Pres.

Description: Voluntary nonpartisan community service agency of civic, professional, business, labor, and religious leaders with a staff of trained social workers and other professionals. Aims to eliminate racial segregation and discrimination in the United States and to achieve parity for blacks and other minorities in every phase of American life. Works to eliminate institutional racism and to provide direct service to minorities in the areas of employment, housing, education, social welfare, health, family planning, mental retardation, law and consumer affairs, youth and student affairs, labor affairs, veterans' affairs, and community and minority business development. Maintains research department in Washington, DC. **Founded:** 1910. **Members:** 50,000. **Budget:** $18,900,000. **Local Groups:** 113. **Regional Offices:** 5. **Publications:** BEEP Newsletter, quarterly. Describes BEEP courses. Includes member news and listing of publications. Community Surveys and Reports, periodic. The Urban League News, quarterly. League program and activities newsletter. **Formerly:** National League on Urban Conditions Among Negroes.

★423★
National Urban/Rural Fellows
55 W. 44th St., Ste. 600
New York, NY 10036
Linda Ruiz Saldibar, Dir.

Ph: (212)921-9400
Fax: (212)921-9572

Description: Program designed to make top leadership opportunities in government and rural development available to minority group members. Recipients of the 14-month fellowships are selected competitively and must be U.S. citizens who: have a bachelor's degree, have experience in solving urban or rural problems; have at least three years of employment experience in an administrative or economic development capacity; have demonstrated ability, leadership qualities, and a commitment to the solution of urban or rural problems. Program is aimed at meeting the need for competent urban and rural administrators, particularly minority group members and women, by combining a nine month, on-the-job assignment as special assistant to an experienced practitioner with several kinds of academic work. A master's degree in public administration or regional planning/rural development is awarded to qualified fellows at the end of the fellowship. **Founded:** 1969. **Fellows:** 530. **Budget:** $1,094,000. **Publications:** Annual Report. Bio/Directory of Class, annual.

★424★
Negro Airmen International
PO Box 1340
Tuskegee Institute, AL 36087
John W. Hicks Jr., Operations Officer

Ph: (205)727-0721

Description: Individuals holding at least a student pilot license who are active in some phase of aviation; members include both aviation professionals and others who are qualified pilots. Seeks greater participation by blacks in the field of aviation through the encouragement of broader job opportunities; promotes awareness by government and industry of the needs, attitudes, and interests of blacks concerning aviation. Encourages black youth to remain in school and to enter the field of aviation. Maintains Summer Flight Academy for teenagers each July at Morton Field, Tuskegee, AL. Sponsors competitions; bestows awards. Operates speakers' bureau, placement service, and library. **Founded:** 1967. **Members:** 912. **Regional Groups:** 10. **Local Groups:** 25. **Computerized Services:** Database on membership and demographics. **Publications:** Newsletter, quarterly. Also publishes informational brochures, and has produced a film on flight basics for youth.

★425★
Newspaper Association of America Foundation
11600 Sunrise Valley Dr.
Dulles International Airport, VA 20041
Rosalind G. Stark, VP & Dir.

Ph: (703)648-1000
Fax: (703)620-1265

Description: Educational arm of the Newspaper Association of America. Seeks to: develop an informed readership; combat illiteracy; educate the public regarding their rights under the First Amendment; increase opportunities for minorities in the industry; foster professionalism in the press. Aids local newspapers with the creation of programs that promote the foundation's objectives and meet the needs of the newspaper and the needs of the community it serves. These programs include: the Newspaper in Education Program, which supplies primary and secondary school systems with curriculum materials and encourages the use of newspapers in the classroom as an educational tool; the Minority Fellowship Program; the Literacy Program. Works with the Accrediting Council on Education in Journalism and Mass Communications. Cosponsors annual Newspaper in Education Week, and International Literacy Day. Bestows awards and fellowships for minority newspaper professionals. Conducts workshops and seminars; provides speakers. **Founded:** 1961. **Publications:** Annual Report. Update, quarterly. Also publishes Bibliography: NIE Publications, Newspaper: What's In It for Me? (career booklet), Family Focus: Reading and Learning Together, The Next Step: Toward Diversity in the Newspaper Business. **Formerly:** (1992) American Newspaper Publishers Association Foundation.

★426★
Nigerian Students Union in the Americas
c/o Granville U. Osuji
654 Girard St. NW, Apt. 512
Washington, DC 20001
Granville U. Osuji, Contact

Ph: (202)462-9124

Description: Nigerian students at institutions of higher learning in North and South America and neighboring islands. Disseminates information about Nigeria and Africa; cooperates with other African student unions in the Americas and with Nigerian student unions in Nigeria and other parts of the world. Maintains placement service and speakers' bureau. Holds teach-ins, symposia, debates, panel discussions, and lectures. Conducts research; bestows awards. **Founded:** 1962. **Members:** 25,000. **Regional Groups:** 4.

★427★
North American Center on Adoption
67 Irving Pl.
New York, NY 10003
Elizabeth S. Cole, Dir.

Ph: (212)254-7410

Description: Resource center dealing with the problems preventing the adoption of older children, minority group children, children with physical, emotional, and/or intellectual problems, and children belonging to a sibling group of three or more. A project of Permanent Families for Children. Works with the media to increase public awareness of the waiting child. Develops training materials and provides technical assistance and consultation to agency staffs and interested groups. Offers resource services and consultation to those interested in establishing or improving state, provincial and regional adoption. Works with specialized agencies. **Founded:** 1974. **Publications:** Permanency Report, quarterly.

★428★
North American Islamic Trust
10900 W. Washington St.
Indianapolis, IN 46231
M. Naziruddin Ali, Gen.Mgr.

Ph: (317)839-9248
Fax: (317)839-2511

Description: Distributes Islamic books and religious supplies. Maintains small library of Arabic and English works on Islam. Sponsors children's services and charitable program. **Founded:** 1973. **Budget:** $1,500,000.

★429★
Office for Advancement of Public Black Colleges - of the National Association of State Universities and Land Grant Colleges
1 Dupont Cir. NW, Ste. 710
Washington, DC 20036-1191
Dr. N. Joyce Payne, Dir.

Ph: (202)778-0818

Description: Collects, organizes, interprets, and disseminates data on 35 predominantly black public colleges. The colleges, located in 18 states, enroll over 135,000 students. Conducts research programs; bestows awards. Compiles statistics; maintains databases. **Founded:** 1968. **Members:** 35. **Regional Groups:** 12. **State Groups:** 18. **Publications:** Key Administrative Personnel, annual. Directory. A National Resource, biennial. Newsletter, periodic. Profiles in Success, quarterly. Also publishes books and booklets. **Formerly:** (1984) Office for Advancement of Public Negro Colleges - of the National Association of State Universities and Land-Grant Colleges.

★430★
Omega Psi Phi
2714 Georgia Ave., NW
Washington, DC 20001
Dr. John S. Epps, Dir.

Ph: (202)667-7158

Description: Social fraternity. **Founded:** 1911. **Members:** 50,000. Active Chapters: 511. Alumni Chapters: 259. **Publications:** Bulletin, quarterly. The Oracle, quarterly.

★431★
Operation Crossroads Africa
475 Riverside Dr., Rm. 242
New York, NY 10115   Ph: (212)870-2106
Willis Logan, Pres.

Description: Students and professionals, mostly from the U.S., who live and work with African counterparts during July and August on selfhelp community development projects in Africa. Opportunities are provided for interaction with village elders, educators, and political and other community leaders. Emphasizes community growth from within a "Third World" structure. Before departure, participants make an intensive study of Africa; after their return, they give speeches about their experiences. Participants pay part of the cost of the project. Organizes workcamp projects for U.S. high school students in the Caribbean and programs the visits of African and Caribbean leaders to the U.S. Sponsors training and exchange programs. Conducts fundraising and relief activities. Maintains liaison with similar groups abroad. **Founded:** 1958. **Members:** 7800. **Budget:** $3,500,000. **Publications:** Annual Report. Crossroads Communique, quarterly. Also publishes brochure.

★432★
Operation PUSH
930 E. 50th St.   Ph: (312)373-3366
Chicago, IL 60615   Fax: (312)924-3571
Att. Jeanette Wilson, Exec.Dir.

Description: National and international human rights organization and movement directed toward educational and economic equity and parity for all, particularly black, Hispanic, and poor people. Seeks to create an ethical atmosphere; encourages self and community motivation and social responsibility. Uses research, education, negotiation, and direct action to achieve its goals. Sponsors Push for Excellence Program to aid the nation's public schools and restore academic excellence and discipline. Conducts conferences; maintains tape and speech library; operates speakers' bureau. (PUSH stands for People United to Serve Humanity.) **Founded:** 1971. **Budget:** $300,000. **Local Groups:** 50. **Publications:** The Push Magazine, quarterly. The Voice of Excellence, bimonthly. Newspaper.

★433★
Operation Sisters United
1104 Allison St. NW
Washington, DC 20011   Ph: (202)726-7365
Eleanore Cox, Dir.

Description: A program of the National Council of Negro Women. Aids teenage girls who have had conflicts with the law; seeks to prevent incarceration and institutionalization of these girls, and help them avoid future legal problems. Works to keep teenage girls with their families. Operates cultural enrichment, counseling, sex education, and family planning programs. Conducts parenting classes for teenage parents. Compiles statistics; maintains placement service. Sponsors competitions and bestows awards. **Founded:** 1972.

★434★
Organization of African-American Veterans
PO Box 873
Ft. Huachuca, AZ 85613   Ph: (602)458-7245
George M. Allen, Pres.

Description: Veterans and active personnel of all branches of the U.S. military. Promotes the physical, mental, social, and economic rehabilitation of veterans; works to obtain compensation, medical care, employment, and business assistance for veterans. Assists and represents veterans and their families in filing benefit claims. Sponsors and supports beneficial legislation. **Founded:** 1978. **Members:** 409.

★435★
Organization of Black Airline Pilots
PO Box 5793   Ph: (201)568-8145
Englewood, NJ 07631   Fax: (201)568-5178
Eddie R. Hadden, Gen.Mgr.

Description: Cockpit crew members of commercial air carriers, corporate pilots, and other interested individuals. Seeks to enhance minority participation in the aerospace industry. Maintains liaison with airline presidents and minority and pilot associations. Conducts lobbying efforts, including congressional examinations into airline recruitment practices. Provides scholarships; cosponsors Summer Flight Academy for Youth at Tuskegee Institute in Alabama. Offers job placement service and charitable program; operates speakers' bureau; compiles statistics on airline hiring practices. **Founded:** 1976. **Members:** 650. **Budget:** Less than $25,000. **Regional Groups:** 5. **Computerized Services:** Job placement bank. **Publications:** Convention Journal, annual. Newsletter, bimonthly.

★436★
Panamerican/PanAfrican Association
PO Box 143   Ph: (315)638-7379
Baldwinsville, NY 13027   Fax: (315)638-0778
Dr. Robert S. Pritchard, Chm.

Description: Supporters include scholars, diplomats, denominations, African-American and inter-American cultural exchange organizations, and persons who promote intercultural, interracial, and inter-group understanding. Maintains Applecrest in Baldwinsville, NY, headquarters and "think tank" for various cultural groups and activities and site of seminars, educational encounters, art exhibits, and music recitals. Coordinated the 7th International Panafricanist congress in Cotonou, Benin, February 1991. Sponsors inter-American, African-American, and Asian-American educational, cultural, and economic exchange, including Royal Ethiopian Philharmonic Orchestra. Maintains public diplomacy program; promotes artistic endeavors including concerts and recitals; conducts public interest civil and humman rights litigation activities; promotes Third World economic development. Administers National and International Black History Month observances each February. Operates library of 2000 items including works from Afro-Brazilian guilds of ecclesiastical music, literature, and specialized studies on multiethnic/multicultural education and curriculum development. **Founded:** 1967. **Publications:** Panamerican/Panafrican Association–Notes, periodic. Newsletter covering association activities and international ethnic and cultural topics. Includes commentary. **Also known as:** Panamerican Association.

★437★
Parker-Coltrane Political Action Committee
669 Federal Bldg.
231 W. Lafayette
Detroit, MI 48226   Ph: (313)961-5670
Hansen Clark, Contact

Description: Political action organization supported by financial contributions of individuals. Organized by Congressman John Conyers and others to encourage and help blacks and progressive candidates to win election to public office in the southern U.S. through direct campaign contributions and technical assistance. Conducts training sessions on methods and techniques of running for office. Initial efforts have been concentrated in Georgia, although the committee now operates throughout the South. Plans to extend operations on a national level. Presently inactive. **Founded:** 1981.

★438★
Partners of the Americas
1424 K St., NW, Ste. 700   Ph: (202)628-3300
Washington, DC 20005   Fax: (202)628-3306
William Reese, Pres.

Description: Volunteer private citizens organized in 60 partnerships linking U.S. states with Latin American and Caribbean countries. Goals are: to encourage innovative, community-based projects and joint planning among local partnerships; to provide a stimulus to local partnerships in generating additional resources for their technical and cultural exchange projects; to assist in the implementation of effective and ongoing development projects in the Latin American, Mexican, and Caribbean partner areas. Partnerships form the basis for exchange projects in agriculture, public health, culture, rehabilitation, community education, sports, and other areas of hemispheric development. Presents grants to partnership projects and travel funds for selected volunteer technicians; bestows awards. **Founded:** 1964. **Members:** 20,000. **Budget:** $6,200,000. **Publications:** Annual Report. Partners, quarterly. Newsletter on technical assistance projects and exchanges between the United States and Latin America in agriculture, public health, education, and development. Also publishes brochures and booklets; makes available A Good Idea That Works (videotape). **Telecommunications Services:** Electronic mail, TYMNET

(CONTYME) DNA.NAPA; telex, 6421 NAPAR. **Formerly:** (1971) National Association of the Partners of the Alliance.

★439★
PFB Project
c/o Robert B. Fitzpatrick
4801 Massachusetts Ave. NW, Ste. 400
Washington, DC 20016-2087   Ph: (202)364-8710
Robert B. Fitzpatrick, Co-Founder
Description: Seeks humane solutions for victims of pseudofolliculitis barbae (PFB). PFB is a skin disorder peculiar to black men in which victims suffer from a bump-like rash on the face which is aggravated by shaving. There is no complete cure for the disorder; the least painful solution is for victims to allow their beards to grow. The project believes that individuals who suffer from the disorder and are forced to shave by employers are victims of racial discrimination. Provides legal assistance to those discriminated against because of PFB. Supports research on PFB; maintains library. **Founded:** 1978.

★440★
Phi Beta Sigma
145 Kennedy St. NW   Ph: (202)726-5424
Washington, DC 20011-5294   Fax: (202)882-1681
Dr. Lawrence E. Miller, Exec.Dir.
Description: Service fraternity. Seeks to develop and translate into functional realities the ideals of brotherhood, service, and scholarship. Promotes three national programs: Bigger and Better Business; Education; Social Action. Sponsors Sigma Beta Club for high school aged males. Maintains political action committee; offers placement service. **Founded:** 1914. **Members:** 90,000. **Publications:** The Crescent, semiannual. The Crescent Extra, periodic. Newsletter.

★441★
Plan of Action for Challenging Times
PACT-Educ. Opportunities Clearinghouse
635 Divisadero St.   Ph: (415)922-2550
San Francisco, CA 94117   Fax: (415)922-6305
W. Charlene Folsom, Project Dir.
Description: Program to benefit minority and/or low-income students who have not, in most cases, utilized their educational potential by reason of circumstances inherent in their background, mainly lack of encouragement, motivation, and finances. Students must be citizens or permanent residents of the U.S. Serves the city and county of San Francisco, CA; African-Americans represent the greatest percentage of students served. Assists Mexican-Americans, Asians, Native Americans, and low-income Caucasians. Students are identified through agency, school, and community referrals offering counseling services, college and financial aid information, and college admissions procedures. Provides college admissions, financial aid, and career counseling services; offers assistance with application forms; organizes campus visits, meetings between college recruiters and students, and visits to corporations and public institutions to observe various professions; conducts financial aid workshops; sponsors presentations to organizations, churches, and clubs. PACT has developed a screening process and a system of commitments from colleges. Supported by U.S. Department of Education under Educational Talent Search Program. **Founded:** 1966.

★442★
Planning and the Black Community
Department of the Army
PO Box C-3755
Seattle, WA 98124-2255   Ph: (206)764-3614
Horace H. Foxall Jr., Treas.
Description: Members of the American Planning Association interested in issues related to planning in the black community. Objectives are to: formulate and articulate positions on national, regional, and statewide policy issues related to blacks for presentation to the APA and the public; provide a forum for exchange of practical experience and knowledge among black planners; establish and strengthen liaison with black professionals and groups such as social workers, economists, lawyers, public administrators, International City Management Association, National Association for the Advancement of Colored People, and National League of Cities. Disseminates employment information and

provides a means for employers to address affirmative action goals regarding planning and planning-related jobs. Encourages and assists black planning students and programs; sponsors planning studies research. **Founded:** 1980. **Members:** 125. **Publications:** Newsletter, quarterly.

★443★
Potomac Institute
1400 20th St. NW, Ste. 5
Washington, DC 20036   Ph: (202)331-0087
Harold C. Fleming, Pres. Emeritus
Description: Research organization concerned with developing human resources by expanding opportunities for racial and economically deprived minorities. Provides advisory and research services to government and private agencies involved in the development of programs to increase opportunities for minorities. Sponsors special purpose conferences to explore problems affecting minority groups. Studies, conferences, and publications have covered such areas as affirmative action in employment, state and local civil rights activities, implementation of federal policies for minorities, school desegregation, police and civil rights, disparities in public education funding, development of black business entrepreneurship, inner-city teacher expectations, and student achievement, inclusionary zoning and housing for lower income families, national youth service, urban growth, and central city technical assistance. Maintains library of 2000 volumes on race relations, civil rights, and urban problems. **Founded:** 1961. **Publications:** none.

★444★
Project Equality
1020 E. 63rd St., Ste. 102   Ph: (816)361-9222
Kansas City, MO 64110   Fax: (816)361-8997
Maurice E. Culver, Pres.
Description: A nationwide interfaith program enabling religious organizations, institutions, and others to support equal opportunity employers with their purchasing power. Services include: validation of hotels for conventions and meetings of organizations, validations of suppliers to member organizations and institutions, and consultant and educational services to assist employers in affirmative action and equal employment opportunity programs. Bestowes awards. **Founded:** 1965. **Members:** 150. **Budget:** $285,000. **Local Groups:** 3. **Computerized Services:** Mailing list of members, prospective members, and participating employers. **Publications:** Project Equality–Buyer's Guide, annual. Directory listing employers that have provided current equal employment opportunity data and have been validated by the project.

★445★
Project US
1945 E. Ridge Rd.
Rochester, NY 14622   Ph: (716)544-8605
Evelyn Scott, Dir.
Description: Attempts to handle the problem of school integration through a totally voluntary two-way urban-suburban transfer program. Makes available transfers to both minority and white children. Maintains Operation Enrichment, a program designed to attract suburban students to urban schools through the offering of specialized courses. Serves as a national model for alternatives to busing. Maintains collection of clippings and materials on integration efforts in Monroe County. Is currently operating in the Rochester and Monroe county school districts of New York state. **Founded:** 1965. **Publications:** Handbook. **Also known as:** Urban-Suburban Interdistrict Transfer Program.

★446★
Project Vote!
1424 16th St., Ste. 101
Washington, DC 20036   Ph: (202)328-1500
Sanford A. Newman, Exec.Dir.
Description: Nonpartisan organization working to increase electoral participation among low-income, minority, and unemployed citizens. Organizes local coalitions and hires local staffs and interns; conducts voter registration and education in order to increase turnout; registers individuals door-to-door and as they wait in food stamp and unemployment lines. Sponsors voter education and training programs. **Founded:** 1982. **Budget:** $1,000,000. **Local Groups:** 3.

Publications: How to Develop a Voter Registration Plan, How to Register Voters at a Central Site, and general information flyer; also produces video training tapes. **Also known as:** Americans for Civic Participation.

★447★
PUSH International Trade Bureau
930 E. 50th St.
Chicago, IL 60615   Ph: (312)373-0992
McNair Grant, Exec.Dir.

Description: A bureau of Operation PUSH. Minority-owned franchises and small businesses; minority individuals who are self-employed. Seeks the creation of a black common market in the U.S. Works to facilitate the opening of new markets for black-owned businesses. Provides technical assistance to members, including market research and analysis, financial counseling, and packaging and marketing services. Negotiates with major U.S. corporations to help create business opportunities for blacks. Conducts workshops on job hunting and business management. Bestows Black Diamond Award to businesses and individuals who have done the most to improve the economic status of blacks in the U.S. Maintains archive. **Founded:** 1982. **Members:** 300. **Publications:** Membership List, quarterly. PUSH International Trade Bureau Economic Viewpoint, monthly. Newsletter. Also publishes brochure.

★448★
Radical Women
523-A Valencia St.
San Francisco, CA 94110   Ph: (415)864-1278
Nancy Reiko Kato, Organizer

Description: Women with a socialist-feminist political orientation who believe that women's leadership is decisive for basic social change. Works toward reform in the areas of reproductive rights, child care, affirmative action, divorce, police brutality, rape, women of color, lesbians, and working women. Opposes efforts of conservative anti-feminist groups. **Founded:** 1967. **Local Groups:** 9. **Publications:** Papers.

★449★
Reporters Committee for Freedom of the Press
1735 Eye St. NW, Ste. 504
Washington, DC 20006   Ph: (202)466-6312
Jane E. Kirtley, Exec.Dir.

Description: Devoted to upholding the First Amendment to the U.S. Constitution and protecting the freedom of information rights of the working press of all media. Conducts studies on the impact of subpoenaing reporters' notes or journalists' testimonies upon their ability to gather news from confidential sources; examines efforts to close criminal justice proceedings to the public and press. Has acted as plaintiff or friend-of-court in most major lawsuits affecting the First Amendment rights of working news reporters and editors since 1972. Provides free legal advice to reporters whose First Amendment Rights are infringed upon by subpoenas or other legal pressures. Sponsors in-house legal fellowships and semester internships for journalism students. Maintains a 200 volume library on media law and the Freedom of Information Service Center to aid journalists in obtaining government information. **Founded:** 1970. **Budget:** $426,000. **Publications:** News Media and the Law, quarterly. News Media Update, biweekly. **Telecommunications Services:** FOI Hotline, (800)336-4243.

★450★
Rhythm and Blues Rock and Roll Society
PO Box 1949
New Haven, CT 06510   Ph: (203)924-1079
William J. Nolan, Dir.

Description: Record collectors, disc jockeys, record dealers, performing artists, and others dedicated to the preservation and promotion of rhythm and blues music and its counterparts (blues, gospel, and jazz) as a part of U.S. cultural heritage. Sponsors benefit concerts for prisoners, fundraising programs for amateur talent, and music concerts and festivals. Conducts workshops on R & B culture with lectures and films on the history of black music. Seeks to encourage the employment of minorities in jobs related to blues music and hopes to offer training programs in the production of educational television shows and films. Sponsors Antique Blues, a cultural radio program presenting, live gospel, blues, and rhythm and

blues performing groups. Bestows awards to artists, authors, and writers. Cooperates with the annual W.C. Handy Blues Music Awards ceremony. Maintains international record review panel. Compiles statistics and conducts research. Operates record and tape-book library and archive; plans to maintain hall of fame and museum. **Founded:** 1974. **Members:** 50,000. **Regional Groups:** 13. **Publications:** Newsletter, periodic. Includes reports on the society's concerts, fundraising events, and festivals; also contains calendar of events, interviews with musicians, research news, and record reviews. **Telecommunications Services:** Telephone referral services.

★451★
Saharan People's Support Committee
217 E. Lehr Ave.
Ada, OH 45810   Ph: (419)634-3666
Anne Lippert, Chwm.

Description: Persons concerned with the right of Sahrawi people of Western Sahara to self-determination. Provides information to the U.S. government and the public on the decolonization and status of Western Sahara. Makes available lectures and slides. Maintains relations with organizations concerned with human rights in Africa. Compiles statistics. **Founded:** 1977. **Publications:** SPSC Letter, quarterly. Newsletter reporting on the war in Western Sahara. Includes information on refugees.

★452★
Scott Joplin Foundation of Sedalia
113 E. 4th St.
Sedalia, MO 65301   Ph: (816)826-2271
John Moore, Festival Coordinator

Description: Fans of ragtime composer and musician Scott Joplin (1868-1917) and of ragtime music. Sponsors concerts featuring ragtime artists. Holds annual educational symposium and panel discussions. Offers children's services; conducts annual research trips to other festivals and historically affiliated sites in the U.S. and Canada. Maintains speakers' bureau, biographical archives, museum, and library of subject biographies, videocassettes of past festivals, and research materials. Bestows awards. **Founded:** 1974. **Budget:** $60,000. **Computerized Services:** Mailing list. **Publications:** Sedalia Rag, 2-3/year. Newsletter. **Formerly:** (1991) Scott Joplin Ragtime Festival; (1983) Scott Joplin Ragtime Festival Committee (the committee reactivated in 1983 to coincide with the issuance of a commemorative stamp in Joplin's honor by the U.S. Postal Service); (1966) Scott Joplin Commemorative Committee.

★453★
Section of Individual Rights and Responsibilities
c/o American Bar Association
1800 M St. NW, South Lobby   Ph: (202)331-2280
Washington, DC 20036   Fax: (202)331-2261
Penny Wakefield, Staff Dir.

Description: A section of the American Bar Association. Lawyers, law students, and other individuals. Concentrates on law and public policy as they relate to civil and constitutional rights, civil liberties, and human rights in the United States and internationally. Projects include representation of the homeless, people with AIDS, and those facing capital sentences. Makes available internships to Soviet and central and eastern European lawyers. Administers ABA International Human Rights Trial Observer Project. **Founded:** 1967. **Members:** 4800. **Publications:** Human Rights Magazine, quarterly.

★454★
Sickle Cell Disease Foundation of Greater New York
127 W. 127, Rm. 421
New York, NY 10027   Ph: (212)865-1500
Dick Campbell, Exec.Dir.

Description: Physicians and professionals in allied fields. A voluntary health agency formed to support and conduct research and educational programs aimed at control and, ultimately, eradication of sickle cell anemia. Activities thus far are conducted primarily in the New York City area, but the group also offers information and guidance to organizations in Europe, Africa, South America, Southeast Asia, London, England, and the Caribbean area. Assists in the establishment of local chapters that establish clinics for screening and genetic counseling; sponsors symposia, seminars, and public school programs; offers professional training for screening and counseling programs. Maintains a speakers' bureau; compiles statistics. Maintains extensive files on research being conducted, individuals and organizations working to overcome the disease, and advocacy services available to families and patients with the disease. Programs include: Outreach, an in-service hospital emergency program which informs hospital personnel of the implications of a crisis in a sickle cell anemia patient; a blood bank; referral services; counseling, social services assistance, and employment and aid services. Bestows awards. Maintains library containing updated reports, pamphlets, and backgrounders-research studies. **Founded:** 1972. **Members:** 1500. **Budget:** $150,000. **Local Groups:** 65. **Publications:** Annual Report. Newsletter, quarterly. Also publishes brochures; makes available educational materials and film.

★455★
Sigma Pi Phi Fraternity
920 Broadway, Ste. 703
New York, NY 10010   Ph: (212)477-5550
Harvey C. Russell, Exec.Sec.

Description: Social fraternity. Promotes social and intellectual camaraderie; supports designated social programs. Maintains the Boule Foundation. **Founded:** 1904. **Members:** 3000. **Regional Groups:** 5. Active Chapters: 91. **Publications:** Boule Journal, quarterly. Roster, biennial.

★456★
Society of Ethnic and Special Studies
Box 1652
Southern Illinois University at Edwardsville
Edwardsville, IL 62026   Ph: (618)692-2042
Dr. Emil F. Jason, Pres.

Description: Faculty, administrators, students, and others interested in the furtherance and preservation of ethnic, environmental, and special programs in secondary and postsecondary education. Sponsors workshops, seminars, publications, and projects that will further the understanding of problems and issues; evaluates special studies and related programs; encourages joint cooperative efforts within regions. Presents awards; sponsors competitions; maintains speakers' bureau. **Founded:** 1973. **Members:** 400. **Local Groups:** 1. **State Groups:** 3. **Publications:** Journal, semiannual.

★457★
South Africa Foundation
1225 19th St. NW, Ste. 700
Washington, DC 20036   Ph: (202)223-5486
Michael Christie, Dir.

Description: Representatives of the private sector of South Africa. Objectives are to: act as a professional international communication network and work with individuals and groups whose decisions affect the lives of South Africans. Does not enter into defense of South African policies or promote any particular ideology or factional interest; favors peaceful change in South Africa through the private sector. Provides policymakers with analyses of South African trends and events. **Founded:** 1960. **Members:** 3000. **Regional Groups:** 2. **Publications:** Information Digest, annual. Review, monthly. South Africa International, quarterly.

★458★
South African Military Refugee Aid Fund
29 Seventh Ave.
Brooklyn, NY 11217

Description: Seeks aid for South African military refugees and war resisters. Provides military dissenters with support and seeks asylum for them in the U.S. Maintains speakers' bureau; offers legal assistance and specialized education. Maintains offices in Brooklyn, NY and San Francisco, CA. **Founded:** 1978. **Publications:** News and Notes, bimonthly.

★459★
Southeastern Regional Office National Scholarship Service and Fund for Negro Students
965 Martin Luther King, Jr. Dr. NW   Ph: (404)577-3990
Atlanta, GA 30314   Fax: (404)577-0089
Geoffrey Heard, Exec.Dir.

Description: Supported by foundation and corporate grants and individual contributions. Maintains a free college advisory and referral service for interested students and those enrolled in Talent Search and Upward Bound projects. Sponsors annual Student-College Interview Sessions and workshops for guidance and admissions counselors (dates and sites available upon request). Participates in professional meetings. Maintains library. **Founded:** 1969. **Computerized Services:** Database of student mailing lists for higher education institutions. **Publications:** Annual Report. Also publishes brochure. **Formerly:** (1987) National Scholarship Service and Fund for Negro Students.

★460★
Southern Africa Project
c/o Lawyers' Comm. for Civil Rights
   Under Law
1400 Eye St. NW, Ste. 400   Ph: (202)371-1212
Washington, DC 20005   Fax: (202)842-3211
Gay McDougall, Dir.

Description: Purpose is to provide competent legal representation to defendants in political and quasi-political trials in South Africa. Concerns include illegal detention, security legislation, and deviations from the law. Provides U.S. government and U.S. organizations with information on human rights violations and conditions in South Africa. **Founded:** 1967. **Publications:** Annual Report. Also publishes Special Reports, reports on trials, and analyses of South African statutes.

★461★
Southern Christian Leadership Conference
334 Auburn Ave. NE
Atlanta, GA 30312   Ph: (404)522-1420
Dr. Joseph E. Lowery, Pres.

Description: Nonsectarian coordinating and service agency for local organizations seeking full citizenship rights, equality, and the integration of African-Americans in all aspects of life in the U.S. and subscribing to the Ghandian philosophy of nonviolence. Works primarily in 16 southern and border states to improve civic, religious, economic, and cultural conditions. Fosters nonviolent resistance to all forms of racial injustice, including state and local laws and practices. Conducts leadership training program embracing such subjects as registration and voting, social protest, use of the boycott, picketing, nature of prejudice, and understanding politics. Sponsors citizenship education schools to teach reading and writing, help persons pass literacy tests for voting, and provide information about income tax forms, tax-supported resources, aid to handicapped children, public health facilities, how government is run, and social security. Conducts Crusade for the the Ballot, which aims to double the Black vote in the South through increased voter registration. Sponsors lectures; disseminates literature. **Founded:** 1957. **Publications:** Newsletter, monthly.

★462★
Southern Coalition for Educational Equity
PO Box 22904   Ph: (601)366-5351
Jackson, MS 39225-2904   Fax: (601)366-5351
Winifred Green, Pres.

Description: Coalition of parents, students, teachers, and administrators that operates in Alabama, Georgia, Louisiana, Mississippi, and North Carolina, with plans to include eight additional states. Works toward developing more efficient educational programs and eliminating racism and sexism within southern schools. Has organized projects including: Arkansas Career Resources Project, which provides minorities and single heads of households with marketable skills and jobs; New Orleans Effective Schools Project, which attempts to increase school effectiveness through high expectations, stressing academic achievement, and quality instruction; Project MiCRO, which seeks to provide computer access for, and sharpen analytical skills of, minority students; Summer Program, which focuses on students' reading comprehension skills. **Founded:** 1978. **Publications:** Annual Report.

★463★
Southern Development Foundation
1006 Surrey St.
Lafayette, LA 70501
Rev. A. J. McKnight CS, Founder
Ph: (318)232-7672
Fax: (318)232-5094

Description: Combats black poverty in the South and helps the poor achieve economic independence. Provides, through its affiliates, money and technical assistance to limited resource co-ops and community controlled organizations. Promotes minority co-ops. Helps to form selfhelp projects. Sponsors National Black Survival Fund. **Founded:** 1972.

★464★
Southern Education Foundation
135 Auburn Ave. NE, 2nd Fl.
Atlanta, GA 30303
Elridge W. McMillan, Pres.
Ph: (404)523-0001

Description: Self-perpetuating, integrated organization created to improve and extend educational opportunities for Southern youth, with special regard to the needs of minorities. Conducts educational programs. **Founded:** 1937. Trustees: 12. **Publications:** Pipeline, quarterly. Newsletter covering issues related to minority teachers; also contains annual report and reviews of educational research publications.

★465★
Southern Poverty Law Center
PO Box 2087
Montgomery, AL 36102
Morris Dees, Exec.Dir.
Ph: (205)264-0286

Description: Seeks to protect and advance the legal and civil rights of poor people, regardless of race, through education and litigation. Does not accept fees from clients. The center is currently involved in several lawsuits representing individuals injured or threatened by activities of the Ku Klux Klan and related groups. Attempts to develop techniques and strategies that can be used by private attorneys. Operates Klanwatch. **Founded:** 1971. **Budget:** $2,000,000. **Publications:** Law Report, 5/year. Klanwatch Intelligence Report, monthly. Also publishes books.

★466★
Southern Regional Council
1900 Rhodes Haverty Bldg.
134 Peachtree St. NW
Atlanta, GA 30303-1925
Stephen T. Suitts, Exec.Dir.
Ph: (404)522-8764
Fax: (404)522-8791

Description: Leaders in education, religion, business, labor, the community, and the professions interested in improving race relations and combatting poverty in the South. Comprises an interracial research and technical assistance center that addresses issues of social justice and political and economic democracy. Seeks to engage public policy as well as personal conscience in pursuit of equality. Develops educational programs; provides community relations consultation and field services when requested by official and private agencies. Distributes pamphlets pertaining to desegregation of various public facilities and fosters elimination of barriers to black voting registration. Acts as official sponsor of overseas government officials, leaders, and othervisitors who wish to view race relations in the South. Maintains extensive library on civil rights, civil liberties, politics, and suffrage, including the largest newspaper collection on civil rights in U.S. Bestows annual Lillian Smith Book Award for best books on the South. **Founded:** 1944. **Computerized Services:** Mailing lists; redistricting services. **Publications:** Legislative Bulletin, quarterly.

★467★
Student National Dental Association
c/o Dr. Robert Knight
Howard University School of Dentistry
600 W. St. NW
Washington, DC 20059
Martin Jordan, Pres.
Ph: (202)806-0301

Description: A section of the National Dental Association. Minority dental students. Addresses the needs of minority dental students; strives to expose and eliminate discriminatory practices encountered by its members. Promotes increased minority enrollment in dental schools. Seeks to improve dental health care delivery to all disadvantaged people. Compiles statistics. **Founded:** 1972. **Members:** 9000. **Budget:** Less than $25,000. **Regional Groups:** 10. **Local Groups:** 46. **Publications:** Convention Bulletin, annual. Help Us to Build Your Dental Career, updated annually. Membership Directory, annual.

★468★
Student National Medical Association
1012 10th St. NW
Washington, DC 20001
Colin Ottey, Chm.
Ph: (202)371-1616

Description: Minority medical students and interns. Seeks to help minority students in recruitment, admission, and retention in medical school and publishes information on problems and achievement in this area. Conducts research forums and medical projects. Sponsors a competition; bestows awards annually. **Founded:** 1964. **Members:** 2600. **Regional Groups:** 10. **Local Groups:** 140. **Publications:** SNMA Journal, quarterly.

★469★
Student National Podiatric Medical Association
c/o Eveleigh W. Bell
Mail Box 637
1001 N. Dearborn
Chicago, IL 60610
Eveleigh W. Bell, Pres.
Ph: (312)335-1458

Description: Minorities in the podiatric medical field furthering podiatric medicine. Promotes minority equality in the podiatric colleges and profession. Conducts charitable and educational programs. Sponsors competitions; bestows awards. Holds ethnic festivals, events, and a Christmas program. Maintains speakers' bureau; compiles statistics. **Founded:** 1973. **Members:** 300. **Publications:** Newsletter, semiannual.

★470★
Tau Gamma Delta
c/o Ernestine Belfield
3152 Greenfield Dr.
Rocky Mount, NC 27804
Ernestine Belfield, Pres.
Ph: (919)443-6786

Description: Service sorority - women in business and the professions. Sponsors Tauettes, for girls ages 13-18, to "help instill good character" and expose them to "the finer cultures"; also sponsors Taugadette, an annual arts program to promote young artists ages 19-35. Presents awards; maintains hall of fame; compiles statistics. **Founded:** 1942. **Members:** 1500. **Regional Groups:** 4. **Local Groups:** 60. **Publications:** Roster, annual. The Star, semiannual.

★471★
Thirdworld Education Outreach
35 Fremont St., Ste. B4
Arlington, MA 02174
Frederick W. Kwoda, Pres.
Ph: (617)648-2535
Fax: (617)661-3502

Description: African nationals in the United States and other concerned individuals. Works to enhance the quality of education in rural areas of developing nations, especially Africa. Supports the idea that the lack of excellence in education is one of the main problems facing Third World countries and that improvement in education will bring about positive change in Africa. Collects and distributes teaching materials; sponsors a "adopt-a-school" program to raise money; operates a volunteer teacher program for student teachers from the United States. Runs a school-to-school linkage program in which high schools in the United States donate excess teaching supplies to schools in Africa. Sponsors research and educational programs. **Founded:** 1988.

★472★
369th Veterans' Association
369th Regiment Armory
1 369th Plz.
New York, NY 10037
Kenneth J. Myles, Pres.
Ph: (212)281-3308

Description: Veterans of World War I, World War II, Korean Conflict, and the Vietnam War. Seeks to support all patriotic endeavors of the

U.S., and to assist members and their families through charitable programs and community activities. Donates funds, equipment, and other supplies to children's camps, needy families, religious institutions, Veterans Administration Hospitals, and community and senior citizen centers. Provides children's services, including: sponsoring Little League baseball teams and a basketball team; a tutorial program; donation of awards to elementary school children at graduation; scholarship assistance for children of members. Sponsored the rehabilitation of apartment buildings in New York City, and a four million dollar housing development for senior citizens and the handicapped. Conducts seminars and counseling sessions to assist unemployed veterans, and offers study classes to adults for preparation in Civil Service examinations. Sponsors the annual Dr. Martin Luther King, Jr. Memorial Parade in New York City. Maintains biographical archives. **Founded:** 1953. **Members:** 2500. **Local Groups:** 10. **State Groups:** 11. **Publications:** 369th News Bulletin, quarterly.

★473★
Trade Union Leadership Council
8670 Grand River Ave.
Detroit, MI 48204   Ph: (313)894-0303
John Brown, Pres.

Description: Primarily black trade unionists in Michigan, but membership is open to anyone. To eradicate injustices perpetrated upon people because of race, religion, sex, or national origin. Seeks increased leadership and job opportunities for blacks. Maintains Nelson Jack Edwards Educational Centre. **Founded:** 1957. **Members:** 2500. **Publications:** Vanguard, quarterly.

★474★
Trade Union Women of African Heritage
530 W. 23rd St., Ste. 4051
New York, NY 10011   Ph: (212)547-5696
Thelma Dailey, Pres.

Description: Black women union members. Supports various causes of ethnic working women; participates in community activities; conducts alternative school programs. Maintains Global Women of African Heritage, Maverick Center for Self Development, and Leaders of the 21st Century. Operates speakers' bureau; compiles statistics; conducts research programs. **Founded:** 1969. **Publications:** The Ethnic Woman, periodic. Magazine.

★475★
TransAfrica
545 8th St. SE, Ste. 200
Washington, DC 20003   Ph: (202)547-2550
Randall Robinson, Exec.Dir.

Description: Concerned with the political and human rights of people in Africa and the Caribbean, and those of African descent throughout the world. Attempts to influence U.S. foreign policy in these areas by informing the public of violations of social, political, and civil rights, and by advocating a more progressive attitude in the U.S. policy stance. Supports the work of the United Nations in Africa. Sponsors TransAfrica Action Alert to mobilize black opinion nationally on foreign policy issues by contacting influential policymakers. **Founded:** 1977. **Members:** 18,000. **Budget:** $300,000. **Publications:** TransAfrica News, semiannual.

★476★
TransAfrica Forum
545 Eighth St. SE, Ste. 200   Ph: (202)547-2550
Washington, DC 20003   Fax: (202)547-7687
Randall Robinson, Exec.Dir.

Description: Research and education arm of TransAfrica. Seeks to provide an independent review of differing perspectives on political, economic, and cultural issues affecting black communities globally through its publications. Conducts seminars with scholars and government officials. **Founded:** 1981. **Publications:** TransAfrica Forum: A Quarterly Journal of Opinion on Africa and the Caribbean. Journal reporting on economic, foreign policy, political, and social issues affecting black Africa and the Caribbean. Includes book reviews and conference and seminar transcriptions.

★477★
Try Us Resources
2105 Central Ave. NE   Ph: (612)781-6819
Minneapolis, MN 55418   Fax: (612)781-0109
Liz Kahnk, Exec.Dir.

Description: Objective is to compile and publish minority business directories to acquaint major corporations and government purchasing agents with the products and services of minority firms. Sponsors minority purchasing seminars. **Founded:** 1968. **Publications:** Guide to Obtaining Minority Business Directories, annual. Directory listing local and regional directories, organized by state.**Formerly:** (1970) National Buy-Black Campaign, (1984) National Minority Business Campaign; (1991) National Minority Business Directories.

★478★
Tuskegee Airmen
65 Cadillac Sq. 3200
Detroit, MI 48226   Ph: (313)965-8858
Elmore M. Kennedy, Pres.

Description: Majority of members are black men and women involved in aviation in the military services, service academies, and ROTC units; former airmen who flew in a segregated U.S. Army Air Corps. Seeks to maintain a relationship among those who fought and served in World War II overseas and at home. Strives to motivate minority students in the proper curriculum for opportunities in high tech society. Provides information about the contributions black Americans have made to aviation history. Has established a scholarship fund for students interested in aviation or aerospace careers. Bestows awards; maintains speakers' bureau and biographical archives. Operates museum at Historic Fort Wayne in Detroit, MI. **Founded:** 1972. **Members:** 1684. **Budget:** $65,000. **Regional Groups:** 3. **Local Groups:** 32. **Publications:** Tuskegee Airmen, quarterly. Tuskegee Airmen, Inc., Membership Roster, annual. Also publishes The Lonely Eagles (book) and historical biography of members. **Formerly:** Do Do Club.

★479★
Twenty-First Century Foundation
10 E. 87 St.   Ph: (212)427-8100
New York, NY 10128   Fax: (212)876-6278
Robert S. Browne, Pres.

Description: For the development of an endowment for the support of black charitable institutions. Grants are bestowed in the areas of education and economic development. **Budget:** $60,000. **Founded:** 1971. **Publications:** none.

★480★
Uncle Remus Museum
PO Box 3184
Eatonton, GA 31024   Ph: (706)485-6856
Madeleine Gooch, Sec.

Description: Persons interested in Joel Chandler Harris (1848-1908) and his folklore tales of Uncle Remus. Purposes are to: honor the memory of Harris; keep his works before the public; distribute the Uncle Remus stories. Maintains museum in an old slave cabin depicting an antebellum Southern plantation and the imaginary world of Uncle Remus. **Founded:** 1962.

★481★
United American Progress Association
701 E. 79th St.
Chicago, IL 60619   Ph: (312)268-1873
Webb Evans, Pres.

Description: Businesses, churches, and organizations in the black community. Promotes and assists black entrepreneurs. Encourages business owners to agree to supply goods and services to black communities whose residents support local black-owned firms. Works in conjunction with Operation PUSH and National Black United Front. **Founded:** 1961. **Members:** 250. **Publications:** Community News, monthly. Newsletter.

★482★
United Black Christians
1380 E. Hyde Park Blvd., No. 815
Chicago, IL 60615
Patricia Eggleston, Pres.
Description: To increase the relevance of United Church of Christ in the struggle for liberation and justice. **Founded:** 1970. **Members:** 70,000. **Formerly:** United Black Churchmen.

★483★
United Black Church Appeal
c/o Christ Church
860 Forest Ave.
Bronx, NY 10456   Ph: (718)665-6688
Hon. Wendell Foster, Pres.
Description: Black clergy and laity. Objective is to awaken the power of the black clergy and the black church to provide leadership for the liberation of the black community. Is concerned with black economic development and political power, and the strengthening of black families and churches. Believes pastors in black churches should reestablish legitimate leadership roles within the black community. Works with troubled black youths in the community; rallies against drugs in urban areas. Supports community betterment projects including surplus food programs and distribution of food to needy families. Raises funds to alleviate hunger in Puerto Rico, Mexico, Colombia, and Africa. Plans to establish Black Church Center to house a hall of fame, museum, and library dedicated to preserving the history and restoring the importance of the black church. **Founded:** 1980. **Members:** 500.

★484★
United Black Fund of America
1012 14th St. NW, Ste. 300
Washington, DC 20005   Ph: (202)783-0430
Dr. Calvin W. Rolark, Pres. & Founder
Description: Nonprofit agencies that provide human care services to low-income or disabled blacks and other minorities. Assists disadvantaged blacks and other minorities in becoming self-sufficient by providing funding to member agencies for the establishment of health and welfare programs. Sponsors fundraising activities to support day care service, education, senior citizens, and drug and alcohol rehabilitation programs; monitors the establishment and development of such programs. **Founded:** 1969. **Publications:** United Black Fund Agency Directory, annual.

★485★
United Church of Christ Commission for Racial Justice
700 Prospect Ave. E., 7th Fl.   Ph: (216)736-2168
Cleveland, OH 44115-1110   Fax: (216)736-2171
Rev.Dr. Benjamin F. Chavis Jr., Exec.Dir.
Description: National civil rights agency of the United Church of Christ. Works to ensure racial justice and social equality for ethic and racial minorities worldwide. Maintains higher education program to provide scholarships to minority college students. **Founded:** 1965. **Publications:** Civil Rights Journal, weekly. Syndicated column. Has also published Toxic Waste and Race in the United States (report).

★486★
United Church of Christ Coordinating Center for Women in Church and Society
700 Prospect Ave.   Ph: (216)736-2150
Cleveland, OH 44115   Fax: (216)736-2156
Mary Sue Gast, Contact
Description: Works to eliminate sexism in the church and society. Promotes advocacy for women's concerns through cooperative projects with United Church of Christ agencies; cooperates in projects by helping to establish a network to respond to legislation affecting women. Promotes consciousness-raising by contributing to other United Church of Christ publications. Maintains 200 volume library on women's issues, theology, economics, and employment. Bestows biennial Antoinette Brown Award to clergy women. Recognizes the contributions of lay women. Provides speakers; conducts workshops. **Founded:** 1980. **Budget:** $495,000. **Publications:** Common Lot, quarterly. Journal. Also publishes Moms Morning Out and Women Pray (books).

★487★
United Golfers' Association
c/o Harriett Powell
1305 Pitner Ave.
Evanston, IL 60201   Ph: (708)475-7581
Harriett Powell, Pres.
Description: Golf clubs with predominantly, though not exclusively, black members. Promotes golf and encourages young people to participate in the sport. Sponsors annual tournament; offers scholarships. **Budget:** Less than $25,000. **Founded:** 1926. **Members:** 60. **Regional Groups:** 7.

★488★
United Mortgage Bankers of America
800 Ivy Hill Rd.
Philadelphia, PA 19150
     Fax: (215)247-1580
Gene Hatton, Exec.Dir. & Pres.
Description: Minority mortgage brokers and mortgage bankers. Purpose is to coordinate and channel mortgage money for all Americans regardless of race, creed, or color, on a non-segregated basis. Arranges discussions with top officials of major insurance companies, savings banks, and pension plans throughout the country. Seeks to ascertain the policies of various companies toward making loans through minority bankers. Provides training for new mortgage brokers; conducts workshops; maintains library of 2000 volumes. **Founded:** 1962. **Members:** 1600. **Budget:** $1,200,000. **Local Groups:** 20. **State Groups:** 8. **Publications:** News Bulletin, monthly.

★489★
United Nations Centre Against Apartheid
United Nations Hdqtrs.   Ph: (212)963-2498
New York, NY 10017   Fax: (212)963-5305
Sotirios Mousouris, Asst.Sec.Gen.
Description: Assists political bodies concerned with apartheid in executing their policy decisions; acts as a clearinghouse of information for the United Nations and specialized agencies involved in the international campaign against apartheid; promotes assistance to the indigenous people of South Africa and their liberation movements; conducts research. Maintains liaisons with anti-apartheid movements, trade unions, religious, student, and youth organizations, and women's groups. Serves the United Nations' Special Committee Against Apartheid, the Advisory Committee on the United Nations Educational and Training Programme for Southern Africa, the International Commission Against Apartheid in Sports, the Intergovernmental Group to Monitor the Supply and Shipping of Oil and Petroleum Products to South Africa, as well as the United Nations General Assembly and Security Council, in their apartheid deliberations. Operates three funds generated by voluntary contributions: the United Nations Trust for South Africa, which is used primarily to provide legal assistance to victims of apartheid and their families; the United Nations Educational and Training Programme for Southern Africa, which provides funds for South Africans seeking postsecondary education outside of South Africa; the Trust Fund for Publicity Against Apartheid, which provides additional means to disseminate publicity material. Provides speakers on apartheid-related issues. **Founded:** 1976. **Telecommunications Services:** Telex, 177642. **Branches:** Committee Servicing and Research; Publicity, Assistance and Promotion of International Action. **Publications:** News Digest, bimonthly. Notes and Documents, 20-25/year. Register of Entertainers, Actors, and Others Who Have Performed in South Africa, semiannual. Register of Sports Contacts with South Africa, semiannual. Also publishes information notes, leaflets, and special reports; makes available posters and films. **Formerly:** (1976) Unit on Apartheid.

★490★
United Nations Special Committee Against Apartheid
United Nations, Rm. 3560   Ph: (212)963-5295
New York, NY 10017   Fax: (212)963-5305
TesFaye Tadesse, Contact
Description: Representatives of member countries of the United Nations. Purposes are to: monitor the racial policies of the South African government and periodically report to the UN General Assembly on these issues; provide consulting services on apartheid

to other UN committees and agencies. Coordinates special studies on the nature, extent, and repercussions of apartheid. Reviews and evaluates the implementation of UN resolutions against apartheid; researches methods of mobilizing effective international action to eliminate apartheid. Advocates sanctions against South Africa including: embargo of arms and oil sales; prohibition of nuclear cooperation; cessation of financial collaboration; institution of general economic and diplomatic sanctions. Encourages and assists South African liberation movements, recognized by the Organization of Africa Unity (see separate entry), namely the African National Congress and Pan Africanist Congress (see separate entries); promotes public observances and opposition campaigns. Investigates the repression of South African opponents of apartheid; seeks the unconditional release of all political prisoners within South Africa. Organizes conferences, seminars, and hearings; compiles statistics; bestows awards. **Founded:** 1962. **Members:** 19. **Publications:** Annual Report. Also publishes other reports and documents. **Telecommunications Services:** Telexes, 232422 UNH UR, 82731, and 62450.

★491★
United Negro College Fund
500 E. 62nd St.
New York, NY 10021   Ph: (212)326-1118
William H. Gray III, CEO & Pres.

Description: Fundraising agency for historically black private colleges and universities and graduate and professional schools, all of which are private and fully accredited. The UNCF Department of Educational Services provides information on a broad range of educational and administrative programs to the member schools; conducts Premedical Summer Institute; sponsors college fairs for high school and community college students; administers scholarship awards and major corporate and foundation programs. **Founded:** 1944. **Members:** 41. **Regional Groups:** 26. **Publications:** A Mind Is, quarterly. Annual Report. Also publishes government affairs, research, and statistical reports.

★492★
U.S. Out of Southern Africa Network
PO Box 1819, Madison Square Sta.
New York, NY 10159   Ph: (212)741-0633
Monica Moorehead, Contact

Description: Seeks to educate the public on the U.S. role in southern Africa, particularly in South Africa. Advocates total U.S. withdrawal and divestiture from that area. Stages demonstrations, provides speakers, and shows films. **Founded:** 1985. **Publications:** History of the Struggle (brochure) and set of fact sheets.

★493★
U.S.-South Africa Leadership Development Program
1730 M St. NW, Ste. 701   Ph: (202)293-5410
Washington, DC 20036   Fax: (202)293-5413
Robert M. Hoen, Exec.Dir.

Description: Supported by U.S. Agency for International Development, private American and South African foundations, corporations, and individuals dedicated to the promotion of a just society through the fostering of communications and interaction across group divisions within and between both countries. A board of directors and a council of American and South African university, business, religious, and civic leaders, a full representation of ethnic, political, vocational, gender, and regional groupings in those countries, supervises the program. Programs include symposia and U.S.-South Africa exchanges by university presidents, jurists, journalists, and other professionals. Assists the midcareer training and counseling of black South African leaders by offering leadership development and training programs in the professi ons, business, science, and the arts. Nominates and finances South African participants in annual Nieman Fellowship in journalism at Harvard and a teaching fellowship at John Hopkins University's Nietze School for Advanced International Studies. Holds symposia on South African sociopolitical dynamics and U.S.-South Africa relations. Maintains library. **Founded:** 1958. **Members:** 50. **Publications:** Newsletter, annual. Contains program highlights and organizational news. Also publishes occasional papers, brochures, and books. **Formerly:** (1992) U.S.-South Africa Leader Exchange Program.

★494★
Urban Environment Conference
c/o Franklin Wallick
7620 Morningside Dr. NW   Ph: (202)726-8111
Washington, DC 20012   Fax: (202)829-6762
Franklin Wallick, Chm.

Description: National labor, minority, and environmental organizations. Lobbies in Washington, DC and at a grass roots level for strong environmental and occupational health laws. Offers educational programs to enable minorities, workers, and others to participate more effectively in decisions affecting their health and interests. **Founded:** 1971. **Budget:** Less than $25,000. **Publications:** America's Forgotten Environment (booklet).

★495★
Visions Foundation
1538 9th St. NW   Ph: (202)462-1779
Washington, DC 20001   Fax: (202)462-3997
Gary A. Puckrein, Exec.Dir.

Description: African Americans. To promote understanding of the Afro-American culture. Conducts media-related and educational programs to educate the public about the contributions of blacks to society and culture in the U.S. Bestows awards. **Founded:** 1983. **Members:** 21,000. **Publications:** American Visions: The Magazine of Afro-American Culture, bimonthly. Lines of Sight, bimonthly. Newsletter. Also publishes Afro-American Art.

★496★
Voter Education Project
604 Beckwith St. SW
Atlanta, GA 30314   Ph: (404)522-7495
Edward Brown, Exec.Dir.

Description: Created as part of the Southern Regional Council to investigate the causes and remedies of low political participation by southern blacks. In June 1970, VEP became an independent corporation, operating in 11 southern states. Through direct grants to local groups for voter registration drives, VEP promotes greater participation and documents the problems and progress of their activities. From 1962 to 1984, black voter registration rose from less than 1,500,000 to more than 5,000,000. Is also concerned with citizenship education and assistance to black elected officials. Maintains statistics on registration and voting, data on black elected officials, and other information concerning black political participation in the South. **Founded:** 1962. **Publications:** Issues publications on political participation, state governments, black political candidates, elected officials, and other issues pertinent to minorities in the South. Undertakes in-depth studies of elections or related events.

★497★
Washington Office on Africa
110 Maryland Ave. NE, Ste. 112
Washington, DC 20002   Ph: (202)546-7961
Imani Countess, Exec.Dir.

Description: To monitor and analyze developments in U.S. policy toward southern Africa and work with national and local groups which support the attainment of majority rule. Lobbies on congressional legislation affecting southern Africa. **Founded:** 1972. **Publications:** Action Alerts, periodic. Legislative Bulletins, periodic. Washington Notes on Africa, quarterly.

★498★
Washington Office on Haiti
110 Maryland Ave. NE, Ste. 310   Ph: (202)543-7095
Washington, DC 20002   Fax: (202)547-9382
Worth Cooley-Prost, Pres.

Description: Works to support the Haitian people's ongoing movement for democracy, social and economic justice, and self-determination through public education and advocacy. Seeks to generate international response to human and labor rights violations in Haiti and create a responsive support network for victims of these violations. Gathers and disseminates information and documentation on development in, and U.S. policy toward, Haiti. Coordinates Haiti National Network, and international network of groups working for peace and justice for Haiti. Sponsors delegations from Haiti and public educational events. Provides resource and referral services for Haitian refugees and for attorneys handling political asylum claims. Maintains speakers' bureau and library. **Founded:** 1984.

Budget: $120,000. **Publications:** The Haiti Beat, quarterly. Newsletter providing information on Haiti, including political analysis and resource availability. Manuscripts welcomed. Haitian News and Resource Service, monthly. Provides documentation and analysis on developments in Haiti.

★499★
Women for Racial and Economic Equality
198 Broadway, Rm. 606
New York, NY 10038   Ph: (212)385-1103
Rudean Leinaeng, Chair

Description: Multiracial and multinational group of working and working class women. Purposes include: to end race and sex discrimination in hiring, pay, and promotion practices; to support quality integrated public education and federally funded comprehensive child care; to promote peace and solidarity with women of all countries; to work for passage of the Women's Bill of Rights, a program of legislative demands that guarantees economic independence and social equality. Lobbies for equal employment, education, child care, and health issues. Conducts community education and action campaigns, conferences, seminars, forums, leadership training, and research projects. Bestows annual Fannielou Hamer Award; maintains speakers' bureau. **Founded:** 1975. **Members:** 1000. MD $20. **Budget:** $30,000. **Local Groups:** 8. **Publications:** WREE-View of Women, quarterly. Tabloid reporting on racism, affirmative action, child care, the environment, housing, and other issues. Includes book reviews.

★500★
Women of Color Partnership Program
100 Maryland Ave. NE, Ste. 307   Ph: (202)543-7032
Washington, DC 20002   Fax: (202)543-7820
Elizabeth Castro, Dir.

Description: A division of the Religious Coalition for Abortion Rights. Educates women about reproductive health issues such as accessibility and cost of health care, role of the church, male responsibility, sterilization, and medical abuse of women. Conducts forums and workshops. Maintains speakers' bureau. **Founded:** 1985. **Publications:** Common Ground - Different Planes, semiannual. Newsletter.

★501★
Women's Africa Committee of the African-American Institute
c/o African-American Institute
833 United Nations Plz.
New York, NY 10017   Ph: (212)949-5666
Warren Rupplel, Sec.-Treas.

Description: Volunteer organization of African and American women. Members seek to become better acquainted through social, educational, and cultural activities. **Founded:** 1959.

★502★
World Institute of Black Communications/CEBA Awards
463 7th Ave.   Ph: (212)714-1508
New York, NY 10018   Fax: (212)714-1563
Adriane T. Gaines, Exec.Dir.

Description: Objectives are to broaden opportunities for blacks in the communications industry; recognize black communications contributions; and establish and quantify the value of the black consumer market to the national advertising community. Sponsors annual Communications Excellence to Black Audience Awards to patronizing corporations and creative entities for most creative, relevant, and professionally executed media efforts. Operates library on advertising directed toward the black consumer market over the last 14 years and slides on black American lifestyles. Compiles demographic and marketing research on the black consumer market. Maintains black media source directory listing: radio and television stations; newspapers; national publications; advertising **Founded:** 1978. **Publications:** Awards Exhibit Journal, annual.

★503★
Young Black Programmers Coalition
PO Box 1051   Ph: (601)631-7191
Vicksburg, MS 39181   Fax: (601)631-7482
Robert Rosenthal, Mgr.

Description: Black professionals in the communications, broadcasting, and music industries. Provides professional training and offers technical assistance to black entrepreneurs in the broadcast and music industries. Conducts lobbying activities pertaining to legislation affecting the music industry. Provides scholarships to attend black colleges and universities. Bestows awards; maintains biographical archives; compiles statistics. **Founded:** 1976. **Members:** 2615. **Budget:** $120,000. **Regional Groups:** 5. **Computerized Services:** Database; mailing list. **Publications:** Book Programming Radio, triennial. The Programmer: YBPC News Letter, monthly. Reports on the communications, broadcasting, and music industries. Includes information on employment opportunities, research, and industry trends.

★504★
Zeta Phi Beta
1734 New Hampshire Ave. NW   Ph: (202)387-3103
Washington, DC 20009   Fax: (202)232-4593
Linda Thompson, Exec.Dir.

Description: Service and social sorority. Maintains Zeta Phi Beta Sorority Educational Foundation. Maintains speakers' bureau and charitable program; sponsors competitions and awards scholarships. **Founded:** 1920. **Members:** 75,000. **Regional Groups:** 8. Alumnae and College Chapters: 550. **Publications:** Archon, semiannual. Journal; includes listing of employment opportunies.

(2) Regional, State, and Local Organizations

───────── Alabama ─────────

★505★
Alabama Black Lawyers Association
c/o Brenda Montgomery
3505 23rd St., N.
Birmingham, AL 35207   Ph: (205)254-0608
Brenda Montgomery, Pres.

★506★
Alabama Lawyers Association
2102 6th Ave., N.
Birmingham, AL 35203   Ph: (205)254-3216
LaVeeda Morgan-Battle, Pres.
Affiliated with: National Bar Association.

★507★
American Association of Blacks in Energy
Birmingham Chapter
c/o Ronald Edwardservices
Alabama Gas Corp.
2101 6th Ave., N.
Birmingham, AL 35203   Ph: (205)326-8433
Ronald Edwards, Pres.

★508★
American Civil Liberties Union
Alabama Affiliate
PO Box 447
Montgomery, AL 36104   Ph: (205)262-0304
Olivia Turner, Contact

★509★
Association for the Study of Afro-American Life and
   History
Birmingham Branch
PO Box 11258
Birmingham, AL 35201   Ph: (205)929-8119
Otis Dismuke, Pres.

★510★
Birmingham Association of Black Journalists
PO Box 185
Birmingham, AL 35201-0185   Ph: (205)322-6666
Art Franklin, Pres.

★511★
Birmingham Brothers
PO Box 55006
Birmingham, AL 35255

★512★
Birmingham Minority Business Development Center
2100 16th Ave., S., Ste. 304
Birmingham, AL 35205   Ph: (205)930-9254

★513★
Birmingham Urban League
1717 4th Ave., N.
PO Box 11269
Birmingham, AL 35202-1269   Ph: (205)326-0162
Charles Wright, Dir. of Operations

★514★
Carver Research Foundation of Tuskegee University
Tuskegee Institute Alabama
Tuskegee, AL 36088   Ph: (205)727-8246
Dr. B. D. Maybarry, Acting Dir.

★515★
Mobile County Criminal Justice Society
5984 Carlisle Dr. N.
Mobile, AL 36608
Herbert McCants, Pres.
Affiliated with: National Black Police Association.

★516★
Mobile Minority Business Development Center
801 Executive Park Dr., Ste. 102
Mobile, AL 36606   Ph: (205)471-5165
Rosalind Allen-Hill, Proj. Dir.

★517★
Mobile Peace Benevolent Association
5928 Heatherwood Ct.
Mobile, AL 36618
Diana Chapman, Pres.
Affiliated with: National Black Police Association.

★518★
Montgomery Minority Business Development Center
770 S. Mc Donough St., Ste. 209
Montgomery, AL 36104   Ph: (205)834-7598

★519★
National Association of Minority Contractors
Alabama Chapter
401 Belt Line Dr. N.
Mobile, AL 36617
Dr. Anthony Carter, Pres.

★520★
National Black MBA Association
Birmingham Chapter
PO Box 370132
Birmingham, AL 35237   Ph: (205)591-1200
Wayman Powell III, Contact

★521★
North Alabama Chapter of Black Professional Fire
   Fighters
4307 Patton Rd. SW, No. 13
Huntsville, AL 35805
Affiliated with: International Association of Black Professional Fire
Fighters.

★522★
Prichard Police Benevolent Association
216 E. Prichard Ave.
Prichard, AL 36610
Leslie Nobles, Pres.
Affiliated with: National Black Police Association.

★523★
United Negro College Fund
Birmingham Office
310 18th St., N., Ste. 400
Birmingham, AL 35023   Ph: (205)322-8623
Territory Includes: All of AL.

Alaska

★524★
Alaska Minority Business Development Center
1577 C St. Plaza, Ste. 200
Anchorage, AK 99501   Ph: (907)274-5400

★525★
American Civil Liberties Union
Alaska Affiliate
PO Box 201844
Anchorage, AK 99520-1844   Ph: (907)276-2258
Jamie Bollenbach, Pres.

★526★
ARCO Alaska, Inc.
700 G St.
PO Box 100360
Anchorage, AK 99510   Ph: (907)265-6123
James M. Posey, Pres.

★527★
Association for the Study of Afro-American Life and
   History
Marianna Branch
Rte. 2, Box 21
Marianna, AK 72360   Ph: (501)295-3273
Carrie P. Anthony, Pres.

★528★
United Minority Coalition
Box 020014
Juneau, AK 99802   Ph: (907)780-6739
Ben E. Holganza, Pres.
Founded: 1984. **Members:** 200. **Publications:** Newsletter, periodic.

Arizona

★529★
American Civil Liberties Union
Arizona Affiliate
2021 N. Central, No. 301
Phoenix, AZ 85004
Louis L. Rhodes, Pres.

★530★
Arizona Alliance of Black Educators
11640 N. 49th Dr.
Glendale, AZ 85304
Darlene M. White, Pres.

★531★
Arizona Association of Blacks in Criminal Justice
PO Box 3665
Phoenix, AZ 85003
Ida Wilber, Exec. Officer

★532★
Arizona Black Lawyers Association
3602 E. Campbell
Phoenix, AZ 85016
Yvonne Evans, Pres.
Affiliated with: National Bar Association.

★533★
Arizona Black United Fund
PO Box 24457
Phoenix, AZ 85074   Ph: (602)268-0666
Carolyn Lowery, Exec.Dir.
Affiliated with: National Black United Fund, Inc.

★534★
Heatwaves
PO Box 8834
Phoenix, AZ 85040
Affiliated with: International Association of Black Professional Fire
Fighters.

★535★
Operation PUSH
Phoenix Chapter
2006 E. Broadway Rd.
Phoenix, AZ 85040   Ph: (602)268-2512
Rev. Bernard Black, Chairman

★536★
Phoenix Black Chamber of Commerce
623 E. Euclid
Phoenix, AZ 85040   Ph: (602)243-1857
Deborah Ellison

★537★
Phoenix Minority Business Development Center
1661 E. Camelback, Ste. 210
Phoenix, AZ 85016   Ph: (602)277-7707

★538★
Phoenix Urban League
1402 S. 7th Ave.
Phoenix, AZ 85007   Ph: (602)254-5611
George Dean, President

★539★
Tucson Minority Business Development Center
181 W. Broadway
Tucson, AZ 85702   Ph: (602)629-9744

★540★
Tucson Urban League
2305 S. Park Ave.
Tucson, AZ 85713
Raymond Clarke, Pres.

Ph: (602)791-9522

───────── **Arkansas** ─────────

★541★
American Association of Blacks in Energy
Arkansas Chapter
c/o Alma Williams
Arkansas Power and Light Co.
PO Box 551
Little Rock, AR 72203
Alma Williams, Pres.

Ph: (501)377-3555

★542★
American Civil Liberties Union
Arkansas Affiliate
103 W. Capitol, No. 304
Little Rock, AR 72201
Joseph L. Jacobson, Pres.

Ph: (501)374-2660

★543★
Arkansas Association of Black School Educators
1823 S. Taylor
Little Rock, AR 72204
Mrs. Othello Faison, Pres.

★544★
Black Little Rock Police Association
3410 Pinewood Loop
Little Rock, AR 72209
Affiliated with: National Black Police Association.

★545★
Little Rock Minority Business Development Center
1 Riverfront Pl., Ste. 740
North Little Rock, AR 72114
Ph: (501)372-7312

★546★
National Association of Minority Contractors
Arkansas Chapter
PO Box 5121
Little Rock, AR 72119
Wall Caradine, Pres.

Ph: (501)375-6262

★547★
National Black Child Development Institute
Magnolia Affiliate
PO Box 236
Emerson, AR 71740
Mary Hanson, Contact

Ph: (501)547-2950

★548★
Operation PUSH
North Little Rock Chapter
5205 S. Woodland
North Little Rock, AR 72117
Dee Bennett, Chairman

Ph: (501)945-7724

★549★
Urban League of Arkansas
2200 Main St.
PO Box 164039
Little Rock, AR 72216
Sandra Key, Interim Pres.

Ph: (501)372-3037

★550★
W. Harold Flowers Law Society
PO Box 2454
Little Rock, AR 72401
Rodney Slater, Pres.
Affiliated with: National Bar Association.

Ph: (501)972-2255

───────── **California** ─────────

★551★
Afro American Community Services Agency
304 N. 6th St.
San Jose, CA 95112
Ph: (408)292-3157

★552★
American Association for Affirmative Action
Region IX
c/o Arthur V.N. Wint
Cal. State Univ.
Fresno, CA 93740-0041
Arthur V.N. Wint J.D., Dir.

Ph: (209)294-2364

★553★
American Association of Blacks in Energy
Los Angeles Chapter
c/o Ezekiel Patten, Jr.
Patten Energy Enterprises
9850 Glenoaks Blvd.
Sun Valley, CA 91352
Ezekiel Patten Jr., Pres.

Ph: (818)504-0982

★554★
American Association of Blacks in Energy
San Francisco Chapter
c/o Danielle T. McGrue
Chevron International Oil Co.
555 Market St., Ste. 732
San Francisco, CA 94105
Danelle T. McGrue, Pres.

Ph: (415)894-2832

★555★
American Civil Liberties Union
Northern California Affiliate
1663 Mission St., No. 460
San Francisco, CA 94103
Dorothy M. Ehrlich, Contact

Ph: (415)621-2488

★556★
American Civil Liberties Union
San Diego Affiliate
1202 Kettner Blvd., No. 6200
San Diego, CA 92101
Linda Hills, Pres.

Ph: (619)232-2121

★557★
American Civil Liberties Union
Southern California Affiliate
633 S. Shatto Pl.
Los Angeles, CA 90005
Ramona Ripston, Pres.

Ph: (213)487-1720

★558★
Anaheim Minority Business Development Center
6 Hutton Center Dr., Ste. 1050
Santa Ana, CA 92707
Ph: (714)434-0444

★559★
Association for the Study of Afro-American Life and History
Los Angeles Branch
Our Authors Study Club
8947 Gramercy Pl.
Los Angeles, CA 90047   Ph: (213)758-4520
Deloris Nehemiah, Pres.

★560★
Association of Black Personnel in City Government
5462 Crenshaw Blvd.
Los Angeles, CA 90043   Ph: (213)290-3070

★561★
Association of Black Psychologists
Southern California Chapter
3731 Stocker St. #107
Los Angeles, CA 90008   Ph: (202)722-0808
Dr. Evelyn Clark, Pres.

★562★
Association of Black Social Workers of Greater Los Angeles
7100 S. Western Ave.
Los Angeles, CA 90047   Ph: (213)752-0223

★563★
Bakersfield Minority Business Development Center
218 S. H St., Ste. 103
Bakersfield, CA 93304   Ph: (805)837-0291

★564★
Bay Area Association of Black Social Workers
PO Box 15254
San Francisco, CA 92115   Ph: (415)982-2716

★565★
Bay Area Black Consortium for Quality Health Care Inc.
1440 Broadway, Ste. 403
Oakland, CA 94612   Ph: (415)763-1872
Dani Taylor, Acting Exec.Dir.

★566★
Bay Area Black Media Coalition
PO Box 2382
Oakland, CA 94614
Rudy Marshall, Contact

★567★
Bay Area Black United Fund
1440 Broadway, Ste. 405
Oakland, CA 94612   Ph: (510)763-7270
Cheryl Garner-Shaw, Exec.Dir.
Affiliated with: National Black United Fund, Inc.

★568★
Bay Area Urban League
2201 Broadway St.
Oakland, CA 94612   Ph: (510)839-8011
Dr. Walter Brame, Pres.

★569★
Berkeley Black Fire Fighters Association
59 Elysian Fields
Berkeley, CA 94605

★570★
Berkeley Black Officers Association
5067 Hartnett Ave.
Richmond, CA 94804
Drucilla H. Cooper, Pres.
Affiliated with: National Black Police Association.

★571★
Bernard S. Jefferson Law Society
2122 N. Broadway, Ste. 200
Santa Anna, CA 92706-2614   Ph: (714)558-1059
Charlotte Adams, Pres.
Affiliated with: National Bar Association.

★572★
Black Agenda
200 E. Slauson Ave.
Los Angeles, CA 90011

★573★
Black Business and Professional Association
119 E. Eighth St.
Long Beach, CA 90813   Ph: (310)499-1038

★574★
Black Christians Political Organizations
PO Box 161659
Sacramento, CA 95816   Ph: (916)363-8583

★575★
Black Federation of San Diego
4291 Dr. Martin Luther King, Jr. Hwy.
San Diego, CA 92102   Ph: (619)263-8161

★576★
Black Journalists Association of Southern California
c/o Linda A. Williams
University Park
Univ. of Southern California
Los Angeles, CA 90089-1695   Ph: (213)740-2311
Linda A. Williams, Pres.

★577★
Black on Black Crime Task Force
2104 Orange Ave.
Long Beach, CA 90806

★578★
Black Peace Officers of Fresno
8871 N. Archie
Fresno, CA 93710   Ph: (209)498-4568
Gregory T. Kelly, Pres.
Affiliated with: National Black Police Association.

★579★
Black Peace Officers of Santa Clara County
PO Box 2275
San Jose, CA 95111
Charles Brown, Pres.
Affiliated with: National Black Police Association.

★580★
Black Police Officers Association - San Diego
PO Box 14320
San Diego, CA 92114
Charles Kindred, Pres.
Affiliated with: National Black Police Association.

★581★
Black Radio Exclusive
6922 Hollywood Blvd., Ste. 110
Hollywood, CA 90028   Ph: (213)469-7262

★582★
Black Sacramento Christian Club Organizers
3301 Broadway
Sacramento, CA 95817

★583★
Black Women Lawyers Association of Northern California
State Bar of California
555 Franklin St.
San Francisco, CA 94102
Phyllis Culp, Pres.

★584★
Black Women Lawyers Association of Southern California
State Bar Court
818 W. 7th St.
Los Angeles, CA 90017
E. Jean Gary, Pres

★585★
Black Women Organized for Educational Development
518 17th St., Ste. 202
Oakland, CA 94612   Ph: (415)763-9501

★586★
Black Women's Forum
PO Box 01702
Los Angeles, CA 90001   Ph: (213)292-3009

★587★
Black Women's Health Project
PO Box 10529 .
Oakland, CA 94601   Ph: (415)533-6923

★588★
Black Women's Resource Center
518 17th St., Ste. 202
Oakland, CA 94612   Ph: (415)763-9501

★589★
Black World Foundation
485 65th St.
Oakland, CA 94609   Ph: (415)547-6633

★590★
Brotherhood Crusade Black United Fund
200 E. Slauson Ave.
Los Angeles, CA 90011
Danny J. Bakewell Sr., Pres.
Affiliated with: National Black United Fund, Inc.

★591★
Brothers United of San Diego
PO Box 14307
San Diego, CA 92114

★592★
Business Equity and Development Corporation
1411 W. Olympic Blvd., #200
Los Angeles, CA 90015   Ph: (213)385-0351

★593★
California Association of Black Lawyers
3580 Wilshire Blvd., Ste. 1920
Los Angeles, CA 90010   Ph: (213)387-6628
Joan Whiteside Green, Pres.
Affiliated with: National Bar Association.

★594★
California Legislative Black Caucus
State Capitol, Rm. 6011
Sacramento, CA 95814   Ph: (916)445-7498
Curtis Tucker, Chairman

★595★
A Central Place
1212 Broadway, Ste. 830
Oakland, CA 94612   Ph: (415)834-7897

★596★
Charles Houston Bar Association
1901 Harrison St., No. 901
Oakland, CA 94612   Ph: (415)465-0368
Felix Stuckey, Pres.
Affiliated with: National Bar Association.

★597★
Compton Black Fire Fighters
1133 W. Rosecrans St.
Compton, CA 90222

★598★
Contra Costa Black Chamber of Commerce
3101 MacDonald Ave.
Richmond, CA 94804   Ph: (415)235-9350
Willie L. Williams, Exec. Officer

★599★
Contra Costa Black Fire Fighters Association
PO Box 2571
Antioch, CA 94531

★600★
Contra Costa Deputies for Better Community Relations
173 Crown Pointe Dr.
Vallejo, CA 94590
Mildred Watkins, Pres.

★601★
Council of Black Nurses
Los Angeles Chapter
PO Box 78338
Los Angeles, CA 90016   Ph: (213)338-0542
Deidre Woods, Pres.

★602★
Earl B. Gilliam Bar Association of San Diego County
3841 4th St.
PO Box 199
San Diego, CA 92103   Ph: (619)557-7047
Randy K. Jones, Pres.

★603★
Ethiopian Refugee Project of the Third Baptist Church
1341 McAllister
San Francisco, CA 94115   Ph: (415)922-9100

★604★
Fair Housing Council of Orange County
1522 E. 17th St., Ste. E
Santa Ana, CA 92701   Ph: (714)835-0160
Maya K. Dunne, Dir.

★605★
Fair Housing Council of San Gabriel Valley
1020 N. Fair Oaks Ave., Rm. 301
Pasadena, CA 91103   Ph: (818)791-0211

★606★
FOCUS
PO Box 50134
Oxnard, CA 93033

★607★
Fresno Minority Business Development Center
2010 N. Fine, Ste.103
Fresno, CA 93727   Ph: (209)252-7551

★608★
Golden State Business League
333 Hagenberger Rd., Ste. 203
Oakland, CA 94021   Ph: (415)635-5900
C.J. Patterson, Pres.
Affiliated with: National Bar Association.

★609★
Golden State Minority Foundation
1999 W. Adams Blvd.
Los Angeles, CA 90018   Ph: (213)731-7771

★610★
Greater Riverside Area Urban League
5225 Canyon Crest Dr., Bldg. 100, Ste.
  105
Riverside, CA 92507   Ph: (714)682-2766
Rose Oliver, Interim Exec.Dir.

★611★
Guardians of Justice
PO Box 163, Sta. A
Richmond, CA 94804

★612★
Hollywood-Mid L.A. Fair Housing Council
7080 Hollywood Blvd., #801
Hollywood, CA 90028   Ph: (213)464-1141
Debra Rodriguez, Exec.Dir.
Founded: 1969.

★613★
Independent School Alliance for Minority Affairs
110 S. LaBrea Ave., Ste. 265
Inglewood, CA 90301   Ph: (213)672-5544
Manasa Hekymara, Exec.Dir.

★614★
Inland Association of Black School Educators
PO Box 7324
San Bernadino, CA 92411
Harriette L. Moore, Pres.

★615★
Inland Empire Peace Officers Association
PO Box 1784
Victorville, CA 92392
Affiliated with: National Black Police Association.

★616★
John Langston Bar Association
360 E. 2nd St., Ste. 600
Los Angeles, CA 90012-4203   Ph: (213)485-4917
Eudon Ferrell, Pres.
Affiliated with: NBA.

★617★
Long Beach Bar Association
11 Golden Shores, Ste. 230
Long Beach, CA 90802   Ph: (310)432-5913

★618★
Los Angeles Black Media Association
1114 W. 99th St.
Los Angeles, CA 90044
Cassandra Jordan, Contact

★619★
Los Angeles Black Media Coalition
PO Box 48899
Los Angeles, CA 90048   Ph: (213)564-2383
Elaine Pounds, Contact

★620★
Los Angeles Council of Black Professional Engineers
4401 Crenshaw Blvd.
Los Angeles, CA 90043   Ph: (213)295-0867

★621★
Los Angeles Equal Rights Congress
4167 S. Normandie Ave.
Los Angeles, CA 900037   Ph: (213)291-1092

★622★
Los Angeles Minority Business Development Center
3807 Wilshire Blvd., Ste. 700
Los Angeles, CA 90010   Ph: (213)380-9471

★623★
Los Angeles Urban League
3450 Mt. Vernon Dr.
Los Angeles, CA 90008   Ph: (213)299-9660
John W. Mack, Pres.

★624★
Minorities Alcoholic Treatment Alternative
1315 Fruitvale Ave.
Oakland, CA 94601   Ph: (510)261-7120

★625★
National Association of Black Social Workers
Los Angeles Chapter
7100 S. W.ern Ave.
Los Angeles, CA 90047   Ph: (213)752-0223

★626★
National Association of Minority Contractors
Northern California Chapter
1177 5th St.
Oakland, CA 94607   Ph: (510)268-1505
Alan Dones, Contact

★627★
National Association of Minority Contractors
Southern California Chapter
11910 Steeplechase Dr.
Moreno Valley, CA 92360   Ph: (714)242-9600

★628★
National Black Child Development Institute
East Bay Affiliate
29150 Ruus Rd.
Hayward, CA 94544   Ph: (510)783-0910
Ms. Larmon Buckner, Pres.

★629★
National Black Child Development Institute
Los Angeles/South Bay Affiliate
8344 Melrose, Ste. 22
Los Angeles, CA 90069   Ph: (213)658-9620
Crystal Stairs, Pres.

★630★
National Black Child Development Institute
Sacramento Affiliate
7505 McMullen Way
Sacramento, CA 95828　　　　　Ph: (916)689-2593
Robin Harrison-Philips, Contact

★631★
National Black Child Development Institute
San Diego Affiliate
6161 El Cajon Blvd., Ste. B-21
San Diego, CA 92115-3922
Gail O. Knight, Pres.

★632★
National Black Child Development Institute
San Francisco Affiliate
1219 Skyline Dr.
Daly City, CA 94015　　　　　Ph: (415)756-5382
Bess Ricketts, Pres.

★633★
National Black Community Fund
Los Angeles Chapter
8344 Melrose Ave
Los Angeles, CA 90069　　　　　Ph: (213)658-9620

★634★
National Black MBA Association
Los Angeles Chapter
PO Box 43009
Los Angeles, CA 90043　　　　　Ph: (213)964-3053
Laurie Murphy, Contact

★635★
National Black MBA Association
San Francisco Chapter
PO Box 3683
San Francisco, CA 94119-3683
Evon Anderson, Contact

★636★
Northern California Black Chamber of Commerce
5741 Telegraph Ave.
Oakland, CA 94609　　　　　Ph: (510)464-8062
Oscar J. Coffey Jr., Pres.

★637★
Oakland Black Firefighters Association
4615 Grass Valley Rd.
Oakland, CA 94605　　　　　Ph: (510)568-8692
Affiliated with: International Association of Black Professional Fire
Fighters.

★638★
Oakland Black Officers Association
1440 Broadway, Ste. 618
Oakland, CA 94612　　　　　Ph: (510)430-8650
Leonard White, Pres.
Affiliated with: National Black Police Association.

★639★
Officers for Justice Peace Officers Association
5126 3rd St.
San Francisco, CA 94124
Joe Williams, Pres.
Affiliated with: National Black Police Association.

★640★
Orange County Urban League
12391 Lewis St., Ste. 102
Garden Grove, CA 92640　　　　　Ph: (714)748-9976
George L. Williams, Pres.

★641★
Oscar Joel Bryant Association
1409 W. Vernon Ave.
Los Angeles, CA 90062
Joseph T. Rouzan III, Pres.

★642★
Oxnard Minority Business Development Center
451 W. 5th St.
Oxnard, CA 93030　　　　　Ph: (805)483-1123

★643★
Pasadena Black Firefighters Association
5623 Bowersfield St.
Los Angeles, CA 90016

★644★
Pasadena Interracial Women's Club
Pilgrim Tower, E., No. 44D
440 N. Madison Ave.
Pasadena, CA 91101　　　　　Ph: (818)791-4942
Clara Epps, Pres.
Founded: 1946. **Publications:** Newsletter, monthly.

★645★
Peace Officers for Better Community Relations
PO Box 5281
Oakland, CA 94605
Del Coleman, Pres.
Affiliated with: National Black Police Association.

★646★
Pomona Association of Black School Educators
PO Box 2274
Pomona, CA 91769　　　　　Ph: (909)397-4568
Brenda Erby, Pres.

★647★
Richmond Black Fire Fighters Association
PO Box 2222
Richmond, CA 94801　　　　　Ph: (510)620-6988
Byron Berhel, President

★648★
Riverside Minority Business Development Center
1060 Cooley Dr., Ste. F
Cotton, CA 92324　　　　　Ph: (714)824-9695

★649★
Sacramento Association of Black School Educators
PO Box 13992
Sacramento, CA 95853
Jerry Payne, Pres.

★650★
Sacramento Black Alcoholism Center
2425 Alhambra Blvd., Ste. F
Sacramento, CA 95817　　　　　Ph: (916)454-4242

★651★
Sacramento Black Chamber of Commerce
1009 22nd St.
Sacramento, CA 95816　　　　　Ph: (916)392-7222
Edward Phillips, Exec.Dir.

★652★
Sacramento Black Women's Network
PO Box 162986
Sacramento, CA 95816   Ph: (916)427-7296

★653★
Sacramento Minority Business Development Center
530 Bercut Dr., Ste. C and D
Sacramento, CA 95814   Ph: (916)443-0700

★654★
Sacramento Urban League
8929 Volunteer Ln., Ste. 220
Sacramento, CA 95826   Ph: (916)368-3280
James C. Shelby, Pres.

★655★
Salinas Minority Business Development Center
123 Capital St., Ste. B
Salinas, CA 93901   Ph: (408)754-1061

★656★
San Bernardino Black Fire Fighters Association
1189 E. Shamrock Ave.
San Bernardino, CA 92410

★657★
San Diego Council of Black Engineers
c/o San Diego Engineering Society
PO Box 2733
San Diego, CA 92112   Ph: (619)222-8641

★658★
San Diego Minority Business Development Center
7777 Alvarado Rd., Ste. 310
La Mesa, CA 91941   Ph: (619)668-6232

★659★
San Diego Urban League
4261 Market St.
San Diego, CA 92102   Ph: (619)263-3115
Eugene Ruffin

★660★
San Francisco Association of Black School Educators
PO Box 27577
San Francisco, CA 94127
Mary Twegdy, Pres.

★661★
San Francisco Black Chamber of Commerce
1426 Filmore St., Ste. 205
San Francisco, CA 94102   Ph: (415)922-8720
Fred Jordan, Pres.

★662★
San Francisco Black Fire Fighters Association
PO Box 12390
San Francisco, CA 94112   Ph: (415)822-3454

★663★
San Francisco/Oakland Minority Business Development Center
1000 Broadway, Ste. 270
Oakland, CA 94607   Ph: (415)465-6756

★664★
San Jose Minority Business Development Center
150 Almaden Blvd., Ste. 600
San Jose, CA 95150   Ph: (408)275-9000

★665★
Santa Barbara Minority Business Development Center
331 N. Milpasst, Ste. G
Santa Barbara, CA 93103   Ph: (805)965-2611

★666★
Santa Clara Black Fire Fighters Association
c/o Bobby Dixon
2264 Shiloh Ave.
Milpitas, CA 95035

★667★
Santa Clara County Association of Black School Educators
PO Box 3134
San Jose, CA 95156
Brenda Smith, Pres.

★668★
Santa Clara Valley Urban League
753 N. 9th St., No. 131
San Jose, CA 95112   Ph: (408)971-0117
Susan Logan, Interim Exec.Dir.

★669★
Sickle Cell Anemia Disease Research Foundation of the Bay Area
1332 Haight St.
San Francisco, CA 94117   Ph: (415)626-5834
Francis Luster, Pres.

★670★
South Bay Black Fire Fighters Association
PO Box 431722
Los Angeles, CA 90043

★671★
South Bay Black Lawyers Association
c/o Moore Law Firm, APC
55 S. Market St., #1020
San Jose, CA 95110
Rodney G. Moore, Pres.
Affiliated with: National Bar Association.

★672★
Stentorians of Los Angeles County
1409 W Vernon Ave.
Los Angeles, CA 90062
Affiliated with: International Association of Black Professional Fire Fighters.

★673★
Stockton Black Fire Fighters Association
9343 Cherbourg Way
Stockton, CA 95210

★674★
Stockton Minority Business Development Center
5361 N. Pershing Ave., Ste. F
Stockton, CA 95207   Ph: (209)467-4774

★675★
Stockton-San Joaquin County Black Chamber of Commerce
11 S. San Joaquim St., Ste. 310
Stockton, CA 95202   Ph: (209)466-7222
Daniel Blue, Pres.

★676★
Unitarian Universalist Association Black Concerns
Working Group
Pacific Central Chapter
2441 LeConte Ave.
Berkeley, CA 94709   Ph: (510)845-6233
Rev. Robbie L. Cranch, District Executive

★677★
Unitarian Universalist Association Black Concerns
Working Group
Pacific Southwest Chapter
12355 Moorpark St.
Studio City, CA 91604   Ph: (818)769-5917
Constance LaFerriere Ed.D., District Executive

★678★
United Negro College Fund
Bay Area Office
1 Sansome St., Ste. 2390
San Francisco, CA 94104   Ph: (415)956-1462
Territory Includes: Oakland, San Francisco, Sacramento, Fresno, San Jose, Salinas/Monterey, CA; All of the Pacific Islands.

★679★
United Negro College Fund
Western Region
Los Angeles Office
725 Fiqueroa, Ste. 800
Los Angeles, CA 90017   Ph: (213)689-0168
Territory Includes: Los Angeles and San Diego, CA; AZ; NV.

★680★
Unity Fellowship Outreach Program
Minority AIDS Project
5149 W. Jefferson Blvd.
Los Angeles, CA 90016   Ph: (213)936-4949

★681★
Vallejo Black Fire Fighters Association
156 Wildberry Ct.
Vallejo, CA 94591

★682★
West Los Angeles Community Service Organization
714 California Ave.
Venice, CA 90291   Ph: (310)823-9254
Flora Chavez, Dir.

★683★
Western States Black Research Center
3617 Montclair St.
Los Angeles, CA 90018   Ph: (213)737-3585
Mayme A. Clayton, Exec.Dir.

★684★
Westside Fair Housing Council
10835 Santa Monica Blvd., Ste. 203
Los Angeles, CA 90025   Ph: (310)475-9671
Stephanie Knapik, Exec.Dir.
Founded: 1968. **Members:** 300. **Publications:** The Center of Things, periodic. Newsletter.

★685★
Wiley M. Manuel Bar Association
449 15th St., Ste. 303
Oakland, CA 94612   Ph: (510)465-0203
Thelma B. Bailey, Pres.
Affiliated with: National Bar Association.

★686★
William H. Hastie Lawyers Association
c/o James & Jeffers
870 Market St., Ste. 1200
San Francisco, CA 94102   Ph: (415)512-7600
Clifton R. Jeffers, Pres.
Affiliated with: National Bar Association.

─────────────── **Colorado** ───────────────

★687★
American Civil Liberties Union
Colorado Affiliate
915 E. 22nd Ave.
Denver, CO 80205   Ph: (303)861-2258
James Jou, Pres.

★688★
American Civil Liberties Union
Mountain States Regional Affiliate
6825 E. Tennessee Ave., Bldg. 2, Ste. 262
Denver, CO 80224   Ph: (303)321-4828
Dorothy Davidson, Pres.

★689★
Colorado Association of Black Journalists
c/o Ray Metoyer
KUSA-TV
1089 Bannock St.
Denver, CO 80231   Ph: (303)893-9000
Ray Metoyer, Pres.

★690★
Colorado Association of Black Law Enforcement
Officers
4800 Troy
Denver, CO 80239
Lynn Foster, Pres.

★691★
Colorado Association of Black School Educators
PO Box 440474
Aurora, CO 80044
Dr. Betty J. Foshee, Pres.

★692★
Colorado Black Chamber of Commerce
517 E. 16th Ave.
Denver, CO 80205   Ph: (303)832-2242
Larry Clayton, Exec.Dir.

★693★
Colorado Black Fire Fighters Association
PO Box 7492
Denver, CO 80277

★694★
Denver Minority Business Development Center
4450 Morrison Rd.
Denver, CO 80219   Ph: (303)937-1005

★695★
National Association of Blacks in Criminal Justice,
Colorado Chapter
13095 E. Elk Pl.
Denver, CO 80239
Vel Gardner, Exec. Officer

★696★
Sam Cary Bar Association
15400 E. 14th Pl.
Aurora, CO 80011
Hon. Robert Russell, Pres.
Affiliated with: National Bar Association.

★697★
Unitarian Universalist Association Black Concerns
  Working Group
Mountain Desert Chapter
1510 Glen Ayr Dr., Ste. 4
Lakewood, CO 80215   Ph: (303)238-4051
Rev. Sue Turner-Kent, District Executive

★698★
Urban League of Metropolitan Denver
1525 Josephine St.
Denver, CO 80206   Ph: (303)388-5861
Thomas Jenkins, Acting Pres.

★699★
Urban League of the Pikes Peak Region
324 N. Nevada
Colorado Springs, CO 80903   Ph: (719)634-1525
Jerome Page, Pres.

——————— Connecticut ———————

★700★
American Civil Liberties Union
Connecticut Affiliate
32 Grand St.
Hartford, CT 06106   Ph: (203)247-9823
William Olds, Pres.

★701★
Association of Black Psychologists
Connecticut Chapter
152 Way Rd.
Salem, CT 06415   Ph: (203)442-3380
Dr. Willie Coleman, Pres.

★702★
Bridgeport Guardians Association
PO Box 9018
Bridgeport, CT 06640
Affiliated with: National Black Police Association.

★703★
Connecticut Association of Black Communicators
c/o The Courant
285 Broad St.
Hartford, CT 06115   Ph: (203)241-6606
Vada O. Crosby, Pres.

★704★
Connecticut Minority Business Development Center
410 Asylum St., Ste. 243
Hartford, CT 06103   Ph: (203)246-5371

★705★
Danbury Guardians Association
36 Tamarack Ave., Ste. 111
Danbury, CT 06811
Elliot Brevard, Pres.

★706★
Firebird Society of Bridgeport
231 Penn Ave.
Bridgeport, CT 06610

★707★
Firebird Society of New Haven
63 Long Meadow Rd.
Hamden, CT 06514
Affiliated with: International Association of Black Professional Fire Fighters.

★708★
George W. Crawford Law Association
PO Box 3291
Hartford, CT 06103   Ph: (203)566-5996
Kimberly Graham, Pres.
Affiliated with: National Bar Association.

★709★
Hartford Guardians
PO Box 1524
Hartford, CT 06144
Carl Henderson, Pres.

★710★
National Association of Minority Contractors
Connecticut Chapter
PO Box 4280
Hartford, CT 06147   Ph: (203)527-1511
George Milward, Pres.

★711★
New Haven Silver Shields
1 Union Ave.
New Haven, CT 06519   Ph: (203)787-6316
Bennie Smith, Pres.
Affiliated with: National Black Police Association.

★712★
Operation PUSH
Hartford Chapter
53 Sharon St.
Hartford, CT 06112   Ph: (203)527-8440
Theodore Hudson, Pres.

★713★
Phoenix Society
PO Box 12481
Hartford, CT 06112

★714★
Southern Connecticut Lawyers Association
106 Ledgebrook Dr.
Norwalk, CT 06854
Gary White, Pres.
Affiliated with: National Bar Association.

★715★
United Negro College Fund
Stamford Office
Soundview Plaza
1266 E. Main St., 4th Fl.
Stamford, CT 06902   Ph: (203)327-5194
Territory Includes: CT; Albany, Rochester, and Buffalo NY.

★716★
Urban League of Greater Bridgeport
285 Golden Hill St.
Bridgeport, CT 06604   Ph: (203)366-1177
William K. Wolfe, Pres.

★717★
Urban League of Greater Hartford
1229 Albany Ave., 3rd Fl.
Hartford, CT 06112   Ph: (203)527-0147
Esther Bush, Pres.

★718★
Urban League of Greater New Haven
1 State St.
New Haven, CT 06510   Ph: (203)624-4168
Pricilla Taylor, Acting Dir.

★719★
Urban League of Southwestern Fairfield County
1 Atlantic St., Ste. 619
Stamford, CT 06901   Ph: (203)327-5810
Dr. Curtiss E. Porter, Pres.

─────────── **Delaware** ───────────

★720★
American Civil Liberties Union
Delaware Affiliate
702 King St., No. 600A
Wilmington, DE 19801   Ph: (302)654-3966
Judith Mellen, Pres.

★721★
Delaware Association of Black School Educators
PO Box 185
Wilmington, DE 19899-0185
Dr. Henry Rose, Pres.

★722★
Unitarian Universalist Association Black Concerns Working Group
Joseph Priestly Chapter
730 Halstead Rd.
Wilmington, DE 19803   Ph: (302)478-1018
Rev. Sidney Peterman, District Consultant

─────────── **District of Columbia** ───────────

★723★
African American Writers Guild
4108 Arkansas Ave., NW
Washington, DC 20002   Ph: (202)678-8462

★724★
Alliance of Black Federal Officers
PO Box 27773
Washington, DC 20038-7773
Ronald E. Stalling, Pres.

★725★
American Association of Blacks in Energy
Washington Chapter
c/o John M. Bush
PEPCO
1900 Pennsylvania Ave., NW
Washington, DC 20068-0001   Ph: (202)872-2399
John M. Bush, Pres.

★726★
American Civil Liberties Union
National Capital Area Affiliate
1400 20th St. NW, No. 119
Washington, DC 20036   Ph: (202)457-0800
Mary Jane DeFrank

★727★
American Civil Liberties Union
National Prison Project
1875 Connecticut Ave. NW, Ste. 410
Washington, DC 20009   Ph: (202)234-4830
Al Bronstein, Pres.

★728★
American Civil Liberties Union
National Washington Office
122 Maryland Ave. NE
Washington, DC 20002   Ph: (202)544-1681
Mort Halperin, Pres.

★729★
Association for the Study of Afro-American Life and History
Capital Branch
1522 Jackson St. NE
Washington, DC 20017   Ph: (202)832-3916
William Steen, Acting Pres.

★730★
Association for the Study of Afro-American Life and History
Carter G. Woodson Branch
3809 17th St. NE
Washington, DC 20018   Ph: (202)526-2247
Lavinia Odejimi, Pres.

★731★
Association for the Study of Afro-American Life and History
Charles H. Wesley Branch
3228 Oliver St. NW
Washington, DC 20015   Ph: (202)966-8760
Col. George Haley, Pres.

★732★
Association for the Study of Afro-American Life and History
Far North East/South East Branch
7238 15th Pl. NW
Washington, DC 20012   Ph: (202)882-3792
Mauree Ayton, Pres.

★733★
Association for the Study of Afro-American Life and History
George E.C. Hayes Branch
440 Buchanan St. NW
Washington, DC 20011   Ph: (202)829-0731
Shirley Hayes Ganao, Pres.

★734★
Black Student Fund
3636 16th St., NW
Ste. AG 15-19
Washington, DC 20010   Ph: (202)387-1414
Barbara Patterson, Exec.Dir.

★735★
Bread for the City
1305 14th St., NW
Washington, DC 20005   Ph: (202)332-0440
Charles Parker, Dir.

★736★
Capitol East Children's Center
315 G St., SE
Washington, DC 20003   Ph: (202)546-6966
Judith Fisher, Dir.

★737★
Capitol Police Chapter of National Black Police Association
PO Box 91907
Washington, DC 20090-1907
Mary J. Rhone, Pres.

★738★
Concerned Black Men
PO Box 33104
Washington, DC 20033   Ph: (202)265-3175
Warner H. Session, Pres.

★739★
District of Columbia American Civil Liberties Union
1400 20th St., NW, Ste. 119
Washington, DC 20036   Ph: (202)457-0800

★740★
District of Columbia Chamber of Commerce
1411 K St., NW, 5th Fl.
Washington, DC 20004   Ph: (202)347-7202
Robert Titus, Pres.
Affiliated with: National Business League.

★741★
District of Columbia City Wide Welfare Rights Organization
PO Box 6951
Washington, DC 20032   Ph: (202)889-3448
Etta Horn Prather, Dir.

★742★
District of Columbia Human Rights Office
2000 14th St., NW
Washington, DC 20009   Ph: (202)939-8740
Maudine R. Cooper, Dir.
Founded: 1977. **Members:** 80. **Publications:** Annual Report. Newsletter, quarterly. Also publishes ad hoc studies, brochures, fact sheets, and human rights laws, regulations, and compilations.

★743★
National Association of Black Social Workers
Metropolitan Washington Chapter
PO Box 2126
Washington, DC 20013   Ph: (202)529-6127
Maxine May, Pres.

★744★
National Black Child Development Institute
Washington/Metro Affiliate
1133 15th St. NW, Ste. 1200
Washington, DC 20005   Ph: (202)466-3952
Doll Gordon, Pres.

★745★
National Black MBA Association
Washington Chapter
PO Box 14042
Washington, DC 20044   Ph: (202)628-0138
Greg Haret, Contact

★746★
National Urban League
Washington Bureau
1111 14th St., NW, 6th Fl., Ste. 600
Washington, DC 20005   Ph: (202)898-1604

★747★
Operation PUSH
Washington Chapter
1612 Buchanan St., NW
Washington, DC 20011   Ph: (202)829-2774
Jerry A. Moore, Pres.

★748★
Progressive Fire Fighters Association of Washington, DC
PO Box 5063
Washington, DC 20019   Ph: (202)529-0638

★749★
United Negro College Fund
Washington Office
700 13th St. NW, Ste. 1180
Washington, DC 20005   Ph: (202)737-8623
Territory Includes: District of Columbia; MD.

★750★
Washington Association of Black Journalists
Washington Post
1150 15th St., NW
Washington, DC 20071   Ph: (202)728-7527
Retha Hill, Pres.

★751★
Washington Bar Association
1819 H St., NW, Ste. 300
Washington, DC 20006   Ph: (202)289-4247
Belva Newsome, Pres.
Affiliated with: National Bar Association.

★752★
Washington Minority Business Development Center
1133-15th St., NW, Ste. 1120
Washington, DC 20005   Ph: (202)785-2886

★753★
Washington Office on Africa
110 Maryland Ave. NE, Ste. 112
Washington, DC 20002   Ph: (202)546-7961
Imani Countess, Executive Director
Founded: 1972. **Publications:** Action Alert, periodic. Legislative Alert, periodic. Washington Notes on Africa, 3/year. Newsletter.

★754★
Washington Urban League
3501 14th St., NW
Washington, DC 20010   Ph: (202)265-8200
Maudine R. Cooper, Pres.

——————————— Florida ———————————

★755★
American Civil Liberties Union
Florida Affiliate
225 NE 34th St., No. 102
Miami, FL 33137   Ph: (305)576-2336
Robyn Blumner, Pres.

★756★
Association for the Study of Afro-American Life and History
Miami-Dade Branch
5400 NW 22 Bldg., Ste. 101
Miami, FL 33142   Ph: (305)636-2390
Dorothy Jenkins Fields, Pres.

★757★
Association of Black Psychologists
Greater Fort Lauderdale Chapter
231 Utah Ave.
Fort Lauderdale, FL 33312   Ph: (202)722-0808
Dr. Timothy R. Moragne, Pres.

★758★
Association of Black Psychologists
Jacksonville Chapter
7202 Eudine Dr., N.
Jacksonville, FL 32210   Ph: (904)725-6662
Larry Richardson

★759★
Association of Black Psychologists
North Florida Chapter
909 Oak Knoll
Tallahasse, FL 32312   Ph: (202)722-0808
Dr. Seward Hamilton, Pres.

★760★
Black Historical Preservation Society of Palm Beach
  County
623 Division Ave.
West Palm Beach, FL 33401   Ph: (407)833-5836

★761★
Black Nurses Association of Tampa Bay
PO Box 310804
Tampa, FL 33680-0804
Florence L. Howell, Pres.

★762★
Blacks in Communications
Tallahassee Chapter
227 N. Magnolia Dr.
Tallahassee, FL 32302   Ph: (904)599-2157
LaNedra A. Carroll, Pres.

★763★
Broward County Law Enforcement Officers
9620 NW 42nd Court
Sunrise, FL 33321
Diane Ramsey, Pres.
Affiliated with: National Black Police Association.

★764★
Florida Association of Voluntary Agencies for
  Caribbean Action
1311 Exec. Center Dr., No. S-202
Tallahassee, FL 32301   Ph: (904)877-4750
David A. Pasquarelli, Exec.Dir.
Founded: 1981. **Members:** 200. **Telecommunications Services:** Fax, (904)656-7944. **Publications:** Communique, quarterly. Newsletter.

★765★
Florida Democratic Black Caucus
PO Box 470518, Martin Luther King, Jr.
  Station
Miami, FL 33247   Ph: (305)284-1023
Dorothy D. Jackson, Sec.
Founded: 1981. **Members:** 250.

★766★
Florida First Coast Chapter/National Business League
8905-A Castle Blvd.
Jacksonville, FL 32208   Ph: (904)765-2339
George F. Carter, Pres.

★767★
Gainesville Guardians Association
205 SE 38th St.
Gainesville, FL 32601   Ph: (904)378-6595
Robert Bryant, Pres.

★768★
Goldcoast Firefighters
PO Box 926
West Palm Beach, FL 33401
Affiliated with: International Association of Black Professional Fire Fighters.

★769★
Greater Tampa Urban League
1405 Tampa Park Plaza
Tampa, FL 33605   Ph: (813)229-8117
Joanna N. Tokley, Pres.

★770★
Jacksonville Association of Black School Educators
1701 Prudential Dr.
Jacksonville, FL 32207
G. Hall, Contact

★771★
Jacksonville Brotherhood Firefighters
PO Box 2728
Jacksonville, FL 32203   Ph: (904)355-3211

★772★
Jacksonville Brotherhood of Police Officers
PO Box 41583
Jacksonville, FL 32203   Ph: (904)766-2038
Anthony R. Rodgers, Pres.
Affiliated with: National Black Police Association.

★773★
Jacksonville Minority Business Development Center
218 W. Adams St., Ste. 300
Jacksonville, FL 32202-3502   Ph: (904)353-3826

★774★
Jacksonville Urban League
233 W. Duval St.
Jacksonville, FL 32202   Ph: (904)356-8336
Dr. Richard Danford, Pres.

★775★
Liberal Fire Fighters of Broward
3871 NW 5th Ct.
Ft. Lauderdale, FL 33311

★776★
Mary McLeod Bethune Community Center
101 Bethune Village
Daytona Beach, FL 32114   Ph: (904)253-9474
Francis Mobley, Exec.Dir.

★777★
Metropolitan Orlando Urban League
2512 W. Colonial Dr.
Orlando, FL 32804   Ph: (407)841-7654
Shirley J. Boykin, Pres.

★778★
Miami Association of Black School Educators
14657 SW 94th Ave.
Miami, FL 33176
George M. Koonce Jr., Pres.

★779★
Miami Community Police Benevolent Association
3261 Venice Way
Miramar, FL 33025
Diane Barnes, Pres.
Affiliated with: National Black Police Association.

★780★
Miami/Ft. Lauderdale Minority Business Development Center
1200 NW 78th Ave., Ste. 301
Miami, FL 38103   Ph: (305)591-7355
Ricardo Martinez, Director

★781★
Minority Builders Coalition of Broward County
771 NW 22nd Rd.
Fort Lauderdale, FL 33311   Ph: (305)792-1121
Lloyd Brown, Pres.

★782★
Minority-Women Business Enterprise
201 S. Rosalind Ave.
Orlando, FL 32801   Ph: (407)836-7317
Veronica Anderson, Manager

★783★
National Association of Minority Contractors
Central State Association of Minority Contractors
2900 Granada Blvd.
Kissimmee, FL 32741   Ph: (407)933-1794
Percival Sewell, Pres.

★784★
National Association of Minority Contractors
Student Chapter
School of Building Construction, SAC 101
Gainesville, FL 32611   Ph: (904)392-5965

★785★
National Bar Association
Florida Chapter
2 S. Orange Plaza
Orlando, FL 32802   Ph: (407)843-4421

★786★
National Black Child Development Institute
Miami Affiliate
395 NW 1st St., Ste. 207
Miami, FL 33128   Ph: (305)253-0992
Regina M. Grace, Pres.

★787★
National Black MBA Association
South Florida Chapter
PO Box 694154
Miami, FL 33269-4154
Sonia A.S. Johnson, Contact

★788★
National Business League
Tri-County Chapter
PO Box 1626
West Palm Beach, FL 33402-1828   Ph: (407)996-0465
Virginia Merriett, Pres.

★789★
National Organization of Black Law Enforcement Executives
Florida Chapter
PO Box 4991
Miami, FL 33269
James L. Bryant, Pres.

★790★
New Breed of Firefighters
PO Box 5512
Tampa, FL 33675
Affiliated with: International Association of Black Professional Fire Fighters.

★791★
Operation PUSH
Pensacola Network
1000 College Blvd.
Pensacola, FL 32514   Ph: (904)484-2130
Joyce Hopson, Pres.

★792★
Organization of Minority Correctional Officers
PO Box 470309
Miami, FL 33147-0309

★793★
Orlando Minority Business Development Center
132 E. Colonial Dr., Ste. 211
Orlando, FL 32801   Ph: (407)422-6234

★794★
Palm Beach Association of Black Journalists
c/o Kenneth Bohannon
The Palm Beach Post
Box 24700
West Palm Beach, FL 33416-4700   Ph: (407)837-4100
Kenneth Bohannon, Pres.

★795★
Pinellas County Urban League
333 31st St., N.
St. Petersburg, FL 33713   Ph: (813)327-2081
James O. Simmons, Pres.

★796★
Professional Black Fire Fighters Association of Miami
6600 NW 27th Ave., No.205
Miami, FL 33142   Ph: (305)596-8675
Charlie Phillips

★797★
Progressive Firefighters Association of Central Florida
PO Box 570966
Orlando, FL 32857

★798★
Progressive Firefighters Association of Dade County
926 Rutland St.
Opa-Locka, FL 33054   Ph: (305)688-3473

★799★
Progressive Officers Club
PO Box 680398
Miami, FL 33168   Ph: (305)624-0099
John Pace, Pres.
Affiliated with: National Black Police Association.

★800★
Society for Black Student Engineers
University of Florida
500 Weil Hall
Gainesville, FL 32611   Ph: (904)392-0937
Candice Williams, Pres.

★801★
South Florida Association of Black Journalists
c/o Daniel C. Holly
The Herald
1 Herald Plaza
Miami, FL 33132
Daniel C. Holly, Pres.

★802★
South Florida Business League
555 NE 15th St., No. 31-A
Miami, FL 33132
Alexis Snyder, Pres.
Affiliated with: National Business League.

★803★
Tallahassee Urban League
923 Old Bainbridge Rd.
Tallahassee, FL 32304   Ph: (904)222-6111
Rev. Ernest Ferrell, Pres.

★804★
**Tampa/St. Petersburg Minority Business Development
Center**
4601 W. Kennedy Blvd., Ste. 200
Tampa, FL 33609   Ph: (813)289-8824

★805★
**Unitarian Universalist Association Black Concerns
Working Group
Southwest Chapter**
4 Cherry Drive Ct.
Ocala, FL 34472   Ph: (813)371-4974
Rev. John and Mary Louise DeWolf-Hurst, Co-Dist. Executives

★806★
**United Negro College Fund
Jacksonville Office**
218 W. Adams, Ste. 301
Jacksonville, FL 32202   Ph: (407)425-3555
Territory Includes: Orlando, Pensacola, Tampa/St. Petersburg,
Tallahassee, Gainesville, Jacksonville/Lake City, FL.

★807★
**United Negro College Fund
Miami Beach Office**
407 Arthur Godfrey Rd.
Miami Beach, FL 33140   Ph: (305)534-1048
Territory Includes: Miami, Platka, and West Palm Beach, FL.

★808★
Urban League of Broward County
11 NW 36th Ave.
Fort Lauderdale, FL 33311   Ph: (305)584-0777
Donald E. Bowen, Exec.Dir.

★809★
Urban League of Greater Miami
8500 NW 25th Ave.
Miami, FL 33147   Ph: (305)696-4450
T. Willard Fair, Pres.

★810★
Urban League of Palm Beach County
1700 Australian Ave.
West Palm Beach, FL 33407   Ph: (407)833-1461
Otehia DuBose, Pres.

★811★
West Palm Beach Minority Development Center
2001 Broadway, Ste. 301
Riveria Beach, FL 33404   Ph: (407)863-0895

──────────── **Georgia** ────────────

★812★
Afro American Patrolmans League
PO Box 92276
Atlanta, GA 30314
Donald Smith, Pres.
Affiliated with: National Black Police Association.

★813★
Afro-American Police Officers of Augusta
PO Box 5337
Augusta, GA 30906

★814★
**American Association of Blacks in Energy
Atlanta Chapter**
c/o Willie J. Green
Georgia Power Co.
333 Piedmont Ave., 6th Fl.
Atlanta, GA 30308   Ph: (404)526-6237
Willie J. Green, Pres.

★815★
**American Civil Liberties Union
Georgia Affiliate**
233 Mitchell St. SW, No. 200
Atlanta, GA 30303   Ph: (404)523-5398
Ellen Spears, Pres.

★816★
**American Civil Liberties Union
Southern Regional Office**
44 Forsyth St. NW, Ste. 202
Atlanta, GA 30303   Ph: (404)523-2721
Laughlin McDonald, Pres.

★817★
Apple Corps
250 Georgia Ave., SE
Atlanta, GA 30312   Ph: (404)522-4662

★818★
**Association for the Study of Afro-American Life and
History
Savannah Chapter**
c/o W. W. Law
502 E. Harris
Savannah, GA 31401   Ph: (912)234-8000
W. W. Law, Pres.

★819★
**Association of Black Psychologists
Atlanta Chapter**
2114 W. Cedar Lane SW
Atlanta, GA 30311   Ph: (202)722-0808
Dr. Arletta Brinson, Pres.

★820★
Association of Law Enforcement Officers of Dekalb
PO Box 370292
Decatur, GA 30037-0972
Darryl Fauly, Pres.
Affiliated with: National Black Police Association.

★821★
Atlanta Black United Fund
75 Piedmont Ave. NE, Ste. 300
Atlanta, GA 30303   Ph: (404)524-4003
Lamont Cassett, Exec. Dir.

★822★
Atlanta Business League
818 Washington St.
Atlanta, GA 30315   Ph: (404)584-6126
Valerie Montague, Pres.
Affiliated with: National Business League.

★823★
**Atlanta Metropolitan Association of Black School
  Educators**
3006 Dodson Dr.
East Point, GA 30344
Dr. Ernest P. Lavender Jr., Pres.

★824★
Atlanta Urban League
100 Edgewood Ave., NE, Ste. 600
Atlanta, GA 30303   Ph: (404)659-1150
Lyndon A. Wade, Pres.

★825★
Black Evangelism and Counseling Association
6635 Doublegate Ln.
Atlanta, GA 30273   Ph: (404)474-0085

★826★
Black Ministerial Association
Statesboro Chapter
c/o Rev. Lee Hunter
135 President Circle
Statesboro, GA 30458   Ph: (912)764-4901
Rev. Lee Hunter, Exec. Officer

★827★
Black Women of Profession
Statesboro Chapter
c/o Carolyn Postell
104 Harris Rd.
Statesboro, GA 30458   Ph: (912)764-4913
Carolyn Postell, Exec. Officer

★828★
Black Women's Coalition of Atlanta
PO Box 11367, Sta. A
Atlanta, GA 30310   Ph: (404)627-6000

★829★
Brother to Brother Firefighters of East Point
2683 Stoneview Terrace
East Point, GA 30344

★830★
Brothers Combined of Atlanta
7528 Old S. Ln.
Jonesboro, GA 30236
Affiliated with: International Association of Black Professional Fire
Fighters.

★831★
Brothers United of Valdosta
516 Troupe St.
Valdosta, GA 31601

★832★
Central Savannah River Area Business League
PO Box 1283
Augusta, GA 30903   Ph: (404)722-0994
Dr. Faye Hargrove, Pres.
Affiliated with: National Business League.

★833★
Dekalb City Fire Department
2687 Elkhorn Dr.
Decatur, GA 30034

★834★
Dekalb County Minority FMA
3858 Natalie Court
Ellenwood, GA 30049

★835★
Dekalb Lawyers Association
PO Box 2403
Decatur, GA 30031-2403   Ph: (404)522-6386
Denise Welch, Pres.
Affiliated with: National Bar Association.

★836★
East Point Association of Black Educators
3006 Dodson Dr.
East Point, GA 30344
Ernest Lavender, Pres.

★837★
Fellowship of Fulton County
PO Box 1051
Red Oak, GA 30272
Affiliated with: International Association of Black Professional Fire
Fighters.

★838★
Fire Fighters United of Augusta
4306 White Pine Ct.
Augusta, GA 30906

★839★
Gate City Bar Association
141 Pryor St., SW
Atlanta, GA 30303   Ph: (404)730-8232
Auarita L. Hanson, Pres.
Affiliated with: National Bar Association.

★840★
Metro Columbus Urban League, Inc.
802 1st Ave.
Columbus, GA 31901   Ph: (706)323-3687
Jessie J. Taylor, Exec.Dir.

★841★
Metro Fair Housing Services
PO Box 5467
Atlanta, GA 30307   Ph: (404)221-0147
Robert Shisalow, Dir.

★842★
National Association of Minority Contractors
Central Savannah River Chapter
PO Box 1442
Augusta, GA 30903   Ph: (706)724-5310
Sandra Bell, Pres.

★843★
National Association of Minority Contractors
Greater Atlanta Chapter
513 Edgewood Ave.
Atlanta, GA 30344　　　　　　Ph: (404)522-7727
Thomas Walton, Pres.

★844★
National Black Child Development Institute
Atlanta Affiliate
5867 Sheldon Ct.
College Park, GA 30349　　　　Ph: (404)669-0884
Sherekaa Osorio, Pres.

★845★
National Black MBA Association
Atlanta Chapter
PO Box 158
Atlanta, GA 30301
Henry Hutchins, Contact

★846★
National Black Media Coalition
Altanta Chapter
6375 Elchaudillo Court
College Park, GA 30349
Joan Lewis, Contact

★847★
Operation PUSH
Columbus Chapter
4601 Old Cusseta Rd.
Columbus, GA 31903　　　　　Ph: (706)687-4567
William B. Howell

★848★
Progressive Firefighters of Columbus
435 Braselman Ave.
Columbus, GA 31907

★849★
Savannah Brotherhood Fire Fighters Association
PO Box 22842
Savannah, GA 31403　　　　　Ph: (912)354-9331

★850★
Savannah Minority Business Development Center
31 W. Congress St., Ste. 201
Savannah, GA 31401　　　　　Ph: (912)236-6708

★851★
Sickle Cell Foundation of Georgia
2391 Benjamin E. Mays Dr., SW
Atlanta, GA 30311　　　　　　Ph: (404)755-1641

★852★
Southeastern Association of Educational Opportunity
　Program Personnel
Atlanta Metro College
1630 Stewart Ave. SW
Atlanta, GA 30310　　　　　　Ph: (404)756-4058
Bobby Olive, Director, Student Support

★853★
Unitarian Universalist Association Black Concerns
　Working Group
Thomas Jefferson-Mid-South Chapter
1534 N. Decatur Rd., NE
Atlanta, GA 30307　　　　　　Ph: (404)377-9275
Roger Comstock, District Executive

★854★
United Negro College Fund
Atlanta Office
229 Peachtree St., Ste. 2505
Atlanta, GA 30303　　　　　　Ph: (404)302-8623
Territory Includes: All of GA; SC; TN.

─────────── **Hawaii** ───────────

★855★
American Civil Liberties Union
Hawaii Affiliate
PO Box 3410
Honolulu, HI 96801　　　　　　Ph: (808)545-1722
Vanessa Y. Chong, Pres.

★856★
Honolulu Minority Business Development Center
1132 Bishop St., Ste. 1000
Honolulu, HI 96813　　　　　　Ph: (808)536-0066

─────────── **Idaho** ───────────

★857★
American Civil Liberties Union
Idaho Affiliate
National Chapter
PO Box 1897
Boise, ID 83701　　　　　　　Ph: (208)344-5243
Jack Van Valkenburg, Pres.

─────────── **Illinois** ───────────

★858★
African American Images
9204 S. Commercial Ave., Ste. 306
Chicago, IL 60617　　　　　　Ph: (312)375-9682

★859★
African-American Police League
80 W. 150th St.
Harvey, IL 60426
Sylvester Jones, Pres.
Affiliated with: National Black Police Association.

★860★
African American Police League of Lake County
PO Box 9204
Waukegan, IL 60079-9204
Timothy Burch, Pres.

★861★
Afro-American Fire Fighters of Chicago
9543 S. University St.
Chicago, IL 60628

★862★
Afro-American Fire Fighters of Peoria
5504 Knoxville St.
Peoria, IL 61614

★863★
Afro-American Police League
9219 S. Elizabeth St.
Chicago, IL 60620
Patricia Hill, Pres.
Affiliated with: National Black Police Association.

★864★
Afro-American Sheriffs League of Cook County
10219 S. Racine Ave.
Chicago, IL 60643
Ms. Leslie Smith, Pres.

★865★
American Association of Blacks in Energy
Chicago Chapter
c/o Frank M. Clark
PO Box 278
Lombard, IL 60148　　　　　　　　Ph: (708)691-4501
Frank M. Clark, Pres.

★866★
American Civil Liberties Union
Illinois Affiliate
20 E. Jackson Blvd., Ste. 1600
Chicago, IL 60604　　　　　　　　Ph: (312)427-7330
Jay Miller, Pres.

★867★
Association for the Study of Afro-American Life and
History
Chicago Branch
6800 S. Wentworth Ave.
Chicago, IL 60621　　　　　　　　Ph: (312)962-3200
Jeanette Williams, Pres.

★868★
Association of Black Law Enforcement Officers
2006 S. 13th Ave.
Broadview, IL 60153
Ronald Reece, Pres.

★869★
Association of Black Social Workers
1525 E. 53rd St.
Chicago, IL 60615　　　　　　　　Ph: (312)753-9583

★870★
Black Police Officers Association - Joliet
PO Box 532
Joliet, IL 60434-0532

★871★
Black Police Officers United for Justice and Equality
7737 S. Phillips Ave.
Chicago, IL 60649
Jerry Crawley, Pres.

★872★
Chicago Association of Black Journalists
c/o Renee Turner
Ebony Magazine
810 S. Michigan Ave.
Chicago, IL 60605　　　　　　　　Ph: (312)322-9258
Renee Turner, Pres.

★873★
Chicago Association of Black School Educators
5127 Greenwood
Chicago, IL 60615
Ida Cross, Pres.

★874★
Chicago Lawyers' Committee for Civil Rights Under
Law
c/o Roslyn C. Lieb
220 S. State St., Ste. 300
Chicago, IL 60604　　　　　　　　Ph: (312)939-5797
Roslyn C. Lieb, Exec.Dir.
Founded: 1969. **Members:** 40. **Publications:** Annual Report.
Newsletter, semiannual.

★875★
Chicago Urban League
4510 S. Michigan Ave.
Chicago, IL 60653　　　　　　　　Ph: (312)285-5800
James W. Compton, Pres.

★876★
Chicago Westside Police Association
5052 W. Huron St.
Chicago, IL 60644
Ernestine Dowell, Pres.

★877★
Coalition of Law Enforcement Officers
5402 Hyde Park Blvd.
Chicago, IL 60615
Jacquelyn Kimber, Pres.

★878★
Cook County Bar Association
25 E. Washington, #1500
Chicago, IL 60602　　　　　　　　Ph: (312)726-5444
Affiliated with: National Bar Association.

★879★
Cosmopolitan Chamber of Commerce
1326 S. Michigan Ave.
Chicago, IL 60605　　　　　　　　Ph: (312)786-0212
Consuelo M. Williams, Exec.Dir.
Founded: 1933. **Members:** 350. **Publications:** Chamber News,
quarterly. **Formerly:** (1954) Chicago Negro Chamber of Commerce.

★880★
Evanston Black Police Association
PO Bos 5244
Evanston, IL 60204-5244
Diane Elam, Pres.

★881★
Evanston Brothers
8415 Central Park
Skokie, IL 60076

★882★
Guardians of Police - Chicago
12609 S. Wentworth
Chicago, IL 60628
Firmin Duplessis, Pres.

★883★
Hope Fair Housing Center
154 S. Main St.
Lombard, IL 60148   Ph: (708)495-4846
Bernard J. Kleina, Exec.Dir.
Founded: 1968. **Budget:** $120,000. **Publications:** Newsletter, periodic. **Formerly:** (1981) Hope/West Suburban Fair Housing Center.

★884★
Illinois Black United Fund
2336 E. 71st St.
Chicago, IL 60649   Ph: (312)324-0494
Henry English, Pres.
Affiliated with: National Black United Fund, Inc.

★885★
Illinois Committee on Black Concerns
Southern Illinois University
411 E. Broadway
East St. Louis, IL 62201   Ph: (618)482-6900
Johnetta Haley, Pres.

★886★
Joint Negro Appeal
2400 S. Michigan Ave.
Chicago, IL 60616   Ph: (312)842-6262
Mr. Robert D. Pruden, President

★887★
Lake County Association of Black School Educators
PO Box 501
North Chicago, IL 60064
Bettye Johnson, Pres.

★888★
Lake County Urban League
122 Madison St.
Waukegan, IL 60085   Ph: (708)249-3770

★889★
League of Black Women
18 S. Michigan Ave.
Chicago, IL 60603   Ph: (312)368-1329

★890★
Madison County Urban League
210 Williams St.
Alton, IL 62002   Ph: (618)463-1906
Dr. Robert C. Green, Director

★891★
Martin Luther King, Jr. Coalition
6430 S. Ashland Ave.
Chicago, IL 60636   Ph: (312)925-5250
Rev. Edgar Jackson, President

★892★
Mega Center
Bankers Bldg
105 W. Adams, Ste. 7
Chicago, IL 60603   Ph: (312)977-9190

★893★
National Black Child Development Institute
Chicago Affiliate
11070 S. W.ern Ave.
Chicago, IL 60643
Dr. George Smith, Pres.

★894★
National Black Child Development Institute
Metro East St. Louis Affiliate
1200 N. 13th St.
East St. Louis, IL 62205   Ph: (618)271-7710
Mary Rhodes, Pres.

★895★
National Black MBA Association
Chicago Chapter
PO Box 8513
Chicago, IL 60680   Ph: (312)236-4480
Mark Smith, Contact

★896★
National Hook-Up of Black Women
Chicago Chapter
1805 W. 107th St.
Chicago, IL 60643
Joyce LeFlore, Pres.

★897★
Neighborhood Fund
1750 E. 71st St.
Chicago, IL 60649   Ph: (312)440-1111

★898★
Neighborhood Institute
1750 E. 71st St.
Chicago, IL 60649   Ph: (312)684-4610

★899★
Oak Park Housing Center
1041 South Blvd.
Oak Park, IL 60302   Ph: (708)848-7150
Roberta L. Raymond, Dir.
Founded: 1972. **Members:** 800. **Budget:** $292,500. **Publications:** Annual Report. From the Center, 3-4/year. Newsletter.

★900★
Operation PUSH
Chicago Chapter
PO Box 5432
Chicago, IL 60680   Ph: (312)287-0422
Rev. Charlie Murray

★901★
Operation PUSH
Joliet Chapter
402 Singleton Pl.
Joliet, IL 60436   Ph: (815)723-9445
Rev. Issac Singleton, Pres.

★902★
Quad County Urban League
305 E. Benton St.
Aurora, IL 60505   Ph: (708)897-5335
Theodia Gillespie, Interim Director

★903★
Society of African American Police
2228 Claremont Dr.
Springfield, IL 62703   Ph: (217)788-8311
Anthony Pettit Sr., Pres.

★904★
Tri-County Urban League
317 S. MacArthur Hwy.
Peoria, IL 61605-3892   Ph: (309)673-7474
Laraine E. Bryson, Pres.

★905★
Unitarian Universalist Association Black Concerns
  Working Group
Central Midwest Chapter
114 S. Marion St.
Oak Park, IL 60302   Ph: (708)383-4344

★906★
United Negro College Fund
Chicago Office
819 S. Wabash, Ste. 202
Chicago, IL 60605   Ph: (312)294-2561
Territory Includes: All of IL.

★907★
Urban League of Champaign County
17 Taylor St.
Champaign, IL 61820   Ph: (217)356-1364
Vernon L. Barkstall, Pres.

★908★
Will County Association of Black School Educators
417 N. Raven Rd.
Shorewood, IL 60435
Dr. Dillard J.F. Harris, Pres.

★909★
YMCA Urban Program West
3600 W. Ogden Ave.
Chicago, IL 60623   Ph: (312)277-4400
Ernie Jenkins, Exec. Dir.

───────────── **Indiana** ─────────────

★910★
American Civil Liberties Union
Indiana Affiliate
445 N. Pennsylvania St., Ste. 991
Indianapolis, IN 46204   Ph: (317)635-4056
Michael Lee Gradison, Pres.

★911★
Association of Black Psychologists
Indiana Chapter
2635 Lincoln Ln.
Indianapolis, IN 46208   Ph: (317)226-4747
Dr. Frankie Cooper

★912★
Black Coalition, Recruitment, and Training
625 E. Bellemeade Ave.
Evansville, IN 47713   Ph: (812)423-5291
Bobby Ogburn, Exec.Dir.

★913★
Community Relations Team
2042 S. Meridan St.
Marion, IN 46953
Thomas J. Wise, Pres.

★914★
Evansville Black Coalition
625 Bellemeade Ave.
Evansville, IN 47713   Ph: (812)423-5291
Bobby Ogbuch, Exec.Dir.

★915★
Fairness in Law Enforcement
6614 Latona Dr.
Indianapolis, IN 46278
Ricky Clark, Pres.

★916★
Ft. Wayne Black Professional Fire Fighters
  Association
906 Drexel Ave.
Ft. Wayne, IN 46806
Affiliated with: International Association of Black Professional Fire
Fighters.

★917★
Ft. Wayne Urban League
Foellinger Community Center
227 E. Washington Blvd.
Fort Wayne, IN 46802   Ph: (219)424-6326
Rick C. Frazier, Pres.

★918★
Gary Minority Business Development Center
567 Broadway
Gary, IN 46402   Ph: (219)883-5802

★919★
Guardians of Police - Fort Wayne
PO Box 11371
Fort Wayne, IN 46857-1371
Jerome Bostwick, Pres.

★920★
Indiana Black Expo
3130 Sutherland Ave.
Indianapolis, IN 46205   Ph: (317)925-2702
Rev. Charles Williams, Pres.

★921★
Indianapolis Association of Black School Educators
5264 Roxbury Rd.
Indianapolis, IN 46226
Dr. Shirl E. Gilbert, Pres.

★922★
Indianapolis Minority Business Development Center
617 Indiana Ave., Ste. 319
Indianapolis, IN 46204   Ph: (317)685-0055

★923★
Indianapolis Plan for Equal Employment
Affirmative Action
445 N. Pennsylvania
Indianapolis, IN 46204   Ph: (317)639-4661

★924★
Indianapolis Professional Association
740 E. 52nd St., Ste. 5
Indianapolis, IN 46205   Ph: (317)542-8540
Leslie Hollingsworth, Pres.

★925★
Indianapolis Urban League
850 Meridian St.
Indianapolis, IN 46204   Ph: (317)639-9404
Sam H. Jones, Pres.

★926★
James Kimbrough Law Association
1345 Wallace St.
Gary, IN 46402   Ph: (219)949-3585
Karen P. Pulliam, Pres.
Affiliated with: National Bar Association.

★927★
Marion County Bar Association
c/o St. Simonsen, Palm and Whitney
127 E. Michigan 5th St.
Indianapolis, IN 46204   Ph: (317)264-6900
Larry G. Whitney, Pres.
Affiliated with: National Bar Association.

★928★
Marion Urban League, Inc.
1221 W. 12th St.
Marion, IN 46953   Ph: (317)664-3933
Cleo Richardson, CEO & President

★929★
Minority Police Officers Association - South Bend
29763 Roycroft Dr.
South Bend, IN 46614
Lynn C. Coleman, Pres.

★930★
National Black Child Development Institute
Indianapolis Affiliate
3737 N. Meridian St., Ste. 403
Indianapolis, IN 46208   Ph: (317)291-0595
Cynthia Renea Oda, Pres.

★931★
National Black MBA Association
Indianapolis Chapter
PO Box 2325
Indianapolis, IN 46206-2325
Darlene Sowell, Contact

★932★
Northwest Indiana Association of Black School
  Educators
401 Rutledge St.
Gary, IN 46404
Leola Rule, Pres.

★933★
Operation PUSH
Anderson Chapter
PO Box 853
Anderson, IN 46015   Ph: (317)643-7952
Rev. Jack Samuels

★934★
Operation PUSH
Indianapolis Chapter
1901 N. Hardy
Indianapolis, IN 46202   Ph: (317)631-5946
Rev. Tommy Brown, Pres.

★935★
Operation PUSH
Michigan City Chapter
PO Box 856
Michigan City, IN 46360   Ph: (219)879-4114
Anita Jordan, Director

★936★
Unitarian Universalist Association Black Concerns
  Working Group
Michigan-Ohio Valley Chapter
1010 E. 86th St., 65H
Indianapolis, IN 46240-1875   Ph: (317)844-0933
Rev. Jerry D. Wright, Interim Dist. Consultant

★937★
United Black Fire Fighters of Michigan City
409 Washington Park
Michigan City, IN 46360
Affiliated with: International Association of Black Professional Fire
Fighters.

★938★
United Negro College Fund
Indianapolis Office
PO Box 88210
Indianapolis, IN 46208   Ph: (317)638-7477
Territory Includes: All of IN.

★939★
Urban League of Northwest Indiana
3101 Broadway
Gary, IN 46408   Ph: (219)887-9621
Eloise Gentry, Pres.

★940★
Urban League of South Bend and St. Joseph County,
  Inc.
PO Box 4043
South Bend, IN 46634   Ph: (219)287-2800

──────────────── **Iowa** ────────────────

★941★
American Civil Liberties Union
Iowa Affiliate
466 Insurance Exchange Bldg.
Des Moines, IA 50309   Ph: (515)243-3576
Cryss D. Farley, Pres.

★942★
Iowa Association of Black School Educators
2210 University Ave.
Des Moines, IA 50311
Alice Clinton Boyd, Pres.

★943★
Iowa National Bar Association
c/o Robin Humphrey
State Attorney General's Office
Hoover State Office Bldg.
Des Moines, IA 50319   Ph: (515)281-7055
Robin Humphrey, Pres.
Affiliated with: National Bar Association.

★944★
National Black Child Development Institute
Des Moines Affiliate
1529 19th St.
Des Moines, IA 50314   Ph: (515)282-4037
Evelyn Davis, Pres.

★945★
Operation PUSH
Waterloo Network
PO Box 2211
Waterloo, IA 50765   Ph: (319)233-0803
Anna Weems

Kansas

★946★
Association for the Study of Afro-American Life and History
Dr. Lorenzo Greene Branch of the Greater Kansas City Area
4836 Sortor Dr.
Kansas City, KS 66104   Ph: (913)287-3247
Dr. Gerald W. Hall, Pres.

★947★
Kansas Association of Black School Educators
2001 Fairlawn Rd.
Topeka, KS 66604
Dr. Robert McFrazier, Pres.

★948★
Kansas City Bar Association
103 Cross Lines Towers
1021 N. 7th St.
Kansas City, KS 66101-2823   Ph: (913)621-1911
Hosea Ellis Sowell, Pres.
Affiliated with: National Bar Association.

★949★
Kansas City Ethical Police Alliance
6618 Sewell Ave.
Kansas City, KS 66104
Burnette Ambler, Pres.
Affiliated with: National Black Police Association.

★950★
Minority Press Association
5121 Parallel Pkwy.
Kansas City, KS 66104   Ph: (913)596-1007
Doretha Jordan, Ed.

★951★
National Business League
Wichita Chapter
1125 E. 13th St.
Wichita, KS 67214   Ph: (316)686-4959
Anderson E. Jackson, Pres.

★952★
PRIDE
1726 Quindaro Blvd.
Kansas City, KS 66104   Ph: (913)321-2733

★953★
Urban League of Wichita, Inc.
1405 N. Minneapolis
Wichita, KS 67214   Ph: (316)262-2463
Otis G. Milton, Pres.

Kentucky

★954★
American Civil Liberties Union
Kentucky Affiliate
425 W. Muhammad Ali Blvd., Ste. 230
Louisville, KY 40202   Ph: (502)581-1181
Jan Phillips, Pres.

★955★
Black Professional Fire Fighters of Louisville
PO Box 11767
Louisville, KY 40211

★956★
BLOOD
553 Ashbury St.
Lexington, KY 40511

★957★
Jefferson County Minority Law Enforcement Association
4515 Brewster Ave.
Louisville, KY 40211
Gwen Lyons, Pres.
Affiliated with: National Black Police Association.

★958★
Louisville Association of Black Communicators
c/o The Courier-Journal
525 W. Broadway
Louisville, KY 40202   Ph: (502)582-7091
Mark McCormick, Pres.

★959★
Louisville Black Police Officers Organization
PO Box 11400
Louisville, KY 40251-0400
Shelby Lanier Jr., Pres.
Affiliated with: National Black Police Association.

★960★
Louisville Minority Business Development Center
611 W. Main St.
Louisville, KY 40202   Ph: (502)589-6232

★961★
Louisville Urban League
1535 W. Broadway
Louisville, KY 40203   Ph: (502)585-4622
Benjamin K. Richmond, Pres.

★962★
National Bar Association
John W. Rowe Chapter
106 W. Vine St.
Lexington, KY 40507   Ph: (606)255-2424
John McNeill, Pres.

★963★
National Bar Association
Kentucky Chapter
436 S. 7th St., Ste. 200
Louisville, KY 40203-2161   Ph: (502)582-1942
Rhonda Richardson, Pres.

★964★
Urban League of Lexington-Fayette County
167 W. Main St., Rm. 406
Lexington, KY 40507   Ph: (606)233-1561
Porter G. Peeples Sr., Pres./CEO

Louisiana

★965★
African Chamber of Commerce
3028 Gentilly Blvd.
New Orleans, LA 70122   Ph: (504)948-9769
Emily Williiams, Dir.

★966★
American Association of Blacks in Energy
New Orleans Chapter
c/o Phillip R. Snowden
Entergy Operations
PO Box 1559
Gretna, LA 70160   Ph: (504)739-6348
Phillip R. Snowden, Pres.

★967★
American Civil Liberties Union
Louisiana Affiliate
921 Canal St., Ste. 1237
New Orleans, LA 70112   Ph: (504)522-0617
Shirley Pedler, Contact

★968★
BANOFF of New Orleans
4301 Macarthur Blvd.
New Orleans, LA 70114

★969★
Baton Rouge Minority Business Development Center
2036 Woodale Blvd., Ste. D
Baton Rouge, LA 70806   Ph: (512)476-9700

★970★
Black and White Communications Task Force
610 Texas
Shreveport, LA 71101

★971★
Black Collegiate Services, Inc.
1240 S. Broad St.
New Orleans, LA 70125   Ph: (504)821-5694

★972★
Black Organization of Police
1540 Canal St., Ste. A
New Orleans, LA 70112   Ph: (504)523-3309
Carl A. Haydel, Acting Dir.
Affiliated with: National Black Police Association.

★973★
Ethnic, Cultural, and Heritage Organization of New
Orleans
c/o Rudolph Ramelli
201 St. Charles   Ph: (504)288-5059
New Orleans, LA 70130   Fax: (206)726-0528
Rudolph Ramelli, Exec. Officer

★974★
Louis A. Martinet Legal Society
New Orleans, LA
Angelique Reed, Pres.
Remarks: No address information available. **Affiliated with:** National
Bar Association.

★975★
Magnolia State Peace Officers Association
Lafayette Chapter
348 Josephine St.
Lafayette, LA 70501
Affiliated with: National Black Police Association.

★976★
Magnolia State Peace Officers Association
Shreveport Chapter
PO Box 913
Shreveport, LA 71101
Sammie Robinson, Pres.

★977★
National Association for Sickle Cell Anemia of Baton
Rouge
2301 N. Blvd.
Baton Rouge, LA 70806   Ph: (504)346-8434

★978★
National Association of Minority Contractors
North Louisiana Chapter
1500 N. Market St., Ste. A-108
Shreveport, LA 71107   Ph: (318)424-4533
Rickey R. Hall, Pres.

★979★
National Black Child Development Institute
New Orleans Affiliate
5725 Providence Pl.
New Orleans, LA 70126   Ph: (504)283-1841
Gladys Robinson, Pres.

★980★
National Society of Black Physicists
Department of Physics
Southern University
Baton Rouge, LA 70810   Ph: (504)771-4130
Eugene Collins

★981★
New Orleans Association of Black School Educators
1400 Camp St.
New Orleans, LA 70130
H. Kenneth Johnson, Pres.

★982★
New Orleans Black Media Coalition
2032 Delachaise St.
New Orleans, LA 70115
C.C. Campbell, Contact

★983★
New Orleans Business League
107 Harbour Circle
New Orleans, LA 70126   Ph: (504)246-1166
Sherman N. Copelin Jr., Pres.
Affiliated with: National Business League.

★984★
New Orleans Minority Business Development Center
1683 N. Claiborne
New Orleans, LA 70116   Ph: (504)523-5400

★985★
Northwest Louisiana Sickle Cell Anemia Foundation
and Research Center
2200 Milam St.
Shreveport, LA 71103   Ph: (318)226-8975

★986★
Operation "X" Cell Minority Fire Fighters
5610 Rickover Dr., No. B
Baton Rouge, LA 70811

★987★
Percy R. Johnson Memorial Fire Fighters Association
2526 Hopewell St.
Shreveport, LA 71104   Ph: (318)798-2643

★988★
Shreveport Bar Association
501 Texas St.
Shreveport, LA 71101   Ph: (318)222-0720

★989★
Southwest Association of Professional Firefighters
PO Box 92592
Lafayette, LA 70509   Ph: (318)989-1328

★990★
Southwest Louisiana Law Association
117 Haymann Blvd., Bldg. No. 10
Lafayette, LA 70503   Ph: (318)232-1707
Robert LaBlanc
Affiliated with: National Bar Association.

★991★
Total Community Action
1420 S. Jefferson Davis Pkwy.
New Orleans, LA 70125   Ph: (504)821-2000

★992★
United Negro College Fund
New Orleans Office
No. 2 Canal St., Ste.900 E
New Orleans, LA 70130   Ph: (504)581-3794
Territory Includes: All of LA.

★993★
Urban League of Greater New Orleans
1929 Bienville Ave.
New Orleans, LA 70112   Ph: (504)524-4667
Clarence L. Barney, Pres.

──────────── **Maine** ────────────

★994★
American Civil Liberties Union
Maine Affiliate
97A Exchange St.
Portland, ME 04101   Ph: (207)774-8087
Sally Sutton, Pres.

★995★
Unitarian Universalist Association Black Concerns
  Working Group
Northeast Chapter
277 Industrial Way
Portland, ME 04103   Ph: (207)797-3246
Rev. Glenn H. Turner, District Minister

──────────── **Maryland** ────────────

★996★
Alliance of Black Women Attorneys
Legal Aid Bureau
714 E. Pratt St.
Baltimore, MD 21202   Ph: (301)539-5340
Harriette Taylor, Pres.

★997★
American Civil Liberties Union
Maryland Affiliate
2219 St. Paul St.
Baltimore, MD 21218   Ph: (301)889-8555
Stuart Comstock-Gay, Pres.

★998★
Association for the Study of Afro-American Life and
  History
Baltimore Branch
PO Box 67582
Baltimore, MD 21215   Ph: (301)484-6686
Richard Andrews, Pres.

★999★
Association for the Study of Afro-American Life and
  History
Julian Branch
3728 Pikeswood Dr.
Baltimore County, MD 21133   Ph: (301)521-3413
Gloria Marrow, Pres.

★1000★
Association of Black Media Workers
Baltimore Chapter
c/o WBAL-TV
3800 Hooper Ave.
Baltimore, MD 21211   Ph: (301)467-3000
Clifton Cox, Pres.

★1001★
Baltimore Council for Equal Business Opportunity
1925 Eutaw Pl.
Baltimore, MD 21217   Ph: (410)669-3400

★1002★
Baltimore Urban League
512 Orchard St.
Baltimore, MD 21201   Ph: (410)523-8150
Roger I. Lyons, Pres.

★1003★
Black Mental Health Alliance
2901 Druid Pk. Dr., Ste. 300
Baltimore, MD 21215   Ph: (410)523-6670

★1004★
Black United Fund of Maryland
2225 St. Paul St.
Baltimore, MD 21218   Ph: (410)366-0494

★1005★
Blue Guardians
PO Box 10004
Towson, MD 21285-0004
Richard I. Flichman Jr., Pres.

★1006★
Business League of Baltimore
1831 W. N. Ave.
Baltimore, MD 21217   Ph: (410)728-1234
Dr. Chester Gregory, Pres.
Affiliated with: National Business League.

★1007★
Citizens for Fair Housing
1004 N. Caroline St.
Baltimore, MD 21205   Ph: (410)522-7474

★1008★
Coalition for Open Doors
Ten N. Calvert St., #405
Baltimore, MD 20202   Ph: (301)576-1103
Susan Goering, Dir.
Founded: 1988. **Members:** 40.

★1009★
Coalition of Black Maryland State Troopers
PO Box 11959
Baltimore, MD 21207
Raymond Grisett, Pres.
Affiliated with: National Black Police Association.

★1010★
Coalition of Black Police Officers
PO Box 1863
Rockville, MD 20850
James A. Fenner, Pres.
Affiliated with: National Black Police Association.

★1011★
Combined Communities in Action of Prince George's County
6200 Annapolis Rd., Ste. 201
Hyattsville, MD 20784   Ph: (301)772-1777
Cora L. Rice, Dir.

★1012★
District of Columbia Afro-American Police Officers Association
900 Cornish St.
Fort Washington, MD 20744
Dewayne Anderson, Pres.
Affiliated with: National Black Police Association.

★1013★
District of Columbia Association of Black School Educators
8601 Manchester Rd., No. 422
Silver Spring, MD 20901
Sharon Godfrey, Pres.

★1014★
Howard County Minority Police Officers
PO Box 1624
Ellicott City, MD 21043
Michael Williams, Pres.

★1015★
J. Franklin Bourne Bar Association
PO Box 1121
Upper Marlboro, MD 20773   Ph: (301)699-5800
Arthur J. Horne Jr., Pres.
Affiliated with: National Bar Association.

★1016★
Maryland Rainbow Coalition
1443 Gorsuch Ave.
Baltimore, MD 21218   Ph: (410)467-9388
Clifford Durand, Co-Chairman

★1017★
Metro Baltimore Association of Black School Educators
1614 Hartsdale Rd.
Baltimore, MD 21239
Annette Howard Hall, Pres.

★1018★
Minority Alliance
1831 W. N. Ave.
Baltimore, MD 21217   Ph: (301)769-2445
Jerome Fenwick, Pres.

★1019★
Montgomery County Association of Black School Educators
PO Box 10278
Rockville, MD 20850
Gerald Johnson, Pres.

★1020★
Monumental City Bar Association
PO Box 2195
Baltimore, MD 21203-2195   Ph: (410)347-8700
Dana Peterson, Pres.
Affiliated with: National Bar Association.

★1021★
National Black Child Development Institute Prince George's County Affiliate
8922 Hillside Ct.
Landover, MD 20785   Ph: (301)336-5844
Dawn A. Johnson, Pres.

★1022★
National Business League Montgomery County Chapter
c/o CIS Inc.
8720 Georgia Ave., Ste. 301
Silver Spring, MD 209110   Ph: (301)588-29777
Michelle Dyson, Pres.

★1023★
National Business League Southern Maryland Chapter
9201 Basil Court, No. 115
Landover, MD 20785   Ph: (301)772-3683
Charlie Partridge, Pres.

★1024★
Progressive Firefighters Association of Montgomery County Maryland
PO Box 10011
Silver Spring, MD 20904

★1025★
Students Assistance Project
5000 Pennsylvania Ave., Ste. J
Suitland, MD 20046   Ph: (301)420-9101
Elois G. Hamilton, Dir.

★1026★
Suburban Maryland Fair Housing
414 Hungerford Dr., Ste. 216
Rockville, MD 20853   Ph: (201)251-1997
Kathy Muehlberger, Dir.

★1027★
United Firefighters TASK
PO Box 3333
Capitol Heights, MD 20791

★1028★
Vanguard Justice Society
4800 Reisterstown Rd.
Baltimore, MD 21215   Ph: (410)542-5777
Barry W. Powell, Pres.

★1029★
Vulcan Blazers
2811 Druid Park Dr.
Baltimore, MD 21215   Ph: (410)367-4157

★1030★
Waring Mitchell Law Society of Howard County
PO Box 651
Columbia, MD 21045   Ph: (410)313-2140
Leslie Turner, Pres.
Affiliated with: National Bar Association.

──────── **Massachusetts** ────────

★1031★
American Academy for Affirmative Action
Region I
Boston University
25 Buick St.
Boston, MA 02215   Ph: (617)353-4475
James W. McClain, Dir.

★1032★
American Civil Liberties Union
Massachusetts Affiliate
19 Temple Pl.
Boston, MA 02111   Ph: (617)482-3170
John Roberts, Pres.

★1033★
Association for the Study of Afro-American Life and
History
Boston Branch
PO Box 5453
Boston, MA 02102   Ph: (617)265-2323
Robert Hayden, Pres.

★1034★
Black Community Information Center
466 Blue Hill Ave.
Dorchester, MA 02121   Ph: (617)445-3098

★1035★
Black Research and Development Foundation
MBA Research Team
2000 Massachusetts Ave.
Cambridge, MA 02140

★1036★
Boston Association of Black Journalists
PO Box 866
Boston, MA 02199   Ph: (617)787-7351
Alexis Yancy George, Pres.

★1037★
Boston Lawyers' Committee for Civil Rights Under
  Law of the Boston Bar
294 Washington St.
Boston, MA 02108   Ph: (617)482-1145
Alan Jay Rom, Interim Dir.
Founded: 1968.

★1038★
Boston Minority Business Development Center
985 Commonwealth Ave.
Boston, MA 02215   Ph: (617)353-7060

★1039★
Boston Society of Vulcans
PO Box 269
Roxbury, MA 02119

★1040★
Cambridge Afro-American Police Association
PO Box 390987
Cambridge, MA 02139
Garfield a. Morrison Jr., Pres.
Affiliated with: National Black Police Association.

★1041★
Lena Park Community Development Corporation
150 American Legion Hwy.
Dorchester, MA 02124   Ph: (617)436-1900

★1042★
MAMLEO
61 Columbia Rd.
Dorchester, MA 02121   Ph: (617)436-6868
Dennis Morrison, Pres.

★1043★
Massachusetts Association of Black School Educators
PO Box 1418
Boston, MA 02104
Dr. Clarence Hoover, Pres.

★1044★
Massachusetts Black Caucus
State House, Rm. 127
Boston, MA 02133   Ph: (617)722-2680
Bettye Robinson, Exec.Dir.

★1045★
Massachusetts Black Lawyers Association
PO Box 2411
Boston, MA 02208   Ph: (617)298-4269
Curt Jackson, Pres.
Affiliated with: National Bar Association.

★1046★
Massachusetts Committee Against Discrimination
Hastings Keith Federal Bldg.
53 N. 6th St.
New Bedford, MA 02740   Ph: (508)997-3191
Publications: Newsletter, quarterly.

★1047★
National Association of Minority Contractors
Massachusetts Chapter
PO Box 275
Dorchester, MA 02121   Ph: (617)265-5500
Theodore Webster, Pres.

★1048★
National Black Child Development Institute
Boston Affiliate
198 Geneva Ave.
Dorchester, MA 02121

★1049★
National Black MBA Association
Boston Chapter
PO Box 3709, JW McCormack Station
Boston, MA 02101
Carole Copeland Thomas, Contact

★1050★
National Business League
Boston Chapter
500-502A Harrison Ave.
Boston, MA 02118   Ph: (617)247-9141
Bob Winstead, Pres.

★1051★
New England Minority Purchasing Council
4 Copley Pl.
Box 145
Boston, MA 02116   Ph: (617)578-8900
May Ling Tong, Exec.Dir.
Founded: 1974. **Members:** 170. **Publications:** Directory, annual.
Newsletter, quarterly.

★1052★
North Shore Afro-American Police Officers Association
PO Box 455
Lynn, MA 02149
Thaddeus Wheeler, Pres.
Affiliated with: National Black Police Association.

★1053★
Unitarian Universalist Association Black Concerns
Working Group
Ballou-Channing Chapter
325 W. Elm St.
Brockton, MA 02401   Ph: (508)559-6650
Rev. Dorothy Boroush, District Executive

★1054★
Unitarian Universalist Association Black Concerns
Working Group
Central Massachusetts-Connecticut Valley Chapter
245 Porter Lake Dr.
Springfield, MA 01106   Ph: (413)788-6140
Rev. William A. DeWolfe, District Executive

★1055★
Unitarian Universalist Churches
Massachusetts Bay Chapter
110 Arlington St.
Boston, MA 02116   Ph: (617)542-3231
Rev. Timothy Ashton, District Executive

★1056★
United Negro College Fund
Boston Office
131 State St., Ste. 30
Boston, MA 02109   Ph: (617)227-0937
Territory Includes: MA; NH; ME; VT; RI; Syracuse/Elmira and
Binghamton, NY.

★1057★
Urban League of Eastern Massachusetts
88 Warren St.
Roxbury, MA 02119   Ph: (617)442-4519
Joan Wallace-Benjamin Ph.D., Pres.

★1058★
Urban League of Springfield
756 State St.
Springfield, MA 01109   Ph: (413)739-7211
Henry M. Thomas III, Pres.

─────── **Michigan** ───────

★1059★
Afro-American Police League
902 Brookhollow Ct., #2B
Flint, MI 48503
Doris Roberts-Henry, Pres.
Affiliated with: National Black Police Association.

★1060★
American Association of Blacks in Energy
Michigan Chapter
c/o Walter Starghill, Jr.
Intervale Fuel Corp.
1411 Livernois
Detroit, MI 48238   Ph: (313)933-4110
Walter Starghill Jr., Pres.

★1061★
American Civil Liberties Union
Michigan Affiliate
1249 Washington Blvd., Ste.2910
Detroit, MI 48226-1822   Ph: (313)961-4662
Howard Simon, Pres.

★1062★
Association for the Study of Afro-American Life and
**   History**
Detroit Branch
2557 W. McNichols Rd., No. 208
Detroit, MI 48221   Ph: (313)862-1938
Arthur Coar, Pres.

★1063★
Association of Black Psychologists
Michigan Chapter
1451 E. Lansing Dr., Ste. 224
East Lansing, MI 48823   Ph: (517)351-9006
Alton Kirk

★1064★
Battle Creek Area Urban League
182 W. Van Buren
Battle Creek, MI 49017   Ph: (616)962-2228
Joyce A. Brown, Pres.

★1065★
Black Educators of Pontiac
50 Dakota Dr.
Pontiac, MI 48341   Ph: (313)334-2751
Joanne Walker, Minority Dir.

★1066★
Black Family Development
15231 W. McNichols
Detroit, MI 48235   Ph: (313)272-3500
Jacqueline Jones, Exec.Dir.

★1067★
Black Police Officers Association - Battle Creek
230 S. Woodrow Ave.
Battle Creek, MI 49015   Ph: (616)966-3656
Charles A. Cooper Jr., Pres.

★1068★
Black Police Officers Association - Kalamazoo
2809 Random Rd.
Kalamazoo, MI 49001
Albert Hampton, Pres.

★1069★
Black Police Officers Association - Saginaw
3231 S. Auburn St.
Saginaw, MI 48601   Ph: (517)754-2375
Alphonso Jamison, Pres.

★1070★
Black United Fund of Michigan
2187 W. Grand Blvd.
Detroit, MI 48208   Ph: (313)894-2200
Brenda L. Rayford, Exec.Dir.
Affiliated with: National Black United Fund, Inc.

★1071★
Booker T. Washington Business Association
2885 E. Grand Blvd.
Detroit, MI 48202   Ph: (313)875-4250
Nicholas Hood III, Pres.
Affiliated with: National Business League.

★1072★
Council on Urban League Executives
208 Mack Ave.
Detroit, MI 48201   Ph: (313)832-4600
Roy Levy Williams, Contact

★1073★
Detroit Minority Business Development Center
65 Cadillac Sq., Ste. 3701
Detroit, MI 48226-2822   Ph: (313)961-2100

★1074★
Detroit Real Estate Brokers Association
15918 W. McNichols
Detroit, MI 48235   Ph: (313)835-2143

★1075★
Detroit Urban League
208 Mack Ave.
Detroit, MI 48201   Ph: (313)832-4600
N. Charles Anderson, Pres.

★1076★
Fair Housing Center of Greater Grand Rapids
1514 Wealthy, SE, Rm. 238
Grand Rapids, MI 49506   Ph: (616)451-2980
Lee Nelson Webber, Exec.Dir.
Founded: 1980. **Budget:** $62,000. **Publications:** Fair Housing
News, 3/year. Newsletter.

★1077★
Fair Housing Center of Metropolitan Detroit
2230 Witherell, Rm. 601
Detroit, MI 48201   Ph: (313)963-1274
Clifford C. Schrupp, Exec.Dir.
Founded: 1977. **Members:** 200. **Budget:** $65,000. **Publications:**
Fair Housing News, 3-4/year. **Formerly:** (1986) Fair Housing Center.

★1078★
Floyd Skinner Bar Association
934 Scibner Ave., NW
Grand Rapids, MI 49504   Ph: (616)774-0003
Stephen R. Drew, Pres.
Affiliated with: National Bar Association.

★1079★
Focus Hope Resource Center
1355 Oakman Blvd.
Detroit, MI 48238   Ph: (313)883-7440

★1080★
Grand Rapids Urban League
745 E.ern St. SE
Grand Rapids, MI 49503   Ph: (616)245-2207
Walter M. Brame Ed.D, Pres.

★1081★
Greater Lansing Urban League
300 N. Washington Sq., Ste. 100
Lansing, MI 48933   Ph: (517)487-3608
Ray Margaret Jackson Ph.D., Interim Exec.Dir.

★1082★
Guardians
14019 Wyoming
Detroit, MI 48238   Ph: (313)273-8600

★1083★
Guardians of Police - Detroit
14009 Warwick St.
Detroit, MI 48223
Herman Hutson Jr., Pres.

★1084★
Kalamazoo Association of Black School Educators
726 Darby Ln.
Kalamazoo, MI 49007
Kai M. Jackson, Pres.

★1085★
Lansing Black Lawyers Association
PO Box 18222
Lansing, MI 48901   Ph: (517)373-1162
Lamont M. Walton, Pres.
Affiliated with: National Bar Association.

★1086★
Mallory, Van-Dyne and Scott Bar Association
432 N. Saganaw, No. 810
Flint, MI 48502   Ph: (313)239-2323
Lyost Fletcher, Pres.

★1087★
Metro Detroit Association of Black School Educators
PO Box 02339 N. End Sta.
Detroit, MI 48202
Tommie L. Burton, Pres.

★1088★
Michigan Coalition for Human Rights
4800 Woodward Ave.
Detroit, MI 48201-1399   Ph: (313)833-4407
Mildred Jeffrey, Interim Chair
Founded: 1980. **Members:** 2400.

★1089★
Michigan State Association of Colored Women's Clubs
1618 Pear St.
Ann Arbor, MI 48105   Ph: (313)995-3603
Mary Taylor, Pres.
Founded: 1895. **Members:** 800. **Publications:** Directory, biennial.
Newsletter, quarterly.

★1090★
Mid-Michigan Association of Black Journalists
c/o Jonesetta Lassiter
The Chronicle
200 E. 1st St.
Flint, MI 48502   Ph: (313)766-6380
Carlton Winfrey, Pres.

★1091★
National Black Child Development Institute
Metro Detroit Affiliate
11000 W. McNichols, Ste. 124
Detroit, MI 48221   Ph: (313)342-4050
Rep. Alma Stallworth, Pres.

★1092★
National Black Child Development Institute
Washtenaw Affiliate
PO Box 7948
Ann Arbor, MI 48107   Ph: (313)662-3627
Zack Allen, Pres.

★1093★
National Black MBA Association
Detroit Chapter
PO Box 02398
Detroit, MI 48202   Ph: (313)972-4832
Bruce Thompson, Contact

★1094★
New Phoenix of Detroit
PO Box 02022
Detroit, MI 48202
Affiliated with: International Association of Black Professional Fire Fighters.

★1095★
Officers of the Shield
142 Alger St. SE
Grand Rapids, MI 49507   Ph: (616)452-2039
Marvin Smith, Pres.

★1096★
Operation PUSH
Detroit Chapter
1465 Balmoral Dr.
Detroit, MI 48202   Ph: (313)368-3600
Rev. Jim Holley, Pres.

★1097★
Operation PUSH
Muskegon Heights Network
3020 Woodcliffe
Muskegon Heights, MI 49444   Ph: (616)739-5247
Dr. Vivian Witherspoon

★1098★
Pontiac Area Urban League
295 W. Huron St.
Pontiac, MI 48341   Ph: (313)335-8730
Jacquelin E. Washington, Pres.

★1099★
Racial Justice Center of Grosse Pointe
17150 Maumee
Grosse Pointe, MI 48230   Ph: (313)882-6464
Jeri Grover, Sec.
Founded: 1967. **Members:** 450. **Budget:** $38,000. **Publications:** Key Notes, monthly. Newsletter. **Formerly:** Grosse Pointe Inter-Faith Center for Racial Justice.

★1100★
Saginaw County Black Fire Fighters Association
PO Box 4838
Saginaw, MI 48601

★1101★
Society of Afro-American Police
211 Auburn St.
Pontiac, MI 48058   Ph: (313)338-2553
Conway Thompson, Pres.
Affiliated with: National Black Police Association.

★1102★
Society of Minority Fire Fighters
PO Box 4129
Flint, MI 48504   Ph: (313)233-0533

★1103★
United Negro College Fund
Detroit Office
417 Penobscot Bldg., Ste. 417
Detroit, MI 48226   Ph: (313)965-5550
Territory Includes: All of MI.

★1104★
Urban League of Flint
202 E. Blvd. Dr., 2nd Fl.
Flint, MI 48503   Ph: (313)239-5111
Melvyn S. Brannon, Pres.

★1105★
Urban League of Flint Housing Center
4401 Detroit St.
Flint, MI 48503   Ph: (313)789-8541
James Richardson, Dir.
Publications: Fair Housing News, 3/year. Newsletter.

★1106★
Urban League of Greater Muskegon
950 W. Norton, Ste. 301
Muskegon, MI 49441   Ph: (616)733-0807
Gloria White Gardner, Executive Director

★1107★
Wolverine Bar Association
645 Griswold, Ste. 1312
Detroit, MI 48226   Ph: (313)962-0250
Darwin Fair, Pres.
Affiliated with: National Bar Association.

─────────── **Minnesota** ───────────

★1108★
American Civil Liberties Union
Minnesota Affiliate
1021 W. Broadway
Minneapolis, MN 55411   Ph: (612)522-2423
William South, Pres.

★1109★
Association of Black Psychologists
Minnesota Chapter
590 Iglehart Ave.
St. Paul, MN 55103   Ph: (202)722-0808
Dr. Pearl Bonner II, Pres.

★1110★
Halie Q. Brown Martin Luther King Center
270 N. Kent St.
St. Paul, MN 55102   Ph: (612)224-4601
Fred Williams, Exec.Dir.

★1111★
Minneapolis Minority Business Development Center
2021 E. Hennepin Ave., LL 35
Minneapolis, MN 55413   Ph: (612)378-0361

★1112★
Minneapolis Urban League
2000 Plymouth Ave., N.
Minneapolis, MN 55411   Ph: (612)521-1099
Gary Sudduth, Pres.

★1113★
Minnesota Association of Black School Educators
701 Printice Ln.
Minneapolis, MN 55411
Joyce A. Lake, Pres.

★1114★
Minnesota Minority Lawyers Association
PO Box 2754, Loop Station
Minneapolis, MN 55402
Jarvis Jones, Pres.
Affiliated with: National Bar Association.

★1115★
National Association of Minority Contractors
Minnesota Chapter
1121 Glenwood Ave.
Minneapolis, MN 55405-1431   Ph: (612)374-5129
Carlo Lachmanfingh, Pres.

★1116★
National Black MBA Association
Twin Cities Chapter
PO Box 2709
Minneapolis, MN 55402
Gregg Smith, Contact

★1117★
St. Paul Association of Centurions
687 Carroll Ave.
St. Paul, MN 55104
Clifford A. Kelly, Pres.

★1118★
St. Paul Urban League
401 Selby Ave.
St. Paul, MN 55102   Ph: (612)224-5771
Willie Mae Wilson, Pres./CEO

★1119★
State Council of Black Minnesotans
Right Bldg., Ste. 426
2233 University Ave.
St. Paul, MN 55114   Ph: (612)642-0811
Lester Collins, Exec. Director

★1120★
Twin Cities Black Journalists
Minneapolis-St. Paul Chapter
c/o Sherrie Marshall
The Star Tribune
Lowry Bldg.
355 N. Wabash, Ste. 275
St. Paul, MN 55102   Ph: (612)298-1540
Sherrie Marshall, Pres.

★1121★
Unitarian Universalist Association Black Conerns
  Working Group
Prairie Star Chapter
122 W. Franklin Ave., Ste. 303
Minneapolis, MN 55404   Ph: (612)870-4823
Rev. Harry C. Green, District Executive

★1122★
United Negro College Fund
Minneapolis Office
401 2nd Ave., S., Ste. 532
Minneapolis, MN 55401   Ph: (612)338-5742
Territory Includes: MN; IA; NE.

Mississippi

★1123★
American Civil Liberties Union
Mississippi Affiliate
PO Box 2242
Jackson, MS 39225   Ph: (601)355-6464

★1124★
Bureau of Business and Economic Research
c/o J.B. Burrell
Jackson State University School of
  Business
PO Box 18525
Jackson, MS 39203   Ph: (601)968-2028
J.B. Burrell, Contact
Affiliated with: National Business League.

★1125★
Firefighters Limited
2650 Livingston Rd., Ste. A
Jackson, MS 39213

★1126★
Jackson Association of Black Journalists
PO Box 2108
Jackson, MS 39205   Ph: (601)961-7000
Eric Stringfellow, Pres.

★1127★
Jackson Concerned Officers for Progress
PO Box 31085
Jackson, MS 39206
Affiliated with: National Black Police Association.

★1128★
Jackson County-Pascagoula-Moss Point Negro Senior
  Club
c/o Roberta Deleah Johnson
5030 Frederick St.
Moss Point, MS 39563   Ph: (601)475-2155
Roberta Deleah Johnson, Pres.

★1129★
Jackson Minority Business Development Center
5285 Galaxie Dr., Ste. 465
Jackson, MS 39206   Ph: (601)362-2260

★1130★
Magnolia Bar Association
2115 W. Capital St.
Jackson, MS 39206   Ph: (601)353-2540
Romaine L. Richards, Pres.
Affiliated with: National Bar Association.

★1131★
Mississippi Action for Community Education
119 S. Theobald St.
Greenville, MS 38701   Ph: (601)335-3523
Larry Farmer, Pres.

★1132★
Mississippi Power and Light
PO Box 1640
Jackson, MS 39215-1640   Ph: (601)949-6409
Bennie F. Paige

★1133★
Natchez Business and Civic League
1044 N. Pine St.
Natchez, MS 39120   Ph: (601)442-6644
Harden Wallace, Pres.
Affiliated with: National Business League.

★1134★
National Association of Minority Contractors
Mississippi Chapter
PO Box 1461
Columbus, MS 39703   Ph: (601)328-0837
Tom Epps, Pres.

★1135★
Operation PUSH
Jackson Chapter
746 Windward Rd.
Jackson, MS 39206   Ph: (601)982-6145
Dr. Leslie McLemore

★1136★
Southern Media Coalition
3322 S. Lamar Blvd.
Oxford, MS 38655   Ph: (601)234-2918
Alvin Chambliss, Contact
Affiliated with: National Black Media Coalition.

★1137★
Urban League of Greater Jackson
3405 Medgar Evers Blvd.
Jackson, MS 39213   Ph: (601)981-4211

───────────── **Missouri** ─────────────

★1138★
American Association of Blacks in Energy
Kansas/Missouri Chapter
c/o Verneda Robinson
Gas Service
2460 Pershing Rd., 2nd Fl.
Kansas City, MO 64108   Ph: (816)346-5504
Verneda Gilbert, Pres.

★1139★
American Civil Liberties Union
Eastern Missouri Affiliate
4557 Lacleda Ave.
St. Louis, MO 39202   Ph: (314)361-2111
Joyce Armstrong, Pres.

★1140★
American Civil Liberties Union
Kansas and Western Missouri Affiliate
201 Wyandotte St., No. 209
Kansas City, MO 64105   Ph: (816)421-4449
Dick Kurtenbach, Pres.

★1141★
Black Economic Union of Greater Kansas City
1601 E. 18th St., Ste. 300
Kansas City, MO 64108   Ph: (816)474-1080
Sylvester Holmes, Exec.Dir.

★1142★
Black Music Society of Missouri
3701 Grandel Sq.
St. Louis, MO 63108   Ph: (314)534-4344

★1143★
Black Nurses Association of Greater St. Louis
5866 Julian Ave.
St. Louis, MO 63112   Ph: (314)367-6599

★1144★
Black United Appeal of Kansas City
3338 Benton Blvd.
Kansas City, MO 64128   Ph: (816)861-1222
Elvis E. Gibson, Pres.
Affiliated with: National Black United Fund, Inc.

★1145★
FIRE
4577 Athlone St.
St. Louis, MO 63115

★1146★
Greater St. Louis Association of Black Journalists
c/o Mary Cannon
KMOV-TV
625 N. Euclid Ave., Ste. 200
St. Louis, MO 63108   Ph: (314)361-7877
Mary Cannon, Pres.

★1147★
Kansas City Association of Black Journalists
1729 Grand Ave.
Kansas City, MO 64108   Ph: (816)234-4300
Gromer Jeffers, Pres.

★1148★
Kansas City Minority Business Development Center
1101 Walnut, Ste. 1600
Kansas City, MO 64106   Ph: (816)471-1520
Stanley Peeples, Director

★1149★
Metro Black Media Coalition
PO Box 5826
St. Louis, MO 63134
Ms. Freddie Lee Thompson, Contact

★1150★
Mound City Bar Association
PO Box 1543
St. Louis, MO 63188   Ph: (314)231-9775
Elaine Spearman, Pres.

★1151★
Mound City Business League
10345 Nashua
Dellwood, MO 63136   Ph: (314)361-2613
Marvin Batey, Pres.
Affiliated with: National Business League.

★1152★
National Black Child Development Institute
St. Louis Affiliate
739 Harvest Ln.
St. Louis, MO 63132
Christine Reams, Pres.
Ph: (314)997-0831

★1153★
National Black MBA Association
Kansas City Chapter
PO Box 410692
Kansas City, MO 64141
Vernita Turner, Contact
Ph: (816)822-7898

★1154★
National Black MBA Association
St. Louis Chapter
PO Box 5296
St. Louis, MO 63115
Kenneth Rowey, Contact

★1155★
Operation PUSH
Kansas City Chapter
2310 E. Linwood Blvd.
Kansas City, MO 64109
Rev. Wallace Hartfields, Pres.
Ph: (816)923-3689

★1156★
Operation PUSH
St. Louis Chapter
1260 Hamilton Ave.
St. Louis, MO 63112

★1157★
St. Louis Black Fire Chiefs Association
6308 Tennessee St.
St. Louis, MO 63111

★1158★
St. Louis County Minority Law Enforcement
  Association
702 W. Caterbury St., Apt. D
University, MO 63132
Craig Franklin, Pres.
Affiliated with: National Black Police Association.

★1159★
St. Louis Ethical Police Society
913 Melvin St.
St. Louis, MO 63137
Rodney Williams, Pres.

★1160★
St. Louis Minority Business Development Center
500 Washington Ave., Ste. 1200
St. Louis, MO 63101
Ph: (314)621-6232

★1161★
United Minority Media Association
5511 Woodland
Kansas City, MO 64110
M.C. Richardson, Contact
Ph: (816)474-8662

★1162★
United Negro College Fund
St. Louis Office
915 Olive St., Ste. 821
St. Louis, MO 64106
Darnell Collins
Ph: (314)241-5958
Territory Includes: All of MO; KS.

★1163★
Urban League of Kansas City
1710 Paseo
Kansas City, MO 64108
William H. Clark, Pres.
Ph: (816)471-0550

★1164★
Urban League of Metropolitan St. Louis
3701 Grandel Sq.
St. Louis, MO 63108
James H. Buford, Pres.
Ph: (314)289-0328

─────────────── **Montana** ───────────────

★1165★
American Civil Liberties Union
Montana Affiliate
PO Box3012
Billings, MT 59103
Scott Crichton, Pres.
Ph: (403)248-1086

─────────────── **Nebraska** ───────────────

★1166★
American Civil Liberties Union
Nebraska Affiliate
633 S. 9th St. LL 10
Lincoln, NE 68508
Bill Schats, Pres.
Ph: (402)476-8091

★1167★
Brotherhood of the Midwest Guardians
2505 N. 24th St., Ste. 468
Omaha, NE 68110
Ph: (402)455-2271

★1168★
Malcolm X Memorial Foundation
2019 20th St.
Omaha, NE 68110
Rowena Moore
Ph: (402)342-4212

★1169★
Omaha Association of Black Professional Fire Fighters
PO Box 11053, Ames Sta.
Omaha, NE 68111

★1170★
Urban League of Nebraska
3022-24 N. 24th St.
Omaha, NE 68110
George H. Dillard, Pres.
Ph: (402)453-9730

—————————— **Nevada** ——————————

★1171★
American Civil Liberties Union
Nevada Affiliate
418 S. Maryland Pkwy.
Las Vegas, NV 89101   Ph: (702)366-1226
Chan Kendrick, Pres.

★1172★
Las Vegas Association of Black School Educators
2300 Alta Dr.
Las Vegas, NV 89107   Ph: (702)734-0019
Daisey Miller, Pres.

★1173★
Las Vegas Black Fire Fighters
PO Box 5027
Las Vegas, NV 89101

★1174★
Las Vegas Minority Business Development Center
2860 E. Flamingo, Ste. K.
Las Vegas, NV 89121   Ph: (702)892-0151
Flo Reijnders, Executive Director

★1175★
National Association of Minority Contractors
Nevada Chapter
4214 Bertsos Dr.
Las Vegas, NV 89103   Ph: (702)876-7699
Claudio Ferreiro, Pres.

★1176★
National Bar Association
Las Vegas Chapter
225 E. Bridger Ave., 8th Fl.
Las Vegas, NV 89155   Ph: (702)455-4761
Michael L. Douglas, Pres.

★1177★
Nevada Black Chamber of Commerce
1048 W. Owens
Las Vegas, NV 89106   Ph: (702)648-6222
Al O'Neal, Pres.

★1178★
Nevada Black Police Association
PO Box 1834
Las Vegas, NV 89125
Cliff E. Davis Jr.
Pres.
Affiliated with: National Black Police Association.

★1179★
Professional Black Fire Fighters of Clark County
Nevada
PO Box 15328
Las Vegas, NV 89114

★1180★
Reno Black Fire Fighters
6091 Banside Way
Reno, NV 89523

—————————— **New Hampshire** ——————————

★1181★
American Civil Liberties Union
New Hampshire Affiliate
11 S. Main St.
Concord, NH 03301   Ph: (603)225-3080
Claire Ebel, Pres.

★1182★
Unitarian Universalist Association Black Concerns
Working Group
New Hampshire-Vermont Chapter
41-A S. State St.
Concord, NH 03301   Ph: (603)228-8704
Rev. Deane Starr, District Executive

—————————— **New Jersey** ——————————

★1183★
American Civil Liberties Union
New Jersey Affiliate
2 Washington Pl.
Newark, NJ 07102   Ph: (201)642-2084
Ed Martone, Pres.

★1184★
Association for the Study of Afro-American Life and
History
Camden County Branch
6 Tulip Ct.
Mt. Laurel, NJ 08054   Ph: (609)235-3758
Christine Blake, Pres.

★1185★
Association for the Study of Afro-American Life and
History
Central New Jersey Branch
137 Central Pl.
East Orange, NJ 07050   Ph: (201)674-2676
Evelyn Claiborne, Pres.

★1186★
Association for the Study of Afro-American Life and
History
Essex County Branch
1060 Broad St., Apt. 606
Newark, NJ 07102   Ph: (201)824-8736
Odelma Hammond, Pres.

★1187★
Association for the Study of Afro-American Life and
History
Franklin/St. John's Branch
260 Meeker Ave.
Newark, NJ 07112   Ph: (201)923-9707
Rev. Lloyd Preston Terrell, Pres.

★1188★
Association for the Study of Afro-American Life and
History
South Jersey Branch
PO Box 283
Berlin, NJ 08009   Ph: (609)629-8483
Elvira Bradford, Pres.

★1189★
Association of Black Psychologists
New Jersey Chapter
111 Livingston Ave.
New Brunswick, NJ 08901   Ph: (202)722-0808
Dr. Abisola Gallagher, Pres.

★1190★
Atlantic City Vulcans
PO Box 161
Atlantic City, NJ 08404

★1191★
Batons
PO Box 974
Newark, NJ 07102
Frank McMickens, Pres.
Affiliated with: National Black Police Association.

★1192★
Black United Fund of New Jersey
50 Park Pl., Ste. 1419
Newark, NJ 07102   Ph: (201)624-0909
Lloyd J. Oxford, Pres.
Affiliated with: National Black United Fund, Inc.

★1193★
Black Youth Organization
308 S. 9th St.
Newark, NJ 07103   Ph: (201)622-1061
W. Leon Moore, Exec.Dir

★1194★
Bronze Shields
PO Box 1144
Newark, NJ 07102
Alonzo Evans, Pres.
Affiliated with: National Black Police Association.

★1195★
Brother Officers Law Enforcement Society
PO Box 914
Trenton, NJ 08606-0914
Ulysses Davis, Pres.
Affiliated with: National Black Police Association.

★1196★
Brotherhood for Unity and Progress
PO Box 641
Camden, NJ 08102
Leonard W. Hall, Pres.

★1197★
Brotherhood of United Fire Fighters
PO Box 753
Camden, NJ 08101

★1198★
Brothers in Blue
450 E. 34th St.
Patterson, NJ 07054
Willie Smoot, Pres.
Affiliated with: National Black Police Association.

★1199★
COFFEE
PO Box 2578
Plainfield, NJ 07062

★1200★
East Orange Kinsmen
PO Box 4075
East Orange, NJ 07017
John W. Lee, Pres.

★1201★
Essex County Education Association
780 Northfield Ave.
West Orange, NJ 07052   Ph: (201)736-5650

★1202★
FAIR
PO Box 99
Montclair, NJ 07042

★1203★
Federation of Afro-American Police Officers
21 Porter Ave.
Newark, NJ 07102
Ron Arbuckle, Pres.
Affiliated with: National Black Police Association.

★1204★
FLAME
518 Arlington Ave.
East Orange, NJ 07017

★1205★
Garden State Bar Association
744 Broad St., #1514
Newark, NJ 07102   Ph: (201)643-5972
Andrew Manns, Pres.
Affiliated with: National Bar Association.

★1206★
Golden Shields Association
PO Box 74
Irvington, NJ 07111
Mike Chase, Pres.

★1207★
IMPAC
PO Box 215
Jersey City, NJ 07302   Ph: (201)435-7115
George Wilson, Pres.

★1208★
Men and Women for Justice
PO Box 1286
Piscataway, NJ 08854
Leonard W. Randolph, Pres.

★1209★
Morris County Urban League Inc.
45 Market St.
Morristown, NJ 07960   Ph: (201)539-2121
Janice S. Johnson, Pres.

★1210★
National Association of Extension Home Economists
Minority Network Committee
2569 E. Landis Ave.
Vineland, NJ 08360   Ph: (609)691-0369
Dianne S. Lennon, Chairman

★1211★
National Association of Minority Contractors
New Jersey Chapter
340 W. 1st Ave.
Roselle, NJ 07203   Ph: (908)241-9500
Tony Singh, Pres.

★1212★
National Black Alcoholism Council
41 Rector St.
Newark, NJ 07102

★1213★
National Black Child Development Institute
Newark/Essex County Affiliate
403 University Ave.
Newark, NJ 07102   Ph: (718)479-4451
Dolores Odom, Pres.

★1214★
National Black MBA Association
Central New Jersey Chapter
PO Box 127
Piscataway, NJ 08854   Ph: (908)246-2878
Donna Johns, Contact

★1215★
National Business League
South Jersey Chapter
PO Box 1382
Atlantic City, NJ 08401   Ph: (609)344-3499
B.A.C. Johnson, Asst. Reg. V. Pres.

★1216★
National Minority Business Council
494 Broad St., Ste. 600
Newark, NJ 07102   Ph: (212)573-2385
William Franklin, Managing Dir.

★1217★
New Brunswick Minority Business Development Center
134 New St., Rm. 102
New Brunswick, NJ 08901

★1218★
New Brunswick Minority Fire Fighters
15 Conger St.
New Brunswick, NJ 08902

★1219★
New York Metropolitan Business League
20 N. Van Brunt St., Ste. 200   Ph: (201)568-8145
Englewood, NJ 07631   Fax: (201)568-5178
E. R. Hadden, Coordinator
Founded: 1976. **Members:** 100. **Publications:** Newsletter, quarterly.

★1220★
Newark Association of Black School Educators
PO Box 32458
Newark, NJ 07102
Dr. Lorenzo, Grant

★1221★
Newark Minority Business Development Center
60 Park Pl., Ste. 1404
Newark, NJ 07102   Ph: (201)623-7712

★1222★
Operation PUSH
Jersey City Chapter
632 Garfield Ave.
Jersey City, NJ 07305
Rev. Edward Allen, Pres.

★1223★
Plainfield Area Ebony Police Association
PO Box 3158
Plainfield, NJ 07063   Ph: (908)753-8835
Siddeeq W. El-Amin, Pres.

★1224★
Sentinel Sixteen - 87, Inc.
PO Box 1192
Montclair, NJ 07042
Benjamin Powell, Pres.

★1225★
Silver Shields Club
23 Williams St.
Newark, NJ 07102
Robert Hubbert, Pres.
Affiliated with: National Black Police Association.

★1226★
United Negro College Fund
Newark Office
24 Commerce St., Ste. 1327
Newark, NJ 07102   Ph: (201)642-1955
Territory Includes: All of NJ.

★1227★
Unity Guardians Association
PO Box 269
Rahway, NJ 07605
Sam Freeman, Pres.

★1228★
Urban League for Bergen County
106 W. Palisade Ave.
Englewood, NJ 07631   Ph: (201)568-4988
William E. Brown, Executive Director

★1229★
Urban League of Essex County
3 Williams St., Ste. 300
Newark, NJ 07102   Ph: (201)624-6660
Lydia D. Barnett, Pres./CEO

★1230★
Urban League of Hudson County
779 Bergen Ave.
Jersey City, NJ 07306   Ph: (201)451-8888
Elnora Watson, Pres.

★1231★
Urban League of Metropolitan Trenton
209 Academy St.
Trenton, NJ 08618   Ph: (609)393-1512
Paul P. Pintella Jr., Pres.

★1232★
Urban League of Union County
272 N. Broad St.
Elizabeth, NJ 07207   Ph: (908)351-7200
Ella S. Teal, Pres.

★1233★
Vulcan Pioneers of Hudson County
PO Box 9104
Jersey City, NJ 07309
Affiliated with: International Association of Black Professional Fire Fighters.

★1234★
Vulcan Pioneers of New Jersey
54 N. Munn Ave., No. 12
Newark, NJ 07106

---------------- **New Mexico** ----------------

★1235★
Albuquerque Minority Business Development Center
718 Central SW
Albuquerque, NM 87102   Ph: (505)843-7114

★1236★
American Civil Liberties Union
New Mexico Affiliate
PO Box 80915
Albuquerque, NM 87108   Ph: (505)266-5915
Grace W. Williams, Pres.

★1237★
Black Officers Association of New Mexico
503 Maddox Loop
Belen, NM 87124
Norman Richard, Pres.
Affiliated with: National Black Police Association.

★1238★
New Mexico Black Lawyers Association
1117 Stanford, NE
Albuquerque, NM 87131   Ph: (505)277-5820
Alfred Matthewson, Pres.
Affiliated with: National Bar Association.

---------------- **New York** ----------------

★1239★
Abeny Association of Black School Educators
GPO Box 1846
Brooklyn, NY 11202
Silverlane Clark, Pres.

★1240★
African Cultural Center of Buffalo
350 Masten Ave.
Buffalo, NY 14209   Ph: (716)884-2013
Agnes M. Bain, Exec.Dir.
Founded: 1958. **Publications:** CenterStage, periodic. Also publishes Carrying on a Heritage of Culture (brochure).

★1241★
Afro-American Police Association
735 Humboldt Pkwy.
Buffalo, NY 14208
Nadine Wilson, Pres.

★1242★
Afro-American Vegetarian Society
PO Box 46, Colonial Park Station
New York, NY 10039   Ph: (914)664-2066
Ron Davis, Pres.
Founded: 1973. **Members:** 150.

★1243★
Albany Area Urban League
95 Livingston Ave.
Albany, NY 12207   Ph: (518)463-3121
Joseph Griggs, Interim

★1244★
American Association of Blacks in Energy
New York Chapter
c/o Leandra H. Abbott
ConEd Co. of New York
4 Irving Pl., Rm. 1634
New York, NY 10003   Ph: (212)460-6918
Leandra H. Abbott, Pres.

★1245★
American Civil Liberties Union
New York Affiliate
132 W. 43rd St., 2nd Fl.
New York, NY 10036   Ph: (212)382-0557
Norman Siegal, Pres.

★1246★
Associated Black Charities
105 E. 22nd St., Ste. 915
New York, NY 10010   Ph: (212)777-6060

★1247★
Association for the Study of Afro-American Life and
  History
American Federation of Teachers Branch, Local 2
15 W. 72nd St., No. 33A
New York, NY 10023   Ph: (212)595-0282
Ponsie Hillman, Pres.

★1248★
Association for the Study of Afro-American Life and
  History
Bronx Branch
3617 Bronxwood Ave.
Bronx, NY 10469   Ph: (212)652-6247
Cheryl Hockaday, Pres.

★1249★
Association for the Study of Afro-American Life and
  History
Sullivan County Branch
PO Box 1351
South Fallsburg, NY 12779   Ph: (914)434-7481
Dorothy Fields, Pres.

★1250★
Association for the Study of Afro-American Life and
  History
Westchester Branch
118 N. Everts Ave.
Elmsford, NY 10523   Ph: (914)592-6425
Yvonne Jones, Pres.

★1251★
Association of Black Lawyers of Westchester County
19 Chestnut Hill Ave.
White Plains, NY 10606   Ph: (914)347-2244
Eric Lamar Harris, Pres.
Affiliated with: National Bar Association.

★1252★
Association of Black Psychologists
New York Chapter
3875 Waldo Ave.
Bronx, NY 10463   Ph: (212)447-0900
Lorraine Maxwell

★1253★
Association of Black Social Workers
1969 Madison Ave.
New York, NY 10035   Ph: (212)348-0035

★1254★
Association of Black Women Attorneys
134 W. 32nd St., Ste. 602
New York, NY 10001   Ph: (212)815-0478
Leslie R. Jones, Pres.

★1255★
Association of Minority Business Enterprises of New York
165 40A Baisle Blvd., Ste. 3
Jamaica, NY 11434   Ph: (718)341-0707
Nathaniel Singleton, Pres.

★1256★
Association of Neighborhood Housing Development
236 W. 27th St.
New York, NY 10001   Ph: (212)463-9600

★1257★
Bi-State Shields
PO Box 382, JFK Station
Jamaica, NY 11430
Howard Walcott, Pres
Affiliated with: National Black Police Association.

★1258★
Black Community Development Project
245 Liberty
Newburgh, NY 12550   Ph: (914)561-2107
Billie McClearn, Exec.Dir.
Publications: Newsletter, monthly.

★1259★
Black Interest Group
Undergraduate Office
Student Union
4245 E. Ave.
Nazareth Coll.
Rochester, NY 14618   Ph: (716)586-2525

★1260★
Black New York Action Committee
1878 Seventh Ave.
New York, NY 10026

★1261★
Black Newspapers Clipping Bureau
68 E. 131st St.
New York, NY 10037   Ph: (212)281-6000

★1262★
Black Radio Network
166 Madison Ave.
New York, NY 10002   Ph: (212)686-6850

★1263★
Black Resources
231 W. 29th St., Rm. 1205
New York, NY 10001   Ph: (212)967-4000

★1264★
Black Resources Inc.
410 Central Park W.
New York, NY 10025   Ph: (212)222-3556

★1265★
Black Theatre Fund
c/o The Black American
545 Eighth Ave., 12th Fl.
New York, NY 10018   Ph: (212)594-0179

★1266★
Black United Fund of New York
2271 7th St.
New York, NY 10030   Ph: (212)234-1695
Kermit Eady, Pres.

★1267★
Black Women's Support Group
280 Valiant Dr.
Rochester, NY 14623   Ph: (716)359-2302
Merlina Moore, Exec. Officer

★1268★
Bronx County Black Bar Association
19828 Pompeii Ave.
Queens, NY 11423   Ph: (212)804-1512
Teresa Mason, Pres.
Affiliated with: National Bar Association.

★1269★
Bronx Minority Business Development Center
349 E. 149th St., Ste. 702
Bronx, NY 10451   Ph: (212)665-8583

★1270★
Bronze Shields of Suffolk County, New York
PO Box 544
Calverton, NY 11933
Clement Snell, Pres.

★1271★
Brooklyn Minority Business Development Center
16 Court St., Rm. 1903
Brooklyn, NY 11201   Ph: (718)522-5880

★1272★
Broome County Urban League
43-45 Carroll St.
Binghamton, NY 13901   Ph: (607)723-7303
Laura C. Keeling, Pres.

★1273★
Brothers of the Shield
PO Box 146
Carle Place, NY 11514
Oscar Powell, Pres.
Affiliated with: National Black Police Association.

★1274★
Buffalo Black Media Coalition
225 Hasting St.
Buffalo, NY 14215
John E. Smith, Contact

★1275★
Buffalo Minority Business Development Center
523 Delaware Ave.
Buffalo, NY 14202   Ph: (716)885-0336

★1276★
Buffalo Urban League
15 E. Genessee St.
Buffalo, NY 14211   Ph: (716)854-7625
Leroy R. Coles Jr., Pres.

★1277★
Catholic Interracial Council of New York
899 10th Ave., Ste. 635
New York, NY 10019   Ph: (212)237-8255
Gerald W. Lynch, Pres.
Founded: 1934. **Members:** 1600. **Budget:** $150,000. **Publications:**
Interracial Review, quarterly. News, quarterly. Also publishes
transcripts of forums, symposia, conferences, and workshops.

★1278★
Concerned Black Film Makers of New York
20 W. 120th St.
New York, NY 10027   Ph: (212)410-2101

★1279★
Council on Economic Development and Empowerment
   of Black People
63 W. 125th St.
New York, NY 10027   Ph: (212)722-1922

★1280★
East Upton Harlem Chamber of Commerce
186 E. 116th St.
New York, NY 10029   Ph: (212)996-2288
Henry Calderon, Pres.

★1281★
Ebony Society
15 Linden St.
Coram, NY 11727
Jeanne Goshay, Pres.

★1282★
Greater New York Business League
491 DeKalb Ave.
Brooklyn, NY 11205   Ph: (718)636-1509
Bryon A. Lee, Pres.
Affiliated with: National Business League.

★1283★
Guardians Association - Long Island Railroad
339 Midward St.
Brooklyn, NY 11225
Stephen Mears, Pres.

★1284★
Guardians Association - New York City Corrections
General Post Office
PO Box 527
Bronx, NY 10451
Ali A. Al-Rahman, Pres.

★1285★
Guardians Association - New York City Housing
Manhattanville Sta.
PO Box 1746
New York, NY 10027
Oubey Jefferson, Pres.

★1286★
Guardians Association - New York Police Department
120-22E Erskine Pl.
Bronx, NY 10475
Roger L. Abel, Pres.

★1287★
Guardians Association - New York State Courts
Lincolnton Sta.
PO Box 524-021
New York, NY 10037
Jay Best Sr., Pres.

★1288★
Harlem Commonwealth Council
361 W. 125th St.
New York, NY 10027   Ph: (212)749-0900

★1289★
Harlem Minority Business Development Center
270 Sylvan Ave.
Englewood Cliffs, NY 07362   Ph: (212)661-8044

★1290★
Harlem Parents Union
271 W. 125th St.
New York, NY 10027   Ph: (212)662-4888

★1291★
Inner-City Scholarship Fund
1011 1st Ave., 14th Fl.
New York, NY 10022   Ph: (212)753-8583
MarieLou Catalano, Director

★1292★
INTERACE
PO Box 582
Forest Hills, NY 11375   Ph: (718)657-2271
Holly Sheeger, Coordinator
Founded: 1983. **Publications:** INTERace, quarterly. Newsletter.

★1293★
Long Island Association of Black School Educators
729 Wilson
Central Islip, NY 11722
Helen D. Brannon, Pres.

★1294★
Long Island Guardians
PO Box 1313M
Bayshore, NY 11706
Wes Daily, Pres.

★1295★
Macon B. Allen Bar Association
112-04 Springfield Blvd.
Queens Village
New York, NY 11429   Ph: (718)465-7415
Claude Steward, Pres.
Affiliated with: National Bar Association.

★1296★
Manhattan Minority Business Development Center
51 Madison Ave., Ste, 2212
New York, NY 10010   Ph: (212)779-4360
Lorraine Kelsey, Vice President

★1297★
Metropolitan Black Bar Association
c/o Le-Roi Gill
363 7th Ave., Ste. 400
New York, NY 10001   Ph: (212)563-1971
Le-Roi Gill, Pres.
Affiliated with: National Bar Association.

★1298★
Minority Bar Association of Western New York
PO Box 211, Niagara Sq. Sta.
Buffalo, NY 14201   Ph: (716)856-4000
Edward D. Peace, Pres.

★1299★
MOCHA
822 N. French Rd.
North Tonawanda, NY 14120

★1300★
Nassau County Guardians
PO Box 100
Uniondale, NY 11553
Larry Hill, Pres.

★1301★
Nassau/Suffolk Minority Business Development Center
150 Broad Hollow Rd., Ste. 304
Melville, NY 11747   Ph: (516)549-5454
Kathleen Percival-Greene, Exec. Dir.

★1302★
National Association of Minority Contractors
New York Chapter
255 Orange St.
PO Box 12
Albany, NY 12210   Ph: (518)449-3192
Herbert Hughes, Pres.

★1303★
National Association of Negro Business, and
Professional Women's Clubs
Rochester Genesee Valley Club
c/o Florella Chandler
49 Alden Rd.
Rochester, NY 14626   Ph: (716)225-6771
Florella Chandler, Pres.

★1304★
National Black Child Development Institute
Buffalo Affiliate
440 W. Adams St.
Buffalo, NY 14212   Ph: (716)845-6157
Odessa Brown, Pres.

★1305★
National Black Child Development Institute
Mid-Hudson Affiliate
PO Box 1383
Newburgh, NY 12550   Ph: (914)297-8933
Linda Melton-Mann, Asst. V.P.

★1306★
National Black Child Development Institute
New York Affiliate
204 W. 136th St.
New York, NY 10030   Ph: (212)926-8000
Dennis Walcott, Pres.

★1307★
National Black MBA Association
New York Chapter
Grand Central Station
PO Box 1602, Grand Central Station
New York, NY 10163   Ph: (212)978-4333
Jennifer Taylor-Smith, Contact

★1308★
National Black MBA Association
Westchester/Greater Connecticut Chapter
PO BOX 552
White Plains, NY 10602
Charles Wade, Contact

★1309★
National Black MBA Association
Western New York Chapter
PO Box 15697
Rochester, NY 14615-0697
Denise Cornwell, Contact

★1310★
National Council for Negro Women of Greater New
York
777 United Nations Plaza, 10th Fl.
New York, NY 10017   Ph: (212)687-5870

★1311★
New American
310 Lenoy Ave.
New York, NY 100127

★1312★
New York Association of Black Journalists
WPIX-TV
220 E. 42nd St.
New York, NY 10017   Ph: (212)210-2420
Sheila D. Stainback, Pres.

★1313★
New York Association of Black School Educators
PO Box 100-449
Brooklyn, NY 11210
Dr. Ronald Frye, Pres.

★1314★
New York Urban Coalition
99 Hudson, 9th Fl.
New York, NY 10013   Ph: (212)219-4500

★1315★
New York Urban League
204 W. 136th St.
New York, NY 10030   Ph: (212)926-8000
Dennis M. Walcott, Pres.

★1316★
Niagra Association of Black School Educators
PO Box 244 Bridge Sta.
Niagra Falls, NY 14305
Gloria Scott, Pres.

★1317★
One Hundred Black Men
105 E. 22nd, 6th Fl.
New York, NY 10010   Ph: (212)777-7070

★1318★
Queens Minority Business Development Center
110-29 Horace Harding Expwy.
Corona, NY 11368   Ph: (516)484-9797

★1319★
Rochester Black Media Coalition
700 N. St.
Rochester, NY 14605
Charles Hatcher, Contact

★1320★
Rochester Minority Business Development Center
350 N. St.
Rochester, NY 14605   Ph: (716)232-6120

★1321★
Schomburg Center for Research in Black Culture
c/o Howard Dodson
New York Public Library
515 Malcolm X Blvd.
New York, NY 10037-1801   Ph: (212)491-2200
Howard Dodson, Chief
Founded: 1925. **Members:** 1200. **Telecommunications Services:** Fax, (212)491-6760. **Publications:** Calendar, periodic. Newsletter, quarterly.

★1322★
Suffolk Housing Services
550 Smithtown Bypass, Rm. 220
Hauppauge, NY 11787   Ph: (516)582-2727
David Berenbaum, Exec.Dir.

★1323★
Syracuse Association of Black Journalists
c/o Saundra Smokes
The Herald-Journal
PO Box 4915
Syracuse, NY 13221
Saundra Smokes, Pres.

★1324★
Syracuse Black Media Coalition
1450 Comstock Ave.
Syracuse, NY 13220   Ph: (315)474-6860
Butch Charles, Contact

★1325★
**Unitarian Universalist Association Black Concerns
   Working Group**
Metropolitan New York Chapter
2 Harvard Rd.
Shoreham, NY 11786   Ph: (516)744-0557
Rev. Howell K. Lind, District Executive

★1326★
**Unitarian Universalist Association Black Concerns
   Working Group**
St. Lawrence Chapter
695 Elmwood Ave.
Buffalo, NY 14222   Ph: (716)882-0430
Rev. Wendy L. Colby, District Consultant

★1327★
United Black Appeal
545 Eighth Ave.
New York, NY 10018   Ph: (212)564-9852

★1328★
United Federation of Black Community Organizations
Child Development Center
474 W. 159th St.
New York, NY 10032   Ph: (212)281-1950

★1329★
Uptown Chamber of Commerce
125th St., Ste. 206
New York, NY 10027   Ph: (212)427-7200
Lloyd Williams, Pres./CEO

★1330★
Urban League of Long Island
219 Carlton
Central Islip, NY 11722   Ph: (516)232-2482
Doris P. Miles, Pres.

★1331★
Urban League of Onondaga County
505 E. Fayette St.
Syracuse, NY 13202   Ph: (315)472-6955
Leon E. Modeste, Pres.

★1332★
Urban League of Rochester
265 N. Clinton
Rochester, NY 14605   Ph: (716)325-6530
William A. Johnson Jr., Pres.

★1333★
Urban League of Westchester County
61 Mitchell Pl.
White Plains, NY 10601   Ph: (914)428-6300
Ernest S. Prince, Pres.

★1334★
Vulcan Society of New York
739 E.ern Pkwy.
Brooklyn, NY 112123

★1335★
Vulcan Society of Westchester County
PO Box 2179
Mt. Vernon, NY 10551
Affiliated with: International Association of Black Professional Fire Fighters.

★1336★
Westchester Association of Black School Educators
1-B Quaker Ridge Rd., No. 101
New Rochelle, NY 10804
Ann Williams, Pres.

★1337★
Westchester Rockland Guardians
PO Box 138
White Plains, NY 10605
Curley Brown, Pres.

★1338★
**Williamsburg/Brooklyn Minority Business Development
   Center**
12 Heywood St.
Brooklyn, NY 11211   Ph: (718)522-5620

——————   **North Carolina**   ——————

★1339★
American Association for Affirmative Action
Region IV
c/o Mary C. Williams
Forsyth Memorial Hospital
Winston-Salem, NC 27103   Ph: (919)760-5469
Mary C. Williams, Dir.

★1340★
American Association of Blacks in Energy
Virginia/North Carolina Chapter
c/o Hilda Pinnix-Ragland
Carolina Power and Light Co.
PO Box 207
Raleigh, NC 27602   Ph: (919)546-7567
Hilda Pinnix-Ragland, Pres.

★1341★
American Civil Liberties Union
North Carolina Affiliate
PO Box 28004
Raleigh, NC 27611   Ph: (919)834-3390
James Shields, Pres.

★1342★
Association of Black Psychologists
North Carolina Chapter
E. Carolina University
Greenville, NC 27834   Ph: (919)757-1531
Dr. Dennis Chestnut, Pres.

★1343★
Black History Research Committee of Henderson
County
733 Third Ave.
Hendersonville, NC 28739   Ph: (704)693-4548
John R. Marable, Dir.

★1344★
Bull City Professional Fire Fighters
1122 Drew St.
Durham, NC 27701

★1345★
Carolinas Minority Supplier Development Council
700 E. Stonewall St., Ste. 340
Charlotte, NC 28202   Ph: (704)372-8731

★1346★
Central Carolina Black Nurses Council
Lorna Harris-School of Nursing
Carrington Hall CB7460
University of N. Carolina at Chapel Hill
Chapel Hill, NC 27599   Ph: (919)966-3648

★1347★
Charlotte Area Association of Black Journalists
PO Box 32574
Charlotte, NC 28232   Ph: (704)289-6576
Cliff Harrington, Pres.

★1348★
Charlotte Meckleburg Urban League
A.M.E. Zion Bldg.
401 E. Second St.
Charlotte, NC 28202   Ph: (704)376-9834
Madine Hester Fails, Pres.

★1349★
Charlotte Minority Business Development Center
700 E. Stonewall St., Ste. 360
Charlotte, NC 28202   Ph: (704)334-7522

★1350★
Durham Business and Professional Chain
PO Box 1088
Durham, NC 27702   Ph: (919)683-1047
Wallace O. Green, Pres.

★1351★
Fayetteville Business and Professional League
PO Box 1387
Fayettville, NC 28302   Ph: (919)483-6252
David C. Brown, Pres.

★1352★
Fayetteville Business League
Fayetteville, NC 28301   Ph: (919)483-6252
David C. Brown, Pres.

★1353★
Fayetteville Minority Business Development Center
114-1/2 Anderson St.
Fayetteville, NC 28302   Ph: (919)483-7513

★1354★
National Association for Sickle Cell Disease
Charlotte Chapter
Independence Bldg
700 E. Stonewall, Ste.320
Charlotte, NC 28208   Ph: (704)332-4184

★1355★
National Black Child Development Institute
Charlotte Affiliate
5822 Rimerton Dr.
Charlotte, NC 28226   Ph: (704)542-0764
Dr. Arthur Griffin, Contact

★1356★
National Black Child Development Institute
Durham Affiliate
1118 Hunstman Dr.
Durham, NC 27713   Ph: (919)544-1050
Nellie F. Riley, Contact

★1357★
National Black Child Development Institute
Greensboro Affiliate
1411 Wayside Dr.
Greensboro, NC 27405   Ph: (919)375-3151
Claudette Burroughs-White, Contact

★1358★
National Black Child Development Institute
High Point Affiliate
1807 Briarcliff Ct.
High Point, NC 27260   Ph: (919)882-2620
Linda Hanes, Contact

★1359★
National Black Child Development Institute
Raleigh (Triangle Area) Affiliate
902 Creech Rd.
Garner, NC
Donald Harris, Contact

★1360★
National Black MBA Association
Raleigh/Durham Chapter
PO Box 728
Durham, NC 27702   Ph: (919)682-9690
Paula Stewart, Contact

★1361★
North Carolina Association of Black Lawyers
c/o Kaye R. Webb
1200 Murchison Rd.
New Bold Station
Lafayetteville, NC 28301-4298   Ph: (919)486-1142
Kaye R. Webb, Pres.
Affiliated with: National Bar Association.

★1362★
Oxford Business and Professional Chain
PO Box 1553
Oxford, NC 27565   Ph: (919)693-8874
Marshall Cooper, Pres.

★1363★
Progressive Firefighters Association of Charlotte
PO Box 16619
Charlotte, NC 28297

★1364★
Raleigh/Durham Minority Business Development Center
817 New Bern Ave., Ste. 8
Raleigh, NC 27601   Ph: (919)833-6122

★1365★
Southern Regional Council on Black American Affairs
c/o Dr. David L. Hunter
Central Piedmont Community College
PO Box 35009
Charlotte, NC 28235   Ph: (704)342-6491
Dr. David Hunter, Pres.

★1366★
United Negro College Fund
Winston-Salem Office
310 W. 4th St., Ste. 630
Winston-Salem, NC 27101   Ph: (919)748-0010
Territory Includes: All of NC.

★1367★
Winston-Salem Urban League
201 W. Fifth St.
Winston-Salem, NC 27101   Ph: (919)725-5614
Delores Smith, CEO

───────── **Ohio** ─────────

★1368★
Afro-American Patrolman's League
1001 Indiana
Toledo, OH 43607
Marlon Shockley, Pres.

★1369★
Akron Association of Black School Educators
BOE 70 N. Broadway
Akron, OH 44308
Johnnette Curry, Pres.

★1370★
Akron Barristers Club
75 E. Market St.
Akron, OH 44308   Ph: (419)867-9028
Orlando Williams, Pres.

★1371★
Akron Community Service Center and Urban League
250 E. Market St.
Akron, OH 44308   Ph: (216)434-3101
Vernon L. Odom, Exec.Dir.

★1372★
American Association of Blacks in Energy
Cleveland Chapter
c/o Elizabeth J Shaw
Centerior Energy Corp.
PO Box 94661
Cleveland, OH 44101-4661   Ph: (216)447-2823
Elizabeth J. Shaw, Pres.

★1373★
American Association of Blacks in Energy
Dayton Chapter
c/o James R. Greene III
Dayton Power and Light Co.
PO Box 8825
Dayton, OH 45401   Ph: (513)259-7114
James R. Greene III, Pres.

★1374★
American Civil Liberties Union
Ohio Affiliate
1223 W. 6th St., 2nd Fl.
Cleveland, OH 44113   Ph: (216)781-6276
Christine Link, Pres.

★1375★
Association for the Study of Afro-American Life and History
Cleveland Branch
3144 Albion Rd.
Shaker Heights, OH 44120   Ph: (216)921-2530
Gail Rose, Pres.

★1376★
Association for the Study of Afro-American Life and History
Columbus Branch
1058 1/2 Fair Ave.
Columbus, OH 43205   Ph: (614)252-4563
Floyd Goode, Pres.

★1377★
Association for the Study of Afro-American Life and History
Dayton Branch
1312 Princeton Dr.
Dayton, OH 45406   Ph: (513)274-8362
Margaret E. Peters, Pres.

★1378★
Association for the Study of Afro-American Life and History
Springfield Branch
424 Willow Dr.
Springfield, OH 45505-2521   Ph: (513)325-4040
Charles Beard, Pres.

★1379★
Association for the Study of Afro-American Life and History
Toledo Branch
c/o the Black Historical Society
1104 Mackow Dr.
Toledo, OH 43607   Ph: (419)531-3759
B. Jeanne Palmer, Treas.

★1380★
Association for the Study of Afro-American Life and History
Tri-County Branch
PO Box 382
Wilberforce, OH 45384   Ph: (513)427-1680
Dr. Joseph Lewis, Pres.

★1381★
Association of Black Psychologists
Central Ohio Chapter
PO Box 8451
Columbus, OH 43201   Ph: (614)292-5766
Dr. Dennis Alexander, Pres.

★1382★
Association of Black Psychologists
Cleveland Chapter
20310 Chagrin Blvd.
Shaker Heights, OH 44122   Ph: (216)491-9405
Dr. Willie Williams, Pres.

★1383★
Association of Black Psychologists
Dayton Chapter
4830 Old Hickory Pl.
Dayton, OH 46226   Ph: (513)837-3961
Dr. Michael Williams, Pres.

★1384★
B-FORCE of Cleveland
PO Box 12729
East Cleveland, OH 44112

★1385★
Bank One
2626 Travis Rd., No. L
Columbus, OH 43209   Ph: (614)248-6488
Lloyd J. McClendon, Pres.

★1386★
Black Economic Union of Ohio
10510 Park Lane Dr.
Cleveland, OH 44106   Ph: (216)231-0080

★1387★
Black Elected Democrats of Ohio
37 W. Broad St., Ste. 430
Columbus, OH 43215   Ph: (614)341-6912
Ray Miller, Pres.

★1388★
Black Focus on the Westside
4115 Bridge Ave.
Cleveland, OH 44113   Ph: (216)631-7660
Willie L. Griffin, Exec.Dir.

★1389★
Black Knights Police Association
PO Box 2052
Youngstown, OH 44506   Ph: (216)743-9100
Louis Averhart, Chairman
Affiliated with: National Black Police Association.

★1390★
Black Law Enforcement Officers Association of Akron
PO Box 66
Akron, OH 44308
Douglas Prade, Pres.
Affiliated with: National Black Police Association.

★1391★
Black Lawyers Association of Cincinnati
230 E. 9th St., Ste. 200
Cincinnati, OH 45202   Ph: (513)352-4663
Ernest F. McAdams, Pres.
Affiliated with: National Bar Association.

★1392★
Black Shield Police Association
4087 E. 131st St.
Cleveland, OH 44105
Andre Haynesworth, Pres.
Affiliated with: National Black Police Association.

★1393★
Canton Black United Fund
1341 Market Ave. N.
Canton, OH 44714-2605
William Dent, Pres.

★1394★
Canton Urban League
Community Center
1400 Sherrick Rd. SE
Canton, OH 44707-3533   Ph: (216)456-3479
Joseph N. Smith, Exec.Dir.

★1395★
Cincinnati African-American Fire Fighters
PO Box 29441
Cincinnati, OH 45229

★1396★
Cincinnati Minority Business Development Center
1821 Summit Rd, Ste. 111
Cincinnati, OH 45237-2810   Ph: (513)679-6000

★1397★
Cleveland Association of Black Journalists
PO Box 5028
Cleveland, OH 44101
Eric D. Stringfellow, Pres.

★1398★
Cleveland Business League
2330 E. 79th St.
PO Box 99556
Cleveland, OH 44199
R. Turner-Hickson, Pres.
Affiliated with: National Business League.

★1399★
Cleveland Council Black Nurses, Inc.
c/o Murtis Taylor Multi-Services Center
13422 Kinsman Rd., #250
Cleveland, OH 13422
Jane Gray, Pres.

★1400★
Cleveland Heights Association of Black School
  Educators
PO Box 18134
Cleveland Hts., OH 44118
Margaret Peacock, Pres.

★1401★
Cleveland Minority Business Development Center No.
  1
601 Lakeside, Ste. 335
Cleveland, OH 44114   Ph: (216)664-4150

★1402★
Columbus Urban League
700 Bryden Rd., Ste. 230
Columbus, OH 43215   Ph: (614)221-0544
Samuel Gresham Jr., Pres.

★1403★
Council for Economic Opportunities in Greater
　Cleveland
668 Euclid Ave.
Cleveland, OH 44114　　　　　　　　Ph: (216)696-9077

★1404★
Dayton Association of Black Professional Fire Fighters
　Paramedics
141 Bank St.
Dayton, OH 45406

★1405★
Dayton Urban League
United Way Bldg., Rm. 200
184 Salem Ave.
Dayton, OH 45406　　　　　　　　　Ph: (513)220-6666
Willie F. Walker, Pres.

★1406★
East Cleveland Black Police Officers Association
PO Box 12429
East Cleveland, OH 44112　　　　　Ph: (216)382-5672
Patricia A. Lane, Pres.
Affiliated with: National Black Police Association.

★1407★
Ebony Police Association of Stark County
377 Hamilton, NE
Canton, OH 44704
John C. Ball, Pres.
Affiliated with: National Black Police Association.

★1408★
Franklin County Association of Black School
　Educators
1850 Bryden Rd.
Columbus, OH 43205
Linda L. Gibson-Tyson, Pres.

★1409★
George A. Martin Gerontology Center
3603 Washington
Cincinnati, OH 45229　　　　　　　Ph: (513)961-0144
John Rogers, Exec.Dir.

★1410★
Greater Cincinnati Association of Black School
　Educators
2133 Crave Ave.
Cincinnati, OH 43205
Dr. Obadiah Williams, Pres.

★1411★
Greater Cleveland Minority Police Officers Association
1869 E. 86th St.
Cleveland, OH 44106
Cheryl M. Tell, Pres.

★1412★
Hamilton County Association for Minority Law
　Enforcement Officers
5355 Tompkins Ave., Apt. No. E-11
Cincinnati, OH 45227
Rudolph Stafford, Pres.

★1413★
Harambee Services to Black Families
1468 E. 55th St.
Cleveland, OH 44103　　　　　　　Ph: (216)391-7044
Iona Willis Hancock, Exec.Dir.

★1414★
Lorain County Association of Black School Educators
PO Box 745
Lorain, OH 44053
Deroy Gorham, Pres.

★1415★
Lorain County Minority Law Enforcement Association
PO Box 1096
Lorain, OH 44052-0096
David Wrice, Pres.
Affiliated with: National Black Police Association.

★1416★
Lorain County Urban League
401 Broad St., Ste. 204-206
Elyria, OH 44035　　　　　　　　　Ph: (216)323-3364
Delbert L. Lancaster, Pres.

★1417★
Massillon Urban League
325 3rd SE
Massillon, OH 44647　　　　　　　Ph: (216)833-2804

★1418★
Metro Cleveland Association of Black School
　Educators
PO Box 1083
Shaker Heights, OH 44120
Dr. Shirley S. Seaton, Pres.

★1419★
Minority Association of Cuyahoga County Corrections
3269 Berkshire Rd.
Cleveland Heights, OH 44118
Varno Harris, Pres.

★1420★
Minority Contracts Assistance Program
20475 Farnsleigh
Shaker Heights, OH 44120　　　　Ph: (216)283-4700
Dr. Michelle Spain, Dir.

★1421★
National Association of Minority Contractors
Dayton Chapter
1705 Guenther Rd.
Dayton, OH 45427　　　　　　　　Ph: (513)854-0281
Warren Wise, Pres.

★1422★
National Association of Minority Contractors
Northern and Central Ohio Chapter
65 E. State St., Ste. 1000
Columbus, OH 43215　　　　　　　Ph: (614)460-3673
Kevin Williams, Pres.

★1423★
National Association of Minority Contractors
Southern Ohio Chapter
1939 Avonlea Ave.
Cincinnati, OH 45237　　　　　　　Ph: (513)351-2114
Sam Moore, Pres.

★1424★
National Black Child Development Institute
Akron Affiliate
1310 Superior Ave.
Akron, OH 44307   Ph: (216)836-8009
Mamie Gardner, Contact

★1425★
National Black Child Development Institute
Cleveland Affiliate
14748 Rider Rd.
Cleveland, OH 44021   Ph: (216)834-4581
Dorothy Cheeks, Contact

★1426★
National Black Child Development Institute
Lorain Affiliate
PO Box 157
Lorain, OH 44052   Ph: (216)246-6359
Sylvia Duvall, Contact

★1427★
National Black Independent Political Party
436 Almeda Ave.
Youngstown, OH 44505   Ph: (216)746-5747
Ron Daniels, Chairperson

★1428★
National Black MBA Association
Cincinnati Chapter
PO Box 3391
Cincinnati, OH 45201   Ph: (513)723-3448
Earl M. Pinkett III, Contact

★1429★
National Black MBA Association
Cleveland Chapter
PO Box 22839
Beachwood, OH 44122
Donald Graham, Contact

★1430★
National Black MBA Association
Dayton Chapter
PO Box 5697
Dayton, OH 45405
Jackie Thornton, Contact

★1431★
National Business League
Dayton Chapter
323 Salem Ave., Ste. 3F
Dayton, OH 45406   Ph: (513)443-4369
Bill Littlejohn Esq., Pres.

★1432★
National Business League
Stark County Chapter
2442 14th St., NE
Canton, OH 44705   Ph: (216)454-8081
Norma Mills, Pres.

★1433★
National Caucus on Black Aged/Senior Employment
   Program
Cleveland Branch
12025 Shaker Blvd., Ste. 208
Cleveland, OH 44120   Ph: (216)721-9197

★1434★
Norman S. Minor Bar Association
8250 Wooster
Cincinnati, OH 45227
Clarence Keller, Pres.
Affiliated with: National Bar Association.

★1435★
Ohio Association of Black School Educators
1114 Gonder SE
Canton, OH 44707
Stephanie Patrick, Pres.

★1436★
Operation PUSH
Akron Network
Tabernacle Baptist Church
795 Russell Ave.
Akron, OH 44307   Ph: (216)762-8810
Rev. Isiah Paul, Contact

★1437★
Operation PUSH
Cincinnati Chapter
5457 Ehrling Rd.
Cincinnati, OH 45227   Ph: (513)272-3631
Barbara Favors, Sec.

★1438★
Operation PUSH
Cleveland Chapter
8712 Quincy Ave.
Cleveland, OH 44106   Ph: (216)721-3585
Rev. Otis Moss, Pres.

★1439★
Operation PUSH
Columbus Chapter
64 S. Highland Ave.
Columbus, OH 43223   Ph: (614)279-3307
Rev. Andy Lewter, Contact

★1440★
Operation PUSH
Shaker Heights Chapter
3646 Rollister Rd.
Shaker Heights, OH 44120   Ph: (216)921-0245
Alfred Warren, Pres.

★1441★
Operation PUSH
Springfield Network
1119 W. Liberty
Springfield, OH 45506
Craig Williams

★1442★
Operation PUSH
Wilberforce Chapter
Central State University
204 Administration Bldg.
Wilberforce, OH 45384   Ph: (513)376-6332
Dr. Arthur Thomas, Pres.

★1443★
Phillis Wheatley Association
4450 Cedar Ave.
Cleveland, OH 44103   Ph: (216)391-4443
Ela H. Becktor, Exec.Dir.

★1444★
Police Officers for Equal Rights
2445 Mason Village Ct.
Columbus, OH 43227   Ph: (614)253-4005
James E. Moss, Pres.

★1445★
Robert B. Elliot Law Club
c/o Attorney General's Office
65 E. State, No. 708
Columbus, OH 43215   Ph: (614)466-6696
Robert Solomon, Asst. Attorney General
Affiliated with: National Bar Association.

★1446★
Sentinel Police Association
3499 Burnette Ave.
Cincinnati, OH 45217   Ph: (513)751-3522
Cheryl Thomas
Founded: 1968. **Members:** 135. **Publications:** Sentinel News, monthly. Newsletter.

★1447★
Springfield Area Association of Black School Educators
1119 W. Liberty Ave.
Springfield, OH 45506
Craig L. Williams, Pres.

★1448★
Springfield Urban League
521 S. Center St.
Springfield, OH 45506   Ph: (513)323-4603
Donna Brino Ph.D., CEO

★1449★
Stonewall Cincinnati Human Rights Organization
Box 954
Cincinnati, OH 45201   Ph: (513)541-8778
Betsy Gressler, Pres.
Founded: 1981. **Members:** 800. **Budget:** $75,000. **Publications:** Stonewall Newsletter, monthly.

★1450★
Thurgood Marshall Law Association
5806 Staghorn Dr.
Toledo, OH 43614
Richard Mitchell, Pres.

★1451★
Thurgood Marshall Law Society
City Hall Municipal Ct.
Dayton, OH 45402
Hon. Alice McCollum, Pres.

★1452★
Unitarian Universalist Association Black Concerns Working Group
Ohio-Meadville Chapter
760 E. Broad St.
Columbus, OH 43205   Ph: (614)224-6688
Rev. Carol Brody, Consultant

★1453★
United Black Fire Fighters of Akron
1020 Winton St.
Akron, OH 44320

★1454★
United Negro College Fund
Cleveland Office
25 W. Prospect Ave., Ste. 705
Cleveland, OH 44115   Ph: (216)781-8623
Territory Includes: Cleveland, Akron, Toledo, OH; All of WV.

★1455★
United Negro College Fund
Columbus Office
50 W. Broad St., Ste. 1308
Columbus, OH 43215   Ph: (614)221-5309
Territory Includes: Columbus, Dayton, Cincinnati, OH; All of KY; SD.

★1456★
Urban League of Greater Cincinnati
2400 Reading Rd., Ste. 407
Cincinnati, OH 45202   Ph: (513)721-2237
Sheila J. Wilson, Exec.Dir.

★1457★
Urban League of Greater Cleveland
1255 Euclid Ave., Ste. 205
Cleveland, OH 44115   Ph: (216)622-0999
Myron Robinson, President/CEO

★1458★
Urban Minority Alcohol Drug Abuse Outreach Program
3807 W. 3rd St.
Dayton, OH 45417   Ph: (513)268-7780
Debra Styles, Exec. Dir.

★1459★
Urban Minority Alcoholism Outreach
2491 E. 59th St.
Cleveland, OH 44104   Ph: (216)881-5533

★1460★
Vanguards of Cleveland
PO Box 1802
Cleveland, OH 44106

★1461★
Warren-Trumbull Urban League
290 W. Market St.
Warren, OH 44481   Ph: (216)394-4316
Marion V. Perkins, Pres.

★1462★
Youngstown Area Urban League
123 E. Rayen
Youngstown, OH 44503   Ph: (216)744-4111
William Ronald Miller, CEO

─────────── Oklahoma ───────────

★1463★
American Civil Liberties Union
Oklahoma Affiliate
1411 Classen, Ste. 318
Oklahoma City, OK 73106   Ph: (405)524-8511
Joann Bell, Pres.

★1464★
Federation of Colored Women's Clubs
Tulsa Chapter
c/o Fannie Bryant
1612 N. Boston
Tulsa, OK 74106   Ph: (918)584-1546
Fannie Bryant, Sec.

★1465★
Greenwood Chamber of Commerce
130 N Greenwood Ave.
Tulsa, OK 74120   Ph: (918)585-2084
Alvarez Allen, Pres.

★1466★
Metropolitan Tulsa Urban League
240 E. Apache St.
Tulsa, OK 74106   Ph: (918)584-0001
Rev. Laverne Hill, Exec.Dir.

★1467★
National Business League
Oklahoma City Chapter
PO Box 11221
Oklahoma City, OK 73136   Ph: (405)843-6400
Anita Arnold, Pres.

★1468★
Northeast Oklahoma Black Lawyers Association
100 Center Plaza, No. 809
Tulsa, OK 74119-1047   Ph: (918)585-3216
Hannibal B. Johnson, Pres.
Affiliated with: National Bar Association.

★1469★
Oklahoma City Metro Area Black Officers Association
PO Box 1674
Oklahoma City, OK 73101-1674
J.W. Martin, Pres.
Affiliated with: National Black Police Association.

★1470★
Oklahoma City Metropolitan Association of Black
  School Educators
3468 Parker Dr.
Del City, OK 73135
Jesse Thompson, Pres.

★1471★
Oklahoma Natural Gas Company
PO Box 871
Tulsa, OK 74102   Ph: (918)588-7365
Elmer Kamphaus, Pres.

★1472★
Operation PUSH
Oklahoma City Network
Jesus Church
2201 NE 15th St.
Oklahoma City, OK 73136   Ph: (405)424-3590
Rev. Clarence E. Davis

★1473★
Tulsa Area Association of Black School Educators
1164 N. Union Pl.
Tulsa, OK 74127   Ph: (918)425-5505
Fred Latimer, Pres.

★1474★
Tulsa Black Officers Coalition
PO Box 1765
Tulsa, OK 74103

★1475★
Tulsa Minority Business Development Center
240 E. Apache St.
Tulsa, OK 74106-3799   Ph: (918)592-1995

★1476★
Urban League of Greater Oklahoma City
3017 Martin Luther King Ave.
Oklahoma City, OK 73111   Ph: (405)424-5243
Leonard D. Benton, Pres.

——————————— **Oregon** ———————————

★1477★
American Association for Affirmative Action
Region X
c/o Stephanie Sanford
Oregon State Univ.
Corvallis, OR 97331   Ph: (503)737-3556
Stephanie Sanford, Dir.

★1478★
American Civil Liberties Union
Oregon Affiliate
705 Board of Trade Bldg.
310 SW 4th Ave.
Portland, OR 73106   Ph: (503)227-3186
Ms. Stevie Remington, Pres.

★1479★
Black United Fund of Oregon
PO Box 12406
Portland, OR 97212   Ph: (503)282-7973
Amina A. Anderson, Exec.Dir.
Affiliated with: National Black United Fund, Inc.

★1480★
National Association of Minority Contractors
Oregon Chapter
PO Box 11233
Portland, OR 97211   Ph: (503)260-9000
Bruce Broussard, Pres.

★1481★
National Business League
Oregon Chapter
6431 Martin Luther King, Jr. Blvd.
Portland, OR 97211   Ph: (503)240-0708
Chad Debnam, Pres.

★1482★
Oregon Association of Black School Educators
PO Box 6067
Portland, OR 97228-6067
Michael L. Grice, Pres.

★1483★
Portland Black Firefighters Association
5630 NE Church St.
Portland, OR 97218

★1484★
Urban League of Portland
Urban Plaza
10 N. Russell
Portland, OR 97227   Ph: (503)280-2600
Dr. Darryl Tukufu, Pres./CEO

─────────── Pennsylvania ───────────

★1485★
Afro-American Automobile Association
5125 Walnut St.
Philadelphia, PA 19139   Ph: (215)472-4250

★1486★
American Association of Blacks in Energy
Philadelphia Chapter
c/o James Banko'le
Philadelphia Electric Co.
2301 Market St., 58-2
Philadelphia, PA 19146   Ph: (215)841-5675
James Banko'le, Pres.

★1487★
American Association of Blacks in Energy
Pittsburgh Chapter
c/o Sylvia Fields
Duquesne Light Co.
1 Oxford Center
301 Grant St.
Pittsburg, PA 15279   Ph: (412)393-6065
Sylvia Fields, Contact

★1488★
American Civil Liberties Union
Pennsylvania Affiliate
PO Box 1161
Philadelphia, PA 19105   Ph: (215)923-4357
Deborah Leavy, Pres.

★1489★
American Civil Liberties Union
Pennsylvania Affiliate
Pittsburgh Chapter
237 Oakland Ave.
Pittsburgh, PA 15213   Ph: (412)681-7736
Marion Demick, Pres.

★1490★
Association for the Study of Afro-American Life and
History
Philadelphia Branch
5403 Angora Terrace
Philadelphia, PA 19143   Ph: (215)748-6164
Othella R. Vaughn, Pres.

★1491★
Barristers Association of Philadelphia
4914 Chancellor St.
Philadelphia, PA 19139   Ph: (215)747-4254
Renee Cardwell Hughes, Pres.
Affiliated with: National Bar Association.

★1492★
Black Clergy of Philadelphia and Vicinity
5238 Chestnut
Philadelphia, PA 19139   Ph: (215)476-9111

★1493★
Black Family Services
115 S. 46th St.
Philadelphia, PA 19138   Ph: (215)662-0533

★1494★
Black United Fund of Pennsylvania
419 S. 15th St.
Philadelphia, PA 19146   Ph: (215)732-9266
Linda Richardson, Pres.
Affiliated with: National Black United Fund, Inc.

★1495★
Business and Professional Association of Pittsburgh
4909 Pennsylvania Ave.   Ph: (412)362-5702
Pittsburgh, PA 15224   Fax: (412)362-9288
Lewis Goodman, Pres.

★1496★
Delaware Valley Association of Black School
Educators
5425 Wynnefield Ave.
Philadelphia, PA 19131-1323
Dr. Edna McCrae, Pres.

★1497★
Fire Power
704 Ward St.
Chester, PA 19013

★1498★
Fund for an Open Society
Social Services Bldg.
311 S. Juniper St., Ste. 400
Philadelphia, PA 19107   Ph: (215)735-6915

★1499★
Garden State Association of Black Journalists
800 Trenton Rd., #95
Longhorne, PA 19047   Ph: (215)741-4673
Pamela E. Judge, Pres.

★1500★
Greater Pittsburgh Association of Black School
Educators
6393 Penn Ave., No. 128
Pittsburgh, PA 15206
Dr. Janet Bell, Pres.

★1501★
Guardian Civic League
1516 W. Girard Ave.
Philadelphia, PA 19130   Ph: (215)763-0490
Ron Oliver, Pres.

★1502★
Guardians of Greater Pittsburgh
PO Box 681
Pittsburgh, PA 15230
Donald G. Page, Pres.

★1503★
Homer S. Brown Law Association
c/o Horace Payne
People's National Gas Co.
625 Liberty Ave.
Pittsburgh, PA 15222   Ph: (412)497-6633
Horace Payne, Pres.
Affiliated with: National Bar Association.

★1504★
Minority Arts Resource Council
1421 W. Girard Ave.
Philadelphia, PA 19130   Ph: (215)236-2688

★1505★
National Bar Association
Erie Chapter
925 French St., Ste. 3
Erie, PA 16501   Ph: (814)454-2139
Melvin T. Toran, Pres.

★1506★
National Black Child Development Institute
Pittsburgh Affiliate
201 Bellefield Ave.
Pittsburgh, PA 15213   Ph: (412)371-1461
Dr. Joan Clark, Contact

★1507★
National Black MBA Association
Philadelphia Chapter
PO Box 1384
Philadelphia, PA 19105   Ph: (215)472-2622
Charlotte Mckines, Contact

★1508★
National Black MBA Association
Pittsburgh Chapter
PO Box 3502
Pittsburgh, PA 15230   Ph: (412)341-7452
Kerry Nelson, Contact

★1509★
Negro Trade Union Leadership Council
929 N. Broad St.
Philadelphia, PA 19123   Ph: (215)787-3600

★1510★
New-Penn-Del Minority Business Resource Council
Monroe Office Center, Ste. 210
1 Winding Dr.
Philadelphia, PA 19131   Ph: (215)578-0964
Thornton Carroll Jr., Pres.
Founded: 1970. **Members:** 1000. **Telecommunications Services:** Fax, (215)878-2832. **Publications:** Listing of Corporate Members and Representatives, periodic.

★1511★
Operation PUSH
Philadelphia Chapter
1204 Paper Mill Rd.
Philadelphia, PA 19118   Ph: (215)424-7855
Ima Jean Anderson, Contact

★1512★
Philadelphia Association of Black Journalists
c/o Vanessa Williams
The Philadelphia Inquirer
Philadelphia, PA 19131   Ph: (215)854-2786
Vanessa Williams, Pres.

★1513★
Philadelphia Black Media Corporation
Temple University
12th & Berks St., Ste. 308
Philadelphia, PA 19122   Ph: (215)204-4322
Molefi Asante, Contact

★1514★
Philadelphia Black Womens Health Project
1231 N. Broad, Rm. 101
Philadelphia, PA 19122   Ph: (215)232-1115

★1515★
Philadelphia Federation of Black Business and
** Professional Organizations**
9200 Bustleton Ave.
2112 Lloyd Bldg.
Philadelphia, PA 19115
Barbara C. Merriweather, Pres.
Founded: 1978. **Members:** 23. **Publications:** Newsletter, quarterly.

★1516★
Philadelphia Minority Business Development Center
125 N. 8th St., 4th Fl.
Philadelphia, PA 19106   Ph: (215)629-9841

★1517★
Philadelphia Urban Coalition
121 N. Broad St., Ste. 618
Philadelphia, PA 19107   Ph: (215)977-2800

★1518★
Pittsburgh Minority Business Development Center
9 Pkwy. Center, Ste. 250
Pittsburgh, PA 15220   Ph: (412)921-1155

★1519★
Pittsburgh Regional Minority Purchasing Council
1 Oliver Plaza, Ste. 3004
Pittsburgh, PA 15222   Ph: (412)391-4423

★1520★
Squirrel Hill Urban Coalition
5604 Solway
Pittsburgh, PA 15217   Ph: (412)422-7666

★1521★
United Negro College Fund
Philadelphia Office
1650 Arch St., Ste. 2770
Philadelphia, PA 19103   Ph: (215)568-4240
Territory Includes: Philadelphia, Harrisburg, and Wilkes-Barre, PA; DE.

★1522★
Urban League of Lancaster County
502 S. Duke St.
Lancaster, PA 17602   Ph: (717)394-1966
Keith Bookert, Pres.

★1523★
Urban League of Metropolitan Harrisburg
25 N. Front St.
Harrisburg, PA 17101   Ph: (717)234-5925
Kinneth W. Washington, Pres.

★1524★
Urban League of Philadelphia
4601 Market St., Ste. 2 South
Philadelphia, PA 19139   Ph: (215)476-4040
Robert W. Sorrell, Pres.

★1525★
Urban League of Pittsburgh
1 Smithville, 3rd Fl.
Pittsburgh, PA 15222   Ph: (412)261-1130
Leon L. Haley Ph.D., Pres.

★1526★
Urban League of Shenango Valley
39 Chestnut St.
Sharon, PA 16146   Ph: (412)981-5310
Phillip E. Smith, Pres.

★1527★
Valiants of Philadelphia
3021 N. 35th St.
Philadelphia, PA 19132   Ph: (215)424-9974

───────── **Puerto Rico** ─────────

★1528★
Mayaguez Minority Business Development Center
70 W. Mendez Bigo
Mayaguez, PR 00708   Ph: (809)833-7783
Yolanda Velez, President

★1529★
Ponce Minority Business Development Center
19 Salud St.
Ponce, PR 00731   Ph: (809)840-8100

★1530★
San Juan Minority Business Development Center
122 Eleanor Roosevelt
Hato Rey, PR 00918   Ph: (809)753-8484

───────── **Rhode Island** ─────────

★1531★
American Civil Liberties Union
Rhode Island Affiliate
212 Union St., Rm. 211
Providence, RI 02903   Ph: (401)831-7171
Steve Brown, Pres.

★1532★
Newport Martin Luther King Center
20 W. Broadway
Newport, RI 02840   Ph: (401)846-4828
Marcia G. Farrar, Exec.Dir.

★1533★
Rhode Island Black Media Coalition
131 Washington St.
Providence, RI 02903
Norman Lincoln, Contact

★1534★
Rhode Island Minority Police Association
950 Eddy St.
Providence, RI 02905   Ph: (401)946-0696
Joseph Almeida, Pres.

★1535★
Urban League of Rhode Island
246 Prairie Ave.
Providence, RI 02905   Ph: (401)351-5000
B. Jae Clanton, Exec. Director

───────── **South Carolina** ─────────

★1536★
American Association of Blacks in Energy
South Carolina Chapter
c/o Vera Steplight Goodson
S. Carolina Electric and Gas
Columbia, SC 29218   Ph: (803)748-3868
Vera Steplight Goodson, Pres.

★1537★
American Civil Liberties Union
South Carolina Affiliate
Middleburg Plaza, Ste. 104
2712 Middleburg Dr.
Columbia, SC 29204   Ph: (803)799-5151
Steven Bates, Contact

★1538★
Association for the Study of Afro-American Life and
   History
Orangeburg Branch
781 Whitman St. SE
Orangeburg, SC 29116   Ph: (803)533-1049
Sarah M. Washington, Pres.

★1539★
Columbia Minority Business Development Center
2711 Middleburg Dr., Ste. 114
Columbia, SC 29204   Ph: (803)256-0528

★1540★
Columbia Urban League
1400 Barnwell St.
PO Drawer J
Columbia, SC 29250   Ph: (803)799-8150
James T. McLawhorn Jr., Pres.

★1541★
Greenville/Spartanburg Minority Business Development
   Center
300 University Ridge, Ste. 200
Greenville, SC 29601   Ph: (803)271-8753

★1542★
Greenville Urban League
15 Regency Hill Dr.
PO Box 10161
Greenville, SC 29603   Ph: (803)244-3862
Myron F. Robinson, Pres.

★1543★
Operation PUSH
Charleston Branch
222 Calhoun St.
Charleston, SC 29401   Ph: (803)722-3470
Rev. Frank Portee III, Chairman

★1544★
Operation PUSH
Marion County Network
Rt. 1, Box 410
Marion, SC 29571   Ph: (803)423-6874
Rev. Joseph Abram Jr., Pres.

★1545★
Palmetto State Law Enforcement Officers
PO Box 515
Summerville, SC 29484   Ph: (803)851-0781
Willie L. Johnson, Pres.

★1546★
Pendleton Foundation for Black History and Culture
PO Box 122
Pendleton, SC 29670   Ph: (803)646-3792
Annie Ruth Morse, Pres.
Founded: 1976. **Members:** 20.

★1547★
South Carolina Association of Black School Educators
103 Bowling Ave.
Columbia, SC 29203
Lemuel C. Stevens, Pres.

★1548★
South Carolina Black Lawyers Association
PO Box 8417
Columbia, SC 29202
Jeremiah Brown, Pres.
Affiliated with: National Bar Association.

─────────── **Tennessee** ───────────

★1549★
Afro-American Police Association
5348 Cosmos Cove
Memphis, TN 38118   Ph: (901)774-5404
Pauline Johnson, Pres.
Affiliated with: National Black Police Association.

★1550★
American Civil Liberties Union
Tennessee Affiliate
PO Box 120160
Nashville, TN 37212   Ph: (615)320-7142
Hedy Weinberg, Pres.

★1551★
Association for the Study of Afro-American Life and
   History
Rosa McGhee/F.A. Dixon Branch
3031 Wilcox Blvd.
Chattanooga, TN 37411   Ph: (615)266-3424
Rev. J. Lloyd Edwards Jr., Pres.

★1552★
Black Business Association
555 Beale St.
Memphis, TN 38103   Ph: (901)527-2222

★1553★
Brothers United of Chattanooga
3864 Mark Twain Circle
Chattanooga, TN 37406

★1554★
Chattanooga Area Urban League
730 Martin Luther King Blvd.
PO Box 11106
Chattanooga, TN 37401   Ph: (615)756-1762
Jerome W. Page, Pres.

★1555★
Clarksville Peace Officers Association
4 Chalemagne Blvd.
Clarksville, TN 37040
George F. Elliott, Pres.

★1556★
Knoxville Area Urban League
2416 Magnolia Ave.
PO Box 1911
Knoxville, TN 37917   Ph: (615)524-5511
Gloria Garner, Interim President

★1557★
Memphis Association of Black School Educators
1844 Kingsview Dr.
Memphis, TN 38114
Dr. James O. Catchings, Pres.

★1558★
Memphis Bar Association
1 Commerce Sq., Ste. 1190
Memphis, TN 38103   Ph: (901)527-3573
Anne Fritze, Director

★1559★
Memphis Black Media Coalition
4796 Coventry Mall
Memphis, TN 38118
Gwen Sneed, Pres.

★1560★
Memphis Minority Business Development Center
5 N. 3rd St., Ste. 2020
Memphis, TN 38103   Ph: (901)527-2298
Gary Rowe, Director

★1561★
Memphis Urban League
2279 Lamar Ave.
Memphis, TN 38114   Ph: (901)327-3591
Herman C. Ewing, Pres.

★1562★
Nashville Bar Association
221 4th Ave. N., Ste. 400
Nashville, TN 37219-2100   Ph: (615)242-9272
Allen Ramsaur, Exec. Dir.

★1563★
Nashville Minority Business Development Center
14 Academy Pl., Ste. 2
Nashville, TN 37210   Ph: (615)255-0432
Marilyn Robinson, Proj. Dir.

★1564★
Nashville Peace Officers Association
PO Box 100109
Nashville, TN 37224
Luther J. Hunter Jr., Pres.
Affiliated with: National Black Police Association.

★1565★
Nashville Urban League
1219 9th Ave.
Nashville, TN 37208   Ph: (615)254-0525
John L. Fair, Pres.

★1566★
National Bar Association
Ben F. Jones Chapter
60 N. Mid-America Mall, Ste. 200
Memphis, TN 38103
Samuel Perkins, Pres.

★1567★
National Bar Association
Napier - Looby Chapter
District Attorney's Office
102 Metro Courthouse
Nashville, TN 38103   Ph: (615)862-5500
Victor Johnson, Pres.

★1568★
National Business League
Mid-South Chapter
918 S. Pkwy., E.
Memphis, TN 38106
M. La Troy Williams, Pres.

★1569★
Operation PUSH
Chattanooga Chapter
PO Box 6221
Chattanooga, TN 37404   Ph: (615)624-6822
Johnny Holloway, Exec.Dir.

★1570★
Operation PUSH
Memphis Chapter
Monumental Baptist Church
704 S. Pkwy., E.
Memphis, TN 38106   Ph: (901)946-2529
Rev. Samuel B. Kyles, Pres.

★1571★
Operation PUSH
Nashville Chapter
Temple Baptist Church
3810 King's Ln.
Nashville, TN 37218   Ph: (615)876-4084
Rev. Michael Graves, Chairman

★1572★
Tennessee Black Caucus
209 War Memorial Bldg.
Nashville, TN 37219   Ph: (615)741-7140

──────────── **Texas** ────────────

★1573★
Afro-American Peace Officers Association
PO Box 943
Arlington, TX 76004
James Hawthorne, Pres.

★1574★
Afro American Police Officers League
4101 San Jacinto, Ste. 225
Houston, TX 77004   Ph: (713)522-2850
Mae Walker, Pres.
Affiliated with: National Black Police Association.

★1575★
American Association of Blacks in Energy
Houston Chapter
c/o Len Taylor
Houston Lighting and Power Co.
PO Box 1700
Houston, TX 77001   Ph: (713)229-7310
Len Taylor, Pres.

★1576★
American Civil Liberties Union
Texas Affiliate
1611 E. 1st St.
Austin, TX 78702-4455   Ph: (512)477-5849
Suzanne Donovan, Pres.

★1577★
American Civil Liberties Union
Texas Affiliate
Dallas Chapter
PO Box 215135
Dallas, TX 75221   Ph: (214)823-1555
Joe Cook, Pres.

★1578★
American Civil Liberties Union
Texas Affiliate
Houston Chapter
1236 W. Gray
Houston, TX 77019   Ph: (713)524-5925
Helen M. Gros, Pres.

★1579★
Association for the Study of Afro-American Life and
**   History**
Houston Branch
3213 Binz St.
Houston, TX 77004   Ph: (713)522-3264
Pearl C. Suel, Pres.

★1580★
Association of Black Psychologists
Dallas Chapter
3625 Cripple Creek Dr.
Dallas, TX 75224   Ph: (202)772-0808
Dr. Linda W. Watson, Pres.

★1581★
Austin Area Urban League
1825 E. 38 1/2 St.
Austin, TX 78722   Ph: (512)478-7176
Linda Moore Smith, Pres.

★1582★
Austin Association of Black School Educators
6101 Highland Hills
Austin, TX 78731
Barbara Williams, Pres.

★1583★
Austin Black Lawyers Association
1309 S. Lamora, Ste. 480
Austin, TX 78704   Ph: (512)448-2911
Velva Price, Pres.
Affiliated with: National Bar Association.

★1584★
Austin Minority Business Development Center
301 Congress Ave., Ste. 1020
Austin, TX 78701   Ph: (512)476-9700

★1585★
Beaumont Minority Business Development Center
550 Fannin, Ste. 106A
Beaumont, TX 77701   Ph: (409)835-1377

★1586★
Black Fire Fighters Association of Dallas
1402 Corinth St., Ste. 113
Dallas, TX 75215

★1587★
Black Registry
1223 A Rosewood Ave.
Austin, TX 78702   Ph: (512)476-0082

★1588★
Black United Fund of Houston
5151 Martin Luther King Blvd.   Ph: (713)644-1461
Houston, TX 77021   Free: 800-332-2834
Cleo Glenn-Johnson, Pres.
Affiliated with: National Black United Fund, Inc.

★1589★
Brownsville Minority Development Center
3649 Leppard St.
Corpus Christi, TX 78408   Ph: (512)887-7961

★1590★
Capitol City Chamber of Commerce
5407 N. IH 35, Ste. 304   Ph: (512)459-1181
Austin, TX 78723   Fax: (512)459-1183
Karen Box, Exec.Dir.

★1591★
Corpus Christi Minority Business Development Center
3649 Leopard, Ste. 301
Corpus Christi, TX 78404   Ph: (512)887-7961

★1592★
Dallas Association of Black School Educators
PO Box 710464
Dallas, TX 75371
Dr. Frederick D. Todd, Pres.

★1593★
Dallas Black Chamber of Commerce
2838 Martin Luther King, Jr. Blvd.
Dallas, TX 75215   Ph: (214)421-5200
Tom Houston, Exec.Dir.

★1594★
Dallas Black Media Coalition
5807 S. Marsalrs St.
Dallas, TX 75241
George Brewer, Contact

★1595★
Dallas-Fort Worth Association of Black Communicators
WFAA-TV
Communications Center
606 Young St.
Dallas, TX 75202   Ph: (214)748-9631
John McCaa, Pres.

★1596★
Dallas/Fort Worth Minority Business/Development Center
1445 Ross Ave., Ste. 800
Dallas, TX 75202   Ph: (214)855-7373

★1597★
Dallas Urban League
2121 Main St., 4th Fl., Ste. 410
Dallas, TX 75201   Ph: (214)747-4734
Dr. Beverly K. Mitchell-Brooks, Exec.Dir.

★1598★
El Paso Minority Business Development Center
1312-A E. Rio Grande St.
El Paso, TX 79902   Ph: (915)544-2700

★1599★
Fort Worth Association of Black School Educators
324 Revere Dr.
Ft. Worth, TX 76134

★1600★
Fort Worth Black Bar Association
777 Main St., #890
Fort Worth, TX 76102-5304   Ph: (817)870-2027
Nelda F. Harris, Pres.
Affiliated with: National Bar Association.

★1601★
Fort Worth Black Fire Fighters
PO Box 19009
Ft. Worth, TX 76119

★1602★
Fort Worth Black Peace Officers Association
PO Box 15907
Fort Worth, TX 76119
Affiliated with: National Black Police Association.

★1603★
Fort Worth Metropolitan Black Chamber of Commerce
2914 E. Rosedale, Ste. 101
Fort Worth, TX 76105   Ph: (817)531-8510
Dezoyd Jennings, Chairman

★1604★
Houston Area Association of Black School Educators
PO Box 660
Houston, TX 77001-0660
Edward Cline, Pres.

★1605★
Houston Area Urban League
3215 Fannin
Houston, TX 77004   Ph: (713)526-5127
Sylvia K. Brooks, Pres.

★1606★
Houston Black Firefighters Association
4101 San Jacinto St., Ste. 229
Houston, TX 77004   Ph: (713)528-7405
Affiliated with: International Association of Black Professional Fire Fighters.

★1607★
Houston Citizens Chamber of Commerce
2808 Wheeler
Houston, TX 77004   Ph: (713)522-9745
Willie Williams, Pres.

★1608★
Houston Lawyers Association
Texas Southern University
Office of General Council
3100 Cleburne
Houston, TX 77004   Ph: (713)527-7950
Renee Smith, Pres.
Affiliated with: National Bar Association.

★1609★
Houston Minority Business Development Center
1200 Smith St., Ste. 2800
Houston, TX 77002   Ph: (713)650-3831

★1610★
J.L. Turner Legal Association
c/o Rick Jordan
132 E. Main St., Ste. 106
Grand Prairie, TX 75050   Ph: (214)922-0100
Rick Jordan, Pres.
Affiliated with: National Bar Association.

★1611★
Laredo Minority Business Development Center
2801 E. Montgomery, Ste. 210
Laredo, TX 78043   Ph: (210)725-5177
Robert Tarney, Director

★1612★
**Lubbock/Midland-Odessa Minority Business
  Development Center**
1220 Broadway, Ste. 509
Lubbock, TX 79401   Ph: (806)762-6232
Lynn O. Castle, Director

★1613★
McAllen Minority Business Development Center
1701 W. Bus. Hwy. 83, Ste. 306
McAllen, TX 78501   Ph: (512)687-5224
Arturo Palacio, Director

★1614★
Men of Color Together
PO 190611
Dallas, TX 72519

★1615★
Minority Assistance National Network
4317 K St.
Houston, TX 77051
Edward Lewis, Exec.Dir.

★1616★
Minority Business Association
625 E. 10th St., Ste. 800
Austin, TX 78701

★1617★
**National Association of Minority Contractors
Houston Chapter**
PO Box 14611
Houston, TX 77221-4611   Ph: (713)747-7206
Edna I.B. Goodie, Pres.

★1618★
**National Black Child Development Institute
Dallas Affiliate**
813 Ryan Rd.
Dallas, TX 75224   Ph: (214)375-8006
Sharon Harris, Contact

★1619★
**National Black Child Development Institute
Houston Affiliate**
8602 Allwood Ave.
Houston, TX 77016   Ph: (713)633-2752
Odessa Sayles, Contact

★1620★
**National Black MBA Association
Dallas Chapter**
PO Box 797174
Dallas, TX 75379   Ph: (214)558-1699
Loretta Barr, Contact

★1621★
**National Black MBA Association
Houston Chapter**
PO Box 56525
Houston, TX 77256
Arnita Gates, Contact

★1622★
**National Business League
Austin Cen-Tex Chapter**
3724 Airport Blvd.
Austin, TX 78722   Ph: (512)476-3506
T.L. Wyatt, Pres.

★1623★
**National Business League
Dallas Chapter**
PO Box 11331
Dallas, TX 75223   Ph: (214)952-9959
Jasper Baccus, Pres.

★1624★
Odessa Black Chamber of Commerce
700 N. Grant, Ste. 200
Odessa, TX 79761   Ph: (915)332-5812
Odel Crawford

★1625★
**Operation PUSH
Austin Network**
Grant Chapel AME Church
1190 Chicon St.
Austin, TX 78702   Ph: (512)472-2827
Rev. William Turner, Contact

★1626★
**Operation PUSH
Dallas Chapter**
3410 S. Polk St.
Dallas, TX 75224   Ph: (214)372-4543
Rev. E. K. Bailey, Contact

★1627★
**Operation PUSH
Fort Worth Chapter**
600 Grove
Fort Worth, TX 76102   Ph: (817)338-4815
Rev. Cedric Britt, Contact

★1628★
San Antonio Bar Association
Court House, 5th Fl.
San Antonio, TX 78205   Ph: (210)227-8822

★1629★
San Antonio Black Lawyers Association
PO Box 830294
San Antonio, TX 78283-0294   Ph: (512)225-3031
Lamont Jefferson, Pres.
Affiliated with: National Bar Association.

★1630★
San Antonio Black Police Officers Coalition
PO Box 1058
San Antonio, TX 78205   Ph: (210)299-7385
Samuel E. Moore, Pres.
Affiliated with: National Black Police Association.

★1631★
San Antonio Minority Business Development Center
801 S. Bowie
San Antonio, TX 78294   Ph: (512)224-1945

★1632★
**Tarrant County Black Historical and Genealogical
  Society**
1020 E. Humbolt
Fort Worth, TX 76104   Ph: (817)332-6049
Don Williams, Pres.

★1633★
Texarkana Black Chamber of Commerce
414 Texas Blvd.
Texarkana, TX 75501-5536   Ph: (903)792-8931
Elridge Robertson, Exec.Vice-Pres.

★1634★
Texas Association of Black School Educators
PO Box 271392
Houston, TX 77277-1393
Joseph Drayton, Pres.

★1635★
Texas Black State Troopers Association
PO Box 472524
Garland, TX 75047-2524

★1636★
Texas Peace Officers Association
PO Box 762353
Dallas, TX 75376-2353   Ph: (214)941-9295
James A. Allen, Pres.
Affiliated with: National Black Police Association.

★1637★
Unitarian Universalist Association Black Concerns
  Working Group
Southwest Chapter
6471 Waverly Way
Fort Worth, TX 76116
Rev. Dwight Brown, District Executive

★1638★
United Negro College Fund
Dallas Office
20001 Ross Ave., Ste. 1500, Lock Box
  113
Dallas, TX 75201   Ph: (214)754-9030
Territory Includes: Dallas, Ft. Worth, Midland/Odessa, Amarillo, Wichita Falls, and Lubbock, TX; OK.

★1639★
United Negro College Fund
Houston Office
6910 Fannin, Ste. 100
2777 Allen Pkwy.
Houston, TX 77030   Ph: (512)224-1674
Territory Includes: Houston, San Antonio, Waco, Beaumont, Hawkins/Longview, Corpus Christi, Tyler, El Paso, TX.

─────────── **Utah** ───────────

★1640★
American Civil Liberties Union
Utah Affiliate
Boston Bldg.
9 Exchange Pl., Ste. 701
Salt Lake City, UT 84111   Ph: (801)521-9289
Michele Parish, Pres.

★1641★
Salt Lake City Minority Business Development Center
350 East 500 South, Ste. 101
Salt Lake City, UT 84111   Ph: (801)328-8181

★1642★
Utah Association of Black School Educators
815 Germaine
Murray, UT 84123
Joyce Gray, Pres.

─────────── **Vermont** ───────────

★1643★
American Civil Liberties Union
Vermont Affiliate
100 State St.
Montepelier, VT 05601   Ph: (802)223-6304
Leslie Williams, Pres.

─────────── **Virgin Islands** ───────────

★1644★
Virgin Islands Minority Business Development Center
81-AB Princess Gade
St. Thomas, VI 00804   Ph: (809)774-7215

─────────── **Virginia** ───────────

★1645★
American Civil Liberties Union
Virginia Affiliate
6 N. 6th St., Ste. 400
Richmond, VA 23219-2419   Ph: (804)644-8022
Kent Willis, Pres.

★1646★
Association for the Study of Afro-American Life and
  History
Louisa County Branch
Rte. 4, Box 62A
Louisa, VA 23093   Ph: (703)894-4818
Pearlie R. Askew, Pres.

★1647★
Black Fire Service Professionals of Alexandria
PO Box 25483
Alexandria, VA 22313-5483
Sam Parker, Pres.

★1648★
Housing Opportunities Made Equal
1218 W. Cary St.
Richmond, VA 23220   Ph: (804)354-0641
Constance K. Chamberlin, Exec.Dir.
Founded: 1971.

★1649★
Metropolitan Business League
121 E. Marshall St.
PO Box 26751
Richmond, VA 23261   Ph: (804)649-7473
Glayds Jackson-Weston, Pres./CEO
Affiliated with: National Business League.

★1650★
National Black Child Development Institute
Hampton Affiliate
671 Bell St.
Hampton, VA 23661   Ph: (804)727-1071

★1651★
National Black Child Development Institute
Williamsburg Affiliate
109 Spring Rd.
Williamsburg, VA 23185   Ph: (804)229-2014
Dr. Elizabeth Morgan, Contact

★1652★
Newport News Minority Business Development Center
6060 Jefferson Ave., Ste. 6016
Newport News, VA 23605   Ph: (804)245-8743

★1653★
Norfolk Minority Business Development Center
355 Crawford Pkwy., Ste. 608
Portsmouth, VA 23704   Ph: (804)399-0888

★1654★
Northern Virginia Urban League
908 King St., Ste. 301
Alexandria, VA 22314   Ph: (703)836-2858
George H. Lambert Jr., Pres.

★1655★
Nothern Virginia Association of Black School
   Educators
Willow Springs Elementary School
12460 Braddock Rd.
Herndon, VA 22070   Ph: (703)741-7977
Mary Roots

★1656★
Old Dominion Bar Association
506 N. Main St.
Suffolk, VA 23434   Ph: (804)539-3007
Dennis Montgomery, Pres.
Affiliated with: National Bar Association.

★1657★
Operation PUSH
Triangle Network
4416 Forestburg Ln.
Triangle, VA 22172
Elsie Queen

★1658★
Progressive Fire Fighters of Fairfax County Virginia
PO Box 404
Fairfax, VA 22030

★1659★
Richmond Black Police Officers Association
PO Box 27201
Richmond, VA 23261
Willie Jones, Pres.
Affiliated with: National Black Police Association.

★1660★
Tidewater Law Enforcement Officers
PO Box 2601
Norfolk, VA 23501   Ph: (804)441-5532
Affiliated with: National Black Police Association.

★1661★
Tidewater Regional Minority Purchasing Council
142 W. York St., Ste. 611
Norfolk, VA 23510   Ph: (804)627-8471
Bernard Big, Exec.Dir.
Founded: 1977. **Members:** 460. **Publications:** Directory of
Membership, periodic. Also issues monthly publication.

★1662★
United Brotherhood Fire Fighters Assocation
PO Box 1734
Norfolk, VA 23501

★1663★
United Negro College Fund
Richmond Office
1001 E. Main St., Ste. 908
Richmond, VA 23219   Ph: (804)644-3157
Territory Includes: All of VA.

★1664★
Urban League of Greater Richmond
101 E. Clay St.
Richmond, VA 23219   Ph: (804)649-8407
Randolph C. Kendall Jr., Pres./CEO

★1665★
Urban League of Hampton Roads
840 Church St., Ste. I
Norfolk, VA 23510   Ph: (804)627-0864
Mary L. Redd, Pres.

★1666★
Virginia Regional Minority Supplier Development
   Council
201 E. Franklin
Richmond, VA 23219   Ph: (804)780-2322
Adele Johnson-Crowley, President

─────────── Washington ───────────

★1667★
American Civil Liberties Union
Washington Affiliate
1720 Smith Tower
Seattle, WA 98104   Ph: (206)624-2180
Kathleen Taylor, Pres.

★1668★
Black Law Enforcement Association of Washington
PO Box 18493
Seattle, WA 98118
Bob Alexander, Contact
Affiliated with: National Black Police Association.

★1669★
Ethnic Heritage Council of the Pacific Northwest
3123 East Lake Ave. E.
Seattle, WA 98102   Ph: (206)328-9204
Peter S. Davenport Jr., Exec.Dir.
Founded: 1980. **Publications:** Contact Directory of Ethnic
Organizations in Washington State, biennial. Northwest Ethnic
News, monthly. Newsletter.

★1670★
Loren Miller Bar Association
PO Box 4233
Seattle, WA 98104   Ph: (206)722-4061
Leah Cattrell, Pres.
Affiliated with: National Bar Association.

★1671★
Port of Seattle Minority Fire Fighters Association
2400 S. 170th St.
Seattle, WA 98188

★1672★
Seattle Association of Black Journalists
2700 4th Ave., #504
Seattle, WA 98121
Rhoda E. McKinney, Pres.

★1673★
Seattle Black Fire Fighters Association
PO Box 22005
Seattle, WA 98118

★1674★
Seattle Minority Business Development Center
155 NE 100th Ave., Ste. 401
Seattle, WA 98125   Ph: (206)525-5617

★1675★
Tacoma-Pierce County Business League
1321 S. K St.
PO Box 5076
Tacoma, WA 98405   Ph: (206)272-7498
Frank H. Russell, Pres.
Affiliated with: National Business League.

★1676★
Tacoma Urban League
2550 S. Yakima Ave.
Tacoma, WA 98405   Ph: (206)383-2006
Thomas Dixon, Pres.

★1677★
United Negro College Fund
Seattle Office
1305 4th Ave., Ste. 608
Seattle, WA 98101   Ph: (206)292-8859
Territory Includes: WA; MT; ID; AK; OR.

★1678★
Urban League of Metropolitan Seattle
105 14th Ave.
Seattle, WA 98122   Ph: (206)461-3792
Rossalind Y. Woodhouse Ph.D., Pres.

★1679★
Washington State Business League and Chamber of Commerce
PO Box 18528
Seattle, WA 98118   Ph: (206)859-8284
James L. McGhee, Pres.
Affiliated with: National Business League.

West Virginia

★1680★
American Civil Liberties Union
West Virginia Affiliate
PO Box 3952
Charleston, WV 25301

★1681★
Mountain State Bar Association
PO Box 1153
Charleston, WV 25304   Ph: (304)346-2272
Duane Tinsley, Pres.
Affiliated with: National Bar Association.

★1682★
West Virginia Black Law Enforcement Officers United
2243 1/2 Oakridge Rd.
Charleston, WV 25311
Dallas Staples, Pres.

★1683★
West Virginia Human Rights Commission
1321 Plaza E., Rm. 106
Charleston, WV 25301-1400   Ph: (304)558-2616
Quewanncuii Stephens, Exec.Dir.
Founded: 1961. **Members:** 9. **Publications:** Annual Report.

Wisconsin

★1684★
Alliance of Black Law Enforcement
3344 N. 39th St.
Milwaukee, WI 53216
Martha Brock, Pres.

★1685★
American Civil Liberties Union
Wisconsin Affiliate
207 E. Buffalo St., No. 325
Milwaukee, WI 53202   Ph: (414)272-4032
Eunice Edgar, Pres.

★1686★
Association for the Study of Afro-American Life and History
Clarence L. and Cleopatra Johnson Branch
3612 N. Rev. Martin Luther King Jr. Dr.
Milwaukee, WI 53212   Ph: (414)265-5300
William Rogers, Pres.

★1687★
League of Martin
PO Box 09628
Milwaukee, WI 53209
Harold Hampton, Pres.

★1688★
Madison Urban League
151 E. Gorham
Madison, WI 53703   Ph: (608)251-8550
Johnny Michler, Exec.Dir.

★1689★
Metro Milwaukee Association of Black School Educators
PO Box 12520
Milwaukee, WI 53212
Dr. Michael Smith, Pres.

★1690★
Milwaukee Bar Association
533 E. Wells
Milwaukee, WI 53202   Ph: (414)274-6760
Arthur J. Harrington, President

★1691★
Milwaukee Black Fire Fighters
6162 N. 35th St., No. 10
Milwaukee, WI 53209

★1692★
Milwaukee Minority Business Development Center
1442 N. Farwell Ave., Ste. 500
Milwaukee, WI 53202   Ph: (414)289-3422
Gregory S. McKinney, Dir.

★1693★
Milwaukee Minority Chamber of Commerce
2821 N. 4th St., Ste. 302
Milwaukee, WI 53212   Ph: (414)264-4111
J. Paul Jordan, Contact
Founded: 1980. **Members:** 350.

★1694★
Milwaukee Urban League
2800 W. Wright St.
Milwaukee, WI 53210   Ph: (414)374-5850

★1695★
National Association for Black Veterans
Milwaukee Chapter
4185 N. Green Bay Ave.
Milwaukee, WI 53209   Ph: (414)562-8387

★1696★
Operation PUSH
Milwaukee Chapter
6985 N. Darien St.
Milwaukee, WI 53209   Ph: (414)228-6779
Rev. Floyd Taylor, Contact

★1697★
Project Equality of Wisconsin
1442 N. Farwell Ave., Ste. 210
Milwaukee, WI 53202   Ph: (414)272-2642
Betty J. Thompson, Exec.Dir.
Founded: 1969. **Members:** 3000. **Budget:** $100,000. **Publications:**
Directory, biennial. PE Wisconsin Update, quarterly. Project Equality
of Wisconsin Buyer's Guide, annual.

★1698★
United Negro College Fund
Milwaukee Office
1730 N. 1st St.
Milwaukee, WI 53212   Ph: (414)374-1900
Territory Includes: All of WI.

★1699★
Urban League of Racine and Kenosha
718-22 N. Memorial Dr.
Racine, WI 53404   Ph: (414)637-8532
Thelma Orr, Interim Pres.

★1700★
Wisconsin Association of Minority Attorneys
230 Westwells
Milwaukee, WI 53202   Ph: (414)271-5888
Carl Ashley, Pres.
Affiliated with: National Bar Association.

Wyoming

★1701★
American Civil Liberties Union
Wyoming Affiliate
PO Box A
Laramie, WY 82070   Ph: (307)742-0945
Laurie Seidenberg, Pres.

(3) Religious Organizations

★1702★
African Methodist Episcopal Church
500 8th Ave. S
Nashville, TN 37203

A short time after the founding of the Methodist Episcopal Church in 1784, friction developed between the blacks and the whites of St. George's Church in Philadelphia. The situation was intensified by the erection of a gallery to which the blacks were relegated. The long-standing grievances came to a head on a Sunday morning in November 1787, when whites tried to pull several blacks from their knees at the altar rail. Richard Allen led the group of blacks out of the church, and they formed a church of their own.

Allen was a former slave whose master had been converted by Freeborn Garrettson (a Methodist preacher). His master allowed Allen to buy his freedom. As a freeman he became a prosperous businessman and a licensed Methodist preacher. After leaving St. George's, Allen purchased an abandoned blacksmith shop, and in 1744 Methodist Bishop Francis Asbury dedicated it as Bethel Church. In 1799 Allen was ordained a deacon, the first black so honored.

Differences continued between the leaders of Allen's Bethel Church and St. George's. The former wished to be independent but with a nominal relation to the Methodists. Finally, in 1816, the issues were settled in a court suit when Bethel was granted full independence.

In Baltimore, blacks at the two white churches formed an independent Colored Methodist Society after they had been put in galleries and not allowed to take communion until after the whites. In 1801 Daniel Coke arrived in Baltimore and took over the leadership of the Society. Through his work an independent Methodist Church, also named Bethel, was formed. A call was issued in 1816 for a national meeting of black Methodists for the purpose of forming an African Methodist Episcopal (AME) Church. The *Discipline*, Articles of Religion, and General Rules of the Methodist Episcopal Church were adopted, and Richard Allen was elected bishop. The AME Church remains close in doctrine, practice and polity to the United Methodist Church, the successor to the Methodist Episcopal Church, with whom it has engaged in some serious merger conversations.

Growth in the church throughout the North and Midwest was steady through 1865. After the Civil War a rapid expansion throughout the South occurred, and conferences were established across the territory of the former confederacy.

A missionary imperative was an early part of African Methodist concern, and in 1827 Scipio Bean was ordained as an elder and sent to Haiti. From that small beginning (and slow growth due to lack of funds), a twentieth-century mission program has emerged with stations in Africa, South America, and the West Indies. The primary work is with other people of African descent.

Publishing was seen as an integral part of the evangelistic, missionary and cultural life of the church from the beginning, and the items published by this church have had a major impact on the black community. The AME Book Concern was the first publishing house owned and operated by black people in America. *The Christian Recorder*, a newspaper begun as *The Christian Herald*, published continuously since 1841, is the oldest black periodical in the world; *The AME Review*, started in 1883, is the oldest magazine published by black people in the world. Education joined publishing as an early concern, and the first AME affiliated college, Wilberforce University, was established in 1856. Educational concerns have been carried to the mission field as well, and the church has established a number of schools from the primary grades through college for its African membership. West Africa Seminary was founded in Sierre Leone.

The church is governed episcopally. An international general conference meets quadrennially. The church is divided into 18 episcopal districts. Districts one through 13 oversee work in the United States, Canada, and Bermuda. The remaining districts oversee foreign work in 20 African countries, Jamaica, Haiti, the Dominican Republic, the Virgin Islands, the Windward Islands, Guyana, and Surinam.

The church is a member of both the National Council of Churches and the World Council of Churches. Affiliated congregations in Barbados and the Caribbean are members of the Caribbean Conference of Churches.

Membership: In 1981 the church reported 2,210,000 members, 6,200 churches, and 6,550 ministers.

Educational Facilities: Payne Theological Seminary, Wilberforce, Ohio.
Wilberforce University, Wilberforce, Ohio.
Allen University, Columbia, South Carolina.
Paul Quinn College, Waco, Texas.
Edward Waters College, Jacksonville, Florida.
Morris Brown College, Atlanta, Georgia.
Kittrell College, Kittrell, North Carolina.
Shorter College, Little Rock, Arkansas.
Campbell College, Jackson Mississippi.
Payne University, Birmingham, Alabama.
Western University, Quindaro, Kansas.

In 1958 Turner Theological Seminary in Atlanta, Georgia joined three other schools to form the Interdenominational Theological Seminary, the largest complex for the education of black Christian ministers in the nation.

Publications: *A.M.E. Christian Recorder.* • *A.M.E. Review.* Send orders to 468 Lincoln Dr. NW, Atlanta, GA 30318. • *The Voice of Missions.*

★1703★
African Methodist Episcopal Zion Church
Box 23843
Charlotte, NC 28232

In the late 1790s, a movement for independence among New York blacks was begun when a group petitioned Bishop Francis Asbury, the first bishop of the Methodist Episcopal Church, to let them hold separate meetings. They complained of not being allowed to preach or join the conference and itinerate. Asbury granted the request, and meetings were held immediately. In 1801 a charter was drawn up for the "African Methodist Episcopal Church (called Zion Church) of the City of New York." It was to be supplied with a minister from the white John's Street Church. Zion Church was thus assured of regular preaching and the sacraments.

In 1813 Zion Church split and Asbury Church was formed as a second black Methodist congregation. Both churches were being served by William Stillwell of John's Street Church in 1820, when Stillwell left the Methodist Episcopal Church with about 300 white members. Blacks, afraid of losing their property to the Methodist Episcopal Church, separated themselves from John's Street Church. They also voted not to join the African Methodist Episcopal Church. Several independent black churches in New Haven and Philadelphia petitioned them for ministers. A *Discipline*, based upon the one of the Methodist Episcopal Church, was drawn up.

Several attempts at reconciliation were made, the most important being a petition to establish the several black congregations as an annual conference within the Methodist Episcopal Church. This request was refused, and the African Methodist Episcopal Zion (AMEZ) Church emerged. Ordination was accepted from William Stillwell, and in 1822 James Varick was elected the first superintendent.

Doctrinally, the AMEZ Church accepts the Twenty-five Articles of Religion common to Methodists and has an episcopal polity similar to the Methodist Episcopal Church. Church boards implement programs of the quadrennial General Conference. The Publishing House and Book Concern are located in the headquarters complex in Charlotte, North Carolina, and publish a complete line of church school material. The church is a member of both the National Council of Churches and the World Council of Churches.

Membership: In 1990 the church reported 1.3 million members, 3,000 churches, and 3,500 ministers.

Educational Facilities: Hood Theological Seminary, Salisbury, North Carolina.
Livingston College, Salisbury, North Carolina.
Clinton Junior College, Rock Hill, South Carolina.
Lomax-Hannon Junior College, Greenville, Alabama.

Publications: *Star of Zion.* • *Quarterly Review.* Send orders for both to PO Box 31005, Charlotte, NC 28231.

★1704★
African Orthodox Church
15801 NW 38th Pl.
Opa Locka, FL 33054
Mt. Rev. Stafford J. Sweeting

The Protestant Episcopal Church, like all American denominations with both episcopal leadership and a significant black membership, faced the problems and pressures related to electing and elevating their first black member to the bishopric. Within the Episcopal Church the cries for a bishop drawn from among black members grew even louder after the Civil War. They were refused, the leadership arguing that, since the church did not recognize racial distinctions, it could not elevate a man to the bishopric just because he was black. A step toward the solution came in 1910 with the creation of black "suffragan" bishops, bishops without right to succession and without vote in the house of bishops.

Among those who complained that suffragans were not enough was Dr. George A. McGuire (1866-1934), an Episcopal priest who had emigrated from the West Indies. In 1921 he left the Protestant Episcopal Church and founded the Independent Episcopal Church. McGuire had had a distinguished career in the Episcopal Church, serving parishes in both the United States and Antigua, and he had been considered for the post of Suffragan Bishop of Arkansas. He declined in order to study medicine at Jefferson Medical College, where he graduated as a Doctor of Medicine in 1910. Upon graduation, he served at St. Bartholomew's Episcopal Church in Cambridge, Massachusetts. He was then called to be the Secretary of the Commission for Work among the Colored People under the Church's Board of Missions.

After several years as Secretary, he moved back to Antigua, where he remained for six years building the church where he was baptized, St. Paul's in Sweets. When fellow West Indian Marcus Garvey formed the United Negro Improvement Association, McGuire returned to the United States to support him. Working with Garvey only strengthened his dissatisfaction in serving a church where black people were systematically denied positions of leadership, and he became determined to pursue an independent course.

On September 2, 1921, in the Church of the Good Shepherd in New York City, a meeting of independent black clergy resolved itself into the first Synod of the African Orthodox Church and designated McGuire as its bishop elect. The Synod then entered into negotiations with the Russian Orthodox Church in America in their search for episcopal orders for their newly elected bishop. The Russians indicated a willingness to consecrate McGuire, but only if they controlled the newly created jurisdiction. The idea of non-Black control had no appeal to either McGuire or his followers. They then turned to the American Catholic Church, headed by Archbishop Joseph Rene Vilatte. Vilatte was willing to confer orders and ask little or nothing in the way of control. On September 29, 1921, Bishop Vilatte, assisted by Carl A. Nybladh, consecrated Dr. McGuire in the Church of Our Lady of Good Death in Chicago.

The church experienced slow but steady growth, although most of the individual congregations were small. The priests were seldom full-time clergy, although every church was encouraged to contribute something to their support. McGuire emphasized education and led in the organization of a seminary for the training of clergy. The first class numbered 14 men. The school provided professional training for its students, while accommodating to the generally lower educational level of its applicants. It has not tried to become an accredited degree-granting institution.

Archbishop McGuire led the Church until his death in 1934, and it enjoyed peace and stability. After his death the leadership of the church fell into the hands of Archbishop W. E. J. Robertson. Shortly after his elevation to the archbishopric, dissatisfaction arose among the group of clergy, and a schism, the Holy African Church, was created. The dissidents were led by Bishop R. G. Barrow, who had been McGuire's closest associate. In time, Barrow was succeeded by Bishop F. A. Toote and then Bishop Gladstone St. Claire Nurse. Bishop Nurse led the efforts to reunite the two factions. On February 22, 1964, the two bodies joined together under Robertson, who adopted the Patriarchal name of Peter IV. Just prior to the merger he consecrated several bishops, an obvious effort to insure his continued control of the church. Nurse did not protest Robertson's action, and upon the death of the Patriarch was elected by the bishops to be the new primate of the church. He quickly brought all the elements of the church together, and upon his death, leadership passed very easily to Archbishop William R. Miller, who served as the church's Primate from 1976 until August 1981. At the Annual Synod of the Church, he resigned and was succeeded by Archbishop Stafford J. Sweeting.

The denomination remains small in the United States, but it has affiliated parishes in the West Indies and Africa (Nigeria, Ghana, and Uganda). Recently, the church lost one of its strongest parishes when Bishop G. Duncan Hinkson of Chicago left to found the African Orthodox Church of the West.

Membership: In 1983 the church reported 17 parishes and 5,100 members in the United States.

Educational Facilities: Endich Theological Seminary, New York, New York.

Publications: *The Trumpet.* Available from Rev. Fr. Harold Furblur, Box 1925, Boston, MA 02105.

★1705★
African Orthodox Church of the West
St. Augustine's African Orthodox Church
5831 S. Indiana St.
Chicago, IL 60637
Most Rev. G. Duncan Hinkson

In 1984 Bishop G. Duncan Hinkson, a physician and pastor of St. Augustine's African Orthodox Church, on the southside of Chicago, left the African Orthodox Church and formed a new jurisdiction. While following the teachings and ritual of its parent body, it is administratively independent. Bishop Hinkson consecrated Bishop Franzo King to lead work in San Francisco.

Membership: In 1992, the church had two parishes, one in Chicago and one in California with several hundred members. **Publications:** *Expression.* Available from One Mind Temple, 351 Divisadero St., San Francisco, CA 94117.

★1706★
African Union First Colored Methodist Protestant Church
2611 N. Claymont St.
Wilmington, DE 19802

The origins of the African Union First Colored Methodist Protestant Church can be traced to 1813 and the formation of the Union Church of Africans, an event that present-day church leaders point to with pride. The Union Church of Africans was the first church in the United States to be originally organized by and afterward wholly under the care of black people.

The Union Church of Africans began in a series of disputes in the Asbury Methodist Episcopal Church, a congregation in Wilmington, Delaware. In 1805, black members under the leadership of Peter Spencer (1782-1843) and William Anderson (d. 1843) withdrew from what had been an integrated congregation, formed an all black congregation, Ezion Church, and erected a building. They cited as reasons for their departure the denial of religious privileges and lack of freedom in exercising their "spiritual gifts." The black members had been segregated in a balcony and made to take communion after white members.

While breaking with the local congregation, Ezion was still a part of the predominantly white Methodist Episcopal Church. However, in 1812, a conflict arose with the white minister who had been assigned to preach to both Wilmington's congregations. The conflict resulted in the minister's dismissing all of Ezion's trustees and class leaders. That action led to a court dispute that ended when the black members withdrew from the church. In 1913, they reorganized independently and elected Spencer and Anderson as their ministers. By 1837, there were 21 congregations.

In the generation after Spencer and Anderson, two events were most important. First, in 1850, a major schism occurred when a group arose in the Union Church that demanded the adoption of an episcopal polity. That group left to found the Union American Methodist Episcopal Church. The Union Church of Africans emerged from this struggle as the African Union Church. Then, after the Civil War, the church merged with the First Colored Methodist Protestant Church to form the present African Union First Colored Methodist Protestant Church.

The First Colored Methodist Protestant Church was formed about 1840 when members of the African Methodist Episcopal Church rejected episcopal leadership and reorganized along the principles of the Methodist Protestant Church, which included no episcopacy and lay representation of local preachers at the general conference. Since the Methodist Protestant Church was very similar to the African Union Church, they united in 1866.

The church accepts the commonly held articles of religion of United Methoidsm, but it has attached the Apostles Creed as the first article and deleted the article on "The Rulers of the United States." It has made a few changes in wording, for example, adding the words "and women" to the article on "The Church," which now reads, "The visible church is a congregation of faithful men and women."

The church is organized congregationally. Congregations are grouped into three districts: the Middle District, which includes New Jersey, Pennsylvania, New York, Delaware, and Canada; the Maryland District, which includes Maryland, the District of Columbia, Virginia, and all states south and southwest of Maryland; and the Southern and Western Missionary District, which includes all the southern and western states. A general conference meets quadrennially.

In 1966, the church moved to replace the titles of general president and general vice president, the two offices elected by the General Conference, with that of senior bishop and junior bishop. In 1971, the office of presiding elder of the combined districts of the church was created, and a second presiding elder was named in 1979.

There is no foreign mission work, and the home mission work is primarily the providence of the women. **Membership:** In 1988, the church reported 6,500 members in 35 congregations served by 50 ministers. There was no membership reported in Canada.

Educational Facilities: AU School of Religion, Wilmington, Delaware.

★1707★
African Universal Church
2336 SW 48th St.
Hollywood, FL 33023

The African Universal Church is one of the two churches which grew out of the ministry of Laura Adorkor Koffey (or Kofi) (1893-1928), generally remembered as Mother Koffey by those who knew her. Mother Koffey was a princess, the daughter of a tribal ruler in what is now Ghana. As a young woman in Africa, she was converted to Pentecostalism and soon afterward felt called to preach. She became a preacher in 1924. Her call was accompanied by a number of dreams and visions in which she was visited by God, whom she referred to as her "Old Man God." God wished her to come to America. She arrived at the beginning of 1926. She made her headquarters in the South, but ocasionally journeyed north and was briefly associated with Marcus Garvey's Universal Negro Improvement Association, then on its final decline. Beginning in the fall of 1926, she preached her way from New Orleans, Louisiana, to Mobile, Alabama, to Jacksonville, Florida. (Koffey's critics told a much different story. They claimed she had been born in Athens, Georgia, and had simply traveled widely prior to her appearance in 1927. It would be the 1960s before the truth of Koffey's own account was definitively verified.)

In 1927, in Jacksonville, the African Universal Church was organized. It is a trinitarian Pentecostal body with a strong emphasis on healing and the imminent return of Jesus Christ. It teaches members to expect four marked spritual experiences: justification, sanctification, the baptism of fire, and the baptism of the Holy Spirit. The baptism of fire is available to the spirit-filled believer. The baptism of the Holy Spirit is for the sanctified. The ordinances of baptism and the Lord's Supper are kept, but water is not used for the baptism and wine is not served during the Lord's Supper.

Along with her religious message, Koffey emphasized the connection of African Americans to the people of contemporary Africa. She had plans to develop a business located in Jacksonville which would provide a commercial tie between America and her homeland. She was arrested in Atlanta on much the same charge that had stopped Garvey, taking money for a fraudulent commercial scheme. Then on March 8, 1928, she was assasinated while preaching to a crowd in Miami, Florida.

Following the assasination, the church reorganized and continued. It is headed by an archbishop (for many years Clarence C. Addison) and regional overseers. There is also a senior mother who oversees district mothers, who in turn oversee parish mothers. Also following the assasination, there was split in the church, with a group in Florida and Alabama separating to form what is now known as the African Universal Church, Inc.

In 1934, the Commercial League Corporation, a self-help company in the spirit of the Universal Negro Improvement Association, was formed. Among other functions, it provides insurance for church members. Addison, who led the chuch for more than 40 years, was a black nationalist and anti-integrationist. As such, during the 1960s, he opposed the goals of the Civil Rights movement and found some approval from the conservative White political groups.

Membership: In 1970, there were approximately 100 congregations, but in recent years, contact has been broken and data on the current status of the group is not available.

★1708★
The Afro-American Social Research Association
Box 2150
Jacksonville, FL 32203

The Afro-American Social Research Association was formed by a black man who has taken the religious name, The Spirit of Truth. In the 1970s he began to receive messages from the Creator, many of which were incorporated into a book entitled "The Spirit of Truth." Doom Days!. The content of the messages was a word of warning and judgment, an important aspect of which was the necessity of doing away with the monetary system. According to The Spirit of Truth, the earth was given as a divine inheritance, but in time the wicked took control of everyone's divine inheritance, the monetary system being a tool in that takeover. He has predicted an astronomic catastrophe in the near future in which a comet will strike the moon which will in turn strike the sun. The earth will then move out of orbit and take a new position in the center of the universe. Most of earth's people will be destroyed in the process and a new world system, the United Countries of the Solar System, will then be established. The

New Jerusalem will be built upon the exact spot where the first Jerusalem was built.

Membership: Not reported.

★1709★
Ahmadiyya Anjuman Ishaat Islam, Lahore, Inc.
36911 Walnut St.
Newark, CA 94560

Following the death of Hazrat Mirza Ghulam Ahmad (1835-1908), founder of the Ahmadiyya Movement in Islam, a disagreement arose among his followers concerning the founder's status. Those who followed Ahmad's family proclaimed him a prophet. However, others, led by Maulawi Muhammad Ali, considered Ahmad the Promised Messiah and the greatest *mujaddid*, i.e., renewer of Islam, but denied that Ahmad had ever claimed the special status of "prophet." Ali asserted that Ahmad's use of that term was entirely allegorical. The claim of prophethood for Ahmad has resulted in the assignment of Ahmadiyya Muslims to a status outside of the Muslim community and resulted in their persecution in several Muslim-dominated countries.

Members of the Ahmadiyya branch founded by Ali came to America in the 1970s and incorporated in California.

Membership: Not reported. There are four centers in the United States and two in Canada. There are an estimated 100,000 people affiliated with the movement worldwide. Centers are found in Indian communities around the world.

Publications: The Islamic Review.

★1710★
Ahmadiyya Movement in Islam
2141 Leroy Pl. NW
Washington, DC 20008

The Ahmadiyya movement was not brought to the United States with the intention of it becoming a black man's religion. Ahmadiyya originated in India in 1889 as a Muslim reform movement. It differs from orthodox Islam in that it believes that Hazrat Mirza Ghulam Ahmad (1835-1908) was the promised Messiah, the coming one of all the major faiths of the world. It has, in the years since its founding, developed the most aggressive missionary program in Islam.

Ahmad had concluded, as a result of his studies, that Islam was in a decline and that he had been appointed by Allah to demonstrate its truth, which he began doing by authoring a massive book, *Barahin-i-Ahmaditah*. He assumed the title of *mujaddid*, the renewer of faith for the present age, and declared himself both Madhi, the expected returning savior of Muslims, and the Promised Messiah of Christians. He advocated the view that Jesus had not died on the cross, but had come to Kashmir in his later life and died a normal death there. The second coming is not of a resurrected Jesus, but the appearance of one who bore the power and spirit of Jesus.

Ahmadiyya came to the United States in 1921 and the first center was in Chicago. Its founder, Dr. Mufti Muhammad Sadiq began to publish a periodical, *Muslim Sunrise*. While recruiting some members from among immigrants, the overwhelming majority of converts consisted of blacks. Only since the repeal of the Asian Exclusion Act in 1965 and the resultant emigration of large numbers of Indian and Pakistani nationals has the movement developed a significant Asian constituency in the United States.

A vast missionary literature demonstrating Islam's superiority to Christianity has been produced. Jesus is widely discussed. He is viewed as a great prophet who only swooned on the cross. He then escaped from the tomb to India and continued many years of ministry. He is buried at Srinagar, India, where the legendary Tomb of Issa (Jesus) is a popular pilgrimage site. The denial of the divinity of Jesus is in line with the assertion of Allah as the one true God. Christianity is seen as tritheistic.

At present, the movement is small. Headquarters were moved to Washington, D.C., in 1950 after a quarter century in Chicago.

Membership: In 1992 the movement reported approximately 10,000 members. Active centers can be found in 37 cities of the United States and 18 in Canada. In addition, Ahmadiyya centers can now be found in most countries of the world.

Publications: The Ahmadiyya Gazette. • The Muslim Sunrise. • Ayesha.

★1711★
Alpha and Omega Pentecostal Church of God of America, Inc.
3023 Clifton Ave.
Baltimore, MD 21216

The Alpha and Omega Pentecostal Church of God of America, Inc., was formed in 1945 by the Rev. Magdalene Mabe Phillips, who withdrew from the United Holy Church of America and, with others, organized the Alpha and Omega Church of God Tabernacles, soon changed to the present name. Like the Church of God (Cleveland, Tennessee), the church's doctrine reserves the baptism of The Holy Spirit for the sanctified.

Membership: Not reported. In 1970 there were three congregations, six missions, and approximately 400 members, all in Baltimore.

★1712★
American Catholic Church (Syro-Antiochean)

Efforts to locate an address for this edition were unsuccessful. In the late 1930s, Abp. Daniel C. Hinton, the third primate of the American Catholic Church, resigned in favor of Bp. Percy Wise Clarkson. Clarkson was the founder-pastor of the jurisdiction's most successful parishes in Laguna Beach, California. However, he had strong theosophical leanings, and strengthened the tendency to move the American Catholic Church into theological alignment with the Liberal Catholic Church. Among those who strongly opposed the direction in which Clarkson was leading was Ernest Leopold Peterson (d. 1959), a black man who had been consecrated in 1927 by the former primate, Abp. Frederick E. J. Lloyd. Peterson authored the liturgy used by the church prior to Clarkson's leadership.

Peterson withdrew from Clarkson's jurisdiction and formed the American Catholic Church (Syro-Antiochean), which continued in the faith and practice of the American Catholic Church. In 1950, Peterson consecrated Herbert F. Wilkie, who succeeded as primate in 1959.

Membership: The church reported 40 churches, 4,663 members, and 66 clergy in 1961, but as of the last report in 1979, three churches, 501 members, and eight clergy remained.

★1713★
American Muslims
Masjid Al-Faatir
1200 E. 47th St.
Chicago, IL 60615
Imam W. Deen Mohammed

Though there are a variety of Muslim groups functioning within the black community, when one reads in the media or hears mention of "Black Muslims," the most likely reference is to the Nation of Islam, founded by Master Wallace Fard Muhammad and headed for many years by its purported prophet, Elijah Muhammad (1897-1975). After Elijah Muhammad's death the organization's name was changed successively to the World Community of Islam in the West and in 1980 the American Muslim Mission. It is the most successful of the Black Muslim bodies, having spread across the nation in the 1960s during the period of the black revolution. Its success and that of one dissident member, Malcolm X, led to numerous books and articles about it.

Following the death of Noble Drew Ali, founder of the Moorish Science Temple of America, there appeared in Detroit, Michigan, one W. D. Fard, a mysterious figure claiming to be Noble Drew Ali reincarnated. He proclaimed that he had been sent from Mecca to secure freedom, justice, and equality for his uncle (the Negroes) living in the wilderness of North America, surrounded and robbed by the cave man. (The white man was also referred to as the "Caucasian devil" and "Satan.") He established a temple in 1930 in Detroit. Among his many converts was Elijah Poole.

The 1930s was a time of intense recruiting activity and dispute with the Nation of Islam. Within Fard's ranks discussion focused on his divinity, legitimacy, and role. In 1934, a second temple was founded in Chicago, and the following year Fard dropped from sight. By this time, Poole, known as Elijah Muhammad, had risen to leadership.

Under Elijah Muhammad's leadership, the Black Muslims emerged as a strong, cohesive unit. Growth was slow, due in part to Muhammad's imprisonment during World War II as a conscientious objector. As the new prophet, he composed the authoritative *Message to the Blackman in America*, a summary statement of the Nation of Islam's position.

The central teaching of the Nation of Islam can be seen as a more sophisticated version of the Moorish Science study of the black man's history. According to Muhammad, Yakub, a mad black scientist, created the white beast, who was then permitted by Allah to reign for six thousand years. That period was over in 1914. Thus the twentieth century is the time for the Nation of Islam to regroup and regain an ascendant position.

Education, economics, and political aspirations were major aspects of the Muslim program. The first University of Islam was opened in 1932, and parochial education (many of the schools being names for Clara Muhammad, Elijah Muhammad's wife) has been a growing and more effective part of the Nation ever since. Besides the common curriculum, Black Muslim history, Islam and Arabic have been stressed. Classes are offered through the twelfth grade. Economically, the Muslims have stressed a work ethic and business development. The weekly newspaper carries numerous ads by businesses owned by Muslims. Politically, Muslims looked to the establishment of a black nation to be owned and operated by blacks.

As Black Muslims, they excluded whites from the movement and imposed a strict discipline on members to accentuate their new religion and nationality. Food, dress, and behavior patterns are regulated; a ritual life based on, but varying from, Orthodox form, was prescribed.

Black Muslims instituted a far-reaching program in furtherance of their aspirations. An evangelizing effort to make the Muslim program known within the black community was sustained in a weekly newspaper, *Muhammad Speaks*. During the 1960 and into the 1970s, growth was spectacular. By the time of Elijah Muhammad's death there were approximately 70 temples across the nation, including the South, and over 100,000 members.

In 1975 Elijah Muhammad died and was succeeded by his son Wallace D. Muhammad. During the decade of Wallace's leadership, a move toward both Orthodox Islam and decentralization of the organization has occurred. These moves have been reflected in the name changes, the schism of conservatives who have left to found movements continuing the peculiar emphasis of the Nation of Islam prior to 1975, and the beginning of acceptance of the American Muslim Mission by orthodox Muslims. *Muhammad Speaks* was renamed *Bilalian News*.

In 1985 Wallace Muhammad, with the approval of the Council of Imans (ministers), resigned his post as leader of the American Muslim Mission and disbanded the movement's national structure. That move represents the establishment of a fully congregational polity by the Muslims whose local centers are now under the guidance of the imans rather than the control of the Chicago headquarters. Wallace D. Muhammad, also known as Warith Deen Muhammad, now operates as an independent Muslim lecturer and a member of the World Council of Masajid which is headquartered in Mecca, Saudi Arabia. His emphasis is upon the proper image of Muslims worldwide.

Membership: Not reported. There were approximately 200 centers in the mission at the time of its disincorporation. Foreign centers were located in Barbados, Belize, Guyana, Bermuda, Jamaica, the Bahamas, Canada, St. Thomas Island, and Trinidad.

Publications: *Muslim Journal*. Send orders to 910 W. Van Buren, Chicago, IL 60607.

★1714★
Ansaaru Allah Community
716 Bushwick Ave.
Brooklyn, NY 11221

Members of the Ansaaru Allah Community, also known as the Nubian Islaamic Hebrew Mission, believe that the nineteenth century Sudanese leader, Muhammed Ahmed Ibn Abdullah (1845-1885), was the True Mahdi, the predicted Khaliyfah (successor) to the Prophet Mustafa Muhammed Al Amin. After his death, Al Mahdi was buried in the Sudan, and the group he founded (the Ansaars) continued under his successors, mainly: 1) As Sayyid Abdur Rahman Muhammad Al Madhi (the first successor); 2) As Sayyid Al Haadi Abdur Muhammad Rahmaan Al Madhi (the second successor); 3) As Sayyid Al Imaan Isa Al Haadi Al Madhi (the third successor). Presently, the third successor, who is also Al Mahdi's great-grandson, leads the mission.

The Community teaches from the Old Testament (Tawrah), the Psalms of David (Zubuwr), the New Testament (Injiyl), and the *Holy Qur'aan*. The last testament, the *Holy Qur'aan*, was given to the last and seal of the Prophets of the line of Adam, Mustafa Muhammad Al

Amin. The group teaches that Allah is Alone in His power, the All (which is Tawhiyd, "Oneness"), and does not use the term "God." They believe that Jesus is the Messiah and that Ali (599-661 C.E.) and Fatima (610-633 C.E.) are the succesors to Mustafa Muhammad Al Amin.

Adam and Hawwah (Eve) are believed to have been Nubians. After the flood, during the prophet Nuwh's (Noah) time, his son Ham desired to commit sodomy while looking at his father's nakedness. This act resulted in the curse of leprosy being put upon Ham's fourth son, Canaan, thus turning his skin pale. In such a manner did the pale races come into existence, including the Amorites, Hittites, Jebusites, Sidonites, all the sons of Canaan and their descendants. Mixing the blood with these "subraces" (so-called because they are no longer pure Nubians), is unlawful for Nubians.

From the seed of Ibrahiym (Abraham), two nations were produced, the nation of Isaac, whose descendants later became known as Israelites, through his son Jacob, and the nation of Ishmael, whose descendants are called the Ishmailites and the nation of Midian, whose descendents are known as Midianites from Ketura, Abraham's third wife. The Israelites were enslaved for 430 years in Egypt. The Ishmailites were predicted to be enslaved in a land not of their own for 400 years. The Nubians of the United States, the West Indies and various other places around the world are the seed of Ishmael (and hence Hebrews). Al Madhi taught that all with straight hair and pale skin were Turks; however, this does not include people of color such as the Latins, Japanese, Koreans, Cubans, Sicilians, etc.

Under As Siddid Al Imaan Isa Al Haahi Al Madhi's guidance, the Nubian Islaamic Hebrew Mission was begun in the late 1960s in New York. In 1970, the prophesies of the "Opening of the Seventh Seal" (Revelation 8:1) commenced with the opening of the Ansaaru Allah Community and the publishing of literature to help remove the veil of confusion from Nubians. In 1972, communities were established in Philadlephia, Pennsylvania; Connecticut; Texas; and Albany, New York. The following year centers were opened in Washington, DC; Baltimore, Maryland; North Carolina; South Carolina; Georgia; Michigan; Florida; and Virginia. In the Carribean, centers were opened in Trinidad, Jamaica, Puerto Rico, Guyana, and Tobago. During the next decade, the movement spread around the world and included South America, Ghana and Hawaii.

Symbol of the community is the six-pointed star (made from two triangles) in an inverted cresent. It is considered to be the seal of Allah.

Membership: Not reported. There are several hundred members in the United States.

Publications: *Ansar Village Bulletin*.

★1715★
Antioch Association of Metaphysical Science

Efforts to locate an address for this edition were unsuccessful. The Antioch Association of Metaphysical Science is a metaphysical church founded in 1932 by Dr. Lewis Johnson of Detroit, Michigan. It serves a predominantly black membership.

Membership: Not reported. In 1965 there were 6 churches.

★1716★
Apostolic Assemblies of Christ, Inc.

Efforts to locate an address for this edition were unsuccessful. The Apostolic Assemblies of Christ was formed in 1970 by former members of the Pentecostal Churches of the Apostolic Faith led by Bishop G. N. Boone. During the term of presiding bishop Willie Lee, questions of his administrative abilities arose. In the midst of the controversy, he died. In the organizational disaray the church splintered, and one group formed around Bishop Boone and Virgil Oates, the vice-bishop. The new body is congregational in organization and continues in the doctrine of the parent body, since no doctrinal controversy accompanied the split.

Membership: In 1980 the Assemblies had approximately 3,500 members, 23 churches and 70 ministers.

★1717★
Apostolic Church of Christ
2044 Martin Luther King, Jr. Dr.
Winston-Salem, NC 27107

The Apostolic Church of Christ was founded in 1969 by Bishop Johnnie Draft and Elder Wallace Snow, both ministers in the Church of God (Apostolic). Draft, for many years an overseer in the church and pastor of St. Peter's Church, the denomination's headquarters congregation, expressed no criticism of the Church of God (Apostolic); rather, he stated that the Spirit of the Lord brought him to start his own organization. The church differs from its parent body in its development of a centralized church polity. Authority is vested in the executive board, which owns all the church property. Doctrine follows that of the Church of God (Apostolic). Bishop Draft serves as the church's Chief Apostle.

Membership: In 1992 the Apostolic Church of Christ had six churches, 400 members, nine ministers, six elders, two licensed missionaries, and one bishop.

★1718★
Apostolic Church of Christ in God
c/o Bethlehem Apostolic Church
1217 E. 15th St.
Winston-Salem, NC 27105

The Apostolic Church of Christ in God was formed by five elders of the Church of God (Apostolic): J. W. Audrey, J. C. Richardson, Jerome Jenkins, W. R. Bryant, and J. M. Williams. At the time of the split, the Church of God (Apostolic) was formally led by Thomas Cox, but, due to his ill health, Eli N. Neal was acting as presiding bishop. The dissenting elders were concerned with the authoritarian manner in which Neal conducted the affairs of the church as well as with some personal problems that Neal was experiencing. Originally, three churches left with the elders, who established headquarters in Winston-Salem, North Carolina. J. W. Audrey was elected the new presiding bishop.

The new church prospered and in 1952 Elder Richardson was elected as a second bishop. In 1956 Audrey resigned and Richardson became the new presiding bishop. Under his leadership the Apostolic Church enjoyed its greatest success. He began The *Apostolic Gazette* (later the *Apostolic Journal*) which served the church for many years. He also instituted a program to assist ministers in getting an education. However, his efforts were frustrated by several schisms that cut into the church's growth, most prominently the 1971 schism led by former-bishop Audrey.

The church retained the doctrine and congregational polity of the Church of God (Apostolic).

Membership: In 1980 the church had 2,150 members in 13 congregations being served by five bishops and 25 ministers.

★1719★
Apostolic Church of Jesus

Efforts to locate an address for this edition were unsuccessful. The Apostolic Church of Jesus was founded by Antonio Sanches, who had been converted in an evangelistic meeting led by Mattie Crawford in Pueblo, Colorado in 1923, and his brother George Sanches. The Sanches brothers began to preach to the Spanish-speaking population of the city and in 1927 organized the first congregation of the Apostolic Church of Jesus. In subsequent years, congregations were established throughout the state and elsewhere and can now be found in Denver, Westminister, Fountain, Walsenbury, and Ft. Garland, Colorado; Palo Alto, California; San Luis, Trinidad; and Velarde, New Mexico. The group, presently under the leadership of Raymond P. Virgil, has a weekly radio ministry.

Membership: Not reported.

Publications: *Jesus Only News of the Apostolic Faith.*

★1720★
Apostolic Faith Mission Church of God
3344 Pearl Ave. N
Birmingham, AL 35207

Among the people who visited the early Pentecostal revival which occurred in 1906-08 in Los Angeles was F. W. Williams (d. 1932), a black man from the deep south. He received the baptism of the Holy Spirit under the ministry of William J. Seymour and returned to Mississippi to establish an outpost of the Apostolic Faith Mission. Not having great success, he moved to Mobile, Alabama, where a revival occurred under his ministry. Among those converted was an entire congregation of the Primitive Baptist Church. The members gave him their building as the first meeting house for the new mission parish. The church was organized on July 10, 1906.

In 1915, Bishop Williams became one of the first to adopt the Oneness or non-Trinitarian theology which had been espoused

through Pentecostal circles. He broke with Seymour and renamed his church the Apostolic Faith Mission Church of God. He incorporated the new church on October 9, 1915. The church continues to place a strong emphasis upon divine healing, allows women preachers, and practices footwashing with communion. Baptism is in the name of the "Lord Jesus Christ," and without the use of the name, the baptism is considered void. Intoxicants, especially tobacco, alcohol, and drugs are forbidden. Members are admonished to marry only those who have been "saved." The church is headed by the Senior Bishop and a Cabinet of Executive Officers composed of the bishops, overseers, and the general secretary.

Membership: In 1989 the church reported 18 congregations (most of which were in Alabama), 6,200 members, and 32 ministers.

★1721★
Apostolic Overcoming Holy Church of God
1120 N. 24th St.
Birmingham, AL 35234
Bishop Jasper C. Roby

The Apostolic Overcoming Holy Church of God was founded by William Thomas Phillips (1893-1973), the son of a Methodist Episcopal Church minister. However, at a tentmeeting service in Birmingham, Alabama, Phillips was converted to the message of pentecost and holiness under the ministry of Frank W. Williams of the Faith Mission Church of God. Williams ordained Phillips in 1913, and three years later Phillips launched his career as an evangelist in Mobile, Alabama. In 1917, he was selected by the people who has responded to his ministry as the bishop of the Ethiopian Overcoming Holy Church of God. The new organization was incorporated in 1920. It adopted its present name in 1941 in realization that the church was for all people, not just Ethiopians, a popular designation for black people in the early twentieth century.

The AOH Church of God follows the Oneness theology,. It believes in One God who subsists in the union of Father, Son, and Holy Spirit. The church, however, rejects any hint of tri-theism and believes that the One God bears the name of Jesus, a name that can express the fulness of the Godhead. Out of this belief, the church baptizes members in the name of Jesus. Baptism is by immersion and considered necessary for salvation.

The church teaches that God acts in the believer both to baptize in the Spirit (which will be signified by speaking-in-tongues) and progressively over a lifetime to sanctify (make holy). Besides baptism, there are two other ordinances—the Lord's supper and foot washing. The church also teaches divine healing and exhorts members to tithe.

Though headed by bishops, the AOH Church of God is basically congregational in polity with each church owning its own property and managing its own affairs. Churches are grouped into districts presided over by bishops and overseers. A General Assembly, to which all churches send representatives, convenes annually. It is led by the presiding bishop. After serving the church for 57 years, Bishop Phillips was succeeded by Bishop Jasper Roby, the present senior presiding bishop. He is assisted by five associate bishops. The church's periodicals are published by the church's publishing board. Missions are supported in Haiti and Africa.

Membership: In 1988, the church reported 12,000 members, approximately 200 churches, and 750 ministers.

Educational Facilities: AOH Theological Seminary, Birmingham, Alabama.

Publications: *People's Mouthpiece.* • *Young Educator.*

★1722★
Associated Churches of Christ (Holiness)
1302 E. Adams Blvd.
Los Angeles, CA 90011

On the West Coast the Church of Christ (Holiness) U.S.A. was formed in 1915 by Bishop William Washington and work was carried on independently of the work in the east and south by the church's founder, C. P. Jones. A few years later, Jones went to Los Angeles and held a revival meeting. At that time the two men worked out an agreement for cooperative endeavor. The agreement was in effect until 1946-47. Because of what the manual of the Associated Churches of Christ (Holiness) calls the "manipulating of some administrative problems in the upper circles of the Church," the West Coast churches withdrew from the Church of Christ (Holiness)

U.S.A. They now continue under the original incorporation of Bishop Washington. Doctrine and polity are identical with the Church of Christ (Holiness) U.S.A.

Membership: Not reported. In the early 1970s there were 6 churches and 1 mission in the Associated Churches.

★1723★
Astrological, Metaphysical, Occult, Revelatory, Enlightenment Church

Efforts to locate an address for this edition were unsuccessful. The Astrological, Metaphysical, Occult, Revelatory, Enlightenment Church (AMORE) was formed in 1972 by the Rev. Charles Robert Gordon, formerly a minister of the African Methodist Episcopal Zion Church. His father was Bishop Buford Franklin Gordon of the AMEZ Church. The church is Bible-based and views Jesus as the embodiment of cosmic consciousness. The AMORE Church believes in using the occult arts as a means to enlightenment in the coming Aquarian Age. Headquarters of the AMORE Church were established in Meriden, Connecticut. In recent years the church has moved and no contact has been made. Its present status (1985) is unknown.

Membership: Not reported.

★1724★
Ausar Auset Society
c/o Oracle of Thoth, Inc.
Box 281
Bronx, NY 10462

The Ausar Auset Society is a Rosicrucian body serving the black community of the United States. It was founded in the mid-1970s by R. A. Straughn, also known by the name Ra Un Nefer Amen, formerly head of the Rosicrucian Anthroposophical League in New York City. He is the author of several occult texts in spiritual science, each offering methods drawn from the Kabbalah and eastern religions to facilitate the orderly transition to the enlightened state.

The Society has directed its program to blacks and *Metu Neter* (formerly *The Oracle of Thoth*) regularly features, alongside of its occult articles, items of general interest and concern to black people. The Society advocates the appropriation of the positive accomplishments of African ancestors by the contemporary black community. The Society offers free public classes in a variety of occult topics. Currently such classes are being held in New York City, Brooklyn, Chicago, Philadelphia, New Haven, Washington, DC, and Norfolk, VA.

Membership: Not reported.

Publications: *Metu Neter.*

★1725★
Bible Way Church of Our Lord Jesus Christ World Wide
1130 New Jersey Ave. NW
Washington, DC 20001

The Bible Way Church of Our Lord Jesus Christ World Wide was founded in 1957 by former members of the Church of the Lord Jesus Christ of the Apostolic Faith. Prior to 1957, some leaders of the Church of Our Lord Jesus Christ of the Apostolic Faith decried what they saw as the autocratic leadership of Robert Clarence Lawson, the church's bishop. They had suggested that Lawson consider sharing the leadership and consecrate more bishops for the growing denomination. Lawson refused and thus a number of the leading ministers and their churches left to form the Bible Way Churches of Our Lord Jesus Christ. Among the leaders of the new church were Smallwood Edmond Williams (1907-1991), John S. Beane, McKinley Williams, Winfield S. Showell, and Joseph Moore. They were consecrated by John S. Holly, a bishop of the Pentecostal Assemblies of the World. They selected Williams, for many years the general secretary of the parent body, as their presiding bishop. The name of the church derives from the name of the congregation Williams had led in Washington, D.C., since the 1920s.

Williams has been credited with taking the lead among Apostolic Pentecostal groups in the development of a social service and social justice ministry. He led the church to become involved in Washington politics, sponsored the construction of a supermarket near his church, encouraged the development of a housing complex, and worked for more job opportunities within the African American community. His book, *Significant Sermons* (1970), was largely concerned with a Christian response to social problems. Williams also emphasized education as signaled by his opening and maintaining a Bible school adjacent to the headquarters church in Washington, D.C. In this effort he was greatly aided by Dr. James I. Clark, remembered as the denomination's great pioneer educator.

The church follows the non-Trinitarian Pentecostal doctrine of its parent body which emphasizes the sole divinity of Jesus and thus baptizes in the name of Jesus only. **Membership:** In 1988 the church reported approximately 250,000 members in 250 churches.

Educational Facilities: Bible Way Training School, Washington, D.C.

Publications: *The Bible Way News Voice.*

★1726★
Bible Way Pentecostal Apostolic Church

Efforts to locate an address for this edition were unsuccessful. The Bible Way Pentecostal Apostolic Church was founded by Curtis P. Jones. Jones began as a pastor in North Carolina in the Church of God (Apostolic), but left that church to join the Church of Our Lord Jesus Christ of the Apostolic Faith under Robert Clarence Lawson. He became pastor of the St. Paul Apostolic Church in Henry County, Virginia. Jones left during the internal disruption within Bishop Lawson's church in 1957, but did not join with Smallwood E. Williams' Bible Way Church of Our Lord Jesus Christ. Rather, in 1960, with two other congregations in Virginia, he founded a new denomination. A fourth church was soon added.

Membership: In 1980 the church had four congregations, all in Virginia.

★1727★
Black Primitive Baptists
c/o Primitive Baptist Library
Rte. 2
Elon College, NC 27244

Until the Civil War, blacks were members of the predominantly white Primitive Baptist associations and worshiped in segregated meeting houses. After the Civil War, the blacks were organized into separate congregations, and associations were gradually formed. In North Alabama, the Indian Creek Association was formed as early as 1869. Among the leaders was Elder Jesse Lee. He was ordained after the War, and in 1868, organized the Bethlehem Church in Washington, Virginia. In 1877, he became the moderator of the newly formed Second Ketocton Association.

Doctrine and practice of the Black Primitive Baptists are like those of the Regulars. They have no periodical. *The Primitive Messenger*, partially underwritten by Elder W. J. Berry, editor of *Old Faith Contender*, lasted only four years in the early 1950s.

Membership: Not reported. In the early 1970s there were 43 associations which averaged approximately five churches per association and 20 members per church. There are approximately 3,000 members.

★1728★
Center of Being

Efforts to locate an address for this edition were unsuccessful. The Center of Being was formed in 1979 by Baba Prem Ananda, also known as "Anandaji" (b. 1949), and Her Holiness Sri Marashama Devi, affectionately known as "Mataji," an American-born black woman considered by her followers to be an avatar (a self-realized master of the highest order). Mataji was born fully Enlightened in her present incarnation and retained that state for the first twelve years of her life. She regressed in order to experience the separation from the Divine and the path to re-union. During this twelve-year period, she retained some communion with the Divine and experienced many unusual powers, among them an ability to see Lord Shiva (considered a major deity by Hindus), who functioned as her guru. At the age of twenty-four, she regained the state of Enlightenment and began to teach privately. One of her first disciples, Anandaji, assisted her in the formation of the Center of Being and her public teaching activity. Anandaji also attained the Enlightened state.

Mataji teaches a path of Enlightenment, a spontaneous way of being beyond intellectual rules and answers. Mataji is considered a divine personage with the ability to bestow the grace which leads to Enlightenment. She offers herself in weekly "darshans," sessions in which disciples sit in her presence, and in "grace intensives" (thrice annually). Darshan sessions include lectures by Mataji and question-

and-answer sessions (satsang). "Pujas," devotional worship services directed to the deities and Mataji, are held quarterly.

Membership: In 1986 there was only one center, in Los Angeles, and less than a hundred disciples.

Publications: *Lila*. Send orders to Box 3384, Los Angeles, CA 90078.

★1729★
Christian Methodist Episcopal Church
564 Frank Ave.
Memphis, TN 38101

From 1844 until the end of the Civil War, slaves formed a large percentage of the membership of the Methodist Episcopal Church. In South Carolina they were in the majority. The proselytizing activity of both the African Methodist Episcopal Church and the African Methodist Episcopal Zion Church claimed many of these former slaves as soon as they were free; others remained with the Methodist Episcopal Church, South (MECS), the southern branch of the Methodist Episcopal Church which had split in 1844. Many white Methodists felt that given the Blacks' new freedom, a new relationship must follow. In 1870, following the wishes of their Black members, the Methodist Episcopal Church, South helped them form a separate church named the Colored Methodist Episcopal Church (CME). In 1954 the church changed its name to the Christian Methodist Episcopal Church.

At the first General Conference nine annual conferences were designated, the *Discipline* of the MEC,S adopted with necessary changes, a publishing house established, and a periodical, *The Christian Index*, begun. Two MEC,S bishops ordained two colored Methodist Episcopal bishops. Throughout its history the Colored Methodist Episcopal Church has been aided financially in its program by the MEC,S and its successor bodies. Today, the church is very similiar to the United Methodist Church in belief and practice.

One of the keys to Colored Methodist Episcopal success was the 41-year episcopate of Isaac Lane. Besides traveling widely and bolstering the poverty-ridden church, he initiated the educational program by founding the CME High School (now Lane College) in 1882. Education of former slaves and their children, a major enterprise of all Methodists, has been carried through the CME Church in the establishment of a number of schools across the South. Paine College, established with the assistance of the MEC,S has been a traditional focus of CME and MEC,S cooperation. Growth and expansion beyond the 200,000 initial members was slowed by lack of funds. Movement northward followed the major migration of Blacks into northern urban centers in the early twentieth century.

The CME Church is a member of both the National Council of Churches and the World Council of Churches.

Membership: In 1983, the church reported 718,922 members, 2,340 churches, and 2,650 ministers.

Educational Facilities: Lane College, Jackson, Tennessee.
Paine College, Augusta, Georgia.
Miles College, Birmingham, Alabama.
Mississippi Industrial College, Holly Springs, Mississippi.
Texas College, Tyler, Texas.

In 1959 Phillips School of Theology moved from Jackson, Tennessee to Atlanta, Georgia to become part of the Interdenominational Theological Center, a complex of four theological schools, the largest educational facility in the nation for the training of black Christian ministers.

Publications: *Christian Index*. Send orders to Box 665, Memphis, TN 38101.

★1730★
Church of Christ (Holiness) U.S.A.
329 E. Monument St.
Jackson, MS 39202

In 1894 C. P. Jones and Charles H. Mason formed the Church of God in Christ as a holiness body, following their exclusion from fellowship with black Baptists in Arkansas. Mason took most of the body into pentecostalism in 1907. Those who remained were reorganized by Jones as the Church of Christ (Holiness) U.S.A. Jones himself, residing in Jackson, Mississippi, became well known as a composer and publisher of holiness gospel songs. Doctrinally, the Church of Christ (Holiness) U.S.A. is very close to the Church of the Nazarene, with which it almost merged. It follows the Methodist

Articles of Religion printed elsewhere in this volume, and stresses the second blessing of the Holy Spirit which imparts sanctification to the believer. Race issues prevented close relations between the Church of Christ (Holiness) U.S.A. and predominantly white holiness churches.

The church is episcopal in structure with a senior bishop as the highest official. There are seven dioceses. A convention held every two years is the highest legislative authority. Missionary work is sponsored in Mexico. There is a publishing house in Los Angeles. Present leader of the church is Bishop M. R. Conic.

Membership: In 1984 the church had over 10,000 members and 170 congregations.

Educational Facilities: Christ Missionary and Industrial College, Jackson, Mississippi.
Boydton Institute, Boydton, Virginia.

★1731★
Church of God and Saints of Christ
10703 Wade Park Ave.
Cleveland, OH 44106
Bp. James R. Grant

Elder William S. Crowdy, a black cook on the Sante Fe Railroad, claimed to have a vision from God calling him to lead his people to the true religion. He left his job and founded the Church of God and Saints of Christ in 1896 at Lawrence, Kansas. In 1900, he moved to Philadelphia, and the first annual assembly was held. Crowdy died in 1908, and Joseph N. Crowdy and William H. Plummer succeeded him as bishops. Joseph N. Crowdy died in 1917, the same year that the headquarters were moved to Bellville, Virginia, where the church had purchased a large farm. In 1931, Calvin S. Skinner, the last leader appointed by the founder, became bishop, but he lived only three months thereafter. He passed the leadership to Howard Z. Plummer, who held it for many years.

The doctrine of the Church of God is a complicated mixture of Judaism, Christianity and black nationalism. Members are accepted into the church by repentance, baptism by immersion, confession of faith in Christ Jesus, receiving communion of unleavened bread and water, having their feet washed by the elder, and agreeing to keep the Ten Commandments. They must also have been taught how to pray according to Matthew 6:9-13, and they must have been breathed upon with a holy kiss. They believe that black people are the descendants of the ten lost tribes of Israel. They believe in keeping the Ten Commandments and adhering literally to the teachings of both the Old and New Testaments as positive guides to salvation., The church observes the Jewish Sabbath and the use of corresponding Hebrew names. The church is a strong advocate of temperance.

The church is headed by its bishop and prophet who is divinely called to his office. He is believed to be in direct communion with God, to utter prophecies, and to perform miracles. When a prophet dies, the office remains vacant until a new call occurs. The prophet presides over the executive board of twelve ordained elders. The church is divided into district, annual, and general assemblies. There are four orders of the ministry: bishops, missionaries, ordained ministers, and nonordained ministers. Deacons care for the temporal affairs of the church. Each local church bears the denominational name and is numbered according to its appearance in the state. The church at Bellville is communalistic, but other churches are not. The Daughters of Jerusalem and Sisters of Mercy is a women's organization whose duty is to look for straying members, to help the sick and needy, and to care for visitors from other local churches.

Membership: Not reported. At last report (1959) there were 217 churches and 38,217 members. There are affiliated congregations in Jamaica.

Educational Facilities: Bellville Industrial Institute, Bellville, Virginia.

★1732★
Church of God (Apostolic)

Efforts to locate an address for this edition were unsuccessful. The Church of God (Apostolic) was formed in 1877 by Elder Thomas J. Cox at Danville, Kentucky, as the Christian Faith Band. It was one of a number of independent holiness associations of the late nineteenth century. In 1915, it voted a name change, and in 1919 became the Church of God (Apostolic). In 1943, Cox was succeeded by M. Gravely and Eli N. Neal as co-presiding bishops. Headquarters were moved to Beckley, West Virginia. Two years later Gravely divorced his wife and remarried. He was disfellowshipped from the church. In

1964 Neal was succeeded by Love Odom who died two years later and was succeeded by David E. Smith. These two bishops did much to put the national church in a firm financial condition. They were suceeded by the present general overseer, Ruben K. Hash.

It is a strict church, opposing worldliness and practicing footwashing with the monthly Lord's Supper. Baptism by immersion is in the name of Jesus. The church is headed by a board of bishops, one of whom is designated the general overseer who serves as the church's executive head. There is a general assembly annually.

Membership: In 1980 the church had 15,000 members, 43 congregations and approximately 75 ministers.

★1733★
Church of God (Black Jews)

Efforts to locate an address for this edition were unsuccessful. The Church of God (Black Jews) was founded in the early twentieth century by Prophet F. S. Cherry, who claimed to have had a vision calling him to his office as prophet. He was sent to America and began the church in Philadelphia. A self-educated man, Prophet Cherry became conversant in both Hebrew and Yiddish. He became famous for his homiletic abilities, colloquialisms, and biting slang.

The Church of God is open only to black people, who are identified with the Jews of the Bible. White Jews are viewed as frauds and interlopers. The church does not use the term synagogue, the place of worship of the white Jews (Rev. 3:9). The church teaches that Jesus was a black man. The first men were also black, the first white man being Gehazi, who received his whiteness as a curse (11 Kings 5: 27). The white man continued to mix with the black people, and the yellow race resulted. Esau was the first red man (Gen. 25:25). God is, of course, black. Black people sprang from Jacob.

The New Year begins with Passover in April. Saturday is the true Sabbath. Speaking in tongues is considered nonsense. Eating pork, divorce, taking photographs, and observing Christian holidays are forbidden. The end of the period that started with creation is approaching, and the Black Jews will return in 2000 A.D. to institute the millennium.

Membership: Not reported.

★1734★
Church of God in Christ
272 S. Main St.
Memphis, TN 38103

The Church of God in Christ was established in 1894 in Jackson, Mississippi, by Charles H. Mason, at that time an independent Baptist minister who four years previously had been affected by the holiness movement and sanctified. With a colleague, Elder C. P. Jones, he had founded the Church of Christ (Holiness) U.S.A.. He had as a child of twelve been healed suddenly of a sickness that almost killed him. In 1907, two events further changed his life. Elder Jones convinced him that he did not yet have the fullness of the Holy Spirit, for, if he did, he would have the power to heal the sick, cast out devils, and raise the dead. He also heard of the meetings at Azusa Street in Los Angeles, went there, was baptized in the Spirit and spoke in tongues.

In August, 1908, the new doctrine and experience was presented to the representatives of the Church of Christ (Holiness) U.S.A. convention in Jackson. At a meeting of those who accepted Pentecostalism, a General Assembly of the Church of God in Christ was organized. Mason was elected general overseer. (This brief history is at odds with the history presented in the item elsewhere in this *Encyclopedia* on the Church of Christ (Holiness) U.S.A.; the two churches involved tell two different stories.)

The Church of God in Christ was organized in an ascending hierarchy of overseer (pastor), state overseer, and general overseer. There are annual state convocations which decide on disputed matters and assign pastors, and a general convocation for matters of the general church.

Upon the death of Bishop Mason in 1961, a series of reorganizational steps began. Power reverted to the seven bishops who made up the executive commission. This group was extended to twelve in 1962 and O. T. Jones, Jr., was named "senior bishop." An immediate controversy began over the focus of power and a constitutional convention was scheduled. In 1967, a court in Memphis ruled that the powers of the senior bishop and executive board should remain intact until the constitutional convention in 1968. That year reorganization took place and power was invested

in a quadrennial general assembly and a general board of twelve with a presiding bishop to conduct administration between meetings of the general assembly.

Doctrine is similar to that of the International Pentecostal Holiness Church. The group believes in the Trinity, holiness, healing, and the premillennial return of Christ. Three ordinances are recognized: baptism by immersion, the Lord's Supper, and foot-washing.

Membership: In 1987 the church reported 3,000,000 members, 10,500 congregations and 31,896 ministers in the United States. There were 21 congregations and 33 ministers in Canada and an additional 700,000 members in 43 countries around the world.

Educational Facilities: Charles H. Mason Theological Seminary, Atlanta, Georgia.

In addition to the seminary in Atlanta (now part of the Interdenominational Theological Center), the church supports the C. H. Mason System of Bible Colleges which includes a number of schools attached to local congregations both in the United States and abroad.

Publications: *Whole Truth.* • *The Voice of Missions.* Send orders to Box 329, Memphis, TN 38101.

★1735★
Church of God in Christ, Congregational
1905 Bond Ave.
East St. Louis, IL 62201

The Church of God in Christ, Congregational, was formed in 1932 by Bishop J. Bowe of Hot Springs, Arkansas, who argued that the Church of God in Christ should be congregational, not episcopal, in its polity. Forced to withdraw, Bowe organized the Church of God in Christ, Congregational. In 1934, he was joined by George Slack. Slack had been disfellowshipped from the church because of his disagreement with the teaching that if a saint did not pay tithes, he was not saved. He was convinced that tithing was not a New Testament doctrine. He became the junior bishop under Bowe. In 1945, Bowe was wooed back into the Church of God in Christ, and Slack became senior bishop.

Doctrine is like that of the Church of God in Christ, but with disagreements on matters of polity and tithing. Members are conscientious objectors.

Membership: Not reported. In 1971 there were 33 churches in the United States, 4 in England, and 6 in Mexico.

★1736★
Church of God in Christ, International
170 Adelphi St.
Brooklyn, NY 11205
Rt. Rev. Carl E. Williams, Presiding Bishop

In 1969, following its constitutional convention and reorganization, a major schism of the Church of God in Christ occurred when a group of fourteen bishops led by Bishop Illie L. Jefferson rejected the polity of the reorganized church, left it and formed the Church of God in Christ, International, at Kansas City. The issue was the centralized authority in the organization of the parent body. The new group quickly set up an entire denominational structure. The doctrine of the parent body remained intact.

Membership: In 1982 the Church reported 200,000 members, 300 congregations and 1,600 ministers.

Publications: *Message.* • *Holiness Code.*

★1737★
Church of God (Sanctified Church)
1037 Jefferson St.
Nashville, TN 37208

In the early years of the Church of Christ (Holiness) U.S.A., discussed elsewhere in this chapter, the church existed as an unincorporated entity called the "Church of God" or the "Holiness Church." It was only after the schism over Pentecostalism in 1907 that the church was incorporated and its present name was adopted. Before the incorporation, one of the ministers, Elder Charles W. Gray, established the church in Nashville, Tennessee, and the surrounding areas. When the Church of Christ (Holiness) U.S.A. incorporated, Gray continued his work independently as the Church of God (Sanctified Church). The doctrine was the same as that of the Church of Christ (Holiness) U.S.A., but the polity was congregational with local churches operating autonomously and appointing their own ministers. The associated churches remained unincorporated. In 1927 there arose a move within the Church of God (Sanctified Church) to incorporate and to consolidate the work under a board of elders. Among those who constituted the newly incorporated church were Elders J. L. Rucker, R. A. Manter, R. L. Martin, M. S. Sowell, B. Smith, and G. A. Whitley. The move to incorporate led to further controversy and a schism. However, under the incorporation, the elders retained the rights to direct the church, and it continues as the Church of God (Sanctified Church). Elder Gray, founder of the church, withdrew to found the Original Church of God (or Sanctified Church).

The Church of God (Sanctified Church) is headed by a general overseer. The first was Elder Rucker. He has been suceeded by Elder Theopolis Dickerson McGhee (d.1965) and Elder Jesse E. Evans. Mission work is conducted in Jamaica.

Membership: Not reported.In the early 1970s the church reported 60 congregations, approximately 5,000 members.

★1738★
Church of the Fuller Concept

The Church of the Fuller Concept is a New Thought group headed by Dr. Bernese Williamson, a doctor of metaphysical science. Dr. Williamson teaches that we live in the God dispensation. God is our Father and Mother, our natural parents being God caring for us. God has a body (I Cor. 11:30) and is manifested in body-form on earth. Man's body is the image and likeness of God. In recognizing God's body, man can have the blessing of a healthy, whole body. Members of the church do not carry insurance, because in God, where man lives and moves and has his being (which is the body of God), there can be no illness. Dr. Williamson teaches that every meal is a communion and that what one visualizes as he eats and drinks will materialize.

Headquarters of the church are at the Hisacres New Thought Center in Washington, D.C. Members live by a pledge to remember their spiritual nature. They greet each other with the word, "Peace." They adopt spiritual names, because they want to acquire the nature, characteristics and attributes of God. All students sign a pledge to give honest service to their employer for their pay, not accepting tips or vacation-with-pay, nor using intoxicants on the job. This pledge is given to the employers.

Membership: Not reported.

★1739★
Church of the Living God (Christian Workers for Fellowship)
434 Forest Ave.
Cincinnati, OH 45229
Bishop W. E. Crumes

The Church of the Living God (Christian Workers for Fellowship) was formed in 1889 by a former slave, the Rev. William Christian (1856-1928) of Wrightsville, Arkansas. Christian was an early associate of Charles H. Mason, also a Baptist minister who left the Baptist Church to form the Church of God in Christ. Christian claimed to have had a revelation that the Baptists were preaching a sectarian doctrine and he left them in order to preach the unadulterated truth. He created the office of "chief." Mrs. Ethel L. Christian succeeded her husband after his death and was, in turn, succeeded by their son, John L. Christian. Mrs. Christian claimed that the original revelation came to both her husband and herself.

The doctrine is trinitarian and somewhat Pentecostal. The group rejects the idea of "tongues" as the initial evidence of the baptism of the Holy Spirit, although "tongues" are allowed. However, "tongues" must be recognizable languages, not "unintelligible utterance." Footwashing is a third ordinance. Salvation is gained by obeying the commandments to hear, understand, believe, repent, confess, be baptized, and participate in the Lord's Supper and in foot-washing.

The Church of the Living God also has a belief that Jesus Christ was of the black race because of the lineage of David and Abraham. David in Psalms 119:83 said he became like a bottle in the smoke (i.e., black). The church members also hold that Job (Job 30:30), Jeremiah (Jer. 8:21), and Moses' wife (Numbers 12:11) were black. These teachings were promulgated at a time when many Baptists were teaching that blacks were not human, but the offspring of a human father and female beast. The Church of the Living God countered with the assertion that the saints of the Bible were black.

The polity is episcopal and the church is modeled along the lines of a fraternal organization. Christian was very impressed with the Masons, and there are reportedly many points of doctrine known only to members of the organization. Tithing is stressed. Churches are called temples.

Membership: In 1985 the church reported 170 churches, 42,000 members, and 170 ministers.

Publications: *The Gospel Truth.* • *Fellowship Echoes.*

★1740★
Church of the Living God, the Pillar and Ground of the Truth, Inc.
4520 Hydes Ferry Pike
Box 80735
Nashville, TN 37208

The Church of the Living God, the Pillar and Ground of the Truth, Inc. traces its beginning to 1903 when Mary Lena Lewis Tate (1871-1930), a black woman, began to preach the gospel first at Steel Springs, Tennessee, and Paducah, Kentucky, and then other states in the South. By 1908, when a number of holiness bands had been formed by people converted under her ministry, she was taken ill. Pronounced beyond cure, she was healed and given the baptism of the Holy Spirit and spoke in tongues. She called an assembly in Greenville, Alabama, during which the Church of the Living God, the Pillar and Ground of Truth was organized. She was selected Chief Apostle Elder and chief overseer. The church grew quickly in the states of Georgia, Florida, Tennessee, and Kentucky and by the end of the next decade had congregations across the eastern half of the United States. Bishops were introduced into the church in 1914.

In 1919, the first of two major schisms occurred. Led by the church in Philadelphia, Pennsylvania, some members left to found the House of God, Which Is the Church of the Living God, the Pillar and Ground of Truth. Then, in 1931, following Mother Tate's death, the church reorganized, and three persons were ordained to fill the office of chief overseer. The three chosen were Mother Tate's son F. E. Lewis, M. F. L. Keith (widow of Bishop W. C. Lewis), and B. L. McLeod. These three eventually became leaders of distinct church bodies. Lewis' following is the continuing Church of the Living God, the Pillar and Ground of the Truth, Inc. Keith's group became known as the House of God Which Is the Church of the Living God, the Pillar and Ground of Truth Without Controversy.

Bishop McLeod's organization is known as the Church of the Living God, the Pillar, and Ground of Truth which He purchased with His Own Blood, Inc. The church affirms the central doctrines of traditional Christianity including the Holy Trinity and salvation through Christ. It teaches that people are justified and cleansed by faith in Christ and glorified and wholly sanctified by receiving the Holy Ghost and Fire. Evidence of the reception of the Holy Ghost is speaking in tongues. The unknown tongue is a sign of God's victory over sin. There are three ordinances: baptism by immersion, the Lord's Supper, and foot washing.

The church is headed by a bishop, designated the chief overseer. After the death of Bishop F. E. Lewis in 1968, Bishop Helen M. Lewis, the present head of the church, became the chief overseer. She administers the affairs of the church with the assistance of the general assembly, which meets annually, a board of trustees, and the supreme executive council consisting of the other bishops and seven elders. The New and Living Way Publishing House is the church's publishing arm. **Membership:** In 1988, the church reported approximately 2,000 members and approximately 100 ministers.

Publications: *The True Report.*

★1741★
Church of Universal Triumph/The Dominion of God
8317 LaSalle Blvd.
Detroit, MI 48206
Rev. James Shaffer

Rivaling Sweet Daddy Grace and Father Divine as charismatic leaders in the black community was the Rev. James Francis Marion Jones, better known as Prophet Jones (1908-1971). Born in Birmingham, Alabama, the son of a railroad brakeman and a school teacher, he was raised in Triumph the Church and Kingdom of God in Christ. Even as a child, he preached (he did so regularly after his eleventh birthday). In 1938 he was sent to Detroit as a missionary and became successful quickly. Tension with headquarters arose before the year was out, however, when members began to shower Jones with expensive gifts. The headquarters claimed them. Rather than surrender his new affluence, Jones left the church and founded the Church of Universal Triumph/the Dominion of God.

The new church, modeled on the parent body, was built upon Jones' charisma. During the 1940s and 1950s he became known for his wealth. His possessions included a white mink coat, a 54-room French chateau which had been built in 1917 by a General Motors executive, five Cadillacs each with its own chauffeur, jewelry, perfumes, and wardrobe of almost 500 ensembles. Jones claimed to be in direct contact with God, who instructed him in the form of a breeze fanning his ear. Among his practices was dispensing solutions to personal problems after inviting individuals to mount his dais and whisper their problems in his ear. Most of Prophet Jones' wealth came from people grateful for Jones' healing ability. Followers were to be found in all the large northern cities. Jones was titled, "His Holiness the Rev. Dr. James F. Jones, D.D., Universal Dominion Ruler, Internationally known as Prophet Jones."

The Church, like the parent body, is very strict. Members are not allowed to smoke, drink, play games of any kind, use coffee or tea, fraternize with non-Dominionitetry, attend another church, or marry without the consent of the ruler of the church. Women must wear girdles and men health belts. The major theological tenet concerns the beginning of the millennium in 2,000 A.D. All alive at that time will become immortal and live in the heaven on earth.

The upward path of Prophet Jones came to an abrupt end in 1956 when a vice raid on his home led to his arrest and trial for gross indecency. He was acquitted, but the damage had been done and his following declined from that time. During the year prior to his death in 1971, he commuted between Detroit and Chicago. Following his death, his assistant, the Rev. Lord James Schaffer became the Dominion Ruler. He was named by the Dominion Council and Board of Trustees. Some 20 ministers and 5,000 members attended the funeral of Prophet Jones in 1971.

Membership: Not reported.

★1742★
Churches of God, Holiness
170 Ashby St. NW
Atlanta, GA 30314

The Churches of God, Holiness, were formed by Bishop King Hezekiah Burruss (d. 1963), formerly of the Church of Christ (Holiness) U.S.A. Burruss began a church in Atlanta in 1914 that belonged to that organization, and by 1920, the Atlanta congregation was large enough that it hosted the national convention of the Church of Christ (Holiness) U.S.A. Shortly after that Atlanta meeting, however, Burruss formed his own church. Doctrine is like the doctrine of the parent body.

The highest authority is the national convention. There are also annual state conventions. Practically speaking the government developed during the period of strong leadership exercised by the founding bishop. The bishop appoints the state overseers who assign all pastors. The present bishop is Titus Paul Burruss.

Membership: Not reported. In 1967 there were 42 churches, 16 ministers and 25,600 members, mostly along the East Coast.

Publications: *The Bethlehem Star.*

★1743★
Commandment Keepers Congregation of the Living God
1 W. 123rd St.
New York, NY 10027

The Commandment Keepers Congregation of the Living God emerged among West Indian blacks who migrated to Harlem. The group began with the Beth B'nai Abraham congregation founded in 1924 by Arnold Josiah Ford, an early black nationalist and leader in the Universal Negro Improvement Association founded by Marcus Garvey. Ford had repudiated Christianity, adopted Judaism, and learned Hebrew. During the years after the congregation began, Ford met Arthur Wentworth Matthew (1892-1973). Matthew was born in Lagos, West Africa, in 1892. His family moved to St. Kitts in the British West Indies and then, in 1911, to New York. Matthew became a minister in the Church of the Living God, the Pillar and Ground of Truth, a black pentecostal church which had endorsed the U.N.I.A. Then in 1919, with eight other men, he organized his own group, the Commandment Keepers: Holy Church of the Living God, over which he became bishop. In Harlem, he had met white Jews for the first time and in the 1920s came to know A. J. Ford. Possibly

from Ford, Matthew began to learn Orthodox Judaism and Hebrew and to acquire ritual materials.

Both also learned of t ie Falashas, the black Jews of Ethiopia, and began to identify with them. In 1930, Ford's congregation ran into financial trouble. Ford turned over the membership to Matthew's care and left for Ethiopia where he spent the rest of his life. The identification with Ethiopia merely increased through the years. In 1935, when Haile Selassie was crowned emperor, Matthew declared himself the Falashas in America and claimed credentials from Haile Selassie.

The Commandment Keepers believe that the black men are really the Ethiopian Falashas and the Biblical Hebrews who had been stripped of the knowledge of their name and religion during the slavery era. It is impossible for a black man to conceive of himself as a "Negro" and retain anything but slave mentality. With other black Jews, adherents believe the biblical patriarchs to have been black. Christianity is rejected as the religion of the Gentiles or whites.

An attempt has been made to align the Commandment Keepers with Orthodox Jewish practice. Hebrew is taught and revered as a sacred language. The Jewish holidays are kept, and the Sabbath services are held on Friday evenings and Saturday mornings and afternoons. Kosher food laws are kept. An Ethiopian Hebrew Rabbinical college trains leaders in Jewish history, the Mishnah, Josephus, the Talmud, and legalism. Elements of Christianity are retained–footwashing, healing, and the gospel hymns. Services are free of what Matthew terms "niggeritions," the loud emotionalism of the holiness groups.

Matthew also taught Kabbalistic Science, a practice derived from conjuring, the folk magic of Southern blacks. By conjuring, Matthew believed that he could heal and create changes in situations. The conjuring is worked through four angels. In order to get results, one must call upon the right angel.

Matthew was succeeded by his grandson, David M. Dore, a graduate of Yeshiva University.

Membership: Not reported. In the early 1970s there were a reported 3,000 members in several congregations in the New York metropolitan area and the Northeast; 300 members attended the synagogue on East 123rd Street in New York City.

★1744★
Deliverance Evangelistic Centers
505 Central Ave.
Newark, NJ 07107

The initial Deliverance Evangelistic Center was formed in Brooklyn, New York in the 1950s by Arturo Skinner (d. 1975). Skinner had been stopped from committing suicide by what he believed to be the voice of God which told him, "Arturo, if you but turn around, I'll save your soul, heal your body, and give you a deliverance ministry." He was twenty-eight years old at the time, and though he had a full gospel background, he had never heard of anything termed a "deliverance ministry." In a period of retreat following his encounter with God, Skinner fasted and had a number of visions and dreams. He also consecrated his life to the ministry to which he had been called. After the founding of the first center, others were founded and pastors ordained to care for them. Women have been accepted into the ordained ministry as both evangelists and pastors.

The statement of belief of the centers includes an affirmation in the authority of the Bible as inspired and infallible, the Trinity, Jesus Christ as redeemer, the Holy Spirit who empowers and baptizes believers, speaking-in-tongues as evidence of the baptism of the Holy Spirit, creation, the necessity of repentence, sanctification, and water baptism by immersion. Skinner was the church's first Apostle. He was succeeded by Ralph Nickels.

Membership: There are centers in Brooklyn and Poughkeepsie, New York; Philadelphia; Washington, D.C.; Orlando, Florida; and Asbury Park and Newark, New Jersey.

Publications: *Deliverance Voice.*

★1745★
Ethiopian Zion Coptic Church

Efforts to locate an address for this edition were unsuccessful. The Ethiopian Zion Coptic Church was founded in Jamaica in 1914 by Marcus Garvey and orginially came to America in 1920 as part of his reformist efforts in the black community. However, the church died out in the United States and became a small body in Jamaica. Then in 1970, several Americans in Jamaica encountered the church, joined it, and brought it back to Star Island, off Miami Beach, Florida.

A second center was started in New Jersey. The leader of the group was Thomas Reilly, Jr., generally known by his religious name, Brother Louv.

Church members believe in a God who is experienced through the smoking of ganja, i.e., marijuana. Smoking marijuana is described as making a burnt sacrifice to the God within. The ceremonies for smoking the ganja utilize a specially made pipe. Coptics smoke ganja in such quantities that they hope it will reorganize their body chemistry around THC, the psycho-active ingredient in the plant, and they will thus survive the end of this world to live in God's new world. The new world is seen as a time in which there will be plenty for all without the necessity of an eight-hour work day. Peace and brotherhood will reign, and life will be lived at the horse-and-buggy pace. Ceremonially smoking ganja is the major sacramental act of church members, and members quote the Bible (Genesis 1:29; Exodus 3:2-4; Psalm 104:14; and Hebrews 6:7) in support of their use of marijuana.

Coptics also have a strong code dictating relations between the sexes. Women sit separately for the sacramental service and are not allowed to fill their own pipe. Sexual activity is strongly regulated. Homosexuality, oral sex, birth control, and abortion are prohibited. The only recognized purpose for sex is procreation.

Even prior to the church being granted tax exemption in 1975, it has fought an intense battle with government authorities. As early as 1973, authorities had seized 105 tons of marijuana from the group. In 1977 tax exemption was revoked. The church filed a lawsuit demanding the religious right of its members to smoke marijuana, a case lost in late 1978. Immediately after the court ruling, Reilly and five other church leaders were arrested in a raid on the Star Island headquarters. They were indicted and in 1981 convicted for drug smuggling. In 1982, Reilly, serving time in the Metropolitan Corrections Center in Miama, sued U.S. Attorney General William French Smith for the right to his daily sacrament of at least an ounce of marijuana.

In 1981, a group of approximately 20 members of the church moved to rural Wisconsin and established a settlement in an isolated valley near Soldiers Grove. They had moved from Iowa because of local harassment as a result of their refusal to have their children immunized as required by state law. Investigation stimulated by the group's use of marijuana led to arrests of church leaders in 1985. The arrest and conviction of church leaders has disrupted the life of the church, and the courts in the United States have persistently refused to allow the use of controlled substances by church organizations (apart from the Native American Church). The present status of the church is in doubt.

International headquarters of the church are in White Horses, Jamaica, where it had incorporated in 1976. They operate a 4,000 acre farm in St. Thomas Parish. Leader of the church in Jamaica is Keith Gordon (religious name, "Nyah").

Membership: Not reported. There are an estimated 200 members in the United States.

Publications: Coptic Time.

★1746★
Fire-Baptized Holiness Church of God of the Americas

Efforts to locate an address for this edition were unsuccessful. W. E. Fuller (1875-1958), the only black man in attendance at the 1898 organizing conference of the Fire-Baptized Holiness Church, became the leader of almost a thousand black people over the next decade. Feelings of discrimination led to their withdrawal and they organized the Colored Fire-Baptized Holiness Church at Anderson, South Carolina, on May 1, 1908. The white body gave them their accumulated assets and property at this time. Reverend Fuller was elected overseer and bishop. Doctrine is the same as in the International Pentecostal Holiness Church, the body that absorbed the Fire-Baptized Holiness Church.

Legislative and executive authority are vested in a general council that meets every four years and in the eleven-member executive council (composed of bishops, district elders, and pastors). Mission work is under one of the bishops.

Membership: Not reported. In 1968 the church reported 53 churches and 9,088 members.

Publications: True Witness.

★1747★
Free Christian Zion Church of Christ
1315 Hutchingson
Nashville, AR 71852

The Free Christian Zion Church of Christ was formed on July 10, 1905, at Redemption, Arkansas, by the Rev. E. D. Brown, a conference missionary of the African Methodist Episcopal Zion Church. He and ministers from other Methodist churches objected to what they considered a taxing of the churches for support of an ecclesiastical system and believed that the primary concern of the church should be the care of the poor and needy.

The doctrine is Wesleyan and the polity Methodist with several minor alterations. The bishop, who is called the chief pastor, presides over the work and appoints the ministers and church officers. Pastors and deacons are the local church officers. There are district evangelists to care for the unevangelized communities.

Membership: In 1965 there were 16,000 members in 60 churches.

Publications: Zion Trumpet.

★1748★
Free Church of God in Christ

Efforts to locate an address for this edition were unsuccessful. The Free Church of God in Christ dates from 1915 when J. H. Morris, a former pastor in the National Baptist Convention of the U.S.A., Inc., and a group of members of his church experienced the baptism of the Holy Spirit and spoke in tongues. The group, mostly members of Morris' family, founded a Pentecostal group which they called the Church of God in Christ. They chose as their leader the founder's son, E. J. Morris, who believed he was "selected" for the role. In 1921, the group united with the larger body led by Bishop Charles H. Mason, which had the same name. The union lasted for only four years, and Morris' group adopted its present name when it again became independent in 1925. It has the same doctrine and polity as the Mason body. By the late 1940s the church had 20 congregations.

Remarks: No direct contact has been made with the Church since the 1940s and its present condition is unknown. It may be defunct.
Membership: Not reported.

★1749★
Fundamental Baptist Fellowship Association

Efforts to locate an address for this edition were unsuccessful. The Fundamental Baptist Fellowship Association was formed in 1962 by black members of the General Association of Regular Baptist Churches (GARBC). The black members came into the GARBC as a result of missionary work but felt that the GARBC would not accept them into the full fellowship. They presently cooperate with the Conservative Baptist Association.

Membership: Not reported. In the early 1970s there were approximately 10 churches.

★1750★
Glorious Church of God in Christ Apostolic Faith

Efforts to locate an address for this edition were unsuccessful. The Glorious Church of God in Christ Apostolic Faith was founded in 1921 by C. H. Stokes, its first presiding bishop. He was succeeded in 1928 by S. C. Bass who was to head the church for over a quarter of a century. However, in 1952, after the death of his first wife, Bass remarried a woman who was a divorcee. It had been taught for many years that marrying a divorced person was wrong. Bass' actions split the fifty-congregation church in half. Those who remained loyal to Bishop Bass retained the name, but the founding charter was retained by the other group, which took the name Original Glorious Church of God in Christ Apostolic Faith.

★1751★
God's House of Prayer for All Nations

Efforts to locate an address for this edition were unsuccessful. God's House of Prayer for All Nations, Inc., was founded in 1964 in Peoria, Illinois, by Bishop Tommie Lawrence, formerly of the Church of God in Christ. The doctrine is "oneness" Pentecostal, identifying Jesus with the Father, and the polity is strongly episcopal. Great stress is placed on healing as one of the signs of the spirit and there is much fellowship with the churches of the Miracle Revival Fellowship founded by the late A. A. Allen.

Membership: Not reported. There are several congregations, all in northern Illinois.

★1752★
Gospel Spreading Church
2030 Georgia Ave. NW
Washington, DC 20003

The Gospel Spreading Church, sometimes called Elder Michaux Church of God or the Radio Church of God, was founded by Lightfoot Solomon Michaux (1885-1968), a minister in the Church of God (Holiness). At one point he served as the church's secretary-treasurer. However, he came into conflict with C. P. Jones, founder of the Church of God (Holiness) and left to found an independent church in Hampton, Virginia, in 1922, retaining the name he had previously used, the Gospel Spreading Tabernacle Association. In 1928 he moved to Washington, D.C., and established the Church of God and Gospel Spreading Association.

His early success continued in the nation's capital, and he had discovered the potential of radio while in Virginia. In 1929 he began broadcasting on WJSV. Shortly thereafter CBS bought the station and his show expanded through the system. By 1934 he was on over 50 stations nationwide, with an estimated audience of 25,000,000. His show was also carried internationally by shortwave. He was the first black person to receive such exposure. He mixed holiness themes with positive thinking. His magazine was entitled *Happy News*.

From his radio audience, congregations began to form in black communities, primarily in the East. However, by the beginning of World War II his radio ministry had declined and he was heard on only a few stations, in those cities where congregations had formed. In 1964 he reorganized his followers as the Gospel Spreading Church, but most of the congregations continued to call themselves the Church of God.

Membership: Not reported.

★1753★
Hanafi Madh-hab Center, Islam Faith
7700 16th St. NW
Washington, DC 20012

The Hanafi Madh-hab Center was first set up in the United States by Dr. Tasibur Uddein Rahman in the late 1920s. In 1947 Khalifa Hammas Abdul Khaalis (born Ernest Timothy McGee) met his teacher, Dr. Rahman, a Mussulman (or Muslim) from Pakistan, who gave him his new name and taught him the *sunnah* (the tradition and practice) of the Prophet Muhammad. In 1950, Dr. Rahman sent Khalifa Hamaas Abdul Khaalis into the Nation of Islam (now the American Muslim Mission) to guide the members into Sunni Islam (that faith and practice recognized by the great majority of Muslims). By 1956 Khalifa Hamaas Abdul Khaalis was the national secretary of the Nation of Islam. He left the Nation of Islam in 1958, after unsuccessfully trying to convince Elijah Muhammad, the leader of the Nation of Islam, to change the direction of the movement. He set-up the Hanafi Madh-hab Center in Washington, D.C.

Again at the beginning of 1973, Khalifa Hamaas Abdul Khaalis wrote letters to the members and leaders of the Nation of Islam asking them to change to Sunni Muslim belief and practice. On January 18, 1973, members of the Nation of Islam came into the center in Washington, D. C., (which also served as Khalifa Hamaas Abdul Khaalis' home) and murdered six of his children and his stepson. His wife was wounded. Subsequently, five members of the Philadelphia Nation of Islam group were convicted of the murders, only to receive relatively light sentences.

In 1977, Khalifa Hamaas Abdul Khaalis and other Al-Hanif Musselman took action against the showing of a motion picture, "Mohammad, Messenger of God," which they considered sacreligious, due to be released in theatres in America. They took over three buildings in Washington, D.C., and held people hostage for 38 hours. In the process, one man was killed. For this action Khalifa Hamaas Abdul Khaalis was sentenced to spend from 41 to 120 years in prison, and 11 of his followers were also convicted and sentenced. Since no believing Musselman was on the the jury, Khalifa Hamaas Abdul Khaalis considers the jury to have lacked impartiality.

The Al-Hanif Hanafi Musselmans uphold the two standards of Islam, *Holy Qur'an* and the Hadiths, and are Sunni (obeying all things as laid down by Allah to the Prophet Muhammad) Muslims. Hanafi means unconditional and uncompromising. They also follow by way of the 124,000 Prophets major and minor, and believe in all holy books according to Allah's knowledge. The *Holy Qur'an* is the final Seal of All Prophets and Prophecy.

The Hanafi Mussulmans have taken a special interest in presenting Islam to African Americans and informing them that Islam is a religion that does not recognize distinctions of race or color.

Authority for Al-Hanif Hanafi Mussulmans is vested in the chief *Iman* (teacher), Khalifa Hammas Abdul Khaalis, and each mosque is headed by an iman appointed by him.

Membership: Not reported. There are estimated to be several hundred Hanafi Muslims in the United States. Mosques are located in Washington, D.C.; New York City; Chicago, Illinois; and Los Angeles, California.

Publications: *Look and See.*

★1754★
Highway Christian Church of Christ
436 W St. NW
Washington, DC 20001

The Highway Christian Church of Christ was founded in 1929 by James Thomas Morris, formerly a minister with the Pentecostal Assemblies of the World. Relations between the two groups remained cordial, and in 1941 Bishop N.J. M. Turpin of the Assemblies consecrated Morris to the episcopal leadership of the Highway Church. Morris died in 1959 and was succeeded by his nephew, J. V. Lomax, formerly a member of the Church of Our Lord Jesus Christ of the Apostolic Faith.

The Highway Church has a reputation as one of the more conservative Pentecostal church bodies. Members are encouraged to wear only black (suits and skirts) and white (shirts and blouses), and to avoid bright colors as too ostentatious. The church will accept ordained women from other denominations, but will neither ordain females nor allow them to pastor congregations.

Membership: In 1980 there were 13 congregations and about 3,000 members.

★1755★
House of God Which Is the Church of the Living God, the Pillar and Ground of Truth

Efforts to locate an address for this edition were unsuccessful. Not to be confused with the church of the same name which derives from the movement begun by Mary L. Tate known as the Church of the Living God, the Pillar and Ground of Truth, the church presently under discussion derives from the work begun by William Christian. In the early twentieth century, the Church of the Living God (Christian Workers for Fellowship), which Christian founded, was splintered on several occasions. In 1902, a group calling itself the Church of the Living God, Apostolic Church, withdrew and, six years later under the leadership of Rev. C. W. Harris, became the Church of the Living God, General Assembly. It united in 1924 with a second small splinter body. In 1925, a number of churches withdrew from the Church of the Living God (Christian Workers for Fellowship) under the leadership of Rev. E. J. Cain and called themselves the Church of the Living God, the Pillar and Ground of Truth. The Harris group joined the Cain group in 1926 and they later adopted the present name. The Church is one in doctrine with the Church of the Living God (Christian Workers for Fellowship). Polity is episcopal and there is an annual general assembly.

Remarks: The last independent source on this body is the 1936 *Census of Religious bodies*. Later sources often confuse it with the Philadelphia-based group of the same name. Its present location and strength is unknown.

Membership: Not reported.

★1756★
House of God Which Is the Church of the Living God, the Pillar and Ground of Truth, Inc.
6107 Cobbs Creek Pkwy.
Philadelphia, PA 19143

In 1919 the Church of the Living God, the Pillar and Ground of Truth founded by Mary L. Tate, experienced a schism led by the congregation in Philadelphia. The new group, the House of God, the Church of the Living God, the Pillar and Ground of Truth continues the doctrine and episcopal polity of the parent body, but is administratively separate. The general assembly meets annually.

Membership: Not reported. In the early 1970 the church reported 103 churches and 25,860 members.

Publications: *The Spirit of Truth Magazine.* Send orders to 3943 Fairmont St., Philadelphia, PA 19104.

★1757★
House of God Which Is the Church of the Living God, the Pillar and Ground of Truth without Controversy (Keith Dominion)
Box 9113
Montgomery, AL 36108
Bishop J. W. Jenkins, Chief Overseer

In 1931, following the death of founder Bishop Mary L. Tate, the Church of the Living God, the Pillar and Ground of the Truth, Inc., appointed three chief overseers. Eventually, each became the head of a distinct segment of the church and then of an independent body called a dominion. One of the three chief overseers was M. F. L. Keith, widow of Bishop Tate's son, W. C. Lewis. Her dominion became known as the House of God Which is the Church of the Living God the Pillar and Ground of Truth Without Controversy (Keith Dominion).

The church is headed by a Chief Overseer (Bishop J. W. Jenkins succeeded Bishop Keith in that post) and a Supreme Executive Council.

Membership: Not reported.

★1758★
House of Judah

Efforts to locate an address for this edition were unsuccessful. The House of Judah is a small Black Israelite group founded in 1965 by Prophet William A. Lewis. Alabama-born Lewis was converted to his black Jewish beliefs (which are similar to those of the Church of God and Saints of Christ) from a street preacher in Chicago in the 1960s. Throughout the decade he gathered a small following out of a storefront on the southside and in 1971 moved the group to a twenty-two-acre tract near Grand Junction, Michigan. The group lived quietly and little noticed until 1983 when a young boy in the group was beaten to death. The incident focused attention on the group for its advocacy of corporal punishment. The mother of the boy was sentenced to prison for manslaughter. By 1985 the group had resettled in Alabama.

The House of Judah teaches that the Old Testament Jews were black, being derived from Jacob and his son Judah, who were black (Jeremiah 14:2). Both Solomon and Jesus were black. Jerusalem, not Africa, is the black man's land. The white Jew is the devil (Rev. 2:9); he occupies the black man's land but will soon be driven out. The House of Judah awaits a deliverer, whom God will send to take the black man from the U.S.A. to Jerusalem. He will be a second Moses to lead his people to the promised land. The group lives communally.

Membership: In 1985 there were approximately 80 members living on the farm in rural Alabama. There is only one center.

★1759★
House of the Lord

Efforts to locate an address for this edition were unsuccessful. The House of the Lord was founded in 1925 by Bishop W. H. Johnson, who established headquarters in Detroit. The doctrine is Pentecostal but departs on several important points. A person who enters the church is born of water and seeks to be born of God by a process of sanctification. The Holy Ghost may be given and is evidenced by speaking in tongues. But sanctification is evidenced by conformity to a very rigid code which includes refraining from worldly amusements, whiskey, policy rackets (the "numbers game"), becoming bell hops, participating in war, swearing, secret organizations, tithing, and life insurance (except as required by an employer). A believer is not sanctified if he owns houses, lands, or goods. Water is used in the Lord's Supper. Members are not to marry anyone not baptized by the Holy Ghost.

The church is governed by a hierarchy of ministers, state overseers, and chief overseer. There is a common treasury at each local church from which the destitute are helped.

Membership: Not reported.

★1760★
Institute of Divine Metaphysical Research

Efforts to locate an address for this edition were unsuccessful. The Institute for Divine Metaphysical Research grew out of a vision of Dr. Henry Clifford Kinley which occurred on June 6, 1931 in Springfield, Ohio. Kinley, a holiness church minister, was given a vision of Yahweh (who others mistakenly call God) and His plan for the ages. He began to give classes on the insight derived from the vision the following year and soon thereafter he founded the Kinley Institute. Among his first students was Carl F. Gross, who became his lifelong associate and president of the institute. In 1958, with approximately seventy of his students, Kinley moved to Los Angeles and incorporated the Institute for Divine Metaphysical Research. In 1961, Elohim the Archetype (Original Pattern of the Universe, the major exposition of the vision) appeared. Copies were immediately sent to a number of prominent world political and religious leaders. In 1971 twelve ministers of the institute were sent out on an Ecclesiastical Peace Mission to countries in Europe and the Middle East. A second such mission to countries on every continent was conducted in 1975.

The intent of the institute has been to spread the message of Kinley's vision as presented in his book. The teachings draw from a variety of sources including both the Sacred Name Movement and theosophy. In the vision he learned the real name of the Holy One of Israel (Yahweh) and of his nature and purposes. Yahweh is Spirit Substance, without form. As Elohim, Yahweh appears in His super incoporeal form and in that form was seen by Moses (Exodus 24), Isaiah (Isaiah 6:1-4), and the disciples at the Mount of Transfiguration (Matthew 17:1-2). Yahweh-Elohim has also taken physical form generally as the material creation (matter is condensed spirit) and specifically as Yahshua the Messiah (generally known as Jesus). After the death and resurrection of Yahshua, Yahweh continued in his physical form as the Comforter or Holy Spirit, and dwells in preachers of the true gospel.

Yahweh-Elohim, as was revealed to Kinley, is the archtypal pattern of the universe, a pattern revealed to Moses and embodied in the Hebrew tabernacle. It is, however, also repeated in numerous earthly structures, among which is the Kaballah, which Kinley terms "theosophy."

Yahweh's purpose is revealed through the ages (i.e., particular periods of history) and dispensations (i.e., the divinely appointed ordering of earthly affairs by Yahweh). The dispensations as recounted by Kinley generally follow that proposed by C. I. Scofield in his reference Bible, and adopt a traditional chronology. The first dispensation begins with Yahweh's covenant with Adam, the second with Noah, the third with Abraham, and the fourth with Noah. Kinley is insistent that the fifth dispensation, that of the "law of the Spirit" or New Testament, this present church age, began not at Jesus' birth but at his resurrection and Pentecost. Most importantly, the present dispensation is swiftly drawing to a close and the next dispensation, that of the Kingdom in Immortality, will begin around the year 2000. The revelation of Yahweh's purposes to Kinley and his work of spreading the information ushered in the last days of the church age.

Membership: In 1984 the institute reported groups in two cities, but with work and members in 38 cities and five countries. Membership of the institute consists predominantly of black Americans.

★1761★
International Council of Community Churches
7808 College Dr., No. 25E
Palos Heights, IL 60463
Rev. J. Ralph Shotwell, Executive Director

The International Council of Community Churches was formally organized in 1946, but possesses a history dating from the early nineteenth century when nonsectarian community churches began to appear as an alternative to the formation of separate denominationally affiliated congregations. Such community churches were especially welcomed in communities too small to support more than one viable congregation. Over the years, such congregations have frequently retained a fiercely independent stance. To their number were added other independent congregations that had separated from denominational structures and adopted a nonsectarian stance.

In the wake of the ecumenical movement in the early twentieth century, the most visible symbol being the Federal Council of Churches of Christ formed in 1908, many congregations merged across denominational lines, some forming independent federated or union churches, dropping all denominational affiliation. During this period, some community churches began to see, in light of their years of existence apart from denominational boundaries, that they had a particular role vis-a-vis Christian unity.

A first attempt to build a network of community churches was known as the Community Church Workers of the United States. At a national conference of individuals serving community churches in Chicago in 1923, a committee formed to hold a second conference and outline plans for a national association. Organization occurred the next year and the Rev. Orvis F. Jordan of the Park Ridge (Illinois) Community Church was named as secretary. He later became the first president of the group. The organization continued for over a decade, but died in the 1930s due to lack of support.

A second organization of community churches was also begun in 1923 among predominantly black congregations. Representatives of five congregations gathered in Chicago, Illinois, in the fall of 1923 to form the National Council of the People's Community Churches (incorporated in 1933 as the Biennial Council of the People's Church of Christ and Community Centers of the United States and Elsewhere). The Rev. William D. Cook, pastor of Metropolitan Community Church in Chicago, served as the first president.

Unable to gain recognition from the Federal Council of Churches, the independent community churches began a second attempt at organization in the last days of World War II. The Rev. Roy A. Burkhart, pastor of First Community Church of Columbus, Ohio, led in the formation of the Ohio Association for Community Churches in 1945. The next year representatives from 19 states and Canada met and formed the National Council of Community Churches.

Almost immediately, the black and white groups began to work toward a merger. The merger, accomplished in 1950, created the International Council of Community Churches with a charter membership of 160 churches. By 1957, the several foreign congregations had ceased their affiliation with the council and the word "International" was dropped. In 1969, the name was changed to National Council of Community Churches. In 1983, however, foreign congregations in Canada and Nigeria affiliated, and in 1984 the original name was again assumed.

There is no doctrinal statement shared by the council or its member churches, though most churches share a liberal, ecumenical-minded, Protestant perspective. The council describes itself as committed to Christian unity and working "toward a fellowship as comprehensive as the spirit and teachings of Christ and as inclusive as the love of God."

The council is a loosely organized fellowship of free and autonomous congregations. The national and regional officers facilitate communication between congregations and serve member congregations in various functions, such as representing them at the Consultation on Church Union and coordinating the securing of chaplains in the armed services.

Membership: In 1990, the council reported 210 member congregations serving 250,000 members and 350 clergy ministers. In addition, the council serves more than 1,000 other congregations (membership unknown). The council allows dual membership, and approximately five percent of the congregations have a denominational affiliation.

Publications: *The Christian Community.* • *The Pastor's Journal.*

★1762★
International Evangelical Church and Missionary Association
c/o Evangel Temple
13901 Central Ave.
Upper Marlboro, MD 20772

The International Evangelical Church and Missionary Association is a charismatic fellowship of churches formed in the early 1980s under the leadership of John Levin Meares, pastor of Evangel Temple in Washington, D.C. Meares was raised in the Church of God (Cleveland, Tennessee), the nephew of the general overseer. After serving several Church of God congregations, Meares went to Washington, D.C., in 1955 to begin the Revival Center (soon renamed the National Evangelistic Center), a new Church of God outreach for the city. However, he soon encountered controversy within the Church of God because he had started an unlicensed ministry. This led to his disfellowshipping in May 1956. He continued his independent ministry, however, which emerged in new quarters

as Evangel Temple in 1957. Membership of the integrated congregation was approximately two-thirds black.

In the early 1960s, Meares became aware of Bethesda Missionary Temple, one of the principle congregations of the Latter-Rain movement. From his observation of the life of the temple, he picked up a new emphasis on praise and the gift of prophecy which he introduced to Evangel Temple. This coincided with the heightened tensions of the civil rights movement which climaxed for Meares and the temple in the rioting that followed the assassination of Martin Luther King. Most of the white members withdrew, and Meares emerged in the early 1970s as the white pastor of a largely black church. Membership dropped to several hundred. The church slowly rebuilt, however, and in 1975 moved into new $3 million facilities. In 1991 Evangel Temple relocated to suburban Maryland. Their new facilities house a 2,000-seat sanctuary and their Bible school.

During his years in Washington, many independent Pentecostal pastors had begun to look to Meares for leadership and guidance. The International Evangelical Churches and Missionary Association emerged out of that relationship. In 1982, Bishops Benson Idahosa of Nigeria, Robert McAleister of Brazil, and Earl P. Paulk, Jr. of Atlanta, Georgia, all members of the International Communion of Charismatic Churches, consecrated Meares a bishop.

Over the years, Meares and Evangel Temple have become major voices in the Pentecostal community speaking to the issues of racism. Since 1984, Evangel Temple has become the site of an annual national Inner City Pastors' Conferences, attended primarily, but by no means exclusively, by black Pentecostal pastors from around the United States and Canada. More than 1,000 pastors attended the 1987 conference.

Membership: Not reported. Evangel Temple has over 1,000 members.

Educational Facilities: Centural Bible School, Upper Marlboro, Maryland.

★1763★
Kodesh Church of Emmanuel
932 Logan Rd.
Bethel Park, PA 15102
Dr. Kenneth O. Barber

The Kodesh Church of Emmanuel is a black holiness sect that was formed by Rev. Frank Russell Killingsworth when he withdrew from the African Methodist Episcopal Church in 1929 along with 120 followers. In common with other holiness churches, this church emphasizes entire sanctification as a second definite work of grace conditioned upon a life of absolute consecration. The church forbids use of alcohol, tobacco and prideful dress; membership in secret societies; and profaning the Sabbath. In 1934, a merger was effected with the Christian Tabernacle Union of Pittsburgh.

The church is governed by a quadrennial general assembly. Regional assemblies meet annually. There is mission work in Liberia.

Membership: In 1980 there were five churches, 326 members, and 28 ministers.

★1764★
Latter House of the Lord for All People and the Church of the Mountain, Apostolic Faith

Efforts to locate an address for this edition were unsuccessful. The Latter House of the Lord for All People and the Church of the Mountain, Apostolic Faith, was founded in 1936 by Bishop L. W. Williams, a former black Baptist preacher from Cincinnati. The founding followed an enlightenment experience and spiritual blessing realized in prayer. The doctrine is Calvinistic, but adjusted to accommodate Pentecostal beliefs. The Lord's Supper is observed, with water being used instead of wine. The Church members are conscientious objectors. The chief overseer is appointed for life.

Membership: Not reported. In 1947 there were approximately 4,000 members.

★1765★
Miracle Life Fellowship International
11052 N. 24th Ave.
Phoenix, AZ 85029

Asa Alonzo Allen was born of a poor Arkansas family, saved in a Methodist revival, and later baptized with the Holy Spirit in a Pentecostal meeting. He joined the Assemblies of God and felt called to preach. In the early 1940s, he began to seek a ministry of signs and wonders, particularly healing. He had what amounted to a theological conversion when, during a prayer time, he formulated the thirteen requirements for a powerful ministry. He became convinced that he could do the works of Jesus, and do more than Jesus did; that he could be flawless and perfect (in the Biblical sense), and should believe all the promises. During World War II, his throat became, according to one throat specialist, "permanently ruined," but Allen was healed.

In 1951, he purchased a tent and began the crusade in earnest. Headquarters of A. A. Allen Revivals, Inc., were established in Dallas and *Miracle Magazine* was begun. From that time until his death, Allen was an immensely popular evangelist speaking both to integrated and predominantly black audiences. As early as 1960, he was holding fully integrated meetings in the South. In 1958, he was given 1,250 acres near Tombstone, Arizona, which were named Miracle Valley and which became the international headquarters. Allen died in 1970 and was succeeded by Don Stewart, who chose the new name for the organization: Miracle Revival Fellowship.

Miracle Valley was created as a totally spiritual community. Allen founded a Bible school and publishing house, located adjacent to radio and television studios, the healing pool of Bethesda, and the headquarters. He also operated a telephone Dial-a-Miracle prayer service. The church seats 2,500. As a result of Allen's accomplishments and success, missionary churches were begun and independent ministers have become associated with him. Miracle Revival Fellowship, (now Miracle Life Fellowship International) at first a department of A. A. Allen Revivals, was established as a ministerial fellowship and licensing agency. After Allen's death, the Bible college was turned over to the Central Latin American District Council of the Assemblies of God and is now known as Southern Arizona Bible College. A. A. Allen Revivals became the Don Stewart Association.

Membership: In 1988, the fellowship of ministers had 350 clergy members in the United States and an additional 50 in other countries.

Publications: *Feed My People Magazine.* • *Miracle Magazine.* Send orders to Box 2960, Phoenix, AZ 85062-9984.

★1766★
Moorish Science Temple of America
762 W. Baltimore St.
Baltimore, MD 21201

Timothy Drew (1886-1929), a black man from North Carolina, had concluded from his reading and travels that black people were not Ethiopians (as some early black nationalists were advocating) but Asiatics, specifically Moors. They were descendants of the ancient Moabites and their homeland was Morocco. He claimed that the Continental Congress had stripped American blacks of their nationality and that George Washington had cut down their bright red flag (the cherry tree) and hidden it in a safe in Independence Hall. Blacks were thus assigned to the role of slaves.

As Noble Drew Ali, Drew emerged in 1913 in Newark, New Jersey, to preach the message of Moorish identity. The movement spread slowly with early centers in Pittsburgh, Detroit, and several southern cities. In 1925, Ali moved to Chicago and the following year incorporated the Moorish Science Temple of America. In 1927 he published *The Holy Koran* (not to be confused with the *Koran* or *Qur'aan* used by all orthodox Moslem groups). Ali's *Koran* was a pamphlet-size compilation of Moorish beliefs which drew heavily upon *The Aquarian Gospel of Jesus Christ*, a volume received by automatic writing by Spiritualist Levi Dowling in the 1890s. The *Koran* delineates the creation and fall of the race, the origin of black people, the opposition of Christianity to God's people and the modern predicament of the Moors.

It was Noble Drew Ali's belief that only Islam could unite the black man. The black race is Asiatic, Moroccan, hence Moorish. Jesus was a black man who tried to redeem the black Moabites and was executed by the white Romans. Moorish Americans must be united under Allah and his holy prophet. Marcus Garvey is seen as forerunner to Ali. Friday has been accepted as the holy day. Worship forms, particularly music, have been drawn from popular black culture and given Islamic content.

Ali died in 1919 and was succeeded by one of his young colleagues, R. German Ali, who still heads the movement. Shortly after Ali's death, one of the members appeared in Detroit as Wallace Fard Muhammad, the reincarnation of Noble Drew Ali, and began the

Nation of Islam (now the American Muslim Mission). In spite of the competition from the Nation of Islam, the temple grew in the years after Ali's death, and during the 1940s temples could be found in Charleston, West Virginia; Hartford, Connecticut; Milwaukee; Richmond, Virginia; Cleveland; Flint, Michigan; Chattanooga, Tennessee; Indianapolis; Toledo and Steubenville, Ohio; Brooklyn; and Indiana Harbor, Indiana. In more recent years, the movement has declined. During the 1970s, the headquarters were moved to Baltimore.

Membership: Not reported.

★1767★
Moorish Science Temple, Prophet Ali Reincarnated, Founder
2119 Aiken St.
Baltimore, MD 21218

In 1975, Richardson Dingle-El, a member of the Moorish Science Temple of America in Baltimore, proclaimed himself Noble Drew Ali 3d, the reincarnation of Noble Drew Ali (1886-1929), the founder of the Moorish Science Temple of America. As such he claimed succession to Noble Drew Ali 2d (d.1945), who had claimed succession in the 1930s. The followers of Noble Drew Ali 3d have established headquarters in Baltimore and have several temples around the United States. A periodical is published by the temple in Chicago. In most ways it follows the beliefs and practices of the Moorish Science Temple of America.

Membership: Not reported.

Publications: *Moorish Guide.* Send orders to 3810 S. Wabash, Chicago, IL 60653.

★1768★
Mount Calvary Holy Church of America

Efforts to locate an address for this edition were unsuccessful. The Mt. Calvary Holy Church is a small black holiness church headquartered in Boston, Massachusetts, founded by Bishop Brumfield Johnson. Its doctrine is similar to that of the United Holy Church of America. Churches are located in North Carolina; Baltimore, Maryland; New York; Boston; and other cities on the east coast.

Membership: Not reported.

★1769★
Mount Hebron Apostolic Temple of Our Lord Jesus of the Apostolic Faith
Mt. Hebron Apostolic Temple
27 Vineyard Ave.
Yonkers, NY 10703

The Mount Hebron Apostolic Temple of Our Lord Jesus of the Apostolic Faith was founded in 1963 by George H. Wiley III, pastor of the Yonkers, New York, congregation of the Apostolic Church of Christ in God. As his work progressed, Wiley came to feel that because of his accomplishments for the denomination he should be accorded the office of bishop. He had had particular success in the area of youth work, and his wife, Sister Lucille Wiley, served as president of the Department of Youth Work. However, the board of the Apostolic Church denied his request to become a bishop. He left with his supporters and became bishop of a new Apostolic denomination.

Wiley has placed great emphasis upon youth work and upon radio work, establishing an outreach in New York, one in North Carolina, and another in South Carolina. The temple continues the doctrine and polity of the Apostolic Church of Christ in God and has a cordial relationship with its parent organization.

Membership: In 1980 the temple reported 3,000 members in nine congregations being served by 15 ministers. There are two bishops.

★1770★
Mount Sinai Holy Church

Efforts to locate an address for this edition were unsuccessful. Ida Robinson grew up in Georgia, was converted at age seventeen, and joined the United Holy Church of America. She moved to Philadelphia where she became the pastor of the Mount Olive Holy Church. Following what she believed to be the command of the Holy Spirit to "Come out on Mount Sinai," she founded the Mount Sinai

Holy Church in 1924. Women have played a prominent role in its leadership from the beginning.

The doctrine is Pentecostal, with sanctification a prerequisite for the baptism of the Holy Spirit. One must be converted before becoming a member. Bishop Robinson believed that God ordained four types of human beings: the elect or chosen of God, the compelled (those who could not help themselves from being saved), the "who so ever will" who can be saved, and the damned (ordained for hell). Spiritual healing is stressed. Foot-washing is practiced. Behavior, particularly sexual, is rigidly codified and rules are strictly observed. Short dresses, neckties, and worldly amusements are frowned upon.

The Mt. Sinai Holy Church is episcopal in government. Bishop Robinson served as senior bishop and president until her death in 1946. She was succeeded by Bishop Elmira Jeffries, the original vice-president, who was, in turn, succeeded by Bishop Mary Jackson in 1964. Assisting the bishops is a board of presbyteries, composed of the elders of the churches. There are four administrative districts, each headed by a bishop. There is an annual conference of the entire church, and one is held in each district. Foreign missions in Cuba and Guinea are supported.

Membership: Not reported. In 1968 there were 92 churches, and approximately 2,000 members.

★1771★
The Nation of Islam (Farrakhan)
Box 20083
Chicago, IL 60620

Of the several factions which broke away from the American Muslim Mission (formerly known as the Nation of Islam and then as the World Community of Islam in the West) and assumed the group's original name, the most successful has been the Nation of Islam headed by Abdul Haleem Farrakhan. Farrakhan was born Louis Eugene Wolcott. He was a nightclub singer in the mid-1950s when he joined the Nation of Islam headed by Elijah Muhammad. As was common among Muslims at that time, he dropped his last name, which was seen as a name imposed by slavery and white society, and became known as Minister Louis X. His oratorical and musical skills carried him to a leading position as minister in charge of the Boston Mosque and, after the defection and death of Malcolm X, to the leadership of the large Harlem center and designation as the official spokesperson for Elijah Muhammad.

In 1975 Elijah Muhammad died. Though many thought Louis X, by then known by his present name, might become the new leader of the nation, Elijah Muhammad's son, Wallace, was chosen instead. At Wallace Muhammad's request, Farrakhan moved to Chicago to assume a national post. During the next three years, the Nation of Islam moved away from many of its distinctive beliefs and programs and emerged as the American Muslim Mission. It dropped many of its racial policies and began to admit white people into membership. It also began to move away from its black nationalist demands and to accept integration as a proper goal of its programs.

Farrakhan emerged as a leading voice among "purists" who opposed any changes in the major beliefs and programs instituted by Elijah Muhammad. Long-standing disagreements with the new direction of the Black Muslim body led Farrakhan to leave the organization in 1978 and to form a new Nation of Islam. He reinstituted the beliefs and program of the pre-1975 Nation of Islam. He reformed the Fruit of Islam, the internal security force, and demanded a return to strict dress standards.

With several thousand followers, Farrakhan began to rebuild the Nation of Islam. He established mosques and developed an outreach to the black community on radio. He was only slightly noticed until 1984 when he aligned himself with the U.S. presidential campaign of Jesse Jackson, a black minister seeking the nomination of the Democratic Party. Jackson's acceptance of his support and Farrakhan's subsequent controversial statements (some claimed by critics to be anti-Semitic) on radio and at press conferences kept Farrakhan's name in the news during the period of Jackson's candidacy and in subsequent months.

Membership: Not reported. There are an estimated 5,000 to 10,000 members of the Nation of Islam.

Publications: *The Final Call.*

★1772★
Nation of Islam (John Muhammad)
14880 Wyoming
Detroit, MI 48238

John Muhammad, brother of Elijah Muhammad, founder of the Nation of Islam, was among those who rejected the changes in the Nation of Islam and the teachings of Elijah Muhammad which led to its change into the American Muslim Mission. In 1978 he left the mission and formed a continuing Nation of Islam designed to perpetuate the programs outlined in Elijah Muhammad's two books, *Message to the Blackman* and *Our Saviour Has Arrived.* According to John Muhammad, who uses the standard title of black Muslim leaders, "Minister" Elijah Muhammad was the last Messenger of Allah and was sent to teach the black man a New Islam.

Membership: Not reported. John Muhammad has support around the United States, but the only temple is in Detroit.

Publications: *Minister John Muhammad Speaks.* Available from Nation of Islam, Temple No. 1, 19220 Conant St., Detroit, MI 48234.

★1773★
The Nation of Islam (The Caliph)

Efforts to locate an address for this edition were unsuccessful. As significant changes within the Nation of Islam founded by Elijah Muhammad proceeded under his son and successor Wallace D. Muhammad, the Nation of Islam became a more orthodox Islamic organization. It was renamed the American Muslim Mission and dropped many of the distinctive features of its predecessor. Opposition among those committed to Elijah Muhammad's ideas and programs led to several schisms in the late 1970s. Among the "purist" leaders, Emmanuel Abdullah Muhammad asserted his role as the Caliph of Islam raised up to guide the people in the absence of Allah (in the person of Wallace Fard Muhammad) and his Messenger (Elijah Muhammad). One Islamic tradition insists that a caliph always follows a messenger.

The Nation of Islam under the caliph continues the beliefs and practices abandoned by the American Muslim Mission. A new school, the University of Islam, was begun and the Fruit of Islam, the disciplined order of Islamic men, reinstituted. A new effort aimed at economic self-sufficiency has been promoted, and businesses have been created to implement the program.

Membership: Not reported. As of 1982, the Nation of Islam under the caliph had only two mosques, one in Baltimore and one in Chicago.

Publications: *Muhammad Speaks.* Available from Muhammad's Temple of Islam No. 1, 1233 W. Baltimore St., Baltimore, MD 21223.

★1774★
Nation of Yahweh (Hebrew Israelites)
c/o Temple of Love
2766 NW 62nd St.
Miami, FL 33147

The Nation of Yahweh, also known as the Hebrew Israelites or the Followers of Yahweh, is a movement founded by Yahweh ben (son of) Yahweh. Yahweh ben Yahweh was born Hulon Mitchell, Jr., considered a slave name, and no longer used. He was the son of a Pentecostal minister who at one point joined the Nation of Islam in which he became the leader of one of the mosques. He began to call together the Followers of Yahweh in the 1970s.

Yahweh ben Yahweh teaches that there is one God, whose name is Yahweh. God is black with woolly hair (Daniel 7:9; Revelation 1:13-15; Dueteronomy 7:21), and has sent his son, Yahweh ben Yahweh to the the Savior and Deliverer of His people, the so-called black people of America. Those who believe in Yahweh ben Yahweh and His name are immortal. Black people are considered the true lost tribe of Judah. They have been chosen by Yahweh, but have yet to be put into their destined office of rulership. Members, upon joining, renounce their slave name and take the surname Israel. Many of then wear white robes as commanded in the Bible (Ecclesiastes 9:8). They believe that all people who oppose God are devils, regardless of race or color. The devil is one who is immoral and follows immoral teachings of wickedness and evilness. Many persons, regardless of their race or color are capable of being and actually are the devil.

While the Nation of Yahweh has a special place for the chosen black people of America, and see white people as especially used by Satan in exercising wicked rulership, in the end salvation is not a matter of color. Any person of any race or color can be saved by faith in Yahweh ben Yahweh.

Along with its particular religious beliefs, the Nation of Yahweh sees itself as establishing a united moral power to benefit the total community of America. It supports voter registration, education, self-help jobs, business opportunities, scholarships for children, health education, better housing, strong family ties, peace, love, and harmony among people regardless of race, creed, or color. Members are taught to practice charity and benevolence, to protect chastity, to respect the ties of blood and friendship, and revere the laws of Yahweh.

The Nation of Yahweh is headed by Yahweh ben Yahweh. In its work, the nation has purchased several hotels and apartment buildings. It owns, through its corporate entity, the Temple of Love, more than 42 (in 1988) businesses which are used to support the organization and its members.

Membership: In 1988, there were congregations in 37 cities and scattered followers in a number of others. The teachings had also spread to 16 countries.

Publications: *Yahweh Magazine.*

★1775★
National Baptist Convention of America
c/o National Baptist Publishing Board
7145 Centennial Blvd.
Nashville, TN 37209

In 1915, an issue arose in the National Baptist Convention of the U.S.A., Inc. over the ownership of the publishing house. Early in the Convention's life, the Rev. R. H. Boyd, a brilliant businessman, was made corresponding secretary of the publication board. Under his leadership, the publishing house did over two million dollars in business in the first decade. As time passed, however, some members of the Convention realized that the publishing interest had been built on Boyd's property, and all the materials had been copyrighted in his name. Further, no proceeds were being donated to other Convention activities.

In a showdown, the 1915 Convention moved to correct its mistake by adopting a new charter which clarified the subservient position of the boards. Refusing to comply, Boyd withdrew the publishing house from the Convention and made it the center of a second National Baptist Convention, called the National Baptist Convention of America. Because of its refusal to accept the charter, it is usually referred to as "unincorporated." Missions are carried on in Jamaica, Panama, and Africa. Ten colleges and seminaries are supported.

Membership: Not reported. The latest statistics are from 1956 when there were a reported 2,668,799 members, 11,398 churches, and 28,574 ministers.

Educational Facilities: Central Baptist Theological Seminary, Indianapolis, Indiana.
Morehouse School of Religion, Atlanta, Georgia.

★1776★
National Baptist Convention, U.S.A.
915 Spain St.
Baton Rouge, LA 70802
Dr. T. G. Jemison, President

The National Baptist Convention of the U.S.A. came into existence after the adoption of a resolution before the Foreign Mission Baptist Convention of the U.S.A. to merge itself, the American National Baptist Convention, and the Baptist National Educational Convention. To these three would be added a publications board for Sunday school literature. The Convention was formed in Atlanta, Georgia, in 1895. Elected president and corresponding secretary of foreign missions were Rev. E. C. Morris and Lewis G. Jordan, respectively. Both were able men; the National Baptist Convention's survival, stability, and success were in no small part due to their long terms in office.

Doctrine and government were taken over from the white Baptists. The congregational form of church life allowed a ready adaptation to the black culture, which used religious forms as a socially accepted way to express their frustration and to protest their conditions. The worship developed a high degree of emotional expression, making little reference to traditional liturgical forms. (While freed from the rituals of their white parents in the faith, the local church developed its own "forms," which seem spontaneous to the occasional visitor. In fact, the black Baptists allowed themselves to create a new

religious culture, the pattern of which they follow weekly in their service.)

Within two years of its founding, the new National Baptist Convention ran into trouble when Jordan moved its offices from Richmond to Louisville. The Virginia Brethren, fearing a loss of power, withdrew support. They formed the Lott Carey Missionary Convention, which still exists as an independent missionary society. A more serious disagreement split the denomination in 1915.

For twenty-nine years (1953-1982) the National Baptists were led by J. H. Jackson. He was succeeded in 1982 by T. J. Jemison, the son of the convention's president from 1941-1953, D. V. Jemison. There is mission work in Africa and the Bahamas. The group operates five colleges, a theological seminary, and a training school for women and girls.

Membership: Not reported. In 1984 there were an estimated 7,000,000 members in over 30,000 congregations.

Educational Facilities: Shaw University, Raleigh, North Carolina.
Shaw Divinity School, Raleigh, North Carolina.
National Baptist College, Nashville, Tennessee.
Central Baptist Theological Seminary, Indianapolis, Indiana.
Morehouse School of Religion, Atlanta, Georgia.
Selma University, Selma, Alabama.
American Baptist Theological Seminary, Nashville, Tennessee.

Publications: *National Baptist Voice.* Send orders to 2900 3rd Ave., Richmond, VA 23222.

★1777★
National Baptist Evangelical Life and Soul Saving Assembly of the U.S.A.
441-61 Monroe Ave.
Detroit, MI 48226

The National Baptist Evangelical Life and Soul Saving Assembly of the U.S.A. was founded by A. A. Banks in 1920 in Kansas City, Missouri. It was begun as a city mission and evangelical movement within the National Baptist Convention of America, with which it remained affiliated for 15 years. Differences arose in the mid-1930s, and in 1936 at Birmingham, Alabama, the Assembly declared itself independent. Centers were established in cities across the nation.

No official statements regulate the doctrine of the Assembly, but generally the doctrine follows that of the National Baptist Convention of America. Relief work, charitable activity, and evangelizing are the main concerns of the Association. Each member hopes to add one member to the kingdom annually. Correspondence courses have been developed in evangelism, missions, pastoral ministry, and the work of deacons and laymen. Degrees are awarded for these studies.

Membership: Not reported. In 1951 there were 57,674 members, 264 churches and 137 ministers.

★1778★
National Colored Spiritualist Association of Churches

Efforts to locate an address for this edition were unsuccessful. Shortly after World War I, the growing black membership in the National Spiritualist Association of Churches separated from the parent body and, in 1922, formed the National Colored Spiritualist Association of Churches. Doctrine and practice follow closely those of the parent body. Churches are located in Detroit, Chicago, Columbus (Ohio), Miami, Charleston (South Carolina), New York City, Phoenix and St. Petersburg.

Membership: Not reported.

Publications: *The Nationalist Spiritualist Reporter.*

★1779★
National Primitive Baptist Convention of the U.S.A.
Box 2355
Tallahassee, FL 32301

Around the turn of the century, there was a movement among the Black Primitive Baptists to organize a national convention. In 1906, Elders Clarence Francis Sams, George S. Crawford, James H. Carey, and others called on their colleagues to join them in a meeting at Huntsville, Alabama, in 1907. Eighty-eight elders from seven Southern states responded. In organizing the convention, of course, the members departed from a main Primitive Baptist concern-that there should be no organization above the loose associations that typically cover several counties.

Doctrinally, the National Primitive Baptist Convention follows the Regular Primitive Baptists. The Convention's creeds profess belief in the "particular election of a definite number of the human race." Footwashing is practiced. The organization is congregational, and at the local level there are two offices-pastor (elder) and deacon or deaconness (mother). The convention meets annually and sponsors Sunday schools and a publishing board.

Membership: Not reported. In 1975, it claimed 606 churches with 250,000 members and 636 ministers.

★1780★
New Bethel Church of God in Christ (Pentecostal)

Efforts to locate an address for this edition were unsuccessful. In 1927, the Rev. A. D. Bradley was admonished by the board of bishops of the Church of God in Christ to refrain from preaching the "Jesus only" doctrine. (The Church of God in Christ was the oldest and among the largest of the predominantly-black trinitarian Pentecostal churches.) He refused, and with his wife and Lonnie Bates established the New Bethel Church of God in Christ (Pentecostal). Bradley became the church's presiding bishop. Doctrine is similar to other "Jesus only" groups. The three ordinances of baptism, the Lord's Supper, and foot-washing are observed. The group is pacifist but allows alternative noncombatant positions to be held by law-abiding church members. The group disapproves of secret societies and of school activities which conflict with a student's moral scruples.

The presiding bishop is the executive officer and presides over all meetings of the general body. A board of bishops acts as a judicatory body and a general assembly as the legislative body.

Membership: Not reported.

★1781★
Original Glorious Church of God in Christ Apostolic Faith

Efforts to locate an address for this edition were unsuccessful. The Glorious Church of God was founded in 1921. However, in 1952 its presiding bishop, S. C. Bass married a divorced woman. Approximately half of the fifty-congregation church rejected Bass and reorganized under the leadership of W. O. Howard and took the name Original Glorious Church of God in Christ Apostolic Faith. The term "Original" signified their claim to the history of the church, demonstrated by their retention of the founding charter. Howard was succeeded by Bishop I. W. Hamiter, under whose leadership the church has grown spectacularly and developed a mission program in Haiti, Jamaica and India. Hamiter has also led in the purchase of a convention center for the church's annual meeting in Columbus, Ohio.

Membership: In 1980 the church had 55 congregations in the United States, 110 congregations overseas, 200 ministers and approximately 25,000 members worldwide.

★1782★
Original Hebrew Israelite Nation

Efforts to locate an address for this edition were unsuccessful. The Black Israelites (members of the Original Hebrew Israelite Nation) emerged in Chicago in the 1960s around Ben Ammi Carter (born G. Parker), a black man who had studied Judaism with a rabbi, and Shaleah Ben-Israel. To the Black Jewish ideas (which were espoused by several groups in Chicago at this time) Carter and Ben-Israel added the concept of Black Zionism and held out the vision of a return to the Holy Land for their members. From headquarters at the A-Beta Cultural Center on Chicago's south side, they began to gather followers. The somewhat anonymous group came into prominence in the late 1960s as a result of their attempts to migrate to Africa and then to Israel. The group moved first to Liberia, seen as analogous to the Hebrew children's wandering in the desert for forty years to throw off the effects of slavery. Soon after their arrival, they approached the Israeli ambassador about a further move to Israel. They were unable to negotiate the move to Israel for members in Liberia. In 1968 Carter and 38 members from Chicago flew directly to Israel. Given temporary sanction and work permits, the group from Liberia joined them. By 1971, when strict immigration restrictions were imposed upon members of the group, over 300 had migrated. Other members of the group continued to arrive, however, using tourist visas which were destroyed upon moving into the colony (which had been established at Dimona). By 1980 between 1,500 and 2,000 had settled in Israel.

The Black Israelites feel they are descendants of the ten lost tribes of Israel and thus Jews by birth. They celebrate the Jewish rituals and keep the Sabbath. However, they are distinguished from traditional Jews by their practice of polygamy (a maximum of seven wives is allowed) and their abandonment of the synagogue structure.

The group is currently headed by Carter, the chief rabbi. He is assisted by a divine council of twelve princes (for each of the twelve ancient tribes of Israel). During the early 1980s, the American following was under the direction of Prince Asiel Ben Israel. Under the princes are seven ministers responsible for providing education, distribution of food, clothing and shelter, economics, transportation, sports, recreation and entertainment, life preservation, and sanitation.

In Israel, the group lives communally. According to most reports, the group (due to lack of legal status), lives under harsh conditions and the continual threat of mass deportation. They have been unable to obtain necessary additional housing (for those many members who immigrated illegally) and the children are not allowed to attend public schools. Within Israel, the group has asked for land to settle in order to create their own community.

Membership: Not reported. In 1980 there were an estimated 1,500 members in Israel (900 at Dimona, 400 at Arad, 100 at Mitzpe Ramon, and 100 at Eilat) and 3,000 living in the United States, scattered in black communities in urban centers such as Chicago, Atlanta, Georgia, and Washington, D.C.

★1783★
Original United Holy Church International
Box 263
Durham, NC 27702
Bishop H. W. Fields

The Original United Holy Church International grew out of a struggle between two bishops of the United Holy Church of America. The conflict led to Bishop James Alexander Forbes and the Southern District being severed from the organization. Those put out of the church met and organized on June 29, 1977, at a meeting in Raleigh, North Carolina. The new body remains in essential doctrinal agreement and continues the polity of the United Holy Church.

The Original United Holy Church is concentrated on the Atlantic coast from South Carolina to Connecticut, with congregations also found in Kentucky, Texas, and California. Bishop Forbes also serves as pastor of the Greater Forbes Temple of Hollis, New York. The church supports missionary work in Liberia. On January 24, 1979, in Wilmington, North Carolina, an agreement of affiliation between the Original United Holy Church and the International Pentecostal Holiness Church was signed, which envisions a close cooperative relationship between the two churches.

Membership: In 1985 the church had approximately 210 congregations and over 15,000 members.

Educational Facilities: United Christian College, Goldsboro, North Carolina.

Publications: *Voice of the World.*

★1784★
Pan African Orthodox Christian Church
13535 Livernois
Detroit, MI 48238

The Pan African Orthodox Christian Church dates to 1953 when 300 members of St. Mark's Presbyterian Church in Detroit walked out and formed Central Congregational Church. In 1957 they moved into facilities at 7625 Linwood in Detroit and over the next decade became intensely involved in community issues, especially those impinging upon the black community. In 1967, the church's pastor, Albert B. Cleage, Jr., preached what has become a famous sermon calling for a new black theology and a black church to articulate it. An 18-foot painting of a black Madonna was unveiled and the Black Christian Nationalist Movement was launched. The church building became known as the Shrine of the Black Madonna No. 1. In 1970 a book store and cultural center were opened. Cleage changed his name to Jaramogi Abebe Agyeman.

The Black Nationalist Creed, printed below, spells out a position which identifies the black man and the Hebrew Nation:

"I Believe that human society stands under the judgment of one God, revealed to all, and known by many names. His creative power is visible in the mysteries of the universe, in the revolutionary Holy Spirit which will not long permit men to endure injustice nor to wear the shackles of bondage, in the rage of the powerless when they struggle to be free, and in the violence and conflict which even now threaten to level the hills and the mountains."

"I Believe that Jesus, the Black Messiah, was a revolutionary leader, sent by God to rebuild the Black Nation Israel and to liberate Black People from powerlessness and from the oppression, brutality, and exploitation of the white gentile world."

"I Believe that the revolutionary spirit of God, embodied in the Black Messiah, is born anew in each generation and that Black Christian Nationalists constitute that living remnant of God's Chosen People in this day, and are charged by him with responsibility for the Liberation of Black People."

"I Believe that both my survival and my salvation depend upon my willingness to reject INDIVIDUALISM, and so I commit my life to the Liberation Struggle of Black people and accept the values, ethics, morals, and program of the Black Nation defined by that struggle and taught by the Black Christian Nationalist Movement."

During the 1970s the organization expanded significantly. Agyeman composed an ordination service and ordained eight ministers, who were given the title "Mwalimu," Swahili for "teacher." Agyemnan's own name means "liberator, blessed man, savior of the nation." Other congregations and centers were established in Detroit. In 1974 a shrine was opened in Atlanta, Georgia and in 1977 in Kalamazoo, Michigan. Also in 1974, a BGN training program to prepare leaders for the liberation struggle of black people was begun.

Membership: Not reported. In 1983 there were six congregations, four in Detroit, one in Kalamazoo, Michigan, and one in Atlanta, Georgia.

★1785★
The Peace Mission Movement
c/o The Woodmont Estate
1622 Spring Mill Rd.
Gladwyne, PA 19035

The Peace Mission Movement was founded as an organization in the early twentieth century by the Rev. Major J. Divine, better known as Father Divine. He was one of the most colorful and controversial leaders of a new religious movement in American history. By his own choosing, and in accord with his own religious conviction, Father Divine's life and activity are veiled in obscurity until just prior to 1919 in Brooklyn, New York, where he was known to be preaching about Jesus Christ and the coming of the kingdom of God.

From his own writings and the testimonies of those who knew him, it is believed that Father Divine left Brooklyn and went south just after the Jim Crow Law was passed in Grover Cleveland's administration. While in the South, he was in the hands of 32 lynch mobs because of his stand for brotherhood, eternal life, and salvation being free and without the payment of money. The first Mother Divine and others were witnesses of his treatment in the hands of lynch mobs. In the name of the Rev. Major J. Divine, he married Mother Penniah Divine on June 6, 1882.

Father Divine appeared as an intinerant preacher on the east coast of the United States who found fellowship with others who were preaching that the Christ could be manifested as God in man. Samuel Morris, known as Father Jehovah, and John Hickerson, known by his followers as Bishop St. John the Divine, were two of these. Because of jealous rivalry, it is believed, Hickerson fabricated the story that Father Divine's name was really George Baker. Hickerson also is responsible for other biographical misinformation.

To remove himself from the turmoil, Father Divine went into seclusion in the little Long Island fishing village of Sayville, New York. It was here that his residence became known as "The Rescue Home for the Poor Only." He attracted those in need of food, clothing, shelter, and employment, as well as seekers who were drawn by the demonstration at the Sayville residence of "supernatural" abundance in the midst of seeming scarcity. Father Divine's work commanded more and more attention, and ever greater numbers flocked to Sayville to banquet with him, listen to his sermons, and receive healings of mind, body, and spirit, all gratis to everyone who came.

The influx of numbers of people into the town disturbed the residents. Their hostility led to a court case against Father Divine in 1931, the events of which created worldwide publicity. Although the local county court convicted Father Divine, fined him, and sent him to jail for 30 days, the appellant court later condemned the proceedings as erroneous and prejudicial.

The vindication notwithstanding, Father Divine chose to move his headquarters to Harlem in 1933, where he could direct his activity to the masses, especially the black people who had gathered there after World War I. While gaining a large following from the Harlem public, he experienced continual harassment from the authorities, so that in 1942 he moved again, this time to Philadelphia, Pennsylvania.

The Peace Mission Movement is primarily of a religious nature, but its tenets have strong social, economic, and patriotic ramifications. Its members believe in the principles of Americanism, brotherhood, Christianity, democracy, and Judaism, and that all true religions are synonymous. Members believe that Father Divine fulfills the scriptural promise of the Second Coming of Christ, is the personification of God in a bodily form, and that heaven is a state of consciousness. This state is being materialized, in as much as the members believe that America is the birthplace of the Kingdom of God on Earth, which will be realized when everyone lives the life of Christ.

Father Divine founded the church under the Peace Mission Movement which was incorporated in 1940 and 1941. Mother Divine, with the recognition of Father Divine's Ever Presence, became the Spiritual Head in 1965. There are no ministers and is no prescribed ritual in the church services. Those in attendance are free to testify, sing, read scripture, repeat the Words of Father Divine or Mother Divine, or offer praise to God as they are led to do from any inner prompting. Services feature congregational singing. The only sacrament is Holy Communion, served daily as a full-course meal to which all are welcome. There are also two holidays: April 29, which is the celebration of Father Divine's marriage to His Spotless Bride (Mother Divine) to bring about the universal brotherhood of man and the propagation of virtue, honesty, and truth; and September 10-12, which is the consecration and dedication of Woodmont to universalize the Woodmont Estate as a symbol of the highest spiritual state of consciousness.

The mission stands for the absolute fatherhood and motherhood of God and the universal brotherhood of man. Its members believe that a person is a person–not a specified race, color, nationality, or religion, and they live integrated together as brothers and sisters in the family of God and as members only of the human race. They avoid all reference to color or race.

Members of the mission live communally in the churches and affiliated sorority and fraternity houses. They are strictly celibate men and women living in separate houses and on separate floors of the larger facilities. They observe Father Divine's International Modest Code which states: "No smoking, No drinking, No obscenity, No vulgarity, No profanity, No undue mixing of sexes, and No receiving of gifts, presents, tips or bribes." It is understood to include abstinence from all drugs.

The Peace Mission Movement was most active in the post-depression era when Father Divine preached peace, health, happiness, and abundance, and demonstrated that his teachings were practical as he provided food and shelter for all those in need at no cost to them. To others in dire circumstances, but who had a poverty-level income or less, Father Divine offered 15-cent meals and one dollar-per-week shelter, so that they could hold up their heads with a sense of individual worth and independence, since they were able to pay for their sustenance. The same abundance was manifested in the churches and extensions in various countries as well as those in the United States, where elaborate banquets are the custom.

After Father Divine's passing, his wife Edna Rose Ritchings, known to members as Mother Divine, assumed leadership of the movement. She had married Father Divine in 1946, and currently resides at Woodmont. The movement has a long history of being integrated, as was the marriage.

Membership: Not reported. In 1992 the movement reported that it owned and operated two hotels in Philadelphia and one in New Jersey. Branches exist in Canada, Germany, Switzerland, Australia, Central America, and Nigeria.

Publications: *The New Day.* Send orders to The New Day Publishing Company, 1600 W. Oxford St., Philadelphia, PA 19121.

★1786★
Pentecostal Assemblies of the World
3939 Meadows Dr.
Indianapolis, IN 46205
James A. Johnson, Presiding Bishop

Oldest of the Apostolic or "Jesus Only" Pentecostal churches, the Pentecostal Assemblies of the World began as a loosely-organized fellowship of trinitarian pentecostals in Los Angeles in 1906. J. J. Frazee (occasionally incorrectly reported as "Frazier") was elected the first general superintendent. Early membership developed along the West Coast and in the Midwest. From 1913 to 1916, the annual convention was held in Indianapolis, soon to become the center of the organization. Growth in the organization was spurred when it became the first group of pentecostals to accept the "Jesus Only" Apostolic theology, which identified Jesus as the Jehovah of the Old Testament and denied the Trinity. Many ministers from other pentecostal bodies joined the Assemblies when the group within which they held credentials rejected Apostolic teachings. In 1918, the General Assemblies of the Apostolic Assemblies, a recently formed Apostolic body, which included such outstanding early movement leaders as D. C. O. Opperman and H. A. Goss, merged into the PAW.

From its beginning the Pentecostal Assemblies of the World was fully integrated racially, though predominantly white in membership. In 1919, following the influx of so many ministers and members, especially the large newly-merged body, the Pentecostal Assemblies reorganized. Four of its 21 field superintendents were black, among whom were Garfield Thomas Haywood (1880-1931), who would later become presiding bishop. In 1924, most of the white members withdrew to form the Pentecostal Ministerial Alliance, now an integral part of the United Pentecostal Church. The remaining members, not totally, but predominantly black, reorganized again, created the office of bishop, and elected Haywood to lead them. He remained presiding bishop until his death in 1931.

Shortly after Haywood's death, the Apostolic Churches of Jesus Christ, a name briefly assumed by the former Pentecostal Ministerial Alliance that was then in a phase of consolidatiing various Apostolic groups into a single organization, invited the Assemblies to consider merger. The merger attempt failed, but the Assemblies again lost individual congregations and members to the Apostolic Churches of Jesus Christ, and a large group who formed a new church, the Pentecostal Assemblies of Jesus Christ, as a prelude to the merger which failed. In the face of the new losses, a third reorganization had to occur in 1932. For several years, the church was led by a small group of bishops, enlarged to seven in 1935. Two years later, Samuel Grimes, a former missionary in Liberia, was elected presiding bishop, a post he retained until his death in 1967. Under his guidance, the Pentecostal Assemblies Church experienced its greatest era of expansion. Contrary to most black Pentecostal bishops, Grimes did not also serve a parish, hence he was able to devote himself full-time to his episcopal duties.

Doctrine of the Assemblies is similar to that of the Assemblies of God except that it does not believe in the Trinity. Holiness is stressed and the group believes that for ultimate salvation, it is necessary to have a life wholly sanctified. Wine is used in the Lord's Supper. Healing is stressed and foot-washing practiced. Members are pacifists, though they feel it is a duty to honor rules. There is a strict dress and behavior code. Divorce and remarriage are allowed under certain circumstances.

There is an annual general assembly which elects the bishops and the general secretary. It also designates the presiding bishop, who heads a board of bishops. The church is divided into 30 districts (dioceses) headed by a bishop. The Assemblies are designated joint members of each local board of trustees. A missionary board oversees missions in Nigeria, Jamaica, England, Ghana, and Egypt.

Membership: In 1980 the Assemblies had reported 1,000,000 members/constituents in 1,556 churches divided into 43 districts, each headed by a bishop. There are approximately 1,000 churches in the foreign missionary field.

Educational Facilities: Aenon Bible School, Indianapolis, Indiana.

Publications: *Christian Outlook.*

★1787★
Pentecostal Church of God
9244 Delmar
Detroit, MI 48211

The Pentecostal Church of God (not to be confused with the Pentecostal Church of God of America headquartered at Joplin, Missouri) is a predominantly black Pentecostal body founded by Apostle Willie James Peterson (1921-1969). Peterson grew up in Florida, and though his family attended the Baptist church there, he was never baptized. The course of his life was interrupted in his early adult years by a dream in which he was in the presence of God and His angels. Peterson began a period of prayer, after which God called him to preach. He became an independent evangelist and had come to believe in the Apostolic or non-Trinitarian position. He began to preach that doctrine in 1955 in Meridian, Mississippi, and to raise up congregations across the South. At the time of his death, Peterson was succeeded by the four bishops of the church, William Duren, J. J. Sears, C. L. Rawls, and E. Rice.

It is the belief of the Pentecostal Church of God that Peterson was an apostle, annointed by God for his task through revelation. The essence of the revelation was an understanding of the Kingdom of God. Peterson taught that conversion meant turning away from worldliness (the kingdom of this world ruled by Satan) to godliness (the kingdom of Heaven). Peterson identified the Roman Catholic Church with Babylon, the Mother of Harlots, spoken of in Revelation 17:3-5. Satanic doctrine was taught in that church and in its daughter churches, Protestantism. To accept the gospel of the kingdom is to turn from the false teachings of the Babylonish churches to God's truths which include repentance as godly sorrow for one's sins; baptism by immersion in the name of Jesus Christ; a rejection of the unbiblical doctrine of the Trinity; an understanding of heaven as the realm of God and his angels and hell as a place of confinement; the nonobservance of holidays such as Christmas, Easter, and New Year's Day; nonparticipation in human government (which includes pacifism, not saluting the flag, and not voting); and holy matrimony performed by a holy minister.

Membership: Not reported.

★1788★
Pentecostal Churches of Apostolic Faith

Efforts to locate an address for this edition were unsuccessful. The Pentecostal Churches of Apostolic Faith was formed in 1957 by former members of the Pentecostal Assemblies of the World under the leadership of Bishop Samuel N. Hancock. Hancock was one of the original men selected as a bishop of the Assemblies following its reorganization in 1925. In 1931 he was one of the leaders in the attempt to unite the Assemblies with the predominantly white Pentecostal Ministerial Alliance, and he helped form the Pentecostal Assemblies of Jesus Christ, a body whose polity was more acceptable to the Alliance. Within a few years, Hancock returned to the Assemblies as an elder and was elected as a bishop for the second time.

However, soon after Hancock's return, it was discovered that he had deviated on traditional Apostolic doctrine in that he taught that Jesus was only the son of God, not that he was God. His position forced the Assemblies to issue a clarifying statement of its position, but Hancock's teachings were tolerated. Hancock also felt that he should have become the presiding bishop. Disappointment at not being elected seems to have fueled the discontent felt throughout the 1950s. Hancock carried two other bishops into the new church formed in 1957, including Willie Lee, pastor of Christ Temple Church, the congregation pastored by Garfield Thomas Haywood, the first presiding bishop of the Assemblies. Lee succeeded Hancock as presiding bishop of the Churches upon the latter's death in 1963. The following year, a major schism occurred when the majority of the Churches rejected the doctrinal position held by Hancock and also taught by Lee. Elzie Young had the charter and claimed the support of the Churches to become the new presiding bishop. The church returned to the traditional Apostolic theology.

The Pentecostal Churches of the Apostolic Faith are congregational in polity, and headed by a presiding bishop (Elzie Young) and a council of bishops. Under Young's leadership, the Churches have grown and stablized their original shaky financial condition. A mission program developed, and the Churches support missionaries in Haiti and Liberia, where they have built a school.

Membership: In 1980 the Churches had approximately 25,000 members, 115 churches and 380 ministers.

★1789★
Progressive National Baptist Convention, Inc.
601 50th St., NE
Washington, DC 20019

The Progressive National Baptist Convention was formed in 1961 following a dispute over the tenure of the presidency at the 1960 meeting of the National Baptist Convention of the U.S.A., Inc. In 1957, Dr. J. H. Jackson, who had been elected president in 1953, declined to step down and ruled the four-year tenure rule out of the Constitution. Prior to the adoption of the rule in 1952, presidents had served for life. At the 1960 Convention session, dissatisfaction came to a head in the attempt to elect Dr. G. C. Taylor as Dr. Jackson's successor. The failure of Dr. Taylor's supporters led in 1961 to the call for a meeting to form a new National Baptist Convention by Dr. L. V. Booth of Zion Baptist Church, Cincinnati, Ohio. He was elected the first president of the new Progressive National Baptist Convention.

Also at issue in the 1961 break was denominational support for the Civil Rights Movement, then gaining momentum in the South. Those who formed the new convention represented the strongest backers of Martin Luther King, Jr., who was among those who left to join the Progressives, who in turn gave King their full support.

The convention is in agreement on doctrine with its parent body, the disagreements being concerned with organization and social policy. It has organized nationally with two-year terms for all officers, except the executive secretary, who has an eight-year term. The women's auxiliary was formed in 1962 and a Department of Christian Education, Home Mission Board, and Foreign Mission Bureau were soon added.

Membership: Not reported. In 1984 there were over 1,000,000 members.

Educational Facilities: Central Baptist Theological Seminary, Indianapolis, Indiana.
Morehouse School of Religion, Atlanta, Georgia.

Publications: *Baptist Progress.* Send orders to 712-14 Quincy St., Brooklyn, NY 11221.

★1790★
Rastafarians

The Rastafarian Movement, a Jamaican black nationalist movement, grew out of a long history of fascination with Africa in general and Ethiopia in particular among the masses in Jamaica. The movement can be traced directly to the efforts of Marcus Garvey, founder of the Universal Negro Improvement Association, who, among other endeavors, promoted a steamship company that would provide transportation for blacks going back to Africa. In 1927 Garvey predicted the crowning of a black king in Africa as a sign that the redemption of black people from white oppression was near. The 1935 coronation of Haile Selassie as emperor of Ethiopia was seen as a fulfillment of Garvey's words.

Haile Selassie was born Ras Tafari Makonnen out of a lineage claimed to derive from the Queen of Sheba and King Solomon. He proclaimed his title as King of Kings, Lord of Lords, His Imperial Majesty the Conquering Lion of the Tribe of Judah. Elect of God. His name Haile Selassie means "Power of the Holy Trinity." Reading about the coronation, four ministers in Jamaica–Joseph Hibbert, Archibald Dunkley, Robert Hinds, and most prominently, Leonard Howell–saw the new emperor as not only the fulfillment of the Garveyite expectation, but also the completion of Biblical prophecies such as those in Revelation 5:2-5 and 19:16 which refer to the Lion of the Tribe of Judah and the King of Kings. The four, independently of each other, began to proclaim Haile Selassie the Messiah of the black people. Their first successes came in the slums of West Kingston, where they discovered each other and a movement began.

Howell began to proselytize around the island. He raised money by selling pictures of Haile Selassie and telling the buyers that they were passports back to Africa. He was arrested and sentenced to two years in jail for fraud. Upon his release he moved into the hill country of St. Catherine's parish and founded a commune, the Pinnacle, which, in spite of government attacks and several moves, became the center of the movement for the next two decades. At the Pinnacle, the smoking of ganga (marijuana) and the wearing of long hair curled to resemble a lion's mane (dread locks) became the marks of identification of the group.

As the Rastafarians matured, they adopted the perspectives of Black Judaism and identified the Hebrews of the Old Testament as

black people. Their belief system was distinctly racial and they taught that the whites were inferior to the blacks. More extreme leaders saw whites as the enemies of blacks and believed that, in the near future, blacks will return to Africa and assume their rightful place in world leadership. Haile Selassie is believed to be the embodiment of God and, though no longer visible, he nevertheless still lives. Some Rastafarians believe Selassie is still secretly alive, though most see him as a disembodied spirit.

Relations with white culture have been tense, lived at the point of "dread," a term to describe the confrontation of a people struggling to regain a denied racial selfhood. Most Rastafarians are pacifists, though much support for the movement developed out of intense antiwhite feelings. Violence has been a part of the movement since the destruction of the Pinnacle, though it has been confined to individuals and loosely organized groups. One group, the Nyabingi Rastas, stand apart from most by their espousal of violence.

Rastafarians came to the United States in large numbers as part of the general migration of Jamaicans in the 1960s and 1970s. They have brought with them an image of violence, and frequent news reports have detailed murders committed by individuals identified as Rastafarians. Rastafarian spokespersons have only complained that many young Jamaican-Americans have adopted the outward appearance of Rastafarians (dread locks and ganga-smoking) without adopting Rastafarian beliefs and lifestyle.

A major aspect of Rastafarian life is the unique music developed as its expression. Reggae, a form of rock music, became popular far beyond Rastafarian circles, and exponents such as Bob Marley and Peter Tosh became international stars. Reggae has immensely helped in the legitimization of Rastafarian life and ideals.

In Jamaica the Rastafarian Movement is divided into a number of organizations and factions, many of which have been brought into the Jamaican community in America. Surveys of American Rastafarians have yet to define the organization in the United States though individual Rastafarians may be found in black communities across America, most noticably Brooklyn, New York, Miami, Florida, and Chicago, Illinois.

Membership: There are an estimated 3,000-5,000 Rastafarians in the United States, though the figures are somewhat distorted by the large number of people who have adopted the outward appearance of Rastafarian life.

Publications: *Arise.* Available from Creative Publishers, Ltd., 8 Waterloo Ave., Kingston, Jamaica, West Indies. • *Jahugliman.* Available from Carl Gayle, 19C Annette Cresent, Kingston 10, Jamaica, West Indies.

★1791★
Redeemed Assembly of Jesus Christ, Apostolic
734 1st St., SW
Washington, DC 20024
Bishop Douglas Williams

The Redeemed Assembly of Jesus Christ, Apostolic was formed by James Frank Harris and Douglas Williams, two bishops of the Highway Christian Church who rejected the leadership of that church by Bishop J. V. Lomax. They complained of his control, bypassing other bishops and pastors and making decisons in conference with the elders of the congregation he headed in Washington, D.C. The new church is headed by a presiding bishop, assistant presiding bishop, and an executive council consisting of the bishops and all the pastors. There was no doctrinal conflict in the split.

Membership: In 1980 the church had six congregations, one in Richmond, Virginia, one in New York City, and four in the Washington, D.C., area.

★1792★
Reformed Methodist Union Episcopal Church
1136 Brody Ave.
Charleston, SC 29407
Rt. Rev. Leroy Gethers

The Reformed Methodist Union Episcopal Church was formed in 1885 by members of the African Methodist Episcopal Church who withdrew after a dispute concerning the election of ministerial delegates to the Annual Conference. The Rev. William E. Johnson was elected the first president. A strong sentiment approving of the non-episcopal nature of the new church was expressed. However, in 1896, steps were taken to alter the polity, and in 1919 after the death of the Reverend Johnson, E. Russell Middleton was elected bishop. He was consecrated by the Rt. Rev. Peter F. Stevens of the Reformed Episcopal Church. Following Middleton's death, a second bishop was elected and consecrated by the laying on of hands of seven elders of the church.

Doctrine was taken from the Methodist Episcopal Church. The polity has moved in the episcopal direction and was fully adopted in 1916. Class meetings and love feasts are also retained. Class meetings are regular gatherings of small groups for exhortation, discussion, confession and forgiveness, Bible study, and prayer. Love feasts are informal services centering on holy communion but also including a light meal, singing, and a talk by the officiating minister.

Membership: In 1983 the church reported 3,800 members, 18 churches, and 33 ministers.

★1793★
Reformed Zion Union Apostolic Church
416 S. Hill Ave.
South Hill, VA 23970
Deacon James C. Feggins

The Reformed Zion Union Apostolic Church was founded by a group from the African Methodist Episcopal Church interested in setting up a religious organization "to aid in bringing about Christian Union, whose fruit will be Holiness unto the Lord." Led by the Rev. James Howell, the group met at Boydton, Virginia, in April 1869, and organized the Zion Union Apostolic Church with the Reverend Howell as the president. Harmony and growth prevailed until 1874, when changes in polity led to the election of the Reverend Howell as bishop with life tenure. Dissatisfaction with this action nearly destroyed the organization, even though Bishop Howell resigned. In 1882 a re-organization was effected, the four-year presidential structure reinstituted, and the present name adopted.

The representative conference structure is maintained with the law-making power invested in the quadrennial General Conference. Over the years the four-year presidency has again been dropped in favor of life-tenure bishops. A Board of Publication has control over church literature and prints the church school material and the *Union Searchlight*, a periodical.

Membership: Not reported. In 1965 the church reported 1,832 members and 27 churches.

Publications: *Union Searchlight.*

★1794★
Sacred Heart Catholic Church (Arrendale)

Efforts to locate an address for this edition were unsuccessful. The Sacred Heart Catholic Church was founded in 1980 by Archbishop James Augustine Arrendale and other former members of Archbishop James Francis Augustine Lashley's American Catholic Church, Archdiocese of New York. Arrendale was consecrated on August 10, 1981 by Bishop Pinachio, who was assisted by Bishops Donald Anthony and William Wren. The group adheres to the teachings of the Seven Ecumenical Councils and the three Ecumenical Creeds. Archbishop Arrendale died in 1985 and the future course of the Archdiocese is in doubt.

Membership: In 1983 the church reported three parishes, two priests, and 50 members.

★1795★
Shiloh Apostolic Temple
1516 W. Master
Philadelphia, PA 19121

The Shiloh Apostolic Temple was founded in 1953 by Elder Robert O. Doub, Jr., of the Apostolic Church of Christ in God. In 1948 Doub had moved to Philadelphia to organize a new congregation for the Apostolic Church of Christ in God. He not only succeeded in building a stable congregation, Shiloh Apostolic Temple, but assisted other congregations throughout the state to organize. In light of his accomplishments, Doub felt that he should be made a bishop and so petitioned the church. He believed that the state overseer was taking all the credit Doub himself deserved. Doub's petition was denied. He left with but a single congregation in 1953 and incorporated separately in 1954.

The energetic work that characterized Doub's years in the Apostolic Church of Christ in God led Shiloh Apostolic Temple to outgrow its parent body. Doub began a periodical and purchased a camp, Shiloh Promised Land Camp, in Montrose, Pennsylvania. He also took over foreign work in England and Trinidad. The doctrine, not at issue in the schism, remains that of the parent Church of God (Apostolic) from which the Apostolic Church of Christ in God came.

Membership: In 1980 the church had 4,500 members of which 500 were in the congregation in Philadelphia. The church reported 23 congregations, of which 8 were in England and 2 in Trinidad.

Publications: *Shiloh Gospel Wave.* Send orders to 1516 W. Master, Philadelphia, PA 19121.

★1796★
Sought Out Church of God in Christ

Efforts to locate an address for this edition were unsuccessful. The Sought Out Church of God in Christ and Spiritual House of Prayer, Inc., was founded in 1947 by Mother Mozella Cook. Mother Cook was converted in a service led by her physical mother, an ecstatic person who was once hauled into court to be examined for lunacy because of her mystical states. Mother Cook's mother seemed to go into trances and was "absent from this world while she talked with God." Mother Cook moved to Pittsburgh and there became a member of the Church of God in Christ founded by Charles H. Mason, but left it to found her own church, which she formed in Brunswick, Georgia, after feeling a divine call.

Membership: Not reported. In 1949 the church had four congregations and 60 members.

★1797★
Sunni Muslims
c/o Islamic Center
2551 Massachusetts Ave. NW
Washington, DC 20008

The Islamic world, though concentrated in the Arab nations of the Middle East, stretches from Yugoslavia to Indonesia and includes not only a large part of the U.S.S.R. but a growing community in Africa south of the Sahara. Since 1965, the Islamic community which had been concentrated in the Midwest and a few Eastern urban centers, has blossomed into a significant religious element of American life in every part of the United States. Literally millions of immigrants from Islamic Asia, Africa and Europe have settled in North America and begun the generation-long process of building ethnic community centers and facilities for worship (often the same building).

Unlike much of Christendom, Islam is organized into a number of autonomous centers. Each center (which may be called a community center, a mosque, a musjid) will tend to be dominated by one ethnic community, though outside the largest urban centers where a variety of mosques can be found, centers will have welcomed people of various nationalities into affiliation. Many of the major centers will have a periodical, which has both a primary local audience and a national circulation. The mosque, headed by the imam (minister-teacher) is the basic center of Islam.

Above the level of the local centers, a variety of national and continental organizations have been formed to mobilize the various local Islamic communities, provide the public (largely ignorant of Islam) with information, and coordinate the activities (particularly the propagation of the faith) of the community at large. These organizations, whose membership will come from a variety of ethnic backgrounds, tend to be divided politically. Each of the different organization will be ideologically aligned to, for example, different factions in the Middle East, and/or atuned to a more-or-less activist role in support of various concerns of the land from which they immigrated. Political activism is particularly noticeable in those groups which serve the large Muslim community on the nation's campuses. Local centers will often affiliate with several of the competing national associations.

Symbolic of Sunni Muslim presence in America is the Islamic Center in Washington, D.C. Begun in 1949, it took seven years to complete. It was officially opened in 1957. While begun as a center for diplomatic personnel, with financial support from seventeen countries, with the growth of Islam in North America it has become a place to which all American Sunnis look as a visible point of unity in the otherwise decentralized Islamic community. The importance of the Center was dramatically underscored in the early 1980s when it was taken over by a group who supported the Iranian Revolution under the Ayatollah Khomeini and opposed the influence of the ambassadors from Saudi Arabia and other Islamic countries. The takeover disrupted the center for several years and led to the withdrawal of its prominent iman, Dr. Muhammad Abdul Rauf, a leading Islamic apologist in North America.

Among the oldest of the Canadian-United States organizations is the Federation of Islamic Organizations in the United States and Canada. It was founded in 1952, largely as a result of the efforts of Abdullah Ingram of Cedar Rapids, Iowa. He called a meeting attended primarily by Lebanese Muslims, representative of the older American Muslim centers, and formed the International Muslim Society, which two years later became the Federation. The Federation has as its goals the perpetuation of Islam and of Muslim culture and the dissemination of correct information about Muslim society worldwide. It publishes a periodical, *The Muslim Star*, and holds annual conventions, usually in the Midwest. The Federation accomplishments have been related to the fellowship of various Muslim centers across national and ethnic boundaries, and more activist groups, while acknowledging the contribution of the Federation, saw the need for further organizations.

The Islamic Society of North America emerged in the early 1980s out of the Muslim Students Association originally founded in 1952. It represents a broadening focus of concern by former students who moved into roles of leadership in the Muslim, academic and professional communities in America. The Society is headquartered at the Islamic Teaching Center, a large complex in suburban Indianapolis, from which it oversees the network of subsidiary organizations it has fostered and nurtured.

From its original goals, developed to assist graduate students temporarily in the United States for study to survive in a non-Muslim environment, the Society has since 1975 refocused its attention on building Islamic structures among a permanent and growing North American Islamic population and actively propagating the faith among the non-Muslim public. To these ends, the society has established the Islamic Medical Association, the Association of Muslim Social Scientists and the Association of Muslim Scientists and Engineers. It has published numerous books (including the proceedings of the many conferences its sponsors) and pamphlets (especially a set designed to introduce Islam to non-Muslims) and several periodicals, most prominently *Al-Ittihad* and *Islamic Horizons*. The Muslim Student Association continues as one department of the Society. The Islamic Teaching Center is the main structure engaged in *dawah*, the propagation of the faith.

Possibly the most inclusive Islamic organization for Sunni Muslims is the Council of Islamic Organizations of America (both the Federation of Islamic Associations and the Islamic Society of North America are affiliates). The idea of the Council emerged in 1973 at a meeting in Saudi Arabia. Then the Muslim World League, an international Muslim organization with offices in New York City, organized the first Islamic Conference of North America which met April 22-24, 1977 at Newark, New Jersey. The Council was organized at that gathering to meet primary needs for unity and co-ordination of the many Islamic centers in North America. In its lengthy list of goals, it set itself the task of fostering unity, establishing and propagating the faith in its fullness, the perpetuation of modest dress codes, assistance in building mosques and other facilities for Muslims, and the funding of various designated projects of broad Muslim interest.

Also formed in the 1970s, the Council of Imams in North America formed as a continent-wide professional organization for the leaders of the various mosques and Islamic centers.

The several organizations mentioned above are but a few of the many new structures being established in the Muslim Community. All of the organizations have been assisted by the development of Muslim publishing concerns, such as American Trust Publications, affiliated with the Islamic Society of North America; Kazi Publications in Chicago; and The Crescent Publications, Tacoma Park, Maryland. As of the mid-1980s, however, the majority of English-language literature produced for the American Muslim community is still published overseas.

Membership: Estimates vary on the size of the Sunni Muslim community. As many as 400 mosques and centers have been counted. Approximately 3,000,000 immigrants from predominantly Muslim countries have come to the United States. Together with converts, including large followings in American black communities, the total number of Muslims approaches the size of the Jewish community.

Educational Facilities: American Islamic College, Chicago, Illinois.

Publications: *Muslim Star*. Available from Federation of Islamic Associations in the U.S.A. and Canada, 25351 Five Mile Rd., Redford Twp., MI 48239. • *Islamic Horizons*. Send orders to Box 38, Plainfield, IN 46168. • *Al-Ittihad*, Box 38, Plainfield, IN 46168. • *The Minaret*. Both available from Islamic Center of Southern California, 434 S. Vermont Ave., Los Angeles, CA 90020. • *Path of*

Righteousness. Available from Council of Imans in North America, 1214 Cambridge Crescent, Sarnia, ON, Canada N7S 3W4. • *Al' Nourl*. Send orders to 2551 Massachusettes Ave., Washington, D.C. 20008. • *Islam Canada*. Available from Council of Muslim Communities of Canada, Box 771, Station B, Willowdale, ON, Canada M2K 2R1.

★1798★
Triumph the Church and Kingdom of God in Christ
Box 77056
Birmingham, AL 35228

Triumph the Church and Kingdom of God in Christ was founded by Elder E. D. Smith in 1902. The founding followed by five years a divine revelation given to Smith. According to the literature of the church, the 1902 organization of the church marked the time when the revelation was "speeded to earth." Finally, in 1904, the content of the revelation was announced. Headquarters for the church were established in Baton Rouge, Louisiana, then were moved to Birmingham, Alabama, and later to Atlanta, Georgia. The founder was in charge of the church until 1920, when he moved to Addis Ababa, Ethiopia.

The church follows the holiness beliefs common to holiness churches, but also believes in fire baptism, a spiritual experience of empowerment by the Holy Spirit. Fire baptism was first received by the Apostles in the upper room on Pentecost, when tongues of fire appeared above their heads (Acts 2). As practiced by the several nineteenth and twentieth century "fire-baptized" churches, fire baptism is similar to the pentecostal experience of the baptism of the Holy Spirit, except it is typically not accompanied by speaking in tongues. (See separate entry on the Fire-Baptized Holiness Church, Wesleyan.)

Triumph the Church and Kingdom of God in Christ holds a unique view of itself as a church in relation to Christendom, traditionally called the church militant. This view is reflected in the following passage from the church's catechism: *Question* Was there another Church in the earth before Triumph *answer*. Yes. Church Militant; *Question* Is there any difference between the Triumph Church and Church Militant *answer* Yes. Church Militant is a Church of warfare, and Triumph is a Church of Peace; *Question* What happened to Church Militant when Triumph was revealed *answer* God turned it upside down and emptied His Spirit into Triumph; *Question* Is Triumph just a Church only *answer* No. It has a Kingdom with it.

Polity is episcopal with bishops elected for life. Under the bishops is a hierarchy of state and local workers. Every four years the church holds an International Religious Congress.

Membership: Not reported. At last report (1972) there were 475 churches, 53,307 members, and 1,375 ministers.

★1799★
True Fellowship Pentecostal Church of God of America
4238 Pimlico Rd.
Baltimore, MD 21215

The True Fellowship Pentecostal Church of God of America was formed in 1964 by the secession of the Rev. Charles E. Waters, Sr., a presiding elder in the Alpha and Omega Pentecostal Church of God of America, Inc.. Doctrine is like the Church of God in Christ, differing only in the acceptance of women into the ministry as pastors and elders. Bishop Waters and his wife operate a mission for those in need in Baltimore.

Membership: Not reported. In 1948 the church reported three congregations and about 120 members, all in Baltimore.

★1800★
True Grace Memorial House of Prayer
205 V St. NW
Washington, DC 20001

In 1960 after Bishop Marcelino Manoel de Graca (Sweet Daddy Grace) died, Walter McCoullough was elected bishop of the United House of Prayer for All People, but approximately six months later criticism was directed at him for his disposal of church monies without explanation to the other church leaders. The elders relieved him of his office and a lawsuit ordered a new election, at which time he was re-elected. Complaints continued that he was assuming false doctrines, such as claiming that he and only he was doing God's work or that he had power to save or condemn people. Shortly after the second election, he dismissed a number of the church leaders. Twelve dissenting members, with Thomas O. Johnson (d. 1970) as their pastor, formed the True Grace Memorial House of prayer in Washington, D.C. (Elder Johnson had been dismissed after 23 years of service as a pastor.) In 1962 the church members adopted a church covenant in which they agreed to assist one another in loving counsel, prayer, and aid in times of sickness and distress; to do all good to all, in part, by assisting them to come under the ministry of the church; to avoid causes of divisions, such as gossip; and to refrain from any activity that might bring disgrace on the cause of Christ. The present head of the church is Elder William G. Easton.

Membership: Not reported. In the 1970s there were eight congregations which could be found in Washington, D.C., Philadelphia, New York City, Baltimore, Savannah, Hollywood, Florida and in North Carolina.

★1801★
Unification Association of Christian Sabbath Keepers
255 W. 131st St.
New York, NY 10027

In the early 1940s in Manhattan a movement was started among black Adventists to unite independent Sabbath-keeping congregations. It was begun by Thomas I. C. Hughes, a former minister in the Seventh-Day Adventist Church and pastor of the Advent Sabbath Church, formed in 1941 in Manhattan. The missionary-minded Hughes conceived the idea of both home and foreign endeavors and began to gather support from his congregation. In 1956, the Unification Association of Christian Sabbath Keepers was formed, bringing together Hughes's parish and the New York United Sabbath Day Advent Church. Others joined, including the Believers in the Commandments of God.

There is a wide range of doctrinal belief in the various churches. Immersion is practiced and the Sabbath kept. A general adventist theology prevails. The polity is congregational. There are annual meetings for fellowship and general conferences every four years for business. At the second general conference, the title "bishop" was created, but there is no episcopal authority accompanying that title. A twenty-three member board of evangelism operates between general conferences.

The Unification Association is very missionary-minded. Missions had been established by its founders even before the Association was formed. Affiliated fellowships can be found in Nigeria, Liberia, Jamaica, Antigua and Trinidad.

Membership: As of 1986 only one congregation remained in the United States, at Elizabeth, New Jersey. There were scattered affiliated congregations in Africa and the West Indies.

Publications: *Unification Leader.*

★1802★
United Church and Science of Living Institute
Box 1000
Boston, MA 02103

The United Church and Science of Living Institute was formed in 1966 by the Rev. Frederick Eikerenkoetter II, a former Baptist minister, popularly known as Reverend Ike. After graduating from the American Bible School in Chicago in 1956, Reverend Ike spent a time in evangelism and faith healing and became influenced by New Thought. "Science of Living" is the term used to describe the teachings of Reverend Ike, which focus upon the prosperity theme in New Thought thinking. He believes the lack of money is the root of all evil.

Reverend Ike emphasizes the use of mind-power. Members are urged to rid the self of attitudes of "pie-in-the-sky," and postponed rewards. Instead, they should begin thinking of God as the real man in the self. Turning one's attention to the self allows God to work. Believing in God's work allows one to see the self as worthy of God's success. Visualization is a popular technique to project desires into the conscious mind as a first step to the abundant life. A prosperity "blessing plan" emphasizes believing, giving, and prospering. Reverend Ike developed an extensive media ministry and is heard over 89 radio and 22 television stations in the Eastern half of the United States and in California and Hawaii.

Membership: Not reported. In 1974 there were two congregations, one in New York (over 5,000 average attendance) and one in Boston. However, Rev. Ike regularly spoke to audiences around the United States.

Publications: *Action.*

★1803★
United Church of Jesus Christ (Apostolic)
5150 Baltimore National Pike
Baltimore, MD 21229
Monroe Saunders, Presiding Bishop

The United Church of Jesus Christ (Apostolic) traces its history to 1945 when Randolph A. Carr an Overseer in the Church of God in Christ, withdrew because of doctrinal differences, and formed the Church of God in Christ (Apostolic). Carr had come to believe in the Apostolic doctrine concerning the Oneness of the Godhead (as opposed to the Church of God in Christ's adherence to the doctrine of the Trinity).

In 1965, Monroe R. Saunders, Sr., then the General Secretary and a member of the Board of Bishops of the church, expressed serious difficulties with some contradictions between belief and action by the church's leadership, specifically as related to the teaching on marriage and divorce and the actions of Bishop Carr. His actions had become a matter of concern throughout the church. Carr forced Saunders out of the church. Many of the members and leaders left with Saunders and joined him in the formation of the United Church of Jesus Christ (Apostolic).

Saunders carefully and prayerfully put together a Book of Church Order and Disciple to guide the administration of the church. The church is operated by a board of bishops, one of which is the presiding bishop or president, and one the vice-bishop or vice-president. The Church observes the ordinances of baptism, holy communion, and foot washing.

Saunders has served as president since the church's founding in 1965. One of the more educated leaders in the Apostolic Movement, Saunders completed his post-graduate studies and has led in the cause of an educated ministry. He formed the Center for a More Abundant Life, which serves as an umbrella for a variety of social and educational services, such as the Center for Creative Learning, an early childhood educational facility; the Monroe R. Saunders School for elementary school children; and two high rise houses for the elderly and handicapped.

Membership: The church reports 80 congregations, 100,000 members, and 150 ministers in the United States and Canada, and it has missions in England, Africa, and the West Indies.

Educational Facilities: Institute of Biblical Studies, Baltimore, Maryland.

★1804★
United Churches of Jesus, Apostolic
Efforts to locate an address for this edition were unsuccessful. The United Churches of Jesus, Apostolic was formed by several bishops of the Apostolic Church of Christ in God who rejected the leadership of presiding bishop J. C. Richardson, Sr. Richardson had married a divorced woman. The church is headed by a general bishop, J. W. Ardrey (one of the founders of the Apostle Church) and a board of bishops. Doctrine is like the parent body.

Membership: In 1980 the United Churches had 2,000 members, 20 churches, 30 ministers and six bishops.

★1805★
United Free-Will Baptist Church
Efforts to locate an address for this edition were unsuccessful. Racial division did not escape the Free Will Baptists, but did wait until the twentieth century. The predominantly black United Free Will Baptist Church was established in 1901. Like its parent body, it is Arminian in theology and practices footwashing and anointing the sick with oil. The congregational polity was modified within a system of district, quarterly, annual, and general conferences. The local church is autonomous in regard to business, elections, and form of government, but the conferences have the power to decide the questions of doctrine.

Membership: Not reported. In 1952 there were 836 churches and 100,000 members.

Educational Facilities: Kingston College, Kingston, North Carolina.

Publications: *The Free Will Baptist Advocate.*

★1806★
United Hebrew Congregation

Efforts to locate an address for this edition were unsuccessful. The United Hebrew Congregation was the name of about a half dozen congregations of black Jews which during the mid-1970s were centered upon the Ethiopian Hebrew Culture Center in Chicago, which were headed by Rabbi Naphtali Ben Israel. It was this group's belief that Ham's sons were black. Included were the Hebrews of which one reads in the Bible. Abraham came from Chaldea, and the ancient Chaldeans were black. The congregation members believe Solomon was black (Song of Solomon 1:5). Sabbath services were held on Saturday. No sign of their continuance into the 1980s has been found.

Membership: Not reported

★1807★
United Holy Church of America

825 Fairoak Ave.
Chillum, MD 20783

The United Holy Church of America was formed as the outgrowth of a holiness revival conducted by the Rev. Isaac Cheshier at Method, North Carolina (near Raleigh), in 1886. In 1900, the group became known as the Holy Church of North Carolina (and as growth dictated, the Holy Church of North Carolina and Virginia). In the early twentieth century, the church became Pentecostal and adopted a theology like the Church of God (Cleveland, Tennessee). The present name was chosen in 1916.

Membership: Not reported. In 1970 there were approximately 50,000 members in 470 churches and over 400 ministers.

Publications: *The Holiness Union.*

★1808★
United House of Prayer for All People

1721 1/2 7th St. NW
Washington, DC 20001

Sweet Daddy Grace, as Bishop Marcelino Manoel de Graca (1884-1960) was affectionately known by his followers, was born in 1884 on Brava, Cape Verde Islands, and was a former railroad cook who began preaching in 1925. He founded the United House of Prayer for All People, which in the 1930s and 1940s was one of the most famous religious groups in the black community.

In doctrine, the church resembles the holiness Pentecostal bodies. It teaches the three experiences-conversion, sanctification, and baptism with the Holy Spirit. There is a strict behavior code. What sets the House of Prayer apart is the role that Daddy Grace assumed in the group, i.e., that of a divine being. In an often repeated quote, he was heard to have admonished his worshippers:

Never mind about God. Salvation is by Grace only. . .Grace has given God a vacation, and since God is on His vacation, don't worry Him. . .If you sin against God, Grace can save you, but if you sin against Grace, God cannot save you.

Thus, while the House of Prayer derives from and continues to grow in relation to the Pentecostal framework, the framework was significantly changed by Grace's assumption of deific powers. Grace reigned supreme as an autocrat until his death. He appointed the ministers and all church officials. A line of Daddy Grace Products included soap, toothpaste, writing paper, face powder, shoe polish, and cookies. There is an annual convocation.

Grace died in 1960 and, after a period of court fights, Bishop Walter McCoullough was acknowledged as head of the church. He has assumed Grace's powers, if not his divine claims. Under his leadership, the church has assumed more traditional Pentecostal stance. In 1974, it launched a $1.5 million housing project in Washington, D.C.

Membership: Not reported. In 1974 Bishop McCollough claimed 4,000,000 members. There were four congregations in Washington, D.C., and others throughout the nation.

★1809★
United Way of the Cross Churches of Christ of the Apostolic Faith

Efforts to locate an address for this edition were unsuccessful. The United Way of the Cross Churches of Christ of the Apostolic Faith was founded by Bishop Joseph H. Adams of the Way of the Cross Church of Christ and Elder Harrison J. Twyman of the Bible Way

Church of Our Lord Jesus Christ World Wide, Inc. The new church was formed when the two founders, both pastors of congregations in North Carolina, discovered that God had given each a similar vision to form a new church. Also, Adams, a bishop in North Carolina for the Way of the Cross Church of Christ, had developed some concerns with the administrative procedures of the church. The church grew, in part, from the addition of pastors and their congregations who had previously left other Apostolic bodies.

Membership: In 1980 the United Way of the Cross Churches had 1,100 members in 14 churches. There were 30 ministers and four bishops.

★1810★
Universal Christian Spiritual Faith and Churches for All Nations

Efforts to locate an address for this edition were unsuccessful. The Universal Christian Spiritual Faith and Churches for All Nations was founded in 1952 by the merger of the National David Spiritual Temple of Christ Church Union (Inc.) U.S.A., St. Paul's Spiritual Church Convocation, and King David's Spiritual Temple of Truth Association. National David Spiritual Temple of Christ Church Union (Inc.) U.S.A. had been founded at Kansas City, Missouri, in 1932 by Dr. David William Short, a former Baptist minister. He became convinced that no man had the right or spiritual power "to make laws, rules or doctrines for the real church founded by Jesus Christ" and that the "denominational" churches had been founded in error and in disregard of the apostolic example. Bishop Short claimed that the temple was the true church, and hence dated to the first century.

The merged church differs from many Pentecostal churches in that it denies that only those who have spoken in tongues have received the Spirit. It does insist, however, that a full and complete baptism of the Holy Ghost is always accompanied by both the gift of "tongues" and other powers. The members of the church rely on the Holy Spirit for inspiration and direction. The church is organized according to I Corinthians 12:1-31 and Ephesians 4:11. It includes pastors, archbishops, elders, overseers, divine healers, deacons, and missionaries. Bishop Short is the chief governing officer. In 1952, he became archbishop of the newly merged body. He is assisted by a national executive board which holds an annual assembly.

Membership: Not reported. In the mid-1960s there were reportedly 60 churches and 40,816 members.

Educational Facilities: St. David Christian Spiritual Seminary.

Publications: *The Christian Spiritual Voice.*

★1811★
Universal Church, the Mystical Body of Christ

Efforts to locate an address for this edition were unsuccessful. The Universal Church, the Mystical Body of Christ, is an interracial Pentecostal group which emerged in the 1970s. It is distinguished by its belief that in order to serve God freely, members must come out of a corrupt government, society, and churches of this land, and establish a separate government on another continent where a theocratic system can be constructed. Only then, can perfection exist in society. Members call upon all Christians to join them. They believe that these are the end-times and that God is calling together his 144,000 mentioned in Revelation.

The church has a strict moral code and disapproves of short dresses for women, long hair for men, and women preachers and elders. Women cover their heads during worship. The group fasts, uses wine and unleavened bread at the Lord's Supper, and believes in baptism for the remission of sins, divine healing, speaking in tongues, and the unity of the church. The Universal Church is headed by Bishop R. O. Frazier. Members do not think of themselves as another denomination, but as the one true body of Christ.

Membership: Not reported.

Publications: *The Light of Life Herald.* Send orders to Box 874, Saginaw, MI 48605.

★1812★
Universal Foundation for Better Living

11901 Ashland Ave.
Chicago, IL 60643

The Universal Foundation for Better Living was founded in 1974, but grew out of the ministry begun in Chicago, Illinois, in 1956 by the Rev. Johnnie Colemon, then a minister with the Unity School of

Christianity and one of the first black New Thought ministers. In 1953 she learned that she had an incurable disease. She moved to Kansas City, Kansas, and enrolled in the Unity School of Christianity. In a few months she was healed and stayed at Unity to become the first black person ordained as a Unity minister (1956). Moving to Chicago, she founded the Christ Unity Temple, which first met in the Y.M.C.A. building on South Cottage Grove. She became a prominent Unity minister and was the first black to be elected president of the Association of Unity Churches. However, in 1974 she withdrew from the association and renamed her congregation Christ Universal Temple. That same year, she founded the Johnnie Colemon Institute as an educational arm of the church for both lay and professional education. The first ministers were graduated and ordained in 1978. In 1981, she began a television ministry with the "Better Living with Johnnie Colemon" show that airs on 13 stations across the United States.

In 1985, the growing ministry reached a major plateau with the opening of the Christ Universal Temple complex on the far south side of Chicago. The church, which also serves as headquarters from the foundation and institute, seats 3,500 in its sanctuary, the largest in Chicago. The building also houses the UFBL Bookstore and the Prayer Ministry, which offers a 24-hour call-in service for those in need.

The beliefs of the foundation are in harmony with that of the Unity School of Christianity, the break being largely a matter of social policy, not doctrine. A statement of belief emphasizes that it is God's will for everyone to live a healthy, happy, and prosperous life and that such a life is attainable for each person. The kingdom within can be brought to visible expression by following the principles of Jesus, the Wayshower. The key is right thinking followed by right action. Specifically cited is a belief that rather than making a primary effort to provide for the needy, the church should provide the teaching which will allow each person to provide for themselves.

The foundation is a member of the International New Thought Alliance (INTA).

Membership: In 1987 the foundation had 17 member churches and study groups in the United States, and one each in Canada, Trinidad, and Guyana.

Educational Facilities: Johnnie Colemon Institute, Chicago, Illinois.

Publications: *Daily Inspiration for Better Living.*

★1813★
Vedantic Center
3528 N. Triunfo Canyon Rd.
Agoura, CA 91301

The Vedantic Center was founded in 1975 in Los Angeles by Alice Coltrane (b. 1937), a former student of Swami Satchidananda, founder of the Integral Yoga Institute, with whom she journeyed in India and Sri Lanka. Raised in Detroit, Coltrane devoted her early life to music, as did her late husband, jazz musician John Coltrane, and like him attained a high level of success and fame. In 1968 at the age of 31, she entered a period described as a time of both spiritual isolation and re-awakening. Directly from the Supreme Lord, she also received an initiation into the renounced order of sannyas, but was instructed not to don the ochre robe, symbolic of the renounced life, until 1975. During the early 1970s she did a series of records expressing her spiritual pilgrimage and devotional life.

In 1975 Coltrane emerged as Swami Turiyasangitananda. A few months later, she organized the Vedantic Center. She authored several books, including *Monument Eternal* and *Endless Wisdom*, and began to build a following. In 1983 the center purchased 48 acres of land in rural southern California near the town of Agoura and established a community, Shanti Anantam, for the center's members.

The Vedantic Center is unique in that it is one of the very few Hindu organizations drawing members predominantly from the American black community and led by a black person (though there are predominantly black centers within large and otherwise predominantly non-black Hindu groups). While beginning with the yoga system passed to her by Swami Satchidananda, Turiyasangitananda has developed an eclectic blend of Eastern philosophy which draws upon Western spiritual traditions as well. She teaches that the purpose of human life is to advance spiritually. The highest stage of life is devotional service (bhakti yoga), rendered unto the Supreme Lord (known in his three aspects as Brahma, Vishnu or Krishna, and Siva). In this light, devotional singing has attained an important role at the ashram, and Turiyasangitananda

has composed new music with a decidedly Western flavor for the traditional bhajans (devotional songs).

The weekly schedule at Shanti Anantam begins with Sunday school for children. There is worship, including satsang discourses by Swami Turiyasangitananda, on Sunday afternoons. An additional satsang occurs on Wednesday evening. Hatha yoga classes are held several times during the week. The center operates a vegetarian restaurant in Westlake Village, California, and a bookstore at the entrance to the ashram grounds. A television show, "Eternity's Pillar", is heard weekly over one station in southern California, and a radio program, "Divine Songs", is heard Wednesday evening on FM radio.

Membership: Approximately 50 people live at Shanti Anantam. A small number of non-residents also attend the ashram's worship services.

Publications: *The Center News.*

★1814★
Way of the Cross Church of Christ
332 4th St., NE
Washington, DC 20003

The Way of the Cross Church of Christ was founded in 1927 by Henry C. Brooks, an independent black Pentecostal minister. Brooks had founded a small congregation in Washington, D.C. which became part of the Church of Our Lord Jesus Christ of the Apostolic Faith founded by Robert Clarence Lawson. At that time there was another small congregation under Bishop Lawson in Washington headed by Smallwood E. Williams, and Lawson wanted Brooks' congregation to join Williams'. Brooks rejected the plan, left Lawson's jurisdiction and founded a separate organization. A second congregation in Henderson, North Carolina, became the first of several along the East Coast. Brooks pastored the mother church for forty years and built a membership of over 3,000.

The Way of the Cross Church is headed by a presiding bishop. John L. Brooks, the son of the founder, succeeded to that post. He is assisted by twelve other bishops. Missions are supported in Ghana and Liberia.

Membership: In 1980 the Way of the Cross Church of Christ had 48 affiliated congregations and approximately 50,000 members.

(4) Library Collections

★1815★
Africa News Service, Inc.
Library
PO Box 3851   Ph: (919)286-0747
Durham, NC 27702   Fax: (919)286-2614
Betsy Hankin

Founded: 1970. **Staff:** 1. **Subjects:** African news - politics, economics, foreign affairs, culture, media, women, sports. **Holdings:** 3000 books; 180 VF drawers of news clippings, documents, radio transcriptions, and other materials. **Subscriptions:** 300 journals and other serials. **Services:** Library open to the public. **Computerized Information Services:** Internal database.

★1816★
African American Historical and Cultural Society
Library of San Francisco
762 Fulton St.
San Francisco, CA 94102   Ph: (415)292-6172
Juliana Haile

Founded: 1963. **Staff:** Prof 3. **Subjects:** African Americans - history, biography, autobiography, fiction. **Holdings:** Figures not available. **Services:** Library open to the public.

★1817★
African-American Institute
Africa Policy Information Center
833 United Nations Plaza   Ph: (212)949-5666
New York, NY 10017   Fax: (212)682-6421
Russell Geekie, Asst.Ed.

Founded: 1974. **Staff:** Prof 1. **Subjects:** Africa - economy, U.S. foreign policy, United Nations, development. **Special Collections:** News clippings from American, European, and African publications, 1974 to present. **Holdings:** Magazines; conference reports; Africa Report (a complete set of the institute's publication). **Subscriptions:** 200 journals and other serials; 50 newspapers. **Services:** Copying; center open to the public.

★1818★
African American Museum
Library
1765 Crawford Rd.
Cleveland, OH 44106   Ph: (216)791-1700
Dr. Joan Baker, Dir./Cur.

Founded: 1953. **Staff:** Prof 3. **Subjects:** African and African-American history and culture. **Special Collections:** African-American music; blacks in aviation; black theology; black church in Cleveland. **Holdings:** 200 books; 200 bound periodical volumes; 10,000 negatives; 100 paintings; 100,000 news clippings; 500 slides; 100 audiotapes; 50 pieces of art; 15 proclamations; 3 Reconstruction maps. **Services:** Library open to the public with restrictions.

★1819★
African Literature Association
Library
Africana Studies and Research Center
Cornell University
310 Triphammer Rd.   Ph: (607)255-4625
Ithaca, NY 14853   Fax: (607)255-0784
Prof. Anne Adams

Staff: Prof 1. **Subjects:** African literature. **Holdings:** 5 VF drawers of business and editorial archives. **Publications:** Directory, annual; Annual Selected Conference Papers.

★1820★
Africare
Library
440 R St. NW   Ph: (202)462-3614
Washington, DC 20001   Fax: (202)387-1034

Subjects: Rural Africa - health, environmental protection, water and agricultural resources, development. **Holdings:** 3300 volumes.

★1821★
Alabama A & M University
J.F. Drake Memorial Learning Resources Center
Box 489   Ph: (205)851-5760
Normal, AL 35762   Fax: (205)851-5768
Dr. Birdie O. Weir, Dir.

Founded: 1904. **Staff:** Prof 8; Other 14. **Subjects:** Education, business and economics, agriculture, the sciences, computer science, literature. **Special Collections:** Black Collection (3278 items); Archival Collection (2965 items); Curriculum Collection (5313 items); Children's Collection (5560 items); Schomburg Collection; Carnegie-Mydral Collection; J.F. Kennedy Memorial Collection; International Studies Collection (1449 items). **Holdings:** 229,646 books; 20,356 bound periodical volumes; 4653 AV programs; 15,926 periodicals on microfilm; 737 college catalogs; 661 telephone directories; 10,921 vertical files; 480,008 ERIC microfiche; 127,481 government documents; Wall Street Journal on microfiche (10,548); NewsBank on microfiche (19,747); Business NewsBank on microfiche (2114). **Subscriptions:** 1572 journals and other serials; 92 newspapers; 652 microfilm subscriptions. **Services:** Interlibrary loan; copying; videotaping; centeropen to the public; courtesy card must be purchased for check out of materials by persons not enrolled at the university or at one of the cooperating institutions. **Automated Operations:** Computerized public access catalog, cataloging, and ILL. **Computerized Information Services:** DIALOG Information Services. Performs searches on fee basis. Contact Person: Prudence W. Bryant, Supv., Ref. & Info.Serv. **Networks and Consortia:** Member of Network of Alabama Academic Libraries (NAAL), Alabama Library Exchange, Inc. (ALEX), SOLINET. **Publications:** Mixed Media (newsletter), annual; In the News (newsletter) - for internal distribution only; LRC Fast Facts; LRC

Handbook of Programs and Services; brochures. **Also known as:** Alabama Agricultural and Mechanical University.

★1822★
Alabama State University
University Library & Learning Resources
Archives & Special Collections
Levi Watkins Learning Center
915 S. Jackson St.
Montgomery, AL 36195-0301   Ph: (205)293-4106
Rubye J. Sullivan, Spec.Coll.Libn.

Staff: Prof 1; Other 6. **Subjects:** Afro-Americans. **Special Collections:** Atlanta University's Black Culture Collection (181 reels of microfilm); George W. Carver Correspondence Collection (67 reels of microfilm); Bibliography of Doctoral Research on the Negro, 1933-1966; E.D. Nixon Collection; Alabama Statewide Oral History Project (10 volumes of transcribed interviews); Montgomery, Alabama Bus Boycott, 1955-1957 (4 volumes). **Holdings:** 11,980 books; 600 bound periodical volumes; 384 reels of microfilm; 435 microfiche; 305 16mm films, cassettes, filmstrip/cassette sets; 2 vertical files of clippings; 200 phonograph records, slides, audiotapes; 1690 theses. **Subscriptions:** 50 journals and other serials; 30 newspapers. **Services:** Copying; collections open to the public. **Special Indexes:** Index to Periodicals by and about Negroes (book); Indexes to Vertical Files (card); Index to Black Cultural Collection (book); Index to Doctoral Research on the Negro (card).

★1823★
Alternative Press Center
Library
Box 33109   Ph: (410)243-2471
Baltimore, MD 21218   Fax: (410)235-5325
Bill Wilson, Coord.

Founded: 1969. **Staff:** Prof 3. **Subjects:** Liberation - women's, gay, black; Third World movement; ecology; alternative life styles. **Holdings:** 420 volumes. **Subscriptions:** 120 journals and other serials; 180 newspapers. **Services:** Library open to the public. **Publications:** Alternative Press Index, quarterly.

★1824★
American Baptist Theological Seminary
T.L. Holcomb Library
1800 Baptist World Center Dr.
Nashville, TN 37207   Ph: (615)228-7877
Dorothy B. Lucas, Libn.

Founded: 1924. **Staff:** Prof 1; Other 4. **Subjects:** Bible, religion, theology, black studies. **Holdings:** 36,214 books; 715 bound periodical volumes; 2576 vertical file materials; 1078 AV programs. **Subscriptions:** 220 journals and other serials. **Services:** Interlibrary loan; copying; library open to the public for reference use only.

★1825★
American Civil Liberties Union
ACLU/CNSS Library
122 Maryland Ave. NE   Ph: (202)544-1681
Washington, DC 20002   Fax: (202)546-0738
Helen Robinson, Libn.

Founded: 1979. **Staff:** Prof 1; Other 2. **Subjects:** Civil rights, religious freedom, reproductive freedom, alien rights and immigration, national security, criminal justice, freedom of speech. **Holdings:** 2500 books; 100 reports. **Subscriptions:** 2000 journals and other serials. **Services:** Interlibrary loan; copying; library open to the public. **Publications:** First Principles: National Security and Civil Liberties. **Also known as:** ACLU Center for National Security Studies.

★1826★
American Civil Liberties Union
Library/Archives
132 W. 43rd St.
New York, NY 10036   Ph: (212)944-9800
Thomas Hilbink, Libn.

Founded: 1920. **Staff:** Prof 1. **Subjects:** Civil liberties, law. **Holdings:** 3000 books; 50 files of ACLU board and committee minutes and reports, affiliate mailings, press releases; annual reports; ACLU pamphlets and newsletters, 1920 to present. **Services:** Copying; library open to the public for research only.

★1827★
Amistad Research Center
Library/Archives
Tulane University
6823 St. Charles Ave.   Ph: (504)865-5535
New Orleans, LA 70118   Fax: (504)865-5580
Dr. Clifton H. Johnson, Exec.Dir.

Founded: 1966. **Staff:** Prof 6; Other 14. **Subjects:** Ethnic minorities of America, Afro-American history and culture, civil rights, Africa, abolitionism, United Church of Christ. **Special Collections:** Manuscript collections (8 million items); Aaron Douglas Art Collection (200 items); Victor DuBois Art Collection (81 items); Amistad Collection of African and American Art (65 items). **Holdings:** 19,000 books; 1600 bound periodical volumes; 15,000 pamphlets; 210 dissertations on microfilm; 2310 reels of microfilm; 500,000 clippings. **Subscriptions:** 650 journals and other serials; 31 newspapers. **Services:** Interlibrary loan; copying; library open to the public. **Computerized Information Services:** OCLC; BITNET (electronic mail service). **Networks and Consortia:** Member of SOLINET. **Publications:** Amistad Reports (newsletter), quarterly; Amistad Log (magazine), annual; Historical Source Research Materials on microfilm, irregular - all free upon request; Amistad Research Center manuscipt holdings, irregular - for sale. **Special Catalogues:** Catalog of the American Missionary Association Archives.

★1828★
Assassination Archives and Research Center
918 F St. NW, Ste. 510
Washington, DC 20004   Ph: (202)393-1917
Jim Lesar

Founded: 1984. **Staff:** Prof 1; Other 3. **Subjects:** Assassinations, including John F. Kennedy, Robert F. Kennedy, and Martin Luther King, Jr.; intelligence operations; organized crime. **Special Collections:** Assassinations scholars and authors research files (20 file cabinets); President Kennedy Assassination Collection (audiotapes; photographs). **Holdings:** 1500 books; 20 bound periodical volumes; 15 file cabinets of government documents; 1000 audiotapes; 25 films; photographs. **Subscriptions:** 12 journals and other serials. **Services:** Interlibrary loan; copying; center open to the public. **Computerized Information Services:** Internal database. Performs searches free of charge. **Publications:** Bibliographies on assassinations.

★1829★
Association for the Study of Afro-American Life and
   History
Carter G. Woodson Library
1407 14th St., N.W.
Washington, DC 20005

Founded: 1915. **Subjects:** Afro-American history. **Special Collections:** Rare books on black involvement in America prior to 1865 (200 books). **Holdings:** 4200 books; 88 bound periodical volumes.

★1830★
Atlanta-Fulton Public Library
Special Collections Department
1 Margaret Mitchell Sq.   Ph: (404)730-1700
Atlanta, GA 30303   Fax: (404)730-1989
Janice White Sikes, Mgr.

Founded: 1925. **Staff:** Prof 5; Other 3. **Subjects:** African-American studies, genealogy, Georgia history and literature, oral history, Margaret Mitchell. **Special Collections:** Hattie Wilson High Memorial Genealogical Collection (6800 books, 372 bound periodical volumes, 129 unbound periodicals, 214 city directories, 1200 maps, 160 reels of microfilm); Samuel Williams Collection of materials by and about Afro-Americans (40,000 books, 1600 bound periodical volumes, 2100 reels of microfilm, 1000 microfiche); Margaret Mitchell Collection (1766 items); Atlanta-Fulton Public Library Archives; rare books. **Holdings:** 54,300 books; 3930 bound periodical volumes; 4396 reels of microfilm; 11,000 microfiche; 300 audiocassettes; 790 other cataloged items. **Subscriptions:** 350 journals and newsletters;

15 newspapers. **Services:** Copying; department open to the public for reference use only. **Publications:** Bibliographies and guides.

★1831★
Baltimore City Community College
Bard Library
2901 Liberty Heights Ave.   Ph: (410)333-5252
Baltimore, MD 21215   Fax: (410)333-5302
Bruce Carroll, Dir., Lib./Media Serv.

Founded: 1947. **Staff:** Prof 4; Other 6. **Subjects:** Black history, health science, Baltimore and Maryland history, technology. **Special Collections:** Baltimore is Best Collection; Baltimore City Community College and its antecedents. **Holdings:** 87,892 books; 125,000 pamphlets (uncataloged); 12,524 reels of microfilm; 20,000 nonprint materials. **Subscriptions:** 752 journals and other serials. **Services:** Interlibrary loan; copying; library open to the public for reference use only. **Automated Operations:** Computerized acquisitions, circulation, and shelflist files. **Computerized Information Services:** ABI/INFORM; CD-ROM (Academic Index, General Periodicals Ondisc, CINAHL-CD, The Baltimore Sun Index); Microcat (internal database). **Formerly:** New Community College of Baltimore.

★1832★
Beloit College
Colonel Robert H. Morse Library
Richard & Marieluise Black Information Center
731 College St.   Ph: (608)363-2481
Beloit, WI 53511   Fax: (608)363-2487
Dennis W. Dickinson, Coll.Libn.

Founded: 1847. **Staff:** Prof 5; Other 7.5. **Subjects:** Anthropology, economics, Shakespeare, international relations, geology, sociology. **Special Collections:** Joseph Rheingold Roosevelt Collection; Irving S. Kull Wilson Collection; Beloit Poetry Journal Collection; Martin Luther King, Jr. Collection. **Holdings:** 226,431 books; 41,515 bound periodical volumes; 4983 reels of microfilm. **Subscriptions:** 868 journals and other serials; 22 newspapers. **Services:** Interlibrary loan; library open to the public for reference use only. **Computerized Information Services:** DIALOG Information Services, Chemical Abstracts Service (CAS), Knowledge Index, WISCAT, First Search, electronic mail service. Performs searches. Contact Person: Christine Nelson, Pub.Serv.Libn.

★1833★
Bennett College
Thomas F. Holgate Library
Special Collections
900 E. Washington
Campus Box M
Greensboro, NC 27401   Ph: (919)273-4431
Dr. Haith

Special Collections: Afro-American Women's Collection (480 books; 2 VF drawers); Norris Wright Cuney Papers (personal and business correspondence, diaries, and newspaper clippings); College Archives (51 boxes; 3 file cabinets; 28 shelves; 1 bookcase). **Services:** Copying; collections open to the public by appointment. **Networks and Consortia:** Member of CCLC.

★1834★
Berean Institute
Library
1901 W. Girard Ave.   Ph: (215)763-4833
Philadelphia, PA 19130   Fax: (215)236-6011
Anthony Thoai Nguyen, Act.Lib.Dir.

Founded: 1920. **Staff:** Prof 1. **Subjects:** Business administration, secretarial science, electronics, cosmetology, data processing, paralegal. **Special Collections:** Edyth Ingraham (black history and education; 600 volumes). **Holdings:** 5000 books; 2000 unbound periodicals; 500 cassette tapes; 100 filmstrips; 125 transparencies; 700 slides; 450 microfiche. **Subscriptions:** 34 journals and other serials. **Services:** Interlibrary loan; copying; library open to the public for reference use only. **Computerized Information Services:** CD-ROM; internal database. **Publications:** Acquisitions list, bimonthly; bibliographies, irregular - for internal distribution only.

★1835★
Bienville Historical Society
Center for Gulf Studies
606 Government St.
Mobile, AL 36602   Ph: (205)457-5242
Johnnie Andrews, Jr., Dir.

Founded: 1955. **Staff:** Prof 4; Other 2. **Subjects:** City of Mobile and Alabama; genealogy; history of Louisiana, Florida, Mississippi, Georgia, and South Carolina; French, Spanish, and English colonial history; black history. **Special Collections:** Colonial Manuscripts,(1500)early church records dating from 1594 from numerous colonial towns; art collection, 1717 to present (1000 prints, etchings, and paintings); Blakeley, Alabama ghost town papers (6000 pages); Pensacola, Florida papers, 1559-1763 (7000 pages); Africa Town, Alabama papers (1000 pages); Overby photomanusripts (200); descriptive catalog of library collection from 1978-1988; Andry-Chastang, Creole Family Papers, 1805-1989 **Holdings:** 37,000 books; 300 railroad manuscripts; 300 early maps; 5000 pamphlets; 60,000 clippings in vertical files; 5000 photographs, 1855 to present; 20,000 copies of colonial archives . **Subscriptions:** 137 journals and other serials; 20 newspapers. **Services:** Copying; translation of holdings; library open to the public by appointment only. **Publications:** 60 publications on Gulf South history and genealogy. **Special Indexes:** Card indexes to library holdings of local history collections in 170 Southern libraries; Index of 150,000 Gulf Coast area residents from 1559-1876 (card). **Formerly:** Cleveland Prichard Memorial Library.

★1836★
Birmingham Public Library
Linn-Henley Library for Southern Historical Research
Department of Archives and Manuscripts
2100 Park Pl.   Ph: (205)226-3645
Birmingham, AL 35203   Fax: (205)226-3743
Marvin Y. Whiting, Archv./Cur., Mss.

Founded: 1976. **Staff:** Prof 1; Other 1. **Subjects:** Birmingham, Alabama - history, civil rights, real estate development, politics and government, private utilities, industry, civic organizations, photographic history, women's history. **Special Collections:** Birmingham Municipal Records (510 linear feet); Jefferson County Public Records (1550 linear feet); Civil Rights in Alabama (90 linear feet and microforms); Robert Jemison, Jr. papers (250 linear feet); Birmingham Water Works Company records (180 linear feet); Southern Women's Archives (500 linear feet). **Holdings:** 1055 books; 405 bound periodical volumes; 9000 linear feet of archives and manuscripts; 923 reels of microfilm of archives and manuscripts; 2106 microfiche; 600 oral history cassette tapes; 215,000 photographic prints and negatives. **Subscriptions:** 9 journals and other serials; 21 newspapers. **Services:** Interlibrary loan; copying; department open to the public for reference use only. **Computerized Information Services:** OCLC; internal databases. **Publications:** A Guide to the Collections of the Department of Archives and Manuscripts, Linn-Henley Research Library - for sale. **Special Catalogues:** Preliminary and Descriptive Inventories for Manuscript Collections and Archival Records Groups, Sub-groups, & Series. **Special Indexes:** Subject file index to photographic collections (card).

★1837★
Birmingham Public Library
Linn-Henley Library for Southern Historical Research
Tutwiler Collection of Southern History and Literature
2100 Park Pl.   Ph: (205)226-3665
Birmingham, AL 35203   Fax: (205)226-3743
Anne F. Knight, Dept.Hd.

Founded: 1927. **Staff:** Prof 5; Other 8. **Subjects:** Birmingham and Alabama history and literature; Southeastern genealogy; Civil War and Reconstruction history; slave history. **Special Collections:** State, county, and municipal documents. **Holdings:** 62,500 books; 7200 bound periodical volumes; 11,500 reels of microfilm; 1800 pamphlets; 6100 microforms; 154 VF drawers. **Subscriptions:** 358 journals and other serials. **Services:** Collection open to the public for reference use only. **Automated Operations:** Computerized cataloging, acquisitions, and serials. **Computerized Information Services:** DIALOG Information Services, OCLC. **Networks and Consortia:** Member of SOLINET. **Publications:** George B. Ward: Birmingham's Urban Statesman; Research in Black History; Genealogical Research in the Tutwiler Collection; Bibliography of

Birmingham, Alabama, 1872-1972 (book); Contemporary Literature in Birmingham; Eyewitness Accounts of the Civil War series - Battle of the Crater, Raid of the Confederate Cavalry, Service in the Cavalry of the Army of the Potomac, and Synopsis of the Military Career of General Joseph Wheeler; The Secret Proceedings and Debates of the Convention to Form the U.S. Constitution; Creek Indian History. **Special Indexes:** Index to the Birmingham News-Birmingham Post Herald, 1978 to present (microfiche).

★1838★
Black Women in Church and Society
Research/Resource Center
Inter Denominational Theological Center
671 Beckwith St., S.W.
Atlanta, GA 30314   Ph: (404)527-7740
Jacqueline Grant

Subjects: Liberation theology, feminism, women's movements, women in ministry. **Holdings:** 250 volumes.

★1839★
Boston College
Graduate School of Social Work Library
McGuinn Hall   Ph: (617)552-3233
Chestnut Hill, MA 02167   Fax: (617)552-3199
Kathleen Boyd, Hd.Libn.

Founded: 1936. **Staff:** Prof 2; Other 4. **Subjects:** Clinical social work; child welfare and families, individuals, and groups; ethnic studies and special populations; gerontology; human behavior; mental health; social policy; administration and research; social planning. **Holdings:** 30,333 books; 5733 bound periodical volumes; 840 masters' theses; 800 doctoral dissertations in social work on microfiche; government documents. **Subscriptions:** 300 journals and other serials. **Services:** Interlibrary loan; copying; library open to the public. **Automated Operations:** Computerized public access catalog, cataloging, acquisitions, serials, and circulation. **Computerized Information Services:** BRS Information Technologies, DIALOG Information Services, CD-ROM. Performs searches on fee basis. Contact Person: Donna L. Ferullo, Ref.Libn.. **Networks and Consortia:** Member of Boston Library Consortium (BLC), Northeast Consortium of Colleges and Universities in Massachusetts (NECCUM), NELINET, Inc.. **Publications:** Periodic acquisitions list; subject bibliographies.

★1840★
Boston University
Department of Special Collections
771 Commonwealth Ave.   Ph: (617)353-3696
Boston, MA 02215   Fax: (617)353-2838
Dr. Howard B. Gotlieb, Dir.

Founded: 1963. **Staff:** Prof 3; Other 8. **Subjects:** Literature - English, American, Afro-American; military history; private presses; Spanish history and literature. **Special Collections:** Twentieth century archives: papers of over 1200 individuals, including Dr. Martin Luther King, Jr. (180 boxes); Bette Davis (18 boxes; 50 scrapbooks); Isaac Asimov (400 boxes); John W. McCormack (200 boxes); Dan Rather (63 boxes); Endowment for Biblical Research: Bibles and Books of Common Prayer (2000 volumes); Robert Frost (6 manuscript boxes; 820 books); Theodore Roosevelt (100 manuscripts; 800 letters; 400 books); Richards Collection of historical and literary manuscripts, 1495-1970 (4000 items); Bortman Collection of Colonial Americana (2000 printed and manuscript items); Abraham Lincoln Collection (4582 books; 100 letters and documents; memorabilia); medieval manuscripts (20 volumes; 80 leaves). **Holdings:** 89,000 books; 30,000 boxes of manuscripts. **Subscriptions:** 35 journals and other serials. **Services:** Copying (limited); department open to the public by appointment. **Automated Operations:** Computerized cataloging and serials. **Networks and Consortia:** Member of Boston Library Consortium (BLC). **Publications:** Special Collections at Boston University (1981); Some Notable Recent Gifts to the Twentieth Century Archives (1984; brochure); Manuscripts Sacred and Secular (1985). **Special Catalogues:** Catalogs to manuscript collections (card); catalogs of printers, presses, illustrators, association copies, and provenance (card). **Special Indexes:** Index to individual collections.

★1841★
Brooklyn Museum
Art Reference Library
200 Eastern Pkwy.   Ph: (718)638-5000
Brooklyn, NY 11238   Fax: (718)638-3731
Deirdre E. Lawrence, Prin.Libn.

OU 1823. **Staff:** Prof 4; Other 4. **Subjects:** American and European painting and sculpture; decorative arts; art - African, Oceanic, Native American; prints and drawings; Asian art; costumes and textiles. **Special Collections:** American fashion sketches, 1900-1950; museum archives. **Holdings:** 140,000 books and exhibition catalogs; 25,000 bound periodical volumes; 100 VF drawers of ephemeral materials; museum archival materials. **Subscriptions:** 400 journals and other serials. **Services:** Interlibrary loan; copying; library open to the public by appointment. **Automated Operations:** Computerized cataloging. **Computerized Information Services:** RLIN; RLIN (electronic mail service). **Networks and Consortia:** Member of New York Metropolitan Reference and Research Library Agency.

★1842★
California State University, Fullerton
Oral History Program
The Library
800 N. State College Blvd.
Fullerton, CA 92634   Ph: (714)773-3580
Gail Gutierrez, Archv.

Founded: 1968. **Staff:** Prof 2. **Subjects:** Local, community, and family history; ethnic groups: Japanese Americans, Chinese Americans, African Americans, Native Americans, Mexican Americans, Swedish Americans; biography; political and university history; Philippine studies; Southeast Utah uranium; Mormon colony. **Holdings:** 825 volumes; 4000 interviews (audio); 15 masters' thesis. **Subscriptions:** 4 journals and other serials. **Services:** Program open to the public by appointment. **Special Catalogues:** Catalog of Oral History Collection, 1985 (addition, 1991).

★1843★
Caribbean Culture Center
Library
408 W. 58th St.   Ph: (212)307-7420
New York, NY 10019   Fax: (212)315-1086
C. Daniel Dawson, Dir., Spec.Proj.

Founded: 1976. **Staff:** 1. **Subjects:** Influence of African traditions in the cultures of the Americas. **Holdings:** Photographs; videotapes. **Services:** Copying; library open to the public by appointment. **Publications:** Caribe Magazine; occasional publications.

★1844★
Carnegie Public Library of Clarksdale and Coahoma
** County**
Delta Blues Museum Collection
114 Delta Ave.
Box 280
Clarksdale, MS 38614   Ph: (601)624-4461
Sid F. Graves, Jr., Dir.

Founded: 1914. **Staff:** Prof 6; Other 5. **Subjects:** Blues music; history - local, state, regional, black. **Holdings:** 15,000 books, periodicals, phonograph records, photographs, videotapes. **Services:** Interlibrary loan; copying; collection open to the public with restrictions. **Publications:** Clarksdale & Coahoma County: A History, 1982.

★1845★
Case Western Reserve University
Lillian and Milford Harris Library
Mandel School of Applied Social Sciences
11235 Bellflower Rd.   Ph: (216)368-2302
Cleveland, OH 44106-7164   Fax: (216)368-2106
Arthur S. Biagianti, Dir./Libn.

Founded: 1927. **Staff:** Prof 1; Other 2. **Subjects:** Social work, social welfare, poverty, alcoholism, corrections, aging, child welfare, minority group relations, community organization, psychiatry and mental health. **Holdings:** 22,000 books; 1500 bound periodical volumes; 7000 pamphlets and monographs; 533 microforms; 274 AV programs. **Subscriptions:** 309 journals and other serials. **Services:** Interlibrary loan; copying; library open to the public for reference use only. **Automated Operations:** Computerized public access catalog, cataloging, and circulation. **Computerized Information Services:** DIALOG Information Services, OCLC. **Networks and Consortia:** Member of Cleveland Area Metropolitan Library System (CAMLS). **Publications:** Acquisitions list. **Special Catalogues:** Catalogs of pamphlet material and minority collection (cards).

★1846★
Center for Cultural Survival
Library

11 Divinity Ave.	Ph: (617)496-8786
Cambridge, MA 02138	Fax: (617)496-8787
Mary Herbert, Asst.Dir.	

Staff: 3. **Subjects:** Indigenous populations, ethnic minorities, human rights, development, social impact, culture change. **Holdings:** 10,000 clippings; 500 unpublished social impact assessments; 1000 reports and documents. **Subscriptions:** 150 journals and other serials; 20 newspapers. **Services:** Library open to the public. **Publications:** Quarterly magazine; occasional reports.

★1847★
Center for Migration Studies
CMS Library

209 Flagg Place	Ph: (718)351-8800
Staten Island, NY 10304-1199	Fax: (718)667-4598
Diana J. Zimmerman, Hd., CMS Lib.	

Founded: 1964. **Staff:** Prof 1; Other 3. **Subjects:** International migration, refugees, ethnicity, ethnic groups in the U.S. **Special Collections:** CMS refugee holdings (2500 entries); 86 archival collections pertaining primarily to the Italian-American experience including L'Archivio del Commissariato Generale dell'Emigrazione (84 reels of microfilm); L'Archivio del Prelato per l'Emigrazione Italiana (28 reels of microfilm); ethnic press (microfilm). **Holdings:** 22,500 volumes; 3600 reports; 285 reels of microfilm of archival material; 500 dissertations on microfilm; manuscripts. **Subscriptions:** 250 journals and other serials; 40 newspapers; 180 newsletters. **Services:** Copying; center open to the public. **Publications:** Directory of International Study Centers, Research Programs and Library Resources, 1987; Refugees: Holdings of the Center for Migration Studies Library/Archives, 1987; Guides to CMS Archives, 1974-1988.

★1848★
Center for Religion, Ethics & Social Policy
Durland Alternatives Library

127 Anabel Taylor Hall	
Cornell University	
Ithaca, NY 14853	Ph: (607)255-6486
Lynn Andersen, Libn.	

Founded: 1974. **Staff:** Prof 2; Other 2. **Subjects:** Afro-America, alternative education, farming & organic gardening, gay & lesbian issues, holistic health, international issues, Native America, disarmament, empowerment, environmental issues, human rights, new age movement, psychology, sexuality, gender, spiritualtiy, women's studies. **Special Collections:** Eco-justice, environment, peace movement, Native Americans, counter-culture; South African investment (2200 periodicals, newsletters, and ephemera). **Holdings:** 6700 books; 550 audio and AV tapes. **Subscriptions:** 260 journals and other serials. **Services:** Interlibrary loan; copying; library open to the public; reserve services for groups committed to contemporary issues; special lending to incarcerated individuals. **Computerized Information Services:** Q&A (internal database).

★1849★
Center for Southern Folklore
Archives

152 Beale St.	
Memphis, TN 38103	Ph: (901)525-3655
Richard Raichelson, Folklorist	

Founded: 1972. **Staff:** Prof 8. **Subjects:** Folklife and ethnic cultures of the Mid-South, folk music and religion, folktales, crafts, folk art and architecture, occupational lore, blues music, ethnic culture, Memphis and Mississippi River history. **Special Collections:** The Reverend L.O. Taylor Collection (documentation of Memphis black community from the late 1920s to 1977); oral histories of Beale Street entertainers and businessmen, and of the Memphis Jewish

community. **Holdings:** 1000 books; 3500 unbound periodical volumes; 2000 newsletters; 1200 phonograph records; 40,000 slides; 200,000 feet of film; 40,000 photographs; 5000 hours of audiotapes. **Services:** Copying; archives open to the public by appointment. **Publications:** Images of the South: Visits with Eudora Welty and Walker Evans (first in the series); Center for Southern Folklore Update, quarterly - to members and media. **Special Catalogues:** American Folklore Films and Videotapes: A Catalog, volume 2. **Special Indexes:** American Folklore Films and Videotapes: An Index, volume 1.

★1850★
Central Michigan University
Clarke Historical Library

Mt. Pleasant, MI 48859	Ph: (517)774-3352
	Fax: (517)774-4499
Frank Boles, Dir.	

Founded: 1955. **Staff:** Prof 3; Other 4. **Subjects:** Michigan, Old Northwest Territory, early travel in the Midwest, Afro-Americana, history of slavery, Native Americans, children's literature, angling. **Special Collections:** Lucile Clarke Memorial Children's Library (6768 volumes); Wilbert Wright Collection Afro-Americana (5000 volumes); Reed T. Draper Angling Collection (1261 volumes); Presidential Campaign Biography Collection (778 volumes); university archives. **Holdings:** 60,000 books; 1440 maps; 3274 manuscripts; 1100 broadsides; 26,400 photographs; 8072 microforms; 3564 pieces of sheet music; 900 newspapers; 12,000 pieces of ephemera; 50 tape recordings; 100 phonograph records. **Subscriptions:** 103 journals and other serials. **Services:** Library open to the public. **Automated Operations:** Computerized public access catalog and cataloging. **Networks and Consortia:** Member of Michigan Library Consortium (MLC). **Publications:** Annual report - to mailing list; Resource Guides; occasional books and bibliographies; Michigan Historical Review, semiannual - by subscription. **Special Indexes:** Indexes to: newspapers on microfilm; Mt. Pleasant death records; manuscripts on microfilm; women's history; Twain Collection.

★1851★
Cheyney University of Pennsylvania
Leslie Pinckney Hill Library
Special Collections

Cheyney, PA 19319	Ph: (215)399-2203
	Fax: (215)399-2491
Lut R. Nero	

Founded: 1837. **Staff:** 11. **Subjects:** Education, economics, business, English and American literature, humanities, industrial management and technology, social and behavioral scienes, textiles. **Special Collections:** Afro-American Collection (3534 volumes); Cheyney Archives and the William Dorsey Collection of Notebooks and Books on Afro-American History (2500 items). **Holdings:** 231,865 volumes; 311,479 ERIC documents; 435,905 microform units; 60,898 documents. **Subscriptions:** 1016 journals and other serials; 31 newspapers. **Services:** Interlibrary loan; copying; collections open to the public with restrictions. **Automated Operations:** Computerized cataloging. **Computerized Information Services:** CD-ROMs. **Networks and Consortia:** Member of Tri-State College Library Cooperative (TCLC), PALINET, State System of Higher Education Libraries Council (SSHELCO).

★1852★
Chicago Public Library
Carter G. Woodson Regional Library
Vivian G. Harsh Research Collection of Afro-American History & Literature

9525 S. Halsted St.	Ph: (312)747-6910
Chicago, IL 60628	Fax: (312)747-3396
Robert Miller, Cur.	

Founded: 1932. **Staff:** Prof 5; Other 1. **Subjects:** Afro-Americans - history, religion, sociology, art, literature, music. **Special Collections:** Illinois Writers Project; Heritage Press Archives; Carl Sang Collection of Afro-American History, 1684 to present; Charlemae Hill Rollins Collection of Children's Literature; Era Bell Thompson Collection; Ben Burns Collection; David P. Ross Collection of Reprints in Afro-Americana and Africana; Horace Revels Cayton Collection; Dr. Majorie Joyner Collection. **Holdings:** 70,000 books; 565 bound periodical volumes; 5000 linear feet of other cataloged items; 10,831 pamphlets; 1146 phonograph records; 1500 cassette tapes; 10,367 reels of microfilm. **Subscriptions:** 70 journals and other serials; 30 newspapers. **Services:** Interlibrary loan; copying; library open to the public. **Automated Operations:** Computerized cataloging. **Computerized Information Services:** OCLC. **Networks and Consortia:** Member of ILLINET. **Publications:** Serials Holding List, biennial; Malcolm X, a Selected Bibliography, biennial; Richard Wright, a Selected Bibliography; Harold Washington, a Selected Bibliography; annual; Dr. Martin Luther King, a Selected Bibliography, biennial; Jazz at Harsh, biennial; Mary Mcleod BethuneBio-Bibliography; Carter Godwin Woodson, Bio-Bibliography; Gwendolyn Brooks, a Selected Bibliographyp Serials Holdings List; Chicago and the African Amer.: A Selected Bibliography **Special Catalogues:** The Dictionary Catalog of the Vivian G. Harsh Collection; Afro-Amer. History & Lit.; The Chicago Afro-Amer. Union Anl. Cat; Union Cat. of Black Music Holdings in Selected Chicago Lib.(on line).

★1853★
Clark Atlanta University Center
Robert W. Woodruff Library
Division of Archives and Special Collections
111 James P. Brawley Dr. SW
Atlanta, GA 30314   Ph: (404)522-8980
Wilson Flemister, Dir.

Founded: 1982. **Staff:** Prof 5; Other 3. **Subjects:** The Afro-American Experience; Afro-Americana in the southeastern United States; materials by and about peoples of African descent. **Special Collections:** Thayer-Lincoln Collection (125 manuscripts, pictures, and artifacts recording the career of Abraham Lincoln); manuscript collections representing outstanding persons in Afro-American history including Arthur Ashe, Clarence A. Bacote, John Brown, Thomas Clarkson, Paul Laurence Dunbar, Grace Towns Hamilton, C. Eric Lincoln, Rose McLendon, Paul and Eslanda Goode Robeson, Henry O. Tanner, George A. Towns, Andrew Young; Countee Cullen-Harold Jackman Collection (black artists and writers); Maud Cuney Hare Music and Musicians Manuscript Collection; Henry P. Slaughter Collection (pre-mid-20th century Afro-American history); archival holdings for academic institutions in the Atlanta University Center consortium (Atlanta University, Clark College, The Interdenominational Theological Center and component seminaries: Gammon Theological Seminary (Methodist), Morehouse School of Religion (Baptist), Charles H. Mason Theological Seminary (Church of God in Christ), Phillips School of Theology (Christian Methodist Episcopal), Johnson C. Smith Seminary, Inc. (Presbyterian), Turner Theological Seminary (African Methodist Episcopal), Morehouse College, Morris Brown College, and Spelman College); archival holdings from race relations and socioeconomic organizations in the South: the Neighborhood Union in Atlanta, Commission on Interracial Cooperation, Association of Southern Women for the Prevention of Lynching, Southern Regional Council, Southern Conference for Human Welfare (manuscripts and archives total approximately 5000 cubic feet); American Missionary Association papers; George Washington Carver papers, 1864-1943; Freedman's Bureau correspondence; Hoyt Fuller Collection on the Afro-American Experience; John and Lugenia Burns Hope Papers, 1888-1947; Martin Luther King, Jr. Memorabilia Collection, 1954 to present; Carl Van Vechten Photograph Collection of internationally known persons of African descent; Black Abolitionists papers, 1830-1865 (microfilm); slavery and antislavery pamphlets from the libraries of Salmon P. Chase and John P. Hale, 1840s and 1850s (microfilm); papers of the Congress of Racial Equality (CORE), records of the Fair Employment Practice Committee, 1941-1946 (microfilm); Johnstown Archeological Collection, 1912-1982 (microfilm); Pennsylvania Abolition Society papers, 1775-1975 (microfilm); Gerrit Smith papers, 1775-1924 (microfilm); Peter Smith papers, 1763-1850 (microfilm); papers of the Student Nonviolent Coordinating Committee (SNCC), 1959-1972 (microfilm); Tuskegee Institute News Clipping File, 1899-1966 (microfilm). **Holdings:** 22,000 books; 1000 bound periodical volumes; 313 college and university catalogs; 94 VF drawers of subject files; 59 audiotapes; 76 microfiche; dissertations on Negros, 1931-1966 on microfilm; Atlanta University and The Interdenominational Theological Center graduate theses and dissertations; pamphlets. **Services:** Interlibrary loan; copying (limited); library open to the public for reference use only for a fee. **Computerized Information Services:** DIALOG Information Services, BRS Information Technologies. **Networks and Consortia:** Member of CCLC, University Center in Georgia, Inc., Georgia Online Database (GOLD). **Publications:** Graduate Theses of Atlanta

University; Guide to Manuscripts and Archives in the Negro Collection of Trevor Arnett Library.

★1854★
Clark Atlanta University
Southern Center for Studies in Public Policy
Research Library
JP Brawley Dr.
Fairstreet SW   Ph: (404)880-8000
Atlanta, GA 30314   Fax: (404)880-8222
Rebecca Ivey, Res.Libn.

Founded: 1968. **Staff:** Prof 2; Other 2. **Subjects:** Economic development, public policy, transportation, employment and labor, blacks and civil rights, poverty. **Special Collections:** Robert Brown Collection; Andrew Brimmer Papers (15). **Holdings:** 5000 books; 325 bound periodical volumes; 6 VF drawers of clippings; 10 tapes each of the National Longitudinal Survey, the Panel Study of Income Dynamics, 1980 Census Report. **Subscriptions:** 185 journals and other serials; 6 newspapers. **Services:** Interlibrary loan; copying; library open to the public for reference use only. **Automated Operations:** Computerized cataloging. **Computerized Information Services:** DIALOG Information Services. **Networks and Consortia:** Member of Georgia Online Database (GOLD). **Publications:** So You Are Doing Research, biennial; Working Papers Series - for sale. **Special Indexes:** Index of journal articles dealing with public policy issues.

★1855★
Cleveland Public Library
Fine Arts and Special Collections Department -
   Special Collections Section
John G. White Collection and Rare Books
325 Superior Ave.
Cleveland, OH 44114-1271   Ph: (216)623-2818
Alice N. Loranth, Dept.Hd.

Founded: 1869. **Staff:** Prof 2; Other 2. **Special Collections:** Orientalia (58,780 volumes); folklore (45,010 volumes); chess and checkers and auxiliary subjects (30,317 volumes); rare books (15,561 volumes); East India Company manuscript collection of official documents and correspondence, 1741-1859 (over 30,000 pages and 200 titles); languages and linguistics (15,360 volumes); India and Southeast Asia (4000 volumes); Near Eastern archeology (7665 volumes); early travel and voyages to the Orient and Africa (7678 volumes); Egyptology (5580 volumes); Chinese, Japanese, and Tibetan religion and philosophy (5440 volumes); Arabic and Persian literature (5695 volumes); Omar Khayyam (1055 editions in 48 languages); Arabian Nights (760 volumes in 57 languages); Sanskrit literature (3311 volumes); Judaica (1730 volumes); manuscript catalogs (720 volumes); Madagascar (510 volumes); proverbs (2870 volumes); gypsies (741 volumes); chapbooks (1730 volumes); Robert Hays Gries Tobacco Collection (1376 volumes); Occult sciences (2625 volumes); witchcraft (1700 volumes); Medieval romance literature (3170 volumes); Celtic and Icelandic language and saga literature (1120 volumes); Tegner (225 19th century editions); Rabelais (245 16th-18th century editions); Castiglione (102 volumes); Vida (106 volumes); Derrydale Press (182 volumes); Cleveland Author Collection (2026 volumes); Cleveland Imprint Collection (458 volumes); 18th-19th century prostitution collection (299 volumes); early children's books (1485 volumes); political pamphlets, 1611 to 20th century (1851); Margaret Klipple Memorial Archives of African Folktales; Newbell Niles Puckett Memorial Archives of Ohio Superstitions and Popular Beliefs, Black Names in America, Religious Beliefs of the Southern Negro, and Canadian Lumberjack Songs. **Holdings:** 165,991 volumes; 1500 bound manuscripts; 342 boxes and 59 VF drawers of clippings and pictorial material on chess; 147 tapes; 2587 reels of microfilm. **Subscriptions:** 799 journals and other serials. **Services:** Interlibrary loan; copying; exhibits; lectures; collection open to the public with valid identification. **Automated Operations:** Computerized public access catalog, cataloging, acquisitions, and circulation. **Computerized Information Services:** OCLC, DIALOG Information Services, BRS Information Technologies, OhioPI (Ohio Public Information Utility), Hannah Information Systems, U.S. Patent Classification System, PFDS Online, WILSONLINE; CD-ROMs (CIRR, ABI/INFORM). **Networks and Consortia:** Member of OHIONET, NEOMARL, Cleveland Area Metropolitan Library System (CAMLS), North Central Library Cooperative (NCLC). **Publications:** Descriptive pamphlets of holdings, irregular; John G. White

Department of Folklore, Orientalia and Chess (2nd ed., 1978). **Special Catalogues:** Black Names in America: Origin and Usage (1975); A Catalog of Folklore, Folklife and Folk Songs (1978); Catalog of the Chess Collection (including checkers), 1964; Popular Beliefs and Superstitions Compendium of American Folklore: From the Ohio Collection of Newbell Niles Puckett (1981). **Special Indexes:** Index to chess biography, tournaments, and historic chess columns; French, Spanish, and Italian folksong and ballad index.

★1856★
Cleveland Public Library
History and Geography Department
325 Superior Ave.
Cleveland, OH 44114-1271   Ph: (216)623-2864
JoAnn Petrello, Dept.Hd.

Founded: 1869. **Staff:** Prof 4; Other 6. **Subjects:** History - ancient, medieval, modern; archaeology; local history; genealogy; heraldry; geography; black history; exploration and travel; numismatics. **Special Collections:** Photograph Collection (900,337); British learned society serials; 19th century travel narratives; English parish register collection. **Holdings:** 215,317 volumes; 12,232 bound periodical volumes; 18,800 Cleveland pictures on microfiche; 6000 maps and brochures with current travel data; local history clipping file; Coat-of-Arms file; 1092 World Wars I and II posters. **Subscriptions:** 935 journals and other serials. **Services:** Interlibrary loan; copying; department open to the public. **Automated Operations:** Computerized public access catalog, cataloging, acquisitions, and circulation. **Computerized Information Services:** OCLC, DIALOG Information Services, BRS Information Technologies, OhioPI (Ohio Public Information Utility), Hannah Information Systems, U.S. Patent Classification System, PFDS Online, WILSONLINE; CD-ROMs (CIRR, ABI/INFORM). **Networks and Consortia:** Member of OHIONET, NEOMARL, Cleveland Area Metropolitan Library System (CAMLS), North Central Library Cooperative (NCLC). **Special Indexes:** Photograph Collection index (movie stills and posters captured on an optical disk).

★1857★
Columbia University
Oral History Research Office
Butler Library
Box 20
New York, NY 10027   Ph: (212)854-2273
Ronald J. Grele, Dir.

Founded: 1948. **Staff:** Prof 3; Other 30. **Subjects:** National affairs, New York history, international relations, culture and the arts, social welfare, business and labor, philanthropy, Afro-American community, law, medicine, education, journalism, religion. **Special Collections:** The New Deal (50,000 pp.); Eisenhower Administration (36,000 pp.); Social Security, origins through Medicare (10,650 pp.); popular arts (7800 pp.); history of Carnegie Corporation (9928 pp.); aviation history (5400 pp.); radio pioneers (4765 pp.); Vietnam Veterans (3720 pp.); Columbia Crisis of 1968 (2450 pp.); psychoanalytic movement (2000 pp.); Nobel Laureates (1500 pp.); Women's History and Population Issues (2500 pp.); Occupation of Japan (1500 pp.); Bennington College Summer School of the Dance (5600 pp.); Adlai E. Stevenson (5600 pp.); Southern Intellectual Leaders (1500 pp.); World Bank (1400 pp.); Robert A. Taft (1600 pp.); United Negro College Fund (2500 pp.); United States-Iranian Relations (1455 pp.); Allard K. Lowenstein Project (6300 pp.); American Craftspeople (7500 pp.).; The Sixties (10,000 pp.). **Holdings:** 6000 volumes of edited transcript; 3400 reels and cassettes of tapes, 1963 to present; microforms of one third of the collection; supporting papers accompany some memoirs; data on other oral history holdings and centers worldwide. **Services:** Research service available; copying (limited); collection open to the public with restrictions. The office provides books on oral history - for sale. **Automated Operations:** Computerized cataloging. **Computerized Information Services:** RLIN. **Networks and Consortia:** Member of Research Libraries Information Network (RLIN). **Publications:** Oral History, annual report, 1949-1987; Report, 1987-1992; The Oral History Collection of Columbia University, 4th edition, 1979 (out of print).

★1858★
Commission on Civil Rights
National Civil Rights Clearinghouse Library
1121 Vermont Ave. NW   Ph: (202)376-8110
Washington, DC 20425   Fax: (202)376-8315
Barbara J. Fontana, Libn.

Founded: 1957. **Staff:** Prof 1; Other 1. **Subjects:** Civil rights, economics, education, sex discrimination, sociology, law. **Special Collections:** The aged and the handicapped; commission publications. **Holdings:** 65,000 books; 1100 bound periodical volumes; 1200 state and federal codes and statutes; 110 legal periodical titles; 500 reels of microfilm of minority periodicals; 300 journals on microfiche. **Subscriptions:** 300 journals and newspapers. **Services:** Interlibrary loan; copying; library open to the public for reference use only. **Automated Operations:** Computerized cataloging. **Computerized Information Services:** DIALOG Information Services, OCLC, LEXIS, NEXIS. **Publications:** Monthly acquisitions list; bibliographies.

★1859★
Compton Community College
Library
Black History Collection
1111 E. Artesia Blvd.   Ph: (213)637-2660
Compton, CA 90221   Fax: (213)638-2401
Saul J. Panski, Hd.Libn.

Founded: 1927. **Staff:** Prof 2.5; Other 1. **Subjects:** Black history. **Holdings:** 40,074 books; 6668 microforms. **Subscriptions:** 193 journals and other serials; 3 newspapers. **Services:** Interlibrary loan; collection open to the public for reference use only. **Networks and Consortia:** Member of Metronet.

★1860★
Cornell University
John Henrik Clarke Africana Library
310 Triphammer Rd.   Ph: (607)255-5229
Ithaca, NY 14850-2599   Fax: (607)255-0784
Thomas Weissinger, Libn.

Founded: 1972. **Staff:** Prof 1; Other 2. **Subjects:** African, Afro-American, Caribbean peoples - history, culture, lifestyles, and economic, social, and political development. **Special Collections:** Civil Rights Microfilm Collection (1,093 microforms). **Holdings:** 13,559 books; 281 videocassettes; 162 sound recordings. **Services:** Interlibrary loan; library open to the public. **Automated Operations:** Computerized public access catalog, cataloging, acquisitions, and circulation. **Computerized Information Services:** DIALOG Information Services, RLIN. **Networks and Consortia:** Member of Research Libraries Information Network (RLIN).

★1861★
Council for Alternatives to Stereotyping in Entertainment
Library
139 Corson Ave.
Staten Island, NY 10301   Ph: (718)720-5378

Subjects: Entertainment - stereotyping, self-image, reality perception, receptivity to accurate performance feedback. **Holdings:** 1000 volumes.

★1862★
County of Los Angeles Public Library
Black Resource Center
A.C. Bilbrew Library
150 E. El Segundo Blvd.   Ph: (213)538-3350
Los Angeles, CA 90061   Fax: (213)327-0824
Louise Parsons, Libn.

Founded: 1974. **Staff:** Prof 1; Other 2. **Subjects:** History and culture of African-Americans, black music and musical artists. **Special Collections:** Pictures/posters of famous black Americans (260). **Holdings:** 10,000 books; 65 bound periodical volumes; 3500 clippings; 2576 reels of microfilm; 1182 microfiche; 360 videocassettes; 378 audiocassettes; 405 phonograph records. **Subscriptions:** 120 journals and other serials; 20 newspapers. **Services:** Interlibrary loan; copying; center open to the public for reference use only. **Automated Operations:** Computerized public access catalog. **Also known as:** A.C. Bilbrew Library.

★1863★
Dallas Museum of Art
Library
1717 N. Harwood   Ph: (214)922-1276
Dallas, TX 75201   Fax: (214)954-0174
Allen Townsend

Founded: 1936. **Staff:** Prof 2. **Subjects:** Art history, painting, sculpture, drawing, prints, decorative arts, pre-Columbian and African art. **Holdings:** 25,000 books; 1000 bound periodical volumes; 60 VF drawers of artist files; art museum annual reports; auction catalogs, 1950 to present. **Subscriptions:** 106 journals and other serials. **Services:** Copying; library open to the public for reference use only. **Computerized Information Services:** OCLC. **Networks and Consortia:** Member of AMIGOS Bibliographic Council, Inc..

★1864★
Denver Art Museum
Frederic H. Douglas Library of Anthropology and Art
100 W. 14th Ave. Pkwy.   Ph: (303)640-1613
Denver, CO 80204   Fax: (303)640-5627
Margaret Goodrich, Libn.

Founded: 1929. **Staff:** 1.5. **Subjects:** American Indians, African and Oceanic art, anthropology, primitive art. **Special Collections:** American Indians. **Holdings:** 6000 volumes; 144 linear feet of clippings; 840 linear feet of journals, serials, and monographs; U.S. government documents from the 19th and early 20th centuries. **Subscriptions:** 21 journals and other serials. **Services:** Copying; library open to the public. **Automated Operations:** Computerized cataloging. **Computerized Information Services:** OCLC. **Networks and Consortia:** Member of Central Colorado Library System (CCLS), Bibliographical Center for Research, Rocky Mountain Region, Inc. (BCR).

★1865★
Detroit Public Library
Film Department
5201 Woodward Ave.
Detroit, MI 48202   Ph: (313)833-1495
Grace Larson, Chf.

Founded: 1947. **Staff:** Prof 3; Other 3. **Subjects:** Film - educational, children's, feature, foreign, black studies. **Holdings:** 17,000 videocassettes. **Subscriptions:** 4 journals and other serials. **Services:** Library open to the public. **Automated Operations:** Computerized circulation. **Computerized Information Services:** Registar II (internal database). **Publications:** Annotated Lists on Parenting and Substance Abuse. **Special Catalogues:** Video Catalog.

★1866★
Detroit Public Library
Music and Performing Arts Department
5201 Woodward Ave.
Detroit, MI 48202   Ph: (313)833-1460
Agatha Pfeiffer Kalkanis, Chf.

Founded: 1921. **Staff:** Prof 5; Other 2. **Subjects:** Music, theater, moving pictures, radio and television, broadcasting, dance, bullfighting, circus, rodeo. **Special Collections:** E. Azalia Hackley Collection (blacks in the performing arts); Michigan Collection (music by Michigan composers or with Michigan associations). **Holdings:** 40,000 books; 8033 bound periodical volumes; 56,000 scores; 30,000 recordings; 20,000 popular sheet music titles; 150 VF drawers; 6 VF drawers of photographs; 3406 cassettes; 1033 reels of microfilm. **Subscriptions:** 344 journals and other serials. **Services:** Interlibrary loan; copying; department open to the public. **Computerized Information Services:** DIALOG Information Services.

★1867★
District of Columbia Public Library
Black Studies Division
Martin Luther King Memorial Library
901 G St., N.W.   Ph: (202)727-1211
Washington, DC 20001   Fax: (202)727-1129
Alice B. Robinson, Chf.

Founded: 1971. **Staff:** Prof 3. **Subjects:** Slavery in the U.S. and Caribbean, biography, business, social conditions, literature, history, science, technology, civil rights. **Special Collections:** Beatrice Murphy Foundation (1860 books); Juvenile Reference Collection (715 books). **Holdings:** 20,655 books; 24 bound periodical volumes; 350 reels of microfilm; 30 VF drawers. **Subscriptions:** 112 journals and other serials; 58 newspapers. **Services:** Copying; division open to the public for reference use only. **Publications:** Booklists on special subject, irregular - free. **Special Indexes:** Index of Black literary magazines (card).

★1868★
Divine Word Seminary of St. Augustine
Library
199 Seminary Dr.
Bay St. Louis, MS 39520   Ph: (601)467-6414

Founded: 1923. **Subjects:** Afro-American history and literature, ethnology, theology, social sciences, pure and applied sciences, literature, geography, history. **Holdings:** 8000 volumes; 500 bound periodical volumes. **Services:** Library open to the public for research purposes only.

★1869★
DuSable Museum of African American History
Library
740 E. 56th Place   Ph: (312)947-0600
Chicago, IL 60637   Fax: (312)947-0677
Theresa Christopher, Reg.

Founded: 1961. **Staff:** Prof 2; Other 3. **Subjects:** Black history, sociology, politics, religion, fiction, biography; Africana. **Holdings:** 7000 volumes; 500 other cataloged items; 100 oral history tapes; 50 manuscripts; 85 VF drawers of clippings. **Services:** Library not open to the public. **Publications:** Calendar, annual.

★1870★
East Texas State University
Oral History Program
James Gilliam Gee Library
East Texas Sta.   Ph: (903)886-5737
Commerce, TX 75429-2953   Fax: (903)886-5039
Dr. James Conrad, Coord. of Oral Hist.

Founded: 1968. **Staff:** Prof 1; Other 1. **Subjects:** History of East Texas - railroad, cotton, blacks, medicine; Texas social work; institutional history. **Special Collections:** Senator A.M. Aikin, Jr. project; Fletcher Warren project; Southwest Dairy project; Dallas Mayors project; Cooper Lake Project; Caddo Lake project. **Holdings:** 301 volumes; 890 cassette tapes of interviews. **Subscriptions:** 3 journals and other serials. **Services:** Copying; program open to the public with restrictions. **Automated Operations:** Computerized cataloging. **Special Catalogues:** Oral history catalog.

★1871★
Eastern Baptist Theological Seminary
Library
6 Lancaster Ave.   Ph: (215)645-9318
Wynnewood, PA 19096   Fax: (215)649-3834
Melody Mazuk, Dir.

Founded: 1925. **Staff:** Prof 2; Other 2. **Subjects:** Theology and allied subjects. **Special Collections:** Russell H. MacBride Collection of Philosophy, Religion and Classical Literature (3750 volumes); J. Pius Barbor Collection in Black Church Studies (1157 volumes); Hispanic Studies Collection (2361 volumes). **Holdings:** 111,247 books; 11,385 bound periodical volumes. **Subscriptions:** 399 journals and other serials. **Services:** Interlibrary loan; copying; library open to graduate students and ministers. **Automated Operations:** Computerized cataloging and acquisitions. **Computerized Information Services:** OCLC. **Networks and Consortia:** Member of

PALINET, Southeastern Pennsylvania Theological Library Association (SEPTLA).

★1872★
ERIC Clearinghouse on Urban Education
Institute for Urban and Minority Education
Teachers College, Columbia University
Box 40   Ph: (212)678-3433
New York, NY 10027   Fax: (212)678-4048
Dr. Erwin Flaxman, Dir.

Founded: 1965. **Staff:** Prof 8; Other 4. **Subjects:** Education of urban and minority children and youths; psychology; sociology. **Holdings:** 1000 books; 15,500 reports, manuscripts, and other documentation; 800,000 titles in ERIC microfiche collection. **Subscriptions:** 60 journals and other serials. **Services:** Reference services by mail in the form of prepared bibliographies and other ERIC/CUE publications; clearinghouse open to the public by appointment. **Computerized Information Services:** DIALOG Information Services, PFDS Online, BRS Information Technologies, CD-ROM (SilverPlatter). Performs searches on fee basis. Contact Person: Dr. Larry Yates, Asst.Dir. **Publications:** Trends and Issues Series - for sale; Urban Diversity Series, irregular - for sale; ERIC/CUE Digests, irregular - single copies free upon request with a self-addressed stamped envelope. **Also known as:** ERIC/CUE.

★1873★
Fisk University
Special Collections Department
17th at Jackson St.
Nashville, TN 37203   Ph: (615)329-8646
Ann Allen Shockley, Assoc.Libn./Archv.

Founded: 1866. **Staff:** Prof 2. **Subjects:** African-American history and culture. **Special Collections:** Negro Collection; Fiskiana Collection (9 VF drawers); Yorkshire Collection; George Gershwin Collection; Langston Hughes Phonograph Collection; Black Oral History Collection (750 tapes); audiotape collection (200 tapes). **Holdings:** 64,000 books; 1565 bound periodical volumes; 3050 reels of microfilm of information by and about blacks; 2300 phonograph records; 4 VF drawers of pictures; 2 VF drawers of newspaper clippings; 4 VF drawers of biographical information by or about blacks; 878 Fisk University masters' theses; 100 archival and manuscript collections. **Subscriptions:** 48 journals and other serials; 7 newspapers. **Services:** Copying; department open to the public with restrictions. **Publications:** Banc! An Annotated Bibliography of the Fisk University Library's Black Oral History Collection. **Special Catalogues:** catalog to Oral History Collection; shelf lists for archives and manuscripts collections; Dictionary Catalog of the Negro Collection, 6 vols. (1974).

★1874★
Fort Hays University
Forsyth Library
Special Collections
600 Park St.   Ph: (913)628-5901
Hays, KS 67601-4099   Fax: (913)628-4096
Esta Lou Riley, Archv./Spec.Coll.Libn.

Staff: Prof 2. **Special Collections:** Center for Ethnic Studies Collection; Western Collection; University Archives (including Kansas Oral History Project and Historian-in-Residence Oral History Project cassettes, reel-to-reel tapes, transcriptions); Folklore Collection; Consortium for Children's and Young Adult's Books Collection (19,000 volumes of children's and juvenile literature). **Holdings:** 22,425 books; 68 boxes of university records and faculty papers; 60 tapes of university events, lectures, speeches; 640 oral history tapes and transcriptions; 87 tapes of folk songs, poems, stories, reminiscences; 32 video cassettes. **Subscriptions:** 7 journals and other serials; 2 newspapers. **Services:** Interlibrary loan; copying; collections open to the public with restrictions. **Automated Operations:** Computerized public access catalog, cataloging, acquisitions, circulation, and serials (NOTIS). **Computerized Information Services:** BRS Information Technologies, OCLC, DIALOG Information Services; BITNET (electronic mail service). Performs searches on fee basis. Contact Person: Phyllis Schmidt, 628-4338. **Special Catalogues:** Catalog for Center for Ethnic Studies Collection . **Special Indexes:** Index to Oral History Collection by interviewer/interviewee and brief subject guide; index to songs and superstitions in the Folklore Collection (card).

★1875★
Great Plains Black Museum
Library
2213 Lake St.
Omaha, NE 68110   Ph: (402)345-2212
Bertha Calloway, Founder/Dir.

Founded: 1976. **Staff:** Prof 2; Other 10. **Subjects:** Blacks in Nebraska and the Great Plains. **Special Collections:** Black women; cowboys; Homesteaders Room. **Holdings:** 2000 books; photographs; archival materials; quilts; military items; rare books. **Subscriptions:** 12 journals and other serials. **Services:** Library open to the public for reference use only.

★1876★
Hampton Institute
William R. & Norma B. Harvey Library
Hampton University
30 Tyler St.
Hampton, VA 23668   Ph: (804)727-5371
Dr. Earl Bean, Dir.

Founded: 1904. **Special Collections:** George Foster Peabody Collection of Negro Literature and History; Hampton University Archives (4 million items); U.S. Government documents (partial depository). **Holdings:** 31,748 volumes. **Services:** Interlibrary loan; copying; collections open to the public with restrictions on circulation. **Automated Operations:** Computerized cataloging. **Computerized Information Services:** DIALOG Information Services, OCLC. Performs searches on fee basis. Contact Person: Mary Marks, Acq. **Networks and Consortia:** Member of SOLINET, Council on Botanical Horticultural Libraries. **Special Catalogues:** Dictionary Catalog of the George Foster Peabody Collection of Negro Literature and History, 1972. **Formerly:** Collis P. Huntington Memorial Library.

★1877★
Harris-Stowe State College Library
3026 Laclede Ave.   Ph: (314)340-3620
St. Louis, MO 63103   Fax: (314)340-3322
Martin Knorr, Dir.

Founded: 1857. **Staff:** Prof 3; Other 4. **Subjects:** Education. **Special Collections:** Elementary education; Education of Exceptional Children; Black Studies; Juvenile Literature; Civil Rights. **Holdings:** 90,000 books; 2400 reels of microfilm of periodicals. **Subscriptions:** 325 journals and other serials; 9 newspapers. **Services:** Interlibrary loan; library open to teachers and education professionals with courtesy card. **Automated Operations:** Computerized circulation. **Computerized Information Services:** DIALOG Information Services. **Networks and Consortia:** Member of St. Louis Regional Library Network.

★1878★
Hatch-Billops Collection, Inc.
491 Broadway, 7th Fl.   Ph: (212)966-3231
New York, NY 10012   Fax: (212)966-3231
Camille Billops, Pres.

Founded: 1975. **Staff:** Prof 1. **Subjects:** African Americana, theater, visual arts. **Special Collections:** Oral history interviews (1210); art slides (14,000); Owen and Edith Dodson Memorial Collection (plays, manuscripts, photos, and letters); Charles and Ellyce Weir Griffin Collection (400 black and white film stills; lobby cards); Theodore Ward plays; Arthur Smith Collection (jewelry designs, photographs, patterns, and business communications). **Holdings:** 4000 books; 1000 black/white photographs; 300 posters; 1200 playbills; 300 art catalogs. **Subscriptions:** 12 journals and other serials. **Services:** Copying; collection open to the public by appointment. **Computerized Information Services:** Internal database (playbills, manuscripts, theater articles). **Publications:** Artist and Influence. **Special Catalogues:** Catalog of oral history holdings with abstracts; catalog of African American theater history; catalog of African American playbills.

★1879★
Hempstead Public Library
Special Collections
115 Nichols Ct.   Ph: (516)481-6990
Hempstead, NY 11550   Fax: (516)481-6719
Irene A. Duszkiewicz, Dir.

Founded: 1898. **Special Collections:** Walt Whitman; Long Island Collection; Foreign Language Collection for Children and Adults; New York State History; Job and Education Information Center; Career Counseling; New York State Documents Reference Center; Black studies; Adult Learning Center; ESL Classes. **Holdings:** 190,000 books. **Subscriptions:** 400 journals and other serials; 75 newspapers. **Services:** Interlibrary loan; copying; collections open to the public. **Automated Operations:** Computerized cataloging, acquisitions, and circulation. **Computerized Information Services:** DIALOG Information Services. Performs searches free of charge for village residents only. **Networks and Consortia:** Member of Nassau Library System.

★1880★
Historical Research Repository, Inc.
Library
PO Box 15364, Fox Creek Sta.   Ph: (313)822-9027
Detroit, MI 48215-0364   Fax: (313)559-6890
John M. Green, Archv.

Founded: 1968. **Staff:** Prof 1. **Subjects:** Black history, Michigan black history. **Special Collections:** Pre-1940 postcards of blacks (115); African American U.S. postal stamps (complete set). **Holdings:** 85 books. **Services:** Library not open to the public. **Publications:** Black Nobel Prize Winners (poster); Michigan Black History Review.

★1881★
Historical Society of Pennsylvania
Library
1300 Locust St.   Ph: (215)732-6201
Philadelphia, PA 19107   Fax: (215)732-2680
Lee Arnold, Lib.Dir.

Founded: 1824. **Staff:** Prof 16. **Subjects:** History - U.S., 1783-1865, Colonial, Revolutionary, Pennsylvania; genealogy; Afro-Americana. **Holdings:** 564,000 volumes; 16 million manuscripts; 2800 microcards; 17,200 microfiche; 14,700 reels of microfilm; maps; prints; drawings; paintings; newspapers; ephemera. **Subscriptions:** 4000 journals and other serials. **Services:** Copying; library open to the public on fee basis. **Automated Operations:** Computerized cataloging. **Computerized Information Services:** OCLC, RLIN. **Networks and Consortia:** Member of PALINET, Research Libraries Information Network (RLIN), Area Consortium of Special Collections Libraries. **Publications:** The Pennsylvania Magazine of History and Biography, quarterly; Guide to the Manuscript Collections of the Historical Society of Pennsylvania; The Pennsylvania Correspondent (newsletter), 5/year - to members.

★1882★
Houston Public Library
Houston Metropolitan Research Center
500 McKinney Ave.
Houston, TX 77002   Ph: (713)247-1661
Louis J. Marchiafava, Ph.D., Archv.

Founded: 1975. **Staff:** Prof 5; Other 1. **Subjects:** Houston - business, politics, architecture, church records, city and county government, agencies. **Special Collections:** John Milsaps Collection (Salvation Army); panoramic photograph collection (500); local photographs (1.8 million); county records for two-county area; Houston African-American Collection; Mexican-American Collection; Oral History Collection; Architectural collection; Texas State Archives regional depository; Texas Jazz Archive. **Holdings:** 18,000 linear feet of archival material. **Services:** Copying; center open to the public. **Networks and Consortia:** Member of Houston Area Library System (HALS), Houston Area Research Library Consortium (HARLIC). **Publications:** The Houston Review, 3/year - by subscription; guide books to the collection.

★1883★
Howard University
African-American Resource Center
2400 6th St. NW
Box 746
Washington, DC 20059   Ph: (202)806-7242
Mr. E. Ethelbert Miller, Dir.

Founded: 1969. **Staff:** Prof 1. **Subjects:** Black studies, economics, history, political science, literature, international relations. **Holdings:** 20,000 books. **Subscriptions:** 50 journals and other serials; 10 newspapers. **Services:** Copying; center open to the public.

★1884★
Howard University
Health Sciences Library
600 W St. NW
Washington, DC 20059   Ph: (202)806-6433
Sekum Boni-Awoti, Act.Supv.

Founded: 1927. **Staff:** Prof 7; Other 11. **Subjects:** Medicine, dentistry, nursing, and allied health sciences. **Special Collections:** Sickle cell anemia (2 drawers of clippings and pamphlets); Negroes in medicine, dentistry, and psychiatry (2 drawers; 20 boxes). **Holdings:** 200,647 books; 84,815 bound periodical volumes; 515 bibliographies; 121 shelves of AV programs; 20 VF drawers of disease, health, medicine files; 6 VF drawers of biographical files; 115 drawers of microfilm. **Subscriptions:** 4810 journals and other serials. **Services:** Interlibrary loan; copying; SDI; library open to the public for reference use only. **Automated Operations:** Computerized cataloging, acquisitions, serials, and circulation. **Computerized Information Services:** MEDLARS, DIALOG Information Services. Performs searches on fee basis. Contact Person: Howertine Farrell-Duncan, Libn./Supv., Ref. **Networks and Consortia:** Member of CAPCON Library Network, Consortium of Academic Health Science Libraries of the District of Columbia, District of Columbia Health Sciences Information Network (DOCHSIN). **Special Catalogues:** Sickle cell anemia; hypertension among Negroes (both card).

★1885★
Howard University
Moorland-Spingarn Research Center
Library Division
500 Howard Pl. NW   Ph: (202)806-7260
Washington, DC 20059   Fax: (202)806-6405
Thomas C. Battle, Dir.

Founded: 1914. **Staff:** Prof 6. **Subjects:** Afro-Americana, Africana, Caribbean, Latin Americana. **Holdings:** 150,000 books; 9564 bound periodical volumes; 10,852 microforms; 563 dissertations. **Subscriptions:** 531 journals and other serials; 130 newspapers. **Services:** Copying; division open to the public. **Networks and Consortia:** Member of CAPCON Library Network.

★1886★
Howard University
Moorland-Spingarn Research Center
Manuscript Division
500 Howard Pl. NW   Ph: (202)806-7480
Washington, DC 20059   Fax: (202)806-6405
Karen L. Jefferson, Cur.

Founded: 1914. **Staff:** Prof 5; Other 2. **Subjects:** Afro-Americana, Africana, Caribbeana. **Special Collections:** Ralph J. Bunche Oral History Collection (individuals involved in 1960s civil rights activities; 700 tapes and transcripts); Music Collection (4000 pieces of sheet music); Prints and Photographs (24,000, including Rose McClendon Collection of Photographs of Celebrated Negroes by Carl Van Vechten, Mary O.H. Williamson Collection, Griffith Davis Collection). **Holdings:** 2000 linear feet of processed manuscripts; 4800 linear feet of unprocessed manuscripts. **Services:** Copying; division open to qualified researchers. **Publications:** Guide to Processed Collections in the Manuscript Division of the Moorland-Spingarn Research Center.

★1887★
Howard University
School of Divinity Library
1400 Shepherd St. NE
Washington, DC 20018   Ph: (202)806-0760
Arthuree M. Wright, Act.Libn.

Founded: 1932. **Staff:** Prof 1; Other 2. **Subjects:** Theology. **Special Collections:** Afro-American religious studies. **Holdings:** 105,996 books; 12,473 bound periodical volumes. **Subscriptions:** 484 journals and other serials. **Services:** Interlibrary loan; copying; library open to the public with restrictions on circulation. **Automated Operations:** Computerized cataloging, acquisitions, serials, and circulation. **Networks and Consortia:** Member of CAPCON Library Network, Washington Theological Consortium. **Publications:** Biographical Directory of Negro Ministers; Afro-American Religious Studies and supplements; The Howard University Bibliography of African and Afro-American Religious Studies. **Special Indexes:** Alphabetical name index of 1800 Negro ministers with addresses.

★1888★
Indiana Historical Society
William Henry Smith Memorial Library
315 W. Ohio St.   Ph: (317)232-1879
Indianapolis, IN 46202-3299   Fax: (317)233-3109
Bruce L. Johnson, Dir.

Founded: 1934. **Staff:** Prof 17; Other 5. **Subjects:** History of Indiana and Old Northwest. **Special Collections:** Architectural history (including Burns & Burns, Bohlen Meyer & Gibson, Russ and Harrison, James & Associates, Rubush and Hunter, and Fenstermaker collections; 161,356 items); black history (including Mme. C.J. Walker, Elijah Roberts, and Herbert Heller manuscript collections, Emmett Brown photograph collection; 6000 items); railroads (including Kauffman Photograph Collection, Preston Collection; 6000 items); Indiana in the Civil War (including Lew Wallace, D.E. Beem, and Jefferson C. Davis manuscript collections; 15,000 items); 19th century Indiana politics (including Charles Fairbanks, William H. English, and John G. Davis manuscript collections; 10,000 items); Old Northwest Territory history (600 manuscripts); William Henry Harrison and Indiana Territory history (500 manuscripts); charitable organizations (including Family Service Association, Pleasant Run Children's Home, and Jewish Welfare Federation manuscript collections; 85,000 items); visual collection (1.5 millionof graphics works, paintings, and photographs). **Holdings:** 65,000 books; 150 bound periodical volumes; 4 million manuscripts; 1000 maps; 1600 reels of microfilm. **Subscriptions:** 360 journals and other serials. **Services:** Limited photocopying; photographic reproductions; preservation consultations; library open to the public. **Computerized Information Services:** OCLC; ARCHIE (internal architectural database). Performs searches free of charge. **Networks and Consortia:** Member of INCOLSA. **Publications:** Indiana Historical Society annual report (accessions); Black History News and Notes, quarterly.

★1889★
Indiana University
Black Culture Center
Library
109 N. Jordan Ave.
Bloomington, IN 47405   Ph: (812)855-3237
Grace Jackson-Brown, Hd.Libn.

Founded: 1972. **Staff:** Prof 1; Other 3. **Subjects:** Blacks - history, reference works, music, literature, drama; black-oriented novels. **Special Collections:** The Arno Press Collection (250 titles). **Holdings:** 3000 books; 75 bound periodical volumes; 100 cassette tapes; 170 titles on 285 tapes; pamphlet files. **Subscriptions:** 22 journals and other serials; 12 newspapers. **Services:** Library open to the public. **Publications:** Shelf list of additions to the Afro-American Collections, 1985-1986; Selected Acquisitions List, 1989-1990; Selected Reference Tools in African American Subject Areas; bibliographies, irregular.

★1890★
Inner City Cultural Center
Langston Hughes Memorial Library
c/o The Ivar Theatre
1605 N. Ivar St.   Ph: (213)962-2102
Los Angeles, CA 90028   Fax: (213)386-9017

Founded: 1967. **Staff:** Prof 2; Other 2. **Subjects:** Ethnic groups, performing and visual arts. **Holdings:** 6500 uncataloged books; 300 bound periodical volumes; 100 manuscripts; 100 sound recordings and tapes; 250 clippings; 175 reports; 200 photographs. **Subscriptions:** 10 journals and other serials. **Services:** Library not open to the public.

★1891★
Johnson Publishing Co., Inc.
Library
820 S. Michigan Ave.
Chicago, IL 60605   Ph: (312)322-9320
Pamela Cash Mensies, Libn.

Founded: 1949. **Staff:** Prof 2; Other 1. **Subjects:** Afro-Americana; black history, literature, biography; Africa. **Special Collections:** Newspaper clippings, 1940s to present; black newspapers, 1846 to present, on microfilm. **Holdings:** 10,000 books; 1000 bound periodical volumes; 300 drawers of newspaper clippings; pamphlets; company publications. **Subscriptions:** 150 journals and other serials; 50 newspapers. **Services:** Library not open to the public.

★1892★
Joint Center for Political and Economic Studies
Office of Information Resources
1301 Pennsylvania Ave. NW, Ste. 400   Ph: (202)626-3530
Washington, DC 20004   Fax: (202)626-3521
Auriel J. Pilgrim, Dir.

Founded: 1979. **Staff:** Prof 1; Other 2. **Subjects:** Blacks - political participation, social and economic conditions, demographic studies; public, education, and economic policies concerning minorities. **Special Collections:** Black elected officials; blacks in the military; black voting and voter registration statistics. **Holdings:** 3606 volumes; 2700 unbound materials; 450 unpublished reports; 111 VF drawers of clippings and archival material; 5 drawers of AV programs. **Subscriptions:** 238 journals and other serials; 4 newspapers. **Services:** Interlibrary loan; copying; office open to the public by appointment for reference use only. **Automated Operations:** Computerized cataloging and acquisitions. **Computerized Information Services:** DIALOG Information Services, NEXIS. **Publications:** Periodical table of contents bulletin, weekly - for internal distribution only.

★1893★
Kansas State University
Farrell Library
Minority Resource Research Center
Manhattan, KS 66506   Ph: (913)532-7453
                                        Fax: (913)532-6144

Founded: 1971. **Staff:** Prof 1; Other 1. **Subjects:** African-American history and literature, American ethnic studies, Kansas minority groups, Native American archeology, 20th century Native American sociology, Chicano studies. **Special Collections:** American Ethnic Studies (100 titles); Kansas State Minority Programs (125 titles). **Holdings:** 5000 volumes; 147 microfiche; 388 reels of microfilm; 15 VF drawers of reports; 4 VF drawers of archives; 732 AV programs. **Subscriptions:** 75 journals and other serials; 22 newspapers. **Services:** ILL; copying; library open to the public. **Automated Operations:** Computerized cataloging, acquisitions, and circulation. **Computerized Information Services:** DIALOG Information Services, BRS Information Technologies, OCLC, STN International, Chemical Abstracts Service (CAS); BITNET (electronic mail service). **Publications:** AV Guide; Minority Children's Bibliography; Minority Reference Collection Bibliography; annotated bibliography of KSU theses and dissertations by and about minorities.

★1894★
Kennedy-King College
Library
6800 S. Wentworth Ave.
Chicago, IL 60621   Ph: (312)602-5449
Mary Jane Rudolph, Chm.

Founded: 1934. **Staff:** Prof 4; Other 5. **Subjects:** Black studies - history, sociology, current issues, nursing. **Holdings:** 47,900 volumes. **Subscriptions:** 400 journals and other serials; 12 newspapers. **Services:** Interlibrary loan; copying; library open to the public with restrictions. **Computerized Information Services:** OCLC. **Networks and Consortia:** Member of ILLINET.

★1895★
Kent State University
Center for the Study of Ethnic Publications and
  Cultural Institutions
University Library, Rm. 318   Ph: (216)672-2782
Kent, OH 44242   Fax: (216)672-7965
Dr. Lubomyr Wynar, Dir.

Staff: Prof 1. **Subjects:** Ethnic bibliography, history, education, and press; ethnic libraries, archives, and museums. **Special Collections:** Ethnic reference files. **Holdings:** 1000 books; 500 pamphlets. **Subscriptions:** 200 journals and other serials. **Services:** Center open to the public with permission. **Publications:** Ethnic Forum: Journal of Ethnic Studies and of Ethnic Bibliography, 2/year - by subscription; Ethnic, Nationality, and Foreign-Language Broadcasting and Telecasting in Ohio (1981); Slavic Ethnic Libraries, Museums and Archives in the United States: A Guide and Directory (1980); Guide to Ethnic Press (1986).

★1896★
Langston University
Melvin B. Tolson Black Heritage Center
Langston, OK 73050   Ph: (405)466-3346
                                     Fax: (405)466-3459
Ronald Keys, Act.Cur.

Founded: 1969. **Staff:** Prof 1. **Subjects:** Afro-American experience in the U.S., Afro-Americans in the humanities and arts since 1900, African history. **Special Collections:** African Art Collection (93 items); Langston University Archives (brochures; programs; yearbooks; presidential papers); Melvin B. Tolson Collection (books; personal items; pictures; awards). **Holdings:** 15,000 books; 1200 bound periodical volumes; 750 recordings; 600 audio cassettes; 150 video cassettes; 100 films; 10,000 VF materials. **Subscriptions:** 90 journals and other serials; 50 newspapers. **Services:** Interlibrary loan; copying; center open to the public. **Publications:** Acquisitions List, monthly; newsletter, quarterly. **Special Indexes:** Biography index; periodical articles index.

★1897★
Lawrence Johnson & Associates, Inc.
Library
13917 Crest Hill Ln.   Ph: (301)236-4433
Silver Spring, MD 20905   Fax: (301)236-4434
Mrs. Tish Nearon, Libn.

Staff: Prof 4; Other 3. **Subjects:** Psychology, race relations, human relations development, child welfare, human factors, education. **Special Collections:** Race relations in the military services (50 volumes). **Holdings:** 2000 books; 2500 technical reports; 700 unbound periodicals; 150 boxes of unpublished manuscripts and dissertations; 200 vuegraphs, slides, audiotapes. **Subscriptions:** 50 journals and other serials; 5 newspapers. **Services:** Interlibrary loan; library not open to the public. **Formerly:** Located in Washington, D.C.

★1898★
Library Company of Philadelphia
1314 Locust St.   Ph: (215)546-3181
Philadelphia, PA 19107   Fax: (215)546-5167
John C. VanHorne, Libn.

Founded: 1731. **Staff:** Prof 6; Other 7. **Subjects:** Pre-1860 Americana, Philadelphia and Pennsylvania, pre-1820 medical material, black history before 1906, women's history. **Special Collections:** Early printed books from Girard College and Christ Church (on deposit). **Holdings:** 450,000 books; 50,000 prints and photographs; 160,000 manuscripts. **Subscriptions:** 130 journals and other serials. **Services:** Interlibrary loan; copying; library open to the public for research. **Computerized Information Services:** RLIN. **Networks and Consortia:** Member of Research Libraries Information Network (RLIN). **Publications:** Annual reports; newsletters - both free to libraries and individuals on request. **Special Catalogues:** Afro-Americana, 1553-1906 in collections of the Library Company and the Historical Society of Pennsylvania; The Library of James Logan: Quarter of a Millennium: The Library Company of Philadelphia, 1731-1981; occasional catalogs of special exhibitions; American Education, 1622-1860; Agriculture in America, 1622-1860; Natural History in America, 1609-1860; American Philanthropy, 1731-1860 (4 volume set covering the collections of the Library Company, Historical Society of Pennsylvania, and the American Philosophical Society).

★1899★
Library of Congress
General Reading Rooms Division
Microform Reading Room Section
Thomas Jefferson Bldg. - LJ-140B
Washington, DC 20540   Ph: (202)707-5471
Betty Culpepper, Hd.

Staff: 11. **Subjects:** Early state records; early English and American periodicals; American fiction to 1905; dime novels; American and British black journals; underground newspapers; oral histories; U.S. nondepository documents; U.S. Department of Education ERIC Reports; copyright records of the U.S. District Courts, 1790-1870; Barbour Collection of Connecticut vital records; State labor reports, 1865-1900; American labor union constitutions and proceedings; English books to 1700; architectural books, 15th-19th centuries; English and American plays, 1516-1830; Western Americana; pre-1900 Canadiana; papers of select British prime ministers; cabinet reports by British foreign ministers, 1837-1916; Journals and Sessional Papers of the British Parliament; papers of the Parliament of Northern Ireland, 1921-1972; manuscripts of American interest filmed by the American Council of Learned Societies; English parish registers, 16th to 19th centuries; Irish genealogical records; British radical periodicals; Modern Language Association reproductions of manuscripts and rare books; manuscripts in St. Catherine's Monastery on Mt. Sinai, in the libraries of the Greek and Armenian Patriarchates in Jerusalem, and in the monasteries of Mt. Athos; early editions of Petrarch and Ronsard; pandects of the Notaries of Genoa to 1300; minutes of the Senate of the Venetian Republic; inventories from the Archives Nationales (Paris) and of numerous German, Austrian, and Italian archives and libraries; Archives of the Austrian Foreign Office, 1848-1918; Spanish drama; early Latin American imprints; papers of Simon Bolivar; Mexican provincial and local archives from Jalisco, Oaxaca, Parral, Pueblo, and other cities; 16th and 17th century Russian imprints; 19th and 20th century Russian history and culture; archives of the Japanese Ministry of the Foreign Affairs and other ministries, 1868-1945; ULTRA intelligence messages, 1939-1945; summaries and translations of world broadcasts since World War II; press summaries and translations from Mainland China, Japan, Indonesia, and Yugoslavia; economic literature prior to 1830; social and economic plans of developing countries; League of Nations documents; United Nations documents; Human Relations Area Files; doctoral dissertations; books from the library's general collections copied for preservation purposes; Early American imprints to 1819; international censuses of population to 1967; contemporary statistics (ASI, IIS, & SRI); women's history and history of U.S. and British woman suffrage; auction and art exhibition catalogs; biographical archives for Great Britain, Germany, and the Soviet Union; photographic archives of art and architecture in France and Germany; Schomburg clipping file on black history; Spanish Civil War pamphlets; inventories of Latin manuscripts published before 1600 A.D.; Organization of American States documents; early science fiction; history and sources for Vietnam War; sources on ecumenical movement; sources on church in Russia and Soviet bloc; records of the Fabian Society; Dutch underground press; publications of Solidarity movement; archives and files relating to Germany in World War II; records of the Oneida community, of Millerites, and of early Adventists and Shakers; Portugese pamphlets, 1610-1921; history of nursing and pharmacy; early Texas imprints; BBC broadcasts during World War II; U.S. Department of State and Central Intelligence Agency reports. **Holdings:** 3.5 million reels and strips of microfilm, microfiche, and micro-opaques. **Services:** Reading room is open to persons above high school age.

★1900★
Lincoln University
Inman E. Page Library
Jefferson City, MO 65101

Ph: (314)681-5512
Fax: (314)681-5511

Elizabeth A. Wilson, Dir.

Founded: 1866. **Staff:** Prof 7; Other 8. **Subjects:** Liberal arts; elementary and secondary education; nursing; corrections and law enforcement. **Special Collections:** Lincoln collection; pro-slavery and antislavery tracts; pre- and post-Civil War period; black and ethnic collections (7000 books). **Holdings:** 138,172 books; 79,711 government documents; 230 theses and dissertations; 21 VF drawers; 4 VF drawers of pictures; 91,945 titles in microform. **Subscriptions:** 625 journasl and newspapers. **Services:** Interlibrary loan; faxing; copying; SDI; library open to the public with restrictions. **Automated Operations:** FirstSearch. **Computerized Information Services:** BRS Information Technologies. Performs online searches on fee basis; performs CD-ROM searches at no charge. Contact Person: Oi-Chi Hui, Ref., 681-5512. **Networks and Consortia:** Member of Missouri Library Network Corp. (MLNC). **Publications:** Lincoln's Page, irregular; Bibliography of Books By and About Blacks, irregular supplement; Monthly Checklist (selected); newsletter; students handbook; annual report; Library Manual.

★1901★
Lincoln University
Langston Hughes Memorial Library
Special Collections
Lincoln University, PA 19352-0999

Ph: (215)932-8300
Fax: (215)932-8317

Staff: Prof 1; Other 2. **Subjects:** Black studies - fine arts, history, civil rights, education; African studies - economics, history, political science, language, literature; antislavery. **Special Collections:** Personal library of Langston Hughes (3300 items); manuscripts of Pennsylvania Colonization Society and Young Men's Colonization Society (6 volumes); rare books (850); rare antislavery pamphlets (200); personal library of Dr. Therman B. O'Daniel (4000 items). **Holdings:** 18,350 books; 1060 bound periodical volumes; 772 reels of microfilm; 100 phonograph records; 250 historical pictures of black performers; 6000 unbound periodicals; 1595 microfiche; 1300 African Government documents; 2500 VF materials; 6000 archival materials and miscellanea. **Subscriptions:** 180 journals and other serials; 7 newspapers. **Services:** Interlibrary loan; copying; collections open to the public for reference use only. **Automated Operations:** Computerized cataloging and ILL. **Computerized Information Services:** OCLC. **Networks and Consortia:** Member of PALINET, Tri-State College Library Cooperative (TCLC). **Publications:** Selected bibliography on Malcolm X; bimonthly accessions lists - both free upon request. **Special Catalogues:** Catalog of the Special Negro and African Collection (2 volumes and supplement, 1970); Computer Output Microfilm Catalog, July 1970 - June 1977; A Survey of the Special Negro Collections; Reference Handbook of Special Collections - all for sale; mimeographed list of periodicals in the African collection; mimeographed reference handbook.

★1902★
Liturgy Library
8000 Hickory Ln.
PO Box 30221
Lincoln, NE 68503-0221

Ph: (402)488-1668

Judy H. Barrick, Dir.

Founded: 1975. **Staff:** 1. **Subjects:** History, theology, and practice of worship in the Judeo-Christian traditions. **Special Collections:** Special needs and contributions of Asian, Black, Hispanic, Native American, aging, disabled, single, and women worshippers. **Holdings:** 5000 books; 125 audio cassettes, filmstrips, kits; 125 sets of choir music; unbound periodicals. **Subscriptions:** 10 journals and other serials. **Services:** Copying (limited); library open to the public for reference use only. **Publications:** Informational brochure; price list.

★1903★
Livingstone College
American Black and African Studies Collection
Andrew Carnegie Library
701 W. Monroe St.
Salisbury, NC 28144
Elizabeth Mosby

Ph: (704)638-5629
Fax: (704)638-5646

Founded: 1908. **Staff:** Prof 4; Other 2. **Special Collections:** Africans and American Blacks; African Methodist Episcopal Zion Church; Ecumenical Methodist Conference, 1881-1956; Livingstone College. **Holdings:** 75,000 books; 4415 bound periodical volumes; 37,226 microfiche; 2752 reels of microfilm. **Subscriptions:** 258 journals and other serials; 28 newspapers. **Services:** Interlibrary loan; copying; collection open to the public. **Computerized Information Services:** DIALOG Information Services.

★1904★
Los Angeles Public Library
Social Sciences, Philosophy and Religion Department
630 W. 5th St.
Los Angeles, CA 90071
Marilyn C. Wherley, Dept.Mgr.

Ph: (213)612-3250
Fax: (213)612-0407

Staff: Prof 10; Other 17. **Subjects:** Philosophy, religion, psychology, social problems, government, foreign affairs, international relations, law, criminology, education, women's movements, family relations, ethnic groups, interpersonal relations. **Special Collections:** California, U.S., and U.N. documents depository; African-American history and culture; Mexican-American Affairs; women; education; the occult; cults and sects; Eastern religions. **Holdings:** 389,000 volumes. **Subscriptions:** 2850 journals and other serials. **Services:** Interlibrary loan; copying; department open to the public. **Automated Operations:** Computerized public access catalog. **Computerized Information Services:** DIALOG Information Services, EasyNet. Performs searches on fee basis. **Networks and Consortia:** Member of Metropolitan Cooperative Library System (MCLS). **Special Indexes:** Superstition; mythology; cults and sects; psychics; metaphysical societies; crime; current affairs; elections; statistics.

★1905★
Lower Merion Library Association
Ardmore Library
Gate Collection on the Black Experience
108 Ardmore Ave.
Ardmore, PA 19003
Peggy Newman, Dir.

Ph: (215)642-5187

Founded: 1899. **Staff:** Prof 1; Other 3. **Subjects:** Black experience - history, literature, personalities. **Holdings:** 30,000 books. **Subscriptions:** 65 journals and other serials; 5 newspapers. **Services:** Interlibrary loan; copying; SDI; collection open to nonresidents with valid Access Pennsylvania affiliation. **Automated Operations:** Computerized cataloging, acquisitions, and circulation.

★1906★
Martin Luther King, Jr. Center for Nonviolent Social Change, Inc.
King Library and Archives
449 Auburn Ave.
Atlanta, GA 30312
Dr. Marshia Turner, Libn.

Ph: (404)524-1956

Founded: 1968. **Staff:** Prof 1; Other 2. **Subjects:** Dr. Martin Luther King, Jr., Civil Rights Movement, African-American history, nonviolence, African-American religion, African-American politics. **Special Collections:** Bilingual materials by Martin Luther King, Jr.; organizational records of the SCLC (1954-1970); SNCL (1959-1972); CORE (1944-1968); MFDP (1964-1965); Delta Ministry (1963-1971); National Lawyers Guild (1936-1968); ESCRU (1959-1970); CCCO (1964-1968); USNSA (1957-1969); Personal papers of Martin Luther King, Jr. (1954-1968), Fred Shuttleworth (1953-1969), Johnnie Carr (1956-1979) and Julian Bond (1964-1968). **Holdings:** 4000 books; over 1 million documents focusing primarily on the American civil rights movement. **Services:** Copying; library open to the public. **Publications:** Martin Luther King Center Newsletter, quarterly; library holdings and services brochures.

★1907★
Mary Holmes College
Barr Library
Oral History Collection
Hwy. 50, W.
Box 1257
West Point, MS 39773   Ph: (601)494-6820
Gail Davis-Peyton   Fax: (601)494-5319

Founded: 1967. **Staff:** 6. **Subjects:** History, sociology, folklore. **Special Collections:** Taped interviews and transcriptions of conversations with rural black Mississippians 70 years of age and older (600); African American Collection (1000 titles). **Holdings:** 14 volumes. **Subscriptions:** 115 journals and other serials; 13 newspapers. **Services:** Interlibrary loan; copying; collection open to the public for reference use only. **Computerized Information Services:** EBSCO Electronic Information. **Networks and Consortia:** Member of SOLINET.

★1908★
McKinney Job Corps
Library
1701 N. Church St.
PO Box 8003
McKinney, TX 75069   Ph: (214)542-2623
Theale McClesky, Libn.

Founded: 1964. **Staff:** Prof 1; Other 1. **Subjects:** Negro history, special education, self-improvement, psychology, careers, guidance and counseling. **Holdings:** 10,500 books; 390 phonograph records. **Subscriptions:** 19 journals and other serials. **Services:** Library not open to the public.

★1909★
Meharry Medical College
Library
1005 D.B. Todd   Ph: (615)327-6728
Nashville, TN 37208   Fax: (615)327-6448
Cheryl Hamberg, Dir.

Founded: 1886. **Staff:** Prof 12; Other 18. **Subjects:** Medicine, dentistry, public health, medical technology, allied health professions. **Special Collections:** Black Medical History Collection (260 books; 100 manuscripts); Meharry Archives Collection (215 books; 65 dissertations; 235 boxes of manuscripts; 98 VF drawers). **Holdings:** 23,155 books; 58,030 bound periodical volumes; 440 audio cassettes; 448 video cassettes; 400 slide/tape sets. **Subscriptions:** 1374 journals and other serials. **Services:** Interlibrary loan (fee); copying; SDI; library open to the public. **Automated Operations:** Computerized cataloging, acquisitions, circulation, and serials. **Computerized Information Services:** MEDLINE, OCLC, DIALOG Information Services; CD-ROMs (MEDLINE, OncoDisc, PsycLIT, Sociofile, Scientific American, CONSULT, ERIC, MAXX); BITNET (electronic mail service). Performs searches on fee basis. **Networks and Consortia:** Member of National Network of Libraries of Medicine - Southeastern/Atlantic Region. **Publications:** Meharry Information Network, bimonthly - to medical libraries. **Special Catalogues:** Library guide.

★1910★
Memphis State University
Special Collections
MSU Libraries
Memphis, TN 38152   Ph: (901)678-2210
Michelle Fagan, Cur.

Founded: 1964. **Staff:** Prof 1; Other 3. **Subjects:** Lower Mississippi Valley - history, culture, literature. **Special Collections:** Memphis multimedia project (race relations); theater collection; sanitation strike of Memphis, 1968 (55 cubic feet); Robert R. Church Family, 1870-1980 (61 cubic feet); U.S. circus history, 1890-1970; university archives (250,000 archival materials); assassination of Martin Luther King, Jr; manuscript collections (315 collections; 6.7 million items). **Holdings:** 33,225 volumes; 7 million manuscript items, including photographs and sheet music; 760 maps; 3271 oral histories on audiotape; 505 videotapes; 228 reels of 16mm film; 77 records. **Services:** Copying; collections open to the public. **Automated Operations:** Computerized cataloging. **Computerized Information Services:** OCLC. **Networks and Consortia:** Member of SOLINET. **Publications:** Brister Library Monograph; Campus Tower News,

both irregular - both on exchange. **Special Catalogues:** Registers and inventories to collections.

★1911★
Metropolitan Council for Educational Opportunity
Library
55 Dimock St.
Roxbury, MA 02119   Ph: (617)427-1545
Jean McGuire, Exec.Dir.

Founded: 1966. **Staff:** Prof 6. **Subjects:** Quality integrated education, Afro-American history, multiculturalism. **Special Collections:** Scrapbooks of clippings on Greater Boston school systems and Boston's desegregation case (40). **Holdings:** 1260 books; 1 dissertation; 26 annual financial reports; 10 unpublished reports; 3 films; photographs. **Subscriptions:** 20 journals and other serials; 10 newspapers. **Services:** Copying; library open to the public. **Automated Operations:** Computerized cataloging. **Computerized Information Services:** Online systems. **Publications:** New Images Newsletter, quarterly; METCO Parent Handbook. **Special Catalogues:** Student enrollment, transportation and routes (both computer printouts).

★1912★
Metropolitan Museum of Art
Robert Goldwater Library
1000 Fifth Ave.   Ph: (212)570-3707
New York, NY 10028-0198   Fax: (212)570-3879

Founded: 1957. **Staff:** Prof 2; Other 1. **Subjects:** Archeology; art - African, Latin American, Indians of North America, Oceania. **Holdings:** 35,000 volumes. **Subscriptions:** 150 journals and other serials. **Services:** Copying; library open to college students and qualified researchers. **Special Catalogues:** Catalog of the Robert Goldwater Library (1982; 4 volumes).

★1913★
Miami University
Humanities and Social Sciences Department
King Library   Ph: (513)529-4141
Oxford, OH 45056   Fax: (513)529-1682
Richard H. Quay, Hd., Hum./Soc.Sci.Dept.

Founded: 1809. **Staff:** Prof 6.5; Other 1.5. **Subjects:** Business, history, education, American literature, political science, geography, sociology, anthropology, gerontology, military and naval science, foreign language, theater, economics, philosophy, psychology, religion, area studies, black world studies, women's studies, American studies. **Holdings:** 865,000 books; 100,000 bound periodical volumes. **Subscriptions:** 5000 journals and other serials; 80 newspapers. **Services:** Interlibrary loan; copying; SDI; library open to library permit holders. **Computerized Information Services:** DIALOG Information Services, BRS Information Technologies, OCLC EPIC, LEXIS/NEXIS, ABI/INFORM; CD-ROMs (Art Index, PsycLIT, ERIC, COMPACT DISCLOSURE, Social Sciences Index, CIRR on Disc, Compustat PC Plus, Business Periodicals Index, MLA International Bibliography, Ulrich's Plus, Thesaurus Linguae Graecae Canon of Greek Authors and Works, InfoTrac, Humanities Index, The British Parliamentary Papers Index, Eighteenth Century Short Title Catalogue, Monarch Notes, The Oxford English Dictionary, World Cruncher Disc, Columbia Granger's World of Poetry); BITNET, InterNet (electronic mail services). Performs searches on fee basis. **Networks and Consortia:** Member of OHIONET, Center for Research Libraries (CRL), Greater Cincinnati Library Consortium (GCLC).

★1914★
Michigan (State) Department of Civil Rights
Civil Rights Library
1200 6th St., 7th Fl.   Ph: (313)256-2622
Detroit, MI 48226   Fax: (313)256-2678
Charles Rouls

Founded: 1964. **Staff:** Prof 1. **Subjects:** Civil rights; discrimination - employment, housing; minority groups. **Holdings:** 10,000 books; 13,000 microfiche; unbound periodicals. **Subscriptions:** 200 journals and other serials; 10 newspapers. **Services:** Interlibrary loan; library open to the public by appointment. **Computerized Information Services:** DIALOG Information Services, VU-TEXT Information Services, ELSS (Electronic Legislative Search System),

WILSONLINE, WESTLAW, LEXIS, NEXIS, Hannah Information Systems, OCLC, Questor, Washington Alert Service, CQ Bill Status.

★1915★
Michigan State University
Labor and Industrial Relations Library
Library E109
East Lansing, MI 48824
Annie M. Cooper, Libn. III
Ph: (517)355-4647
Fax: (517)353-9806

Founded: 1956. **Staff:** Prof 1; Other 2. **Subjects:** Labor unions, public employee unionism, labor law, employment and training, minorities. **Special Collections:** Union constitutions and proceedings; public sector agreements for State of Michigan. **Holdings:** 50,000 books; 5000 bound periodical volumes; 200 VF drawers of pamphlets and mimeographed materials, by subject. **Subscriptions:** 125 journals and other serials; 75 newspapers. **Services:** Interlibrary loan; copying; library open to the public. **Computerized Information Services:** DIALOG Information Services; InterNet (electronic mail service). Performs searches on fee basis.

★1916★
Millersville University
Helen A. Ganser Library
Special Collections
Millersville, PA 17551
Ph: (717)872-3624
Fax: (717)872-3854
Robert E. Coley, Univ.Archv./Spec.Coll.Libn.

Founded: 1855. **Staff:** Prof 1; Other 1. **Special Collections:** Local History and Culture Collection (5000 titles); Wickersham Pedagogical Collection (3500 titles); Pennsylvania Imprint Collection (2150 titles); Rare Book Collection (1725 titles); University Archives (3500 linear feet; 450 volumes); Archives of the International Technological Education Association (340 linear feet), Pennsylvania Industrial Arts Association (microfilm), Pennsylvania Sociological Association (3 linear feet), and Pennsylvania State Modern Language Association (9 linear feet); Leo Ascher Center for the Study of Operetta Music (4000 items); Davison Collection on Weaving and Textiles (450 volumes); Amish and Mennonites (1300 titles); Carl Van Vechten Memorial Collection of Afro-American Arts and Letters (900 items). **Holdings:** 16,000 books; 600 manuscripts; 3600 linear feet of archives; 100 microfiche; 400 reels of microfilm. **Subscriptions:** 15 journals and other serials. **Services:** Copying; collections open to the public. **Automated Operations:** Computerized cataloging. **Computerized Information Services:** DIALOG Information Services, OCLC; Dynix (internal database). **Networks and Consortia:** Member of PALINET, Associated College Libraries of Central Pennsylvania (ACLCP). **Special Indexes:** Indices to the various collections maintained in department.

★1917★
Minneapolis Public Library & Information Center
Special Collections Department
300 Nicollet Mall
Minneapolis, MN 55401-1992
Edward R. Kukla, Dept.Hd.
Ph: (612)372-6648

Founded: 1987. **Staff:** Prof 3; Other 1. **Special Collections:** Minneapolis Athenaeum Collections (North American Indians, Spencer Natural History, Early American Exploration and Travel, Heffelfinger Aesop's and Others' Fables, History of Books and Printing; 5000 volumes); Minneapolis Collection (city of Minneapolis; 4000 volumes; 10,000 photographs; 150 archival collections; pictures; maps; VF materials); Kittleson World War II Collection (World War II - military and naval operations, social and economic aspects, personal narratives, anti-Semitism and the Holocaust; 8000 books; 400 pamphlets; 14 volumes of scrapbooks; 3 VF drawers of clippings; 2000 posters; 400 unbound periodicals; 1500 leaflets and pictures); Huttner Abolition and Anti-Slavery Collection (Abolitionist movement, slavery, black writers and reformers of the 19th century; 550 books; 50 letters and documents; 250 pamphlets, broadsides, newspapers); 19th Century American Studies Collection (materials by and about 19th century American writers, antislavery movement, New England descriptive and historical writings; Truman Nelson letters; John Greenleaf Whittier-Evelina Bray Downey correspondence; manuscript "Ode to France," James Russell Lowell; 4500 books; 200 bound periodical volumes; 150 pamphlets; 150 autograph letters; 150 pictures; 250 unbound periodicals, pamphlets, newspapers; 1 VF drawer of clippings); Hoag Mark

Twain Collection (250 books and pamphlets). **Subscriptions:** 24 journals and other serials. **Services:** Copying; collections open to the public with restrictions. **Computerized Information Services:** DataTimes; Photos I (internal database).

★1918★
Minneapolis Public Schools
Special School District 1
School Media/Professional Library
807 NE Broadway
Minneapolis, MN 55413
Susan Kranz, Media Spec.
Ph: (612)627-2179
Fax: (612)627-2164

Staff: Prof 1; Other 4. **Subjects:** Education - preschool through 12th grade, educational psychology, disadvantaged children and youth, child and adolescent psychology, sociology, minorities, school media centers, information technology. **Special Collections:** Multicultural and gender-fair materials; Special Education Institutional Materials Center. **Holdings:** 3000 books; 160 archival materials. **Subscriptions:** 140 journals and other serials. **Services:** Interlibrary loan; copying; library open to the public. **Computerized Information Services:** DIALOG Information Services, BRS Information Technologies. **Networks and Consortia:** Member of Metronet. **Special Catalogues:** Union List of Serials in Minneapolis Public Schools, annual.

★1919★
Mississippi Valley State University
James Herbert White Library
Special Collections
Itta Bena, MS 38941
Ph: (601)254-9041
Fax: (601)254-6704
Dr. Robbye R. Henderson, Dir.

Founded: 1952. **Staff:** 16. **Special Collections:** Education; Martin Luther King, Jr.; Mississippi history, Mississippi Valley State University Archival Collection. **Holdings:** 119,822 books; 12,949 bound periodical volumes; 240 reports; 205 feet of archival materials; 270,929 microfiche; 6116 microfilm. **Subscriptions:** 671 journals and other serials; 42 newspapers. **Services:** Interlibrary loan; copying; collections open to the public for reference use only. **Computerized Information Services:** InfoTrac; CLSI (internal database).

★1920★
National Archives & Records Administration
Still Picture Branch
8th St. & Pennsylvania Ave. NW
NNSP-18N
Washington, DC 20408
Ph: (202)501-5455

Founded: 1935. **Staff:** Prof 9; Other 14. **Subjects:** AV materials; still photography; posters; United States - history, politics, government. **Special Collections:** Included in the wide-ranging files are historical photographs from such agencies as: American Commission for the Protection and Salvage of Artistic and Historic Monuments in War Areas, 1943-1946 (German destruction of monuments; vandalism of historic buildings; architectural damage caused by war activities in Europe and Japan; works of art); Department of Defense, 1775-1982 (Army, Navy, Air Force, Marine Corps personnel, activities, installations, ordnance, transport); includes Revolutionary War, Mathew Brady Civil War photographs, western exploration, surveys, settlement, minor military expeditions, Spanish-American War, World War I, history of flight, scenic photographs, recruiting and war loan posters, effects of atomic bombing of Japan, occupation of Germany and Japan, U.S. Navy and U.S. Army photographs of World War II, the Korean War, and Vietnam War; Harmon Foundation Collection of Photographs, 1922-1966 (art works by black American and African artists; prominent black Americans; foreign art objects; activities of blacks on campuses of southern colleges; exhibits of black artists' works and art workshops); Department of the Interior, 1850-1973 (geological surveys; western land development; coastal fishing; wildlife; power, irrigation, soil conservation projects; national parks and recreation; U.S. territories; Indian affairs; Antarctic exploration; Bureau of Mines activities and Russell Lee photographs of coal mining activities in 1946); NASA, 1920-1965 (history of aviation and rocketry research and development; lunar surface photographs); Tennessee Valley Authority, 1933-1941 (dams, scenery, recreational areas; Lewis Hine photographs of families forced to leave their land); Department of the Treasury, 1917-1977 (posters for war bonds and E bonds campaigns; stills from World War I promotional movies;

Bureau of Engraving and printing activities); Office of War Information, 1940-1950 (World War II military operations and U.S. home front; U.S. and foreign posters; international conferences and personalities; views of American life and culture for foreign distribution). **Holdings:** 7 million archival photographs from U.S. Federal Government agencies which document American and world cultural, social, environmental, economic, technological, political history of a nongovernmental nature as well as activities of military and civilian governmental agencies; historical photographs of precursors of contemporary governmental activity. **Services:** Copying; branch open to the public for reference use only. **Computerized Information Services:** TextBank (internal database). **Publications:** Guide to the Holdings of the Still Pictures Branch of the National Archives (1990). **Special Catalogues:** War and Conflict: Selected Images from the National Archives, 1795-1970.

★1921★
National Association for the Advancement of Colored People
NAACP Legal Defense and Educational Fund
Law Library
99 Hudson St., 16th Fl.
New York, NY 10013
Donna Gloeckner   Ph: (212)219-1900

Subjects: Civil rights law - discrimination against blacks, other racial minorities, and women in employment, education, housing, and other areas. **Holdings:** 15,000 volumes.

★1922★
New College of California
New College Library
50 Fell St.
San Francisco, CA 94102-5298   Ph: (415)241-1300

Founded: 1973. **Staff:** Prof 2; Other 3. **Subjects:** Law, alternative humanities, psychology, poetics, women's studies, homosexuality/lesbianism, minorities, Third World. **Special Collections:** Modern American poetry. **Holdings:** 30,000 books; unbound periodicals. **Subscriptions:** 100 journals and other serials. **Services:** Interlibrary loan; library not open to the public. **Automated Operations:** Computerized cataloging, serials, and circulation. **Computerized Information Services:** DIALOG Information Services, WESTLAW, OCLC; internal database. Performs searches on fee basis. Contact Person: Dale Soules, Ref./Comp..

★1923★
New York City Human Resources Administration
Library
109 E. 16th St.
New York, NY 10003
Harold W. Benson, Libn.   Ph: (212)420-7652

Founded: 1945. **Staff:** Prof 1; Other 1. **Subjects:** Public welfare, social work, child welfare, poverty, homeless, ethnic studies, public administration, employment, income maintenance. **Holdings:** 14,500 volumes; 75 VF drawers; 5000 titles of uncataloged reports and pamphlets. **Subscriptions:** 200 journals and other serials; 6 newspapers. **Services:** Interlibrary loan; copying; library open to the public. **Computerized Information Services:** DIALOG Information Services, OCLC. **Publications:** Library Bulletin, bimonthly.

★1924★
New York City Technical College of City University of New York
Library
300 Jay St.
Brooklyn, NY 11201
Darrow Wood, Chf.Libn. & Dept.Chm.   Ph: (718)260-5470   Fax: (718)260-5467

Founded: 1947. **Staff:** Prof 14; Other 6. **Subjects:** Paramedical sciences, graphic arts, hotel and restaurant management, Afro-American studies, engineering technology, business fields. **Holdings:** 161,041 books; 5276 bound periodical volumes; 108 VF drawers of pamphlet material; 3 VF drawers of menus; 15 VF drawers of pictures; 15 VF drawers of career material; 15 VF drawers of company history; 10,415 reels of microfilm; 1950 phonograph records; 803 8mm film loops; 342 audio tapes; 909 videocassettes. **Subscriptions:** 890 journals and other serials; 11 newspapers. **Services:** Interlibrary loan; copying; library open to the public for reference use only. **Automated Operations:**

Computerized public access catalog and cataloging. **Computerized Information Services:** OCLC, BRS Information Technologies, ACADEMIC INDEX, MAGAZINE ASAP; CD-ROM (Newspaper Abstracts Ondisc). **Networks and Consortia:** Member of New York Metropolitan Reference and Research Library Agency, Academic Libraries of Brooklyn (ALB). **Publications:** Library Notes, irregular; Library Basics; Library Alert, irregular - all to faculty and to others on request.

★1925★
New York Public Library
Countee Cullen Regional Branch Library
African-American Heritage Collection
104 W. 136th St.
New York, NY 10030
Phyllis G. Mack, Reg.Libn.   Ph: (212)491-2070   Fax: (212)491-6541

Founded: 1905. **Staff:** Prof 7; Other 6. **Subjects:** Ethnic heritage, African and African-American heritage and culture. **Special Collections:** James Weldon Johnson Collection of Children's Books on the Black Experience. **Holdings:** 58,347 books; 1,495 recordings; 1,298 videocassettes; 109 non-circulating software. **Subscriptions:** 134 journals and other serials; 16 newspapers. **Services:** Interlibrary loan; copying; library open to the public. **Formerly:** Its Ethnic Heritage Collection.

★1926★
New York Public Library
The Research Libraries
Schomburg Center for Research in Black Culture
515 Malcolm X Blvd.
New York, NY 10037-1801
Howard Dodson, Chf.   Ph: (212)491-2200   Fax: (212)491-6760

Founded: 1926. **Staff:** Prof 30; Other 33. **Subjects:** Social sciences, humanities, the black experience throughout the world. **Special Collections:** Haitian Collection; African and Caribbean music; works of Harlem Renaissance authors and artists. **Holdings:** 102,000 volumes; 3200 archival record groups; 10,000 recordings; 300,000 photographs; 600 videotapes; 5000 hours of oral history; 30,000 reels of microfilm; 40,000 microfiche; paintings; sculpture; drawings; prints; African artifacts. **Subscriptions:** 1000 journals and other serials. **Services:** Copying; center open to adults for reference use. **Computerized Information Services:** RLIN. **Networks and Consortia:** Member of Research Libraries Information Network (RLIN), New York Metropolitan Reference and Research Library Agency, New York State Interlibrary Loan Network (NYSILL). **Publications:** The Schomburg Center Journal, quarterly. **Special Indexes:** Kaiser Index to Black Resources, 1940 to present (card, online); clipping files (microfiche); local data bases; vertical file holdings, 1925-1974 (microfiche), 1975 to present (paper).

★1927★
New York Theological Seminary
Library
5 W. 29th St.
New York, NY 10001
Eleanor Soler, Libn.   Ph: (212)532-4012

Founded: 1900. **Staff:** Prof 1; Other 1. **Subjects:** Bible, theology, pastoral counseling, parish ministry, African-American, Hispanic American, and Korean American church studies, women in the church. **Holdings:** 20,000 volumes; 700 audio cassettes; 20 video cassettes; 300 Spanish books; 200 Korean books; 2 drawers of periodicals on microfiche. **Subscriptions:** 40 journals and other serials. **Services:** Interlibrary loan; copying; library open to the public for reference use only.

★1928★
Newark Public Library
Humanities Division
5 Washington St.
Box 630
Newark, NJ 07101-0630
Sallie Hannigan, Supv.Libn.   Ph: (201)733-7820   Fax: (201)733-5648

Founded: 1889. **Staff:** Prof 4; Other 1. **Subjects:** Literature, language, literary criticism, biography, bibliography, religion, philosophy, history, geography, psychology, librariana, travel, film, theater, television, sports and recreation, encyclopedias, dictionaries. **Special Collections:** Black literature, history, and biography; Granger Collection of Poetry and Anthologies; Travel Collection; collective biography (books; pamphlets; clippings). **Holdings:** 130,000 books; 1000 bound periodical volumes; 1000 maps; dictionaries and encyclopedias in Spanish, Italian, French, German, Russian; information file. **Subscriptions:** 630 journals and other serials. **Services:** Interlibrary loan; copying; telephone and in-person reference available in Spanish; division open to the public. **Automated Operations:** Computerized public access catalog, cataloging, acquisitions, and circulation. **Computerized Information Services:** BRS Information Technologies, DIALOG Information Services, ORBIT Search Service, NEXIS, WILSONLINE, OCLC EPIC, DataTimes. Performs searches on fee basis. **Networks and Consortia:** Member of New Jersey Library Network, Essex Hudson Regional Library Cooperative.

★1929★
Newark Public Library
Popular Library Division
5 Washington St.
Box 630
Newark, NJ 07101-0630
Anthony Lardieri, Supv.Libn.

Ph: (201)733-7784
Fax: (201)733-5648

Staff: Prof 9; Other 10. **Subjects:** General fiction, popular nonfiction, black studies, foreign languages, job and career information. **Special Collections:** African American room, Sala Hispanoamericana; French, German, Italian, Polish, Portuguese, Russian, and Yiddish language collections; 20,000 volumes in Spanish. **Holdings:** 60,000 books; 30 films; 2000 video cassettes; 500 phonograph records; 1500 audio cassettes; 550 large print titles. **Subscriptions:** 25 journals and other serials; 10 newspapers. **Services:** Interlibrary loan; copying; division open to the public. **Automated Operations:** Computerized public access catalog, cataloging, acquisitions, and circulation. **Computerized Information Services:** DIALOG Information Services, BRS Information Technologies, NEXIS, OCLC EPIC, ORBIT Search Service, VU-TEXT Information Services, WILSONLINE, DataTimes. Performs searches on fee basis. Contact Person: James #Capuano, Prin.Libn., 733-7814. **Networks and Consortia:** Member of New Jersey Library Network, Essex Hudson Regional Library Cooperative. **Publications:** Monthly film list - to registered borrowers. **Special Indexes:** Index of books into films.

★1930★
North Carolina A&T State University
F.D. Bluford Library
Greensboro, NC 27411
Ph: (919)334-7782
Fax: (919)334-7783
Alene C. Young, Dir., Lib.Serv.

Founded: 1894. **Staff:** Prof 17; Other 28. **Subjects:** Agriculture, business, nursing, engineering, education. **Special Collections:** Collections of Black Studies; Film Collection; Chemistry Library. **Holdings:** 365,288 volumes; 496,544 microforms; archival materials; government documents; theses; pictures; maps; modules. **Subscriptions:** 1804 journals and other serials. **Services:** Interlibrary loan; copying; cooperative lending; library open to the public. **Automated Operations:** Computerized cataloging and circulation. **Computerized Information Services:** OCLC, DIALOG Information Services, LS/2000. Performs searches on fee basis. Contact Person: Evelyn Blount, 334-7159. **Networks and Consortia:** Member of SOLINET. **Publications:** Newsletter. **Special Indexes:** Local newspaper index (online).

★1931★
North Carolina Central University
School of Library and Information Sciences Library
J.E. Shepard Library
Durham, NC 27707
Ph: (919)560-5212
Fax: (919)560-6402
Alice S. Richmond, Libn.

Staff: Prof 2; Other 1. **Subjects:** Librarianship, children's literature. **Special Collections:** William Tucker Collection (materials for children by black authors and illustrators; 302 items; 190 volumes); Black Librarians' Collection (1200 items). **Holdings:** 24,940 books; 4875 bound periodical volumes; 455 reels of microfilm; 15,500 microfiche; 15 VF drawers. **Subscriptions:** 429 journals and other serials. **Services:** Interlibrary loan; library open to the public with restrictions. **Automated Operations:** Computerized public access catalog and cataloging. **Computerized Information Services:** DIALOG Information Services, WILSONLINE. **Networks and Consortia:**

Member of SOLINET. **Publications:** Acquisitions list, irregular - for internal distribution only.

★1932★
Northeastern Illinois University
Ronald Williams Library
5500 N. St. Louis Ave.
Chicago, IL 60625-4699
Bradley F. Baker, Univ.Libn.

Ph: (312)794-2615
Fax: (312)794-2550

Founded: 1961. **Staff:** Prof 21; Other 53. **Subjects:** Education, business and management, social sciences, literature and languages. **Special Collections:** U.S. and Illinois document depositories; Illinois Regional Archive Depository (IRAD) for Chicago and Cook County; African-American literature; William Gray Reading Collection; curriculum guides; textbooks. **Holdings:** 546,056 books; 68,977 bound periodical volumes; 3259 linear feet of archival materials; 29,573 reels of microfilm; 648,245 microfiche. **Subscriptions:** 4617 journals and other serials; 42 newspapers. **Services:** Interlibrary loan; copying; library open to the public. **Automated Operations:** Computerized public access catalog, acquisitions, and serials. **Computerized Information Services:** DIALOG Information Services, OCLC, WILSONLINE, OCLC EPIC, CARL UnCover; InfoTrac; CD-ROMs (ERIC, PAIS on CD-ROM, MLA International Bibliography, Disclosure Incorporated, PsycLIT, Computer Library); BITNET (electronic mail service). Performs searches on fee basis. Contact Person: Mary Jane Hilburger, Hd.Ref.Libn., 794-2614. **Networks and Consortia:** Member of ILLINET. **Publications:** Annual Report; departmental bibliographies and handouts. **Special Catalogues:** Library shelf lists for special collections, documents, and curriculum materials. **Special Indexes:** Periodicals holding list.

★1933★
Oakland Public Library
History/Literature and Oakland History Room
125 14th St.
Oakland, CA 94612
Ph: (510)273-3136
Sherrill Reeves, Sr.Libn.

Staff: Prof 5; Other 3. **Subjects:** History, travel, biography, English and foreign languages and literature, genealogy, maps. **Special Collections:** Jack London collection (autographed first editions; signed letters; photographs, letters from literary friends; artifacts); logbooks of the cutter BEAR; Ina Coolbrith materials; U.S. Geological Survey Topographical Maps; Schomberg Collection of Black Literature and History (in microform); Negroes of New York, 1939 (Writers Program; in microform); Library of American Civilization (in microform); Sutro Library Family History and Local History Subject Catalogs (in microform); Index to Biographies in State and Local Histories in the Library of Congress (in microform). **Holdings:** 100,663 books; genealogy microfilms. **Subscriptions:** 114 journals and other serials. **Services:** Interlibrary loan; copying; division open to the public. **Networks and Consortia:** Member of Bay Area Library and Information System (BALIS). **Publications:** New Releases. **Special Indexes:** Indexes for Drama, Short Story, Poetry, Literary Criticism (on cards); local newspapers, 1978 to present; Local History.

★1934★
Oberlin College - Library
Archives
420 Mudd Center
Oberlin, OH 44074-1532
Ph: (216)775-8014
Fax: (216)775-8739
Roland M. Baumann, Coll.Archv.

Founded: 1966. **Staff:** Prof 2; Other 1. **Subjects:** Higher education, 19th century reform, temperance, women's history, black education, architecture, Ohio history. **Special Collections:** Missions, the antislavery movement, and temperance in Oberlin; papers of Oberlin College faculty and graduates; Congressman Charles Mosher papers; Congressman Don J. Pease papers; Oberlin municipal government records; photographs of Oberlin College and Oberlin. **Holdings:** 5000 linear feet of manuscripts and archival materials. **Subscriptions:** 6 journals and other serials. **Services:** Copying; archives open to the public. **Automated Operations:** Computerized public access catalog, cataloging, acquisitions, serials, and circulation. **Computerized Information Services:** DIALOG Information Services, BRS Information Technologies; InterNet (electronic mail service). Performs searches free of charge. Contact Person: Cynthia Comer, Assoc.Hd., Ref. **Networks and Consortia**

Member of NEOMARL, OHIONET. **Publications:** Library of Congress Rule Interpretation for AACR2; Guide to the Women's History Sources in the Oberlin College Archives (1990); Current Scholarship in Women's Studies (1987); Oberlin History Bibliography, a partial listing of published titles bearing on the history of the College and Community, 1833-1992. **Special Catalogues:** Catalog of the Antislavery Collection.

★1935★
Ohio State University
Black Studies Library

1858 Neil Ave. Mall	Ph: (614)292-2393
Columbus, OH 43210-1286	Fax: (614)292-7859
Eleanor M. Daniel, Hd.Libn.	

Founded: 1971. **Staff:** Prof 1; Other 1. **Subjects:** African-American studies, African studies. **Special Collections:** Schomburg Collection; Atlanta University Black Culture Collection; Black Newspaper Collection (Bell & Howell); Black Woman: Oral History Project; Black Women in United States History; W.E.B. DuBois papers; Black Biographical Dictionaries; papers of the National Association for the Advancement of Colored People (NAACP), parts 1-8; papers of the Congress of Racial Equality, 1941-1967. **Holdings:** 30,000 books; 13,000 microforms; 70 major black U.S. newspapers. **Subscriptions:** 177 journals and other serials; 16 newspapers. **Services:** Interlibrary loan; collection open to the public. **Automated Operations:** Computerized cataloging, serials, and circulation. **Computerized Information Services:** Online systems; BITNET (electronic mail service). **Publications:** Selected List of Titles Received by the Black Studies Library, monthly.

★1936★
Payne Theological Seminary
R.C. Ransom Memorial Library

PO Box 474	Ph: (513)376-2946
Wilberforce, OH 45384-0474	Fax: (513)376-2948
J. Dale Balsbaugh, Dir. of the Lib.	

Founded: 1844. **Staff:** Prof 1; Other 1. **Subjects:** Philosophy, Biblical studies, pastoral theology, doctrinal theology, black studies, African Methodist Episcopal Church history. **Special Collections:** Arno Press Black Studies Program - The American Negro, His History and Literature (150 volumes). **Holdings:** 25,000 books; 500 archival materials. **Subscriptions:** 35 journals and other serials; 2 newspapers. **Services:** Interlibrary loan; copying; library open to the public. **Computerized Information Services:** OPAC (internal database). **Special Catalogues:** Union Serials List of Seminaries, every 4 years.

★1937★
Prairie View A & M University
Special Collections/University Archives

John B. Coleman Library, Rm. 505	
PO Box 519	Ph: (409)857-3119
Prairie View, TX 77446	Fax: (409)857-2755
Dudley V. Yates, Dir.	

Founded: 1912. **Staff:** 1; Other 2. **Special Collections:** T.K. Lawless Collection; Black Heritage of the West Collection; university archives; rare books collection; Blacks in the Military Collection. **Holdings:** 2059 books; 74 bound periodical volumes; 761 reels of microfilm; VF drawers; 1254 folders, pictures, memorabilia; 164 cubic feet of official records; 114 cubic feet of papers; 44 cubic feet of university publications; 19 cubic feet of clippings and pamphlets. **Services:** Interlibrary loan; copying; collections open to the public. **Automated Operations:** Computerized public access catalog (NOTIS) and cataloging. **Computerized Information Services:** DIALOG Information Services, OCLC; internal databases. Performs searches on fee basis. **Networks and Consortia:** Member of Houston Area Research Library Consortium (HARLIC), AMIGOS Bibliographic Council, Inc.. **Publications:** Annual report. **Special Catalogues:** Record series control (card).

★1938★
Prince George's County Memorial Library System
Sojourner Truth Room

6200 Oxon Hill Rd.	
Oxon Hill, MD 20745	Ph: (301)839-2400
Teresa M. Stakem, Libn. II	

Founded: 1968. **Staff:** Prof 2. **Subjects:** African American history - women, family, slavery, civil rights; literary criticism; military. **Special Collections:** Slave narratives (30). **Holdings:** 5000 books; 130 bound periodical volumes; 12 VF drawers of clippings, pamphlets, government documents; 100 reels of microfilm and 35 microfiche of periodicals. **Subscriptions:** 30 journals and other serials. **Services:** Copying; room open to the public with restrictions. **Automated Operations:** Computerized circulation. **Computerized Information Services:** CLSI (internal database).

★1939★
Providence College
Phillips Memorial Library

River Ave. at Eaton St.	Ph: (401)865-2377
Providence, RI 02918	Fax: (401)865-2057
Jane Jackson, Dir. of Archv.	

Founded: 1917. **Staff:** Prof 10; Other 31. **Subjects:** Works of St. Thomas Aquinas, Thomistic philosophy and theology, Dominican Order. **Special Collections:** John E. Fogarty Papers (500,000 pieces); Dennis J. Roberts Papers (3000 pieces); William Henry Chamberlin Papers (120 pieces and 40 diaries on microfilm); Louis Francis Budenz Papers (9500 pamphlets and periodicals); Rhode Island Constitutional Convention Collection, 1964-1968 (1000 pieces); Cornelius Moore Papers (250 pieces); J. Lyons Moore Collection (3000 pieces); Robert E. Quinn Papers and Oral History Project; Rhode Island Urban League Papers (200,000 items); Nazi Bund Collection (300 pieces); John J. Fawcett Collection (3000 drawings); Limited Constitutional Convention, 1973 (500 pieces); Quonset Point Collection (9500 pieces); Blackfriars' Guild Collection (2500 pieces); Joseph A. Doorley, Jr. Collection (60,000 pieces); Black Regiment Collection (600 pieces); Bonniwell Liturgical Collection (2100 books); Coutu Genealogy; Aime J. Forand Collection (4500 pieces); Irish Literature Collection (100 pieces); John O. Pastore Collection (100,000 pieces); Social Justice Collection, 1936-1942 (325 pieces); Walsh Civil War Diary (30 pages); Black Newspapers, 1932-1957 (8 reels of microfilm); Confederation Period in Rhode Island Newspapers Collection (48 pieces); Reunification of Ireland Clippings (7 pieces); National Association for the Advancement of Colored People Collection (pending); English and Colonial 18th Century Trade Statistics Collection (500,000 I.B.M. cards); Alice Lafond Altieri Collection (925 pieces); J. Howard McGrath Collection (62,100 pieces); Thomas Matthew McGlynn, O.P. Collection (5000 pieces and art objects); Edward J. Higgins Collection; Edward P. Beard Collection (75,100 pieces); Patrick T. Conley Photograph Collection (460 reprints); Rhode Island Football Officials' Association Collection (900 pieces); Rhode Island Constitutional Convention, 1986 (2300 pieces); Frank Lanning Collection (57 drawings); Providence College Archives. **Holdings:** 253,250 books; 52,913 bound periodical volumes; 123,976 government documents; 26,143 microforms. **Subscriptions:** 1877 journals. **Services:** Interlibrary loan (books only); copying; library open to the public for reference use only. **Automated Operations:** Computerized cataloging, acquisitions, circulation, and ILL. **Computerized Information Services:** DIALOG Information Services, BRS Information Technologies, OCLC, LEXIS, NEXIS, Knowledge Index, OCLC EPIC; CD-ROM. **Networks and Consortia:** Member of Consortium of Rhode Island Academic and Research Libraries, Inc. (CRIARL), NELINET, Inc., Association of Rhode Island Health Sciences Librarians (ARIHSL).

★1940★
Prudence Crandall Museum
Library

PO Box 58	
Canterbury, CT 06331	Ph: (203)546-9916
Kazimiera Kozlowski, Musm.Cur.	

Staff: Prof 1. **Subjects:** Black history, life of Prudence Crandall, state and local history, women's history. **Holdings:** 1000 books. **Services:** Library open to the public by appointment for reference use only.

★1941★
Queens Borough Public Library
History, Travel & Biography Division
89-11 Merrick Blvd.   Ph: (718)990-0762
Jamaica, NY 11432   Fax: (718)658-8312
Deborah Hammer, Hd.

Founded: 1930. **Staff:** Prof 6; Other 2. **Subjects:** History, Indians of North America, biography, geography, travel, exploration. **Special Collections:** Carter G. Woodson Collection of Afro-American Culture and Life; Schomburg microfilm collection; U.S. Geographic Survey topographic maps (10,300); physical/thematic maps of countries of the world (126); nautical charts (8 kits); jet/ocean/world navigation charts (520); national forest maps (75); Latin American topographic maps (97); New York State planimetric maps (968); New York state, county, road maps (78); railroad transportation zone maps (82); historic/city maps (442). **Holdings:** 143,000 books; 3550 bound periodical volumes; 6800 microforms; 1 drawer of microfiche; 36 VF drawers of pamphlets; New York Daily News, 1950 to present; newspapers on microfilm. **Subscriptions:** 71 journals and other serials; 32 newspapers. **Services:** Interlibrary loan; copying; division open to the public. **Automated Operations:** Computerized public access catalog and circulation. **Computerized Information Services:** ALANET (electronic mail service). **Special Indexes:** Collective biography analytics (card).

★1942★
Queens Borough Public Library
Library Action Committee of Corona-East Elmhurst, Inc.
Langston Hughes Community Library and Cultural Center
102-09 Northern Blvd.   Ph: (718)651-1100
Corona, NY 11368   Fax: (718)651-6258
Andrew P. Jackson, Exec.Dir.

Founded: 1969. **Staff:** Prof 6; Other 17. **Subjects:** Third World, children's literature. **Special Collections:** Langston Hughes Collection (books by and about the author); Black Heritage Reference Collection; Langston Hughes Music Collection; Langston Hughes Video Club; Langston Hughes Art Collection. **Holdings:** 110,000 books; 150 documents, manuscripts, reels of microfilm. **Subscriptions:** 105 journals and other serials; 15 newspapers. **Services:** Copying; library open to the public. **Publications:** Library Center Brochure.

★1943★
Queens College of City University of New York
Ethnic Materials Information Exchange
Graduate School of Lib. & Info. Studies
NSF 316
65-30 Kissena Blvd.   Ph: (718)997-3626
Flushing, NY 11367   Fax: (718)793-8049
David Cohen, Prog.Dir.

Founded: 1980. **Staff:** Prof 1; Other 1. **Subjects:** Ethnic studies resources, minority groups in America, multicultural librarianship. **Holdings:** 2000 volumes; 40 filmstrips; 10 tapes; 250 pamphlets; curriculum materials; vertical file of clippings for each group and information area. **Subscriptions:** 6 journals and other serials. **Services:** Center open to the public.

★1944★
Radcliffe College
Arthur and Elizabeth Schlesinger Library on the History of Women in America
10 Garden St.
Cambridge, MA 02138   Ph: (617)495-8647
Dr. Patricia M. King, Dir.

Founded: 1943. **Staff:** Prof 11; Other 8. **Subjects:** Women - suffrage, medicine, education, law, social service, labor, family, organizations; history of American women in all phases of public and private life. **Special Collections:** Beecher-Stowe; Woman's Rights; Blackwell Family; Charlotte Perkins Gilman; Emma Goldman; Somerville-Howorth; Dr. Martha May Eliot; Jeannette Rankin; National Organization for Women; National Women's Political Caucus; Black Women Oral History Project; Culinary Collection (9000 volumes); etiquette books; picture collection (50,000). **Holdings:** 47,000 volumes; 3000 bound periodical volumes; 950

major collections of papers on individual American women, families, women's organizations; 9500 reels of microfilm; 2250 magnetic tapes; 400 oral history transcripts; 70 VF drawers; 2500 reels of audio- and videotapes; 6500 linear feet of manuscripts; 50,000 photographs. **Subscriptions:** 475 journals and other serials. **Services:** Interlibrary loan; copying; library open to the public. **Automated Operations:** Computerized public access catalog, cataloging and serials. **Publications:** Occasional Reports; Newsletters, both sent on request. **Special Catalogues:** Manuscript Inventories; Catalogs of the Manuscripts, Books and Periodicals, 1984 (10 volumes); Women of Courage exhibition catalog, 1984.

★1945★
Richmond Public Library
Special Collections
325 Civic Center Plaza
Richmond, CA 94804   Ph: (510)620-6561
Adelia Lines, Dir.

Founded: 1905. **Special Collections:** Local history; job information center; AV collection (film; video cassettes); motor manuals; art prints; Afro-American history; LEAP (literacy program). **Services:** Interlibrary loan; collections open to the public. **Automated Operations:** Computerized cataloging and circulation. **Computerized Information Services:** DIALOG Information Services, WILSONLINE; CLSI (internal database); OnTyme Electronic Message Network Service (electronic mail service). Performs searches on fee basis. Contact Person: Douglas Holtzman. **Networks and Consortia:** Member of Bay Area Library and Information Network, Bay Area Library and Information System (BALIS).

★1946★
Rockefeller University
Rockefeller Archive Center
15 Dayton Ave.
Pocantico Hills   Ph: (914)631-4505
North Tarrytown, NY 10591   Fax: (914)631-6017
Dr. Darwin H. Stapleton, Dir.

Founded: 1975. **Staff:** Prof 10; Other 6. **Subjects:** American philanthropy; Rockefeller family; education; medicine; physical, natural, and social sciences; public health; arts; humanities; agriculture; Black history; international relations and economic development; labor; politics; population; religion; social welfare; women's history. **Special Collections:** Rockefeller Foundation (7200 cubic feet); General Education Board (350 cubic feet); Laura Spelman Rockefeller Memorial (58 cubic feet); Bureau of Social Hygiene (32 cubic feet); Sealantic Fund (48 cubic feet); John D. Rockefeller (550 cubic feet); Nelson A. Rockefeller papers; John and Mary R. Markle Foundation records (52 cubic feet); Office of the Messrs. Rockefeller (580 cubic feet); International Education Board (37 cubic feet); Spelman Fund of New York (42 cubic feet); Rockefeller University (3500 cubic feet); The Commonwealth Fund (600 cubic feet); International Basic Economy Corporation (94 cubic feet; microforms); Russell Sage Foundation (43 cubic feet); Products of Asia (27 cubic feet); Asia Society (264 cubic feet); China Medical Board (82 cubic feet); Rockefeller Brothers Fund (520 cubic feet); Agricultural Development Council (225 cubic feet); American International Association for Economic and Social Development (143 cubic feet); Population Council (657 cubic feet); Arts, Education and Americans Panel (21 cubic feet); Davison Fund, Inc. (16 cubic feet); JDR 3rd Fund (143 cubic feet); Memorial Sloan-Kettering Cancer Center (582 cubic feet); Martha B. Rockefeller Fund for Music (118 cubic feet); Rockefeller Sanitary Commission for the Eradication of Hookworm Disease (6.5 cubic feet); Union Tank Car Company (6 cubic feet); Lawrence B. Dunham (2 cubic feet); Frederick T. Gates (2 cubic feet); Lewis W. Hackett (20 cubic feet); J. George Harrar (15 cubic feet); John H. Knowles (23 cubic feet); William Rockefeller (12 cubic feet). **Holdings:** 26,000 cubic feet of archival and manuscript collections; 250,000 photographs; 4000 microfiche; 1600 films. **Services:** Copying; center open to scholars by appointment. **Computerized Information Services:** RLIN. **Networks and Consortia:** Member of Research Libraries Information Network (RLIN). **Publications:** Newsletter, annual; occasional papers; Research Reports from the Rockefeller Archive Center. **Special Catalogues:** A Guide to Archives and Manuscripts at the Rockefeller Archive Center, 1989 (pamphlet); Photograph Collections in the Rockefeller Archive Center, 1986.

★1947★
St. Joseph's Seminary
Library
1200 Varnum St., N.E.
Washington, DC 20017   Ph: (202)526-4231
Laurence A. Schmitt, Libn.

Founded: 1930. **Staff:** Prof 1; Other 1. **Subjects:** Philosophy and theology, black studies. **Holdings:** 24,000 volumes. **Subscriptions:** 75 journals and other serials. **Services:** Interlibrary loan (limited); library open to the public by appointment.

★1948★
St. Louis Community College at Forest Park
Instructional Resources
Special Collections
5600 Oakland Ave.   Ph: (314)644-9209
St. Louis, MO 63110   Fax: (314)644-9240
Carol S. Warrington

Founded: 1968. **Staff:** Prof 5.5; Other 20.5. **Subjects:** African Americans, allied health, tourism. **Services:** Interlibrary loan; collection open to the public. **Automated Operations:** Computerized cataloging (NOTIS). **Computerized Information Services:** DIALOG Information Services, BRS Information Technologies, WILSONLINE. Performs searches. Contact Person: Carol Shahriary, Ref.Libn.

★1949★
Seattle Public Library
Douglass-Truth Branch Library
2300 E. Yesler Way   Ph: (206)684-4704
Seattle, WA 98122   Fax: (206)684-4346
Irene Haines, Team Ldr. & Young Adult Libn.

Founded: 1914. **Staff:** Prof 3; Other 4. **Subjects:** African-American history and literature - the African-American experience in the Pacific Northwest, the portrayal of blacks in children's literature. **Special Collections:** African-American Collection; Children's Literature Research Collection. **Holdings:** 6477 books; 346 bound periodical volumes; 5 VF drawers of pictures and pamphlets; 95 sound recordings; 3 boxes of microfiche; 200 video recordings. **Subscriptions:** 17 journals and other serials; 6 newspapers. **Services:** Interlibrary loan; copying; library open to the public. **Automated Operations:** Computerized public access catalog, serials, and circulation. **Computerized Information Services:** InfoTrac. **Networks and Consortia:** Member of Western Library Network (WLN). **Special Indexes:** Afro-American History Index (card).

★1950★
Southern California Library for Social Studies and
  Research
6120 S. Vermont Ave.   Ph: (213)759-6063
Los Angeles, CA 90044   Fax: (213)759-2252
Sarah Cooper, Dir.

Founded: 1963. **Staff:** Prof 3; Other 8. **Subjects:** Labor; Marxism; socialism; black, Chicano, and women's movements; Southern California grassroots organizations. **Special Collections:** Civil Rights Congress (Los Angeles area) archival records; Harry Bridges papers on deportation trials; Los Angeles Committee for the Protection of the Foreign Born records; personal manuscript collections from Charlotta A. Bass, Richard Gladstein, Robert W. Kenny, and Earl Robinson. **Holdings:** 35,000 books; 30,000 pamphlets; 3500 tapes; 500,000 news clippings; 3000 periodicals titles; files from labor, peace, and civil rights organizations, 1930s to present; 100 documentary films, 1930s-1970s. **Services:** Copying; library open to the public. **Publications:** Heritage (newsletter), quarterly.

★1951★
Stanford University
Hoover Institution on War, Revolution and Peace
Library
Stanford, CA 94305   Ph: (415)723-2058
                                             Fax: (415)723-1687
Charles G. Palm, Dp.Dir.

Founded: 1919. **Staff:** Prof 31; Other 62. **Subjects:** 20th century economic, political, and social problems with special emphasis on World Wars I and II and the following geographical areas: Africa, China, Eastern Europe, U.S.S.R., Japan, North and Latin America, Middle East, United States, Central and Western Europe. **Special Collections:** American Relief Administration records; military journals; international organizations; communist party materials; Paris Peace Conference records; propaganda and psychological warfare; underground movements. **Holdings:** 1.6 million volumes; 66,607 reels of microfilm; 60,777 microfiche; 4016 archival collections of national and international organizations, military government, political personnel; 1105 videotapes; 165,511 photographs; 4047 slides; 71,055 posters; pamphlets; government documents; newspaper and periodical file in Slavic, Western, and East Asian languages (38,770 titles). **Subscriptions:** 3756 journals and other serials; 404 newspapers. **Services:** Interlibrary loan; copying; library open to the public. **Automated Operations:** Computerized public access catalog and cataloging. **Computerized Information Services:** DIALOG Information Services, RLIN; Socrates (internal database); BITNET (electronic mail service). **Networks and Consortia:** Member of Research Libraries Information Network (RLIN). **Publications:** List of publications - available on request. **Special Catalogues:** The Library Catalogs of the Hoover Institution; surveys of area collections.

★1952★
State Community College
Senator Kenneth Hall Learning Resource Center
Special Collections
601 James R. Thompson Blvd.   Ph: (618)583-2566
East St. Louis, IL 62203   Fax: (618)583-2660
Dr. W.J. Van Grunsven, Dir.

Founded: 1969. **Staff:** Prof 3; Other 4. **Subjects:** African-Americans - general, history. **Holdings:** 31,250 books; 2305 reels of microfilm; bound periodical volumes. **Subscriptions:** 112 journals and other serials; 11 newspapers. **Services:** Interlibrary loan; copying; library open to the public for reference use only. **Computerized Information Services:** CD-ROM (InfoTrac). **Networks and Consortia:** Member of ILLINET.

★1953★
State Historical Society of Wisconsin
Library
816 State St.   Ph: (608)264-6534
Madison, WI 53706-1482   Fax: (608)264-6520
R. David Myers, Dir.

Founded: 1846. **Staff:** Prof 20; Other 13. **Subjects:** History - American, Canadian, Wisconsin, local, labor; radical/reform movements and groups in the U.S. and Canada; ethnic and minority groups in North America; genealogy; women's history; military history; religious history. **Special Collections:** African American History Collection (newspapers; periodicals); Native American History Collection (12,000 items; government documents; Native American publications); Women's Collection (pamphlets; periodicals; newspapers; publications of Phyllis Wheatley, Lydia Child, Harriet Jacobs, Jane Addams, Susan B. Anthony, Carrie Chapman Catt, Emma Goldman, etc.). **Holdings:** 1.5 million books and bound periodical volumes; 100,000 cubic feet of archives; 1.3 million microfiche and reels of microfilm. **Subscriptions:** 8500 periodicals; 500 newspapers. **Services:** Interlibrary loan; copying; library open to the public. **Automated Operations:** Computerized public access catalog. **Computerized Information Services:** OCLC; CD-ROMs; America: History & Life (internal database); electronic mail. **Networks and Consortia:** Member of Wisconsin Interlibrary Services (WILS), Center for Research Libraries (CRL). **Publications:** Native American Periodicals and Newspapers, 1828-1982; Wisconsin Public Documents (checklist of state government documents) - free upon request; bibliographies; guides. **Special Indexes:** Indian Culture and History (micoform); Index to Wisconsin Native American Periodicals, 1897-1981; Index to names in Wisconsin federal census, 1820-1870 and 1905 state census; Wisconsin necrology index; index of names in Wisconsin county histories.

★1954★
State University of New York
Syracuse Educational Opportunity Center
Paul Robeson Library
100 New St.   Ph: (315)472-0130
Syracuse, NY 13202   Fax: (315)472-1241
Florence Beer, Dir.

Founded: 1969. **Staff:** Prof 2. **Subjects:** Afro-Americans, job preparation, women, African fiction, business skills, minorities. **Special Collections:** Frazier Library of Afro-American Books (500 volumes); National Archives Collection of Afro-American Artists (23 trays of slides). **Holdings:** 11,000 books and bound periodical volumes; 40 VF drawers. **Subscriptions:** 139 journals and other serials; 20 newspapers. **Services:** Interlibrary loan; copying; library open to the public. **Networks and Consortia:** Member of Central New York Library Resources Council (CENTRO). **Publications:** Periodical Holdings, annual - for internal distribution only; New Acquisitions Listings, semiannual. **Special Catalogues:** Catalog to audiovisual collection.

★1955★
Staten Island Institute of Arts and Sciences
Archives and Library
75 Stuyvesant Place
Staten Island, NY 10301   Ph: (718)727-1135
John-Paul Richiuso, Archv./Hist.

Founded: 1881. **Staff:** Prof 2; Other 1. **Subjects:** Natural history, Staten Island history, archeology, black history, women's history, urban planning. **Special Collections:** Architecture; N.L. Britton; G.W. Curtis; J.P. Chapin; W.T. Davis (total of 1000 cubic feet); photographs and prints of old Staten Island; local black history; repository for U.S. Geological Survey publications; complete list of special collections available on request. **Holdings:** 12,000 books; 22,000 bound periodical volumes; 3000 maps; 1200 prints; 50,000 photographs; 1500 art museum and gallery catalogs; 1500 cubic feet of manuscripts, letters, and documents; 80 reels of microfilm of Staten Island newspapers. **Subscriptions:** 200 journals and other serials. **Services:** Copying; library open to the public by appointment. **Publications:** Proceedings, 2/year - by subscription and exchange; Guide to Special Collections, 16 volumes. **Special Indexes:** Guide to Institute Archives, 2 vol umes; indexes to newspapers, iconography of Staten Island, special collections (all on cards).

★1956★
Suffolk University
Mildred F. Sawyer Library
Collection of African-American Literature
8 Ashburton Pl.
Boston, MA 02108   Ph: (617)573-8532
E.G. Hamann, Dir.

Founded: 1937. **Staff:** Prof 6; Other 6. **Subjects:** African-American literature - bibliography, history, biography, literary criticism; New England African-American writers. **Holdings:** 5000 books; 200 bound periodical volumes. **Subscriptions:** 20 journals and other serials. **Services:** Interlibrary loan; copying; collection open to the public for reference use only. **Automated Operations:** Computerized cataloging and indexing. **Computerized Information Services:** BRS Information Technologies, ABI/INFORM, Academic Index. **Networks and Consortia:** Member of NELINET, Inc., Fenway Library Consortium (FLC). **Publications:** Black Writers in New England, a Bibliography, 1985 - for sale; Acquisitions List, annual - free upon request.

★1957★
Talladega College
Savery Library
Historical Collections
627 W. Battle St.   Ph: (205)362-0206
Talladega, AL 35160   Fax: (205)362-3870
Frances Baker Dates, Dir.

Founded: 1939. **Staff:** 6. **Subjects:** American blacks; missions in Angola, Mozambique, Zaire, and South Africa; the black church; civil rights; education. **Special Collections:** College archives (includes the activities of Talladega alumni); Historical Collections (the black church, African missions, southern Africa, civil rights, education). **Holdings:** 120 linear feet of archival items. **Subscriptions:** 4 journals

and other serials. **Services:** Interlibrary loan; copying; collections open to serious researchers and noncampus undergraduates with letter from supervising faculty. **Computerized Information Services:** NCS (internal database). **Publications:** A Guide to the Archives of Talladega College, 1981; A Guide to the Collections, 1981.

★1958★
Temple University
Charles L. Blockson Afro-American Historical
Collection
Sullivan Hall, 1st Fl.   Ph: (215)787-6632
Philadelphia, PA 19122   Fax: (215)787-5197
Charles L. Blockson, Cur.

Founded: 1983. **Staff:** Prof 1; Other 3. **Subjects:** Afro-American history, literature, and religion; African history; blacks in sports; Caribbean; sociology; education. **Special Collections:** History of blacks in Pennsylvania; underground railroad; John Mosley Photo Collection; Paul Robeson Collection; Bishop R.R. Wright, Jr. Collection. **Holdings:** 40,000 books; 169 bound periodical volumes; 20,000 other cataloged items. **Subscriptions:** 22 journals and other serials. **Services:** Copying; collection open to the public for reference use only. **Automated Operations:** Computerized cataloging and circulation. **Computerized Information Services:** RLIN. **Networks and Consortia:** Member of Association of Research Libraries (ARL). **Publications:** Afro-Americana: An Exhibition of Selected Books, Manuscripts & Prints, 1984; The Charles L. Blockson Afro-American Collection Newsletter, semiannual. **Special Catalogues:** Catalogue of the Charles L. Blockson Afro-American Collection, 1990.

★1959★
Tennessee (State) Human Rights Commission
Resource Library
Cornerstone Sq. Bldg., Ste. 400
530 Church St.
Nashville, TN 37243-0745   Ph: (615)741-5825

Staff: 1. **Subjects:** Race relations; discrimination in employment, housing, and public accommodations; legislation and decisions rendered in discrimination cases. **Holdings:** 75 books; 500 bound periodical volumes; commission-related materials. **Subscriptions:** 10 journals and other serials. **Services:** Library open to the public with restrictions. **Publications:** Annual Report.

★1960★
Tennessee State University
Lois H. Daniel Memorial Library
Special Collections
3500 John Merritt Blvd.   Ph: (615)320-3682
Nashville, TN 37209-1561   Fax: (615)320-3364
Mrs. Yildiz B. Binkley, Dir.

Founded: 1912. **Staff:** Prof 16; Other 23. **Special Collections:** Tennessee State University Archives (66.5 linear feet); Thomas Poag Manuscript Collection (1.54 linear feet); Daniel E. Owens Jazz Collection (1934 recordings); papers of prominent African-Americans; Herman McNeil LP Collection (560 LPs). **Holdings:** 358,515 books; 76,325 bound periodical volumes; 685,875 microfiche; 14,703 reels of microfilm. **Subscriptions:** 1752 journals and other serials; 23 newspapers. **Services:** Interlibrary loan; copying; library open to the public for reference use only. **Computerized Information Services:** DIALOG Information Services; CD-ROMs (PsycLIT, ABI/INFORM, Cinahl, AGRICOLA, CRIS, ERIC); InfoTrac; BITNET (electronic mail service). Performs searches. **Publications:** Bibliographies; staff and student handbooks; Library Newsletter, grants, book reviews.

★1961★
Texas Southern University
Library
Heartman Collection
3100 Cleburne St.   Ph: (713)527-7149
Houston, TX 77004   Fax: (713)639-1875
Dorothy H. Chapman, Libn.

Founded: 1948. **Staff:** Prof 2; Other 2. **Subjects:** Black culture and history, slavery. **Special Collections:** Barbara Jordan Archives (24 square feet); Texas Southern University Archives (12 square feet); Jazz Archives; Traditional African Art Gallery. **Holdings:** 35,000 books; 487 bound periodical volumes; 10,000 pamphlets; 66 VF drawers of clippings; 1 VF drawer of pictures; 1 VF drawer of sheet music. **Subscriptions:** 163 journals and other serials; 26 newspapers. **Services:** Interlibrary loan; copying; collection open to the public. **Automated Operations:** Computerized cataloging and acquisitions.

★1962★
Tri-County Technical College
Learning Resource Center
Box 587
Pendleton, SC 29670   Ph: (803)646-8361
Nancy C. Griese, Hd.Libn.

Founded: 1963. **Staff:** Prof 2; Other 6. **Subjects:** Industrial electronics, business administration, secretarial science, machine shop, marketing, management, radio and television broadcasting, electronics engineering, veterinary technology, textile management, quality assurance, automated manufacturing, computer technology, criminal justice, dental assisting, surgical technology, practical nursing, nursing, medical lab, heating, venilating, air conditioning, industrial mechanics. **Special Collections:** Black studies (300 items); Child Development (3000 items); Medical Lab Technicians (200 items). **Holdings:** 39,439 books; 4565 bound periodical volumes; 3868 AV programs. **Subscriptions:** 170 journals and other serials; 12 newspapers. **Services:** Interlibrary loan; copying; comprehensive audiovisual production services; center open to residents of Anderson, Oconee, and Pickens Counties, South Carolina. **Computerized Information Services:** OCLC. **Networks and Consortia:** Member of South Carolina Library Network. **Publications:** Quarterly and annual reports. **Special Catalogues:** Printed catalog of AV materials.

★1963★
Trinity College
Watkinson Library
300 Summit St.   Ph: (203)297-2268
Hartford, CT 06106   Fax: (203)297-2251
Dr. Jeffrey H. Kaimowitz, Cur.

Founded: 1857. **Staff:** Prof 5; Other 2. **Subjects:** Americana (especially 19th century), American Indians, black history, U.S. Civil War, British history and topography, folklore, witchcraft, graphic arts, history of printing, natural history, horology, philology (especially American Indian languages), early voyages and travels, maritime history. **Special Collections:** Incunabula and 16th century imprints (especially Trumbull-Prime Collection of illustrated books); private press books (especially Ashendene Press); English and American first editions (especially Frost, E.A. Robinson, Walter Scott); 18th and 19th century English and American periodicals; ornithology (6000 volumes); Barnard Collection of early American school books (7000 volumes); manuscripts of Charles Dudley Warner, Samuel Clemens (Mark Twain Memorial deposit collection), Frost, E.A. Robinson, Walter Scott, Henry Barnard, Ely Halperine-Kaminsky, Sibour, Nathan Allen, Watkinson family, Hartford families, and other historical and literary figures; American music (including jazz and blues and 18th and 19th century religious and secular works in printed and manuscript form; 1100 song sheets; 26,000 pieces of sheet music. **Holdings:** 165,000 books and bound periodical volumes; atlases; 500 maps; printed ephemera including 100 indexed scrapbooks, advertisements, fashion plates, music and theater programs, and valentines. **Subscriptions:** 40 journals and other serials. **Services:** Copying; library open to the public for reference use only. **Automated Operations:** Computerized cataloging. **Computerized Information Services:** OCLC. **Networks and Consortia:** Member of NELINET, Inc.. **Publications:** Bibliographies, irregular. **Special Catalogues:** Exhibition catalogs.

★1964★
Tuskegee University
Architecture Library
Willcox Bldg. A
Tuskegee, AL 36088   Ph: (205)727-8351
Linda K. Harvey, Hd.Libn.

Founded: 1964. **Staff:** Prof 1; Other 6. **Subjects:** Architecture, construction, science management, planning, historic preservation. **Special Collections:** Rare architectural book collection (520); African-American architects and architecture. **Holdings:** 8100 books; 525 bound periodical volumes; 89 theses; 22,678 slides; microfiche. **Subscriptions:** 125 journals and other serials. **Services:**

Interlibrary loan; copying; SDI; library open to the public for reference use only. **Computerized Information Services:** Access to DIALOG Information Services. Performs searches on fee basis. Contact Person: Edna L. Williams, 727-8892. **Networks and Consortia:** Member of SOLINET. **Special Catalogues:** Library's Periodical Holdings (book). **Special Indexes:** Index to African-American architects and architecture collection.

★1965★
Tuskegee University
Hollis Burke Frissell Library-Archives
Main Library   Ph: (205)727-8888
Tuskegee, AL 36088   Fax: (205)727-9282
Daniel T. Williams, Archv.

Staff: Prof 1; Other 1. **Subjects:** African-American history, Tuskegee University history, civil rights, oral history. **Special Collections:** Washington Collection; Tuskegee University archives; Booker T. Washington papers (155 containers); George W. Carver papers (159 containers). **Holdings:** 25,000 books; 625 bound periodical volumes; 101 cabinets of Tuskegee University clipping files. **Subscriptions:** 39 journals and other serials; 19 newspapers. **Services:** Interlibrary loan; library open to the public on a limited schedule. **Computerized Information Services:** OCLC. **Networks and Consortia:** Member of Network of Alabama Academic Libraries (NAAL), CCLC. **Publications:** A Guide to the Special Collection and Archives of Tuskegee University (1974).

★1966★
United Mortgage Bankers of America
Library
800 Ivy Hill Rd.
Philadelphia, PA 19150
                                                   Fax: (215)247-1580
Gene Hatton, Exec.Dir.

Founded: 1962. **Subjects:** Minority mortgage brokering and banking. **Holdings:** 2000 volumes. **Publications:** Newsletter, monthly.

★1967★
United Negro College Fund, Inc.
Department of Archives and History
500 E. 62nd St.
New York, NY 10021   Ph: (212)326-1285
Paula Williams, Asst.Archv.

Staff: Prof 2. **Subjects:** Higher education for blacks, history of philanthropy and fund raising. **Holdings:** 750 cubic feet. **Services:** Copying; department open to the public with restrictions. **Special Indexes:** United Negro College Fund Archives: A Guide and Index.

★1968★
U.S. Equal Employment Opportunity Commission
Library
1801 L St. NW, Rm. 6502   Ph: (202)663-4630
Washington, DC 20507   Fax: (202)663-4629
Susan D. Taylor, Lib.Dir.

Founded: 1964. **Staff:** Prof 2; Other 3. **Subjects:** Employment discrimination, minorities, women, aged, handicapped, testing, labor law, civil rights. **Special Collections:** Equal Employment Opportunity Commission Publications. **Holdings:** 25,000 books. **Subscriptions:** 300 journals and other serials; 8 newspapers. **Services:** Interlibrary loan; copying; SDI; library open to the public by appointment. **Computerized Information Services:** LEXIS, DIALOG Information Services, WESTLAW, LEGI-SLATE, OCLC. **Networks and Consortia:** Member of FEDLINK. **Publications:** Library service and selected bibliographies, brochure. **Also known as:** EEOC.

★1969★
U.S. National Park Service
Booker T. Washington National Monument
Library
Rte. 3, Box 310
Hardy, VA 24101   Ph: (703)721-2094
Richard Saunders, Chf.Interp. & Rsrcs.Mgt.

Subjects: Booker T. Washington, black history, local agriculture in the mid-19th century, Appalachian culture. **Special Collections:** Correspondence and documents relating to Burroughs plantation, birthplace of Booker T. Washington. **Holdings:** 600 books; photographs. **Services:** Interlibrary loan; copying (limited); library open to the public.

★1970★
U.S. National Park Service
Fort Davis National Historic Site
Library
Box 1456   Ph: (915)426-3224
Fort Davis, TX 79734   Fax: (915)426-3122
Jerry R. Yarbrough, Supt.

Founded: 1963. **Subjects:** Frontier military history. **Special Collections:** Colonel Benjamin H. Grierson Manuscript Collection (10,000 letters and documents, 1840-1920, on microfilm); Lt. Henry Flipper Collection; materials on "Buffalo Soldiers" (African-American regiments organized after the Civil War). **Holdings:** 2000 books; 100 pamphlets and magazines; 60 copies of frontier military maps; 10 manuscripts and theses; 185 reels of microfilm of records of Fort Davis. **Subscriptions:** 5 journals and other serials; 3 newspapers. **Services:** Library open to the public by appointment for reference use only.

★1971★
U.S. National Park Service
George Washington Carver National Monument
Library
Box 38   Ph: (417)325-4151
Diamond, MO 64840   Fax: (417)325-4231
Lisa Curtis, Pk.Ranger

Staff: Prof 1. **Subjects:** George Washington Carver, black history, national parks. **Special Collections:** Carver Collection (3019 archives and artifacts); original Carver letters (97 items). **Holdings:** 246 books; 130 documents and technical reports; 50 maps and charts; 1505 pictures and study prints; 16 VF drawers of park administrative records. **Subscriptions:** 14 journals and other serials. **Services:** Interlibrary loan; copying; library open to the public for historic research. **Publications:** Monumental News (newsletter), quarterly - free upon request. **Special Catalogues:** Carver Collection.

★1972★
U.S. National Park Service
Martin Luther King, Jr. National Historic Site
Library
522 Auburn Ave. NE   Ph: (404)331-3920
Atlanta, GA 30312   Fax: (404)331-1064
John Huth, Pk. Ranger

Subjects: Dr. Martin Luther King, Jr., Civil Rights Movement, black history, black Atlanta history, historic preservation. **Holdings:** 600 books, 200 audiocassettes; 40 videocassettes; vertical files; photographic files. **Subscriptions:** 13 journals and other serials; 4 newspapers. **Services:** Library open to the public by appointment.

★1973★
U.S. Navy
Naval Institute
Oral History Office
118 Maryland Ave.   Ph: (410)268-6110
Annapolis, MD 21402-5035   Fax: (410)269-7940
Paul Stillwell, Dir., Oral Hist.

Founded: 1969. **Staff:** Prof 3. **Subjects:** Naval biography, Coast Guard biography, naval aviation. **Special Collections:** Admiral Nimitz Collection; POLARIS interviews; WAVE interviews; early black naval officers. **Holdings:** 175 bound volumes containing 90,000 pages of transcripts; tapes of 215 individual memoirs. **Services:** Library open to researchers.

★1974★
University of Arkansas, Pine Bluff
John Brown Watson Memorial Library
N. University Blvd.
U.S. Hwy. 79
Pine Bluff, AR 71601   Ph: (501)541-6825
E.J. Fontenette, Libn.

Founded: 1938. **Staff:** 1. **Subjects:** History and biography, emigration, sociology, literature, slavery and emancipation, education, music, religion, economics. **Special Collections:** Afro-American Literature; Paul Laurence Dunbar papers (9 reels of microfilm). **Holdings:** 4615 books; 65 bound periodical volumes; 73 reels of microfilm of the Pittsburgh Courier; 4 recordings; 4 films; 18 overhead transparencies; periodicals on microfilm. **Subscriptions:** 41 journals and other serials; 10 newspapers. **Services:** Interlibrary loan; copying; library open to the public. **Computerized Information Services:** OCLC. **Networks and Consortia:** Member of AMIGOS Bibliographic Council, Inc..

★1975★
University of California, Los Angeles
Center for Afro-American Studies
Library
44 Haines Hall
405 Hilgard Ave.   Ph: (310)825-6060
Los Angeles, CA 90024-1545   Fax: (310)206-3421
Itibari Zulu, Lib.Hd.

Founded: 1969. **Staff:** Prof 1; Other 4. **Subjects:** Afro-American studies. **Special Collections:** African-American photograph collection (250 items). **Holdings:** 5265 volumes; 540 35mm slides; 283 photographs; 78 videotapes; 410 audiocassettes; 2350 pamphlets; 34 audio reels; 35 mongraphs. **Services:** Copying; library open to the public.

★1976★
University of California, Los Angeles
Department of Special Collections
University Research Library, Fl. A   Ph: (310)825-4879
Los Angeles, CA 90024-1575   Fax: (310)206-1864
David Zeidberg, Hd.Libn.

Founded: 1946. **Staff:** Prof 6; Other 16. **Subjects:** Californiana; motion pictures; radio; television; dance; blacks in entertainment and literature; Japanese in America; history of photography; folklore, including broadside ballads, songsters, hymnals, American almanacs; university archives; popular culture, including pulp magazines and comic books. **Special Collections:** Michael Sadleir Collection of 19th century English fiction; Ahmanson-Murphy Collections of Aldines and Early Italian Printing; Sir Maurice Holmes Collection of Captain Cook; English and American auction catalogs; early children's books; Bodoni imprints; Spinoza Collection; 1500 manuscript collections, including papers of William Starke Rosecrans, Franz Werfel, Henry Stevens, John Houseman, Ralph Bunche; oral history interviews; Near Eastern manuscripts (Arabic, Turkish, Persian, Armenian); books and manuscripts of Henry Miller, Norman Douglas, Aldous Huxley, Edward Gordon Craig, Gertrude Stein, Maria Edgeworth, Raymond Chandler. **Holdings:** 182,555 volumes; 19.7 million manuscripts; 632 volumes of newspapers; 238,409 pieces of ephemera and clippings; 46,730 pamphlets; 673,225 pictorial items; 2188 historical maps; 12,684 reels of microfilm; 205 sound recordings; 4719 slides; 3028 videotapes. **Subscriptions:** 339 journals and other serials. **Services:** Copying (limited); department open to the public for reference use only. **Automated Operations:** Computerized cataloging, acquisitions, serials, and circulation. **Computerized Information Services:** OCLC; ORION (internal database); InterNet (electronic mail service). Performs searches free of charge. **Publications:** Bibliographies of Henry Miller, Kenneth Rexroth, and Lawrence Durrell.

★1977★
University of California, Santa Barbara
Black Studies Library Unit
Santa Barbara, CA 93106   Ph: (805)893-2922
                                             Fax: (805)893-4676
Sylvia Y. Curtis, Black Studies Libn.

Founded: 1971. **Staff:** Prof 1; Other 1. **Subjects:** African-American studies, African area studies, Caribbean studies, Black literature and history. **Holdings:** 7000 books; 5 VF drawers of newspaper clippings; 5 VF drawers of pamphlets; 100 posters; catalogs from black colleges and universities. **Subscriptions:** 101 journals and other serials. **Services:** Interlibrary loan; SDI; library open to the public. **Automated Operations:** Computerized cataloging, acquisitions, serials, and circulation. **Computerized Information Services:** DIALOG Information Services, BRS Information Technologies, WILSONLINE; BITNET (electronic mail service). Performs searches on fee basis to members of the University of California community. **Publications:** New Acquisitions List & Announcements - to researchers, patrons, and on request.

★1978★
University of Florida
Center for Latin American and Tropical Art
Library
University Art Gallery
102 FAB   Ph: (904)392-0201
Gainesville, FL 32611   Fax: (904)392-3802
Karen Valdes, Dir.

Founded: 1965. **Staff:** 2. **Subjects:** Art - Latin American, African, Asian, Indian. **Holdings:** 100 catalogs. **Subscriptions:** 4 journals and other serials. **Services:** Interlibrary loan (limited); library not open to the public.

★1979★
University of Iowa
Iowa Urban Community Research Center
Reference Library
W170 Seashore Hall   Ph: (319)335-2525
Iowa City, IA 52242   Fax: (319)335-2509
Prof. Lyle W. Shannon, Dir.

Founded: 1958. **Staff:** 3. **Subjects:** U.S. Census, vital statistics and public health, population and demography, minority groups, juvenile delinquency and crime. **Special Collections:** Selected series of U.S. Census, 1910 to present. **Holdings:** 1000 books; 25 drawers of reprints, publications; punched cards and tapes on all studies conducted, 1958 to present. **Subscriptions:** 30 journals and other serials. **Services:** Library open to the public. **Publications:** Monograph series - for sale.

★1980★
University of Kansas
Kansas Collection
220 Spencer Research Library
Lawrence, KS 66045-2800
Sheryl K. Williams, Cur.   Ph: (913)864-4274

Founded: 1892. **Staff:** Prof 4; Other 3. **Subjects:** Kansas and Great Plains - social movements, business and economic history, social and cultural history, politics, travel; regional African-American history. **Special Collections:** Overland diaries; Kansas State documents depository; J.J. Pennell Collection of photographs and negatives, 1891-1923 (40,000 items); Wilcox Collection of Contemporary Political Movements, 1960 to present (6500 books; 6000 serials; 84,000 pieces of ephemera); Jules Bourquin Collection of photographs, 1898-1959 (30,000); J.B. Watkins Land Mortgage Company Records, 1864-1946 (627 linear feet); regional African-American history. **Holdings:** 107,744 volumes; 9416 linear feet of manuscripts; 1.4 million photographs; 81,866 glass negatives; 9399 sheets and volumes of maps; 4260 cartoons. **Subscriptions:** 1211 journals and other serials; 50 newspapers. **Services:** Interlibrary loan; copying; collection open to the public. **Automated Operations:** Computerized cataloging and serials. **Computerized Information Services:** OCLC; BITNET (electronic mail service). **Networks and Consortia:** Member of Bibliographical Center for Research, Rocky Mountain Region, Inc. (BCR), Kansas Library Network.

★1981★
University of Maine
Raymond H. Fogler Library
Special Collections Department
Orono, ME 04469   Ph: (207)581-1686
                                     Fax: (207)581-1653
Muriel Sanford, Spec.Coll.Libn.

Founded: 1970. **Staff:** Prof 1.5; Other 2. **Subjects:** State of Maine, maritime history. **Special Collections:** State of Maine Collection (16,000 volumes); Maine State Documents Collection (8500 titles);

University Collection (13,725 items); Clinton L. Cole Marine Library (4550 volumes); O'Brien Collection of American Negro History and Culture (1600 items); Philip H. Taylor Collection of Modern History, War, and Diplomacy (1200 volumes); Thoreau Fellowship Papers. **Holdings:** 35,000 books; 475 bound periodical volumes; 1700 archive boxes of manuscripts on Maine; 2500 maps of Maine; 5600 reels of microfilm. **Subscriptions:** 75 journals and other serials; 36 Maine newspapers. **Services:** Interlibrary loan; copying; library open to the public. **Automated Operations:** Computerized public access catalog, acquisitions, serials, and indexing. **Special Catalogues:** A Catalog of the Clinton L. Cole Collection (1972). **Special Indexes:** Maine Times Index; Down East Magazine Index; Maine Campus Index; Elderberry Times Index; Maine Fish and Wildlife Index (each in card or book form); Shaker Quarterly Index.

★1982★
University of Massachusetts
Library
Special Collections and Archives
Amherst, MA 01003   Ph: (413)545-2780
Linda Seidman, Act.Lib.Hd.

Founded: 1867. **Staff:** Prof 1; Other 2. **Subjects:** History of botany and entomology to 1900; historical geography and cartography of Northeastern United States to 1900; history of Massachusetts and New England; antislavery movement in New England; travel and tourism in New England, New York, and eastern Canada; Massachusetts; African-American studies; labor and business history. **Special Collections:** Alspach Yeats Collection (600 items); Federal Land Bank Collection (cartography, county maps and atlases; 270 items); Robert Francis Collection (100 items); Binet French Revolution Collection (1524 items); Massachusetts Pamphlet Collection (985 items); Benjamin Smith Lyman Collection (Japan; 2000 items); Papers of W.E.B. Du Bois, Horace Mann Bond, Erasmus Darwin Hudson, John Haigis, Maurice Donahue, Sol Barkin, J. William Belanger, Kenyon Butterfield, Harvey Swados, Robert Francis, Joseph Obrebski, William Smith Clark, Thomas Copeland; Records of American Writing Paper Co., Northampton Cutlery Co., George H. Gilbert Co., Rodney HuntCo., Granite Cutters International Association, Carpenters unions of Western Massachusetts, New England Joint Board of Textile Workers Union of America, American Dialect Society, University of Massachusetts. **Holdings:** 19,000 books; 7000 linear feet of records, manuscripts, clippings, photographs, maps, building plans, microfilm, audiotapes. **Services:** Copying; collections open to the public. **Computerized Information Services:** OCLC. **Networks and Consortia:** Member of NELINET, Inc., HILC, Inc..

★1983★
University of Minnesota
Special Collections and Rare Books Library
466 Wilson Library
309 19th Ave. S.   Ph: (612)624-3855
Minneapolis, MN 55455   Fax: (612)626-9353
Austin J. McLean, Cur.

Staff: Prof 2; Other 1. **Subjects:** History, literature, philosophy, astronomy, 17th century England and Holland, private press books, fortification, Scandinavian travel, art, Austrian history. **Special Collections:** Walter de la Mare; Henry Miller; John Galsworthy; Franklin Delano Roosevelt; Sinclair Lewis; John Steinbeck; Sherlock Holmes; Charles Dickens - Edwin Drood; modern Greek literature; Thomas Wolfe; World War I pamphlets (6000); black literature; Swedish Americana; Vincent Starrett; August Strindberg; photomechanics collection; ballooning; silent film scores. **Holdings:** 125,000 books and bound periodical volumes. **Subscriptions:** 20 journals and other serials. **Services:** Copying; library open to the public for reference use only. **Automated Operations:** Computerized public access catalog. **Computerized Information Services:** Interal database. **Networks and Consortia:** Member of Research Libraries Information Network (RLIN), MINITEX Library Information Network. **Publications:** Exhibit Catalogues. **Special Indexes:** Card indexes to places, dates, printers of books before 1700; card index to private press books by press, printer, designers; card indexes of provenance, manuscripts, signed bindings.

★1984★
University of Mississippi
Archives & Special Collections/Mississippiana
J.D. Williams Library
University, MS 38677   Ph: (601)232-7408
Dr. Thomas M. Verich, Univ.Archv.

Founded: 1975. **Staff:** Prof 1; Other 3. **Subjects:** Mississippi and Southern subjects and authors, Afro-American fiction. **Special Collections:** Lumber archives of lumber industry of southern Mississippi (268 linear feet); William Faulkner Collection (2000 volumes); Wynn Collection of Faulkner editions; Senator Pat Harrison Collection (51 linear feet including photographs); Arthur Palmer Hudson Folklore Collection (5 linear feet); David L. Cohn Collection (12 linear feet); Stark Young Collection (3.5 linear feet); Seymour Lawrence Publilshing Archive (35 linear feet); Revolutionary War Letters (1 linear foot); Rayburn Collection of Paper Americana (36 linear feet); Herschel Brickell Collection (4000 manuscript items; 3400 volumes; 150 linear feet); William Faulkner Rowan Oak Literary Manuscript Collection; literary papers of Ellen Douglas, Barry Hannah, and Beth Henley (33 linear feet); James Silver papers (20 linear feet); Aldrich Collection (10 linear feet); William R. Ferris Collection (350 linear feet). **Holdings:** 32,000 books; 3000 bound periodical volumes; 2000 manuscripts; 525 linear feet of University of Mississippi archival materials; 221 linear feet of Thomas G. Abernathy papers; 67 linear feet of Carroll Gartin papers, 1913-1966; 485 linear feet of John E. Rankin papers, 1882-1960; 164 linear feet of William M. Whittington papers, 1878-1962; 9.5 linear feet of Henry H. Bellamann papers, 1882-1945; 80 linear feet of James W. Garner papers. **Subscriptions:** 150 journals and other serials. **Services:** Copying; archives open to the public.

★1985★
University of Mississippi
John Davis Williams Library
Music Library/Blues Archive
Farley Hall   Ph: (601)232-7753
University, MS 38677   Fax: (601)232-7753

Founded: 1984. **Staff:** Prof 2; Other 1. **Subjects:** Music - blues, gospel, American traditional; folklore. **Special Collections:** Goldstein Folklore Collection (10,000 volumes; 5600 recordings); B.B. King Collection (9100 recordings); Living Blues Archival Collection (22 feet of archives; 20,000 recordings); Trumpet Record Company (10 feet of archives). **Holdings:** 12,000 books; 200 bound periodical volumes; 38,000 phonograph records; 39 feet of manuscripts and archives; 525 posters; 6.5 feet of photographs; 400 audiocassettes; 150 videocassettes; 2000 pamphlets; 175 feet of unbound periodicals. **Subscriptions:** 40 journals and other serials. **Services:** Copying; archive open to the public. **Automated Operations:** Computerized cataloging. **Computerized Information Services:** Public access catalog and circulation; OCLC. **Networks and Consortia:** Member of SOLINET. **Special Catalogues:** Finding aids to manuscript and archival collections.

★1986★
University of Pittsburgh
Afro-American Library
Hillman Library, First Floor   Ph: (412)648-7714
Pittsburgh, PA 15260   Fax: (412)648-1245
Pearl E. Woolridge

Founded: 1969. **Staff:** Prof 1; Other 1. **Subjects:** History, political science, literature, literary criticism, social sciences, culture and the arts, blacks in Western Pennsylvania. **Special Collections:** Atlanta University Black Culture Collection (microfilm); W.E.B. Dubois papers (microfilm); papers of the Congress of Racial Equality (microfilm); black history and landmarks in Western Pennsylvania (80 slides). **Holdings:** 16,936 volumes; 6 VF drawers of clippings and pamphlets. **Subscriptions:** 82 journals and other serials; 27 newspapers. **Services:** Interlibrary loan; library open to the public. **Automated Operations:** Computerized public access catalog, cataloging, acquisitions, serials, and circulation. **Networks and Consortia:** Member of Pittsburgh Regional Library Center (PRLC), Oakland Library Consortium.

★1987★
University of Rochester
Government Documents and Microtext Center
Rush Rhees Library   Ph: (716)275-4484
Rochester, NY 14627   Fax: (716)473-1906
Kathleen E. Wilkinson, Govt.Docs.Libn.

Founded: 1880. **Staff:** Prof 1; Other 3. **Subjects:** Documents - U.S. Congress, U.S. Bureau of the Census, New York State, women's studies, black studies, North American Indians, American and British literature. **Special Collections:** Goldsmiths'-Kress Collection (economic literature); slavery; papers of William Henry Seward and of the National Association for the Advancement of Colored People (NAACP); Early English Books; American Fiction; History of Women; Early British Periodicals. **Holdings:** 380 books; 428,000 uncataloged government documents in paper; 914,200 uncataloged government documents in microform; 2.4 million other microforms. **Subscriptions:** 10 journals and other serials. **Services:** Interlibrary loan; copying; center open to the public. **Computerized Information Services:** DIALOG Information Services, BRS Information Technologies.

★1988★
University of the District of Columbia
Georgia/Harvard Campus
Harvard Street Library
1100 Harvard St. NW
Washington, DC 20009   Ph: (202)673-7018
Melba Broome, Supv.

Staff: Prof 3; Other 1. **Subjects:** Education, human ecology. **Special Collections:** Trevor Arnett Library of Black Culture (8000 reels of microfilm); Miner-Wilson Collection (2000 rare books); legislative history of Federal City College. **Holdings:** 111,000 books; 10,000 bound periodical volumes; 150,000 microforms; archives. **Subscriptions:** 500 journals and other serials; 6 newspapers. **Services:** Interlibrary loan; copying; library open to the public with restrictions. **Networks and Consortia:** Member of Consortium of Universities of the Washington Metropolitan Area. **Special Catalogues:** Catalog of Miner-Wilson Collection; District of Columbia Teachers College Library (book catalog).

★1989★
University of the District of Columbia
Learning Resources Division
4200 Connecticut Ave. NW
MB 4102   Ph: (202)282-7536
Washington, DC 20008   Fax: (202)282-3102
Albert J. Casciero, Dir.

Staff: 68. **Special Collections:** Human Relations Area Files (microfiche); Atlanta University Black Culture Collection; Water Resources (625 items); University of D.C. archives (513 linear feet); slavery source materials (962 microfiche); Schombury Clipping File (9500 microfiche). **Holdings:** 507,472 books; 591,739 microfiche. **Subscriptions:** 2,583 journals and other serials; 25 newspapers. **Services:** Interlibrary loan; copying; SDI; division open to the public with restrictions. **Automated Operations:** Computerized cataloging and circulation. **Computerized Information Services:** DIALOG Information Services, OCLC. Performs searches on fee basis. Contact Person: Veronica Nance, 282-3091. **Networks and Consortia:** Member of CAPCON Library Network, Washington Research Library Consortium. **Publications:** Access brochures.

★1990★
University of Toledo
Ward M. Canaday Center
William S. Carlson Library   Ph: (419)537-4480
Toledo, OH 43606   Fax: (419)537-2726
Barbara L. Floyd, Act.Dir.

Staff: Prof 3; Other 2. **Subjects:** 20th century American poetry, Southern authors, and black American literature; university history; history of books and printing; Toledo glass industry. **Special Collections:** Ezra Pound Collection (400 volumes); William Faulkner Collection (500 volumes); Black American Poetry, 1920 to present (1000 volumes); William Dean Howells Collection (150 volumes); Herbert W. Martin Collection (15 feet); Etheridge Knight Collection (10 feet); Libbey-Owens-Ford Corporation archives (150 feet); Richard T. Gosser Collection (20 feet); Jean Gould Collection (11 feet); university archives (2000 feet); J.H. Leigh Hunt (100 volumes);

Scott Nearing (50 volumes); T.S. Eliot (200 volumes); William Carlos Williams (75 volumes); Marianne Moore (75 volumes); Broadside Press (200 items); Women's Social History, 1840-1920 (1200 volumes). **Holdings:** 25,000 books; 3000 linear feet of archives and manuscripts. **Services:** Copying; center open to the public. **Automated Operations:** Computerized public access catalog and cataloging. **Computerized Information Services:** BITNET (electronic mail service). **Publications:** Friends of the University of Toledo Libraries; exhibition catalogs. **Special Catalogues:** Catalog to special collections (card).

★1991★
Virginia State University
Johnston Memorial Library
Special Collections
1 Hayden St.
Box 9406
Petersburg, VA 23806   Ph: (804)524-5040
Catherine V. Bland, Act. Dean, Lib.Serv.

Founded: 1882. **Special Collections:** U.S. Government document depository; black studies; instructional materials; manuscripts. **Holdings:** Figures not available. **Services:** Interlibrary loan; copying; collections open to the public with restrictions. **Automated Operations:** Computerized cataloging. **Computerized Information Services:** DIALOG Information Services, OCLC. **Networks and Consortia:** Member of SOLINET.

★1992★
Virginia Union University
William J. Clark Library
Special Collections
1500 N. Lombardy St.   Ph: (804)257-5820
Richmond, VA 23220   Fax: (804)257-5818
Vonita W. Dandridge, Libn.

Founded: 1865. **Staff:** 9. **Subjects:** Social sciences, natural sciences, mathematics, education, psychology, business, and humanities. **Special Collections:** African-American materials, with emphasis on Richmond Black history; L.D. Wilder Collection. **Holdings:** 18,941 volumes. **Subscriptions:** 310 journals and other serials; 14 newspapers. **Services:** Interlibrary loan; copying; collections open to the public with special permit for reference use only. **Automated Operations:** Computerized cataloging, acquisitions, circulation, and serials. **Computerized Information Services:** Cooperative College Library Center (CCLC), OCLC. **Publications:** Library Newsletter.

★1993★
Wayne State University
Folklore Archive
448 Purdy Library   Ph: (313)577-4053
Detroit, MI 48202   Fax: (313)577-8618
Janet L. Langlois, Dir.

Founded: 1939. **Staff:** Prof 2; Other 2. **Subjects:** Oral, customary, and material culture of urban, occupational, and ethnic groups. **Special Collections:** Afro-American Folklore Collections; German and German-American Folklore Collections; Italian and Italian-American Folklore Collection; Greek and Greek-American Folklore Collections; Polish and Polish-American Folklore Collections; Armenian Collection; International Library of African Music (authentic tribal music); Ivan Walton Collection of Michigan Folklore (Great Lakes folk music); Michigan State University Collection of Folk Narrative; Southern Upland Folklife Oral Histories (Southern whites in Detroit); Greek American Families in Detroit (oral histories; 75 tapes); Great Lakes Lighthouse Keepers (oral histories; 26 tapes); Bruce L. Harkness Poletown Photographic Exhibit (urban ethnic neighborhood; 487 black/white photographs); Urban Legends: Video Anecdotes of Contemporary Folklore; Wayne State University Folklore Archive Studies Series; recitations and sayings; medical collection; college folksongs. **Holdings:** 200 books; 3000 manuscripts; 1000 audiotape recordings; 460 phonograph records; 350 slides; 5 videotapes. **Services:** Copying; archive open to the public. **Publications:** Triennial Report; annotated holdings lists; Holiday Pamphlet Series; Archive Study Series (1st volume: Italian Folktales in America, 1985).

★1994★
West Virginia (State) Library Commission
Film Services Department
Cultural Center
1900 Kanawha Blvd.,E.   Ph: (304)558-3976
Charleston, WV 25305   Fax: (304)558-2044
Steve Fesenmaier, Hd. Film Serv.

Founded: 1976. **Staff:** Prof 2; Other 3. **Special Collections:** Appalachia (250 films); astronomy (10 films); women (100 films); feature films (2000); Les Blank Collection (30 films); foreign feature films (300); black history and culture (200 films); independent animation (500 titles); 1992 Pickflik Video. **Holdings:** 5000 16mm sound films; 3000 videocassettes. **Subscriptions:** 12 journals and other serials. **Services:** Interlibrary loan (within state); department open to the public. **Publications:** WVLC Film Services Newsletter, quarterly - to WV public libraries; Pickflick Papers (online); Library Trustees Manual, 1989. **Special Catalogues:** Video Catalog, 1989. **Special Indexes:** Pickflick Papers III and supplements; filmographies on energy, women, Appalachia, features.

★1995★
Western Historical Manuscript Collection
Thomas Jefferson Library
University of Missouri, St. Louis
8001 Natural Bridge Rd.
St. Louis, MO 63121   Ph: (314)553-5143
Ann Morris, Assoc.Dir.

Founded: 1968. **Staff:** Prof 3; Other 2. **Subjects:** History - state and local, women's, Afro-American, ethnic, education, immigration; socialism; 19th century science; environment; peace; religion; Missouri politics; social reform and welfare; photography; journalism; business; labor. **Special Collections:** Socialist Party of Missouri records; Oral History Program (1000 tapes); Photograph Collection (200,000 images); League of Women Voters of Missouri; papers of Irving Dilliard, Dr. Thomas A. Dooley, Margaret Hickey, Leo Drey, Judge Noah Weinstein, Charles Guenther, Marlin Perkins, Ernest and Deverne Calloway, Theodore Lentz, Alberta Slavin, Rep. William Hungate, Rep. Robert Young, Rep. James Symington, Lt. Governor Harriet Woods, Paul Preisler, Joseph Pulitzer (copy), Virginia Irwin, and Kay Drey; Coalition for the Environment; Committee for Environmental Information; KETC-TV; Metropolitan Church Federation; Sierra Club - Ozark Chapter; Nuclear Weapons Freeze Campaign; Health and Welfare Council; Bureau for Men; Dismas House; St. Louis Labor Council; Family and Children's Service of Greater St. Louis; Regional Commerce and Growth Association; Missouri Public Interest Research Group; Ethical Society of St. Louis; YMCA and YWCA of St. Louis; Amalgamated Clothing and Textile Workers Union - Southwest Region. **Holdings:** 5500 linear feet of manuscripts, photographs, oral history tapes, and university archives. **Services:** Interlibrary loan (limited); copying of manuscripts and photographs; library open to the public with restricted circulation. **Publications:** Western Historical Manuscript Collection - St. Louis (1993 Guide). **Special Indexes:** Unpublished inventories to collections in repository.

★1996★
Western Historical Manuscript Collection
University of Missouri, Columbia
23 Ellis Library
Columbia, MO 65201   Ph: (314)882-6028
Nancy Lankford, Assoc.Dir.

Founded: 1943. **Staff:** Prof 13; Other 3. **Subjects:** History - Missouri, political, economic, agricultural, urban, labor, black, women's, frontier, religious, literary, social, science, steamboating, social reform and welfare, business. **Holdings:** 13,100 linear feet of manuscripts; 7300 reels of microfilm; 3725 audiotapes and audiocassettes; 700 phonograph records; 190 video materials. **Services:** Interlibrary loan; copying; collection open to the public. **Publications:** Guide to the Western Historical Manuscripts Collection, 1952; supplement, 1956; finding aids (index, shelf list, and chronological file).

★1997★
Western Interstate Commission for Higher Education
Library

Drawer P   Ph: (303)541-0285
Boulder, CO 80301   Fax: (303)541-0291
Eileen Conway, Cons.Dir.

Founded: 1955. **Staff:** Prof 1; Other 1. **Subjects:** Higher education, mental health and human services, nursing, minority education. **Holdings:** 7000 books and documents; 1000 volumes of unbound periodicals; 2000 documents on microfiche. **Subscriptions:** 280 journals and other serials; 10 newspapers. **Services:** Interlibrary loan; copying; SDI; library open to the public. **Automated Operations:** Computerized public access catalog, serials, and circulation. **Computerized Information Services:** DIALOG Information Services. Performs searches on fee basis. **Publications:** Acquisitions List, monthly - for internal distribution only.

★1998★
Western Reserve Historical Society
Library

10825 E. Blvd.   Ph: (216)721-5722
Cleveland, OH 44106   Fax: (216)721-0645
Kermit J. Pike, Dir.

Founded: 1867. **Staff:** Prof 7; Other 7. **Subjects:** Ohio history, American genealogy, Civil War, slavery and abolitionism, ethnic history, African Americans. **Special Collections:** Wallace H. Cathcart Shaker Collection; William P. Palmer Civil War Collection; David Z. Norton Napoleon Collection. **Holdings:** 235,950 books; 25,506 volumes of newspapers; 50,300 pamphlets; 6 million manuscripts; 32,500 reels of microfilm. **Subscriptions:** 325 journals and other serials; 50 newspapers. **Services:** Interlibrary loan; copying; library open to the public. **Networks and Consortia:** Member of OHIONET. **Special Catalogues:** Catalogs to manuscript, genealogy, and Shaker collections (all on cards).

★1999★
Wilberforce University
Rembert Stokes Learning Center
Archives and Special Collections

Wilberforce, OH 45384-1003   Ph: (513)376-2911
Jean Mulhern, Lib.Dir.

Staff: Prof 2; Other 3. **Subjects:** African Methodist Episcopal (A.M.E.) Church history; books by and about blacks, 19th century; history of Wilberforce University. **Special Collections:** A.M.E. Church conference minutes; papers of Bishop Reverdy Cassius Ransom, university president W.S. Scarborough, and Wilberforce professor Milton S.J. Wright. **Holdings:** 2000 books; 20 reels of microfilm; 10,000 uncataloged items. **Services:** Copying; collections open to the public by appointment. **Computerized Information Services:** DIALOG Information Services. **Networks and Consortia:** Member of Southwestern Ohio Council for Higher Education (SOCHE). **Publications:** Printed guides to some parts of collection.

★2000★
Xavier University of Louisiana
Library Archives and Special Collections Department

7325 Palmetto St   Ph: (504)483-7304
New Orleans, LA 70125-1098   Fax: (504)488-3320
Robert E. Skinner, Univ.Libn.

Founded: 1937. **Staff:** Prof 10; Other 13. **Special Collections:** African-American History and Culture (1000 volumes; 50 linear feet of manuscripts); Southern Culture and Literature (1000 volumes; 25 linear feet of manuscripts); Southern Catholica and Religion (200 volumes; 15 linear feet of manuscripts). **Services:** Interlibrary loan; copying; SDI; library open to the public. **Automated Operations:** Computerized cataloging (VTLS). **Computerized Information Services:** DIALOG Information Services, NASA/RECON. Performs searches. Contact Person: Laura D. Turner, Hd., Pub.Serv.Div. **Networks and Consortia:** Member of AMIGOS Bibliographic Council, Inc.. **Publications:** African-American and Other Historic Serials Held in the Xavier University Archives; pathfinders; information brochures; Xavier Library News, monthly.

(5) Museums and Other Cultural Organizations

Alabama

★2001★
George Washington Carver Museum
PO Drawer 10
Tuskegee Institute, AL 36087   Ph: (205)727-6390
Willie C. Madison, Superintendent and CEO

★2002★
Macon County Fine Arts Manifesto
104 Frazier St.
Tuskegee, AL 36083   Ph: (205)727-3029
Barbara Danner, President
Remarks: Provides workshops in dance, drama, and the visual arts.

★2003★
Tuskegee Institute National Historic Site
1212 Old Montgomery Rd.
PO Drawer 10
Tuskegee Institute, AL 36088   Ph: (205)727-6390
Willie C. Madison, Superintendent
/REM Collections include items pertaining to Dr. George Washington Carver and Booker T. Washington.

Arizona

★2004★
Black Theater Troupe
333 E. Portland St.
Phoenix, AZ 85004   Ph: (602)258-8128
Brenda Williams, Managing Director
Remarks: Presents four to five productions a year. Conducts workshops and an eight week workshop/touring program in the summer.

California

★2005★
Africa House
3463 State St.
Santa Barbara, CA 93105   Ph: (805)565-1314
Magnolia Raine, Pres.

★2006★
African American Drama Company of California
195 Ney St.
San Francisco, CA 94112   Ph: (415)333-2232
Phillip Walker, Director
Remarks: Touring company specializing in Black history.

★2007★
African American Historical and Cultural Society
Fort Mason Center Bldg. C, Rm. 165
San Francisco, CA 94123   Ph: (415)441-0640
Julian Haile, Director
Remarks: Interested in the role of the African American in art and history. Houses a museum and gallery.

★2008★
Afro American Cultural Center
2560 W. 54th St.
Los Angeles, CA 90043   Ph: (213)299-6124
Dr. Karenga, Director

★2009★
Black Filmmakers Hall of Fame, Inc.
447 15th St., Ste. 200
Oakland, CA 94612   Ph: (510)465-0804
Mary P. Smith, Executive Director
Remarks: A media arts organization whose primary purpose is to recognize, honor, and support the achievements of Blacks in cinema.

★2010★
Black Repertory Group
3201 Adeline St.
Berkeley, CA 94703   Ph: (510)652-2120
Nora Vaughn, Executive Director
Remarks: Presents five productions a year by Black playwrights and presents a series of one-act plays by local writers. Conducts workshops in acting, dance, and creative writing.

★2011★
Brockman for the Cultural Arts
3401 W. 43rd St.
Los Angeles, CA 90008   Ph: (213)294-5201
Dale Davis, Contact
Remarks: Formerly known as Brockman Gallery.

★2012★
California Afro-American Museum
600 State Dr., Exposition Park
Los Angeles, CA 90037   Ph: (213)744-7432
Rick Moss, Director
Remarks: Exhibitions include items relating to Afro-American heritage.

★2013★
Center for African-American History
5606 San Pablo Ave.
Oakland, CA 94608   Ph: (510)658-3158
Lawrence Crouchett, Director
Remarks: Researches national and international Black history. Collections include books, pictures, documents, and artifacts.

★2014★
Dunbar Hotel Cultural and Historical Museum
4225 S. Central Ave.
Los Angeles, CA 90011   Ph: (213)462-3475
Bernard Johnson, Dir.

★2015★
Ebony Museum of Art
30 Alice St.
Jack London Village, Sts. 208 & 209
Oakland, CA 94607   Ph: (510)763-0141
Aissatoui Vernita, Executive Director
Remarks: Black oriented exhibitions.

★2016★
Harambee Dance Ensemble
3026 57th Ave.
Oakland, CA 94605   Ph: (510)532-8558
Remarks: Performs African dance and music from the west coast of Africa, the Caribbean, and the United States.

★2017★
Museum of African American Art
4005 Crenshaw Blvd., 3rd Fl.
Los Angeles, CA 90008   Ph: (213)294-7071
Remarks: Exhibits art of Africans and African decendants. Collections include: traditional sculpture from Southeast, West and East Africa; paintings, prints, and sculptures of contemporary American artists; and Harlem Renaissance art.

★2018★
Oakland Ensemble Theater
1428 Alice St., Ste. 306
Oakland, CA 94612   Ph: (510)763-7774
Sharon Walton, Producing Director
Remarks: Explores contemporary American life through the sensibilities, idiom, and world-view of Black Americans.

Colorado

★2019★
Black American West Museum and Heritage Center
3091 California St.
Denver, CO 80207   Ph: (303)292-2566
Geraldine Stepps, Gen. Mgr.
Remarks: Collections include items relating to Black culture.

★2020★
EDEN Theatrical Workshop
1570 Gilpin St.
Denver, CO 80218   Ph: (303)321-2320
Lucy M. Walker, President
Remarks: Provides funds in support of visual, performing, and literary arts projects with an emphasis on Black culture.

Connecticut

★2021★
Connecticut Afro-American Historical Society
444 Orchard St.
New Haven, CT 06511   Ph: (203)776-4907
Khalid Lum, President
Remarks: Museum exhibits reflect the Afro-American cultural experience.

Delaware

★2022★
Afro-American Historical Society of Delaware
512 E. 4th St.
Wilmington, DE 19801   Ph: (302)984-1421
Harmon R. Carey, President

District of Columbia

★2023★
African Cultural Foundation
731 Rock Creek Church Rd., N.W.
Washington, DC 20010   Ph: (202)882-2232

★2024★
African Heritage Center for African Dance and Music
4018 Minnesota Ave., N.E.
Washington, DC 20019   Ph: (202)399-5252
Melvin Deal, Founding Director
Remarks: Serves as a multicultural center for instruction and training in traditional West African dance, music, and dramatic ritualistic forms. Receives traveling artists from abroad for workships and exchange. Maintains art gallery and a collection of traditional African musical instruments.

★2025★
Anacostia Museum
1901 Fort Pl. SE
Washington, DC 20020   Ph: (202)287-3306
Steven Cameron Newsome, Director
Remarks: Explores American history in relation to the Afro-American experience and culture.

★2026★
Andrew Cacho African Drummers and Dancers
PO Box 15282
Washington, DC 20003-0282   Ph: (202)889-0350
Andrew Cacho, Director
Remarks: Teaches African dance and drumming aimed primarily at youth.

★2027★
Bethune Museum-Archives
1318 Vermont Ave. NW
Washington, DC 20005   Ph: (202)332-1233
Tracye McQuirter, Site Managerrector
Remarks: Offers permanent and changing exhibitions and preserves the records of Black women and their organizations. Interested in promoting the role of Black women in America through educational programs.

★2028★
Black Film Institute
University of the District of Columbia
Carnegie Bldg.
800 Mt. Vernon Pl. NW, Rm. 210
Washington, DC 20001　　　　　　　Ph: (202)727-2396
Dr. Anthony Gittens, Director
Remarks: Exhibition and discussion forum on Blacks and the Third World. Shows films and presents lectures on campus and at community sites, prisons, schools, and senior centers.

★2029★
**Carter G. Woodson Center/Association for Afro-
　American Life and History**
1407 14th St. NW
Washington, DC 20005　　　　　　　Ph: (202)667-2822
Karen McRae, Executive Director
Remarks: Promotes study of Black history.

★2030★
Evans-Tibbs Collection
1910 Vermont Ave., NW
Washington, DC 20001　　　　　　　Ph: (202)234-8164
Thurlow E. Tibbs Jr., Director

★2031★
Frederick Douglass National Historic Site
1411 W St. SE
Washington, DC 20020　　　　　　　Ph: (202)426-5961
Carnell Poole, Site Manager
Remarks: Furnishings, documents, and personal items of Frederick Douglass.

★2032★
Howard University Gallery of Art
2455 6th St., NW
Washington, DC 20059　　　　　　　Ph: (202)806-7070
Tritobia H. Benjamin, Director
Remarks: Collections include Afro-American paintings, sculpture, and graphic art.

★2033★
**Howard University Museum
Moorland-Springarn Research Center**
500 Howard Pl. NW
Washington, DC 20059　　　　　　　Ph: (202)806-7239
Thomas C. Battle, Director
Remarks: Black history museum. Exhibits African artifacts and historic documents pertaining to the Black experience in America.

★2034★
National Museum of African Art - Smithsonian Institute
950 Independence Ave., SW
Washington, DC 20560　　　　　　　Ph: (202)357-4600
Sylvia H. Williams, Director
Remarks: Collections include film footage on African art and culture, wood metal, ceramic, ivory, and fiber objects of African art.

★2035★
Pin Points Traveling Theater
4353 Dubois Pl., SE
Washington, DC 20019　　　　　　　Ph: (202)582-0002
Ersky Freeman Jr., President
Remarks: Uses academic subjects such as biology, history, and math and puts them into theatrical formats that "edu-tain." The play "1001 Black Inventions" illustrates the lives of Black inventors.

★2036★
Sign of the Times Cultural Art Center
605 56th St., NE
Washington, DC 20019　　　　　　　Ph: (202)399-3400
James Griggs, Director
Remarks: :Provides art and drama education to at-risk minority youth in the Washington, DC, area.

──────────── **Florida** ────────────

★2037★
African American Caribbean Cultural Center
1601 S. Andrews Ave.
Ft. Lauderdale, FL 33316　　　　　　Ph: (305)467-4056
Aina Olomo, Director
Remarks: Formerly known as Afro-American Cultural Center.

★2038★
Appleton Museum of Art/The Appleton Cultural Center
4333 E. Silver Springs Blvd.
Ocala, FL 34470　　　　　　　　　　Ph: (904)236-5050
Sandra Talarico, Director
Remarks: Collections include African arts.

★2039★
Black Archives Research Center and Museum
c/o Florida A & M University
Tallahassee, FL 32307　　　　　　　Ph: (904)599-3020
James N. Eaton, Executive Director
Remarks: Collections include documents and other items relating to the Afro-Americann experience.

★2040★
Black Heritage Museum
PO Box 570327
Miami, FL 33257-0327　　　　　　　Ph: (305)252-3535
Priscilla G. Stephens Kruize, President
Remarks: Contains artifacts of Black heritage, including tribal artifacts from Africa and New Guinea, and Black Americana.

★2041★
Gallery Antiqua
5130 Biscayne Blvd.
Miami, FL 33137　　　　　　　　　　Ph: (305)759-5355
Caleb A. Davis, Director
Remarks: Displays Black and African art.

★2042★
Museum of African-American Art
1308 Marion St.
Tampa, FL 33602　　　　　　　　　　Ph: (813)272-2466
Deirdre Bibby, Director
Remarks: Collections include works of African-American artists from the 1800s to present.

──────────── **Georgia** ────────────

★2043★
Apex Museum
135 Auburn Ave. NE　　　　　　　　Ph: (404)521-2739
Atlanta, GA 30303　　　　　　　　　Fax: (404)521-3086
Bethany J. Campbell, Director
Remarks: Collection includes West African artifacts, and a permanent African-American art collection which includes pieces by nationally renowned artists.

★2044★
Atlanta African Film Society
PO Box 50319
Atlanta, GA 30302   Ph: (404)525-1136

★2045★
Harriet Tubman Historical and Cultural Museum
340 Walnut St.
Macon, GA 31208   Ph: (912)743-8544
Dorothy Hardman, Dir.

★2046★
Herndon Home
587 University Pl. NW
Atlanta, GA 30314   Ph: (404)581-9813
Carole Merritt, Director
Remarks: Home of slave-born Alonzo Herndon, who founded the Atlanta Life Insurance Company. The home contains various artifacts and furnishings.

★2047★
Jomandi Productions
1444 Mayson St., NE
Atlanta, GA 30324   Ph: (404)876-6346
Thomas W. Jones II, Co-Artistic Director
Remarks: Presents four productions a year on universal themes viewed from the Black perspective.

★2048★
Just Us Theater Company
PO Box 42271
Atlanta, GA 30311   Ph: (404)753-2399
Zaron W. Burnett Jr., Executive Producer
Remarks: Presents and tours works by Black dramatists. Supports new works fpr the Black theatre.

★2049★
Martin Luther King, Jr. Center
449 Auburn Ave., NE
Atlanta, GA 30312   Ph: (404)524-1956
Coretta Scott King, President
Remarks: Collections include furnishings and personal belongings of Dr. King, manuscript collection, and artwork commemorating Dr. King.

★2050★
Martin Luther King, Jr. National Historic Site and Preservation District
522 Auburn Ave., NE
Atlanta, GA 30312   Ph: (404)331-5190
Troy Lissimore, Superintendent
Remarks: Neighborhood of Dr. Martin Luther King, Jr.; includes birthplace, childhood home, church, and gravesite. Research is carried out on the Civil Rights Movement and Black history.

★2051★
Ruth Hall Hodges Art Gallery
Morris Brown College
643 Martin Luther King Jr., Dr. SW
Atlanta, GA 30314   Ph: (404)525-7831
Dr. Lee A. Ransaw, Chairperson

─────────── **Illinois** ───────────

★2052★
African-American Arts Alliance of Chicago
1805 E. 71st St.
Chicago, IL 60649   Ph: (312)288-5100
Remarks: Consortium of art groups and individuals. Publishes a newsletter, provides technical assistance, and sponsors performances.

★2053★
Ancient Egyptian Museum
3849 S. Michigan Ave.
Chicago, IL 60653   Ph: (312)268-3700
Jerry Parker, Exec. Dir.
Remarks: Displays artifacts, paintings, and other works of art depicting the culture of the ancient Egyptians.

★2054★
Center for Black Music Research
Columbia College
600 S. Michigan Ave.
Chicago, IL 60605-1996   Ph: (312)663-1600
Dr. Samuel Floyd, Director
Remarks: Maintains archives on the history of all forms of black music, from the era of slavery, to the present.

★2055★
Chicago City Theater Company/Joel Hall Dancers
1225 W. School
Chicago, IL 60613   Ph: (312)880-1002
Joel Hall, Co-Director
Remarks: Multi-racial, ethnic dance and theater companies featuring jazz and contemporary styles. Features new works by Black choreographers.

★2056★
Downstate Afro-American Hall of Fame—Museum
309 S. DuSable
Peoria, IL 61605   Ph: (309)673-2206
Andre Bohannon, President

★2057★
DuSable Museum of African-American History
740 E. 56th Pl.
Chicago, IL 60637   Ph: (312)947-0600
Dr. Gwendolyn Robinson, Director
Remarks: Collections include African and Afro-American art, sculpture, photographs, and books.

★2058★
Malcolm X College
1900 W. Van Buren St.
Chicago, IL 60612   Ph: (312)942-3000
Zerrie Campbell, President
Remarks: Houses African cultural artifacts.

★2059★
Southside Community Art Center
3831 S. Michigan Ave.
Chicago, IL 60653   Ph: (312)373-1028
Gerald Sanders, Managing Dir.

─────────── **Indiana** ───────────

★2060★
Madame Walker Urban Life Center
617 Indiana Ave.
Indianapolis, IN 46202   Ph: (317)236-2099
Josephine Weathers-Rogers, Director
Remarks: Now a historic landmark, originally this structure housed Madame Walker's cosmetic company.

Iowa

★2061★
Gateway Dance Theater
1225 Stephenson Way
Des Moines, IA 50314   Ph: (515)282-8696
Lee Furgerson, Director
Remarks: A Black dance group that presents performances and workshops.

Kansas

★2062★
First National Black Historical Society of Kansas
PO Box 2695
Wichita, KS 67201   Ph: (316)262-7651
Ruby Parker, Director
Remarks: Exhibits include African and historical artifacts, doll collection, and paintings by John Allen. Also offers traveling exhibitions.

Louisiana

★2063★
Alliance for Community Theaters
PO Box 50575
New Orleans, LA 70150   Ph: (504)595-8411
Deborah Smith
Remarks: Acts as a support organization for local Black theater programs.

Maryland

★2064★
Baltimore's Black American Museum
1765 Carswell St.
Baltimore, MD 21218   Ph: (410)243-9600
Frank Richardson, Director

★2065★
Banneker-Douglass Museum
84 Franklin St.
Annapolis, MD 21401   Ph: (410)974-2893
Dr. Ronald Sharps, Director
Remarks: Exhibits art dealing with the Black experience in America.

★2066★
Eubie Blake National Museum
409 N. Charles St.
Baltimore, MD 21201   Ph: (301)396-3181
Norman E. Ross, Coordinator

★2067★
Great Blacks in Wax Museum
1601 E. North Ave.
Baltimore, MD 21213   Ph: (410)563-3404
Joanne Martin, Director

★2068★
Lillie Carroll Jackson Museum, Inc.
Civil Rights Museum
1320 Eutaw Pl.
Baltimore, MD 21217   Ph: (301)523-1634
Gail Mitchell, Dir.

★2069★
Maryland Museum of African Art
5430 Vantage Point Rd.
PO Box 1105
Columbia, MD 21044   Ph: (410)730-7105
Claude M. Ligon, Director
Remarks: Exhibits traditional African art, including sculpture, textiles, masks, jewelry, musical instruments, and household items.

★2070★
Morgan State University Gallery of Art
Morgan State University
Carl Murphy Fine Arts Center
Hillen & Coldspring Ln.
Baltimore, MD 21239   Ph: (410)444-3030
James Lewis, Dir.

★2071★
Orchard Street Cultural Museum
24 S. Abington Ave.
Baltimore, MD 21229   Ph: (410)669-3100
Marguerite Campbell, Dir.

Massachusetts

★2072★
African-American Museum and Cultural Center of Western Massachusetts
PO Box 4033
Springfield, MA 01101   Ph: (413)737-9209

★2073★
Harriet Tubman Gallery and Resource Center
United SouthEnd Settlement
566 Columbus Ave.
Boston, MA 02118   Ph: (617)536-8610
Guadulesa, Director
Remarks: Exhibits items relating to Afro-American history during Harriet Tubman's lifetime.

★2074★
Museum of Afro-American History
46 Joy St.
Boston, MA 02114   Ph: (617)742-1854
Leona Martin, Exexutive Director
Remarks: A charitable nonprofit institution established "to locate, collect, conserve, preserve, and secure for exhibition and research, historical material pertaining to the life, thought, material culture, and heritage of Afro-Americans in New England." The majority of the collection pertains to 19th and 20th century history. Maintains library of films and filmstrips on Afro-American history. Provides guided tours of a 19th century black neighborhood 9the Black Heritage Trail and a 20th century Black community (Roxbury Heritage Trail).

★2075★
Museum of the National Center for Afro-American Artists
300 Walnut Ave.
Boston, MA 02119   Ph: (617)442-8014
Barry Gaither, Director and Curator
Remarks: Collections include paintings, prints, and graphics of Afro-American artists.

★2076★
National Center for Afro-American Artists
122 Elm Hill Ave.
Dorchester, MA 02121   Ph: (617)442-8820
Edmond B. Gaither
Remarks: Multi-disciplinary cultural institution committed to the celebration of global African-American heritage. Offers museum specializing in contemporary African-American artists.

★2077★
Parting Ways; The Museum of Afro-American
   Ethnohistory
130 Court St., Rear
Plymouth, MA 02361   Ph: (617)746-6028
Diane Haynes, Executive Director
Remarks: Black history collections include documents and photographs of an early Black family in the Plymouth area, underground railroad collection, and a manuscript collection.

★2078★
Wendell Street Gallery
17 Wendell St.
Cambridge, MA 02138   Ph: (617)864-9294
Constance Brown, Director
Remarks: Features the work of distinguished African-American artists.

──────────── Michigan ────────────

★2079★
Afrikan American Studio Theater Co.
PO Box 05339
Detroit, MI 48205   Ph: (313)885-5222
James Reed-Faulkner
Remarks: Offers performances exploring the concerns of the area's black community.

★2080★
Black Theatre Network
PO Box 11502
Fisher Bldg. Sta.
Detroit, MI 48211
Addell Austin Anderson, President

★2081★
Detroit Black Arts Alliance
13217 Livernois
Detroit, MI 48238-3162   Ph: (313)931-3427
David Rambeau, Director
Remarks: A coalition of independent Black art organizations.

★2082★
Detroit Historical Museum
African-American Businesses in Detroit Exhibit
5401 Woodward
Detroit, MI 48202   Ph: (313)833-1805
Vicki Kruckeberg, Chief Curator
Remarks: Exhibit of historical artifacts and memorabilia from early Black businesses in Detroit.

★2083★
Graystone International Jazz Museum
1521 Broadway
Detroit, MI 48226   Ph: (313)963-3813
James T. Jenkins, President

★2084★
Harmonie Park Playhouse and Actors Lab
230 E. Grand River, 5th Fl.
Detroit, MI 48226   Ph: (313)965-2480
Maggie Porter, Founder/Executive Director
Remarks: Offers studio workshops for a professional interracial acting ensemble. Minority playwrights are highlighted, although all works are considered.

★2085★
Henry Ford Museum and Greenfield Village
African-American Family Life and Culture Center
20900 Oakwood Blvd.
PO Box 1970
Dearborn, MI 48121-1970   Ph: (313)271-1620
Harold Skramstad, Director
Remarks: Features a memorial to George Washington Carver, two brick slave houses, recordings from the 1930s of former slaves describing their lives, and a house owned by a free Black family during the slavery era.

★2086★
Historic Fort Wayne
6325 W. Jefferson
Detroit, MI 48207   Ph: (313)297-9360
Remarks: An 83-acre former military post which includes the National Museum of the Tuskegee Airmen.

★2087★
McCree Theater and Performing Arts Center
115 E. Pierson Rd.
Flint, MI 48505   Ph: (313)232-1665
Charles Winfrey, Executive Director
Remarks: Conducts workshops in the arts serving the area's African-American community.

★2088★
Michigan Ethnic Heritage Center
60 Farnsworth
Detroit, MI 48202   Ph: (313)832-7400
Germaine Strobel, Director
Remarks: Conducts series of briefings, training, and community outreach programs dealing with ethnic issues.

★2089★
Michigan Opera Theater
6519 2nd Ave.
Detroit, MI 48202   Ph: (313)874-7850
David Di-Chiera, General Director
Remarks: Offers a Black outreach program for schools, audiences, and teachers. Program explores the Black Heritage in Western music.

★2090★
Motown Museum Historical Foundation
2648 W. Grand Blvd.
Detroit, MI 48208   Ph: (313)867-0991
Dr. Rowena Stewart
Remarks: Exhibits include photographs of African-American recording artists and other Motown memorabilia.

★2091★
Museum of African American History
301 Frederick Douglass St.
Detroit, MI 48202   Ph: (313)833-9800
James Wyatt, Deputy Director
Remarks: Dedicated to preserving, documenting, interpreting, and exhibiting the cultural heritage of African-Americans and their ancestors. Serves as a learning and resource center; collects and documents contributions of Black people. Offers permanent and traveling exhibits. Conducts workshops, seminars, and lecture series. Maintains reference library containing books, films and audiotapes of African world history, art, and culture.

★2092★
Project BAIT
13217 Livernois
Detroit, MI 48238-3162   Ph: (313)931-3427
David Rambeau, Director
Remarks: Black media production and training organization.

★2093★
TABS Center
2226 S. Westnedge Ave.
Kalamazoo, MI 49008   Ph: (616)342-1382
Leandre Jones Ph.D., President and Director
Remarks: Presents four theater and TV programs for community organizations. Goal is to build morale and encourage talent in the Black community.

★2094★
Your Heritage House
110 E. Ferry
Detroit, MI 48202   Ph: (313)871-1667
Josephine H. Love, Director
Remarks: Exhibits a Black heritage collection.

---------------- **Minnesota** ----------------

★2095★
Gospel Workshop of America
3029 3rd Ave., S.
Minneapolis, MN 55408   Ph: (612)823-8706
K. L. Robinson, Chapter Representative
Remarks: Presents five major gospel concerts a year highlighting mostly Black gospel composers. A division of the Gospel Music Workshop of America.

★2096★
Pillsbury House
3501 Chicago Ave., S.
Minneapolis, MN 55407   Ph: (612)824-0708
Helen McElroy-Freese, Director
Remarks: Provides art programming for predominately Black neighborhoods.

★2097★
Whittier Writers' Workshop
PO Box 1042
Minneapolis, MN 55440   Ph: (612)822-1914
Carolyn Holbrook-Montgomery, Director
Remarks: Offers specialized programming for Black American writers in the Minneapolis-St. Paul area.

---------------- **Mississippi** ----------------

★2098★
Black Arts Music Society
PO Box 3214
Jackson, MS 39207   Ph: (601)354-1049
John Reese, President
Remarks: Books jazz concerts featuring top regional artists.

★2099★
Smith Robertson Museum and Cultural Services Center
528 Bloom St.
PO Box 3259
Jackson, MS 39207   Ph: (601)960-1457
David Taylor, Director
Remarks: Collections include artwork with Afro-American themes and artwork of Black artists.

---------------- **Missouri** ----------------

★2100★
Black Archives of Mid-America
2033 Vine St.
Kansas City, MO 64108   Ph: (816)483-1300
Ruby Jackson, Director
Remarks: Collections include Black art, paintings, and sculptures.

★2101★
Black Repertory Company
634 N. Grand, 10th Fl., Ste. F
St. Louis, MO 63103   Ph: (314)534-3807
Rons Hines, Director
Remarks: Offers theater and dance performances. Sponsors acting and dance classes and tours.

★2102★
Charlie Parker Memorial Foundation
Academy of the Arts
4605 The Paseo
Kansas City, MO 64110   Ph: (816)924-2200
Eddie Baker, Executive Director
Remarks: Preserves jazz heritage through studies, performances, and workshops by internationally recognized artists. Offers youth study programs.

★2103★
St. Louis Science Center
5050 Oakland Ave.
St. Louis, MO 63110   Ph: (314)289-4400
Dwight S. Crandell, Executive Director
Remarks: Collections include ethinic miniatures.

★2104★
Vaughn Cultural Center
525 N. Grand
St. Louis, MO 63103   Ph: (314)535-9227
Almetta Jordan, Director
Remarks: Cultural arts center providing performances, art, and literature featuring African-Americans.

---------------- **Nebraska** ----------------

★2105★
Emmy Gifford Children's Theater
3504 Center St.
Omaha, NE 68105   Ph: (402)345-4849
Mark Hoeger, Executive Director
Remarks: Presents original productions by Black performers and playwrights. Sponsors a theater school and institute.

★2106★
Great Plains Black Museum
2213 Lake St.
Omaha, NE 68110   Ph: (402)345-2212
Bertha Calloway, Executive Director
Remarks: Founded by the Negro Historical Society. Contains gallery rooms and offers special ehibits, lectures, tours, and resource material.

New Jersey

★2107★
African Art Museum of the S.M.A. Fathers
23 Bliss Ave.
Tenafly, NJ 07670   Ph: (201)567-0450
Dr. Richard Barrows S.M.A

Remarks: Explores the transition of African art to the Americas. Exhibits sculpture, masks, textiles, household utensils, musical instruments, and other items from more than 40 West African groups.

★2108★
Afro-American Historical Society Museum
1841 Kennedy Blvd.
Jersey City, NJ 07305   Ph: (201)547-5262
Theodore Brunson, President

Remarks: Displays 1800-present, New Jersey African American history, civil rights posters, African musical instruments, and other artifacts. Formerly known as Afro-American Historical & Cultural Society of Jersey City, Inc.

★2109★
Afro-One Dance, Drama, and Drum Theater
Park Plaza Mall, Rt. 130 S.
Willingboro Plaza
Willingboro, NJ 08046   Ph: (609)871-8340
Patricia Reid-Bookhart, Founder and Artistic Director

Remarks: Presents performances depicting the Black experience in America featuring dancers, drummers, and poets.

★2110★
Carter G. Woodson Foundation
69 Lincoln Park
Newark, NJ 07101   Ph: (201)242-0500
Jean Wesley, President

★2111★
Crossroads Theater Company
7 Livingston Ave.
New Brunswick, NJ 08901   Ph: (908)249-5581
Ricardo Khan, Artistic Director

Remarks: A professional Black company that produces mainstage productions and co-productions with TV and New York theater.

★2112★
Merabash Museum
Museum for Education and Research in
  American Black Art, Science and History
PO Box 752
Willingboro, NJ 08046   Ph: (609)877-3177
Mark Henderson Jr., Executive Director

★2113★
Newark Museum
43-49 Washington St.
Newark, NJ 07101   Ph: (201)596-6550
Samuel C. Miller, Director

Remarks: Exhibits an ethnology collection. Also sponsors the Newark Black Film Festival comprised of films by Black filmakers and films about the history and culture of Black people.

New York

★2114★
African-American Cultural and Arts Network
2090 Adam Clayton Powell, Jr. Blvd.
New York, NY 10027   Ph: (212)749-4408

★2115★
African-American Cultural Center - Buffalo
350 Masten Ave.
Buffalo, NY 14209   Ph: (716)884-2013
Agnes Bain, Director

Remarks: Exhibits items pertaining to Afro-American history and art.

★2116★
African-American Institute
833 United Nations Plaza
New York, NY 10017   Ph: (212)949-5666
Vivian Derryck, President

Remarks: Displays loan exhibitions of traditional and contemporary Africans arts and crafts. Museum also houses an African affairs library.

★2117★
African American Museum of Nassau County
110 N. Franklin St.
Hempstead, NY 11550   Ph: (516)485-0470
Willy Houston, Acting Dir.

Remarks: Exhibits and programs reflect the history and culture of Afro-Americans in the Long Island area.

★2118★
Afrikan Poetry Theater
176-03 Jamaica Ave.
Jamaica, NY 11432   Ph: (718)523-3312
John Watusi Branch, Executive Director

Remarks: A predominantly Black, multicultural center which offers poetry readings and workshops, musical and cultural performances, lecturers, educational programs, and a children's workshop.

★2119★
Afro-American Cultural Foundation
180 Sheridan Ave.
Mt. Vernon, NY 10552   Ph: (914)665-0784
Charles Smith, Director

Remarks: Sponsors lectures and seminars. Operates library of 500 volumes on history, literature, and sociology. Maintains a museum of Black hostory in honor of Black businesswoman Madam C.J. Walker (1967-1919) and a mobile exhibit on the Black history of Westchester County, New York.

★2120★
Artists Doing Business Worldwide
874 Brooklyn Ave.
Brooklyn, NY 11206   Ph: (718)693-1274
Al Browne, Director

Remarks: Offers entertainment skills of talented Black performing artists.

★2121★
Aunt Len's Doll and Toy Museum
6 Hamilton Terr.
New York, NY 10031   Ph: (212)281-4143
Lenon H. Hoyte, Director

Remarks: Collection of national and international dolls.

★2122★
**Bedford-Stuyvesant Restoration Center for Arts and
  Culture**
1368 Fulton, Ste. 4G
Brooklyn, NY 11218   Ph: (718)636-7791
Ted Gunn, President

Remarks: Offers special cultural events, community programs, workshops, and outreach activities which delve into the American Black-African experience. Exhibitions held on a continual basis.

★2123★
Billie Holiday Theater
1368 Fulton St.
Brooklyn, NY 11216   Ph: (718)636-0919
Marjorie Moon, Executive Director
Remarks: Produces a 40-week season of original work by Black Playwrights. Presents a Little Folk series of performances for children, workshops, and a college internship program.

★2124★
Black Arts Research Center
30 Marion St.
Nyack, NY 10960   Ph: (914)358-2089
John Gray, Dir.
Remarks: An archival resource center dedicated to the documentation, preservation, and dissemination of the African cultural legacy.

★2125★
Black Experience Ensemble
5 Homestead Ave.
Albany, NY 12203   Ph: (518)457-5651
Mars Hill, Executive Director
Remarks: Conducts drama and dance workshops 12-30 weeks per year and produces 1-3 plays per year.

★2126★
Black Experimental Theater
47 McKeever Pl. 6H
Brooklyn, NY 11225   Ph: (718)735-4290
Van Fisher, President/Artistic Director
Remarks: Presents theater productions using community members. Performs plays and musicals dealing with Caribbean and Black American culture.

★2127★
Black Fashion Museum
157 W. 126 St.
New York, NY 10027   Ph: (212)666-1320
Lois K. Alexander, Founder-Director
Remarks: Presents two exhibitions per year of costumes and other fashion memorabilia designed, made, or worn by Blacks in the U.S.

★2128★
Black Filmmaker Foundation
Tribeca Film Center
375 Greenwich St.
New York, NY 10013   Ph: (212)941-3944
Andre Robinson, Executive Director
Remarks: Media arts center established to support the independently produced work of Black media artists. Programs and services include production, distribution, exhibition, programming, newsletter, and membership screenings.

★2129★
Black Spectrum Theater Co.
Roy Wilkins Park of Southern Queens
119th Ave. & Merrick Blvd.
Jamaica, NY 11434   Ph: (718)723-1800
Carl Clay, Executive Director
Remarks: Presents works that are socially significant to the Black community. Company performs four to five productions per year. Conducts acting and technical theater classes and produces original films.

★2130★
Boys Choir of Harlem
127 W. 127th St.
New York, NY 10027   Ph: (212)749-1717
Walter J. Turnbull, Founder and Executive Director
Remarks: A touring choir of boys, ranging in ages from nine to nineteen. Choristers study voice and piano with a program of counseling and academic tutoring.

★2131★
Charles Moore Dance Theater
1043 President St.
Brooklyn, NY 11225   Ph: (718)467-7127
Pam Mitchell, Manager
Remarks: Performs African, Caribbean, and other Black related dance in concert in New York. Researches dance and dance styles from the past and operates a school for dance in New York.

★2132★
The Cinque Gallery
560 Broadway, Ste. 504
New York, NY 10012   Ph: (212)966-3464
Ruth Jett, Director
Remarks: Exhibits the works of Afro-American artists.

★2133★
Community Folk Art Gallery
2223 E. Genessee St.
Syracuse, NY 13210   Ph: (315)424-8487
Herbert Williams, Director

★2134★
Dance Theater of Harlem
215 E. 94th St.
New York, NY 10128   Ph: (212)690-2800
Charmaine Jefferson, Executive Director
Remarks: A ballet company which performs an annual New York Season and tours nationally and internationally. Operates a school of classical ballet for children three years and older.

★2135★
Frederick Douglass Creative Arts Center
270 W. 96th St.
New York, NY 10025   Ph: (212)864-3375
Fred Hudson, President
Remarks: Holds writing workshops. Features Off-Broadway Equity Showcases and the Black Roots Festival of Poetry and Music.

★2136★
Genesis II Museum of International Black Culture
509 Cathedral Pwy.
New York, NY 10025   Ph: (212)666-7222
Andi Owens, Director

★2137★
Grinnell Gallery
800 Riverside Dr., Studio 5E
New York, NY 10032   Ph: (212)927-7941
Ademola Olugebesola, Co-Director
Remarks: Displays original African, African-American, and Caribbean works of art.

★2138★
Harlem Cultural Council
215 W. 125 St., Ste. 400A
New York, NY 10027   Ph: (212)316-6277
Jeane Faulkner, Director
Remarks: Sponsors a Dancemobile, Black filmmaking projects, and poetry festivals. Offers technical assistance in securing grants to artists and arts organizations.

★2139★
Harlem Institute of Fashion
157 W. 126th St.
New York, NY 10027   Ph: (212)666-1320
Lois K. Alexander, Founder-Director
Remarks: Offers courses in dressmaking, millinery, tailoring, and related fashion courses. Conducts workshops with an emphasis on the above subjects, as well as reading, math, ethnic studies, and computer technology as it relates to fashion.

★2140★
Harlem School of the Arts
645 St. Nicholas Ave.
New York, NY 10030   Ph: (212)926-4100
Betty Allen, Executive Director
Remarks: Exposes children to the arts and offers professional arts training. Provides classical arts education (music, dance, drama, and visual arts) primarily to minority youngsters.

★2141★
Hatch-Billops Collection
491 Broadway
New York, NY 10012   Ph: (212)966-3231
Camille Billops, Director
Remarks: Concerned with the collection and preservation of historical and contemporary articles relating to the cultural experiences of Afro-Americans.

★2142★
Henry Street Settlement's Art Center
466 Grand St.
New York, NY 10002   Ph: (212)598-0400
Daniel Kronenfeld
Remarks: Presents six predominatly Black and four Ethnic Heritage productions each season. Offers workshops in Black theater for adults and drama classes for children. Formerly known as Henry Street Settlement Arts for Living Center.

★2143★
International Agency for Minority Artists Affairs
147 W. 42nd St., Ste. 603
New York, NY 10036   Ph: (212)873-5040
Gregory Javan Mills, Chairman/CEO
Remarks: Provides technical and arts managerial training to Black artists. Sponsors a year-round Black Film Festival.

★2144★
Langston Hughes Institute
25 High St.
Buffalo, NY 14203   Ph: (716)881-3266
Ora Lee Lewis-Delgado, Director
Remarks: Houses the Kush Museum which contains Arfican artifacts.

★2145★
Museum for African Art
593 Broadway
New York, NY 10012   Ph: (212)966-1313
Carol Braide, Contact
Remarks: Exhibits include historic art originating in Africa.

★2146★
National Black Theater Institute
2033 5th Ave.
New York, NY 10035   Ph: (212)722-3800
Barbara Ann Teer, Executive Producer
Remarks: Organizes workshops in acting and creative development in the theater. Tours in the East. Operates a children's school and develops children's plays.

★2147★
National Black Touring Circuit
417 Convent Ave.
New York, NY 10031   Ph: (212)283-0974
Woodie King, Producer
Remarks: Produces Black theater and film. Co-produces and assists other organizations with touring projects.

★2148★
Negro Ensemble Co., Inc.
155 W. 46 St., 5th Fl.
New York, NY 10036   Ph: (212)575-5860
Douglas Turner Ward, Director
Remarks: Black professional theater company that produces new plays based on the Black experience. Sponsors playwrighters' workshops to foster the development of new plays.

★2149★
New Muse Community Museum of Brooklyn
1530 Bedford Ave.
Brooklyn, NY 11216   Ph: (718)774-2900
Remarks: Permanent exibitions, traveling exhibits, numerous workshops, and classes in music, dance, and the arts. Special events in the cultural center are dedicated to the Black experience in America.

★2150★
Schomburg Center for Research in Black Culture
135th St. & Malcolm X Blvd.
New York, NY 10037   Ph: (212)491-2202
Howard Dodson, Chief
Remarks: Collections include literature on Afro-Americans and African life, paintings, sculpture, photographs, and historical artifacts.

★2151★
Society for the Preservation of Weeksville and Bedford-Stuyvesant History
PO Box 130120, St. John's Sta.
Brooklyn, NY 11213-0002   Ph: (718)756-5250
Joan Maynard, Executive Director
Remarks: Working to develop a neighborhood museum of African-American history at a New York City national register site. Films and slide-lecture presentation available.

★2152★
Storefront Museum
48 Alder Dr.
Mastic Beach, NY 11951   Ph: (516)281-7585
Tom Lloyd, Exec. Dir.

★2153★
Studio Museum in Harlem
144 W. 125th St.
New York, NY 10027   Ph: (212)864-4500
Kinshasha H. Conwill, Executive Director
Remarks: Presents exhibitions featuring black artists, conducts research in black art, publishes exhibition catalogues, schedules tours, workshops, lectures, symposia, seminars, and concerts.

★2154★
Wayne County Minority Performing Arts Series
PO Box 181
Alton, NY 14413   Ph: (315)483-4092
Gloria Battle, President
Remarks: Plans a series of arts events representing Black-American and Haitian cultures.

★2155★
Westchester African-American Historical Society
1126 Howard St.
Peekskill, NY 10566
Kay Amory-Mosier, Pres.

──────────── North Carolina ────────────

★2156★
Afro-American Cultural Center
401 N. Myers St.
Spirit Square
Charlotte, NC 28202   Ph: (704)374-1565
Wanda Montgomery, Interim Director
Remarks: Preserves, promotes, and presents Afro-American culture and history. Provides multicultural, multiethnic, and multifaceted programming.

★2157★
Black Artists' Guild
100 Adkin St.
PO Box 2162
Kinston, NC 28501   Ph: (919)523-0003
Milton R. Pollock, Executive Director
Remarks: Seeks to alleviate problems concerning Black artists and to preserve Afro-American heritage.

★2158★
Harambee Arts Festival
Lenoir Recreation Department
PO Box 958
c/o Viewmont Community Center
Lenoir, NC 28645   Ph: (704)754-3278
Dwight Perkins, Center Director
Remarks: Promotes a greater awareness of Black culture through the performing arts, art exhibits, and crafts.

★2159★
Mattye Reed African Heritage Center
North Carolina A & T State University
Greensboro, NC 27411   Ph: (919)379-7874
Frank Eguaroje, Curator
Remarks: Collections include arts and crafts from over 31 African nations, New Guinea and Haiti; manuscript collections.

★2160★
North Carolina Black Repertory Company
610 Coliseum Dr.
Winston-Salem, NC 27106   Ph: (919)723-7907
Larry Leon Hamlin, Artistic Director
Remarks: Produces four mainstage and two second stage productions per year. Offers a four-year acting training program and a children's Acting for Television Commercials Workshop.

★2161★
North Carolina Central University Art Museum
North Carolina Central University
PO Box 19555
Durham, NC 27707   Ph: (919)560-6211
Norman E. Pendergraft, Director
Remarks: Exhibits contemporary Afro-American art. Collection includes work of R.S. Duncanson, Henry Tanner, and Elizabeth Catlett.

★2162★
Somerset Place State Historic Site
Rt. 1, Box 337
Creswell, NC 27928   Ph: (919)797-4560
Dorothy Redford, Curator
Remarks: Collections include plantation slave records. Conducts research on Afro-American history.

★2163★
Young Men's Institute Cultural Center
PO Box 7301
Asheville, NC 28802   Ph: (704)252-4614
Wanda Henry-Coleman, Director
Remarks: Seeks to enhance the cultural lives of the minority population of Asheville.

──────────── Ohio ────────────

★2164★
African American Museum
1765 Crawford Rd.
Cleveland, OH 44106   Ph: (216)791-1700
Joyce Morrow-Jones, Director
Remarks: Persons in the Cleveland area who are interested in building a national Afro-American history museum in that city. Goals are: to promote genealogical research; to study the Afro-American and minority race achievements and contributions; to bring about a harmonious relationship between the races through better understanding. Furnishes speakers for school and civic organizations; holds history classes and workshops. Maintains library of 1200 volumes and Alexander E. Pushkin exhibit.

★2165★
Afro-American Cultural and Historical Society Museum
1765 Crawford Rd.
Cleveland, OH 44106   Ph: (216)791-1700
Joyce Morrow-Jones, Director
Remarks: Promotes genealogical research and studies Afro-American and minority race relations. Also furnishes speakers for school and civic organizations and holds history classes and workshops.

★2166★
Afro-American Cultural Center
Cleveland State University
Black Studies Program
2121 Euclid Ave., UC 103
Cleveland, OH 44115   Ph: (216)687-3655
Dr. Howard Mims, Director

★2167★
Afro American Music Hall of Fame and Museum
1870 Goleta
Youngstown, OH 44504   Ph: (216)783-9922
Frank Halssacre, Director
Remarks: Exhibits items relating to the lives of Black usicians and composers.

★2168★
Art for Community Expressions
1937 Clay Court
Columbus, OH 43205   Ph: (614)252-3036
Kojo Kamau, Executive Director
Remarks: Sponsors art exhibitions featuring Afro-American artists. Offers two annual projects.

★2169★
Arts Consortium
1515 Linn St.
Cincinnati, OH 45214   Ph: (513)381-0645
Ernest O. Britton, Executive Director
Remarks: Brings the arts to some of Cincinnati's minority neighborhoods through a museum/art gallery featuring minority artists, and providing education activities in art, dance, and theatre. Formerly known as Resident Art and Humanities Consortium.

★2170★
Cincinnati Art Museum
Eden Park
Cincinnati, OH 45202   Ph: (513)721-5204
Millard F. Rogers Jr., Director
Remarks: Exhibits primitive art of Africa.

★2171★
Dunbar House State Memorial
PO Box 1872
Dayton, OH 45401   Ph: (513)224-7061
LaVerne Sci, Director
Remarks: Last home of Paul Lawrence Dunbar, the first African-American widely accepted in literary circles. On display are artifacts including clothing and furniture.

★2172★
Harriet Tubman Museum and Cultural Association
PO Box 20178
Cleveland, OH 44120-0178   Ph: (216)663-1115
Hanif Wahab, Dir./Curator

★2173★
Karamu House
2355 E. 89th St.
Cleveland, OH 44106   Ph: (216)795-7070
Margaret Ford Taylor, Director
Remarks: Black theater featuring a resident acting company, classes, and a music series focusing on Black artists. Provides workshops and gallery spaces.

★2174★
National Afro-American Museum and Cultural Center
1350 Brush Row Rd.
PO Box 578
Wilberforce, OH 45384   Ph: (513)376-4944
Dr. John E. Fleming, Director
Remarks: Separately incorporated, nonprofit organization affiliated with the Ohio Historical Society, operating under a state and general board. Studies the role of Afro-American in America through preservation and conservation of Afro-American culture. Collections include manuscripts and rare books on Black history and culture and art and historical objects.

★2175★
National Conference of Artists
PO Box 1287 MCS
Dayton, OH 45402   Ph: (513)278-6793
Michael L. Sampson, President
Remarks: Goals include the promotion, production, and encouragement of Black visual artists working in diverse media. Sponsors exhibits of African-American visual artists. Offers free public workshops, seminars, and artist demonstrations.

★2176★
Watkins Academy Museum of Cultural Arts
724 Mineola Ave.
Akron, OH 44320   Ph: (216)864-0673
James Watkins, Director

Oklahoma

★2177★
Kirkpatrick Center Museum Complex
2100 NE 52nd
Oklahoma City, OK 73111   Ph: (405)427-5461
William T. Bowden, Director
Remarks: Exhibits Arican art and sponsors ethnic festivals.

★2178★
NTU Art Association
2100 NE 52nd St.
Oklahoma City, OK 73111   Ph: (405)424-7760
Sylvia Lewis, President
Remarks: Offers an educational program, sponsors receptions with community organizations, provides tour guides, sponsors seminars for teachers, and presents special exhibitions and programs.

★2179★
Sanamu African Art Museum
2100 NE 52nd St.
Oklahoma City, OK 73111   Ph: (405)424-7760
Mary Ann Haliburton, Dir.

★2180★
Theater North
PO Box 6255
Tulsa, OK 74148   Ph: (918)587-8937
Maybelle Wallace, Director
Remarks: Black community theater producing dramatic presentations, gospel, and jazz concerts. Screens films with an emphasis on Black culture.

Pennsylvania

★2181★
African Cultural Art Forum
237 S. 60 St.
Philadelphia, PA 19139   Ph: (215)476-0680
Rashid Samad
Remarks: Interested in promoting Black artists and their work.

★2182★
Afro-American Historical and Cultural Museum
701 Arch St.
Philadelphia, PA 19106   Ph: (215)574-0380
Nannette Acker-Clark, Acting Director
Remarks: Conducts research on Black history in Pennsylvania 1660-1976. Collections include prints and sculptures, African sculpture and artifacts, and artifacts pertaining to the American Revolution and slave trade.

★2183★
Minority Arts Resource Council
1421 W. Girard Ave.
Philadelphia, PA 19130   Ph: (215)236-2688
Curtis E. Brown, Executive Director
Remarks: Consortium or Black and Hispanic professional arts groups. Sponsors performances and exhibitions throughout the Delaware Valley.

★2184★
New Freedom Theater
1346 N. Broad St.
Philadelphia, PA 19121   Ph: (215)765-2793
Walter Dallas, Director
Remarks: Produces repertory and new plays. Offers classes in drama and dance, and produces plays using young actors.

Rhode Island

★2185★
Rhode Island Black Heritage Society
46 Aborn St.
Providence, RI 02903   Ph: (401)751-3490
Linda Deishinni, Director
Remarks: Exhibits documents, photographs, and an art collection pertaining to the Afro-American in Rhode island; organizes touring exibitions, lecture series, and arts workshops.

South Carolina

★2186★
Avery Research Center for Afro-American History and Culture
College of Charleston
125 Bull St.
Charleston, SC 29424   Ph: (803)727-2009
Harriet Cochran, Interim Director
Remarks: Collections include materials, manuscripts, and artifacts illustrating the history and culture of the Afro-American in South Carolina.

★2187★
I.P. Stanback Museum and Planetarium
South Carolina State University
Orangeburg, SC 29117   Ph: (803)536-7174
Dr. Leo F. Twiggs, Executive Director
Remarks: Exhibits include contemporary African and Afro-American art including 300-400 photographs, Harlem On My Mind Exhibit, and over 60 pieces from Cameroon and parts of Western Africa.

★2188★
Mann-Simons Cottage: Museum of African-American Culture
1403 Richland St.
Columbia, SC 29201   Ph: (803)252-1450
Pat Middleton, Coordinator
Remarks: An historic house museum which is also operated as a cultural center for the preservation of African-American culture.

★2189★
Old Slave Mart Museum
PO Box 459
Sullivans Island, SC 29482   Ph: (803)883-8900
Judith Wragg Chase, Educational Dir.

★2190★
Oyotunji African Village
PO Box 51
Sheldon, SC 29941   Ph: (803)846-8900
Oseijeman Adefunmi, Dir.

★2191★
Pendleton Foundation for Black History and Culture
116 W. Queen St.
Pendleton, SC 29670   Ph: (803)646-3792
Annie Ruth Webb-Morse, Dir.

Tennessee

★2192★
Beck Cultural Exchange Center
1927 Dandridge Ave.
Knoxville, TN 37915   Ph: (615)524-8461
Robert J. Booker, Executive Director
Remarks: Explores local Black history. Collections include Black weekly newspapers, books, and artwork by local artists.

★2193★
Blues City Cultural Center
415 S. Main St.
Memphis, TN 38103   Ph: (901)525-3031
Deborah Glass-Frazier, Founder/General Manager
Remarks: Exhibits and produces original and historic works related to the Southern Black experience.

★2194★
Institute for African Affairs
Tennessee State University
PO Box 828
Nashville, TN 37209   Ph: (615)320-3035
Dr. Levi Jones, Director
Remarks: Disseminates information about African nations, including lifestyles, religious values, and culture.

★2195★
Memphis Black Arts Alliance
PO Box 40854
Memphis, TN 38174-0854   Ph: (901)274-8134
Martin A. Wakefield, Executive Director
Remarks: Houses a gallery, theater/dance studio, classrooms, and offices. Also provides literary and screenwriting workshops, a slide registry, directory, and administrative services.

★2196★
National Civil Rights Museum
450 Mulberry St.
Memphis, TN 38103   Ph: (901)521-9699
Juanita Moore, Exec. Dir.
Remarks: Exhibits include recreations of turbulent events during the Civil Rights Movement.

★2197★
The University Galleries
Fisk University
D.B. Todd Blvd. & Jackson St. N.   Ph: (615)329-8543
Nashville, TN 37208   Fax: (615)329-8715
Dr. Henry Ponder, CEO & Pres.
Remarks: Collections include African-American paintings, sculpture, graphics, and photography.

Texas

★2198★
Black Art Gallery
5408 Almeda Rd.
Houston, TX 77004   Ph: (713)529-7900
Robert Lee, President

★2199★
Black Arts Alliance
1157 Navasota St.
Austin, TX 78702   Ph: (512)477-9660
Michelle Bocknite, Director
Remarks: Arts organization serving both artists and communities in Texas with a visual and performing arts registry, multi-arts performances, workshops, and exhibitions of Texas artists.

★2200★
Black Texan Cultural Museum and Hall of Fame
920 E. 11th St.
Austin, TX 78702   Ph: (512)472-5731

★2201★
Community Music Center of Houston
5613 Almeda
Houston, TX 77004   Ph: (713)523-9710
Anne Lundy, Executive Director
Remarks: Conducts research on Afro-American music and seeks to educate the community through performances of Afro-American music.

★2202★
George Washington Carver Museum and Cultural Center
1165 Angelina St.
Austin, TX 78702   Ph: (512)472-4809
Bernadette M. Phifer, Director

Remarks: Collections include manuscripts, maps, books, and photographs documenting the history of Blacks.

★2203★
Museum of African-American Life and Culture
PO Box 150153
Dallas, TX 75315-0153   Ph: (214)565-9026
Dr. Harry Robinson, Director

Remarks: Sponsors approximately six exhibitions per year, including a Youth Symphony Orchestra, a biannual Black Woman's Conference, and the Annual Southwest Black Art Exhibition.

Virginia

★2204★
Alexandria Black History Resource Center
638 N. Alfred St.
Alexandria, VA 22314   Ph: (703)838-4356
Eugene Thompson, Director

★2205★
Black History Museum and Cultural Center of Virginia
00 Clay St.
Richmond, VA 23219   Ph: (804)780-9093
Brian Little, Executive Director

Remarks: Commemorates accomplishments of Black people through community education efforts. Formerly known as Virginia Museum for Black History and Archives.

★2206★
Booker T. Washington National Monument
Rte. 3, Box 10
Hardy, VA 24101   Ph: (703)721-2094
Alice Hanawalt, Curator

Remarks: Displays plantation equipment, furniture, and blacksmith tools.

★2207★
Harrison Museum of African American Culture
PO Box 194
Roanoke, VA 24002   Ph: (703)345-4818
Melody Stovall Jr., Director

Remarks: Repository for the history of Blacks in the Roanoke Valley.

★2208★
Task Force on Historical Preservation and Minority Communities
W. Lee St., No. 12
Richmond, VA 23220   Ph: (804)788-1709
Preddy Ray, Director

Wisconsin

★2209★
Hedzoleh African Dance Troupe
2630 Smithfield Dr.
Madison, WI 53719   Ph: (608)274-9769
Malzern Akyea, Artistic Director

Remarks: African drum and dance company choreographing West African dance by recreating events and rituals of traditional African society. Offers lecture-demonstrations, performances, and residencies.

★2210★
Ko-Thi Dance Company
PO Box 1093
Milwaukee, WI 53201   Ph: (414)442-6844
Margo Mazur, Managing Director

Remarks: Professional Black ensemble specializing in traditional and contemporary African-American performing arts. Offers concerts, lecture-demonstrations, and master classes.

(6) Historically Black Colleges and Universities

★2211★
Alabama A & M University
PO Box 908   Ph: (205)851-5245
Normal, AL 35762   Fax: (205)851-9747
                 Free: 800-533-0816
Dr. David B. Henson, President
Founded: 1875. State-supported university. **Cost:** $3,900.00 in-state; $5,450.00 out-of-state. **Application Deadline:** Rolling admissions policy. **Number of Students:** 5215. **Tests Required:** SAT or ACT. **Admissions Director:** James O. Heyward.

★2212★
Alabama State University
915 S. Jackson St.
Montgomery, AL 36101   Ph: (205)293-4291
Dr. C.C. Baker, President
Founded: 1874. State-supported university. **Cost:** $3,151.00 in-state; $4,311.00 out-of-state. **Application Deadline:** July 31 (fall). **Number of Students:** 4,800. **Tests Required:** SAT or ACT. **Admissions Director:** Debbie Moore.

★2213★
Albany State College
504 College Dr.
Albany, GA 31705-2797   Ph: (912)430-4646
Dr. Billy C. Black, President
Founded: 1903. State-supported college. **Cost:** $4,554.00 in-state; $7,134.00 out-of-state. **Application Deadline:** September 1 (fall). **Number of Students:** 2746. **Tests Required:** SAT (preferred) or ACT. **Admissions Director:** Patricia Price.

★2214★
Alcorn State University
New Administration Bldg.
Lorman, MS 39096   Ph: (601)877-6147
Dr. Walter Washington, President
Founded: 1871. State-supported university. **Cost:** $3,600.00 in-state; $4,782.00 out-of-state. **Application Deadline:** August 15 (fall). **Number of Students:** 3256. **Tests Required:** SAT or ACT. **Admissions Director:** Albert Z. Johnson.

★2215★
Allen University
1530 Harden St.
Columbia, SC 29204   Ph: (803)254-4165
Dr. Collie Coleman, President
Founded: 1870. Independent university. **Cost:** $8,702.00. **Application Deadline:** Rolling applications policy. **Number of Students:** 223. **Tests Required:** Open admissions policy. **Admissions Director:** Rev. Romeo Leonard.

★2216★
Arkansas Baptist College
1600 Bishop St.
Little Rock, AR 72202   Ph: (501)374-7856
Dr. William Keaton, President
Founded: 1884. Independent four-year college. **Cost:** $4,258.00. **Application Deadline:** Rolling admissions policy. **Number of Students:** 408. **Tests Required:** Open admissions policy. **Admissions Director:** Annie A. Hightower, Registrar.

★2217★
Atlanta Metropolitan College
Atlanta, GA 30310   Ph: (404)756-4004
Dr. Edwin A. Thompson, President
Founded: 1974. State-supported two-year college. **Cost:** $1,257.00 in-state; $3,183.00 out-of-state. **Application Deadline:** August 30 (fall). **Number of Students:** 1785. **Tests Required:** SAT or ACT. **Admissions Director:** Verle V. Wilson.

★2218★
Barber-Scotia College
145 Cabarrus Ave. W.
Concord, NC 28025   Ph: (704)786-5171
Dr. Joel Nwagbaraocha, President
Founded: 1867. Independent four-year college affiliated with the Presbyterian Church. **Cost:** $6,487.00. **Application Deadline:** Rolling applications policy. **Number of Students:** 600. **Tests Required:** SAT or ACT. **Admissions Director:** Dr. Bruce Smith, Executive Director of Enrollment Management/Registrar.

★2219★
Benedict College
1600 Harden St.   Ph: (803)253-5143
Columbia, SC 29204   Fax: (803)253-5085
Dr. Marshall C. Grigsby, President
Founded: 1870. Private Baptist four-year college. **Cost:** $7,376.00. **Application Deadline:** Rolling applications policy. **Number of Students:** 1422. **Tests Required:** SAT or ACT. **Admissions Director:** Virginia McKee.

★2220★
Bennett College
900 E. Washington St.
Greensboro, NC 27401-3239   Ph: (919)370-8624
Dr. Gloria R. Scott, President
Founded: 1873. Private undergraduate women's college. **Cost:** $11,275.00. **Application Deadline:** Rolling applications policy. **Number of Students:** 568. **Tests Required:** SAT or ACT. **Admissions Director:** Susan Gibson.

★2221★
Bethune-Cookman College
640 2nd Ave.   Ph: (904)255-1401
Daytona Beach, FL 32115   Free: 800-448-0228
Dr. Oswald B. Bronson, President
Founded: 1904. Independent four-year Methodist college. **Cost:** $8,459.00. **Application Deadline:** July 30 (fall). **Number of Students:** 2273. **Tests Required:** SAT or ACT. **Admissions Director:** Gloria Bartley.

★2222★
Bishop State Community College
351 N. Broad St.   Ph: (205)690-6419
Mobile, AL 36603   Free: 800-523-7235
Dr. Yvonne Kennedy, President
Founded: 1965. State-supported junior college. **Cost:** $891.00 in-state; $1,559.00 out-of-state. **Application Deadline:** Rolling admissions policy. **Number of Students:** 2144. **Tests Required:** Open admissions policy.

★2223★
Bluefield State College
219 Rock St.   Ph: (304)327-4065
Bluefield, WV 24701   Fax: (304)327-7747
Dr. Gregory D. Adkins, Pres.
Founded: 1895. **Cost:** $1,454.00 in-state; $3,424.00 out-of-state. **Application Deadline:** Rolling applications policy. **Number of Students:** 2907. **Tests Required:** ACT. **Admissions Director:** John C. Cardwell.

★2224★
Bowie State University
14000 Jericho Park Rd.
Bowie, MD 20715-9465   Ph: (301)464-6563
Dr. James E. Lyons Sr., President
Founded: 1865. State-supported university. **Cost:** $6,648.00 in-state; $8,862.00 out-of-state. **Application Deadline:** April 1 (fall). **Number of Students:** 4437. **Tests Required:** SAT. **Admissions Director:** Lawrence A. Waters.

★2225★
Central State University
Norman Ward University Center
Wilberforce, OH 45384   Ph: (513)376-6348
Dr. Arthur E. Thomas, President
Founded: 1887. State-supported four-year university. **Cost:** $6,291.00 in-state; $9,087.00 out-of-state. **Application Deadline:** June 15 (fall). **Number of Students:** 3266. **Tests Required:** ACT. **Admissions Director:** Robert E. Johnson.

★2226★
Charles R. Drew University of Medicine and Science
1621 E. 120th St.
Los Angeles, CA 90059   Ph: (213)563-4960
Dr. Reed V. Tuckson, President
Founded: 1978. Federally funded private university. **Cost:** $10,230.00 in-state; $15,230.00 out-of-state. **Application Deadline:** November 15 (fall). **Number of Students:** 24. **Tests Required:** MCAT. **Admissions Director:** Dr. Alice Faye-Singleton.

★2227★
Cheyney University of Pennsylvania
Cheyney, PA 19319   Ph: (215)399-2275
                                                  Fax: (215)399-2415
Dr. Valarie Swain Cade, Interim President
Founded: 1837. State-supported university. **Cost:** $5,794.00 in-state; $8,058.00 out-of-state. **Application Deadline:** Rolling applications policy. **Number of Students:** 1607. **Tests Required:** SAT or ACT. **Admissions Director:** Earl E. Acker.

★2228★
Chicago State University
95th St. at King Dr.
Chicago, IL 60628   Ph: (312)995-2516
Dr. Dolores Cross, President
Founded: 1867. State-supported university. **Cost:** $1,856.00 in-state; $5,168.00 out-of-state. **Application Deadline:** Rolling applications policy. **Number of Students:** 8004. **Tests Required:** SAT or ACT. **Admissions Director:** Romi Lowe.

★2229★
City University of New York - Medgar Evers College
1650 Bedford Ave.
Brooklyn, NY 11225   Ph: (718)270-6024
Dr. Edison O. Jackson, President
Founded: 1969. State-supported four-year college. **Cost:** $1,702.00 in-state; $2,378.00 out-of-state. **Application Deadline:** Rolling applications policy. **Number of Students:** 4400. **Tests Required:** SAT. **Admissions Director:** Lincoln Sessoms, Assistant Dean of Enrollment Services.

★2230★
Claflin College
700 College St., NE
Orangeburg, SC 29115   Ph: (803)534-2710
Dr. Oscar A. Rogers Jr., President
Founded: 1869. Independent, four-year United Methodist college. **Cost:** $6,430.00. **Application Deadline:** Rolling applications policy. **Number of Students:** 885. **Tests Required:** SAT or ACT. **Admissions Director:** George F. Lee.

★2231★
Clark Atlanta University
240 James P. Brawley Dr., SW   Ph: (404)880-8784
Atlanta, GA 30314   Free: 800-688-7228
Dr. Thomas W. Cole Jr., President
Founded: 1869. Independent four-year college affiliated with the United Methodist Church. **Cost:** $10,100.00. **Application Deadline:** Rolling applications policy. **Number of Students:** 3996. **Tests Required:** SAT or ACT. **Admissions Director:** Peggy Wade, Associate Director of Admissions.

★2232★
Clinton Junior College
1020 Crawford Rd.
PO Box 968
Rock Hill, SC 29730   Ph: (803)327-5587
Dr. Sallie V. Moreland, President
Founded: 1894. Private two-year college. **Cost:** $3,140.00. **Application Deadline:** Rolling applications policy. **Number of Students:** 76. **Tests Required:** Open applications policy. **Admissions Director:** Patrice Dixon.

★2233★
Coahoma Community College
Rt. 1, Box 616
Clarksdale, MS 38614   Ph: (601)627-2571
Dr. Vivian M. Presley, Interim President
Founded: 1949. State and locally supported two-year college. **Cost:** $2,946.00 area; $3,346.00 in-state; $4,346.00 out-of-state. **Number of Students:** 1478. **Admissions Director:** Rita Hanfor. **Application Deadline:** Rolling applications policy. **Tests Required:** ACT.

★2234★
Concordia College
1804 N. Green St.   Ph: (205)874-5736
Selma, AL 36701   Fax: (205)875-5755
Dr. Julius Jenkins, President
Founded: 1922. Private two-year college. **Cost:** $5,956.00. **Application Deadline:** September 2 (fall). **Number of Students:** 383. **Tests Required:** ACT. **Admissions Director:** Evelyn Pickens.

★2235★
Coppin State College
2500 W. North Ave.
Baltimore, MD 21216   Ph: (410)383-5990
Dr. Calvin W. Burnett, President

Founded: 1900. State-supported college. **Cost:** $3,104.00 in-state; $5,000.00 out-of-state. **Application Deadline:** July 30 (fall). **Number of Students:** 2816. **Tests Required:** SAT. **Admissions Director:** Allen D. Mosley.

★2236★
Delaware State College
1200 N. Dupont Hwy.
Dover, DE 19901   Ph: (302)739-4917
Dr. William B. DeLauder, President

Founded: 1891. State-supported college. **Cost:** $4,826.00 in-state; $7,050.00 out-of-state. **Application Deadline:** June 1 (fall); December 1 (spring). **Number of Students:** 2882. **Tests Required:** SAT (preferred) or ACT. **Admissions Director:** Jethro C. Williams.

★2237★
Denmark Technical College
Solomon Blatt Blvd.   Ph: (803)793-3301
Denmark, SC 29042   Fax: (803)793-5942
Dr. Curtis E. Bryan, President

Founded: 1948. State-supported two-year college. **Cost:** $3,412.00 in-state; $4,492.00 out-of-state. **Application Deadline:** Rolling applications policy. **Number of Students:** 725. **Tests Required:** Open admissions policy. **Admissions Director:** Pamela Felheim.

★2238★
Dillard University
2601 Gentilly Blvd.
New Orleans, LA 70122   Ph: (504)283-8822
Dr. Samuel Cooke, President

Founded: 1869. Independent, interdenominational four-year college. **Cost:** $9,150.00. **Application Deadline:** July 15 (fall). **Number of Students:** 1651. **Tests Required:** SAT or ACT. **Admissions Director:** Vernese B. O'Neal.

★2239★
Edward Waters College
1658 Kings Rd.
Jacksonville, FL 32209   Ph: (904)366-2528
Dr. Robert L. Mitchell, President

Founded: 1866. Private four-year college. **Cost:** $6,966.00. **Application Deadline:** Rolling application policy. **Number of Students:** 634. **Tests Required:** Open admissions policy. **Admissions Director:** Mercedes Cullins, Acting Registrar.

★2240★
Elizabeth City State University
PO Box 901 ECSU
Elizabeth City, NC 27909   Ph: (919)335-3299
Dr. Jimmy R. Jenkins, President

Founded: 1891. State-supported four-year college. **Cost:** $4,062.00 in-state; $8,536.00 out-of-state. **Application Deadline:** August 1 (fall). **Number of Students:** 1762. **Tests Required:** SAT or ACT. **Admissions Director:** Tommy M. Foust.

★2241★
Fayetteville State University
1200 Murchison Rd.   Ph: (919)486-1371
Fayetteville, NC 28301   Fax: (919)486-6024
Dr. Lloyd V. Hackley, President   Free: 800-222-2594

Founded: 1867. State-supported institution; part of the University of North Carolina System. **Cost:** $3,518.00 in-state; $8,572.00 out-of-state. **Application Deadline:** Rolling applications policy. **Number of Students:** 3736. **Tests Required:** SAT. **Admissions Director:** Charles A. Darlington.

★2242★
Fisk University
1000 17th Ave., N.
Nashville, TN 37208   Ph: (615)329-8665
Dr. Henry Ponder, President

Founded: 1866. Independent university affiliated with the United Church of Christ. **Cost:** $8,865.00. **Application Deadline:** June 15 (fall). **Number of Students:** 875. **Tests Required:** SAT or ACT. **Admissions Director:** Harrison F. DeShields, Jr.

★2243★
Florida A&M University
Tallahassee, FL 32307   Ph: (904)599-3796
Dr. Frederick S. Humphries, President

Founded: 1887. State-supported university. **Cost:** $4,197.00 in-state; $8,336.00 out-of-state. **Application Deadline:** June 1 (fall). **Number of Students:** 9196. **Tests Required:** SAT or ACT. **Admissions Director:** Barbara Cox.

★2244★
Florida Memorial College
15800 Florida Memorial College Ave.   Ph: (305)625-4141
Miami, FL 33054   Free: 800-822-1362
Dr. Bennie L. Reeves, President

Founded: 1879. Independent four-year college affiliated with the Baptist Church. **Cost:** $7,250.00. **Application Deadline:** Rolling applications policy. **Number of Students:** 2000. **Tests Required:** SAT or ACT. **Admissions Director:** Peggy Kelly.

★2245★
Fort Valley State College
1005 State College Dr.
Fort Valley, GA 31030-3298   Ph: (912)825-6307
Dr. Oscar L. Prater, President

Founded: 1895. State-supported college. **Cost:** $3,960.00 in-state; $6,540.00 out-of-state. **Application Deadline:** September 1 (fall). **Number of Students:** 2368. **Tests Required:** SAT or ACT. **Admissions Director:** Delia W. Taylor.

★2246★
Grambling State University
100 Main St.   Ph: (318)274-2330
Grambling, LA 71245   Fax: (318)274-2777
Dr. Harold Lundy, President

Founded: 1901. State-supported university. **Cost:** $5,303.00 in-state; $6,853.00 out-of-state. **Admissions Director:** Irene S.A. Thomas, Registrar. **Application Deadline:** Rolling applications policy. **Number of Students:** 6485. **Tests Required:** SAT or ACT.

★2247★
Hampton University
Hampton, VA 23668   Ph: (804)727-5328
          Fax: (804)727-5084
Dr. William R. Harvey, President

Founded: 1868. Private university. **Cost:** $9,550.00. **Application Deadline:** February 15 (fall). **Number of Students:** 5704. **Tests Required:** SAT or ACT. **Admissions Director:** Dr. Ollie M. Bowman.

★2248★
Harris-Stowe State College
3026 Laclede Ave.
St. Louis, MO 63103   Ph: (314)533-3366
Dr. Henry Givens Jr., President

Founded: 1857. State-supported four-year college. **Cost:** $1,728.00 in-state; $3,296.00 out-of-state. **Application Deadline:** Rolling applications policy. **Number of Students:** 1850. **Tests Required:** SAT or ACT. **Admissions Director:** Valerie A. Beeson.

★2249★
Hinds Community College - Utica Campus
Utica, MS 39715   Ph: (601)885-6062
Dr. George Barnes, Vice-President
Founded: 1903. State-supported two-year college. **Application Deadline:** August 23 (fall); January 10 (spring). **Number of Students:** 1030. **Admissions Director:** Ellestene Turner, Registrar.

★2250★
Howard University
2400 Sixth St., NW
Washington, DC 20059   Ph: (202)806-2750
Dr. Franklyn G. Jenifer, President
Founded: 1867. Private university. **Cost:** $10,564.00. **Application Deadline:** April 1 (fall). **Number of Students:** 10,871. **Tests Required:** SAT or ACT. **Admissions Director:** Emmett R. Griffin, Jr.

★2251★
Huston-Tillotson College
1820 E. 8th St.   Ph: (512)476-7421
Austin, TX 78702   Fax: (512)474-0762
Dr. Joseph T. McMillan Jr., President
Founded: 1875. Independent religious four-year college. **Cost:** $8,100.00. **Application Deadline:** Rolling admissions policy. **Number of Students:** 653. **Tests Required:** SAT or ACT. **Admissions Director:** Donnie J. Scott.

★2252★
Interdenominational Theological Center
671 Beckwith St., SW
Atlanta, GA 30314   Ph: (404)527-7709
Dr. James H. Laston, President
Founded: 1958. Private graduate center. **Cost:** $5,754.00. **Application Deadline:** August 1 (fall). **Number of Students:** 300. **Tests Required:** None (GRE required for file). **Admissions Director:** Dr. Edith D. Thomas.

★2253★
Jackson State University
1400 John R. Lynch St.   Ph: (601)968-2911
Jackson, MS 39217   Free: 800-848-6817
Dr. Herman B. Smith, Interim President
Founded: 1877. State-supported university. **Cost:** $4,314.00 in-state; $5,776.00 out-of-state. **Application Deadline:** August 1 (fall). **Tests Required:** SAT. **Admissions Director:** Curtis Johnson, Admissions Counselor.

★2254★
Jarvis Christian College
Hwy. 80 West
Drawer G
Hawkins, TX 75765   Ph: (903)769-2174
Dr. Sebetha Jenkins, President
Founded: 1912. Independent four-year college affiliated with the Christian Church. **Cost:** $6,343.00. **Application Deadline:** Rolling admissions policy. **Number of Students:** 543. **Tests Required:** ACT. **Admissions Director:** Linda Rutherford, Assistant Director of Admissions.

★2255★
J.F. Drake State Technical College
3421 Meridian St. N.
Huntsville, AL 35811   Ph: (205)539-8161
Dr. Johnny L. Harris, Pres.
Founded: 1961. **Cost:** $920.00 in-state; $1,520.00 out-of-state. **Application Deadline:** Rolling appliations policy. **Number of Students:** 953. **Tests Required:** Open admissions policy. **Admissions Director:** Mary Malone.

★2256★
Johnson C. Smith University
100-152 Beatties Ford Rd.
Charlotte, NC 28216   Ph: (704)378-1010
Dr. Robert L. Albright Jr., President
Founded: 1867. Independent four-year college. **Cost:** $8,034.00. **Application Deadline:** August 1 (fall). **Number of Students:** 1256. **Tests Required:** SAT or ACT. **Admissions Director:** Marvin K. Dunlap.

★2257★
Kentucky State University
PO Box PG-92
Frankfort, KY 40601   Ph: (502)227-6813
Dr. John T. Wolfe Jr., President
Founded: 1886. State-supported university. **Cost:** $3,900.00 in-state; $6,500.00 out-of-state. **Application Deadline:** Rolling admissions policy. **Number of Students:** 2518. **Tests Required:** SAT. **Admissions Director:** Tava T. Clay. **Toll-free phone:** (800)633-9415 (Kentucky only); (800)325-1716 (out-of-state).

★2258★
Knoxville College
901 College St., NW
Knoxville, TN 37921   Ph: (615)524-6525
Dr. John Turner, President
Founded: 1875. Private undergraduate college. **Cost:** $8,800.00. **Application Deadline:** Rolling applications policy. **Number of Students:** 1266. **Tests Required:** SAT or ACT. **Admissions Director:** Earl Nash. **Remarks:** Knoxville College acquired Morristown College, Morristown, TN, in the fall of 1988.

★2259★
Lane College
545 Lane Ave.
Jackson, TN 38301   Ph: (901)426-7532
Dr. Alex A. Chambers, President
Founded: 1882. Private four-year college. **Cost:** $6,850.00. **Application Deadline:** Rolling applications policy. **Number of Students:** 562. **Tests Required:** SAT or ACT. **Admissions Director:** E. Ruth Maddox.

★2260★
Langston University
Langston, OK 73050   Ph: (405)466-2231
Dr. Ernest L. Holloway, President
Founded: 1897. State-supported four-year university. **Cost:** $3,999.00 in-state; $5015.00 out-of-state. **Application Deadline:** August 18 (fall). **Number of Students:** 2030. **Tests Required:** ACT or SAT. **Admissions Director:** JoAnn R. Clark.

★2261★
Lawson State Community College
3060 Wilson Rd., SW   Ph: (205)925-2515
Birmingham, AL 35221   Fax: (205)929-6316
Dr. Perry Ward, President
Founded: 1965. State-supported two-year college. **Cost:** $792.00 in-state; $1,368.00 out-of-state. **Application Deadline:** Rolling applications policy. **Number of Students:** 1959. **Admissions Director:** Myra P. Davis, Coordinator Admissions/Records.

★2262★
LeMoyne-Owen College
807 Walker Ave.   Ph: (901)942-7302
Memphis, TN 38126   Fax: (901)942-7810
Dr. Burnett Joiner, President
Founded: 1870. Private four-year college. **Cost:** $6,500.00. **Application Deadline:** August 15 (fall). **Number of Students:** 1064. **Tests Required:** ACT. **Admissions Director:** Melvin Hughes.

★2263★
Lewis College of Business
17370 Meyers Rd.
Detroit, MI 48235   Ph: (313)862-6300
Dr. Marjorie Harris, President
Founded: 1929. Independent two-year college. **Cost:** $2,250.00. **Application Deadline:** Rolling applications policy. **Number of Students:** 386. **Tests Required:** Open admissions policy. **Admissions Director:** Francis Ambrose, Admissions Secretary.

★2264★
Lincoln University - Missouri
820 Chestnut St.
Jefferson City, MO 65102   Ph: (314)681-5024
Dr. Wendell G. Rayburn, President
Founded: 1866. State-supported university. **Cost:** $4,308.00 in-state; $5,992.00 out-of-state. **Number of Students:** 3698. **Tests Required:** ACT. **Admissions Director:** Marguerite R. McPike.

★2265★
Lincoln University - Pennsylvania
Lincoln University, PA 19352   Ph: (215)932-8300
Dr. Niara Sudarkasa, President
Founded: 1854. State-related university. **Cost:** $5,410.00 in-state; $6,730.00 out-of-state. **Application Deadline:** Rolling applications policy. **Number of Students:** 1458. **Tests Required:** SAT or ACT. **Admissions Director:** Jimmy Arrington.

★2266★
Livingstone College
Salisbury, NC 28144   Ph: (704)638-5502
Dr. Bernard W. Franklin, President
Founded: 1879. Private four-year college. **Cost:** $7,844.00. **Number of Students:** 683. ** Rolling applications policy. **Tests Required:** SAT or ACT. **Admissions Director:** Grady Deese.

★2267★
Mary Holmes College
Hwy. 50 West
West Point, MS 39773   Ph: (601)494-6820
Dr. Sammie Potts, President
Founded: 1892. Private two-year college. **Cost:** $7,900.00. **Application Deadline:** Rolling applications policy. **Number of Students:** 742. **Tests Required:** Open admissions policy. **Admissions Director:** Natalie Raleigh, Admissions Counselor. **Toll-free phone:** (800)634-2749 (Mississippi only).

★2268★
Meharry Medical College
1005 D. B. Todd Blvd.
Nashville, TN 37208   Ph: (615)327-6223
Dr. David Satcher, President
Founded: 1876. Private professional college. **Cost:** $14,256.00. **Application Deadline:** December 15 (fall). **Number of Students:** 562. **Tests Required:** MCAT, DAT, or GRE. **Admissions Director:** Dr. James Story.

★2269★
Miles College
Bell Bldg.
Birmingham, AL 35208   Ph: (205)923-2771
Dr. Albert Sloan II, President
Founded: 1905. Independent, four-year Christian Methodist Episcopal college. **Cost:** $6,550.00. **Application Deadline:** Rolling admissions policy. **Number of Students:** 700. **Tests Required:** SAT or ACT. **Admissions Director:** Gloria Beverly.

★2270★
Mississippi Valley State University
Itta Bena, MS 38941   Ph: (601)254-9041
Dr. William W. Sutton, President
Founded: 1946. State-supported university. **Cost:** $3,578.00 in-state; $5,040.00 out-of-state. **Application Deadline:** Rolling admissions policy. **Number of Students:** 1675. **Tests Required:**

SAT or ACT (preferred). **Admissions Director:** Maxcine B. Rush. **Toll-free phone:** (800)821-2743 (Mississippi only).

★2271★
Morehouse College
830 Westview Dr., SW
Atlanta, GA 30314   Ph: (404)681-2800
Dr. Leroy Keith Jr., President
Founded: 1867. Independent four-year men's college. **Cost:** $11,426.00. **Application Deadline:** March 15 (fall). **Number of Students:** 2992. **Tests Required:** SAT or ACT. **Admissions Director:** Sterling H. Hudson, III.

★2272★
Morehouse School of Medicine
720 Westview Dr., SW
Atlanta, GA 30310-1495   Ph: (404)752-1651
Dr. James A. Goodman, President
Founded: 1975. Independent graduate institution. **Cost:** $14,212.00. **Application Deadline:** December 1. **Number of Students:** 145. **Admissions Director:** Dr. Angela Franklin, Assistant Dean for Student Affairs.

★2273★
Morgan State University
Cold Spring Ln. and Hillen Rd.   Ph: (410)319-3000
Baltimore, MD 21239   Free: 800-332-6674
Dr. Earl S. Richardson, President
Founded: 1867. State-supported university. **Cost:** $7,077.00 in-state; $9,329.00 out-of-state. **Application Deadline:** Rolling applications policy. **Number of Students:** 5034. **Tests Required:** SAT or ACT. **Admissions Director:** Chelseia Harold-Miller.

★2274★
Morris Brown College
643 Martin Luther King Jr. Dr., NW   Ph: (404)220-0270
Atlanta, GA 30314   Fax: (404)220-0267
Calvert H. Smith, President
Founded: 1881. Private four-year college. **Cost:** $12,240.00. **Application Deadline:** Rolling applications policy. **Number of Students:** 2000. **Tests Required:** SAT or ACT. **Admissions Director:** Col. Tyrone P. Fletcher.

★2275★
Morris College
100 W. College St.   Ph: (803)775-9371
Sumter, SC 29150-3599   Fax: (803)773-3687
Dr. Luns C. Richardson, President
Founded: 1908. Private four-year college. **Cost:** $6,570.00. **Application Deadline:** Rolling applications policy. **Number of Students:** 701. **Tests Required:** Open admissions policy. **Admissions Director:** Queen W. Spann.

★2276★
Natchez College
1010 N. Union St.
Natchez, MS 39120   Ph: (601)445-9702
Dr. James E. Gray Sr., President
Founded: 1885. Private two-year college. **Application Deadline:** September 15 (fall); January 15 (spring). **Number of Students:** 100. **Tests Required:** Open admissions policy. **Admissions Director:** L. G. Rucker.

★2277★
Norfolk State University
2401 Corprew Ave.
Norfolk, VA 23504   Ph: (804)683-8391
Dr. Harrison B. Wilson, President
Founded: 1935. State-supported university. **Cost:** $5,680.00 in-state; $8,510.00 out-of-state. **Application Deadline:** Rolling applications policy. **Number of Students:** 8298. **Tests Required:** SAT. **Admissions Director:** Dr. Frank Cool.

★2278★
North Carolina A&T State University
1601 E. Market St.   Ph: (919)334-7946
Greensboro, NC 27411   Fax: (919)334-7136
Dr. Edward B. Fort, Chancellor
Founded: 1891. State-supported university. **Cost:** $3,508.00 in-state; $8,562.00 out-of-state. **Application Deadline:** June 1 (fall). **Number of Students:** 7119. **Tests Required:** SAT or ACT. **Admissions Director:** John Smith.

★2279★
North Carolina Central University
PO Box 19717
Durham, NC 27707   Ph: (919)560-6326
Dr. Donna J. Benson, Interim President
Founded: 1910. State-supported university. **Cost:** $4,084.00 in-state; $9,138.00 out-of-state. **Application Deadline:** June 1 (fall). **Number of Students:** 5385. **Tests Required:** SAT or ACT. **Admissions Director:** Nancy R. Rowland.

★2280★
Oakwood College
Oakwood Rd., NW
Huntsville, AL 35896   Ph: (205)726-7000
Dr. Benjamin F. Reaves, President
Founded: 1896. Private four-year college. **Cost:** $9,411.00. **Application Deadline:** Rolling admissions policy. **Number of Students:** 1223. **Tests Required:** SAT or ACT. **Admissions Director:** Lovey Verdun.

★2281★
Paine College
1235 15th St.   Ph: (404)821-8320
Augusta, GA 30910   Fax: (404)821-8293
                                      Free: 800-746-7703
Dr. Julius S. Scott Jr., President
Founded: 1882. Private four-year college. **Cost:** $7,916.00. **Application Deadline:** August 1 (fall). **Number of Students:** 582. **Tests Required:** SAT or ACT. **Admissions Director:** Phyllis Wyatt-Woodruff, Director of Enrollment Management.

★2282★
Paul Quinn College
1020 Elm Ave.
Waco, TX 76704   Ph: (817)753-6415
Dr. Warren W. Morgan, President
Founded: 1872. Independent, four-year African Methodist Episcopalian college. **Cost:** $5,650.00. **Application Deadline:** Rolling admissions policy. **Number of Students:** 577. **Tests Required:** Open admissions policy. **Admissions Director:** Marilyn Marshall.

★2283★
Philander-Smith College
812 W. 13th
Little Rock, AR 72202   Ph: (501)375-9845
Dr. Myer L. Titus, President
Founded: 1877. Independent, four-year United Methodist college. **Cost:** $3,300.00. **Application Deadline:** Rolling admissions policy. **Number of Students:** 620. **Tests Required:** SAT or ACT. **Admissions Director:** Annie Carson.

★2284★
Prairie View A & M University
PO Box 2610   Ph: (409)857-2626
Prairie View, TX 77446-2610   Free: 800-334-1807
Dr. Julius W. Becton Jr., President
Founded: 1878. State-supported university. **Cost:** $4,596.00 in-state; $8,856.00 out-of-state. **Application Deadline:** Rolling applications policy. **Number of Students:** 5590. **Tests Required:** SAT or ACT. **Admissions Director:** Linda Berry.

★2285★
Roxbury Community College
1234 Columbus Ave.
Roxbury Crossing, MA 02120   Ph: (617)541-5310
Dr. Walter C. Howard, President
Founded: 1973. State-supported two-year college. **Cost:** $1,107.00 in state; $4,779.00 out-of-state. **Application Deadline:** September 1 (fall). **Number of Students:** 2500. **Tests Required:** Open admissions policy. **Admissions Director:** Rosie Quashie.

★2286★
Rust College
150 Rust Ave.   Ph: (601)252-8000
Holly Springs, MS 38635   Fax: (601)252-6107
Dr. William A. McMillan, President
Founded: 1866. Private, four-year college. **Cost:** $6,100.00. **Application Deadline:** Rolling applications policy. **Number of Students:** 1075. **Tests Required:** ACT. **Admissions Director:** Jo Ann Scott.

★2287★
St. Augustine's College
1315 Oakwood Ave.   Ph: (919)828-4451
Raleigh, NC 27610-2298   Fax: (919)834-6473
Dr. Prezell R. Robinson, President
Founded: 1867. Independent, four-year Episcopalian college. **Cost:** $8,700.00. **Application Deadline:** August 10 (fall). **Number of Students:** 1907. **Tests Required:** SAT. **Admissions Director:** Wanzo Hendrix.

★2288★
St. Paul's College
406 Windsor Ave.   Ph: (804)848-3984
Lawrenceville, VA 23868   Free: 800-678-7071
Dr. Thomas M. Law, President
Founded: 1888. Independent, four-year Episcopalian college. **Cost:** $7,986.00. **Application Deadline:** Rolling applications policy. **Number of Students:** 700. **Tests Required:** SAT. **Admissions Director:** Larnell R. Parker.

★2289★
Savannah State College
James A. Colston Administration Bldg.
Savannah, GA 31404   Ph: (912)356-2181
Dr. Ann Brock, Acting President
Founded: 1890. State-supported college. **Cost:** $6,096.00 in-state; $8,676.00 out-of-state. **Application Deadline:** September 1 (fall). **Number of Students:** 2656. **Tests Required:** SAT or ACT. **Admissions Director:** Dr. Roy A. Jackson.

★2290★
Selma University
1501 Lapsley
Selma, AL 36701   Ph: (205)872-2533
Dr. B. W. Dawson, President
Founded: 1878. Independent, four-year Baptist college. **Cost:** $4,015.00. **Application Deadline:** August 20 (fall). **Number of Students:** 207. **Tests Required:** Open admissions policy. **Admissions Director:** Ovetta C. Williams.

★2291★
Shaw University
118 E. South St.   Ph: (919)546-8275
Raleigh, NC 27611   Fax: (919)546-8301
Dr. Talbert O. Shaw, President
Founded: 1865. Independent, four-year Baptist college. **Cost:** $11,708.00. **Application Deadline:** August 10 (fall). **Number of Students:** 2149. **Tests Required:** SAT or ACT. **Admissions Director:** Alfonzo Caster.

★2292★
Shorter College
604 Locust St.
North Little Rock, AR 72114   Ph: (501)374-6305
Dr. Katherine Mitchell, President
Founded: 1886. Private two-year college. **Cost:** $4,300.00.
Application Deadline: Rolling applications policy. **Number of
Students:** 120. **Tests Required:** Open admissions policy.
Admissions Director: Delores Voliber.

★2293★
Simmons Bible College
1811 Dumesnil St.
Louisville, KY 40210   Ph: (502)776-1443
Dr. W. J. Hodge, President
Founded: 1879. Denomination-supported four-year college. **Cost:**
$900.00. **Application Deadline:** September 1 (fall); January 26
(spring). **Number of Students:** 115. **Tests Required:** Open
admissions policy. **Admissions Director:** Charles E. Price.

★2294★
Sojourner-Douglass College
500 N. Caroline St.   Ph: (401)276-0306
Baltimore, MD 21205   Fax: (410)675-1810
Dr. Charles W. Simmons, President
Founded: 1980. Independent four-year college. **Cost:** $3,305.00.
Application Deadline: Rolling applications policy. **Number of
Students:** 350. **Tests Required:** Open admissions policy.
Admissions Director: Clyde Hatcher.

★2295★
South Carolina State College
300 College St., NE
Orangeburg, SC 29117   Ph: (803)536-7185
Dr. Carl A. Carpenter, Interim President
Founded: 1896. State-supported college. **Cost:** $4,832.00 in-state;
$6,622.00 out-of-state. **Application Deadline:** July 31 (fall). **Number
of Students:** 5145. **Tests Required:** SAT or ACT. **Admissions
Director:** Benny Mayfield, Dean of Enrollment Management.

★2296★
Southern University & A & M College - Baton Rouge
T.H. Harris Hall
Baton Rouge, LA 70813   Ph: (504)771-2430
Dr. Marvin L. Yates, President
Founded: 1880. State-supported college; part of the Southern
University System. **Cost:** $4,374.00 in-state; $5,896.00 out-of-state.
Application Deadline: August 26 (fall). **Number of Students:**
10,000. **Tests Required:** SAT or ACT. **Admissions Director:** Henry
J. Bellaire.

★2297★
Southern University - New Orleans
6400 Press Dr.
New Orleans, LA 70126   Ph: (504)286-5314
Dr. Robert Gex, Chancellor
Founded: 1956. State-supported college; part of the Southern
University System. **Cost:** $1,452.00 in-state; $3,010.00 out-of-state.
Application Deadline: July 1 (fall). **Number of Students:** 2179.
Tests Required: ACT. **Admissions Director:** Melvin Hodges,
Registrar.

★2298★
Southern University - Shreveport
3050 Martin Luther King, Jr. Dr.
Shreveport, LA 71107   Ph: (318)674-3342
                              Fax: (318)674-3489
Dr. Robert H. Smith, Chancellor
Founded: 1964. State-supported two-year college; part of the
Southern University System. **Cost:** $830.00 in-state; $1,860.00 out-
of-state. **Application Deadline:** Rolling applications policy. **Number
of Students:** 928. **Tests Required:** ACT. **Admissions Director:**
Clifton Jones.

★2299★
Southwestern Christian College
Jack Evans Administration Bldg.
Terrell, TX 75160   Ph: (214)563-3341
Dr. Jack Evans, President
Founded: 1949. Private four-year college. **Cost:** $5,926.00.
Application Deadline: July 15 (fall). **Number of Students:** 244.
Tests Required: Open admissions policy. **Admissions Director:**
Gerald E. Lee.

★2300★
Spelman College
350 Spelman Ln., SW   Ph: (404)681-3643
Atlanta, GA 30314   Free: 800-241-3421
Dr. Johnnetta Cole, President
Founded: 1881. Private, four-year women's college. **Cost:**
$11,727.00. **Application Deadline:** February 1 (fall). **Number of
Students:** 1850. **Tests Required:** SAT or ACT. **Admissions
Director:** Aline A. Rivers.

★2301★
Stillman College
PO Box 1430   Ph: (205)349-4240
Tuscaloosa, AL 35403   Fax: (205)758-0821
Dr. Cordell Wynn, President
Founded: 1876. Private four-year college. **Cost:** $7,214.00.
Application Deadline: Rolling admissions policy. **Number of
Students:** 822. **Tests Required:** SAT or ACT (preferred).
Admissions Director: Mason Bonner.

★2302★
Talladega College
627 W. Battle St.
Talladega, AL 35160   Ph: (205)362-0206
Dr. Joseph Johnson, President
Founded: 1867. Private four-year college. **Cost:** $6,737.00.
Application Deadline: Rolling admissions policy. **Number of
Students:** 751. **Tests Required:** SAT or ACT. **Admissions Director:**
Monroe Thorton.

★2303★
Tennessee State University
3500 John Merritt Blvd.   Ph: (615)320-3420
Nashville, TN 37209-1561   Fax: (615)320-3114
Dr. James Hefner, President
Founded: 1912. State-supported university. **Cost:** $4,008.00 in-
state; $6,772.00 out-of-state. **Application Deadline:** August 1 (fall).
Number of Students: 7405. **Tests Required:** SAT or ACT.
Admissions Director: Dr. Anne Mitchell-Hinton, Director of High
School Relations.

★2304★
Texas College
2404 N. Grand Ave.
Tyler, TX 75702   Ph: (903)593-8311
Dr. A.C. Mitchell Patton, Acting President
Founded: 1894. Independent four-year college affiliated with the
Christian Methodist Episcopalian Church. **Cost:** $6,220.00.
Application Deadline: August 15 (fall). **Number of Students:** 353.
Tests Required: ACT or SAT. **Admissions Director:** Dr. William
Ammons.

★2305★
Texas Southern University
3100 Cleburne Ave.   Ph: (713)527-7474
Houston, TX 77004   Fax: (713)527-7842
Dr. William H. Harris, President
Founded: 1947. State-supported university. **Application Deadline:**
August 10 (fall). **Number of Students:** 10,269. **Cost:** $4,384.00 in-
state; $7,624.00 out-of-state. **Tests Required:** SAT or ACT.
Admissions Director: Collie Chambers, Coordinator of Recruitment.

★2306★
Tougaloo College
Tougaloo, MS 39174
Ph: (601)977-7764
Fax: (601)977-7739

Dr. Adib Shakir, President

Founded: 1869. Private four-year college. **Cost:** $6,930.00. **Application Deadline:** Rolling applications policy. **Number of Students:** 1003. **Tests Required:** SAT or ACT. **Admissions Director:** Washington Cole, Director of Student Enrollment Management Center.

★2307★
Trenholm State Technical College
1225 Air Base Blvd.
Ph: (205)832-9000
Montgomery, AL 36108
Fax: (205)832-9777
Dr. Thad McClammy, Pres.

Founded: 1965. **Cost:** $1,308.00 in-state; $1,962.00 out-of-state. **Application Deadline:** Rolling applications policy. **Number of Students:** 823. **Tests Required:** ACT. **Admissions Director:** Jean Taylor.

★2308★
Tuskegee University
Office of Admissions and Enrollment
Services
Carnegie Hall, 4th Fl.
Tuskegee, AL 36088
Ph: (205)727-8500
Dr. Benjamin F. Payton, President

Founded: 1881. Independent university. **Cost:** $9,250.00. **Application Deadline:** April 15 (fall). **Number of Students:** 3687. **Tests Required:** SAT or ACT. **Admissions Director:** Ann R. Ware.

★2309★
University of Arkansas, Pine Bluff
PO Box 31
University Dr.
Pine Bluff, AR 71601
Ph: (501)541-6500
Dr. Lawrence A. Davis, President

Founded: 1873. State-supported four-year university. **Cost:** $3,382.00 in-state; $5,206.00 out-of-state. **Application Deadline:** August 1 (fall). **Number of Students:** 3626. **Tests Required:** ACT. **Admissions Director:** Katherine King.

★2310★
University of Maryland - Eastern Shore
Princess Anne, MD 21853
Ph: (410)651-2200
Fax: (410)651-2270

Dr. William P. Hytche, President

Founded: 1886. State-supported university. **Cost:** $6,704.00 in-state; $11,068.00 out-of-state. **Application Deadline:** Rolling applications policy. **Number of Students:** 2397. **Tests Required:** SAT or ACT. **Admissions Director:** Edwina Morse, Assistant Director.

★2311★
University of the District of Columbia
4200 Connecticut Ave. NW
Washington, DC 20008
Ph: (202)282-7300
Dr. Tilden J. LeMelle, President

Founded: 1976. State- and locally-supported university. **Cost:** $720.00 in-state; $2,880.00 out-of-state. **Application Deadline:** August 1 (fall). **Number of Students:** 12,000. **Tests Required:** Open admissions policy. **Admissions Director:** Alfred Taylor.

★2312★
Virginia State University
20708 4th Ave.
Ph: (804)524-5695
Petersburg, VA 23806
Fax: (804)524-5055
Dr. Wesley Cornelious McClure, President

Founded: 1882. State-supported university. **Cost:** $7,040.00 in-state; $10,442.00 out-of-state. **Application Deadline:** May 1 (fall). **Number of Students:** 4585. **Tests Required:** SAT. **Admissions Director:** Karen Winston.

★2313★
Virginia Union University
1500 N. Lombardy St.
Richmond, VA 23220
Ph: (804)257-5600
Dr. S. Dallas Simmons, President

Founded: 1865. Private Baptist University. **Cost:** $9,933.00. **Application Deadline:** June 15 (fall). **Number of Students:** 1360. **Tests Required:** SAT or ACT. **Admissions Director:** Gil Powell. **Toll-free phone:** (800)368-3227.

★2314★
Voorhees College
1411 Voorhees Rd.
Ph: (803)793-3351
Denmark, SC 29042
Fax: (803)793-4584
Dr. Leonard E. Dawson, President

Founded: 1897. Private four-year college. **Cost:** $5,992.00. **Application Deadline:** Rolling applications policy. **Number of Students:** 613. **Tests Required:** Open admissions policy. **Admissions Director:** Marian Thompson, Director, Enrollment Management.

★2315★
West Virginia State College
Farrell Hall, Rm. 106
Institute, WV 25112
Ph: (304)766-3221
Dr. Hazo W. Carter, President

Founded: 1891. State-supproted four-year college. **Cost:** $4,528.00 in-state; $6,638.00 out-of-state. **Application Deadline:** August 1 (fall). **Number of Students:** 4986. **Tests Required:** ACT or SAT. **Admissions Director:** John L. Fuller.

★2316★
Wilberforce University
Wilberforce, OH 45384
Ph: (513)376-2911
Free: 800-367-8568
Dr. John L. Henderson, President

Founded: 1856. Independent four-year college affiliated with the African Methodist Episcopalian Church. **Cost:** $10,038.00. **Application Deadline:** June 1 (fall). **Number of Students:** 758. **Tests Required:** SAT or ACT. **Admissions Director:** Karen Preston, Assistant Director of Admissions.

★2317★
Wiley College
711 Wiley Ave.
Marshall, TX 75670
Ph: (214)938-8341
Dr. David L. Beckley, President

Founded: 1873. Private four-year college. **Cost:** $6,490.00. **Application Deadline:** March 15 (fall); October 15 (spring). **Number of Students:** 400. **Tests Required:** SAT or ACT recommended. **Admissions Director:** Edward Morgan.

★2318★
Winston-Salem State University
601 Martin Luther King Jr. Dr.
Ph: (919)750-2070
Winston Salem, NC 27110
Fax: (919)750-2459
Dr. Cleon F. Thompson Jr., President

Founded: 1892. State-supported four-year university. **Cost:** $3,690.00 in-state; $8,164.00 out-of-state. **Application Deadline:** Rolling applications policy. **Number of Students:** 2604. **Tests Required:** SAT or ACT. **Admissions Director:** Van C. Wilson.

★2319★
Xavier University of Louisiana
7325 Palmetto St.
New Orleans, LA 70125
Ph: (504)483-7651
Dr. Norman C. Francis, President

Founded: 1925. Private university. **Cost:** $9,720.00. **Application Deadline:** March 1 (fall). **Number of Students:** 3099. **Tests Required:** SAT or ACT. **Admissions Director:** Winston D. Brown.

(7) Black Studies Programs

Two-Year Colleges

★2320★
Bronx Community College of the City University of New York
Cultural Affairs
Blacks and Puerto Rician Study Options
181st & University Ave.
Bronx, NY 10453   Ph: (212)220-6121
Ismay Taylor, Coordinator

★2321★
City College of Chicago - Olive-Harvey College
African-American Studies
Chicago, IL 60628   Ph: (312)568-3700
Glenn Nance, Chairperson

★2322★
City College of San Francisco
Afro-American Studies Department
San Francisco, CA 94112   Ph: (415)239-3000
Robert Balestreri, Dean of Adm.

★2323★
Compton Community College
Ethnic Studies
Compton, CA 90221   Ph: (310)637-2660
Dr. David Horne, Div. Chair of Soc. Science/Ethnic Stud.

★2324★
Contra Costa College
San Pablo, CA 94806   Ph: (510)235-7800
Jim Lacy, Chairperson

★2325★
De Anza College
Intercultural Studies
Cupertino, CA 95014   Ph: (408)864-8419
Duane Kubo, Acting Dean

★2326★
East Los Angeles College
Africana-American Studies
Monterey Park, CA 91754   Ph: (213)265-8864
David Wells, Chairperson

★2327★
El Camino College
African-American History
Torrance, CA 90506   Ph: (310)532-3670
Joseph Georges, Acting Dean

★2328★
Fresno City College
African American Studies
Fresno, CA 93741   Ph: (209)442-8240
Kehinde Solwazi, Dept. Head

★2329★
Laney College
African-American Studies
Oakland, CA 94607   Ph: (510)464-3154
Ronald Moore, Chairperson

★2330★
Los Angeles Harbor College
Afro-American History
Wilmington, CA 90744   Ph: (310)522-8200
Dr. Maria Mateo, Director

★2331★
Los Angeles Valley College
Afro-American Studies
Van Nuys, CA 91401   Ph: (818)781-1200
Billy Reid, Asst. Dean of Adm.

★2332★
Merritt College
African-American Studies
Oakland, CA 94619   Ph: (510)436-2477
Dr. Celicia Arrington, Director

★2333★
Nassau Community College
Afro-American Studies Department
Garden City, NY 11530   Ph: (516)222-7157
Prof. Kenneth Jenkins, Chairperson

★2334★
Pasadena City College
African-American Studies
Pasadena, CA 91106   Ph: (818)585-7748
Carol Kaser, Supr. Adm.

★2335★
Rancho Santiago College
Santa Ana, CA 92706   Ph: (714)564-6000
Dr. Harold Bateman, Dean of Adm.

★2336★
St. Louis Community College at Forest Park
St. Louis, MO 63110   Ph: (314)644-9131
Bart S. Devoti, Dir. of Adm. & Registrar
John Dickerson, Coordinator, Social Studies

★2337★
San Diego City College
San Diego, CA 92101   Ph: (619)230-2475
Leticia Peters, Student Svc. Technician

★2338★
San Diego Mesa College
San Diego, CA 92111   Ph: (619)560- 2689
Wiletta Tomlinson, Adm./Records Officer

★2339★
Santa Barbara City College
Ethnic Studies Department
Santa Barbara, CA 93109   Ph: (805)965-0581
Jane G. Craven, Asst. Dean of Adm.

★2340★
Solano Community College
Ethnic Studies
Suisun City, CA 94585   Ph: (707)864-7113
Gerald Fisher, Asst. Dean of Adm. and Records

★2341★
South Suburban College
African-American Studies
South Holland, IL 60473   Ph: (708)596-2000
Ellis Falk, Dean of Admin.

★2342★
South Suburban College
Urban Studies
South Holland, IL 60473   Ph: (708)596-2000
Larry Polselli, Dean of Adm.

★2343★
Triton College
School of Arts and Sciences
River Grove, IL 60171   Ph: (708)456-2500
Gwen E. Kanelos, Dean of Students

★2344★
Yuba College
Afro-American Studies
Marysville, CA 95901   Ph: (916)741-6705
Susan Singhas, Dean of Adm.

Four-Year Colleges and Universities

★2345★
Amherst College
Department of Black Studies
Amherst, MA 01002   Ph: (413)542-5832
Rhonda Cobham-Fander, Chairperson

★2346★
Antioch College
African-American Studies
Yellow Springs, OH 45387   Ph: (513)767-6400
                                        Free: 800-543-9436
Joseph Jordan, Exec. Dir.

★2347★
Ball State University
Afro-American Studies
Muncie, IN 47306   Ph: (317)285-8288
Ruth Vedvik, Dir. of Adm.

★2348★
Bowdoin College
Africana-American Studies Program
Brunswick, ME 04011   Ph: (207)725-3272
Randolph Stakeman, Dir of Africana-American Studies Program

★2349★
Bowling Green State University
Ethnic Studies Department
Bowling Green, OH 43403   Ph: (419)372-2796
Robert Perry Ph.D., Dir. of Adm.

★2350★
Brandeis University
Department of African and African-American Studies
Waltham, MA 02254   Ph: (617)736-2000
Ibirahim Sundiata, Chairman

★2351★
Brown University
AfroAmerican Studies Program
Providence, RI 02912   Ph: (401)863-3137
Henry Paget, Dir. of Adm.

★2352★
Bryn Mawr College
Africana Studies
Bryn Mawr, PA 19010   Ph: (215)526-5000
Elizabeth G. Vermey, Dir. of Adm.

★2353★
California State University
Ethnic Studies
San Bernardino, CA 92407   Ph: (714)880-5202
Khare Brig, Dir.

★2354★
California State University - Dominquez Hills
African-American Studies Program
Carson, CA 90747   Ph: (310)516-3600
Anita Gash, Dir. of Adm.

★2355★
California State University - Fullerton
Department of Afro-Ethnic Studies
Fullerton, CA 92634   Ph: (714)773-2370
J. Owens Smith, Chairperson

★2356★
California State University - Hayward
Afro-American Studies Program
Hayward, CA 94542   Ph: (510)881-3817
Glenn Perry, Dir. of Admission & Records

★2357★
California State University - Long Beach
Department of Black Studies
Long Beach, CA 90840   Ph: (310)985-4111
James F. Menzel, Dir. of Adm.

★2358★
California State University - Los Angeles
Department of Pan-African Studies
Los Angeles, CA 90032   Ph: (213)343-3000
Dr. Aida Pakla O'Reilly, Chairperson

★2359★
California State University - Northridge
Pan-African Studies Department
Northridge, CA 91330   Ph: (818)885-3311
Dr. Selase Williams, Chairperson

★2360★
California State University - Sacramento
Pan-African Studies Program
Sacramento, CA 95819   Ph: (916)278-6011
Larry Glasmire, Adm. Officer

★2361★
Central State University
Department of Political Science
African and African-American Studies
Wilberforce, OH 45384   Ph: (513)376-6464
Lois Pelekoudas Ph.D., Chairperson of Political Science

★2362★
Chatham College
African-African American Studies
Pittsburgh, PA 15232   Ph: (412)365-1290
Emma T. Lucas, Dir.

★2363★
City College of City University of New York
Department of African and Afro-American Studies
New York, NY 10031   Ph: (212)650-7000
Edmond Gordon, Chairman

★2364★
Claremont McKenna College
Black Studies Department
Claremont, CA 91711   Ph: (714)621-8000
Richard Vos, V.P./Dean of Adm. and Fin. Aid

★2365★
Clark Atlanta University
Afro-American Studies
Atlanta, GA 30314   Ph: (404)880-8427
Ken Baird, Chair

★2366★
Coe College
Afro-American Studies
Cedar Rapids, IA 52402   Ph: (319)399-8000
James Randall, Chairman

★2367★
Colgate University
Africana Studies
Hamilton, NY 13346   Ph: (315)824-7401
Thomas S. Anthony, Dean of Adm.

★2368★
College of Staten Island of City University of New
  York
Institute for African American Studies
130 Styvesant Pl.
Staten Island, NY 10301   Ph: (718)390-7990
Ramon H. Hulsey, Dir. of Adm.

★2369★
College of the Holy Cross
African-American Studies
Worcester, MA 01610   Ph: (508)793-2443
Thomas Stokes, Chair

★2370★
College of Wooster
Black Studies Program
Wooster, OH 44691   Ph: (216)263-2000
Dr. Josephine Wright, Chairperson

★2371★
Columbia University
Institute of African Studies
New York, NY 10027   Ph: (212)854-4633
George Bond, Dir. of African Studies

★2372★
Cornell University
African Studies and Research Center
Ithaca, NY 14853   Ph: (607)255-5241
Susan Murphy, Dean of Adm.

★2373★
Dartmouth College
African and Afro-American Studies Program
Hanover, NH 03755   Ph: (603)646-3397
Keith Walker, Chairperson

★2374★
Denison University
Center for Black Studies
Granville, OH 43023   Ph: (614)587-6594
John L. Jackson, Dir. of Adm.

★2375★
DePaul University
African-American Studies
Chicago, IL 60604   Ph: (312)362-8300
Dr. Gary Smith, Program Dir.

★2376★
Duke University
Black Studies
2138 Campus Drive
Durham, NC 27706   Ph: (919)684-4736
Leonard C. Beckum Ph.D., Chairperson

★2377★
Earlham College
African and African-American Studies
Richmond, IN 47374   Ph: (317)983-1200
Phyllis Boanes, Program Dir.

★2378★
Eastern Illinois University
Afro-American Studies
Charleston, IL 61920   Ph: (217)581-5719
Dr. William Colvin, Dir. of Adm.

★2379★
Eastern Michigan University
Department of Afro-American Studies
Ypsilanti, MI 48197   Ph: (313)487-3460
James Olsen, Admission Coor.

★2380★
Edinboro University of Pennsylvania
History Department
African History
Edinboro, PA 16444   Ph: (814)732-2000
Andrew Rusnak, Chairperson

★2381★
Emory University
African American and African Studies Program
Atlanta, GA 30322   Ph: (404)727-6036
Daniel C. Walls, Dean of Adm.

★2382★
Florida A&M University
Afro-American Studies
Tallahassee, FL 32307   Ph: (904)599-3374
Theodore Hemmingway, Director

★2383★
Fordham University
Afro-American Studies Department
Bronx, NY 10458   Ph: (212)579-2133
Dr. Claude Mangum, Chairperson

★2384★
Friends World College
African Studies
Huntington, NY 11743   Ph: (516)283-4000
Dr. Jeff Halper, Chairperson

★2385★
Grambling State University
Afro-American Studies Program
Grambling, LA 71245   Ph: (318)247-3811
Karen Lewis, Dir. of Adm.

★2386★
Grinnell College
Afro-American Studies
Grinnell, IA 50112-0807   Ph: (515)269-3600
Dr. Kesho Scott, Chairperson

★2387★
Hamilton College
African-American Studies Program
Clinton, NY 13323   Ph: (315)859-4421
Vincent Odamtten, Director

★2388★
Hampshire College
Social Science Dept.
Amherst, MA 01002   Ph: (413)549-4600
Fran White, Dean of School of Social Science

★2389★
Harvard University
Afro-American Studies Department
Cambridge, MA 02138   Ph: (617)495-4113
Dr. Henry Louis Gates Jr., Dept. Chairperson

★2390★
Hobart College
African & Latin Studies
Geneva, NY 14456   Ph: (315)781-3791
Marilyn Jimenez, Coordinator

★2391★
Hofstra University
Africana Studies
Hempstead, NY 11550   Ph: (516)463-6700
David Powell, Dean of Liberal Arts & Sciences

★2392★
Howard University
Department of Afro-American Studies
Washington, DC 20059   Ph: (202)806-7242
Russel L. Adams, Chairperson

★2393★
Hunter College of City University of New York
Black and Puerto Rician Studies Dept.
New York, NY 10021   Ph: (212)772-5035
Jose Manuel Torres Santiango, Chairperson

★2394★
Indiana State University
Center for Afro-American Studies
Terre Haute, IN 47809   Ph: (812)237-2550
Dr. Warren C. Swindell, Dir.

★2395★
Indiana University Bloomington
Afro-American Studies Department
814 E. Third St.
Bloomington, IN 47405   Ph: (812)855-3875
Mellonee Burnim, Chairperson

★2396★
Indiana University Northwest
Department of Minority Studies
Gary, IN 46408   Ph: (219)980-6821
William D. Lee, Dir. of Adm.

★2397★
Kent State University
Institute of African American Affairs
Kent, OH 44242   Ph: (216)672-2300
Dr. Kwame Nantambu, Dir., Institute of Afro-American Affairs

★2398★
Kenyon College
African and African-American Studies Concentration
Gambier, OH 43022   Ph: (614)427-5778
John W. Anderson, Dean of Adm.

★2399★
Knox College
Black Studies Department
Galesburg, IL 61401   Ph: (309)343-0112
Paul Stennis, Acting Dir. of Adm.

★2400★
Lehigh University
African-American Studies
Bethlehem, PA 18015   Ph: (215)758-3100
William Scott, Dir.

★2401★
Lehman College of City University of New York
Black Studies Department
Bronx, NY 10468   Ph: (212)960-8283
Dr. James Jervis, Chairperson

★2402★
Loyola Marymount University
Department of Afro-American Studies
Los Angeles, CA 90045   Ph: (310)642-2750
Dr. John Davis, Chairperson

★2403★
Loyola University of Chicago
Afro-American Studies Program
Chicago, IL 60626   Ph: (312)508-3670
Allen V. Lentino, Director of Admissions

★2404★
Luther College
African-American Studies
Decorah, IA 52101   Ph: (319)387-1158
Lawrence Williams, Chairperson

★2405★
Martin University
African-American Studies
Indianapolis, IN 46218   Ph: (317)543-3241
Sister Jane Schilling, V.P. of Academic Affairs

★2406★
Mercer University - Macon
Afro-American Studies
Macon, GA 31207
                        Free: 800-637-2378
Catherine Meeks, Director

★2407★
Metropolitan State College
Department of Afro-American Studies
Denver, CO 80204   Ph: (303)556-2543
Akbarali Thobhani, Director of Interculture Studies

★2408★
Miami University
Afro-American Studies
Oxford, OH 45056   Ph: (513)529-2531
Rodney Coates, Chief Departmental Advisor

★2409★
Morgan State University
Department of History
Baltimore, MD 21239   Ph: (410)319-3190
Dr. Charles Johnson, Chairperson

★2410★
Mount Holyoke College
African-American Studies
South Hadley, MA 01075   Ph: (413)538-2577
Samba Gadjigo, Chairperson

★2411★
New York University
African Studies
New York, NY 10012   Ph: (212)998-3970
Manphia Diawara, Dir. of African Studies

★2412★
Northeastern University
Department of African and Afro-American Studies
Boston, MA 02115   Ph: (617)437-3148
Dr. Ronald Bailey, Chairperson

★2413★
Northwestern University
African American Studies Department
Evanston, IL 60201   Ph: (708)491-5122
Leon Forrest, Chairperson

★2414★
Oakland University
African and African-American Studies Program
Rochester, MI 48309   Ph: (313)370-3364
Vincent Khapoya, Coord.

★2415★
Oberlin College
Black Studies Department
Oberlin, OH 44074   Ph: (216)775-8923
Adrienne Jones, Chairperson

★2416★
Occidental College
Department of History
Los Angeles, CA 90041   Ph: (213)259-2700
Charlene Liebau, Dean of Adm.

★2417★
Ohio State University
Department of Black Studies
Columbus, OH 43210   Ph: (614)292-3700
James Upton, Chairperson

★2418★
Ohio University - Athens
Afro-American Studies
Athens, OH 45701   Ph: (614)593-4546
Dr. Vattel T. Rose, Chairperson

★2419★
Ohio Wesleyan University
Black World Studies
Delaware, OH 43015   Ph: (614)369-4431
Trace Regan, Director

★2420★
Pomona College
Black Studies
Claremont, CA 91711   Ph: (714)621-8134
Bruce Poch, Dean of Adm.

★2421★
Princeton University
Afro-American Studies Program
Princeton, NJ 08544   Ph: (609)258-6150
Cornell West, Dir.

★2422★
Purdue University
Afro-American Studies Center
West Lafayette, IN 47907   Ph: (317)494-5680
Dr. Leonard Harris, Dir. of Adm.

★2423★
Rhode Island College
African and Afro-American Studies Program
Providence, RI 02908   Ph: (401)456-8000
Dr. Richard Logan, Director

★2424★
Roosevelt University
African, Afro-American, and Black Studies
Chicago, IL 60605   Ph: (312)341-3515
Christopher Reed, Chairperson

★2425★
Rutgers State University of New Jersey - Camden
   College of Arts and Sciences
Africana-American Studies
Camden, NJ 08102   Ph: (609)225-6246
Joseph Walker, Director

★2426★
Rutgers State University of New Jersey - Douglas
   College
Africana Studies
New Brunswick, NJ 08903   Ph: (201)932-3770
Dr. Gerald Davis, Chairperson

★2427★
Rutgers State University of New Jersey - Newark
   College of Arts and Sciences
Afro-American and African Studies Department
Newark, NJ 07102   Ph: (201)648-5586
Wendell Holbrook, Chair

★2428★
St. Olaf College
American Minority Studies Program
Northfield, MN 55057   Ph: (507)646-3025
John Ruohoniemi, Dir. of Adm.

★2429★
San Diego State University
Department of Afro-American Studies
San Diego, CA 92182   Ph: (619)594-5200
Nancy C. Sprotte, Dir. of Adm.

★2430★
San Jose State University
Afro-American Studies Department
San Jose, CA 95192   Ph: (408)924-1000
Dr. Millner, Advisor

★2431★
Scripps College
Claremont, CA 91711   Ph: (714)621-8149
Leslie Miles, Dean of Adm.

★2432★
Seton Hall University
African American Studies
South Orange, NJ 07079   Ph: (201)761-9332
Patricia L. Burgh, Dean of Adm.

★2433★
Shaw University
Afro-American Studies
Raleigh, NC 27611   Ph: (919)546-8200
Gloria Smith, Asst. Dir. of Student Affairs

★2434★
Simmons College
Afro-American Studies Program
Boston, MA 02115   Ph: (617)738-2107
Debra Wright, Assoc. Dean of Adm.

★2435★
Smith College
Department of Afro-American Studies
Northampton, MA 01063   Ph: (413)584-0515
Juliet Brigham, Dir. of Adm.

★2436★
Sonoma State University
American Multi-Cultural Studies
Rohnert Park, CA 94928   Ph: (707)664-2326
Dr. Frank Tansey, Dean of Adm.

★2437★
Southern Illinois University - Carbondale
Black American Studies Program
Carbondale, IL 60091   Ph: (618)536-4405
Thomas McGinnis, Director of Admissions

★2438★
Southern Methodist University
Department of Anthropology
Dallas, TX 75275   Ph: (214)768-2058
Ron Moss, Dir. of Adm.

★2439★
Stanford University
African and Afro-American Studies Program
Stanford, CA 94305   Ph: (415)725-0104
Horace Porter, Chairperson

★2440★
State University of New York at Albany
African and Afro-American Studies
Albany, NY 12222   Ph: (518)442-3300
Dr. Micheileen Treadwell, Dir. of Adm.

★2441★
State University of New York at Binghamton
Afro-American and African Studies Department
Binghamton, NY 13901   Ph: (607)777-2171
Geoffrey D. Gould, Dir. of Adm.

★2442★
State University of New York at Brockport
Department of African and Afro-American Studies
Brockport, NY 14420   Ph: (716)395-2751
Mr. Cook, Acting Dir. of Adm.

★2443★
State University of New York at Cortland
Black Studies Program
Cortland, NY 13045   Ph: (607)753-4711
Michael K. McKeon, Dir. of Adm.

★2444★
State University of New York at Geneseo
Geneseo, NY 14454   Ph: (716)245-5571
Jill Conlin, Dean of Adm.

★2445★
State University of New York at New Paltz
Black Studies Department
New Paltz, NY 12561   Ph: (914)257-2121
Robert J. Seaman, Dean of Adm.

★2446★
State University of New York at Oneonta
Department of Black and Hispanic Studies
Oneonta, NY 13820   Ph: (607)436-2524
Richard Burr, Dir. of Adm.

★2447★
Syracuse University
Afro-American Studies Department
Syracuse, NY 13244   Ph: (315)443-1870
David C. Smith, Dean of Adm.

★2448★
Temple University
Pan-African Studies
Philadelphia, PA 19122   Ph: (215)204-7200
Dr. Randy Miller, Dir. of Undergrd. Adm.

★2449★
Tougaloo College
African-American Studies
Tougaloo, MS 39174   Ph: (601)977-7700
Washington Cole, Dir. of Student Enrollment

★2450★
Towson State University
African-American Studies
Towson, MD 21204   Ph: (410)830-2112
Linda J. Collins, Dir. of Adm.

★2451★
Trenton State College
African-American Studies
Hillwood Lakes, CN4700
Trenton, NJ 08625   Ph: (609)771-2138
Gloria H. Dickinson, Director

★2452★
Tuskegee University
Tuskegee, AL 36088   Ph: (205)727-8500
Lee Young, Dir. of Adm.

★2453★
University of California - Berkeley
Afro-American Studies Department
Berkeley, CA 94720   Ph: (510)642-6000
Andre Bell, Dir. of Adm.

★2454★
University of California - Davis
African-American Studies Program
Davis, CA 95616   Ph: (916)752-1011
Dr. Gary Tudor, Dir. of Adm.

★2455★
University of California - Los Angeles
Center for Afro-American Studies
Los Angeles, CA 90024   Ph: (310)825-4321
Dr. Rae Lee Siporin, Dir. of Adm.

★2456★
University of California - Santa Barbara
Department of Black Studies
Santa Barbara, CA 93106   Ph: (805)893-8000
William Villa, Dir. of Adm.

★2457★
University of Chicago
African and African-American Studies
Chicago, IL 60637   Ph: (312)702-1234
Theodore O'Neill, Dean of Adm.

★2458★
University of Cincinnati
Afro-American Studies
Cincinnati, OH 45221   Ph: (513)556-6000
Mary Ellen Ashley, Acting Director

★2459★
University of Colorado at Boulder
Black Studies Program
Boulder, CO 80309   Ph: (303)492-6301
Gary Kelsey, Dir. of Adm.

★2460★
University of Colorado at Boulder
Center for Studies of Ethnicity and Race in America
Boulder, CO 80309-0339   Ph: (303)492-8852
Dr. Evelyn Hu-DeHart, Director

★2461★
University of Delaware
Black American Studies
Newark, DE 19716   Ph: (302)831-8123
James Newton, Dir.

★2462★
University of Hartford
African-American Studies
West Hartford, CT 06117   Ph: (203)243-4296
Richard A. Zeiser, Dir. of Adm.

★2463★
University of Illinois at Chicago
Black Studies Program
Chicago, IL 60680   Ph: (312)996-4350
Marge Gockel, Assoc. Dir. of Adm.

★2464★
University of Illinois at Urbana-Champaign
Afro-American Studies and Research Center
Urbana, IL 61801   Ph: (217)333-0302
Martha H. Moore, Asst. Dir. of Adm.

★2465★
University of Iowa
African-American World Studies Program
Iowa City, IA 52242   Ph: (319)335-3847
Michael Barron, Acting Dir. of Adm.

★2466★
University of Kansas
African and African American Studies Department
Lawrence, KS 66045   Ph: (913)864-3054
Arthur D. Drayton, Chair

★2467★
University of Maryland - Baltimore County
Department of African-American Studies
Catonsville, MD 21228   Ph: (410)455-2291
Mindy Hand, Dir. of Adm.

★2468★
University of Maryland - College Park
Afro-American Studies
College Park, MD 20742   Ph: (301)405-1000
Dr. Linda M. Clement, Dir. of Adm.

★2469★
University of Massachusetts at Amherst
W.E.B. DuBois Department of Afro-American Studies
Amherst, MA 01003   Ph: (413)545-0222
Ruth Green, Acting Dir. of Adm.

★2470★
University of Massachusetts at Boston
Black Studies
Boston, MA 02125   Ph: (617)287-5000
David Norris, Dir. of Adm.

★2471★
University of Michigan - Ann Arbor
Center for Afro American and African Studies
Ann Arbor, MI 48109   Ph: (313)764-7433
Dr. Theodore Spencer, Dir. of Adm.

★2472★
University of Michigan - Flint
Afro-American and African Studies Program
Flint, MI 48502   Ph: (313)762-3300
David James, Director of Adm.

★2473★
University of Minnesota - Twin Cities Campus
Afro-American and African Studies Program
Minneapolis, MN 55455   Ph: (612)625-5000
Wayne Sigler, Dir. of Adm.

★2474★
University of Missouri—Columbia
Black Studies Program
Columbia, MO 65211   Ph: (314)882-7651
Dr. Gary L. Smith, Dir. of Adm.

★2475★
University of Nebraska - Lincoln
African-American Studies
Lincoln, NE 68588   Ph: (402)472-2480
Robert Hitchcock, Director

★2476★
University of Nevada, Las Vegas
Ethnic Studies Program
Las Vegas, NV 89154   Ph: (702)739-3443
Roosevelt Fitzgerald, Chair

★2477★
University of New Mexico
African-American Studies Department
1130 Mesa Vista Hall
Albuquerque, NM 87131   Ph: (505)277-3430
Tony Franklin, Director

★2478★
University of North Carolina at Chapel Hill
Afro-American Studies
Chapel Hill, NC 27514   Ph: (919)966-3621
Dr. Walters, Dir. of Adm.

★2479★
University of North Carolina at Charlotte
Afro-American and African Studies
Charlotte, NC 28223   Ph: (704)547-2211
Kathi Baucom, Dir. of Adm.

★2480★
University of North Carolina at Greensboro
Anthropology Department
Black Studies Program
Greensboro, NC 27412   Ph: (919)334-5243
Chuck Richard, Director of Admissions

★2481★
University of Northern Colorado
Afro-American Studies
Greeley, CO 80639   Ph: (303)351-2881
Gary Gullickson, Dir. of Adm.

★2482★
University of Notre Dame
African-American Studies Program
Notre Dame, IN 46556   Ph: (219)631-7505
Frederick Wright, Dir.

★2483★
University of Pennsylvania
Afro-American Studies Program
Philadelphia, PA 19104   Ph: (215)898-7507
Willis J. Stetson Jr., Dean of Adm.

★2484★
University of Pittsburgh
Department of Black Studies
Pittsburgh, PA 15260   Ph: (412)624-7488
Dr. Betsy A. Porter, Dir. of Adm. and Financial Aid

★2485★
University of South Carolina - Columbia
Afro-American Studies
Columbia, SC 29208   Ph: (803)777-7700
Terry Davis, Dir. of Adm.

★2486★
University of South Florida
Department of African and Afro-American Studies
Tampa, FL 33620   Ph: (813)974-3350
Vicki W. Ahrens, Dir. of Adm.

★2487★
University of Tennessee, Knoxville
Afro-American Studies Program
Knoxville, TN 37996   Ph: (615)974-2184
Dr. Gordon Stanley, Acting Dir. of Adm.

★2488★
University of Texas at Austin
Center for African and Afro-American Studies
Austin, TX 78712   Ph: (512)471-1711
Shirley Binder, Dir. of Adm.

★2489★
University of the Pacific
Department of Black Studies
Stockton, CA 95211   Ph: (209)946-2211
Ed Schoenberg, Dir. of Adm.

★2490★
University of Toledo
Minority Affairs
Toledo, OH 43606   Ph: (419)537-2696
Richard J. Eastop, Dean of Adm.

★2491★
University of Virginia
Carter G. Woodson Institute for Afro-American and
African Studies
Charlottesville, VA 22903   Ph: (804)924-3109
Armistad Robinson, Director

★2492★
University of Washington
Afro-American Studies Program
Seattle, WA 98195   Ph: (206)543-9686
Stephanie Preston, Asst. Dir. of Adm.

★2493★
University of Wisconsin—Milwaukee
Afro-American Studies Department
Milwaukee, WI 53201   Ph: (414)229-1122
Beth L. Weckmueller, Dir. of Adm.

★2494★
Upsala College
Black Studies
East Orange, NJ 07019   Ph: (201)266-7191
Susan Chalfin, Dir. of Adm.

★2495★
Vanderbilt University
Nashville, TN 37240   Ph: (615)322-2561
Dr. Neill Sanders, Dean of Adm.

★2496★
Virginia Polytechnic Institute and State University
Black Studies Program
Blacksburg, VA 24061-0202   Ph: (703)231-5812
Dr. H.D. Flowers II, Coord.

★2497★
Washington State University
Heritage House
Pullman, WA 99164   Ph: (509)335-5586
Terry Flynn, Acting Dir. of Adm.

★2498★
Washington University
Black Studies
St. Louis, MO 63130   Ph: (314)935-5000
Dr. Harold Wingood, Dean of Adm.

★2499★
Wayne State University
Black Americana Studies Center
Detroit, MI 48202   Ph: (313)577-3501
Michael Martin, Director

★2500★
Wellesley College
African Studies Department
Wellesley, MA 02181   Ph: (617)235-0320
Robin Gaynor, Assoc. Dir. of Adm.

★2501★
Wesleyan University
Center for Afro-American Studies
Middletown, CT 06457   Ph: (203)347-9411
Barbara Jan Wilson, Dean of Adm.

★2502★
Western Illinois University
African-American Studies Program
Currens Hall, Rm. 500
Macomb, IL 61455   Ph: (309)298-1181
Dr. J.Q. Adams, Acting Director

★2503★
Western Michigan University
Black Americana Studies
Kalamazoo, MI 49008　　　　Ph: (616)387-2000
Leroy Ray, Director

★2504★
William Paterson College of New Jersey
Department of African and Afro-American Studies
Wayne, NJ 07470　　　　Ph: (201)595-2126
Leo DeBartolo, Dir. of Adm.

★2505★
Williams College
African-American Studies Program
Williamstown, MA 01267　　　　Ph: (413)597-3131
Dennis Dickerson, Chair

★2506★
Yale University
Afro-American Studies Department
New Haven, CT 06520　　　　Ph: (203)432-1900
Richard Shaw, Dean of Adm.

★2507★
York College of City University of New York
Afro-American Studies
9420 Guy R. Brewer Blvd.
Jamaica, NY 11451　　　　Ph: (718)262-2165
Sally Nelson, Dir. of Adm.

★2508★
Youngstown State University
Black Studies Program
Youngstown, OH 44555　　　　Ph: (216)742-3158
Mrs. Marie Cullen, Assoc. Dir. of Adm.

Graduate Programs

★2509★
Atlanta University
Department of Afro-American Studies
James P. Brawley Dr. at Fer　　　　Ph: (404)880-8000
Atlanta, GA 30314　　　　Fax: (404)681-0251
Peggy Wade, Registrar and Dir. of Adm.

★2510★
Boston University
Africana-American Studies Program
Boston, MA 02215　　　　Ph: (617)353-2795
Herbert Otter Ph.D., Dir.

★2511★
Clark Atlanta Universtiy
Center for Africana-American Studies
Atlanta, GA 30314-4389　　　　Ph: (404)880-8784
Keith Baird Ph.D., Chair.

★2512★
Cornell University
Africana Studies and Research Center
Ithaca, NY 14853　　　　Ph: (607)255-4626
Locksley Egmondson, Dir.

★2513★
Emory University
African and Afro-American Studies Program
Atlanta, GA 30322　　　　Ph: (404)727-6847
Dr. Rudolph Byrd, Dir., Grad. Lib. Arts

★2514★
Morgan State University
Afro-American Studies
Baltimore, MD 21239　　　　Ph: (410)319-3400
Dr. Rosalyn Terborg-Penn, Coordinator of Graduate Program in Hist.

★2515★
North Carolina A&T State University
English and Afro-American Literature Program
Greensboro, NC 27411　　　　Ph: (919)334-7771
Dr. Joe Benson, Chair, Dept. of Eng.

★2516★
Ohio State University
Department of Black Studies
Columbus, OH 43210　　　　Ph: (614)292-3700
Dr. William E. Nelson, Chairperson

★2517★
Princeton University
Afro-American Studies Program
Princeton, NJ 08544　　　　Ph: (609)258-4270
Cornel West, Dir.

★2518★
San Francisco State University
School of Ethnic Studies
Black Studies Department
San Francisco, CA 94132　　　　Ph: (415)338-1693
Dr. Jim Okutsu, Graduate Coor.

★2519★
State University of New York at Albany
Department of African & Afro-American Studies
Albany, NY 12222　　　　Ph: (518)442-4730
Leonard Slade, Chairperson

★2520★
Temple University
African American Studies
Philadelphia, PA 19122　　　　Ph: (215)204-7200

★2521★
University of California - Los Angeles
Afro-American Studies Program
Los Angeles, CA 90024　　　　Ph: (310)825-7462
Eugene Grigsby, Director

★2522★
University of Iowa
African-American World Studies Program
Iowa City, IA 52242　　　　Ph: (319)335-0317
Fred Woodward, Chairperson

★2523★
University of Maryland Graduate School
African-American Studies
Baltimore, MD 21228　　　　Ph: (410)455-2538
Angela Walton-Raji, Asst. Dir.

★2524★
University of Wisconsin—Madison
Department of Afro-American Studies
Madison, WI 53706　　　　Ph: (608)263-1642
Prof. Freda Tesfagiorgis, Chairperson

★2525★
Yale University
African and Afro-American Studies Program
New Haven, CT 06520　　　　Ph: (203)432-1170
John Blassingame, Chairman

(8) Scholarships, Fellowships, and Loans

★2526★
AACP-AFPE Gateway Scholarships for Minorities
American Foundation for Pharmaceutical
  Education
618 Somerset St.
PO Box 7126
North Plainfield, NJ 07060   Ph: (201)561-8077
Study Level: Graduate. **Award Type:** Scholarship. **Purpose:** To encourage minority undergraduates in pharmacy colleges to continue their education and pursue a Ph.D. in one of the pharmaceutical sciences. **Applicant Eligibility:** Applicants must have participated in the American Association of Colleges of Pharmacy (AACP) Undergraduate Research Participation Program for Minorities. Candidates must be U.S. citizens or permanent residents and demonstrate proof of acceptance into a graduate program leading to a Ph.D. degree in any pharmaceutical discipline. **Selection Criteria:** Selection by the AFPE Boards of Grants. **Funds Available:** Four scholarhips at $5,000 each funded through a grant from GLAXO, Inc. are available. **Application Details:** Applicants must send the following information: letter providing a summary of research conducted as a recipient of the Research Participation Program award, additional research experience gained while a pharmacy undergraduate, and reasons for wishing to earn a Ph.D. degree; letter of recommendation from the pharmacy college/school dean; name of the graduate school applicant has been accepted into and the major area of study to be undertaken, e.g. pharmaceutics, pharmacy administration, pharmaceutical chemistry, etc; transcript of all completed pharmacy course work; list of special honors, awards, accomplishments in high school and pharmacy college reflecting achievement and an ability to succeed in graduate school. **Application Deadline:** All information must be received by AFPE by July 1. Recipients will be notified by August 1. Award will be provided anytime after September 1 and after confirmation that the student is enrolled in a graduate program for the Ph.D.

★2527★
AAUW Focus Professions Fellowships
American Association of University Women
Educational Foundation
1111 16th St. NW   Ph: (202)728-7603
Washington, DC 20006   Fax: (202)872-1425
Study Level: Graduate. **Award Type:** Fellowship. **Applicant Eligibility:** Awarded to minority women who are citizens or permanent residents of the United States and who are graduate professional degree candidates completing their final year of study in the fellowship year in the fields of business administration, law, or medicine. No restrictions exist on the age of the applicant or place of study (among accredited U.S. institutions). **Selection Criteria:** Special consideration will be given to applicants who demonstrate professional promise in innovative or neglected areas of research and/or practice, public interest concerns, or those specialties in which women remain underrepresented. **Funds Available:**

Fellowships stipends range from $5,000 to $9,500 for full-time study. **Application Details:** Applications available August 1 - December 1 (except M.B.A.); August 1 - December 15 (M.B.A. only). **Application Deadline:** December 15; February 1 (M.B.A. only).

★2528★
ABF Summer Research Fellowships in Law and Social Science for Minority Undergraduate Students
American Bar Foundation
750 N. Lake Shore Dr.
Chicago, IL 60611
Study Level: Undergraduate. **Award Type:** Fellowship. **Purpose:** To acquaint undergraduate minority students with research in the field of law and social science. **Applicant Eligibility:** Applicants must be citizens or permanent residents of the United States. They must be American Indians, Blacks, Mexicans, or Puerto Ricans. Candidates should have completed at least the sophomore year of college and must not have received a bachelor's degree by the time the fellowship begins. Applicants must have a grade point average of at least 3.0 on a 4.0 scale and be moving toward an academic major in one of the social science disciplines. **Funds Available:** Four summer fellowships are awarded. The fellowship lasts 10 weeks and pays a stipend of $3,300. **Application Details:** A formal application must be submitted, along with a personal statement, official transcripts, and one letter of reference from a faculty member familiar with the student's work. **Application Deadline:** March 1. Recipients are announced by April 15.

★2529★
ADHA Minority Scholarship Program
American Dental Hygienists' Association
  Institute
Institute for Oral Health
444 N. Michigan Ave., Ste. 3400   Ph: (312)440-8944
Chicago, IL 60611   Fax: (312)440-8929
Study Level: Undergraduate. **Award Type:** Scholarship. **Purpose:** Minority scholarships provide financial assistance for minority groups currently underrepresented in the dental hygiene program. **Applicant Eligibility:** Applicants must be members of minority groups, including Native Americans, African-Americans, Hispanics, Asians, and males. Male applicants are not required to be members of minority groups. Applicants must have completed a minimum of one year in a dental hygiene curriculum. They must have a minimum grade point average of 3.0 on a 4.0 scale for the time they have been enrolled in a dental hygiene curriculum. Applicants must be full-time students during the academic year for which they are applying. Candidates must be able to document financial need of at least $1,500. **Funds Available:** Funds for financial assistance are limited because they consist of donations and grants from various sources. **Application Details:** A formal application must be filed. Upon request, a scholarship application packet is sent to interested candidates. **Application**

Deadline: Completed packets and all other application materials must be filed by May 1. All applicants are notified in September whether or not they have been selected as recipients.

★2530★
AEJ Summer Internships for Minorities
Institute for Education in Journalism
New York University
Institute of Afro-American Affairs
289 Mercer St., Ste. 601   Ph: (212)998-2130
New York, NY 10003   Fax: (212)995-4040

Study Level: Undergraduate. **Award Type:** Internship. **Applicant Eligibility:** The program is for undergraduates; preference is for full-time juniors or full-time seniors going on to graduate schools. The students' credentials must reflect an interest in journalism. Students must be members of a minority group, e.g., Black, Puerto Rican, American Indian, Mexican American, Eskimo. **Funds Available:** As an AEJ intern, the candidate is placed for 10 weeks in an entry level position with news publications, primarily in the New York/New Jersey area. As a full-time writer the minimum stipend is $200 a week for a 35-hour week. **Application Details:** Formal application requires information about the applicant's reasons for pursuing a career in journalism; what he/she would like to gain from the internship; an autobiographical essay of less than 500 words; college transcript; samples of work; resume; and two recommendations. **Application Deadline:** Application must be filed by mid-December.

★2531★
AFDH Dental Scholarships for Minority Students
American Fund for Dental Health
211 E. Chicago Ave., Ste. 820   Ph: (312)787-6270
Chicago, IL 60611   Fax: (312)787-9114

Study Level: Doctorate. **Award Type:** Scholarship. **Purpose:** The American Fund for Dental Health recognizes the fact that the cost of a dental education has prevented many promising students from disadvantaged minorities from considering dentistry as a career. It is also acutely aware of the need for many more dentists to provide basic dental care for all Americans. In 1968, the AFDH received a three-year challenge grant from the W.K. Kellogg Foundation to establish a dental scholarship program for Black students. Since then the program has been expanded to include students from three aditional minority groups. **Applicant Eligibility:** Candidates must be United States citizens from a minority group which is currently under-represented in the dental profession, i.e., African Americans, Hispanics, Blacks, Native Americans and Puerto Ricans. Only minority students who are entering their first year of dental school are eligible. **Selection Criteria:** Candidates are considered on the basis of their academic records, financial need, and character. While scholastic achievement is important, any student with an interest in dentistry is encouraged to apply. **Funds Available:** Up to $1,000 is awarded for first year dental school only. Scholarships are intended to be used for school expenses and living costs. Grants will not be made to anyone receiving a full scholarship from another source. **Application Details:** Each candidate must submit a formal application, transcripts of all and college records, and a financial aid form. Each applicant must arrange for two persons to send letters of reference addressing the candidate's character, personality, and academic ability. No application is considered unless it is completely filled out and accompanied by required supporting documents. **Application Deadline:** May 1. Recipients are announced in July.

★2532★
Agnes Jones Jackson Scholarship
National Association for the Advancement
  of Colored People
4805 Mt. Hope Dr.
Baltimore, MD 21215-3297   Ph: (410)358-8900

Study Level: Graduate; Undergraduate. **Award Type:** Scholarship. **Applicant Eligibility:** Applicants must be undergraduate and graduate students who have not reached the age of 25 by April 30 of the year of application. They must have been current regular members for at least one year or fully paid life members. Undergraduates must possess a grade point average of at least 2.5 and graduate students must possess a 3.0 or "B" average. **Funds**

Available: The undergraduate award is $1,500; the graduate award is $2,500. **Application Details:** Application forms will be available from the NAACP in January. **Application Deadline:** April 30.

★2533★
AHA Minority Scientist Development Award
American Heart Association
National Center
7320 Greenville Ave.
Dallas, TX 75231

Study Level: Postdoctorate. **Award Type:** Grant. **Purpose:** To assist promising minority scientists in the early stages of research careers and minority clinical faculty seeking basic research training to develop independent research programs. These five-year awards combine rigorous full-time training in a highly qualified preceptor's laboratory for two years, and project support for three years of independent research. **Applicant Eligibility:** Applicants must hold an M.D., Ph.D., D.O., or equivalent degree, and must be members of ethnic groups underrepresented in the field of cardiovascular research. Underrepresented minority investigators are defined as persons who are Black, Hispanic, Native American, or Pacific Islander. Candidates must have between two and five years of relevant postdoctoral experience. Those having attained the rank of Assistant Professor and clinical faculty wishing to resume or embark upon research careers are eligible to apply if this criterion is met. Applicants must demonstrate a strong commitment to a career of investigative science. At the time of application, candidates must be citizens or permanent residents of the United States. Student and exchange visas are not acceptable. During the preceptorship period, the awardee will be expected to spend virtually 100 percent of his or her time in research. After the preceptorship, no less than 80 percent of his or her time must be spent in research. The applicant and sponsor must make all arrangements necessary for the proposed program of training and research, including those with the scientific preceptor. The sponsor should be familiar with the applicant's area of research, committed to the independent professional development of the applicant, and must indicate a willingness to protect the applicant's time so that the necessary time is devoted to the research project. Sponsor and preceptor shall not be the same person. Institutional commitment is limited to the duration of the award. However, evidence of willingness to give support to the candidate after the award would be considered favorably. The institution is expected to provide the awardee with a sabbatical/leave of absence for the preceptorship training. The sponsoring department must commit itself to provide the space and equipment required and to honor the applicant's commitment of time for research. **Selection Criteria:** Factors which enter into the committee's judgement include: probability of recruiting a potential investigator who otherwise might not establish an independent research program; applicant's need for research training; qualifications and commitment of the preceptor; growth potential for the applicant implicit in the preceptorship; scientific merit of the studies proposed for the preceptorship; estimate of the potential of the applicant; and institutional commitment. The initiation of independent research will be based upon: a detailed account of the work done during the preceptorship; an evaluation of the candidate's potential as an independent investigator by the preceptor; a detailed plan of the work to be undertaken in the sponsoring institution; and possibly an interview with a member of the Research Committee. **Funds Available:** Total salary paid to awardee will be determined by the awardee's department head and/or institutional sponsor. The Association's annual portion of the total stipend will not exceed $40,000 in the first year of the award. $1,000 incremental increases will be given annually thereafter during the term of the award. No indirect costs are provided. After satisfactory completion of the preceptorship, an Initiation Grant of $33,000 plus 10 percent overhead will be provided to the awardee for initiation of independent research at the sponsoring institution. Moving expenses, up to $2,500 each way, may be provided if justified, if the preceptor's laboratory is more than 50 miles from the sponsoring institution. **Application Details:** Applicants must furnish a specific plan for the development of an independent research program. Statements and commitments are required from three participants in that plan: the applicant, a sponsor at the applicant's institution, and a research preceptor. Applicants without home institutions must identify a facility where they will conduct independent research by the end of the preceptorship period. A sponsor at such a facility must also be identified by this time. **Application Deadline:** June 1; award activation July of the following year.

★2534★
AICPA Scholarships for Minority Undergraduate Accounting Majors
American Institute of Certified Public
  Accountants
1211 Avenue of the Americas
New York, NY 10036-8775

Study Level: Undergraduate. **Award Type:** Scholarship. **Applicant Eligibility:** Applicant must be a minority student who is an undergraduate accounting major, and a United States citizen or permanent resident. **Funds Available:** The maximum individual scholarship is $2,000 for an academic year. More than five hundred scholarships may be awarded annually. Scholarships may be renewed if recipients are making satisfactory progress toward completing their degree; reapplication forms and transcripts must be submitted. **Application Details:** Application forms call for information on personal background, individual and family financial needs, academic background, expected college expenses and income from other sources. A current transcript of all academic grades must also be submitted. The application must be signed by the responsible financial aid officer of the student's college or university. **Application Deadline:** Applications must be filed by July 1 for consideration of scholarships for the full academic year or fall semester and by December 1 for the spring semester.

★2535★
Albert W. Dent Scholarship
American College of Healthcare Executives
  Foundation
840 N. Lake Shore Dr.   Ph: (312)943-0544
Chicago, IL 60611   Fax: (312)943-3791

Study Level: Graduate. **Award Type:** Scholarship. **Purpose:** To provide financial aid and increase the enrollment of minority and physically disabled students in healthcare management graduate programs and to encourage them to obtain middle- and upper-level positions in healthcare management. **Applicant Eligibility:** Candidates are Student Associates in good standing in the American College of Healthcare Executives. They must be either minority or physically disabled undergraduate students who either have been accepted for full-time study for the fall term in a healthcare management graduate program accredited by the Accrediting Commission on Education for Health Services Administration, or who are enrolled full-time and are in good academic standing in an accredited graduate program in healthcare management. Candidates must be United States or Canadian citizens. Previous recipients are not eligible. Financial need must be demonstrated. **Funds Available:** Each scholarship is $3,000. The number of awards varies from year to year. **Application Deadline:** Completed applications must be filed between January 1 and March 31.

★2536★
Alphonso Deal Scholarship Award
National Black Police Association
3251 Mt. Pleasant St. NW, 2nd Fl.
Washington, DC 20010   Ph: (202)986-2070

Study Level: Undergraduate. **Award Type:** Scholarship. **Purpose:** To enhance the higher educational opportunities among qualified high school graduates in the area of law enforcement or other related fields for the betterment of the criminal justice system. **Applicant Eligibility:** Applicant must be a U.S. citizen, a high school senior accepted by a college or university prior to the date of award, and have maintained at least a 2.5 GPA. **Selection Criteria:** Selection is based upon GPA, recommendations, and extra-curricular activities. **Funds Available:** $500 per recipient. **Application Details:** Candidates should submit information regarding their educational background, biographical information, and transcripts. **Application Deadline:** June 1.

★2537★
American Architectural Foundation - Minority/Disadvantaged Scholarship
American Architectural Foundation
1735 New York Ave. NW   Ph: (202)626-7511
Washington, DC 20006-5292   Fax: (202)626-7420

Study Level: Undergraduate; Postgraduate. **Award Type:** Scholarship. **Purpose:** To financially assist minority and disadvantaged students in their pursual of a professional degree in architecture at schools of architecture accredited by The National Architectural Accrediting Board (NAAB). **Applicant Eligibility:** Qualified applicants will be high school seniors, technical school/junior college students transferring to an NAAB school, or college freshmen beginning a program that will lead to either a bachelor's or master's degree. **Selection Criteria:** Students who have completed their first year of a standard four-year curriculum are not eligible. **Funds Available:** The award amount is determined by the financial need of the student and in cooperation with the scholarship program director and the directors of financial aid at the school. The scholarship is not intended to cover the full cost of education. **Application Details:** Candidates must first submit a nomination in order to receive an application. Suitable nominations may be made by the following: an architect or architectural firm; a local chapter of The American Institute of Architects; a community design center; a guidance counselor or teacher; a dean, department head, or professor from an accredited school of architecture; or a director of a community, civic, or religious organization. **Application Deadline:** Nominations must be received by December 4, 1992. Completed applications must be received by January 15, 1993. ** For nomination forms, write: The Minority/Disadvantaged Scholarship, AIA/AAF Scholarship Program Director, at the above address.

★2538★
American Economic Association/Federal Reserve System Minority Graduate Fellowships in Economics
American Economic Association
2014 Broadway, Ste. 305
Nashville, TN 37203

Study Level: Doctorate. **Award Type:** Fellowship. **Applicant Eligibility:** Candidates must be U.S. citizens who are Black, Hispanic, or Native American and are enrolled in an accredited graduate program in economics in the United States. They should be doctoral students who have completed their comprehensive examinations and, if applicable, their field examinations, and are about to begin their dissertation research. **Selection Criteria:** Awards will be based on academic performance. Preference will be given to applicants whose area of concentration is of special interest to the Federal Reserve System, for instance financial markets and monetary policy, nonfinancial macroeconomics, forecasting, banking markets and financial structure, regional studies, the external sector of the U.S. economy, the conomies of other countries, foreign exchange markets, and international banking and financial markets. **Funds Available:** A monthly stipend of $900 during the academic year and the institution nominating the student must provide tuition relief. **Application Details:** Write for application materials. **Application Deadline:** March 1. ** Dr. Margaret C. Simms, Chair, AEA Committee on the Status of Minority Groups in the Economics Profession, c/o The Joint Center for Political and Economic Studies, 1090 Vermont Ave., NW, Suite 1100, Washington, DC 20005. Telephone: (202)789-3500.

★2539★
American Economic Association Summer Minority Program at Stanford University
American Economic Association
2014 Broadway, Ste. 305
Nashville, TN 37203

Study Level: Undergraduate. **Award Type:** Other. **Applicant Eligibility:** Candidates must be minority juniors and qualified sophomores majoring in economics and who are interested in pursuing a doctorate degree in economics. **Funds Available:** All students admitted into the program will receive a scholarship that pays a stipend of $1,500 and covers tuition, room and board, books, student health benefits, and the cost of transportation. As part of the regular summer quarter at Stanford, students attending this program will receive grades and transcripts reflecting 12 units of credit. **Application Details:** Write for an application. **Application Deadline:**

March 1. ** Susan A. Maher, AEA Program Administrator, Food Research Institute, Stanford University, Stanford, CA 94305-6084. Telephone: (415)723-3653.

★2540★
**American Psychological Association Minority
   Fellowship in Neuroscience**
American Psychological Association
1200 17th St. NW
Washington, DC 20036   Ph: (202)995-7600

Study Level: Doctorate. **Award Type:** Fellowship. **Purpose:** To increase the number of ethnic minority students who are trained at the doctorate level in the neuroscience field. **Applicant Eligibility:** Must be American citizens or permanent visa residents including, but not limited to, those who are Black, Hispanic, American Indian, Alaskan Native, Asian American, and Pacific Islanders, and those who show an interest in and commitment to careers in neuroscience research. This program is open to students beginning study leading to the doctoral degree in neuroscience as listed in the *Society for Neuroscience Training Prgrams in North America* handbook. New students must gain admission to a graduate program and express a commitment to neuroscience research. **Selection Criteria:** Based on scholarship, research potential, research experience, commitment to research career in neuroscience, writing ability, and financial need. **Funds Available:** $8,500 for twelve months; cost-sharing arrangements with unversities often include full tuition scholarships and additional stipends. Students can receive up to three years of funding, contingent upon their continued good standing in the school's graduate program and the availability of funding. **Application Details:** Write or phone for application form. **Application Deadline:** January 15; announcements are made in March.

★2541★
**American Psychological Association Minority
   Fellowships in Psychologv-Clinical Training**
American Psychological Association
1200 17th St. NW
Washington, DC 20036   Ph: (202)995-7600

Study Level: Doctorate. **Award Type:** Fellowship. **Purpose:** To increase the number of ethnic minority students who are trained in psychology at the doctorate level. The ultimate goal of the program is that upon completion of training, these persons will provide services in their respective ethnic minority communities as clinicians or will conduct research that will increase the base of knowledge related to ethnic minority mental health issues. **Applicant Eligibility:** Must be American citizens or permanent visa residents including, but not limited to, those who are Black, Hispanic, American Indian, Alaskan Native, Asian American, and Pacific Islanders, and those who show an interest in and commitment to careers in mental health, research, and/or services relevant to ethnic and racial minority groups. This program is open to students beginning or continuing study leading to the doctoral degree in psycholgy and students must be enrolled in a training program that is APA accredited. New students must gain admission to a graduate program and express a commitment to research, delivery of clinical services, and involvement in minority issues in mental health and behavioral sciences. **Selection Criteria:** Based on clinical and/or research potential, scholarship, writing ability, ethnic minority identification, knowledge of broad issues in psychology, professional commitment, and financial aid. **Funds Available:** $8,500 for twelve months; cost-sharing arrangments with universities often include full tuition scholarships and additional stipends. Fellowship is an annual award that may be extended up to three years contingent on satisfactory academic progress. **Application Details:** Call or write for application form beginning in August. **Application Deadline:** January 15.

★2542★
**American Psychological Association Minority
   Fellowships in Psychology-Research Training**
American Psychological Association
1200 17th St. NW
Washington, DC 20036   Ph: (202)995-7600

Study Level: Doctorate. **Award Type:** Fellowship. **Purpose:** To increase the number of ethnic minority students who are trained in psychology at the doctorate level. The ultimate goal of the program is that upon completion of training, these persons will conduct

research that will increase the base of knowledge related to ethnic minority mental health issues. **Applicant Eligibility:** Must be American citizens or permanent visa residents including, but not limited to, those who are Black, Hispanic, American Indian, Alaskan Native, Asian American, and Pacific Islanders, and those who show an interest in and commitment to careers in mental health, research, and/or services relevant to ethnic and racial minority groups. This program is open to students beginning or continuing study leading to the doctoral degree in psychology and students must be enrolled in a training program that is APA accredited. New students must gain admission to a graduate program and express a commitment to research, delivery of clinical services, and involvement in minority issues in mental health and behavioral sciences. **Selection Criteria:** Based on research potential, scholarship, writing ability, ethnic minority identification, knowledge of broad issues in psychology, professional commitment, and financial aid. **Funds Available:** $8,500 for twelve months; cost-sharing arrangements with universities often include full tuition scholarships and additional stipends. Fellowship is an annual award that may be extended for up to three years contingent on satisfactory academic progress. **Application Details:** Call or write for application form beginning in August. **Application Deadline:** January 15.

★2543★
**American Society for Microbiology Predoctoral
   Fellowships in Microbiology for Minority Students**
American Society for Microbiology
1325 Massachusetts Ave. NW
Washington, DC 20005

Study Level: Doctorate. **Award Type:** Fellowship. **Purpose:** To help increase the number of underrepresented minorities who complete doctoral degrees in microbiology and related fields thus elevating the pool of highly qualified individuals in these areas. **Applicant Eligibility:** Applicants must be U.S. citizens or permanent residents who have been formally admitted as a candidate for a doctorate in microbiology at an accredited U.S. institution at the time of application. They must alos be a member of one of the following minority groups: African American, Hispanic, Native Alaskan, Native American, or Native Pacific Islander. **Funds Available:** The total award is $10,000, a portion of which must be used for tuition and fees. If a fellowship awardee leaves the approved program during an award year, he or she will forfeit that portion of the stipend and tuition and fees remaining to be disbursed and the balance will be returned to the ASM. As part of the acceptance agreement, each awardee will be asked to provide an accounting of predoctoral progress at the end of each semester in the year for which he or she has fellowship support. **Application Deadline:** May 1.

★2544★
APA Planning Fellowships
American Planning Association
1776 Massachusetts Ave. NW
Washington, DC 20036   Ph: (202)872-0611

Study Level: Graduate. **Award Type:** Fellowship. **Applicant Eligibility:** Applicants must be citizens of the United States or Canada and must be members of African-American, Hispanic, or Native American minority groups. Candidates must be enrolled or accepted for enrollment as first and second year students in a graduate planning program that has been accredited by the Planning Accreditation Board. **Selection Criteria:** Preference is given to full-time schedules. **Funds Available:** Several fellowships ranging from $1,000 to $4,000 are awarded annually. One-half of the award is paid to the school in September; the second half in January, contingent upon a written report from the school stating that the student is still enrolled and doing satisfactory work. Recipients of first year Fellowships may reapply for the second year. **Application Details:** The application must include a letter of nomination from a professor or school official unless self-nominated. A maximum of two other letters of recommendation may be submitted to enhance the application. A two to five page statement by the applicant describing how his or her graduate education will be applied to career goals and why the student has chosen planning as a career as well as a resume must also be provided. Transcripts of all previous collegiate and graduate work must be sent directly from the office of the registrar. The following materials must be also submitted: an APA financial aid application form; a notarized statement of financial independence; a photocopy of the university's acceptance letter for graduate study in planning; and written verification from the university's financial officer or copies of a school publication indicating the average cost of one academic year of graduate school. **Application Deadline:** May 15. Awards decisions are made by mid-June.

★2545★
APA Undergraduate Minority Scholarships
American Planning Association
1776 Massachusetts Ave. NW
Washington, DC 20036   Ph: (202)872-0611
Study Level: Undergraduate. **Award Type:** Scholarship. **Purpose:** To recognize outstanding minority undergraduate planning programs in the United States. **Applicant Eligibility:** Must be students in their second or third year of study. **Selection Criteria:** Based on academic merit, leadership potential, and evidence of responsible citizenship. An advisory board consisting of seven members of the American Planning Association will screen the applications. **Application Details:** Application will ask for: grade point average; participation in university activities, participtin in community, city, state and/or national activities; involvement in minority community affairs; and career objectives. Applicants must also submit a brief essay, copy of college transcript, and at least two letters of recommendations. Applications will be distributed to both degree and non-degree planning programs that offered curricula programs. **Application Deadline:** May 15.

★2546★
APSA Graduate Fellowships for African-American Students
American Political Science Association
1527 New Hampshire Ave. NW
Washington, DC 20036
Study Level: Graduate. **Award Type:** Fellowship. **Purpose:** To identify and to aid prospective African-American political science graduate students; encourage other institutions to provide financial assistance to these prospective students; and to increase the number of African-American Ph.D.'s in political science. **Applicant Eligibility:** Applicants must be African-American students who qualify for acceptance at accredited institutions of higher learning and who have a potential for graduate work in political science. Priority is given to persons about to enter graduate school. Applicants with the greatest financial need are given preference. Students are free to attend the university of their choice. **Funds Available:** APSA Fellows are chosen and ranked. The first three are offered stipends of approximately $6,000 each for one year of study. These Fellows usually receive a waiver of tuition and fees. The graduate school attended by the recipient is encouraged to support the future years of study. The remaining Fellows are designated as Fellows without stipend and are recommended to graduate departments of political science for fellowships at the department level. **Application Deadline:** Applications must be received prior to December 1.

★2547★
ASC Fellowship for Ethnic Minorities
The American Society of Criminology
1314 Kinnear Rd., Ste. 212   Ph: (614)292-9207
Columbus, OH 43212   Fax: (614)292-6767
Study Level: Doctorate. **Award Type:** Fellowship. **Purpose:** To encourage minority students to enter the field of criminology. **Applicant Eligibility:** Applicants should be minority students, especially African Americans, Hispanics, Native Americans, and Asian Americans. They need not be members of The American Society of Criminology. The winner must be accepted in a program of doctoral studies in criminology or criminal justice. Individuals studying in social sciences or public policy are encouraged to apply. **Funds Available:** The ASC offers a one year fellowship for $12,000. **Application Details:** Applicants must provide: an up-to-date curriculum vita; evidence of academic excellence (e.g., copies of undergraduate and/or graduate transcripts); three letters of reference; and a letter or statement describing career plans, salient experiences, and the nature of the applicant's interest in criminology or criminal justice, as well as an indication of race/ethnicity and of need and prospects for financial assistance for graduate study.

Application materials should be sent to Sarah Hall, Administrator, American Society of Criminology. **Application Deadline:** June 1.

★2548★
AT&T Bell Laboratories Cooperative Research Fellowships for Minorities
AT&T Bell Laboratories
Special Programs
Crawfords Corner Rd., Rm. 1E-209   Ph: (908)949-4301
Holmdel, NJ 07733-1988   Fax: (908)949-6800
Study Level: Graduate. **Award Type:** Fellowship. **Purpose:** To identify and develop scientific and engineering research ability among members of underrepresented minority groups, and to increase their representation in the sciences and engineering. **Applicant Eligibility:** Applicants must be members of underrepresented minority groups (Blacks, Native American Indians, and Hispanics) who are graduate students in programs leading to doctoral degrees in the following disciplines: chemistry, chemical engineering, communications science, computer science and engineering, electrical engineering, information science, materials science, mathematics, mechanical engineering, operations research, physics, and statistics. Awards are made only to U.S. citizens or permanent residents, and who are admitted to full-time study in a graduate program approved agreed to by AT&T Bell Laboratories. **Selection Criteria:** Candidates are selected on the basis of scholastic attainment in their field of specialization, and other evidence of their ability and potential as research scientists. A personal interview with AT&T Bell Laboratories scientists and engineers is arranged to select an appropriate summer mentor. **Funds Available:** Nine to 12 fellowships are awarded annually. The fellowship provides full tuition, an annual stipend of $13,200 (paid bi-monthly September through May), books, fees, and related travel expenses. Fellowship recipients may not accept any other fellowship support. Fellowships may be renewed on a yearly basis for four years, contingent upon satisfactory progress toward the doctoral degree. If needed, the fellowship will be renewed after four years subject to an annual review by the CRFP committee. Fellowship holders are invited to resume employment at AT&T Bell Laboratories during subsequent summers, but may elect to continue supervised university study or research; fellowship support would be continued (with the exception of the living stipend). During periods of summer employment, fellowship holders receive salaries commensurate with those earned by employees at approximately the same level of training. **Application Details:** Applications should include: a completed application form; official transcripts of grades from all undergraduate schools attended; a statement of interest; letters of recommendation from college professors who can evaluate the applicant's scientific aptitude and potential for research (additional letters of recommendation are also invited); Graduate Record Examination scores on the Aptitude Test and the appropriate Advanced Test (scores are required and should be submitted by listing on the GRE registration form Institution Code R2041-2-00, AT&T Bell Laboratories). **Application Deadline:** Applications and all supporting documentation, preferably in one package, must be received by January 15.

★2549★
Aura E. Severinghaus Award
National Medical Fellowships
254 W. 31 St., 7th Fl.
New York, NY 10001
Study Level: Doctorate. **Award Type:** Scholarship. **Applicant Eligibility:** Candidates must be American Blacks, mainland Puerto Ricans, Mexican-Americans, and American Indians who are enrolled in accredited schools of allopathic or osteopathic medicine in the United States and who are United States citizens. **Selection Criteria:** Severinghaus Award is for a student at Columbia University College of Physicians and Surgeons who has academic excellence and leadership. **Funds Available:** One-renewable Severinghaus Award of $2000 is awarded annually. **Application Details:** Application by nomination by the committee of faculty at Columbia University College of Physicians and Surgeons only. **Application Deadline:** Nominations requested in September.

★2550★
Baxter Foundation Scholarships
National Medical Fellowships
254 W. 31 St., 7th Fl.
New York, NY 10001

Study Level: Doctorate. **Award Type:** Scholarship. **Applicant Eligibility:** Candidates must be American Blacks, mainland Puerto Ricans, Mexican-Americans, and American Indians who are enrolled in accredited schools of allopathic or osteopathic medicine in the United States and who are United States citizens. Baxter Scholarship applicants are second-year students who have previously received NMF financial assistance and have outstanding academic achievement. **Funds Available:** Two non-renewable Baxter Scholarships of $2500 each are awarded annually. **Application Details:** Applications by Dean's nomination only. **Application Deadline:** Nominations requested in September.

★2551★
The Benjamin E. Mays Scholarships for Ministry
The Fund for Theological Education, Inc.
475 Riverside Dr., Ste. 832
New York, NY 10115-0008   Ph: (212)870-2058

Study Level: Graduate. **Award Type:** Scholarship. **Purpose:** To support Black North Americans who hold high promise for effectiveness in the ministries of the Christian churches and to recruit women and men in the United States and Canada who are ordained or committed to the ordained ministry. **Applicant Eligibility:** Nominees shall be ordained or an official candidate for ordination. They shall be Black citizens of the United States or Canada. They shall be at least graduating seniors from an accredited college or university. Candidates must be enrolled or prepared to enroll full-time in a Master of Divinity program at a theological school fully accredited by The Association of Theological Schools in the United States and Canada. A person who has already attended a theological school is not eligible. **Selection Criteria:** Academic competence and promise for ministry. **Funds Available:** The amount of the scholarship will vary according to individual need. The scholarship is not intended to replace financial aid normally offered by the student's church or school. Scholarships are not renewable. **Application Details:** A person must be nominated by a church administrator, minister, member of a faculty or administration, or FTE alumni/ae. The letter of nomination must provide the person's name, address, and indicate some of the qualities for ministry which the person exemplifies. **Application Deadline:** Nominations must be received by FTE by November 10 of each year. An application will be sent directly to nominees and must be returned by December 15. Early nominations are encouraged. Awards will be announced in April of each year.

★2552★
Benjamin E. Mays Scholarships for Ministry for Part-Time Students
The Fund for Theological Education, Inc.
475 Riverside Dr., Ste. 832
New York, NY 10115-0008   Ph: (212)870-2058

Study Level: Graduate. **Award Type:** Scholarship. **Purpose:** To identify and support Black North American men and women who demonstrate effectiveness in Christian ministry and intend to complete the Master of Divinity degree on a part-time basis. **Applicant Eligibility:** Nominees shall be ordained or are official candidates for ordination. They must have demonstrated identification with and commitment to the practice of ministry in Spanish speaking communites in the United States, Canada, or Puero Rico. They must be in circumstances, either professional or personal, which preclude full-time theological education. Candidates must be enrolled or prepared to enroll full-time in a Master of Divinity program at a theological school fully accredited by The Association of Theological Schools in the United States and Canada. Consideration will be given to persons pursuing other first level seminary degrees (such as the M.R.E. and the M.A.R.). **Selection Criteria:** Academic competence and promise for ministry. **Funds Available:** The amount of the scholarship will vary according to individual need. The scholarship is not intended to replace financial aid normally offered by the student's church or school. Persons selected Scholars are eligible for renewal of the scholarship. **Application Details:** A person must be nominated by a church administrator, minister, member of a faculty or administration, or FTE alumni/ae. The letter of nomination must provide the person's

name, address, and indicate some of the qualities for ministry which the person exemplifies. **Application Deadline:** Nominations must be received by FTE by November 10 of each year. An application will be sent directly to nominees and must be returned by December 15. Early nominations are encouraged. Awards will be announced in April of each year.

★2553★
Big Apple Engineering Scholarship Program
National Action Council for Minorities in
    Engineering
3 W. 35th St.
New York, NY 10001-2281   Ph: (212)279-2626

Study Level: Undergraduate. **Award Type:** Scholarship. **Applicant Eligibility:** Applicants must be African American, Hispanic, and American Indian students who are studying engineering in the state of New York. **Funds Available:** These supplemental awards may be used toward the costs of tuition and other educational and out-of-pocket expenses. **Application Details:** Scholarships are administered by participating colleges and universities. Students should apply to the dean of admissions or call NACME.

★2554★
Black American Cinema Society Grants
Black American Cinema Society
3617 Montclair St.   Ph: (213)737-3292
Los Angeles, CA 90018   Fax: (213)737-2842

Study Level: Undergraduate; Graduate; Other. **Award Type:** Grant. **Purpose:** To encourage and support Black filmmakers in their attempt to make or finish films. **Applicant Eligibility:** College students and independent filmmakers are eligible. **Funds Available:** Awards of up to $3,000 are given. **Application Details:** Applicants must submit works on 16mm film or 3/4-inch videotape. Each film must be created, produced, and directed by black filmmakers. Applications must be requested before February 10.

★2555★
Carole Simpson Scholarship
Radio and Television News Directors
    Foundation
1000 Connecticut Ave. NW, Ste. 615   Ph: (202)659-6570
Washington, DC 20036   Fax: (202)223-4007

Study Level: Undergraduate; Graduate. **Award Type:** Scholarship. **Applicant Eligibility:** Applicants may be any sophomore or more advance undergraduate or graduate minority student whose career objectives are broadcast or cable news, and who have declared a major in electronic journalism at an accredited or nationally recognized college or university. Applicants must have at least one full year of school remaining. **Funds Available:** $2,000 for one year of study. **Application Details:** Application may be obtained from the faculty advisor, dean's office, or from the Foundation. **Application Deadline:** March 15.

★2556★
Central Intelligence Agency Undergraduate Scholarship
Central Intelligence Agency
Office of Student Programs
Dept. S, Rm. 4N2OJ
1925
Washington, DC 20013   Ph: (703)482-7303

Study Level: Undergraduate. **Award Type:** Internship; Scholarship. **Purpose:** To give financial assistance to disabled or minority undergraduates who wish to complete postsecondary education and gain experience at the CIA. **Applicant Eligibility:** Applicants must be minority or disabled, must have 3.0 GPA, and must major in engineering, computer science, mathematics, physics, cartography, imagery science, Russian, Chinese, or Japanese. **Funds Available:** Five or more scholarships/internships are awarded each year and provide tuition; summer internships provide competitive salaries. **Application Deadline:** January.

★2557★
Chicago Association of Black Journalists Scholarships
Chicago Association of Black Journalists
c/o Dr. Lillian S. Bell
802 York Woods Dr., Apt F
Elkhart, IN 46516   Ph: (219)293-1122

Study Level: Undergraduate; Graduate. **Award Type:** Scholarship. **Purpose:** To financially assist minorities in journalism during the 1993-1994 academic year. **Applicant Eligibility:** Applicants must be minorities and full-time undergraduate juniors, seniors, or full-time graduate students attending an accredited college or univeristy in the Chicago metropolitan area. In addition, candidates must be majoring in print or broadcast journalism, or show a strong interest in a journalism career. **Funds Available:** $2,000. **Application Details:** Send: completed application form; resume, including candidate's contact information and career goals; three reference letters (two from college faculty and one from a non-faculty person), including address/telephone of writer; college transcript; and a 500-word essay discussing how and why applicant was drawn to journalism, and what applicant expects to contribute to journalism in general and as a minority journalist specifically. **Application Deadline:** February 28, 1993.

★2558★
CIC Predoctoral Fellowship
Committee on Institutional Cooperation
  (CIC)
Kirkwood Hall
Indiana University   Ph: (812)855-0822
Bloomington, IN 47405   Fax: (812)855-9943

Study Level: Doctorate; Graduate. **Award Type:** Fellowship. **Purpose:** To increase minority representation in areas of study leading toward the Ph.D., and to increase minority presence on "Big Ten" campuses. **Applicant Eligibility:** Applicants should hold a bachelors degree from an accredited institution. To be eligible for the fellowship, applicants should be admitted into an approved masters or doctorate program leading to a Ph.D. **Selection Criteria:** Selections are based entirely upon merit as demonstrated on the application and supporting materials. **Funds Available:** CIC awards 10, 4-year fellowships to minority candidates in the humanities and 25, 5-year fellowships to minority candidates in the social sciences. The award amount for the 1990-91 school year was full tuition waiver plus a $9,000 stipend. **Application Details:** Students can apply to graduate study at any of the "Big Ten" universities through CIC by submitting the fellowship/graduate admission application. They are required to provide three letters of recommendation, all official transcripts, GRE scores, and a statement of purpose. Inquiries about specific fields covered by the fellowship should be directed to the CIC office. **Application Deadline:** January 1.

★2559★
Clinical Training Fellowship for Registered Nurses
American Nurses Association
Ethnic/Racial Minority Fellowships
  Programs
600 Maryland Ave. SW, Ste. 100 W
Washington, DC 20024-2571

Study Level: Doctorate. **Award Type:** Fellowship. **Purpose:** To increase the number of ethnic minority psychiatric nurses. To increase the number of clinicians skilled in the prevention, treatment, and study of mental health problems affecting ethnic minority populations. **Applicant Eligibility:** Applicants must be American citizens or permanent visa residents. They must be members of an ethnic or racial minority group, including but not limited to Blacks, Hispanics, American Indians, Asian Americans, Pacific Islanders and/or demonstrate a commitment to career in psychiatric nursing related to ethnic minority health. They must also be registered nurses, enrolled full-time in an ANA-approved academic program leading to a doctoral degree in psychiatric nursing by the time a fellowship is awarded. Students not yet enrolled in a doctoral program may apply but are encouraged to apply to a doctoral program as soon as possible. **Selection Criteria:** Selection is based upon clinical and/or research potential, scholarship, writing ability, ethnic or racial minority orientation, knowledge of broad issues in psychiatric health care, and professional commitment. **Funds Available:** The amounts vary but will not exceed $7,500 per year. An award may be extended for a maximum of three years and is contingent on satisfactory academic progress. Students who accept an award are obligated to provide clinical services to underserved populations within 24 months after the completion of their training and for a period equal to the length of the award. This obligation may not be fulfilled in private clinical practice. **Application Deadline:** January 15.

★2560★
Corporate Sponsored Scholarships for Minority Undergraduate Physics Majors
American Physical Society
335 E. 45th St.
New York, NY 10017-3483   Ph: (212)682-7341

Study Level: Undergraduate. **Award Type:** Scholarship. **Purpose:** To significantly increase the level of underrepresented minority participation in physics in this country. **Applicant Eligibility:** Any Black, Hispanic, or American Indian U.S. citizen who is majoring or plans to major in physics and who is a high school senior, or college freshman or sophomore is eligible. **Selection Criteria:** A Selection Committee of the APS Committee on Minorities in Phyics and appointed by the APS President will select the scholarship recipients and match the recipient with an available scholarship from a host corporate sponsor. The Selection committee will provide an accomplished physicist as a mentor for each scholarship recipient. It is the intention of the Selection Committee to give approximately half the awards to students in institutions with historically or predominatly Black, Hispanic, or American Indian enrollment. **Funds Available:** $2,000 for tuition, room, or board, and $500 awarded to each college or university physics department that hosts one or more APS minority undergraduate scholars. The scholarship may be renewed one time. **Application Details:** Applicants must submit a completed application form with a personal statement. Three completed reference forms and a copy of applicant's high school and/or college transcripts should be mailed directly to the APS office. ACT, SAT, and any other scholastic aptitude test scores must be sent directly to the APS office by the testing service. **Application Deadline:** February 26.

★2561★
Cox Minority Journalism Scholarship
Cox Newspapers
Minority Journalism Scholarship
PO Box 4689
Atlanta, GA 30302

Study Level: Undergraduate. **Award Type:** Scholarship. **Applicant Eligibility:** Must be graduating high school seniors in need of financial assistance, who are racial minorities from the public schools of the Atlanta, Georgia area. They must have at least a B average and an interest in journalism. The recipient will attend either Georgia State University or one of the colleges in the Atlanta University Center. The recipient must major or minor in journalism. **Funds Available:** All education expenses will be paid for four years of college, including room, board, books and tuition. Only one student will be awarded a scholarship each year. **Application Deadline:** April 30. ** Mrs. Alexis Scott Reeves.

★2562★
Detroit Free Press Minority Journalism Scholarship
Detroit Free Press
Publishers Office
321 W. Lafayette Blvd.   Fax: (313)222-8874
Detroit, MI 48226   Free: 800-678-6400

Study Level: Undergraduate. **Award Type:** Scholarship. **Purpose:** To encourage outstanding minorities to enter journalism. **Applicant Eligibility:** Black, Asian, Hispanic and Native American high school seniors in the Free Press circulation area who plan to become writers, editors, or photohournalists and to attend a four-year college majoring in journalism or related field. A 3.0 cumulative average is mandatory. **Selection Criteria:** Based on grades, essay (on why student wants to become a journalist), extracurricular activities (particularly those related to journalism) and recommendations from high school. Finalists are interviewed in person. **Funds Available:** First place winners (2) win $1,000, second place winner receives $750. First place winners automatically compete for three $20,000 scholarships offered nationally by Knight Ridder, Inc. **Application Details:** Application form must be accompanied by 3-5 page essay, high school transcript, two letters of recommendation from students' school, and copy of ACT or SAT scores. **Application Deadline:** January 6.

★2563★
Doctoral Fellowships in Sociology
American Sociological Association
Minority Fellowship Program
1722 N St. NW
Washington, DC 20036

Study Level: Doctorate. **Award Type:** Fellowship. **Purpose:** The program's purpose is to contribute to the development of sociology by recruiting individuals who will add differing orientations and creativity to the field. Persons who can approach research on mental health issues relating to minorities from an indigenous perspective are sought. **Applicant Eligibility:** Candidates must be American citizens or permanent visa residents from minority backgrounds. Applicants include but are not limited to persons who are Black, Latino-Hispanic (Chicano, Cuban, Puerto Rican), American Indian, Asian American (Chinese, Japanese, Korean), and Pacific Islanders (Filipino, Samoan, Hawaiian, Guamanian). Candidates may be beginning or continuing study in sociology departments. New students must qualify for acceptance at accredited institutions of higher learning and indicate a commitment to teaching, research, and service careers on the sociological aspects of mental health issues. Recipients are expected, upon completion of their program, to engage in behavioral research or teaching for a period equal to the period of support beyond 12 months. **Selection Criteria:** Financial need and potential for success in graduate studies are considered. **Funds Available:** Depending upon the availability of funds, approximately ten fellowships a year are awarded. Maximum stipend is $8,800. Arrangements are made with the universities for payment of tuition. A limited number of awards to support dissertation research are also provided. **Application Details:** Official transcripts for each college and university attended are required. Three references, at least two of whom must have taught the applicant, must be supplied. An essay of not more than three double-spaced pages must include a statement of career goals and aspirations, anticipated date of receipt of doctorate, and how the candidate thinks the attainment of the Ph.D. relates to his/her goals. **Application Deadline:** A formal application and all supporting materials must be received by January 15th; recipients are announced by April 15th.

★2564★
Dow Jones Newspaper Fund Minority Reporting Scholarships
The Dow Jones Newspaper Fund
P.O. Box 300
Princeton, NJ 08543-0300   Ph: (609)452-2820

Study Level: Undergraduate. **Award Type:** Scholarship. **Applicant Eligibility:** Must be a college minority sophomore who completes a reporting internship during the summer at the end of their sophomore year. **Selection Criteria:** Scholarship recipients will be judged on the writing they did during their internship, an essay, and recommendation from their supervisor. **Funds Available:** 20 scholarships of $1,000 each. **Application Details:** Students must be nominated by their newspaper supervisors. Details will be availabe at the beginning of December. Applications will be available between March 1 and August 15. **Application Deadline:** September 1.

★2565★
Earl Warren Legal Training Scholarships
Earl Warren Legal Training Program
99 Hudson St., Ste. 1600   Ph: (212)219-1900
New York, NY 10013   Fax: (212)226-7592

Study Level: Graduate. **Award Type:** Scholarship. **Purpose:** To increase the number of black lawyers in the U.S. by roughly one-third the current number. **Applicant Eligibility:** Must be an entering law student and a U.S. citizen. Emphasis is placed on scholarships for applicants who wish to enroll in law schools in the South. Preferred consideration is given to applicants in financial need, under 35 years of age, and to those who plan to participate where there is a dearth of black lawyers. Each recipient must attend law school full-time and will be expected to graduate within the normally prescribed time of three years. Applicants must take the Law School Admission Test

(LSAT). **Selection Criteria:** High LSAT score, undergraduate record, and need. **Funds Available:** $1,500 per student per year. **Application Details:** Unconditional acceptance in an accredited law school is necessary for review of the application. A copy of the acceptance letter must accompany the application. Write for an application form. **Application Deadline:** March 15.

★2566★
Edward D. Stone Jr. and Associates Minority Scholarship
Landscape Architecture Foundation
4401 Connecticut Ave. NW, Ste. 500
Washington, DC 20008   Ph: (202)686-0068

Study Level: Undergraduate. **Award Type:** Scholarship. **Purpose:** To help continue the education of students entering their final years of undergraduate study in landscape architecture. **Applicant Eligibility:** Applicants must be minority students in their final years study. **Funds Available:** Two $1,000 scholarships are awarded. **Application Details:** Applications consist of the following: a typed, double-spaced 500-word essay; between four and eight 35mm color slides neatly arranged in a plastic folder or three to five 8x10 black and white or color photographs that demonstrate the student's best work; two letters of recommendation; a completed application form; and a completed Financial Aid Form. **Application Deadline:** May 4.

★2567★
Equal Opportunity Publications Scholarship
Career Opportunities Through Education
PO Box 2810   Ph: (609)573-9400
Cherry Hill, NJ 08034   Fax: (609)573-9799

Study Level: Undergraduate. **Award Type:** Scholarship. **Applicant Eligibility:** Applicants must be minorities, women, or disabled college students who are pursuing a career in engineering. They must be enrolled in a full-time undergraduate program leading to a Bachelor's degree in any engineering discipline at an accredited four-year college or university. Applicants should have a minimum grade point average of 3.0 out of 4.0. **Selection Criteria:** The preliminary selection procedure will be based solely on the applicant's GPA as verified by an official transcript. The top students will be selected and receive applications on or about April 1. The final selection procedure will be based on cumulative GPA, participation in extracurricular activities, a personal statement, and a recommendation. **Funds Available:** Two $500 non-renewable scholarships. **Application Deadline:** February 15.

★2568★
Evangelical Lutheran Church in America Scholarships
Evangelical Lutheran Church in America
Division for Higher Education and Schools
8765 W. Higgins Rd.
Chicago, IL 60631

Study Level: Undergraduate. **Award Type:** Scholarship. **Purpose:** To encourage ELCA colleges and universities to become more inclusive communities, with particular attention to their recruitment of African American, Hispanic, Asian and Native American students. **Applicant Eligibility:** Applicants must be African American, Hispanic, Asian, and Native American students who are members of Evangelical Lutheran Church in America congregations. They must also be United States citizens, or have immigrant status, and be enrolled or accepted for admission as an undergraduate student at an accredited college or university. **Selection Criteria:** Awards are given based on applicant's financial need and availability of funds. **Funds Available:** Awards are $800 and are renewable for up to four years. Recipients' congregations are asked to provide 20 percent of the scholarship award. **Application Details:** Candidates must be nominated by an ELCA congregation. Applicants must complete a financial aid application at the institution they are attending. **Application Deadline:** August 31.

★2569★
Flemmie P. Kittrell Fellowship for Minorities
American Home Economics Association
  Foundation
1555 King St.
Alexandria, VA 22314   Ph: (703)706-4600

Study Level: Graduate. **Award Type:** Fellowship. **Applicant Eligibility:** This fellowship is available to members of minority groups in the United States and to home economists from developing countries. Applicants must be members of the American Home Economics Association and be United States citizens, permanent residents of the United States, or foreign nationals who wish to study home economics in the United States. Candidates must have completed at least one year of professional home economics experience (which may include a graduate assistantship, traineeship, or internship) by the beginning of the year for which the award is granted. In addition, candidates must show clearly defined plans for full-time graduate study during the award period. Exceptions in qualifications requirements may be made for applicants from countries which offer little or no college training in home economics. The recipient of this fellowship must submit an annual progress report to the Foundation, and upon completing the required investigation or study, must submit its title, date of completion, and the location where a written report is available. **Selection Criteria:** Applicants are evaluated on the basis of the following criteria: scholarship and special aptitudes for advanced study; proposed research problems or areas; educational and/or professional experiences; professional and personal characteristics; and professional contributions to home economics. **Funds Available:** One award of $3,000. **Application Details:** An application fee ($10 for AHEA members, $30 for nonmembers) must accompany each request for fellowship materials. International students living outside the United States at the time of application are not assessed an application fee. Six copies of the application must be filed. **Application Deadline:** January 15; recipient is notified in April.

★2570★
Ford Foundation Dissertation Fellowships for
Minorities
National Academy of Sciences
National Research Council
2101 Constitution Ave.
Washington, DC 20418   Ph: (202)334-2860

Study Level: Doctorate. **Award Type:** Fellowship. **Purpose:** To increase the presence of underrepresented minorities on the nation's college and university faculties by offering doctoral fellowships to members of those groups. Fellowships can be used for study in research-based doctoral programs in the behavioral and social sciences, humanities, engineering, mathematics, physical sciences, and biological sciences, as well as for interdisciplinary programs comprised of two or more eligible disciplines. **Applicant Eligibility:** Applicants must be U.S. citizens or nationals at the time of application and must be members of one of the following minority groups: Alaskan Natives (Eskimo or Aleut), Native American Indians, Black or African Americans, Mexican Americans or Chicanos, native Pacific Islanders (Polynesian or Micronesian), and Puerto Ricans. Students must have finished all required course work and examinations except for the defense of the dissertation. They must be admitted to degree candidacy by January 13 and expect to complete the dissertation during the academic year. **Selection Criteria:** Achievement and ability as determined via academic records, letters of recommendation, the suitability of the proposed institution for the plan of study, and the applicants's ability to present a well-written, thoughtfully prepared application. **Funds Available:** Approximately 20 fellowships are awarded annually. Tenure is from 9 to 12 months; stipends of $18,000 are disbursed through the sponsoring institution. **Application Details:** Application materials are available in September from the Fellowship Office of the NRC. Applications are comprised of two parts. Completed applications must be submitted along with the following: verification of doctoral degree status; abstract of dissertation prospectus; official copies of all undergraduate and graduate transcripts; at least two reference reports, one of which must be from applicant's dissertation advisor; description of previous research experience; and proposed plan for completion of doctoral degree. Also required for the second part of the application process are two additional reference reports; a resume; and a working dissertation bibliography. **Application Deadline:** November.

★2571★
Ford Foundation Predoctoral Fellowships for Minorities
National Academy of Sciences
National Research Council
2101 Constitution Ave.
Washington, DC 20418   Ph: (202)334-2860

Study Level: Doctorate. **Award Type:** Fellowship. **Purpose:** To increase the presence of underrepresented minorities on the nation's college and university faculties by offering doctoral fellowships to members of those groups. Fellowships can be used for study in research-based doctoral programs in the behavioral and social sciences, humanities, engineering, mathematics, physical sciences, and biological sciences, as well as for interdisciplinary programs comprised of two or more eligible disciplines. **Applicant Eligibility:** Applicants must be U.S. citizens or nationals at the time of application and must be members of one of the following minority groups: Alaskan Natives (Eskimo or Aleut), Native American Indians, Black or African Americans, Mexican Americans or Chicanos, native Pacific Islanders (Polynesian or Micronesian), and Puerto Ricans. Students must be at or near the begining of their graduate study and plan to work toward the Ph.D. or Sc.D. degree; persons holding a doctoral degree earned at any time in any field are not eligible to apply. Applicants must have taken the GRE (Graduate Record Examinations) General Test. **Selection Criteria:** Fellowships are awarded to candidates who have demonstrated superior scholarship and who show the greatest promise for future achievement as scholars, researchers, and teachers in institutions of higher education. Applications are evaluated for achievement and ability as measured by academic records, letters of recommendation, suitability of proposed institution for the graduate study plan, and applicants's ability to present a well-written, thoughtfully prepared application. **Funds Available:** Approximately 55 fellowships are awarded annually, each including an annual stipend of $11,500 for each of three years; an annual institutional grant of $6,000 to the fellowship institution in lieu of tuition and fees is also awarded. Continuation of fellowship support for second and third years is contingent upon satisfactory progress toward the Ph.D. or Sc.D. degree. **Application Details:** Application materials are available in September from the Fellowship Office of the NRC. Applications are comprised of two parts. Completed applications must be submitted along with the following: GRE General Test scores; official copies of all undergraduate and graduate transcripts; at least two reference reports, one of which must be from a faculty member in the applicant's major academic field; and a proposed plan of graduate study. Also requried at the second stage of the application process are course reports from which the applicant's GPA is derived; official transcript of any work completed during the current Fall term; two additional reference reports; description of previous research experience; and resume. **Application Deadline:** November.

★2572★
Franklin C. McLean Award
National Medical Fellowships
254 W. 31 St., 7th Fl.
New York, NY 10001

Study Level: Doctorate. **Award Type:** Scholarship. **Applicant Eligibility:** Candidates must be American Blacks, mainland Puerto Ricans, Mexican-Americans, and American Indians who are enrolled in accredited schools of allopathic or osteopathic medicine in the United States and who are United States citizens. McLean Awards are for senior medical students in recognition of outstanding academic achievement, leadership, and community service. **Application Details:** After students have received acceptance from at least one medical school, they are urged to request National Medical Scholarship applications. They should also obtain information about the additional special funds listed above that the National Medical Fellowships, Inc. administers so that they may apply for those for which they are also eligible. Scholarship applications for NMF Scholarships become available in March. **Application Deadline:** New applicants must submit their applications by August 31; renewals are due by April 30.

★2573★
Freda A. DeKnight Memorial Fellowship
American Home Economics Association
  Foundation
1555 King St.
Alexandria, VA 22314   Ph: (703)706-4600
Study Level: Graduate. **Award Type:** Fellowship. **Applicant Eligibility:** This fellowship is available to Black American graduate students. Preference is given to qualified applicants who plan careers in home economics communications or in cooperative extension. Candidates must show clearly defined plans for full-time graduate study during the award period. Applicants must be members of the American Home Economics Association and be citizens or permanent residents of the United States. In addition, candidates must have completed at least one year of professional home economics experience (which may include a graduate assistantship, traineeship, or internship) by the beginning of the year for which the award is granted. The recipient of this fellowship must submit an annual progress report to the Foundation, and upon completing the required investigation or study, must submit its title, date of completion, and the location where a written report is available. **Selection Criteria:** Applicants are evaluated on the basis of the following criteria: scholarship and special aptitudes for advanced study and research; educational and/or professional experiences; professional and personal characteristics; professional contributions to home economics; and significance of the proposed research problem or area to the public well-being and the advancement of home economics. **Funds Available:** One award of $2,500 is granted annually. **Application Details:** An application fee ($15 for AHEA members, $30 for nonmembers) must accompany each request for fellowship materials. **Application Deadline:** Nine copies of the application must be filed by January 15th. Recipient is notified in April.

★2574★
FTE Black North American Dissertation Year
  Scholarships
The Fund for Theological Education, Inc.
475 Riverside Dr., Ste. 832
New York, NY 10115-0008   Ph: (212)870-2058
Study Level: Doctorate. **Award Type:** Scholarship. **Purpose:** To strengthen Christian theological education in the United States and Canada by supporting Black North American women and men who demonstrate high promise for academic excellence and teaching effectiveness and to enable Black North American graduate students within the field of religious studies to complete their Ph.D., Th.D., or Ed.D. dissertation. **Applicant Eligibility:** Nominees must be members of a Christian church. They must be Black citizens of the United States or Canada. They must have a prospectus or dissertation proposal approved by the appropriate faculty committee by the time the candidate is interviewed by the Final Selection Committee. **Selection Criteria:** Academic excellence and promise for scholarship and teaching effectiveness. **Funds Available:** The amount of the scholarship will vary according to individual need. Scholarships may be supplemented with financial aid. Scholarships are for one year, with the expectation of a completed dissertation by the end of the scholarship year. **Application Details:** Direct applications are not accepted. Each candidate must be nominated by a vote of the appropriate faculty committee of the school admitting the candidate. The faculty must be reasonably certain that the candidate will complete the dissertation during the scholarship year. There is no limit to the number of candidates an institution may nominate. **Application Deadline:** Nominations must be received by FTE by February 10 of each year. An application will be sent directly to nominees and must be returned by March 15. Early nominations are encouraged. Awards will be announced in early May.

★2575★
FTE Black North American Doctoral Scholarships for
  the Study of Religion
The Fund for Theological Education, Inc.
475 Riverside Dr., Ste. 832
New York, NY 10115-0008   Ph: (212)870-2058
Study Level: Doctorate. **Award Type:** Scholarship. **Purpose:** To strengthen Christian theological education in the United States and Canada by supporting Black North American women and men who demonstrate high promise for academic excellence and teaching effectiveness and also to encourage theological schools and graduate departments of religious studies to recruit and support Black doctoral students. **Applicant Eligibility:** Nominees must be members of a Christian church. They must have demonstrated identification with and commitment to theological scholarship and teaching from an Hispanic American perspective in the United States, Canada, or Puerto Rico. They must be at least a graduating senior in an accredited college, university, or seminary degree program, or enrolled in or applying to a Ph.D., Th.D., or Ed.D. program in a field of religious study. They must have completed no more than one year of coursework. **Selection Criteria:** Academic excellence and promise for scholarship and teaching effectiveness. **Funds Available:** The amount of the scholarship will vary according to individual need. Scholarships may be supplemented with financial aid. The scholarship is renewable if the student has not completed more than one year of coursework. **Application Details:** Direct applications are not accepted. Each candidate must be nominated by a vote of the appropriate faculty committee of the school admitting the candidate. There is no limit to the number of candidates an institution may nominate. **Application Deadline:** Nominations must be received by FTE by February 10 of each year. An application will be sent directly to nominees and must be returned by March 15. Early nominations are encouraged. Awards will be announced in early May.

★2576★
GE Foundation Minority Student Scholarships
General Electric Foundation
Fairfield, CT 06431
Study Level: Undergraduate. **Award Type:** Scholarship. **Purpose:** To assist minority engineering and business students. **Selection Criteria:** GE Foundation does not provide scholarships directly to individuals. Awards are made to universities and organizations, who then select the individuals. **Funds Available:** $1,000,000 in funds available.

★2577★
GEM Master's Fellowships
National Consortium for Graduate Degrees
  for Minorities in Engineering and Science
PO Box 537   Ph: (219)287-1097
Notre Dame, IN 46556   Fax: (219)287-1486
Study Level: Graduate. **Award Type:** Fellowship. **Purpose:** To provide opportunities for ethnic minority students to obtain a master's degree in engineering through a program of paid summer engineering internships and financial aid. **Applicant Eligibility:** Candidate must be an American citizen and belong to one of the ethnic groups underrepresented in engineering: American Indian, Black American, Mexican-American, or Puerto Rican. At the time of application the student must have attained at least junior year status in an accredited engineering discipline. Individuals currently in their senior year or who have received a B.S. degree in engineering are encouraged to apply. They must have an undergraduate record which indicates the ability to pursue graduate studies in engineering. **Funds Available:** Graduate fellowships pay tuition, fees, and a stipend of $6,000 per graduate academic year. The summer internship brings the total award value to between $20,000 and $40,000, depending upon academic class, summer employer, and graduate school involved. **Application Details:** Applications are available August 15 of each year. Awards are made by February 1 of the following year. **Application Deadline:** December 1.

★2578★
GEM Ph.D. Engineering Fellowships
National Consortium for Graduate Degrees
  for Minorities in Engineering and Science
PO Box 537   Ph: (219)287-1097
Notre Dame, IN 46556   Fax: (219)287-1486
Study Level: Doctorate. **Award Type:** Fellowship. **Purpose:** To provide opportunities for ethnic minority students to obtain a doctoral degree in engineering through a program of paid tuition, fees, and a stipend. **Applicant Eligibility:** Candidates must be American citizens and belong to one of the ethnic groups underrepresented in engineering: American Indian, Black American, Mexican-American, or Puerto Rican. They must be applicants to the Ph.D. engineering component and must have or be in the process of attaining a master's degree. The academic records of applicants to all programs must indicate the ability to pursue doctoral studies in engineering. **Funds Available:** Graduate fellowships are awarded

that pay tuition, fees, and a stipend of $12,000 per calendar year. The total award value is between $60,000 and $100,000, depending upon the graduate school involved. **Application Details:** Applications are available August 15 of each year. Awards are made by February 1 of the following year. **Application Deadline:** December 1.

★2579★
GEM Ph.D. Science Fellowships
National Consortium for Graduate Degrees
  for Minorities in Engineering and Science
PO Box 537   Ph: (219)287-1097
Notre Dame, IN 46556   Fax: (219)287-1486

Study Level: Doctorate. **Award Type:** Fellowship. **Purpose:** To provide opportunities for ethnic minority students to obtain a Ph.D. degree in the natural sciences through a program of paid summer internship and financial aid. **Applicant Eligibility:** Candidates must be American citizens and belong to one of the ethnic groups underrepresented in engineering: American Indian, Black American, Mexican-American, or Puerto Rican. At the time of application, they should have a minimum academic status of junior year enrollment in an accredited science discipline. Their general undergraduate record should indicate the ability to pursue doctoral studies in the natural sciences. **Funds Available:** Graduate fellowships pay tuition, fees, and a stipend of $12,000 per calendar year. The summer internship brings the total award value to between $60,000 and $100,000, depending upon academic class, summer employer, and graduate school involved. **Application Details:** Applications are available August 15 of each year. Awards are made by February 1 of the following year. **Application Deadline:** December 1.

★2580★
General Hospital No. 2 Nurses Alumnae Scholarships
General Hospital No. 2
Nurses Alumnae
PO Box 413657
Kansas City, MO 64141

Study Level: Undergraduate. **Award Type:** Scholarship. **Purpose:** To honor General Hospital No. 2, School of Nursing, where professional nursing was taught to Black students from 1911 to 1957. **Applicant Eligibility:** Candidates must be Black students who are enrolled in any accredited School of Nursing in the United States. **Selection Criteria:** Students must display motivation, maturity, commitment, and financial need. **Funds Available:** $500 each. Awards are renewable annually if the student remains in good academic standing. **Application Details:** Required materials include an autobiographical statement, two references, an official copy of academic standing and grade point average, and a recent passport photograph. Application forms are sent upon request. **Application Deadline:** March 31.

★2581★
George A. Strait Minority Stipend
American Association of Law Libraries
53 W. Jackson Blvd., Ste. 940   Ph: (312)939-4764
Chicago, IL 60604   Fax: (312)431-1097

Study Level: Graduate. **Award Type:** Scholarship. **Applicant Eligibility:** Candidate must be a member of a minority group as defined by current guidelines of the United States Government who are college graduates, college seniors, or matriculated graduate library school students and who have an interest in law librarianship. They must be working toward an advanced degree that will further their law/library career. Applicants must be citizens of the United States or Canada or submit evidence of becoming naturalized at the beginning of the award period. A definite interest and aptitude for law library work and financial need are required. **Selection Criteria:** Preference is given to those with previous service in law librarianship. **Funds Available:** The stipend is $3500 a year. **Application Deadline:** April 1.

★2582★
GOALS Fellowships
Industrial Relations Council on GOALS
PO Box 4363   Ph: (517)351-6122
East Lansing, MI 48826-4363   Fax: (517)351-1960

Study Level: Graduate. **Award Type:** Fellowship. **Applicant Eligibility:** Applicants must be African American, Hispanic, Native Alaskan, Native American, or Native Hawaiian who are U.S. citizens. They must use the fellowship for full-time graduate study in Human Resource Mangement**ustrial Relations at any one of the 12 participating consortium universities. Candidates must also have an undergradate degree in one of the social sciences, such as economics, psychology, sociology, or political science, or have concentrations in business administration, communications, or social work. **Selection Criteria:** Candidates are ranked according to overall academic ability by a selection committee. **Funds Available:** Fellowships include either whole or partial waiver of tuition and fees and stipends of up to $7,800 per academic year. The number of fellowships awarded each year varies depending on funds donated by corporate sponsors. **Application Details:** Students must be accepted at one of the 12 consortium graduate schools to be eligible. Candidates must then apply directly to the school for the GOALS fellowship and be nominated by the school's director. **Application Deadline:** Depends on university. Many graduate programs require that necessary documents be received by the middle of January for the following fall term.

★2583★
Golden State Minority Foundation Scholarships
Golden State Minority Foundation
1999 W. Adams Blvd.
Los Angeles, CA 90018

Study Level: Undergraduate. **Award Type:** Scholarship. **Applicant Eligibility:** Applicants must attend school in or be a resident of California or Michigan, study business, be a qualified minority (African-American, Hispanic, Native American, or other underrespresented minority), have minimum 3.0 GPA, be a U.S. citizen or legal resident, be of at least junior standing (60 units of college credit), work not more than 20 hours per week, and have full-time status at an accredited four-year college or university. **Application Details:** Applications are on file at most schools' financial aid offices or can be obtained by sending a self-addressed stamped envelope.

★2584★
Henry G. Halladay Awards
National Medical Fellowships
254 W. 31 St., 7th Fl.
New York, NY 10001

Study Level: Doctorate. **Award Type:** Scholarship. **Applicant Eligibility:** Candidates must be American Blacks who are enrolled in accredited schools of allopathic or osteopathic medicine in the United States and who are United States citizens. National Medical Fund Scholarships are for students enrolled in the first or second year of medical school. Halladay Awards are for black male medical school students who are enrolled in the first year of medical school, have overcome significant obstacles, and have exceptional financial need. **Funds Available:** Five new supplemental Halladay Scholarships of $760 each are awarded annually. **Application Details:** After students have received acceptance from at least one medical school, they are urged to request National Medical Scholarship applications. They should also obtain information about the additional special funds that National Medical Fellowships, Inc. administers so that they may apply for those for which they are also eligible. Scholarship applications for NMF Scholarships become available in March. **Application Deadline:** New applicants must submit their applications by August 31; renewals are due by May 30.

★2585★
Herbert Lehman Scholarship
Herbert Lehman Education Fund
99 Hudson St., No. 1600
New York, NY 10013   Ph: (212)219-1900

Study Level: Undergraduate. **Award Type:** Scholarship. **Purpose:** To promote goodwill and understanding by providing educational scholarships and financial assistance to needy students entering recently desegregated and publicly supported undergraduate colleges and universities in the deep South. **Applicant Eligibility:** Applicants must be highly qualified high school graduates planning to begin undergraduate study at one of the institutions described above. Applicants must be citizens of the United States. **Funds Available:** A limited number of scholarship awards are available. Support for each scholar may continue through the completion of the full normal four-year course of study if funds continue to be available. **Application Details:** All requests for application forms must be requested in writing by the applicant. **Application Deadline:** April 15.

★2586★
HRSA-BHP MARC Honors Undergraduate Research Training Awards
Health Resources and Services
  Administration
Bureau of Health Professions
Parklawn Bldg., Rm. 8-38
5600 Fishers Ln.
Rockville, MD 20857
Study Level: Graduate. **Award Type:** Award. **Purpose:** To help prepare minority students for careers in biomedical research and to increase the number of minorities successfully completing Ph.D. in biomedical research. **Applicant Eligibility:** Must be third or fourth year undergraduate honor students in a college or university whose enrollment is drawn substantially from ethnic minority groups. **Selection Criteria:** Based on potential for success in biomedical sciences and demonstration of intent to enter graduate programs leading to a Ph.D. **Funds Available:** Each school will give five to ten awards for tuition and stipend. Travel expenses to one national meeting closely related to the project may be included. **Application Deadline:** January 10, May 10 or September 10. ** United State Health and Human Services, National Institute of Health, National Institute of General Medical Sciences, Westwood Bldg., Rm. 9A18, Bethesda, MD, 20892.

★2587★
Hugh J. Andersen Memorial Scholarships
National Medical Fellowships
254 W. 31 St., 7th Fl.
New York, NY 10001
Study Level: Doctorate. **Award Type:** Scholarship. **Applicant Eligibility:** Candidates must be American Blacks, mainland Puerto Ricans, Mexican-Americans, and American Indians who are enrolled in accredited schools of allopathic or osteopathic medicine in the United States and who are United States citizens. National Medical Fund Scholarships are for students enrolled in the first or second year of medical school. Andersen Scholarship candidates must attend Minnesota medical schools and exhibit outstanding leadership, community service, and financial need. Minnesota residents attending out-of-state schools are also eligible. **Funds Available:** Up to 7 new Andersen Scholarships are awarded annually; they are renewable and range from $2500 to $4000. **Application Details:** Applications by Dean's nomination only. **Application Deadline:** Nominations requested in October.

★2588★
IBM Minority Fellowships
International Business Machines
T.J. Watson Research Center
P.O. Box 218
Yorktown Heights, NY 10598
Study Level: Graduate. **Award Type:** Fellowship. **Purpose:** To assist universities in training graduate students in areas of central interest to the electronics industry. **Applicant Eligibility:** Applicants must be minority graduate students in the following fields: computer science; electrical engineering; mechanical engineering; mathematics; physics; manufacturing engineering; industrial engineering; materials science; chemistry; chemical engineering. **Selection Criteria:** Academic excellence; relevance to ongoing research in the electronics industry. **Funds Available:** 15 fellowships are awarded. Duration of award is one year. **Application Deadline:** February 1.

★2589★
Indiana Minority Teacher & Special Education Scholarships
Indiana State Student Assistance
  Commission
150 W, Market St., 5th Fl.   Ph: (317)232-2350
Indianapolis, IN 46204   Fax: (317)232-3260
Study Level: Undergraduate. **Award Type:** Scholarship. **Purpose:** The Minority Teacher Scholarship was created by the 1988 Indiana General Assembly to address the critical shortage of Black and Hispanic teachers in Indiana. Later, in response to critical shortages in the areas of special education, physical therapy, and occupational therapy, the Special Education Scholarship was formed. **Applicant Eligibility:** Applicants must be Indiana residents who are either minority students (defined as Black or Hispanic) seeking teacher certification or students (of any background) seeking certification in special education, occupational therapy, or physical therapy. Residency is defined by the colleges students plan to attend. Candidates must also be admitted to or attend eligible institutions as full-time students (at least 12 credit hours), intend to pursue or be pursuing a course of study that would enable them, upon graduation, to teach in an accredited elementary or secondary school in Indiana, and have a mimimum College GPA of at least 2.0/4.0, or meet the minimum GPA requirements established at the college or its school of education. **Selection Criteria:** The college is responsible for making the actual awards. They may not base the awards solely on merit-based factors. Financial need may be considered but is not a requirement. Preference will be given to minority students and students enrolling in college for the first time. **Funds Available:** The maximum annual scholarship is $1,000. The college will determine the actual amount when reviewing the scholar's financial aid package. The college may not reduce the scholar's state or federal gift (free) financial aid, if any, when awarding the scholarship. The scholar must agree to: pursue a program leading to an Indiana teacher certification; complete the teacher certification program within six years of the time the first scholarship is received; following certification, teach on a full-time basis for three out of five years in an accredited Indiana elementary or secondary school or schools. Unless the student has already completed a baccalaureate degree, the completion of the teacher certification program must coincide with graduation from the baccalaureate program. Failure to fulfill these conditions will result in a review by SSACI and may bring further action. **Application Details:** Applications may be obtained from the college or university financial aid office or college of education, high school guidance office, or SSACI. The student must submit the application to financial aid office of the college or university the student plans to attend.

★2590★
Iowa Minority Academic Grants for Economic Success
Iowa College Student Aid Commission
914 Grand Ave., Ste. 201   Ph: (515)281-3501
Des Moines, IA 50309   Fax: (515)242-5996
Study Level: Undergraduate. **Award Type:** Grant. **Purpose:** To assist needy Iowa minority students attending an eligible Iowa private college or state university. **Selection Criteria:** Financial need, with priority given to the neediest applicants and those holding college-bond vouchers. **Application Details:** Applicants must follow the same application procedures as stated for all Iowa-sponsored grants. Students attending one of the three state universities should contact the financial aid administrator at the institution to determine the application procedures. **Application Deadline:** Applications must be received by April 22 to be given first priority.

★2591★
Irving Graef Memorial Scholarship
National Medical Fellowships
254 W. 31 St., 7th Fl.
New York, NY 10001
Study Level: Doctorate. **Award Type:** Scholarship. **Applicant Eligibility:** Candidates must be American Blacks, mainland Puerto Ricans, Mexican-Americans, and American Indians who are enrolled in accredited schools of allopathic or osteopathic medicine in the United States and who are United States citizens. Graef Scholarship is for third year medical students who have previously received NMF financial assistance and demonstrated academic achievement, leadership, and community service. **Funds Available:** One new Graef Scholarship is awarded annually. Stipend is $2,000 and is

renewable. **Application Deadline:** Contact Special Programs, National Medical Fellowships, Inc. for deadline.

★2592★
James H. Robinson Memorial Prizes
National Medical Fellowships
254 W. 31 St., 7th Fl.
New York, NY 10001

Study Level: Doctorate. **Award Type:** Scholarship. **Applicant Eligibility:** Candidates must be American Blacks, mainland Puerto Ricans, Mexican-Americans, and American Indians who are enrolled in accredited schools of allopathic or osteopathic medicine in the United States and who are United States citizens. Robinson prizes given to senior medical for outstanding achievement in surgery. **Funds Available:** Two non-renewable Robinson Awards of $500 each are awarded annually. **Application Details:** Students apply by dean's nomination. **Application Deadline:** Nominations requested in January.

★2593★
Jimmy A. Young Memorial Scholarships
American Respiratory Care Foundation
11030 Ables Lane   Ph: (214)243-8892
Dallas, TX 75229   Fax: (214)484-2720

Study Level: Undergraduate. **Award Type:** Scholarship. **Purpose:** To assist minority students in respiratory therapy programs based on academic achievement. Applicants must be United States citizens or submit a copy of their immigrant visa. They must be members of minority groups, which include American Indians, Asian or Pacific Islanders, Black-Americans, Spanish-Americans, and Mexican-Americans. They must provide evidence of enrollment in an AMA-approved respiratory care program. Candidates must have a minimum grade point average of 3.0 on a 4.0 scale. **Funds Available:** One scholarship of $1,000 is awarded annually. **Application Details:** Candidates must submit official transcripts of grades, two letters of recommendation from the program director and medical director that verifies the applicant is deserving and a member of a designated minority group. A budget must be submitted. An original essay on some facet of respiratory care is also required. **Application Deadline:** Applications are accepted between April 1 and June 1. Scholarships are awarded by September 1.

★2594★
KNTV Minority Scholarship
KNTV Television
645 Park Ave.
San Jose, CA 95110

Study Level: Undergraduate. **Award Type:** Scholarship. **Applicant Eligibility:** Students must be either Black, Hispanic, Asian/Pacific Islander, or American Indian. They must be residents of either Santa Clara, Santa Cruz, Monterey, or San Benito Counties. The award is contingent on the acceptability of student for admission to an accredited California four-year college or university. The major should be television production or journalism or a related field (marketing, public relations, advertising, graphics, or engineering with demonstrated interest in television). Students must have one full year of undergraduate work remaining and must carry a minimum of 12 semester units during each semester of the 1991-92 school year. **Selection Criteria:** These scholarships are given to students with financial need who demonstrate interest and potential in the field of television production and television journalism. **Funds Available:** Two $750 scholarships will be awarded. **Application Details:** Contact KNTV for applications. **Application Deadline:** April.

★2595★
Lauranne Sams Scholarship Award
National Black Nurses' Association
PO Box 1823   Ph: (202)393-6870
Washington, DC 20013   Fax: (202)347-3808

Study Level: Undergraduate. **Award Type:** Scholarship. **Applicant Eligibility:** At the time of application candidates must be enrolled in an A.D., Diploma, B.S.N. or L.P.N./L.V.N. nursing program and be in good academic standing. They must be members of the Association and/or active members of a Local Chapter if there is one in their area. They are expected to exhibit any or all of the following: academic excellence, professional nursing commitment, active

involvement in the Black community, personal integrity, and financial need. **Funds Available:** The amount of scholarships is individually determined. **Application Details:** Transcript from the school of nursing, two letters of recommendation, an essay written by the candidate about his/her goals in nursing and particular qualifications for the award, as well as documented evidence of participation in student nurse activities and in the Black community must accompany the application. Where there is a local chapter, candidates must be recommended by a chapter; the initial screening is done at the local level. If there is no local chapter in the candidate's area, the application can be sent directly to national headquarters. Applicants affirm on the application that if they receive a scholarship they will remain a member of the Association and work diligently toward achieving its goals and objectives.

★2596★
Leonard M. Perryman Communications Scholarship for Ethnic Minority Students
United Methodist Communications
475 Riverside Dr., Ste. 1901
New York, NY 10115

Study Level: Undergraduate. **Award Type:** Scholarship. **Applicant Eligibility:** Applicants must be college juniors or seniors who are members of an ethnic minority, intend to pursue a career in religious communication in an accredited institution of higher education, and are United States citizens. Communications covers various mediums such as audiovisual, electric and print journalism. **Selection Criteria:** Applicants are judged on five criteria: Christian commitment and involvement in the life of the church; academic achievement as revealed by transcripts, grade point averages, and letters of reference; journalistic experience and/or evidence of journalistic talent; clarity of purpose in plans and goals for the future; and potential professional usefulness as a journalist in the field of religion. **Funds Available:** $2,500 scholarship. Half of the award will be paid in August or September after the recipient is enrolled in an undergraduate program in an accredited school or department of journalism in the United States, and the remainder of the grant will be paid in December. There are no grants for summer sessions. **Application Details:** A formal application must be submitted with official transcripts from the institution of higher learning that the applicant is attending or any previous attended colleges or universities; an essay of no more than 500 words about the candidates interest in religious journalism; three samples of applicants work; and a recent black and white glossy photograph, preferably head and shoulders, suitable for publicity use should the applicant win. In addition, three letters of recommendation must also be submitted: one from the applicant's local church pastor or a denominational official; one from the chairperson of the department in which the candidate is majoring as an undergraduate; and one from an employer for whom the applicant has worked as a journalist. If any of these are not available, a letter from a knowledgeable person related to journalism may be substituted. All letters of recommendation should be sent by the writer directly to New York. **Application Deadline:** The 1993 deadline was March 1.

★2597★
LITA/OCLC Minority Scholarship in Library and Information Science
American Library Association
Library and Information Technology
  Association
50 E. Huron St.   Ph: (312)944-6780
Chicago, IL 60611   Fax: (312)440-9374

Study Level: Graduate. **Award Type:** Scholarship. **Purpose:** To encourage qualified students, who hold a strong commitment to the use of automation in libraries, to enter library automation. **Applicant Eligibility:** Applicants must be master's students who are members of principal minority groups. **Funds Available:** $2,500. **Application Deadline:** April 1.

★2598★
Louise Giles Minority Scholarship
American Library Association
Office for Library Personnel Resources
50 E. Huron St.
Chicago, IL 60611　　　　　　　　Ph: (312)944-6780
Study Level: Graduate. **Award Type:** Scholarship. **Purpose:** To permit a worthy minority student to begin an MLS degree at an ALA-accredited program. **Applicant Eligibility:** Applicants must be members of a minroity group, and must be U.S. or Canadian citizens. **Funds Available:** $3,000.

★2599★
Lucy Dalbiac Luard Scholarship
The English-Speaking Union of the United
　States
16 E. 69th St.
New York, NY 10021　　　　　　　Ph: (212)879-6800
Study Level: Undergraduate. **Award Type:** Scholarship. **Purpose:** To enable college students to spend their junior years studying in the United Kingdom. **Applicant Eligibility:** Applicants must have completed their sophomore year at Howard or Hampton university, or a United Negro College Fund school. **Funds Available:** Awards cover transportation, tuition, room and board, and books at a university in the United Kingdom. **Application Details:** Applications must be submitted to a participating school in the United States. **Application Deadline:** November.

★2600★
Martin Luther King, Jr. Memorial Scholarships
California Teachers Association
1705 Murchison Dr.
PO Box 921
Burlingame, CA 94011-1400　　　　Ph: (415)697-1400
Study Level: Graduate. **Award Type:** Scholarship. **Purpose:** To provide scholarship aid for graduate studies to qualifying racial and ethnic minorities. **Applicant Eligibility:** Minority applicants should be one or more of the following: active CTA members; dependent children of active CTA members; dependent children of deceased CTA members; or student CTA members. **Funds Available:** Scholarships vary each year depending on the amount of contributions and on the financial need of individual applicants. **Application Details:** Applications are available in January of each year. They may be obtained by contacting the CTA Human Rights Department in Burlingame or any CTA Regional Resource Center Office. **Application Deadline:** March 15.

★2601★
Maxwell House Coffee Minority Scholarship
Maxwell House Coffee
250 North St.
White Plains, NY 10625　　　　　　Ph: (914)335-2361
Study Level: Undergraduate. **Award Type:** Scholarship. **Purpose:** To encourage minority students to pursue postsecondary education through financial assistance. **Applicant Eligibility:** Applicants must be minority students who are high school seniors or have recently graduated. They must reside in: New York, Philadelphia, Detroit, Chicago, St. Louis/East St. Louis, Baltimore, or Newark and must be willing to attend an historically black college that participates in the Maxwell House sponsored black college fairs. **Selection Criteria:** Applicants are evaluated based on the following: financial need, GPA, academic record, class ranking, community involvement. **Funds Available:** Five recipients will be awarded $1,000 per year for four years. **Application Details:** The following must accompany the completed application: biography, photo, and letters of recommendation from principal and 3 teachers. High school transcripts including GPA and class ranking must be sent by school. Applicant will also have an interview. **Application Deadline:** Mid-April.

★2602★
Minority Advertising Internships
American Association of Advertising
　Agencies
666 Third Ave.
New York, NY 10017
Study Level: Undergraduate. **Award Type:** Internship. **Purpose:** The Program, a ten week (June-August) summer experience in Chicago, Detroit, Los Angeles, San Francisco and New York, is designed to provide student interns with a realistic job experience in an advertising agency and to help prepare a student for an entry-level professional position in advertising. Advertising agencies also gain an opportunity to identify talented minority students with an interest in advertising. **Applicant Eligibility:** Applicants must be racial minority students in an undergraduate or graduate program who will have completed at least their junior year by the summer for which they are applying. They must plan to return to school in the fall to complete their studies. There are no restrictions in major or concentration. **Funds Available:** Undergraduates receive a salary of $250 per week for a ten week internship. A higher salary is set for graduate students. Sixty percent of dormitory housing and transportation expenses are paid for students who do not live in the cities where they are placed. **Application Details:** Candidates must submit an application form, undergraduate school transcript, letters of recommendation from a professor and a previous employer, and other supporting material, e.g., sample art work. Initial screening is conducted by the A.A.A.A. Equal Employment Opportunities Committee. Semi-finalists are interviewed by the participating agencies. **Application Deadline:** January 15.

★2603★
Minority Student Scholarships in Earth, Space, and Marine Sciences
American Geological Institute　　　Ph: (703)379-2480
4220 King St.　　　　　　　　　　Fax: (703)379-7563
Alexandria, VA 22302-1507　　　　Free: 800-336-4764
Study Level: Graduate; Undergraduate. **Award Type:** Scholarship. **Applicant Eligibility:** The scholarships are open to graduate and undergraduate students in earth, space, and marine sciences, and Earth science education. Eligible are members of Black, Native American and Hispanic ethnic groups, who are United States citizens. **Selection Criteria:** Geoscience students, particularly marine science students who are enrolled in or applying to accredited institutions and who have good academic records are urged to apply. **Funds Available:** Approximately 80 scholarships each ranging from $500-$10,000 are awarded annually. **Application Details:** These fellowships are a cooperative program of the American Geophysical Union, the American Geological Institute's Minority Participation Program and the NOAA Sea Grant Program. **Application Deadline:** Completed applications must be filed by February 1.

★2604★
MLA Scholarship for Minority Students
Medical Library Association
Six North Michigan Ave., Suite 300
Chicago, IL 60602
Study Level: Graduate. **Award Type:** Scholarship. **Purpose:** Scholarships are part of the Medical Library Association's effort to encourage candidates showing excellence in scholarship and potential for accomplishment in health sciences librarianship. **Applicant Eligibility:** Applicants must be minority students entering an ALA accredited graduate library school or having at least one-half of his or her academic requirements to complete during the year following the granting of the scholarship. Competition is open only to citizens of or those having permanent resident status in the United States or Canada. Previous winners of MLA Scholarships or the MLA Scholarships for Minority Students are ineligible. Minority group is defined as Black, Hispanic, Asian, Native American or Pacific Island American. **Funds Available:** One scholarship of $2,000 is awarded annually. Funds are disbursed in four equal installments over the course of a year. **Application Details:** Applicants must submit a formal application form, three letters of reference, official transcripts, and a statement of career objectives. **Application Deadline:** Applications are due by February 1.

★2605★
NAA Foundation Minority Fellowships
Newspaper Association of America
 Foundation
11600 Sunrise Valley Dr.   Ph: (703)648-1000
Reston, VA 22091   Fax: (703)620-1265
Study Level: Professional Development. **Award Type:** Fellowship.
Purpose: To widen opportunities for racial and ethnic minority professionals to enter into or advance in newspaper management. **Selection Criteria:** Based on supervisors' recommendations and panel's belief that the applicants are candidates for advancement newspaper management. **Funds Available:** Thirty fellowships cover seminar and workshop registration fees, travel, meals, and hotel expenses. Fifteen winners are selected in winter and fifteen more in the summer. **Application Details:** Newspaper executives are asked to nominate candidates who demonstrate managerial potential. Self-nomination, with a supervisor's recommendation, also is encouraged. Application must be submitted. **Application Deadline:** Varies.

★2606★
NAACP Willems Scholarship
National Association for the Advancement
 of Colored People
4805 Mt. Hope Dr.
Baltimore, MD 21215-3297   Ph: (410)358-8900
Study Level: Graduate; Undergraduate. **Award Type:** Scholarship.
Applicant Eligibility: This scholarship is awarded to students who are majoring in Engineering, Chemistry, Physics, or Computer and Mathematical Sciences. Applicants must possess a cumulative grade point average of at least 3.0 or "B" average and must be members of the NAACP. **Funds Available:** Undergraduates will receive a maximum award of $8,000 to be paid in annual installments of $2,000. Graduates will be awarded a $3,000 scholarship which can be renewed. **Application Details:** Updated application forms will be available in January. **Application Deadline:** April 30.

★2607★
NABJ Scholarship Awards
National Association of Black Journalists
Box 17212   Ph: (703)648-1270
Washington, DC 20041   Fax: (703)476-6245
Study Level: Graduate; Undergraduate. **Award Type:** Scholarship.
Purpose: To support Black students with the potential to succeed in a journalism career. **Applicant Eligibility:** Candidates must be Black college students who are United States citizens with a minimum 2.5 grade point average and enrolled in a four-year college or university, and who will be either an undergraduate or graduate student the following academic year. Eligible students must either major in journalism print, photography, radio-television or be planning a career in one of these fields. **Selection Criteria:** Application materials will be judged on the basis of quality, completeness of reporting, writing ability and originality. **Funds Available:** Ten scholarships of $2,500 each are available each year. Previous winners are not eligible. **Application Details:** Applicants must be nominated by letter by their school adviser, dean or faculty member who is familiar with the student's work. Nominating letters must be accompanied by a resume, glossy black and white photo and a one-page autobiography. The resume shall include student's campus and home addresses and telephone numbers and should indicate the student's career goals and journalistic activities. Applicants must also write a 500- to 800-word article on a black journalist in the student's home or campus community. Three other samples of the student's work are to be included: articles, photos, broadcast scripts, etc. No tapes are to be submitted. All materials must be typewritten, double-spaced and will not be returned. **Application Deadline:** Nominations must be received by March 31. Recipients will be notified by May 31.

★2608★
NABJ Summer Internships
National Association of Black Journalists
Box 17212   Ph: (703)648-1270
Washington, DC 20041   Fax: (703)476-6245
Study Level: Undergraduate; Graduate. **Award Type:** Internship.
Applicant Eligibility: Candidates are black sophomores or juniors who are enrolled at an accredited four-year college or university and have a 2.5 gradepoint average. They must be majoring in print or broadcast journalism or planning a career in the communications field, and plan to be enrolled in school for the school year following submission of the application. **Selection Criteria:** Applications will be considered by the NABJ Internship Committee on the basis of the candidate's writing ability, scholarship, and originality and completeness of materials submitted. **Funds Available:** Internship payments vary. **Application Details:** Candidates must submit the following typewritten documents: letter of nomination from the journalism dean or appropriate faculty member; a completed application form; a resume giving basic facts of identity of the applicant; a 500-word autobiography; and a 150-200 word essay on why the candidate is interested in journalism. In addition, print candidates must submit copies of at least five published by-line stories; broadcast candidates, an audio or video cassette of at least three news oriented programs produced by the candidate from actual local happening; and photography candidates, a minimum of five published news photographs. For references, each candidate must submit two letters of recommendation from school faculty members or professional journalists. ** Applications must be filed by November 1. Students selected for internships are notified no later than January 31.

★2609★
NABWA Scholarship Award
National Association of Black Women
 Attorneys
3711 Macomb St. NW, 2nd Fl.   Ph: (202)966-9693
Washington, DC 20016   Fax: (202)244-6648
Study Level: Graduate. **Award Type:** Scholarship. **Purpose:** To provide financial assistance to black female law students. **Applicant Eligibility:** Applicant must be a black female in her first, second, or third year of a four year program at an accredited law school. **Selection Criteria:** Applicants are judged through a writing competition. **Application Deadline:** Information must be submitted to law school deans and BLSA offices of all accredited law schools on October 1 of each year with a submission deadline of mid-February of the next year.

★2610★
NACA Multi-Cultural Scholarship
National Association for Campus Activities
Educational Foundation
13 Harbison Way   Ph: (803)732-6222
Columbia, SC 29212-3401   Fax: (803)749-1047
Study Level: Professional Development. **Award Type:** Scholarship.
Purpose: To increase the participation of ethnic minorities in the field of campus activities by providing economic assistance to qualified minority group members to allow attendance at NACA-sponsored training workshops, regional conferences or national conventions. **Applicant Eligibility:** Applicants must be identified as members of Black, Latino, Native American, Pacific Islander, or Asian-American ethnic minority groups who are interested in training in campus activities. **Funds Available:** Up to three scholarships are available for registration to NACA-sponsored training workshops, regional conferences and national conventions. Travel is not included. **Application Details:** In addition to a completed application form, candidates must submit documentation attesting to minority status, financial need and intention to engage in campus activities for at least one year following the workshop for which a scholarship is being sought. At least one letter of recommendation is required from a person well-acquainted with the applicant's campus involvements. Also needed is a statement of future goals in this field. **Application Deadline:** Applications must be filed by May 1.

★2611★
NACME Corporate Scholars Program
National Action Council for Minorities in
  Engineering
3 W. 35th St.
New York, NY 10001-2281   Ph: (212)279-2626
Study Level: Undergraduate. **Award Type:** Scholarship. **Applicant Eligibility:** Applicants must be African American, Hispanic, and American Indian students who are studying engineering. **Selection Criteria:** Students must demonstrate engineering leadership potential in areas where imminent need is anticipated. **Funds Available:** Scholars receive between $12,000 and $20,000 each during their college careers. They also receive summer internship opportunities with their corporate sponsors. **Application Details:** Scholarships are administered by paricipating colleges and universities. Students should apply to the dean of admissions or contact NACME.

★2612★
NACME Incentive Grants Program
National Action Council for Minorities in
  Engineering
3 W. 35th St.
New York, NY 10001-2281   Ph: (212)279-2626
Study Level: Undergraduate. **Award Type:** Scholarship. **Applicant Eligibility:** Applicants must be African American, Hispanic, and American Indian students who are studying engineering. **Selection Criteria:** Selection is based on the student's potential for success in engineering. **Funds Available:** Between $3,000 and $18,000 is available to each student over the course of their education. **Application Details:** Scholarships are administered by participating colleges and universities. Students should contact the dean of admissions for application information or contact NACME.

★2613★
National Achievement Scholarship Program for Outstanding Negro Students
National Merit Scholarship Corporation
1560 Sherman Ave., Ste. 200
Evanston, IL 60201-4897
Study Level: Undergraduate. **Award Type:** Scholarship. **Purpose:** The National Merit Scholarship Corporation administers the National Merit Scholarship Program and the National Achievement Scholarship Program for Outstanding Negro Students. The Achievement Program, established in 1964, is a compensatory activity that seeks to identify academically able high school students who are Black Americans and increase their college admission and financial aid opportunities. **Applicant Eligibility:** Black students request consideration in the Achievement Program at the time they take the Preliminary Scholastic Aptitude Test/National Merit Scholarship Qualifying Test (PSAT/NMSQT). They indicate on the test answer sheet that they are Black Americans and wish to be considered in the Achievement Program. Such students participate simultaneously in both the Achievement Program and the Merit Program, which are separately administered by the National Merit Scholarship Corporation (NMSC). The PSAT/NMSQT performance required to receive recognition in the Merit Program is independent of the level required for a student to be honored in the Achievement Program. A student who takes the qualifying test to enter the competition for Achievement Scholarships must: request entry to the Achievement Program ; be a United States citizen or taking steps to become a United States citizen as soon as qualified; be enrolled full time in a secondary school progressing normally toward meeting the requirements for graduation or completion of high school requirements; plan to attend a regionally accredited college in the United States upon completing high school and to enroll full time in a course of study leading to one of the traditional baccalaureate degrees; and take the PSAT/NMSQT at the proper time in high school, regardless of grade classification. Students who complete grades 9 through 12 in four years take the PSAT/NMSQT as juniors and compete for Achievement Scholarships to be awarded in the spring of their senior year. Students who plan to go directly to college after three years or less in grades 9 through 12 will either take the PSAT/NMSQT in their second (sophomore) year of high school and compete for scholarships awarded in the spring of their third and final year of secondary school, or take the PSAT/NMSQT in their third and final year of secondary school and compete for

scholarships awarded in the spring that they complete their freshman year in college. **Funds Available:** About 750 Achievment Scholarships have been awarded annually in recent competitions. They are financed by Achievement Program sponsors, by contributions from donors, and by the Achievement Program's own funds. The three types of scholarships offered are: National Achievement $2,000 Scholarships which is a single-payment scholarship; Corporate-sponsored Achievement Scholarships; and the College-sponsored Achievement Scholarships worth $250 to $2,000 or more per year for four years. **Application Details:** Black students who qualify as Achievement Program Semifinalists are notified through their schools the fall after taking the PSAT/NMSQT. Achievement Program Semifinalists who meet further requirements and advance to Finalist standing in the Achievement Program competition are notified of their standing through their high schools. All Achievement Scholarship stipends must be used exclusively to pay college costs at a regionally accredited United States college or university, and the winner must follow a course of study leading to one of the usual baccalaureate degrees. Both the corporate-sponsored and college-sponsored Achievement Scholarships may be renewed for up to four years of full-time undergraduate study or until baccalaureate degree requirements are met, whichever occurs first. Throughout the undergraduate years the winner must continue to meet all the terms of the scholarship.

★2614★
National Consortium for Educational Access Fellowship
National Consortium for Educational
  Access
Georgia Institute of Technology
Alumni Faculty House   Ph: (404)894-2389
Atlanta, GA 30332   Fax: (404)853-0446
Study Level: Doctorate. **Award Type:** Fellowship. **Purpose:** To provide financial support to minorities who are pursuing Ph.D.s, particularly in the scientific, technological, and business-related fields and to increase the number of minorities with Ph.D.s who are teaching on the university and college level. **Applicant Eligibility:** Applicants must be enrolled full-time in Ph.D. program at a NCEA member institution. **Selection Criteria:** Applicants will be judged on the bases of GPA, standardized test scores, recommendations, and academic discipline. **Funds Available:** $3,000 for students; $5,000 for faculty members. Member schools waive tuition and fees and provide assistantships. **Application Details:** Candidates must submit original applications plus four copies directly to the NCEA. Transcripts and test scores must be forwarded when available. **Application Deadline:** December 1.

★2615★
National FFA Foundation Minority Scholarships
National FFA Foundation
310 N. Midvale Blvd.
P.O. Box 5117   Ph: (608)238-4222
Madison, WI 53705-0117   Fax: (608)238-6350
Study Level: Undergraduate. **Award Type:** Scholarship. **Applicant Eligibility:** Applicants must be FFA members pursuing college degrees in any area of agriculture and must represent a minority ethnic group (American Indian or Alaskan Native, Asian or Pacific Islander, Black, or Hispanic). FFA members from any state, Puerto Rico, the Virgin Islands, or the District of Columbia are eligible. **Funds Available:** Four $10,000 scholarships and three $5,000 scholarships. Winners of the $10,000 scholarship will have to provide documentation of college expenses (tuition, books, room and board) to the National FFA in order to receive allotment of funds and maintain full-time student status and a GPA of 2.0/4.0. A copy of quarter, trimester, or semester grades will be sent to FFA after each grading period. **Application Details:** Application material is available from the FFA. **Application Deadline:** March 1.

★2616★
National Physical Science Consortium Fellowships

National Physical Sciences Consortium for
  Minorities and Women
c/o New Mexico State University
O'Loughlin House
University Blvd.
Box 30001, Dept. 3 NPS   Ph: (505)646-6037
Las Cruces, NM 88003   Fax: (505)646-6097

Study Level: Graduate; Doctorate. **Award Type:** Fellowship. **Purpose:** To expand the pool of women and minorities in graduate physical science studies. **Applicant Eligibility:** Applicants must be U.S. citizens who are African American, Hispanic, Native American, and/or female. They must also have an undergraduate standing as a senior with at least a 3.0 GPA, be eligible to pursue graduate study at a participating member university, and be an entering or returning student. Study must be in the fields of astronomy, chemistry, computer science, geology, materials science, mathematics, or physics. **Selection Criteria:** Selection is based on grade point average, GRE scores, transcripts, letters of recommendation, and prior research and/or employment experience. Photocopies of each candidate's application are sent to major research laboratories, national corporations, and leading Ph.D. granting universities. Two review committees, consisting of scientists, academic deans, and sponsoring employers, review the applications.**Funds Available:** Fellowships are worth from $150,000 to $180,000 depending on the cost of graduate school for a period of six years. They pay for tuition, fees, and a stipend $10,000 to $15,000 for each graduate year. **Application Details:** Applications must be submitted along with official transcripts for each post-secondary school attended, GRE test scores, and a one-page statement regarding applicant's research experience, educational objectives, and professional goals. **Application Deadline:** November 15. ** Jean Garcia, administrator, National Physical Science Consortium, at the above address, or at the University of California, San Diego, D-016, La Jolla, CA, 92093. For information about the application process students may call the NPSC student recruitment office collect at: (505)646-6038 or (505)646-6849; or toll-free: 800-952-4118. The NPSC headquarters office toll-free number is: 800-854-NPSC; or students may call collect at: (619)534-7183 or (619)534-7327.

★2617★
National Science Foundation - Minority Graduate
Fellowship

Consulat General de France Service
  Culturel
737 N. Michigan Ave., Ste. 1170   Ph: (312)664-3525
Chicago, IL 60611   Fax: (312)664-9528

Study Level: Postgraduate; Doctorate. **Award Type:** Fellowship. **Purpose:** To provide assistance for study or work leading to master's or doctoral degrees in the mathematical, biological, engineering, and social sciences, and in the history and philosophy of science. **Applicant Eligibility:** Those proposing research/study outside the United States must be United States citizens. The fellowship is only open to applicants who are members of an ethnic minority underrepresented at the advanced levels of the United States science and engineering pool. **Selection Criteria:** The fellowship is intended for students at or near the beginning of their graduate study. **Funds Available:** For 1992-93, $13,500. An additional $1000 International Travel Allowance is also available. **Application Details:** Applications are available starting in September. **Application Deadline:** Early November. ** Write: National Research Council, Fellowship Office, 2101 Constitution Ave. NW, Washington, D.C. 20418. Telephone: (202)334-2872.

★2618★
New York Philharmonic Music Assistance Fund
Scholarships

New York Philharmonic
Music Assistance Fund
Avery Fisher Hall
10 Lincoln Center Plaza   Ph: (212)875-5735
New York, NY 10023-6973   Fax: (212)875-5717

Study Level: Undergraduate; Graduate; High School. **Award Type:** Scholarship. **Purpose:** To provide merit scholarships to students throughout the country to attend schools of music and summer institutes that provide concentrated study and performance opportunities. **Applicant Eligibility:** Applicants must be United States citizens of African descent, including but not limited to African-American, Afro-Caribbean, and similar heritages. They must also pursue degrees at conservatories and university schools of music. The scholarships are for orchestral instruments only; piano is not included. Candidates may be high school students if they demonstrate accomplishment and promise. **Selection Criteria:** Grants are awarded based on an audition, financial need, and written recommendations. **Funds Available:** From $500 to $3,000 each. **Application Details:** Applicants are required to complete an application form, file a Financial Aid Form (FAF) or a Graduate and Professional Scholarship Financial Aid Service Form (GAPSFAS) with the College Scholarship Service of the College Board (using the code 2501 to release scores to the Music Assistance Fund), solicit a letter of recommendation from an instrumental teacher, and write a brief essay. Candidates must also perform a personal audition and must contact the Music Assistance Fund office for an audition consultation. **Application Deadline:** January 29.

★2619★
New York Telephone Scholarship for Black and
Hispanic Students

Career Opportunities Through Education
PO Box 2810   Ph: (609)573-9400
Cherry Hill, NJ 08034   Fax: (609)573-9799

Study Level: Undergraduate. **Award Type:** Scholarship. **Applicant Eligibility:** Applicants must be Black or Hispanic, residents of New York State, and enrolled full-time in a post-secondary school located in New York State. Specific eligibilities are listed in applications. **Funds Available:** Thirty-five renewable awards ranging from $1,000 to $2,000. **Application Details:** Application must be obtained from Career Opportunities Through Education no later than February 15.

★2620★
Newsday Scholarship in Communications for Minorities

Newsday
Melville, NY 11747   Ph: (516)845-2183

Study Level: Undergraduate. **Award Type:** Scholarship. **Purpose:** To provide financial assistance to minority students from Nassau and Suffolk counties. **Applicant Eligibility:** Applicant must be graduating from high school in Queens, Nassau, or Suffolk County, New York, must be interested in communications, and must intend to enroll in a 4-year college in one of the above mentioned counties. **Funds Available:** Full tuition is provided for one year and may be renewed for up to 3 years if student maintains a 3.0 GPA and remains interested in communications. **Application Deadline:** March.

★2621★
NIH Postdoctoral Fellowship Awards for Minority
Students

National Institute of General Medical
  Sciences   Ph: (301)496-7137
Bethesda, MD 20892   Fax: (301)402-3665

Study Level: Doctorate. **Award Type:** Fellowship. **Purpose:** To make fellowships available to minority doctoral candidates. **Applicant Eligibility:** Applicants must be currently enrolled in a Ph.D. or M.D./Ph.D. graduate program in the biomedical sciences, or have been accepted by and agreed to enroll in such a graduate program the following academic year. **Selection Criteria:** Selection is based upon academic records and research experience, which is evaluated for scientific merit and training potential as well as originality of proposed research. **Funds Available:** 30 fellowships. **Application Details:** Fellowship application PHS 416-1 should be used when applying. It is available through the Office of Grants Inquiries, Division of Research Grants, National Institutes of Health, Westwood Bldg., Rm. 449, Bethesda, MD 20892. **Application Deadline:** The deadline for 1993 was April 27.

★2622★
NSF Minority Graduate Fellowships featuring the special component Women in Engineering
National Science Foundation
2101 Constitution Ave.   Ph: (202)334-2872
Washington, DC 20418   Fax: (202)334-2759
Study Level: Doctorate; Graduate. **Award Type:** Fellowship. **Purpose:** To increase the number of practicing female scientists and engineers who are members of ethnic minority groups that traditionally have been underrepresented in the advanced levels of the Nation's engineering talent pool. NSF annually awards 15 fellowships to support graduate studies in engineering leading to master's or doctoral degrees. Fellowships are intended for students at or near the beginning of their graduate study in engineering. **Applicant Eligibility:** Applicants must be female citizens or nationals of the U.S. and members of minority groups underrepresented in the advanced levels of the U.S. engineering pool. Such groups currently include American Indian, Black, Hispanic, Native Alaskan (Eskimo or Aleut), and Native Pacific Islander (Polynesian or Micronesian). They must have, by the begining of the Fall term of the application year, completed no more than 30 semester hours, 45 quarter hours, or the equivalent of graduate study in the science and engineering fields since completion of their last baccalaureate degree in science or engineering. Applicants who have earned any medical degree are not eligible. **Selection Criteria:** Ability and special aptitude for advanced training in science or engineering as judged by considering academic records, recommendations regarding applicant's qualifications, and GRE scores. **Funds Available:** Fellowships for a three-year tenure (usable over a five-year period). Stipends for 12 months periods are $14,000. Additionally, cost-of-educations allowances of $7,500 per fellow are awarded to sponsoring institutions, as well as a special international research travel allowance for Fellows who qualify. **Application Details:** In addition to completed applications (comprised of two parts), candidates are required to provide a proposed plan of study/research, description of previous research experience, course reports and academic transcripts, reference reports, and GRE scores. **Application Deadline:** Part 1 of the application is due in early November; part 2 in early December. ** The Fellowship Office, National Research Council, 2101 Constitution Ave., Washington, DC 20418; (202) 334-2872.

★2623★
NSNA Breakthrough to Nursing Scholarships for Ethnic People of Color
The Foundation of the National Student
 Nurses' Association, Inc.
555 W. 57th St., Ste. 1325
New York, NY 10019   Ph: (212)581-2215
Study Level: Undergraduate. **Award Type:** Scholarship. **Applicant Eligibility:** Applicants must be minority students who are currently enrolled in a state-approved school of nursing or pre-nursing in a program leading to an associate or baccalaureate degree, a diploma, or a generic doctorate or master's degree. **Selection Criteria:** Awards are based on academic achievement, financial need, and involvement in nursing student organizations and community activities related to health care. **Funds Available:** Scholarships range from $1,000 to $2,500 each. In 1992-93, over $100,000 in scholarship funds were awarded. **Application Details:** Students must submit a copy of their recent nursing school and college transcripts or grade reports and a $5 processing fee along with completed applications. Those members of NSNA must submit proof of their membership. Application forms are available by sending a self-addressed, legal-size envelope with 52 cents postage. They are available from September until January. **Application Deadline:** February 1.

★2624★
Organization of Black Airline Pilots Summer Flight Academy
Organization of Black Airline Pilots
PO Box 86
La Guardia Airport
Flushing, NY 11371
Study Level: Other. **Award Type:** Scholarship. **Purpose:** To provide a concentrated introduction to flying including a ground school and flight training at the Tuskegee Institute in Alabama. Two weeks usually results in a solo flight by participants. **Applicant Eligibility:**

Must be between the ages of 16 and 19 years of age. **Application Details:** Application forms may be requested. An essay will be required with the application. **Application Deadline:** May 1.

★2625★
Ortho/McNeil Predoctoral Minority Fellowship in Antimicrobial Chemotherapy
American Society for Microbiology
1325 Massachusetts Ave., NW
Washington, DC 20005
Study Level: Doctorate. **Award Type:** Fellowship. **Purpose:** To support a graduate student conducting research in antimicrobial chemotherapy who is a member of a recognized racial or ethnic minority group in the United States. **Applicant Eligibility:** To be eligible, an applicatn must be a U.S. citizen or a permanent resident, be a member of the African American, Hispanic, Native Alaskan , Native American, or Native Pacific Islander group, and be formally admitted as a candidate for a doctoral degree in microbiology at an accredited U.S. institution at the time of application. **Funds Available:** A two-year fellowship of $10,000 per year is awarded. A portion of the fellowship must be used for tuition and fees. If an awardee leaves the approved program during an award year, he or she forfeits that portion of the stipend, tuition, and fees remaining to be disbursed. The awardee will be required to provide an accounting of pre-doctoral progress at the end of each semester for which he or she receives the fellowship support. **Application Details:** Applications must consist of a nomination cover page, a nominating letter, proof of admission to a doctoral program in microbiology at an accredited U.S. institution, a one to two page description of the research project, a copy of the nominee's undergraduate and graduate transcripts and a copy of GRE scores supplied by the university, and three letters of recommendation, one of which should be from the nominee's research advisor. **Application Deadline:** May 1.

★2626★
Presbyterian Church Racial/Ethnic Leadership Supplemental Grants
Presbyterian Church (U.S.A.)
Office of Financial Aid for Studies
100 Witherspoon St.
Louisville, KY 40202-1396   Ph: (502)569-8056
Study Level: Graduate. **Award Type:** Grant. **Applicant Eligibility:** Candidates must be United States citizens, members of the Presbyterian Church (U.S.A.) under care of a presbytery for a church occupation, and be enrolled at least half-time in a prescribed program of study approved by their presbytery. Applicants must be Asian, Black, Hispanic, or Native American. **Funds Available:** Under normal circumstances, the maximum grant is $1,000 for a one year period. **Application Details:** Applicants should contact the Financial Aid Officer at their seminary or other institution of study who will make recommendations to the Office of Financial Aid for Studies.

★2627★
Presbyterian Church Student Opportunity Scholarships
Presbyterian Church (U.S.A.)
Office of Financial Aid for Studies
100 Witherspoon St.
Louisville, KY 40202-1396   Ph: (502)569-8056
Study Level: Undergraduate. **Award Type:** Scholarship. **Purpose:** Student Opportunity Scholarships have been established for young persons of limited opportunities from ethnic minority groups. **Applicant Eligibility:** Applicants must be Asian, Black, Hispanic, Native American and members of the Presbyterian Church (U.S.A.). Candidates must be entering college as incoming full-time freshmen and must have applied to the college for financial aid. They must be United States citizens or permanent residents. **Funds Available:** Scholarships range from $100 to $1,400 and are individually determined based on financial need and funds available. They may be renewed during a student's undergraduate years depending upon continued financial need and satisfactory academic progress. **Application Deadline:** April 1 of the candidate's senior year in high school.

★2628★
Racial Ethnic Scholarship Program
The Synod of The Trinity
3040 Market St.
Camp Hill, PA 17011
Study Level: Undergraduate. **Award Type:** Scholarship. **Applicant Eligibility:** Applicants must be members of racial minority groups (e.g., Asians, African Americans, Hispanics, and Indigenous Americans) who are residents of Pennsylvania, West Virginia, or the Ohio counties of Belmont, Harrison, Jefferson, Monroe, and Columbiana. They must also be enrolled in or are applying for enrollment as a full-time student in an undergraduate program at an accredited college or vocational school. **Application Details:** Application forms are available from the Synod. **Application Deadline:** March 1.

★2629★
REC Educational Grant
Racine Environment Committee Educational
  Fund
310 5th St., Rm. 101
Racine, WI 53403   Ph: (414)631-5600
Study Level: Undergraduate. **Award Type:** Grant. **Purpose:** To provide financial assistance to low-income, minority students in order for them to attend a college or university. **Applicant Eligibility:** Applicant must be a minority member, resident of the city of Racine, and show financial need. **Funds Available:** Funds vary. **Application Details:** Application is available upon request. **Application Deadline:** June 30 for the first semester; October 31 for the second semester.

★2630★
Research Training Fellowship for Registered Nurses
American Nurses Association
Ethnic/Racial Minority Fellowships
  Programs
600 Maryland Ave., SW, Ste. 100 W
Washington, DC 20024-2571
Study Level: Doctorate. **Award Type:** Fellowship. **Purpose:** To increase the number of ethnic minority research scientists. To increase the data on issues related to ethnic minority mental health. **Applicant Eligibility:** Candidates must be registered nurses pursuing careers as research scientists on mental health issues related to minority populations. They must be American citizens or permanent visa residents. Applicants should be members of an ethnic or racial minority group, including but not limited to Blacks, Hispanics, American Indians, Asian Americans, Pacific Islanders and/or demonstrate a commitment to careers in behavioral science research related to ethnic minority mental health. They must also be registered nurses, enrolled full-time in an ANA-approved academic program leading to a doctoral degree in the behavioral sciences by the time a fellowship is awarded. Students not yet enrolled in a doctoral program may apply but are encouraged to apply to a doctoral program as soon as possible. **Selection Criteria:** Selection is based upon research potential, scholarship, writing ability, ethnic or racial minority orientation, knowledge of broad concepts in health science, and professional commitment. **Funds Available:** The amounts vary but the award does not exceed $7,500 per year. The award may be extended for a maximum of three years but is contingent on satisfactory academic performance. Students who accept an award have no obligation for the first year of the award. However, if funding is received beyond one year, the student is obliged to engage in biomedical or behavioral research and/or teaching with a minority mental health orientation for a period equal to the length of the award was received beyond the first year. **Application Deadline:** January 15.

★2631★
Robert A. Hine Memorial Scholarship
Southern California Edison Company
The Edison Scholarship Committee
PO Box 800
Rosemead, CA 91770   Ph: (818)302-0284
Study Level: Undergraduate. **Award Type:** Scholarship. **Purpose:** To recognize and reward the achievement of an outstanding student from an underrepresented ethnic group. **Applicant Eligibility:** Applicants must be high school seniors who are members of an underrepresented ethnic group, live in or attend school in an area served by Southern California Edison, and be a citizen or a permanent resident of the United States. Students must also plan to attend a four-year university as a full-time student and demonstrate academic achievement. **Selection Criteria:** Candidates are ranked by SAT scores. The 100 highest scoring candidates are asked to complete an application and return it to an independent scholarship organization. A judging panel selects the winner based on educational performance, leadership skills, extracurricular activities, and potential to succeed. **Funds Available:** One $20,000 award. **Application Details:** Candidates must take the Scholastic Aptitude Test (SAT) of the College Board Admissions Testing Program by the first Saturday in December of their senior year. Scores may be released by marking "No. 0043–Robert A. Hine Memorial Scholarship" on the registration form. Applications are sent to the top-scoring 100 students.

★2632★
RTNDF Six-month Internships for Minority Students
Radio and Television News Directors
  Foundation
1000 Connecticut Ave., NW, Ste. 615   Ph: (202)659-6570
Washington, DC 20036   Fax: (202)223-4007
Study Level: Graduate. **Award Type:** Internship. **Applicant Eligibility:** Minority students who have recently graduated with a degree in electronic journalism and who are pursuing a career in news management may apply. **Funds Available:** Three paid six-month entry level internships in production or news management are available. **Application Details:** Applications may be obtained from the applicant's faculty advisor, dean's office, or from the Foundation. **Application Deadline:** March 15.

★2633★
RTNDF Summer Internships for Minority Students
Radio and Television News Directors
  Foundation
1000 Connecticut Ave., NW, Ste. 615   Ph: (202)659-6570
Washington, DC 20036   Fax: (202)223-4007
Study Level: Undergraduate. **Award Type:** Internship. **Applicant Eligibility:** Minority students in their junior year who have declared a major in broadcast or cable news and are interested in a career in news management may apply. **Funds Available:** Three paid summer internships in production or news management. **Application Details:** Applications may be obtained from the applicant's faculty advisor, dean's office, or from the Foundation. **Application Deadline:** March 15. ** Scholarships/Internships, Radio and Television News Directors Foundation, 1000 Connecticut Ave., Ste. 615, Washington, DC 20036.

★2634★
Sachs Foundation Grant
Sachs Foundation
United Bank Tower
90 S. Cascade Ave., Ste. 1410
Colorado Springs, CO 80903   Ph: (719)633-2353
Study Level: Undergraduate. **Award Type:** Grant. **Applicant Eligibility:** Applicants must be Black residents of Colorado. **Selection Criteria:** Preference will be given to those who demonstrate financial and have grade point averages of 3.4 or higher. **Funds Available:** The amount of scholarships is dependent on the Board of Directors. **Application Details:** Applications are available from the Foundation between January 1 and March 1. **Application Deadline:** March 1.

★2635★
Santa Fe Pacific Achievement Scholarships for
  Outstanding African American Students
Santa Fe Pacific Foundation
1700 E. Golf Rd.
Schaumburg, IL 60173-5860
Study Level: Undergraduate. **Award Type:** Scholarship. **Applicant Eligibility:** Candidates are African American students who are

finalists in the NMSC's Achievement competition. They must be children of SFP employees. **Application Details:** To be considered for the four-year scholarship, students must take the PSAT/NMSQT in the fall of their junior year.

★2636★
Sara Lee National Achievement Scholarships
Sara Lee Foundation
3 First National Plaza
Chicago, IL 60602-4260   Ph: (312)558-8448
Study Level: Undergraduate. **Award Type:** Scholarship. **Applicant Eligibility:** Must be a black student who is the child of an employee and meets the selection criteria of the National Merit Scholarship Corporation.

★2637★
SBNA Scholarship
Sacramento Black Nurses Association
PO Box 5171
Sacramento, CA 95817   Ph: (916)392-8230
Study Level: Undergraduate. **Award Type:** Scholarship. **Purpose:** To help African American nursing students further their education. **Applicant Eligibility:** Applicants must be African Americans currently enrolled in nursing programs. **Selection Criteria:** Selection is based on financial need, academic records, an essay, and a personal interview. **Funds Available:** $1,000. **Application Details:** Applicants must submit an essay explaining the need for the scholarship, and appear for a committee interview. **Application Deadline:** September 30.

★2638★
SLA Affirmative Action Scholarships
Special Libraries Association
1700 Eighteenth St. NW
Washington, DC 20009   Ph: (202)234-4700
Study Level: Graduate. **Award Type:** Scholarship. **Purpose:** To assist graduate students attain a master's degree in libraianship at a recognized school of library or information science. **Applicant Eligibility:** Applicants must be members of a minority group (Black, Hispanic, Asian or Pacific Islander, or American Indian or Alaskan Native). **Selection Criteria:** Preference is given to applicants who display an aptitude for and interest in special library work. Extra consideration is given to members of SLA and to persons who have worked in and for special libraries. **Funds Available:** Number and value of scholarships depend on the availability of funds. Students may receive only one SLA scholarship during their graduate library school career. **Application Details:** Candidates must submit the following: completed application form; evidence of financial need; statement (500 to 1,000 words) describing experience in special libraries and expected contribution to special librarianship; and a statement of provisional acceptance by a recognized library school or information science program. Matriculated school applicants must submit an official transcript of their library school record to date. Applicants must also arrange to have reference letters sent directly to SLA from three persons not related to applicant. **Application Deadline:** October 31. Reference letters must be received by SLA by November 6. Scholarship winners are notified in May. Official announcement and presentation is made at the Association's Annual Conference in June.

★2639★
Smithsonian Institution Minority Fellowships
Smithsonian Institution
Office of Fellowships and Grants
955 L'Enfant Plaza, Ste. 7300
Washington, DC 20560   Ph: (202)287-3271
Study Level: Graduate; Undergraduate. **Award Type:** Internship. **Applicant Eligibility:** Applicants must be minority undergraduate or graduate students. **Funds Available:** Internships carry a cash stipend and a travel allowance.

★2640★
SOCHE/PGA Scholarship
Southwestern Ohio Council for Higher
  Education
2900 Acosta St., Ste. 141
Dayton, OH 45420
Study Level: Undergraduate. **Award Type:** Scholarship. **Purpose:** To Assist minority students who have enrolled in one of the Council institutions. **Selection Criteria:** Recipients are selected on a needs basis by the Financial Aid Officers of SOCHE.

★2641★
**Society of Actuaries/Casualty Actuarial Society
  Scholarships for Minority Students**
Society of Actuaries
475 N. Martingale Rd., Ste. 800
Schaumburg, IL 60173   Ph: (708)706-3500
Study Level: Undergraduate. **Award Type:** Scholarship. **Purpose:** The scholarship program is designed to aid minority students interested in pursuing actuarial careers. **Applicant Eligibility:** Candidates must be members of a minority group (i.e., Black, Hispanic, Oriental, or Native North American). They must be either U.S. citizens or have permanent resident visas. Candidates must be admitted to a college or university offering either a program in Actuarial Science or courses which will serve to prepare the student for an actuarial career. All applicants must have demonstrated mathematical ability and evidence some understanding of the field. Applicants must have taken Exam 100 of the Actuarial Examinations, the Scholastic Aptitude Test (SAT), or the ACT. **Selection Criteria:** Scholarships are awarded on the basis of individual merit and financial need. **Funds Available:** The number and amount of the scholarships are determined by a committee of members of the Society of Actuaries and the Casualty Actuarial Society. The number and amount of the awards vary from year to year. **Application Details:** Applicants must submit the Financial Aid Form (FAF) to the College Scholarship Service (CSS) of the College Board not later than March 31 and give CSS permission to forward information to the Society. Applicants must also submit two nomination forms, completed by their instructors or academic advisors. **Application Deadline:** May 1.

★2642★
**Southern California Edison Company Independent
  Colleges of Southern California Scholarships**
Southern California Edison Company
The Edison Scholarship Committee
PO Box 800
Rosemead, CA 91770   Ph: (818)302-0284
Study Level: Undergraduate. **Award Type:** Scholarship. **Purpose:** To recognize and reward the achievement of outstanding students from underrepresentated ethnic groups. **Applicant Eligibility:** Applicants must be members of an underrepresented minority group living in an area serviced by Southern California Edison. Students should also be U.S. citizens or permanent residents planning to enter college as full-time undergraduate students at an Independent Colleges of Southern California (ICSC) school, in one of its regular programs, and under its usual academic standards. Each applicant must demonstrate financial need, as verified by college administration, and academic achievement. Dependents of SCEcorp employees are not eligible. **Selection Criteria:** Each member college submits two candidate choices based on the student's academic performance, extracurricular activities, and demonstrated leadership skills. Their names are submitted to ICSC for selection of finalists. The finalists are interviewed by a panel of community leaders, who select two recipients based on educational performance, leadership skills, extracurricular activites, and potential to succeed. Preference is given to students who are the first generation in their families to attend college. **Funds Available:** Two $20,000 scholarships. **Application Details:** Member colleges nominate two candidates each. Interested students must obtain an application from the Financial Aid Office of their school.

★2643★
Star Supporter Scholarship/Loan
Christian Church (Disciples of Christ)
Homeland Ministries
222 S. Downey Ave.
PO Box 1986
Indianapolis, IN 46206   Ph: (317)353-1499

Study Level: Graduate. **Award Type:** Scholarship Loan. **Applicant Eligibility:** This scholarship is limited to Black or African-American ministerial students who plan to prepare for a professional ministry in the Christian Church (Disciples of Christ). Applicants must be members of the Christian Church (Disciples of Christ) with Regional Representation; be above average scholastically; provide evidence of financial need; be enrolled in an accredited college, university, or seminary; and provide a transcript of academic work. **Funds Available:** Scholarship/loans call for a promissory note to be signed by the recipient. Two methods of repayment are provided. The first method is a service option in which each complete year of fulltime professional ministry reduces the scholarship/loan by one-third. Three such years of service in a full-time professional ministry will cancel the entire scholarship/loan. The second method is for those who do not enter the ministry. They are expected to repay the scholarship/loan either in one cash payment or on a monthly installment basis of $100 at the rate of 6 percent annual interest on the principal. These payments begin three months after leaving school. Scholarship/Loans are renewable upon application. **Application Details:** Candidates must file a formal application which includes an estimate of income and expenses; parents' financial information for dependent students; and five references, one of which must be from the pastor of the congregation in which the applicant is a member, one from candidate's regional minister; and one from the church school superintendent. References must be persons who can vouch for candidate's academic ability and potential for the ministry. Candidates must describe as briefly as possible their present vocational direction, plans for further education and any additional information about themselves that may be helpful to the scholarship committee. **Application Deadline:** March 15.

★2644★
TechForce Scholarships
National Action Council for Minorities in
  Engineering
3 W. 35th St.
New York, NY 10001-2281   Ph: (212)279-2626

Study Level: Undergraduate. **Award Type:** Scholarship. **Applicant Eligibility:** Candidates must be exceptional high school seniors who plan to pursue careers in engineering. **Selection Criteria:** Students must demonstrate academic excellence, leadership skills, and commitment to engineering as a career. **Funds Available:** Ten primary finalists receive awards of $1,000 each per year, renewable for four years. Two top scholars receive an additional $2,500 per year for four years. Also, ten semifinalists each receive $500. A total of 20 awards are given annually.

★2645★
Tennessee Community College Education Recruitment Scholarship
Tennessee Student Assistance Corp.
Parkway Towers, Ste. 1950
404 James Robertson Pkwy.
Nashville, TN 37243-0820   Ph: (615)741-1346

Study Level: Undergraduate. **Award Type:** Scholarship. **Purpose:** To attract members of Tennessee minorities into teacher education programs at Tennessee community colleges. **Applicant Eligibility:** Applicants must be U.S. citizens and Tennessee residents. They must be freshmen enrolled full-time in an eligible Tennessee community college. The courses that they are enrolled in full-time must be documented to be transferable to a teacher education program at a senior institution. The receiving community college cannot enroll more than ten awardees per academic year and must have a transfer agreement in place with a senior institution that has a state-approved teacher education program. **Funds Available:** $2,000 per academic year, renewable for a second year. **Application Details:** Applications are available through TSAC.

★2646★
Tennessee Teaching Fellowships
Tennessee Student Assistance Corp.
Parkway Towers, Ste. 1950
404 James Robertson Pkwy.
Nashville, TN 37243-0820   Ph: (615)741-1346

Study Level: Undergraduate. **Award Type:** Scholarship Loan. **Purpose:** To encourage qualified minority students to enter the teaching profession. **Applicant Eligibility:** Only entering freshmen who are minority Tennesseans are eligible for first-time awards. To be considered, they must have earned at least a 3.5 GPA in high school through the seventh semester level, and either have scored at least an 18 on the ACT or 780 on the SAT or be in the top 25 percent of their high school graduating class. They must be U.S. citizens and agree in writing to teach at some K-12 level in a Tennessee public school upon college graduation. **Funds Available:** $5,000 for each year eligible. $20,000 maximum. Those who fail to fill the obligation by teaching must repay the award balance plus 12 percent interest. **Application Details:** Application forms will be sent to Tennessee high schools only if awards are to be made in a given year (funds must be made available by the state legislature).

★2647★
Texas Black Scholarships
Baptist General Convention of Texas
Black Church Relations Sector
333 North Washington St., Ste. 371   Ph: (214)828-5131
Dallas, TX 75246-1798   Fax: (214)828-5284

Study Level: Undergraduate. **Award Type:** Scholarship. **Purpose:** The Texas Black Baptist Scholarship Program recognizes worthy, capable young men and women and offers them continuing opportunities afforded by a Christian education. **Applicant Eligibility:** Candidates must: be Black and hold active membership in a Baptist church; give evidence of being a genuine Christian; be graduates of Texas schools; have acceptable recommendations from pastors and teachers; have maintained a B average in high school, or have a minimum of 2.0 on a 4.0 grading scale from a credited college or university; be residents of Texas for at least 12 months before being eligible for consideration for a scholarship; possess a vital interest in the advance of the Kingdom of God; and attend a Texas Baptist Educational Institution, or a Baptist Institution agreed upon by the scholarship committee. **Selection Criteria:** Each person making an application for a scholarship will be carefully considered. Final selection of scholarship students is made by the scholarship committe. Applicants should look upon preliminary interviews merely as steps toward a final interview with the committee. The committee receives recommendations from many sources. Papers, mission personnel, high school teachers and advisors, and many others send names of worthy students to the committee for consideration. **Funds Available:** Scholarship grants are $400 per semester, or $266.66 per quarter. Scholarships are for one year and may be renewed each year. **Application Details:** Applicants must write the Black Church Relations Section requesting application for Texas Black Baptist Scholarship. The completed application must be returned. A confidential file is compiled which includes letters of recommendation, transcript, biographical data, and other basic information. If applicants qualify under scholarship policy limitations, they will be invited to meet with the scholarship committee, during which time the final decision regarding scholarship shall be made.

★2648★
Texas State Scholarship Program for Ethnic Recruitment
Texas Higher Education Coordinating
  Board
PO Box 12788
Capitol Station
Austin, TX 78711-2788   Ph: (512)462-6325

Study Level: Undergraduate. **Award Type:** Scholarship. **Applicant Eligibility:** Applicant must be a resident minority student enrolling for the first time either as freshmen or new transfer student and whose ethnic group comprises less than 40 percent of the enrollment at a particular school. Entering freshmen must score at least 800 on the SAT or at least 18 on the ACT, and transfer students must have a GPA of at least 2.75. **Selection Criteria:** A judgement of financial need by the financial aid director at the institution and recommendations of the admissions officer or minority affairs officer help determine eligibility for the scholarship. **Funds Available:** One time awards range from $500 to $1,000. **Application Details:** Interested students should contact the financial aid director at the public senior college.

★2649★

Virgil Hawkins Fellows Scholarships
Florida Department of Education
Office of Student Financial Assistance
1344 Florida Education Center
Tallahassee, FL 32399-0400   Ph: (904)487-0049

Study Level: Graduate. **Award Type:** Scholarship. **Purpose:** Provides financial assistance to first-year minority law students. **Applicant Eligibility:** Applicants must: be a member of an ethnic group that was by law and custom previously denied access to a law school at a predominately white institution in Florida; meet the registration requirements of the Selective Service Administration; be admitted to the law school at Florida State University or the University of Florida; and be recommended by the law school dean. A renewal applicant must continue studies toward completion of a Jurist Doctor degree, be considered to be in good standing by the law school, and be recommended by the law school dean for continuation of the scholarship. **Funds Available:** $5,000 per academic year or as specified in the General Appropriations Act for a maximum of six semesters. Scholarships are limited to 10 new awards each at Florida State University and the University of Florida. ** The Dean of the Law School at Florida State University, 425 W. Jefferson St., Tallahassee, FL 32306, or at the University of Florida, 164 Holland Law Center, Gainsville, FL 32611.

★2650★

Virginia Undergraduate Student Financial Assistance
Virginia Council of Higher Education
James Monroe Building
101 N. 14th St.
Richmond, VA 23219   Ph: (804)225-2137

Study Level: Undergraduate. **Award Type:** Grant. **Purpose:** To assist undergraduate, black Virginia students to attend state-supported colleges and universities on at least a half-time basis. **Applicant Eligibility:** Must be a black, domiciliary resident of Virginia. **Selection Criteria:** Need based. **Funds Available:** The minimum USFAP/Last Dollar grant is $200 for any one academic term.

★2651★

William and Charlotte Cadbury Award
National Medical Fellowships
254 W. 31 St., 7th Fl.
New York, NY 10001

Study Level: Doctorate. **Award Type:** Scholarship. **Applicant Eligibility:** Candidates are American Blacks, mainland Puerto Ricans, Mexican-Americans, and American Indians who are enrolled in accredited schools of allopathic or osteopathic medicine in the United States and who are United States citizens. Cadbury Award candidates are senior medical students who have exhibited superior scholastic achievement and leadership. **Funds Available:** One Cadbury Award of $2000 is awarded annually. **Application Details:** Applications by Dean's nomination only. **Application Deadline:** Nominations requested in October.

★2652★

Wisconsin Minority Retention Grants
Wisconsin Higher Education Aids Board
131 W. Wilson St.
PO Box 7885
Madison, WI 53707   Ph: (608)266-0888

Study Level: Undergraduate. **Award Type:** Grant. **Purpose:** To provide financial assistance to Black, Hispanic, and Native American students, and students who were admitted to the United States after December 31, 1975, and who are either a former citizen of Laos, Vietnam, or Cambodia or whose ancestor was a citizen of Laos, Vietnam, or Cambodia. The goal of the Grant is to improve the rate of retention and graduation.

★2653★

Wisconsin Minority Teacher Loans
Wisconsin Higher Education Aids Board
131 W. Wilson St.
PO Box 7885
Madison, WI 53707   Ph: (608)266-0888

Study Level: Undergraduate. **Award Type:** Loan. **Applicant Eligibility:** Must be Wisconsin resident minority students attending private colleges or universities in Wisconsin who are in their junior or senior year majoring in education. **Funds Available:** Recipients may borrow up to $2,500 per academic year for a total of $5,000. Loans are forgiven when the borrower is employed as a teacher in an eligible Wisconsin school district. For each year so employed, 25 percent of the amount borrowed is forgiven. **Application Details:** Interested students should contact the financial aid office of the school at which they are enrolled.

★2654★

Woodrow Wilson Program in Public Policy and International Affairs Graduate Fellowships
Woodrow Wilson National Fellowship
Foundation
PO Box 642   Ph: (609)924-4713
Princeton, NJ 08542   Fax: (609)497-9064

Study Level: Graduate. **Award Type:** Fellowship. **Applicant Eligibility:** Must have successfully completed a junior year institute, and have been accepted by one of the participating schools of public policy or international affairs. **Funds Available:** Fellowship is for the first year of graduate study. Financial support, based on need, is provided by participating institutions in a student's second year.

★2655★

Woodrow Wilson Program in Public Policy and International Affairs Junior Year Summer Institutes
Woodrow Wilson National Fellowship
Foundation
PO Box 642   Ph: (609)924-4713
Princeton, NJ 08542   Fax: (609)497-9064

Study Level: Undergraduate. **Award Type:** Other. **Applicant Eligibility:** Must have completed the junior year in college and have at least one full semester of coursework left before graduation. Must be U.S. citizens or permanent residents and members of minority groups historically underrepresented in public policy and international careers, especially African Americans, Hispanics, Native Americans, Asian Americans, and Alaska Natives. No particular major is required. Students must, however, demonstrate strong interest in public policy and internationl affairs. **Application Details:** Write for current information. Applications are made directly to the summer institutes at participating universities. **Application Deadline:** March 15.

★2656★

Woodrow Wilson Program in Public Policy and International Affairs Senior Year Summer Programs
Woodrow Wilson National Fellowship
Foundation
PO Box 642   Ph: (609)924-4713
Princeton, NJ 08542   Fax: (609)497-9064

Study Level: Graduate. **Award Type:** Other. **Purpose:** The programs consist of Senior Year Institutes, which are designed to further strengthen skills in math, economics, and communications; Internships, which provide practical experience in policy or international work between college and graduate school; and Language Institutes, which offer intensive summer language study programs at institutions such as the Paul A. Nitze School of Advanced International Studies, the Johns Hopkins University, and the Monterey Institute of International Studies. **Applicant Eligibility:** Must have successfully completed a junior year institute and have been accepted into an approved graduate program in public policy or international affairs.

(9) Research Centers

★2657★
Amistad Research Center
Tulane Univ.
6823 St. Charles Ave.   Ph: (504)865-5535
New Orleans, LA 70118   Fax: (504)865-5580
Dr. Frederick Stielow, Dir.

Founded: 1966. **Research Activities and Fields:** Collects primary source materials pertaining to the history of American ethnic minorities, race relations, civil rights, and various religious denominations. **Publications:** Amistad Reports (quarterly). **Library:** Maintains a reference collection of about 20,000 books, 1,000 serials, 30,000 pamphlets, 1,500,000 press clippings, and 2,400 reels of microfilm; Andrew Simon, contact.

★2658★
Association for the Study of Afro-American Life and History
1407 14th St. NW   Ph: (202)667-2822
Washington, DC 20005   Fax: (202)387-9802
Gail A. Hansberry, Exec. Dir.

Founded: 1915. **Research Activities and Fields:** Afro-American life and history. Collects historical manuscripts and materials relating to black people and promotes study of black history through schools, colleges, churches, homes, fraternal groups, and clubs. Publishes books on Afro-American life and history and originated Negro History Week (now observed as Afro-American History Month each February). **Publications:** Journal of Negro History (quarterly); Negro History Bulletin (bimonthly). **Meetings/Educational Activities:** Holds professional conferences and conventions annually. Ford Foundation grant is used to fund the Carter G. Woodson Scholar in Residence and the Essay Contest for graduate and undergraduate students. **Library:** Private collection of 2,100 volumes on black history and culture. **Formerly:** Association for Study of Negro Life and History.

★2659★
Balch Institute for Ethnic Studies
18 S. 7th St.
Philadelphia, PA 19106   Ph: (215)925-8090
Dr. John Tenhula, Pres.

Founded: 1971. **Research Activities and Fields:** Immigration, race, and ethnicity. Activities focus on documenting and interpreting the American multicultural experience. **Publications:** New Dimensions (semiannually). Also publishes monographs on the history of immigration and ethnic groups in North America. Maintains a press in cooperation with associated universities. **Meetings/Educational Activities:** Sponsors occasional conferences. Offers educational programs to the public. **Library:** 50,000 volumes on American ethnic groups.

★2660★
Black Music Archives
8615 Central Park Ave.   Ph: (312)663-1600
Skokie, IL 60076-2933   Fax: (312)663-9019
Dr. Dominique-Rene de Lerma, Dir.

Founded: 1976. **Research Activities and Fields:** Identification, documentation, and bibliographic and discographic registration of various manifestations of black music cultures and black composers, including books, scores and parts, journals, recordings, letters, photographs, and similar items. Cooperates with other departments and divisions of the University and the city and serves as nucleus for recording, publication, concert, and broadcasting projects. Provides public reference services for educators, researchers, and performers. **Publications:** Sonorities in Black Music (irregularly). **Library:** 30,000 books, records, and scores on black music (international). **Formerly:** Morgan Center for Black Music Research(1978); Sonorities in Black Music (1985).

★2661★
Black Periodical Literature Project, 1827-1940
Harvard Univ.
77 Dunster St.   Ph: (617)496-7404
Cambridge, MA 02138   Fax: (617)496-8547
Prof. Henry Louis Gates Jr., Dir.

Founded: 1981. **Research Activities and Fields:** Collects periodical fiction, poetry, and book reviews, published in African-American periodicals between 1827 and 1940. **Formerly:** Black Periodical Fiction Project(1987).

★2662★
Boston Sickle Cell Center
Boston City Hospital
818 Harrison Ave., FGH 2   Ph: (617)534-5727
Boston, MA 02118   Fax: (617)534-5739
Dr. Lillian E.C. McMahon, Dir.

Founded: 1973. **Research Activities and Fields:** Sickle cell trait and sickle cell anemia/disease, including molecular, cellular, tissue, and organ studies. Investigates glucose 6-phosphate dehydrogenase deficiency, coagulation and carbomylation of hemoglobin S, anti-sickling compounds, red cell membrane alterations, fetal jeopardy, fetal hemoglobin synthesis, cardiac manifestations, lung function, and infection. Conducts ultrastructural and clinical studies and seeks to translate basic and clinical research to improved health care at the community level. **Publications:** Educational Booklets. **Meetings/Educational Activities:** Holds Annual Directors Conference, sponsored by National Institutes of Health for staff members from participating centers. Offers initial training and on-going, weekly, in-service training to the Center's staff. **Library:** BSCC Audio-Visual Library, containing a variety of films, slide collections, and slide-tape presentations.

★2663★
Boston University
African American Studies Center
138 Mountfort St.   Ph: (617)353-2795
Brookline, MA 02146   Fax: (617)353-2053
Founded: 1969. **Research Activities and Fields:** African-American history, sociology, and literature. **Publications:** Occasional Paper Series. **Meetings/Educational Activities:** Offers a master's degree in African-American studies and hosts workshops, seminars, discussion groups, conferences, and conferences series. Sponsors the Roxbury-Birmingham Lecture Series. **Formerly:** Afro-American Studies Center(1991).

★2664★
Boston University
African Studies Center
270 Bay State Rd.   Ph: (617)353-7308
Boston, MA 02215   Fax: (617)353-4975
Dr. Allan Hoben, Dir.
Founded: 1953. **Research Activities and Fields:** Anthropology, archeology, economics, geography, history, sociology, and political science as related to basic facets of African life. Also studies African art, literature, and law, with particular emphasis placed upon areas of health care delivery, rural development, and population distribution and migration. **Publications:** International Journal of African Historical Studies (quarterly); Discussion Papers in the African Humanities. **Meetings/Educational Activities:** Provides a program of instruction in African languages, including Hausa and Swahili through third year level, Yoruba and Sesotho/Setwsana through second year, and less commonly taught African languages on demand. Sponsors seminars on African history, politics, and problems of population and administration in relation to development in Africa. **Library:** 30,000 volumes, 22,000 documents, 2,000 pamphlets, 700 periodicals, and 120 newspapers on anthropology, economics, history, sociology, geography, political sciences, education, languages, and religion; Gretchen Walsh, head.

★2665★
Brooklyn College of City University of New York
Africana Research Center
3105 James Hall Bldg.
Brooklyn, NY 11210   Ph: (718)780-5485
Dr. George Cunningham, Head
Founded: 1968. **Research Activities and Fields:** History, economics, sociology, psychology, education, political science, and the arts as they relate to black people. Studies are being conducted on African-American history, Southern Africa, and the Caribbean. **Publications:** Black Prism (annually). **Formerly:** Africana Research Institute (1985).

★2666★
Brown University
AfroAmerican Studies Program
Box 1904   Ph: (401)863-3137
Providence, RI 02912   Fax: (401)863-3700
Prof. Anani Dzidzienyo, Chm.
Research Activities and Fields: History, culture, psychology, and literature of Afro-Americans in the Caribbean and North, Central, and South America and their historic and present linkages to continental Africa. **Publications:** The Langston Hughes Review (biennially). **Meetings/Educational Activities:** Offers courses and extracurricular activities in Afro-American studies.

★2667★
Brown University
Center for the Study of Race and Ethnicity in America
Box 1886   Ph: (401)863-3080
Providence, RI 02912   Fax: (401)863-7589
Rhett S. Jones, Dir.
Research Activities and Fields: Racial and ethnic minorities in America, focusing on African Americans, Asian Americans, Latinos, and Native Americans. Emphasis is on interdisciplinary, comparative, and analytical studies of race, gender, and class. **Publications:** Newsletter (quarterly). **Meetings/Educational Activities:** Sponsors public lectures, faculty seminars, faculty study groups, presentation of papers by graduate and undergraduate students interested in race and ethnicity.

★2668★
Brown University
Rites and Reason
Box 1148   Ph: (401)863-3558
Providence, RI 02912   Fax: (401)863-3700
Karen Baxter, Managing Dir.
Founded: 1970. **Research Activities and Fields:** Examines Afro-American issues and culture and seeks to investigate and portray the realities of black life in the Americas for theatre. **Publications:** The Langston Hughes Review (journal). **Meetings/Educational Activities:** Offers courses in the arts, humanities, and social sciences dealing with Africa, the Caribbean, South America, and the United States.

★2669★
Brown University
Thomas J. Watson Jr. Institute for International Studies
2 Stimson Ave.
Box 1970   Ph: (401)863-2809
Providence, RI 02912   Fax: (401)863-1270
Founded: 1986. **Research Activities and Fields:** North-South/East-West relations, regional security, transnational organization, U.S.-Soviet relations, security studies, world hunger, population, comparative study of development, geographical medicine, primary health care, Latin American studies, humanitarianism and war, international military operations, Portuguese and Brazilian studies, Afro-American studies, East Asian studies, and South Asian studies. **Publications:** Annual Report; Newsletters; Conference Reports; Occasional Papers; also publishes books. **Meetings/Educational Activities:** Offers international relations undergraduate major, and foreign exchange programs for faculty and students. Sponsors selected teaching positions in academic departments, conferences, seminars, and lectures. **Formerly:** Institute for International Studies (1991).

★2670★
Center for Applied Jurisprudence
Pacific Research Institute for Public Policy
177 Post St., Ste. 500   Ph: (415)989-0833
San Francisco, CA 94108   Fax: (415)989-2411
Sally C. Pipes, Pres.
Founded: 1986. **Research Activities and Fields:** Civil rights, property rights, First Amendment, and litigation strategy development.

★2671★
Center for Blood Research
800 Huntington Ave.
Boston, MA 02115   Ph: (617)731-6470
Dr. Chester A. Alper, Scientific Dir.
Founded: 1953. **Research Activities and Fields:** Human blood, including multidisciplinary studies on heart disease, diabetes, cancer, AIDS, hemophilia, sickle cell anemia, mental illness, hepatitis, Rh factor in pregnancy, serum proteins, blood collection methods, preservation of formed elements, methods of plasma fractionation, and characterization of plasma components. **Library:** Maintains a reference collection of current journals. **Formerly:** Until 1967 known as the Protein Foundation and subsequently as Blood Research Institute until its merger in 1972 with Blood Grouping Laboratory, formed in 1942.

★2672★
Center for Conflict Resolution
731 State St.
Madison, WI 53703   Ph: (608)255-0479
Lance Smith, Contact
Founded: 1970. **Research Activities and Fields:** Conflict resolution, group dynamics, democratic management, program or project planning, organizational skills, communication, power, education, and change. **Library:** Maintains a resource center of 400 books, periodicals, and other publications related to conflict, group

process, peace and conflict education, and current social issues; Hal Witteman, contact.

★2673★
Center for the Study of Social Policy
1250 I St. NW, Ste. 503   Ph: (202)371-1565
Washington, DC 20005   Fax: (202)371-1472
Tom Joe, Dir.
Founded: 1979. **Research Activities and Fields:** Social policy, including studies on children and youth, income support, long-term care, health, disability, and minorities. Focus on children and family services and policy. **Formerly:** Center for the Study of Welfare Policy (1982).

★2674★
Charles R. Drew University of Medicine and Science
Hypertension Research Center
1621 E. 120th St., MP 11
Los Angeles, CA 90059   Ph: (213)563-5927
Clarence E. Grim M.D., Dir.
Founded: 1984. **Research Activities and Fields:** Epidemiology, causes, and treatment of high blood pressure in blacks. Analyzes twin studies to assess genetic and environmental factors in blood pressure variations. Conducts cross-cultural studies in Barbados and Nigeria. **Meetings/Educational Activities:** Offers pre- and postdoctoral training in hypertension research.

★2675★
Children's Hospital Oakland Research Institute
747 52nd St.   Ph: (415)428-3502
Oakland, CA 94609   Fax: (415)428-3608
Dr. Bertram Lubin, Dir. of Medical Research
Founded: 1959. **Research Activities and Fields:** Biochemical studies on in vivo, intact tissue, including cellular, homogenate, enzyme, and molecular levels of a variety of metabolic pathways. Directs programs in control mechanisms of carbohydrate and lipid metabolism in normal and abnormal tissues, deranged metabolic relationships in various diseased states, carcinogenesis, growth and development, cardiovascular physiology, hypertension, vascular disease, hematology, platelet aggregation, thrombosis, gestation, experimental surgery, and nutrition as these relate to pediatric problems. Special research focuses include problems in sickle cell anemia, cystic fibrosis, cancer gene markers, nutritional/metabolic analytical method, and toxic chemical exposure. **Library:** Maintains a reference collection of over 2,500 volumes on medical and biochemical subjects. **Formerly:** Children's Hospital Research Laboratory (1986).

★2676★
City University of New York
Center for Social Research
33 W. 42nd St.
New York, NY 10036   Ph: (212)642-1600
Dr. William Kornblum, Dir.
Founded: 1966. **Research Activities and Fields:** Basic and applied research in such areas as art, culture, mass media, race and ethnicity, political economy, urban politics and anthropology, women, and comparative social research.

★2677★
Clark Atlanta University
Southern Center for Studies in Public Policy
Brawley St. & Fair St., SW   Ph: (404)880-8085
Atlanta, GA 30314   Fax: (404)880-8222
Dr. Robert A. Holmes, Dir.
Founded: 1968. **Research Activities and Fields:** Labor market, education, welfare, rural transportation, and rural political and economic development studies emphasizing strategies, policies, and programs to improve the political and economic position of black and minority populations. **Publications:** Monographs; Newsletter; Occasional Papers; Research Reports. **Library:** Maintains a research library of 12,000 volumes, a microfiche collection, and computer tapes.

★2678★
Clemson University
Center for the Study of the Black Experience
  Affecting Higher Education
30F Martin St.
PO Box 345405
Clemson, SC 29634-5404   Ph: (803)656-0313
Herman G. Green, Dir.   Fax: (803)656-0314
Founded: 1988. **Research Activities and Fields:** Issues related to the recruitment and retention of graduate and undergraduate African-American students and African-American faculty and staff at institutions of higher education in South Carolina and the southeastern and southern regions of the U.S. Promotes access and equity at all educational levels. **Publications:** Challenge (quarterly newsletter). **Meetings/Educational Activities:** Sponsors seminars, roundtables, and symposia. **Formerly:** Center for the Study of the Black Experience in Higher Education.

★2679★
College of Staten Island of City University of New
  York
Institute for African American Studies
130 Stuyvesant Pl.
Staten Island, NY 10301   Ph: (718)390-7990
Dr. Calvin B. Holder, Professor
Founded: 1969. **Research Activities and Fields:** African and Afro-American studies, including selected aspects of African civilization, sociocultural and political institutions, contributions of Afro-Americans to American civilization, and role of Afro-Americans in the U.S. **Publications:** Research Review (semiannually). **Meetings/Educational Activities:** Provides instruction. **Formerly:** Institute for Afro-American Studies.

★2680★
Columbia University
Center for American Culture Studies
603 Lewisohn Hall
New York, NY 10027   Ph: (212)854-8253
Jack Salzman, Dir.
Founded: 1982. **Research Activities and Fields:** American culture studies, with special emphasis on ethnic communities. **Publications:** Prospects: An Annual of American Cultural Studies; The Dispatch (biennial newsletter). Coordinating the Encyclopedia of African American Culture and History (five volumes). **Meetings/Educational Activities:** Sponsors conferences, lectures, and panel discussions; also sponsors international scholars. Hosts Summer Institute in American Culture Studies.

★2681★
Columbia University
Comprehensive Sickle Cell Center
Harlem Hospital
Sickle Cell Dept., Rm. 6146
506 Lenox Ave.
New York, NY 10037   Ph: (212)491-8074
Dr. Jeanne A. Smith, Dir.
Founded: 1972. **Research Activities and Fields:** Sickle cell disease, including studies of pathophysiological and biochemical aspects, rheological studies of the blood, studies on intellectual growth and development of children with sickle cell and allied diseases, biochemical factors involved in the clinical severity of the disease, and synthesis of normal hemoglobin in vitro.

★2682★
Columbia University
ERIC Clearinghouse on Urban Education
Institute for Urban & Minority Education
Teachers College
Box 40   Ph: (212)678-3433
New York, NY 10027   Fax: (212)678-4048
Dr. Erwin Flaxman, Dir.
Founded: 1965. **Research Activities and Fields:** Information collection and dissemination regarding urban education, with an aim to better serve the populations in urban school districts, including education of minorities, women, immigrants, and refugees.

Publications: Monographs; Fact Sheets; Urban Diversity Series; Trends and Issues Series; ERIC/CUE Digests. Enters documents into ERIC educational database, indexed in published volumes of Resources in Education and Current Index to Journals in Education. **Meetings/Educational Activities:** Offers workshops on using the ERIC system. **Library:** Maintains a complete ERIC microfiche collection and a library of more than 16,000 items. **Formerly:** ERIC Clearinghouse for the Urban Disadvantaged; IUME/ERIC Clearinghouse on Urban Education.

★2683★
Columbia University
Institute of African Studies
420 W. 118th St.   Ph: (212)854-4633
New York, NY 10027   Fax: (212)864-4847
Dr. George Bond, Dir.

Research Activities and Fields: African politics, history, anthropology, art history, linguistics, literature, economic development, and education. **Meetings/Educational Activities:** Offers students instruction on peoples and problems of the African continent, particularly those of tropical Africa.

★2684★
Columbus Minority Business Development Center
233 12th St., Ste. 621
PO Box 1696   Ph: (706)324-4253
Columbus, GA 31902-1696   Fax: (706)324-0335
Edward G. Dawson, Project Dir.

Founded: 1982. **Research Activities and Fields:** Marketing research on economic and general business conditions of minority businesses, especially in the area of construction. **Meetings/Educational Activities:** Sponsors seminars and workshops in management training, taxes, procurement, finance, and bonding.

★2685★
Comprehensive Sickle Cell Center (Cincinnati)
Children's Hospital Research Foundation
Elland & Bethesda Aves.
Cincinnati, OH 45229   Ph: (513)559-4543
Donald Rucknagel M.D.,, Dir.

Founded: 1972. **Research Activities and Fields:** Sickle cell disease, including molecular, cellular, tissue, and organ studies. Conducts clinical trials and seeks to translate research to improved health care. **Meetings/Educational Activities:** Offers postgraduate training courses and continuing medical education.

★2686★
Cornell University
Africana Studies and Research Center
310 Triphammer Rd.   Ph: (607)255-5218
Ithaca, NY 14850   Fax: (607)255-0784
Prof. Locksley Edmondson, Dir.

Founded: 1969. **Research Activities and Fields:** Africa, America, and Caribbean. **Publications:** Monograph Series. Sponsors postdoctoral faculty humanities fellowships in African cultural studies. **Meetings/Educational Activities:** Offers lectures and graduate and undergraduate instruction. **Library:** Houses a collection of reference materials and research guides.

★2687★
Designs for Change
220 S. State St., Ste. 1900   Ph: (312)922-0317
Chicago, IL 60604   Fax: (312)922-6993
Dr. Donald R. Moore, Exec.Dir.

Founded: 1977. **Research Activities and Fields:** Improving the quality of public schools, particularly for low-income, minority, and handicapped children. Projects include assisting with the restructuring of the Chicago Public Schools; training local school councils, parents, and community residents to improve their local schools; and assisting parents of handicapped students. **Publications:** Reports; All Our Kids Can Learn to Read: A Guide to Parent and Citizen Action (in English and Spanish); Caught in the Web: Misplaced Children in Chicago's Classes for the Mentally Retarded; Child Advocacy and the Schools: Past Impact and Potential for the 1980's; Helping Schools Change: Ideas for Assistance Groups.

★2688★
Duke University
Center for Documentary Studies
331 W. Main St., Ste. 511
Durham, NC 27701   Ph: (919)687-0486
Iris Tillman Hill, Exec.Dir.

Founded: 1990. **Research Activities and Fields:** American history and culture, focusing on oral history and documentary photography and film. Specific areas of study include the American family, African-American life and race relations, law and politics, and ecology and environment. **Meetings/Educational Activities:** Offers courses in the documentary tradition.

★2689★
Duke University
Comprehensive Sickle Cell Center
Medical Center
Morris Bldg., Box 3934   Ph: (919)684-3724
Durham, NC 27710   Fax: (919)681-8477
Wendell F. Rosse M.D., Dir.

Research Activities and Fields: Sickle cell disease, including molecular, cellular, tissue, and organ studies. Conducts clinical trials. Seeks to translate basic and clinical research to improved health care at the community level.

★2690★
Education Commission of the States
707 17th St., Ste. 2700   Ph: (303)299-3600
Denver, CO 80202-3427   Fax: (303)296-8332
Dr. Frank Newman, Pres.

Founded: 1965. **Research Activities and Fields:** Policy research, surveys, and special studies on all phases of state education policy for all levels of education, including restructuring of the education system, at-risk youth, school finance, teacher education, the quality of undergraduate education, and minority success. Maintains cooperative relationships with many education-related organizations and a broad network of information contacts and sources. **Publications:** Special Reports; Working Papers; State Education Leader (three times per year). **Meetings/Educational Activities:** Sponsors a Steering Committee Meeting in fall and spring, an annual meeting in summer, and special topical and network meetings.

★2691★
Emory University
Carter Center
1 Copenhill   Ph: (404)331-3900
Atlanta, GA 30307   Fax: (404)420-5145
Dr. William H. Foege, Exec.Dir.

Founded: 1982. **Research Activities and Fields:** Policy-oriented research on conflict resolution, human rights and international law, African governance, Middle Eastern affairs, domestic and international health policy, Latin America and Caribbean studies, U.S.-Soviet media, and urban poverty and social problems. **Publications:** Carter Center News (fall and spring); Conference Report Series; Occasional Paper Series. **Meetings/Educational Activities:** Sponsors conferences. **Library:** Houses the Jimmy Carter Library and Museum, open to the public and operated by the National Archives.

★2692★
Florida A&M University
Developmental Research School
PO Box A-19   Ph: (904)599-3325
Tallahassee, FL 32307   Fax: (904)561-2211
Dr. Ada Puryear Burnette, Dir.

Founded: 1919. **Research Activities and Fields:** African-American students who do not drop-out, math and science technology, self-esteem, computer education, minority engineering for middle schools, pharmaceutical apprenticeships, multicultural education, health identification and treatment, nutrition education, physical education improvements, and relationships between uniform outfits and academic improvement. **Publications:** Administrative Bulletin.

★2693★
Florida International University
Center for Multilingual & Multicultural Studies
Univ. Park Campus, DM 274   Ph: (305)348-3207
Miami, FL 33199   Fax: (305)559-7251
Dr. Tanya Saunders-Hamilton, Act.Dir.

Founded: 1981. **Research Activities and Fields:** Migration, language policy, ethnicity, cross-cultural education, multicultural communication, linguistics, and international studies. Employs basic, field, survey, historical, and analytical research methods. **Publications:** FIU Special Language Series; Haitian Publications; Paper Series; Cuban Heritage (magazine). **Meetings/Educational Activities:** Sponsors Hispanic conference (biennially in February), African-New World Studies conference (biennially in March or April), Haitian conference (annually), and Native American conference (annually).

★2694★
Florida State University
Black Abolitionist Papers Project
Dept. of History
Tallahassee, FL 32306   Ph: (904)644-4527
Dr. C. Peter Ripley, Dir.

Founded: 1976. **Research Activities and Fields:** Conducts research and collects documents on free blacks and fugitive slaves in the U.S., Canada, and the British Isles who worked to promote the emancipation of enslaved fellow blacks from 1830 to 1865. **Publications:** Black Abolitionist Papers, a five volume letterpress series.

★2695★
Fordham University
Langenfeld Research and Demonstration Center
Graduate School of Social Service
Fordham at Lincoln Center   Ph: (212)636-6621
New York, NY 10023   Fax: (212)636-6613
Dr. Eugene B. Shinn, Dir.

Founded: 1968. **Research Activities and Fields:** Develops and implements social research methodologies related to gerontology, international social service policy, and family, children, and minority services, substance abuse, and family violence. **Formerly:** Research Center-Graduate School of Social Service; Research and Demonstration Center.

★2696★
Harvard University
W.E.B. DuBois Institute for AfroAmerican Research
44 Brattle St.   Ph: (617)495-4192
Cambridge, MA 02138   Fax: (617)496-8547
Henry L. Gates Jr., Dir.

Founded: 1975. **Research Activities and Fields:** Postdoctoral research on Afro-American history and culture, emphasizing the humanities, social sciences, and an international perspective. **Publications:** Transition Magazine; The Newsletter of the Afro-American Religious History Group (semiannually); Monograph Series; and brochures and application procedures available upon request. **Meetings/Educational Activities:** Sponsors working groups and research conferences.

★2697★
Howard University
Bureau of Educational Research
School of Education
2441 4th St. NW   Ph: (202)806-8120
Washington, DC 20059   Fax: (202)806-8130
Dr. Ruth Palmer, Dir.

Founded: 1932. **Research Activities and Fields:** Education of African Americans.

★2698★
Howard University
Center for Sickle Cell Disease
2121 Georgia Ave. NW
Washington, DC 20059   Ph: (202)806-7930
Dr. Oswaldo Castro, Dir.

Founded: 1972. **Research Activities and Fields:** Sickle cell disease, including basic and clinical investigations of its nature, causes, effects, and potential control. Develops and implements high quality total care for victims of the disease. Develops and evaluates methods of prevention through screening for sickle and other abnormal hemoglobins and participates in the Mid-Atlantic Regional Genetic Counseling Program. **Publications:** Annual Report. **Meetings/Educational Activities:** Offers educational and training programs for medical professionals and allied health personnel, including bimonthly staff meetings, an annual symposium on sickle cell disease and other related abnormal hemoglobins, an annual postgraduate conference, monthly scientific seminars, and sickle cell grand rounds.

★2699★
Howard University
Department of African Studies
PO Box 231   Ph: (202)806-7115
Washington, DC 20059   Fax: (202)806-5523
Sulayman S. Nyang Ph.D., Dir.

Founded: 1953. **Research Activities and Fields:** Africa, with particular reference to social science, language training studies, professional sciences, and natural sciences, including studies of African development, policy planning, and history. **Publications:** African Monograph Series. **Meetings/Educational Activities:** Sponsors noon seminar series, monthly seminar series, rural/urban development conference, and national conference (annually). **Formerly:** Formed by merger of former African Studies Program and African Language and Area Center; African Studies and Research Program (1989).

★2700★
Howard University
Housing and Community Studies Center
2900 Van Ness St. NW, HC310   Ph: (202)806-8770
Washington, DC 20008   Fax: (202)806-8782
Ms. J. McRae, Program Dir.

Founded: 1983. **Research Activities and Fields:** Conducts research on high priority problems in the area of housing and community development, including homelessness and substance abuse, housing characteristics of black householders, elderly housing alternatives, public housing policy, multi-ethnic neighborhoods, community surveys, workshop suitability and viability, fair housing, and related topics. **Publications:** The Right to Housing: Final Report; Management Workbook for CDBG Organizations; Housing Research: Monograph I; African Americans, Public Housing, and Drug-Related Evictions: A Structural Analysis; Housing Characteristics of Black Female Householders; An Annotated Bibliography of Research Methods Used to Study the Homeless; Correlates of Drug Abuse Among the Homeless. **Formerly:** Housing and Community Development Studies Center.

★2701★
Howard University
Institute for Urban Affairs and Research
2900 Van Ness St. NW   Ph: (202)806-8770
Washington, DC 20008   Fax: (202)806-8782
Lawrence E. Gary Ph.D., Dir.

Founded: 1972. **Research Activities and Fields:** Psychology, sociology, social work, demography, and public health studies in the urban environment. Specific areas of research include the following: well being at midlife for women; housing and African-Americans; health and social behavior of African-American males; clinical training and services for mentally ill ethnic minorities; mental health of African-Americans; African-American family life; and infant mortality. **Publications:** Newsletter (semiannually); Occasional Papers; Monographs; books; resource guides and directories. Disseminates information and bibliographies upon request. **Meetings/Educational Activities:** Sponsors a series of conferences covering such topics as stress at the workplace and African-American fathers and families; open to lay persons and professionals. **Library:** 10,000 volumes on mental health, administration of justice, social support networks, child abuse and neglect, and human resources development. Lloyd S.

★2702★
Howard University
Moorland-Spingarn Research Center
500 Howard Pl. NW   Ph: (202)806-7239
Washington, DC 20059   Fax: (202)806-6405
Dr. Thomas C. Battle, Dir.

Founded: 1914. **Research Activities and Fields:** Repository for collections documenting history and culture of people of African descent in the Americas, Africa, and Europe. **Library:** 150,000 volumes on Afro-American history and culture, Africa, the Caribbean and Afro-Brazilian culture, also artifacts, manuscripts, newspapers, photographs, prints, recordings, and other materials documenting from antiquity to the present the history and culture of black people in Africa, Europe, Latin America, the Caribbean, and United States. **Formerly:** Moorland Foundation (1946); Moorland-Spingarn Collection (1973).

★2703★
Indiana University Bloomington
African Studies Program
Bloomington, IN 47405   Ph: (812)855-6825
                           Fax: (812)855-6734
Dr. Patrick O'Meara, Dir.

Founded: 1961. **Research Activities and Fields:** Emerging nations of sub-Saharan Africa, including interdisciplinary studies in anthropology and ethnography, comparative literature, economics, fine arts, music and folklore, geography, government, history, politics, and linguistics, with emphasis on West Africa and southern Africa. **Meetings/Educational Activities:** Provides graduate and undergraduate instruction.

★2704★
Indiana University Bloomington
Afro-American Arts Institute
109 N. Jordan Ave.
Bloomington, IN 47405   Ph: (812)855-9501
Dr. Charles Sykes, Dir.

Founded: 1974. **Research Activities and Fields:** Afro-American performing arts: black dance, black choral music, and urban popular music. Reflects upon the historical development of black people through research and performance. Consists of three performance groups which present live performances and lecture-demonstrations. **Meetings/Educational Activities:** Supports undergraduate curriculum in Afro-American studies. **Library:** Maintains 1,000 volumes on black studies; Grace Jackson-Brown, library director.

★2705★
Institute for African-American Writing
PO Box 50172
Washington, DC 20004   Ph: (202)727-4047
Joseph Jordan, Dir.

Founded: 1978. **Research Activities and Fields:** Local African-American authors and the history of African-American writing in Washington, D.C. (1800-present). **Publications:** Antti-Talk (summer and spring publication); Bywords (quarterly newsletter); Monographs; Anthologies. **Meetings/Educational Activities:** Sponsors creative writing workshops, photo-literary exhibits, and fall, winter, and spring colloquiums, open to the public. **Formerly:** Institute for the Preservation and Study of African-American Writing.

★2706★
Institute for American Pluralism
American Jewish Committee
55 E. Jackson Blvd., Ste. 1880
Chicago, IL 60604   Ph: (312)663-5400
David Roth, Dir.

Founded: 1967. **Research Activities and Fields:** Issues affecting American pluralism in areas such as the humanities, communications, immigration, foreign and coalition building, leadership, and education. Research topics chosen by Institute's staff and leaders of Illinois Ethnic Consultation, affiliated with the

Institute. Professionals from across the country conduct the research. **Formerly:** Institute on Pluralism and Group Identity.

★2707★
Institute for Policy Studies
1601 Connecticut Ave. NW
Washington, DC 20009   Ph: (202)234-9382
Marcus Raskin, Codir.

Founded: 1963. **Research Activities and Fields:** National security, foreign policy, human rights, international economic order, knowledge and politics, and domestic reconstruction, including studies of the security alternatives in the 1990s, U.S./U.S.S.R. exchange on disarmament, Europe, nuclear and conventional arms, crisis monitoring, intervention and revolution, human rights in Latin America, women in developing countries, feminism and socialism, transnational corporations, international aid, race and class, science and technology, and Blacks and Hispanics in the U.S. **Meetings/Educational Activities:** Sponsors a network of study groups which explores elements of ethical inquiry into current disciplines and myths of value-free science while formulating alternatives.

★2708★
Institute for Public Policy Advocacy
1730 Rhode Island Ave. NW, Ste. 600   Ph: (202)659-8475
Washington, DC 20036-3118   Fax: (202)659-8484
David Cohen, Codirector

Founded: 1984. **Research Activities and Fields:** Conducts research on the role of public interest advocacy, especially in the areas of civil, children, and human rights, public health, arms control, foreign affairs, environment, consumerism, tax justice, and economic opportunity. **Publications:** Advocate's Advocate (monthly newsletter). **Meetings/Educational Activities:** Conducts workshops and seminars on advocacy skills.

★2709★
Institute for Scientific Analysis
2235 Lombard St.
San Francisco, CA 94123   Ph: (415)749-6595
Dr. Dorothy L. Miller, Pres.

Founded: 1966. **Research Activities and Fields:** Fulfills research contracts for public or private agencies, and oversees research projects on social problems in the fields of education, social welfare, criminology, alcoholism, drug addiction, mental health, population, runaways, child rearing, status of women and ethnic minorities, and transportation.

★2710★
Institute for Southern Studies
PO Box 531   Ph: (919)419-8311
Durham, NC 27702   Fax: (919)419-8315
Isaiah Madison, Exec.Dir.

Founded: 1970. **Research Activities and Fields:** Labor, civil rights, energy, land use, environment, banking and finance, campaign finances, community economic development, and social change movements in the South. **Publications:** Southern Exposure (quarterly); Special Reports.

★2711★
Institute for Women's Policy Research
1400 20th St. NW, Ste. 104
Washington, DC 20036   Ph: (202)785-5100
Heidi I. Hartmann Ph.D., Dir.

Founded: 1987. **Research Activities and Fields:** Causes and consequences of women's poverty, particularly of minority women; costs and benefits of family and work policies; pay equity; wages and employment opportunities; impact of tax policy on women and families; and access to and costs of health care. Specific issues include the impact of the Pregnancy Discrimination Act, the costs and benefits of family and medical leave, pay equity in 20 state civil service systems, the wage gap between women of color and white women, low-wage work, and welfare reform. **Meetings/Educational Activities:** Offers workshops, conferences, and speeches.

★2712★
Institute of Comparative Social and Cultural Studies
6935 Wisconsin Ave., Ste. 500
Chevy Chase, MD 20815
Ph: (301)656-7996
Fax: (301)652-9020
Dr. Lorand B. Szalay, Dir.

Founded: 1976. **Research Activities and Fields:** Tests and compares the differences in perceptions and values of different social and cultural groups in the U.S. and abroad using the Associative Group Analysis Technique, and other empirical methods. Produces new perceptual and motivational insights into psycho-cultural dispositions, which shape people's views and behavior without their conscious awareness, for utilization in international education, substance abuse treatment and prevention programs, mental health service, conflict resolution, cross-cultural problem solving, and management in multi-cultural settings.

★2713★
Intercultural Development Research Association
5835 Callaghan Rd., Ste. 350
San Antonio, TX 78228-1190
Ph: (210)684-8180
Dr. Maria Robledo Montelel, Exec.Dir.

Founded: 1973. **Research Activities and Fields:** Minority and bilingual education, school finance, desegregation, and compensatory education. **Publications:** IDRA Newsletter (monthly). **Meetings/Educational Activities:** Sponsors conferences, seminars, and workshops for school and related personnel. **Library:** 20,000 items on minority, compensatory, and early childhood education and school finance.

★2714★
International Center
731 8th St. SE
Washington, DC 20003
Ph: (202)547-3800
Fax: (202)546-4784
Lindsay Mattison, Exec.Dir.

Founded: 1977. **Research Activities and Fields:** U.S. and Soviet foreign policy toward developing nations, including studies on Latin America, Africa, and Asia. The New Forests Project works to curb deforestation in the developing world. **Publications:** Briefing Books; New Forests News (quarterly newsletter). **Meetings/Educational Activities:** Sponsors international delegations and fellowships, and round-table discussions focusing on issues relating to Burma and Taiwan.

★2715★
International Organization for the Study of Group Tensions, Inc.
240 E. 76th St., Apt. 1-B
New York, NY 10021
Ph: (212)628-1797
Dr. Benjamin B. Wolman, Pres.

Founded: 1970. **Research Activities and Fields:** Causes of and solutions to human conflict and violence. Members' professions include anthropology, economics, history, political science, psychiatry, psychoanalysis, psychology, and sociology. **Publications:** International Journal of Group Tensions (quarterly). **Meetings/Educational Activities:** Sponsors or cosponsors international conferences; topics have included the college campus of the future as a source of multicultural experience, and problems of racial, ethnic, and other special groups from both national and international perspectives.

★2716★
Investor Responsibility Research Center, Inc.
1755 Massachusetts Ave. NW, Ste. 600
Washington, DC 20036
Ph: (202)234-7500
Fax: (202)332-8570
Margaret Carroll, Exec.Dir.

Founded: 1972. **Research Activities and Fields:** Social, public policy, and corporate governance issues and their impact on major corporations and institutional investors. Issues studied have included anti-takeover measures, U.S. and foreign business in South Africa, energy and the environment, the electric utility industry, military contracting, executive compensation, South Africa-related divestment, business in Northern Ireland, plant closings, global shareholder rights, animal testing, and voting and other actions by institutional investors. Also offers consulting and contract research. **Publications:** News for Investors (monthly); Corporate Governance Bulletin (bimonthly); South Africa Reporter (quarterly); Global Shareholder (quarterly); Investor's Environmental Report (bimonthly). **Meetings/Educational Activities:** Sponsors seminars, briefings and workshops.

★2717★
James N. Gamble Institute of Medical Research
2141 Auburn Ave.
Cincinnati, OH 45219
Ph: (513)369-2582
Fax: (513)241-3899
Gilbert M. Schiff M.D., Pres.

Founded: 1927. **Research Activities and Fields:** Virology and immunology, including studies on rubella and rubella vaccines, anti-influenza agents, basic virology of influenza, herpes virus latency, role of complement in sickle cell disease and burn wounds, and basic and clinical studies on rotaviruses, hepatitis, and human immunodeficiency virus. **Library:** 5,200 volumes, 290 current journal titles, and 8,000 bound journal volumes on virology, immunology, medicine, and surgery. **Formerly:** Christ Hospital Institute of Medical Research (1984).

★2718★
Joint Center for Political and Economic Studies
1090 Vermont Ave. NW, Ste. 1100
Washington, DC 20005-4961
Ph: (202)789-3500
Milton Morris, V.P. of Research

Founded: 1970. **Research Activities and Fields:** Politics and public policy, including issues which have impact on minorities and the disadvantaged. Collects, analyzes, and disseminates data on all aspects of black political participation. Also works with minority elected officials and pinpoints resources that can be used to solve problems besetting socially and economically disadvantaged communities. **Publications:** Focus (monthly); Roster of Black Elected Officials (annually). **Meetings/Educational Activities:** Holds forums, seminars, and conferences. **Library:** Maintains a reference and periodical collection, including 4,000 volumes on black politics and urban affairs; Basheba Valentine, information director. **Formerly:** Joint Center for Political Studies, Inc.

★2719★
Kent State University
Center for the Study of Ethnic Publications and Cultural Institutions
School of Library Science
Kent, OH 44242-0001
Ph: (216)672-2782
Fax: (216)672-7965
Prof. Lubomyr R. Wynar, Dir.

Founded: 1971. **Research Activities and Fields:** Promotes bibliographical and historical research on ethnic publications and cultural institutions in the U.S. in cooperation with various scholarly, professional, and governmental organizations and agencies. Surveys ethnic press as well as ethnic serials, books, libraries, archives, and museums. Activities focus on developing a curriculum for library schools, emphasizing library services to ethnic communities and ethnic publicatons. **Publications:** Ethnic Forum; Journal of Ethnic Studies and Ethnic Bibliography (semiannually); Monographs. **Library:** 1,200 volumes on major ethnic studies. **Formerly:** Program for Study of Ethnic Publications (1980); Center for the Study of Ethnic Publications (1988).

★2720★
Kent State University
Institute for African American Affairs
Dept. of African Studies
18 Ritchie Hall
Kent, OH 44242
Ph: (216)672-2300
Dr. Mohan Kaul, Dir.

Founded: 1969. **Research Activities and Fields:** African and American affairs. **Publications:** Monograph Series; Kitabu Newsletter; Occasional Papers. **Meetings/Educational Activities:** Offers teacher training workshops, public forums on black community issues, biweekly research-in-progress colloquia, grantsmanship seminars, and a speakers bureau.

★2721★
Louisiana State University
Center for French and Francophone Studies
Dept. of French & Italian
225 Prescott Hall   Ph: (504)388-6589
Baton Rouge, LA 70803   Fax: (504)388-6620
Prof. Edouard Glissant, Dir.

Founded: 1983. **Research Activities and Fields:** French and francophone culture of the southern U.S., Caribbean, and Caribbean coast of Latin America, including studies of the mores and customs, work, law and commerce, slave trade, role of women in the system, Creole languages, musics of silence, and literature in the South and Caribbean. In association with the French Education Project in the College of Education, the Center supports research on the teaching of the French language in Louisiana and throughout the world.

★2722★
Louisiana State University
Public Administration Institute
3171 CEBA   Ph: (504)388-6743
Baton Rouge, LA 70803   Fax: (504)388-3807
James A. Richardson, Dir.

Research Activities and Fields: Public administration, including studies on health policy, minority health care, economics and taxes, state and local governments, and public finance. **Meetings/Educational Activities:** Offers graduate instruction and administers a master's degree program.

★2723★
Martin Luther King, Jr. Center for Nonviolent Social Change, Inc.
449 Auburn Ave. NE   Ph: (404)524-1956
Atlanta, GA 30312   Fax: (404)522-6932
Coretta Scott King, Pres./CEO

Founded: 1968. **Research Activities and Fields:** Nonviolence, violence, resolution of conflict, current social and economic issues, and civil rights leader Martin Luther King, Jr. (1929-1968). **Publications:** Annual Report. **Meetings/Educational Activities:** Sponsors King Week (annually); Youth and Adult Workshops on Nonviolence (annually in July); Kingfest; Gandhi Day, in honor of the Indian nationalist, spiritual leader, and nonviolent activist whom Dr. King emulated; "I have a Dream" Celebration, in memory of noted speech by Dr. King; and over 20 other programs, including continuing education seminars, conferences, and workshops on nonviolent conflict resolution. **Library:** Collection of reference material on Dr. Martin Luther King, Jr.

★2724★
Medical College of Georgia
Comprehensive Sickle Cell Center
1435 Laney-Walker Blvd.   Ph: (404)721-3091
Augusta, GA 30912-2200   Fax: (404)721-6611
Dr. Titus H.J. Huisman, Dir.

Founded: 1972. **Research Activities and Fields:** Hemoglobinopathy detection, identification, and characterization, including studies of factors determining severity of sickle cell anemia in adults and the young child, cardiac evaluation of children with sickle cell anemia, thalassemia in association with sickle cell syndromes, biochemical studies in sickle cell anemia and related disorders with special emphasis on heterogeneity of Hb F, immunological identification, DNA gene mapping of hemoglobin variants, nucleotide sequence, and thalassemia genes, and characterization of hemoglobin variants. **Publications:** SPHERE (six times per year); Hemoglobin: International Journal for Hemoglobin Research (six times per year). **Meetings/Educational Activities:** Sponsors Hemoglobin Research Club (semimonthly), open to interested personnel, and a weekly conference on DNA research for personnel involved. Sponsors three workshops per year in basic hemoglobin techniques, HPLC methodology, and DNA mapping. **Library:** 3,000 volumes on hemoglobinopathies and related topics.

★2725★
Meharry Medical College
Clinical Research Center
1005 D.B. Todd Blvd.
PO Box 115-A   Ph: (615)327-6353
Nashville, TN 37208   Fax: (615)327-5835
Mary Ann South M.D., Dir.

Founded: 1988. **Research Activities and Fields:** Clinical research, including pulmonary studies, AIDS, sickle cell disease, hypertension, body composition, coronary artery disease, infectious diseases, and oncology.

★2726★
Meharry Medical College
Comprehensive Sickle Cell Center
1005 D.B. Todd Blvd.   Ph: (615)327-6763
Nashville, TN 37208   Fax: (615)327-5835
Ernest A. Turner M.D., Dir.

Founded: 1972. **Research Activities and Fields:** Basic, clinical, and psychosocial research in sickle cell disease and variants of the disease in the fields of biochemistry, biology, molecular biology, medicine, pediatric medicine, social science, and psychiatry. Specific research includes hearing loss and sickle cell anemia, hemoglobinopathies in Southeast Asians, complement activation in sickle cell anemia, recombinant human parvoviruses for gene therapy of hemoglobinopathies, vitamin E and sickle cell disease, and isolation and characterization of glycophorin. **Meetings/Educational Activities:** Sponsors National Conference on Sickle Cell Disease, and in-service training for health care professionals. Also participates in sickle cell grand rounds, sickle cell conferences, seminars, and training workshops for public health nurses.

★2727★
Meiklejohn Civil Liberties Institute
PO Box 673   Ph: (415)848-0599
Berkeley, CA 94701   Fax: (415)848-6008
Prof. Ann Fagin Ginger, Pres.

Founded: 1965. **Research Activities and Fields:** Constitutional, international, U.N. Charter, First Amendment, human rights, and peace law. Collects and documents material for attorneys and non-attorneys. **Publications:** Newsletter (semiannually); Peace Net Bulletins (monthly); Human Rights Organizations and Periodicals Directory (biennially); Human Rights & Peace Law Docket (annually); Peace Law Packets; Studies in law and Social Change (book series). **Meetings/Educational Activities:** Sponsors annual symposium on civil liberties and peace law issues.

★2728★
Memphis State University
Center for Research on Women
Clement Hall-339
Memphis, TN 38152   Ph: (901)678-2770
Lynn Weber, Dir.

Founded: 1982. **Research Activities and Fields:** Southern women and women of color (Black, Latina, Asian American, and Native American) in the U.S., including critical examination of the intersection of gender, class, and racial oppression; perception of class among Americans; mobility strategies of minority women; working class women in the South; rural poverty; and comparative study of Black and White professional and managerial women in the Memphis area. **Publications:** Newsletter (twice per year); Southern Women: The Intersection of Race, Class and Gender (co-sponsored with the Duke University–University of North Carolina Women's Studies Research Center); Research Papers Curriculum Integration Publications; a printed version of the database (updated annually). **Meetings/Educational Activities:** Sponsors Workshop on Women in the Curriculum (annually) and summer research institutes (occasionally).

★2729★
Memphis State University
Center for Voluntary Action Research
Memphis, TN 38152   Ph: (901)678-2080
Dr. Stanley E. Hyland, Contact

Founded: 1981. **Research Activities and Fields:** Provides research assistance to groups, agencies, and industries interested in developing collaborative social science projects. Activities include establishing neighborhood associations for the transfer of information, developing mutual aid societies, investigating minority and small business concerns, analyzing urban renewal, evaluating community health, studying alcoholism and minorities, establishing a neighborhood health association for Shelby County Health Department, and weatherization in low-income neighborhoods and rural areas. **Publications:** Journal for Voluntary Action Research (quarterly).

★2730★
Michigan State University
African Studies Center (ASA)
East Lansing, MI 48824-1035   Ph: (517)353-1700
                                     Fax: (517)336-1209
David Wiley, Dir.

Founded: 1960. **Research Activities and Fields:** Coordinates and fosters teaching/research and public service programs in African area studies throughout the University and the region. Courses offered through departments of the University include 25 African languages, African anthropology, art history, sociology, geography, history, linguistics, literature, political science, economics, agricultural economics, business, education, ecology, agriculture, tropical agriculture, public health, animal science and veterinary medicine, medicine, criminal justice, tropical medicine, and communication, with emphasis on sub-Saharan Africa, including islands and Republic of South Africa. Administers Title VI, South African, and Zimbabwean fellowships for African language and area studies at the graduate level. **Publications:** African Urban Studies (quarterly journal); Rural Africana (quarterly journal); Northeast African Studies (quarterly journal); ASC Newsletter; Africana: Select Recent Acquisitions (three times yearly). The Center also publishes an Africana Monograph Series and a Monograph Series in Northeast African Studies. **Meetings/Educational Activities:** Sponsors annual national conference on Africa and an African Cultural Festival. **Library:** Maintains African collection of 170,000 volumes; Onuma Ezera, head.

★2731★
Michigan State University
Center for Advanced Study of International
   Development
306 Berkey Hall   Ph: (517)353-5925
East Lansing, MI 48824-1111   Fax: (517)355-1912
Prof. Tom W. Carroll, Dir.

Founded: 1981. **Research Activities and Fields:** International social, economic, and technological change from a social science and humanities perspective with special focus on reducing inequalities within and among nations. Current activities focus on environment and development, ethnic relations, social justice, and development; global restructuring (trends towards privatization and public-private partnerships); regional security, military expenditures and development; and urban development in developing countries. Additional research focuses on the African diaspora; food security in Africa; microenterprise institutions and investment; improvement of primary schools in developing countries; agro-forestry management systems in Jamaica; agricultural surveys and policy analysis in Rwanda; multidisciplinary research program on the great lakes of East Africa; and edible bean/cowpeas collaborative research support. **Publications:** CASID Occasional Papers; CASID Distinguished Speaker Monographs. **Meetings/Educational Activities:** Sponsors seminars, lectures, and conferences, open to the public. Coordinates faculty-student interest groups on selected development topics. Disseminates information on academic department seminars (biweekly). Acts as Secretariat for MSU/Lansing Area Chapter of the Society for International Development (weekly seminar series). Conducts the annual Summer Institute for Curriculum Improvement in International Development Studies for faculty from community and four-year collages.

★2732★
Michigan State University
Center for Urban Affairs
East Lansing, MI 48824   Ph: (517)353-9035
Dr. Marvel Lang, Dir.

Founded: 1968. **Research Activities and Fields:** Problems of urban communities, with particular emphasis on improvement of life chances for poor and disadvantaged minorities, including studies on fiscal affairs and urban development. Also urban research designed to generate new knowledge about the changing condition of cities and to aid private and public policy decisions that will affect the future of urban areas. Initiates experimental community action and development programs and develops cooperative relationship with other University programs and community groups. **Publications:** Monographs; Research Papers (series).

★2733★
Morehouse College
Morehouse Research Institute
830 Westview Dr.
Atlanta, GA 30314   Ph: (404)681-2800
Waldon Jackson, V.P. for Academic Affairs

Founded: 1990. **Research Activities and Fields:** Interdisciplinary studies designed to generate, disseminate, and exchange information on public policy and programs which impact black males in American society. **Publications:** Journal; Newsletter. **Meetings/Educational Activities:** Sponsors conferences and workshops.

★2734★
National Afro-American Museum and Cultural Center
Box 578   Ph: (513)376-4944
Wilberforce, OH 45384   Fax: (513)376-2007
John E. Fleming, Dir.

Founded: 1972. **Research Activities and Fields:** Twentieth century black America, and the African-American experience. **Meetings/Educational Activities:** Produces primary and middle school curriculum; sponsors performances, exhibitions, workshops, and educational and cultural programs. **Formerly:** National Center for the Study of Afro-American History and Culture.

★2735★
National Black Child Development Institute
1023 15th St. NW, Ste. 600   Ph: (202)387-1281
Washington, DC 20005   Fax: (202)234-1738
Evelyn K. Moore, Dir.

Founded: 1970. **Research Activities and Fields:** Policy issues affecting black children, with emphasis on child care, child welfare, health, and education. Studies foster care and tutoring/mentoring programs, include after-school care, teenage pregnancy, health care policy, and juvenile justice. **Publications:** Black Child Advocate (quarterly newsletter); Child Health Talk (quarterly newsletter); Reports. **Meetings/Educational Activities:** Sponsors an annual conference and convenes forums.

★2736★
National Caucus and Center on Black Aged, Inc.
1424 K St. NW, Ste. 500   Ph: (202)637-8400
Washington, DC 20005   Fax: (202)347-0895
Samuel J. Simmons, Pres.

Founded: 1970. **Research Activities and Fields:** Elderly black Americans, including studies on job placement, medical services in the Southwest U.S., and older women in the workplace. **Publications:** Reports. **Meetings/Educational Activities:** Sponsors National Conference (annually in June).

★2737★
National Institute Against Prejudice and Violence
31 S. Greene St.   Ph: (410)328-5170
Baltimore, MD 21201   Fax: (410)328-7551
Howard J. Ehrlich Ph.D., Contact

Founded: 1984. **Research Activities and Fields:** Causes of prejudice and violence and their effects on individuals and society, including studies of the news media. Special focus is on college campus, housing, and workplace violence involving race, religion, ethnicity, gender, or sexual orientation. **Publications:** Forum (newsletter); Reports. **Meetings/Educational Activities:** Sponsors conferences and prejudice reduction workshops.

★2738★
National Institute for Women of Color
624 9th St. NW
Washington, DC 20001-5303
Sharon Parker, Chair

Founded: 1981. **Research Activities and Fields:** Women of color, including studies on demographic trends, education, sports, and sex equity. Assists in the formulation and implementation of public policy. **Publications:** NIWC Network News. **Meetings/Educational Activities:** Developed and distributes a resource packet on reproductive freedom for women of color.

★2739★
National Urban Coalition
1875 Connecticut Ave., 4th Fl.   Ph: (202)986-1460
Washington, DC 20009   Fax: (202)986-1468
Ramona H. Edelin, Pres. & CEO

Founded: 1967. **Research Activities and Fields:** Housing and neighborhood revitalization, employment, youth employment, urban education, income maintenance, and economic development. **Publications:** Alert (monthly); Neighborhood Exchange (quarterly); Urban Policy Watch (quarterly); and Network (annual magazine). **Meetings/Educational Activities:** Sponsors workshops, and seminars, by invitation only. **Library:** 1,000 volumes.

★2740★
National Urban League, Research Department
1111 14th St. NW, 6th Fl.   Ph: (202)898-1604
Washington, DC 20005   Fax: (202)408-1965
Dr. Billy J. Tidwell, Dir. of Research

Research Activities and Fields: U.S. social and economic conditions, blacks, and poor minorities. Studies are undertaken from a black perspective and are directed at influencing policy. Answers inquiries and makes referrals. **Publications:** Urban League Review (semiannually); The State of Black America (annually); Monographs; Papers; Quarterly Economic Report on the African American Worker. **Meetings/Educational Activities:** The National Urban League Conference (annually in July/August), open to public.

★2741★
New Jersey Public Policy Research Institute
1188 Raymond Blvd.
Box 244
Newark, NJ 07102   Ph: (609)989-3331
Gwendolyn Long, Dir.

Founded: 1978. **Research Activities and Fields:** Public policy issues as they impact African Americans in New Jersey. **Publications:** Annual Report series. **Meetings/Educational Activities:** Sponsors forums, and offers technical assistance and consultation.

★2742★
New York University
Institute of Afro-American Affairs
269 Mercer St., Ste. 601
New York, NY 10003   Ph: (212)998-2130

Founded: 1969. **Research Activities and Fields:** Afro-American life, heritage, and thought. Focuses on historical conflicts as well as contemporary issues faced by the African-American community and promotes cultural awareness among people of the United States, South America, the Caribbean, Oceania, and Africa. **Publications:** Monograph Series. **Meetings/Educational Activities:** Sponsors conferences and symposiums on social, political, cultural, and economic issues related to African Americans, and cosponsors annual meetings for the National Association of Black Counselors and Black Women in Higher Education. Sponsors the Association for Education in Journalism Summer Internship for Minorities. **Library:**

★2743★
Niagara University
Center for the Study and Stabilization of the Black Family
PO Box 367
Niagara University, NY 14109   Ph: (716)285-1212
Umeme Sababu, Dir.

Research Activities and Fields: Black family, including studies on moral values, academic achievements, educational goals, parenting skills, and social relationships.

★2744★
North Carolina Central University
Institute on Desegregation
214 Taylor Education Bldg.
Durham, NC 27707   Ph: (919)560-6367
Dr. Beverly W. Jones, Dir.

Founded: 1972. **Research Activities and Fields:** Desegregation and postsecondary education, including studies on housing, health, employment, and private and public secondary education. **Publications:** Journal on Minority Issues (semiannually). **Meetings/Educational Activities:** Sponsors annual conference on desegregation, open to the public.

★2745★
North Carolina Central University
Office of Research, Evaluation and Planning
Fayetteville St.
Durham, NC 27707   Ph: (919)560-6367
Dr. Linda K. Pratt, Assoc. V. Chancellor

Founded: 1951. **Research Activities and Fields:** Higher education, including institutional studies with particular reference to attitudes and achievements of students attending predominantly black colleges, evaluation of remedial instruction, curriculum evaluation, institutional goals, and planning. **Publications:** Journal of Minority Issues. **Formerly:** Bureau of Educational Research.

★2746★
Northern Illinois University
Center for Black Studies
DeKalb, IL 60115   Ph: (815)753-1709
Dr. Admasu Zike, Dir.

Founded: 1970. **Research Activities and Fields:** All areas of interest and concern affecting blacks and other minorities, including Afro-American history, Afro-American education, multicultural education, African political systems, African history, and African oral and written literature. **Publications:** Reports. **Meetings/Educational Activities:** Sponsors lectures, seminars, and conferences, open to the public. **Library:** 6,000 volumes on Afro-American studies, black education, and African studies; Rob Ridinger, librarian. **Formerly:** Center for Minority Studies.

★2747★
Northwestern University
Center for Urban Affairs and Policy Research
2040 Sheridan Rd.   Ph: (708)491-3395
Evanston, IL 60208-4100   Fax: (708)491-9916
Burton A. Weisbrod, Dir.

Founded: 1968. **Research Activities and Fields:** Interdisciplinary public policy studies, including programs on poverty, race, and inequality (housing, education, crime, and unemployment); community development; law, society, and the economy; philanthropy, voluntarism, and nonprofit organizations; communications, media, and public policy; health care technology; and urban data systems. Maintains working groups on environmental policy, the state of the family over the life course, and urban ethnography. **Publications:** Working Paper Series; Monographs; Center Research & Policy Reports; Urban Affairs News (a periodic newsletter); Center Brochure. **Meetings/Educational Activities:** Sponsors a graduate training program in advanced urban poverty research in cooperation with University of Chicago. **Formerly:** Center for Urban Affairs.

★2748★
Northwestern University
Institute for the Advanced Study and Research in African Humanities
620 Library Pl.   Ph: (708)491-7323
Evanston, IL 60208   Fax: (708)491-3739
Prof. David William Cohen, Dir.

Research Activities and Fields: Interdisciplinary studies in African humanities. Aims to dispel myths regarding the continent. Promotes theoretical and empirical research of African cultural practices. **Publications:** Passages, a Chronicle of the Humanities (twice per year). **Meetings/Educational Activities:** Sponsors lecturers, weekly seminars, workshops, and performances.

★2749★
Northwestern University
Program of African Studies
620 Library Pl.   Ph: (708)491-7323
Evanston, IL 60208   Fax: (708)491-3739
David William Cohen, Dir.

Founded: 1948. **Research Activities and Fields:** Economics, political science, anthropology, history, performance studies, sociology, art history, music, literature, religions, education, law, and African languages and linguistics, including interdisciplinary study of African peoples and cultures in the past and in their contemporary settings. Research program maintains a regional emphasis on Africa south of the Sahara. Activities are centered in Africa House on the University campus; library and field research are conducted in Africa by faculty and graduate students. **Publications:** P.A.S. News and Events; Inter/Notes; Arabic Literature in Africa; Fontes; Asantesem: The Asante Collective Biography Project. **Meetings/Educational Activities:** Provides graduate and undergraduate instruction and research opportunities at the University and in Africa. Holds research seminars and public lecture series during the academic year, an annual interdisciplinary seminar on approaches to study of Africa, and national conferences. **Library:** Maintains a special collection of 187,000 volumes in University library and 2,000 periodicals dealing with Africa, as well as most newspapers from Africa; David Easterbrook, curator.

★2750★
Northwestern University
Program on International Cooperation in Africa
Program of African Studies
620 Library Pl.   Ph: (708)491-7323
Evanston, IL 60208   Fax: (708)491-3739
David W. Cohen, Chair

Founded: 1988. **Research Activities and Fields:** Interdisciplinary program focusing on the borderland areas of African countries and the economic, cultural, political, and social processes which are distinctive to these areas. Topics of study include refugees, labor migration, famine and drought, environmental management, epidemic diseases, and cross-border languages and economies. **Meetings/Educational Activities:** Sponsors quarterly workshops and offers graduate-level seminars. **Library:** Melville J.

★2751★
Office of Postsecondary Research
State Education Dept.
Cultural Education Center, Rm. 5B44
Albany, NY 12230   Ph: (518)474-5093
Dr. Thomas McCord, Dir.

Research Activities and Fields: Fiscal analysis of higher education and enrollment studies and projections in New York state. Also studies student financial aid, simulation of costing out legislative proposals, and minority access to higher education. **Meetings/Educational Activities:** Sponsors internships. **Library:** 500-700 volumes on education.

★2752★
Ohio University
African Studies Program
56 E. Union St.   Ph: (614)593-1834
Athens, OH 45701   Fax: (614)593-1837
Prof. W. Stephen Howard, Dir.

Founded: 1964. **Research Activities and Fields:** Politics, geography, history, economics, philosophy, and literature of Africa. Provides instruction in these fields at the University. **Publications:** African Studies Series (four per year).

★2753★
Ohio University
Center for Afro-American Studies
300 Lindley Hall
Athens, OH 45701   Ph: (614)593-4546
Dr. Vattel T. Rose, Dir.

Founded: 1969. **Research Activities and Fields:** Afro-American politics, education, family, and culture. Studies include urban politics, comparison analyses of Afro-American and African political thought, multicultural education issues, socialization patterns, impact of technology, strength of the family structure, single parent families, portrayal of black males in media and effects on the family, race and ethnicity, and aesthetics in black media, film, and literature. **Meetings/Educational Activities:** Sponsors conferences (annually).

★2754★
Princeton University
Afro-American Studies Program
112 Dickinson Hall   Ph: (609)258-4270
Princeton, NJ 08544-1017   Fax: (609)258-5095
Prof. Cornel West, Dir.

Research Activities and Fields: Position and experience of people of African ancestry in the United States, seen in relation to the experience of black peoples in other parts of the world.

★2755★
Purdue University
Afro-American Studies Center
326 Stone Hall   Ph: (317)494-5680
West Lafayette, IN 47907   Fax: (317)494-3660
Carolyn E. Johnson Ph.D., Sr. Res. Assoc.

Founded: 1974. **Research Activities and Fields:** Identity and community studies of African, African-American, and Caribbean culture. **Publications:** NOMMO (quarterly). **Meetings/Educational Activities:** Holds Martin Luther King Lecture Series (spring), W.E.B. DuBois Lecture Series (fall), a Brown Bag Seminar Series (spring and fall), an annual Symposium on Afro-American Culture and Philosophy (March), a film festival, and a Malcolm X Tribute (February). Sponsors an outreach program and offers a bachelor's degree in Afro-American Studies.

★2756★
Queens College of City University of New York
Africana Studies and Research Institute
65-30 Kissena Blvd.
Flushing, NY 11367   Ph: (718)520-7545
Prof. Omayemi Agbeyebe, Dir.

Founded: 1973. **Research Activities and Fields:** Promotes Africana scholarship and publications, supports the teaching of African studies at the College, and related academic research and teaching to the needs and interests of the black community. **Meetings/Educational Activities:** Offers an interdisciplinary curriculum with a major, minor, and electives in Africana studies. Sponsors monthly seminars, open to students, faculty, staff, and the public. **Library:** Maintains volumes on African, African-American, and Caribbean studies.

★2757★
Rutgers University
Institute for Research on Women
Douglass College
27 Clifton Ave.
New Brunswick, NJ 08903   Ph: (908)932-9072
Cora L. Kaplan, Dir.   Fax: (908)932-1180

Founded: 1976. **Research Activities and Fields:** Feminist theory and methodology, women's leadership, gender integration and curricular reform, reproductive laws, women and war and peace, and Black women writers. Currently developing an archive on women. **Publications:** NETWORC (semiannual newsletter); Women, War & Peace Bibliography and Filmography; Women & Gender Directory; New Jersey Project Handbook. **Meetings/Educational Activities:** Sponsors Consortium for Educational Equity; Thinking About Women Lecture Series (monthly); a Celebration of Our Work Conference (annually, open to the public); and a fortnightly seminar, Towards 2000, open to faculty, graduate students, and visiting scholars. Also sponsors a Visiting Scholar residency program. **Formerly:** Women's Studies Institute (1982).

★2758★
San Diego State University
Bureau of Business and Economic Research
School of Business Administration
San Diego, CA 92182   Ph: (619)594-6838
Dr. Oliver Galbraith III, Dir.

Founded: 1957. **Research Activities and Fields:** Business administration and health economics, particularly studies of minority business and small business in the Pacific coast and the southwest. **Publications:** Operation of MBDC in San Diego and Los Angeles.

★2759★
Schomburg Center for Research in Black Culture
515 Malcolm X Blvd.   Ph: (212)491-2200
New York, NY 10037-1801   Fax: (212)491-6760
Howard Dodson, Chief

Founded: 1925. **Research Activities and Fields:** Collects and preserves materials on black people, including books, rare books, microforms, photographs, oral histories, video tapes, manuscripts, archives, paintings, sculpture, and U.S. Census reports (1790-1900). **Publications:** Schomburg Center Journal (quarterly). **Meetings/Educational Activities:** Sponsors scholar-in-residence program, forums, exhibitions, and book parties. **Library:** 100,000 volumes, available to the public. **Formerly:** Schomburg Collection of Negro Literature and History (1972).

★2760★
Sickle Cell Association of the Texas Gulf Coast
2626 S. Loop W., Ste. 245   Ph: (713)666-0300
Houston, TX 77054   Fax: (713)666-0217
Rebecca Jasso, Exec.Dir.

Founded: 1971. **Research Activities and Fields:** Performs laboratory tests to identify persons with sickle cell disease. **Publications:** Sickle Cell Anemia Fast Facts. **Meetings/Educational Activities:** Conducts support groups and offers sickle cell anemia education programs on request. Holds residential summer camp programs and tutorial programs. **Formerly:** Sickle Cell Disease Research Foundation of Texas, Inc. (1990).

★2761★
Social Science Research Council
605 3rd Ave.   Ph: (212)661-0280
New York, NY 10158   Fax: (212)370-7896
David L. Featherman, Pres.

Founded: 1923. **Research Activities and Fields:** Seeks to advance research in the social sciences by providing fellowships and grants such as the MacArthur Foundation Fellowship in International Security, Public Policy Research on Contemporary Hispanic Issues, and Research on the Urban Underclass. Maintains the following committees with the American Council of Learned Societies (ACLS): African Studies, Chinese Studies, Eastern Europe Studies, Japanese Studies, Korean Studies, Latin American Studies, South Asian Studies, Southeast Asian Studies, Soviet Studies, Western Europe Studies, and Scholarly Communication with the People's Republic of China. **Publications:** Items (quarterly); Annual Report.

★2762★
South Dakota State University
Census Data Center
Brookings, SD 57007   Ph: (605)688-4132
Dr. James Satterlee, Dir.

Founded: 1981. **Research Activities and Fields:** Population census, agriculture census, minorities, and migration. The Center responds to out-state needs of public and private agencies for census data and is a repository for all census data for South Dakota. Participates in the U.S. Census Bureau State Data Center program. **Publications:** Update Series; monthly Newsletter. Sponsors Census Users Workshops (two or three per year). **Library:** Maintains a collection of census data on microfiche, computer tape, and printed materials; Don Arwood, librarian.

★2763★
Spelman College
Women's Research and Resource Center
Box 115   Ph: (404)223-7528
Atlanta, GA 30314   Fax: (404)753-8383
Dr. Beverly Guy-Sheftall, Dir.

Founded: 1981. **Research Activities and Fields:** Black women, particularly history, literature, higher education, and health care studies. Coordinates curriculum development project in black women's studies at selected southern colleges. **Publications:** Exhibit Catalogs; Sage: A Scholarly Journal on Black Women (semiannually). **Meetings/Educational Activities:** Sponsors conferences on black women, brown bag luncheon seminars, and cosponsors workshops, symposia, and a lecture series.

★2764★
State University of New York at Albany
Center for Women in Government
Draper 310
135 Western Ave.   Ph: (518)442-3900
Albany, NY 12222   Fax: (518)442-5232
Judith R. Saidel Ph.D., Dir.

Founded: 1978. **Research Activities and Fields:** Brings together unions, women's organizations, advocacy organizations, and government officials to address public sector employment issues of interest to women and minorities, including studies on career ladders, promotion processes, pay equity, and other barriers preventing full participation of women and minorities in public service. Other areas of study include access to public sector jobs for economically disadvantaged women, and women's public policy leadership development. **Publications:** Women in Public Service Bulletin; Working Paper Series; News on Women in Government (newsletter); Technical Reports; Guidebooks. **Meetings/Educational Activities:** Sponsors seminars and special programs, including training seminars.

★2765★
State University of New York at Binghamton
Fernand Braudel Center for the Study of Economies,
   Historical Systems, and Civilizations
Binghamton, NY 13902-6000   Ph: (607)777-4924
                                Fax: (607)777-4315
Prof. Immanuel Wallerstein, Dir.

Founded: 1976. **Research Activities and Fields:** Center is organized into research working groups, which study the following topics: hegemony and rivalry in the world-system, 1500-2025 AD; commodity chains; world labor; southern Africa and the world-system, 1975-2000 AD; institutionalization of the social sciences; households and labor force formation in the world economy; and gender, race, and ethnicity in the world-system. Administers a postdoctoral training and research program in the historical social sciences, titled "Beyond Multidisciplinary, Toward Unidisciplinary." **Publications:** Review (quarterly journal); Studies in Modern Capitalism (book series); Southern Africa (pamphlet series); Annual Newsletter; Newsletter on Long Waves; Research Bulletin on Southern Africa. **Meetings/Educational Activities:** Sponsors conferences in coordination with research programs and monthly seminars.

★2766★
State University of New York Health Science Center at Brooklyn
Sickle Cell Center
450 Clarkson Ave., Box 20
Brooklyn, NY 11203   Ph: (212)735-2249
Dr. R.F. Rieder, Program Dir.

Founded: 1972. **Research Activities and Fields:** Sickle cell disease, including studies on natural history of sickle cell disease, and genetic basis for variations in disease severity.

★2767★
Temple University
Center for African American History and Culture
Weiss Hall, Ste. B18
13th & Cecil B. Moore Ave.   Ph: (215)787-4851
Philadelphia, PA 19122   Fax: (215)787-3794
Dr. Bettye Collier-Thomas, Dir.

Founded: 1989. **Research Activities and Fields:** African American social, political, and economic history and culture, focusing on African-Americans in Pennsylvania, women, and religion. **Publications:** Heritage (semiannual newsletter). **Meetings/Educational Activities:** Offers graduate programs, hosts postdoctoral fellows and visiting scholars, and sponsors exibitions, symposia, and conferences.

★2768★
Tennessee State University
Office of Business and Technology Research
College of Business
330 10th Ave. N.
Nashville, TN 37203   Ph: (615)251-1505

Research Activities and Fields: Business and economic research concentrating on economy and minority-owned businesses in Nashville. **Formerly:** Bureau of Business and Economic Research.

★2769★
Thomas Jefferson University
Cardeza Foundation for Hematologic Research
1015 Walnut St.   Ph: (215)955-7786
Philadelphia, PA 19107   Fax: (215)955-2366
Sandor S. Shapiro M.D., Dir.

Founded: 1939. **Research Activities and Fields:** Conducts basic and clinical hematologic research. Maintains a blood bank, hemophilia and sickle cell centers, and a photographic unit. **Meetings/Educational Activities:** Sponsors weekly seminars for interested workers in the field. **Library:** 1,500 volumes on hematology; Doris Riso, librarian.

★2770★
TransAfrica Forum
1744 R St. NW   Ph: (202)547-2550
Washington, DC 20009   Fax: (202)547-7687
Randall Robinson, Exec.Dir.

Research Activities and Fields: U.S. foreign policy studies, focusing on aid to Africa and the Caribbean.

★2771★
University of Alabama
Center for Southern History and Culture
PO Box 870342
University, AL 35487-0342   Ph: (205)348-7467
Dr. Robert J. Norrell, Dir.

Founded: 1976. **Research Activities and Fields:** History and culture of the South, including regional and urban studies, economic history, and race relations. Supports research and writing and aids the University library in discovering and preserving important documents. **Publications:** The Alabama Review (quarterly) for the Alabama Historical Association; Alabama Heritage (popular history magazine). **Meetings/Educational Activities:** Trains students in research and writing. Conducts teacher education activities, including in-service workshops and residential institutes. **Formerly:** Center for the Study of Southern History and Culture.

★2772★
University of Alabama
Institute of Higher Education Research and Services
Wilson Hall, Rm. 209
PO Box 870302
Tuscaloosa, AL 35487-0302   Ph: (205)348-1173
Prof. David Masoner, Dir.

Founded: 1970. **Research Activities and Fields:** Development of postsecondary education, with special attention given to Alabama and surrounding states, including institutional self-studies and long-range planning activities, studies of interinstitutional cooperative arrangements, single and multi-institution goal-setting efforts, postsecondary educational needs by state or area within state, international education, and black community in Alabama. **Publications:** Progress Report (annually, mimeographed). **Meetings/Educational Activities:** Trains college teachers and administrators in working with work with disadvantaged students. Holds periodic seminars for college administrators and faculty members, also workshops on community services, developing human potential, and improvement of instruction.

★2773★
University of California, Los Angeles
Center for Afro-American Studies
160 Haines Hall
405 Hilgard Ave.   Ph: (310)825-7403
Los Angeles, CA 90024-1545   Fax: (310)206-3421
Dr. J. Eugene Grigsby III, Act.Dir.

Founded: 1969. **Research Activities and Fields:** Conducts and coordinates academic and research programs in Afro-American studies designed to expand the knowledge of the history, life styles, and sociocultural systems of persons of African descent and to investigate problems that have bearing on the psychological, social, and material well-being of Afro-Americans throughout the Western Hemisphere. Current research includes examination of mate availability as related to social structure and social psychological adaptation, interracial dating and marriage, the socioeconomic well-being of ethnic communities in Los Angeles, high risk sexual behavior related to risk of AIDS in sociocultural context, and African-American entrepreneurship. **Publications:** Afro-American Culture and Society Monograph Series; The Community Classic Series; CAAS Special Publication Series; Annual Report; CAAS Report (semiannually). **Meetings/Educational Activities:** Administers B.A. and M.A. degree programs and provides fellowships and scholarships. Sponsors a wide variety of scholarly and cultural programs with Afro-American themes, including Thurgood Marshall Lecture (annually), symposia, exhibits, and concerts. **Library:** 5,000 volumes on black history, literature, and culture, plus subscriptions to leading black newspapers and video cassettes of events affecting the Afro-American experience.

★2774★
University of California, Los Angeles
Higher Education Research Institute
Graduate School of Education   Ph: (310)825-1925
Los Angeles, CA 90024   Fax: (310)206-2228
Dr. Alexander W. Astin, Dir.

Founded: 1973. **Research Activities and Fields:** Higher education institutions, federal and state policy assessment, minority access to higher education, student and faculty development, retention, and women, leadership, and values in higher education. Conducts the Annual Survey of American College Freshmen. Survey data is collected on 280,000 freshmen from 600 institutions each fall, since 1966. Follow-up surveys on each cohort are conducted after 2-4 years. Nationally faculty surveys are conducted every three years. **Publications:** American Freshman: National Norms for Fall (annually).

★2775★
University of California, Los Angeles
National Study of Black College Students
Dept. of Sociology
405 Hilgard Ave.   Ph: (213)206-7107
Los Angeles, CA 90024-1551   Fax: (213)206-9838
Prof. Walter R. Allen, Dir.

Research Activities and Fields: Analyzes experiences of black students attending predominantly white or predominantly black schools, including studies of psychological stress and social groups. **Meetings/Educational Activities:** Sponsors American Educational Research Association Meetings.

★2776★

University of California, Los Angeles
Research Center on the Psychobiology of Ethnicity
1000 W. Carson St.
B-4 S.
Torrance, CA 90504   Ph: (213)212-4266
Keh-Ming Lin, Dir.

Founded: 1990. **Research Activities and Fields:** Role of ethnicity (including culture) and biological variables in the mental health of ethnic minority populations. Conducts studies using pharmacokinetical, pharmacodynamical, and pharmacogenetical research techniques to examine ethnic and individual differences in responses to psychotropic drugs. **Meetings/Educational Activities:** Provides research training to psychiatric residents and other trainees.

★2777★

University of California, San Francisco
Northern California Comprehensive Sickle Cell Center
San Francisco General Hospital
1001 Potrero Ave., 6J5   Ph: (415)206-5169
San Francisco, CA 94110   Fax: (415)206-3071
William C. Mentzer M.D., Dir.

Research Activities and Fields: Sickle cell disease, including molecular, cellular, tissue, and organ studies. Conducts clinical trials. Seeks to translate research on sickle cell disease to improved health care at the community level. **Formerly:** Comprehensive Sickle Cell Center.

★2778★

University of California, Santa Barbara
Center for Black Studies
Santa Barbara, CA 93106-3140   Ph: (805)893-3914
Dr. Charles H. Long, Dir.

Founded: 1969. **Research Activities and Fields:** Social, historical, political, and economic forces that have affected African people throughout the world. Sponsors a faculty development program, which supports dissertation research.

★2779★

University of Chicago
Committee on African and African-American Studies
5828 S. University Ave.   Ph: (312)702-8344
Chicago, IL 60637   Fax: (312)702-2587
Prof. Jean Conaroff, Chm.

Research Activities and Fields: Serves as a supporting and coordinating body for research on African and African-American history, culture, economy, and society conducted by faculty and students of the University. **Formerly:** Committee on African Studies (1986).

★2780★

University of Colorado at Boulder
Center for Comparative Politics
Dept. of Political Science, CB 333   Ph: (303)492-7064
Boulder, CO 80309   Fax: (303)492-5105
William Safran, Dir.

Founded: 1983. **Research Activities and Fields:** Ethnic and class-based groups, social and economic policies, growth of state powers and resources, ethnic conflicts, political terrorism and revolution, political institutions, and group-institution relationships in democratic, authoritarian, and revolutionary situations. Projects conducted on the global level, including areas of western Europe, Latin America, and Africa.

★2781★

University of Colorado at Boulder
Center for Studies of Ethnicity and Race in America
Ketchum 30
CB 339   Ph: (303)492-8852
Boulder, CO 80309-0339   Fax: (303)492-7799
Dr. Evelyn Hu-DeHart, Dir.

Founded: 1988. **Research Activities and Fields:** Comparative race and ethnicity and specific ethnic groups, including Afro-American, American Indian, Asian-American, and Chicano studies; African and Asian diasporal studies. **Meetings/Educational Activities:** Offers public lectures, art exhibits, and conferences.

★2782★

University of Connecticut
Institute for African-American Studies
241 Glenbrook Rd., U-162
Storrs Mansfield, CT 06269-2162   Ph: (203)486-3630
Prof. Donald Spivey, Dir.

Research Activities and Fields: History, culture, experiences, and contributions of African-Americans, including socioeconomic condition and political life.

★2783★

University of Florida
Center for African Studies
427 Grinter Hall   Ph: (904)392-2183
Gainesville, FL 32611   Fax: (904)392-2435
Dr. Peter R. Schimdt, Dir.

Founded: 1964. **Research Activities and Fields:** Directs and coordinates African studies at the University, including tropical rural development, constitutionality and governance, food supply, languages and literature, prehistory, agroforestry, and wildlife ecology. **Publications:** Annual volume based on its Carter Lecture Series. **Meetings/Educational Activities:** Offers certificates at the undergraduate, M.A., and Ph.D. levels. Sponsors Carter Lecture Series, conferences, and seminars. **Library:** 80,000 volumes, 500 periodicals, and an extensive map collection; Peter Malanchuk, Africana bibliographer.

★2784★

University of Houston
African American Studies Program
College of Humanities, Fine Arts, &
   Communications
Agnes Arnold Hall   Ph: (713)743-2811
Houston, TX 77204-3783   Fax: (713)743-2818
Dr. Linda Reed, Dir.

Founded: 1969. **Research Activities and Fields:** Public policy-related issues and topics focused on African Americans in Houston, Texas, and throughout the U.S. **Meetings/Educational Activities:** Provides instruction emphasizing cultural and historical heritage of black Americans, analyzing and critically examining sociological, psychological, economic, and political aspects of black community as it exists in the U.S. and Africa. **Library:** 800 volumes; Audrey Taylor, librarian.

★2785★

University of Illinois at Chicago
UIC Eye Center
1855 W. Taylor   Ph: (312)996-6590
Chicago, IL 60612   Fax: (312)996-7770
Dr. J. Chandler, Head

Founded: 1858. **Research Activities and Fields:** Various diseases affecting the eye, including diabetic retinopathy, retinitis pigmentosa, branch vein occlusion, sickle cell eye disease, ocular trauma, ocular and corneal immunology, genetic eye diseases, glaucoma, vitreous fluorophotometry, external eye diseases, retinopathy of prematurity, optic neuritis, ocular melanoma, herpes simplex virus, macular degeneration, and uveitis. **Publications:** Eyewitness News; Eye Facts, Annual Report. **Meetings/Educational Activities:** Sponsors clinical conferences (weekly), UIC Eye Center Horizons in Ophthalmology Meeting featuring the Dr. Marvin D. Henry Memorial Lecture and Peter Kronfeld Memorial Lectures (annually), and special teaching workshops on new eye procedures and treatment techniques. Offers active teaching program at all levels of medical training, provides medical residency for 10 physicians per year, and sponsors continuing education courses for practicing ophthalmologists. Holds patient education seminars on a variety of eye care topics. **Library:** Maintains collections on eye diseases and research; Mary Winnike, librarian.

★2786★
University of Illinois at Urbana-Champaign
Afro-American Studies and Research Program
606 S. Gregory   Ph: (217)333-7781
Urbana, IL 61801   Fax: (217)244-4809
Prof. Dianne M. Pinderhughes, Dir.

Founded: 1969. **Research Activities and Fields:** Subjects related to Afro-Americans, including the African diaspora in the Americas, educational policy, intellectual history, curriculum development, critical social theory, social sciences, and the humanities. **Publications:** The Afro-Americanist Newsletter. Sponsors colloquia. **Library:** Maintains a reference collection.

★2787★
University of Illinois at Urbana-Champaign
Center for African Studies
210 International Studies Bldg.
910 S. 5th St.   Ph: (217)333-6335
Champaign, IL 61820   Fax: (217)244-2429
Dr. D.E. Crummey, Dir.

Founded: 1970. **Research Activities and Fields:** Coordinates research, instructional, and outreach activities at the University in Sub-Saharan Africa, including agriculture, education, social science, language studies, and the humanities. **Meetings/Educational Activities:** Offers a noon lunch series, including guest lecturers, on topical political matters and current research. Sponsors a spring symposium. **Library:** Yvette Scheven, librarian. **Formerly:** African Studies Program.

★2788★
University of Kansas
Institute for Black Leadership Development and
    Research
1028 Dole   Ph: (913)864-3990
Lawrence, KS 66045-0048   Fax: (913)864-5323
Jacob U. Gordon, Exec.Dir.

Founded: 1986. **Research Activities and Fields:** Studies, develops, and disseminates data and information on African Americans, including research on alcohol and drug abuse, community development, race relations, and quality of life. **Meetings/Educational Activities:** Sponsors Black Leadership Symposium (annually), as well as other symposiums, seminars, workshops, and conferences.

★2789★
University of Massachusetts at Boston
William Monroe Trotter Institute for the Study of Black
    Culture
Harbor Campus
Boston, MA 02125-3393   Ph: (617)287-5880
Dr. James Jennings, Dir.

Founded: 1984. **Research Activities and Fields:** Black issues nationally and locally, including economics, history, black service institutions, demographic and political trends, community development, black artists, housing, education, Africa, women, family, criminal justice, black image in media, psychology, and research and technical assistance to community groups. **Publications:** Trotter Institute Review (semiannually); Research Report Series; Occasional Paper Series. **Meetings/Educational Activities:** Sponsors Forums and panel discussions.

★2790★
University of Miami
Innovation and Entrepreneurship Institute
PO Box 249117
Coral Gables, FL 33124   Ph: (305)284-4692
Carl McKeney, Exec.Dir.

Founded: 1984. **Research Activities and Fields:** Entrepreneurship and innovation in Florida, including studies on high-technology ventures and black and Cuban-American entrepreneurs. Promotes

interaction of entrepreneurs and capital and service providers. **Publications:** Research Report Series; Friends of the Forum Directory. **Meetings/Educational Activities:** Sponsors the University of Miami Venture Council Forum, a series of programs to assist small entrepreneurial companies that include company case studies, seminars, workshops, and lectures.

★2791★
University of Miami
Institute for the Study of Culture and Nursing
School of Nursing
Royce Bldg., D2-5
1755 NW 12th Ave.   Ph: (305)547-3707
Miami, FL 33136   Fax: (305)547-3808
Dr. Lydia DeSantis, Dir.

Research Activities and Fields: Clinical nursing, focusing on serving multicultural populations and managing multicultural organizations. **Meetings/Educational Activities:** Sponsors continuing education sessions for health care providers and conference planning.

★2792★
University of Michigan - Ann Arbor
Center for Afro-American and African Studies
W. Engineering Bldg., Rm. 200
550 E. Univ.   Ph: (313)764-5513
Ann Arbor, MI 48109-1092   Fax: (313)764-0543
Prof. Earl Lewis, Dir.

Founded: 1970. **Research Activities and Fields:** Conducts interdisciplinary studies on the African-American experience in Africa and throughout the diaspora. Projects include a national study of African-American college students, immigration and acculturation of Falashas in Israel, comparative black family organization, Africa's triple heritage, urban political systems and racial transitions in Detroit, west African women, African agriculture and trade, and post-emancipation societies in the Caribbean and North America. **Publications:** Voices of the African Diaspora (newletter, published three times per year). **Meetings/Educational Activities:** Sponsors the Zora Neale Hurston Speakers Series and the Speakers Colloquia.

★2793★
University of Michigan - Ann Arbor
Program for Research on Black Americans
5118 Institute for Social Research
426 Thompson St.
PO Box 1248   Ph: (313)763-0045
Ann Arbor, MI 48106-1248   Fax: (313)763-0044
Prof. James S. Jackson, Dir.

Founded: 1976. **Research Activities and Fields:** Aging and human development of Black Americans, including race and cultural factors in marital formation and dissolution, race and sociocultural factors in productive activities across the life course, intergenerational family influences on adolescent pregnancy, and health and coping in elderly blacks; race attitudes and political behavior, including archived datasets, National Survey of Black Americans (NSBA, 1979-80) and a black election study (1984 and 1988); psychiatric epidemiology and mental health of blacks, including a survey conducted in a community based mental health treatment facility and a probability survey of risk factors, mental health status, and treatment in Michigan prisons. Activities include investigations on the correlation of religious participation and family and friendship networks of Black Americans. **Publications:** Research and Training Activities. **Meetings/Educational Activities:** Provides education and research opportunities at the undergraduate, graduate, and postdoctoral levels.

★2794★
University of Missouri—Kansas City
Center for Study of Metropolitan Problems in
    Education
5100 Rockhill Rd.
Kansas City, MO 64110   Ph: (816)276-2251
Dr. Eugene E. Eubanks, Dir.

Founded: 1964. **Research Activities and Fields:** Educational problems in metropolitan areas, including studies on relation between census data and school achievement. Emphasizes studies involving compensatory education and desegregation.

★2795★
University of North Carolina at Charlotte
Urban Institute
Charlotte, NC 28223   Ph: (704)547-2307
    Fax: (704)547-3178
Dr. William J. McCoy, Dir.

Founded: 1969. **Research Activities and Fields:** Economic development and planning, survey research, and low income neighborhood development. The Institute maintains a Survey Center, which analyzes retail marketing, housing needs, medical insurance availability, recycling, and hazardous waste systems. **Publications:** Annual Report; Newsletter; Research and News. **Meetings/Educational Activities:** Employs graduate assistants from the University and provides support services for summer internships for students.

★2796★
University of Notre Dame
Institute for Urban Studies
Law School
Notre Dame, IN 46556   Ph: (219)239-8129
Dr. Thomas F. Broden, Dir.

Founded: 1969. **Research Activities and Fields:** Neighborhoods in the U.S., minority educational opportunity, and minority community development, including Hispanic community development in the Midwest. **Library:** Maintains a small collection on neighborhoods, youth advocacy, social indicators, and urban affairs; Theodessa Earles, librarian.

★2797★
University of Oklahoma
Center for Research on Multi-Ethnic Education
455 W. Lindsey St., Rm. 804   Ph: (405)325-4529
Norman, OK 73019-0535   Fax: (405)325-4991
Prof. Wanda Ward, Dir.

Founded: 1986. **Research Activities and Fields:** Needs of and opportunities for minorities in education and the nature of minority participation in education and the workforce. Activities focus on higher education, including minority graduate education, effect of various admission standards upon minority student access, factors affecting academic success and the cultural identity of minority students on college and university campuses, and minority faculty career development. **Publications:** Cultural Diversity (newsletter). **Meetings/Educational Activities:** Administers senior scholar and postdoctoral scholar programs. **Formerly:** Center for Research on Minority Education (1991).

★2798★
University of Pennsylvania
Center for Cultural Studies
420 Williams Hall   Ph: (215)898-6836
Philadelphia, PA 19104   Fax: (215)898-0933
Dr. Gerald Prince, Codirector

Founded: 1986. **Research Activities and Fields:** Cross-disciplinary studies of systems of cultural expression. Activities focus on anthropology, art history, communications, literature, folklore, linguistics, black studies, women's studies, musicology, psychology, American studies, drama, film, history, and history of science.

★2799★
University of Pennsylvania
Center for the Study of Black Literature and Culture
3400 Walnut St., Bennett Hall
Philadelphia, PA 19104-6273   Ph: (215)898-5141
Dr. Houston A. Baker, Dir.

Founded: 1987. **Research Activities and Fields:** Afro-American and African diasporic literary and cultural study. Sponsors practical programs and theoretical projects on the study and teaching of black (including Caribbean) literature and intellectual history. **Meetings/Educational Activities:** Sponsors faculty seminars, a distinguished speakers program, summer seminars, a residency fellowship program, and an Afro-American Studies program.

★2800★
University of Pennsylvania
Institute for Research on Higher Education
4200 Pine St., 5th Fl.
Philadelphia, PA 19104-4090   Ph: (215)898-4585
Dr. Robert Zemsky, Dir.

Founded: 1979. **Research Activities and Fields:** Enrollment planning, demographic research, and minority participation in higher education. Also conducts collegiate curriculum analysis, strategic planning, postsecondary education finance studies, and research on institutional decision making. **Publications:** Policy Perspectives (quarterly). **Meetings/Educational Activities:** Sponsors a higher education seminar.

★2801★
University of Rochester
Frederick Douglass Institute for African and African-American Studies
Rochester, NY 14627   Ph: (716)275-7235
    Fax: (716)442-5769
Karen Fields, Dir.

Founded: 1986. **Research Activities and Fields:** Politics in Africa and its diaspora, world economics, social history, and environmental issues. **Publications:** Undergraduate Perspectives in African and African-American Studies. **Meetings/Educational Activities:** Maintains predoctoral and postdoctoral fellowship programs.

★2802★
University of Southern California
Comprehensive Sickle Cell Center
2025 Zonal Ave., Rm. 304   Ph: (213)342-1259
Los Angeles, CA 90033   Fax: (213)342-2644
Dr. Cage S. Johnson, Dir.

Founded: 1972. **Research Activities and Fields:** Sickle cell disease, including studies on molecular biology of red cells, fetal hemoglobin identification, and renal, cardiovascular, and endocrine functions.

★2803★
University of Tennessee
Clinical Research Center
951 Court Ave., Rm. 326B
Memphis, TN 38163   Ph: (901)528-5802
Williams B. Applegate M.D., Program Dir.

Founded: 1965. **Research Activities and Fields:** Provides general clinical research facilities for controlled inpatient and outpatient studies on human subjects with various disorders, including sickle cell anemia, diabetes mellitus, hyperandrogenism and other endocrine disorders, kidney disease, liver disorders, hypertension, brain tumors, muscular dystrophy, obesity, metabolic bone diseases, psychiatric disorders, osteoporosis, Reye's syndrome, hirsutism, sexual disorders, problems of reproduction, thyroid disorders, cancer of the breast, and leukemia. **Publications:** Annual Report. **Meetings/Educational Activities:** Holds scientific advisory committee meetings and investigators conferences, to which all faculty members of the College are invited. Provides training to science students in community colleges and conducts lectures for students interested in health science careers. **Library:** Maintains all research publications generated by the Center.

★2804★
University of Tennessee, Knoxville
Society for the Study of Social Problems
901 McClung Tower
Knoxville, TN 37996-0490   Ph: (615)974-6021
Dr. Thomas C. Hood, Exec.Dir.

Founded: 1951. **Research Activities and Fields:** Community research and development; crime and juvenile delinquency; drinking and drugs; racial and ethnic minorities; international conflict and cooperation; the family; poverty, class, and inequality; psychiatric sociology; social problems theory; sociology and social welfare; youth, aging, and the life course; educational problems; environmental problems; environment and technology; labor studies; sexual behavior; and health and health policy and services. **Publications:** Social Problems (journal); Newsletters. **Meetings/Educational Activities:** Offers training workshops, symposia, and panels. Sponsors an annual meeting and bestows awards.

★2805★
University of Texas at Austin
Center for African and Afro-American Studies
Jester A232A   Ph: (512)471-1784
Austin, TX 78712   Fax: (512)471-1798
Prof. John Sibley Butler, Act.Dir.

Founded: 1969. **Research Activities and Fields:** African and Afro-American cultures, including studies in African geography and history. Studies include African-American history, literature, historical figures, music, institutional racism, roles of African-American women, the black family, minority education, entrepreneurial activities in the community, black movements in the Caribbean, sociological perspectives of black Americans, and Black English (linguistics). **Publications:** Newsletter (bimonthly); Working Paper Series; Reprint Series. **Meetings/Educational Activities:** Sponsors Heman Sweatt Symposium on Civil Rights (annually in spring).

★2806★
University of Texas Southwestern Medical Center at Dallas
Sickle Cell Case Management Program
1935 Motor St.
Dallas, TX 75235   Ph: (214)688-3111
Dr. George Buchanan, Dir.

Research Activities and Fields: Researches morbidity and mortality of pediatric sickle cell patients.

★2807★
University of Virginia
Carter G. Woodson Institute for Afro-American and African Studies
1512 Jefferson Park Ave.
Charlottesville, VA 22903   Ph: (804)924-3109
Prof. Armstead L. Robinson, Dir.

Founded: 1981. **Research Activities and Fields:** African studies, including persons of African descent in the Americas, Europe, and the Caribbean, across the spectrum of social science and humanistic disciplines. **Formerly:** Institute for Afro-American Studies and African Studies (1982).

★2808★ ·
University of Wisconsin—La Crosse
Office of Minority Affairs
223 Main Hall
1725 State St.
La Crosse, WI 54601   Ph: (608)785-8225
Ronald B. Shaheed, Act.Dir.

Founded: 1981. **Research Activities and Fields:** Student retention and prediction equations for student success. **Library:** Carol Miller, librarian. **Formerly:** Institute of Minority Studies.

★2809★
University of Wisconsin—Madison
African Studies Program
1454 Van Hise Hall
1220 Linden Dr.
Madison, WI 53706   Ph: (608)262-2380
Prof. Edris Makward, Dir.

Founded: 1961. **Research Activities and Fields:** Individually determined studies on Africa by 60 faculty members in 23 departments of the University, including African art, African languages and literature, Afro-American studies, art history, comparative literature, economics, educational policy, curriculum and instruction, geography, history, journalism, law, music, politics, sociology, anthropology, women's studies, and agricultural and development sciences. **Publications:** News and Notes (semiannually). Also publishes bibliographies and language materials. **Meetings/Educational Activities:** Provides instruction, with emphasis on postgraduate studies on Africa and outreach assistance to kindergarten through twelfth grade teachers in Wisconsin and other states of the upper Midwest. Holds weekly Africanist seminars and occasional conferences for educators in schools and colleges.

★2810★
Urban Institute
2100 M St. NW   Ph: (202)833-7200
Washington, DC 20037   Fax: (202)223-3043
William Gorham, Pres.

Founded: 1968. **Research Activities and Fields:** Domestic, social, and economic affairs, including multidisciplinary studies and government program evaluations in the areas of tax and budget reform, health policy, housing and community development, human resources, income security and pension, international activities, public finance, productivity and economic development, social services, and immigration. Also conducts research programs on employment and training, children's issues and family policy, minorities and social policy, poverty, state and local governments, transportation, and community impact and demography. **Publications:** Policy and Research Report (three times yearly); Annual Report; Policy Bites (bimonthly); supplements and summaries of reports, papers, reprints, and other communications of the Institute. **Meetings/Educational Activities:** Conducts press briefings, policy seminars, and interdisciplinary conferences. **Library:** 32,000 volumes, 650 journals, and 5,000 reels of microfilm on social and economic issues; Camille Motta, librarian.

★2811★
Wayne State University
Archives of Labor and Urban Affairs
Walter P. Reuther Library
5401 Cass Ave.   Ph: (313)577-4024
Detroit, MI 48202   Fax: (313)577-4300
Dr. Leslie S. Hough, Dir.

Founded: 1959. **Research Activities and Fields:** American labor movement, urban affairs, African-American and women's studies, social welfare, and medical history, and movements for social, political, and economic reform. Serves as a depository for major international labor unions and related organizations, including personal papers of public and private citizens pertaining to these fields; such materials are made available to qualified researchers. **Publications:** Occasional Newsletter. **Meetings/Educational Activities:** Annual Labor and Local History Conferences, open to the public, and intermittent public presentations and exhibits of episodes in labor history. **Library:** Maintains a collection on labor and other movements for social, political, and economic reforms, 35,000 official union publications, contracts, constitutions, and convention proceedings, 13,000 books, and 900,000 photographs of union officials and significant events; Carrolyn Davis, librarian. **Formerly:** Labor History Archives.

★2812★
Wayne State University
Comprehensive Sickle Cell Center
Curricular Affairs Office
Scott Hall, Rm. 1206
540 E. Canfield   Ph: (313)577-1546
Detroit, MI 48201   Fax: (313)577-8777
Charles F. Whitten M.D., Dir.

Research Activities and Fields: Sickle cell disease, including molecular, cellular, tissular, and organic studies. Seeks to apply sickle cell research to improved health care at the community level.

★2813★
Wayne State University
Folklore Archive
Purdy Library, Rm. 448
Detroit, MI 48202   Ph: (313)577-4053
Janet L. Langlois, Dir.

Founded: 1939. **Research Activities and Fields:** Folklore and urban tradition, especially of Michigan and Detroit, including oral traditions in urban centers and among ethnic and occupational groups. Sponsors collection, classification, and cross-indexing of field data, maintains and prepares collections for use by researchers, solicits field collections from individuals and institutions, develops questionnaires and forms for use by collectors, provides consulting services for the mass media, and advises institutions developing folklore archive materials. **Publications:** Annotated Holdings List (occasionally); Holiday Pamphlet Series; Triennial Report. **Meetings/Educational Activities:** Sponsors a Folklore and Mythology Interest Group Lecture Series. **Library:** 200 volumes on folklore, ethnographic data, and history of Michigan and Detroit, 350 slides, and 5 videos. **Formerly:** Folklore Archive and Center for Study of Urban Tradition; merged with the University's Archive of Ethnomusicology (1966).

★2814★
Wayne State University
Race Relations Institute
College of Urban, Labor & Metropolitan
   Affairs
656 W. Kirby, Rm. 3208 FAB
Detroit, MI 48202   Ph: (313)577-5071
Leon Chestang, Contact

Founded: 1991. **Research Activities and Fields:** Basic and applied research on race relations, focusing on the Detroit metropolitan area.

★2815★
Wesleyan University
Center for Afro-American Studies
Middletown, CT 06457   Ph: (203)344-7943
Marshall Hyatt, Dir.

Research Activities and Fields: Interdisciplinary study of black life in the Americas, focusing on the African-American experience and black expression from various perspectives.

★2816★
Western Michigan University
Black Americana Studies
814 Sprau Tower
Kalamazoo, MI 49008   Ph: (616)387-2661
Dr. Leroi Ray Jr., Dir.

Research Activities and Fields: Black Americans, particularly students.

★2817★
William O. Douglas Institute
PO Box 45745, University Sta.
Seattle, WA 98145   Ph: (206)522-2388
Prof. Hubert G. Locke, Dir.

Founded: 1972. **Research Activities and Fields:** Race and ethnicity, social pathology, democratic theory, the administration of justice, and the quality of urban life. The Institute's current program focuses on the problems that were dominant under German national socialism and which persist as critical issues in contemporary America: economic instability, race, technology, ideological extremism, and the integrity of the political process. **Publications:** Occasional Papers. **Library:** 1,000 volumes on race and ethnicity and law and justice. **Formerly:** The Institute for the Study of Contemporary Social Problems.

★2818★
Wisconsin Policy Research Institute, Inc.
3107 N. Shepard Ave.
Milwaukee, WI 53211   Ph: (414)963-0600
James H. Miller, Pres.

Founded: 1987. **Research Activities and Fields:** State public policy issues focusing on education, including minority education, educational finance, and programs for gifted and talented children. Also studies welfare reform, criminal justice, and economic development. **Formerly:** Wisconsin Public Policy Research Institute, Inc.

(10) Awards, Honors, and Prizes

★2819★
A. Philip Randolph Achievement Award
A. Philip Randolph Institute
260 Park Ave. S., 6th Fl.
New York, NY 10010   Ph: (212)533-8000

For recognition of a ranking black trade unionist who has achieved high excellence and has made a major contribution to the improvement of the lives of workers. Candidate must hold a high ranking responsible position in the American trade union movement. A medallion is presented annually. Established in 1968 by A. Philip Randolph.

★2820★
A. Philip Randolph/Bayard Rustin Freedom Award
A. Philip Randolph Institute
260 Park Ave. S., 6th Fl.
New York, NY 10010   Ph: (212)533-8000

For recognition of outstanding contributions to the advancement of human rights and civil rights nationally and internationally. A medallion of A. Philip Randolph and Bayard Rustin is presented annually. Established in 1968 by A. Philip Randolph. Renamed in 1988 in honor of A. Philip Randolph and Bayard Rustin.

★2821★
Adam Clayton Powell Award for Black Political Empowerment
Congressional Black Caucus Foundation
Special Events Director
1004 Pennsylvania Ave. SE   Ph: (202)675-6735
Washington, DC 20003   Fax: (202)547-3806

To recognize an individual in the political arena who has contributed substantially to Black political awareness and empowerment. Members of the Congressional Black Caucus nominate individuals for the award. A plaque is awarded annually. Established in 1972.

★2822★
Affirmative Action and Equal Employment Opportunity Award
Western Reserve Historical Society
10825 East Blvd.   Ph: (216)721-5722
Cleveland, OH 44106-1788   Fax: (216)721-0645

To recognize individuals and organizations that have distinguished themselves in the area of affirmative action. A plaque is awarded annually at the Martin Luther King, Jr. Celebration Program. Established in 1991 in memory of Dr. Martin Luther King, Jr. Administered by the African American Archives Auxiliary of the Society.

★2823★
Aggrey Medal
Phelps-Stokes Fund
10 E. 87th St.
New York, NY 10028   Ph: (212)427-8100

To recognize individuals who have made significant contributions in one of the charter areas of interest of the Phelps-Stokes Fund, i.e., education for Africans, African Americans, and American Indians. A silver medal is awarded from time to time by the Board of Trustees of the Phelps-Stokes Fund. Established in 1986 to honor Dr. J.E.K. Aggrey, the renowned African educator who was a member of the first Phelps-Stokes African Education Commission (1920-21), and one of the period's foremost proponents of racial equality.

★2824★
Alan Barth Service Award
American Civil Liberties Union of the
   National Capital Area
1400 20th St. NW, Ste. 119
Washington, DC 20036   Ph: (202)457-0800

For recognition of volunteer service to the American Civil Liberties Union of the National Capital Area. The candidate must be a member, must have contributed volunteer service to the ACLU Fund of the National Capital Area, and must have been nominated by the board of ACLU/NCA. A plaque is presented annually at an awards dinner. Established in 1980 in memory of Alan Barth, former editorial writer for the Washington Post, for recognition of a lifetime of service to civil liberties.

★2825★
Alice C. Browning Award
International Black Writers
PO Box 1030
Chicago, IL 60690   Ph: (312)924-3818

To recognize excellence in writing. Published writers who are 18 years or older and members of the organization are eligible. A plaque and a certificate are presented annually. Established in 1986 by Mable Terrell in honor of Alice C. Browning, founder of the International Black Writers Conference.

★2826★
American Black Achievement Awards
Johnson Publishing Co., Inc.
820 S. Michigan Ave.
Chicago, IL 60605   Ph: (312)322-9352

To honor Black accomplishment in the fields of public service, religion, dramatic arts, fine arts, music, business and the professions, and athletics. The awards are open to any persons who have achieved monumental success in their field during a given year. A trophy is awarded in the following categories: (1) Jackie Robinson Award for Athletics; (2) Business and the Professions Award; (3)

Dramatic Arts Award; (4) Fine Arts Award; (5) Music Award; (6) Martin Luther King, Jr. Award For Public Service; (7) Religion Award; (8) *EBONY* Lifetime Achievement Award; (9) Trailblazer Award; and (10) Thurgood Marshall Black Education Fund Educational Achievement Award. Awarded annually in the fall in Hollywood. Established in 1978. Sponsored by *Ebony*. Additional information is available from Lydia J. Davis.

★2827★
American Jazz Masters Fellowship Awards
National Endowment for the Arts
Nancy Hanks Center
1100 Pennsylvania Ave. NW
Washington, DC 20506   Ph: (202)682-5400
To recognize distinguished jazz masters who have made a significant contribution to the jazz art form in the African-American tradition. Recipients of these one-time awards are nominated by the jazz community and the general public. Recipients must be citizens or permanent residents of the United States. Monetary awards of $20,000 for a project of the recipient's choice are presented. Up to five awards are given annually. Established in 1982. Additional information is available from the Music Program, phone: (202) 682-5445.

★2828★
Anisfield - Wolf Book Awards/Exploring Human
  Diversity and Prejudice
Cleveland Foundation
1422 Euclid Ave., Ste. 1400   Ph: (216)861-3810
Cleveland, OH 44115-2001   Fax: (216)861-1729
To recognize books published during the previous year which have made outstanding contributions to our appreciation for the richness or achievements of diverse human cultures or to our understanding of the mechanisms and injustices of racism. Books (in English or English translation) published during the previous calendar year may be submitted by January 31. Stipends totaling $6,000 are usually divided between two works: one of a scholarly nature, the other of creative literature (fiction, poetry, biography). Awarded annually in February or early March. Established in 1934 by Edith Anisfield Wolf, a Cleveland philanthropist, in memory of her husband Eugene E. Wolf and father, John Anisfield.

★2829★
Ann Tanneyhill Award
National Urban League
500 E. 62nd St.
New York, NY 10021   Ph: (212)310-9000
To recognize an employee of the National Urban League with ten years or more of service for excellence and extraordinary commitment to the Urban League Movement. A monetary award of $1,000 and a plaque are presented annually. Established in 1970.

★2830★
Artists-in-Residence Program
Studio Museum in Harlem
144 W. 125th St.   Ph: (212)864-4500
New York, NY 10027   Fax: (212)666-5753
To serve emerging African American artists and other emerging artists from African derived cultures (e.g., African, Puerto Rican, Caribbean et al). Awards are presented in the following categories: sculpture, painting, printmaking, fiber arts or assemblage. A fellowship and studio space for a period of 12 months are awarded annually. Established in 1967.

★2831★
Audelco Recognition Award
Audience Development Committee
PO Box 30
Manhattanville Sta.
New York, NY 10027   Ph: (212)189-5900
For recognition of outstanding contributions to Black theater. Awards are given in the following categories: (1) Lighting Design; (2) Sound Design; (3) Scenic Design; (4) Costume Design; (5) Director/Dramatic Production; (6) Director/Musical Production; (7) Choreography; (8) Playwright; (9) Supporting Actress; (10) Supporting Actor; (11) Outstanding Performance in a

Musical/Female; (12) Outstanding Performance in a Musical/Male; (13) Outstanding Musical Creator; (14) Musical Production of the Year; (15) Lead Actress in a Dramatic Role; (16) Lead Actor in a Dramatic Role; and (17) Dramatic Production of the Year. In addition, the Pioneer Award recognizes an individual, who by foresight and dedication, has built the foundation on which black theatre stands. Eligibility is limited to productions mounted by professional, not-for-profit organizations, in existence at least two years and providing a minimum of 500 hours of rehearsal, performance and/or training. To be eligible, productions must have been performed 12 or more times between September 1 and August 31. Friends of Audelco, in good financial standing, receive ballots reflecting the final list of nominations in each category from the Nominating Committee. They are eligible to vote only in categories in which they have seen at least three of the nominees. The Audelco Awards Selection Committee evaluates, counts, and makes a final tally of the ballots. Plaques are awarded annually. Established in 1973.

★2832★
Aura E. Severinghaus Award
National Medical Fellowships
254 W. 31st St., 7th Fl.
New York, NY 10001-2813   Ph: (212)714-0933
To recognize and honor an outstanding minority medical student at Columbia University College of Physicians and Surgeons for outstanding academic achievement, leadership, and community service. A $2,000 stipend and a certificate of merit are awarded annually. Established in 1975 by Mr. Chauncey Waddell and the Charles Evans Hughes Memorial Foundation, Inc., in memory of Aura E. Severinghaus, a long-time NMF Board member and Associate Dean Emeritus of Columbia University's College of Physicians and Surgeons.

★2833★
Bayard Rustin Humanitarian Award
A. Philip Randolph Institute
260 Park Ave. S., 6th Fl.
New York, NY 10010   Ph: (212)533-8000
For recognition of achievement in the areas of human rights and social justice. Nomination is by the Executive Committee of the Institute and approval by the National Board. A specially designed trophy is awarded annually. Established in 1989 in honor of Bayard Rustin, civil rights leader and champion for human rights and dignity.

★2834★
Beatrice G. Konheim Award
American Association of University
  Professors
1012 14th St. NW, Ste. 500   Ph: (202)737-5900
Washington, DC 20005   Fax: (202)737-5526
To recognize a chapter of the Association for distinctive achievement in advancing the objectives of AAUP in academic freedom, student rights and freedoms, the status of academic women, the elimination of discrimination against minorities, or the establishment of equal opportunity for members of college and university faculties. A monetary prize of $1,000 is awarded annually. Established in 1974.

★2835★
Bertha Maxwell Award
National Council for Black Studies
115 A Independence Hall
Ohio State Univ.
1923 Neil Ave. Mall
Columbus, OH 43210   Ph: (614)292-1035
To recognize and facilitate outstanding student scholarship through National Student Essay Contest participation. Undergraduate and graduate students at a university or college are eligible to participate in both creative and scholastic writing categories. The deadline varies from year to year. A monetary prize of $500, a plaque, and publication of the noted essays in a leading journal of black studies are awarded. First and second prizes are awarded annually at the convention. Established in 1978 in honor of Dr. Bertha Maxwell, first chairperson of NCBS.

★2836★
Black Engineer of the Year Awards
Career Communications Group
729 E. Pratt St., Ste. 504
Baltimore, MD 21202   Ph: (301)244-7101

To recognize black engineers who have excelled in their field. Awards are given in the following categories: (1) Black Engineer of the Year; (2) Technical Contribution; (3) Outstanding Achievement in Government; (4) President's Award; (5) Lifetime Achievement; (6) Entrepreneur; (7) Promotion of Engineering Education; (8) Affirmative Action; (9) Most Promising Engineer; (10) Higher Education; (11) Student Leadership; (12) Community Service; (13) Professional Achievement; and (14) Honorable Mention. Trophies are awarded in each category annually at the Award Conference. Established in 1987. Co-sponsored by Mobil Oil Corporation, *US Black Engineer* magazine, and the Council of Engineering Deans of the Historically Black Colleges and Universities.

★2837★
C. Francis Stradford Award
National Bar Association
1225 11th St. NW   Ph: (202)842-3900
Washington, DC 20001-4217   Fax: (202)289-6170

To recognize a person who has performed outstanding service in the furtherance of the Association's objectives. Nominations are accepted by June 1. A plaque is presented at the NBA Annual Convention each summer. Awarded in honor of C. Francis Stradford, NBA co-founder.

★2838★
Candace Award
National Coalition of 100 Black Women
300 Park Ave., Ste. 2
New York, NY 10022-7401   Ph: (212)974-6140

To recognize leadership and achievements of black women in various fields of endeavor. Named after the ancient Ethiopian word for queen. Sponsored by Bailey's Irish Cream.

★2839★
Carter G. Woodson Award
Berea College
Appalachian Center
PO Box 2336
Berea, KY 40404   Ph: (606)986-9341

For recognition of efforts to foster either the development of unity, culture or research of Black communities or equality and understanding in interracial and multicultural education. Individuals from the United States with special emphasis on the Southern Appalachian region and adjacent urban areas are eligible for consideration. A plaque is awarded annually in February (Black History Month). Established in 1983 in memory of Carter G. Woodson, Berea alumnus and founder of Black History Month. Additional information is available from Andrew Baskin, Director of the Black Cultural Center, Berea College, CPO Box 134, Berea, KY 40404.

★2840★
CBCF Lifetime Achievement Award
Congressional Black Caucus Foundation
Special Events Director
1004 Pennsylvania Ave. SE   Ph: (202)675-6735
Washington, DC 20003   Fax: (202)547-3806

For recognition of a lifetime of contributions to the human and civil rights movement.

★2841★
CEBA Awards (Communications Excellence to Black Audiences)
World Institute of Black Communications
c/o CEBA Awards
463 7th Ave.   Ph: (212)714-1508
New York, NY 10018   Fax: (212)307-0635

To recognize excellence in communications directed at black audiences. Awards are presented in the following categories: (1) Consumer Print - newspapers, campaign, consumer magazine, public service, and public relations; (2) Radio - product messages, public relations, campaign, public service, non-entertainment programming; (3) Television - product message, campaign, public service; (4) Film and Video - single feature segments, interview, public relations, dramatic productions, music videos; and (5) Merchandizing and Sales Promotion - posters, album covers, brochures, newsletters, sales promotion, etc. A bronze statuette designed by Valerie Maynard is awarded annually. Established in 1978 by the National Black Network.

★2842★
Chapter Award for Minority Enhancement
American Physical Therapy Association
APTA Awards Program
1111 N. Fairfax St.   Ph: (703)684-2782
Alexandria, VA 22314   Fax: (703)684-7343

To recognize outstanding efforts of an APTA chapter in fostering minority representation and participation in physical therapy. The recipient must be a chapter organization of the APTA. The deadline for entry is December 1. Chapters must demonstrate exceptionally valuable contributions that enhance minorities in any area of the Profession, including but not limited to education, chapter activities, and Association activities. A plaque is awarded. Established in 1984.

★2843★
Charles D. Henry Award
American Alliance for Health, Physical
   Education, Recreation, and Dance
1900 Association Dr.
Reston, VA 22091   Ph: (703)476-3405

For recognition of essential contributions of its members who, through distinguished service to the Alliance (or its component structures): (1) increase involvement of ethnic minorities in AAHPERD; (2) increase communication with greater numbers of ethnic minority members; and (3) extend meaningful services to AAHPERD ethnic minorities. Members who have held such membership for at least five years and have served professionally in school (preschool, elementary, secondary), college, or community programs in AAHPERD for a period of at least five years may be nominated. A plaque is presented annually in a ceremony at the National Convention. Not more than one award is given each year. Established in 1984.

★2844★
Charles H. and N. Mildred Nilon Excellence in Minority Fiction Award
Fiction Collective Two
English Dept. Publications Center
Campus Box 494
Univ. of Colorado   Ph: (303)492-8947
Boulder, CO 80309-0494   Fax: (303)492-5105

To recognize works of fiction by American writers from U.S. ethnic and racial minorities. In addition to recognizing individual writers, the award is intended to draw broad public attention to the growing number of excellent books by minority fiction writers. Eligibility for the award is limited to citizens of the United States of America who belong to one or more of the following U.S. racial and ethnic minorities: African-American, Hispanic, Native American or Alaskan native, and Asian or Pacific Islander. Only original, unpublished, English language, book-length fiction such as novels, novellas, and short story collections are considered. Minimum book length is approximately 200 double-spaced typed or printed pages. The deadline is November 30. A monetary award of $1,000 and joint publication of the winning manuscript by the University of Colorado at Boulder and *Fiction Collective Two* are awarded annually in October. Established in 1988.

★2845★
Clarence L. Holte Literary Prize
Phelps-Stokes Fund
10 E. 87th St.
New York, NY 10028   Ph: (212)427-8100

To recognize a living writer for a significant contribution to the cultural heritage of Africa and the African diaspora made through published writings in the humanities. Nominations for this international prize are open to the public. A monetary prize of $7,500 is awarded biennially from the earnings of an endowment established anonymously in 1977 in honor of Clarence L. Holte, a writer and editor who is a collector of books about the African heritage and diaspora. The prize was conceived by Cliff Lashley, scholar, book collector, and former Jamaican diplomat. Co-sponsored by the Schomburg Center for Research in Black Culture, the New York Public Library, and the Fund. Additional information is available from Harold Anderson, Schomburg Center, (212) 862-4000.

★2846★
Commonwealth Fund Medical Fellowship Program
National Medical Fellowships
254 W. 31st St., 7th Fl.
New York, NY 10001-2813   Ph: (212)714-0933

To encourage academically outstanding minority medical students to pursue careers in biomedical research and academic medicine. The program fosters mentor relationships between these students and prominent biomedical scientists. NMF annually names up to twenty minority medical students as Commonwealth Fund Medical Fellows. Competition is open to minority students attending accredited U.S. medical schools who have demonstrated outstanding academic achievement and show promise for careers in research and academic medicine. Candidates must be nominated by the medical school deans. Up to twenty $5,000 fellowships are awarded annually. Each Fellow spends eight to twelve weeks working in a major research laboratory under the tutelage of a well-known biomedical scientist. Established in 1983with grant support from The Commonwealth Fund of New York, New York.

★2847★
Coretta Scott King Book Award
American Library Association
Social Responsibilities Round Table
50 E. Huron St.
Chicago, IL 60611   Ph: (312)944-6780

To recognize African American authors and illustrators for outstanding contributions to children's literature which promote better understanding and appreciation of the culture and contribution of all peoples to the realization of the American Dream. The noted book must be published in the calendar year preceding the year of award presentation. The deadline for nominations is December 31. The winners are announced during the ALA's midwinter meeting in January and presented with an honorarium of $250, a plaque, and a set of Encyclopedia Britannica or World Book Encyclopedias. Certificates are awarded to those chosen for Honorable Mention. Awarded annually. Established in 1969 by Glyndon Flynt Greer to commemorate the life and works of Dr. Martin Luther King, Jr., and to honor Mrs. Coretta Scott King for her courage and determination in continuing work for peace and world brotherhood.

★2848★
Cornerstone Competition: A National Playwrighting Competition
Penumbra Theatre Company
The Martin Luther King Bldg.
270 N. Kent St.
Saint Paul, MN 55102-1794   Ph: (612)224-4601

To encourage the development of plays and playwrights which, and who are directly concerned with the Pan African and African American experience as it relates to realistic portrayals on the American stage. Full-length drama or comedy must address the Pan African and African American experience, and may be submitted by March 1. Entries should not have been previously produced. The winning play and playwright receive a monetary award of $2,000, a workshop-reading of the play, and a full production as part of Penumbra's mainstage season. Established in 1984. Partially sponsored by The Jerome Foundation.

★2849★
Corporate Leadership Award
Western Reserve Historical Society
10825 East Blvd.   Ph: (216)721-5722
Cleveland, OH 44106-1788   Fax: (216)721-0645

For recognition of outstanding corporate leadership in Cleveland. A plaque is awarded annually at the Martin Luther King, Jr. Celebration Program. Established in 1991 in memory of Dr. Martin Luther King, Jr. Administered by the African American Archives Auxiliary of the Society.

★2850★
David L. Clendenin Award
Workers Defense League
218 W. 40th St., Ste. 203   Ph: (212)730-7412
New York, NY 10018   Fax: (212)730-0151

To recognize distinguished service by prominent labor, religious or political figures to the labor movement and civil rights. A plaque is awarded annually in memory of David L. Clendenin, co-founder of the League and a strong advocate of democratic trade unionism. Established in 1941.

★2851★
Denali Press Award
American Library Association
Reference and Adult Services Division
50 E. Huron St.   Ph: (312)280-4395
Chicago, IL 60611   Fax: (312)280-3257

To recognize achievement in creating reference works, outstanding in quality and significance, that provide information about ethnic and minority groups in the United States. Contributions are judged on accuracy, scope, usefulness, format, special features, and access, as well as the gap in the literature filled by the work. A monetary award of $500 and a citation are presented annually, at the ALA Conference. Established in 1989 by Denali Press, Alan Edward Schorr, President.

★2852★
Distinguished Contribution to Ethnic Minority Psychology Award
Society for the Psychological Study of
Ethnic Minority Issues
1000 Bascom Mall
Education Bldg., Box 56, 3rd Fl.
Madison, WI 53706

To recognize contributions to ethnic minority psychology through research and service. Individuals who have a Ph.D. and are leaders in the field of ethnic minority psychology are eligible. A plaque is awarded annually. Established in 1990.

★2853★
Distinguished Officer of the Year
Blacks in Law Enforcement
256 E. McLemore Ave.
Memphis, TN 38106   Ph: (901)774-1118

To recognize officers who have gone above and beyond the call of duty and employment obligation with service to their department and concern for their community. Officers submitted by their department heads for entry in the BLE publication during the award year are eligible. A plaque is awarded annually. Established in 1987 by Clyde R. Venson.

★2854★
Elliott Rudwick Prize
Organization of American Historians
112 N. Bryan St.
Bloomington, IN 47408-4199   Ph: (812)855-7311

To recognize a book on the experience of racial and ethnic minorities in the United States. The deadline for receipt of entries is September 1 of even-numbered years. No book that has won the James A. Rawley Prize is eligible for the Elliott Rudwick Prize. A monetary award of $2,000 and a certificate are presented biennially beginning in 1991 and continue thereafter until the final prize is given in 2001. The prize is given in memory of Elliott Rudwick, professor of history and sociology at Kent State University.

★2855★
Equal Employment Opportunity Award
United States Department of State
Rm. 431, Annex 6   Ph: (703)516-1665
Washington, DC 20520   Fax: (703)516-1677

For recognition of outstanding contributions toward improving employment opportunities for minorities and women. It is given to an employee of the Department of State who has made the most significant achievements in the furtherance of affirmative action and equal employment opportunity. The award consists of a certificate signed by the Secretary and $5,000 in cash. Awarded annually.

★2856★
Equal Opportunity Day Award
National Urban League
500 E. 62nd St.
New York, NY 10021   Ph: (212)310-9000

To recognize contributions made by individuals, corporations, labor unions and other organizations to equal opportunity for all. A plaque is awarded annually. Established in 1957.

★2857★
Fellowship Program in Health Policy and Management for Minority Medical Students
National Medical Fellowships
254 W. 31st St., 7th Fl.
New York, NY 10001-2813   Ph: (212)714-0933

To encourage minority medical students to enter careers in health policy and management. Blacks, mainland Puerto Ricans, Mexican-Americans, and American Indians who are U.S. citizens attending M.D. degree-granting programs in the United States accredited by the Liaison Committee on Medical Education of the Association of American Medical Colleges, or in D.O. degree-granting programs at colleges of osteopathic medicine in the United States accredited by the Bureau of Professional Education of the American Osteopathic Association, are eligible. Deans of medical schools may nominate up to two candidates. Five funded fellowships of $4,000 each to rising second-, third-, or fourth-year minority students are awarded. Each fellow studies a policy issue which is of particular concern to the Health and Hospitals Corporation, and works with high-level administrators in the New York City Health and Hospitals Corporation's central office, or with executive directors or designees of HHC's municipal hospitals. Additional information is available from: Maritza E. Myers.

★2858★
Ford Foundation Postdoctoral Fellowships for Minorities
National Research Council
2101 Constitution Ave. NW
Washington, DC 20418   Ph: (202)334-2860

To provide for one-year postdoctoral fellowships to teacher-scholars preparing for or already engaged in college or university teaching and research. Awards are made in the behavioral and social sciences, humanities, engineering, mathematics, physical sciences, and biological sciences, or for interdisciplinary programs comprised of two or more eligible disciplines. Applicants must be U.S. citizens or nationals who are members of the following minority groups: American Indian or Alaskan Native (Eskimo or Aleut), Black American, Mexican American/Chicano, Native Pacific Islander (Micronesian or Polynesian), and Puerto Rican. A stipend of $22,500 for Postdoctoral Fellows; and $26,000 for Senior Postdoctoral Fellows are awarded. The National Research Council also offers the Ford FoundationPredoctoral and Dissertation Fellowships for Minorities.

★2859★
Founders Award
Indiana Black Expo
3130 Sutherland Ave.   Ph: (317)925-2702
Indianapolis, IN 46205   Fax: (317)925-6624

To recognize an African-American citizen of Indiana for outstanding achievement.

★2860★
Franklin C. McLean Award
National Medical Fellowships
254 W. 31st St., 7th Fl.
New York, NY 10001-2813   Ph: (212)714-0933

This, the oldest and most prestigious honor of NMF, is given to recognize a senior minority medical student for distinguished academic achievement, leadership ability, and community service. A monetary prize of $3,000 and a certificate of merit are awarded annually. Established in 1968 in memory of NMF's founder, Franklin C. McLean.

★2861★
Frederick Douglass Award
New York Urban League
218 W. 40th St., 6th Fl.
New York, NY 10018   Ph: (212)730-5200

To recognize New Yorkers for distinguished leadership in the fight for equal opportunity. Three engraved medallions are awarded annually. Established in 1966 to honor Frederick Douglass, father of the Protest Movement.

★2862★
Freedom Award
Indiana Black Expo
3130 Sutherland Ave.   Ph: (317)925-2702
Indianapolis, IN 46205   Fax: (317)925-6624

To recognize the individual whom Indiana Black Expo, Inc. feels has contributed the most effective service in promoting goodwill to all mankind through performance, accomplishments and contributions to our world. Awarded annually. Established in 1981.

★2863★
George Hill Memorial Scholarship Program
National Medical Fellowships
254 W. 31st St., 7th Fl.
New York, NY 10001-2813   Ph: (212)714-0933

To recognize a black medical student from Westchester County, New York for outstanding academic achievement, leadership and community service. Black residents of Westchester County, New York, who have been accepted into first-year classes of accredited U.S. medical schools are eligible to apply. One new scholarship is awarded each year. The Hill Scholar receives $4,000 annually for the length of undergraduate medical education. Established in 1975 by Chesebrough-Pond's Inc. of Westport, Connecticut, in memory of the black physician who pioneered in the testing, screening and counseling of persons suffering from sickle-cell anemia.

★2864★
George Thomas "Mickey" Leland Humanitarian Award
Congressional Black Caucus Foundation
Special Events Director
1004 Pennsylvania Ave. SE   Ph: (202)675-6735
Washington, DC 20003   Fax: (202)547-3806

To recognize an individual for exceptional work in the struggle for human rights and social justice. Members of the Congressional Black Caucus nominate individuals for the award. A plaque is awarded annually. Established in 1972.

★2865★
George W. Collins Award for Community Service
Congressional Black Caucus Foundation
Special Events Director
1004 Pennsylvania Ave. SE   Ph: (202)675-6735
Washington, DC 20003   Fax: (202)547-3806

To recognize the individual or group of individuals on the local level who exemplify the dedication and work styles of the late Honorable George W. Collins in the areas of young people, senior citizens and minorities. Members of the Congressional Black Caucus nominate individuals for the award. An engraved plaque is awarded annually. Established in 1973.

★2866★
Gertrude E. Rush Award
National Bar Association
1225 11th St. NW   Ph: (202)842-3900
Washington, DC 20001-4217   Fax: (202)289-6170

To recognize individuals who have demonstrated leadership ability in the community within their profession; a pioneer spirit in the pursuit of civil and human rights; and excellence in legal education and perseverance in the law, public policy or social activism. Nominations are accepted. A trophy is awarded annually during the NBA Mid-Year Conference. Established in 1982 in honor of Gertrude Rush, NBA's only woman co-founder.

★2867★
Gertrude Johnson Williams Writing Contest
Johnson Publishing Co., Inc.
820 S. Michigan Ave.
Chicago, IL 60605   Ph: (312)322-9352

To recognize short stories by Black Americans. Monetary awards of $5,000 for the winning story and $1,000 for each of five runners-up are presented annually. Established in 1988 in honor of *EBONY* editor and publisher John H. Johnson's late mother.

★2868★
Hall of Fame
National Association of Black Women
  Attorneys
3711 Macomb St. NW   Ph: (202)966-9693
Washington, DC 20016   Fax: (202)244-6648

For recognition of civic and community leadership. Contributions to the black community are considered. Induction into the Hall of Fame is awarded annually at the Red Dress Ball at the Convention. Established in 1987.

★2869★
Harold Washington Award for Excellence in Coalition Building
Congressional Black Caucus Foundation
Special Events Director
1004 Pennsylvania Ave. SE   Ph: (202)675-6735
Washington, DC 20003   Fax: (202)547-3806

To recognize an individual who has demonstrated excellence in coalition building. Members of the Congressional Black Caucus nominate individuals for the award. Established in 1988 in memory of Harold Washington.

★2870★
Henry G. Halladay Awards
National Medical Fellowships
254 W. 31st St., 7th Fl.
New York, NY 10001-2813   Ph: (212)714-0933

To recognize the achievement of black males in the first year of medical school who have overcome significant obstacles to obtain a medical education. Five supplemental scholarships of $760 each are awarded annually. Established in 1970 by an endowment from Mrs. Henry G. Halladay in memory of her husband.

★2871★
Henry J. Kaiser Family Foundation Merit Awards
National Medical Fellowships
254 W. 31st St., 7th Fl.
New York, NY 10001-2813   Ph: (212)714-0933

To recognize the achievements of about 25 outstanding graduating minority medical students. Students are nominated by medical schools on the basis of academic achievement, leadership, social consciousness, and potential for significant contributions to the medical profession. Monetary awards and certificates of merit are awarded annually. Established in 1980. Sponsored by the Henry J. Kaiser Family Foundation, Menlo Park, California.

★2872★
Herskovits Award
African Studies Association
Credit Union Bldg.
Emory Univ.
Atlanta, GA 30322   Ph: (404)329-6410

To recognize the author of a distinguished work on Africa published or distributed in the United States during the preceding year. The winning work must be an original scholarly publication. Edited collections, symposia, new editions of previously published books, bibliographies, and dictionaries are not eligible. A monetary prize is awarded annually.

★2873★
Hugh J. Andersen Memorial Scholarships
National Medical Fellowships
254 W. 31st St., 7th Fl.
New York, NY 10001-2813   Ph: (212)714-0933

To provide need-based scholarships for outstanding leadership and community service. These scholarships are available to rising second-, third-or fourth-year minority students attending Minnesota medical schools. In addition to demonstrating leadership and community involvement, students must have financial need. Up to seven new scholarships are presented each year. Students must be nominated by their medical school deans. Stipends of $2,500 to $4,000 and certificates are awarded.Nominations are requested in August. Established in 1982 with an endowment from the Andersen family of Minnesota to honor the memory of Hugh J. Andersen, a long-time contributor and active member of NMF's Minneapolis/St. Paul Advisory Committee.

★2874★
Ida B. Wells Award
University of Kansas
William Allen White School of Journalism
  and Mass Communication
208 Stauffer-Flint Hall   Ph: (913)864-4755
Lawrence, KS 66045   Fax: (913)864-5261

For recognition of exemplary leadership in providing minorities with employment opportunities in journalism. Applications or nominations showing the leadership and achievements reflected in the purpose of the award are accepted from anyone. An original bust of Ida B. Wells with inscription of the winner's exemplary achievements is awarded. Scholarships in the name of the winner are awarded for journalism training of minority students. Awarded annually at the convention of one of the sponsoring organizations: National Association of Black Journalists; National Conference of Editorial Writers; and National Broadcast Editorial Association. Established in 1983 by Michael Richardson and Samuel Adams. The award honors Ida B. Wells (1866-1932), pioneer black editor and anti-lynching leader. She was co-owner of a newspaper, a candidate for Congress, and a founding member of the NAACP.

★2875★
Image Awards
National Association for the Advancement
  of Colored People
4805 Mt. Hope Dr.
Baltimore, MD 21215-3297   Ph: (410)358-8900

To recognize entertainers and sports figures who have made positive contributions to minority images in movies, television, the music business and sports. Included in this program is the Jackie Robinson Sports Award for high achievement in athletics and contributions to black youth. Awarded annually by the Hollywood California Chapter of NAACP. Established in 1979. Additional information is available from the Press Office, (213) 734-6108.

★2876★
Indiana State Senator Carolyn Mosby Above and Beyond Award
Indiana Black Expo
3130 Sutherland Ave.   Ph: (317)925-2702
Indianapolis, IN 46205   Fax: (317)925-6624

To recognize an African-American public figure for outstanding contributions and achievements. Awarded annually. Established in 1970.

★2877★
James Comer NIMH Minority Fellowship Awards (Comer Awards)
American Academy of Child and
  Adolescent Psychiatry
3615 Wisconsin Ave. NW   Ph: (202)966-7300
Washington, DC 20016   Fax: (202)966-2891

To help stimulate minorities to participate in research in child and adolescent psychiatry. Stipends of $3,000 each are awarded to support participation in research in child and adolescent psychiatry during the summer. Awarded annually. Established in 1991 to honor James Comer, M.D., child and adolescent psychiatrist who developed an innovative school-based management approach used in economically disadvantaged areas of New Haven, CT. The Success of "the Comer Process" has made it a model increasingly used throughout the United States.

★2878★
James H. Robinson, M.D. Memorial Prizes in Surgery
National Medical Fellowships
254 W. 31st St., 7th Fl.
New York, NY 10001-2813   Ph: (212)714-0933

To recognize senior, minority medical students selected in a national competition for outstanding performance in surgery. Eligible candidates must be minority students enrolled in accredited U.S. schools of medicine who will graduate during the academic year in which the awards are made available. Students must be nominated by medical school deans and the chairmen of the departments of Surgery at the medical schools in which they are enrolled by December. Each prize includescertificate of merit and a $500 stipend. Established in 1986 in memory of James H. Robinson, M.D. who was clinical professor of Surgery and associate dean of Student Affairs at Jefferson Medical College of Thomas Jefferson University in Philadelphia, Pennsylvania.

★2879★
James J. and Jane Hoey Award for Interracial Justice
Catholic Interracial Council of New York
John Jay College
899 10th Ave.   Ph: (212)237-8255
New York, NY 10019   Fax: (212)237-8607

To recognize outstanding contributions in the cause of human rights and social justice. Engraved silver medals are presented to Catholic and non-Catholic recipients annually. Established in 1942.

★2880★
Jane Addams Children's Book Award
Jane Addams Peace Association
777 United Nations Plaza
New York, NY 10017   Ph: (212)682-8830

To promote the cause of peace, social justice, world community, and the equality of the sexes and all races. Children's books published in English in the preceding year are eligible. A certificate is awarded annually in September. Established in 1953 by Marta Teele of Ithaca, NY. Co-sponsored by the Women's International League for Peace and Freedom. Additional information is available from Jean Gore, 980 Lincoln Place, Boulder, CO 80302.

★2881★
John LaFarge Memorial Award for Interracial Justice
Catholic Interracial Council of New York
John Jay College
899 10th Ave.   Ph: (212)237-8255
New York, NY 10019   Fax: (212)237-8607

To recognize outstanding contributions for furthering interracial justice. Outstanding public figures are eligible. A hand-lettered scroll is awarded annually. Established in 1965 in memory of Father John LaFarge, founder of the Council.

★2882★
Kelly M. Alexander, Sr., NAACP State Conference President's Award
National Association for the Advancement
 of Colored People
4805 Mt. Hope Dr.
Baltimore, MD 21215-3297   Ph: (410)358-8900

To recognize a State Conference president for outstanding achievement in the following areas: (1) programs; (2) membership; (3) fund raising; (4) growth of branches; (5) leadership; and (6) youth and college leadership development. Nominations may be submitted by December 31. A monetary award of $1,000 and a gold medal are awarded annually. Established in 1987 to honor Kelly M. Alexander, Sr., who served as a State Conference President for 27 years and chairman of the NAACP Board of Directors.

★2883★
Kitty Cole Human Rights Award
American Association for Counseling and
 Development
5999 Stevenson Ave.   Ph: (703)823-9800
Alexandria, VA 22304   Fax: (703)823-0252

To honor a member who has made significant contributions in one or more areas of the broad spectrum of human rights. Human rights contributions include, but are not limited to, services to people with special needs or handicaps, abused and neglected children, minority groups, economically disadvantaged, or other underserved populations. Nominees should have contributed to the field of human rights either through a special project, direct services, or a life's work and role. Nominees should have contributed a significant amount of time and effort to the area or project for which they were nominated, thus demonstrating a long-term commitment to the field of human rights. Nominations of current members must be submitted by December 15. Awarded annually. Established in honor of Kitty Cole, an active leader in the counseling and human development profession.

★2884★
Labor Affairs Award
National Urban League
500 E. 62nd St.
New York, NY 10021   Ph: (212)310-9000

To recognize organized labor's commitment to forging links and strengthening bonds between the trade union movement and the black community. Two plaques are awarded annually. Established in 1986.

★2885★
Lifetime Achievement in Education and Research Award
Association of Black Nursing Faculty in
 Higher Education
5823 Queens Cove
Lisle, IL 60532   Ph: (708)969-3809

To recognize an individual for a significant contribution to nursing and/or the health care of African-American patients. ABNF members may nominate members or non-members. A plaque is awarded annually at the annual meeting. Established in 1988.

★2886★
LITA/OCLC Minority Scholarship in Library and Information Technology
American Library Association
Library and Information Technology
 Association
50 E. Huron St.   Ph: (312)280-4270
Chicago, IL 60611   Fax: (312)280-3257

To encourage a member of principal minority groups with a strong commitment to library automation to choose library automation as a career. U.S. or Canadian citizens who are enrolled at or accepted in an ALA-accredited master program and who are members of a principal minority may apply by April 1. A scholarship of $2,500 is awarded annually, usually midsummer. Established in 1990.

★2887★
Living Legacy Award
National Caucus and Center on Black
 Aged
1424 K St. NW, Ste. 500   Ph: (202)637-8400
Washington, DC 20005   Fax: (202)347-0895

To honor Black Americans for outstanding contributions to society and for achievement in the arts, sciences and humanities. Candidates must be 60 years of age or older and U.S. citizens. Nominations may be submitted by national, state or local civic or non-profit organizations. A plaque is presented annually to six awardees at the Living Legacy Awards Banquet in Washington, D.C. Hotel and travel expenses for awardees are paid by NCBA. Established in 1979.

★2888★
Living Legends Award
National Urban League
500 E. 62nd St.
New York, NY 10021   Ph: (212)310-9000

To recognize Black Americans who have made a significant contribution in their particular field of endeavor. Ten trophies are awarded annually. In addition, Special Legend Awards are presented posthumously. Established in 1987.

★2889★
Lorraine Hansberry Playwriting Award
American College Theatre Festival
John F. Kennedy Center for the
  Performing Arts
Washington, DC 20566   Ph: (202)254-3437

To recognize an outstanding, original play on the Black experience in America written by a student in an undergraduate or graduate program. Plays entered in the Michael Kanin Playwriting Awards Program are eligible. The following monetary prizes are awarded: first prize - $2,500 to the playwright and $750 to the drama department presenting the play; and second prize - $1,000 and $500 to the Theatre Departments of the college(s) and university(ies) producing the play. Awarded annually. Established in 1977. Funded by Penn State University.

★2890★
Martin Luther King, Jr. - Abraham Joshua Heschel Award
B'nai B'rith International
Don King Center for Black-Jewish
  Relations
1640 Rhode Island Ave. NW
Washington, DC 20036   Ph: (202)857-6545

To recognize individuals for continuing commitment to the advancement of equality, human rights and a meaningful relationship between the Black and Jewish communities. A plaque is awarded periodically. Established in 1988 to honor Martin Luther King and Abraham Joshua Heschel, two distinguished clergymen from the Black and Jewish communities who struggled together in the American civil rights movement.

★2891★
Martin Luther King, Jr. Achievement Award
Congress of Racial Equality
30 Cooper Sq.   Ph: (212)598-4000
New York, NY 10003   Fax: (212)982-0184

For recognition of individuals who have accomplished within their chosen field and maintained a commitment to civil and human rights. A sculpture bust of Martin Luther King, Jr. is awarded annually at the King Holiday Dinner. Established in 1985 to commemorate Dr. Martin Luther King, Jr.

★2892★
Martin Luther King, Jr. Nonviolent Peace Prize
Martin Luther King, Jr. Center for
  Nonviolent Social Change, Inc.
449 Auburn Ave. NE   Ph: (404)524-1956
Atlanta, GA 30312   Fax: (404)526-8969

This, the highest award of the Center, is given to honor those persons and/or organizations whose continuing activities have made outstanding contributions to nonviolent social change in the spirit and tradition of Martin Luther King, Jr. The prize recognizes achievements in the eradication of poverty and racism, and the successful quest for alternatives to war. A monetary award of $1,000, a medal depicting Dr. King, a diploma and a citation are awarded annually. Established in 1973 and often presented during the celebration of Dr. King's birthday.

★2893★
Mary Mahoney Award
American Nurses' Association
2420 Pershing Rd.   Ph: (816)474-5720
Kansas City, MO 64108   Fax: (816)471-4903

To honor an individual or group of nurses for significant contributions to opening and advancing equal opportunities in nursing to members of minority groups and who have also made a significant contribution to nursing. The deadline for nominations is October. Awarded biennially. Established in 1936 by the National Association of Colored Graduate Nurses in honor of Mary Eliza Mahoney, the first black graduate nurse in the United States, and her efforts to raise the status of black nurses in professional life. Awarded by the ANA since 1952, following dissolution of the NACGN.

★2894★
McKnight Doctoral Fellowship Program in Arts and Sciences, Mathematics, Business and Engineering
Florida Endowment Fund
201 E. Kennedy Blvd., Ste. 1510   Ph: (813)221-2772
Tampa, FL 33602   Fax: (813)272-2784

To provide up to $5,000 in tuition and fees plus an annual tax-free stipend of $11,000 to 25 African-American citizens to pursue Ph.D. degrees at participating Florida universities. Applicants must hold or be receiving a bachelor's degree from a regionally-accredited college or university. The deadline for applications is January 15. Contingent upon successful academic progress, the maximum length of awards is five years. The Florida Endowment Fund funds the first three years and the student's university continues funding at the same level of support, if required, for a fourth and fifth year. Established in 1984.

★2895★
Metropolitan Life Foundation Award Program for Academic Excellence in Medicine
National Medical Fellowships
254 W. 31st St., 7th Fl.
New York, NY 10001-2813   Ph: (212)714-0933

To recognize and reward minority medical students for outstanding academic achievement and demonstrated leadership. Candidates must be second-or third-year students enrolled in accredited, degree-granting programs leading to the M.D. or D.O. degrees, and must be members of minority groups considered to be underrepresented in medicine by the Association of American Medical Colleges: blacks, American Indians, Mexican-Americans and mainland Puerto Ricans. Medical schools may nominate one candidate for these awards by January 16. Criteria for selection include: (1) Outstanding academic achievement; (2) Leadership; (3) Potential for Distinguished Contributions to Medicine; and (4) Documented Financial Need. Minority students must attend medical school or have legal residence in the following cities or designated surrounding areas: San Francisco, CA; Tampa, FL; Atlanta, GA; Aurora, IL; Wichita, KS; New York, NY; Tulsa, OK; Pittsburgh, PA; Scranton, PA; Warwick, RI; Greenville, SC; and San Antonio, TX. Up to ten need-based awards, valued at $2,500 each, are awarded.

★2896★
Minority Achievement Award
American Physical Therapy Association
APTA Awards Program
1111 N. Fairfax St.   Ph: (703)684-2782
Alexandria, VA 22314   Fax: (703)684-7343

To recognize continuous achievement by an entry-level accredited physical therapy program in the recruitment, admission, retention, and graduation of minority students. The applicant must be accredited by the American Physical Therapy Association. The efforts for minority students must have been ongoing for at least three years. The deadline for entry is December 1. A certificate and monetary award of $1,000 are presented. Established in 1984.

★2897★
Minority Initiatives Award
American Physical Therapy Association
APTA Awards Program
1111 N. Fairfax St.
Alexandria, VA 22314

Ph: (703)684-2782
Fax: (703)684-7343

To recognize the efforts of a physical therapy education program in the initiation and/or improvement of recruitment, admission, retention, and graduation of minority students, and the provision of services for students from racial and ethnic minority groups. Eligible applicants are accredited education programs in physical therapy and physical therapy education programs which have been granted accreditation candidacy status. The deadline for entry is December 1. A monetary prize of $1,000 and a certificate are awarded. Established in 1984.

★2898★
Minority Screenwriter's Development and Promotional Program
American Film Institute Alumni Association
Writers Workshop
PO Box 69799
Los Angeles, CA 90069

Ph: (213)559-4512

To recognize outstanding minority writers and to bring them to the attention of the Hollywood filmmaking community. Ethnic minority screenwriters (Black, Latino, Asian, Native American and Eskimo) may submit screenplays by November 9. Scripts for television pilots and on-going television series are not eligible. Five screenwriters are selected annually to receive tuition, a $500 stipend and a plaque. Established in 1990 by Willard Rodgers, founder/director. Sponsored by the Los Angeles City Office of Cultural Affairs and Walt Disney Studios.

★2899★
Miss Black America
J. Morris Anderson Production Company
PO Box 25668
Philadelphia, PA 19144

Ph: (215)844-8872

To recognize outstanding pageant participants in the categories of swimwear, talent, and personality projection. Cash awards, merchandise, trips, and public appearances are awarded annually in July. Established in 1968. Sponsored by Luster Products.

★2900★
Multicultural Playwrights' Festival
Seattle Group Theatre Company
3940 Brooklyn Ave. NE
Seattle, WA 98105

Ph: (206)545-4969

To develop new plays and to nurture young playwrights. American citizens of Asian, Black, Chicano, Hispanic or Native American descent may submit previously unproduced scripts. A monetary award of $1,000, travel expenses and a two week residency with workshop productions of the winning play are awarded annually to two playwrights. Established in 1984.

★2901★
National Association of Black Journalists Salute to Excellence Awards
National Association of Black Journalists
11600 Sunrise Valley Dr.
Reston, VA 22091

Ph: (703)648-1270

To recognize outstanding stories and photographs that highlight Black people or programs and issues of special concern to the Black community. Entries are judged for impact, sensitivity, quality and significance. An entry can be a single news story, photo or TV or radio program or a series of stories, photos or TV or radio programs on a related subject. Newspaper entries for each category are grouped and judged according to circulation, entries from papers with a circulation of less than 75,000 and entries from papers of a circulation of 75,000 or more. Television entries for each category are judged based on market ranking. Monetary awards of $100 are given in the following categories: (1) Radio Categories: (a) Spot News Reporting; and (b) Public Affairs-Documentary; (2) Print Categories: (a) International Reporting; (b) General News; (c) Feature; (d) Sports; (e) Commentary; and (f) Photojournalism; and (3) Television Categories: (a) International Reporting; (b) General News;

(c) Features; (d) Sports; (e) Documentary; and (f) Photojournalism. The following special awards are also presented: (1) Journalist of the Year Award; (2) Lifetime Achievement Award; and (3) Percy Qoboza Award for Foreign Journalists. Established in 1975. Additional information is available from Carl E. Morris, Sr., Executive Director, PO Box 17212, Washington, DC 20041, phone: (703) 648-1270 or Jackie Greene, *USA Today*, 1000 Wilson Boulevard, Arlington, VA 22209.

★2902★
National Equal Employment/Affirmative Action Exemplary Practices Award
American Society for Public Administration
1120 G St. NW, Ste. 500
Washington, DC 20005

Ph: (202)393-7878

To recognize a person or organization making an outstanding contribution to a more equal society. The emphasis is on achievements and results, not simply effort. The following criteria are considered: (1) Complexity of the problems addressed and organizations directed; (2) Severity of the problems addressed; (3) Use of original/innovative/effective approaches; (4) Impact of contributions, i.e., extent of long-term or lasting benefits of the nominee's accomplishments; and (5) Contributions to the attainment of the goals of ASPA's EO/AA national policy positions. Nominations may be submitted by December 2. Up to four awards are presented to individuals or organizations representing the following categories: (1) Federal, state or local government units; (2) Educational institutions; (3) Non-profit institutions; and (4) Private sector organizations. Plaques are presented annually at the ASPA National Conference.

★2903★
National Medical Fellowships/New York City Health and Hospitals Corporation Health Policy and Management Fellowship Program
National Medical Fellowships
254 W. 31st St., 7th Fl.
New York, NY 10001-2813

Ph: (212)714-0933

To encourage minority medical students to enter careers in health policy, planning and management. Competition for fellowships is open to minority students attending accredited U.S. medical schools who are in good academic standing and show promise for leadership positions in health policy, planning and management. Candidates must be nominated by the medical school deans. Nominations are requested in the summer. Five $4,000 fellowships are presented annually. Fellows spend eight to twelve weeks working with top-level executives of the New York City Health and Hospitals Corporation or with executive directors of HHC municipal hospitals. Established in 1985 with grant support from the Medical Trust of Philadelphia, Pennsylvania and the Booth Ferris Foundation of New York, New York.

★2904★
Paul Robeson Awards
Newark Black Film Festival
The Newark Museum
49 Washington St.
PO Box 540
Newark, NJ 07101

Ph: (201)596-6637
Fax: (201)642-0459

For recognition of excellence in independent filmmaking. The Newark Black Film Festival screens films by black filmmakers and films featuring the history and culture of black people in America and elsewhere. Films completed in the two-year period between awards may be entered in the following categories: (1) documentary; (2) long narrative; (3) short narrative; and (4) experimental. A monetary prize is awarded biennially. Established in 1985 in honor of Paul Robeson. Sponsored by The Newark Museum; Newark Public Library; New Jersey Institute of Technology; Rutgers, The State University, Newark Campus; and Newark Symphony Hall.

★2905★
President's Postdoctoral Fellowship Program
University of California
Office of the President
President's Fellowship Program
300 Lakeside Dr., 18th Fl.   Ph: (510)987-9500
Oakland, CA 94612-3550   Fax: (510)987-9612

To enhance the competitiveness of outstanding minority and women scholars for academic appointments at major research universities. U.S. citizens or permanent residents who hold or will receive a Ph.D. from an accredited university are eligible. Preference is given to minority and women candidates historically underrepresented in higher education. A stipend, research and travel funds, health benefits and intercampus travel are awarded annually. Established in 1984 by the Regents of the University of California.

★2906★
Prized Pieces Competition
National Black Programming Consortium
929 Harrison Ave., Ste. 104
Columbus, OH 43215   Ph: (614)299-5355

For recognition of superior artistic achievement in the development, production, and presentation of programming that depicts black people and their cultures from throughout the world positively. Awards are given in the following categories: (1) Public Affairs/News; (2) Cultural Affairs; (3) Children/Teens; (4) Drama; (5) Documentary; (6) Innovative; and (7) Comedy. Producers, distributors or individuals may submit any Black-oriented television programs with Blacks in primary roles that enrich the understanding of lifestyles, culture, and the concerns of Blacks. The deadline is October 3. Monetary prizes and plaques are awarded annually at the Prized Pieces Awards Ceremony. Established in 1981.

★2907★
Ralph J. Bunche Award
American Political Science Association
1529 New Hampshire Ave. NW
Washington, DC 20036   Ph: (202)483-2512

For recognition of the best scholarly work in political science published within the previous year that explores the phenomenon of ethnic and cultural pluralism. Books must be nominated by the publisher. A monetary prize of $500 is awarded annually. Established in 1978 in memory of Ralph J. Bunche, a prominent black world statesman and diplomat.

★2908★
Reginald H. Jones Distinguished Service Award
NACME
Reginald H. Jones Award
3 W. 35th St., Third Fl.   Ph: (212)279-2626
New York, NY 10001-2281   Fax: (212)279-5178

To recognize individuals whose efforts have resulted in increased minority participation in the nation's engineering workforce. A $10,000 grant donated in the name of the recipient to a tax-exempt organization working in the minority engineering effort and a plaque are awarded annually. Established in 1983 to honor Reginald H. Jones, the former chairman and CEO of the General Electric Company, whose pioneering leadership helped initiate the minority engineering effort.

★2909★
Renault Robinson Award
National Black Police Association
1919 Pennsylvania Ave. NW, Ste. 300
Washington, DC 20006   Ph: (202)457-0563

To recognize a member who has served the black community during the year. A plaque is awarded annually. Established to honor Renault Robinson, for his courageous efforts to provide equal rights and justice to all citizens and for being outspoken on equal employment opportunities for black police officers nationwide.

★2910★
Rhythm and Blues Award Show
Baruch Entertainment
1331 F St. NW, Ste. 800   Ph: (202)833-1777
Washington, DC 20004   Fax: (202)737-0725

To recognize outstanding black rhythm and blues and rap artists. Awards are presented in numerous categories, including: (1) Top Rap Artist; (2) Top Male Vocalist; (3) Top Single and Top Album; (4) Most Promising Male Vocal Group; (5) Most Promising Female Group; (6) Top New Female Group; (7) Most Promising New Male Vocalist; and (8) Top Female Rap Vocalist. Winnes are chosen by *Black Radio Exclusive Magazine*. Established in 1980. Additional information is available from WAQT Productions, c/o John Jackson, 200 E. 94th St., Ste. 910, New York, NY 10128, phone: (212) 722-4463.

★2911★
Robie Award for Achievement in Industry
Jackie Robinson Foundation
80 8th Ave., 20th Fl.   Ph: (212)675-1511
New York, NY 10011   Fax: (212)675-9157

To recognize outstanding corporate leaders who have worked to improve the plight of minorities in economic development. Chief executive officers who have guided their company to improve the plight of minorities in economic development are eligible. A medallion is awarded annually at the Awards Dinner Dance. Established in 1980 in memory of Jackie Robinson.

★2912★
Robie Award for Humanitarianism
Jackie Robinson Foundation
80 8th Ave., 20th Fl.   Ph: (212)675-1511
New York, NY 10011   Fax: (212)675-9157

To recognize outstanding individuals who have devoted their lives to the promotion of human dignity and social justice. Individuals who have contributed through their advocacy of human rights and/or social justice to enrich lives and secure a more equitable world are eligible. Awarded annually. Estblished in 1979 to honor Jackie Robinson.

★2913★
Rosetta LeNoire Award
Actors' Equity Association
165 W. 46th St.   Ph: (212)869-8530
New York, NY 10036   Fax: (212)921-8454

To recognize those theatres and producing organizations under an Equity contract which are exemplary in the hiring of ethnic minority and female actors through affirmative action, multi-racial and non-traditional casting. Nominations are of a theatre producing organization are accepted by October 31. Established in 1989 by the Ethnic Minorities Committee.

★2914★
Rosina Tucker Award
A. Philip Randolph Institute
260 Park Ave. S., 6th Fl.
New York, NY 10010   Ph: (212)533-8000

For recognition of the contribution to the strengthening of the Black-labor alliance in the spirit of A. Philip Randolph. Nomination is by the Executive Committee of the Institute and approval by the National Board. A plaque is awarded annually. Established in 1989 in honor of Rosina Tucker, former President of Ladies' Auxillary of the Brotherhood of Sleeping Car Porters.

★2915★
S. Randolph Edmonds Playwriting Award
National Association of Dramatic and
  Speech Arts
309 Cherokee Dr.
Blacksburg, VA 24060-1823   Ph: (703)552-6862

To honor the best play written on the black experience. Established in 1975 by S. Randolph Edmonds, Founder of NADSA.

★2916★
Samuel Z. Westerfield Award
National Economic Association
School of Business
University of Michigan   Ph: (313)763-0121
Ann Arbor, MI 48109-1234   Fax: (313)763-5688

To recognize and encourage scholarly work by black economists. Selection is based on outstanding contributions as both a scholar and an economist. A plaque is awarded periodically, usually every two years.

★2917★
Scholarship Award
National Association of Black Women
 Attorneys
3711 Macomb St. NW   Ph: (202)966-9693
Washington, DC 20016   Fax: (202)244-6648

To provide a scholarship for black women law students. Several scholarships are presented annually at the Red Dress Ball at the Convention. Established in 1978 by Attorney Mabel D. Haden, Washington, DC, with contributions from various businesses, lawyers and concerned citizens.

★2918★
Small Business Advocates of the Year
U.S. Small Business Administration
c/o Office of Public Communicators
1441 L St. NW
Washington, DC 20416   Ph: (202)653-6365

To recognize individuals in various professions who have significantly increased awareness of small business concerns or created opportunities for small business to succeed. Advocates of the Year are recognized in each of the 50 states, the District of Columbia, and Puerto Rico for their efforts in the following areas of importance to small businesses: (1) accountant advocate; (2) banker advocate; (3) media advocate; (4) minority advocate; (5) veteran advocate; and (6) women in business advocate. State winners are then eligible for national recognition. The criteria for selection are: engaging in civic and community activities that promote small business; volunteering services to assist small firms experiencing management, financial, or legal problems; sponsoring or participating in legislative or regulatory initiatives; communicating publicly through speech or the written word; actively participating in small business organizations; or pursuing initiatives that will help a large number of small businesses. Nominations are accepted. Awards are presented during Small Business Week in May. Established in 1978.

★2919★
Social Justice Award
Western Reserve Historical Society
10825 East Blvd.   Ph: (216)721-5722
Cleveland, OH 44106-1788   Fax: (216)721-0645

To recognize individuals and organizations that have distinguished themselves in the area of social justice as promulgated by Dr. King. A plaque is awarded annually at the Martin Luther King, Jr. Celebration Program. Established in 1991 in memory of Dr. Martin Luther King, Jr. Administered by the African American Archives Auxiliary of the Society.

★2920★
Spingarn Medal
National Association for the Advancement
 of Colored People
4805 Mt. Hope Dr.
Baltimore, MD 21215-3297   Ph: (410)358-8900

To recognize the highest achievement of an American Negro. The purpose of the medal is twofold: to call the attention of the American people to the existence of distinguished merit and achievement among American Negroes; and to serve as a reward for such achievement, and as a stimulus to the ambition of colored youth. Men and women of African descent and American citizenship who shall have made the highest achievement during the preceding year or years in any honorable field of human endeavor are eligible. Nominations may be submitted by January 1. A gold medal is presented at the annual convention of the National Association for the Advancement of Colored People, and the presentation speech is delivered by a distinguished citizen. Established in 1914 by the late J.E. Spingarn, then Chairman of the Board of Directors of the National Association for the Advancement of Colored People. The award honors Joel E. Spingarn, President of the NAACP, 1930-1939.

★2921★
Unity Awards in Media
Lincoln University - Missouri
Dept. of Communications
201 Elliff Hall
Jefferson City, MO 65101   Ph: (314)681-5436

To recognize the media for excellence in reporting on issues affecting minorities and the disadvantaged, and to emphasize the national goals the media serves in improving understanding among all peoples. In the past, the Human Relations Citation was basically restricted to coverage of the Black American. Entries may be submitted from print and broadcast media in the United States in the following categories: (1) Reporting of Economics; (2) Reporting of Education; (3) Investigative Reporting; (4) Reporting of Politics; (5) Editorial Writing; and (6) Public Affairs/Social Issues Reporting. The contest is open to any print or broadcast person working for a recognized daily, weekly, monthly or quarterly publication including newspapers and magazines as well as radio and television stations. Submissions are evaluated in both regional and national categories. The deadline for submission is January 6. A trophy is presented annually. Established in 1949 by Armistead S. Pride, Professor Emeritus of Journalism and former Head of the Department.

★2922★
Western Political Science Association Awards
Western Political Science Association
c/o Dept. of Political Science
Univ. of Utah   Ph: (916)278-7737
Salt Lake City, UT 84112   Fax: (916)278-6959

To recognize outstanding unpublished papers in the field of political science. The following awards are presented: (1) Dissertation Award - $250 for the best doctoral dissertation completed at a university within the regional groupings of the WPSA between July 1 and June 30 of the previous academic year; (2) Pi Sigma Alpha Award - $200 for the best paper presented at the last WPSA annual meeting; (3) WPSA Women and Politics Awards - $100 for an outstanding paper on women and politics; (4) WPSA Best Paper Award on Chicano Politics - $100 for an outstanding paper by a Chicano scholar on Chicano politics and its relative aspects; and (5) Award by Committee on the Status of Blacks - $100 for an outstanding paper discussing issues and problems which concern most Black Americans.

★2923★
**Whitney M. Young, Jr. Memorial Football Classic
 Award**
New York Urban League
218 W. 40th St., 6th Fl.
New York, NY 10018   Ph: (212)730-5200

To recognize an individual for the ideals of leadership, character, and sportsmanship that honor the memory of Whitney M. Young, Jr. A plaque is awarded at the Annual Football Classic in the fall. Established in 1971. Sponsored by the New York Yankees in association with the New York Urban League and the New York Daily News. The proceeds from the Football Classic help support scholarships at the participating schools - Grambling and North Carolina Central - and fund the New York Urban League's Whitney M. Young Jr. Memorial Scholarship Program, which was established in 1978. Traditionally ten students are awarded scholarships of $1,500 each.

★2924★
William and Charlotte Cadbury Award
National Medical Fellowships
254 W. 31st St., 7th Fl.
New York, NY 10001-2813   Ph: (212)714-0933

To recognize the outstanding achievement of a fourth year minority medical student. Academic achievement, leadership, and social consciousness are criteria for the award. A monetary prize of $2,000 and a certificate of merit are awarded annually. Established in 1977 by Dr. Irving Graef in honor of the organization's former Executive Director and Staff Associate.

★2925★
William Edward Burghardt Du Bois Medal
National Association for the Advancement
  of Colored People
4805 Mt. Hope Dr.
Baltimore, MD 21215-3297   Ph: (410)358-8900

To recognize individuals who are not citizens of the United States for exceptional contributions to the protection of human rights and furtherance of international understanding, fraternity and fundamental freedoms. Men or women whose lives exemplify the tradition of service to mankind; who perform extraordinary acts of moral courage; and whose work promotes civil rights and democratic principles are eligible. Nominations may be submitted by May 15. A medal is awarded annually. Established in 1985.

★2926★
William L. Dawson Award for Legislative Development
Congressional Black Caucus Foundation
Special Events Director
1004 Pennsylvania Ave. SE   Ph: (202)675-6735
Washington, DC 20003   Fax: (202)547-3806

To recognize an individual who has made significant research, organizational and leadership contributions in the development of legislation that addresses the needs of minorities in the United States. Members of the Congressional Black Caucus nominate individuals for the award. A plaque is awarded annually. Established in 1981.

★2927★
**William T. Grant Behavior Development Research
  Fellowship Program**
National Medical Fellowships
254 W. 31st St., 7th Fl.
New York, NY 10001-2813   Ph: (212)714-0933

To foster minority student research interest in the areas of stress and coping among school-age children. The program also encourages pursuit of academic careers in child psychiatry, behavior development research and health policy. The fellowship competition is open to minority students attending accredited U.S. medical schools who are in good academic standing and show promise for careers in child psychiatry, behavior development research or mental health policy. Candidates must be nominated by the medical school deans by September. National Medical Fellowships annually selects five students through a national competition. Fellows will spend eight to twelve weeks working with senior staff of the Prevention Research Center, a project of the Department of Mental Hygiene at The Johns Hopkins University School of Hygiene and Public Health in Baltimore, Maryland. Five fellowships of $3,500 each are presented annually. Established in 1986 with grant support from the William T. Grant Foundation of New York, New York.

★2928★
Young Publisher Award
Association of Black Nursing Faculty in
  Higher Education
5823 Queens Cove
Lisle, IL 60532   Ph: (708)969-3809

To recognize members for a manuscript which addresses either the health care needs of African-American patients/communities/families or is related to the educational needs of African-American faculty/students. Manuscripts published during the preceding year are eligible. A plaque is awarded annually at the national convention. Established in 1989.

★2929★
Young Researcher Award
Association of Black Nursing Faculty in
  Higher Education
5823 Queens Cove
Lisle, IL 60532   Ph: (708)969-3809

To recognize members who have received funding for research related to either the African-American patient/family/community or

faculty/student. A plaque is awarded annually at the annual meeting. Established in 1989.

★2930★
Youth Leadership Award
Western Reserve Historical Society
10825 East Blvd.   Ph: (216)721-5722
Cleveland, OH 44106-1788   Fax: (216)721-0645

For recognition of outstanding youth in Cleveland. A plaque is awarded annually at the Martin Luther King, Jr. Celebration Program. Established in 1991 in memory of Dr. Martin Luther King, Jr. Administered by the African American Archives Auxiliary of the Society.

(11) Federal Government Agencies

★2931★
U.S. Commission on Civil Rights
1121 Vermont Ave., N.W.
Washington, DC 20425   Ph: (202)523-5571
Arthur A. Fletcher, Chairman

★2932★
U.S. Commission on Civil Rights
Central Region
Old Federal Bldg.
911 Walnut St., Rm. 3103
Kansas City, MO 64106   Ph: (816)426-5253
Melvin Jenkins, Regional Director

Territory Includes: AL, AK, IA, KS, LA, MS, MO, NE.

★2933★
U.S. Commission on Civil Rights
Eastern Region
624 9th St., NW, Rm. 500
Washington, DC 20425   Ph: (202)376-7533
John I. Binkley, Regional Director

Territory Includes: CT, DE, DC, ME, MD, MA, NH, NJ, NY, PA, RI, VT, VA, WV.

★2934★
U.S. Commission on Civil Rights
Midwestern Region
175 W. Jackson St.
Chicago, IL 60604   Ph: (312)353-8311
Constance D. Davis, Reg. Dir.

Territory Includes: Illinois, Indiana, Michigan, Minnesota, Ohio, and Wisconsin.

★2935★
U.S. Commission on Civil Rights
Rocky Mountain Region
1700 Broadway
Denver, CO 80290   Ph: (303)866-1040
William Muldrow, Reg. Dir.

Territory Includes: Colorado, Montana, North Dakota, South Dakota, Utah, and Wyoming.

★2936★
U.S. Commission on Civil Rights
Southern Region
101 Marietta St.
Atlanta, GA 30303   Ph: (404)730-2476
Bobby Doctor, Reg. Dir.

Territory Includes: Florida, Georgia, Kentucky, North Carolina, South Carolina, and Tennessee.

★2937★
U.S. Commission on Civil Rights
Western Region
3660 Wilshire Blvd., Suite 810
Los Angeles, CA 90010   Ph: (213)894-3437
Philip Montez, Regional Director

Territory Includes: AL, AR, CA, HI, NV, NM, OK, OR, TX, WA.

★2938★
U.S. Department of Agriculture
Food and Nutrition Service
Civil Rights/Equal Employment Opportunity Division
3101 Park Center Dr.
802 Parkoffice Ctr.
Alexandria, VA 22302   Ph: (703)305-2195
Larry A. Brantley, Director

★2939★
U.S. Department of Agriculture
Office of Advocacy and Enterprise
Equal Opportunity Services
14th St. and Independence Ave., SW
1349 S. Agriculture Bldg.
Washington, DC 20250   Ph: (202)720-5681
Robert Franco, Associate Director

★2940★
U.S. Department of Agriculture
Office of Small and Disadvantaged Business
   Utilization
14th St. and Independence Ave., SW,
1323 S. Agriculture Bldg.
Washington, DC 20250   Ph: (202)720-7117
Belinda Ward, Acting Associate Director

★2941★
U.S. Department of Commerce
Economic Development Administration
Office of Program Support
Compliance Review Division—Civil Rights
Herbert Clark Hoover Bldg.
14th St. and Constitution Ave., NW, Rm.
  7019
Washington, DC 20230   Ph: (202)482-5575
David E. Lasky, Chief

★2942★
U.S. Department of Commerce
Minority Business Development Agency
Herbert Clark Hoover Bldg.
14th St. and Constitution Ave., NW, Rm.
  5055
Washington, DC 20230   Ph: (202)482-5061
Jose Lira, Director

★2943★
U.S. Department of Commerce
Minority Business Development Agency
Atlanta Region
The Summit Bldg.
401 Peachtree, Ste. 1930
Atlanta, GA 30308-3516   Ph: (404)730-3300
Carlton L. Eccles, Regional Director
Territory Includes: AL, FL, GA, KY, MS, NC, SC, TN.

★2944★
U.S. Department of Commerce
Minority Business Development Agency
Chicago Region
55 E. Monroe St., Ste. 1440
Chicago, IL 60630   Ph: (312)353-0182
David Vega, Regional Director
Territory Includes: IL, IN, IA, KS, MI, MN, MO, NE, OH, WI.

★2945★
U.S. Department of Commerce
Minority Business Development Agency
Dallas Region
1100 Commerce St., Rm. 7-B23
Dallas, TX 75242   Ph: (214)767-8001
Melda C. Cabrera, Regional Director
Territory Includes: AR, CO, LA, MT, NM, ND, OK, SD, TX, UT, WY.

★2946★
U.S. Department of Commerce
Minority Business Development Agency
New York Region
26 Federal Plaza, Rm. 3720
Jacob K. Javits Federal Bldg.
New York, NY 10278   Ph: (212)264-3262
John F. Inglehart, Regional Director
Territory Includes: CT, ME, MA, NH, NJ, NY, PR, RI, VT, VI.

★2947★
U.S. Department of Commerce
Minority Business Development Agency
San Francisco Region
221 Main St., Rm. 1280
San Francisco, CA 94105   Ph: (415)744-3001
Xavier Mena, Regional Director
Territory Includes: AK, American Samoa, AZ, CA, HI, ID, NV, OR,
WA.

★2948★
U.S. Department of Commerce
Minority Business Development Agency
Washington, DC Region
1255 22nd St., Rm. 701
Washington, DC 20230   Ph: (202)377-1356
Georginia A. Sanchez, Regional Director
Territory Includes: DE, DC, MD, PA, VA, WV.

★2949★
U.S. Department of Commerce
Office of Civil Rights
14th St. and Constitution Ave., NW, Rm.
  6010
Washington, DC 20230   Ph: (202)482-0625
Gerald R. Lucas, Director

★2950★
U.S. Department of Commerce
Office of Civil Rights
Equal Employment Opportunity Programs
14th St. and Constitution Ave., N.W.
Washington, DC 20230   Ph: (202)377-5691

★2951★
U.S. Department of Commerce
Office of Small and Disadvantaged Business
  Utilization
14th St. and Constitution Ave., NW, Rm.
  6411
Washington, DC 20230   Ph: (202)482-3387
James P. Maruca, Director

★2952★
U.S. Department of Education
Assistant Secretary for Postsecondary Education
Higher Education Programs
Minorities and Women/Howard University
7th and D Sts., SW, Rm. 3915
Washington, DC 20202   Ph: (202)708-5656
Cosette Ryan, Program Director

★2953★
U.S. Department of Education
Assistant Secretary for Postsecondary Education
Higher Education Programs
Minority Science Improvement Program
7th and D Sts., SW
Washington, DC 20202   Ph: (202)708-4662
Argelia Velez-Rodriquez, Sr. Science Education Officer

★2954★
U.S. Department of Education
Assistant Secretary for Postsecondary Education
Historically Black Colleges and Universities
7th and D Sts., SW, Rm. 3682
Washington, DC 20202   Ph: (202)708-8667
Hazel Mingo, Director

★2955★
U.S. Department of Education
Civil Rights Office
Region I, Boston
McCormack Post Office and Courthouse,
  Rm. 222
Boston, MA 02109   Ph: (617)223-9667
Thomas Habino, Regional Director
Territory Includes: CT, ME, MA, NH, RI, VT.

★2956★
U.S. Department of Education
Civil Rights Office
Region II, New York
26 Federal Plaza, Rm. 36-118
New York, NY 10278   Ph: (212)264-4633
Paula Kuebler, Regional Director
Territory Includes: NY, NJ, PR, VI.

★2957★
U.S. Department of Education
Civil Rights Office
Region III, Philadelphia
3535 Market St., Rm. 6300
Philadelphia, PA 19104-3326   Ph: (215)596-6787
Dr. Robert Smallwood, Regional Director
Territory Includes: DE, DC, MD, PA, VA, WV.

★2958★
U.S. Department of Education
Civil Rights Office
Region IV, Atlanta
101 Marietta St., Ste. 2702
Atlanta, GA 30301   Ph: (404)331-2954
Achier B. Meyer, Regional Director
Territory Includes: AL, FL, GA, NC, SC, TN.

★2959★
U.S. Department of Education
Civil Rights Office
Region V, Chicago
401 S. State St., Rm. 700C
Chicago, IL 60605   Ph: (312)886-3456
Kenneth Mines, Regional Director
Territory Includes: IL, IN, MI, MN, OH, WI.

★2960★
U.S. Department of Education
Civil Rights Office
Region VI, Dallas
1200 Main Tower Bldg.
Dallas, TX 75202   Ph: (214)767-3959
Taylor D. August, Regional Director
Territory Includes: AR, LA, MS, NM, OK, TX.

★2961★
U.S. Department of Education
Civil Rights Office
Region VII, Kansas City
10220 N. Executive Hills Blvd., 8th Fl.
Kansas City, MO 64153-1367   Ph: (816)891-8026
Charles J. Nowell, Regional Director
Territory Includes: IA, KS, KY, MO, NE.

★2962★
U.S. Department of Education
Civil Rights Office
Region VIII, Denver
1244 Speer Blvd., Rm. 310
Denver, CO 80204   Ph: (303)844-5695
Cathy Louis, Regional Director
Territory Includes: CO, MT, ND, NV, NM, SD, UT, WY.

★2963★
U.S. Department of Education
Civil Rights Office
Region IX, San Francisco
50 U.N. Plaza, Rm. 205
San Francisco, CA 94102   Ph: (415)556-7000
John E. Palomino, Regional Director
Territory Includes: CA.

★2964★
U.S. Department of Education
Civil Rights Office
Region X, Seattle
915 2nd Ave., Rm. 3310
Seattle, WA 98174-1099   Ph: (206)220-7900
Gary Jackson, Regional Director
Territory Includes: AK, HI, ID, NV, OR, WA, Guam, American Somoa, Pacific Islands.

★2965★
U.S. Department of Education
Office of Hearings and Appeals
Civil Rights Reviewing Authority
490 E. L'Enfant Plaza
Washington, DC 20202   Ph: (202)732-1828
Frank Furey, Director

★2966★
U.S. Department of Education
Office of Small and Disadvantaged Business
  Utilization
400 Maryland Ave., SW, Rm. 3120, R0B3
Washington, DC 20202-0521   Ph: (202)708-9820
Daniel L. Levin, Director

★2967★
U.S. Department of Education
Office of the Secretary
Assistant Secretary for Civil Rights
330 C St., SW, Rm. 5000
Mary E. Switzer B1
Washington, DC 20202   Ph: (202)205-5413
Jeanette Lim, Acting Assistant Secretary

★2968★
U.S. Department of Energy
Office of Administration and Management
Office of Equal Opportunity
Affirmative Action Programs Division
Forrestal Bldg.
1000 Independence Ave., SW, Rm. 4B-
  112
Washington, DC 20585   Ph: (202)586-8010
John J. Pagano, Director

★2969★
U.S. Department of Energy
Office of Minority Economic Impact
Forrestal Bldg.
1000 Independence Ave., SW
Washington, DC 20585   Ph: (202)586-8383
Gloria B. Smith, Director

★2970★
U.S. Department of Energy
Office of Minority Economic Impact
Minority Energy Information Clearinghouse
Forrestal Bldg.
1000 Independence Ave., S.W., Rm. 5B-
  110
Washington, DC 20585   Ph: (202)586-5876
Ann Young, Officer

★2971★
U.S. Department of Energy
Office of Small and Disadvantaged Business
  Utilization
1707 H St., NW, Rm. 905
Washington, DC 20585   Ph: (202)254-5583
Leonel V. Miranda, Director

★2972★
U.S. Department of Health and Human Services
Administration for Children and Families
Office of Equal Opportunity and Civil Rights
370 L'Enfant Promenade SW, Rm. 701
Washington, DC 20447   Ph: (202)401-4784
David L. Shorts, Director

★2973★
U.S. Department of Health and Human Services
Administration on Children, Youth and Families
Head Start Bureau
330 C St., SW, Rm. 2054
Washington, DC 20201   Ph: (202)245-8572
Douglas Klafehn, Acting Associate Commissioner

★2974★
U.S. Department of Health and Human Services
Assistant Secretary for Management and Budget
Office of Budget
Office of Equal Employment Opportunity
330 Independence Ave., SW, Rm. 4317
Washington, DC 20201   Ph: (202)619-1564
Barbara Aulenbach, Director

★2975★
U.S. Department of Health and Human Services
Assistant Secretary for Management and Budget
Small and Disadvantaged Business Utilization and
   Civil Rights
200 Independence Ave., SW, Rm. 513D
Humphrey Bldg.
Washington, DC 20201   Ph: (202)690-7300
Verl Zanders, Acting Director

★2976★
U.S. Department of Health and Human Services
Assistant Secretary for Personnel
   Administration/Director of Equal Employment
   Opportunity
200 Independence Ave. SW, Rm. 522A
Washington, DC 20201   Ph: (202)690-7284
Thomas S. McFee, Asst. Secretary and Dir.

★2977★
U.S. Department of Health and Human Services
Civil Rights Office
Region I, Boston
J.F. Kennedy Federal Bldg., Rm. 1875
Government Center
Boston, MA 02203   Ph: (617)565-1340
Caroline Chang, Regional Manager

★2978★
U.S. Department of Health and Human Services
Civil Rights Office
Region II, New York
26 Federal Plaza, Rm. 3312
New York, NY 10278   Ph: (212)264-3313
John J. Gomez, Regional Manager

★2979★
U.S. Department of Health and Human Services
Civil Rights Office
Region III, Philadelphia
3535 Market
Philadelphia, PA 19101   Ph: (215)596-1262
Paul Cushing, Regional Manager

★2980★
U.S. Department of Health and Human Services
Civil Rights Office
Region IV, Atlanta
101 Marietta Tower
Atlanta, GA 30323   Ph: (404)331-2779
Marie A. Chretien, Regional Manager

★2981★
U.S. Department of Health and Human Services
Civil Rights Office
Region V, Chicago
105 W. Adams, 16th Fl.
Chicago, IL 60603   Ph: (312)886-2359
Charlotte Irons, Regional Manager

★2982★
U.S. Department of Health and Human Services
Civil Rights Office
Region VI, Dallas
1200 Main Tower Bldg., Ste. 1360
Dallas, TX 75202   Ph: (214)767-4056
Davis Sanders, Regional Manager

★2983★
U.S. Department of Health and Human Services
Civil Rights Office
Region VII, Kansas City
601 E. 12th St.
Federal Bldg.
Kansas City, MO 64106   Ph: (816)426-7277
Lois Carter, Regional Manager

★2984★
U.S. Department of Health and Human Services
Civil Rights Office
Region VIII, Denver
Federal Bldg.
1961 Stout St.
Denver, CO 80294   Ph: (303)844-2024
Vada Kyle-Holmes, Regional Manager

★2985★
U.S. Department of Health and Human Services
Civil Rights Office
Region IX, San Francisco
50 United Nations Plaza, Rm. 322
San Francisco, CA 94102   Ph: (415)556-8586
Virginia Apodaca, Regional Manager

★2986★
U.S. Department of Health and Human Services
Civil Rights Office
Region X, Seattle
2201 6th Ave., Mailstop RX-11
Seattle, WA 98121   Ph: (206)553-7483
Carmen Palomera-Rockwell, Regional Manager

★2987★
U.S. Department of Health and Human Services
Office for Civil Rights
330 Independence Ave., SW, Rm. 5400
Washington, DC 20201   Ph: (202)619-0403
Edward Mercado, Director

★2988★
U.S. Department of Health and Human Services
Office for Civil Rights
Equal Employment Opportunity/Affirmative Action
330 Independence Ave., SW, Rm. 5400,
   Cohen Bldg.
Washington, DC 20201   Ph: (202)619-0585
Ronald Copeland, Acting Director

★2989★
U.S. Department of Health and Human Services
Office of Human Development Services
Office of Equal Opportunity and Civil Rights
200 Independence Ave., SW, Rm. 339
Washington, DC 20201   Ph: (202)245-1787
David L. Shorts, Director

★2990★
U.S. Department of Health and Human Services
Office of the General Counsel
Civil Rights Division
330 Independence Ave., SW, Rm. 5059
Washington, DC 20201   Ph: (202)619-0900
George Lyon, Associate General Counsel

★2991★
U.S. Department of Health and Human Services
Public Health Service
Assistant Secretary for Health
Office of Minority Health
5515 Security Lane, Ste. 1102
Rockville, MD 20852   Ph: (301)443-5084
Claudia R. Baquet, Director

★2992★
U.S. Department of Health and Human Services
Public Health Service
Centers for Disease Control and Prevention
Minority Health
Bldg. 1, 1600 Clifton Rd., NE, Rm. 2122
Atlanta, GA 30333   Ph: (404)639-3703
Rueben C. Warren, Associate Director

★2993★
U.S. Department of Health and Human Services
Public Health Service
Food and Drug Administration
Office of Equal Employment and Civil Rights
Park Lawn Bldg., 5600 Fishers Lane, Rm.
  894
Rockville, MD 20857   Ph: (301)443-5541
Rosamelia De la Rocha, Director

★2994★
U.S. Department of Health and Human Services
Public Health Service
National Institutes of Health
Equal Opportunity Office
9000 Rockville Pike, Bldg. 31, Rm. 2B40
Bethesda, MD 20892   Ph: (301)496-6301
Diane E. Armstrong, Director

★2995★
U.S. Department of Health and Human Services
Public Health Service
National Institutes of Health
Office of Minority Health
9000 Rockville Pike, Bldg. 1, Rm. 260
Bethesda, MD 20892   Ph: (301)402-1366
John Ruffin, Associate Director

★2996★
U.S. Department of Health and Human Services
Public Health Service
Office of Equal Opportunity and Civil Rights
Park Lawn Bldg., 5600 Fishers Lane, Rm.
  14-25
Rockville, MD 20857   Ph: (202)443-5636
J. Calvin Adams, Administrator

★2997★
U.S. Department of Housing and Urban Development
Assistant Secretary for Community Planning and
  Development
Office of Block Grant Assistance
451 7th St., SW, Rm. 7286
Washington, DC 20410   Ph: (202)708-3587
Don Patch, Director

★2998★
U.S. Department of Housing and Urban Development
Assistant Secretary for Fair Housing and Equal
  Opportunity
451 7th St., SW, Rm. 5100
Washington, DC 20410   Ph: (202)708-4252
Roberta Achtenberg, Assistant Secretary

★2999★
U.S. Department of Housing and Urban Development
Assistant Secretary for Fair Housing and Equal
  Opportunity
Office of Operations and Management
Office of Affirmative Action and Equal Employment
  Opportunity
451 7th St. SW, Rm. 5246
Washington, DC 20201   Ph: (202)708-2033
William O. Anderson, Dir.

★3000★
U.S. Department of Housing and Urban Development
Office of Fair Housing and Equal Opportunity
Region I, Boston
O'Neill Federal Bldg
10 Causeway St.
Boston, MA 02222-1092   Ph: (617)565-5304
Robert W. Laplante, Director

★3001★
U.S. Department of Housing and Urban Development
Office of Fair Housing and Equal Opportunity
Region II, New York
26 Federal Plaza
New York, NY 10278-0068   Ph: (212)264-1290
Stanley Seidenfeld, Director

★3002★
U.S. Department of Housing and Urban Development
Office of Fair Housing and Equal Opportunity
Region III, Philadelphia
105 S. Seventh St.
Philadelphia, PA 19106-3392   Ph: (215)597-2338
Walter Valentine, Acting Director

★3003★
U.S. Department of Housing and Urban Development
Office of Fair Housing and Equal Opportunity
Region IV, Atlanta
75 Spring St., SW, Ste. 230
Atlanta, GA 30303   Ph: (404)331-5140
Katheline Coughlin, Director

★3004★
U.S. Department of Housing and Urban Development
Office of Fair Housing and Equal Opportunity
Region V, Chicago
77 W. Jackson
Chicago, IL 60604   Ph: (312)353-7776
Thomas Higginbothan, Director

★3005★
U.S. Department of Housing and Urban Development
Office of Fair Housing and Equal Opportunity
Region VI, Ft. Worth
PO Box 2905
Ft. Worth, TX 76113-2905   Ph: (817)885-5491
John E. Wright, Director

★3006★
U.S. Department of Housing and Urban Development
Office of Fair Housing and Equal Opportunity
Region VII, Kansas City
400 State Ave.
Gateway 2 Bldg.
Kansas City, KS 66101   Ph: (913)236-3958
Floyd May, Director

★3007★
U.S. Department of Housing and Urban Development
Office of Fair Housing and Equal Opportunity
Region VIII, Denver
1405 Curtis St., 27th Fl.
Executive Tower N.
Denver, CO 80202   Ph: (303)844-4751
Lloyd R. Miller, Director

★3008★
U.S. Department of Housing and Urban Development
Office of Fair Housing and Equal Opportunity
Region IX, San Francisco
450 Golden Gate Ave.
San Francisco, CA 94102   Ph: (415)556-6826
LaVera Gillespie, Director

★3009★
U.S. Department of Housing and Urban Development
Office of Fair Housing and Equal Opportunity
Region X, Seattle
1321 2nd
Mailstop 10-E
Seattle, WA 98101   Ph: (206)220-5170
James Brown, Director

★3010★
U.S. Department of Housing and Urban Development
Office of Small and Disadvantaged Business
  Utilization
Minority Business
451 7th St., SW, Rm. 10234
Washington, DC 20410   Ph: (202)708-3350
Clarence White, Coordinator

★3011★
U.S. Department of Housing and Urban Development
Office of the General Counsel
Office of Equal Opportunity and Administrative Law
451 7th St., SW Rm. 10244
Washington, DC 20410   Ph: (202)708-2203
Carole W. Wilson, Associate General Counsel

★3012★
U.S. Department of Housing and Urban Development
Office of the Secretary
Martin Luther King, Jr. Federal Holiday Commission
449 Auburn Ave. NE
Atlanta, GA 30312   Ph: (404)730-3155
Lloyd Davis, Exec. Dir.

★3013★
U.S. Department of Justice
Civil Rights Division
10th St. and Constitution Ave., NW, Rm.
  5643
Washington, DC 20530   Ph: (202)514-2151

★3014★
U.S. Department of Justice
Justice Management Division
Office of Small and Disadvantaged Business
  Utilization
12 Pennsylvania Ave. NW, Rm. 3235
Washington, DC 20530   Ph: (202)616-0521
Joseph Bryan, Director

★3015★
U.S. Department of Justice
Office of Justice Programs
Office for Civil Rights
633 Indiana Ave. NW, Rm. 600C
Washington, DC 20530   Ph: (202)307-0690
Inez Alfonzo-Lasso, Dir.

★3016★
U.S. Department of Labor
Office of Administration and Management
Directorate of Civil Rights
200 Constitution Ave., NW
Washington, DC 20210   Ph: (202)219-8927
Annabelle T. Lockhart, Director

★3017★
U.S. Department of Labor
Office of Administration and Management
Directorate of Civil Rights
Office of Equal Employment Opportunity and
  Affirmative Action
200 Constitution Ave., NW, Rm. N4123
Washington, DC 20210   Ph: (202)219-6362
Andre Carl Whisenton, Division Chief

★3018★
U.S. Department of Labor
Office of Small Business and Minority Affairs
200 Constitution Ave., NW, Rm. C2318
Washington, DC 20210   Ph: (202)219-9148
June M. Robinsen, Director

★3019★
U.S. Department of Labor
Office of the Solicitor
Civil Rights Division
200 Constitution Ave. NW
Washington, DC 20210   Ph: (202)219-8286
James D. Henry, Associate Solicitor

★3020★
U.S. Department of State
Bureau of Human Rights and Humanitarian Affairs
2201 C St., N.W., Rm. 7802
Washington, DC 20520   Ph: (202)647-2126
Patricia Diaz Dennis, Assistant Secretary

★3021★
U.S. Department of State
Office of Small and Disadvantaged Business
  Utilization
SA-6, Rm. 633.
Washington, DC 20520   Ph: (703)875-6824
Durie N. White, Acting Operations Director

★3022★
U.S. Department of State
Office of the Secretary
Equal Employment Opportunity and Civil Rights Office
2201 C St., NW, Rm. 4216
Washington, DC 20520   Ph: (202)647-9294
Thomas Jefferson, Associate Director

★3023★
U.S. Department of State
Office of the Secretary
Equal Employment Opportunity and Civil Rights Office
Affirmative Action Outreach
2201 C St., NW, Rm. 4216
Washington, DC 20520   Ph: (202)647-7824
Gloria J. Jackson, Coordinator

★3024★
U.S. Department of the Interior
Policy, Management, and Budget
Office of Small and Disadvantaged Business
  Utilization
1849 C St. NW, Rm. 272
Washington, DC 20240   Ph: (202)208-3493
Kenneth T. Kelly, Director

★3025★
U.S. Department of the Interior
Policy, Management, and Budget
Office of the Assistant Secretary
Office of Equal Opportunity
1849 C Street NW, Rm. 1324
Washington, DC 20240   Ph: (202)208-5693
Carmen R. Maymi, Director

★3026★
U.S. Department of the Interior
Policy, Management, and Budget
Office of the Assistant Secretary
Office of Historically Black College and University
  Programs and Job Corps
1849 C St. NW, Rm. 2759
Washington, DC 20240   Ph: (202)208-6403
Ira J. Hutchison, Director

★3027★
U.S. Department of Transportation
Coast Guard, United States
Office of Acquisition
Contract Support Division—Small and Minority
  Business
2100 2nd St., SW, Rm. 5218
Washington, DC 20593   Ph: (202)267-2499
Danni S. Wildason, Specialist

★3028★
U.S. Department of Transportation
Coast Guard, United States
Office of Civil Rights
2100 2nd St., SW, Rm. 2400
Washington, DC 20593   Ph: (202)267-1562
Walter R. Somerville, Chief

★3029★
U.S. Department of Transportation
Federal Aviation Administration
Assistant Administrator for Civil Rights
800 Independence Ave., SW, Rm. 1030
Washington, DC 20590   Ph: (202)267-3254
Leon C. Watkins, Assistant Administrator

★3030★
U.S. Department of Transportation
Federal Aviation Administration
Office of Civil Rights
Historically Black Colleges and Universities
800 Independence Ave., SW, Rm. 1030
Washington, DC 20590   Ph: (202)267-3267
George Thomas, Program Manager

★3031★
U.S. Department of Transportation
Federal Highway Administration
Office of Civil Rights
400 7th St., SW, Rm. 4132
Washington, DC 20590   Ph: (202)366-0693
Edward W. Morris Jr., Director

★3032★
U.S. Department of Transportation
Federal Highway Administration
Office of Civil Rights
Program Operations Division
400 7th St., SW, Rm. 4132
Washington, DC 20590   Ph: (202)366-2925
George F. Duffy, Division Chief

★3033★
U.S. Department of Transportation
Federal Railroad Administration
Civil Rights Office
400 7th St., SW
Washington, DC 20590   Ph: (202)366-0482
Miles S. Washington Jr., Officer

★3034★
U.S. Department of Transportation
Federal Transit Administration
Office of Civil Rights
400 7th St., SW
Washington, DC 20590   Ph: (202)366-4018
Susan Schruth, Acting Director

★3035★
U.S. Department of Transportation
National Highway Traffic Safety Administration
Office of Civil Rights
400 7th St., SW, Rm. 5201
Washington, DC 20590   Ph: (202)366-4762
George Anick, Director

★3036★
U.S. Department of Transportation
Office of Civil Rights
400 7th St., SW, Rm. 10215
Washington, DC 20590   Ph: (202)366-4648
William T. Hudson, Director

★3037★
U.S. Department of Transportation
Office of Civil Rights
Minority Colleges and Universities
400 7th St., SW, Rm. 10215
Washington, DC 20590   Ph: (202)366-5997
William T. Hudson, Director

★3038★
U.S. Department of Transportation
Office of Small and Disadvantaged Business
  Utilization
Minority Business Resource Center
400 7th St., SW, Rm. 9410
Washington, DC 20590   Ph: (202)366-2852
Joe Capuano, Chief

★3039★
U.S. Department of Transportation
Research and Special Programs Administration
Office of Civil Rights
400 7th St., SW, Rm. 8419
Washington, DC 20590   Ph: (202)366-9638
Judith Foist, Director

★3040★
U.S. Environmental Protection Agency
Office of Civil Rights
401 M St., SW, Rm. W206
Washington, DC 20460   Ph: (202)260-4575
Dan J. Rondeau, Director

★3041★
U.S. Environmental Protection Agency
Office of Civil Rights
National Black Employment Programs
401 M St., SW, Rm. W206
Washington, DC 20460   Ph: (202)260-7495
Ronald Blakely, Manager

★3042★
U.S. Environmental Protection Agency
Office of Small and Disadvantaged Business
  Utilization
401 M St., SW, Mailstop A-149C
Washington, DC 20460   Ph: (703)305-7777
Leon Hampton Jr., Director

★3043★
U.S. Equal Employment Opportunity Commission
1801 L St., NW, Rm. 10006
Washington, DC 20507   Ph: (202)663-4001
Evan J. Kemp Jr., Chairman

★3044★
U.S. Equal Employment Opportunity Commission
Atlanta District Office
75 Piedmont Ave., NE, Ste. 1100
Atlanta, GA 30335   Ph: (404)331-0604
Chris Roggerson, Director
Territory Includes: GA.

★3045★
U.S. Equal Employment Opportunity Commission
Baltimore District Office
111 Market Pl., Ste. 4000
Baltimore, MD 21202   Ph: (301)962-3932
Issie L. Jenkins, Director
Territory Includes: MD, VA.

★3046★
U.S. Equal Employment Opportunity Commission
Birmingham District Office
1900 3rd Ave., N., Ste. 101
Birmingham, AL 35203   Ph: (205)731-0082
Warren A. Bullock, Director

★3047★
U.S. Equal Employment Opportunity Commission
Charlotte District Office
5500 Central Ave.
Charlotte, NC 28212   Ph: (704)567-7100
Marsha Drane, Director
Territory Includes: NC, SC.

★3048★
U.S. Equal Employment Opportunity Commission
Chicago District Office
536 S. Clark St., Rm. 930-A
Chicago, IL 60605   Ph: (312)353-2713
John P. Rowe, Director
Territory Includes: Nothern IL.

★3049★
U.S. Equal Employment Opportunity Commission
Cleveland District Office
1375 Euclid Ave., Rm. 600
Cleveland, OH 44115   Ph: (216)522-2001
Harold Ferguson, Director
Territory Includes: OH.

★3050★
U.S. Equal Employment Opportunity Commission
Dallas District Office
8303 Elmbrook Dr., 2nd Fl.
Dallas, TX 75247   Ph: (214)767-7015
Jacqueline R. Bradley, Director
Territory Includes: OK, TX (northern).

★3051★
U.S. Equal Employment Opportunity Commission
Denver District Office
1845 Sherman St., 2nd Fl.
Denver, CO 80203   Ph: (303)866-1300
Francisco J. Flores, Director
Territory Includes: CO, MT, NE, ND, SD, WY.

★3052★
U.S. Equal Employment Opportunity Commission
Detroit District Office
477 Michigan Ave., Rm. 1540
Detroit, MI 48226   Ph: (313)226-7636
A. William Schukar, Director
Territory Includes: MI.

★3053★
U.S. Equal Employment Opportunity Commission
Houston District Office
1919 Smith St., 7th Fl.
Houston, TX 77002   Ph: (713)653-3373
Harriet J. Ehrlich, Director

★3054★
U.S. Equal Employment Opportunity Commission
Indianapolis District Office
101 W. Ohio St., 18th Fl.
Indianapolis, IN 46204   Ph: (317)266-7212
Thomas P. Hadfield, Director
Territory Includes: IN, KY (Louisville only).

★3055★
U.S. Equal Employment Opportunity Commission
Los Angeles District Office
255 E. Temple St., 4th Fl.
Los Angeles, CA 90010   Ph: (213)894-1000
Dr. Dorothy Porter, Director
Territory Includes: CA (southern), NV.

★3056★
U.S. Equal Employment Opportunity Commission
Memphis District Office
1407 Union Ave., Ste. 621
Memphis, TN 38104   Ph: (901)722-2617
Walter S. Grabon, Director
Territory Includes: KY (except Louisville), TN.

★3057★
U.S. Equal Employment Opportunity Commission
Miami District Office
1 NE First St., 6th Fl.
Miami, FL 33132   Ph: (305)536-4491
Frederico Costales, Director
Territory Includes: FL, Panama Canal Zone.

★3058★
U.S. Equal Employment Opportunity Commission
Milwaukee District Office
310 W. Wisconsin Ave., Ste. 800
Milwaukee, WI 53203 Ph: (414)297-1111
Chester V. Bailey, Director
Territory Includes: IA, MN, WI.

★3059★
U.S. Equal Employment Opportunity Commission
New Orleans District Office
701 Loyola Ave., Ste. 600
New Orleans, LA 70113 Ph: (504)589-2329
Patricia Fields Bivins, Director
Territory Includes: AR, LA.

★3060★
U.S. Equal Employment Opportunity Commission
New York District Office
90 Church St., Rm. 1501
New York, NY 10007 Ph: (212)264-7161
Spencer H. Lewis Jr., Director
Territory Includes: CT, ME, MA, NH, NY, PR, VT, VI.

★3061★
U.S. Equal Employment Opportunity Commission
Office of Federal Operations
Federal Sector Programs
Affirmative Employment Programs Division
2401 E St., NW
Washington, DC 20507 Ph: (202)634-7833
Louis Jones, Branch Chief

★3062★
U.S. Equal Employment Opportunity Commission
Office of Program Operations
Federal Sector Programs
Affirmative Employment Programs Division
1801 L St. NW
Washington, DC 20507 Ph: (202)663-7039
James Troy, Director

★3063★
U.S. Equal Employment Opportunity Commission
Philadelphia District Office
1421 Cherry St., 10th Fl.
Philadelphia, PA 19102 Ph: (215)656-7020
Johnny J. Butler, Director
Territory Includes: DE, NJ, PA, WV.

★3064★
U.S. Equal Employment Opportunity Commission
Phoenix District Office
4520 N. Central Ave., Ste. 300
Phoenix, AZ 85012 Ph: (602)640-5000
Charles D. Burtner, Director
Territory Includes: AZ, NM, UT.

★3065★
U.S. Equal Employment Opportunity Commission
St. Louis District Office
625 N. Euclid St., 5th Fl.
St. Louis, MO 63108 Ph: (314)425-6585
Lynn Bruner, Director
Territory Includes: KS, MO.

★3066★
U.S. Equal Employment Opportunity Commission
San Antonio District Office
5410 Fredericksburg Rd., Ste. 200
San Antonio, TX 78229 Ph: (210)229-4810
Pedro Esquivel, Director
Territory Includes: TX(southern).

★3067★
U.S. Equal Employment Opportunity Commission
San Francisco District Office
901 Market St., Ste. 500
San Francisco, CA 94103 Ph: (415)744-6500
Paul Montanez, Director
Territory Includes: AS, CA(northern), Commonwealth of the Northern Mariana Islands, GU, HI, Wake Islands.

★3068★
U.S. Equal Employment Opportunity Commission
Seattle District Office
2815 Second Ave., Ste. 500
Seattle, WA 98121 Ph: (206)553-0968
Jeanette M. Leino, Director
Territory Includes: AK, ID, OR, WA.

★3069★
U.S. Equal Employment Opportunity Commission
Washington District Office
1400 L St., NW, Ste. 200
Washington, DC 20005 Ph: (202)275-7377
Susan Reilly, Director
Territory Includes: DC.

★3070★
U.S. General Accounting Office
Civil Rights Office
441 G St., NW, Rm. 3019
Washington, DC 20548 Ph: (202)512-6388
Nilda Aponte, Director

★3071★
U.S. Information Agency
Bureau of Management
Office of Equal Employment Opportunity and Civil Rights
301 4th St., SW, Rm. 365
Washington, DC 20547 Ph: (202)619-5151
Brenda Johnson, Acting Director

★3072★
U.S. National Aeronautics and Space Administration
Office of Equal Opportunity Programs
300 E St. SW, Rm. 3A20
Washington, DC 20546 Ph: (202)358-2167
Yvonne B. Freeman, Associate Administrator

★3073★
U.S. National Aeronautics and Space Administration
Office of Equal Opportunity Programs
Affirmative Action
300 E St. SW, 3rd Fl.
Washington, DC 20546 Ph: (202)358-0963
James R. Cole Sr., Program Manager
Alfonso Ludi

★3074★
U.S. National Aeronautics and Space Administration
Office of Equal Opportunity Programs
Discrimination Complaints Division
300 E St. SW., 3rd Fl.
Washington, DC 20546 Ph: (202)358-0942
Oceola S. Hall, Director

★3075★
U.S. National Aeronautics and Space Administration
Office of Equal Opportunity Programs
Minority University Research and Education Programs
300 E St., SW, 2nd Fl.
Washington, DC 20546 Ph: (202)358-0971
Samuel E. Massenberg, Director

★3076★
U.S. National Aeronautics and Space Administration
Office of Equal Opportunity Programs
Minority University Research and Education Programs
Historically Black Colleges and Universities
300 E St., SW, 2nd Fl.
Washington, DC 20546   Ph: (202)358-0948
Sheree Stovall Alexander, Program Manager

★3077★
U.S. National Aeronautics and Space Administration
Office of Equal Opportunity Programs
Minority University Research and Education Programs
Other Minority Universities
300 E St., SW, 2nd Fl.
Washington, DC 20546   Ph: (202)453-2173
Bettie L. White, Program Manager

★3078★
U.S. National Aeronautics and Space Administration
Office of Small and Disadvantaged Business
  Utilization
Minority Business
300 E St. SW, Rm 9K70
Washington, DC 20546   Ph: (202)358-2088
Rae C. Martel, Advisor

★3079★
U.S. Office of Personnel Management
Office of Equal Employment Opportunity
1900 E St., NW, Rm. 5431
Washington, DC 20415   Ph: (202)606-2460
Teresa Alzamora del Rio, Assistant Director

★3080★
U.S. Office of Personnel Management
Office of the Deputy Director
Administration Group
1900 E St. NW
Washington, DC 20415   Ph: (202)606-2180
Leutrell Osborne, Small/Disadvantaged Bus. Utilization Sp.

★3081★
U.S. Small Business Administration
Associate Deputy Administrator for Management and
  Administration
Office of Civil Rights Compliance
Ofice of Equal Opportunity and Compliance
409 3rd St. SW, 4th Fl.
Washington, DC 20416   Ph: (202)205-6750
J. Arnold Feldman, Chief

★3082★
U.S. Small Business Administration
Associate Deputy Administrator for Management and
  Administration
Office of Equal Employment Opportunity and
  Compliance
409 3rd St. SW, 4th Fl.
Washington, DC 20416   Ph: (202)205-6750
George H. Robinson, Director

★3083★
U.S. Small Business Administration
Minority Small Business and Capital Ownership
  Development
409 3rd St. SW
Washington, DC 20416   Ph: (202)205-6410
Judith A. Watts, Associate Administrator

★3084★
U.S. Small Business Administration
Minority Small Business and Capital Ownership
  Development
Minority Small Business Outreach Division
409 3rd St. SW
Washington, DC 20416   Ph: (202)205-6421
Bernita M. Kane, Dir.

★3085★
U.S. Small Business Administration
Minority Small Business and Capital Ownership
  Development
Region I, Boston
155 Federal St., 9th Fl.
Boston, MA 02110   Ph: (617)451-2036
Barbara Manning, Assistant Administrator

★3086★
U.S. Small Business Administration
Minority Small Business and Capital Ownership
  Development
Region II, New York
26 Federal Plaza, Rm. 3100
New York, NY 10278   Ph: (212)264-1046
Sheila Thomas, Assistant Administrator

★3087★
U.S. Small Business Administration
Minority Small Business and Capital Ownership
  Development
Region III, Philadelphia
475 Allendale Rd., Ste. 201
King of Prussia, PA 19406   Ph: (215)962-3758
Dayton Watkins, Assistant Administrator

★3088★
U.S. Small Business Administration
Minority Small Business and Capital Ownership
  Development
Region IV, Atlanta
1375 Peachtree St., NE
Atlanta, GA 30367-8102   Ph: (404)347-4089
Isaiah Washington, Assistant Administrator

★3089★
U.S. Small Business Administration
Minority Small Business and Capital Ownership
  Development
Region V, Chicago
230 S. Dearborn St., Rm. 570
Chicago, IL 60604   Ph: (312)353-4361
Gary Peele, Assistant Administrator

★3090★
U.S. Small Business Administration
Minority Small Business and Capital Ownership
  Development
Region VI, Dallas
8625 King George Dr., Bldg. C
Dallas, TX 75235-3391   Ph: (214)767-7631
Lavan Alexander, Assistant Administrator

★3091★
U.S. Small Business Administration
Minority Small Business and Capital Ownership
  Development
Region VII, Kansas City
911 Walnut St., 13th Fl.
Kansans City, MO 64106   Ph: (816)426-3516
Art Seibert, Assistant Administrator

★3092★
U.S. Small Business Administration
Minority Small Business and Capital Ownership
  Development
Region VIII Denver
999 18th St., Ste. 701
Denver, CO 80202   Ph: (303)294-7076
Ralph Layman, Acting Assistant Administrator

★3093★
U.S. Small Business Administration
Minority Small Business and Capital Ownership
  Development
Region IX, San Francisco
71 Stevenson St., 20th Fl.
San Francisco, CA 94105   Ph: (415)774-6429
R. Stephen Bangs, Assistant Regional Administrator

★3094★
U.S. Small Business Administration
Minority Small Business and Capital Ownership
  Development
Region X, Seattle
2615 4th Ave., Ste. 440
Seattle, WA 98121   Ph: (206)553-0391
Carol Colpitts, Assistant Regional Administrator

★3095★
U.S. Smithsonian Institute
National Museum of African Art
950 Independence Ave., SW, Rm. 2127
Washington, DC 20560   Ph: (202)357-4600
Sylvia H. Williams, Director

★3096★
U.S. Smithsonian Institute
National Museum of American History
Department of Social and Cultural History
Community Life Division—Black American Culture
14th St. and Constitution Ave. NW, Rm.
  4112
Washington, DC 20560   Ph: (202)357-2735
Ann C. Golovin

★3097★
U.S. Smithsonian Institute
National Museum of American History
Department of Social and Cultural History
Political History Division—Black History and Civil
  Rights
14th St. and Constitution Ave. NW, Rm.
  4108
Washington, DC 20560   Ph: (202)357-2008
Lonnie G. Bunch, Curator

★3098★
U.S. Smithsonian Institution
Office of Equal Opportunity and Minority Affairs
915 L'Enfant Plaza, SW
Washington, DC 20560   Ph: (202)287-3487
Era Marshall, Director

★3099★
U.S. Smithsonian Institution
Office of Equal Opportunity and Minority Affairs
Affirmative Action Program
915 L'Enfant Plaza, SW
Washington, DC 20560   Ph: (202)287-3508
Carol Gover, Manager

(12) Federal Domestic Assistance Programs

★3100★
Georgia Equal Opportunity Commission
710 Cain Tower, Peachtree Center
229 Peachtree St. NE   Ph: (404)656-1736
Atlanta, GA 30303   Fax: (404)656-4399
Carla A. Ford, Administrator

★3101★
U.S. Commission on Civil Rights
Clearinghouse Services, Civil Rights Discrimination
   Complaints (29.001)
1121 Vermont Ave., NW
Washington, DC 20425   Ph: (202)376-8177

Types of Assistance: Dissemination of technical information.
Applicant Eligibility: Anyone can seek information; no criteria must
be satisfied. **Beneficiary Eligibility:** General public. **Range and
Average of Financial Assistance:** Not applicable.

★3102★
U.S. Department of Agriculture
Office of Advocacy and Enterprise
Special Emphasis Outreach Programs Grants (10.140)
14th and Independence Ave., SW
Washington, DC 20250   Ph: (202)447-2019
Obie Patterson

Types of Assistance: Project Grants, Advisory Services, and
Counseling. **Applicant Eligibility:** Public, private, state, and other
colleges, universities and related institutions of higher learning
whose activities meet the required criteria of encouraging minority
participation in agricultural sciences. **Beneficiary Eligibility:** Same
as above. **Range and Average of Financial Assistance:** 5,000.00
to 25,000.00.

★3103★
U.S. Department of Commerce
Economic Development Administration
Economic Development - Business Development
   Assistance (11.301)
Herbert C. Hoover Bldg., Rm. H7844
Washington, DC 20230   Ph: (202)377-5067
Steven R. Brennen, Deputy Assistant Secretary, Loan Program

Types of Assistance: Loan guarentees/grants. **Applicant
Eligibility:** Private lending institutions lending to private borrowers
whose projects have been approved for assistance by the state or
political sub-division in which the project to be finanaced is located.
Beneficiary Eligibility: Borrowers must be privately owned firms,
which may include, but is not limited to, sole proprietorships,
partnerships, public or private corporations, or employee stock
ownership trust. **Range and Average of Financial Assistance:**
$500,000.00 to $111,100,000.00; $2,000,000.00.

★3104★
U.S. Department of Commerce
Economic Development Administration
Economic Development - Grants for Public Works and
   Development Facilities (11.300)
Public Works Division
Herbert C. Hoover Bldg., Rm. H7326
Washington, DC 20230   Ph: (202)482-5265
David L. McIlwain, Director

Types of Assistance: Project grants. **Applicant Eligibility:** States,
cities, counties, and other political subdivisions, and private or public
nonprofit organizations or associations representing a
redevelopment area or a designated Economic Development Center
are eligible to receive grants. Corporations and associations
organized for profit are not eligible. **Beneficiary Eligibility:**
Unemployed and underemployed persons and/or members of low-
income families. **Range and Average of Financial Assistance:** No
specific minimum or maximum project amount - $80,160.00 to
$2,316,572.00; $742,831.00.

★3105★
U.S. Department of Commerce
Economic Development Administration
Special Economic Development and Adjustment
   Assistance Program - Sudden and Severe Economic
   Dislocation and Long-term Economic Deterioration
   (11.307)
Economic Adjustment Division
Herbert C. Hoover Bldg., Rm. H7327
Washington, DC 20230   Ph: (202)482-2659
David L. McIlwain, Director

Types of Assistance: Project grants. **Applicant Eligibility:** States,
cities, counties or other political subdivisions of a State, consortia of
such political subdivisions, public or private nonprofit organizations
representing redevelopment areas designated under the Public
Works and Economic Development Act of 1965. **Beneficiary
Eligibility:** Grants may be used in direct expenditures by the eligible
recipient or through redistribution by the recipient to public and
private entities, in the form of grants, loans, loan guarantees, or
other appropriate assistance except that grants may not be made to
for-profit entities. **Range and Average of Financial Assistance:** No
specific minimum or maximum size.

★3106★
U.S. Department of Commerce
Independent Education and Science Projects and
**   Programs (11.449)**
Environmental Research Laboratories
1335 East-West Hwy.
Silver Spring, MD 20910   Ph: (301)713-2458

Types of Assistance: Project Grants. **Applicant Eligibility:**
Nonprofit community organizations administering a Math,
Engineering, Science Achievement (MESA) program, or a math and
science volunteer tutoring program. **Beneficiary Eligibility:**
Organizations and individuals with interests in improving college
enrollment in math and science, as well as math and science
competency of primary and secondary students. **Range and**
Average of Financial Assistance: $5,000.00 to $10,000.00.

★3107★
U.S. Department of Commerce
Minority Business Development Agency
Minority Business Development Centers (11.800)
Office of Operations, Rm. 5063
14th and Constitution Ave., NW
Washington, DC 20230   Ph: (202)377-8015
Bharat Bhargava, Assistant Director

Types of Assistance: Project grants. **Applicant Eligibility:** No
restrictions. **Beneficiary Eligibility:** Recipient is to provide
assistance to minority-owned businesses or minorities interested in
starting a business. **Range and Average of Financial Assistance:**
$165,000.00 to $622,000.00; $212,000.00.

★3108★
U.S. Department of Commerce
Minority Business Development Agency
Minority Business Resource Development (11.802)
Office of Program Development, Rm. 5096
14th and Constitution Ave., NW
Washington, DC 20230   Ph: (202)377-5770
Theresa Speake, Assistant Director

Types of Assistance: Project grants (cooperative agreements).
Applicant Eligibility: Restricted to established business, industry,
professional and trade associations, and chambers of commerce.
Beneficiary Eligibility: Same as above. **Range and Average of**
Financial Assistance: $25,000.00 to $320,000.00.

★3109★
U.S. Department of Education
Office of Assistant Secretary for Elementary and
**   Secondary Education**
Desegregation Assistance, Civil Rights Training, and
**   Advisory Services (84.004)**
Equity and Educational Excellence Division
400 Maryland Ave., SW
Washington, DC 20202-6438   Ph: (202)408-0360
Sylvia Wright

Types of Assistance: Project grants. **Applicant Eligibility:** State
educational agencies, and for desegregation assistance centers, any
private nonprofit organization or any public agency (other than SEA
or school board). **Beneficiary Eligibility:** Educational personnel and
elementary and secondary students in eligible local school districts.
Range and Average of Financial Assistance: For DACs:
$500,000.00 to $900,000.00; $720,000.00; For SEAs: $71,500.00
to $700,000.00; $268,811.00.

★3110★
U.S. Department of Education
Office of Assistant Secretary for Elementary and
**   Secondary Education**
Magnet Schools Assistance in Desegregating Districts
**   (84.165)**
Equity and Educational Excellence Division
Rm. 2040, FB6
400 Maryland Ave., SW
Washington, DC 20202-6440   Ph: (202)401-0360
Sylvia Wright

Types of Assistance: Project grants. **Applicant Eligibility:** Local
educational agencies. **Beneficiary Eligibility:** Local educational

agencies and participating students. **Range and Average of**
Financial Assistance: $210,018.00 to $3,592,891.00.

★3111★
U.S. Department of Education
Office of Assistant Secretary for Postsecondary
**   Education**
Grants to Institutions to Encourage Women and
**   Minority Participation in Graduate Education (84.202)**
Division of Higher Education Incentive
    Programs
Washington, DC 20202-5251   Ph: (202)708-9393
Walter T. Lewis

Types of Assistance: Project grants. **Applicant Eligibility:**
Accredited institutions of higher education and consortia of such
institutions. **Beneficiary Eligibility:** Institutions receiving the awards
will provide direct fellowship aid to undergraduate students accepted
and approved by the institution to prepare them for graduate
studies. **Range and Average of Financial Assistance:** Estimated
range of awards: $30,989.00 to $100,000.00; $82,000.00.

★3112★
U.S. Department of Education
Office of Assistant Secretary for Postsecondary
**   Education**
Minority Science Improvement (84.120)
Division of Higher Education Incentive
    Programs
Washington, DC 20202-5251   Ph: (202)708-4662
Argelia Velez-Rodriguez

Types of Assistance: Project grants. **Applicant Eligibility:** Private
and public accredited two- and four-year institutions of higher
education whose enrollments are predominantly (50% or more)
American Indian, Alaskan Native, Black (not Hispanic origin),
Hispanic, Pacific Islander, or any combination of these or other
ethnic minorities who are underrepresented in science and
engineering. Proposals may also be submitted by professional
scientific societies, and all nonprofit accreditied colleges and
universities. **Beneficiary Eligibility:** Same as above; also nonprofit
science-oriented organizations, professional scientific societies, and
all nonprofit accredited colleges and universities. **Range and**
Average of Financial Assistance: $19,500.00 to $467,256.00;
$254,124.00 for Institutional; $448,400.00 for Cooperative;
$19,500.00 for Design Projects, and $55,431.00 for Special
Projects.

★3113★
U.S. Department of Education
Office of Assistant Secretary for Postsecondary
**   Education**
Upward Bound (84.047)
Division of Student Services
Education Outreach Branch
400 Maryland Ave., SW, Rm. 3060
Regional Office Bldg. 3
Washington, DC 20202-5249   Ph: (202)708-4804
Goldia Hodgdon

Types of Assistance: Project grants. **Applicant Eligibility:**
Institutions of higher education, public and private agencies and
organizations, and in exceptional cases, secondary public schools.
Beneficiary Eligibility: Low-income individuals and potential first
generation college students who have a need for academic support
in order to successfully pursue a program for postsecondary
education. Two-thirds of the participants must be low-income
individuals who are also potential first generation college students.
The remaining participants must be either low-income individuals or
potential first generation college students. Except for veterans, who
can be served regardless of age, project participants must be
between 13 and 19 years old and have completed the eighth grade,
but have not entered the twelfth grade (exceptions allowed). **Range**
and Average of Financial Assistance: $118,103.00 to
$575,590.00; $236,842.00. Math/Science Regional Centers:
$88,347.00 to $241,144.00; $180,3 58.00.

★3114★
U.S. Department of Energy
Office of Minority Economic Impact
Management and Technical Assistance for Minority
  Business Enterprises (81.082)
Forrestal Bldg., Rm. 5B-110
Washington, DC 20585   Ph: (202)586-1594
Sterling Nichols

Types of Assistance: Advisory services and counseling. **Applicant Eligibility:** Minority business enterprises. **Beneficiary Eligibility:** Minority business enterprises wanting to do business with the Department of Energy. **Range and Average of Financial Assistance:** Not applicable.

★3115★
U.S. Department of Energy
Office of Minority Economic Impact
Minority Educational Institution Research Travel Fund
  (81.083)
Forrestal Bldg., Rm. 5B-110
Washington, DC 20585   Ph: (202)586-1593
Isiah O. Sewell

Types of Assistance: Direct payments for specified use. **Applicant Eligibility:** Minority postsecondary educational institutions personnel. **Beneficiary Eligibility:** Faculty members and graduate students involved in an energy research related planning project. **Range and Average of Financial Assistance:** $200.00 to $800.00; $500.00.

★3116★
U.S. Department of Energy
Office of Minority Economic Impact
Minority Energy Information Clearinghouse (81.085)
Forrestal Bldg., Rm. 5B-110
Washington, DC 20585   Ph: (202)586-5876
Effie A. Young

Types of Assistance: Dissemination of techinical information. **Applicant Eligibility:** No restrictions. **Beneficiary Eligibility:** Scholars and members of organizations doing energy-related research and minority business enterprises. **Range and Average of Financial Assistance:** Not applicable.

★3117★
U.S. Department of Energy
Office of Minority Economic Impact
Minority Honors Training and Industrial Assistance
  Program (81.084)
Forrestal Bldg., Rm. 5B-110
Washington, DC 29585   Ph: (202)586-1593
Isiah O. Sewell

Types of Assistance: Project grants. **Applicant Eligibility:** Limited to minority honor students attending participating two-year postsecondary institutions offering programs in at least four energy-related areas of study. **Beneficiary Eligibility:** Financially needy minority honor students. **Range and Average of Financial Assistance:** $33,000.00 to $78,500.00; $59,000.00.

★3118★
U.S. Department of Energy
Office of Minority Economic Impact
Office of Minority Economic Impact Loans (81.063)
Forrestal Bldg., Rm. 5B-110
Washington, DC 20585   Ph: (202)586-1594
Sterling Nichols

Types of Assistance: Direct loans. **Applicant Eligibility:** A firm, including sole proprietorship, corporation, association, or partnership, which is at least 50% owned or controlled by a member of a minority or a group of members of a minority. Control means direct or indirect possession of the power to direct or cause the direction of management and policies, whether through the ownership of voting securities, by contract or otherwise. **Beneficiary Eligibility:** Minority business enterprises. **Range and Average of Financial Assistance:** Program temporarily suspended.

★3119★
U.S. Department of Health and Human Services
Family Support Administration
Work Incentive Program (93.790)
Office of Family Assistance
Washington, DC 20201   Ph: (202)535-0174
Ronald E. Putz, Executive Director

Types of Assistance: Formula grants. **Applicant Eligibility:** WIN services are available in all States as well as in Washington, DC, Puerto Rico, the Virgin Islands, and Guam. **Beneficiary Eligibility:** Applicants and recipients of Aid to Families with Dependent Children (AFDC) who are required by law to register with WIN or who choose to register voluntarily. **Range and Average of Financial Assistance:** $94,000.00 to $12,677,000.00; $1,713,907.00.

★3120★
U.S. Department of Health and Human Services
National Institutes of Health, Public Health Service
Minority Biomedical Research Support (93.375)
National Institute of General Medical
  Sciences
Bethesda, MD 20892   Ph: (301)496-6745
Dr. Ciriaco Gonzales, Director

Types of Assistance: Project grants. **Applicant Eligibility:** Four-year colleges, universities, and health professional schools with over 50% minority enrollment; four-year institutions with significant, but not necessarily over 50% minority enrollment, provided they have a history of encouragement and assistance to minorities; two-year colleges with 50% minority enrollment. **Beneficiary Eligibility:** Minority students and facutly, and investigators at eligible institutions. **Range and Average of Financial Assistance:** $50,000.00 to $1,200,000.00 per year for three to four years.

★3121★
U.S. Department of Health and Human Services
Office of Human Development Services
Head Start (93.600)
PO Box 1182
Washington, DC 20013   Ph: (202)205-8569

Types of Assistance: Project grants. **Applicant Eligibility:** Any local government, federally-recognized Indian tribe, or, public or private nonprofit agency which meets the requirements may apply for a grant. Grantee agencies may subcontract with other child-serving agencies to provide service to Head Start children. **Beneficiary Eligibility:** Head Start programs are primarily for children from age 3 up to the age when the child enters the school system, but may include some younger children. No less than 10% of the total enrollment opportunities in Head Start programs in each State shall be available for children with disabilities. **Range and Average of Financial Assistance:** $7,490.00 to $68,067,055.00.

★3122★
U.S. Department of Health and Human Services
Office of the Secretary
Civil Rights Compliance Activities (93.675)
Office of Director
5032 Cohen Bldg.
330 Independence Ave., SW
Washington, DC 20201   Ph: (202)245-6403

Types of Assistance: Investigation of complaints; dissemination of techinical information. **Applicant Eligibility:** Anyone who believes he or she has been discriminated against and recipients of Federal financial assistance who desire technical assistance and information of the purpose of assuring their compliance with nondiscrimination laws. **Beneficiary Eligibility:** Individual subject to discrimination and recipients who require technical assistance and information. **Range and Average of Financial Assistance:** Not applicable.

★3123★
U.S. Department of Health and Human Services
Public Health Service
Epidemiologic Research Studies of (AIDS) and (HIV)
Infection in Selected Population Groups (93.943)
Center for Disease Control
1600 Clifton Rd. NE
MS-E-45
Atlanta, GA 30333   Ph: (404)639-6130

Types of Assistance: Project Grants. **Applicant Eligibility:** States, political subdivisions of states or their agents or instrumentalities, and other public and private nonprofit organizations. **Beneficiary Eligibility:** State and local health agencies; public and private nonprofit organizations; minority groups; and persons physically afflicted with AIDS/HIV infection. **Range and Average of Financial Assistance:** $83,766.00 to $2,036,531.00; $380,000.00.

★3124★
U.S. Department of Health and Human Services
Public Health Service
National Institutes of Health
Minority Access to Research Careers (93.880)
National Institute of General Medical
  Sciences
Bethesda, MD 20892   Ph: (301)496-7941
Elward Bynum, Program Director

Types of Assistance: Project grants. **Applicant Eligibility:** Any non-federal public or private nonprofit four-year university or college with substantial enrollment of ethnic minority students may apply for the institutional National Research Service Awards. To be eligible for funding, a proposal must first receive favorable recommendations from a scientific review committee and a national advisory council. Individual National Research Service awardees must be nominated and sponsored by a public or nonprofit private institution having staff and facilities appropriate to the proposed research training program. All awardees must be citizens or have been admitted to the United States for permanent residence. **Beneficiary Eligibility:** Any non-federal public or private nonprofit four-year university or college with a substantial enrollment of ethnic minorities. **Range and Average of Financial Assistance:** $21,000.00 to $503,000.00; $64,088.00.

★3125★
U.S. Department of Health and Human Services
Public Health Service
Office of the Assistant Secretary for Health
Minority Community Health Coalition Demonstration
(93.137)
Office of Minority Health
Rockwall II Bldg., Ste. 800
5515 Security Ln.
Rockville, MD 20852   Ph: (301)227-8769
Joan S. Jacobs

Types of Assistance: Project grants. **Applicant Eligibility:** Public and private nonprofit organizations. **Beneficiary Eligibility:** Members of the four major minority groups: Asian/Pacific Islanders, Blacks, Hispanics, Native American, or a subgroups of any of these groups. **Range and Average of Financial Assistance:** $200,000.00.

★3126★
U.S. Department of Housing and Urban Development
Office of Fair Housing and Equal Opportunity
Equal Opportunity in Housing (14.400)
Assistant Secretary for Fair Housing and
  Equal Opportunity   Ph: (202)708-4252
Washington, DC 20410   Free: 800-669-9777

Types of Assistance: Investigation of complaints. **Applicant Eligibility:** Any aggrieved person, or the Assistant Secretary, may file a complaint after an alleged discriminatory housing practice occurs because of a person's race, color, religion, sex, familial status, handicap, or national origin. **Beneficiary Eligibility:** Individuals. **Range and Average of Financial Assistance:** Not applicable.

★3127★
U.S. Department of Housing and Urban Development
Office of Fair Housing and Equal Opportunity
Fair Housing Assistance Program - State and Local
(14.401)
451 7th St., SW
Washington, DC 20410   Ph: (202)708-0455
Jacquelyn J. Shelton

Types of Assistance: Project grants (cooperatie agreements). **Applicant Eligibility:** State and local governments administering State and local fair housing laws and ordinances which have been certified by HUD as providing substantially equivalent rights and remedies as those provided by the Fair Housing Act, and which have executed formal written agreements with HUD to process Title VIII complaints. **Beneficiary Eligibility:** Any person or group of persons aggrieved by a discriminatory housing practice because of race, color, religion, sex, handicap, familial status, or national origin. **Range and Average of Financial Assistance:** Contribution for capacity building and complaint processing - $20,000.00 to $250,000.00; training - $6,000.00.

★3128★
U.S. Department of Housing and Urban Development
Office of Fair Housing and Equal Opportunity
Non-Discrimination in Federally Assisted Programs (On
the Basis of Race, Color, or National Origin)
(14.405)
451 7th St., SW
Washington, DC 20410   Ph: (202)708-0404
Roy J. Rodriguez

Types of Assistance: Investigation of complaints. **Applicant Eligibility:** Any individual feeling aggrieved because of an alleged discriminatory action on the basis of race, color, or national origin may file a complaint with the Department of Housing and Urban Development. **Beneficiary Eligibility:** Aggrieved individuals. **Range and Average of Financial Assistance:** Not applicable.

★3129★
U.S. Department of Housing and Urban Development
Office of Fair Housing and Equal Opportunity
Non-Discrimination in the Community Development
Block Grant Program (On the Basis of Race, Color,
National Origin, Sex, Handicap, or Age) (14.406).
451 7th St., SW
Washington, DC 20410   Ph: (202)619-8045
Roy J. Rodriguez

Types of Assistance: Investigation of complaints. **Applicant Eligibility:** Any individual feeling aggrieved because of an alleged discriminatory action in a Title I program on the basis of race, color, national origin, handicap, or age may file a complaint with the Department of Housing and Urban Development. **Beneficiary Eligibility:** Aggrieved individuals. **Range and Average of Financial Assistance:** Not applicable.

★3130★
U.S. Department of Justice
Civil Rights Division
Civil Rights Prosecution (16.109)
Criminal Section
Washington, DC 20530   Ph: (202)514-3204

Types of Assistance: Investigation of complaints. **Applicant Eligibility:** All persons. **Beneficiary Eligibility:** All persons. **Range and Average of Financial Assistance:** Not applicable.

★3131★
U.S. Department of Justice
Civil Rights Division
Desegregation of Public Education (16.100)
Educational Opportunities Litigation Section
Washington, DC 20530   Ph: (202)514-2007
Amy Casner, Office of Public Affairs

Types of Assistance: Provision of specialized services. **Applicant Eligibility:** Parent or group of parents in the case of public schools. An individual or his/her parents in the case of a public college.

Beneficiary Eligibility: Same as above. **Range and Average of Financial Assistance**: Not applicable.

★3132★
U.S. Department of Justice
Civil Rights Division
Equal Employment Opportunity (16.101)
Employment Litigation Section
Washington, DC 20530   Ph: (202)514-2007
Amy Casner, Office of Public Affairs

Types of Assistance: Provision of specialized services. **Applicant Eligibility**: All persons. **Beneficiary Eligibility**: All persons. **Range and Average of Financial Assistance**: Not applicable.

★3133★
U.S. Department of Justice
Civil Rights Division
Fair Housing and Equal Credit Opportunity (16.103)
Housing and Civil Enforcement
Washington, DC 20530   Ph: (202)514-2007
Amy Casner, Office of Public Affairs

Types of Assistance: Provision of specialized services. **Applicant Eligibility**: All persons. **Beneficiary Eligibility**: All persons. **Range and Average of Financial Assistance**: Not applicable.

★3134★
U.S. Department of Justice
Civil Rights Division
Protection of Voting Rights (16.104)
Voting Section
Washington, DC 20530   Ph: (202)514-2007
Amy Casner, Office of Public Affairs

Types of Assistance: Provision of specialized services. **Applicant Eligibility**: All U.S. citizens of voting age. **Beneficiary Eligibility**: Same as above. **Range and Average of Financial Assistance**: Not applicable.

★3135★
U.S. Department of Justice
Community Relations Service (16.200)
Washington, DC 20530   Ph: (301)492-5929

Types of Assistance: Provision of specialized services. **Applicant Eligibility**: Any person, group, community, or State of local governmental unit that seeks to alleviate tensions related to race, color, or national origin may be considered for CRS assistance. **Beneficiary Eligibility**: Any group, person, or community, or State or local governmental unit that experiences tensions involving race, color, or national origin. **Range and Average of Financial Assistance**: Not applicable.

★3136★
U.S. Department of Labor
Employment Standards Administration
Non-discrimination and Affirmative Action By Federal Contractors and Assisted Construction Contractors (17.301)
Office of Federal Contract Compliance
  Programs
Washington, DC 20210   Ph: (202)523-9475
Jaime Ramon, Director

Types of Assistance: Dissemination of technical information and investigation of complaints. **Applicant Eligibility**: Complaints against Federal contractors and federally assisted construction contractors which allege employment discrimination on the basis of race, sex, religion, or national origin may be filed. **Beneficiary Eligibility**: Employees, former employees, or applicants with a Government contractor or federally involved contractor, including construction contractors. **Range and Average of Financial Assistance**: Not applicable.

★3137★
U.S. Department of Transportation
Federal Transit Administration
Human Resource Programs (20.511)
Office of Civil Rights
400 7th St., SW, Rm. 7412
Washington, DC 20590   Ph: (202)366-4018

Types of Assistance: Project grants (cooperative agreements) and dissemination of technical information. **Applicant Eligibility**: Grants and Cooperative Agreements; public bodies, State and local agencies, other legally constituted public agencies, institutions of higher learning, nonprofit institutions. Contracts: the same as for Grants and Cooperative Agreements as well as for profit business endeavors. **Beneficiary Eligibility**: All public and private sector bodies and organizations, universities, and individuals. **Range and Average of Financial Assistance**: None established.

★3138★
U.S. Equal Employment Opportunity Commission
Employment Discrimination - Equal Pay Act (30.010)
Office of Communications and Legislative
  Affairs
Public Information Unit
1801 L St., NW
Washington, DC 20507
          Free: 800-USA-EEOC

Types of Assistance: Advisory services and counseling; investigation of complaints. **Applicant Eligibility**: Individuals who believe they have been paid in violation of the Equal Pay Act or who believe that other persons are being paid in violation of the Act in any State of the United States, the District of Columbia, or any territory or possession of the United States. **Beneficiary Eligibility**: Individuals covered by the Fair Labor Standards Act of 1938, as amended. **Range and Average of Financial Assistance**: Not applicable.

★3139★
U.S. Equal Employment Opportunity Commission
Employment Discrimination - Private Bar Program (30.005)
Office of General Counsel
1801 L St., NW
Washington, DC 20507   Ph: (202)663-4798
Phillip B. Sklover

Types of Assistance: Provision of specialized services. **Applicant Eligibility**: Any individual who has received a notice of right to sue from the Commission. **Beneficiary Eligibility**: Same as above. **Range and Average of Financial Assistance**: Not applicable.

★3140★
U.S. Equal Employment Opportunity Commission
Employment Discrimination - State and Local Fair Employment Practices Agency Contracts (30.002)
Office of Program Operations
Charge Resolution and Review Program
1801 L St., NW, Rm. 8030
Washington, DC 20556   Ph: (202)663-4862
Lawrence E. Koziarz, Director

Types of Assistance: Direct payments for specified use. **Applicant Eligibility**: Official State and local government agencies charged with the administration and enforcement of fair employment practices laws. **Beneficiary Eligibility**: Employees, potential employees, and former employees covered by Title VII of the Civil Rights Act of 1964 as amended, or the Age Discrimination in Employment Act of 1967. **Range and Average of Financial Assistance**: $18,450.00 to $2,035,800.00; $233,106.00.

★3141★

U.S. Equal Employment Opportunity Commission
Employment Discrimination - Title VII of the Civil
Rights Act of 1964 (30.001)
Public Information Unit
Office of Communication and Legislative
Affairs
1801 L St., NW
Washington, DC 20507   Ph: 800-USA-EEOC

Types of Assistance: Investigation of complaints. **Applicant Eligibility:** Any aggrieved individual or individuals, labor union, association, legal representative, or unincorporated organization, filing on behalf of an aggrieved individual who has reason to believe that an unlawful employment practice within the meaning of Title VII, as amended, has been committted by an employer with more than 15 employees, employment agency, labor organization, or joint labor-management committee. **Beneficiary Eligibility:** Potential employees, employees and former employees of the named respondents in a charge who have been subject to unlawful employment practices. **Range and Average of Financial Assistance:** Not applicable.

★3142★

U.S. General Services Administration
Business Services (39.001)
Office of Small and Disadvantaged
Business Utilization
Washington, DC 20405   Ph: (202)501-1021

Types of Assistance: Advisory services and counseling. **Applicant Eligibility:** Any business concern is eligible. **Beneficiary Eligibility:** Business concerns. **Range and Average of Financial Assistance:** Not applicable.

★3143★

U.S. Office of Personnel Management
Federal Employment for Disadvantaged Youth - Part-
time (27.003)
Career Entry Group
Office of Affirmative Recruiting and
Employment
1900 E St., NW
Washington, DC 20415   Ph: (202)606-0870
Helen Lee

Types of Assistance: Federal employment. **Applicant Eligibility:** Disadvantaged young people 16 years of age and older; must be accepted for or enrolled in an accredited secondary school or institution of higher learning pursuing an education no higher than a baccalaureate level; maintain an acceptable school standing; and meet the financial need criterion of the program which is divided into income levels based upon the Department of Health and Human Services Poverty Level. **Beneficiary Eligibility:** Disadvantaged youth 16 years of age and older. **Range and Average of Financial Assistance:** Not applicable.

★3144★

U.S. Office of Personnel Management
Federal Employment for Disadvantaged Youth -
Summer (27.004)
Career Entry Group
Office of Affirmative Recruiting and
Employment
1900 E St., NW
Washington, DC 20415   Ph: (202)606-0870

Types of Assistance: Federal employment. **Applicant Eligibility:** Youth must meet the program's economic needs criteria, which is divided into income levels based upon the Department of Health and Human Services Poverty Level. **Beneficiary Eligibility:** Disadvantaged youth 16 years of age and older. **Range and Average of Financial Assistance:** Not applicable.

★3145★

U.S. Small Business Administration
Management and Technical Assistance for Socially
and Economically Disadvantaged Businesses
(59.007)
Minority Small Businesses and Capital
Ownership Development
409 3rd St., SW
Washington, DC 20416   Ph: (202)205-6423

Types of Assistance: Project grants (cooperative agreements). **Applicant Eligibility:** State and local governments, education institutions, public or private organizations and individuals that have the capability to provide the necessary assistance. **Beneficiary Eligibility:** Socially and economically disadvantaged persons; businesses which are owned and operated by economically and socially disadvantaged; or businesses operating in low-income or high-unemployment areas, or firms owned by low-income individuals. **Range and Average of Financial Assistance:** $1,800.00 to $388,000.00; $78,620.00.

★3146★

U.S. Small Business Administration
Microloan Demonstration Program (59.046)
Office of Financing, Loan Policy and
Procedures Branch
409 3rd St. SW, 8th Fl.
Washington, DC 20416   Ph: (202)205-6570

Types of Assistance: Formula Grants; Project Grants; Direct Loans. **Applicant Eligibility:** Must meet definition of an intermediary lender as a private nonprofit entity or a private nonprofit community development corporation that seeks to borrow or has borrowed funds from SBA to make microloans to small business concerns under this program; has a minimum of one year experience making and servicing microloans to start up, newly established, growing, or other small business concerns; has the capability to service microloans in-house and without the assistance of affiliates or outside contractors or contracting organizations; has a minimum of one year experience providing intensive marketing, management and technical assistance to its borrowwers. **Beneficiary Eligibility:** Small businesses, minority entrepreneurs, nonprofit entities, business owners, women and low-income, and other individuals possessing the capability to operate successful business concerns. **Range and Average of Financial Assistance:** New program, information not yet available.

★3147★

U.S. Small Business Administration
Minority Business Development (59.006)
Office of AA/MSBDCOD
1441 L St., NW, Rm. 602
Washington, DC 20416   Ph: (202)653-6407

Types of Assistance: Provision of specialized services. **Applicant Eligibility:** Qualification as a socially and economically disadvantaged person on the basis of clear and convincing evidence. **Beneficiary Eligibility:** Socially and economically disadvantaged individuals. **Range and Average of Financial Assistance:** Not applicable.

★3148★

U.S. Small Business Administration
Small Business Investment Companies (59.011)
Investment Division
Office of Investments
409 3rd St., SW
Washington, DC 20416   Ph: (202)205-6510

Types of Assistance: Direct loans, guaranteed and insured loans, and advisory services and counseling. **Applicant Eligibility:** Any chartered small business investment company having a combined paid-in capital and paid-in surplus of not less than $2,500,000.00 ($1,000,000.00 for SSBICs),having qualified management, and giving evidence of sound operation, and establishing the need for SBIC financing in the geographic area in which the applicant proposes to operate. **Beneficiary Eligibility:** Individual businesses (single proprietorship, partnership, or corporation) which satisfy the established criteria of a small business. SSBICs beneficiary must also be a business owned and operated by socially or economically disadvantaged individuals. **Range and Average of Financial Assistance:** Guarantee loans: $50,000.00 to $35,000,000.00; $1,000,000.00.

(13) State and Local Government Agencies

─────── Alabama ───────

★3149★
Alabama Attorney General
Civil Rights Division
11 S. Union St.
Montgomery, AL 36130   Ph: (205)242-7384
Milt Belcher, Director

★3150★
Alabama Department of Public Health
Division of Minority Health
434 Monroe St.
Montgomery, AL 36130-3017   Ph: (205)242-5839
Sharon Rose, Director

★3151★
Alabama Development Office
Minority Business Enterprises
401 Adams Ave.   Ph: (205)242-0488
Montgomery, AL 36104   Fax: (205)242-0486
Jack Crittenden, Manager

─────── Alaska ───────

★3152★
Alaska Dept. of Administration
Division of Personnel/Equal Employment Opportunity
PO Box 110201
Juneau, AK 99811-0201   Ph: (907)465-3570
Kevin Ritchie, Director

★3153★
Alaska Office of the Governor
Human Rights Commission
800 A. St., Ste. 202
Anchorage, AK 99501-3669   Ph: (907)276-7474
Paula Haley, Executive Director

─────── Arizona ───────

★3154★
Affirmative Action Department
Minority Business Enterprise Program
550 W. Washington St.
Phoenix, AZ 85003   Ph: (602)262-6790
Rose Newsome, Director

★3155★
Arizona Attorney General
Civil Rights Division
1275 W. Washington
Phoenix, AZ 85007   Ph: (602)542-5263
Richard Martinez, Chief Counsel

★3156★
Arizona Department of Administration
Affirmative Action Office
1700 W. Washington, Ste. 156
Phoenix, AZ 85007   Ph: (602)542-3711
Victor Melendez, Director

★3157★
Arizona Department of Commerce
Community Development Block Grant
3800 N. Central
Phoenix, AZ 85012   Ph: (602)280-1300
Rivco Knox, Director

★3158★
Arizona Department of Health Services
Office of Planning, Evaluation and Public Health
 Statistics
1740 W. Adams St., Rm. 312
Phoenix, AZ 85007   Ph: (602)542-1216
Joanne Gersten Ph.D., Manager

★3159★
Arizona Health Services Department
Affirmative Action Office
1740 W. Adams
Phoenix, AZ 85007   Ph: (602)542-1085

★3160★
Phoenix Economic Security Department
EEO Office (Equal Employment Opportunity)
550 W. Washington St.
Phoenix, AZ 85003   Ph: (602)262-7716

★3161★
Phoenix Equal Opportunity Department
Community Relations Committee
Fair Housing Services
550 W. Washington St.
Phoenix, AZ 85003   Ph: (602)261-8242

★3162★
Scottsdale Human Resources Department
7575 E. Main St.
Scottsdale, AZ 85251   Ph: (602)994-2491

★3163★
Tucson Minority Business Enterprise
110 E. Pennington
Tucson, AZ 85701   Ph: (602)791-4593
Clarence Boykins, Director

Arkansas

★3164★
Arkansas Education Department
Affirmative Action
Bldg. 4 Capitol Mall
Little Rock, AR 72201-1071   Ph: (501)682-5753
Clemetta Hood, Director

★3165★
Arkansas Industrial Development Commission
Minority Business Division
1 Capitol Mall
Little Rock, AR 72201   Ph: (501)682-5060
James Hall, Director

California

★3166★
California Attorney General (Justice Department)
Affirmative Action
1515 K St., Ste. 511
PO Box 944255   Ph: (916)324-5482
Sacramento, CA 94244-2550   Fax: (916)324-5205
Aisha Martin-Walton, Officer

★3167★
California Business, Transportation, and Housing
  Agency
California Highway Patrol
Equal Employment Opportunity Office
2555 1st Ave.
PO Box 942898   Ph: (916)657-7426
Sacramento, CA 94298-0001   Fax: (916)657-7324
B. Witman, Commander

★3168★
California Business, Transportation, and Housing
  Agency
Transportation Department
Affirmative Action and Equal Opportunity
1120 N St.   Ph: (916)654-4958
Sacramento, CA 95814   Fax: (916)654-2393
Jose Perez, Asst. Dir.

★3169★
California Business, Transportation, and Housing
  Agency
Transportation Department
Civil Rights Division
1120 N St.   Ph: (916)654-2393
Sacramento, CA 95814   Fax: (916)654-6608
Algerine McCray, Chief

★3170★
California Community Colleges
Civil Rights Office
1107 9th St., 9th Fl.
Sacramento, CA 95814   Ph: (916)327-5491
Nancy Davenport, Director

★3171★
California Department of Fair Employment and
  Housing
2014 T St., Ste. 210
Sacramento, CA 95814   Ph: (916)227-2873
Steve Owyang
Nancy Gutierrez, Director

★3172★
California Department of Health Services
Primary Health Services Development Program
714 P St., Rm. 599
Sacramento, CA 95814   Ph: (916)654-0238
Arthur E. Jordan, Chief

★3173★
California Education Department
Equal Employment Opportunity Office
PO Box 944272   Ph: (916)657-4562
Sacramento, CA 94244-2720   Fax: (916)657-5101
Sharon Felix, Director

★3174★
California Health and Welfare Agency
1600 9th St., Rm. 460
Sacramento, CA 95814   Ph: (916)654-3454
Russell S. Gould, Secretary

★3175★
California Health and Welfare Agency
Employment Development Department
Equal Employment Opportunity Office
800 Capitol Mall
PO Box 826880
Sacramento, CA 94280-0001   Ph: (916)653-0707
Thomas Nagle, Director

★3176★
California Health and Welfare Agency
Health Services Department
Civil Rights Office
714/744 P St.   Ph: (916)657-1411
Sacramento, CA 95814   Fax: (916)657-1156
Pliney Young, Chief

★3177★
California Health and Welfare Agency
Mental Health Department
Affirmative Action Division
1600 9th St.
Sacramento, CA 95814   Ph: (916)654-3454
Russell S. Gould, Secretary

★3178★
California State and Consumer Services Agency
Fair Employment and Housing Commission
1390 Market St., Ste. 410   Ph: (415)557-2325
San Francisco, CA 94102-5377   Fax: (415)557-0855
Steven C. Owyang, Exec. and Legal Aff. Sec.

★3179★
California State and Consumer Services Agency
Small and Minority Business Office
1531 I St., 2nd Fl.   Ph: (916)322-5060
Sacramento, CA 95814   Fax: (916)442-7855
Denise Alvarado-Vazquez, Special Asst. to the Director

★3180★
California State Lottery Commission
Minority Affairs
600 N. 10th St.   Ph: (916)324-9638
Sacramento, CA 95814-0393   Fax: (916)327-1345
Terri Fontenette, Dir.

★3181★
State Personnel Board
Affirmative Action and Exam Services
PO Box 944201
801 Capitol Mall
Sacramento, CA 94244-2010   Ph: (916)653-1705
Gloria Harmon, Executive Officer

──────────── **Colorado** ────────────

★3182★
Colorado Department of Health
Alcohol and Drug Abuse Division
4300 Cherry Creek Dr., S.
Denver, CO 80222-1530   Ph: (303)692-2930
Linda Garrett, Minority Resource Information Specialist

★3183★
Colorado Regulatory Agencies Department
Civil Rights Division
1560 Broadway, Ste. 1550   Ph: (303)894-7822
Denver, CO 80202   Fax: (303)894-7885
Jack Lang Y. Marquez, Director

──────────── **Connecticut** ────────────

★3184★
Connecticut Administrative Services Department
Personnel and Labor Relations Bureau
Affirmative Action and Employee Relations
165 Capitol Ave.   Ph: (203)566-4669
Hartford, CT 06106   Fax: (203)566-7606
Thelma Ball, Dir.

★3185★
Connecticut Commission on Human Rights and
  Opportunities
90 Washington St.
Hartford, CT 06106   Ph: (203)566-4895
Louis Martin, Director

★3186★
Connecticut Education Department
Affirmative Action
165 Capitol Ave.   Ph: (203)566-7619
Hartford, CT 06106   Fax: (203)566-8964
Robert Babcock Sr., Administrator

★3187★
Connecticut Human Resources Department
Affirmative Action
1049 Asylum Ave.   Ph: (203)566-3375
Hartford, CT 06105   Fax: (203)566-7613
Mary Priestman, Officer

──────────── **Delaware** ────────────

★3188★
Delaware Department of State
Human Relations Division
820 N. French St., 4th Fl.
Wilmington, DE 19801   Ph: (302)577-3485
Andrew J. Turner Jr., Director

★3189★
Delaware Labor Department
Industrial Affairs Division
Discrimination Review Board
820 N. French St.
Wilmington, DE 19801   Ph: (302)577-2877
John F. Kirk Jr., Director

★3190★
Delaware Transportation Department
Disadvantaged Business Enterprise
PO Box 778
Dover, DE 19903   Ph: (302)739-4359
Willie Jones, Director

──────────── **District of Columbia** ────────────

★3191★
Commission on Human Rights
1 Judiciary Sq.
441 4th St. NW, Ste. 290
Washington, DC 20001   Ph: (202)727-0656
James Loots, Chairperson

★3192★
District of Columbia Arts and Humanities Commission
Human Rights and Minority Business Opportunity
  Commission
2000 14th St., NW
Washington, DC 20009   Ph: (202)939-8740
Margie A. Utley, Director

★3193★
District of Columbia Economic Development
Human Rights and Minority Business Development
  Department
2000 14th St. NW, 3rd Fl.   Ph: (202)939-8740
Washington, DC 20009   Fax: (202)673-7054
Marge Utlely, Dir.

★3194★
District of Columbia Human Rights Office
2000 14th St. NW   Ph: (202)939-8742
Washington, DC 20009   Fax: (202)939-7133
Margie Utley, Dir.

★3195★
District of Columbia Human Services Department
801 N. Capitol St., NE, Ste. 700
Washington, DC 20002   Ph: (202)727-0310
Vincent Gray, Director

★3196★
District of Columbia Human Services Department
Social Services Commission
801 N. Capitol St., NE, Ste. 700
Washington, DC 20002   Ph: (202)727-5930
Vincent Gray, Director

───────────── Florida ─────────────

★3197★
Florida Commission on Human Relations
325 John Knox Rd., Bldg F, Ste. 240
Tallahassee, FL 32303   Ph: (904)488-7082
Ronald McElrath, Director

★3198★
Florida Health and Rehabilitative Services Department
Civil Rights Office
1317 Winewood Blvd., Bldg. 3
Tallahassee, FL 32399-0700   Ph: (904)487-1901
Melvin Herring, Director

★3199★
Florida Labor and Employment Security Department
Civil Rights Office
303 Hartman Bldg.
2012 Capital Circle SE   Ph: (904)488-5905
Tallahassee, FL 32399-2152   Fax: (904)488-8930
Deirdre Kyle, Dir.

★3200★
Hillsborough County Equal Opportunity Office
412 E. Madison, Ste. 913
Tampa, FL 33602   Ph: (813)272-5969
Cretta Johnson, Director

★3201★
Jacksonville Minority Business
220 E. Bay St., 4th Fl.
Jacksonville, FL 32202   Ph: (904)630-1165
Connell Heyward, Director

★3202★
Tampa Administration Department
Women and Minority Business Enterprise
306 E. Jackson St.
Tampa, FL 33602   Ph: (813)223-8192
George Davis, Director

───────────── Hawaii ─────────────

★3203★
Hawaii Health Department
Affirmative Action Office
1250 Punchbowl St.   Ph: (808)586-4616
Honolulu, HI 96813   Fax: (808)586-4444
Gerald Ohta, Affirmative Action Officer

★3204★
Hawaii Human Services Department
PO Box 339   Ph: (808)586-4997
Honolulu, HI 96809   Fax: (808)586-4890
Winona E. Rubin, Director

★3205★
Hawaii Labor and Industrial Relations Department
Equal Employment Opportunity Officer
830 Punchbowl St.
Honolulu, HI 96813   Ph: (808)548-4533
Alice Hong, Director

★3206★
Hawaii Office of the Governor
Affirmative Action Office
5 State Capitol   Ph: (808)586-0070
Honolulu, HI 96813   Fax: (808)586-0006
Joan Lindsey, Coordinator

───────────── Idaho ─────────────

★3207★
Idaho Human Rights Commission
450 W. State St.
Boise, ID 83720   Ph: (208)334-2873
Marilyn T. Shuler, Director

───────────── Illinois ─────────────

★3208★
Illinois Central Management Services Department
Minority and Female Business Enterprises Office
100 W. Randolph, Ste. 4400
Chicago, IL 60601   Ph: (312)814-4190
Irene Cualoping, Director

★3209★
Illinois Commerce and Community Affairs Department
Equal Employment Opportunity and Affirmative Action
620 E. Adams
Springfield, IL 62701   Ph: (217)785-7360
Jan Grayson, Director

★3210★
Illinois Department of Public Health
Division of Health Promotion
535 W. Jefferson
Springfield, IL 62761   Ph: (217)785-2060
Edie Sternberg, Chief

★3211★
Illinois Human Rights Commission
William G. Stratton Bldg., Rm. 404   Ph: (217)785-4350
Springfield, IL 62706   Fax: (217)524-4877
Gail Bradshaw, Exec. Dir.

★3212★
Illinois Human Rights Department
100 W. Randolph, Ste. 10-100   Ph: (312)814-6245
Chicago, IL 60601   Fax: (312)814-6251
Rosemary Bombela, Director

★3213★
Illinois Revenue Department
Equal Employment Opportunity Office
101 W. Jefferson
Springfield, IL 62794   Ph: (217)785-0959
Sherry Pittman, Officer

★3214★
Illinois Secretary of State
Affirmative Action Officer
State of Illinois Bldg.
100 W. Randolph, Rm. 5-400
Chicago, IL 60601   Ph: (312)814-3321
Carlos J. Salazar, Director

——————————— Indiana ———————————

★3215★
Department of Workforce Development
Indiana Employment and Training Services Department
10 N. Senate Ave., Rm. 103
Indianapolis, IN 46204
David Shaheed, Director
Ph: (317)232-7482

★3216★
Indiana Administration Department
Minority Business Development Division
402 W. Washington St., Rm. W479
Indianapolis, IN 46204
Addison Simpson, Commissioner
Ph: (317)232-3061

★3217★
Indiana Civil Rights Commission
Indiana Government Center N.
100 N. Senate Ave., Rm.N-103
Indianapolis, IN 46204
Sandra D. Leek, Director
Ph: (317)232-2614
Fax: (317)232-6580

★3218★
Indiana Family and Social Administration
Division of Disability, Aging, and Rehabilitative
  Services
Government Center S., Rm. W451
Indianapolis, IN 46204
Bobby Comner, Director
Ph: (317)232-1147

★3219★
Indiana Personnel Department
Affirmative Action Division
402 W. Washington St., Rm. W161
Indianapolis, IN 46204
Steven Jones, Dir.
Ph: (317)232-8029
Fax: (317)232-3089

★3220★
Indiana State Department of Health
Office of Special Populations
Interagency Council on Black and Minority Health
1330 W. Michigan St.,
PO Box 1964
Indianapolis, IN 46206-1964
Z. May Jimison, Director
Ph: (317)633-0683

★3221★
Indianapolis Equal Opportunity Division
129 E. Market St., Ste. 300
Indianapolis, IN 46204
Robert Ransom, Director
Ph: (317)327-5262

——————————— Iowa ———————————

★3222★
Iowa Attorney General
Civil Rights Division
Hoover State Office Bldg., 2nd Fl.
Des Moines, IA 50319
Teresa Baustian, Director
Ph: (515)281-4121

★3223★
Iowa Civil Rights Commission
211 E. Maple St.
Grimes State Office Bldg., 2nd Fl.
Des Moines, IA 50319
Don Grove, Acting Director
Ph: (515)281-4121

★3224★
Iowa Human Rights Department
Status of Blacks Division
321 12th St.
Lucas State Office Bldg.
Des Moines, IA 50319
Gary Lawson, Administrator
Ph: (515)281-7283

★3225★
Iowa Human Services Department
Policy Coordination Division
Affirmative Action Bureau
Hoover State Office Bldg., 5th St.
Des Moines, IA 50319
Barb Oliver Hall, Chief
Ph: (515)281-6090

——————————— Kansas ———————————

★3226★
Kansas Administration Department
Equal Employment Opportunity Office
Landon State Office Bldg.
900 SW Jackson St.
Topeka, KS 66612
Clyde Howard, Director
Ph: (913)296-4288

★3227★
Kansas Commerce and Housing Department
Minority Business Office
700 SW Harrison, Ste. 1300
Topeka, KS 66603-3712
Tony Augusto, Director
Ph: (913)296-2954

★3228★
Kansas Human Resources Department
Equal Employment Opportunity Office
401 Topeka Ave.
Topeka, KS 66603
Janet Palmer, Director
Ph: (913)296-2667

★3229★
Kansas Human Rights Commission
851-S Landon State Office Bldg.
900 SW Jackson St.
Topeka, KS 66612-1252
Michael J. Brungardt, Exec. Dir.
Ph: (913)296-3206
Fax: (913)296-0589

★3230★
Kansas Social and Rehabilitation Services Department
Civil Rights/Equal Employment Opportunity Section
300 S. West Oakley
State Complex W.
Biddle Bldg.
Topeka, KS 66606
Gene Wilson, Director
Ph: (913)296-4766

——————————— Kentucky ———————————

★3231★
Kentucky Commission on Human Rights
500 Mero St., Ste. 832
Capital Plaza Tower
Frankfort, KY 40601
Beverly Watts, Director
Ph: (502)564-3550

★3232★
Kentucky Economic Development Cabinet
Community Development Department
Small and Minority Business Division
Capitol Plaza Tower
500 Mero St.   Ph: (502)564-2064
Frankfort, KY 40601   Fax: (502)564-3256
Floyd C. Taylor, Director

★3233★
Kentucky Finance and Administration Cabinet
Equal Opportunity Contract Compliance
383 State Capitol Annex   Ph: (502)564-2874
Frankfort, KY 40601   Fax: (502)564-6785
Ventra Remson, Exec. Dir.

★3234★
Kentucky Human Rights Commission
332 W. Broadway, 7th Fl.
PO Box 69
Louisville, KY 40202-0069   Ph: (502)595-4024
Beverly L. Watts, Executive Director

★3235★
Kentucky Transportation Cabinet
Minority Affairs Office
State Office Bldg.
501 High St.   Ph: (502)564-3601
Frankfort, KY 40622   Fax: (502)564-4809
Maurice Sweeney, Exec. Director

Louisiana

★3236★
Louisiana Economic Development Department
Minority and Women's Business Enterprise Division
PO Box 94185   Ph: (504)342-5373
Baton Rouge, LA 70804-9185   Fax: (504)342-5389
Henry Stamper, Exec. Dir.

★3237★
Louisiana Health and Hospitals Department
Human Rights Bureau
PO Box 629   Ph: (504)342-3417
Baton Rouge, LA 70821-0629   Fax: (504)342-9508
George Clark, Dir.

★3238★
Louisiana Office of the Governor
Minority Business Development Office
101 France St.
Baton Rouge, LA 70804   Ph: (504)342-5373
Henry Stamper, Director

★3239★
Louisiana Social Services Department
Civil Rights Section
546 Main St.
Baton Rouge, LA 70821   Ph: (504)342-2700
Paula Braxton, Director

★3240★
New Orleans Human Resources
Policy and Planning
Administrative Unit
Human Rights
1300 Perdido St.
City Hall Rm. 1W-06
New Orleans, LA 70112   Ph: (504)565-7120
Tommie Lockhart, Director

★3241★
Office of the Mayor
Kenner Minority Affairs
1801 Williams Blvd.
Kenner, LA 70062   Ph: (504)468-7295
Joseph James, Asst. to the Mayor/Minority Affairs

Maine

★3242★
Maine Human Rights Commission
State House Sta. 51   Ph: (207)289-2326
Augusta, ME 04333-0051   Fax: (207)624-6063
Brian E. Thibeau, Chairman

★3243★
Maine Human Services Department
Management, Budget, and Policy Office
Affirmative Action
State House, Sta. 11   Ph: (207)287-3488
Augusta, ME 04333   Fax: (207)626-5555
Ann Twombly, Officer

★3244★
Maine Transportation Department
Public Affairs and Human Resources Management
Equal Opportunity and Employee Relations
State House Station 16
Augusta, ME 04333   Ph: (207)287-3576
Jane Gilbert, Director

Maryland

★3245★
Baltimore City Housing Authority
Fair Housing and Equal Opportunity
417 E. Fayette St.
Baltimore, MD 21202   Ph: (410)396-3246
Barbara Snow, Special Asst. to the Commissioner

★3246★
Baltimore Social Services Department
1510 Guilford Ave.
Baltimore, MD 21202   Ph: (410)361-4700
Alvin Collins, Director

★3247★
Maryland Department of Health and Mental Hygiene
Community Relations
201 W. Preston St., Rm. 519A
Baltimore, MD 21201   Ph: (410)225-6600
Michael Carter, Director

★3248★
**Maryland Economic and Employment Development
   Department**
Equal Employment Opportunity Office
217 E. Redwood St.   Ph: (410)333-6626
Baltimore, MD 21202-3316   Fax: (410)333-6911
Dale Webb, Director

★3249★
Maryland Education Department
Equity Assurance and Compliance
200 W. Baltimore St.
Baltimore, MD 21201   Ph: (410)333-2228
Woodrow Grant, Director

★3250★
Maryland Higher Education Commission
Affirmative Action
16 Francis St.
Annapolis, MD 21401
Debbie Mason, Director
Ph: (410)974-2971

★3251★
Maryland Human Relations Commission
20 E. Franklin St.
Baltimore, MD 21202-2274
Jennifer Burdick, Executive Director
Ph: (410)333-1715
Fax: (410)333-1841

★3252★
Maryland Human Resources Department
Equal Opportunity Division
311 W. Saratoga St.
Baltimore, MD 21201
Bruce Moore, Director
Ph: (410)333-0350
Fax: (410)333-0392

★3253★
Maryland Minority Affairs Office
301 W. Preston St., Ste. 1008E
Baltimore, MD 21201
Mitchell Smith, Exec. Dir.
Ph: (410)225-1843

★3254★
Maryland Personnel Department
Equal Opportunity Officer
301 W. Preston St.
Baltimore, MD 21201
Cathy Austin, Asst. Secretary Personnel
Ph: (410)225-4792

★3255★
Maryland Transportation Department
Minority Business Enterprise and Equal Opportunity
Office
PO Box 8755
B W I Airport, MD 21240
Ruth Roberts Webbon, Dir.
Ph: (410)859-7327
Fax: (410)859-7318

Massachusetts

★3256★
Boston Fair Housing Commission
Boston City Hall, Rm. 957
Boston, MA 02201
Victoria Williams, Executive Director
Ph: (617)635-4408

★3257★
Cambridge Affirmative Action Office
795 Massachusetts Ave.
Cambridge, MA 02139
William Gomes, Director
Ph: (617)349-4332

★3258★
Massachusetts Administration and Finance Executive
Office
Affirmative Action Central Regional Office
455 Main St.
City Hall
Worcester, MA 01608
Ph: (508)799-1186

★3259★
Massachusetts Administration and Finance Executive
Office
Affirmative Action Office
1 Ashburton Pl., Rm. 303
Boston, MA 02108
Rachel Kemp, Director
Ph: (617)727-7441
Fax: (617)727-2779

★3260★
Massachusetts Administration and Finance Executive
Office
Commission Against Discrimination
One Ashburton Pl.
Boston, MA 02108
Michael T. Duffy, Chairman
Ph: (617)727-3990

★3261★
Massachusetts Attorney General's Office
Public Protection Bureau
Civil Rights and Civil Liberties Division
1 Ashburton Pl., Rm. 2010
Boston, MA 02108
Richard Cole, Director
Ph: (617)727-2200
Fax: (617)727-5768

★3262★
Massachusetts Bay Transportation Authority
Affirmative Action and Equal Employment Opportunity
Division
10 Park Plaza, Rm. 3510
Boston, MA 02116-3969
Mary A. Fernandes, Director
Ph: (617)722-3305

★3263★
Massachusetts Education Equity Department
1385 Hancock St.
Quincy, MA 02169
Ph: (617)770-7321

★3264★
Massachusetts Human Services Executive Office
Corrections Department
Affirmative Action Office
100 Cambridge St.
Boston, MA 02202
Kim Battle, Director
Ph: (617)727-1238

★3265★
Massachusetts Minority and Women's Business
Assistance Office
100 Cambridge St., Rm. 1305
Boston, MA 02202
Lynn Wachtel, Executive Director
Ph: (617)727-8692

★3266★
Massachusetts State of Minority and Women Business
Assistance
100 Cambridge St., Rm. 1305
Boston, MA 02202
Lynn Wachtel, Executive Director
Ph: (617)727-3220

★3267★
Office of Personnel Management
Affirmative Action Program
City Hall Plaza, Rm. 612
1 City Hall Square
Boston, MA 02201
Roscoe Marvis, Director
Ph: (617)635-3361

Michigan

★3268★
Michigan Agriculture Department
Affirmative Action Office
PO Box 30017
Lansing, MI 48909
Sandy Svec, Dir.
Ph: (517)373-9264
Fax: (517)373-9146

★3269★
Michigan Attorney General's Office
Civil Rights Division
PO Box 30212   Ph: (313)256-2557
Lansing, MI 48909   Fax: (517)373-4916
Robert Willis, Assistant in Charge

★3270★
Michigan Civil Rights Department
303 W. Kalamazoo, 4th Fl.   Ph: (517)373-1189
Lansing, MI 48913   Fax: (517)335-6513
James H. Horn II, Public Information Director

★3271★
Michigan Civil Rights Department
Contractual Services Division
Minority/Woman Business Certification
State Plaza Bldg.
1200 6th Ave.
Detroit, MI 48226   Ph: (313)256-2651
Winifred Avery, Director

★3272★
Michigan Civil Rights Department
Detroit Office
Michigan Plaza Bldg.
1200 6th St.   Ph: (313)256-2663
Detroit, MI 48226   Fax: (313)256-2709

★3273★
Michigan Department of Public Health
Office of Minority Health
3423 Martin Luther King Blvd.
Box 30195   Ph: (517)335-9287
Lansing, MI 48909   Fax: (517)335-9476
Cheryl Anderson-Small, Chief

★3274★
Michigan Social Services Department
Affirmative Action and Equal Opportunity Office
235 S. Grand Ave., Ste. 506
Lansing, MI 48909   Ph: (517)373-8520
James Newsom, Director

★3275★
Michigan Transportation Department
Executive Bureau
Equal Opportunity Programs Office
PO Box 30050   Ph: (517)373-6732
Lansing, MI 48909   Fax: (517)373-6457
Charles E. Ford, Exec.

——————— **Minnesota** ———————

★3276★
Minneapolis Civil Rights Department
350 S. 5th St.
City Hall, Rm. 239
Minneapolis, MN 55415   Ph: (612)673-3012
Emma Hixson, Director

★3277★
Minneapolis Community Development Agency
105 5th Ave. S.
Minneapolis, MN 55401   Ph: (612)673-5095
Jay Jensen, Executive Director

★3278★
Minnesota Attorney General's Office
Human Rights Division
State Capitol Bldg., Rm. 102
75 Constitution Ave.   Ph: (612)296-9417
St. Paul, MN 55155   Fax: (612)297-4193
Richard L. Vario Jr., Manager

★3279★
Minnesota Education Department
Human Resources Department
Affirmative Action Office
Capitol Square Bldg.
550 Cedar St.
St. Paul, MN 55101   Ph: (612)296-0347
Lourie Asumma, Director

★3280★
Minnesota Employee Relations Department
Equal Opportunity Division
658 Cedar St., 2nd Fl.   Ph: (612)296-8272
St. Paul, MN 55155   Fax: (612)296-5445
Steven Zachary, Director

★3281★
Minnesota Housing Finance Agency
Fair Housing and Equal Opportunity Division
400 Sibley St., Rm. 300   Ph: (612)296-9825
St. Paul, MN 55101   Fax: (612)296-8139
Charles Williams, Dir.

★3282★
Minnesota Human Rights Department
500 Bremer Tower   Ph: (612)296-5665
St. Paul, MN 55101   Fax: (612)296-9042
David Beaulieu, Commissioner

★3283★
Minnesota Human Rights Department
Equal Employment Opportunity Commission Office
500 Bremer Tower
7th Pl. and Minnesota
St. Paul, MN 55101   Ph: (612)296-9061
Karen Ferguson, Director

★3284★
Minnesota Human Services Department
Affirmative Action and Civil Rights Office
444 Lafayette Rd.
St. Paul, MN 55155   Ph: (612)296-3510
Mary Jean Anderson, Director

★3285★
Minnesota Jobs and Training Department
Affirmative Action Office
390 N. Robert St.
St. Paul, MN 55101   Ph: (612)296-1823
Linda Sloan, Director

——————— **Mississippi** ———————

★3286★
Mississippi Human Services Department
421 W. Pascagoula
Jackson, MS 39203   Ph: (601)960-4246
Greg Phillips, Director

★3287★
Mississippi Office of the Governor
Human Services Department
421 W. Pascagoula St.
Jackson, MS 39203   Ph: (601)960-4245
Greg Phillips, Director

★3288★
Mississippi State Department of Health
Office of Health Education and Health Promotion
2423 N. State St.
PO Box 1700
Jackson, MS 39215   Ph: (601)960-7499
Ellen Jones, Director

─────────── **Missouri** ───────────

★3289★
Missouri Administration Office
Affirmative Action Office
111 N. 7th St.
St. Louis, MO 63101   Ph: (314)340-7028

★3290★
Missouri Administration Office
Minority Business Development Commission
PO Box 809
Jefferson City, MO 65102   Ph: (314)751-2249
Mark Miller, Director

★3291★
Missouri Department of Health
Office of Minority Health
1738 E. Elm St.
PO Box 570
Jefferson City, MO 65102   Ph: (314)751-6064
Jacquelin Horton, Chief

★3292★
Missouri Housing Development Commission
Human Rights
3770 Broadway
Kansas City, MO 64111   Ph: (816)756-3790
Richard Grose, Director

★3293★
Missouri Labor and Industrial Relations Department
Human Rights Commission
3315 W. Truman Blvd.
PO Box 504   Ph: (314)751-3325
Jefferson City, MO 65102   Fax: (314)751-7973
Alvin A. Plummer, Executive Director

★3294★
St. Louis Civil Rights Enforcement Agency
Civil Courts Bldg., 1 Mezzanine N.
10 N. Tucker
St. Louis, MO 63101   Ph: (314)622-3301
Claude Rogers, Dir.

★3295★
St. Louis Human Services Department
121 S. Merrimac
Clayton, MO 63105   Ph: (314)889-3453
Judith Parker, Director

─────────── **Montana** ───────────

★3296★
Montana Labor and Industry Department
Human Rights Division
PO Box 1728   Ph: (406)444-3870
Helena, MT 59624-1728   Fax: (406)444-2699
Ann MacIntyre, Administrator

─────────── **Nebraska** ───────────

★3297★
Nebraska Equal Opportunity Commission
PO Box 94934   Ph: (402)471-2024
Lincoln, NE 68509-4934   Fax: (402)471-2597
Lawrence R. Myers, Executive Director

★3298★
Nebraska Personnel Department
Affirmative Action/Recruitment
PO Box 94905
Lincoln, NE 68509-4905   Ph: (402)471-3680
Rodney Moore, Admin.

─────────── **Nevada** ───────────

★3299★
Nevada Equal Rights Commission
1515 E. Tropicana Ave., Ste. 590   Ph: (702)486-7161
Las Vegas, NV 89158   Fax: (702)486-7054
Fernando Romero, Executive Director

★3300★
Nevada Human Resources Department
505 E. King St.
Carson City, NV 89710   Ph: (702)687-4400
Jerry G. Carlin, Director

─────────── **New Hampshire** ───────────

★3301★
New Hampshire Human Rights Commission
163 Loudon Rd.   Ph: (603)271-2767
Concord, NH 03301   Fax: (603)271-6339
Raymond S. Perry Jr., Executive Director

─────────── **New Jersey** ───────────

★3302★
New Jersey Attorney General's Office (Law and
  Public Safety Department)
Civil Rights Division
383 W. State St.
CN 089   Ph: (609)984-3100
Trenton, NJ 08625   Fax: (609)777-0466
C. Gregory Stewart, Dir.

★3303★
New Jersey Commerce and Economic Development
  Department
Development for Small Business, Women and Minority
  Business Division
CN 820, 20 W. State St.   Ph: (609)292-3860
Trenton, NJ 08625   Fax: (609)292-9145
Chuck Jones, Director

★3304★
New Jersey Health Department
Minority Health Office
Health and Agriculture Bldg.
CN 360   Ph: (609)292-6962
Trenton, NJ 08625-0360   Fax: (609)984-5474
Rosalind Thigpen-Rodd M.H.A., Dir.

★3305★
New Jersey Human Services Department
Family Development Division
CN716
Trenton, NJ 08625   Ph: (609)588-2401
Marion Reitz, Director

★3306★
New Jersey Law and Public Safety Department
Civil Rights Division
31 Clinton St., 3rd Fl.
Newark, NJ 07102   Ph: (201)648-2700
C. Gregory Stewart, Director

★3307★
New Jersey Office of Legislative Services
Institutions, Health and Welfare Committee
Legislative Office Bldg. CN068
Trenton, NJ 08625   Ph: (609)292-1646
Eleanor Seel, Chair

★3308★
New Jersey Personnel Department
Equal Employment Opportunity Affirmative Action
  Division
3 Station Plaza, CN 317   Ph: (609)777-0919
Trenton, NJ 08625   Fax: (609)984-3631
Howard Woodson, Director

─────────── **New Mexico** ───────────

★3309★
Minority Business Enterprises
Albuquerque Affirmative Action Office
PO Box 1293
Albuquerque, NM 87103   Ph: (505)768-3540
Eugene Sanchez, Director

★3310★
New Mexico Highway and Transportation Department
Equal Opportunity Program
PO Box 1149   Ph: (505)827-5602
Santa Fe, NM 87504-1149   Fax: (505)827-3214
Rudy Maestas, Bur. Chf.

★3311★
New Mexico Labor Department
Human Rights Division
1596 Pacheco St.   Ph: (505)827-6838
Santa Fe, NM 87502   Fax: (505)827-6812
Virginia D. Hendley, Director

─────────── **New York** ───────────

★3312★
New York Agriculture and Markets Department
Affirmative Action Program
Capital Plaza
1 Winners Circle
Albany, NY 12235   Ph: (518)457-3880
Richard McGuire, Director

★3313★
New York Alcoholism and Substance Abuse Division
Affirmative Action Bureau
194 Washington Ave.
Albany, NY 12210   Ph: (518)474-5418
Margorite Saunders, Director

★3314★
New York Attorney General's Office (Law Department)
New York City Office
Civil Rights Bureau
120 Broadway   Ph: (212)416-8240
New York, NY 10271   Fax: (212)416-6005
Sanford Cohen, Asst. Atty. Gen.

★3315★
New York Division of Human Rights
Albany Regional Office
State Office Bldg., 25th Fl.
Albany, NY 12225   Ph: (518)474-2705
Carol Praylor, Director

★3316★
New York Division of Human Rights
Binghamton Regional Office
State Office Bldg. Annex
164 Hawley St.
Binghamton, NY 13901   Ph: (607)773-7713
John H. Petersen, Director

★3317★
New York Division of Human Rights
Buffalo Regional Office
65 Court St., Ste. 506
Buffalo, NY 14202   Ph: (716)847-7632
Richard E. Clark, Director

★3318★
New York Division of Human Rights
Nassau County Regional Office
175 Fulton Ave.
Hempstead, NY 11550   Ph: (516)538-1360
Ralph Seskine, Director

★3319★
New York Division of Human Rights
New York City (Brooklyn - Staten Island) Regional
  Office
55 Hanson Pl.
Brooklyn, NY 11217   Ph: (718)260-2856
Wilson P. Ortez, Director

★3320★
New York Division of Human Rights
New York City (Lower Manhattan) Regional Office
State Office Bldg., 9th Fl.
270 Broadway
New York, NY 10007   Ph: (212)417-5041
John A. Cooper, Director

★3321★
New York Economic Development Department
Minority and Women's Business Division
1515 Broadway
New York, NY 10036   Ph: (212)827-6181
Heyward B. Davenport, Dir.

★3322★
New York General Services Office
Minority and Women-Owned Business Enterprises
Mayor Erastus Corning II Tower
Empire State Plaza   Ph: (518)473-8337
Albany, NY 12242   Fax: (518)474-1546
Lartharee Jones, Asst. Commissioner

★3323★
New York Housing and Community Renewal Division
Community Affairs and Affirmative Action Office
1 Fordham Plaza
Bronx, NY 10458   Ph: (212)519-5848
Hector Del Toro, Deputy Commissioner

★3324★
New York Housing and Community Renewal Division
Community Affairs and Affirmative Action Office
Minority Business Affairs and Contract Compliance
1 Fordham Plaza   Ph: (212)519-5928
Bronx, NY 10458   Fax: (212)519-5840
Anthony Shaw, Dir.

★3325★
New York Human Rights Commission
55 W. 125th St.   Ph: (212)870-8400
New York, NY 10027   Fax: (212)870-8552
Margarita Rosa, Commissioner

★3326★
New York Human Rights Division
55 W. 125th St.   Ph: (212)870-8400
New York, NY 10027   Fax: (212)870-8552
Margarita Rosa, Commissioner

★3327★
New York Insurance Department
New York City Office
Affirmative Action
160 W. Broadway   Ph: (212)602-0432
New York, NY 10013   Fax: (212)602-0437
Miriam Boggio, Supt.

★3328★
New York Social Services Department
Minority Program Development Office
40 N. Pearl St.   Ph: (518)473-8555
Albany, NY 12243   Fax: (518)474-7870
Judith Stewart, Dir.

★3329★
New York Transportation Department
Equal Opportunity Development and Compliance
Office
W.A. Harriman Campus, Bldg. 5   Ph: (518)457-1134
Albany, NY 12232   Fax: (518)457-6506
Howard Sheffey, Dir.

North Carolina

★3330★
North Carolina Department of Environment, Health and
  Natural Resources
State Health Director's Office
PO Box 27687
Raleigh, NC 27611   Ph: (919)733-4984
Jonathan Howes, Secretary

★3331★
North Carolina Office of the Governor
Human Relations Council
121 W. Jones St.
Raleigh, NC 27603   Ph: (919)733-7996
William Barber, Director

★3332★
North Carolina State Personnel Office
Equal Opportunity Services Division
116 W. Jones St.   Ph: (919)733-0205
Raleigh, NC 27603-8004   Fax: (919)733-0653
Nelly Riley, Director

North Dakota

★3333★
North Dakota Human Services Department
600 E. Blvd.
State Capitol
Bismarck, ND 58505   Ph: (701)224-2310
Henry Wessman, Executive Director

★3334★
North Dakota Labor Department
Equal Employment Opportunity Division
State Capitol, 6th Fl.
600 E. Boulevard Ave.   Ph: (701)224-2660
Bismarck, ND 58505   Fax: (701)224-3000
John E. Lynch, Officer

Ohio

★3335★
Commission on Minority Health
77 S. High St., Ste. 745
Columbus, OH 43215   Ph: (614)466-4000
Cheryl Boyce, Executive Director

★3336★
Cuyahoga County Office of Equal Opportunity
County Administration Annex Bldg., 5th Fl.
112 Hamilton
Cleveland, OH 44114   Ph: (216)443-7230
Douglas R. Peck, Director

★3337★
Ohio Administrative Services Department
Equal Opportunity Center
77 S. High St., 24th Fl.   Ph: (614)466-8380
Columbus, OH 43266-0408   Fax: (614)644-1795
Booker T. Hall, Deputy Director

★3338★
Ohio Attorney General's Office
Civil Rights Section
50 W. Broad St., 17th Fl.   Ph: (614)466-7900
Columbus, OH 43215   Fax: (614)466-5087
Sherrie Passmore, Chief

★3339★
Ohio Civil Rights Commission
220 Parsons Ave.   Ph: (614)466-2785
Columbus, OH 43206-0543   Fax: (614)644-8776
Joseph Carmichaels, Executive Director

★3340★
Ohio Commerce Department
Equal Employment Opportunity Office
77 S. High St., 23rd Fl.
Columbus, OH 43266   Ph: (614)466-3636
Nancy Childs Dix, Director

★3341★
Ohio Development Department
Minority Business Division
Vern Riffe Center
PO Box 1001   Ph: (614)466-5700
Columbus, OH 43266-0101   Fax: (614)644-5167
Anthony Whitmore, Dir.

★3342★
Ohio Education Department
Equal Employment Opportunity Division
65 S. Front St., Rm. 808
Columbus, OH 43266-0308   Ph: (614)466-3304
Ted Sanders, Superintendent of Public Instruction

★3343★
Ohio Employment Services Bureau
Affirmative Action Office
145 S. Front St.
Columbus, OH 43216   Ph: (614)481-5797

★3344★
Ohio Health Department
Minority Health Affairs Office
246 N. High St.
PO Box 118   Ph: (614)466-8694
Columbus, OH 43266-0118   Fax: (614)644-8526
Morrie Thorington, Chief

★3345★
Ohio Industrial Relations Department
Equal Employment Opportunity Office
2323 W. 5th Ave.
PO Box 825   Ph: (614)644-2229
Columbus, OH 43266-0567   Fax: (614)644-2618
Lynnette Riley, Director

★3346★
Ohio Natural Resources Department
Office of Employee Services
1930 Belcher Dr., Bldg. D1
Columbus, OH 43224   Ph: (614)265-6981
Charles Schultz, Director

★3347★
Ohio Transportation Department
Administration Division
Equal Opportunity Office
25 S. Front St.
Columbus, OH 43215   Ph: (614)466-1163
Melanie M. Lackland, Dir.

--- **Oklahoma** ---

★3348★
Oklahoma Central Services Department
Minority Business Assistance Program
104 State Capitol   Ph: (405)521-4846
Oklahoma City, OK 73105   Fax: (405)521-6403

★3349★
Oklahoma Education Department
Multicultural Equity and Counseling
2500 N. Lincoln Blvd.
Oklahoma City, OK 73105   Ph: (405)521-2841
Shirley Marntinson, Director

★3350★
Oklahoma Education Department
Professional Services Division
Minority Teacher Recruitment Center
2500 N. Lincoln Blvd.   Ph: (405)521-3460
Oklahoma City, OK 73105-4599   Fax: (405)521-6205
Ruby Nichols, Dir.

★3351★
Oklahoma Employment Security Commission
Equal Employment Opportunity Office
212 Will Rogers Memorial Bldg.   Ph: (405)557-7255
Oklahoma City, OK 73105   Fax: (405)557-7256
Barbara Williams, Director

★3352★
Oklahoma Health Department
Affirmative Action Division
1000 NE 10th St.
PO Box 53551   Ph: (405)271-4171
Oklahoma City, OK 73152   Fax: (405)271-3431
Charles Smith, Director

★3353★
Oklahoma Human Rights Commission
2101 N. Lincoln Blvd., Rm. 480
Oklahoma City, OK 73105   Ph: (405)521-3441
Ronald L. Johnson, Director

★3354★
Oklahoma State Department of Health
PO Box 53551
1000 NE 10th St.
Oklahoma City, OK 73152   Ph: (405)271-5600
Thomas Peace, Commissioner of Health

--- **Oregon** ---

★3355★
Oregon Human Resources Department
Affirmative Action Unit
417 Public Service Bldg.
Salem, OR 97310   Ph: (503)378-4342
Linda Topping, Personnel Officer

★3356★
Oregon Labor and Industries Bureau
Civil Rights Division
800 NE Oregon St., No. 32   Ph: (503)731-4873
Portland, OR 97232   Fax: (503)731-4069
Johnnie Bell, Administrator

★3357★
Oregon Office of the Governor
Affirmative Action Director
775 Court St., NE
Salem, OR 97310   Ph: (503)378-5336
Jeanne Pai, Director

--- **Pennsylvania** ---

★3358★
Pennsylvania Commerce Department
Bureau of Minority Business Development
1400 Spring Garden St., Rm 1704
Philadelphia, PA 19130   Ph: (215)560-3236
Kelvin Carolina, Regional Representative

★3359★
Pennsylvania Corrections Department
Affirmative Action Office
PO Box 598
Camp Hill, PA 17011-0598   Ph: (717)975-4906
Eugene Smith, Director

★3360★
Pennsylvania Education Department
Postsecondary/Higher Education Office
Equal Employment Opportunity Office (EEO)
333 Market St.   Ph: (717)783-9531
Harrisburg, PA 17126-0333   Fax: (717)783-4517
Alvin Revell, Dir.

★3361★
Pennsylvania General Services Department
Minority Construction Information Center
210 S. Bouquet St.
Pittsburgh, PA 15213-4098   Ph: (412)565-2365

★3362★
Pennsylvania General Services Department
Minority Development Office
Rm. 515, N. Office Bldg.
Harrisburg, PA 17125   Ph: (717)787-7629
Brenda Blake, Director

★3363★
Pennsylvania Human Relations Commission
PO Box 3145
101 2nd St., Ste. 300
Harrisburg, PA 17105-3145   Ph: (717)787-4410
Homer Floyd, Executive Director

★3364★
Pennsylvania Human Relations Commission
Harrisburg Regional Office
Uptown Shopping Center
2971-E, N. 7th St.
Harrisburg, PA 17110-2123   Ph: (717)787-9780
Howard L. Tucker Jr., Regional Director

★3365★
Pennsylvania Human Relations Commission
Philadelphia Regional Office
711 State Office Bldg.
1400 Spring Garden St.
Philadelphia, PA 19130   Ph: (215)560-2496
Sandra Bacote, Regional Director

★3366★
Pennsylvania Human Relations Commission
Pittsburgh Regional Office
300 Liberty Ave.
State office Bldg., Ste. 1100
Pittsburgh, PA 15222   Ph: (412)565-5395
George A. Simmons, Regional Director

★3367★
Pennsylvania Minority Business Enterprise Council
1600 Arch St.
Philadelphia, PA 19103   Ph: (215)686-6372
Marla Hamilton, Director

★3368★
Pennsylvania Office of the Governor
Administration Office
Affirmative Action Bureau
207 Finance Bldg.
Harrisburg, PA 17120   Ph: (717)783-1130
Richard James, Director

★3369★
Pennsylvania Public Welfare Department
Civil Rights Compliance
PO Box 2675
Harrisburg, PA 17105-2675   Ph: (717)787-3336
Robert L. Lane, Director

★3370★
Pennsylvania Transportation Department
Administration
Equal Opportunity Bureau
Transportation and Safety Bldg., Rm.
  1200   Ph: (717)787-5891
Harrisburg, PA 17120   Fax: (717)787-5491
Leroy Jamison, Dir.

Rhode Island

★3371★
Rhode Island Administration Department
Human Resources Division
Equal Opportunity Office
1 Capitol Hill
Providence, RI 02908-5890   Ph: (401)277-3090
A. Vincent Igliozzi, Director

★3372★
Rhode Island Human Rights Commission
10 Abbott Park Pl.   Ph: (401)277-2661
Providence, RI 02903-3768   Fax: (401)277-2616
Eugene L. Booth, Executive Director

South Carolina

★3373★
South Carolina Department of Health and
  Environmental Control
Office of Minority Health
c/o Division of Maternal Health
2600 Bull St.
Columbia, SC 29201   Ph: (803)734-4972
Gardenia Ruff, Director

★3374★
South Carolina Health and Human Services Finance
  Commission
1801 Main St.
Columbia, SC 29202   Ph: (803)253-6100
Eugene A. Laurent, Director

★3375★
South Carolina Human Affairs Commission
PO Box 4490   Ph: (803)253-6336
Columbia, SC 29240   Fax: (803)253-4191
Willis C. Ham, Commissioner

South Dakota

★3376★
South Dakota Commerce and Regulations Department
Human Rights Division
500 E. Capitol
State Capitol
Pierre, SD 57501-5070   Ph: (605)773-4493

★3377★
South Dakota Personnel Bureau
Equal Employment Opportunity
500 E. Capitol
Pierre, SD 57501   Ph: (605)773-4919
Pamela Roberts, Director

Tennessee

★3378★
Tennessee Attorney General's Office
Civil Rights and Claims Division
450 James Robertson Pkwy.   Ph: (615)741-2091
Nashville, TN 37243-0485   Fax: (615)741-2009
Kimberly Dean, Attorney General

★3379★
Tennessee Economic and Community Development
Department
Minority Business Enterprise Division
320 6th Ave., N., 8th Fl.   Ph: (615)741-2545
Nashville, TN 37243-0405   Fax: (615)741-5829
John Birdsong, Director

★3380★
Tennessee Human Rights Commission
400 Cornerstone Sq. Bldg.
530 Church St.   Ph: (615)741-5825
Nashville, TN 37243-0745   Fax: (615)532-2197
Warren Moore, Executive Director

★3381★
Tennessee Human Services Department
400 Deaderick St.   Ph: (615)741-3241
Nashville, TN 37248   Fax: (615)741-4165
Robert A. Grunow, Commissioner

★3382★
Tennessee Personnel Department
Human Resources Development
Affirmative Action Division
James K. Polk Bldg., 2nd Fl.
Nashville, TN 37243-0635   Ph: (615)741-4845
Rose Wilson, Dir.

Texas

★3383★
Houston Affirmative Action Office
500 Jefferson, Ste. 1400
Houston, TX 77002   Ph: (713)658-3800
Lee Elliot-Brown, Director

★3384★
Houston Housing and Community Development Office
Fair Housing Section
601 Sawyer St., 2nd Fl.
Houston, TX 77007   Ph: (713)868-8300
Annie R. Hill, Administrator

★3385★
Texas Department of Health
Tuberculosis Elimination
1100 W. 49th St.
Austin, TX 78756   Ph: (512)458-7447
John Byber, Director

★3386★
Texas Employment Commission
Equal Employment Opportunity Division
101 E. 15th St.   Ph: (512)463-2400
Austin, TX 78778   Fax: (512)475-1133
Marc Korb, Director

★3387★
Texas Health Department
Civil Rights Office
1100 W. 49th St.   Ph: (512)458-7627
Austin, TX 78756   Fax: (512)458-7750
Charles W. Pankey, Dir.

★3388★
Texas Human Services Department
701 W. 51st St.
PO Box 149030   Ph: (512)450-3030
Austin, TX 78714-9030   Fax: (512)450-3884
Burton F. Raiford, Commissioner

★3389★
Texas Transportation Department
Civil Rights Division
125 E. 11th St.   Ph: (512)475-0688
Austin, TX 78701-2483   Fax: (512)463-0032
Charles Bailey, Dir.

Utah

★3390★
Utah Community and Economic Development
Department
Black Affairs Division
324 S. State St., Ste. 500   Ph: (801)538-8816
Salt Lake City, UT 84111   Fax: (801)538-8888
Betty Sawyer, Director

★3391★
Utah Department of Health
Division of Community Health Services
Ethnic Minority Health Committee Program
PO Box 16660
288 North 1460 West
Salt Lake City, UT 84116-0660   Ph: (801)538-6305
Gar Elison, Director

★3392★
Utah Transportation Department
Civil Rights Office
4501 South 2700 West   Ph: (801)965-4208
Salt Lake City, UT 84119   Fax: (801)965-4338
Mario Blanco, Dir.

Vermont

★3393★
Vermont Human Rights Commission
133 State St.
Montpelier, VT 05633-6301   Ph: (802)828-2480
Susan Sussman, Executive Director

Virginia

★3394★
Virginia Administration Office
Personnel and Training Department
Equal Employment Services
Monroe Bldg.
101 N. 14th St.   Ph: (804)225-2135
Richmond, VA 23219   Fax: (804)371-7401
George Gardner, Director

★3395★
Virginia Department of Health
Main Street Station
PO Box 2448
Richmond, VA 23218   Ph: (804)786-3561
Robert Stroube, Health Commissioner

★3396★
Virginia Economic Development Secretariat
Commerce Department
Fair Housing
3600 W. Broad St.
Richmond, VA 23230   Ph: (804)367-8530
Susan Scovill, Dir.

★3397★
Virginia Economic Development Secretariat
Minority Business Enterprises
1100 9th St. Office Bldg.
Richmond, VA 23219   Ph: (804)786-5560
Esther H. Vasser, Dir.

★3398★
Virginia Health and Human Resources Office
Health Department
Equal Employment Opportunity Division
PO Box 2448   Ph: (804)225-4059
Richmond, VA 23218   Fax: (804)786-4616
Alexis Thorton-Crump, Director

★3399★
Virginia Health and Human Resources Office
Social Services Department
Civil Rights Division
8007 Discovery Dr.   Ph: (804)662-9292
Richmond, VA 23229-8699   Fax: (804)622-7022
Brenda Macklin, Coordinator

★3400★
Virginia Human Rights Council
PO Box 717   Ph: (804)225-2292
Richmond, VA 23206   Fax: (804)225-3294
Mona L. Adkins-Easley, Executive Director

---------- **Washington** ----------

★3401★
King County Affirmative Action
Minority/Women's Business Enterprise
406 S. Water
Olympia, WA 98504   Ph: (206)753-9693

★3402★
King County Office of Civil Rights and Complaints
Fair Employment Office
516 3rd Ave.
King County Courthouse, Rm. E-224
Seattle, WA 98104-2312   Ph: (206)296-7592
Manford Lee, Director

★3403★
King County Office of Civil Rights and Compliance
Fair Housing Office
516 3rd Ave.
King County Courthouse, Rm. E-224
Seattle, WA 98104-2312   Ph: (206)296-7592
Manford Lee, Director

★3404★
King County Office of Human Resource Management
  Affirmative Action
500 4th Ave., Ste. 450
Seattle, WA 98104   Ph: (206)296-7340
Jim Yearby, Director

★3405★
Washington Human Rights Commission
711 S. Capitol Way, Ste. 402
PO Box 42490   Ph: (206)753-2558
Olympia, WA 98504-2490   Fax: (206)586-2282
Merritt Long, Executive Director

★3406★
Washington Human Rights Commission
Seattle Office
1511 3rd Ave., Ste. 921
Seattle, WA 98101   Ph: (206)464-6500
Idolina Reta, District Manager

★3407★
Washington Human Rights Commission
Spokane Office
W. 905 Riverside, Ste. 416
Spokane, WA 99201   Ph: (509)456-4473

★3408★
Washington Human Rights Commission
Yakima Office
32 N. 3rd St., Ste. 441
Yakima, WA 98901   Ph: (509)575-2772

★3409★
Washington Social and Health Services Department
Equal Opportunity Office
PO Box 45839
Olympia, WA 98504-5839   Ph: (206)753-4070
Dan Lundsford, Office Chief

★3410★
Washington Transportation Department
Equal Opportunity Office
Transportation Bldg.
PO Box 47300   Ph: (206)705-7090
Olympia, WA 98504-7300   Fax: (206)705-6806
Brenda Richardson, Dir.

---------- **West Virginia** ----------

★3411★
Community and Industrial Development
Economic Opportunity Office
1204 Kanawha Blvd., E. 2nd Fl.
Charleston, WV 25301   Ph: (304)558-8860
Ralph Goolsby, Director

★3412★
Community and Industrial Development
Minority and Small Business Development Agency
1115 Virginia St., E.
Charleston, WV 25301   Ph: (304)558-2960
Hazel Kroesser, Director

★3413★
West Virginia Attorney General's Office
Civil Rights Division
State Capitol 26 E.   Ph: (304)558-8986
Charleston, WV 25305-0220   Fax: (304)558-0140
Mary Kay Buchmelter, Deputy Attorney General

★3414★
West Virginia Human Rights Commission
1321 Plaza E.   Ph: (304)558-2616
Charleston, WV 25301   Fax: (304)558-2248
Quewannocoii C. Stephens, Executive Director

---------- **Wisconsin** ----------

★3415★
Wisconsin Employment Relations Department
Affirmative Action Division
PO Box 7855   Ph: (608)266-3017
Madison, WI 53707-7855   Fax: (608)267-1020
Gregory Jones, Administrator

★3416★
Wisconsin Health and Social Services Department
Affirmative Action/Civil Rights Office
PO Box 7850   Ph: (608)266-3465
Madison, WI 53707   Fax: (608)266-7882
Georgina Taylor, Director

★3417★
Wisconsin Industry, Labor, and Human Relations
  Department
201 E. Washington Ave.
PO Box 7946
Madison, WI 53707   Ph: (608)266-7552
Carol Skornicka, Secretary

★3418★
Wisconsin Industry, Labor, and Human Relations
  Department
Equal Rights Division
PO Box 7946   Ph: (608)266-0946
Madison, WI 53707   Fax: (608)266-1784
J. Sheehan Donoghue, Admin.

─────────── **Wyoming** ───────────

★3419★
Wyoming Employment Department
Division of Labor Standards
Herschler Bldg.
122 W. 25th St.
Cheyenne, WY 82002   Ph: (307)777-7261
Mike Sullivan, Administration

(14) Businesses (Top 100 Companies)

★3420★
TLC Beatrice International Holdings, Inc.
9 W. 57th St., 48th Fl.
New York, NY 10009   Ph: (212)756-8900
Jean S. Fugett Jr., CEO

Founded: 1987. **Type of Business:** International food processor and distributor. **1992 Sales (in millions of dollars):** 1665.000. **Staff:** 5,000. **Current Rank:** 1. **Previous Rank:** 1.

★3421★
Johnson Publishing Co., Inc.
820 S. Michigan Ave.
Chicago, IL 60605   Ph: (312)322-9200
John H. Johnson, CEO

Founded: 1942. **Type of Business:** Publishing; broadcasting; TV production; cosmetics; hair-care. **1992 Sales (in millions of dollars):** 274.197. **Staff:** 2,785. **Current Rank:** 2. **Previous Rank:** 2.

★3422★
Philadelphia Coca-Cola Bottling Co., Inc.
725 E. Erie Ave.
Philadelphia, PA 19134   Ph: (215)427-4500
J. Bruce Llewellyn, CEO

Founded: 1985. **Type of Business:** Soft-drink bottler. **1992 Sales (in millions of dollars):** 266.000. **Staff:** 1,000. **Current Rank:** 3. **Previous Rank:** 3.

★3423★
H.J. Russell & Co.
504 Fair St. SW
Atlanta, GA 30313   Ph: (404)330-1000
Herman J. Russell, CEO

Founded: 1952. **Type of Business:** Construction and development; food services. **1992 Sales (in millions of dollars):** 145.610. **Staff:** 825. **Current Rank:** 4. **Previous Rank:** 4.

★3424★
The Anderson-Dubose Co.
6195 Davis Industrial Pkwy.
Solon, OH 44139   Ph: (216)248-8800
Warren Anderson, CEO

Founded: 1991. **Type of Business:** Food distributor. **Previous Rank:** Not in Top 100. **1992 Sales (in millions of dollars):** 110.000. **Current Rank:** 5. **Staff:** 80.

★3425★
RMS Technologies, Inc.
5 Eves Dr.
Marlton, NJ 08053   Ph: (609)596-5775
David W. Huggins, CEO

Founded: 1977. **Previous Rank:** 8. **1992 Sales (in millions of dollars):** 103.300. **Current Rank:** 6. **Staff:** 1,176. **Type of Business:** Computer and technical services.

★3426★
Gold Line Refining Ltd.
7324 Southwest Fwy., Ste. 600
Houston, TX 77074   Ph: (713)271-3550
Earl Thomas, CEO

Founded: 1990. **Previous Rank:** 28. **1992 Sales (in millions of dollars):** 91.880. **Current Rank:** 7. **Staff:** 51. **Type of Business:** Oil refinery.

★3427★
Soft Sheen Products, Inc.
1000 E. 87th St.
Chicago, IL 60619   Ph: (312)978-0700
Edward G. Gardner, CEO

Founded: 1964. **Type of Business:** Hair-care products manufacturer. **1992 Sales (in millions of dollars):** 91.700. **Staff:** 547. **Current Rank:** 8. **Previous Rank:** 7.

★3428★
Garden State Cable TV
1250 Haddonfield-Berlin Rd
Cherry Hill, NJ 08034   Ph: (609)354-1880
J. Bruce LLewellyn, CEO

Founded: 1989. **Type of Business:** Cable TV operator. **1992 Sales (in millions of dollars):** 91.000. **Staff:** 300. **Current Rank:** 9. **Previous Rank:** 6.

★3429★
Threads 4 Life Corp.
PO Box 91-1091
Commerce, CA 90091   Ph: (213)890-4700
Carl Jones, CEO

Founded: 1990. **Previous Rank:** 80. **1992 Sales (in millions of dollars):** 89.000. **Current Rank:** 10. **Staff:** 250. **Type of Business:** Apparel manufacturer.

★3430★
Barden Communications, Inc.
243 W. Congress, 10th Fl.
Detroit, MI 48226   Ph: (313)963-5010
Don H. Barden, CEO

Founded: 1981. **Type of Business:** Communications and real estate development. **1992 Sales (in millions of dollars):** 78.600. **Staff:** 328. **Current Rank:** 11. **Previous Rank:** 5.

★3431★
The Bing Group
1130 W. Grand Blvd.
Detroit, MI 48208   Ph: (313)895-3400
David Bing, CEO

Founded: 1980. **Type of Business:** Steel processing and metal stamping distribution. **1992 Sales (in millions of dollars):** 77.634. **Staff:** 210. **Current Rank:** 12. **Previous Rank:** 10.

★3432★
Burrell Communications Group
20 N. Michigan Ave.
Chicago, IL 60602   Ph: (312)443-8600
Thomas J. Burrell, CEO

Founded: 1971. **Type of Business:** Advertising; public relations; consumer promotions. **1992 Sales (in millions of dollars):** 77.007. **Staff:** 115. **Current Rank:** 13. **Previous Rank:** Not in Top 100.

★3433★
Uniworld Group, Inc.
100 Avenue of the Americas
New York, NY 10013   Ph: (212)219-1600
Byron E. Lewis, CEO

Founded: 1969. **Type of Business:** Advertising. **1992 Sales (in millions of dollars):** 72.419. **Staff:** 85. **Current Rank:** 14. **Previous Rank:** Not in Top 100.

★3434★
Pulsar Systems, Inc.
2 Reads Way, Ste. 218
New Castle, DE 19720   Ph: (302)325-3484
William W. Davis Sr., CEO

Founded: 1982. **Previous Rank:** 14. **1992 Sales (in millions of dollars):** 67.000. **Current Rank:** 15. **Staff:** 65. **Type of Business:** Systems integration; office automation; computer resaler.

★3435★
Stop Shop and Save
4514 Edmondson Ave.
Baltimore, MD 21229   Ph: (410)233-7152
Henry T. Baines Sr., CEO

Founded: 1978. **Type of Business:** Supermarkets. **1992 Sales (in millions of dollars):** 66.000. **Staff:** 600. **Current Rank:** 16. **Previous Rank:** 9.

★3436★
Black Entertainment Television Holdings
1232 31st St. NW
Washington, DC 20007   Ph: (202)337-5260
Robert Johnson, CEO

Founded: 1980. **Previous Rank:** 15. **1992 Sales (in millions of dollars):** 61.655. **Current Rank:** 17. **Staff:** 328. **Type of Business:** Cable TV network and magazine publishing.

★3437★
Mays Chemical Co., Inc.
7760 E. 89th St.
Indianapolis, IN 46256   Ph: (317)842-8722
William G. Mays, CEO

Founded: 1980. **Previous Rank:** 13. **1992 Sales (in millions of dollars):** 60.800. **Current Rank:** 18. **Staff:** 75. **Type of Business:** Industrial chemical distributors.

★3438★
Essence Communications, Inc.
1500 Broadway
New York, NY 10036   Ph: (212)642-0600
Edward Lewis, CEO

Founded: 1969. **Type of Business:** Magazine publishing; TV production; direct-mail catalog. **1992 Sales (in millions of dollars):** 56.345. **Staff:** 87. **Current Rank:** 19. **Previous Rank:** 23.

★3439★
Community Foods, Inc.
2936 Remington Ave.
Baltimore, MD 21211   Ph: (410)235-9800
Oscar A. Smith Jr., CEO

Founded: 1970. **Type of Business:** Supermarkets. **1992 Sales (in millions of dollars):** 47.500. **Staff:** 400. **Current Rank:** 20. **Previous Rank:** 18.

★3440★
Technology Applications, Inc.
6101 Stevenson Ave.
Alexandria, VA 22304   Ph: (703)461-2000
James I. Chatman, CEO

Founded: 1977. **Type of Business:** Systems integration and software engineering. **1992 Sales (in millions of dollars):** 46.500. **Staff:** 525. **Current Rank:** 21. **Previous Rank:** 11.

★3441★
Surface Protection Industries, Inc.
3411 E. 15th St.
Los Angeles, CA 90023   Ph: (213)269-9231
Robert C. Davidson Jr., CEO

Founded: 1978. **Type of Business:** Paint and specialty coatings manufacturer. **1992 Sales (in millions of dollars):** 46.200. **Staff:** 200. **Current Rank:** 22. **Previous Rank:** 20.

★3442★
Johnson Products Co., Inc.
8522 S. Lafayette Ave.
Chicago, IL 60620   Ph: (312)483-4100
Joan B. Johnson, CEO

Founded: 1954. **Type of Business:** Hair and personal care products manufacturer. **1992 Sales (in millions of dollars):** 46.000. **Staff:** 215. **Current Rank:** 23. **Previous Rank:** 20.

★3443★
Luster Products Co.
1625 S. Michigan Ave.
Chicago, IL 60616   Ph: (312)431-1150
Jory Luster, CEO

Founded: 1957. **Previous Rank:** 20. **1992 Sales (in millions of dollars):** 46.000. **Current Rank:** 23. **Staff:** 315. **Type of Business:** Hair care products manufacturer and distributor.

★3444★
The Maxima Corp.
4200 Parliament Pl.
Lanham, MD 20706   Ph: (301)459-2000
Joshua I. Smith, CEO

Founded: 1978. **Type of Business:** Systems engineering and computer facilities management. **1992 Sales (in millions of dollars):** 45.098. **Staff:** 752. **Current Rank:** 25. **Previous Rank:** 16.

★3445★
Wesley Industries, Inc.
c/o Flint Coatings Inc.
40221 James P. Cole Blvd.
Flint, MI 48505   Ph: (313)787-3077
Delbert W. Mullens, CEO

Founded: 1983. **Type of Business:** Makers of industrial coatings and foundry products. **1992 Sales (in millions of dollars):** 45.000. **Staff:** 395. **Current Rank:** 26. **Previous Rank:** 35.

★3446★
Pepsi-Cola of Washington, DC, L.P.
PO Box 10520
Washington, DC 20020   Ph: (202)337-3774
Earl G. Graves, CEO

Founded: 1990. **Previous Rank:** 19. **1992 Sales (in millions of dollars):** 43.869. **Current Rank:** 27. **Staff:** 138. **Type of Business:** Soft-drink distributor.

★3447★
Integrated Systems Analysts, Inc.
2800 Shirlington Rd., Ste. 1100
Arlington, VA 22206   Ph: (703)824-0700
C. Michael Gooden, CEO

Founded: 1980. **Type of Business:** Systems engineering; computer systems services. **1992 Sales (in millions of dollars):** 43.600. **Staff:** 595. **Current Rank:** 28. **Previous Rank:** 34.

★3448★
Granite Broadcasting Corp.
1 Dag Hammarskjold Plaza
New York, NY 10017   Ph: (212)826-2530
W. Don Cornwell, CEO

Founded: 1988. **Type of Business:** Network TV affiliates. **1992 Sales (in millions of dollars):** 43.108. **Staff:** 364. **Current Rank:** 29. **Previous Rank:** 24.

★3449★
The Mingo Group
228 E. 45th St., 2nd Fl.
New York, NY 10017   Ph: (212)697-4515
Samuel J. Chisholm, CEO

Founded: 1977. **Type of Business:** Advertising and public relations. **1992 Sales (in millions of dollars):** 42.733. **Staff:** 40. **Current Rank:** 30. **Previous Rank:** Not in Top 100.

★3450★
Crest Computer Supply
7855 Gross Point Rd., Ste. H-1
Skokie, IL 60077   Ph: (708)982-1030
Gale Sayers, CEO

Founded: 1984. **Type of Business:** Computer hardware and software supplier. **1992 Sales (in millions of dollars):** 42.000. **Staff:** 60. **Current Rank:** 31. **Previous Rank:** 41.

★3451★
Beauchamp Distributing Co.
1911 S. Santa Fe Ave.
Compton, CA 90221   Ph: (310)639-5320
Patrick L. Beauchamp, CEO

Founded: 1971. **Type of Business:** Beverage distributor. **1992 Sales (in millions of dollars):** 40.200. **Staff:** 100. **Current Rank:** 32. **Previous Rank:** 29.

★3452★
Rush Communications
New York, NY
Russell Simmons, CEO

** Efforts to locate an address for this edition were unsuccessful. **Founded:** 1990. **Previous Rank:** 32. **1992 Sales (in millions of dollars):** 40.000. **Current Rank:** 33. **Staff:** 65. **Type of Business:** Music publishing; TV, film, radio production.

★3453★
Grimes Oil Co., Inc.
165 Norfolk
Boston, MA 02124   Ph: (617)825-1200
Calvin M. Grimes, CEO

Founded: 1940. **Previous Rank:** 26. **1992 Sales (in millions of dollars):** 38.700. **Current Rank:** 34. **Staff:** 18. **Type of Business:** Petroleum products distributor.

★3454★
Westside Distributors
2405 Southern Ave.
South Gate, CA 90280   Ph: (213)758-3133
Edison R. Lara Sr., CEO

Founded: 1974. **Type of Business:** Beer and snack foods distributor. **1992 Sales (in millions of dollars):** 37.131. **Staff:** 115. **Current Rank:** 35. **Previous Rank:** 25.

★3455★
Pro-Line Corp.
2121 Panoramic Circle
Dallas, TX 75212   Ph: (214)631-4247
Comer J. Cottrell Jr., CEO

Founded: 1970. **Type of Business:** Hair-care products manufacturer and distributor. **1992 Sales (in millions of dollars):** 36.874. **Staff:** 236. **Current Rank:** 36. **Previous Rank:** 33.

★3456★
Thacker Engineering, Inc.
101 Marietta St. NW, Ste. 3402
Atlanta, GA 30303   Ph: (404)223-3404
Floyd G. Thacker, CEO

Founded: 1970. **Type of Business:** Construction; construction management; engineering. **1992 Sales (in millions of dollars):** 36.500. **Staff:** 140. **Current Rank:** 37. **Previous Rank:** 36.

★3457★
Calhoun Enterprises
4155 Lomac St., Ste. G
Montgomery, AL 36106   Ph: (205)272-4400
Greg Calhoun, CEO

Founded: 1984. **Type of Business:** Supermarkets. **1992 Sales (in millions of dollars):** 36.479. **Staff:** 578. **Current Rank:** 38. **Previous Rank:** 27.

★3458★
The Gourmet Companies
1100 Spring St., Ste. 450
Atlanta, GA 30309   Ph: (404)876-5700
Nathaniel R. Goldston III, CEO

Founded: 1975. **Type of Business:** Food services; golf facilities management. **1992 Sales (in millions of dollars):** 36.200. **Staff:** 813. **Current Rank:** 39. **Previous Rank:** 30.

★3459★
Capsonic Group
Division of Gabriel Inc.
460 S. 2nd St.
Elgin, IL 60123   Ph: (708)888-7300
Jim Liautaud, CEO

Founded: 1968. **Previous Rank:** Not in Top 100. **1992 Sales (in millions of dollars):** 36.000. **Current Rank:** 40. **Staff:** 232. **Type of Business:** Maker of electrical components.

★3460★
Drew Pearson Companies
15006 Beltway Dr.
Dallas, TX 75244   Ph: (214)702-8055
Drew Pearson, CEO

Founded: 1985. **Type of Business:** Sports licensing and sportswear manufacturer. **1992 Sales (in millions of dollars):** 36.000. **Staff:** 85. **Current Rank:** 40. **Previous Rank:** 79.

★3461★
Trumark, Inc.
1820 Sunset Ave.
Lansing, MI 48917   Ph: (517)482-0795
Carlton L. Guthrie, CEO

Founded: 1985. **Type of Business:** Metal stampings; manufacturing; welding. **1992 Sales (in millions of dollars):** 35.300. **Staff:** 300. **Current Rank:** 42. **Previous Rank:** 44.

★3462★
Network Solutions, Inc.
505 Huntmar Park Dr.
Herndon, VA 22070   Ph: (703)742-0400
Emmit J. McHenry, CEO

Founded: 1979. **Type of Business:** Systems integration. **1992 Sales (in millions of dollars):** 35.000. **Staff:** 380. **Current Rank:** 43. **Previous Rank:** 17.

★3463★
Am-Pro Protective Agency, Inc.
PO Box 23829
Columbia, SC 29224   Ph: (803)741-0287
John E. Brown, CEO

Founded: 1982. **Previous Rank:** 30. **1992 Sales (in millions of dollars):** 32.127. **Current Rank:** 44. **Staff:** 1,082. **Type of Business:** Security guard services.

★3464★
Metters Industries, Inc.
8200 Greensboro Dr., Ste. 500
Mc Lean, VA 22102   Ph: (703)821-3300
Samuel Metters, CEO

Founded: 1981. **Type of Business:** Systems engineering; telecommunications. **1992 Sales (in millions of dollars):** 31.597. **Staff:** 494. **Current Rank:** 45. **Previous Rank:** 43.

★3465★
Input Output Computer Services, Inc.
400 Totten Pond Rd.
Waltham, MA 02254   Ph: (617)890-2299
Thomas A. Farrington, CEO

Founded: 1969. **Type of Business:** Computer software and systems integrations. **1992 Sales (in millions of dollars):** 31.000. **Staff:** 200. **Current Rank:** 46. **Previous Rank:** 37.

★3466★
Advantage Enterprises, Inc.
5030 Advantage Blvd.
Toledo, OH 43612   Ph: (419)727-0027
Levi Cook Jr., CEO

Founded: 1980. **Previous Rank:** Not in Top 100. **1992 Sales (in millions of dollars):** 30.134. **Current Rank:** 47. **Staff:** 250. **Type of Business:** Project integrator for health care and construction.

★3467★
Automated Sciences Group Inc.
1010 Wayne Ave., Ste. 700
Silver Spring, MD 20910   Ph: (301)587-8750
Arthur Holmes Jr., CEO

Founded: 1974. **Previous Rank:** 37. **1992 Sales (in millions of dollars):** 30.000. **Current Rank:** 48. **Staff:** 300. **Type of Business:** Maker of information and sensor technologies.

★3468★
Dudley Products Inc.
7856 McCloud Rd.
Greensboro, NC 27409   Ph: (919)668-3000
Joe Louis Dudley Sr., CEO

Founded: 1968. **Previous Rank:** Not in Top 100. **1992 Sales (in millions of dollars):** 30.000. **Current Rank:** 48. **Staff:** 501. **Type of Business:** Beauty products manufacturer.

★3469★
Brooks Sausage Co., Inc.
7600 95th St.
Kenosha, WI 53142   Ph: (414)947-0320
Frank B. Brooks, CEO

Founded: 1985. **Type of Business:** Sausage manufacturer. **1992 Sales (in millions of dollars):** 29.000. **Staff:** 148. **Current Rank:** 50. **Previous Rank:** 39.

★3470★
Inner City Broadcasting Corp.
801 2nd Ave.
New York, NY 10017   Ph: (212)661-3344
Pierre Sutton, CEO

Founded: 1972. **Type of Business:** Radio, TV, cable TV franchise. **1992 Sales (in millions of dollars):** 28.000. **Staff:** 200. **Current Rank:** 51. **Previous Rank:** 45.

★3471★
Yancy Minerals
1768 Litchfield Tpke.
Woodbridge, CT 06525   Ph: (203)624-8067
Earl Yancy, CEO

Founded: 1977. **Type of Business:** Industrial metals, minerals and coal distributor. **1992 Sales (in millions of dollars):** 28.000. **Staff:** 8. **Current Rank:** 51. **Previous Rank:** 42.

★3472★
Cimarron Express, Inc.
21883 State Rte. 51
PO Box 185
Genoa, OH 43430   Ph: (419)855-7010
Glenn G. Grady, CEO

Founded: 1984. **Previous Rank:** Not in Top 100. **1992 Sales (in millions of dollars):** 27.773. **Current Rank:** 53. **Staff:** 85. **Type of Business:** Interstate trucking.

★3473★
Queen City Broadcasting, Inc.
7 Broadcast Plaza
Buffalo, NY 14202   Ph: (716)845-6100
J. Bruce Llewellyn, CEO

Founded: 1985. **Type of Business:** Network TV affiliate. **1992 Sales (in millions of dollars):** 26.350. **Staff:** 130. **Current Rank:** 54. **Previous Rank:** 48.

★3474★
Integrated Steel Inc.
12301 Hubbell St.
Detroit, MI 48227   Ph: (313)273-4000
Geralda L. Dodd, CEO

Founded: 1990. **Previous Rank:** Not in Top 100. **1992 Sales (in millions of dollars):** 26.000. **Current Rank:** 55. **Staff:** 305. **Type of Business:** Automotive stamping and steel services.

★3475★
Premium Distributors Inc. of Washington, D.C.
3350 New York Ave. NE
Washington, DC 20002   Ph: (202)526-3900
Henry Neloms, CEO

Founded: 1984. **Previous Rank:** 45. **1992 Sales (in millions of dollars):** 26.000. **Current Rank:** 55. **Staff:** 75. **Type of Business:** Beer distributor.

★3476★
African Development Public Investment Corp.
1635 N. Cahuenga Blvd.
Hollywood, CA 90028   Ph: (213)461-0390
Dick Griffey, CEO

Founded: 1985. **Type of Business:** African commodities and air charter service. **1992 Sales (in millions of dollars):** 25.500. **Staff:** 12. **Current Rank:** 57. **Previous Rank:** 53.

★3477★
Restoration Supermarket Corp.
1360 Fulton St.
Brooklyn, NY 11216   Ph: (718)636-6900
Roderick B. Mitchell, CEO

Founded: 1977. **Type of Business:** Supermarket and drugstore. **1992 Sales (in millions of dollars):** 25.457. **Staff:** 178. **Current Rank:** 58. **Previous Rank:** 47.

★3478★
Navcom Systems Inc.
7203 Gateway Ct.
Manassas, VA 22110   Ph: (703)361-0884
Elijah "Zeke" Jackson, CEO
Founded: 1986. **Previous Rank:** 61. **1992 Sales (in millions of dollars):** 25.000. **Current Rank:** 59. **Staff:** 139. **Type of Business:** Electronic engineering system design and integration.

★3479★
Lockhart & Pettus
79 5th Ave., 10th Fl.
New York, NY 10003   Ph: (212)366-3200
Keith E. Lockhart, CEO
Founded: 1977. **Previous Rank:** Not in Top 100. **1992 Sales (in millions of dollars):** 24.893. **Current Rank:** 60. **Staff:** 32. **Type of Business:** Advertising agency.

★3480★
Parks Sausage Co.
PO Box 854
Baltimore, MD 21203   Ph: (410)664-5050
Raymond V. Haysbert Sr., CEO
Founded: 1951. **Type of Business:** Sausage manufacturer. **1992 Sales (in millions of dollars):** 24.800. **Staff:** 230. **Current Rank:** 61. **Previous Rank:** 49.

★3481★
Dick Griffey Productions
1635 N. Cahuenga Blvd.
Los Angeles, CA 90028   Ph: (213)461-0390
Dick Griffey, CEO
Founded: 1975. **Type of Business:** Entertainment. **1992 Sales (in millions of dollars):** 24.200. **Staff:** 78. **Current Rank:** 62. **Previous Rank:** 55.

★3482★
R.O.W. Sciences Inc.
1700 Research Blvd., Ste. 400
Rockville, MD 20850   Ph: (301)294-5400
Ralph Williams, CEO
Founded: 1983. **Previous Rank:** 55. **1992 Sales (in millions of dollars):** 24.000. **Current Rank:** 63. **Staff:** 365. **Type of Business:** Biomedical and health services; research.

★3483★
American Development Corp.
1930 Hanahan Rd.
North Charleston, SC 29406   Ph: (803)572-0010
W. Melvin Brown Jr., CEO
Founded: 1972. **Type of Business:** Manufacturing and sheet metal fabrication. **1992 Sales (in millions of dollars):** 23.000. **Staff:** 175. **Current Rank:** 64. **Previous Rank:** 50.

★3484★
Sylvest Management Systems Corp.
10001 Derek Wood Ln., Ste. 225
Lanham, MD 20706   Ph: (301)459-2700
Gary S. Murray, CEO
Founded: 1987. **Previous Rank:** 74. **1992 Sales (in millions of dollars):** 22.600. **Current Rank:** 65. **Staff:** 42. **Type of Business:** Computer systems and engineering.

★3485★
Regal Plastics Co., Inc.
15700 Common Rd.
PO Box 246
Roseville, MI 48066   Ph: (313)772-7120
William F. Pickard, CEO
Founded: 1985. **Type of Business:** Custom plastic injection molding. **1992 Sales (in millions of dollars):** 21.711. **Staff:** 222. **Current Rank:** 66. **Previous Rank:** 54.

★3486★
Simmons Enterprises, Inc.
c/o Simmons Carvel Insurance Agency
7781 Cooper Rd., Ste. 2
Cincinnati, OH 45242   Ph: (513)791-4446
Carvel Simmons, CEO
Founded: 1970. **Type of Business:** Trucking; farm operations; day care centers. **1992 Sales (in millions of dollars):** 21.475. **Staff:** 52. **Current Rank:** 67. **Previous Rank:** 65.

★3487★
Earl G. Graves, Ltd.
130 5th Ave.
New York, NY 10011   Ph: (212)242-8000
Earl G. Graves, CEO
Founded: 1970. **Type of Business:** Magazine publishing. **1992 Sales (in millions of dollars):** 21.418. **Staff:** 65. **Current Rank:** 68. **Previous Rank:** 73.

★3488★
H.F. Henderson Industries, Inc.
45 Fairfield Pl.
West Caldwell, NJ 07006   Ph: (201)227-9250
Henry F. Henderson Jr., CEO
Founded: 1954. **Type of Business:** Industrial process controls and defense electronics. **1992 Sales (in millions of dollars):** 20.662. **Staff:** 150. **Current Rank:** 69. **Previous Rank:** 66.

★3489★
Stephens Engineering Co., Inc.
4601 Forbes Blvd., Ste. 300
Lanham, MD 20706   Ph: (301)306-9355
Wallace O. Stephens, CEO
Founded: 1979. **Type of Business:** System integration, facility and computer maintenance. **1992 Sales (in millions of dollars):** 20.500. **Staff:** 140. **Current Rank:** 70. **Previous Rank:** 61.

★3490★
D-Orum Hair Products
1075 Grant St.
Gary, IN 46404   Ph: (219)882-2922
Ernest Daurham Jr., CEO
Founded: 1979. **Previous Rank:** Not in Top 100. **1992 Sales (in millions of dollars):** 20.000. **Current Rank:** 71. **Staff:** 150. **Type of Business:** Minority hair products manufacturer.

★3491★
Bronner Brothers
600 Bronner Brothers Way
Atlanta, GA 30310   Ph: (404)577-4321
Nathaniel Bronner Sr., CEO
Founded: 1947. **Type of Business:** Hair-care products manufacturer. **1992 Sales (in millions of dollars):** 19.500. **Staff:** 250. **Current Rank:** 72. **Previous Rank:** 67.

★3492★
Dual Inc.
2101 Wilson Blvd., Ste. 600
Arlington, VA 22201   Ph: (703)527-3500
J. Fred Dual Jr., CEO
Founded: 1983. **Type of Business:** Engineering and technical services. **1992 Sales (in millions of dollars):** 19.306. **Staff:** 241. **Current Rank:** 73. **Previous Rank:** 69.

★3493★
C.H. James & Co.
3990 Dunbar Ave.
Dunbar, WV 25064   Ph: (304)744-0880
Charles H. James III, CEO
Founded: 1883. **Type of Business:** Wholesale food distribution. **1992 Sales (in millions of dollars):** 18.702. **Staff:** 22. **Current Rank:** 74. **Previous Rank:** 72.

★3494★
Consolidated Beverage Corp.
235 W. 154th St.
New York, NY 10039   Ph: (212)926-5865
Albert N. Thompson, CEO

Founded: 1978. **Type of Business:** Beverage exporter and importer. **1992 Sales (in millions of dollars):** 18.500. **Staff:** 24. **Current Rank:** 75. **Previous Rank:** 82.

★3495★
Watiker & Son, Inc.
PO Box 2688
Zanesville, OH 43702   Ph: (614)454-7958
Al Watiker Jr., CEO

Founded: 1973. **Type of Business:** Heavy highway, bridges, mine reclamation. **1992 Sales (in millions of dollars):** 18.000. **Staff:** 200. **Current Rank:** 76. **Previous Rank:** 87.

★3496★
Terry Manufacturing Co., Inc.
PO Box 648
Roanoke, AL 36274   Ph: (205)863-2171
Roy Terry, CEO

Founded: 1963. **Type of Business:** Apparel manufacturing. **1992 Sales (in millions of dollars):** 17.500. **Staff:** 300. **Current Rank:** 77. **Previous Rank:** 76.

★3497★
J.E. Ethridge Construction Inc.
5270 E. Pine St.
Fresno, CA 93727   Ph: (209)454-0500
John E. Ethridge, CEO

Founded: 1971. **Previous Rank:** Not in Top 100. **1992 Sales (in millions of dollars):** 17.300. **Current Rank:** 78. **Staff:** 25. **Type of Business:** Commercial construction.

★3498★
Burns Enterprises
822 S. 15th St.
Louisville, KY 40210   Ph: (502)585-4548
Tommie Burns Jr., CEO

Founded: 1969. **Type of Business:** Janitorial services and supermarkets. **1992 Sales (in millions of dollars):** 17.000 **Staff:** 460. **Current Rank:** 79. **Previous Rank:** 61.

★3499★
Ozanne Construction Co., Inc.
1635 E. 25th St.
Cleveland, OH 44114   Ph: (216)696-2876
Leroy Ozanne, CEO

Founded: 1956. **Type of Business:** General construction and construction management. **1992 Sales (in millions of dollars):** 17.000. **Staff:** 130. **Current Rank:** 79. **Previous Rank:** 88.

★3500★
UBM Inc.
212 W. Van Buren St., 8th Fl.
Chicago, IL 60607   Ph: (312)939-0505
Sandra Dixon Jiles, CEO

Founded: 1975. **Previous Rank:** Not in Top 100. **1992 Sales (in millions of dollars):** 16.674. **Current Rank:** 81. **Staff:** 53. **Type of Business:** General contracting and construction management.

★3501★
AMSCO Wholesalers Inc.
6525 Best Friend Rd., Ste. A
Norcross, GA 30071   Ph: (404)447-5100
Thurmond B. Woodard, CEO

Founded: 1990. **Previous Rank:** Not in Top 100. **1992 Sales (in millions of dollars):** 16.200. **Current Rank:** 82. **Staff:** 86. **Type of Business:** Wholesale distributor to apartment industry.

★3502★
Systems Engineering & Management Associates, Inc.
2000 N. Beauregard St., Ste. 600
Alexandria, VA 22311   Ph: (703)845-1200
James C. Smith, CEO

Founded: 1985. **Type of Business:** ADP technical support services. **1992 Sales (in millions of dollars):** 16.000. **Staff:** 260. **Current Rank:** 83. **Previous Rank:** 80.

★3503★
American Urban Radio Networks
New York, NY
Sydney Small, CEO

** Efforts to locate an address for this edition were unsuccessful. **Founded:** 1973. **Previous Rank:** 83. **1992 Sales (in millions of dollars):** 15.000. **Current Rank:** 84. **Staff:** 65. **Type of Business:** Radio network; radio station; telemarketing.

★3504★
Mid-Delta Home Health Inc.
PO Box 373
Belzoni, MS 39038   Ph: (601)247-1254
Clara Taylor Reed, CEO

Founded: 1978. **Previous Rank:** Not in Top 100. **1992 Sales (in millions of dollars):** 15.000. **Current Rank:** 84. **Staff:** 345. **Type of Business:** Home health care medical equipment and supplies.

★3505★
Urban Constructors Inc.
4128 N. Miami Ave.
Miami, FL 33127   Ph: (305)576-1408
Jacque E. Thermilus, CEO

Founded: 1988. **Previous Rank:** Not in Top 100. **1992 Sales (in millions of dollars):** 15.000. **Current Rank:** 84. **Staff:** 60. **Type of Business:** General contracting and construction management.

★3506★
Specialized Packaging International, Inc.
3190 Whitney Ave., Bldg. 1
Hamden, CT 06518   Ph: (203)287-8561
Carlton L. Highsmith, CEO

Founded: 1983. **Type of Business:** Packaging design; engineering; brokerage. **1992 Sales (in millions of dollars):** 14.860. **Staff:** 7. **Current Rank:** 87. **Previous Rank:** 89.

★3507★
A Minority Entity, Inc.
PO Box 397
Norco, LA 70079   Ph: (504)764-2422
Burnell K. Moliere, CEO

Founded: 1978. **Type of Business:** Janitorial and food services. **1992 Sales (in millions of dollars):** 14.753. **Staff:** 1,200. **Current Rank:** 88. **Previous Rank:** 78.

★3508★
Tresp Associates Inc.
4900 Seminary Rd., Ste. 700
Alexandria, VA 22311   Ph: (703)845-9400
Lillian B. Handy, CEO

Founded: 1981. **Previous Rank:** 94. **1992 Sales (in millions of dollars):** 14.000. **Current Rank:** 89. **Staff:** 220. **Type of Business:** Military logistics; systems engineering; computers.

★3509★
Solo Construction Corp.
15251 NE, 18th Ave., Ste. 12
North Miami, FL 33162   Ph: (305)944-3922
Randy Pierson, CEO

Founded: 1978. **Type of Business:** General engineering construction. **1992 Sales (in millions of dollars):** 13.959. **Staff:** 46. **Current Rank:** 90. **Previous Rank:** Not in Top 100.

★3510★
RPM Supply Co., Inc.
621 N. 2nd St.
Philadelphia, PA 19123   Ph: (215)627-7106
Robert P. Mapp, CEO

Founded: 1977. **Type of Business:** Electrical and electronic components distributor. **1992 Sales (in millions of dollars):** 13.891. **Staff:** 20. **Current Rank:** 91. **Previous Rank:** 99.

★3511★
Powers & Sons Construction Co., Inc.
2636 W. 15th St.
Gary, IN 46404   Ph: (219)949-3100
Mamon Powers Sr., CEO

Founded: 1967. **Type of Business:** Construction. **1992 Sales (in millions of dollars):** 13.721. **Staff:** 60. **Current Rank:** 92. **Previous Rank:** 57.

★3512★
Williams-Russell and Johnson, Inc.
771 Spring St. NW
Atlanta, GA 30308   Ph: (404)853-6800
Pelham Williams CEO

Founded: 1976. **Type of Business:** Engineering, architecture and construction management. **1992 Sales (in millions of dollars):** 13.600. **Staff:** 125. **Current Rank:** 93. **Previous Rank:** 95.

★3513★
Black River Manufacturing, Inc.
2625 20th St.
Port Huron, MI 48060   Ph: (313)982-9812
Isaac Lang Jr., CEO

Founded: 1977. **Type of Business:** Auto parts manufacturer. **1992 Sales (in millions of dollars):** 13.400. **Staff:** 77. **Current Rank:** 94. **Previous Rank:** 96.

★3514★
Eltrex Industries
65 Sullivan St.
Rochester, NY 14605   Ph: (716)454-6049
Matthew Augustine, CEO

Founded: 1968. **Type of Business:** Office furniture manufacturer fulfillment services. **1992 Sales (in millions of dollars):** 12.976. **Staff:** 155. **Current Rank:** 95. **Previous Rank:** 93.

★3515★
Advanced Systems Technology Inc.
3490 Piedmont Rd., Ste. 1410
Atlanta, GA 30305   Ph: (404)240-2930
Wayne H. Knox, CEO

Founded: 1981. **Previous Rank:** Not in Top 100. **1992 Sales (in millions of dollars):** 12.700. **Current Rank:** 96. **Staff:** 200. **Type of Business:** Nuclear, environmental, and corrosion technology.

★3516★
Advanced Consumer Marketing Corp.
810 Burlway Rd.
Burlingame, CA 94010   Ph: (415)340-7134
Harry W. Brooks Jr., CEO

Founded: 1984. **Type of Business:** Information systems and telecommunications. **1992 Sales (in millions of dollars):** 12.380. **Staff:** 35. **Current Rank:** 97. **Previous Rank:** 59.

★3517★
Spiral Distribution Inc.
7100 W. Erie St.
Chandler, AZ 85226   Ph: (602)940-0441
Reggie Fowler, CEO

Founded: 1987. **Previous Rank:** Not in Top 100. **1992 Sales (in millions of dollars):** 12.300. **Current Rank:** 98. **Staff:** 24. **Type of Business:** Packaging suppliers to the grocery industry.

★3518★
Systems Management American Corp.
254 Monticello Ave.
Norfolk, VA 23510   Ph: (804)627-9331
Herman Valentine, CEO

Founded: 1970. **Type of Business:** Computer systems integration. **1992 Sales (in millions of dollars):** 12.000. **Staff:** 130. **Current Rank:** 99. **Previous Rank:** 52.

★3519★
Wise Construction Co. Inc.
1705 Guenther Rd.
Dayton, OH 45417   Ph: (513)854-0281
Warren C. Wise, CEO

Founded: 1983. **Previous Rank:** Not in Top 100. **1992 Sales (in millions of dollars):** 12.000. **Current Rank:** 99. **Staff:** 75. **Type of Business:** General construction.

(15) Publications

Newspapers

★3520★
Afro-American
429 Central Ave.
East Orange, NJ 07108   Ph: (201)672-9102

Text: Black community newspaper. **Contact(s):** Robert Queen, Editor.

★3521★
Afro-American Times
The Challenge Group
1360 Fulton St.   Ph: (718)636-9500
Brooklyn, NY 11216   Fax: (718)857-9115

Text: Black community newspaper. **Frequency:** Weekly. **Contact(s):** Thomas H. Watkins, Jr., Editor and Publisher. **Circulation:** 55,000.

★3522★
Afro-Americans in New York Life and History
Afro-American Historical Association of the
  Niagara Frontier, Inc.
PO Box 63
Buffalo, NY 14207   Ph: (716)878-5412

Established: 1977. **Column Depth:** 7 1/2 in. **Frequency:** 2x/yr. **Trim Size:** 6 x 9. **Number of Columns Per Page:** 1. **Column Width:** 4 1/2 in. **Print Method:** Offset. **Contact(s):** Monroe Fordham, Editor. **ISSN:** 0364-2437. **Subscription:** $8. $5 single issue. **Circulation:** 600.

★3523★
The Akron Reporter
1046 S. Arlington
PO Box 2042   Ph: (216)773-4196
Akron, OH 44309   Fax: (216)773-2992

Text: Black community newspaper. **Established:** 1969. **Frequency:** Weekly (Thurs.). **Contact(s):** William R. Ellis, Sr., Editor and Publisher. **Circulation:** 17,000.

★3524★
The Alexandria News Weekly
1746 Mason
Alexandria, LA 71301   Ph: (318)443-7664

Text: General newspaper for the black community. **Established:** 1975. **Column Depth:** 294 agate lines. **Frequency:** Weekly (Thurs.). **Number of Columns Per Page:** 6. **Column Width:** 26 nonpareils. **Print Method:** Offset. **Contact(s):** Rev. C.J. Bell, Editor; H. Nicholas

Stull, Publisher and Advertising Mgr. **Subscription:** $15. **Circulation:** 13,750.

★3525★
Amsterdam News
2340 Fredrick Douglas Blvd.   Ph: (212)932-7400
New York, NY 10027   Fax: (212)222-3842

Text: Black community newspaper. **Established:** 1909. **Column Depth:** 200 agate lines. **Frequency:** Weekly (Sat.). **Number of Columns Per Page:** 6. **Column Width:** 18 nonpareils. **Print Method:** Offset. **Contact(s):** William Egyir, Publisher. **Subscription:** $18. **Circulation:** 32,701.

★3526★
Arizona Informant
1746 E. Madison, No. 2   Ph: (602)257-9300
Phoenix, AZ 85034   Fax: (602)257-0547

Text: Black community newspaper. **Established:** 1958. **Column Depth:** 116 agate lines. **Frequency:** Weekly (Wed.). **Trim Size:** 9 3/4 x 16. **Number of Columns Per Page:** 6. **Column Width:** 20 nonpareils. **Print Method:** Web offset. **Contact(s):** Charles R. Campbell, Editor and Publisher; Cloves C. Campbell, Sr., Publisher; Cloves C. Campbell, Jr., Advertising Mgr. **ISSN:** 051-770. **Subscription:** $15; $18 out of area. **Circulation:** 10,000.

★3527★
Arkansas State Press
PO Box 164037   Ph: (501)371-9991
Little Rock, AR 72216   Fax: (501)371-9128

Text: Statewide black newspaper. **Established:** 1941. **Column Depth:** 13 1/2 in. **Frequency:** Weekly (Thurs.). **Trim Size:** 11 3/4 x 14 1/2. **Number of Columns Per Page:** 4. **Column Width:** 2 1/8 in. **Print Method:** Offset. **Contact(s):** Janis Kearney, Publisher. **Subscription:** $20. **Circulation:** 5,000.

★3528★
Atlanta Daily World
145 Auburn Ave. NE
Atlanta, GA 30335-1201   Ph: (404)659-1110

Text: Black community newspaper. **Established:** 1928. **Column Depth:** 21 in. **Frequency:** 4x/wk. (Tues., Thurs., Fri., and Sun.). **Number of Columns Per Page:** 6. **Column Width:** 1 5/8 in. **Print Method:** Offset. **Contact(s):** C.A. Scott, Editor and Publisher. **Subscription:** $65. **Circulation:** 18,000.

★3529★
The Atlanta Inquirer
947 Martin Luther King Jr. Dr. NW
Atlanta, GA 30314   Ph: (404)523-6086
Text: Black community newspaper. Distributed each Thursday with a Saturday publication date. **Established:** 1960. **Column Depth:** 21 in. **Frequency:** Weekly (Thurs.). **Number of Columns Per Page:** 6. **Column Width:** 2 1/16 in. **Print Method:** Offset. **Contact(s):** John B. Smith, Publisher; Irene Ireland, Admin. Assist.; Christopher Weems, Asst. Editor. **Subscription:** $14. **Circulation:** 60,000.

★3530★
The Atlanta Voice
633 Pryor St. SW   Ph: (404)524-6426
Atlanta, GA 30312   Fax: (404)523-7853
Text: Black community newspaper. **Established:** 1966. **Column Depth:** 21 1/2 in. **Frequency:** Weekly (Thurs.). **Number of Columns Per Page:** 6. **Print Method:** Web. **Contact(s):** Stan Washington, Editor; Janis Ware, Publisher. **Subscription:** $39. **Circulation:** 103,000.

★3531★
Bakersfield News Observer
1219 20th St.   Ph: (805)324-9466
Bakersfield, CA 93301   Fax: (805)324-9472
Text: Black community newspaper. **Frequency:** Weekly (Wed.). **Contact(s):** Opal Buchanan, Managing Editor; Joseph L. Coley, Publisher.

★3532★
Baltimore Afro-American
The Afro-American Co.
628 N. Eutaw St.   Ph: (301)728-8200
Baltimore, MD 21201   Fax: (301)383-3213
Text: Black community newspaper. **Established:** 1892. **Column Depth:** 301 agate lines. **Frequency:** Weekly (Sat.). **Number of Columns Per Page:** 6. **Column Width:** 24 nonpareils. **Print Method:** Letterpress. **Contact(s):** John J. Oliver, Jr. Chairman/Publisher. **Subscription:** $26; $46 two years; $58 three years. **Circulation:** 13,385.

★3533★
Bay State Banner
925 Washington St.
Dorchester, MA 02124   Ph: (617)288-4900
Text: Newspaper serving the black community. **Established:** 1965. **Column Depth:** 224 agate lines. **Frequency:** Weekly (Thurs.). **Number of Columns Per Page:** 5. **Column Width:** 23 nonpareils. **Print Method:** Offset. **Contact(s):** Melvin B. Miller, Editor and Publisher; Kim Rogers, Advertising Mgr. **Subscription:** $15. **Circulation:** 11,500.

★3534★
Bayou Talk
Jo Val, Inc.
PO Box 1344
West Corinaey, CA 91793-1344   Ph: (714)247-1316
Text: Cajun Creole community newspaper. **Established:** 1987. **Column Depth:** 13 in. **Frequency:** Monthly (first Thurs.). **Column Width:** 12 picas. **Number of Columns Per Page:** 5. **Contact(s):** Velma V. Conant Metoyer, Editorial Advisor. **Subscription:** $13.

★3535★
Berkeley Tri City Post
The Alameda Publishing Corp.
PO Box 1350   Ph: (510)763-1120
Oakland, CA 94604   Fax: (510)763-9670
Text: Black community newspaper. **Established:** 1963. **Column Depth:** 21 1/2 in. **Frequency:** 2x/wk. (Wed. and Sun.). **Number of Columns Per Page:** 6. **Column Width:** 1 1/16 in. **Print Method:** Offset. **Contact(s):** Gail Berkley, Editor; Thomas Berkley, Publisher; Donald V. Welcher, Advertising Mgr. **Subscription:** $42. **Circulation:** 20,000.

★3536★
Birmingham Times
The Birmingham Times Publishing Co.
115 3rd Ave. W.
PO Box 10503   Ph: (205)251-5158
Birmingham, AL 35202   Fax: (205)323-2294
Text: Black community newspaper. **Established:** February 1964. **Column Depth:** 21 in. **Frequency:** Weekly. **Number of Columns Per Page:** 6. **Column Width:** 13 picas. **Print Method:** Offset. **Contact(s):** James E. Lewis, Editor and Publisher; Jesse J. Lewis, Sr., Advertising Mgr. **Subscription:** $20.

★3537★
Birmingham World
407 15th St. N.   Ph: (205)251-6523
Birmingham, AL 35203-1877   Fax: (205)328-6729
Text: Black community newspaper. **Established:** April 1930. **Column Depth:** 21 1/2 in. **Frequency:** Weekly. **Number of Columns Per Page:** 6. **Column Width:** 2 4/5 in. **Print Method:** Offset. **Contact(s):** Joe N. Dickson, Editor and Publisher. **ISSN:** 0006-3754. **Subscription:** $26. **Circulation:** 12,600.

★3538★
Black American
Cool Magazine, Inc.
310 Lenox Ave., No. 304
New York, NY 10027-4411
Text: Black-oriented newspaper reporting on movies, theatre, African and local politics, and interviews. **Established:** 1960. **Column Depth:** 14 1/4 in. **Frequency:** Weekly (Thurs.). **Trim Size:** 10 1/4 x 14 1/4. **Number of Columns Per Page:** 5. **Column Width:** 2 in. **Print Method:** Offset. **Contact(s):** Hope Offord, Editor; Carl Offord, Publisher; Carlton Brown, Advertising Mgr. **ISSN:** 0890-5983. **Subscription:** $33.

★3539★
The Black Chronicle
PO Box 17498   Ph: (405)424-4695
Oklahoma City, OK 73136   Fax: (405)424-6708
Text: Black community newspaper. **Established:** April 1979. **Column Depth:** 301 agate lines. **Frequency:** Weekly. **Trim Size:** 12 1/2 x 21 1/2. **Number of Columns Per Page:** 8. **Column Width:** 10 picas. **Print Method:** Offset. **Contact(s):** Albert J. Lindsey, Managing Editor; Russell M. Perry, Editor and Publisher. **Subscription:** $19.60. **Circulation:** 28,927.

★3540★
Black Miami Weekly
PO Box F
Miami, FL 33147
Text: Black community newspaper. **Contact(s):** Joel B. Dyer, Publisher.

★3541★
Black Voice/Carta Boricua
Rutgers University
Student Activities Center
Box 28
George St.   Ph: (908)463-1626
New Brunswick, NJ 08903   Fax: (908)463-1702
Text: Collegiate newspaper aimed at a black and Hispanic audience. **Established:** 1969. **Column Depth:** 224 agate lines. **Frequency:** Weekly (Tues.). **Number of Columns Per Page:** 5. **Column Width:** 21 nonpareils. **Print Method:** Offset. **Contact(s):** Kim Robinson, Editor-in-Chief; Saniah M. Johnson, Business Mgr.. **Circulation:** 4,000.

★3542★
Black Voice News
PO Box 1581
Riverside, CA 92502   Ph: (714)682-6070
Text: Newspaper serving African-American communities in what is commonly called the "Inland Empire": Riverside, Moreno Valley, Perris, Banning, Palm Springs, San Bernardino, Ontario, Redlands, and Fontana. **Established:** 1972. **Column Depth:** 294 agate lines.

Frequency: Weekly (Thurs.). **Number of Columns Per Page:** 6. **Column Width:** 24 nonpareils. **Print Method:** Offset. **Contact(s):** Hardy Brown, Publisher. **Subscription:** $32.33; $37.71 out of area. **Circulation:** 7,500.

★3543★
Blazer News
PO Box 806   Ph: (517)787-0450
Jackson, MI 49204   Fax: (517)787-2907
Text: Black community newspaper. **Established:** 1963. **Column Depth:** 224 agate lines. **Frequency:** Weekly (Wed.). **Number of Columns Per Page:** 5. **Column Width:** 23 nonpareils. **Print Method:** Offset. **Contact(s):** Ruth Wade, Editor; Ben Wade, Publisher. **Subscription:** $15. **Circulation:** 6,100.

★3544★
Boston Greater News
PO Box 497
Roxbury, MA 02119-0004   Ph: (617)445-7063
Text: Black community newspaper. **Established:** September 1983. **Column Depth:** 14 in. **Frequency:** Weekly. **Trim Size:** 11 x 15. **Number of Columns Per Page:** 5. **Column Width:** 2 in. **Print Method:** Offset. **Contact(s):** Fred J. Clark, Editor and Publisher; Edwin Sumpter, Advertising Mgr. **Subscription:** $18.

★3545★
Brooklyn New York Recorder
86 Bainbridge St.
Brooklyn, NY 11233   Ph: (718)493-4616
Text: Black community newspaper. **Established:** 1953. **Frequency:** Weekly. **Contact(s):** Dale T. Watkins, Publisher.

★3546★
The Buckeye Review
William Publishing Co.
626 Belmont Ave.
Youngstown, OH 44502   Ph: (216)743-2250
Text: Black community newspaper. **Established:** 1937. **Column Depth:** 182 agate lines. **Frequency:** Weekly (Fri.). **Number of Columns Per Page:** 5. **Column Width:** 24 nonpareils. **Print Method:** Offset. **Contact(s):** Crystal A. Williams, Editor. **Subscription:** $15.

★3547★
Buffalo Criterion
623 William St.
Buffalo, NY 14206   Ph: (716)882-9570
Text: Black community newspaper. **Established:** 1925. **Frequency:** Weekly (Thurs.). **Print Method:** Offset. **Trim Size:** 13 x 19 1/2. **Number of Columns Per Page:** 8. **Column Width:** 1 7/8 in. **Contact(s):** Frank E. Merriweather, Editor and Publisher. **Subscription:** $14.95; $19.95 out of area.

★3548★
Buffalo Fine Print News
806 Fillmore Ave.   Ph: (716)855-3810
Buffalo, NY 14212   Fax: (716)855-3810
Text: Black community newspaper. **Established:** February 20, 1970. **Frequency:** Weekly. **Print Method:** Offset. **Number of Columns Per Page:** 5. **Contact(s):** Ronald H. Fleming, Editor and Publisher; Carolyn Fleming, Advertising Mgr. **Subscription:** $12. **Circulation:** 10,000.

★3549★
The Bulletin
2490 Dr. M.L. King, Jr. Way
PO Box 2560
Sarasota, FL 34230-2560   Ph: (813)953-3990
Text: Black community newspaper. **Established:** 1959. **Column Depth:** 126 agate lines. **Frequency:** Weekly (Fri.). **Number of Columns Per Page:** 6. **Column Width:** 2 1/16 in. **Print Method:** Offset. **Contact(s):** Richard Wright, Editor; Rosalind J. Bacon, Mng. Editor; Fred L. Bacon, Publisher; Ralph Pompey, Advertising Mgr. **Subscription:** $26. $.25 single issue. **Circulation:** 18,000.

★3550★
California Advocate
452 Fresno St.
PO Box 11826   Ph: (209)268-0941
Fresno, CA 93775   Fax: (209)266-6947
Text: Black community newspaper. **Established:** 1967. **Frequency:** 2x/mo. **Contact(s):** Pauline Kimber, Editor; Lesly H. Kimber, Publisher. **Circulation:** 22,500.

★3551★
California Voice
2956 Sacramento St., Ste. C   Ph: (510)644-2446
Berkeley, CA 94702   Fax: (510)644-0603
Text: Black community newspaper. **Established:** 1919. **Frequency:** Weekly (Fri.). **Print Method:** Letterpress. Uses mats. **Contact(s):** Dr. Ruth C. Love, Editor and Publisher. **Subscription:** $9. **Circulation:** 37,325.

★3552★
Call
Kansas City Call Inc.
PO Box 410-477   Ph: (816)842-3804
Kansas City, MO 64141   Fax: (816)842-4420
Text: Black community newspaper. **Established:** 1919. **Column Depth:** 294 agate lines. **Frequency:** Weekly (Fri.). **Number of Columns Per Page:** 8. **Column Width:** 18 nonpareils. **Print Method:** Offset. **Contact(s):** Lucille Bluford, Editor and Publisher. **Subscription:** $17.50.

★3553★
Call and Post
1949 E. 105 St.   Ph: (216)791-7600
Cleveland, OH 44106   Fax: (216)791-6568
Text: Black community newspaper. **Established:** 1919. **Column Depth:** 294 agate lines. **Frequency:** Weekly (Thurs.). **Number of Columns Per Page:** 6. **Column Width:** 26 nonpareils. **Print Method:** Letterpress and offset. **Contact(s):** Harry Alexander, Editor and Publisher. **Subscription:** $20. **Circulation:** 43,283.

★3554★
Campus Digest
Tuskegee University
Tuskegee, AL 36083   Ph: (205)727-8263
Text: Black collegiate newspaper. **Established:** 1931. **Column Depth:** 196 agate lines. **Frequency:** Every other week (Fri..). **Number of Columns Per Page:** 5. **Column Width:** 20 nonpareils. **Print Method:** Offset. **Contact(s):** Derrick T. Darteh, Editor. **Subscription:** $3.50. **Circulation:** 2,000.

★3555★
Capital Outlook
417 N. Duval St.   Ph: (904)681-1852
Tallahassee, FL 32301   Fax: (904)681-1093
Text: Black community newspaper. **Established:** 1964. **Column Depth:** 21 1/2. **Frequency:** Weekly. **Column Width:** 2. **Number of Columns Per Page:** 6. **Contact(s):** Roosevelt Wilson, Editor and Publisher. **Subscription:** $30. **Circulation:** 11,333.

★3556★
Carolina Peacemaker
400 Summit Ave.   Ph: (919)274-6210
Greensboro, NC 27405   Fax: (919)273-5103
Text: Black community newspaper. **Established:** April 3, 1967. **Column Depth:** 301 agate lines. **Frequency:** Weekly (Thurs.). **Number of Columns Per Page:** 6. **Column Width:** 26 nonpareils. **Print Method:** Offset. **Contact(s):** John Marshall Kilimanjaro, Editor and Publisher; Thomas E. Price, Advertising Mgr. **Subscription:** $15; $18 out of state. **Circulation:** 5,490.

★3557★
The Carolina Times
PO Box 3825
Durham, NC 27702   Ph: (919)682-2913
Text: Black community newspaper. **Established:** 1926. **Column Depth:** 301 agate lines. **Frequency:** Weekly (Thurs.). **Number of**

Columns Per Page: 6. Column Width: 24 nonpareils. Print Method: Offset. Contact(s): Mrs. V.A. Edmonds, Editor and Publisher; Kenneth W. Edmonds, Advertising Mgr. Subscription: $12.60; $18.90 out of area. Circulation: 5,300.

★3558★
The Carolinian
518 E. Martin St.
PO Box 25308
Raleigh, NC 27601

Ph: (919)834-5558
Fax: (919)832-3243

Text: Black community newspaper. Established: October 1940. Column Depth: 294 agate lines. Frequency: 2x/wk. (Mon. and Thurs.). Number of Columns Per Page: 6. Column Width: 25 nonpareils. Print Method: Offset. Contact(s): P.J. Monroe, contact. Subscription: $25.

★3559★
Carson Bulletin
Rapid Publishing
PO Box 4248
Compton, CA 90224

Ph: (213)774-0018

Text: Black community newspaper. Column Depth: 21 1/2 in. Frequency: Weekly (Wed.). Column Width: 12 1/2 picas. Number of Columns Per Page: 6. Contact(s): O. Ray Watkins, Publisher.

★3560★
The Catholic Mentor
Winston Derek Publishers, Inc.
PO Box 90883
Nashville, TN 37209

Ph: (615)321-0535

Text: Newspaper for black Catholics. Established: 1986. Frequency: 6x/yr. Contact(s): James W. Peebles, Editor-in-Chief.

★3561★
Central Star/Journal Wave
Central News-Wave Publications
2621 W. 54th St.
Los Angeles, CA 90043

Ph: (213)290-3000
Fax: (213)291-0219

Text: Black community newspaper. Established: 1919. Column Depth: 21 1/2 in. Frequency: Weekly (Wed.). Trim Size: 13 3/4 x 21 1/2. Number of Columns Per Page: 6. Column Width: 5 nonpareils. Print Method: Offset. Contact(s): C.Z. Wilson, Publisher. Subscription: $78. Circulation: 39,900.

★3562★
The Challenger
1303 Fillmore Ave.
Buffalo, NY 14211

Ph: (716)897-0442
Fax: (716)897-3307

Text: Black community newspaper featuring political editorials. Established: 1963. Frequency: Weekly (Wed.). Print Method: Offset. Column Width: 22 nonpareils. Column Depth: 196 agate lines. Number of Columns Per Page: 5. ** 1 7/8 in. ** 1 in. Contact(s): Barbara Banks, Editor and Publisher. Subscription: $15. Circulation: 10,000.

★3563★
Charleston Black Times
South Carolina Black Media Group
1310 Harden
Columbia, SC 29204

Ph: (803)799-5252
Fax: (803)799-7709

Text: Black community interest newspaper. Established: 1970. Column Depth: 224 agate lines. Frequency: Weekly (Wed.). Number of Columns Per Page: 6. Column Width: 24 nonpareils. Print Method: Offset. Contact(s): Zack Weston, Editor; Isaac Washington, Publisher; Cynthia Bowden, Advertising Mgr. Subscription: $25. Circulation: 6,883.

★3564★
The Charleston Chronicle
Chronicle Communications Corp.
534 King St.
PO Box 20548
Charleston, SC 29413-0548

Ph: (803)723-2785
Fax: (803)577-6099

Text: Black community newspaper. Established: 1971. Column Depth: 294 agate lines. Frequency: Weekly (Wed.) Number of

Columns Per Page: 6. Column Width: 26 nonpareils. Print Method: Offset. Contact(s): J. John French, Editor and Publisher. Subscription: $18.

★3565★
The Charlotte Post
1531 Camden Rd.
PO Box 30144
Charlotte, NC 28230

Ph: (704)376-0496
Fax: (704)342-2160

Text: Black community newspaper. Established: 1887. Column Depth: 301 agate lines. Frequency: Weekly (Thurs.). Number of Columns Per Page: 6. Column Width: 25 nonpareils. Print Method: Offset. Contact(s): Herbert White, Editor; Gerald Johnson, Publisher; Bob Johnson, Publisher; Fran Farrer-Bradley, Advertising Mgr. Subscription: $21; $18 senior citizens. Circulation: 11,500.

★3566★
Chatham-Southeast Citizen
Citizen Newspapers
412 E. 87th St.
Chicago, IL 60619

Ph: (312)487-7700
Fax: (312)487-7931

Text: Newspaper serving Chicago's black community. Established: 1965. Column Depth: 196 agate lines. Frequency: Weekly (Thurs.). Number of Columns Per Page: 5. Column Width: 25 nonpareils. Print Method: Offset. Contact(s): William Garth, Pres./Publisher/Advertising Mgr.; Lisa Ely, Mng. Editor. Subscription: $25.

★3567★
Chicago Citizen
Citizen Newspapers
412 E. 87th St.
Chicago, IL 60619

Ph: (312)487-7700
Fax: (312)487-7931

Text: Black community newspaper. Established: 1965. Frequency: Weekly (Thurs.). Contact(s): John Williams, Jr., Editor; William A. Garth, Publisher.

★3568★
Chicago Crusader
Crusader Newspapers
6429 S. Martin Luther King Dr.
Chicago, IL 60637

Ph: (312)752-2500
Fax: (312)752-2817

Text: Black community newspaper (tabloid). Established: June 1940. Column Depth: 14 in. Frequency: Weekly (Sat.). Trim Size: 10 x 14. Number of Columns Per Page: 5. Column Width: 2 in. Print Method: Offset. Contact(s): Dorothy R. Leavell, Editor and Publisher; John Smith, Advertising Mgr. Subscription: $12. Circulation: 57,000.

★3569★
Chicago Independent Bulletin
2037 W. 95th St.
Chicago, IL 60643

Ph: (312)783-1040

Text: Black community newspaper. Established: 1958. Frequency: Weekly (Thurs.). Contact(s): Hurley Green, Sr., Editor and Publisher. Circulation: 64,000.

★3570★
Chicago Metro News
3437 S. Indiana Ave.
Chicago, IL 60616-3840

Text: Newspaper for the black community. Established: 1965. Column Depth: 301 agate lines. Frequency: Weekly (Sat.). Number of Columns Per Page: 6. Column Width: 26 nonpareils. Print Method: Offset. Contact(s): Ruth Armstrong, Editor and Publisher; Judith M. Armstrong, Advertising Mgr.; Patricia Armstrong, Advertising Mgr. Subscription: $20.

★3571★
Chicago Shoreland News
AJA Enterprise
11740 S. Elizabeth
Chicago, IL 60643

Ph: (312)568-7091
Fax: (312)928-6056

Text: Black community newspaper. Established: 1974. Column Depth: 14 in. Frequency: Weekly (Thurs.). Trim Size: 9 3/4 x 14.

Number of Columns Per Page: 5. Column Width: 11 picas. Print Method: Offset. Contact(s): Al Johnson, Publisher; Donna Weathersby, Editor Subscription: $21.

★3572★
Chicago South Shore Scene
7426 S. Constance
Chicago, IL 60649   Ph: (312)363-0441
Text: Community newspaper (Black). Established: 1959. Column Depth: 224 agate lines. Frequency: Weekly (Thurs.). Number of Columns Per Page: 4. Column Width: 18 nonpareils. Print Method: Offset. Contact(s): Dr. Claudette McFarland, Editor and Publisher. Subscription: $50.

★3573★
Chicago Standard News
Standard Newspapers
615 S. Halsted   Ph: (708)755-5021
Chicago Heights, IL 60411   Fax: (708)755-5020
Text: Black community newspaper. Established: 1984. Column Depth: 16 in. Frequency: Weekly. Number of Columns Per Page: 5. Column Width: 11 picas. Print Method: Offset. Contact(s): Lorenzo Martin, Editor and Publisher; Pat Rush Martin, Advertising Mgr. Subscription: $30. Circulation: 15,000.

★3574★
Chicago Weekend
Citizen Newspapers
412 E. 87th St.   Ph: (312)487-7700
Chicago, IL 60619   Fax: (312)487-7931
Text: Weekend newspaper serving Chicago's black community. Established: 1974. Column Depth: 196 agate lines. Frequency: Weekly (Thurs.). Number of Columns Per Page: 5. Column Width: 25 nonpareils. Print Method: Offset. Contact(s): William Garth, Pres./Publisher/Advertising Mgr.; Lisa Ely, Mng. Editor. Subscription: $25.

★3575★
Cincinnati Herald
Porter Publishing
836 Lincoln Ave.   Ph: (513)221-5440
Cincinnati, OH 45206   Fax: (513)221-2959
Text: Black community newspaper. Established: 1955. Column Depth: 294 agate lines. Frequency: Weekly. Trim Size: 15 x 22. Number of Columns Per Page: 6. Column Width: 2 3/16 in. Print Method: Offset. Contact(s): Donald Anthony, Editor; William Spillers, Jr., Publisher; Jermaine Hill, Advertisingand Promotion Dir. Subscription: $20. Circulation: 24,500.

★3576★
The City Sun
The City Sun Publishing Co., Inc.
GPO 560   Ph: (718)624-5959
Brooklyn, NY 11202   Fax: (718)596-7429
Text: Newspaper with black orientation. Established: June 6, 1984. Column Depth: 198 agate lines. Frequency: Weeky (Wed.). Number of Columns Per Page: 6. Column Width: 9 1/2 picas. Print Method: Letterpress. Contact(s): Utrice C. Leid, Editor; Andrew W. Cooper, Publisher and Advertising Mgr. Subscription: $26. Circulation: 20,000.

★3577★
The Coastal Times
701 E. Bay St.
BTC Box 1407
Charleston, SC 29403   Ph: (803)723-5318
Text: Community newspaper (Black oriented). Established: July 1983. Column Depth: 21 in. Frequency: Weekly (Wed.). Number of Columns Per Page: 6. Column Width: 2 1/16 in. Print Method: Offset. Contact(s): Mignon Clyburn, Editor; James E. Clyburn, Publisher. Subscription: $15.

★3578★
Columbia Black News
S.C. Black Media Group
PO Box 11128   Ph: (803)799-5252
Columbia, SC 29211   Fax: (803)799-7709
Text: Black community newspaper. Established: 1970. Column Depth: 224 agate lines. Frequency: Weekly (Wed.). Number of Columns Per Page: 6. Column Width: 24 nonpareils. Print Method: Offset. Contact(s): Issac Washington, Publisher. Subscription: $25. Circulation: 22,834.

★3579★
The Columbus Times
Columbus limes
2230 Buena Vista Rd.
PO Box 2845   Ph: (404)324-2404
Columbus, GA 31993-2999   Fax: (404)596-0657
Text: Black community newspaper. Established: 1970. Column Depth: 21 1/2 in. Frequency: Weekly (Wed.). Trim Size: 13 x 21 1/2. Number of Columns Per Page: 6. Column Width: 2 1/16 in. Print Method: Offset. Broadsheet. Contact(s): Ophelia Devore Mitchell, Editor and Publisher; Helmut Gerdes, Advertising Mgr. Subscription: $16.80. Circulation: 20,000.

★3580★
Communicade
Okang Communications Corp.
104 Magnolia St.
PO Box 60739
Rochester, NY 14606
Text: Regional newspaper (Black). Established: 1972. Column Depth: 224 agate lines. Frequency: Every other week. Number of Columns Per Page: 5. Column Width: 24 nonpareils. Print Method: Offset. Contact(s): Frank B. Willis, Editor. Subscription: $4.95.

★3581★
Community Leader
1210 North Blvd.
Baton Rouge, LA 70802
Text: Black community newspaper. Contact(s): Alfonso Lankster, General Manager.

★3582★
Compton Bulletin
Rapid Publishing
PO Box 4248
Compton, CA 90224   Ph: (213)774-0018
Text: Black community newspaper. Column Depth: 21 1/2 in. Frequency: Weekly (Wed.). Column Width: 12 1/2 picas. Number of Columns Per Page: 6. Contact(s): O. Ray Watkins, Publisher.

★3583★
Compton/Carson Wave
Central News-Wave Publications
2621 W. 54th St.   Ph: (213)290-3000
Los Angeles, CA 90043   Fax: (213)291-0219
Text: Black community newspaper. Column Depth: 21 1/2 in. Frequency: Weekly (Wed.). Trim Size: 13 3/4 x 21 1/2. Number of Columns Per Page: 6. Column Width: 5 nonpareils. Print Method: Offset. Contact(s): C.Z. Wilson, Publisher. Subscription: $78. Circulation: 38,200.

★3584★
Compton Metropolitan Gazette
First-Line Publishers
17939 Chatsworth St., Ste. 429   Ph: (818)782-8695
Granada Hills, CA 91344   Fax: (818)782-2924
Text: Black community newspaper serving Compton and Carson. Established: 1966. Frequency: Weekly (Thurs.). Print Method: Offset. Trim Size: 13 x 21 1/2. Number of Columns Per Page: 6. Column Width: 2 in. Contact(s): Hillary Hamm, Publisher; Hillard Hamm, C.E.O. Subscription: Free; $25. Circulation: 60,000.

★3585★
Culver City/Westchester Star
Central News-Wave Publications
2621 W. 54th St.   Ph: (213)290-3000
Los Angeles, CA 90043   Fax: (213)291-0219
Text: Black community newspaper. **Established:** 1980. **Column Depth:** 21 1/2 in. **Frequency:** Weekly (Wed.). **Number of Columns Per Page:** 6. **Column Width:** 5 nonpareils. **Print Method:** Offset. **Contact(s):** C.Z. Wilson, Publisher. **Subscription:** $78. **Circulation:** 33,750.

★3586★
Daily Challenge
1360 Fulton St.   Ph: (718)636-9500
Brooklyn, NY 11216   Fax: (718)857-9115
Text: Black community newspaper. **Frequency:** Daily. **Contact(s):** Thomas H. Watkins, Jr., Publisher. **Circulation:** 79,000.

★3587★
Dallas Examiner
424 Centre St.   Ph: (214)948-9175
Dallas, TX 75208   Fax: (214)948-9176
Text: Black community newspaper. **Established:** 1986. **Frequency:** Weekly (Thurs.). **Contact(s):** Charles O'Neal, Editor; Finch Belt, Publisher. **Circulation:** 50,000.

★3588★
Dallas Post Tribune
2726 S. Beckley   Ph: (214)946-7678
Dallas, TX 75224   Fax: (214)946-6823
Text: Black community newspaper. **Established:** 1947. **Column Depth:** 294 agate lines. **Frequency:** Weekly (Thurs.). **Number of Columns Per Page:** 6. **Column Width:** 24 nonpareils. **Print Method:** Offset. **Contact(s):** Dorothy Lee, Editor; T.R. Lee, Publisher; Doris Green, Advertising Mgr. **Subscription:** $20. **Circulation:** 30,000.

★3589★
The Dallas Weekly Newspaper
Ad-Mast Publishing, Inc.
Anthony T. Davis Bldg.
3101 Martin Luther King, Jr. Blvd.   Ph: (214)428-8958
Dallas, TX 75215   Fax: (214)428-2807
Text: Black community newspaper. **Established:** 1955. **Column Depth:** 175 agate lines. **Frequency:** Weekly (Wed.). **Trim Size:** 9 7/8 x 13. **Number of Columns Per Page:** 5. **Column Width:** 143 agate lines. **Print Method:** Offset. **Contact(s):** Steven Scott, Gen. Mgr.; James Washington, Publisher. **ISSN:** 0895-1271. **Subscription:** Free; $60. **Circulation:** 20,300.

★3590★
Daytona Times
Daytona Times, Inc.
429 S. Dr. M. L. King Blvd.
PO Box 1110   Ph: (904)253-0321
Daytona Beach, FL 32115   Fax: (904)254-7510
Text: Black community newspaper. **Established:** August 1978. **Column Depth:** 21 in. **Frequency:** Weekly (Thurs.). **Number of Columns Per Page:** 6. **Column Width:** 2 1/16 in. **Print Method:** Offset. **Contact(s):** Charles W. Cherry II, Editor and Publisher. **Subscription:** $25. **Circulation:** 20,150.

★3591★
Decatur Voice
625 E. Wood St.   Ph: (217)423-2231
Decatur, IL 62523   Fax: (217)423-2231
Text: Black community newspaper. **Established:** 1968. **Column Depth:** 16 in. **Frequency:** Weekly. **Trim Size:** 10 x 16. **Number of Columns Per Page:** 5. **Column Width:** 2 in. **Print Method:** Offset. **Contact(s):** Horace G. Livingston, Jr., Publisher; Mildred Covington, Advertising Mgr. **Subscription:** $24.

★3592★
The Defender
1702 Locust St.   Ph: (302)656-3252
Wilmington, DE 19802   Fax: (215)471-1130
Text: Black community newspaper. **Established:** 1962. **Column Depth:** 16 in. **Frequency:** Weekly. **Trim Size:** 15 x 17. **Number of Columns Per Page:** 6. **Column Width:** 1 1/2 in. **Print Method:** Offset. **Contact(s):** Earl Brown, Publisher. **Subscription:** $25.

★3593★
Denver Weekly News
PO Box 38939   Ph: (303)839-5800
Denver, CO 80238-0939   Fax: (303)839-5891
Text: Black community newspaper serving Denver and surrounding areas. **Frequency:** Weekly (Thurs.). **Contact(s):** F. Cosmo Harris, Editor and Publisher; Ms. Tommie Thomas, Advertising Mgr. **Circulation:** 17,500.

★3594★
The Detroit Journal
B&Y Publications
11000 W. McNichols, Ste. 19   Ph: (313)342-1717
Detroit, MI 48221   Fax: (313)312-9078
Text: Black community newspaper (tabloid). **Established:** 1992. **Frequency:** Monthly. **Print Method:** Offset. **Contact(s):** Walter Johnson, Editor and Publisher. **Subscription:** Free. **Circulation:** 20,000.

★3595★
East St. Louis Crusader
10th & State St.   Ph: (618)271-2000
East Saint Louis, IL 62205   Fax: (618)271-2045
Text: Black community newspaper. **Frequency:** Weekly. **Print Method:** Heatset web. **Contact(s):** Joe Lewis, Sr., Publisher.

★3596★
East St. Louis Monitor
East St. Louis Monitor Publishing, Inc.
1501 State St.
Box 2137
East Saint Louis, IL 62205   Ph: (618)271-0468
Text: Black community newspaper. **Established:** 1963. **Column Depth:** 21 1/2 in. **Frequency:** Weekly. **Trim Size:** 13 1/8 x 21 1/2. **Number of Columns Per Page:** 6. **Column Width:** 2 in. **Print Method:** Offset. **Contact(s):** Ernest Mercer, Acting Editor; Anne E. Jordan, Publisher; George Laktzian, Advertising Mgr. **Subscription:** $21.80. **Circulation:** 22,500.

★3597★
Ecorse Telegram
4122 10th St.
PO Box 4585   Ph: (313)928-2955
Ecorse, MI 48229   Fax: (517)787-2907
Text: Black community newspaper. **Established:** 1945. **Column Depth:** 16 in. **Frequency:** Weekly. **Number of Columns Per Page:** 5. **Column Width:** 23 nonpareils. **Print Method:** Offset. Uses mats. **Contact(s):** J.C. Wall, Editor and Publisher; Dorothy Wall, Advertising Mgr. **Subscription:** $25. **Circulation:** 12,000.

★3598★
The Evening Whirl
Thomas Publication Co.
PO Box 5088 Nagel Sta.   Ph: (314)383-3875
Saint Louis, MO 63115   Fax: (314)383-7335
Text: Black community newspaper. **Established:** 1938. **Column Depth:** 294 agate lines. **Frequency:** Weekly (Tues.). **Number of Columns Per Page:** 8. **Column Width:** 21 nonpareils. **Print Method:** Offset. **Contact(s):** A.C. Clay, Editor; Benjamin Thomas, Publisher. **Subscription:** $50; $40 6 months; $30 3 months. **Circulation:** 40,000.

★3599★
Every Wednesday
Afro-American Newspapers
628 N. Eutaw St.   Ph: (301)728-8200
Baltimore, MD 21201   Fax: (301)383-3213
Text: Black community newspaper. **Established:** 1984. **Frequency:** Weekly (Wed.). **Print Method:** Offset. **Trim Size:** 11 x 14. **Number of Columns Per Page:** 2. **Contact(s):** Robert Matthews, Editor; John Oliver, Publisher; Marsha White, Advertising Mgr. **Circulation:** 42,777.

★3600★
Facts Newspaper
2765 E. Cherry St.
PO Box 22015   Ph: (206)324-0552
Seattle, WA 98122   Fax: (206)324-1007
Text: Black community newspaper. **Established:** 1961. **Column Depth:** 224 agate lines. **Frequency:** Weekly. **Trim Size:** 17 X 21. **Number of Columns Per Page:** 6. **Column Width:** 20 nonpareils. **Print Method:** Offset. **Contact(s):** Elizabeth Beaver, Editor and Publisher. **Subscription:** $52.

★3601★
The Famuan
Florida A&M University   Ph: (904)599-3159
Tallahassee, FL 32307   Fax: (904)561-2570
Text: College newspaper. **Established:** 1919. **Column Depth:** 196 agate lines. **Frequency:** Weekly. **Trim Size:** 11 1/2 x 17 1/2. **Number of Columns Per Page:** 4. **Column Width:** 26 nonpareils. **Print Method:** Offset. **Contact(s):** Gale A. Workman, Faculty Adviser. **Subscription:** Free; $15 (mail). **Circulation:** 4,000.

★3602★
The Fayetteville Black Times
The Black Press, Inc.
108 Webb St.
PO Box 863
Fayetteville, NC 28302
Text: Black community newspaper. **Frequency:** Weekly (Wed.). **Number of Columns Per Page:** 6. **Contact(s):** Thelma H. Kinney, Sharing Editor; Dr. Johnny Gaston, Contributing Editor; Bro. J.D. Marshall, Contributing Editor.

★3603★
The Final Call
734 W. 79th St.   Ph: (312)602-1230
Chicago, IL 60620   Fax: (312)602-1013
Text: Newspaper serving the black community. **Established:** 1979. **Column Depth:** 13 in. **Frequency:** Every other week **Trim Size:** 11 3/8 x 13 3/4. **Number of Columns Per Page:** 5. **Column Width:** 11.5 picas. **Print Method:** Web offset. **Contact(s):** Abdul Wali Muhammed, Editor-in-Chief. **Subscription:** Free; $18.

★3604★
Firestone Park News/Southeast News Press
PO Box 19027A   Ph: (213)291-9486
Los Angeles, CA 90019   Fax: (213)291-2123
Text: Newspaper serving the black community of L.A. **Established:** 1924. **Column Depth:** 294 agate lines. **Frequency:** Weekly (Thurs.). **Trim Size:** 13 x 21 1/2. **Number of Columns Per Page:** 6. **Column Width:** 29 nonpareils. **Print Method:** Offset. **Contact(s):** Lela Ward Oliver, Editor; John H. Holoman, Publisher; Eric L. Holoman, Advertising Mgr. **ISSN:** 8550-2038. **Subscription:** $20; $40 national.

★3605★
Fisk News
Fisk University
1000 17th Ave. N.
Nashville, TN 37208   Ph: (615)329-8710
Text: Black collegiate newspaper. **Established:** 1950. **Column Depth:** 84 agate lines. **Frequency:** Weekly. **Number of Columns Per Page:** 2. **Column Width:** 36 nonpareils. **Print Method:** Offset. **Circulation:** 1,000.

★3606★
Florence Black Sun
1310 Harden   Ph: (803)799-5252
Columbia, SC 29204   Fax: (803)799-7709
Text: Black community interest newspaper. **Established:** 1970. **Column Depth:** 224 agate lines. **Frequency:** Weekly (Wed.). **Number of Columns Per Page:** 6. **Column Width:** 24 nonpareils. **Print Method:** Offset. **Subscription:** $18. **Circulation:** 5,734.

★3607★
Florida Sentinel-Bulletin
2207-21st Ave.
PO Box 3363   Ph: (813)248-1921
Tampa, FL 33601   Fax: (813)248-4507
Text: Black community newspaper (tabloid). **Established:** 1945. **Column Depth:** 15 in. **Frequency:** 2x/wk. (Tues. and Fri.). **Trim Size:** 10 x 15. **Number of Columns Per Page:** 5. **Column Width:** 2 in. **Print Method:** Offset. **Contact(s):** C. Blythe Andrews, Jr., Publisher; Sybil Andrews Wells, Gen. Mgr. **Subscription:** $31. **Circulation:** 23,345.

★3608★
Florida Star Times
PO Box 40629   Ph: (904)354-8880
Jacksonville, FL 32203 Fax: (904)358-2821
Text: Black community newspaper. **Contact(s):** Eric O. Simpson, Editor.

★3609★
Florida Sun Review
LMH Publications
702 18th St.
PO Box 2348
Orlando, FL 32802   Ph: (407)423-1156
Text: Black-oriented newspaper. **Established:** 1931. **Column Depth:** 231 agate lines. **Frequency:** Weekly (Thurs.). **Number of Columns Per Page:** 6. **Column Width:** 19 nonpareils. **Print Method:** Offset. **Contact(s):** James A. Madison, Editor and Publisher; James W. Macon, Publisher. **Subscription:** $12.50. **Circulation:** 16,500.

★3610★
Ft. Pierce Chronicle
1527 Avenue D
Fort Pierce, FL 34950
Text: Black community newspaper. **Established:** 1957. **Frequency:** Weekly (Wed.). **Contact(s):** C.E. Bolen, Editor and Publisher. **Circulation:** 10,500.

★3611★
Fort Valley Herald
Atlantic Communications of Georgia, Inc.
315 N. Camellia Blvd.
PO Box 899   Ph: (912)825-7000
Fort Valley, GA 31030   Fax: (912)232-8666
Text: Black community newspaper. **Established:** 1986. **Frequency:** Weekly (Wed.). **Print Method:** Offset. **Trim Size:** 13 x 21 1/2 in. **Number of Columns Per Page:** 6. **Column Width:** 2 in. **Contact(s):** Robert E. James, Editor and Publisher. **Subscription:** $15; $17 out of state. **Circulation:** 6,000.

★3612★
Frost Illustrated
Frost, Inc.
3121 S. Calhoun
Fort Wayne, IN 46807-1901   Ph: (219)745-0552
Text: Black community newspaper. **Established:** November 1968. **Column Depth:** 13. **Frequency:** Weekly (Wed.). **Number of Columns Per Page:** 5. **Print Method:** Offset. **Contact(s):** Edna M. Smith, Editor; Edward N. Smith, Sr., Publisher; Edward N. Smith, Jr., Advertising Mgr. **Subscription:** $12; $15 out of area.

★3613★
Gary American
2268 Broadway
Gary, IN 46407   Ph: (219)883-4903

Text: Black community newspaper. **Established:** 1927. **Column Depth:** 224 agate lines. **Frequency:** Weekly (Fri.). **Number of Columns Per Page:** 5. **Column Width:** 27 nonpareils. **Print Method:** Offset. **Contact(s):** Fred Harris, Editor and Publisher. **Subscription:** $12; $16 out of state.

★3614★
Gary New Crusader
1549 Broadway   Ph: (219)885-4357
Gary, IN 46407   Fax: (219)885-4359

Text: Black community newspaper. **Established:** 1961. **Column Depth:** 1 in. **Frequency:** Weekly (Thurs.). **Column Width:** 2 in. **Number of Columns Per Page:** 5. **Contact(s):** Dorothy R. Leavell, Editor and Publisher. **Subscription:** $15. **Circulation:** 27,000.

★3615★
The Grand Rapids Times
PO Box 7258   Ph: (616)245-8737
Grand Rapids, MI 49510   Fax: (616)245-1026

Text: Newspaper targeted for black population in Grand Rapids, Muskegon, Battle Creek and Kalamazoo, Michigan. **Established:** 1959. **Column Depth:** 15 in. **Frequency:** Weekly. **Trim Size:** 9 5/16 x 15. **Number of Columns Per Page:** 5. **Column Width:** 2 in. **Print Method:** Web offset. **Contact(s):** Patricia Pulliam, Editor and Publisher; Yergan Pulliam, Publisher and Advertising Mgr. **Subscription:** $12.

★3616★
Greene County Democrat
Greene County Newspaper Co.
214 Boligee St.
PO Box 598   Ph: (205)372-3373
Eutaw, AL 35462   Fax: (205)372-2243

Text: Black community newspaper. **Established:** 1890. **Column Depth:** 294 agate lines. **Frequency:** Weekly (Wed.). **Number of Columns Per Page:** 6. **Column Width:** 21 nonpareils. **Print Method:** Offset. **Contact(s):** John Zippert, Publisher; Carol Zippert, Publisher; Laddi Jones, Advertising Mgr. **ISSN:** 0889-518X. **Subscription:** $15; $18 out of area; $20 out of state. **Circulation:** 3,500.

★3617★
Greenville Black Star
1310 Harden   Ph: (803)799-5252
Columbia, SC 29204   Fax: (803)799-7709

Text: Black community interest newspaper. **Column Depth:** 224 agate lines. **Frequency:** Weekly (Wed.). **Number of Columns Per Page:** 6. **Column Width:** 24 nonpareils. **Print Method:** Offset. **Contact(s):** Zack Weston, Editor; Isaac Washington, Publisher; Cynthia Bowden, Advertising Mgr. **Subscription:** $25. **Circulation:** 6,849.

★3618★
Hartford Inquirer
Inquires Newspaper Group
PO Box 1260   Ph: (203)522-1462
Hartford, CT 06143   Fax: (203)522-3014

Text: Black community newspaper. **Established:** 1975. **Column Depth:** 16. **Trim Size:** 11 X 17. **Number of Columns Per Page:** 6. **Column Width:** 9 1/2. **Print Method:** Offset. **Contact(s):** Edward Laiscell, Editor; William R. Hales, Publisher. **Subscription:** $27. **Circulation:** 125,000.

★3619★
The Herald
1803 Barnard St.
PO Box 486   Ph: (912)232-4505
Savannah, GA 31402   Fax: (912)232-4079

Text: Black community newspaper. **Established:** 1945. **Column Depth:** 14 in. **Frequency:** Weekly (Wed.). **Number of Columns Per Page:** 5. **Column Width:** 11 picas. **Print Method:** Offset. **Contact(s):** Floyd Adams, Editor and Publisher. **Subscription:** $15.90. **Circulation:** 8,000.

★3620★
Herald Dispatch
4053 Marlton Ave.
PO Box 19027A   Ph: (213)291-9486
Los Angeles, CA 90008   Fax: (213)291-2123

Text: Black community newspaper. **Established:** 1952. **Column Depth:** 294 agate lines. **Frequency:** Weekly (Thurs.). **Number of Columns Per Page:** 6. **Column Width:** 29 nonpareils. **Print Method:** Offset. **Contact(s):** Lela Ward Oliver, Editor; John H. Holoman, Publisher. **Subscription:** $20. **Circulation:** 35,000.

★3621★
Houston Defender
PO Box 8005   Ph: (713)663-7716
Houston, TX 77288   Fax: (713)663-7116

Text: Black community newspaper. **Established:** October 1930. **Column Depth:** 294 agate lines. **Frequency:** Weekly (Wed.). **Number of Columns Per Page:** 6. **Column Width:** 25 nonpareils. **Print Method:** Offset. **Contact(s):** Lucious New, Editor; Sonceria Messiah-Jiles, Publisher; Sonny Jiles, Advertising Mgr. **Subscription:** $30.

★3622★
Houston Forward Times
Forward Times Publishing Co.
4411 Almeda Rd.
PO Box 8346   Ph: (713)526-4727
Houston, TX 77288-8346   Fax: (713)526-3170

Text: Black community newspaper. **Established:** 1960. **Column Depth:** 303 agate lines. **Frequency:** Weekly (Sat.). **Number of Columns Per Page:** 6. **Column Width:** 20 nonpareils. **Print Method:** Offset. **Contact(s):** Bud Johnson, Editor; Lenora Carter, Publisher; Henrietta Smith, Advertising Mgr. **Subscription:** $25. **Circulation:** 52,260.

★3623★
Houston Informer
PO Box 3086   Ph: (713)527-8261
Houston, TX 77253   Fax: (713)524-7028

Text: Black community newspaper. **Established:** 1893. **Frequency:** Weekly (Tues.). **Contact(s):** George McElroy, Editor and Publisher. **Circulation:** 23,000.

★3624★
Houston Sun
1520 Isabella   Ph: (713)524-4474
Houston, TX 77004   Fax: (713)524-0089

Text: Black community newspaper. **Established:** 1983. **Column Depth:** 21 in. **Frequency:** Weekly (Thurs.). **Number of Columns Per Page:** 6. **Column Width:** 11 picas. **Print Method:** Web offset. **Contact(s):** Doris Ellis, Editor and Publisher. **Subscription:** Free; $35 (mail). **Circulation:** 80,000.

★3625★
Hudson Valley Black Press
PO Box 2160
Newburgh, NY 12550   Ph: (914)562-1313

Text: Black community newspaper. **Established:** 1983. **Column Depth:** 224 agate lines. **Frequency:** Weekly (Wed.). **Number of Columns Per Page:** 6. **Column Width:** 18 nonpareils. **Print Method:** Offset. **Contact(s):** Chuck Stewart, Editor and Publisher. **Subscription:** $22. **Circulation:** 42,500.

★3626★
Hyde Park Citizen
Citizen Newspapers
412 E. 87th St.   Ph: (312)487-7700
Chicago, IL 60619   Fax: (312)487-7931

Text: Newspaper serving Chicago's black community. **Established:** 1987. **Column Depth:** 196 agate lines. **Frequency:** Weekly (Thurs.). **Number of Columns Per Page:** 5. **Column Width:** 25 nonpareils. **Print Method:** Offset. **Contact(s):** William Garth,

Pres./Publisher/Advertising Mgr.; Lisa Ely, Mng. Editor. **Subscription:** $25. **Circulation:** 15,000.

★3627★
The Indianapolis Recorder
The George P. Stewart Printing, Inc.
2901 N. Tacoma Ave.
PO Box 18499   Ph: (317)924-5143
Indianapolis, IN 46218   Fax: (317)924-5148
Text: Black community newspaper. **Established:** 1895. **Column Depth:** 298 agate lines. **Frequency:** Weekly (Thurs.). **Number of Columns Per Page:** 6. **Column Width:** 13 picas. **Print Method:** Offset. **Contact(s):** Bill Mays, Publisher; Pam Beene, Advertising Mgr.; Audrey Gadzekpo, Mgr Editor. **Subscription:** $23; $20 out of area. **Circulation:** 10,281.

★3628★
Info
Info Printing & Publishing, Inc.
1953 Broadway   Ph: (219)882-5591
Gary, IN 46407   Fax: (219)886-1090
Text: Black newspaper with a Democratic orientation. **Established:** 1963. **Column Depth:** 14 in. **Frequency:** Weekly (Thurs.). **Trim Size:** 10 1/2 x 14 1/2. **Number of Columns Per Page:** 6. **Column Width:** 1 5/8 in. **Print Method:** Offset. **Contact(s):** Imogene Harris, Editor and Publisher; Huston Pugh, Advertising Mgr. **Subscription:** $12.

★3629★
Inglewood/Hawthorne Wave
Central News-Wave Publications
2621 W. 54th St.   Ph: (213)290-3000
Los Angeles, CA 90043   Fax: (213)291-0219
Text: Black community newspaper. **Established:** 1978. **Column Depth:** 21 1/2 in. **Frequency:** Weekly (Wed.). **Number of Columns Per Page:** 6. **Column Width:** 5 nonpareils. **Print Method:** Offset. **Contact(s):** C.Z. Wilson, Publisher. **Subscription:** $78. **Circulation:** 44,075.

★3630★
Inglewood Tribune
Rapid Publishing
349 W. Compton
PO Box 4248
Compton, CA 90244   Ph: (213)774-0018
Text: Black community newspaper. **Column Depth:** 21 1/2 in. **Frequency:** Weekly (Wed.). **Column Width:** 12 1/2 picas. **Number of Columns Per Page:** 6. **Contact(s):** O. Ray Watkins, Publisher.

★3631★
Inner City News
Inner City Enterprises, Inc.
PO Box 1545
Mobile, AL 36633-1545   Ph: (205)452-9329
Text: African-American community-oriented newspaper. **Established:** January 1977. **Column Depth:** 21 1/2 in. **Frequency:** Weekly (Thurs.). **Trim Size:** 13 x 23. **Number of Columns Per Page:** 6. **Column Width:** 2 in. **Print Method:** Offset. **Contact(s):** Charles W. Porter, Editor and Publisher. **Subscription:** $25. **Circulation:** 8,000.

★3632★
Iredell County News
PO Box 407
Statesville, NC 28687   Ph: (704)873-1054
Text: Black community newspaper. **Established:** 1980. **Column Depth:** 21 1/2 in. **Frequency:** Weekly. **Number of Columns Per Page:** 6. **Column Width:** 12 1/2 picas. **Print Method:** Offset. **Contact(s):** Mason McCullough, Publisher. **Subscription:** $15.

★3633★
Jackson Advocate
PO Box 3708   Ph: (601)948-4122
Jackson, MS 39207-3708   Fax: (601)948-4125
Text: Black community newspaper. **Established:** 1937. **Column Depth:** 21 in. **Frequency:** Weekly. **Number of Columns Per Page:** 6. **Column Width:** 2 1/8 in. **Print Method:** Offset. **Contact(s):**

Charles W. Tisdale, Editor and Publisher; Alice Thomas, Advertising Mgr. **Subscription:** $20.

★3634★
Jamaica Shopping & Entertainment Guide
North American Publications
164-11 89th Ave., Ste. 190
Jamaica, NY 11432   Ph: (718)591-7777
Text: Black community newspaper. **Established:** Nov. 1989. **Frequency:** Every other week (Thurs.). **Print Method:** Web offset. **Trim Size:** 11 1/2 x 16. **Contact(s):** Joseph Wallace, Editor; Aaron Slaughter, Editor. **Subscription:** Free. **Circulation:** 30,000.

★3635★
Journal & Guide
362 Campostella Rd.
Norfolk, VA 23523-2204
Text: Black community newspaper. **Established:** 1900. **Column Depth:** 129 agate lines. **Frequency:** Weekly (Wed.). **Number of Columns Per Page:** 6. **Column Width:** 2 1/16 in. **Print Method:** Offset. **Contact(s):** Brenda Andrews, Publisher; Martha Pritchard, Advertising Mgr. **Subscription:** $18.20. **Circulation:** 25,000.

★3636★
Kansas City Globe
Jordan Communications Co., Inc.
615 E. 29th St.
PO Box 090410   Ph: (816)531-5253
Kansas City, MO 64109   Fax: (816)531-5256
Text: Black community newspaper. **Established:** 1972. **Frequency:** Weekly (Fri.). **Contact(s):** Marion Jordan, Editor and Publisher. **Circulation:** 30,000.

★3637★
The Kansas City Voice
2727 N. 13th St.
Kansas City, KS 66104
Text: Black community newspaper. **Contact(s):** Gladys Adams, Publisher.

★3638★
L.A. Metropolitan Gazette
First-Line Publishers/L.A. Metro Group
14621 Titust St., Ste. 228   Ph: (818)782-8695
Van Nuys, CA 91402   Fax: (818)782-2924
Text: Black community newspaper serving Los Angeles, Compton, Carson, Pasadena, Lynwood, and North Long Beach. **Established:** 1966. **Frequency:** Weekly (Thurs.). **Print Method:** Offset. **Trim Size:** 13 x 21 1/2. **Number of Columns Per Page:** 6. **Column Width:** 2 in. **Contact(s):** Beverly Hamm, Publisher; Hillard Hamm, C.E.O. **Subscription:** $25. **Circulation:** 60,000.

★3639★
Las Vegas Sentinel-Voice
1201 S. Eastern Ave.   Ph: (702)383-3114
Las Vegas, NV 89104   Fax: (702)383-3114
Text: Black community newspaper. **Frequency:** Weekly (Thurs.). **Contact(s):** Ed Brown, Editor and Publisher; Betty Brown, Editor and Publisher. **Subscription:** $25. **Circulation:** 5,000.

★3640★
The Lincolnian
Lincoln University
English Dept
Lincoln University, PA 19352   Ph: (215)932-8300
Text: Collegiate newspaper. **Established:** 1929. **Frequency:** 14x/yr. (during the academic year). **Print Method:** Letterpress and offset. **Trim Size:** 17 x 22. **Number of Columns Per Page:** 5. **Subscription:** $12. **Circulation:** 1,300.

★3641★
Long Beach Express
First-Line Publishers
17939 Chatsworth St.
Ste. 429   Ph: (818)782-8695
Granada Hills, CA 91344   Fax: (818)782-2924
Text: Black community newspaper serving Long Beach.
Established: 1966. **Frequency:** Weekly (Thurs.). **Print Method:**
Offset. **Trim Size:** 13 x 21 1/2. **Number of Columns Per Page:** 6.
Column Width: 2 in. **Contact(s):** Victoria Turner, Publisher; Hillard
Hamm, C.E.O. **Subscription:** Free; $25. **Circulation:** 60,000.

★3642★
Los Angeles Sentinel
1112 E. 43rd St.
PO Box 11456   Ph: (213)232-3261
Los Angeles, CA 90011   Fax: (213)232-8035
Text: Black community newspaper. **Established:** January 26, 1934.
Column Depth: 294 agate lines. **Frequency:** Weekly (Thurs.). **Trim
Size:** 13 x 22 1/2. **Number of Columns Per Page:** 6. **Column Width:**
26 nonpareils. **Print Method:** Offset. **Contact(s):** Kenneth R.
Thomas, Publisher. **Subscription:** $25. **Circulation:** 28,000.

★3643★
Louisiana Weekly
616 Baronne St.   Ph: (504)524-5563
New Orleans, LA 70150   Fax: (504)527-5826
Text: Black community newspaper. **Established:** September 25,
1925. **Column Depth:** 21 in. **Frequency:** Weekly (Sat.). **Number of
Columns Per Page:** 6. **Column Width:** 2 1/8 in. **Print Method:**
Offset. Uses mats. **Contact(s):** C.C. Dejoie, Jr., Publisher.
Subscription: $15. **Circulation:** 4,156.

★3644★
Louisville Defender
PO Box 2557   Ph: (502)772-2591
Louisville, KY 40201   Fax: (502)775-8655
Text: Black community newspaper. **Established:** March 1933.
Column Depth: 21 1/2 in. **Frequency:** Weekly (Thurs.). **Trim Size:**
13 x 21 1/2. **Number of Columns Per Page:** 6. **Column Width:** 2
1/16 in. **Print Method:** Offset. **Contact(s):** Yvonne D. Coleman,
Acting Editor; Clarence Leslie, Advertising Mgr./Exec. V.P.
Subscription: $16; $18 out of state.

★3645★
Lubbock Southwest Digest
902 E. 28th St.
Lubbock, TX 79404   Ph: (806)762-3612
Text: Black community newspaper. **Established:** September 8,
1977. **Column Depth:** 22 1/2 in. **Frequency:** Weekly (Thurs.). **Trim
Size:** 13 x 22 1/2. **Number of Columns Per Page:** 6. **Column Width:**
1 3/4 in. **Print Method:** Letterpress and offset. **Contact(s):** T.J.
Patterson, Editor and Publisher; Eddie P. Richardson, Publisher.
Subscription: $15.

★3646★
Lynwood Journal
Rapid Publishing
349 W. Compton
PO Box 4248
Compton, CA 90224   Ph: (213)774-0018
Text: Black community newspaper. **Column Depth:** 21 1/2 in.
Frequency: Weekly (Wed.). **Column Width:** 12 1/2 picas. **Number of
Columns Per Page:** 6. **Contact(s):** O. Ray Watkins, Publisher.

★3647★
Lynwood Wave
Central News-Wave Publications
2621 W. 54th St.   Ph: (213)290-3000
Los Angeles, CA 90043   Fax: (213)291-0219
Text: Black community newspaper. **Established:** 1919. **Column
Depth:** 21 1/2 in. **Frequency:** Weekly (Wed.). **Number of Columns
Per Page:** 6. **Column Width:** 5 nonpareils. **Print Method:** Offset.
Contact(s): C.Z. Wilson, Publisher. **Subscription:** $78. **Circulation:**
24,020.

★3648★
Memphis Silver Star News
3144 Park Ave.
Memphis, TN 38111
Text: Black community newspaper. **Frequency:** Weekly (Wed.).
Contact(s): J. Delnoah Williams, Editor and Publisher.

★3649★
Mesa Tribune Wave
Central News-Wave Publications
2621 W. 54th St.   Ph: (213)290-3000
Los Angeles, CA 90043   Fax: (213)291-0219
Text: Black community newspaper. **Established:** 1919. **Column
Depth:** 21 1/2 in. **Frequency:** Weekly (Wed.). **Number of Columns
Per Page:** 6. **Column Width:** 5 nonpareils. **Print Method:** Offset.
Contact(s): C.Z. Wilson, Publisher. **Subscription:** $78. **Circulation:**
30,100.

★3650★
Metro Chronicle
529 14th St., Ste. 1143
Washington, DC 20045
Text: Black commmunity newspaper. **Contact(s):** Paris D. Davis,
Publisher.

★3651★
The Metro Courier
PO Box 2385   Ph: (404)724-6556
Augusta, GA 30903   Fax: (404)722-7104
Text: Black community newspaper. **Established:** 1983. **Column
Depth:** 294 agate lines. **Frequency:** Weekly (Wed.). **Trim Size:** 6 x
21. **Number of Columns Per Page:** 6. **Column Width:** 24 nonpareils.
Print Method: Offset. **Contact(s):** Barbara A. Gordon, Editor and
Publisher. **Subscription:** $20. **Circulation:** 19,040.

★3652★
Metro Reporter
270 Francisco St.   Ph: (415)391-2030
San Francisco, CA 94133-2120   Fax: (415)391-2527
Text: Black community newspaper. **Established:** 1973. **Column
Depth:** 21 in. **Frequency:** Weekly (Sun.). **Number of Columns Per
Page:** 6. **Column Width:** 2 1/16 in. **Print Method:** Offset.
Contact(s): Charles E. Belle, Editor; Carlton B. Goodlett, Publisher.
Subscription: $10. **Circulation:** 108,895.

★3653★
Metro Star
42353 47th St. W.
Quartz Hill, CA 93534
Text: Black community newspaper. **Contact(s):** Leon Hudson,
Publisher.

★3654★
The Miami Times
900 NW 54th St.   Ph: (305)757-1147
Miami, FL 33127   Fax: (305)756-0771
Text: Black community newspaper. **Established:** September 1,
1923. **Column Depth:** 21 in. **Frequency:** Weekly (Thurs.). **Trim Size:**
13 3/4 x 22. **Number of Columns Per Page:** 6. **Column Width:** 2
1/16 in. **Print Method:** Offset. **Contact(s):** Rachel J. Reeves,
Executive Editor; Mohamed Hamaludin, Managing Editor; Garth C.
Reeves, Publisher. **Subscription:** $35.

★3655★
Michigan Chronicle
Sengestacke Newspaper Corp.
479 Ledyard St.   Ph: (313)963-5522
Detroit, MI 48201   Fax: (313)963-8788
Text: Black community newspaper. **Established:** 1936. **Column
Depth:** 294 agate lines. **Frequency:** Weekly (Sat.). **Number of
Columns Per Page:** 6. **Column Width:** 26 nonpareils. **Print Method:**
Offset. **Contact(s):** John H. Stengstacke, Publisher; Samuel Logan,
Gen. Mgr. **Circulation:** 35,000.

★3656★
Michigan Citizen
New Day Publishing Enterprises
12541 2nd St.
Highland Park, MI 48203
Ph: (313)869-0033
Fax: (313)869-0430
Text: Newspaper serving African-American communities in Michigan. **Established:** November 25, 1978. **Column Depth:** 21 in. **Frequency:** Weekly. **Number of Columns Per Page:** 6. **Column Width:** 12 picas. **Print Method:** Offset. **Contact(s):** Teresa Maxwell-Kelly, Editor; Charles D. Kelly, Publisher/Advertising Mgr. **Subscription:** $21; $36 two years.

★3657★
The Michigan Sentinel
27350 Southfield Rd., No. 127
Lathrup Village, MI 48076
Ph: (313)559-1010
Text: Black community newspaper. **Established:** July 1991. **Frequency:** Monthly. **Print Method:** Offset. **Contact(s):** Elaine Campbell, Editor and Publisher. **Circulation:** 18,000.

★3658★
Milwaukee Community Journal
Community Journal, Inc.
3612 N. Martin Luther King Dr.
Milwaukee, WI 53212
Ph: (414)265-5300
Fax: (414)265-1536
Text: Black community newspaper. **Established:** 1976. **Column Depth:** 189 agate lines. **Frequency:** 2x/wk. (Wed. and Fri.). **Number of Columns Per Page:** 6. **Column Width:** 20 nonpareils. **Print Method:** Offset. **Contact(s):** Mikel Holt, Editor; Patricia O'Flynn Thomas, Publisher; Robert Thomas, Gen. Mgr. **Subscription:** Free; $20 (mail).

★3659★
Milwaukee Courier
2431 W. Hopkins St.
Milwaukee, WI 53206
Ph: (414)449-4866
Fax: (414)449-4872
Text: Black community newspaper. **Established:** 1964. **Column Depth:** 126 agate lines. **Frequency:** Weekly (Sat.). **Number of Columns Per Page:** 6. **Column Width:** 21 nonpareils. **Print Method:** Offset. **Contact(s):** Joni Alston, Editor; Carole Geary, Publisher; Faithe Colas, Assoc. Publisher. **Subscription:** $25. **Circulation:** 15,000.

★3660★
Milwaukee Star
3815 N. Teutonia Ave.
Milwaukee, WI 53206
Ph: (414)449-4870
Fax: (414)449-4872
Text: Black community newspaper. **Established:** 1961. **Frequency:** Weekly (Thurs.). **Print Method:** Offset. **Number of Columns Per Page:** 5. **Column Width:** 14. **Contact(s):** Joni Alston, Editor; Carole Geary, Publisher; Faithe Colas, Assoc. Publisher. **Subscription:** Free; $12.50 (mail). **Circulation:** 5,000.

★3661★
Milwaukee Times
2183 N. Sherman Blvd.
PO Box 16489
Milwaukee, WI 53216-0489
Ph: (414)444-8611
Fax: (414)871-7634
Text: Black community newspaper. **Frequency:** Weekly. **Contact(s):** Nathan Conyers, Publisher.

★3662★
Minneapolis Spokesman
3744 4th Ave. S.
Minneapolis, MN 55409
Ph: (612)827-4021
Fax: (612)827-0577
Text: Black community newspaper. **Established:** 1934. **Column Depth:** 218 agate lines. **Frequency:** Weekly (Thurs.). **Number of Columns Per Page:** 6. **Column Width:** 21 nonpareils. **Print Method:** Offset. **Contact(s):** Launa Newman, Editor and Publisher; Lynda Jackman, Advertising Mgr. **Subscription:** $14; $19 other states.

★3663★
The Mississippi Enterprise
540 1/2 N. Farish St.
PO Box 87236
Chicago, IL 60680-0236
Text: Black community newspaper. **Established:** July 7, 1933. **Column Depth:** 21 in. **Frequency:** Weekly (Fri.). **Number of Columns Per Page:** 8. **Column Width:** 11 picas. **Print Method:** Offset. **Contact(s):** Lee Lyon, Editor/Advertising Mgr.; LeFloris Lyon, Publisher. **Subscription:** $17.

★3664★
Mississippi Memo Digest
2511 5th St.
Box 5782
Meridian, MS 39301
Ph: (601)693-2372
Text: Black community newspaper. **Established:** January 14, 1961. **Column Depth:** 13 in. **Frequency:** Weekly (Wed.). **Number of Columns Per Page:** 6. **Column Width:** 9 1/2 picas. **Print Method:** Offset. **Contact(s):** Robert E. Williams, Editor and Publisher; Mary Jones, Advertising Mgr. **Subscription:** $9.80. **Circulation:** 3,050.

★3665★
Mobile Beacon
2311 Costarides St.
PO Box 1407
Mobile, AL 36633
Ph: (205)479-0629
Text: Black community newspaper. **Established:** 1943. **Column Depth:** 21 in. **Frequency:** Weekly (Sat.). **Number of Columns Per Page:** 6. **Column Width:** 2 1/8 in. **Print Method:** Offset. **Contact(s):** Cleretta T. Blackmon, Editor/Advertising Mgr.; Lancie M. Thomas, Publisher. **Subscription:** $19. **Circulation:** 4,952.

★3666★
Montgomery-Tuskegee Times
3900 University Hwy.
Montgomery, AL 36108
Text: Black community newspaper. **Established:** 1977. **Frequency:** Weekly. **Contact(s):** Rev. Alvin Dixon, Editor. **Circulation:** 10,000.

★3667★
New Bayview
Double Rock Press
1624 Oakdale Ave.
PO Box 24477
San Francisco, CA 94124-0477
Ph: (415)826-1484
Fax: (415)826-1485
Text: Black community newspaper (tabloid). **Established:** September 1, 1976. **Column Depth:** 14 in. **Frequency:** Weekly. **Trim Size:** 8 x 10 3/4. **Number of Columns Per Page:** 5. **Column Width:** 1 7/8 in. **Print Method:** Offset. **Contact(s):** Muhammad Al-Kareem, Editor and Publisher. **Subscription:** $15.

★3668★
The New Iowa Bystander
PO Box 762
Des Moines, IA 50303
Text: Newspaper serving the Black community. **Established:** 1893. **Column Depth:** 210 agate lines. **Frequency:** Weekly (Thurs.). **Number of Columns Per Page:** 6. **Column Width:** 21 nonpareils. **Print Method:** Offset. **Contact(s):** Loren T. Sampson, Editor and Publisher. **Subscription:** $7.50.

★3669★
New Jersey Afro-American
PO Box 22162
Newark, NJ 07103
Ph: (201)242-5364
Text: Black community newspaper. **Established:** 1892. **Frequency:** Weekly. **Print Method:** Offset. **Number of Columns Per Page:** 6. **Contact(s):** Deborah P. Smith, Editor and Advertising Mgr.; Frances Murphy Draper, Publisher (301/728-8200). **Subscription:** $26. **Circulation:** 20,000.

★3670★
New Observer
811 Florida Ave. NW
Washington, DC 20001

Ph: (202)232-3060
Fax: (202)232-1711

Text: Black community newspaper. **Contact(s):** Michael Angelo Graham, Editor.

★3671★
New Orleans Data News Weekly
Data Enterprises, Inc.
1001 Howard Ave., Ste. 2309
PO Box 51933
New Orleans, LA 70151

Ph: (504)522-1418
Fax: (504)523-7364

Text: Black community newspaper. **Established:** 1966. **Column Depth:** 14 in. **Frequency:** Weekly (Sat.). **Number of Columns Per Page:** 5. **Column Width:** 2 in. **Print Method:** Offset. **Contact(s):** June Hazeur, Editor; Terry Jones, Publisher; Keith Brown, Circulation Mgr.. **ISSN:** 1043-4445. **Subscription:** $13.

★3672★
New Pittsburgh Courier
315 E. Carson St.
Pittsburgh, PA 15219

Ph: (412)481-8302
Fax: (412)481-1360

Text: Black community newspaper. **Established:** 1910. **Column Depth:** 294 agate lines. **Frequency:** 2x/wk. (Wed. and Sat.). **Number of Columns Per Page:** 6. **Column Width:** 26 nonpareils. **Print Method:** Offset. **Contact(s):** Ed Davis, Mng. Editor; John H. Sehgstacke, Publisher; Rod Doss, V.P./Gen. Mgr.; Stephan A. Broadus, Advertising Mgr. **Subscription:** $35. **Circulation:** 30,000.

★3673★
The New Times
The New Times Group, Inc.
156 S. Broad St.
Mobile, AL 36602-0356

Ph: (205)432-0356
Fax: (205)432-8320

Text: Black community newspaper. **Established:** 1981. **Column Depth:** 294 agate lines. **Frequency:** Biweekly. **Number of Columns Per Page:** 6. **Column Width:** 26 nonpareils. **Print Method:** Offset. **Contact(s):** Vivian Davis Figures, Editor/Advertising Mgr. **Subscription:** $11 (mail).

★3674★
The New York Beacon
Smith Haj Publishing
155 Water St., 5th Fl.
Brooklyn, NY 11201

Ph: (718)852-6001
Fax: (718)852-7846

Text: Black community newspaper. **Established:** 1976. **Column Depth:** 196 agate lines. **Frequency:** Weekly (Sat.). **Number of Columns Per Page:** 5. **Column Width:** 26 nonpareils. **Print Method:** Offset. Uses mats. **Contact(s):** Walter Smith, Jr., Publisher. **Subscription:** $26.50. **Circulation:** 53,766.

★3675★
The New York Voice-Harlem U.S.A.
75-43 Parsons Blvd.
Flushing, NY 11366

Ph: (718)591-6600

Text: Black community newspaper. **Established:** 1959. **Column Depth:** 200 agate lines. **Frequency:** Weekly (Fri.). **Number of Columns Per Page:** 4. **Column Width:** 32 nonpareils. **Print Method:** Offset. **Contact(s):** Tom Sinclair, Editor; Kenneth Drew, Publisher. **Subscription:** $25. **Circulation:** 1,624.

★3676★
News Reporter
1610 N. Howard Ave.
Tampa, FL 33607

Ph: (813)254-2608

Text: Black community newspaper. **Contact(s):** James Jackson, Editor. **Circulation:** 9,694.

★3677★
The Northwest Dispatch
PO Box 5637
Tacoma, WA 98415

Ph: (206)272-7587
Fax: (206)272-4418

Text: Black community and legal newspaper. **Established:** July 1982. **Column Depth:** 21 1/2 in. **Frequency:** Daily. **Number of Columns Per Page:** 6. **Column Width:** 2 1/16 in. **Print Method:** Offset. **Contact(s):** Lu Taylor, Editor/Advertising Mgr.; Virginia Taylor, Publisher. **ISSN:** 1058-9627 **Subscription:** $60.

★3678★
NY Carib News
Carib News
15 W. 39th St.
New York, NY 10018

Ph: (212)944-1991
Fax: (212)944-2089

Text: Newspaper (tabloid) with black orientation, providing Caribbean news and features. **Established:** June 29, 1982. **Column Depth:** 194 agate lines. **Frequency:** Weekly (Wed.). **Trim Size:** 11 1/2 x 15. **Number of Columns Per Page:** 6. **Column Width:** 18 nonpareils. **Print Method:** Offset. **Contact(s):** Karl B. Rodney, Publisher; Faye A. Rodney, Advertising Mgr. **Subscription:** $30.

★3679★
Oakland Post
The Alameda Publishing Corp.
PO Box 1350
Oakland, CA 94604

Ph: (415)763-1120
Fax: (415)763-9670

Text: Black community newspaper. **Established:** 1963. **Column Depth:** 21 1/2 in. **Frequency:** 2x/wk. (Wed. and Sun.). **Number of Columns Per Page:** 6. **Column Width:** 1 1/16 in. **Print Method:** Offset. **Contact(s):** Gail Berkley, Editor; Thomas Berkley, Publisher; Donald V. Welcher, Advertising Mgr. **Subscription:** $42. **Circulation:** 62,496.

★3680★
Observer
6040 S. Harper St.
Chicago, IL 60637

Ph: (312)288-5840

Text: Black community newspaper. **Established:** 1964. **Column Depth:** 196 agate lines. **Frequency:** Weekly (Thurs.). **Number of Columns Per Page:** 5. **Column Width:** 24 nonpareils. **Print Method:** Offset. **Contact(s):** Leon D. Finney, Jr. Publisher; Carolyn Fortier, Advertising Mgr. **Subscription:** $8. **Circulation:** 30,000.

★3681★
Ocean State Grapevine
PO Box 16333
Providence, RI 02916-0693

Text: Black community newspaper. **Contact(s):** Douglas Terry, Editor.

★3682★
The Oklahoma Eagle
PO Box 3267
Tulsa, OK 74101

Ph: (918)582-7124

Text: Black community newspaper. **Established:** 1921. **Column Depth:** 21 1/2 in. **Frequency:** Weekly (Thurs.). **Number of Columns Per Page:** 6. **Column Width:** 2 1/16 in. **Print Method:** Offset. **Contact(s):** James O. Goodwin, Co-Publisher; E.L. Goodwin, Co-Publisher. **Subscription:** $21. **Circulation:** 12,800.

★3683★
Orangeburg Black Voice
1310 Harden
Columbia, SC 29204

Ph: (803)799-5252
Fax: (803)799-5252

Text: Black community interest newspaper. **Established:** 1970. **Column Depth:** 224 agate lines. **Frequency:** Weekly (Wed.). **Number of Columns Per Page:** 6. **Column Width:** 24 nonpareils. **Print Method:** Offset. **Contact(s):** Zack Weston, Editor; Isaac Washington, Publisher; Cynthia Bowden, Advertising Mgr. **Subscription:** $25. **Circulation:** 5,365.

★3684★
The Orlando Times
PO Box 555339
Orlando, FL 32855-5339   Ph: (407)841-3710

Text: Black community newspaper. **Established:** 1975. **Frequency:** Weekly (Thurs.). **Contact(s):** Lottie Collins, Editor; Calvin Collins, Jr., President and Publisher. **Circulation:** 5,710.

★3685★
Pasadena Gazette
First-Line Publishers/L.A. Metro Group
14621 Titus St., Ste. 228   Ph: (818)782-8695
Van Nuys, CA 91402   Fax: (818)782-2924

Text: Black community newspaper serving Pasadena, Altedena, Monrovia, and Duarte. **Established:** 1966. **Frequency:** Weekly (Thurs.). **Print Method:** Offset. **Trim Size:** 13 x 21 1/2. **Number of Columns Per Page:** 6. **Column Width:** 2 in. **Contact(s):** K.R. Hamm, Publisher; Hillard Hamm, C.E.O. **Subscription:** Free; $25. **Circulation:** 60,000.

★3686★
Pensacola Voice
213 E. Yonge St.   Ph: (904)434-6963
Pensacola, FL 32503   Fax: (904)469-8745

Text: Black community newspaper. **Established:** 1966. **Column Depth:** 21 in. **Frequency:** Weekly. **Column Width:** 2 in. **Number of Columns Per Page:** 6. **Subscription:** $10. **Circulation:** 35,896.

★3687★
Philadelphia New Observer
1930 Chestnut St., Ste. 900
PO Box 30092   Ph: (215)665-8400
Philadelphia, PA 19103   Fax: (215)665-8914

Text: Newspaper (tabloid) with features for Black and Hispanic audience. **Established:** 1975. **Column Depth:** 224 agate lines. **Frequency:** Weekly (Wed.). **Trim Size:** 11 x 17 **Number of Columns Per Page:** 6. **Column Width:** 1 9/16 in. **Print Method:** Offset. **Contact(s):** J. Hugo Warren III, Editor and Publisher. **Subscription:** $30.

★3688★
The Philadelphia Tribune
524-526 S. 16th St.   Ph: (215)893-4050
Philadelphia, PA 19146   Fax: (215)735-3612

Text: Newspaper with an Independent orientation (Black). **Established:** 1884. **Column Depth:** 200 agate lines. **Frequency:** 3x/wk. (Tues., Thurs., and Fri.). **Number of Columns Per Page:** 6. **Column Width:** 25 nonpareils. **Print Method:** Offset. **Contact(s):** Paul A. Bennett, Editor; Robert W. Bogle, President. **Subscription:** $36.

★3689★
The Philadelphia Tribune (Metro Edition)
Philadelphia Tribune Co.
522 S. 16th St.   Ph: (215)893-4050
Philadelphia, PA 19146   Fax: (215)735-3612

Text: Black community newspaper. **Established:** 1978. **Column Depth:** 182 agate lines. **Frequency:** Weekly (Thurs.). **Number of Columns Per Page:** 5. **Column Width:** 25 nonpareils. **Print Method:** Offset. **Contact(s):** Paul A. Bennett, Editor; Robert W. Bogle, Pres. **Circulation:** 88,000.

★3690★
Portland Observer
PO Box 3137
Portland, OR 97211   Ph: (503)288-0033

Text: Black community newspaper. **Frequency:** Weekly (Thurs.). **Contact(s):** A.L. Henderson, Editor and Publisher. **Circulation:** 10,000.

★3691★
The Portland Skanner
PO Box 5455   Ph: (503)287-3562
Portland, OR 97228-5455   Fax: (503)284-5677

Text: Black community newspaper. **Established:** 1975. **Column Depth:** 224 agate lines. **Frequency:** Weekly (Wed.). **Trim Size:** 6 x 16. **Number of Columns Per Page:** 6. **Column Width:** 20 nonpareils. **Print Method:** Offset. **Contact(s):** Bernard V. Foster, Editor and Publisher. **Subscription:** $25. **Circulation:** 20,000.

★3692★
Precinct Reporter
1677 W. Baseline St.   Ph: (714)889-0597
San Bernardino, CA 92411   Fax: (714)889-1706

Text: Black community newspaper. **Established:** July 26, 1965. **Column Depth:** 294 agate lines. **Frequency:** Weekly (Thurs.). **Number of Columns Per Page:** 6. **Column Width:** 18 nonpareils. **Print Method:** Offset. **Contact(s):** Brian Townsend, Publisher. **Subscription:** $20. **Circulation:** 55,000.

★3693★
The Public Post
PO Box 1951
Laurinburg, NC 28352   Ph: (919)875-8938

Text: Black community interest newspaper. **Established:** 1981. **Column Depth:** 21 in. **Frequency:** Weekly (Wed.). **Number of Columns Per Page:** 6. **Column Width:** 2 1/16 in. **Print Method:** Offset. **Contact(s):** Roosevelt McPherson, Editor and Publisher. **Subscription:** $10.

★3694★
Richmond Afro-American
The Afro-American Co.
628 N. Eutaw St.   Ph: (410)554-8200
Baltimore, MD 21218   Fax: (410)554-8213

Text: Black community newspaper. **Established:** 1882. **Column Depth:** 308 agate lines. **Frequency:** Weekly (Wed.). **Number of Columns Per Page:** 6. **Column Width:** 25 nonpareils. **Print Method:** Letterpress and offset. **Contact(s):** Frances L. Murphy II, Publisher. **Subscription:** $26; $46 two years; $58 three years. **Circulation:** 13,385.

★3695★
Richmond Post
The Alameda Publishing Corp.
PO Box 1350   Ph: (415)763-1120
Oakland, CA 94604-1350   Fax: (415)763-9670

Text: Black community newspaper. **Established:** 1963. **Column Depth:** 21 1/2 in. **Frequency:** 2x/wk. (Wed. and Sun.). **Number of Columns Per Page:** 6. **Column Width:** 2 1/16 in. **Print Method:** Offset. **Contact(s):** Gail Berkley, Editor; Thomas Berkley, Publisher; Donald V. Welcher, Advertising Mgr. **Subscription:** $42. **Circulation:** 13,661.

★3696★
Roanoke Tribune
PO Box 6021
Roanoke, VA 24017   Ph: (703)343-0326

Text: Black community newspaper. **Established:** 1938. **Column Depth:** 294 agate lines. **Frequency:** Weekly (Thurs.). **Number of Columns Per Page:** 6. **Column Width:** 25 nonpareils. **Print Method:** Offset. **Contact(s):** Claudia A. Whitworth, Editor and Publisher. **Subscription:** $10. **Circulation:** 5,200.

★3697★
Rock Hill Black View
South Carolina Black Media Group
1310 Harden   Ph: (803)799-5252
Columbia, SC 29204   Fax: (803)799-7709

Text: Black community interest newspaper. **Established:** 1970. **Column Depth:** 224 agate lines. **Frequency:** Weekly (Wed.). **Number of Columns Per Page:** 6. **Column Width:** 24 nonpareils. **Print Method:** Offset. **Contact(s):** Bernard Legette, Editor; Isaac Washington, Publisher; Melody Harris, Advertising Mgr. **Subscription:** $25. **Circulation:** 5,164.

★3698★
Sacramento Observer
The Observer Newspapers
PO Box 209
Sacramento, CA 95801
Ph: (916)452-4781
Fax: (916)452-7744
Text: Black community newspaper. **Established:** 1962. **Frequency:** Weekly (Thurs.). **Print Method:** Offset. **Trim Size:** 10 x 15. **Number of Columns Per Page:** 5 and 6. /CLD 21 in. **Contact(s):** Kathryn C. Lee, Mng. Editor; Dr. William H. Lee, Publisher. **Subscription:** $20. **Circulation:** 49,090.

★3699★
The St. Louis American
American Publishing Co.
4144 Lindell Blvd.
Saint Louis, MO 63108
Ph: (314)533-8000
Fax: (314)533-0038
Text: Black community newspaper. **Established:** 1928. **Column Depth:** 194 agate lines. **Frequency:** Weekly (Thurs.). **Trim Size:** 13 1/2 x 22 3/4. **Number of Columns Per Page:** 6. **Column Width:** 26 nonpareils. **Print Method:** Offset. **Contact(s):** Dr. Donald M. Suggs, Publisher. **Subscription:** $12.50.

★3700★
St. Louis Argus
4595 Martin Luther King Dr.
Saint Louis, MO 63113
Ph: (314)531-1323
Text: Black community newspaper. **Frequency:** Weekly. **Contact(s):** Donald Thompson, Editor; Dr. Eugene Mitchell, Publisher. **Circulation:** 15,000.

★3701★
St. Louis Crusader
4371 Finney Ave.
Saint Louis, MO 63113
Text: Black community newspaper. **Frequency:** Weekly. **Contact(s):** William P. Russell, Pres./Chm. of the Board.

★3702★
St. Louis Sentinel Newspaper
Woods Publications
2900 N. Market
Saint Louis, MO 63106
Ph: (314)531-2691
Fax: (314)531-4442
Text: Black community newspaper with a Republican orientation. **Established:** April 1968. **Frequency:** Weekly (Thurs.). **Print Method:** Offset. **Trim Size:** 13 x 21 1/2. **Number of Columns Per Page:** 6. **Column Width:** 2 1/16 in. **Contact(s):** Michael Williams, Editor; Jane E. Woods, Publisher; Roy Cheatham, Advertising Mgr. **Subscription:** Free; $25 (mail).

★3703★
St. Paul Recorder
590 Endicott Ave.
St. Paul, MN 55407
Ph: (612)827-4021
Fax: (612)827-0577
Text: Black community newspaper. **Contact(s):** Cecil Newman, Editor.

★3704★
San Antonio Register
PO Box 1598
San Antonio, TX 78296-1598
Ph: (512)222-1721
Text: African-American community newspaper. **Established:** 1931. **Column Depth:** 21 in. **Frequency:** Weekly. **Trim Size:** 13 1/2 X 22 3/4. **Number of Columns Per Page:** 6. **Column Width:** 12 picas. **Print Method:** Web offset. **Contact(s):** Kathy Little, Editor/Advertising Mgr.. **Subscription:** $22.

★3705★
The San Bernardino American News
The American News
1583 W. Baseline St.
San Bernardino, CA 92411-1756
Ph: (714)889-7677
Fax: (714)889-2882
Text: Black community newspaper. **Established:** 1969. **Column Depth:** 294 agate lines. **Frequency:** Weekly (Thurs.). **Number of Columns Per Page:** 6. **Column Width:** 26 nonpareils. **Print Method:**

Offset. **Contact(s):** Samuel Martin, Publisher. **Subscription:** $12. **Circulation:** 5,000.

★3706★
The San Diego Voice and Viewpoint
1729 N. Euclid Ave.
San Diego, CA 92105
Ph: (619)266-2233
Fax: (619)266-0533
Text: Black American newspaper. **Established:** 1960. **Column Depth:** 224 agate lines. **Frequency:** Weekly (Thurs.). **Number of Columns Per Page:** 5. **Column Width:** 23 nonpareils. **Print Method:** Offset. Uses mats. **Contact(s):** Earl Davis, Jr., Editor and Publisher. **Subscription:** $25. **Circulation:** 13,000.

★3707★
San Fernando Gazette Express
First-Line Publishers/L.A. Metro Group
14621 Titus St., Ste. 228
Van Nuys, CA 91402
Ph: (818)782-8695
Fax: (818)782-2924
Text: Black community newspaper serving Pacoima, Arleta, and Panorama City. **Established:** 1966. **Frequency:** Weekly (Thurs.). **Print Method:** Offset. **Trim Size:** 13 x 21 1/2. **Number of Columns Per Page:** 6. **Column Width:** 2 in. **Contact(s):** Hillard Hamm, C.E.O. **Subscription:** Free; $25. **Circulation:** 60,000.

★3708★
San Francisco Post
The Alameda Publishing Corp.
PO Box 1350
Oakland, CA 94604
Ph: (415)763-1120
Fax: (415)763-9670
Text: Black community newspaper. **Established:** 1963. **Column Depth:** 21 1/2 in. **Frequency:** 2x/wk.(Wed. and Sun.). **Number of Columns Per Page:** 6. **Column Width:** 1 1/16 in. **Print Method:** Offset. **Contact(s):** Gail Berkley, Editor; Thomas Berkley, Publisher; Donald V. Welcher, Advertising Mgr. **Subscription:** $42. **Circulation:** 18,289.

★3709★
The Savannah Tribune
Savannah Tribune, Inc.
916 Montgomery St.
PO Box 2066
Savannah, GA 31402
Ph: (912)233-6128
Fax: (912)232-8666
Text: Black community newspaper. **Established:** 1875. **Column Depth:** 21 1/2 in. **Frequency:** Weekly (Thurs.). **Trim Size:** 13 x 21 1/2. **Number of Columns Per Page:** 6. **Column Width:** 2 in. **Print Method:** Offset. **Contact(s):** Shirley B. James, Editor and Publisher. **Subscription:** $15; $17 out of area.

★3710★
Seaside Post News-Sentinel
The Alameda Publishing Corp.
1244A Broadway Ave.
PO Box 670
Seaside, CA 93955
Ph: (408)394-6632
Text: Black community newspaper. **Established:** 1947. **Column Depth:** 301 agate lines. **Frequency:** Weekly (Wed.). **Number of Columns Per Page:** 6. **Column Width:** 26 nonpareils. **Print Method:** Offset. Uses mats. **Contact(s):** Willie L. Harrell, Editor and Publisher. **Subscription:** $20.

★3711★
Seattle Medium
Piloven Publishing
2600 S. Jackson
Seattle, WA 98144
Ph: (206)323-3070
Fax: (206)322-6518
Text: Black community newspaper. **Established:** 1970. **Frequency:** Weekly (Wed.). **Contact(s):** Angela Jenkins, Editor; Chris Bennett, Publisher. **Circulation:** 37,000.

★3712★
Shoals News Leader
PO Box 427
Florence, AL 35631   Ph: (205)766-5542
Text: Black community newspaper. **Established:** 1980. **Frequency:** Weekly. **Contact(s):** William R. Liner, Editor and Publisher. **Circulation:** 10,000.

★3713★
The Shreveport Sun
The Shreveport Sun, Inc.
PO Box 38357
Shreveport, LA 71133-8357   Ph: (318)631-6222
Text: Black community newspaper. **Established:** 1920. **Column Depth:** 301 agate lines. **Frequency:** Weekly (Wed.). **Number of Columns Per Page:** 6. **Column Width:** 25 nonpareils. **Print Method:** Offset. **Contact(s):** Sonya Collins Landry, Editor; Ronald Collins, Advertising Mgr. **Subscription:** $15.

★3714★
South East Times
3249 E. 137th St.
Cleveland, OH 44120   Ph: (216)921-2788
Text: Black community newspaper. **Contact(s):** Michael L. Potts, President.

★3715★
South End Citizen
Citizen Newspapers
412 E. 87th St.   Ph: (312)487-7700
Chicago, IL 60619   Fax: (312)487-7931
Text: Newspaper serving Chicago's black community. **Established:** 1966. **Column Depth:** 196 agate lines. **Frequency:** Weekly (Thurs.). **Number of Columns Per Page:** 5. **Column Width:** 25 nonpareils. **Print Method:** Offset. **Contact(s):** William Garth, Pres./Publisher/Advertising Mgr.; Lisa Ely, Mng. Editor. **Subscription:** $25.

★3716★
South Suburban Citizen
Citizen Newspapers
412 E. 87th St.   Ph: (312)487-7700
Chicago, IL 60619   Fax: (312)487-7931
Text: Newspaper serving Chicago's suburban black community. **Established:** 1983. **Column Depth:** 196 agate lines. **Frequency:** Weekly (Thurs.). **Number of Columns Per Page:** 5. **Column Width:** 25 nonpareils. **Print Method:** Offset. **Contact(s):** William Garth, Pres./Publisher. **Subscription:** $15.

★3717★
South Suburban Standard
615 S. Halsted   Ph: (708)755-5021
Chicago Heights, IL 60411   Fax: (708)755-5020
Text: Black community newspaper. **Established:** 1979. **Column Depth:** 225 agate lines. **Frequency:** Biweekly. **Number of Columns Per Page:** 6. **Column Width:** 19 nonpareils. **Print Method:** Offset. **Contact(s):** Charles R. Gordon, Editor; Lorenzo Martin, Publisher; Pat Rush Martin, Advertising Mgr. **Subscription:** $30. **Circulation:** 25,000.

★3718★
Southeastern News
W Retvland Pub.
PO Box 489   Ph: (912)273-6714
Cordele, GA 31015   Fax: (912)273-6714
Text: Black community newspaper. **Contact(s):** Eugene Rutland, General Manager.

★3719★
Southwest News Wave
Central News-Wave Publications
2621 W. 54th St.   Ph: (213)290-3000
Los Angeles, CA 90043   Fax: (213)291-0219
Text: Black community newspaper. **Established:** 1919. **Column Depth:** 21 1/2 in. **Frequency:** Weekly (Wed.). **Trim Size:** 13 3/4 x 21 1/2. **Number of Columns Per Page:** 6. **Column Width:** 5 nonpareils. **Print Method:** Offset. **Contact(s):** C.Z. Wilson, Publisher. **Subscription:** $78. **Circulation:** 40,450.

★3720★
Southwest Topics/Sun Wave
Central News-Wave Publications
2621 W. 54th St.   Ph: (213)290-3000
Los Angeles, CA 90043   Fax: (213)291-0219
Text: Black community newspaper. **Established:** 1919. **Column Depth:** 21 1/2 in. **Frequency:** Weekly (Wed.). **Trim Size:** 13 3/4 x 21 1/2. **Number of Columns Per Page:** 6. **Column Width:** 5 nonpareils. **Print Method:** Offset. **Contact(s):** C.Z. Wilson, Publisher. **Subscription:** $78. **Circulation:** 30,000.

★3721★
Speakin' Out News
2006 Poole Ave. NW, Ste. A
PO Box 2826   Ph: (205)852-9449
Huntsville, AL 35804   Fax: (205)852-9484
Text: Black community newspaper. **Established:** 1980. **Column Depth:** 15 in. **Frequency:** Weekly (Wed.). **Trim Size:** 10 1/4 x 15. **Number of Columns Per Page:** 6. **Column Width:** 1 1/2 in. **Print Method:** Offset. **Contact(s):** William Smothers, Editor and Publisher. **Subscription:** $20. **Circulation:** 16,500.

★3722★
Star of Zion
A.M.E. Zion Publishing House
PO Box 31005   Ph: (704)377-4329
Charlotte, NC 28231-1005   Fax: (704)333-1769
Text: Religious newspaper (tabloid) for the black community. **Established:** October 1876. **Column Depth:** 140 agate lines. **Frequency:** Weekly (Thurs.). **Number of Columns Per Page:** 4. **Column Width:** 26 nonpareils. **Print Method:** Offset. **Contact(s):** Dr. Morgan W. Tann, Editor; Thad Garrett, Advertising Mgr. **ISSN:** 0038-9820. **Subscription:** $22.

★3723★
Sumter Black Post
PO Box 11128   Ph: (803)799-5252
Columbia, SC 29211   Fax: 800-799-7709
Text: Black community interest newspaper. **Established:** 1970. **Column Depth:** 224 agate lines. **Frequency:** Weekly (Wed.). **Number of Columns Per Page:** 6. **Column Width:** 24 nonpareils. **Print Method:** Offset. **Contact(s):** Zack Weston, Editor; Isaac Washington, Publisher; Cynthia Bowden, Advertising Mgr. **Subscription:** $25. **Circulation:** 5,355.

★3724★
Sun-Reporter
Reporter Publications
1366 Turk St.   Ph: (415)931-5778
San Francisco, CA 94115   Fax: (415)931-0214
Text: Black community newspaper (tabloid). **Established:** 1943. **Column Depth:** 14 in. **Frequency:** Weekly (Wed.). **Number of Columns Per Page:** 5. **Column Width:** 2 1/16 in. **Print Method:** Offset. **Contact(s):** Amelia-Ashley Ward, Editor; Carlton B. Goodlett, Ph.D., M.D., Publisher; Jack Kisbey, Advertising Mgr. **Subscription:** $11. **Circulation:** 11,249.

★3725★
The Suspension Press
PO Box 2064
Covington, KY 41012
Text: Black community newspaper. **Established:** August 21, 1982. **Column Depth:** 210 agate lines. **Frequency:** Every other week. **Number of Columns Per Page:** 5. **Column Width:** 22 nonpareils.

Print Method: Offset. **Contact(s):** Pamela Mullins, Editor; Patricia Humphries Fann, Publisher; Robert Humphries, Advertising Mgr.. **Subscription:** $12.

★3726★
Tacoma True Citizen
Pilovbin Publishing
2600 S. Jackson St.   Ph: (206)627-1103
Seattle, WA 98144   Fax: (206)322-6518

Text: Black community newspaper. **Frequency:** Weekly (Thurs.). **Contact(s):** Connie Cameron, Editor; Chris Bennett, Publisher. **Circulation:** 13,500.

★3727★
The Toledo Journal
3021 Douglas Rd.
PO Box 2536   Ph: (419)472-4521
Toledo, OH 43606   Fax: (419)472-1604

Text: African-American newspaper. **Established:** 1975. **Column Depth:** 10 1/4 x 16. **Frequency:** Weekly (Wed.). **Trim Size:** 10 1/4 x 16. **Print Method:** Offset. **Number of Columns Per Page:** 6. **Contact(s):** Myron A. Stewart, Editor; Sandra S. Stewart, Publisher. **Subscription:** $25. **Circulation:** 17,000.

★3728★
Tri-City Journal
8 S. Michigan Ave., Ste. 1111   Ph: (312)346-8123
Chicago, IL 60603   Fax: (312)236-2221

Text: Black community newspaper. **Established:** 1978. **Column Depth:** 14 in. **Frequency:** Weekly (Thurs.). **Trim Size:** 10 x 14 in. **Number of Columns Per Page:** 5. **Column Width:** 11 1/2 in. **Print Method:** Offset. **Contact(s):** Ibn Sharrieff, Editor and Publisher. **Circulation:** 50,000.

★3729★
Tri-State Defender
PO Box 2065   Ph: (901)523-1818
Memphis, TN 38101-2065   Fax: (901)523-1820

Text: Black community newspaper. **Established:** 1951. **Column Depth:** 21 in. **Frequency:** Weekly (Thurs.). **Trim Size:** 13 1/2 x 22 1/2. **Number of Columns Per Page:** 6. **Column Width:** 2 1/16 in. **Print Method:** Web offset. **Contact(s):** P.McGhee, Editor; John H. Sengstacke, Publisher. **Subscription:** $20. **Circulation:** 15,000.

★3730★
Twin Cities Courier
84 S. 6th St., Ste. 501
Minneapolis, MN 55402   Ph: (612)332-3211

Text: Black community newspaper. **Contact(s):** Mary J. Kyle, Editor.

★3731★
View South News
PO Box 1849   Ph: (803)531-1662
Orangeburg, SC 29116   Fax: (803)531-1662

Text: Black community newspaper (tabloid). **Established:** 1979. **Frequency:** Weekly. **Trim Size:** 11 x 16. **Number of Columns Per Page:** 4. **Contact(s):** Cecil J. Williams, Editor and Publisher. **Circulation:** 5,000.

★3732★
The Villager
1223-A Rosewood Ave.   Ph: (512)476-0082
Austin, TX 78702   Fax: (512)476-0179

Text: Black community newspaper. **Established:** May 13, 1973. **Column Depth:** 294 agate lines. **Frequency:** Weekly (Fri.). **Trim Size:** 13 x 21. **Number of Columns Per Page:** 6. **Column Width:** 26 nonpareils. **Print Method:** Offset. **Contact(s):** Bobbie J. Hall, Managing Editor; T.L. Wyatt, Publisher/Advertising Mgr. **Subscription:** $20 (mail). **Circulation:** 6,000.

★3733★
Voice
Bethune-Cookman College
640 2nd Ave.   Ph: (904)255-1401
Daytona Beach, FL 32115   Fax: (904)257-4832

Text: Black collegiate newspaper. **Established:** 1974. **Column Depth:** 196 agate lines. **Frequency:** Monthly. **Trim Size:** 11 x 17. **Number of Columns Per Page:** 4. **Column Width:** 22 nonpareils. **Print Method:** Offset. **Contact(s):** N.T. Kabugi, Publisher; Terri D. Baker, Editor; Tenecia Bradley, Acting Advertising Dir. **Subscription:** Free; $10. **Circulation:** 3,000.

★3734★
The Waco Messenger
Smith Printing Co.
PO Box 2087
Waco, TX 76703   Ph: (817)799-6911

Text: Black community newspaper. **Established:** 1929. **Column Depth:** 20 in. **Frequency:** Weekly (Fri.). **Trim Size:** 22 x 30. **Number of Columns Per Page:** 6. **Column Width:** 13 picas. **Print Method:** Letterpress. **Contact(s):** M.P. Harvey, Editor and Publisher. **Subscription:** $10; $12.75 out of state. **Circulation:** 3,000.

★3735★
Washington Afro-American
The Afro-American Co.
2519 N. Charles St.   Ph: (410)554-8200
Baltimore, MD 21218   Fax: (410)554-8213

Text: Newspaper serving the black community. **Established:** 1933. **Column Depth:** 301 agate lines. **Frequency:** Weekly (Sat.). **Number of Columns Per Page:** 6. **Column Width:** 24 nonpareils. **Print Method:** Letterpress. **Contact(s):** Olive Vassell, Editor; Frances L. Murphy II, Publisher; Kevin E. Peck, Advertising Mgr. **Subscription:** $26; $46 two years; $58 three years. **Circulation:** 5,500.

★3736★
The Washington Capital Spotlight Newspaper
1264 National Press Bldg.   Ph: (202)628-0700
Washington, DC 20045   Fax: (202)662-8725

Text: Black community newspaper. **Established:** 1953. **Column Depth:** 14 in. **Frequency:** Weekly (Thurs.). **Column Width:** 1 9/16 in. **Number of Columns Per Page:** 6. **Contact(s):** Norman Robinson, Editor; Ike Kendrick, Publisher. **Subscription:** $25. **Circulation:** 60,000.

★3737★
The Washington Informer
3117 Martin Luther King Jr. Ave. SE   Ph: (202)561-4100
Washington, DC 20032   Fax: (202)574-3785

Text: Newspaper (tabloid) serving Washington's metropolitan area black community. **Established:** October 16, 1964. **Column Depth:** 12 1/2 in. **Frequency:** Weekly (Thurs.). **Number of Columns Per Page:** 6. **Column Width:** 1 1/2 in. **Print Method:** Offset. **Contact(s):** Calvin W. Rolark, Editor and Publisher. **Subscription:** $15. **Circulation:** 27,000.

★3738★
The Washington New Observer
811 Florida Ave. NW   Ph: (202)232-3060
Washington, DC 20001   Fax: (202)232-1711

Text: Black community newspaper. **Established:** 1957. **Column Depth:** 196 agate lines. **Frequency:** Weekly (Thurs.). **Number of Columns Per Page:** 5. **Column Width:** 24 nonpareils. **Print Method:** Tabloid. Offset. **Contact(s):** Robert T. Newton, Editor; Lauren Newton Johnson, Advertising Mgr. **Subscription:** $24. **Circulation:** 20,000.

★3739★
Watts Star Review
PO Box 19027A   Ph: (213)291-9486
Los Angeles, CA 90019   Fax: (213)291-2123

Text: Black community newspaper. **Established:** 1875. **Column Depth:** 194 agate lines. **Frequency:** Weekly (Thurs.). **Number of Columns Per Page:** 6. **Column Width:** 29 nonpareils. **Print Method:**

Offset. **Contact(s):** Lela Ward Oliver, Editor; John H. Holoman, Publisher. **Subscription:** $20. **Circulation:** 30,000.

★3740★
The Weekly Challenger
2500 9th St. S.
Saint Petersburg, FL 33705   Ph: (813)896-2922

Text: Black community newspaper. **Established:** September 1967. **Column Depth:** 21 1/2 in. **Frequency:** Weekly. **Trim Size:** 8 x 21 1/2. **Number of Columns Per Page:** 8. **Column Width:** 1 1/2 in. **Print Method:** Offset. **Contact(s):** Cynthia Armstrong, Editor; Cleveland Johnson, Publisher; William Blackshear, Advertising Mgr. **Subscription:** $15; $22 out of county. **Circulation:** 32,000.

★3741★
West Virginia Beacon Digest
PO Box 981
Charleston, WV 25324   Ph: (304)342-4600

Text: Black community newspaper. **Established:** 1957. **Column Depth:** 21 1/4 in. **Frequency:** Weekly. **Number of Columns Per Page:** 6. **Column Width:** 2 in. **Print Method:** Web press. **Contact(s):** Stephen R. Starks, Editor and Publisher. **Subscription:** $13. **Circulation:** 35,861.

★3742★
Westchester County Press
PO Box 1631   Ph: (914)684-0006
White Plains, NY 10602   Fax: (914)694-5150

Text: Newspaper directed to the total community, with special emphasis on the positive issues about the Black community. **Established:** 1928. **Column Depth:** 14 in. **Frequency:** Weekly (Thurs.). **Trim Size:** 11 x 14. **Number of Columns Per Page:** 4. **Column Width:** 2 3/8 in. **Print Method:** Offset. Uses mats. **Contact(s):** Orial A. Redd, Exec. Editor; Tanya Lewis Mng. Editor; Alvin J. Nall, Editor; M. Paul Redd, Publisher; Paula A. Zeman, Advertising Mgr. **ISSN:** 0043-3373. **Subscription:** $25. **Circulation:** 20,000.

★3743★
Westchester Observer
542 E. 3rd St.
Mount Vernon, NY 10553

Text: Black community newspaper. **Contact(s):** Ben Anderson, Editor.

★3744★
Westside Gazette
PO Box 5304   Ph: (305)523-5115
Fort Lauderdale, FL 33310   Fax: (305)522-2553

Text: Black community newspaper. **Established:** 1971. **Column Depth:** 294 agate lines. **Frequency:** 2x/wk. (Thurs. and Sun.). **Number of Columns Per Page:** 6. **Column Width:** 24 nonpareils. **Print Method:** Offset. **Contact(s):** Yvonne Henry, Editor; Levi Henry, Jr., Publisher. **Subscription:** $20.

★3745★
Wilmington Beacon
Rapid Publishing
349 W. Compton
PO Box 4248
Compton, CA 90224   Ph: (213)774-0018

Text: Black community newspaper. **Column Depth:** 21 1/2 in. **Frequency:** Weekly (Wed.). **Column Width:** 12 1/2 picas. **Number of Columns Per Page:** 6. **Contact(s):** O. Ray Watkins, Publisher.

★3746★
The Wilmington Journal
412 S. 7th St.
PO Box 1618   Ph: (919)762-5502
Wilmington, NC 28401   Fax: (919)343-1334

Text: Black community newspaper. **Established:** 1927. **Column Depth:** 294 agate lines. **Frequency:** Weekly (Thurs.). **Number of Columns Per Page:** 6. **Column Width:** 25 nonpareils. **Print Method:** Offset. **Contact(s):** T.C. Jervay, Editor and Publisher. **ISSN:** 0049-7649. **Subscription:** $15. **Circulation:** 8,600.

★3747★
Winston-Salem Chronicle
617 N. Liberty St.
PO Box 1636   Ph: (919)722-8624
Winston-Salem, NC 27102   Fax: (919)723-9173

Text: Black community newspaper. **Established:** 1974. **Column Depth:** 294 agate lines. **Frequency:** Weekly (Thurs.). **Number of Columns Per Page:** 6. **Column Width:** 24 nonpareils. **Print Method:** Offset. **Contact(s):** Ernest H. Pitt, Publisher. **Subscription:** $30.72. **Circulation:** 7,500.

Periodicals

★3748★
A&T Register
North Carolina Agricultural & Technical
University
Box E25
Greensboro, NC 27411   Ph: (919)334-7700

Text: Collegiate magazine with a black orientation. **Established:** 1892. **Column Depth:** 210 agate lines. **Frequency:** Weekly (Fri.). **Number of Columns Per Page:** 5. **Column Width:** 22 nonpareils. **Print Method:** Offset. **Contact(s):** Esther Woods, Editor; Warren McNeill, Advertising Mgr. **Subscription:** $12.

★3749★
About...Time
About...Time Magazine, Inc.
283 Genesee St.   Ph: (716)235-7150
Rochester, NY 14611   Fax: (716)235-7195

Text: Magazine providing a chronicle of minority history and achievement. **Established:** December 1972. **Frequency:** Monthly. **Print Method:** Offset. **Trim Size:** 8 1/2 x 11. **Number of Columns Per Page:** 2 and 3. **Contact(s):** Carolyne S. Blount, Editor; James M. Blount, Publisher and Advertising Mgr. **Subscription:** $11.

★3750★
Africa Today
Africa Today Associates
University of Denver
Graduate School of International Studies   Ph: (303)871-3678
Denver, CO 80208   Fax: (303)871-2456

Text: Journal on political, social, and economic conditions in Africa. **Established:** March 1954. **Column Depth:** 119 agate lines. **Frequency:** Quarterly. **Trim Size:** 5 x 8. **Number of Columns Per Page:** 1. **Column Width:** 66 nonpareils. **Print Method:** Offset. **Contact(s):** Jendayi Frazer, Exec. Editor. **ISSN:** 0001-9887. **Subscription:** $48.

★3751★
African American Review
Department of English
Indiana State University   Ph: (812)237-2968
Terre Haute, IN 47809   Fax: (812)287-4382

Text: Journal presenting essays on African-American literature and culture. Contains interviews, poems, fiction, and book reviews. **Established:** Fall 1967. **Column Depth:** 54 picas. **Frequency:** 4x/yr. **Trim Size:** 7 x 10. **Number of Columns Per Page:** 2. **Column Width:** 14 picas. **Print Method:** Offset. **Contact(s):** Joseph Weixlmann, Editor. **ISSN:** 1062-4783. **Subscription:** $20; $40 institutions; $27 other countries; $47 institutions, other countries.

★3752★
Aim—America's Intercultural Magazine
Aim Publications
7308 S. Eberhart Ave.
Chicago, IL 60619   Ph: (312)874-6184

Text: Magazine promoting intercultural awareness and understanding in America. **Established:** 1974. **Column Depth:** 9 3/4 in. **Frequency:** Quarterly. **Number of Columns Per Page:** 3. **Column Width:** 2 1/4 in. **Trim Size:** 8 1/2 x 11. **Contact(s):** Myron

Apilado, Mng. Editor; Ruth Apilado, Editor and Publisher. **Subscription:** $10.

★3753★
Alternative Press Index
PO Box 33109
Baltimore, MD 21218   Ph: (410)243-2471

Text: Alternative index including Black, Hispanic, and women's listings. **Established:** 1969. **Column Depth:** 130 agate lines. **Frequency:** Quarterly. **Trim Size:** 8 1/2 x 11. **Number of Columns Per Page:** 3. **Column Width:** 27 nonpareils. **Print Method:** Offset. **Contact(s):** Bill Wilson, Editor. **ISSN:** 0002-662X. **Subscription:** $35; $175 institutions.

★3754★
American Visions: The Magazine of Afro-American Culture
Dialogue Diaspora, Inc.
2101 S St. NW   Ph: (202)462-1779
Washington, DC 20008   Fax: (202)462-3997

Established: January 1986. **Column Depth:** 50 picas. **Frequency:** 6x/yr. **Trim Size:** 8 1/4 x 10 7/8. **Number of Columns Per Page:** 3. **Column Width:** 13 picas. **Print Method:** Offset. **Contact(s):** Gary Puckrein, Editor-in-Chief; Joanne Harris, Editor; Timothy Jenkins, Publisher **ISSN:** 0884-9390. **Subscription:** $18.

★3755★
AUC Digest
Atlanta University Center
PO Box 3191   Ph: (404)523-6136
Atlanta, GA 30302   Fax: (404)523-5467

Text: Collegiate magazine (tabloid). **Established:** 1973. **Column Depth:** 196 agate lines. **Frequency:** Weekly (Mon.). **Number of Columns Per Page:** 4. **Column Width:** 27 nonpareils. **Print Method:** Offset. **Contact(s):** Lo Jelks, Editor and Publisher; Tim Williams, Advertising Mgr. **Subscription:** $12.

★3756★
Black Books Bulletin: Words Work
7524 S. Cottage Grove Ave.   Ph: (312)651-0700
Chicago, IL 60619   Fax: (312)651-7286

Text: Consumer magazine. **Frequency:** Quarterly. **Subscription:** $2.95 single issue.

★3757★
BLACK CAREERS
Project Magazine, Inc.
PO Box 8214
Philadelphia, PA 19101-8214   Ph: (215)387-1600

Text: Business news magazine for minority college graduates and working professionals in business, industry, and government. Provides job search information and career guidance and development. **Established:** 1965. **Frequency:** 6x/yr. **Print method:** Offset. **Trim size:** 8 1/2 x 11. **Number of columns per page:** 3. **Column width:** 27 nonpareils. **Column depth:** 140 agate lines. **Contact(s):** Emory W. Washington, Editor and Publisher; Herbert Bass, Advertising Mgr.; D. Gooden, Circulation Mgr. **Subscription:** $20.

★3758★
Black College Sports Review
Winston-Salem Chronicle
617 N. Liberty St.   Ph: (919)723-9026
Winston-Salem, NC 27102   Fax: (919)723-9173

Text: Magazine covering black college sports. **Contact(s):** Ernest H. Pitt, Publisher.

★3759★
The Black Collegian
Black Collegiate Services, Inc.
1240 S. Broad St.   Ph: (504)821-5694
New Orleans, LA 70125-2091   Fax: (504)821-5713

Text: Career opportunity magazine featuring job searching role models, interviews, entertainment, art, and African-American history. **Established:** 1970. **Column Depth:** 9 in. **Frequency:** 4x/yr. **Trim

Size: 8 x 10 3/4. **Number of Columns Per Page:** 3. **Column Width:** 13.5 picas. **Print Method:** Offset. **Contact(s):** Kuumba Ferrouillett, Editor; Preston J. Edwards, Publisher; Carter Womack, Sr. V.P. Adv. **ISSN:** 0192-3757. **Subscription:** $10; $5 students. $2.50 single issue.

★3760★
Black Employment and Education Magazine
Hamdani Communications Inc.
Bldg. 56, Ste. 282
2625 Piemont Rd.
Atlanta, GA 30324   Ph: (404)469-5891

Text: Periodical for black college and trade school students and professors. **Established:** 1990. **Column Depth:** 9 1/2 in. **Frequency:** 6x/yr.. **Number of Columns Per Page:** 3. **Column Width:** 2 1/8 in. **Trim Size:** 8 1/2 x 11. **Contact(s):** S. Barry Hamdani, Editor and Publisher. **ISSN:** 1053-704X. **Subscription:** $15. $3 single issue.

★3761★
Black Enterprise
Earl G. Graves Publishing Co.
130 5th Ave.   Ph: (212)242-8000
New York, NY 10011   Fax: (212)886-9610

Text: Black-oriented business magazine. **Established:** 1970. **Column Depth:** 134 agate lines. **Frequency:** Monthly. **Trim Size:** 8 1/8 x 10 7/8. **Number of Columns Per Page:** 3. **Column Width:** 27 nonpareils. **Print Method:** Offset. **Contact(s):** Earl G. Graves, Editor and Publisher. **Subscription:** $12.95. $1.95 single issue. **Circulation:** 251,983.

★3762★
Black Family
Kent Enterprises, Inc.
Box 1046
Herndon, VA 22070-1046

Text: Magazine focusing and shaping positive lifestyles for middle to upper-middle income black consumers. **Established:** 1980. **Column Depth:** 140 agate lines. **Frequency:** 6x/yr. **Trim Size:** 8 1/8 x 10 7/8. **Number of Columns Per Page:** 3. **Print Method:** Offset. **Contact(s):** Evelyn Ivery, Managing Editor; Frank C. Kent, Publisher; Mai Ling Poole, Advertising Mgr.

★3763★
Black Health
Altier & Maynard Communications, Inc.
6 Farmingville Rd.
Ridgefield, CT 06877   Ph: (203)431-3454

Established: 1988. **Frequency:** 4x/yr. **Print Method:** Web offset. **Trim Size:** 8 1/8 x 10 3/4. **Contact(s):** Bonnie Maynard, Publisher; Carlos Maynard, Publisher. **Subscription:** Free to qualified subscribers; $10. $2.50 single issue.

★3764★
Black Lace
PO Box 83912
Los Angeles, CA 90083   Ph: (213)410-0808

Text: Magazine published by and for African-American lesbians. Includes erotica and politically focused articles and analysis. **Frequency:** Quarterly.

★3765★
Black News Digest
U.S. Dept. of Labor
Office of Information & Public Affairs
200 Constitution Ave. NW
Washington, DC 20210   Ph: (202)606-7828

Text: Government publication containing news and feature material about the U.S. Department of Labor and its programs for black Americans. **Frequency:** Weekly. **Trim Size:** 8 1/2 x 11. **Contact(s):** Sue Blumenthal, Editor; Paul S. Williams, Chief, Division of Media and Editorial Services. **Subscription:** Free.

★3766★
The Black Scholar
Black World Foundation
PO Box 2869   Ph: (510)547-6633
Oakland, CA 94609   Fax: (510)547-6679

Established: November 1969. **Column Depth:** 8 1/2 in. **Frequency:** Quarterly. **Trim Size:** 7 x 10. **Number of Columns Per Page:** 2. **Column Width:** 2 5/8 in. **Print Method:** Offset. **Contact(s):** Robert Chrisman, Editor and Publisher. **ISSN:** 0006-4246. **Subscription:** $30; $50 institutions; $65 other countries. $6 single issue.

★3767★
Black Tennis Magazine
PO Box 210767   Ph: (214)670-7618
Dallas, TX 75211   Fax: (214)330-1318

Text: Sports magazine featuring black tennis players, clubs, and parks. **Established:** August 1977. **Column Depth:** 140 agate lines. **Frequency:** Monthly. **Trim Size:** 8 1/2 x 11. **Number of Columns Per Page:** 3. **Column Width:** 27 nonpareils. **Print Method:** Offset. **Contact(s):** Marcus A. Freeman, Jr., Editor and Publisher. **Subscription:** $15; $28 two years. **Circulation:** 5,000.

★3768★
The Black Writer
Terrell Associates
PO Box 1030   Ph: (312)995-5195
Chicago, IL 60690   Fax: (312)924-3818

Text: Magazine offering information to Afro-American writers and serving as a forum for publishing works by black writers. **Established:** 1974. **Frequency:** Quarterly. **Print Method:** Offset. **Trim Size:** 8 1/2 x 11. **Number of Columns Per Page:** 2. **Contact(s):** Mable Terrell, Editor and Publisher; Cary D. Boykin, Advertising Mgr. **Subscription:** $19; $15.20 institutions.

★3769★
Botswana Review
PO Box 278
Ivoryton, CT 06442

Text: Pan-African scholarly journal dealing with cultural matters. **Established:** 1989. **Column Depth:** 9 1/2 in. **Frequency:** Quarterly. **Number of Columns Per Page:** 1. **Column Width:** 7 1/4 in. **Trim Size:** 8 1/2 x 11. **Contact(s):** William C. Bendig, Editor; Dan Claffey, Managing Editor; Nicholas Russell, Publisher. **Subscription:** $85. $25 single issue.

★3770★
Callaloo
The Johns Hopkins University Press
701 W. 40th St., Ste. 275   Ph: (410)516-6982
Baltimore, MD 21211   Fax: (410)516-6998

Text: Journal covering critical studies and original works by Blacks worldwide. **Established:** 1978. **Column Depth:** 45 picas. **Frequency:** Quarterly. **Trim Size:** 6 7/8 x 10. **Number of Columns Per Page:** 1. **Column Width:** 30 picas. **Print Method:** Offset. **Contact(s):** Charles H. Rowell, Editor (University of Virginia); Tara Dorai-Berry, Advertising Mgr. **ISSN:** 0161-2492. **Subscription:** $22; $47 institutions. **Circulation:** 1,650.

★3771★
Caribbean Review
Caribbean Review Inc.
9700 SW 67th Ave.   Ph: (305)284-8466
Miami, FL 33156   Fax: (305)284-1019

Text: Magazine dedicated to the Caribbean, Latin America, and their emigrant groups. **Established:** January 1969. **Frequency:** Quarterly. **Print Method:** Offset. **Trim Size:** 8 1/2 x 11. **Number of Columns Per Page:** 3. **Contact(s):** Barry B. Levine, Editor and Publisher. **ISSN:** 0008-6525. **Subscription:** $20.

★3772★
Chocolate Singles
Chocolate Singles Enterprises, Inc.
PO Box 333   Ph: (718)978-4800
Jamaica, NY 11413   Fax: (718)978-4819

Text: Magazine for black singles. **Contact(s):** Barbara Miles, Publisher.

★3773★
The Christian Index
Christian Methodist Episcopal Church
PO Box 665
Memphis, TN 38101   Ph: (901)345-1173

Text: Religious magazine covering the predominantly black Christian Methodist Episcopal denomination. **Established:** 1868. **Frequency:** 2x/mo. **Print Method:** Letterpress and offset. **Trim Size:** 8 1/2 x 11. **Number of Columns Per Page:** 2 and 3. **Contact(s):** Lawrence L. Reddick III, Editor and Publisher. **ISSN:** 0744-4060. **Subscription:** $15; $28 two years. **Circulation:** 6,000.

★3774★
Class Magazine
900 Broadway   Ph: (212)677-3055
New York, NY 10003   Fax: (212)677-3341

Text: Magazine serving black America. **Established:** 1979. **Column Depth:** 9 in. **Frequency:** Monthly. **Trim Size:** 8 1/4 x 10 7/8. **Number of Columns Per Page:** 3. **Column Width:** 13 1/2 picas. **Print Method:** Web offset. **Contact(s):** Rene John-Sandy, Publisher; Constance M. Weaver, Exec. Editor; Andrew Alsuran, Circulation Mgr. **ISSN:** 0747-3826. **Subscription:** $15; $20 other countries. $2.50 single issue.

★3775★
Clubdate Magazine
1826 E. 93rd St.
Cleveland, OH 44106-2052

Text: Magazine for upper income blacks. **Established:** 1979. **Column Depth:** 140 agate lines. **Frequency:** 6x/yr. **Trim Size:** 8 1/2 x 11. **Number of Columns Per Page:** 3. **Column Width:** 27 nonpareils. **Print Method:** Web offset. **Contact(s):** Madelyne B. Blunt, Publisher; Carol Evyans, Advertising Mgr. **Subscription:** $14. $2.50 single issue.

★3776★
CORPORATE HEADQUARTERS
HQ Publications
516 North Ave. E.   Ph: (201)233-8837
Westfield, NJ 07090   Fax: (201)233-8230

Text: Magazine for Black professionals; containing personal, professional, and career development editorial. **Established:** July 1985. **Frequency:** Quarterly. **Trim Size:** 8 1/2 x 11. **Contact(s):** Mrs. Terri Fisher, Editor; Dr. Harold E. Fisher, Publisher. **Subscription:** $12.

★3777★
Creole Magazine
PO Box 91496   Ph: (318)269-1956
Lafayette, LA 70509   Fax: (318)332-4775

Text: Community magazine discussing the cultural heritage, customs, music, cuisine, and language of southwest Louisiana. **Established:** 1990. **Column Depth:** 9 1/2 in. **Frequency:** Monthly. **Number of Columns Per Page:** 3. **Column Width:** 3 3/4 in. and 2 1/2 in. **Trim Size:** 8 1/4 x 10 1/2. **Contact(s):** Ruth Foote, Editor and Publisher; Emmette J. Jacob, Jr., Exec. Publisher; Dianne Dupas, Advertising Dir. **Subscription:** Free; $15 out of distribution area; $30 other countries. $1.50 single issue.

★3778★
The Crisis
NAACP/Crisis Publishing
260 5th Ave., 6th Fl.   Ph: (212)481-4100
New York, NY 10001   Fax: (212)779-9277

Text: Magazine covering civil rights, current events, and the arts. **Established:** November 1910. **Frequency:** Monthly. **Print Method:** Offset. **Trim Size:** 8 1/2 x 11. **Number of Columns Per Page:** 3.

Column Width: 13 picas. **Contact(s):** Fred Beauford, Editor; Benjamin L. Hooks, Publisher; Harriett H. Diles, Advertising Mgr. **Subscription:** $10. **Circulation:** 350,000.

★3779★
Cultural Survival Quarterly
Cultural Survival, Inc.
215 1st St.   Ph: (617)374-1650
Cambridge, MA 02142   Fax: (617)621-3814
Text: Magazine for general public and policy makers intended to stimulate action for ethnic minorities. **Established:** 1976. **Frequency:** Quarterly. **Print Method:** Web. **Trim Size:** 8 1/2 x 11. **Number of Columns Per Page:** 3. **Column Width:** 13 1/2 picas. **Contact(s):** Marc S. Miller, Editor. **ISSN:** 0740-3291. **Subscription:** $45. $5 single issue. **Circulation:** 10,000.

★3780★
Dollars & Sense Magazine
1610 E. 79th St.   Ph: (312)375-6800
Chicago, IL 60649   Fax: (312)375-7149
Text: Magazine covering black history and development in business and other professions. **Established:** 1974. **Column Depth:** 54 picas. **Frequency:** 6x/yr. **Trim Size:** 8 1/8 x 10 7/8. **Number of Columns Per Page:** 3. **Column Width:** 13 picas. **Print Method:** Offset. **Contact(s):** Cheryl Evans, Editorial Dir; Donald C. Walker, Publisher. **Subscription:** $14.95. **Circulation:** 286,000.

★3781★
Ebony
Johnson Publishing
820 S. Michigan Ave.
Chicago, IL 60605   Ph: (312)322-9200
Text: General editorial magazine geared toward African-Americans. **Established:** 1945. **Column Depth:** 140 agate lines. **Frequency:** Monthly. **Number of Columns Per Page:** 3 **Column Width:** 30 nonpareils. **Print Method:** Offset **Contact(s):** John H. Johnson, Publisher. **Subscription:** $16. **Circulation:** 1,887,595.

★3782★
EM: Ebony Man
Johnson Publishing Co.
820 S. Michigan Ave.
Chicago, IL 60605   Ph: (312)322-9200
                                                     Fax: (312)322-0918
Text: Black men's magazine featuring regular columns on health, fashion, and sports. **Frequency:** Monthly. **Contact(s):** Ooloong J. Smith, Editor; John H. Johnson, Publisher; Errol Griffiths, Advertising Dir. **ISSN:** 0884-4879. **Subscription:** $16. $2 single issue. **Circulation:** 200,000.

★3783★
Emerge
Emerge Communications Inc.
170 Varick St., 12th Fl.   Ph: (212)627-4151
New York, NY 10013   Fax: (212)627-4157
Text: General interest news magazine for sophisticated black readers. **Established:** 1989. **Column Depth:** 66 picas. **Frequency:** 10x/yr. **Trim Size:** 8 1/8 x 10 7/8. **Number of Columns Per Page:** 3. **Column Width:** 13 picas. **Print Method:** Web offset. **Contact(s):** Wilmer C. Ames, Jr., Editor-in-Chief; Catherine Hennessey, Assoc. Publisher. **ISSN:** 0899-1154. **Subscription:** $16.97. $2.50 single issue.

★3784★
Essence
Essence Communications, Inc.
1500 Broadway 6th fl.   Ph: (212)642-0600
New York, NY 10036   Fax: (212)921-5173
Text: Magazine for contemporary black women. **Established:** 1970. **Column Depth:** 140 agate lines. **Frequency:** Monthly. **Trim Size:** 8 x 10 7/8. **Number of Columns Per Page:** 3. **Column Width:** 26 nonpareils. **Print Method:** Offset. **Contact(s):** Susan Taylor, Editor-in-Chief; Edward Lewis, Publisher/CEO; Clarence O. Smith, President. **ISSN:** 0014-0880. **Subscription:** $12.96. $2 single issue. **Circulation:** 950,000.

★3785★
Feelin' Good
Ware Publishing, Inc.
1142 Manhattan Ave., No 112
Manhattan Beach, CA 90266-5398
Text: Magazine covering healthy lifestyles for black women. **Established:** 1988. **Frequency:** 6x/yr. **Print Method:** Web offset. **Trim Size:** 8 1/4 x 10 3/4. **Contact(s):** Reginald D. Ware, Publisher. **Subscription:** $2.95 single issue. **Circulation:** 250,000.

★3786★
Gladiator
135 W. 50th St.   Ph: (212)307-8000
New York, NY 10020   Fax: (212)307-8060
Text: Magazine featuring professional black athletes. **Established:** April 1989. **Frequency:** Quarterly. **Print Method:** Web offset. **Trim Size:** 8 1/2 x 11 1/2. **Contact(s):** Vinette Pryce, Editor; Flo Anthony, Publisher. **Subscription:** $14 two years. $2 single issue. **Circulation:** 30,000.

★3787★
Harmony Magazine
PO Box 81, Pratt Sta.
Brooklyn, NY 11205   Ph: (718)875-7448
Text: Magazine featuring African studies and cross-cultural experiences. **Established:** 1982. **Frequency:** Quarterly. **Print Method:** Offset. **Trim Size:** 8 1/2 x 11. **Contact(s):** Shirley Ademu-John, Editor; Ekundayo Ademu-John, Assoc. Editor. **ISSN:** 0741-1804. **Subscription:** $16; $30 libraries/institutions. $3.50 single issue. **Circulation:** 5,000.

★3788★
Impartial Citizen
PO Box 98   Ph: (315)638-7868
Syracuse, NY 13205-0098   Fax: (315)638-0778
Text: Newspaper for multi-ethnic communities. **Established:** September 1980. **Column Depth:** 294 agate lines. **Frequency:** 2x/mo. **Trim Size:** 14 x 23. **Number of Columns Per Page:** 6. **Column Width:** 24 nonpareils. **Print Method:** Offset. **Contact(s):** Antoine J. Polgar, Editor and Advertising Mgr.; Robert S. Pritchard, Publisher. **ISSN:** 0738-9116. **Subscription:** $15.

★3789★
In a Word
Society of the Divine Word
199 Seminary Drive   Ph: (601)467-1097
Bay Saint Louis, MS 39520   Fax: (601)466-4393
Text: Magazine on black Catholics in the U.S.A. **Established:** 1983. **Frequency:** Monthly. **Contact(s):** Rev. James A. Pawlicki, S.U.D., Editor. **Circulation:** 38,500.

★3790★
International Journal of Intercultural Relations
Pergamon Press, Inc.
600 White Plains Road   Ph: (914)524-9200
Tarrytown, NY 10591-5153   Fax: (914)333-2444
Frequency: 4x/yr. **Contact(s):** Dan Landis, Editor: Susan Rosenthal, Advertising Sales Representative. **ISSN:** 0147-1767. **Subscription:** $270.

★3791★
The International Review of African American Art
Museum of African American Art
4005 Crenshaw Blvd., 3rd Fl.
Los Angeles, CA 90008-2534   .   Ph: (213)294-7071
Text: Magazine disseminating information about the contemporary black artist internationally. **Frequency:** Quarterly. **Contact(s):** Samella Lewis, Ph.D., Art Editor.

★3792★
Interrace
PO Box 15566
Beverly Hills, CA 90209

Text: Magazine covering interracial and transcultural adoption, and interracial dating and marriage. **Frequency:** Bimonthly. **Subscriptions:** $20. **Editor(s):** Candace Mills. **ISSN:** 1047-5370.

★3793★
Ivy Leaf
Alpha Kappa Alpha Sorority, Inc.
5656 S. Stony Island Ave.   Ph: (312)684-1282
Chicago, IL 60637   Fax: (312)288-8251

Text: Sorority publication for Black women. **Established:** December 1921. **Column Depth:** 140 agate lines. **Frequency:** Quarterly. **Trim Size:** 8 1/2 x 11. **Number of Columns Per Page:** 3. **Column Width:** 14 picas. **Print Method:** Offset. **Contact(s):** Alison A. Harris, Executive Director. **ISSN:** 0021-3276. **Subscription:** $10. **Circulation:** 37,000.

★3794★
Jet
Johnson Publishing Co., Inc.
820 S. Michigan Ave.
Chicago, IL 60605   Ph: (312)322-9200

Text: Newsmagazine for the black community. **Established:** 1951. **Column Depth:** 90 agate lines. **Frequency:** Weekly (Mon.). **Number of Columns Per Page:** 2. **Column Width:** 30 nonpareils. **Print Method:** Offset. **Contact(s):** John H. Johnson, Publisher. **Subscription:** $36. $1.25 single issue. **Circulation:** 968,545.

★3795★
Journal of Asia-Pacific Business
The Haworth Press, Inc.
10 Alice St.   Ph: (607)722-5857
Binghamton, NY 13904-1580   Fax: (607)722-1424

Text: Journal featuring managerially oriented as well as academic articles centered on the Asia-Pacific region. **Established:** Spring 1993. **Frequency:** Quarterly. **Contact(s):** Zahir A. Quraeshi, Editor; Bill Cohen, Publisher. **ISSN:** 1059-9231. **Subscription:** $24; $48 institutions; $75 libraries.

★3796★
Journal of Black Studies
Sage Periodicals Press
2455 Teller Rd.   Ph: (805)499-0721
Newbury Park, CA 91320   Fax: (805)499-0871

Text: Journal containing economic, historical, and philosophical research on Black people. **Established:** 1970. **Column Depth:** 100 agate lines. **Frequency:** Quarterly. **Trim Size:** 5 1/2 X 8 1/2. **Number of Columns Per Page:** 1. **Column Width:** 50 nonpareils. **Print Method:** Offset. **Contact(s):** Molefi K. Asante, Editor; Sara Miller McCune, Publisher; Valerie Giramberk, Circulation Mgr.. **ISSN:** 0021-9347. **Subscription:** $45; $121 institutions; $90 two years; $242 two years, institutions. $16 single issue; $34 single issue, institutions.

★3797★
Journal of Ethnic Studies
Western Washington University   Ph: (206)647-4861
Bellingham, WA 98225   Fax: (206)676-3037

Text: Journal covering interdisciplinary scholarship, opinion, and creative expression in ethnic matters. **Established:** Spring 1973. **Frequency:** Quarterly. **Print Method:** Offset. **Trim Size:** 6 x 8 1/4. **Number of Columns Per Page:** 1. **Contact(s):** Jesse Hiraoka, Editor. **ISSN:** 0091-3219. **Subscription:** $12; $15 institutions and libraries.

★3798★
Journal of Modern African Studies
Cambridge University Press
40 W. 20th St.
New York, NY 10011   Ph: (914)937-9600

Text: Journal surveying politics, economics, and related topics in contemporary Africa. **Frequency:** Quarterly. **Contact(s):** David

Kimble, Editor; Alan Winter, Press Dir., U.S. **ISSN:** 0022-278X. **Subscription:** $49; $114 institutions. $32 single issue.

★3799★
The Journal of Negro Education
Howard University
PO Box 311   Ph: (202)806-8120
Washington, DC 20059   Fax: (202)806-2130

Text: Educational research journal devoted to black and minority education. **Established:** 1932. **Column Depth:** 18 in. **Frequency:** Quarterly. **Trim Size:** 7 x 10. **Number of Columns Per Page:** 1. **Column Width:** 5 in. **Print Method:** Letterpress. **Contact(s):** Dr. Sylvia T. Johnson, Editor; Mahmoud Gudarzi, Advertising Mgr. **ISSN:** 0022-2984. **Subscription:** $16; $20 institutions; $24 other countries. $6 single issue.

★3800★
Journal of Negro History
Association for the Study of Afro-American
   Life and History
Morehouse College
Box 20
Atlanta, GA 30314   Ph: (404)681-2650

Text: Afro-American history journal. **Established:** 1916. **Column Depth:** 112 agate lines. **Frequency:** Quarterly. **Number of Columns Per Page:** 1. **Column Width:** 51 nonpareils. **Print Method:** Offset. **Contact(s):** Dr. Alton Hornsby, Jr., Editor. **Subscription:** $30.

★3801★
Journal of Pan African Studies
PO Box 13063
Fresno, CA 93794-3063   Ph: (209)266-2550

Text: Journal. **Established:** 1987. **Frequency:** Quarterly. **Print Method:** Offset. **Trim Size:** 8 1/2 x 11. **Number of Columns Per Page:** 4. **Contact(s):** Itibari M. Zulu, Editor. **ISSN:** 0888-6601. **Subscription:** $12; $20 other. $4 single issue.

★3802★
Journal of the National Medical Association
Slack, Inc.
6900 Grove Rd.   Ph: (609)848-1000
Thorofare, NJ 08086-9447   Fax: (609)853-5991

Text: Journal on specialized clinical research related to the health problems in the urban environment; recognizing significant contributions by black physicians and others towards inner city health care improvement. **Established:** 1909. **Column Depth:** 140 agate lines. **Frequency:** Monthly. **Trim Size:** 8 1/8 x 10 7/8. **Number of Columns Per Page:** 3 and 2. **Column Width:** 27 and 42 nonpareils. **Print Method:** Web offset. **Contact(s):** Calvin C. Sampson, M.D., Editor; Richard N. Roash, V.P./Publisher; Susan Walker, Natl. Advertising Sales Mgr. **ISSN:** 0027-9684. **Subscription:** $76; $91 institutions. $15 single issue.

★3803★
Journal of the National Technical Association
Black Collegiate Services, Inc.
1240 S. Broad St.   Ph: (504)821-5694
New Orleans, LA 70125-2091   Fax: (504)821-5713

Text: Journal covering jobs, careers, and technical interchange for experienced African-American technical professionals. **Established:** 1926. **Column Depth:** 140 agate lines. **Frequency:** 2x/yr, plus Technical papers supplement. **Trim Size:** 8 x 10 3/4. **Number of Columns Per Page:** 3. **Column Width:** 26 nonpareils. **Print Method:** Offset. Uses mat. **Contact(s):** Sonya Stinson, Editor; Melba R. Lemieux, Publisher; Carter D. Womack, Sr. V.P. Advertising. **ISSN:** 0271-776X. **Subscription:** $30; $50 two years.

★3804★
Lincoln Review
Lincoln Institute for Research and
   Education
1001 Connecticut Ave. NW, Ste. 1135
Washington, DC 20036   Ph: (202)223-5112

Text: Black public policy journal. **Established:** 1979. **Frequency:** Quarterly. **Print Method:** Offset. **Trim Size:** 6 x 9. **Number of

Columns Per Page: 1. **Contact(s):** J.A. Parker, Editor and Publisher. **ISSN:** 0192-5083. **Subscription:** $12. **Circulation:** 7,000.

★3805★
Living Blues
Center for the Study of Southern Culture
University of Mississippi   Ph: (601)232-5518
University, MS 38677   Fax: (601)232-5740
Text: Magazine covering the African-American blues tradition. **Established:** 1970. **Column Depth:** 60 picas. **Frequency:** 6x/yr. **Trim Size:** 8 1/2 x 11. **Number of Columns Per Page:** 3. **Column Width:** 14 picas. **Print Method:** Offset. **Contact(s):** David Nelson, Editor; Brett Bonner, Advertising Mgr. **ISSN:** 0024-5232. **Subscription:** $18. $3.50 single issue. **Circulation:** 16,000.

★3806★
Message Magazine
Review and Herald Publishing Assoc.
55 W. Oak Ridge Dr.   Ph: (301)791-7000
Hagerstown, MD 21740   Fax: (301)791-7012
Text: Religious magazine for African-Americans. **Established:** 1898. **Column Depth:** 9 1/4 in. **Frequency:** 6x/yr. **Trim Size:** 8 1/8 x 10 5/8. **Number of Columns Per Page:** 3. **Column Width:** 2 1/8 in. **Print Method:** Offset. **Contact(s):** Stephen P. Ruff, Editor; Mark Thomas, Advertising Mgr. **ISSN:** 0026-0231. **Subscription:** $11.95.

★3807★
Minorities and Women in Business
Venture X, Inc.
PO Drawer 210   Ph: (919)229-1462
Burlington, NC 27216   Fax: (919)222-7455
Text: Magazine networks with major corporations and small businesses owned and operated by minority and female entrepreneurs. **Established:** October 1984. **Frequency:** 6x/yr. **Trim Size:** 8 3/8 x 10 3/4. **Number of Columns Per Page:** 3. **Column Width:** 2 1/2 in. **Contact(s):** John D. Enoch, Editor and Publisher; Karen C. Bassler, Managing Editor; Cynthia A. McCray, Art Dir.. **Subscription:** Free to qualified subscribers; $15; $36 three years.

★3808★
Minority Business Entrepreneur
924 N. Market St.   Ph: (310)673-9398
Inglewood, CA 90302   Fax: (310)673-0170
Text: Business magazine for the Ethnic Minority Business owner. **Established:** Fall 1984. **Column Depth:** 10 in. **Frequency:** 6x/yr. **Trim Size:** 8 x 10 7/8. **Number of Columns Per Page:** 3. **Column Width:** 13 picas. **Print Method:** Offset. **Contact(s):** Jeanie M. Barnett, Editor; Ginger Conrad, Publisher. **ISSN:** 1048-0919. **Subscription:** Free to qualified subscribers; $12. **Circulation:** 26,851.

★3809★
Minority Business Social and Cultural Directory
PO Box 10112   Ph: (706)722-7327
Augusta, GA 30903   Fax: (706)724-6969
Text: Minority directory. **Established:** 1989. **Column Depth:** 13 in. **Frequency:** Quarterly. **Trim Size:** 10 1/4 x 13. **Number of Columns Per Page:** 5. **Column Width:** 2 in. **Print Method:** Web offset. **Contact(s):** Frederick Benjamin, Editor; Charles W. Walker, Publisher; Tanya Barnhill, Mktg. Mgr. **Subscription:** $15.

★3810★
National Scene Magazine
22 E. 41st St.
New York, NY 10017   Ph: (212)862-3700
Text: Magazine serving black Americans. **Contact(s):** William Decker Clarke, Publisher.

★3811★
The Negro Educational Review
The Negro Educational Review, Inc.
Box 2895, General Mail Center
Jacksonville, FL 32203   Ph: (904)646-2860
Text: Education journal. **Established:** 1950. **Frequency:** Quarterly. **Contact(s):** R. Lloyd, Editor. **Subscription:** $15. **Circulation:** 5,000.

★3812★
Negro History Bulletin
The Association for the Study of Afro-
American Life & History, Inc.
1407 14th St. NW   Ph: (202)667-2822
Washington, DC 20005-3704   Fax: (202)387-9802
Text: Magazine profiling black history through feature articles and biographies. **Established:** 1937. **Frequency:** Quarterly. **Trim Size:** 8 1/2 x 11. **Contact(s):** Karen Robinson, Exec. Dir. **ISSN:** 0028-2529. **Subscription:** $25. **Circulation:** 10,000.

★3813★
The New Research Traveler & Conventioneer
11717 S. Vincennes Ave.
Chicago, IL 60643   Ph: (312)881-3712
Text: Magazine containing travel and convention news for black professionals. **Established:** November 1942. **Column Depth:** 133 agate lines. **Frequency:** 6x/yr.. **Trim Size:** 8 1/2 x 11 1/4. **Number of Columns Per Page:** 3. **Column Width:** 27 nonpareils. **Print Method:** Offset. **Contact(s):** C.M. Markham, Jr., Editor and Publisher; C.M. Markham III, Advertising Mgr. **Subscription:** $7.50. **Circulation:** 88,550.

★3814★
New Visions
16360 Broadway   Ph: (216)581-7070
Maple Heights, OH 44137   Fax: (216)581-7072
Text: Magazine covering Cleveland's black community developments, activities, and leaders. **Established:** July 1989. **Frequency:** 6x/yr. **Contact(s):** Jane Littleton, Editor; Rodney Reynolds, Publisher. **Subscription:** $7.50. $2.50 single issue.

★3815★
Nightmoves
Nightmoves Publishing Co.
105 W. Madison, Ste. 1100
Chicago, IL 60602
Text: Black newspaper (tabloid): half politics, and half entertainment. **Established:** July 1980. **Column Depth:** 13 in. **Frequency:** 2x/mo. **Trim Size:** 10 1/4 x 13. **Number of Columns Per Page:** 4. **Column Width:** 2 1/4 in. **Print Method:** Offset. **Contact(s):** Lise Wilson, Editor; Gloria Golden, Publisher; Tom Drake, Advertising Mgr. **Subscription:** $18. **Circulation:** 100,000.

★3816★
Northwest Ethnic News
Ethnic Heritage Council
3123 Eastlake Ave. E.   Ph: (206)328-9204
Seattle, WA 98102   Fax: (206)726-0528
Text: Newspaper (tabloid) for local ethnic communities, presenting calendar of events, listings of ethnic art on exhibit, profiles, and political issues. **Established:** 1984. **Column Depth:** 224 agate lines. **Frequency:** Monthly. **Trim Size:** 11 1/2 x 17 1/2. **Number of Columns Per Page:** 5. **Column Width:** 22 nonpareils. **Print Method:** Web offset. **Contact(s):** Sarah Sarai, Editor. **Subscription:** $12; $30 institutions.

★3817★
The NSBE Bridge
National Society of Black Engineers
1454 Duke St.   Ph: (703)549-2207
Alexandria, VA 22314   Fax: (703)683-5312
Text: Magazine for high school students devoted to raising interest in the technical disciplines among minority students. **Established:** 1990. **Frequency:** Quarterly. **Contact(s):** Norris Hite, Jr., Publisher/Managing Editor. **Circulation:** 100,000.

★3818★
NSBE Magazine
NSBE Publications
1454 Duke St.   Ph: (703)549-2207
Alexandria, VA 22314   Fax: (703)683-5312
Text: Journal providing information on engineering careers, self-development, and cultural issues for recent graduates with technical majors. **Established:** October 1985. **Column Depth:** 140 agate

lines. **Frequency:** 5x/yr. **Trim Size:** 8 x 10 3/4. **Number of Columns Per Page:** 3. **Column Width:** 13 picas. **Print Method:** Offset. **Contact(s):** Norris Hite, Publisher. **ISSN:** 0888-0573. **Subscription:** $10. $2 single issue.

★3819★
PHYLON
Atlanta University
223 James P. Brawley Dr. SW
Atlanta, GA 30314   Ph: (404)880-8680

Text: Race and culture review magazine. **Established:** 1940. **Column Depth:** 105 agate lines. **Frequency:** Quarterly. **Number of Columns Per Page:** 1. **Column Width:** 58 nonpareils. **Print Method:** Letterpress. **Contact(s):** Wilbur H. Watson, Editor. **Subscription:** $14; $24 institutions. **Circulation:** 2,200.

★3820★
Players
Players International Publications
8060 Melrose Ave.   Ph: (213)653-8060
Los Angeles, CA 90046   Fax: (213)655-9452

Text: Entertainment magazine for the 18-40 year old black American male. **Established:** 1973. **Column Depth:** 10 in. **Frequency:** Monthly. **Trim Size:** 8 3/8 x 10 7/8. **Number of Columns Per Page:** 3. **Column Width:** 2 1/4 in. **Print Method:** Web offset. **Contact(s):** Joe Nazel, Editor. **Subscription:** $45; $36 institutions; $46 other countries. $4.95 single issue. **Circulation:** 175,000.

★3821★
The Review of Black Political Economy
Transaction Periodicals Consortium
Rutgers - The State University of New
  Jersey
Dept. 3092   Ph: (908)932-2280
New Brunswick, NJ 08903   Fax: (908)932-3138

Text: Journal covering the economic status of Black and Third World peoples by identifying and analyzing policies designed to reduce racial economic inequality. **Established:** 1970. **Column Depth:** 101 agate lines. **Frequency:** Quarterly. **Trim Size:** 6 x 9. **Number of Columns Per Page:** 1. **Column Width:** 54 nonpareils. **Print Method:** Offset. **Contact(s):** James Stewart, Editor; Mary E. Curtis, Sr. V.P./Publisher; Alicja Garbie, Advertising Mgr.. **ISSN:** 0034-6446. **Subscription:** $36; $68 institutions. **Circulation:** 1,100.

★3822★
Right On!
Sterling Macfadden Partnership
355 Lexington Ave.   Ph: (212)973-3200
New York, NY 10017   Fax: (212)986-5926

Text: Black young adult entertainment magazine. **Established:** October 1971. **Column Depth:** 143 agate lines. **Frequency:** Monthly. **Trim Size:** 8 1/4 x 10 7/8. **Number of Columns Per Page:** 3. **Column Width:** 27 nonpareils. **Print Method:** Offset. **Contact(s):** Cynthia Horner, Editor; John Plunkett, Publisher; Allen Tuller, National Advertising Dir. **ISSN:** 0048-8305. **Subscription:** $17.99. $2.25 single issue. **Circulation:** 350,000.

★3823★
Sage: A Scholarly Journal on Black Women
SAGE Women's Educational Press, Inc.
PO Box 42741   Ph: (404)223-7528
Atlanta, GA 30311-0741   Fax: (404)753-8383

Text: Journal for African-American women. Contains articles, interviews, profiles, documents, book reviews, and bibliographies. **Established:** 1984. **Frequency:** 2x/yr. **ISSN:** 0741-8639. **Subscription:** $15; $21 outside U.S.; $25 institutions; $31 institutions outside U.S.

★3824★
SENGA
Megasin Publications
7501 Morrison Rd.
New Orleans, LA 70126   Ph: (504)242-6022

Text: Journal focusing on issues relating to the assessment and education of black children. **Established:** 1989. **Column Depth:** 10 in. **Frequency:** Quarterly. **Trim Size:** 8 1/2 x 11. **Number of**

Columns Per Page: 3. **Column Width:** 13 1/4 picas. **Print Method:** Web offset. **Contact(s):** Dorothy J. Aramburo, Editor-in-Chief. **ISSN:** 1044-0275. **Subscription:** $25; $30 other countries. $9 single issue; $11 single issue other countries.

★3825★
SISTERS
National Council of Negro Women, Inc.
1667 K. St. NW, Ste. 700   Ph: (202)659-0006
Washington, DC 20006   Fax: (202)785-8733

Text: Magazine covering diverse issues that affect the African-American woman and her community. **Established:** 1988. **Frequency:** Quarterly. **Print Method:** Offset. **Trim Size:** 8 1/4 x 11. **Contact(s):** Dorothy I. Height, Publisher. **ISSN:** 0899-935X. **Subscription:** $20. $5 single issue.

★3826★
Sophisticate's Black Hairstyles and Care Guide
Associated Publications, Inc.
1165 N. Clark St., No. 607
Chicago, IL 60610   Ph: (312)266-8680

Text: Black hairstyle magazine. **Established:** 1984. **Frequency:** 6x/yr. **Print Method:** Web Offset. **Contact(s):** James Spurlock, Publisher; Bonnie L. Krueger, Publishing Director, Cynthia Hill, Advertising Mgr. **Subscription:** $15.36. $3.25 single issue. **Circulation:** 182,250.

★3827★
Transition
Oxford University Press
200 Madison Ave.   Ph: (212)679-7300
New York, NY 10016   Fax: (212)725-2972

Text: Magazine on African and African-American issues. **Established:** 1961. **Column Depth:** 7 13/16 in. **Frequency:** Quarterly. **Number of Columns Per Page:** 2. **Column Width:** 2 1/2 in. **Trim Size:** 6 7/8 x 9 3/4. **Contact(s):** Henry Louis Gates, Jr., Editor; Kwame Anthony Appiah, Editor. **Subscription:** $24. $8.95 single issue.

★3828★
U.S. Black Engineer
Career Communications Group, Inc.
729 E. Pratt St., Ste. 504   Ph: (410)244-7101
Baltimore, MD 21202   Fax: (410)752-1837

Text: Magazine for black engineers. **Established:** 1980. **Frequency:** 5x/yr. **Print Method:** Offset. **Trim Size:** 8 1/2 x 11. **Contact(s):** Diane Hayes, Editor; Keith Clinkscales, Publisher; Hayward Henderson, Promotion Dir.; Floyd Sowell, Production Mgr./Art Dir.; Linda Hummell, Advertising Dir.; Norris Smith, Circulation Dir.; Tonya Carol, Contributing Editor. **Subscription:** Free to qualified subscribers; $15.

★3829★
Upscale
Upscale Communications
594 Fielding Ln.   Ph: (404)758-7467
Atlanta, GA 30311   Fax: (404)758-2314

Text: Periodical covering entertainment and lifestyle. **Established:** 1989. **Frequency:** 6x/yr. **Print Method:** Web offset. **Trim Size:** 8 1/8 x 11. **Contact(s):** Sheila Fowler, Editor; Bernard Bronner, Publisher. **ISSN:** 1047-2592. **Subscription:** Controlled. **Circulation:** 200,000.

★3830★
Urban Profile Magazine
Urban Profile Communications, Inc.
729 E. Pratt St., Ste. 504   Ph: (410)244-7101
Baltimore, MD 21202   Fax: (410)752-1837

Text: Magazine covering African-American student interests. **Established:** 1988. **Frequency:** Monthly. **Contact(s):** Keith T. Clinkscales, Publisher/Editor-In-Chief; Leonard E. Burnett, Jr., Exec. Dir.. **ISSN:** 1049-9695. **Subscription:** $10; $18 two years.

★3831★
Voice of Missions
A.M.E. Sunday School Union
475 Riverside Dr., Rm 1926   Ph: (212)870-2258
New York, NY 10115   Fax: (212)870-2242

Text: Black Methodist Episcopal Church magazine. **Established:** 1898. **Column Depth:** 133 agate lines. **Frequency:** 6x/yr. **Number of Columns Per Page:** 2. **Column Width:** 27 nonpareils. **Print Method:** Uses mats. Letterpress. **Contact(s):** Frederick Harrison, Publisher. **Subscription:** $10.

★3832★
Washington View
Viewcomm, Inc.
6856 Eastern Ave. NW, No. 309
Washington, DC 20012-2165

Text: Magazine for upscale blacks living in the Washington area. **Established:** June 1989. **Frequency:** 6x/yr. **Print Method:** Web offset. **Trim Size:** 8 1/4 x 10 3/4. **Number of Columns Per Page:** 3. **Contact(s):** Effie Upshaw, Mng. Editor; Malcolm Beech, Publisher. **ISSN:** 1042-4229. **Subscription:** $12. $2.95 single issue. **Circulation:** 40,000.

★3833★
The Western Journal of Black Studies
Cooper Publication   Ph: (509)335-8681
Pullman, WA 99164-5910   Fax: (509)335-8568

Text: Journal covering the universal black experience. **Established:** 1977. **Column Depth:** 113 agate lines. **Frequency:** Quarterly. **Trim Size:** 8 x 10. **Number of Columns Per Page:** 2. **Column Width:** 36 nonpareils. **Print Method:** Offset. **Contact(s):** Prof. Talmadge Anderson, Editor; Fred C. Bohm, Advertising Mgr.; Nancy Grunewald, Circulation Mgr.. **ISSN:** 0197-4327. **Subscription:** $20; $30 institutions; $27.50 other countries; $37.50 institutions other countries. $7.50 single issue.

★3834★
Word Up!
Word Up! Publications, Inc.
63 Grand Ave.   Ph: (201)487-6124
River Edge, NJ 07661   Fax: (201)487-7965

Text: Black entertainment magazine. Coverage includes film, television, music. **Established:** 1987. **Frequency:** Monthly. **Print Method:** Offset. **Subscription:** $24. $2.95 single issue.

★3835★
Young Horizons Indigo
2897 Bradmoor Ct.   Ph: (404)241-5003
Decatur, GA 30034   Fax: (404)241-2668

Text: Newsmagazine for parents and teachers of African-American children, ages 0-13. **Subscriptions:** $12. **Circulation:** 15,000.

★3836★
YSB
Paige Publications, Inc.
3109 M St., NW
Washington, DC 20007

Text: Magazine discussing the interest and concerns of African-American youth. **Frequency:** 10x/yr. **Contact(s):** Frank Dexter Brown, Editor; Debra L. Lee, Publisher. **Subscription:** $11.95. $1.95 single issue.

Newsletters

★3837★
AAAA News
American Association for Affirmative Action
 (AAAA)
11 E. Hubbard St., Ste. 200
Chicago, IL 60611   Ph: (312)329-2512

Edited by: Gwendolyn Combs. **Description:** Reports on Association news and activities as well as pertinent civil rights legislation and Equal Employment Opportunity Commission (EEOC) decisions. Recurring features include book reviews, notices of publications available, and a calendar of events. **Illustrations:** Contains black and white photographs and graphics. **Editorial policies:** Accepts display advertising. **Size:** 8-1/2 x 11, 12 pages. **Price:** Included in membership. **ISSN:** 0896-8217.

★3838★
AALC Reporter
African-American Labor Center
1400 K St. NW, Ste. 700   Ph: (202)789-1020
Washington, DC 20005   Fax: (202)842-0730

Edited by: John T. Sarr. **Description:** Covers activities of the AALC for the promotion of free and democratic trade unions on the African continent. **Illustrations:** Includes black and white photographs. Audience: African, American, and international labor organizations. **First published:** 1965. **Frequency:** Bimonthly. **Indexed:** Every 3-5 yrs. **Size:** 4-6 pages. **Price:** Free. **Circulation:** 3,800. Also available in French and Arabic.

★3839★
ACAS Bulletin
Association of Concerned Africa Scholars
 (ACAS)
St. Augustine's College
Political Science Dept.   Ph: (919)828-4451
Raleigh, NC 27610   Fax: (919)834-6473

Edited by: Allan Cooper. **Description:** Concerned with U.S. policy toward Africa. Relates the Association's intent to formulate and communicate alternatives to U.S. Africa policies and to develop a communication action network among Africa scholars. Recurring features include book reviews, news of research, reports on political action, and notes and resources. Audience: Activist scholars. **First published:** 1977. **Frequency:** 3/yr. **Size:** 8-1/2 x 11, 30-40 pages. **Price:** Included in membership. **ISSN:** 1051-0842. **Circulation:** 350.

★3840★
ACOA Action News
American Committee on Africa (ACOA)
198 Broadway
New York, NY 10038   Ph: (212)962-1210

Edited by: Jennifer Davis. **Description:** Reports on the activities of the Committee, which supports African independence and majority rule. Carries news of events in Africa, news of members, and brief descriptions of recent publications from The African Fund. **Illustrations:** Includes black and white photographs. Audience: Anti-apartheid activists. **Frequency:** Semiannually. **Size:** 8-1/2 x 11, 4 pages. **Price:** $25/yr. **Circulation:** 5,000.

★3841★
Affirmative Action Compliance Manual for Federal Contractors
Bureau of National Affairs, Inc. (BNA)   Ph: (202)452-4200
1231 25th St. NW   Fax: (202)822-8092
Washington, DC 20037   Free: 800-372-1033

Edited by: Susan L. Sala. **Description:** Provides text of the compliance manual issued by the Office of Federal Contract Compliance Programs and information on developments affecting affirmative action programs. Audience: Businesses contracting with the federal government. **First published:** 1975. **Frequency:** Monthly. **Indexed:** Quarterly. **Size:** 8-1/2 x 11. **Price:** $270/yr. **ISSN:** 0148-8147. **Remarks:** Telex number is 285656 BNAI WSH.

★3842★
Africa Insider
Matthews Associates
Box 53398, Temple Heights Sta.
Washington, DC 20009   Ph: (301)493-4852

Edited by: Dan Matthews. **Description:** Reports on U.S.-African affairs, with special emphasis on developments in Washington, DC. Focuses on Congress and Africa, and the American media and Africa. Audience: Policy makers and researchers in American foreign policy. **First published:** 1984. **Frequency:** Semimonthly. **Size:** 8-1/2 x 11, 8 pages. **Price:** $75/yr. for individuals; $150 for non-profit organizations and African institutions, $300 for corporations, U.S. and Canada; $180 for non-profit organizations, individuals, and

African institutions, $330 for corporations elsewhere. **ISSN:** 0748-4356.

★3843★
Africa News
Africa News Service, Inc.
720 9th St.
PO Box 3851　　　　　　　　　Ph: (919)286-0747
Durham, NC 27702　　　　　　　Fax: (919)286-2614
Edited by: Reed Kramer. **Description:** Covers political, economic, and other news about the continent of Africa. Focuses particularly on U.S. policy and relations with African nations and personalities. Recurring features include reports from correspondents in Africa, statistics, book reviews, and background material. **Illustrations:** Includes black and white graphics. **First published:** June 1973. **Frequency:** Semimonthly. Indexed: Annually. **Size:** 8-1/2 x 11, 12 pages. **Price:** $30/yr. for individuals; $48 for institutions. **ISSN:** 0191-6521. **Circulation:** 3,800. **Online through:** NewsNet Inc., 945 Haverford Rd., Bryn Mawr, PA 19010, (215) 527-8030; Nexis, Mead Data Central, Inc., 9393 Springboro Pike, P.O. Box 933, OH 43401, (513) 865-6800.. **Remarks:** Reprints are available from Univeristy Micro-films International, 300 N. Zeeb Rd., Ann Arbor, MI 48106, (313) 761-4700.

★3844★
African American Museum—Newsletter
African American Museum
1765 Crawford Rd.
Cleveland, OH 44106　　　　　　Ph: (216)791-1700
Edited by: H.E. Murray. **Description:** Informs members about activities at the Museum. Seeks to stimulate interest in African and African American history and culture. **Frequency:** Bimonthly. **Size:** 8-1/2 x 11, ca. 4 pages. **Price:** Included in membership.

★3845★
African-American Traveler
TUBW Press
328 Sterling Pl., No. 2B　　　　Ph: (718)398-8941
Brooklyn, NY 11238　　　　　　Fax: (718)398-8941
Edited by: Linda Cousins. **Description:** Describes Black cultural and historical sites, as well as Black-owned, travel-related businesses in the Caribbean and Africa. Focuses on the literature of African authors throughout the world. Recurring features include book reviews, notices of publications available, and a section titled Armchair Travel. **Illustrations:** Contains black and white photographs. **Editorial policies:** Accepts advertising. Considers articles for publication. **First published:** 1987. **Frequency:** Quarterly. **Size:** 8-1/2 x 11, 4-8 pages. **Price:** $20/yr., U.S.; $25, Canada. **Subscription:** PO Box 5, Radio City Sta., New York, NY 10101-0005, (718) 398-8941. **Circulation:** 1,000.

★3846★
African Americanews
Museum of African American History
301 E. Frederick Douglass　　　Ph: (313)833-9800
Detroit, MI 48202-4024　　　　Fax: (313)832-7933
Edited by: Lenda Jackson. **Description:** Describes and carries interpretive articles on the Museum's exhibits and acquisitions. Recurring features include listings of workshops, seminars, and lecture series conducted by the Museum. **First published:** December 1990. **Frequency:** Quarterly. Indexed: 8-1/2 x 11. **Price:** Included in membership. **Circulation:** Ca. 5,000. **Former Title(s):** The Gallery.

★3847★
African Studies Center—Newsletter
African Studies Center (ASC)
Michigan State University
100 Center for International Programs
East Lansing, MI 48824　　　　Ph: (517)353-1700
Edited by: David Wiley. **Description:** Provides current news and information on Africa and African studies. Contains news of faculty, new courses in African studies, outreach activities, sources of funding information, and grants and awards. Recurring features include announcements of employment, travel, and educational opportunities. Audience: Persons interested in Africa. **First**

published: October 21, 1976. **Frequency:** 2/yr. **Size:** 8-1/2 x 11, 10-16 pages. **Price:** Free. **Circulation:** 1,400. **Former Title(s):** Michigan Information on Africa–Newsletter, 1979.

★3848★
Africana Libraries Newsletter
Africana Library
Michigan State University Libraries　Ph: (517)355-2366
East Lansing, MI 48824-1048　　Fax: (517)336-1445
Edited by: Joseph J. Lauer. **Description:** Concerned with librarianship in African studies. Announces recent publications and other African resources, particularly those "not readily available through regular trade channels." Recurring features include news of professionals in the field, inquiries from readers, and reports from the African Studies Association, its Archives-Library Committee, and the Cooperative Africana Microform Project. Audience: Librarians. **First published:** July 1975. **Frequency:** Quarterly. **Size:** 8-1/2 x 11, 8 pages. **Price:** Free. **ISSN:** 0148-7868. **Circulation:** 600.

★3849★
The Afroamericanist Newsletter
Afro-American Studies and Research
　Program
University of Illinois
606 S. Gregory
Urbana, IL 61801　　　　　　　Ph: (217)333-7781
Edited by: Valinda Littlefield. **Description:** Focuses on issues and research concerning the Afro-American community. **Illustrations:** Includes photographs. Audience: Afro-American Studies Program participants, high school teachers and counselors, and media personnel. **First published:** 1986. **Frequency:** 2/yr. Indexed: Annually. **Size:** 8-12 pages. **Price:** Free. **Circulation:** 1,800. **Online through:** Contact publisher.

★3850★
ASA News
African Studies Association
ASA
Credit Union Bldg.
Emery University
Atlanta, GA 30322　　　　　　　Ph: (404)329-6410
Edited by: Eric D. Wright and John Distefano. **Description:** Reports news of interest to Africanists. Includes notices of employment opportunities, Association activities, grants and awards, meetings, publications, and information about foreign research institutes. **First published:** 1967. **Frequency:** Quarterly. **Size:** 6 x 9, 32-64 pages. **Price:** Included in membership. **Circulation:** 2,400. **Former Title(s):** African Studies Newsletter.

★3851★
ASC Newsletter
African Studies Center (ASC)
Michigan State University
100 Center for International Programs
East Lansing, MI 48824　　　　Ph: (517)353-1700
Edited by: David Wiley. **Description:** Provides news of activities of the Center. Audience: Persons interested in Africa or its culture. **Frequency:** Semiannual. **Price:** Free. **Circulation:** 1,000.

★3852★
BEEP Newsletter
Black Executive Exchange Program (BEEP)
National Urban League, Inc.
500 E. 62nd St.
New York, NY 10021　　　　　　Ph: (212)310-9195
Edited by: Renee Du Jean. **Description:** Describes BEEP courses at black universities in which black executives serve as professors to link the classroom with the working world. Recurring features include news of members, notices of publications available, and a column titled The Inside Line. **Illustrations:** Includes black and white graphics and photographs. Audience: Administrators at traditionally black universities and black executives in the public and private sectors. **First published:** September 1970. **Frequency:** Semiannual. **Size:** 8-1/2 x 11, 4-6 pages. **Price:** Free. **Circulation:** 5,000.

★3853★
Best of Health—Newsletter
Best of Health
PO Box 40-1232
Brooklyn, NY 11240-1232   Ph: (718)756-2245

Edited by: Janice Harvin-Norris. **Subtitle:** Building Healthier Black Families. **Description:** Covers African American health issues. Contains news on nutrition and fitness. Recurring features include letters to the editor; interviews; a calendar of events; book reviews; notices of new products, videos, and audio cassettes available; and columns titled Kaye's Health Vine and Newsline. **Illustrations:** Contains black and white graphics. **Audience:** African Americans between 25 and 49 years of age. **Editorial policies:** Accepts advertising. Considers articles for publication. **First published:** April 1987. **Frequency:** Quarterly. **Indexed:** Annually. **Size:** 8 x 12, 12 pages. **Price:** $14/yr., U.S.; $28, Canada. **ISSN:** 1055-3398. **Circulation:** 1,000.

★3854★
Bill of Rights Journal
National Emergency Civil Liberties
  Committee
175 Fifth Ave., Rm. 814
New York, NY 10160   Ph: (212)673-2040

Edited by: Jeff Kisseloff. **Description:** Focuses on civil liberties and rights issues. Discusses legislation and other pertinent national developments, and carries book reviews. **Illustrations:** Includes black and white photographs and cartoons. **Audience:** Civil libertarians, social and political scientists, lawyers, and libraries. **Editorial policies:** Considers articles for publication. **First published:** 1953. **Frequency:** 3/yr. **Size:** 8-1/4 x 11, 16 pages. **Price:** Included in membership. **Circulation:** 8,500. **Former Title(s):** Rights.

★3855★
Black Caucus Newsletter
BCALA Newsletter
Campus Box 2654
Rollins College
Winter Park, FL 32789   Ph: (407)646-2676

Edited by: Dr. George C. Grant. **Description:** Reports news of interest about black librarians in library work and library education. Recurring features include notices of professional opportunities and activities of individuals within the Caucus and the American Library Association. **Illustrations:** Includes black and white graphics. **Audience:** Library and information science professionals and students. **Editorial policies:** Accepts advertising. Considers articles for publication. **First published:** June 1972. **Frequency:** Bimonthly. **Size:** 8-1/2 x 11, 8 pages. **Price:** Included in membership; $7.50/yr. for nonmembers. **ISSN:** 8755-9277. **Circulation:** 900.

★3856★
Black Child Advocate
National Black Child Development Institute
1023 15th St. NW, Ste. 600
Washington, DC 20005   Ph: (202)387-1281

Description: Discusses current issues facing the black child and family. Also contains public policy updates and internal news of the Institute, and promotes publications and conferences. Recurring features include letters to the editor, interviews, book reviews, and issues analyses. **Illustrations:** Includes black and white photographs, tables, and charts. **Audience:** Parents, educators, health professionals, and service providers. **Editorial policies:** Accepts display advertising. **First published:** 1972. **Frequency:** Quarterly. **Size:** 8-1/2 x 11, 8 pages. **Price:** Included in membership. **Circulation:** 3,500.

★3857★
Black Congressional Monitor
Len Mor Publications
PO Box 75035
Washington, DC 20013   Ph: (202)488-8879

Edited by: Lenora Moragne, Ph.D. **Subtitle:** A Monthly Report of Legislative Initiatives From the U.S. Congress. **Description:** Reports on legislative initiatives of African-Americans in Congress and provides information regarding minority set-asides and executive branch action relevant to minorities. **Audience:** Elected officials, librarians, political scientists, historians, and the general public. **First published:** 1987. **Frequency:** Monthly. **Size:** 8-1/2 x 11, 8 pages. **Price:** $16.95/yr. **ISSN:** 0895-1780.

★3858★
Black Issues in Higher Education
Cox, Matthews, & Associates, Inc.
10521 Warwick Ave., Ste. B-8   Ph: (703)385-2981
Fairfax, VA 22030   Fax: (703)385-1839

Edited by: Ed Wiley, III. **Description:** Reports on news affecting minorities and major issues in U.S. higher education. Includes articles on school reform proposals, profiles of successful educators and students, summaries of research reports on ethnicity and education, employment opportunities, and analysis of critical trends and developments in academic and related environments. **Illustrations:** black and white graphics and photographs. **Audience:** Higher education professionals. **First published:** March 1984. **Frequency:** Biweekly. **Indexed:** Annually. **Size:** 8-1/2 x 11, 48-72 pages. **Price:** $40/yr. **ISSN:** 0742-0277. **Circulation:** 38,000. **Online through:** NewsNet Inc., 945 Haverford Rd., Bryn Mawr, PA 19010, (215) 527-8030.

★3859★
BNA's Employee Relations Weekly
Bureau of National Affairs, Inc. (BNA)   Ph: (202)452-4200
1231 25th St. NW   Fax: (202)822-8092
Washington, DC 20037   Free: 800-372-1033

Edited by: Susan J. Sala. **Description:** Monitors employee and labor relations cases. Follows developments in compensation, health benefits, Equal Employment Opportunity (EEO), labor economics, legislation, and regulatory issued. Recurring features include a calendar of events. **Audience:** Employee relations practitioners. **Frequency:** Weekly. **Indexed:** Every 6 weeks; cumulated quarterly. **Size:** 8-1/2 x 11, 32 pages. **Price:** $772/yr. **ISSN:** 0739-3016. **Online through:** Human Resource Information Network (HRIN), Executive Telecom System, Inc., College Park N., 9585 Valparaiso Ct., Indianapolis, IN 46268, (317) 872-2045. **Former Title(s):** September 5, 1983. **Remarks:** Telex number is 285656 BNAI WSH.

★3860★
Building Blocks
National Center for Urban Ethnic Affairs
Box 20, Cardinal Station
Washington, DC 20064   Ph: (202)232-3600

Edited by: Dr. John Kromkowski. **Description:** Provides community action information. **Circulation:** 16,000.

★3861★
Building Concerns
National Association of Minority
  Contractors
1333 F St. NW, Ste. 500
Washington, DC 20004   Ph: (202)347-8259

Edited by: Ralph C. Thomas, III. **Description:** Concentrates on national and regional news regarding minority construction contractors. Contains articles on issues generally affecting the industry–especially issues affecting minorities–including topics such as legislative and regulatory activity and reports on major corporation developments. Recurring features include reports of meetings, news of educational opportunities, a calendar of events, and news of NAMC chapters and members. **Audience:** Minority construction contractors, majority-owned construction firms, government contract compliance officers, and all interested in minority business affairs. **Editorial policies:** Accepts feature articles for publication. **First published:** 1981. **Frequency:** Monthly. **Size:** 8-1/2 x 11, 8 pages. **Price:** Included in membership. **Circulation:** 3,500.

★3862★
CAAS Report
Center for Afro-American Studies
University of California, Los Angeles
160 Haines Hall   Ph: (213)825-7403
Los Angeles, CA 90024-1545   Fax: (213)206-3421
Edited by: M. Belinda Tucker and N. Cherie Francis. **Description:** Features news of the Center and its work in Afro-American Studies. Covers news of research; information on visiting professors, programs, and awards; and special Center programs. Recurring features include notices of publications available. **Illustrations:** Includes black and white graphics. Audience: Faculty, staff, and students of Afro-American Studies and concerns. **First published:** Ca. 1977. **Frequency:** Semiannually. **Size:** 8-1/2 x 11, 20 pages. **Price:** Free. **ISSN:** 0197-5579. **Circulation:** 6,600.

★3863★
CALC Report
Clergy and Laity Concerned (CALC)
PO Box 1987
Decateur, GA 30031
Edited by: Mark Reeve. **Description:** Provides information on justice and peace movement in the U.S. and internationally and about U.S. military presence around the world. Addresses human rights issues in the U.S., Central America and the Caribbean, South Africa, the Phillines, and the Middle East. Recurring features include news of the association. **Illustrations:** Includes black and white graphics. Audience: "People of faith and conscience working for justice and peace." **First published:** Fall 1975. **Frequency:** 4/yr. **Size:** 8-1/2 x 11, 24 pages. **Price:** Included in membership. **Circulation:** 17,000. **Former Title(s):** CALC Report/TWC Bulletin.

★3864★
Catholic League Newsletter
Catholic League for Religious and Civil
  Rights   Ph: (414)476-8911
6324 W. North Ave.   Fax: (414)476-9511
Wauwatosa, WI 53213   Free: 800-927-0056
Edited by: John C. Pantuso. **Description:** Discusses Catholic perspectives on social, moral, and ethical issues. **Illustrations:** Includes black and white graphics. **First published:** 1973. **Frequency:** Monthly. **Size:** 8-1/2 x 11, 16 pages. **Price:** Included in membership. **Circulation:** 26,000.

★3865★
Center for Democratic Renewal—Monitor
Center for Democratic Renewal
PO Box 50469
Atlanta, GA 30302   Ph: (404)221-0025
Edited by: Daniel Levitas. **Description:** Reports on Ku Klux Klan activities and anti-Klan movements around the U.S. Carries commentary on racial and religious violence and bigotry. Recurring features include highlights of legislative and police actions, news of research, and letters to the editor. **Illustrations:** Includes black and white graphics. Audience: Educators, civil rights activists, law enforcement personnel, and elected officials. **First published:** 1980. **Frequency:** Bimonthly. **Size:** 8 x 10-1/2, 16 pages. **Price:** Included in membership; $15/yr. for nonmembers. **Circulation:** 10,000.

★3866★
Center for Sickle Cell Disease—Newsletter
Center for Sickle Cell Disease
Howard University
2121 Georgia Ave. NW   Ph: (202)806-7930
Washington, DC 20059   Fax: (202)806-4517
Edited by: Roland B. Scott. M.D. **Description:** Focuses on sickle cell disease. Reports on research, fundraising and community activities, and people in the field. Recurring features include news of the Center and its staff, letters from readers, profiles of sickle cell patients, reports of seminars and appointments, and notices of awards and continuing education opportunities. **Illustrations:** Includes black and white graphics. Audience: Patients, relatives, friends, researchers, and clinicians. **Editorial policies:** Considers articles for publication. **First published:** January 1973. **Frequency:** Quarterly. Indexed: Quarterly. **Size:** 8-1/2 x 11, 6 pages. **Price:** Free. **Circulation:** 8,000.

★3867★
Chapter to Chapter
National Association of Black Accountants
220 I St. NE, Ste. 150   Ph: (202)546-6222
Washington, DC 20002   Fax: (202)547-1041

★3868★
The Chicago Reporter
Community Renewal Society
332 S. Michigan Ave.
Chicago, IL 60604   Ph: (312)427-4830
Edited by: Laura Washington. **Description:** Serves as a voice for Chicago's poor. Addresses issues on race relations, ethnic stereotypes, and health hazards and sanitation problems in public housing. **Illustrations:** Includes black and white graphics. Audience: Civic leaders, politicians, and editors. **First published:** 1972. **Frequency:** Monthly, July/August issues are combined. Indexed: Periodically. **Size:** 12-16 pages. **Price:** $19/11 issues. **ISSN:** 0300-6921. **Circulation:** 4,400.

★3869★
Child Health Talks
National Black Child Development Institute
1023 15th St. NW, Ste. 600   Ph: (202)387-1281
Washington, DC 20005   Fax: (202)234-1738
Description: Provides information and guidance to parents on health issues facing black children. **Illustrations:** Includes black and white photographs. Audience: Parents, educators, and health professionals. **Frequency:** Quarterly. **Size:** 8-1/2 x 11, 8 pages. **Price:** Included in membership; $8/yr for nonmembers. **Circulation:** 3,500.

★3870★
The Children's Voice
National Coalition to End Racism in
  America's Child Care System
22075 Koths
Taylor, MI 48180   Ph: (313)295-0257
Edited by: Frank Ehlers. **Description:** Reflects the aims of the Coalition, whose purpose is to assure that all children requiring placement outside the home through foster care or adoption are placed in the earliest available home most qualified to meet the child's needs. Encourages recruitment of foster and adoptive homes of all races and cultures. Recurring features include news of legislation, foster care and adoptive programs, and legal advancements. **First published:** 1984. **Frequency:** Quarterly. **Price:** $10/yr. for individuals; $25 for organizations. **Circulation:** 1,000.

★3871★
Civil Liberties
American Civil Liberties Union Foundation
  (ACLU)
132 W. 43rd St.
New York, NY 10036   Ph: (212)944-9800
Edited by: Jean Carey Bond. **Description:** Supplies news of the legal defense, research, and public education projects of the ACLU, conducted to enable citizens to know and assert their rights. Focuses on civil liberties issues relating to freedom of expression, due process of law, equality, and privacy. Recurring features include news of significant legislation. **Illustrations:** Contains black and white graphics. **First published:** June 1931. **Frequency:** Periodic. **Size:** Tabloid. **Price:** Included in membership. **ISSN:** 0009-790X. **Circulation:** 275,000.

★3872★
Civil Rights: From the State Capitals
Wakeman/Walworth, Inc.
300 N. Washington St., Ste. 204   Ph: (703)549-8606
Alexandria, VA 22314   Fax: (703)549-1372
Edited by: Keyes Walworth. **Description:** Covers state civil rights and affirmative action legislation, including ethnic, race, and sex discrimination; judicial decisions regarding desegregation; discrimination compensation; gay rights; and civil rights of the disabled. **First published:** 1946. **Frequency:** Weekly. **Price:** $215/yr. **ISSN:** 0741-353X.

★3873★

Commission for the Catholic Missions Among the Colored People and the Indians—Quarterly

Commission for the Catholic Missions
Among the Colored People and the
Indians
2021 H St. NW   Ph: (202)331-8542
Washington, DC 20006   Fax: (202)331-8544

Edited by: Monsignor Paul A. Lenz. **Description:** Concerned with evangelism in church programs for the Black and Indian communities in the U.S. Publishes news and updates the financial status of the Commission. Reports the ordination of priests and the activities of individuals from Black and Indian communities. Recurring features include a letter from the editor and statistics. **Illustrations:** Includes black and white graphics. Audience: Catholic priests. **First published:** 1977. **Frequency:** Annual. **Size:** 8-1/2 x 11, 4 pages. **Price:** Free. **Circulation:** Ca. 40,000.

★3874★

Con Brio

National Black Music Caucus
Music Educators National Conference
c/o Dr. Willis Patterson
University of Michigan
2308 More St.
Ann Arbor, MI 48109   Ph: (313)764-0586

Description: Monitors the activities of the Caucus, whose purpose is to foster the creation, study, and promotion of black derived music in education. Helps to heighten awareness of the problems faced by black music educators and students and provides a forum for the discussion of concerns. Recurring features include reports on regional conferences, collegiate and high school gospel choir competitions, and news of members. **Frequency:** Quarterly. **Price:** Included in membership.

★3875★

The Corporate Examiner

Interfaith Center on Corporate
Responsibility (ICCR)
475 Riverside Dr., Rm. 566
New York, NY 10115   Ph: (212)870-2293

Edited by: Diane Bratcher. **Description:** Examines "policies and practices of major U.S. corporations with regard to South Africa, labor, environment, equal employment, minorities, women, military production, government, and foreign investment." Recurring features include editorials, news of research, news of members, news of corporate activities, reviews of resource materials, and a supplement titled ICCR Brief. **Illustrations:** Includes black and white graphics. Audience: Churches, organizations, and individuals "concerned about the social impact of corporations and the application of social criteria to investments." **Editorial policies:** Considers articles for publication upon editor's request. **First published:** 1971. **Frequency:** 10/yr. **Size:** 8-1/2 x 11, 8 pages. **Price:** Included in membership. $35/yr. for nonmembers, U.S. and Canada; $40 elsewhere. **ISSN:** 0361-2309. **Circulation:** 1,500.

★3876★

The Correspondent

Congress of Racial Equality
30 Cooper Sq.   Ph: (212)598-4000
New York, NY 10003   Fax: (212)982-0184

Edited by: George W. Holmes. **Description:** Preserves and promotes the philosophical tenets initiated by Marcus Garvey (1887-1940), the Jamaican-born black nationalist leader. Provides news and information concerning the right of black people to govern themselves in areas which are demographically and geographically defined as theirs. Emphasizes the inspirational role of Africa and social concerns such as drug abuse, education, employment, housing, prison reform, and senior citizens. Recurring features include news of members, and news of Congress programs and activities. **Illustrations:** Includes black and white graphics. Audience: Persons of African ancestry. **First published:** January 1980. **Frequency:** Quarterly. **Size:** 11 x 17. **Price:** Included in membership. **Circulation:** 50,000.

★3877★

County Compass

National Organization of Black County
Officials
440 1st St. NW
Washington, DC 20001   Ph: (202)347-6953

Edited by: Rosemary Davis. **Description:** Provides information and technical assistance on a range of economic development and other issues. **Illustrations:** Includes photographs. Audience: Elected and appointed county officials and other interested groups. **First published:** 1984. **Frequency:** Quarterly. **Size:** 8 pages. **Price:** Included in membership. **Circulation:** 2,000.

★3878★

Courier

Caribbean American Intercultural
Organization
PO Box 27099   Ph: (202)829-7468
Washington, DC 20038   Fax: (202)842-0215

Edited by: Shirley Hamburg and Helen Madison-Kinard. **Description:** Intended to promote, encourage, and maintain intercultural relations between the various peoples of the Caribbean and the people of the U.S. Profiles outstanding individuals of Caribbean ancestry who have made significant contributions to the development of the U.S., Caribbean, or Third World. Recurring features include announcements of exhibitions, forums, and audiovisual educational programs sponsored by the Organization. **First published:** 1968. **Frequency:** Quarterly. **Size:** 8-1/2 x 11. **Price:** Included in membership. **Circulation:** 400.

★3879★

CTS Network

Center for Transportation (CTS)
Morgan State University
PO Box 924
Baltimore, MD 21239   Ph: (301)444-3394

Edited by: Dr. Moges Ayele. **Description:** Serves as an information exchange among HBCUs (Historically Black Colleges and Universities) concerning issues in transportation education and research. Recurring features include information on the Center's studies, projects, and educational programs, plus reports on other research of interest; notices of symposia, workshops, internships, and research assistantships; a calendar of events; and columns titled Workshop Development, Minority Job Bank in Transit, and Faculty, Student, and Alumni News. **Illustrations:** Includes two-color and black and white graphics. Audience: HBCUs interested in transportation education and research, and other transportation agencies, organizations, and institutions. **Editorial policies:** Considers articles for publication. **First published:** Summer 1984. **Frequency:** Semiannually. **Size:** 8-1/2 x 11, 4 pages. **Price:** Free. **Circulation:** 1,500.

★3880★

Cultural Diversity at Work Newsletter

The Gil Deane Group
13751 Lake City Way NE, Ste. 105   Ph: (206)362-0336
Seattle, WA 98125-3615   Fax: (206)368-6850

Edited by: Barbara R. Deane. **Description:** Designed to advise professionals who manage, train, and conduct business with culturally diverse people. Discusses such issues as cultural sensitivity, stereotypes, cultural differences between genders, and cultural representations in the media. Recurring features include letters to the editor, a calendar of events, reports of meetings, news of educational opportunities, and notices of publications available. **Illustrations:** Contains black and white graphics. **Editorial policies:** Accepts display advertising. Considers articles for publication. **Frequency:** Bimonthly with 11 monthly Bulletins. **Size:** 8-1/2 x 11, ca. 12 pages. **Price:** $39/yr. for individuals and $59 for organizations, U.S.; $44 and $64, Canada and Mexico; $69 elsewhere. **ISSN:** 1043-1322. **Former Title(s):** Training and Culture Newsletter, September 1991.

★3881★
Cultural Survival Quarterly
Cultural Survival, Inc.
53A Church St.   Ph: (617)495-2562
Cambridge, MA 02138   Fax: (617)495-1396
Edited by: Marc Miller. **Description:** Provides information on indigenous peoples and the threats posed to their cultures by modern civilization. Designed to "publicize and mitigate the more violent infringements of human rights as well as the more subtle and ongoing ones." Recurring features include news of research, annual review of projects, a list of Cultural Survival publications, and editorials. **Illustrations:** Includes black and white graphics. **Editorial policies:** Considers articles for publication. **First published:** 1976. **Frequency:** Quarterly. Indexed: Annually. **Size:** 8-1/2 x 11, 60-80 pages. **Price:** Included in membership. **ISSN:** 0740-3291. **Circulation:** 15,000.

★3882★
Educating in Faith
Catholic Negro-American Mission Board
2021 H St. NW   Ph: (202)331-8542
Washington, DC 20006   Fax: (202)331-8544
Edited by: Monsignor Paul A. Lenz. **Description:** Publishes news and concerns of the Board and of the schools and programs they sponsor. Focuses on the needs of the black community in the U.S., including daycare and other educational programs. Recurring features include a letter from the editor, news of meetings, and a calendar of events. **Illustrations:** Includes black and white graphics. **Audience:** Catholic and non-Catholic blacks and the religious community. **Frequency:** Quarterly. **Size:** 8-1/2 x 11, 4 pages. **Price:** Free. **Circulation:** 20,000.

★3883★
EEOC Compliance Manual
Bureau of National Affairs, Inc. (BNA)
1231 25th St. NW
Washington, DC 20037   Ph: (202)452-4200
Edited by: Susan J. Sala. **Description:** Summarizes and analyzes policies, procedures, and standards followed by the staff of the Equal Employment Opportunity Commission (EEOC). Contains text of compliance procedures, interpretive manual, conciliation standards, and EEOC regional attorneys' deskbook. Supplemented with official information as issued by the Commission. **First published:** 1975. **Frequency:** Periodic. Indexed: Every 4 months. **Size:** 8-1/2 x 11. **Price:** $180/yr.

★3884★
EMIE Bulletin
Ethnic Materials & Information Exchange
   Round Table
American Library Association (ALA)
Queens College, NSF 300   Ph: (718)997-3626
Flushing, NY 11367   Fax: (718)793-8049
Edited by: David Cohen. **Description:** Reports on programs and activities of the Round Table and news of related ethnic organizations. Presents articles by members on ethnicity and librarianship topics. Recurring features include book reviews and book lists. **Audience:** Individuals interested in ethnic outreach programs, members, and librarians. **Editorial policies:** Considers articles for publication. **First published:** 1983. **Frequency:** Quarterly. **Size:** 8-1/2 x 11, 12 pages. **Price:** $10/yr.; $15 for ALA institutional members. **ISSN:** 0737-9021. **Circulation:** Ca. 600.

★3885★
The Equal Employer
Y.S. Publications, Inc.
PO Box 2172
Silver Spring, MD 20915   Ph: (301)649-1231
Edited by: Gilbert Ginsburg and Donald P. Miller. **Description:** "Contains concise, accurate and complete digests of the latest critical decisions of all courts and United States government agencies bearing on employment discrimination." Analyzes recent developments in fair employment practices, especially within the Equal Employment Opportunity Commission (EEOC) and the Office of Federal Contract Compliance Programs (OFCCP). Recurring features include columns titled Cases and Decisions and Miscellany.

Audience: Labor lawyers, general counsel, Equal Employment officers, personnel officers of corporations and government agencies, and librarians. **First published:** 1977. **Frequency:** Biweekly. Indexed: Annually. **Size:** 8-1/2 x 11, 8 pages. **Price:** $245/yr. **Circulation:** 200.

★3886★
Fair Employment Practices
Bureau of National Affairs, Inc. (BNA)   Ph: (202)452-4200
1231 25th St. NW   Fax: (202)822-8092
Washington, DC 20037   Free: 800-372-1033
Edited by: Bill L. Manville. **Description:** Provides a notification and reference service covering developments affecting fair employment practices. Includes federal laws, orders, and regulations; policy guides and discussions of federal court decisions; and state and local fair employment practice laws. **Illustrations:** Has charts. **Audience:** Human resource professionals, equal employment officals, and labor lawyers. **First published:** July 2, 1965. **Frequency:** Biweekly. Indexed: Biennially. **Size:** 8-1/2 x 11, 6-8 pages. **Price:** $501/yr. **ISSN:** 0149-2683. **Circulation:** 13,000. **Online through:** Human Resource Information Network (HRIN), Executive Telecom System, Inc., College Park N., 9585 Valparaiso Ct., Indianapolis, IN 46268, (317) 872-2045. **Remarks:** Telex number is 285656 BNAI WSH. **Former Title(s):** Fair Employment Practice Service.

★3887★
Fair Employment Practices Guidelines
Bureau of Business Practice   Ph: (203)442-4365
24 Rope Ferry Rd.   Fax: (203)434-3341
Waterford, CT 06386   Free: 800-243-0876
Edited by: Emily Mitchell. **Description:** Provides information on legislative, administrative, and judicial developments in the fair employment practices field. Covers one specific fair employment case per issue, and includes three in-depth court cases regarding that topic. **Audience:** Personnel executives. **Frequency:** Monthly. Indexed: Semiannually. **Size:** 8 pages. **Price:** $84/yr. **ISSN:** 0093-7630.

★3888★
Fair Employment Practices Summary of Latest
   Developments
Bureau of National Affairs, Inc. (BNA)   Ph: (202)452-4200
1231 25th St. NW   Fax: (203)343-3341
Washington, DC 20037   Free: 800-372-1033
Edited by: Bill L. Manville. **Description:** Highlights developments in employment opportunity and affirmative actions, and affirmative action programs. Reports on federal and state court decisions, Equal Employment Opportunity Commission (EEOC) rulings and Office of Federal Contract Compliance Programs (OFCCP) decisions, new laws, regulations, and agency directives. Also provides information on special programs for minorities, the handicapped, women, and older workers. **Illustrations:** Includes graphs. **Audience:** Human resource professionals, equal employment officials, and labor lawyers. **First published:** March 4, 1965. **Frequency:** Biweekly. Indexed: Quarterly. **Size:** 8-1/2 x 11, 6 pages. **Price:** $96/yr. **ISSN:** 0525-2156. **Circulation:** 13,000. **Online through:** Human Resource Information Network (HRIN), Executive Telecom System, Inc., College Park N., 9585 Valparaiso Ct., Indianapolis, IN 46268, (317) 872-2045. **Remarks:** Telex number is 285656 BNAI WSH.

★3889★
Fair Employment Report
Business Publishers, Inc.   Ph: (301)587-6300
951 Pershing Dr.   Fax: (301)587-1081
Silver Spring, MD 20910   Free: 800-274-0122
Edited by: Steve Lash. **Description:** Focuses on developments on the state and national levels regarding employment practices and discrimination. Emphasizes important legal decisions and governmental activities, particularly those of the Equal Employment Opportunity Commission, the Civil Rights Commission, and the Office of Federal Contract Compliance. **Audience:** Personnel executives, union officials, consultants, and government agencies. **First published:** 1964. **Frequency:** Biweekly. Indexed: Annually. **Size:** 8-1/2 x 11, 8-10 pages. **Price:** $234.54/yr. **ISSN:** 0014-6919. **Former Title(s):** Civil Rights Employment Reporter.

★3890★
Heritage
Southern California Library for Social
  Studies and Research
6120 S. Vermont Ave.
Los Angeles, CA 90044   Ph: (213)759-6063

Description: Reports news of the Library, "a leading resource center specializing in radical, progressive, labor and minorities literature." Provides information on Library-sponsored conferences and programs, new collections, research services, issues of social history, and plans for future development. Recurring features include news of research and a calendar of events. Audience: Community activists, scholars, and the general public. **Editorial policies:** Considers articles for publication. **First published:** Fall 1982. **Frequency:** Quarterly. **Size:** 7 x 8-1/2, 4 pages. **Price:** Donation requested. **Circulation:** 3,600.

★3891★
HMP Newsletter
Hemispheric Migration Project (HMP)
Center for Immigration Policy and Refugee
  Assistance
Georgetown University
Box 2298, Hoya Sta.   Ph: (202)298-0213
Washington, DC 20057   Fax: (202)338-0572

Edited by: Mary Ann Larkin. **Description:** Reviews the progress and results of research projects concerning international migration, refugee flows, and related policy issues throughout North America, Latin America, and the Caribbean. Includes news of members, a calendar of events, and recent bibliography. **Illustrations:** Includes black and white photographs. Audience: Scholars and policymakers in the area of migration. **Editorial policies:** Considers articles for publication. **First published:** December 1, 1984. **Frequency:** Quarterly. **Size:** 8-1/2 x 11, 10 pages. **Price:** Free. **Circulation:** Ca. 600.

★3892★
IBCA Scope
Institute on Black Chemical Abuse (IBCA)
2616 Nicollet Ave. S.   Ph: (612)871-7878
Minneapolis, MN 55408   Fax: (612)871-2567

Edited by: David Grant. **Description:** Views alcohol and drug abuse from an African-American perspective. Recurring features include interviews, news of research, a calendar of events, reports of meetings, book reviews, and notices of publications available. **Illustrations:** Contains black and white graphics. Audience: Individuals interested in African-Americans and chemical dependency. **First published:** 1979. **Frequency:** Quarterly. **Size:** 8-1/2 x 11, 4 pages. **Price:** $5/yr. for individuals, U.S.,; $8 for institutions, U.S.; $6 and $10, Canada. **ISSN:** 0895-8661. **Circulation:** 15,000.

★3893★
IDRA Newsletter
Intercultural Development Research
  Association
5835 Callaghan Rd., Ste. 350
San Antonio, TX 78228   Ph: (512)684-8180

Edited by: Jose A. Cardenas. **Description:** Furnishes educational and social policy concepts emphasizing advocacy for minority groups. Focuses on research and technological implementation related to education and the delivery of other human services. Concentrates on the particular educational needs of children in Texas. Recurring features include news of research. **Illustrations:** Includes black and white graphics and tables. Audience: Educators, school board members, and the community. **Editorial policies:** Considers articles for publication. **First published:** May 1973. **Frequency:** Monthly. **Size:** 8-1/2 x 11, 8-12 pages. **Price:** Free. **Circulation:** 6,000. **Former Title(s):** Tee Newsletter, September 1974.

★3894★
Immigration Newsletter
National Immigration Project
National Lawyers Guild
14 Beacon St., Ste. 506   Ph: (617)227-9727
Boston, MA 02108   Fax: (617)227-5495

Description: Discusses immigration issues from the legal viewpoint. Concerned with the protection of civil rights and liberties, the elimination of racism, and the extension of the rights of workers, women, farmers, and minority groups. Recurring features include a listing of available publications, accounts of recent cases, and a column titled Brief Bank. **Illustrations:** Includes black and white graphics. **First published:** January 1973. **Frequency:** Quarterly. **Size:** 8-1/2 x 11, 20 pages. **Price:** $40/yr. for individuals; $50 for institutions. **Circulation:** 700.

★3895★
Indialantic
Tuskegee Airmen Inc.
156 Sugar Tom's Ln. E.
East Norwich, NY 11732   Ph: (516)922-1198

Edited by: John D. Silvera. **Description:** Contains news of reunions and other member activites of the Tuskegee Airmen. **Illustrations:** Includes black and white photographs. Audience: Primarily black men and women involved in aviation in the military services. **Frequency:** Quarterly. **Size:** 8-10 pages. **Circulation:** 1,400.

★3896★
Interracial Family Alliance—Communique
Interracial Family Alliance (IFA)
PO Box 16248
Houston, TX 77222   Ph: (713)454-5018

Edited by: Elizabeth Radcliffe. **Description:** Promotes the purposes of the IFA, which seeks to "stengthen and support the interracial family unit and promote its acceptance by the public." Explores the concerns of interracial families and proposes positive solutions to problems. Focuses on the development of self-esteem in biracial children. Recurring features include editorials, news of members, letters to the editor, news of members, book reviews, a calendar of events, and columns titled A Closer Look, Have You Read, and Adoption. **Illustrations:** Includes black and white photographs and tables. Audience: Interracial families, biracial individuals, interracial dating couples, mental health professionals and educators. **Editorial policies:** Considers articles for publication. **First published:** December 1, 1983. **Frequency:** Quarterly. **Size:** 8-1/2 x 11, 8 pages. **Price:** Included in membership; $15/yr. for nonmembers. **Circulation:** 150.

★3897★
Iowa Civil Rights Communicator
Iowa Civil Rights Commission   Ph: (515)281-4121
211 E. Maple St., 2nd Fl.   Fax: (515)242-5840
Des Moines, IA 50319   Free: 800-457-4416

Edited by: Carol Anne Leach. **Description:** Serves as the official newsletter of the Commission, which seeks to "eliminate discrimination and to establish equality and justice for all persons within the state through civil rights enforcement and advocacy." Features news of civil rights legislation and court decisions. Identifies civil rights issues of particular interest to Iowa residents, as well as discussing issues of general interest. Includes articles written by civil rights professionals. **Illustrations:** Includes black and white photographs, charts, and graphs. Audience: Iowa residents, civil rights professionals, advocacy groups, civil rights attorneys, employers, labor unions, and real estate/management companies. **First published:** 1980. **Frequency:** Quarterly. **Size:** 8-1/2 x 11, 6 pages. **Price:** Free. **Circulation:** 2,500.

★3898★
Jack and Jill of America Foundation—Intercom
Jack and Jill of America Foundation, Inc.
PO Drawer 3689
Chattanooga, TN 37404   Ph: (615)622-4476

Edited by: Violet D. Greer. **Description:** Furnishes information about the Foundation and its chapters, which "increase opportunities for children in the areas of education, cultural growth and civic responsibility." Provides news of Foundation activities and reports on the fundraising events of various chapters. Recurring features include editorials, news of research, news of members, a calendar of events, and columns titled President's Message, Chapter Contributions, and National Projects. **Illustrations:** Includes black and white photographs and charts. **First published:** 1973. **Frequency:** Biennially. **Size:** 8-1/2 x 11, 8-10 pages. **Price:** Free. **Circulation:** 8,000.

★3899★
Joint Center for Political and Economic Studies— Focus
Joint Center for Political and Economic
  Studies
1301 Pennsylvania Ave. NW, Ste. 400
Washington, DC 20004   Ph: (202)626-3500
Edited by: David Ruffin. **Description:** Reports on black and other minority participation in electoral politics. Offers public policy analysis on other issues that affect minorities. Recurring features include announcements of available publications, a column titled Perspective, and a supplement titled Political TrendLetter. **Illustrations:** Includes black and white graphics. **First published:** November 1970. **Frequency:** Monthly. Indexed: Annually. **Size:** 8-1/2 x 11, 8-12 pages. **Price:** $15/yr. **Circulation:** 11,500. **Former Title(s):** Joint Center for Political Studies–Focus.

★3900★
Juluka
1625 Q St. NW, Ste. 206   Ph: (202)387-7744
Washington, DC 20009   Fax: (202)387-0065
Edited by: Cliff Matheson, Tladi Kekana, and Victor Miller. **Subtitle:** A Newsletter for Southern Africans in North America. **Description:** Covers issues of special interest to Southern Africans living elsewhere. Contains news and commentary as well as coverage of Southern African products and services. Recurring features include letters to the editor, interviews, a calendar of events, reports of meetings, book reviews, notices of publications available, and columns titled Newsbriefs from South Africa, U.S. & Canadian News, Opinion, Profile, and Travel. **Illustrations:** Incorporates black and white photographs, graphs, and sketches. Audience: South Africans in North America and Americans interested in South African issues. **Editorial policies:** Accepts display and classified advertising. Considers articles for publication. **First published:** August 1991. **Frequency:** 6/yr. **Size:** 8-1/2 x 11, 10 pages. **Price:** $20/yr., U.S.; $24, Canada. **Circulation:** 3,500.

★3901★
Lawyers' Committee for Civil Rights Under the Law— Committee Report
Lawyers' Committee for Civil Rights Under
  Law
1400 I St. NW, Ste. 400
Washington, DC 20005   Ph: (202)371-1212
Edited by: Douglas B. Farquhar. **Description:** Discusses Supreme, Federal, and State Court cases that concern the rights of minorities and the poor. Covers civil rights litigation in numerous areas such as education, voting rights, employment discrimination, and equalization of municipal services and other governmental services and benefits. Informs readers of legislation and new programs that affect the civil rights of American citizens and about anti-apartheid work in South Africa and Namibia. Contains information on the Committee's activities and staff members as well as other civil rights issues. **First published:** November 1970. **Frequency:** Quarterly. **Size:** 8-1/2 x 11, 4-14 pages. **Price:** $20/yr. **Circulation:** 5,000.

★3902★
Let's Be Human
National Labor Service
11 Wedgewood Lane
Wantagh, NY 11793   Ph: (516)731-3069
Edited by: Harry Fleischman. **Description:** Presents articles on labor and civil rights. **First published:** August 1953. **Frequency:** Quarterly. **Size:** 8-1/2 x 11. **Price:** $10/yr. **Circulation:** 2,100.

★3903★
Making Success Happen Newsletter
National Association of Black Women
  Entrepreneurs
PO Box 1375   Ph: (313)341-7400
Detroit, MI 48231   Fax: (313)342-3433
Description: Acts as a national support system for Black businesswomen in the U.S. and focuses on the unique problems they face. Promotes the Association's objective to enhance business, professional, and technical development of both present and future Black businesswomen. Recurring features include announcements of symposia, workshops, and forums aimed at increasing the business awareness of Black women, profiles of successful Black businesswomen, and news of resources available. Audience: Upscale business and professional women. **First published:** 1978. **Frequency:** Bimonthly. **Size:** 8-1/2 x 11, 8 pages. **Price:** Included in membership. **Circulation:** Ca. 5,000.

★3904★
Michigan Civil Rights Commission—Newsletter
Michigan Civil Rights Commission
Information Division
Department of Civil Rights
303 W. Kalamazoo, Fourth Fl.   Ph: (517)373-1189
Lansing, MI 48913   Fax: (517)335-6513
Edited by: James H. Horn. **Description:** Informs the public of specific issues affecting the Civil Rights Commission's jurisdiction, including legislative developments. Covers news of the Commission regarding elections and appointments. Recurring features include notices of publications. **Illustrations:** Includes black and white graphics, charts, and graphs. **First published:** 1970. **Frequency:** Quarterly. **Size:** 8-1/2 x 11, 4 pages. **Price:** Free. **Circulation:** 8,000.

★3905★
Minorities in Business Insider
CD Publications   Ph: (301)588-6380
8204 Fenton St.   Fax: (301)588-6385
Silver Spring, MD 20910   Free: 800-666-6380
Edited by: Ken Silverstone. **Description:** Covers affirmative action, employment, government contracting, and education in relation to minorities in business. Audience: Prime contractors, government agencies, and minority business ownwers. **First published:** 1987. **Frequency:** Semimonthly. Indexed: Annually. **Size:** 8-1/2 x 11, 8-10 pages. **Price:** $250/yr.

★3906★
Minorities in the Newspaper Business
Task Force on Minorities in the
  Newspaper Business
Dulles Airport
PO Box 17401
Washington, DC 20041   Ph: (703)648-1285
Edited by: Walterene Swanston. **Description:** Provides a forum for articles and points of view on promotion, retention, management, and education issues throughout the newspaper industry. Keeps readers abreast of industry trends and programs relating to Asians, African-Americans, Hispanics, and Native Americans. **Editorial policies:** Considers articles for publication. **Frequency:** Quarterly. **Size:** 8-1/2 x 11. **Price:** Free. **Circulation:** 15,000. **Remarks:** Publication temporarily suspended.

★3907★
Minority Funding Report
Government Information Services, Inc.
1611 N. Kent St., Ste. 508
Arlington, VA 22209   Ph: (703)528-1082
Edited by: David Lytle. **Description:** Reports on federal and private-sector financial aid opportunities for disadvantaged minority groups. Audience: Government agencies and nonprofit minority and disadvantaged organizations. **First published:** April 1989. **Frequency:** Monthly. **Size:** 12 pages. **Price:** $128/yr. **ISSN:** 1047-3300.

★3908★
Minority Markets Alert
EPM Communications Inc.
488 E. 18th St.
Brooklyn, NY 11226   Ph: (718)469-9330
Edited by: Eric Miller. **Description:** Contains reports of research on minority consumers. Profiles the Black, Hispanic and Asian American populations. Recurring features include news of research, book reviews, and notices of publications available. **First published:** 1989. **Frequency:** Monthly. **Size:** 8-1/2 x 11, 8 pages. **Price:** $189/yr., U.S. and Canada; $229 elsewhere. **ISSN:** 1041-7524. **Online through:** NewsNet Inc., 945 Haverford Rd., Bryn Mawr, PA 19010, (215) 527-8030; Predicasts, 11001 Cedar Ave., Cleveland, OH 44106, (216) 795-3000. **Remarks:** Formerly published by Alert Publishing.

★3909★
The Minority Trendsletter
Center for Third World Organizing
3861 Martin Luther King Way
Oakland, CA 94609   Ph: (415)654-9601
Edited by: John Anner and Gary Delgado. **Description:** Analyzes issues and trends of particular concern in the Black, Asian, Latino, and Native American communities by surveying "mainstream" media coverage and issuing a different perspective. **Frequency:** Quarterly. **Size:** 24 pages. **Price:** $20/yr. for individuals, U.S.; $50 for institutions. **Circulation:** 15,000. **Former Title(s):** Third Force.

★3910★
Montgomery Business View
R&D Village
Montgomery County
Office of Economic Development
101 Monroe St., Ste. 1500
Rockville, MD 20850   Ph: (301)217-2345
Edited by: DeVance Walker, Jr. **Description:** Contains information on services, programs, and technical assistance for small and minority-owned businesses. **Illustrations:** Includes black and white photographs. Audience: Major employers and small and minority-owned businesses. **First published:** January 1988. **Frequency:** Monthly. **Size:** 11-1/2 x 15, 4-8 pages. **Price:** Free. **Circulation:** Ca. 7,000.

★3911★
Multicultural Leader
Educational Materials and Services Center
PO Box 802
Edmonds, WA 98020   Ph: (206)542-4218
Description: Contains articles on multiculturalism. Includes book reviews, news of research, and reports. **Frequency:** 4/yr. **Price:** $35/yr.

★3912★
Multicultural Publishers Exchange
Praxis Publications, Inc.
2215 Atwood Ave.   Ph: (608)244-5633
Madison, WI 53704   Fax: (608)244-3255
Edited by: Charles Taylor. **Subtitle:** A bimonthly newsletter for networking with independent minority owned self-publishers. **Description:** Offers advice on selling books, networking, improving efficiency, computerizing the office, and growing. **Illustrations:** Includes black and white graphics. Audience: Minority (African, Asian, Hispanic, and Native American) independent publishers. **Editorial policies:** Accepts classified advertising. **First published:** November 1989. **Frequency:** Bimonthly. Indexed: Annually. **Size:** 8-1/2 x 11, 10 pages. **Price:** $48/yr. **ISSN:** 1049-5428. **Circulation:** 2,000. **Former Title(s):** Praxis Publishing Pointers; Minority Publishers Exchange.

★3913★
NAFEO Inroads
National Association for Equal Opportunity
   in Higher Education (NAFEO)
400 12th St. NE   Ph: (202)543-9111
Washington, DC 20002   Fax: (202)543-9113
Edited by: Johnson Niba. **Description:** Focuses on "research on Blacks in higher education." Includes campus, presidential, and RFP news. Audience: Educators, students, researchers, foundation representatives, corporate officials, federal agencies, Association institutional representatives, and general subscribers. **First published:** June 1986. **Frequency:** Bimonthly. **Size:** 16-28 pages. **Price:** Included in membership; $30/yr. for nonmembers. **Circulation:** Ca. 2,000. **Former Title(s):** Inroads.

★3914★
National Association for the Advancement of Black
   Americans in Vocational Education—Newsletter
National Association for the Advancement
   of Black Americans in Vocational
   Education
c/o Dr. Ethel O. Washington
5057 Woodward, Rm. 976
Detroit, MI 48202   Ph: (313)494-1660
Edited by: Dr. Ethel O. Washington. **Description:** Provides a forum for the expression of minority concerns within the American Vocational Association. Discusses equity issues and successful programs in vocational education. Facilitates the exchange of Chapter news among states. Recurring features include meeting announcements, notice of job vacancies, and a commentary. **Illustrations:** Includes black and white graphics. **Editorial policies:** Considers articles for publication. **First published:** Spring 1980. **Frequency:** Quarterly. Indexed: Periodic. **Size:** 8-1/2 x 11, 4-6 pages. **Price:** $10/yr. **Circulation:** 600.

★3915★
National Association of Black Accountants—Chapter
   to Chapter
National Association of Black Accountants
220 I St. NE, Ste. 150   Ph: (202)546-6222
Washington, DC 20002   Fax: (202)547-1041
Edited by: Chanetta A. Ramey. **Description:** Serves as a means of communication among the Association's student chapters. Covers student programs and events sponsored by the Association. **Illustrations:** Includes black and white photographs. Audience: Black accounting students. **First published:** October 1991. **Frequency:** 3/yr. **Size:** 8-1/2 x 11, 8 pages. **Price:** Included in membership.

★3916★
National Association of Black Accountants—News
   Plus
National Association of Black Accountants
220 I St. NE, Ste. 150   Ph: (202)546-6222
Washington, DC 20002   Fax: (202)547-1041
Edited by: Beverly L. Everson-Jones. **Description:** Addresses concerns of black business professionals, especially in the accounting profession. Reports on accounting education issues, developments affecting the profession, and the Association's activities on the behalf of minorities in the accounting profession. Recurring features include member profiles, job listings, reports of meetings, news of research, and a calendar of events. Audience: CPAs, accountants, and accounting students. **Editorial policies:** Accepts classified advertising and corporate image advertisements. Accepts "technical notes" on topics such as tax issues for publication. **Frequency:** Ca. 1978. Frequency: Bimonthly. **Size:** 8-1/2 x 11, 8-12 pages. **Price:** Included in membership; $20/yr. for nonmembers. **Circulation:** Ca. 3,500.

★3917★
National Association of Investment Companies—
   Newsletter
1111 14th St., Ste. 700
Washington, DC 20005   Ph: (202)289-4336
Description: Presents "issues, events and trends of vital concern to the MESBIC industry and to minority small business." Focuses on legislative trends and actions. Audience: Minority small business entrepreneurs. **First published:** 1976. **Frequency:** Monthly. **Size:** 8-1/2 x 11, 2 pages. **Price:** $38.64/yr. **Former Title(s):** National Association of Minority Enterprise Small Business Investment Companies–Perspective.

★3918★
National Black MBA Association—Newsletter
National Black MBA Association
180 N. Michigan, Ste. 1820
Chicago, IL 60601

Ph: (312)236-2622
Fax: (312)236-4131

Edited by: Joleen Spencer and Eyvette Jones. **Description:** Serves as a communication network for members who hold masters degrees in business administration. Reports on chapter activities, other national MBA programs, and on the efforts of the Association to further the skills of the minority manager through continuing business education. Recurring features include news of research, a calendar of events, reports of meetings, and columns titled MBAs on the Move, Letter From the National President, and Message From the Editor-In-Chief. **Illustrations:** Includes black and white photographs. Audience: Members, corporate sponsors including Fortune 100 H.R. professionals, colleges and universities with business programs, and the Congressional Black Caucus. **Editorial policies:** Accepts advertising. Accepts for publication items on chapter activities or national business programs. **First published:** 1981. **Frequency:** Bimonthly. **Size:** 8-1/2 x 11, 8 pages. **Price:** Free. **Circulation:** 3,500.

★3919★
National Business League—National Memo
National Business League
1629 K St. NW, Ste. 605
Washington, DC 20006

Ph: (202)466-5483

Edited by: Barry L. Hudson. **Description:** Discusses minority business development, especially the role of the League in furthering continued advances. Features news about economic trends, government policies and issues, private sector trends, minority business trade association activity, and chapter activities. Recurring features include reports of meetings, news of educational opportunities, book reviews, notices of publications available, a calendar of events, and a column titled From the President's Desk. **Illustrations:** Includes black and white graphics. Audience: Corporate constituents, government agencies, minority business enterprises, minority business and trade associations, and members of the National Business League. **Editorial policies:** Accepts advertising. Considers articles for publication. **First published:** 1963. **Frequency:** Quarterly. Indexed: Semiannually. **Size:** 8-1/2 x 11, 8 pages. **Price:** Included in membership. **Circulation:** 5,000. **Remarks:** Publication temporarily suspended.

★3920★
NBPA Advocate
National Black Police Association
3251 Mt. Pleasant St. NW
Washington, DC 20010-2103

Ph: (202)457-0563
Fax: (202)223-6739

Edited by: Fran L. Lassiter. **Description:** Furthers the Association's goals to improve relationships between police departments and the Black community; to recruit minority police officers on a national scale; and to eliminate police corruption, brutality, and racial discrimination. Recurring features include profiles of outstanding Black police officers and news of research. Audience: Male and female Black police officers. **First published:** 1987. **Frequency:** Quarterly. **Price:** Included in membership. **Circulation:** Ca. 35,000. **Former Title(s):** Grapevine Newsletter; NBPA Newsletter.

★3921★
New Images
Metropolitan Council for Educational
  Opportunity
55 Dimock St.
Roxbury, MA 02119

Ph: (617)427-1545

Edited by: J. Marcus Mitchell. **Description:** Reports on the Council's integration program placing black children from Boston, Massachusetts, in suburban schools. Discusses educational and integration issues and promotes quality integrated education for urban children, new learning experiences for suburban children, and cooperation between parents and other citizens. Audience: Parents and the educational community. **First published:** April 1978. **Frequency:** Quarterly. **Size:** 8-1/2 x 11, 4 pages. **Price:** Free. **Circulation:** 3,000.

★3922★
New York African Studies Association—Newsletter
New York African Studies Association
STL-614
State University College
New Paltz, NY 12561

Ph: (914)257-3681
Fax: (914)257-3670

Edited by: Thomas E. and Corinne E. Nyquist. **Description:** Acts as an information exchange that promotes African studies at all educational levels in New York and the region. Contains news of the Association and its members, special reports, and summaries of past and current events in Africa. Recurring features include notices of work, study, and travel opportunities, poetry, book reviews, a calendar of events, news of members, papers, and columns titled African Studies in New York, Africana Materials, People and Events, and NYASA Guide. **Illustrations:** Includes black and white graphics, charts, and tables. **First published:** Spring 1974. **Frequency:** 3/yr. **Size:** 8-1/2 x 11, 8 pages. **Price:** Included in membership; $10/yr. for nonmembers. **ISSN:** 0148-7264. **Circulation:** Ca. 250. **Also known as:** NYASA Newsletter.

★3923★
The Newsletter of the Afro-American Religious History
Group
W.E.B. DuBois Institute for Afroamerican
  Research
Harvard University
44 Brattle St.
Cambridge, MA 02138

Ph: (617)495-4192
Fax: (617)496-8547

Edited by: Randall K. Burkett. **Description:** Serves as an informal means of scholarly communication among librarians, academicians, and others interested in Afro-American religious history. Audience: Historians, religious studies faculty, American studies faculty, and research librarians. **First published:** Fall 1976. **Frequency:** Semiannual. **Size:** 8-16 pages. **Price:** $4/yr. **ISSN:** 0889-6178. **Circulation:** Ca. 450.

★3924★
NMRLS Notes
North Mississippi Rural Legal Services
  (NMRLS)
PO Box 767
Oxford, MS 38655

Ph: (601)234-8731
Fax: (601)236-3263

Edited by: Joseph D. Delaney, Jr. **Description:** Reports on health, housing, economics, education, and other social and legal issues affecting clients of NMRLS. Examines new federal and state laws and court decisions that affect minorities and the poor. Includes news of staff members and of NMRLS conferences and events. **Illustrations:** Includes black and white graphics. Audience: Clients and staff of NMRLS and other interested individuals. **Editorial policies:** Considers articles for publication. **First published:** November 1976. **Frequency:** Bimonthly. **Size:** 8 x 11, 4-6 pages. **Price:** Free. **Circulation:** 1,500.

★3925★
Nommo: The Power of the Word
Afro-American Studies Center
Purdue University
326 Stone Hall
West Lafayette, IN 47907

Ph: (317)494-5680

Edited by: Winston Napier. **Description:** Reports on and discusses significant events, guest lectures, community matters, and activities in the arts related to Afro-American studies. Recurring features include summaries of Center activities, listings of course offerings and of other educational and professional opportunities, and columns titled What's the Word, Women's Desk, News From Africa, and Caribbean. **Illustrations:** Includes black and white graphics. Audience: Black students, staff and faculty. **First published:** 1976. **Frequency:** 3/academic yr. **Size:** 8-1/2 x 11, 8-12 pages. **Price:** Free. **Circulation:** 1,500.

★3926★
The Nonviolent Activist
War Resisters League
339 Lafayette St.   Ph: (212)228-0450
New York, NY 10012   Fax: (212)228-6139

Edited by: Ruth Benn. **Description:** Monitors League activities and the peace movement in general. Analyzes issues of concern from a pacifist perspective, including disarmament, civil rights, feminism, and various political philosophies. Recurring features include letters to the editor, book reviews, and member news. **Illustrations:** Includes black and white graphics, tables, and graphs. **Editorial policies:** Accepts advertising. Considers articles for publication. **First published:** November 1984. **Frequency:** 8/yr. **Size:** 8-1/2 x 11, 24 pages. **Price:** $15/yr. for individuals; $25 for institutions. **ISSN:** 8755-7428. **Circulation:** 15,000.

★3927★
NOW Newsletter
National Black Methodists for Church
  Renewal
601 W. Riverview Ave.
Dayton, OH 45406   Ph: (513)227-9460

Description: Addresses concerns of black clergy and lay members of the United Methodist Church. Discusses issues such as revival of the black church, involvement of blacks within the structure of the church, the church's social and political position, community approach to the drug crisis through the Church, and support for black education. Recurring features include news of the organization and its members. **Frequency:** 11/yr. **Price:** Included in membership. **Circulation:** 3,000.

★3928★
Operation Big Vote Newsletter
National Coalition on Black Voter
  Participation
1629 K St. NW, Ste. 801
Washington, DC 20006   Ph: (202)659-4929

Description: Focuses on Operation Big Vote, a program to increase black voter registration and participation in electoral voting. Also reports on the local independent coalitions developed and funded by the Coalition to increase nonpartisan voter participation and citizenship empowerment programs. Recurring features include news of research and information on voter education. Audience: Program directors and convenors, and the general public. **First published:** 1983. **Frequency:** Periodic. **Size:** 8-1/2 x 11. **Price:** Free. **Circulation:** 2,000.

★3929★
The Organizer
National Alliance Against Racist and
  Political Repression
11 John St., Rm. 702   Ph: (212)406-3330
New York, NY 10038   Fax: (212)406-3542

Edited by: Mike Welch. **Description:** Reports on the activities of task forces within the Alliance concerned with issues such as repressive legislation, political prisoners, police crimes, labor rights, prisoners' rights, racism, and political repression. Recurring features include information on the Alliance's national priority cases and activities planned around each case. **Illustrations:** Includes black and white graphics. **First published:** 1973. **Frequency:** Quarterly. **Size:** 8-1/2 x 11, 8 pages. **Price:** Included in membership; $10/yr. for nonmembers. **Circulation:** 10,000.

★3930★
Peacework
American Friends Service Committee
  (AFSC)
2161 Massachusetts Ave.   Ph: (617)661-6130
Cambridge, MA 02140   Fax: (617)354-2832

Edited by: Pat Farren. **Subtitle:** A New England Peace Movement Newsletter. **Description:** Concerned with social issues such as disarmament, peace and social justice, anti-draft and anti-nuclear movements, alternative economics, feminism, civil liberties, racial equality, community empowerment, and nonviolence. Recurring features include news items, book and resource listings, and a calendar of events. **Illustrations:** Includes black and white graphics

and maps. Audience: Persons interested in nonviolent social change. **Editorial policies:** Considers articles for publication. **First published:** June 1972. **Frequency:** Monthly. Indexed: Annually. **Size:** 8-1/2 x 11, 16 pages. **Price:** $12/yr. **ISSN:** 0748-0725. **Circulation:** 2,500.

★3931★
Police Misconduct and Civil Rights Law Report
Clark Boardman Callaghan
375 Hudson St.   Ph: (212)929-7500
New York, NY 10014   Free: 800-221-9428

Edited by: Elizabeth Brooks. **Description:** Monitors current research and court cases related to police misconduct, civil rights law, and actions under section 1983 of 42 U.S.C. Audience: Attorneys engaged in police misconduct and civil cases and other concerned professionals. **First published:** April 1983. **Frequency:** 6/yr. Indexed: Annually. **Size:** 8-1/2 x 11, 12 pages. **Price:** $100/yr. **ISSN:** 0738-0623. **Circulation:** 2,500. **Remarks:** Fax number is (212) 924-0460. Prepared under the auspices of the National Lawyers Guild Civil Liberties Committee.

★3932★
Positive Energy
Positive Energy Communications
1533 Marion St. NW
Washington, DC 20001   Ph: (202)328-0707

Edited by: Ayo Handy. **Subtitle:** The Information Bridge of Positive People. **Description:** Presents positive ideas, images, and cultural, health, spiritual, and entrepreneurial information from an African perspective. **Illustrations:** Includes black and white photographs and graphics. **First published:** 1981. **Frequency:** 11/yr. **Size:** 13 x 10. **Price:** $20/yr. **ISSN:** 1042-3788. **Circulation:** 15,000.

★3933★
Profits
Small Business Development Center
Howard University
PO Box 748   Ph: (202)806-1653
Washington, DC 20059   Fax: (202)806-1777

Edited by: Desiree L. Robinson. **Description:** Carries news of current programs in the public and private sectors relating to minority business assistance. Also covers the activities of the Center. **Illustrations:** Includes black and white graphics. Audience: Business owners. **First published:** 1970. **Frequency:** Irregular. Indexed: Quarterly. **Size:** 8-1/2 x 11, 8 pages. **Price:** Free. **Circulation:** 2,000.

★3934★
Project Equality—Update
Project Equality
1020 E. 63rd St., Ste. 102   Ph: (816)361-9222
Kansas City, MO 64110   Fax: (816)361-8997

Edited by: Maurice E. Culver. **Description:** Reports on program activities of the Project and Advocacy issues. Focuses on issues related to the achievement of equal employment opportunities. Recurring features include list of new employers accepted. **Illustrations:** Includes black and white graphics, charts, and graphs. **First published:** 1974. **Frequency:** Quarterly. **Size:** 7 x 8-1/2, 12 pages. **Price:** $10/yr. **Circulation:** Ca. 2,500. **Remarks:** Incorporates the former Project Equality–EEO News and Project Equality–Action. **Former Title(s):** Project Equality–News, 1976; Project Equality–Newsletter, 1977.

★3935★
Psych Discourse
Association of Black Psychologists
PO Box 55999   Ph: (202)722-0808
Washington, DC 20040   Fax: (202)722-5941

Edited by: Halford H. Fairchild, Ph.D. **Description:** Publishes news of the Association, whose aim is to "address the long neglected needs of Black professionals and begin to positively impact upon the mental health of the national Black community by means of planning, programs, services, training, and advocacy." Recurring features include editorials, news of research, letters to the editor, a calendar of events, and columns titled Social Actions, Chapter News, Publications, and Members in the News. **Illustrations:** Includes black and white graphics. Audience: Members, colleges, universities, and persons in the behavioral sciences. **Editorial policies:** Accepts advertising. Considers articles for publication. **First published:** 1970. **Frequency:** Bimonthly. **Size:** 8-1/2 x 11, 24 pages. **Price:** Included in membership; $90 for institutions; $75 for individuals. **Circulation:** 1,500. **Former Title(s):** Association of Black Psychologists–Newsletter.

★3936★
Rural Southern Voice for Peace Journal
Rural Southern Voice for Peace
1898 Hannah Branch Rd.
Burnsville, NC 28714   Ph: (704)675-5933
Edited by: Clare Hanrahan. **Description:** Emphasizes the "political, spiritual, and social alternatives that will help build a just and sustainable future." Promotes nonviolent efforts for social and economic justice, environmental protection and restoration, and global communication and cooperation. Reports on Grassroots Listening and Organizing (GLO) projects and activities of volunteers and Board of Directors. **Illustrations:** Includes black and white graphics. Audience: Activists and organizers in rural communities and small cities in southeastern United States. **First published:** November 1981. **Frequency:** Bimonthly. **Size:** 8-1/2 x 11, 20 pages. **Price:** $25/yr. **ISSN:** 1055-3908. **Circulation:** 2,500. **Remarks:** Affiliated with Fellowship of Reconciliation. **Former Title(s):** Rural Southern Voice for Peace–Newsletter.

★3937★
Save Our Sons and Daughters—Newsletter
Save Our Sons and Daughters (SOSAD)
453 Martin Luther King Blvd.
PO Box 32421
Detroit, MI 48201   Ph: (313)833-3030
Edited by: Grace Lee Boggs. **Description:** Serves as a forum for the organization, a group of parents and supporters of children killed in street violence who began working together "to create positive alternatives for young people." Provides commentaries, news of neighborhood coalitions, concerts, rallies, and other social activities. **Illustrations:** Includes black and white graphics. Audience: Churches, activists, agencies, and political leaders. **First published:** June 1987. **Frequency:** Monthly. **Size:** 8-1/2 x 11, 8 pages. **Price:** Free. **Circulation:** 4,000.

★3938★
Sickle Cell Disease Foundation of Greater New York—Newsletter
Sickle Cell Disease Foundation of Greater
New York
127 W. 127th St., Rm. 421
New York, NY 10027   Ph: (212)865-1500
Subtitle: Authoritative Sickle Cell News. **Description:** Provides information on sickle cell anemia and the Foundation's programs and services. Recurring features include editorials, news of research, news of members, and a calendar of events. **Illustrations:** Includes black and white photographs. Audience: Individuals and families with sickle cell anemia or the sickle cell trait. **First published:** 1972. **Frequency:** Quarterly. Indexed: Annually. **Size:** 8-1/2 x 11, 8 pages. **Price:** Free. **Circulation:** 15,000. **Online through:** Contact publisher.

★3939★
South Africa Reporter
Investor Responsibility Research Center,
Inc.
1755 Massachusetts Ave. NW, Ste. 600   Ph: (202)939-6500
Washington, DC 20036   Fax: (202)332-8570
Edited by: Meg Voorhes. **Description:** Reports on events and trends that will shape the future of South Africa and analyzes how these developments affect multinational corporations with investments in South Africa. **First published:** February 1983. **Frequency:** 4/yr. **Size:** 8-1/2 x 11, 16 pages. **Price:** $100/yr. **ISSN:** 1053-5497. **Circulation:** 1,250.

★3940★
Southern Poverty Law Center—Law Report
Southern Poverty Law Center
PO Box 548
Montgomery, AL 36101-0548   Ph: (205)264-0286
Edited by: Sara Bullard and Dave Watson. **Description:** Reviews advances in the legal rights of the poor, monitors Ku Klux Klan and militant right-wing group activities nationwide, and provides model statutes for municipalities or states seeking to regulate racial and religious violence or violations of citizens' civil rights. Recurring features include summaries of significant law suits and court decisions, notices of publications available, and occasional state-by-state surveys of relevant legislation. **Illustrations:** Includes black and white graphics. **First published:** March 1981. **Frequency:** Bimonthly. **Size:** 8-1/2 x 11, 8 pages. **Price:** Donation requested. **Circulation:** 140,000. **Also known as:** Intelligence Report.

★3941★
Spotlight on Africa
American-African Affairs Association
1001 Connecticut Ave. NW, No. 1135
Washington, DC 20036   Ph: (202)223-5110
Description: Supports the aim of the Association, which is "to further the cause of knowledge concerning Africa among the people of the United States." Covers such topics as foreign involvement in Africa, famine relief, and African economic issues. **Frequency:** Bimonthly. **Size:** 8-1/2 x 11, 4 pages. **Price:** $10/yr.

★3942★
Statement
National Coalition of 100 Black Women
50 Rockefeller Plaza, Ste. 46
New York, NY 10020   Ph: (212)974-6140
Description: Reports on the activities and achievements of Black women involved with such issues as economic development, health, employment, education, voting, housing, criminal justice, the status of Black families, and the arts. Comments on the problems encountered by Blacks in cities and operates as a forum for the exchange of ideas on improving the conditions for Black communities. **Frequency:** Periodic. **Price:** Included in membership. **Circulation:** 3,500.

★3943★
Today
National Association of Minority Women in
Business
906 Grand Ave., Ste. 200
Kansas City, MO 64106   Ph: (816)421-3335
Description: Serves as a network for the exchange of ideas and information on business opportunities for minority women in the public and private sectors. Discusses topics of concern to minority women in business ownership and management positions. Recurring features include highlights of pertinent legislative developments, news of members, news of research, notices of educational opportunities, and a calendar of events. Also includes items on women who have made significant contributions to the field. **Frequency:** Bimonthly. **Price:** Included in membership. **Circulation:** Ca. 5,000.

★3944★
Trends in Housing
1629 K St. NW, Ste. 802   Ph: (202)833-4456
Washington, DC 20006   Fax: (202)775-7465
Edited by: Natalie P. Shear. **Description:** Covers developments in fair housing issues, with articles on financing, redlining, low-income projects, consequences of regulations and legislation, and related subjects. Serves national, metropolitan, and local fair-housing advocacy and other civil rights groups. **Illustrations:** Includes black and white graphics. Audience: Persons involved in Human Relations Commissions, realtors, bankers, community redevelopment specialists, architects, planners, and lawyers. **First published:** August 1950. **Frequency:** Bimonthly. **Size:** 8-1/2 x 11, 8-12, pages. **Price:** $18/yr. **Circulation:** 20,000.

★3945★
Turning the Tide
People Against Racist Terror (PART)
PO Box 1990
Burbank, CA 91507   Ph: (818)509-3435

Edited by: Michael Novick. **Description:** Serves to expose racist, anti-semetic, homophobic, and anti-woman violence. Monitors the activities of the Populist Pary, Ku Klux Klan, Christian Identity Movement, White Aryan Resistance, Jewish Defense League, and other related organizations and associated individuals. Contains notices of publications available. **Illustrations:** Includes black and white photographs and cartoons. **Frequency:** Bimonthly. **Size:** 11 x 17, 4 pages. **Price:** Included in membership.

★3946★
The Tuskegee Airmen
Tuskegee Airmen Inc.
PO Box 1623
Melbourne, FL 32902   Ph: (305)727-3772

Edited by: Col. John D. Silvera. **Subtitle:** Official National Publication. **Description:** Promotes the recognition of the role of blacks in military and civilian aviation. Profiles the careers of prominent blacks who served in the armed forces. Recurring features include news items of interest to members in Tuskegee's 36 chapters, a calendar of events, research news, and a column titled Along the Tai Line. **Illustrations:** Contains black and white photographs and graphics. Audience: Personnel at black newspapers in major cities as well as Tuskegee members. **Editorial policies:** Accepts display and classified advertising. Considers articles for publication. **First published:** 1978. **Frequency:** Quarterly. **Size:** 8-1/2 x 11, 8 pages. **Price:** Included in membership. **Circulation:** 1,800.

★3947★
UCC Courage in the Struggle for Justice and Peace
Office for Church in Society
United Church of Christ (UCC)
110 Maryland Ave.
Washington, DC 20002   Ph: (202)543-1517

Edited by: Rev. Rubin Tendai. **Description:** Monitors congressional legislation in the areas of current social issues. Considers such topics as U.S. involvement in Central America, the role of women and blacks in the elections, tax relief for the disabled, and the fight of clerical and pastoral groups against racism. Reports on denominational justice and peace activities nationally, regionally, and locally. **Illustrations:** Includes black and white graphics. Audience: Church lay people and clergy interested in social issues. **First published:** 1977. **Frequency:** Monthly. **Size:** 8-1/2 x 11, 4 pages. **Price:** Free to UCC members. **Circulation:** 15,000. **Former Title(s):** UCC Network; UCC Peace Priority.

★3948★
The Urban Banker
National Association of Urban Bankers
810 1st St. NE, Ste. 530
Washington, DC 20002   Ph: (202)783-4743

Description: Monitors trends in the provision of financial services products for member minority professionals in the banking industry and related fields. Provides coverage of legislative and regulatory actions affecting the industry, of Association programs, and of the professional accomplishments of members. Recurring features include chapter updates, reports on national and regional conferences and expositions, a calendar of events, results of financial industry surveys, news of educational opportunities, and the column Message From the President. **Illustrations:** Contains black and white photographs. Audience: Minority professionals in financial services. **Editorial policies:** Accepts summaries of chapter activities for publication. **First published:** 1978. **Frequency:** Quarterly. **Size:** 8-1/2 x 11, 4-6 pages. **Price:** Free. . **Circulation:** Ca. 2,300.

★3949★
Urban Research Review
Institute for Urban Affairs and Research
2900 Van Ness St. NW
Washington, DC 20008   Ph: (202)686-6770

Edited by: Ms. Eva M. Bell **Description:** Publishes research findings related to physical and mental health, violence and criminal justice, human resource development, community services, religion, and education, focusing primarily on Blacks. Recurring features include statistical data, interviews with research scholars, book reviews, reference citations, listings of educational and job opportunities, and announcements of research grants, conferences, workshops, and other events. **Illustrations:** Contains black and white graphics. Audience: Social researchers, social workers, psychologists, psychiatrists, public administrators, political and civic leaders, college students, and other laypersons. **Editorial policies:** Considers articles for publication. **First published:** March 1974. **Frequency:** Semiannually. **Size:** 8-1/2 x 11, 12-16 pages. **Price:** Free. **Circulation:** 3,000.

★3950★
Vital Signs
National Black Women's Health Project
1237 Gordon St. SW
Atlanta, GA 30310   Ph: (404)753-0916

Edited by: Lisa Diane White. **Description:** Encourages mutual and self-help activism among women to bring about a reduction in health care problems prevalent among black women. Reports on research conducted on the health problems of black women and discusses black women's health issues. Recurring features include news of upcoming conferences and lectures sponsored by the Project. Audience: African-American women and their supporters, health program planners, advocates and providers, and grass root organizations. **First published:** 1984. **Frequency:** Quarterly. **Size:** 11 x 17. **Price:** Included in membership. **Circulation:** 10,000.

★3951★
VOICES of the African Diaspora: The CAAS Research Review
Center for Afroamerican and African
  Studies
University of Michigan
200 W. Engineering Bldg.
550 E. University
Ann Arbor, MI 48109-1092   Ph: (313)764-5513

Edited by: Susanne Kocsis. **Description:** Contains in-depth articles from current research on the African diaspora from a cross-cultural perspective. Provides book reviews, intervies, poetry, and announcements. **Illustrations:** Includes black and white photographs. Audience: Scholars and librarians. **First published:** October 1984. **Frequency:** 3/yr. **Size:** 8 x 10-1/2, 32-44 pages. **Price:** $18/yr. for individuals; $24 for institutions; $15 for students. **ISSN:** 1054-4238. **Circulation:** 2,000. **Former Title(s):** CAAS Newsletter.

Directories

★3952★
Affirmative Action Register
Affirmative Action, Inc.   Ph: (314)991-1335
8356 Olive Blvd.   Fax: (314)997-1788
St. Louis, MO 63132   Free: 800-537-0655

Description: In each issue, about 300 positions at a professional level (most requiring advanced study) available to women, minorities, veterans, and the handicapped; listings are advertisements placed by employers with affirmative action programs. **Entries include:** Company or organization name, address, contact name; description of position including title, requirements, duties, application procedure, salary, etc. **Arrangement:** Classified by profession. **Pages (approx.):** 50. **Frequency:** Monthly. **Editor(s):** Joyce R. Green. **Price:** $1.50 per issue; distributed free to women, minority, and handicapped candidate sources (ISSN 0146-2113).

★3953★
African-American Blackbook International Reference Guide
National Publications Sales Agency, Inc.
1610 E. 79th St.
Chicago, IL 60649

Ph: (312)375-6800
Fax: (312)375-7149

Description: About 6,000 African-American businesses and organizations, including local affiliates; African-Americans on boards of major corporations; in the food, beverage, and tobacco industries; elected officials and in the defense industry. **Entries include:** Firm name, address, phone, key personnel, history. **Pages (approx.):** 300. **Frequency:** Annual, March. **Editor(s):** Donald C. Walker. **Price:** $9.95. plus $3.00 shipping. **Other Information:** Supersedes "Blackbook Business and Reference Guide," which covered only Chicago, Illinois. **Former Title(s):** Blackbook International Reference Guide; Blackbook National Resource Guide.

★3954★
Alabama's Black Heritage: A Tour of Historic Sites
Alabama Bureau of Tourism & Travel
532 S. Perry Street
Montgomery, AL 36104

Description: Sites of significance in Black American history in Alabama. **Other Information:** Formerly published by DCI.

★3955★
American League of Financial Institutions—Directory of Members and Associate Members
U.S. League of Financial Institutions
1709 New York Ave. NW, Ste. 801
Washington, DC 20006

Ph: (202)628-5624

Description: About 49 minority owned savings and loan associations in 25 states and the District of Columbia. **Entries include:** Association name, address, phone, name of principal executive. **Arrangement:** Geographical. **Pages (approx.):** 5. **Frequency:** Irregular; previous edition August 1986; latest edition June 1988. **Editor(s):** John Harshaw. **Price:** $3.50. **Other Information:** Former association name is American Savings and Loan League. Previously cited as "American League of Financial Institutions–Membership Roster." **Former Title(s):** Directory of Minority Owned Savings and Loan Institutions.

★3956★
ArtSourceBook Minority Artists and Organizations in Pennsylvania
Pennsylvania Council on the Arts
Finance Building, Room 216
Harrisburg, PA 17120

Ph: (717)787-6883

Description: About 1,100 minority artists in Pennsylvania, including visual artists, filmmakers, performing arts companies, individual performing artists, and literary artists; also includes more than 550 sponsors of the arts and approximately 155 publishers. **Entries include:** For artists - Name, medium, accomplishments, education, address, and phone. For others - Name, address, phone. **Arrangement:** Artists are classified by medium; sponsors are geographical by region; publishers are alphabetical. **Pages (approx.):** 140. **Frequency:** Every four years; latest edition October 1988. **Editor(s):** S. Damon Kletzien. **Price:** Free. **Also Includes:** Bibliography of resource publications.

★3957★
Black Americans Information Directory
Gale Research Inc.
835 Penobscot Bldg.
Detroit, MI 48226-4094

Ph: (313)961-2242
Fax: (313)961-6083
Free: 800-877-GALE

Description: Approximately 4,800 sources of information on a variety of aspects of Black American life and culture, including national, state, and local organizations; publishers of newspapers, periodicals, newsletters, and other publications and videos; television and radio stations; traditionally Black colleges and universities; library collections; museums and other cultural institutions; Black studies programs and research centers; federal and state government agencies; Black religious organizations; and awards, honors, and prizes. **Entries include:** Name, address, phone, name and title of contact, description of services, activities, etc. **Arrangement:** Classified by type of organization, activity, service, etc. **Indexes:** Name/keyword. **Pages (approx.):** 514. **Frequency:** Biennial, odd years. **Editor(s):** Wendy S. Van de Sande. **Price:** $75.00.

★3958★
Black Clergy Directory
Episcopal Commission for Black Ministries
Episcopal Church Center
815 2nd Ave.
New York, NY 10017

Ph: (212)867-8400

Description: About 495 Black Episcopal clergy. **Entries include:** Name, address, phone, diocese. **Arrangement:** Alphabetical. **Pages (approx.):** 60. **Frequency:** Annual, January. **Editor(s):** Reverend Canon Harold T. Lewis. **Price:** Free.

★3959★
Black Elected Officials: A National Roster
Joint Center for Political Studies
1090 Vermont Ave. NW, Ste. 1100
Washington, DC 20005

Ph: (202)789-3500
Fax: (202)626-8774

Description: Over 6,600 Black Americans who hold elective public office in all 50 states, the District of Columbia, and the Virgin Islands. **Entries include:** Name, title, address, jurisdiction in which person serves, date term ends. **Arrangement:** Geographical, by state; then by level of office. **Pages (approx.):** 470. **Frequency:** Reported as annual; latest edition February 1989. **Editor(s):** Carolyn Barnett-Jones, Research Analyst. **Price:** $48.00, cloth; $32.50 paper. **Send orders to:** University Press of America, 4720 Boston Way, Lanham, MD 20706 (301-459-3366). **Former Title(s):** National Roster of Black Elected Officials.

★3960★
Black Enterprise—Top Black Businesses Issue
Earl G. Graves Publishing Co.
130 5th Ave., 10th Fl.
New York, NY 10011

Ph: (212)242-8000
Fax: (212)989-8410
Free: 800-727-7777

Description: Lists of 100 Black-owned industrial/service companies with sales of $5 million or above, more than 35 banks with total assets of $1.6 billion or more, nearly 35 savings and loan associations with total assets of $1.15 billion or more, about 30 insurance companies with total assets of about $830 million or more, and 100 auto dealers with sales of $10 million or above. **Entries include:** Company name, city and state, name of chief executive, year founded, number of employees, financial data. **Arrangement:** In categories, with rankings by financial size. **Frequency:** Annual, June. **Editor(s):** Earl G. Graves. **Price:** $3.50; back issues $4.50 each. **Also Includes:** Analyses of the lists and of the industries in which firms listed operate. **Other Information:** Cover title, "Black Enterprise–The Top 100 Businesses Issue."

★3961★
The Black Pages of New England
Thelma Sullivan
PO Box 1848
Brockton, MA 02403

Ph: (508)584-5656

Description: Approximately 300 paid listings of Black-owned businesses in New England. **Entries include:** Business name, address, phone. **Arrangement:** Classified by type of product/service. **Pages (approx.):** 90. **Frequency:** Annual, January. **Editor(s):** Thelma Sullivan. **Price:** $3.00. **Other Information:** Liquor stores and bar rooms are not included. Supersedes The Black Business Directory of New England.

★3962★
Black Resource Guide
Black Resource Guide, Inc.
501 Oneida Pl. NW
Washington, DC 20011

Ph: (202)291-4373
Fax: (202)291-4373

Description: Over 4,500 organizations and individuals especially relevant to or comprised primarily of Black Americans, including adoption agencies, business and bar associations, colleges, public administrators, book publishers, church denominations, financial institutions, sports agents, Urban League directors, hospitals, museums, embassies and consulates, and others; also included are Blacks in federal elected and appointed positions; individuals are chosen for their prominence in Black America. **Entries include:** Generally, listings show name, address, and phone; name and title of chief executive officer may also be included. **Arrangement:** Classified by line of business or activity. **Pages (approx.):** 393. **Frequency:** Biennial, September of even years. **Editor(s):** R. Benjamin Johnson and Jacqueline L. Johnson, Publishers. **Price:** $69.00, plus $3.50 shipping. **Also Includes:** Population, business, and census statistics.

★3963★
Black Student's Guide to Colleges
Beckham House Publishers, Inc.   Ph: (301)681-3024
PO Box 8008   Fax: (301)681-3024
Silver Spring, MD 20907-8008   Free: 800-444-2524
Description: Nearly 182 colleges, including about 75 considered to be "the most selective residential colleges," 25 historically Black colleges, and others selected for general popularity, etc. **Entries include:** Name, location, number of Black students, number of Black faculty, total number of faculty, library holdings, tuition, costs, majors often selected by Black students, support services specifically for Black students, and comments by recent alumni or current Black students regarding the general atmosphere and environment of the college. **Arrangement:** Alphabetical. **Indexes:** Geographical. **Pages (approx.):** 512. **Frequency:** Biennial. **Editor(s):** Barry Beckham. **Price:** $16.95. **Other Information:** A library edition containing additional indexes is also available; $35.00. Formerly published by E. P. Dutton, Inc.

★3964★
Black Student's Guide to Scholarship
Beckham House Publishers, Inc.   Ph: (301)681-3024
PO Box 8008   Fax: (301)681-3024
Silver Spring, MD 20907-8008   Free: 800-444-2524
Description: Providers of financial aid for Black students pursuing a college education. **Entries include:** Organization name, address, phone, name and title of contact, eligibility requirements, description of award or grant. **Arrangement:** By category. **Pages (approx.):** 145. **Frequency:** Irregular; previous edition August 1990; latest edition December 1991. **Editor(s):** Barry Beckham, President. **Price:** $9.95. **Former Title(s):** 75 Scholarships Every Black High School Student Should Know About.

★3965★
Black Theatre Directory
Audience Development Committee
Box 30, Manhattanville Sta.
New York, NY 10027   Ph: (212)534-8776
Description: Nearly 1,000 individuals interested in or pursuing a career in Black theater.

★3966★
Black Writers
Gale Research Inc.   Ph: (313)961-2242
835 Penobscot Bldg.   Fax: (313)961-6083
Detroit, MI 48226-4094   Free: 800-877-GALE
Description: Over 400 Black authors of the twentieth century from the U.S. or of interest to American readers. Entries are selected and updated from "Contemporary Authors" (see separate entry). The 1993 edition will include 200 newly covered authors as well as update selected entries from the 1988 edition. **Entries include:** Author's name; home and office addresses, agent's name and address; date and place of birth, names of parents, spouse, and children, colleges attended and degrees earned, political beliefs; description of career, awards and honors, memberships; chronological bibliography of books written, list of other notable publications such as screenplays and periodical articles; description of works in progress; "Sidelights" section discussing author's literary development, personal interests and attitudes, and reception of author's works by critics; list of publications containing more information on author. **Arrangement:** Alphabetical. **Pages (approx.):** 600. **Frequency:** First edition November 1988; new edition expected October 1993. **Editor(s):** Sharon Malinowski. **Price:** $85.00 (1988 edition); $89.00 (1993 edition).

★3967★
Burrelle's Black Media Directory
Burrelle's Media Directories
75 E. Northfield Rd.
Livingston, NJ 07039   Ph: (201)992-6600
Description: Newspapers, magazines, newsletters, radio and television programs, and other media serving the interests of the Black population. **Entries include:** Publication or station name, address, phone, names and titles of key personnel, description of publication or program. **Arrangement:** Geographical. **Indexes:** Geographical. **Pages (approx.):** 295. **Frequency:** Irregular; latest edition 1989. **Price:** $50.00, plus $3.75 shipping.

★3968★
Buyers' Guide to Minority Business
Arizona Minority Supplier Development
  Council
5151 N. 16th St., Ste. 124   Ph: (602)274-4647
Phoenix, AZ 85016   Fax: (602)277-8599
Description: Minority commercial and industrial firms in Arizona. **Entries include:** Company name, address, phone, name of contact, date established, number of employees, facilities, product or service provided, references. **Arrangement:** Classified by line of business. **Indexes:** Alphabetical. **Pages (approx.):** 300. **Frequency:** Annual, November. **Editor(s):** Patsy DiRuzza. **Price:** $50.00, plus $3.50 shipping.

★3969★
Career Opportunities for Minority College Graduates
Paoli Publishing, Inc.
1708 E. Lancaster Ave., Ste. 287   Ph: (215)640-9889
Paoli, PA 19301   Fax: (215)296-9266
Description: Over 900 companies, organizations and schools representing 24 occupational fields and five continuing educational alternatives. **Entries include:** Name, address, personnel contact name or department; phone listed in many entries. **Arrangement:** Classified by occupation then geographical. **Pages (approx.):** 83. **Frequency:** Annual. **Editor(s):** J. William Wrigley. **Price:** $2.75. **Also Includes:** For some entries, display advertisements which provide company details and employment opportunities.

★3970★
Caribbean Business Directory & Yellow Pages
Caribbean Publishing Co.
9500 S. Dadeland Blvd., Ste. 500   Ph: (305)670-4899
Miami, FL 33156   Free: 800-227-4835
Description: 40,000 business firms, government offices, and medical and legal practices in 30 Caribbean countries; also includes listings in Miami, Florida. **Entries include:** Name of firm, address, phone, telex, fax. **Arrangement:** Classified by type of firm. **Indexes:** Product/service. **Pages (approx.):** 950. **Frequency:** Annual, December. **Editor(s):** Rafael Sangiovanni, Production Manager. **Price:** $49.95, plus $4.95 shipping. **Send orders to:** Caribbean Imprint Directory Services, 410 W. Falmouth Hwy., Falmouth, MA 02574 (508-540-5378). **Former Title(s):** Caribbean Telephone Directory; Caribbean Business Directory.

★3971★
Caribbean Exporters, Importers and Business Services Directory
Caribbean Business Development Group,
  Inc.
67 Wall St., Ste. 2411   Ph: (212)323-7952
New York, NY 10005   Fax: (212)432-9366
Description: Over 5,500 exporters, importers, and business service companies in 23 Caribbean countries. **Entries include:** Company name, address, phone, telex, name and title of contact, number of employees, line of business activity. **Arrangement:** Classified by product, service or SIC code. **Indexes:** Standard Industrial Classification (SIC) code, geographical, and numerical. **Pages (approx.):** 400. **Frequency:** Annual. **Editor(s):** Lloyd Pilgrim Spooner. **Price:** $79.95.

★3972★
Certified Minority Business Enterprises & Women Business Enterprises in Rhode Island

Small Business Division
Rhode Island Department of Economic
Development
7 Jackson Walkway
Providence, RI 02903   Ph: (401)277-2601

Description: About 300 professional, commercial, industrial, and consumer firms in Rhode Island. **Entries include:** Company name, address, phone, name of principal officer, line of business, certification and recertification dates. **Arrangement:** Classified by line of business. **Indexes:** Alphabetical. **Pages (approx.):** 49. **Frequency:** Latest edition October 1992. **Editor(s):** Charles Newton, Coordinator. **Price:** Free. **Other Information:** Publishing office was formerly the Business and Industry Division. **Former Title(s):** Rhode Island Minority Businesses; Rhode Island Minority Business Enterprises.

★3973★
Cleveland Ethnic Directory

Nationalities Services Center of Cleveland
1836 Euclid Ave., Ste. 200
Cleveland, OH 44115   Ph: (216)781-4560

Description: Several thousand ethnic organizations, societies, cultural and political organizations, and performing groups in the Cleveland, Ohio area. **Entries include:** Organization name, address, phone, names and titles of key personnel, subsidiary and branch names and locations. **Arrangement:** Classified by nationality. **Indexes:** Subject. **Frequency:** Irregular; latest edition 1990.

★3974★
Contemporary Black American Playwrights & Their Plays: A Biographical Directory & Dramatic Index

Greenwood Publishing Group, Inc.
88 Post Rd. W.
PO Box 5007   Ph: (203)226-3571
Westport, CT 06881   Fax: (203)222-1502

Pages (approx.): 651. **Frequency:** Latest edition May 1988. **Editor(s):** Bernard L. Peterson, Jr. **Price:** $75.00.

★3975★
Contemporary Black Biography

Gale Research Inc.   Ph: (313)961-2242
835 Penobscot Bldg.   Fax: (313)961-6083
Detroit, MI 48226-4094   Free: 800-877-GALE

Description: In each volume, approximately 70 notable Black persons of the 20th Century. **Entries include:** Name, portrait, date and place of birth, family names, educational background, career data, memberships, awards, essay detailing career and achievements, books written and other works, mailing address (as available). **Arrangement:** Alphabetical. **Indexes:** Nationality, occupation, subject, name. **Pages (approx.):** 275 per volume. **Frequency:** Twice yearly. **Editor(s):** Barbara Carlisle Bigelow. **Price:** $42.00 per volume.

★3976★
Dallas/Fort Worth Black Pages

Dallas/Fort Worth Black Pages
3606 Marvin D. Love Fwy., Ste. 130
Dallas, TX 75224   Ph: (214)375-5200

Description: About 3,000 minority firms offering professional, commercial, and industrial products and services in the greater Dallas/Ft. Worth, Texas area. **Entries include:** Firm name, address, phone, name and title of owner or chief executive, products or services. **Arrangement:** Alphabetical. **Indexes:** Product/service. **Frequency:** Annual, October. **Editor(s):** Arnette D. French. **Price:** Free.

★3977★
Directory of African American Design Firms

San Francisco Redevelopment Agency
770 Golden Gate Ave.   Ph: (415)749-2423
San Francisco, CA 94102-3120   Fax: (415)749-2526

Description: Over 80 architectural, engineering, planning, and landscape design firms. **Entries include:** Firm name, address, phone names and titles of key personnel, particular type of work. **Arrangement:** Alphabetical. **Pages (approx.):** 10. **Frequency:** Annual, December. **Editor(s):** Benson Hattem. **Price:** Free. **Former Title(s):** Directory of Black Architects and Engineers in the West; Directory of Black Design Firms in the West; Directory of Black Design Firms.

★3978★
Directory of African American Religious Bodies

Howard University School of Divinity
Research Center   Ph: (202)806-0750
1400 Shepherd St. NE   Fax: (202)806-4946
Washington, DC 20017   Free: 800-441-1303

Description: Approximately 1,000 African American religious denominations; resource and service agencies that serve the African American community; religious educational institutions, research organizations, and professional religious organizations; African American colleges and universities founded by religious bodies; African American religious scholars. **Entries include:** For religious denominations–Institution name, address, phone, names and titles of key personnel, description of institution, group type, year founded, number of members, publications, meeting dates. For resource and service agencies–Company name, address, phone. For religious educational institutions, research organizations, and professional religious organizations–Organization name, address, phone, name and title of contact, description of organization. For colleges and universities–School name, address, phone. For individuals–Personal name, address, phone, biographical data. **Arrangement:** Separate sections for religious denominations, resource and service agencies; religious educational institutions, research organizations, and professional religious organizations; colleges and universities, and scholars. **Indexes:** Religious bodies, personal name, geographical, group type, religious category, publications. **Pages (approx.):** 363. **Frequency:** First edition published 1991. **Editor(s):** Dr. Wardell J. Payne, Research Director. **Price:** $49.95, cloth; $29.95, paper. **Send orders to:** Marketing Department, Howard University Press, 1240 Randolph St., NW, Washington, DC 20017 (202-806-4935).

★3979★
Directory of African and Afro-American Studies in the United States

African Studies Association
Credit Union Bldg.
Emory University   Ph: (404)329-6410
Atlanta, GA 30322   Fax: (404)329-6433

Description: About 425 institutions offering programs in African and Afro-American studies. **Entries include:** For principal institutions–Name, address, courses offered, faculty, library collections available, financial aid, and area of specialized study, and courses. **Arrangement:** Geographical. **Indexes:** Institution name, faculty and staff, program, title and degree offerings, African language. **Pages (approx.):** 275. **Frequency:** Irregular; previous edition spring 1988; latest edition 1993. **Editor(s):** AnneMarie Christy and Beth Pearce. **Price:** $20.00, plus $2.00 shipping; payment with order. **Former Title(s):** Directory of Third World Studies in the United States.

★3980★
Directory of Black Americans in Political Science

American Political Science Association
1527 New Hampshire Ave. NW
Washington, DC 20036   Ph: (202)483-2512

Description: Over 500 Black advanced graduate students, academics, and professionals in the field of political science. A list of about 75 predominantly Black colleges and universities with political science programs is included. **Entries include:** For individuals–Name, title, affiliation, address, degree, fields of specialization, publications. For colleges–Name, address; many listings also include phone. **Arrangement:** Alphabetical. **Indexes:**

Field of interest. **Pages (approx.):** 200. **Frequency:** Irregular; previous edition 1977 (out of print); latest edition January 1988. **Editor(s):** Maurice C. Woodard. **Price:** $15.00. **Other Information:** An index of Black member political scientists appears in "American Political Science Association–Membership Directory".

★3981★
Directory of Certified Minority and Women-Owned Business Enterprises
Minority and Women's Business
  Development
New York State Department of Economic
  Development
1 Commerce Plaza
Albany, NY 12245   Ph: (518)473-0582
Description: Officially certified minority-owned and woman-owned construction, professional, service, manufacturing, distributing, and retail firms in New York State. **Entries include:** Firm name, address, phone, contact name, Standard Industrial Classification (SIC) number, products or services, sales figure. **Arrangement:** Classified by major industry group, then in four-digit SIC code order (numerical) within 10 economic development regions. **Indexes:** Company name, product/service (four-digit SIC). **Pages (approx.):** 700. **Frequency:** Annual, periodic updates. **Price:** $59.00. **Fax:** (518)473-0665. **Other Information:** Variant title, "Directory of Minority and Women-Owned Business Enterprises." **Former Title(s):** Register of Minority Business Enterprise; Registry of Business Enterprise.

★3982★
Directory of Certified Minority Business Enterprises
Minority Business Opportunity Commission
2000 14th Street, NW
Washington, DC 20009   Ph: (202)939-8780
Description: About 550 suppliers of professional, commercial, and industrial products and services, and construction services, all firms in which minority ownership and control has been certified by the District of Columbia Minority Business Opportunity Commission in accordance with D.C. Law I-95. **Entries include:** Firm name, address, phone, name and title of owner or chief executive, products or services. **Arrangement:** Alphabetical. **Indexes:** Product/service, personal name. **Pages (approx.):** 140. **Frequency:** Annual. **Editor(s):** Faith Roland.

★3983★
Directory of Certified Minority, Women, and Disadvantaged Business Enterprise
Washington Office of Minority and
  Women's Business Enterprises
406 S. Water St.
PO Box 41160   Ph: (206)753-9693
Olympia, WA 98504-1160   Fax: (206)586-7079
Description: More than 3,500 professional, commercial, industrial, and consumer firms in Washington state. **Entries include:** Company name, address, phone, name and title of contact, status of certification as a minority- or woman-owned firm, product/service provided. **Arrangement:** Classified by commodity code. **Pages (approx.):** 200. **Frequency:** Annual, July; three addenda per year. **Editor(s):** Randall Daley. **Price:** $40.00 per year; payment must accompany order. **Other Information:** Combines four previously separate directories which were published by the City of Seattle Human Rights Department, King County Minority & Women's Business Enterprises Business Program, City of Spokane - Affirmative Action Department, and the above office. **Former Title(s):** Directory of Certified State and Federal Minority and Women's Business Entertprises (1990).

★3984★
Directory of Ethnic Minority Professionals in Psychology
American Psychological Association
Office of Ethnic Minority Affairs
750 1st St. NE
Washington, DC 20002-4242   Ph: (202)336-5500
Description: Over 2,000 ethnic minority psychologists nationwide and in Puerto Rico. **Entries include:** Company name, address, phone, language spoken. **Arrangement:** Classified by race/ethnicity and geographic area. **Indexes:** Name, ethnicity, major field of study.

Pages (approx.): 264. **Frequency:** Previous edition January 1990; latest edition 1993. **Price:** $20.00. **Former Title(s):** Ethnic Minority Directory of Professionals in Psychology.

★3985★
Directory of Financial Aids for Minorities
Reference Service Press
1100 Industrial Rd., Ste. 9   Ph: (415)594-0743
San Carlos, CA 94070   Fax: (415)594-0411
Description: Over 2,150 financial aid programs and awards available to members of minority groups; includes scholarships, fellowships, loans, grants, awards, and internships; state government agencies with related information. **Entries include:** Program title, sponsor name, address, phone, eligibility requirements, purpose, duration, application deadline, financial data, etc. **Arrangement:** Programs are classified by type of aid, then by minority group; state agencies are geographical. **Indexes:** Program title, sponsor name, geographical, subject, month of application deadline. **Pages (approx.):** 600. **Frequency:** Biennial, January of odd years. **Editor(s):** Gail Ann Schlachter. **Price:** $47.50, plus $4.00 shipping. **Other Information:** Former publisher, ABC-Clio Information Services.

★3986★
Directory of Minority- and Women-Owned Business Enterprises
New York City Office of Business
  Development
17 John St., 10th Fl.   Ph: (212)513-6466
New York, NY 10038   Fax: (212)267-2598
Description: About 600 New York city businesses that are at least 51% owned by women or members of minority groups. **Entries include:** Company name, address, phone, name and title of contact, description of products or services. **Arrangement:** Classified by line of business. **Indexes:** Alphabetical. **Pages (approx.):** 100. **Frequency:** Annual, January. **Editor(s):** Edmund Yu. **Price:** Free.

★3987★
Directory of Minority and Women Owned Businesses
Louisiana Office of Minority and Women's
  Business Enterprise
Department of Economic Development
Box 94185
Baton Rouge, LA 70804   Ph: (504)342-5373
Description: Firms offering professional, commercial, and industrial products and services. **Entries include:** Firm name, address, phone, name and title of contact, number of employees, products or services, geographical area served, financial data, Standard Industrial Classification (SIC) code. **Arrangement:** Alphabetical. **Pages (approx.):** 250. **Frequency:** Irregular; previous edition 1987; latest edition February 1989. **Editor(s):** Angelisa M. Harris, Executive Director. **Price:** $10.00. **Former Title(s):** Minority Entrepreneur Directory; Minority and Women's Business Directory.

★3988★
Directory of Minority and Women-Owned Investment Bankers
San Francisco Redevelopment Agency
770 Golden Gate Ave.   Ph: (415)749-2423
San Francisco, CA 94102   Fax: (415)749-2526
Description: About 16 minority-owned investment banking firms. **Entries include:** Company name, address, phone, owner's name and title, fax and toll free numbers if available. **Arrangement:** Alphabetical. **Pages (approx.):** 1. **Frequency:** Approximately biennial, even years. **Editor(s):** Benson I. Hattem.

★3989★
Directory of Minority Arts Organizations
Civil Rights Division
National Endowment for the Arts
1100 Pennsylvania Ave. NW, Rm. 812
Washington, DC 20506   Ph: (202)682-5454
Description: Almost 1,000 performing groups, presenters, galleries, art and media centers, literary organizations, and community centers with significant arts programming that have leadership and constituency that is predominantly Asian-American, Black, Hispanic, Native American, or multi-racial. **Entries include:** Organization

name, address, phone, name and title of contact, description of activities. **Arrangement:** Geographical. **Indexes:** Organization name, activity. **Pages (approx.):** 120. **Frequency:** Irregular; previous edition 1982; latest edition February 1987. **Editor(s):** Nellie Fowler. **Price:** Free.

★3990★
Directory of Minority Business in Wisconsin
Wisconsin Office of Minority Business
  Enterprise
Box 7970
Madison, WI 53707   Ph: (608)267-9550

Description: About 300 non-retail minority firms. **Entries include:** Name, address, phone, name of chief executive or contact, type of minority, year established, number of employees, employer's identification number, Standard Industrial Classification (SIC) code, description of business, including history, capabilities, major customers, geographic territory covered, annual gross sales or income. **Arrangement:** Classified by service. **Pages (approx.):** 100. **Frequency:** Approximately annual; previous edition June 1987; latest edition May 1988. **Price:** Free. **Former Title(s):** Minority Architectural-Engineering Firms and Construction Supply Distributors in Wisconsin; Wisconsin Minority Business Directory (1981).

★3991★
Directory of Minority Construction Contractors and Subcontractors
San Francisco Redevelopment Agency
939 Ellis St.
San Francisco, CA 94109   Ph: (415)771-8800

Description: Over 1,000 firms in northern California which offer products and services to the construction industry. **Entries include:** Company name, address, phone, license number, name of contact. **Arrangement:** Classified by product or trade. **Pages (approx.):** 115. **Frequency:** Irregular; previous edition 1983; latest edition December 1987. **Editor(s):** Benson Hattem. **Price:** $15.00.

★3992★
Directory of Minority Management Consulting Firms
San Francisco Redevelopment Agency
939 Ellis St.
San Francisco, CA 94109   Ph: (415)771-8800

Description: More than 70 management and tax consultants and appraisers. **Entries include:** Firm name, address, phone, name and title of contact, services, clients. **Arrangement:** Alphabetical. **Pages (approx.):** 10. **Frequency:** Annual. **Editor(s):** Benson I. Hattem, Affirmative Action Officer. **Price:** Free.

★3993★
Directory of Minority Media
San Francisco Redevelopment Agency
770 Golden Gate Ave.   Ph: (415)749-2423
San Francisco, CA 94102-3120   Fax: (415)749-2423

Description: More than 50 radio stations, television stations, and publications oriented to Asian Americans, Blacks, Native Americans, and Hispanic Americans in northern California. **Entries include:** Name of medium, name of contact, address, phone. **Arrangement:** Classified by medium. **Pages (approx.):** 4. **Frequency:** Annual. **Editor(s):** Benson I. Hattem. **Price:** Free.

★3994★
Directory of Minority Public Relations Professionals
Public Relations Society of America
33 Irving Pl., 3rd Fl.
15th and 16th Sts.
New York, NY 10003   Ph: (212)995-2230

Description: About 190 minority individuals in the field of public relations. **Entries include:** Individual name, title, company name, address, phone. **Arrangement:** Geographical. **Pages (approx.):** 15. **Frequency:** Irregular; latest edition 1990. **Price:** $10.00.

★3995★
Directory of Minority Suppliers
Indiana Regional Minority Supplier
  Development Council
300 E. Fall Creek Pkwy., N. Drive, No.
  403
Indianapolis, IN 46205

Description: About 450 firms offering professional, commercial, and industrial products and services. **Entries include:** Firm name, address, phone, name of contact, services, capabilities. **Arrangement:** Alphabetical. **Indexes:** Product/service. **Pages (approx.):** 80. **Frequency:** Annual, October. **Editor(s):** Jeffery L. Donald, Business Development Specialist. **Price:** $25.00, plus $2.00 shipping. **Also Includes:** List of local and national minority assistance agencies.

★3996★
Directory of Minority Truckers
San Francisco Redevelopment Agency
939 Ellis St.
San Francisco, CA 94109   Ph: (415)771-8800

Entries include: Company name, address, phone, license number, name of contact, list of equipment. **Arrangement:** Alphabetical. **Pages (approx.):** 30. **Frequency:** Irregular; previous edition 1981; latest edition 1984; new edition expected late 1989. **Editor(s):** Benson Hattem. **Price:** $3.00.

★3997★
Directory of Operating Small Business Investment Companies
Small Business Administration
1441 L St. NW, Rm. 808
Washington, DC 20416   Ph: (202)653-6672

Description: About 570 operating small business investment companies holding regular licenses and licenses under the section of the Small Business Investment Act covering minority enterprise SBICs. **Entries include:** Company name, address, phone, branch offices, type of ownership, date licensed by SBA, license number, amount of obligation to the Small Business Administration, amount of private capital held, and type of investments made. **Arrangement:** Separate geographical sections for each type of license. **Pages (approx.):** 90. **Frequency:** Semiannual, June and December. **Editor(s):** John R. Wilmeth. **Price:** Free.

★3998★
Directory of Special Programs for Minority Group Members: Career Information Services, Employment Skills Banks, Financial Aid Sources
Garrett Park Press
PO Box 190F
Garrett Park, MD 20896   Ph: (301)946-2553

Description: About 2,000 private and governmental agencies offering financial aid, employment assistance, and career guidance programs for minorities. **Entries include:** Organization or agency name, address, phone, contact name, type of organization, purpose, description of services and activities in the equal opportunity employment area. **Arrangement:** Alphabetical. **Indexes:** Alphabetical, type of program. **Pages (approx.):** 350. **Frequency:** Irregular; latest edition 1990. **Editor(s):** Willis L. Johnson. **Price:** $27.00, payment with order; $30.00, billed.

★3999★
Ebony—100 Most Influential Black Americans Issue
Johnson Publishing Co., Inc.
820 S. Michigan Ave.
Chicago, IL 60605   Ph: (312)332-9200

Entries include: Name, profession, brief career notes. **Frequency:** Annual, May. **Editor(s):** John H. Johnson and Lerone Bennett Jr. **Price:** $2.00.

★4000★
Editor & Publisher International Year Book
Editor & Publisher Co., Inc.
11 W. 19th St., 10th Fl.   Ph: (212)675-4380
New York, NY 10011   Fax: (212)929-1259
Description: Daily and Sunday newspapers in the United States and Canada; weekly newspapers; foreign daily newspapers; special service newspapers; newspaper syndicates; news services; journalism schools; foreign language and Black newspapers in the United States; news, picture, and press services; feature and news syndicates; comic and magazine services; advertising clubs; trade associations; clipping bureaus; house organs; journalism awards; also lists manufacturers of equipment and supplies. **Entries include:** For daily papers–Publication name, address, phone, names of executives and departmental editors (business, financial, book, food, etc.), circulation and advertising data, production information including format of paper and equipment used. Similar but less detailed information for other publications. **Arrangement:** Publications and schools are geographical; most other lists are alphabetical. **Pages (approx.):** 600. **Frequency:** Annual, April. **Editor(s):** Colin Philips. **Price:** $90.00.

★4001★
Educating Tomorrow's Engineers: A Guide to Precollege Minority Engineering Programs
National Action Council for Minorities in Engineering
3 W. 35th St.   Ph: (212)279-2626
New York, NY 10001-2281   Fax: (212)629-5178
Description: More than 100 precollege engineering programs for minority students. **Entries include:** Program name, address, phone, names and titles of key officials, description of activities. **Arrangement:** Geographical. **Pages (approx.):** 146. **Frequency:** Irregular; latest edition 1990. **Editor(s):** Ronni Denes, Vice President of Communications and Public Affairs. **Price:** $12.00. **Also Includes:** Student profiles. **Other Information:** Supersedes "MEPs/USA: The Directory of Precollege and University Minority Engineering Programs."

★4002★
EEO Resource Directory: Technical Assistance Guide for Southern California Personnel Practitioners
Institute of Industrial Relations
1001 Gayley Ave., 2nd Fl.   Ph: (310)825-9191
Los Angeles, CA 90024   Fax: (310)825-3731
Description: About 180 agencies, organizations, subscription and information service companies, sponsors of seminars, and suppliers of audiovisual or printed materials related to equal employment opportunity issues, such as affirmative action, recruitment, sexual harassment, the handicapped, and age discrimination. **Entries include:** Company, organization, or agency name, address, phone, name and title of contact, geographical area served, subsidiary and branch names and locations, description of services or products. **Arrangement:** Classified by subject area. **Pages (approx.):** 65. **Frequency:** Irregular; latest edition 1988. **Editor(s):** Rosalind Schwartz, Director, Management Center, IIR. **Price:** $3.00, plus $1.00 shipping. **Also Includes:** State and federal laws related to equal employment opportunity issues.

★4003★
Ethnic Genealogy: A Research Guide
Greenwood Publishing Group, Inc.
88 Post Rd. W.
PO Box 5007
Westport, CT 06881   Ph: (203)226-3571
Description: Genealogical organizations and societies, and libraries and historical societies with significant collections for research in genealogy of American Indians, Asian Americans, Black Americans, Hispanic Americans, and other ethnic groups. **Frequency:** Published 1983. **Editor(s):** Jessie Carney Smith. **Price:** $55.00; payment must accompany order from individuals.

★4004★
Ethnic Groups in California: A Guide to Organizations and Information Resources
California Institute of Public Affairs
517 19th St.
PO Box 189040   Ph: (916)442-CIPA
Sacramento, CA 95818   Fax: (916)442-2478
Description: Organizations that provide services and information to ethnic groups in California; publishers of related publications. **Entries include:** Organization or publisher name, address, product or service. **Arrangement:** Classified by ethnic group. **Pages (approx.):** 80. **Frequency:** Irregular; previous edition 1981; latest edition 1988. **Price:** $21.50, plus $2.00 shipping.

★4005★
Ethnic Periodicals in Contemporary America: An Annotated Guide
Greenwood Publishing Group, Inc.
88 Post Rd. W.
PO Box 5007   Ph: (203)226-3571
Westport, CT 06881   Fax: (203)222-1502
Description: Approximately 290 U.S. ethnic-interest periodicals. **Pages (approx.):** 256. **Frequency:** Published 1990. **Editor(s):** Sandra Jones Ireland. **Price:** $39.95.

★4006★
Financial Aid for Minorities in...Series on Occupations
Garrett Park Press
PO Box 190F
Garrett Park, MD 20896   Ph: (301)946-2553
Description: In 6 volumes, sources of financial aid for minorities. Volume 1 covers health occupations; volume 2 covers business and law; volume 3 covers education; volume 4 covers engineering and science; volume 5 covers journalism and mass communications; volume 6 covers financial aid for students with any major. **Entries include:** Organization, institution, or agency name, address, type of assistance, amounts available, application deadline and procedures. **Arrangement:** Alphabetical. **Pages (approx.):** 80 per volume. **Frequency:** Irregular; latest edition 1992. **Price:** $4.95 per volume; $25.00 per set; postpaid.

★4007★
Financial Aid Unscrambled: A Guide for Minority Engineering Students
National Action Council for Minorities in Engineering
3 W. 35th St.   Ph: (212)279-2626
New York, NY 10001-2281   Fax: (212)629-5178
Description: Over 80 state financial aid and Guaranteed Student Loan (GSL) offices; over 40 private grants and scholarships; and 10 publications on financial aid for African American, Hispanic, and Native American engineering students. **Entries include:** For state financial aid or GSL offices–Program name, address, phone. For private grants and scholarships–Program name, description, requirements, deadline, sponsor name, address, phone. For publications–Title, publisher name, address, phone. **Arrangement:** Classified by type of agency or publication. **Pages (approx.):** 24. **Frequency:** Biennial, even years. **Editor(s):** Trina V. Brooks. **Price:** $1.00. **Also Includes:** Information on obtaining financial aid. **Other Information:** Also available in a Spanish-language edition titled "Pasos pora Obtener Ayuda Economica: Guia para Estudiantes de Engenieria."

★4008★
Gebbie Press All-in-One Directory
Gebbie Press, Inc.
Box 1000
New Paltz, NY 12561   Ph: (914)255-7560
Description: 1,700 daily newspapers, 8,500 weekly newspapers, 7,000 radio stations, 900 television stations, 250 general-consumer magazines, 430 professional business publications, 2,900 trade magazines, 320 farm publications, list of the Black press and radio, Hispanic press and radio, and a list of news syndicates. **Entries include:** For periodicals–Name, address, phone, frequency, editor, circulation, readership. For newspapers–Name, address, phone, circulation. For radio and television stations–Call letters, address,

phone, network affiliations. **Arrangement:** Classified by type of media. **Pages (approx.):** 510. **Frequency:** Annual, November. **Editor(s):** Amalia Gebbie. **Price:** $78.00, payment with order; $85.00, billed.

★4009★
Gospel Music Association Official Resource Guide
Gospel Music Association
PO Box 23201   Ph: (615)242-0303
Nashville, TN 37202-3201   Fax: (615)254-9755
Description: Gospel musicians, composers, and artists; recording companies, studios, and production companies; booking agencies; publishers; performing rights organizations; television and radio broadcasting stations; book stores, Bible supply stores, and other retailers/managers; publications; ministry organizations. **Entries include:** All listings include name, address; some listings include phone. Broadcasting station listings include contact, program title, format. **Arrangement:** Broadcasting stations are geographical; others are alphabetical. **Pages (approx.):** 160. **Frequency:** Annual, October. **Editor(s):** Bruce Koblish, Executive Director. **Price:** $21.95. **Also Includes:** Sections of the guide titled ''The How To Series,'' ''The Dove Award Recipients,'' and ''Gospel Platinum & Gold List.'' **Former Title(s):** Gospel Music.

★4010★
Grants for Minorities
The Foundation Center   Ph: (212)620-4230
79 5th Ave.   Fax: (212)807-3677
New York, NY 10003-3050   Free: 800-424-9836
Description: Foundations and organizations which have awarded grants in the preceding year for ethnic groups and minority populations, including African-Americans, Hispanics, Asian-Americans, Native Americans, gays and lesbians, and immigrants and refugees. **Entries include:** Foundation name, address, limitations on grants; recipient name and location, grant amount, date authorized, duration and purpose of grant, data source. **Arrangement:** Geographical by state, then alphabetical by foundation name. **Indexes:** Recipient name, foundation's preferred subject areas, geographical location of foundation. **Frequency:** Annual, October. **Editor(s):** Ruth Kovacs. **Price:** $60.00, plus $4.50 shipping; payment must accompany order. **Also Includes:** A concise overview of foundation spending patterns within the specified field. **Other Information:** Part of ''Grant Guides'' series, which supersedes the ''COMSEARCH Printouts'' series.

★4011★
Guide to Multicultural Resources
Praxis Publications, Inc.   Ph: (608)244-5633
2215 Atwood Ave.   Fax: (414)563-7395
Madison, WI 53704   Free: 800-558-2110
Description: Over 4,000 minority and multicultural organizations and associations involved with the Asian, Black, Hispanic, and Native American communities. **Entries include:** Organization name, address, phone, contact names, description of organization, information or publications available, whether willing to network with other groups. **Arrangement:** Classified by racial/minority group. **Indexes:** Alphabetical, subject, geographical. **Pages (approx.):** 500. **Frequency:** Biennial, January of odd years. **Editor(s):** Charles Taylor, Publisher. **Price:** $49.00. **Other Information:** Published jointly with Highsmith Press.

★4012★
Higher Education Opportunities for Minorities and Women: Annotated Selections
U.S. Office of Postsecondary Education
400 Maryland Ave., Rm. 3915
Washington, DC 20202-5151   Ph: (202)708-9180
Description: Programs of public and private organizations and state and federal government agencies that offer loans, scholarships, and fellowship opportunities for women and minorities. **Entries include:** Organization name, address, brief description of program. **Arrangement:** Classified by subject. **Pages (approx.):** 143. **Frequency:** Latest edition 1991. **Editor(s):** William C. Young and Edward L. Hicks. **Price:** $5.00. **Send orders to:** Superintendent of Documents, U.S. Government Printing Office, Washington, DC 20402 (202-783-3238). **Former Title(s):** Selected List of Postsecondary Education Opportunities for Minorities and Women.

★4013★
Historic Black Landmarks: A Traveler's Guide
Visible Ink Press
Gale Research Inc.   Ph: (313)961-2242
835 Penobscot Bldg.   Fax: (313)961-6083
Detroit, MI 48226-4094   Free: 800-776-6265
Description: Sites significant in African-American history and culture in the U.S. and Ontario. **Entries include:** Site name, location, mailing address, description of site and its significance, season, days and hours of operation, handicap access, exhibits and facilities, special programs. **Arrangement:** Geographical. **Indexes:** Alphabetical. **Pages (approx.):** 408. **Frequency:** Published spring 1991. **Price:** $17.95. **Also Includes:** Timeline of events related to sites described in the book; essay on the history of Black America; bibliography.

★4014★
Historic Landmarks of Black America
Gale Research Inc.   Ph: (313)961-2242
835 Penobscot Bldg.   Fax: (313)961-6083
Detroit, MI 48226-4094   Free: 800-877-GALE
Description: 300 sites significant in African-American history. **Entries include:** Name, location, mailing address, phone, season, days and hours of operation, discussion of site and its significance, admission fees, accessibility to handicapped, exhibits and facilities, special programs. **Arrangement:** Geographical by region, then by state. **Pages (approx.):** 372. **Frequency:** Published May 1991. **Price:** $35.00.

★4015★
How and Where to Research Your Ethnic-American Cultural Heritage
Robert D. Reed
PO Box 2008   Ph: (408)866-6303
Saratoga, CA 95070   Fax: (408)866-0825
Description: Historical societies, cultural institutes, libraries, archives, publishers, and other sources for genealogical research into German, Russian, Native American, Polish, Black, Japanese, Jewish, Irish, Mexican, Italian, Chinese, and Scandinavian backgrounds; 12 separate volumes cover each ethnic group. **Entries include:** Institution name, address, phone. **Pages (approx.):** 30. **Frequency:** Most volumes first published 1979; latest edition January 1993. **Editor(s):** Robert D. Reed. **Price:** $4.50, plus $1.50 shipping per volume. **Also Includes:** Bibliographies.

★4016★
HRI Reporter—Master List Issue
Human Rights Internet
c/o Human Rights Centre
University of Ottawa
57 Louis Pasteur   Ph: (613)564-3492
Ottawa, ON, Canada K1N 6N5   Fax: (613)564-4054
Description: List of nongovernmental organizations, publishers, researchers, and producers of educational material concerned with human rights; listing of serial publications on human rights, including information on publisher, frequency, and cost. **Entries include:** Organization name, address, publications. **Arrangement:** Alphabetical. **Frequency:** Reported as annual; latest edition 1990-91; new edition expected 1993. **Editor(s):** Laurie S. Wiseberg. **Price:** $20.00; or included in subscription, $80.00 per year to institutions; $60.00 per year to individuals (ISSN 0275-049X).

★4017★
Illinois Minority and Female Business Enterprise Directory
Minority and Female Business Enterprise Bureau
Illinois Department of Central Management Services
801 Stratton Bldg., North End
Springfield, IL 62706   Ph: (217)785-4320
Description: About 900 firms offering professional, commercial, and industrial products and services. **Entries include:** Firm name, address, phone, name and title of owner or chief executive, products or services, year established. **Arrangement:** Alphabetical. **Pages (approx.):** 810. **Frequency:** Irregular; latest edition May 1988. **Price:**

Restricted circulation. **Former Title(s):** Illinois Minority Vendors Directory.

★4018★
International Business in South Africa
Investor Responsibility Research Center,
    Inc.
1755 Massachusetts Ave. NW, Ste. 600   Ph: (202)234-7500
Washington, DC 20036   Fax: (202)332-8570
Description: Non-U.S. companies with business links to South Africa. **Entries include:** Name and address of parent company, line of business, names and locations of South African subsidiaries, number of employees by race, policies. **Arrangement:** Alphabetical by parent company. **Indexes:** Subsidiary company name, company by number of employees, industry sector, company headquarters location. **Pages (approx.):** 354. **Frequency:** Annual, November. **Price:** $250.00 (ISSN 1048-5880). **Also Includes:** Lists of companies that do business in South Africa but do not own any assets there; companies that have recently left South Africa; companies with "non equity" links to South Africa; an appendix on international sanctions against South Africa. **Other Information:** Companies based in the United States are listed in "U.S. Business in South Africa".

★4019★
Jazz Referral Service
Arts Midwest
528 Hennepin Ave., Ste. 310   Ph: (612)341-0755
Minneapolis, MN 55403   Fax: (612)341-0902
Description: Over 400 jazz musicians and ensembles, support organizations and presenters, educators, radio and television stations that program jazz, jazz writers and publications, and record stores and distributors in Illinois, Indiana, Iowa, Michigan, Minnesota, North Dakota, Ohio, South Dakota, and Wisconsin. **Entries include:** Company, organization, or personal name, address, phone; name and title of contact, biographical data, description of services or products. **Arrangement:** Geographical. **Pages (approx.):** 500. **Editor(s):** Linda Carlson, Program Associate. **Price:** $50.00 (inside Midwest region); $65.00 (outside Midwest region).

★4020★
Kansas Minority-Owned & Women-Owned Directory
Office of Minority Business
Kansas Department of Commerce &
    Housing
400 W. 8th St., 5th Fl.   Ph: (913)296-3805
Topeka, KS 66603-3957   Fax: (913)296-5055
Description: Approximately 1,000 minority and women-owned businesses and professional firms in Kansas. **Entries include:** Company name, address, phone, name of principal executive, code for number of employees, line of business, product/service provided, code indicating ethnic group. **Arrangement:** Classified by product/service. **Indexes:** Geographical, alphabetical. **Pages (approx.):** 75. **Frequency:** Annual, January. **Editor(s):** Antonio Augusto. **Price:** Free. **Other Information:** Former name of publishers, Kansas Department of Economic Development and Kansas Department of Commerce. **Former Title(s):** Directory of Kansas Minority Businesses; Directory of Minority-Owned & Women-Owned Businesses; Kansas Minority Business Directory (1990).

★4021★
Kentucky Directory of Black Elected Officials
Kentucky Commission on Human Rights
701 W. Muhammad Ali Blvd.
Box 69   Ph: (502)588-4024
Louisville, KY 40201   Free: 800-292-5566
Description: About 75 Blacks serving in elective positions in Kentucky. **Entries include:** Name, party affiliation, personal and career data, photograph. **Arrangement:** Classified by office held. **Pages (approx.):** 40. **Frequency:** Irregular; previous edition September 1982; latest edition June 1988; new edition expected 1990. **Editor(s):** Andrea Brooks, Research Assistant. **Price:** Free.

★4022★
Latin America and Caribbean: A Directory of
    Resources
Third World Resources   Ph: (510)835-4692
464 19th St.   Fax: (510)835-3012
Oakland, CA 94612   Free: 800-735-3741
Description: Organizations or companies that publish, compile, or distribute publications, audiovisual productions, and other information resources about Latin America and the Caribbean; international organizations with interests in Latin America and the Caribbean. **Entries include:** Publisher, supplier, or organization name, address, phone; description of publication, production, or purpose; geographical area covered; price; distributor name, branch office or subsidiaries. **Arrangement:** Organization or resource. **Indexes:** Organization name, individual name, title, geographical, subject. **Pages (approx.):** 160. **Frequency:** Published 1986. **Editor(s):** Tom Fenton and Mary Heffron. **Price:** $12.95, plus $2.00 shipping. **Other Information:** Formerly published by Orbis Books. Part of a 10 volume series (updated in a quarterly magazine titled "Third World Resources"), each volume covering a single region or issue.

★4023★
List of 8(a) Approved Contractors
Seattle Regional Office
Small Business Administration
2615 4th Ave., Rm. 440   Ph: (206)553-2872
Seattle, WA 98121   Fax: (206)553-4155
Description: More than 150 minority contractors offering industrial and commercial services and products in the Region Ten districts of Anchorage, Alaska; Boise, Idaho; Portland, Oregon; and Seattle and Spokane, Washington. **Entries include:** Company name, address, phone, name of contact, line of business. **Arrangement:** Geographical. **Pages (approx.):** 45. **Frequency:** Semiannual, January and June. **Editor(s):** Carol Colpitts. **Price:** Free.

★4024★
List of Minority Firms in North & South Carolina
Carolinas Minority Supplier Development
    Councils
Hatteras Bldg., Ste. 10640
5624 Executive Center Dr., Ste. 106   Ph: (704)536-2884
Charlotte, NC 28212   Fax: (704)536-8856
Description: About 430 minority-owned firms offering professional, commercial, and industrial products and services. **Entries include:** Firm name, address, phone, name and title of owner or chief executive, products or services, year established. **Arrangement:** Classified by affiliate council name. **Indexes:** Product/service, SIC code. **Pages (approx.):** 75. **Frequency:** Annual. **Editor(s):** Katrina D. Crowder, Administrative Assistant. **Price:** $50.00. **Former Title(s):** Minority Business Enterprise (MBE) Directory (1992).

★4025★
List of 96 Ethnic and Religious Genealogical and
    Historical Societies and Archives
Summit Publications
Box 222
Munroe Falls, OH 44262
Frequency: Irregular; latest edition March 1989. **Editor(s):** J. Konrad. **Price:** $4.00, postpaid.

★4026★
Maryland/DC Minority Supplier Development Council
    Minority Business Directory
Maryland/DC Minority Supplier
    Development Council
9150-5B Rumsey Rd.
PO Box 2069   Ph: (410)997-7599
Columbia, MD 21045   Fax: (410)997-2040
Description: Approximately 500 businesses in the District of Columbia and Maryland. **Entries include:** Company name, address, phone, name and title of contact, subsidiary and branch names and locations, description of products and services. **Arrangement:** Classified by product or service. **Indexes:** Product/service, company name, subject. **Pages (approx.):** 100. **Frequency:** Annual, June.

Editor(s): Charles R. Owens, Executive Director. Price: Available to members only.

★4027★
Michigan Ethnic Organizations Directory
Michigan Ethnic Heritage Center
Rackham Bldg., Ste. 120
Detroit, MI 48202
Ph: (313)832-7400
Fax: (313)831-5633
Description: About 2,000 ethnic organizations and institutions in Michigan. **Entries include:** Organization name, address, phone, name and title of contact, description of activities and purpose. **Arrangement:** Classified by ethnic group. **Indexes:** Organization name. **Pages (approx.):** 100. **Frequency:** Irregular; latest edition October 1991; new edition expected 1994. **Editor(s):** O. Feinstein. **Price:** $15.00. **Other Information:** Supersedes "Peoples of Michigan: A Two Volume Guide to Ethnic Michigan."

★4028★
Minorities and Women: A List of Major Organizations in Librarianship
American Library Association (ALA)
50 E. Huron St.
Chicago, IL 60611
Ph: (312)280-4277
Fax: (312)280-3256
Free: 800-545-2433
Description: About 10 minority and women librarian organizations. **Entries include:** Organization name, address, phone, names and titles of key personnel, publications. **Arrangement:** Classified by interest group. **Frequency:** Annual, summer. **Price:** Free.

★4029★
Minority and Women Business Directory
Massachusetts Office of Minority and
   Women Business Assistance
100 Cambridge St., Rm. 1300
Boston, MA 02202
Ph: (617)727-8692
Description: About 1,000 minority- and women-owned firms offering professional, commercial, and industrial products and services; includes contractors and national firms operating in Massachusetts. **Entries include:** Firm name, address, phone, name of owner or chief executive, line of business, whether minority- or woman-owned. **Arrangement:** Alphabetical. **Indexes:** Product/service. **Pages (approx.):** 125. **Frequency:** Annual, October; quarterly supplements. **Price:** $5.00; free to federal and state purchasing agents. **Send orders to:** Massachusetts State Book Store, Room 116, Boston, MA 02133. **Former Title(s):** Minority Business Directory.

★4030★
Minority & Women Business Directory
Minority and Women Business
   Development
Indiana Department of Commerce
One N. Capitol, Ste. 501
Indianapolis, IN 46204
Ph: (317)232-8820
Description: About 300 firms offering professional, commercial, industrial, and consumer products and services. **Entries include:** Company name, address, phone, name of contact or owner, services or products, area covered. **Arrangement:** Classified by service or line of business, then geographical. **Pages (approx.):** 70. **Frequency:** Monthly. **Editor(s):** Andrew Thomas, Jr., Construction Manager Engineer. **Price:** Free. **Other Information:** Publisher was formerly named Office of Minority Business Enterprise. **Former Title(s):** Minority Purchasing Guide; Indiana Minority Business Directory.

★4031★
Minority Business Development Agency—Directory of Regional & District Offices and Funded Organizations
U.S. Minority Business Development
   Agency
Washington, DC 20230
Ph: (202)377-2414
Description: About 10 regional and district offices of the Minority Business Development Agency; approximately 110 agency-funded minority business development centers which offer business services for a nominal fee to current and prospective minority business operators. **Entries include:** For regional offices–Office name, address, phone, states served, director name. For district offices–Office address and phone, names of district officers. For development centers–Center name, address, phone, project director name. **Arrangement:** Separate geographical lists for regional offices, district offices, and development centers. **Pages (approx.):** 15. **Price:** Free.

★4032★
Minority Business Directory
Nevada Economic Development
   Commission
3770 Howard Hughes Pkwy.
Las Vegas, NV 89109
Ph: (702)486-7282
Description: About 500 firms offering professional, commercial, and industrial products and services. **Entries include:** Firm name, address, phone; name and title of owner, chief executive, or contact; line of business, corporate structure, product or service, number of employees, year established. **Arrangement:** Alphabetical. **Indexes:** Product/service. **Pages (approx.):** 75. **Frequency:** Biennial, May. **Editor(s):** Marilyn D. Cherry. **Price:** Free.

★4033★
Minority Business Information System (MBISYS)
National Minority Supplier Development
   Council (NMSDC)
15 W. 39th St., 9th Fl.
New York, NY 10018
Ph: (212)944-2430
Description: Approximately 15,000 companies that are certified by the NMSDC as minority owned. **Entries include:** Company name, address, phone, parent company name, Standard Industrial Classification (SIC) code, description of products and services, year founded, ownership structure, number of employees; name, title, ethnicity, and sex of owners; major customers, annual sales, geographical area served, most recent certification date and accrediting council. **Frequency:** Updated as needed. **Editor(s):** Terri Myers. **Other Information:** Previously cited as "National Minority Purchasing Council Data Bank–Minority Vendor Information Service" and "Supplier Development Council." **Former Title(s):** Minority Business Enterprise Network (MBENET) (1988).

★4034★
Minority CPAs
San Francisco Redevelopment Agency
939 Ellis St.
San Francisco, CA 94109
Ph: (415)771-8800
Fax: (415)771-3005
Description: Over 90 Spanish-speaking, Asian, Black or native American certified public accounting (CPA) firms in Northern California; minority CPA associations. **Entries include:** For firms - Name, address, phone. For associations - Name, address, phone, name of president. **Arrangement:** Alphabetical. **Pages (approx.):** 5. **Frequency:** Irregular; latest edition November 1988. **Price:** Free.

★4035★
Minority Employment Report
Federal Communications Commission
1919 M St. NW
Washington, DC 20554
Ph: (202)632-7000
Description: Television and radio stations with ten or more full-time employees. **Entries include:** Station name (call letters or channel), city and state, class of station; total, female, and minority full-time employment in higher and lower pay occupations, and part-time employment for previous five years. **Arrangement:** By state and community. **Pages (approx.):** 1,480. **Frequency:** Annual, December. **Price:** Free.

★4036★
Minority Engravers, Graphic Artists and Printers
San Francisco Redevelopment Agency
939 Ellis St.
San Francisco, CA 94109
Ph: (415)771-8800
Fax: (415)771-3005
Description: About 50 minority firms in Northern California. **Entries include:** Firm name, address, phone, contact name. **Arrangement:** Alphabetical. **Price:** Free.

★4037★
Minority Law Firms
San Francisco Redevelopment Agency
939 Ellis St.   Ph: (415)771-8800
San Francisco, CA 94109   Fax: (415)771-3005
Description: Over 200 Spanish-speaking, Asian, Black, or native American law firms and lawyers in Northern California; minority bar associations. **Entries include:** For firms - Name, address, phone. For associations - Name, address, phone, name of president. **Arrangement:** Alphabetical. **Price:** Free.

★4038★
Minority Organizations: A National Directory
Garrett Park Press
PO Box 190F
Garrett Park, MD 20896   Ph: (301)946-2553
Description: Over 9,700 groups composed of or intended to serve members of minority groups, including Alaska Natives, American Indians, Blacks, Hispanics, and Asian Americans. **Entries include:** Organization name, address, description of activities, purpose, publications, etc. **Arrangement:** Alphabetical. **Indexes:** Organization name, geographical, program, defunct organization. **Pages (approx.):** 514. **Frequency:** Irregular; previous edition 1987; latest edition 1992. **Editor(s):** Robert Calvert, Jr. **Price:** $50.00.

★4039★
Minority Student Guide to American Colleges
Paoli Publishing, Inc.
1708 E. Lancaster Ave., Ste. 287   Ph: (215)640-9889
Paoli, PA 19301   Fax: (215)296-9266
Description: In three separate sections, colleges, military education programs, and financial aid information for minority students. **Entries include:** Institution name, contact name, address, phone, description. **Arrangement:** Alphabetical. **Pages (approx.):** 89. **Frequency:** Annual. **Editor(s):** J. William Wrigley. **Price:** $2.75. **Also Includes:** In Section 1, brief tutorials covering a variety of education-related topics. In Section 3, display advertisements from several schools.

★4040★
Minority Student Opportunities in United States Medical Schools
Association of American Medical Colleges
  (AAMC)
2450 N St. NW   Ph: (202)828-0400
Washington, DC 20037-1126   Fax: (202)828-1125
Description: Programs for minority group students at nearly 130 medical schools. **Entries include:** Name of school, name of parent institution, if applicable, address, phone, name of contact; descriptions of recruitment, admissions, financial aid, and academic assistance programs for the minority student; statistical table on minority admissions and enrollment. **Arrangement:** Geographical. **Indexes:** School name, geographical. **Pages (approx.):** 325. **Frequency:** Biennial, August of even years. **Editor(s):** Mary T. Cureton-Russell, Staff Associate. **Price:** $7.50, plus $2.50 shipping; payment must accompany order. **Also Includes:** List of schools offering summer programs.

★4041★
Minority Supplier Directory
Rio Grande Minority Purchasing Council
5000 Marble NE, Ste. 317
Albuquerque, NM 87110   Ph: (505)265-7677
Description: Approximately 460 firms offering professional, commercial, and industrial products and services. **Entries include:** Company name, address, phone, name of contact, capability number and description of product, number of employees, date established. **Arrangement:** Classified by type of product. **Indexes:** Product/service. **Pages (approx.):** 70. **Frequency:** Irregular; latest edition summer 1989. **Editor(s):** C. M. Davis, Associate Director. **Price:** $25.00, including updates, to New Mexico residents; $35.00 to others. **Other Information:** Former name of publisher, New Mexico Minority Supplier Development Council. **Former Title(s):** New Mexico Minority Suppliers Directory.

★4042★
Minority Supplier Directory
Michigan Minority Business Development
  Council
2990 W. Grand Blvd., Ste. 408
Detroit, MI 48202   Ph: (313)873-3200
Description: Firms offering professional, commercial, and industrial products and services. **Entries include:** Firm name, address, phone, name and title of owner or chief executive, products or services, year established, etc. **Arrangement:** Alphabetical. **Indexes:** Product/service. **Pages (approx.):** 100. **Frequency:** Quarterly. **Price:** Available to members only.

★4043★
Minority Supplier Directory
New England Minority Purchasing Council
4 Copley Pl.
Box 145
Boston, MA 02116-6504   Ph: (617)578-8900
Description: Over 400 firms offering professional, commercial, and industrial products and services in Maine, Massachusetts, New Hampshire, Rhode Island, and Vermont. **Entries include:** Firm name, address, phone, name and title of contact, number of employees, geographical area served, product or service, year established, Standard Industrial Classification (SIC) code. **Arrangement:** Classified by product/service. **Indexes:** Alphabetical. **Pages (approx.):** 126. **Frequency:** Annual, winter. **Editor(s):** May Ling Tong, Executive Director. **Price:** $45.00, postpaid. **Former Title(s):** Minority Vendor Directory (1991).

★4044★
NACME Students' Guide to Engineering Schools
National Action Council for Minorities in
  Education (NACME)
3 W. 35th St.   Ph: (212)279-2626
New York, NY 10001   Fax: (212)629-5178
Description: Engineering colleges and universities in the United States with at least one curriculum accredited by the Accreditation Board for Engineering and Technology. **Entries include:** Institution name, location, financial data, outline of admission dates and requirements, minority enrollment, engineering curricula offered, description of program, and support activities. **Arrangement:** Alphabetical. **Pages (approx.):** 45. **Frequency:** Irregular; latest edition 1988, out of print. **Price:** $10.00 per 30 copies; $25.00 per 100.

★4045★
National Association of College Deans, Registrars and Admissions Officers—Directory
National Association of College Deans,
  Registrars and Admissions Officers
917 Dorsett Ave.
Albany, GA 31701   Ph: (912)435-4945
Description: About 325 member deans, registrars, and admissions officers at nearly 90 predominantly Black schools. **Entries include:** Institution name, address, phone, names and titles of key personnel, enrollment, whether a public or private institution. **Arrangement:** Alphabetical. **Pages (approx.):** 15. **Frequency:** Annual, February. **Editor(s):** Helen M. Mayes, Executive Secretary. **Price:** $5.00.

★4046★
National Association of Investment Companies— Membership Directory
National Association of Investment
  Companies
111 14th St. NW, Ste. 700   Ph: (202)289-4336
Washington, DC 20005   Fax: (202)289-4329
Description: About 130 venture capital firms for minority small businesses; licensed by the Small Business Administration. **Entries include:** Company name, address, phone, president; investment policy, industry preference, preferred limit of loans and investments. **Arrangement:** Geographical. **Pages (approx.):** 23. **Frequency:** Annual, June. **Editor(s):** Angela Johnson, Publications Director. **Price:** $5.00, postpaid. **Other Information:** Association formerly named American Association of Minority Enterprise Small Business Investment Companies.

★4047★
National Bankers Association—Roster of Minority Banking Institutions
National Bankers Association
1802 T St. NW
Washington, DC 20009
Ph: (202)588-5432
Fax: (202)588-5443
Description: About 140 banks owned or controlled by minority group persons or women. **Entries include:** Bank name, address, phone, name of one executive. **Arrangement:** Geographical. **Pages (approx.):** 60. **Frequency:** Annual, October. **Editor(s):** Nathaniel W. Thomas. **Price:** $5.00.

★4048★
National Black Health Leadership Directory
NRW Associates
1315 Hamlin St. NE
Washington, DC 20017
Ph: (202)635-4804
Description: Approximately 500 Black health professionals serving in leadership roles in private and public sector organizations, including the Department of Health and Human Services, public health departments, hospitals and hospital systems, associations, agencies, educational institutions, health maintenance organizations, long-term health care administration, community and family care centers, health policy, planning, and research. **Entries include:** Name, title, organization, address, phone, fax. **Arrangement:** Classified by by organizational setting. **Indexes:** Personal name, geographical. **Pages (approx.):** 212. **Frequency:** Annual, January. **Editor(s):** Nathaniel Wesley, Jr., Publisher. **Price:** $65.00.

★4049★
National Black Talent Directory
Shooting Gallery Company
6223 Sunset Blvd.
Hollywood, CA 90028
Ph: (213)466-0570
Description: More than 3,000 Black screen actors, athletes, singers, models, commentators, and those involved in production and promotion in the entertainment industry. **Entries include:** Personal name, name and phone of contact, professional society memberships. **Arrangement:** Classified by typical role or line of business, then alphabetical. **Pages (approx.):** 500. **Frequency:** Annual. **Editor(s):** J. J. Jones, Publisher. **Price:** $85.00. **Other Information:** Publisher also cited as The National Black Talent Directory, Inc.

★4050★
National Directory of Minority-Owned Business Firms
Business Research Services, Inc.
4201 Connecticut Ave. NW, Ste. 610
Washington, DC 20008
Ph: (202)364-6473
Fax: (202)686-3228
Free: 800-325-8720
Description: Over 40,000 minority-owned businesses. **Entries include:** Company name, address, phone, name and title of contact, minority group, certification status, date founded, number of employees, description of products or services, sales volume, government contracting experience, references. **Arrangement:** Standard Industrial Classification (SIC) code, geographical. **Indexes:** Alphabetical **Pages (approx.):** 1,500. **Frequency:** Biennial, even years. **Editor(s):** Tom Johnson. **Price:** $245.00, plus $5.00 shipping (ISSN 0886-3881). **Other Information:** Also available from Gale Research Inc., 835 Penobscot Bldg., Detroit, MI 48226 (800-887-GALE). This and "National Directory of Woman-Owned Business Firms" were formerly combined in "National Directory of Minority and Women-Owned Business Firms."

★4051★
National Insurance Association—Member Roster
National Insurance Association
PO Box 53230
Chicago, IL 60653-0230
Ph: (312)924-3308
Fax: (312)285-0064
Description: About 18 insurance companies owned or controlled by Blacks. **Entries include:** Company name, address, phone, date founded, states in which licensed, officers. **Arrangement:** Alphabetical. **Pages (approx.):** 10. **Frequency:** Annual, June. **Editor(s):** Josephine King, President. **Price:** Available to members only.

★4052★
National Minority Chamber Directory
National Association of Black and Minority Chambers of Commerce
c/o Oscar J Coffey Jr.
117 Broadway
Oakland, CA 94607-3715
Description: About 100 affiliated minority chambers of commerce. **Frequency:** Annual.

★4053★
Nationwide Black Radio Directory
CDE
PO Box 310551
Atlanta, GA 30331
Description: About 500 Black-owned radio stations, broadcasting firms, radio stations with Black programming, Black college radio stations, syndicated radio shows, music organizations, Black music publications, and other music and broadcasting companies with strong Black influence or ownership. **Entries include:** Company name, address, phone. **Arrangement:** Classified by line of business. **Pages (approx.):** 35. **Frequency:** Annual, January. **Editor(s):** Charles Edwards, Publisher. **Price:** $50.00, plus $2.50 shipping.

★4054★
The Negro Almanac: A Reference Work on the African American
Gale Research Inc.
835 Penobscot Bldg.
Detroit, MI 48226-4094
Ph: (313)961-2242
Fax: (313)961-6083
Free: 800-877-GALE
Description: Lists of civil rights organizations and black power advocates; African Americans in law, politics; highly capitalized black companies; predominantly black colleges and universities in the U.S.; blacks in the military; outstanding black athletes, literary figures, artists, scientific pioneers, astronauts, entertainers, publishers, and journalists, etc. **Entries include:** Contact information, biography where applicable. **Arrangement:** Chapters by major subjects. **Indexes:** Name. **Pages (approx.):** 1,625. **Frequency:** Latest edition December 1989; new edition expected November 1993; expected to be triennial thereafter. **Editor(s):** Kenneth Estell. **Price:** $110.00 (1989 edition); $120.00 (1993 edition). **Other Information:** Principal content of publication is an all-in-one resource to significant dates, movements, legislation, and people in African American history and culture in America. Title of 1993 edition will be "The African-American Almanac."

★4055★
NUCEA Directory of Black Professionals in Continuing Higher Education
National University Continuing Education Association (NUCEA)
1 Dupont Circle, NW, Ste. 615
Washington, DC 20036
Ph: (202)659-3130
Fax: (202)785-0374
Description: Black continuing higher education professionals employed in NUCEA institutions. **Entries include:** Name, address, phone. **Arrangement:** Alphabetical. **Pages (approx.):** 12. **Frequency:** Annual, April. **Price:** $10.00.

★4056★
Ohio Minority Business Directory
Minority Business Development Division
Ohio Department of Development
Box 1001
Columbus, OH 43266
Ph: (614)466-5700
Free: 800-848-1300
Description: More than 5,500 minority firms in Ohio offering professional, commercial, construction, industrial, and consumer products and services. **Entries include:** Company name, address, phone, name and ethnic origin of owner, state certification, geographical area served, product or service codes. **Arrangement:** Classified by product or service, then geographical. **Indexes:** Product/service. **Pages (approx.):** 1,450. **Frequency:** Irregular; latest edition December 1988; new edition expected February 1990. **Editor(s):** Deborah Archie. **Price:** $30.00. **Other Information:** Also cited as "Ohio Minority Business Guide".

★4057★
Refugee and Immigrant Resource Directory
Denali Press
PO Box 021535   Ph: (907)586-6014
Juneau, AK 99802   Fax: (907)463-6780

Description: About 2,000 organizations offering assistance to refugees and immigrants. **Entries include:** Organization name and address, phone, fax, number of employees, geographical area served, financial data, name and title of contact, hours of operation, description of services, publications, U.S. Board of Immigration Appeals recognition, date of establishment, statement of purpose, and coded list of activities. **Arrangement:** Alphabetical. **Indexes:** Product/service, name, religion, population of clientele. **Pages (approx.):** 350. **Frequency:** Approximately triennial; latest edition January 1990; new edition expected November 1993. **Editor(s):** Alan Edward Schorr. **Price:** $37.50, plus $2.50 shipping (current edition); $47.50 (1993 edition). **Also Includes:** List of U.S. government offices concerned with refugees and immigrants; essay on U.S. immigration and refugee policy by the Refugee Policy Group; chronologies, texts of documents, and statistical charts/tables. **Former Title(s):** Directory of Services for Refugees and Immigrants, (1987).

★4058★
Refugee Resettlement Program—Annual Report to the Congress
Office of Refugee Resettlement
Administration for Children and Families
370 L'Enfant Promenade, SW   Ph: (202)401-9253
Washington, DC 20447   Fax: (202)401-4683

Description: Lists of state refugee coordinators. **Entries include:** Coordinator name, address, phone. **Arrangement:** Geographical. **Frequency:** Annual, August. **Editor(s):** Loren W. Bussert. **Price:** Free. **Other Information:** Principal content includes a report on the activities of the Refugee Resettlement Program, including federal, state, and private refugee programs in placement, education, job training, health, and social services; and a list of grants awarded by the Refugee Health Program of the Centers for Disease Control showing awardee name and amount of grant. Administration formerly known as U.S. Family Support Administration (1992).

★4059★
Regional Directory of Minority & Woman-Owned Business Firms
Business Research Services, Inc.   Ph: (202)364-6473
4201 Connecticut Ave. NW, Ste. 610   Fax: (202)686-3228
Washington, DC 20008   Free: 800-325-8720

Description: Published in 3 regional volumes: Eastern, with 25,000 listings; Central, with 23,000 listings; and Western, with 21,000 listings. Based on "National Directory of Minority-Owned Business Firms" and "National Directory of Woman-Owned Business Firms". **Entries include:** Company name, address, phone, name and title of contact, minority group, certification status, date founded, number of employees, description of products or services, sales volume, government contracting experience, references. **Arrangement:** Alphabetical; Standard Industrial Classification (SIC) code, geographical. **Pages (approx.):** Eastern, 600; Central, 560; Western, 500. **Frequency:** Biennial, even years. **Price:** $195.00 each, plus $5.00 shipping. **Other Information:** Also available from Gale Research Inc., 835 Penobscot Bldg., Detroit, MI 48226 (800-877-GALE).

★4060★
Roster of Minority Financial Institutions
U.S. Department of the Treasury
401 14th St. SW
Washington, DC 20227   Ph: (202)874-6799

Description: About 190 commercial, minority-owned and controlled financial institutions participating in the Department of the Treasury's Minority Bank Deposit Program. **Entries include:** Name of institution, name and title of chief officer, address, phone. **Arrangement:** Geographical. **Frequency:** Biennial. **Editor(s):** Joann Hassell. **Price:** Free.

★4061★
Society of Newspaper Design—Internship Project
Society of Newspaper Design
The Newspaper Center
Box 17290 Dulles International Airport   Ph: (703)620-1083
Washington, DC 20041   Fax: (703)620-4557

Description: About 75 organizations offering 150 internships in the graphic arts and design fields, including paid and minority internships; limited international coverage. **Entries include:** Organization name, address, phone, name and title of contact. **Arrangement:** Geographical. **Pages (approx.):** 15. **Frequency:** Annual, fall. **Price:** Free.

★4062★
Standard Rate & Data Service—Newspaper Rates & Data
Standard Rate & Data Service   Ph: (708)441-2235
3004 Glenview Rd.   Fax: (708)441-2400
Wilmette, IL 60091   Free: 800-323-4588

Description: More than 1,800 newspapers and newspaper groups, including newspaper-distributed magazines, comics, religious newspapers, Black newspapers, and specialized newspapers. **Entries include:** Publication name, address, phone, names and titles of key personnel, advertising rates, special features, contract and copy regulations, mechanical requirements, and circulation. Information on classified advertising for each publication in separate section. **Arrangement:** Geographical. **Pages (approx.):** 775. **Frequency:** Monthly. **Editor(s):** Jodi Miller. **Price:** $218.00 per issue; $485.00 per year. **Also Includes:** Market and census data. **Other Information:** "Circulation" supersedes "Newspaper Circulation Analysis."

★4063★
Student National Dental Association—Directory
Student National Dental Association
c/o Dr. Robert Knight
Howard University School of Dentistry
600 W St., NW
Washington, DC 20059   Ph: (202)806-0301

Description: About 1,000 minority dental students. **Entries include:** Name, address, phone, minority classification. **Arrangement:** Alphabetical. **Pages (approx.):** 50. **Frequency:** Annual. **Price:** Available to members only. **Other Information:** Affiliated with the National Dental Association.

★4064★
Talent Roster of Outstanding Minority Transfer Students from Two-Year Colleges
The College
45 Columbus Ave.
New York, NY 10023-6992   Ph: (212)713-8000

Description: 5,000 minority graduates of two-year colleges selected by their colleges on the basis of grade point average. **Entries include:** Name, address, grade point average, intended major. **Arrangement:** Geographical, then by name of college presently attending. **Pages (approx.):** 200. **Frequency:** Annual, fall. **Price:** Free. **Other Information:** Former name of publisher, "College Entrance Examination Board". **Former Title(s):** "Talent Roster of Outstanding Minority Community College Graduates".

★4065★
Try Us: National Minority Business Directory
Try Us Resources, Inc.   Ph: (612)781-6819
2105 Central Ave. NE   Fax: (612)781-0109
Minneapolis, MN 55418   Free: 800-627-4347

Description: Over 6,000 minority-owned companies capable of supplying their goods and services on national or regional levels. **Entries include:** Company name, address, phone, name of principal executive, number of employees, date established, trade and brand names, financial keys, products or services, names of three customers, certification status, minority identification, gross sales. **Arrangement:** Classified by product or service, then geographical and alphabetical. **Indexes:** Company, product/service. **Pages (approx.):** 500. **Frequency:** Annual, January. **Editor(s):** Liz Kahnk, Executive Director. **Price:** $45.00. **Other Information:** Former name of publisher National Minority Business Directories.

★4066★
Venture Capital Directory
Forum Publishing Co.
383 E. Main St.
Centerport, NY 11721   Ph: (516)754-5000
Description: Over 500 members of the Small Business Administration and the Small Business Investment Company that provide funding for small and minority businesses. **Entries include:** Company name, address, phone, names and titles of key personnel, geographical area served, financial data, branch office or subsidiary names, description of services and projects. **Arrangement:** Alphabetical. **Pages (approx.):** 50. **Frequency:** Annual, February. **Editor(s):** Raymond Lawrence. **Price:** $12.95.

★4067★
West Virginia Minority Business Directory
West Virginia Small Business Development
    Center
1115 Virginia St. E.   Ph: (304)558-2960
Charleston, WV 25301   Fax: (304)558-0127
Description: Over 150 firms offering professional, commercial, and industrial products and services; coverage is not limited to West Virginia. **Entries include:** Firm name, address, phone, name and title of owner or chief executive, product or service, minority ownership classification. **Arrangement:** Alphabetical. **Indexes:** Product/service. **Pages (approx.):** 50. **Frequency:** Updated continuously, printed as requested. **Editor(s):** Juanita D. Graves. **Price:** Free.

★4068★
Who's Who among Black Americans
Gale Research Inc.   Ph: (313)961-2242
835 Penobscot Bldg.   Fax: (313)961-6083
Detroit, MI 48226-4094   Free: 800-877-GALE
Description: Over 20,000 African-American leaders in government, business, education, religion, communications, civic affairs, the arts, law, medicine, science, sports, and entertainment. **Entries include:** Name, home and/or business address and phone (at listees' discretion), education, career, and personal data; organizational affiliations; honors, awards, military service, special achievements, and biographical sources. **Arrangement:** Alphabetical. **Indexes:** Geographical, occupational. **Pages (approx.):** 1,800. **Frequency:** Biennial, odd years. **Editor(s):** Shirelle Phelps; William C. Matney, Consulting Editor. **Price:** $115.00 (1991 edition); $120.00 (1993 edition). **Also Includes:** Obituary section. **Other Information:** Formerly published by Educational Communications, Inc.

★4069★
Who's Who in Business, A Guide for Doing Business in St. Croix, U.S. Virgin Islands
St. Croix Chamber of Commerce
16A Church St.
Christiansted
St. Croix, VI 00820   Ph: (809)773-1435
Description: About 1,600 member businesses and professionals in St. Croix, U.S. Virgin Islands. **Entries include:** Company or individual name, address, phone. **Arrangement:** Alphabetical. **Indexes:** Product/service. **Pages (approx.):** 105. **Frequency:** Annual, summer. **Price:** $10.00.

★4070★
Who's Who in Music
Mid-South Management, Inc.
PO Box 1051
Vicksburg, MS 39181-1051   Ph: (601)631-7191
Description: About 20,000 musicians, singers, music associations, broadcasting organizations, record companies, producers, representatives, and others in the Black music industry. **Entries include:** Individual, organization, or company name, address, phone, key personnel; listings for individuals include biographical data. **Arrangement:** Alphabetical. **Indexes:** Subject. **Pages (approx.):** 210. **Frequency:** Irregular; latest edition 1987. **Editor(s):** Robert Rosenthal. **Price:** $40.00, plus $2.00 shipping. **Former Title(s):** Who's Who in Black Music.

★4071★
Who's Who of Black Millionaires
Who's Who of Black Millionaires, Inc.
PO Box 12092
Fresno, CA 93776   Ph: (209)233-1346
Description: Black Americans whose net worth is approximately $1 million or more. **Entries include:** Personal name, location, biographical and financial data. **Arrangement:** Classified by line of profession. **Indexes:** Personal name. **Pages (approx.):** 185. **Frequency:** Irregular; previous edition 1984; latest edition 1993. **Editor(s):** Frank Johnson, President. **Price:** $9.95.

★4072★
World Directory of Minorities
St. James Press
Gale Research Inc.   Ph: (313)961-2242
835 Penobscot Bldg.   Fax: (313)961-6083
Detroit, MI 48226-4094   Free: 800-877-GALE
Description: Major minorities that are, by definition, a numerically inferior portion of a national population differing from the majority in ethno-religio-linguistic ways; worldwide coverage. **Entries include:** Description of the minority including population, percentage of national population, location, language, religion. **Arrangement:** Geographical. **Indexes:** Subject and keyword. **Pages (approx.):** 430. **Frequency:** Published 1990. **Price:** $85.00. **Also Includes:** Maps; bibliographies of further references.

(16) Publishers

★4073★
A. G. Halldin Publishing Co., Inc.
PO Box 667   Ph: (412)463-8450
Indiana, PA 15701   Fax: (412)463-0621

Description: Publishes books on African-Americans, geography, and cookbooks. Offers magazines, newsletters, and calendars. Accepts unsolicited manuscripts. Reaches market through direct mail. **Principal Officers and Managers** Arthur G. Halldin, President; Walter Halldin, Vice-President. **Discounts:** Bookstores - 40%; Libraries - 20%; Individuals - 10% (10). **Percentage of Sales to:** Bookstores - 10%; Libraries - 10%; Individuals - 80%. **Selected Titles:** *Black Americans* by Axford; *Dowser's Primer* by Steffy; *Buy Yourself a Minute* by Smith and DeBiaso; *Into the Deep Misty Woods of Ardennes* by Niedermayer; *Mr. Buckleberry* by Delfavero; *Women of Cambria County* by AAUW Staff.

★4074★
A. J. Muste Memorial Institute
339 Lafayette St.
New York, NY 10012   Ph: (212)533-4335

Description: Reprints classical and modern writings on non-violence, disarmament, race, labor, and women's issues. Reaches market through direct mail and advertising. **Principal Officers and Managers** Murray Rosenblith, Executive Director. **Discounts:** Universal Schedule - 30%. **Percentage of Sales to:** Bookstores - 20%; Non-Book Retail Outlets - 30%; Individuals - 50%. **Selected Titles:** *Peace Agitator: The Story of A. J. Muste* by Nat Hentoff; *Three Essays* by Martin Luther King, Jr.; *On Civil Disobedience* by H. D. Thoreau.

★4075★
Adrienne Publications
123 Cheshire Rd.
Bethany, CT 06525   Ph: (203)393-2323

Principal Officers and Managers Richard Kaletsky, President and Treasurer; Laurie Kaletsky, Vice-President and Secretary. **Discounts:** Bookstores - 40%. **Percentage of Sales to:** Libraries - 5%; Bookstores - 20%; Individuals - 75%. **Selected Titles:** *Ali and Me: Through the Ropes* by Richard Kaletsky.

★4076★
Afram Press
PO Box 2262
Philadelphia, PA 19101   Ph: (609)871-6992

Description: Publishes on the Afro-American experience. Also produces newsletters, greeting cards, calendars, and a magazine for black children. Reaches market through commission representatives, direct mail, and trade sales. **Principal Officers and Managers** Albert Pitts, Publisher; Yahya Karim, Editor; Linda Richardson, Office Manager. **Discounts:** Bookstores - 40% (10). **Percentage of Sales to:** Bookstores - 80%; Non-Book Retail Outlets - 10%; Individuals - 10%. **Selected Titles:** *Haitian Creole Cookery, Ethiopian Cookery, Afro-Brazilian Cookery, Yoruba Names, Baby Book, Swahili Coloring Book.*

★4077★
Africa Fund
198 Broadway, 4th Fl.   Ph: (212)962-1210
New York, NY 10038   Fax: (212)964-8570

Description: Conducts research and publishes resources on southern Africa concerning apartheid and colonialism. Also publishes *Southern Africa Perspectives.* Offers *ACOA Action News.* Distributes titles from other publishers. **Principal Officers and Managers** Jennifer Davis, Executive Secretary; Richard Knight, Literature Director. **Discounts:** Please inquire. **Selected Titles:** *Unified List of United States Companies Doing Business in South Africa* by Richard Knight; *A Woman's Place Is in the Struggle–Not Behind Bars* by the Federation of Transvaal Women; *Apartheid Whitewash: South African Disinformation in the United States* by Richard Leonard; *South Africa Fact Sheet.*

★4078★
Africa World Press
PO Box 1892   Ph: (609)771-1666
Trenton, NJ 08607   Fax: (609)771-1616

Description: Publishes on the social, political, and economic development, problems, and prospects of Africa. Reaches market through direct mail and trade sales. **Principal Officers and Managers** Kassahun Checole, Publisher and President; Pamela A. Sims, Administrative Assistant. **Number of New Titles:** 1992 - 64, 1993 (est.) - 50; Total Titles in Print - 194. **Discounts:** Bookstores - 40%; Jobbers - 20%. **Percentage of Sales to:** Libraries - 25%; Bookstores - 45%; Individuals - 30%. **Selected Titles:** *Adam Clayton Powell: Portrait of a Marching Black, Always Movin' On: The Life of Langston Hughes,* both by James Haskins; *Black People Who Made the Old West* by William L. Katz; *Research on Wole Soyinka* by Gibbs and Lindfors; *Black Man in the Old Testament* by Alfred Dunston, Jr.; *St. Eustatius: The Treasure Island of the Caribbean* by Eric O. Ayisi.

★4079★
African-American Institute
833 United Nations Plaza
New York, NY 10017   Ph: (212)949-5666

Description: Promotes African-American understanding and assists African development. Conducts conferences, facilitative and informational services, cultural projects, and educational and development training programs. Reports and documents available from the organization directly. Also offers a bimonthly magazine on African political and economic development and U.S.-African policy analysis. **Principal Officers and Managers** Vivian Lowery Derryck, President. **Selected Titles:** *Toward a New Africa Policy, Africa Policy in the 1980's,* both by Margaret A. Novicki; *African*

Development and Policy Issues: Implications for California; Higher Education and Rural Development in Africa; Africa and the United States, Williamsburg, Virginia 1981; African-American Relations in the '80's, Freetown, Sierra Leone 1981.

★4080★
African & Caribbean Imprint Library Services
236 Main St.   Ph: (508)540-5378
Falmouth, MA 02540   Fax: (508)548-6801

Description: Distributor. Handles all types of publications from Africa and the Caribbean. Offers microfilm and microfiche, monographs, periodicals, maps, newspapers, and government documents. Reaches market through direct mail. **Principal Officers and Managers** Allen R. Boyd, Director; Christopher W. Boyd, Managing Director. **Discounts:** Libraries - 10% (no returns). **Percentage of Sales to:** Bookstores - 1%; Libraries - 99%.

★4081★
African Studies Association/Crossroads Press
Credit Union Bldg.
Emory University
Atlanta, GA 30322   Ph: (404)329-6410

Description: Publishes scholarly and bibliographical material on African studies. **Principal Officers and Managers** Edna Bay, Executive Secretary.

★4082★
Africana Publishing Co.
30 Irving Pl.   Ph: (212)254-4100
New York, NY 10003   Fax: (212)254-4104
                         Free: 800-437-7840

Description: Publishes books in the humanities and social sciences related to Africa. **Principal Officers and Managers** Miriam H. Holmes, Managing Director. **Discounts:** Please inquire. **Selected Titles:** Governing in Black Africa: Perspectives on New States, 2nd rev. ed. edited by Marion E. Doro and Newell M. Stulz; Africa Contemporary Record, Vol. XXI: 1988-89 edited by Marion E. Doro; A History of Southern Africa, rev. ed. by Neil Parsons.

★4083★
Afro-Am Publishing/Distributing Co., Inc.
407 E. 25th St., Ste. 600
Chicago, IL 60616   Ph: (312)791-1611

Description: Publishes African and Afro-American educational materials for grades pre-kindergarten through high school. Distributes Black-oriented titles for grades kindergarten through twelve, from Harper & Row, Random House, Chelsea House, and Doubleday. Reaches market through direct mail. Formerly known as Afro-Am Publishing Co., Inc. **Principal Officers and Managers** Richard Walker, President; Loretta Rivers, Secretary-Treasurer. **Subjects:** Black studies. **Discounts:** Bookstores - 20-40%; Libraries - 15%; Catalog Jobbers - 40%. **Percentage of Sales to:** Libraries - 10%; Bookstores - 5%; Individuals - 5%; Educational Institutions - 80%. **Selected Titles:** Great Negroes, Past and Present by Russell Adams; Afro-Americans '76 by Eugene Winslow.

★4084★
Akili Books of America
PO Box 1291
South Gate, CA 90280   Ph: (213)635-7191

Description: Publishes books concerning cultural heritage of African-Americans, adults and children alike, on any subject. **Principal Officers and Managers** Issy K. Tindimwebwa, Publishing Manager. **Subjects:** Folklore, philosophy, traditions. **Discounts:** Bookstores - Please inquire; Libraries - 20% (10); Others - Please inquire. **Selected Titles:** Names from East Africa, Meaning and Pronunciation by I. K. Tindimwebwa and H. McCkinzie; A Book of African Sayings and Their Meanings, Children's Stories from Africa, both by Issy K. Tindimwebwa.

★4085★
A.L.A. Black Caucus Publications Committee
499 Wilson Library
University of Minnesota Libraries
Minneapolis, MN 55455   Ph: (612)373-3097

Description: Publishes a quarterly newsletter and a biennial directory. Reaches market through direct mail. **Principal Officers and Managers** Barbara Williams-Jenkins, Black Caucus Chairor; Thomas Weissinger, Chairor, Publications Committee. **Selected Titles:** A.L.A. Black Caucus Directory.

★4086★
Alpha Kappa Alpha Sorority, Inc.
5656 S. Stony Island Ave.
Chicago, IL 60637   Ph: (312)684-1282

Description: Publishes on education and reading. Also publishes Ivy Leaf Magazine. **Principal Officers and Managers** Nan Johnson, Executive Director; Janet J. Ballard, National President. **Selected Titles:** Reading and the Black Child by M. Tamao Denniston; When Is Reading Reading by Mattie Claybrook Williams; Toward a Better Start in Reading by Dorothy S. Strickland; Teen-Age Reading: Achieving Competence in Written Communication by Carolyn Troupe; The 3M Crisis: Miseducating Millions of Minorities by Shirley A. Jackson.

★4087★
Amen-Ra Publishing Co.
PO Box 328642
Columbus, OH 43232   Ph: (614)863-5189

Description: Publishes on the history, religion, and culture of African-Americans. Reaches market through direct mail. **Principal Officers and Managers** Barbara Johnson, Publisher. **Number of New Titles:** 1991 - 2, 1992 - 3; Total Titles in Print - 1. **Discounts:** Wholesalers - 40% (2-199), 50% (200-499), 55% (500). **Percentage of Sales to:** Bookstores - 25%; Libraries - 25%; Individuals - 50%. **Selected Titles:** The Last Days by Fred Ahmed Evans; The Black Holocaust by Khaz Rael; The Poison Book, Muslims or Muhammadans, Universal Law, Book of the Living Dead, all by Hassan Omowale.

★4088★
Andre's and Co.
289 Varick St.
Jersey City, NJ 07302   Ph: (201)451-3804

Description: "Grew out of a need in the Black academic community for a place to publish (unabriged) works dealing with new (Black) prospectives in the psychological, anthropological, economic, and political realms." Concerns are academic, not exclusively Black. **Principal Officers and Managers** Andre Joseph, President and Editor; Lawrence C. Joseph, Vice-President; Reginald L. Ardrey, Associate Editor; Vincent Thompson, Copy Editor. **Subjects:** Black concerns, math, English, poetry. **Discounts:** Bookstores & Libraries - 10%. **Selected Titles:** The Psycho-mathematical Basic Skills Learning Workbooklet, The Psycho-mathematical Mini Math Packs, The White Lie: Black Inferiority, all by Andre Joseph; Basic College Writing: A Workbook by Bessie Waites-Black.

★4089★
Ankh Enterprises
PO Box 46085
Los Angeles, CA 90046   Ph: (213)850-7203

Description: Self-publisher of poetry. Does not accept unsolicited manuscripts. Reaches market through direct mail. **Principal Officers and Managers** Raymond A. Maxwell, Proprietor. **Number of New Titles:** 1992 - 1, 1993 (est.) - 2; Total Titles in Print - 1. **Subjects:** Afrocentrism. **Selected Titles:** Dress Black: A Collection of Poetry by Raymond A. Maxwell.

★4090★
Arts & Communications Network Inc.
PO Box 435
Rosendale, NY 12440   Ph: (914)687-0767

Description: Publishes on African-American arts and culture, including children's workbooks. Also offers cards and games. Accepts unsolicited manuscripts; query first for guidelines. Reaches market through direct mail and workshops. **Principal Officers and**

Managers Erika Wheatley, Creative Director. **Number of New Titles:** 1991 - 2, 1992 - 2; Total Titles in Print - 7. **Discounts:** Bookstores & Libraries - 2-10%. **Percentage of Sales to:** Libraries - 40%; Individuals - 60%. **Selected Titles:** *African Americans and Visual Arts: Resource Guide, Aspects of African American Creativity: Annotated Bibliography of the Arts,* both by F. J. Staats; *Multicultural Activity Workbook: Africa, Asia, and the Americas; African American Workbook for Children,* both by J. Monteith; *Your Destiny Profile: Activity Workbook for Children* by Topaz; *Resource Guide to African American Art: 1952-1992.*

★4091★
Asante Publications
218 Main St., No. 425
Kirkland, WA 98033-6199   Ph: (619)287-7926

Description: "Specializes in literature on the struggles of African-Americans and Africans in the Caribbean." Reaches market through direct mail and speaking tours. **Principal Officers and Managers** Leslie Robinson, Publisher; Michael Grigsby, Editor. **Subjects:** African-American history, politics, and culture. **Discounts:** Bookstores - 40%; Libraries - 40%. **Percentage of Sales to:** Libraries - 10%; Bookstores - 70%; Individuals - 20%. **Selected Titles:** *More than a Dream: The Revolutionary Life of Martin Luther King, Reflections on Liberation, Black Art, Good Morning Revolution: A Tribute to Langston Hughes, For the People: Black Socialists in the United States, Africa, and the Caribbean,* all by Daryl Grigsby.

★4092★
Associated Publishers, Inc.
1407 14th St. NW   Ph: (202)265-1441
Washington, DC 20005-3704   Fax: (202)328-8677

Description: Publishes on Afro-American life and history. Also produces Annual Black History Kits. Reaches market through exhibits and direct mail. **Principal Officers and Managers** Edgar A. Toppin, President; Willie L. Miles, Managing Director; Janet Sims-Wood, Treasurer; Roland McConnell, Secretary. **Number of New Titles:** 1991 - 3, 1992 - 2, 1993 (est.) - 30; Total Titles in Print - 65. **Discounts:** Bookstores - 25-40%; Libraries & Schools - 20%. **Percentage of Sales to:** Libraries - 20%; Bookstores - 25%; Non-Book Retail Outlets - 20%; Individuals - 5%. **Selected Titles:** *History of Negro Church, Negro in Our History,* both by Carter G. Woodson, revised by C. H. Wesley; *Black Americans in Cleveland* by Russell H. Davis; *Economic Development: International and African Perspectives* by Andrew F. Brimmer; *R. Nathaniel Dett: His Life and Works, 1882-1943* by Vivian Flagg McBrier; *Women Builders* by Sadie Daniels.

★4093★
Association of Caribbean Universities and Research Institutes (UNICA)
PO Box 11532, Caparra Heights Sta.
San Juan, PR 00922   Ph: (809)764-0000

Description: "UNICA publishes educational material related to the universities and univerity research programs related to the Caribbean region." Reaches market through direct mail. **Principal Officers and Managers** Thomas Mathews, Secretary General. **Percentage of Sales to:** Libraries - 90%; Individuals - 10%. **Selected Titles:** *El Caribe de la Pesca, Vols. I-II* by Kaldone Nweihed; *Curacao* by Rene Romer; *Agricultural Production and the Small Farmer in the Caribbean* edited by Luis Marcano; *Improvement of University Teaching* in Spanish and English, edited by Claudio and Pinero.

★4094★
Aye-Aye Press
31 Queen St.
PO Box 1122
St. Croix, VI 00821   Ph: (809)778-8465
                              Fax: (809)778-8465

Description: Publishes local topics and reference indexes. Offers microform publications and a computer search service. Reaches market through direct mail and trade sales. **Principal Officers and Managers** Robert V. Vaughn, Proprietor. **Number of New Titles:** 1991 - 5, 1992 - 10, 1993 (est.) - 8; Total Titles in Print - 5. **Subjects:** Journalism, education, library science, computer services. **Discounts:** 25-40% depending upon title. **Percentage of Sales to:** Libraries - 10%; Bookstores - 40%; Individuals - 50%. **Selected Titles:** *Virgin Islands in. . .Periodical Literature, Education in the Virgin Islands, Virgin Islands Newspapers–Substantive Index, Virgin Islands Acronyms, The Air Transport Industry. . ., Quotable Quotes from the Virgin Islands,* all by R. V. Vaughn.

★4095★
Balamp Publishing
4205 Fullerton
Detroit, MI 48238   Ph: (313)491-1950

Principal Officers and Managers James M. Jay, President. **Subjects:** Biographies, autobiographies. **Discounts:** Bookstores - 40% (trade); Libraries - 10%. **Selected Titles:** *Robeson: Labor's Forgotten Champion* by Charles H. Wright; *You Don't Look Like a Musician* by Bud Freeman; *Walk Quietly through the Night and Cry Softly* by Burniece Avery; *Eubie Blake: Keys of Memory* by Lawrence T. Carter; *My World of Reality* by Hildrus A. Poindexter; *Black American Scholars: A Study of Their Beginnings* by Horace Mann Bond.

★4096★
Beckham House Publishers, Inc.
PO Box 177
Hampton, VA 23669   Ph: (804)851-9598

Description: Publishes books by and about Blacks and guidance materials on the college selection process. Also publishes a newsletter *Black Student Advisor.* Accepts unsolicited manuscripts. Reaches market through direct mail and Talman Co. **Principal Officers and Managers** Barry E. Beckham, President. **Discounts:** Bookstores - 40-55%. **Percentage of Sales to:** Libraries - 25%; Bookstores - 25%; Non-Book Retail Outlets - 50%. **Selected Titles:** *Black Student's Guide to Colleges, College Selection Workbook,* both by Barry Beckham; *1999 Facts about Blacks* by Raymond Corbin.

★4097★
Bell Enterprises, Inc.
PO Box 9054
Pine Bluff, AR 71611   Ph: (501)247-1922

Description: Publishes materials on self-help, English, speech, accomplishments of Black leaders. Reaches market through direct mail. **Principal Officers and Managers** Ida R. Bellegarde, President and Owner. **Discounts:** Bookstores - 20%. **Selected Titles:** *Black Heroes and Heroines, Vols. 1-5; Idylls of the Seasons, Lisping Leaves, Easy Steps to Correct Speech, Easy Steps to Good Grammar, Easy Steps to a Large Vocabulary,* all by Bellegarde.

★4098★
Benin Press Ltd.
5225 S. Blackstone Ave.
Chicago, IL 60615   Ph: (312)643-2363

Description: Reprints out-of-print Africana. **Principal Officers and Managers** Herbert Biblo, President. **Discounts:** Bookstores - 20%. **Selected Titles:** *The Tshi-Speaking Peoples of the Gold Coast of West Africa, The Ewe-Speaking Peoples of the Slave Coast of West Africa, The Yoruba-Speaking Peoples of the Slave Coast of West Africa,* all by Alfred B. Ellis.

★4099★
Benin Publishing Co.
802 Columbus Dr.
Teaneck, NJ 07666   Ph: (201)837-8641

Description: Publishes business books for minorities. Reaches market through direct mail. **Principal Officers and Managers** Robert M. Waite, President. **Discounts:** Bookstores - 30%. **Percentage of Sales to:** Bookstores - 100%. **Selected Titles:** *Daddy Big Bucks* by Robert Waite.

★4100★
Best Western Press
PO Box 494
Bakersfield, CA 93302   Ph: (805)323-0738

Description: Publishes a book on Black history. Reaches market through direct mail. **Principal Officers and Managers** Samuel Barnes, President; William McCulland, Sales Manager. **Discounts:** Please inquire. **Selected Titles:** *Identity* by Samuel Barnes.

★4101★
Black Classic Press
PO Box 13414
Baltimore, MD 21203   Ph: (410)602-0980
Description: Publishes African and American studies. "Our intent is to bring to light obscure and significant works by and about people of African descent." Reaches market through direct mail. **Principal Officers and Managers** W. Paul Coates, Director. **Number of New Titles:** 1991 - 6, 1992 - 12; Total Titles in Print - 26. **Discounts:** Bookstores - 10-40%. **Percentage of Sales to:** Bookstores - 70%; Libraries - 20%; Individuals - 10%. **Selected Titles:** *African Glory* by J. C. DeGraft-Johnson; *100 Years of Lynchings* by Ralph Ginzburg; *The Life and Adventure of Nat Love* by Nat Love; *Coltrane* by C. O. Simpkins; *Black Man of the Nile* by Yosef ben-Jochannan; *Your History: From the Beginning of Time to the Present* by J. A. Rogers.

★4102★
Black Economic Research Team Inc.
PO Box 13513
Baltimore, MD 21203
Description: Purpose is "to bridge the gap between large businesses and small businesses." Reaches market through commission representatives and direct mail. **Principal Officers and Managers** Cleveland C. Washington, Jr., President. **Selected Titles:** *Minority Business Directory: State of Maryland.*

★4103★
Black Entrepreneurs Press
4502 S. Congress Ave., Ste. 254
Austin, TX 78745
Description: Publishes self-help books for African-Americans in business. Offers a newsletter, *Black Entrepreneur's Wealth Builders.* Reaches market through direct mail and Baker & Taylor. **Principal Officers and Managers** Derek A. Broadnax, President. **Subjects:** Personal finance. **Discounts:** Bookstores - 20%, 25% (2-9), 40% (10-99), 45% (100); Libraries - 10%. **Percentage of Sales to:** Libraries - 5%; Bookstores - 1%; Individuals - 94%. **Selected Titles:** *The Black Entrepreneur's Guide to Money, The Black Entrepreneur's Guide to Starting and Building a Million Dollar Business of Your Own!, Directory of African-American Owned Savings and Loan Institutions, What Every Black American Should Know to Gain Financial Success in the 90's,* all by Derek A. Broadnax.

★4104★
Black Graphics International
PO Box 732, Linwood Sta.
Detroit, MI 48206   Ph: (313)890-1128
Description: Publishers and distributors of revolutionary literature and art. **Principal Officers and Managers** Ibn Pori, Publisher and Editor; Julian Richardson, Publisher; Adebayo Ni Youn, Public Relations. **Discounts:** Bookstores - 30%. **Selected Titles:** *Fire Music* by Rob Backus; *Assassin Poems* by Vajava Mogumbo and Brothers.

★4105★
Black Resource Guide, Inc.
501 Oneida Pl. NW   Ph: (202)291-4373
Washington, DC 20011   Fax: (202)291-4373
Description: Performs research for organizations interested in making contact with various elements in the national Black community. Publishes an annual directory and offers mailing labels of prominent members of the Black community. Audience includes educational institutions, members of the media, and general public. Reaches market through commission representatives, direct mail, telephone sales, trade sales, and wholesalers. **Principal Officers and Managers** Robert B. Johnson, President; Jacqueline L. Johnson, Secretary-Treasurer. **Number of New Titles:** 1991 - 1, 1992 - 1, 1993 (est.) - 1; Total Titles in Print - 8. **Discounts:** Bookstores - 40%; Libraries - 20% (10 prepaid). **Percentage of Sales to:** Libraries - 35%; Bookstores - 20%; Individuals - 45%. **Selected Titles:** *The Black Resource Guide: A National Black Directory.*

★4106★
Black Student Fund
3636 16th St. NW, Ste. AG 15-19
Washington, DC 20010   Ph: (202)387-1414
Description: "Encourages positive racial and economic diversity in the independent schools of Washington." Publishes a directory of independent schools. Reaches market through direct mail. **Principal Officers and Managers** Barbara Patterson, Executive Director. **Selected Titles:** *A History Deferred* by Susan Rice, *The Black Student Fund Independent School Directory; Black Student Fund Symposium.*

★4107★
Blacklight Fellowship
2859 W. Wilcox St.
Chicago, IL 60612   Ph: (312)722-1441
Description: Publishes Black Christian biblical literature. Offers seminars. Accepts unsolicited manuscripts. Reaches market through direct mail, trade sales, and Baker & Taylor. **Principal Officers and Managers** Rev. Walter Arthur McCray, Director. **Number of New Titles:** 1991 - 3; Total Titles in Print - 7. **Discounts:** Bookstores - 40%; Libraries - None. **Percentage of Sales to:** Libraries - 5%; Bookstores - 70%; Individuals - 20%. **Selected Titles:** *The Black Presence in the Bible, How to Stick Together During Times of Tension, Reaching and Teaching Black Young Adults,* all by McCray; *By Your Traditions* by Arthur D. Griffin.

★4108★
Blue Diamond Press
Tilden Towers II
801 Tilden St.
Bronx, NY 10467   Ph: (212)882-8160
Description: Reaches market through Bookazine Co., Inc. Presently inactive. **Principal Officers and Managers** Joseph Mason Andrew Cox, President; Richard L. Baltimore, Jr., Chairman; Marshall J. Mohammad. **Subjects:** History, poetry, drama, prose. **Selected Titles:** *New and Selected Poems, Great Black Men of Masonry 1723-1988, Vols. I-III, Land Dimly Seen, Ode to Dr. Martin Luther King, Jr., History of Port-au-Prince 1492-1936, Vols. I-II,* all by Joseph Mason Andrew Cox.

★4109★
Boston University
African Studies Center
270 Bay State Rd.   Ph: (617)353-3673
Boston, MA 02215   Fax: (617)353-4975
Description: "The African Studies Center began a more vigorous publishing program of its own after the Boston University Press was officially closed, in order to publish research monographs, collected articles, edited historical documents, and a series of working papers, and to achieve greater circulation for work going on at the Center." Reaches market through direct mail. Publishes *International Journal of African Historical Studies.* **Principal Officers and Managers** Allen Hoben, Center Director; Jean Hay, Publications Editor. **Subjects:** African studies. **Percentage of Sales to:** Libraries - 50%; Bookstores - 10%; Individuals - 40%. **Selected Titles:** *School, Work, and Equity: Educational Reform in Rwanda* by Susan Hober; *Lamu in the Nineteenth Century: Land, Trade and Politics* by Marguerite Ylvisaker; *Precolonial Senegal: The Jolof Kingdom* by Eunice Charles; *Nama/Namibia: The Diary and Letters of Nama Chief Hendrik Witbooi* edited by Georg M. Gugelberger; *Discovering the African Past: Essays in Honor of Daniel McCall* edited by Norman Bennett; *Agrarian Reform in Ethiopia* by Allan Hober.

★4110★
Broadside Press
PO Box 04257
Detroit, MI 48204   Ph: (313)934-1231
Description: Publishes poetry by Black authors. Reaches market through direct mail, telephone sales, and Baker & Taylor. Formerly Broadside/Crummel Press. **Principal Officers and Managers** Hilda Vest, Publisher; Donald Vest, Business Manager; Gloria House, Editor; Willie D. Williams, Photographer; Ernest Tanks, Board Member. **Subjects:** Poetry, criticism. **Discounts:** Bookstores and Wholesalers - 40%; Libraries - 20%. **Percentage of Sales to:** Libraries - 15%; Bookstores - 80%; Individuals - 5%. **Selected Titles:** *Upside Down Tapestry Mosaic History* by Leslie Reese;

Report from Part One by Gwendolyn Brooks; *Safari of African Cooking* by Bill Odarty; *Abstract Blues* by Rayfield Waller; *Rainrituals* by Aneb Kgositsile.

★4111★
Burrelle's Information Services
75 E. Northfield Rd.
Livingston, NJ 07039   Ph: (201)992-6600
Description: Publishes media directories to several eastern states. Also publishes directories pertaining to specific groups, including Hispanics, Blacks, and women. Reaches market through direct mail. **Principal Officers and Managers** Fred Wynne, Arthur Wynne, Jr., Robert Waggoner. **Selected Titles:** *1989 Hispanic Media Directory; 1989 Black Media Directory; 1987 New York State Media Directory; 1989 Washington, DC Directory; 1988 New England Media Directory; 1989 Chicago, Illinois (Metro Area) Media Directory.*

★4112★
Calaloux Publications
PO Box 812028
Wellesley, MA 02181-0012   Ph: (617)237-2230
Description: Publishes original works or noteworthy reprints of important works by or about Caribbean, African-American, African, and other Third World people. Offers brochures, videotapes of interviews, and documentaries. Distributes for New Beacon Books and Aquarela Galleries. Accepts unsolicited manuscripts. **Principal Officers and Managers** Selwyn R. Cudjoe, President; Sharon Holas-Huggins, Vice-President; Ronald Thomas, Secretary. **Number of New Titles:** 1992 - 3; Total Titles in Print - 10. **Discounts:** Bookstores - 35%. **Selected Titles:** *Movement of the People, A Just and Moral Society,* both by Selwyn R. Cudjoe; *Labour Law in Trinidad and Tobago* by Roy D. Thomas; *Growing Up with Miss Milly* by Sybil Seaforth; *Those That Be in Bondage* by A. R. F. Webber; *The Still Cry* by Noor Kumar Mahabir.

★4113★
Cape of Good Hope Foundation
1201 E. California   Ph: (818)356-4469
Pasadena, CA 91125   Fax: (818)795-1547
Description: Publishes on Southern Africa. Offers an annual, *IMVO News.* Reaches market through direct mail. Formerly listed as California Institute of Technology, Munger Africana Library. **Principal Officers and Managers** Edwin S. Munger, President; Helga Harrison, Financial Officer. **Number of New Titles:** 1993 (est.) - 1; Total Titles in Print - 7. **Discounts:** Bookstores - 20%. **Selected Titles:** *The Hunter and His Art* by Jalmar and Ione Rudner; *Report on Portugal's War in Guinea-Bissau* by Al J. Venter; *Africana Byways* by Anna H. Smith.

★4114★
Capitol Press
PO Box 60583   Ph: (202)726-4233
Washington, DC 20011   Fax: (703)764-2589
Description: Publishes on the history of Blacks in sports. Reaches market through baseball organizations. Presently inactive. **Principal Officers and Managers** John B. Holway, President. **Discounts:** Please inquire. **Percentage of Sales to:** Individuals - 100%. **Selected Titles:** *Bullet Joe and the Monarchs, Smokey Joe and the Cannonballs,* both by John B. Holway.

★4115★
Carib House (USA)
11305 Goleta St.
Los Angeles, CA 91342   Ph: (818)890-1056
Description: Publishes and distributes books on all subjects relevant to the Caribbean region; manuscripts also solicited. **Principal Officers and Managers** Rupert Singh, Owner and Manager; P. D. Sharma, Editor; Lynn Franklin, Sales and Promotion. **Discounts:** Bookstores - 50%; Libraries - 25%; Distributors - 60%. **Selected Titles:** *The New Caribbean Man* by P. D. Sharma.

★4116★
Caribbean Studies Association
Dept. of Social Sciences
Inter American University   Ph: (809)892-6055
San German, PR 00931   Fax: (809)892-6350
Description: A multidisciplinary professional society. Publishes a quarterly newsletter, a directory of scholars, and proceedings of annual conference. Reaches market through direct mail. **Principal Officers and Managers** Jacqueline Braveboy-Wagner, President; Gilberte Arroyo, Secretary-Treasurer; James Wessman, Newsletter Editor. **Discounts:** None. **Selected Titles:** *Directory of Caribbeanists,* 2nd ed. compiled and edited by Sylvia Potter.

★4117★
Carlisle Press
201 Gale St., No. 303
Mechanicsburg, PA 17055   Ph: (717)697-1642
Description: Publishes a biographical book on famous Black Americans. Reaches market through direct mail and wholesalers and distributors, including Quality Books, Inc., Harrisburg News Co., and Baker & Taylor. **Principal Officers and Managers** E. J. Machamer, Publisher. **Number of New Titles:** 1992 - 1, 1993 (est.) - 1; Total Titles in Print - 2. **Discounts:** Bookstores - 40%; Libraries - 30%. **Percentage of Sales to:** Libraries - 20%; Bookstores - 30%; Non-Book Retail Outlets - 40%; Individuals - 10%. **Selected Titles:** *The Illustrated Black American Profiles* by Gene Machamer; *101 Uses for a Crooked Politician.*

★4118★
Carver Publishing, Inc.
PO Box 9353
Hampton, VA 23670-0353   Ph: (804)838-1244
Description: Publishes the history of contributions of Black men and women to U.S. military defense since 1619. Formerly known as Ebony Publishing Inc. **Principal Officers and Managers** Jesse J. Johnson LTC, Ret., Publisher. **Subjects:** Military history. **Selected Titles:** *Ebony Brass, A Pictorial History of the Black Soldier in the United States in Peace and War, A Pictorial History of Black Servicemen, Black Armed Forces Officers, Roots of Two Black Marine Sergeants Major, Black Women in the Armed Forces,* all by Jesse J. Johnson.

★4119★
Center for Nation Management Economics, Inc.
PO Box 834, University Sta.
Syracuse, NY 13210   Ph: (315)478-1985
Description: Publishes economic strategies to end poverty in Africa. Reaches market through direct mail and bookstores. **Principal Officers and Managers** Agbeko Katapu, President; Prof. Ethel H. Fine, Director of Studies. **Discounts:** Libraries - 15%; Bookstores - 15% (negotiable). **Percentage of Sales to:** Libraries - 60%; Bookstores - 40%. **Selected Titles:** *Workable Strategies to End Africa's Poverty* by Agbeko Katapu.

★4120★
Charill Publishers
4468 San Francisco Ave.   Ph: (314)382-4998
St. Louis, MO 63115   Fax: (314)531-2627
Description: Publishes materials aimed at African-American children on building self-esteem and discipline through poetry. Offers children's posters. Reaches market through direct mail and telephone sales. **Principal Officers and Managers** Fred D. Hill, President; Charlotte M. Hill, Owner. **Number of New Titles:** 1991 - 4, 1992 - 3; Total Titles in Print - 6. **Discounts:** Bookstores - 40%. **Percentage of Sales to:** Libraries - 9%; Bookstores - 48%; Non-Book Retail Outlets - 4%; Individuals - 39%. **Selected Titles:** *Poetry for Wee Folks, Wee Folks Learn to Read: Book 1,* both by Charlotte M. Hill; *Christopher & Cumulus Cloud* by Fred D. Hill; *Wee Folks Inching On: Book 2; Wee Folks Moving Up: Book 3; Wee Folks Soaring High: Book 4.*

★4121★
Chatham Bookseller
8 Green Village
Madison, NJ 07940   Ph: (201)822-1361
Description: Publishes hardcover reprints of novels by Black writers. **Principal Officers and Managers** Frank Deodene, President. **Discounts:** Bookstores - 20%. **Selected Titles:** *The Heat's On, Pinktoes, Run Man Run,* all by Chester Himes; *Banana Bottom* by Claude McKay; *One for New York* by John A. Williams; *Savage Holiday* by Richard Wright.

★4122★
CIL, Inc., Books
860 SW 9th St. Circle, Ste. 201
Boca Raton, FL 33486   Ph: (407)392-3936
Description: Publishes on legends and lore of the Bahamas and the Caribbean Islands. Reaches market through direct mail, telephone sales, and trade sales. **Principal Officers and Managers** A. N. Campbell, President and Author. **Number of New Titles:** 1993 (est.) - 1; Total Titles in Print - 2. **Discounts:** Bookstores - 50%. **Percentage of Sales to:** Libraries - 15%; Bookstores - 15%; Individuals - 50%. **Selected Titles:** *Railroad Sirens, Voodoo: Treasurer in Bootle Bay, Ten Sails in the Sunrise, Scion,* all by A. N. Campbell.

★4123★
City University of New York
Caribbean Research Center
Medgar Evers College
1150 Carroll St.   Ph: (718)270-6418
Brooklyn, NY 11225   Fax: (718)270-6496
Description: Publishes academic research and creative writing on Caribbean and Caribbean-American themes. Accepts unsolicited manuscripts; include a self-addressed, stamped envelope. Reaches market through commission representatives, telephone sales, and Ingram Book Co. **Principal Officers and Managers** J. A. George Irish, Director. **Number of New Titles:** 1991 - 5, 1992 - 5; Total Titles in Print - 22. **Discounts:** Bookstores - 40%; Libraries - 20%. **Percentage of Sales to:** Prior permission required; books in resalable condition accepted within 90 days for credit. **Selected Titles:** *Native Landscapes: An Anthology of Caribbean Short Stories* edited by Clarke; *Political Behaviour and Social Interaction among Caribbean and Black American Residents in Brooklyn* edited by Irish and Riviere; *Life in Colonial Crucible* by J. A. G. Irish; *The Fever of Years* by E. B. Baisden; *An Immigrant Handbook on the Educational and Social System in the USA* by McNicol, Thomas, and J. A. G. Irish; *Establishing New Lives: Selected Readings on Caribbean Immigrants in New York City* edited by Clarke and Riviere.

★4124★
Clarity Press
3277 Roswell Rd. NE, Ste. 469   Ph: (404)231-0649
Atlanta, GA 30305   Fax: (404)231-3899
                                 Free: 800-247-6553
Description: Publishes scholarly works relating to political, minority, and human rights issues. Accepts unsolicited nonfiction manuscripts; query for guidelines. Reaches market through direct mail, trade sales, and wholesalers. **Number of New Titles:** 1991 - 3, 1992 - 4, 1993 (est.) - 3; Total Titles in Print - 12. **Discounts:** Bookstores - 40%; Libraries - 20% (10); Jobbers - 20%. **Percentage of Sales to:** Libraries - 30%; Bookstores - 30%; Individuals - 40%. **Selected Titles:** *The Anti-Social Contract, The Black Book: The True Political Philosophy of Malcolm X (El Hajj Malik El Shabazz), International Law and the Black Minority in the U.S.,* all by Dr. Y. N. Kly; *The Invisible Women of Washington* by Diana G. Collier; *Dalit: The Black Untouchables of India* by V. T. Rajshekar; *The End of Zionism* edited by Eibie Weizfeld.

★4125★
Cobblestone Communications
PO Box 552
Malden, MA 02148   Ph: (617)322-3998
Description: Publishes an African-American travel guide resource and business directory. **Principal Officers and Managers** Linda Cline, Publisher. **Selected Titles:** *Access: The Black Patron's Directory of Metropolitan Boston's Business, Professional, and Specialized Services.*

★4126★
Communicators Press
221 Sheridan St. NW   Ph: (202)726-8618
Washington, DC 20011   Fax: (202)291-9149
Description: Publishes on the philosophy of the Afrocentric culture. Offers audio and video cassettes. Reaches market through direct mail and telephone sales. **Principal Officers and Managers** Clarence Ellis, Owner; Leon Dobbs, President. **Number of New Titles:** 1992 - 5; Total Titles in Print - 1. **Subjects:** African culture. **Discounts:** Bookstores - 40%; Libraries - 50%. **Percentage of Sales to:** Bookstores - 50%; Non-Book Retail Outlets - 50%. **Selected Titles:** *God, the Black Man, and Truth* by Ben Ammi.

★4127★
Contemporary Crafts, Inc.
5271 W. Pico Blvd.
Los Angeles, CA 90019   Ph: (213)933-6622
Description: Black art history, black art. **Principal Officers and Managers** Mildred Sanders, Director; Samella Lewis, President. **Discounts:** Bookstores - 25-41%; Libraries - 10-15%. **Selected Titles:** *Black Artists on Art, Vols. 1-2; Earthbook; Who Took the Weight.*

★4128★
CORE Publications
1457 Flatbush Ave.
Brooklyn, NY 11210   Ph: (718)434-3580
Description: Promotes human rights. **Principal Officers and Managers** Roy Innis, Chairor; Wendall Garnett, Director of Operations; Cyril Boynes, Jr., Editor; George Holmes, Communications; Theresa Alexander, Finance Director. **Subjects:** Civil rights, sports, government. **Selected Titles:** *The Correspondent* by George Holmes; *Profiles in Black* by Doris Innis.

★4129★
Cottage Books
PO Box 2071
Silver Spring, MD 20902   Ph: (301)649-5123
Principal Officers and Managers Samuel F. Yette, Publisher; Brend Bland, Editor; Frederick Walton Yette, General Counsel; Michael Lewis Yette, Secretary-Treasurer. **Subjects:** Black history and culture, American politics, the world in pictures. **Discounts:** Bookstores - Up to 40%; Individuals - 25% (volume orders); Libraries - 20%. **Percentage of Sales to:** Libraries - 30%; Bookstores - 30%; Individuals - 30%; Non-Book Retail Outlets - 10%. **Selected Titles:** *The Choice: The Issue of Black Survival in America* by Samuel F. Yette; *Washington and Two Marches, 1963 and 1983* by Frederick Walton Yette and Samuel F. Yette.

★4130★
Council on Interracial Books for Children, Inc.
1841 Broadway
New York, NY 10023   Ph: (212)757-5339
Description: Publishes "to identify–and more recently to counteract–racism, sexism, and other anti-human values in children's learning materials and society." Offers books, maps, filmstrips, catalogs, and booklists. Reaches market through direct mail. **Principal Officers and Managers** Melba Kgositsile, Executive Director. **Discounts:** Bookstores - 20%. **Percentage of Sales to:** Libraries - 20%; Bookstores - 10%; Individuals - 20%; Schools & Universities - 50%. **Selected Titles:** *Embers: Stories for a Changing World; Guidelines for Selecting Bias-Free Textbooks and Storybooks; Stereotypes, Distortions and Omissions in U.S. History Textbooks; Violence, the Ku Klux Klan and the Struggle for Equality; Chronicles of American Indian Protest; Unlearning "Indian" Stereotypes,* all by the CIBC.

★4131★
Crescent Imports & Publications
PO Box 7827   Ph: (313)665-3492
Ann Arbor, MI 48107   Fax: (313)677-1717
                                 Free: 800-521-9744
Description: Distributor and wholesaler. Imports Black literature and Afro-American and Islamic titles. Reaches market through direct mail and telephone sales. **Principal Officers and Managers** Ashfaq Ibrahim, Owner. **Discounts:** Bookstores - 25-30%. **Percentage of**

Sales to: Bookstores - 10%; Libraries - 5%; Non-Book Retail Outlets - 10%; Individuals - 75%.

★4132★
Cultural Survival, Inc.
53A Church St. Ph: (617)495-2562
Cambridge, MA 02138 Fax: (617)495-1396
Description: A nonprofit organization founded by a group of social scientists concerned with the fate of tribal peoples and ethnic minorities around the world. Publications serve to inform the general public, educators, and policy makers in the U.S. and abroad to stimulate action on behalf of these societies. Reaches market through direct mail and distributors. **Principal Officers and Managers** David Maybury-Lewis, President; Marc S. Miller, Editor; Pam Solo, Executive Director. **Subjects:** Human rights, anthropology, social sciences. **Discounts:** Bookstores - 40%; Colleges - 20%; Libraries - None.

★4133★
Dayton Human Relations Council
40 S. Main St., Ste. 721
Dayton, OH 45402 Ph: (513)225-5336
Description: Makes large segment of the community aware of the services and programs of the Human Relations Council. Reaches market through direct mail and distribution points. **Principal Officers and Managers** Jerald L. Steed, Executive Director. **Subjects:** Unlawful discriminatory practices in employment, public accommodations, housing, credit transactions. **Discounts:** All publications are free to the general public. **Selected Titles:** *Rules and Regulations for Filing a Complaint of Alleged Discrimination; Your Rights Are Protected by Law; Human Relations Council Ordinances Prohibiting Discrimination; Guide to Complainant; Guide to Respondent.*

★4134★
Detroit Black Writers' Guild, Inc.
5601 W. Warren
Detroit, MI 48210 Ph: (313)897-2551
Description: Publishes material by Black Americans with an emphasis on children's books. Also produces *Westside Journal.* Offers greeting cards, posters, and African statues. Accepts unsolicited manuscripts with a self-addressed, stamped envelope. Reaches market through commission representatives, direct mail, telephone sales, and personal contact. **Principal Officers and Managers** Peggy A. Moore, Executive Director; Harry M. Anderson, Assistant Director; Patsy Douglas, Executive Secretary and Treasurer; Peggy Sue Moore, Marketing. **Discounts:** Bookstores - 25-40%; Libraries - 25%. **Percentage of Sales to:** Libraries - 20%; Bookstores - 20%; Non-Book Retail Outlets - 10%; Individuals - 50%. **Selected Titles:** *How Not to Abuse Your Child, The Saga of John Hunley, Neighbors and Friends Coloring Book,* all by Peggy A. Moore; *Detroit '64* by Harry M. Anderson; *How to Celebrate Kwanza; Through Ebony Eyes.*

★4135★
Dr. G. Carlo Jean
2110 Newkirk Ave., Apt. 5C
Brooklyn, NY 11226 Ph: (718)859-8913
Description: Publishes books on linguistics of Haitian creole. Reaches market through commission representatives. **Percentage of Sales to:** Libraries - 12%; Bookstores - 30%; Non-Book Retail Outlets - 14%; Corporations - 13%; Individuals - 22%; Others - 9%. **Selected Titles:** *La Linguistique Moderne appliquee a L'Education: Regard et Reflexion sur lescas du Francais de L'Anglais et du Creole haitien, Prises de Position sur l'Enseignement et la Question Linguistique Haitienne,* both by G. Carlo Jean.

★4136★
Duncan & Duncan, Inc.
2809 Pulaski Hwy.
Edgewood, MD 21040 Ph: (410)538-5579
  Fax: (410)538-5584
  Free: 800-487-5580
Description: Publishes books for the African and African-American markets. Also offers puzzles. Accepts unsolicited manuscripts; must cover a pertinent subject. Reaches market through direct mail, telephone sales, trade sales, and major distributors. Formerly known as M. E. Duncan & Co., Inc. **Principal Officers and Managers** Mike Duncan, President; Shirley E. Duncan, Vice-President. **Number of New Titles:** 1991 - 2, 1992 - 5, 1993 (est.) - 6; Total Titles in Print - 6. **Subjects:** Biography, careers, entreprenuership, children's books. **Discounts:** Bookstores - 40%; Libraries - None. **Percentage of Sales to:** Libraries - 15%; Bookstores - 30%; Non-Book Retail Outlets - 5%; Individuals - 50%. **Selected Titles:** *A Mind for Money* by John B. Slaughter, II; *And Still, I Cry* by Barbara A. Robinson; *Reach Your Goals in Spite of the Old Boy Network* by Mike Duncan; *Each Night, I Die* by David Belton; *Beyond the Timberline* by T. M. Alexander, Sr.; *Black Wealth through Black Entrepreneurship* by Robert L. Wallace.

★4137★
Eastern Caribbean Institute
PO Box 1338 Ph: (809)772-1011
Frederiksted, VI 00841 Fax: (809)772-3665
Description: Publishes on economics and politics of the eastern Caribbean. Also publishes poetry. Distributes for Caribbean Research Institute, University of the Virgin Islands, and University of the West Indies, Institute of Social and Economic Research. Accepts unsolicited manuscripts. Reaches market through direct mail. **Principal Officers and Managers** S. B. Jones-Hendrickson, President. **Number of New Titles:** 1991 - 2, 1992 - 3; Total Titles in Print - 8. **Discounts:** Bookstores & Libraries - 20% (1-5), 30% (6-24), 40% (25-49), 50% (50). **Percentage of Sales to:** Libraries - 50%; Bookstores - 40%; Non-Book Retail Outlets - 10%. **Selected Titles:** *Public Finance and Monetary Policy in Open Economies; Sonny Jim of Sandy Point,* both by S. B. Jones-Hendrickson; *Readings in Caribbean Public Sector Economics* edited by Fuat Andic and S. B. Jones-Hendrickson; *Caribbean Visions; A Profile of Frederiksted, St. Croix, U.S. Virgin Islands; Interviews With Lee L. Moore.*

★4138★
ECA Associates
PO Box 15004
Chesapeake, VA 23320 Ph: (804)547-5542
Description: An educational and human resources agency that specializes in providing publications and services for African-Americans. Distributes material from Cottage Books and Open Hand. Reaches market through direct mail. **Principal Officers and Managers** E. Curtis Alexander, President; Edward Alexander II, Vice-President; Barbara Alexander, Secretary-Treasurer. **Subjects:** African and African-American history, religion, and education. **Discounts:** Bookstores - 42%; Libraries - 20%. **Percentage of Sales to:** Libraries - 5%; Bookstores - 65%; Individuals - 25%; Wholesalers - 5%. **Selected Titles:** *Who's Who in African Heritage Book Publishing, Education: A Guide for African and African-American Studies Programs, African Foundations of Judaism and Christianity, How to Publish and Market Your Own Book as an Independent Black Publisher, Elijah Muhammed on African American,* all by Alexander; *Cheikh Anta Diop: On History, Culture, and Technology.*

★4139★
Eliza Washington
614 Wilshire Ave.
Waterloo, IA 50701 Ph: (319)234-1460
Percentage of Sales to: Individuals - 100%. **Selected Titles:** *Tomorrow Is Another Day: Hope of a Better Future for Black Americans* by Eliza Washington.

★4140★
Elramco Enterprises, Inc.
257 Osborne Rd.
Albany, NY 12211 Ph: (518)489-1771
Description: Publishes poetry and social issue books in paperback. Offers minority group greeting cards. Reaches market through direct mail, trade sales, and Baker & Taylor. **Principal Officers and Managers** Leroy L. Ramsey, President; Westmore Wolfe, Vice-President, Sales Promotions; Marjorie A. Mussman, Vice-President, Editor. **Discounts:** Bookstores & Libraries - 40%. **Selected Titles:** *Deni: The Loving Soul of a Woman* by Denise Norman; *Struggle to Survive* by Marguerite Guerrero; *The Anglo-African in the Melting Pot* by Ramsey and C. B. Thorpe; *Story of Desire and Determination; The Weight of the Shadow; Black American Victory in World War II; Venice: Bride of the Adriatic.*

★4141★
Essai Seay Publications
PO Box 55
East St. Louis, IL 62202-0055   Ph: (618)271-7890

Description: Founded to promote literature about Black people, living now, who are role models in their community. **Principal Officers and Managers** Sheryl Clayton, President. **Number of New Titles:** 1992 - 1, 1993 (est.) - 1; Total Titles in Print - 4. **Discounts:** Bookstores - 40% (20); Quantity - 50% (200). **Percentage of Sales to:** Libraries - 50%; Individuals - 50%. **Selected Titles:** *Black Men Role Models of Greater St. Louis, Black Women Role Models of Greater St. Louis,* both by Sheryl H. Clayton; *Burning the Years and Lobo* by William Childress.

★4142★
Evangelist Association
700 W. 55th Ave.
Merrillville, IN 46410

Principal Officers and Managers Rev. Herbert Mitchell, Owner and Manager; Willa Mitchell, Secretary; John Prince, Curtiss Watkins, Associates; Herman Mitchell, Editor. **Subjects:** Science, technology, Black American cooking. **Discounts:** Bookstores & Libraries - 20%. **Selected Titles:** *Black-American Cookbook, Vols. 1-3* by Willa Mitchell.

★4143★
Fire!! Press
241 Hillside Rd.
Elizabeth, NJ 07208   Ph: (201)964-8476

Description: Publishes works from the Harlem Renaissance. Reaches market through direct mail. **Principal Officers and Managers** Thomas H. Wirth, Publisher. **Number of New Titles:** 1991 - 1; Total Titles in Print - 1. **Subjects:** African-American literature. **Discounts:** Bookstores - 40%. **Percentage of Sales to:** Libraries - 10%; Bookstores - 40%; Non-Book Retail Outlets - 10%; Individuals - 40%. **Selected Titles:** *Fire!!* edited by Wallace Thurman.

★4144★
Freeland Publications
PO Box 18941
Philadelphia, PA 19119   Ph: (215)226-2507

Description: Publishes on African-American culture. Also produces calendars. Reaches market through direct mail. **Principal Officers and Managers** Skobi Matunde, Chairor. **Percentage of Sales to:** Bookstores - 70%; Non-Book Retail Outlets - 15%; Individuals - 15%. **Selected Titles:** *Do You Play the Drum or Does the Drum Play You, Makini's Coming of Age, National Afrikan-Amerikan Calendar,* all by S. Matunde; *Child of Life Reader, Children's Stories for Teenage Adults, The Web That Binds,* all by R. Brooks.

★4145★
General Hall, Inc.
5 Talon Way
Dix Hills, NY 11746   Ph: (516)243-0155

Description: Publishes college level text and supplemental books on sociology, Black studies, education, and communications. Offers computer typesetting and book production services. Accepts unsolicited manuscripts. Reaches market through direct mail and wholesalers, including Baker & Taylor and Blackwell North America. **Principal Officers and Managers** Ravi Mehra, President; Lata Mehra, Vice-President; Leota Lamb, Treasurer; Valerie Kressner, Larry Reynolds, Editors. **Number of New Titles:** 1991 - 12, 1992 - 10, 1993 (est.) - 10; Total Titles in Print - 90. **Discounts:** Bookstores - 20%; Libraries - None; Wholesalers - 20%. **Percentage of Sales to:** Libraries - 30%; Bookstores - 70%. **Selected Titles:** *A New Look at Black Families* by Charles V. Willie; *Terrorism in Northern Ireland* by Alfred McClung Lee; *Seven Deadly Sins* by Stanford M. Lyman; *Mainstreaming Outsiders: The Production of Black Professionals* by James E. Blackwell; *Pursuit of Equality in Higher Education* by Anne S. Pruitt; *Classes: A Marxist Critique* by Paul Kamolnick.

★4146★
Georgia A. Johnson Publishing Co.
2608 Darien Dr.   Ph: (517)372-9642
Lansing, MI 48912   Fax: (517)669-1265

Description: Publishes nonfiction concerning Blacks and women. Reaches market through Partner's Distributor, Baker & Taylor, and Quality Books, Inc. **Principal Officers and Managers** Georgia A. Johnson, Proprietor. **Number of New Titles:** 1991 - 1, 1993 (est.) - 2; Total Titles in Print - 3. **Subjects:** Black history, U.S. gold rush history. **Discounts:** Bookstores - 40%; Libraries - 20%; Others - 55%. **Percentage of Sales to:** Libraries - 10%; Bookstores - 40%; Individuals - 40%; Others - 10%. **Selected Titles:** *Towpath to Freedom, Webster's Gold,* both by Georgia A. Johnson.

★4147★
Georgian Press Co.
2620 SW Georgian Pl.
Portland, OR 97201   Ph: (503)223-9899

Description: Publishes books on Portland history (business and politics) and Black history. Reaches market through direct mail, reviews, and Pacific Pipeline. **Principal Officers and Managers** E. Kimbark MacColl, President and Treasurer; Leeanne G. MacColl, Vice-President; E. Kimbark MacColl, Jr., Secretary. **Discounts:** Bookstores - 40% (no returns); Libraries - 20%; Others - 20% (with the option to return). **Percentage of Sales to:** Libraries - 20%; Individuals - 10%. **Selected Titles:** *A Peculiar Paradise: A History of Blacks in Oregon* by Elizabeth McLagan; *Merchants, Money and Power: The Portland Establishment 1843-1913* by Kim MacColl and Harry H. Stein.

★4148★
Good Hope Enterprises, Inc.
4300 N. Central, Ste. 201   Ph: (214)823-7666
Dallas, TX 75206   Fax: (214)823-7373

Description: Publishes nonfiction novels and cultural and political books about Africa and other countries. Also publishes a monthly newspaper, *African Herald.* Reaches market through commission representatives. **Principal Officers and Managers** Richard O. Nwachukwu, President; Victoria Nwachukwu, Vice-President. **Discounts:** Bookstores - 40-55%. **Percentage of Sales to:** Libraries - 10%; Bookstores - 45%; Non-Book Retail Outlets - 30%. **Selected Titles:** *The Agony: The Untold Tale of the Nigerian Society, The Dark and Bright Continent: Africa in the Changing World,* both by Richard O. Nwachukwu.

★4149★
Guild Press
PO Box 22583
Robbinsdale, MN 55422   Ph: (612)566-1842

Description: Publishes works of minority authors in Minnesota. Reaches market through direct mail. **Principal Officers and Managers** Ginny Knight, Maurice W. Britts, Leon Knight, P. J. Sloan. **Number of New Titles:** 1991 - 3, 1992 - 3; Total Titles in Print - 27. **Subjects:** Poetry, short prose. **Discounts:** Bookstores - 40%. **Selected Titles:** *A Distant Land: Near* by Leon Knight and Zhang Yun; *A Most Defiant Act* by Hazel Clayton Harrison and Ginny Knight; *Vera's Return* by Leon Knight; *Butterflies on the Wind* (Chinese and English); *Black Men Still Singing; Fragrant African Flowers.*

★4150★
Gumbs & Thomas Publishers, Inc.
142 W. 72nd St., Ste. 9   Ph: (212)769-8022
New York, NY 10023   Fax: (212)283-4306

Description: Publishes materials on Black history and culture from around the world. Offers greeting cards. Distributes for Culture Expressions. Reaches market through direct mail, trade sales, and wholesalers. **Principal Officers and Managers** Verl Thomas, President; Bob Gumbs, Vice-President. **Number of New Titles:** 1991 - 3, 1992 - 7; Total Titles in Print - 6. **Discounts:** Bookstores - 30-50%. **Percentage of Sales to:** Libraries - 10%; Bookstores - 50%; Individuals - 5%; Distributors - 35%. **Selected Titles:** *Kwanzaa: Everything You Always Wanted to Know but Didn't Know Where to Ask* by Cedric McClester; *Harlem Today: A Cultural and Visitors Guide* by A. Peter Bailey; *Let's Celebrate Kwanzaa: An Activity Book for Young Readers* by Helen Davis Thompson; *On the Real Side* by Shirley Riley; *The Caribbean: A Cultural Journey* by Linda Cousins.

★4151★
Harlem Institute of Fashion
155-157 W. 126th St.
New York, NY 10027 Ph: (212)666-1320

Description: Publishes on the history of Black fashion from slavery to present times. Offers art post cards. Reaches market through direct mail. **Principal Officers and Managers** Lois K. Alexander, Founder and Director; Julius F. Lane, Administrator; Alma Goss, National President; J. Lane, Department Director. **Percentage of Sales to:** Libraries - 50%; Bookstores - 10%; Non-Book Retail Outlets - 10%; Individuals - 30%. **Selected Titles:** *Blacks in the History of Fashion* by L. K. Alexander; *Portrait of the Black Designer: 1880-1988; Modiste Elizabeth Heckley: From Slaverey to the White House.*

★4152★
Helga M. Rogers
4975 59th Ave. S.
St. Petersburg, FL 33715 Ph: (813)864-3292

Description: Publishes on Black Americans. **Principal Officers and Managers** Helga M. Rogers, Owner. **Subjects:** History. **Discounts:** Bookstores - Please inquire. **Selected Titles:** *Sex and Race, Vols. I-III; 100 Amazing Facts about the Negro; The Five Negro Presidents; From Superman to Man; Nature Knows No Color Line; Africa's Gift to America,* all by J. A. Rogers.

★4153★
Heritage Press
PO Box 18625
Baltimore, MD 21216 Ph: (301)728-8521

Description: Publishes books on the Black perspective of life in America. **Principal Officers and Managers** Wilbert L. Walker, President. **Discounts:** Bookstores - 40% (2); Libraries - 30%; Others - Up to 50% (quantity). **Percentage of Sales to:** Bookstores - 10%; Libraries - 15%; Individuals - 50%; Schools & Colleges - 25%. **Selected Titles:** *Stalemate at Panmunjon, We Are Men: Memoirs of World War II and the Korean War, Servants of All, The Deputy's Dilemma,* all by Wilbert L. Walker.

★4154★
Holistic Academy
PO Box 1621
Muncie, IN 47308

Description: Publishes books, videos, and catalogs on holistic health, women, and Black studies. Offers a quarterly newsletter and *Nature's Aid First Aid Kits.* Also offers herbs, vitamins, and health products. Distributes for Nature's Sunshine, Carlton Press, Earth Pride, and Nutrition Express. Reaches market through direct mail, wholesalers, and trade sales. Formerly known as Holistic Exchange. **Principal Officers and Managers** Melvia F. Miller, President. **Number of New Titles:** 1992 - 2; Total Titles in Print - 20. **Discounts:** Bookstores - Please inquire. **Percentage of Sales to:** Libraries - 10%; Bookstores - 40%; Individuals - 50%. **Selected Titles:** *Black History Comic Books* by Baylor; *An Apple A Day, Road to Riches, New and Different Friends,* all by Miller; *System Guide to Natural Health; The Seven Basic Lesson of Black History.*

★4155★
Holloway House Publishing Co.
8060 Melrose Ave. Ph: (213)653-8060
Los Angeles, CA 90046 Fax: (213)655-9452

Description: Publishes books written by Blacks, about the Black lifestyle, and history. Offers a calendar. Reaches market through commission representatives and telephone sales. **Principal Officers and Managers** Ralph Weinstock, President; Mitchell Neal, General Manager; Marc K. Morriss, Systems Manager; Marian O'Farrell, Vice-President Operations. **Percentage of Sales to:** Libraries - 20%; Bookstores - 40%; Individuals - 2%; Mass Market Outlets - 50%. **Selected Titles:** *Trick Baby* by Robert Beck; *Daddy Cool* by Donald Goines; *How to Win* by Mike Goodman; *Paul Robeson, Richard Pryor,* both by Joe Nazel; *Passion's Surrender* by K. Norton.

★4156★
Impact! Publications
5517 Secrest Dr.
Los Angeles, CA 90043 Ph: (213)298-0266

Description: Publishes on social issues. Offers a newsletter, *Ofari's Bimonthly.* Does not accept unsolicited manuscripts. Reaches market through trade sales and wholesalers and distributors, including Baker & Taylor, Inland Books, and Red Sea Press. **Principal Officers and Managers** Barbara Bramwell, Publisher. **Number of New Titles:** 1992 - 1, 1993 (est.) - 1; Total Titles in Print - 3. **Subjects:** Black studies. **Percentage of Sales to:** Libraries - 15%; Bookstores - 75%; Non-Book Retail Outlets - 1%; Individuals - 5%. **Selected Titles:** *Crime: Why It Exists, What Can Be Done; Crime, Drugs, and African Americans; Black Fatherhood: The Guide to Male Parenting,* all by Earl Ofari Hutchinson.

★4157★
Indiana University Bloomington African Studies Program
Woodburn Hall 221
Bloomington, IN 47405 Ph: (812)335-6825

Description: Publishes monographs, papers, and lecture texts by scholars in the field of African studies. Reaches market through wholesalers and library exchange. **Principal Officers and Managers** Patrick O'Meara, Director; N. Brian Winchester, Associate Director. **Subjects:** African studies, including political science, folklore, anthropology, fine arts, music, linguistics, history. **Discounts:** Bookstores - 10% (10, single title). **Percentage of Sales to:** Bookstores - 40%; Non-Book Retail Outlets - 40%; Individuals - 10%. **Selected Titles:** *Security Problems: An African Predicament* by Francis Deng; *Short Time to Stay: Comments on Time, Literature, and Oral Performance* by Ruth Finnegan; *Films on Africa* by Paul Lazar; *Speaking of Art: A Giriama Impression* by David Parkin; *The Dialects of Mandekan* by Charles Bird.

★4158★
Institute for Liberian Studies
4719 Chester Ave.
Philadelphia, PA 19143

Principal Officers and Managers Svend E. Holsoe. **Subjects:** Liberia. **Selected Titles:** *Immigrants to Liberia, 1820-1843: An Alphabetical Listing* by Tom W. Shick; *Immigrants to Liberia, 1844-1864; An Alphabetical Listing* by Robert T. Brown; *Essays on the Economic Anthropology of Liberia and Sierra Leone* by Darjahn and Isaac; *Immigrants to Liberia, 1865-1904: An Alphabetical Listing* by Peter J. Murdza, Jr.; *Ethnohistorical Studies on the Kru Coast* by Ronald W. Davis; *A Bibliography on Liberia, Parts 1-2* by Svend E. Holsoe.

★4159★
Institute for Southern Studies
2009 Chapel Hill Rd.
Durham, NC 27707 Ph: (919)419-8311

Description: Founded by civil rights and peace groups, the Institute sponsors programs and publications to assist organizations and individuals working for progressive change in this region. Also publishes a journal of southern politics, *Southern Exposure.* Reaches market through commission representatives and direct mail. **Principal Officers and Managers** Eric Bates, Managing Editor. **Number of New Titles:** 1991 - 5, 1992 - 4; Total Titles in Print - 80. **Subjects:** Black studies, energy, politics, economics, labor history, women's studies, culture. **Discounts:** Bookstores - 40%. **Percentage of Sales to:** Libraries - 10%; Bookstores - 4%; Non-Book Retail Outlets - 1%; Individuals - 85%. **Selected Titles:** *The Encyclopedia of Southern Life and Change* by Hall; *Elections: Grassroots Strategies for Change/A User's Manual* by Miller; *Changing Scene: Theater in the South* by Ranson; *Older, Wiser, Stronger: Aging and Elders* by Eldridge; *Tower of Babel: The Nuclear Power Industry* by Overton; *Through the Hoop: The Sporting South* by Wood and Okun.

★4160★
Investor Responsibility Research Center, Inc.
1755 Massachusetts Ave. NW, Ste. 600 Ph: (202)234-7500
Washington, DC 20036 Fax: (202)332-8570

Description: An independent, not-for-profit corporation that conducts research and publishes reports on contemporary business and public policy issues that affect corporations and institutional investors. Offers software and five newsletters, *News for Investors, Corporate Governance Bulletin, South Africa Reporter, Investor's Environmental Report,* and *Global Shareholder.* Accepts manuscripts. Reaches market through direct mail. **Principal Officers and Managers** Margaret Carroll, Executive Director; Carolyn Mathiasen, Social Issues Director; Meg Voorhes, South Africa Director; Peg O'Hara, Director, Corporate Communications; Patrick McGurn, Corporate Governance Director. **Number of New Titles:** 1991 - 12, 1992 - 15, 1993 (est.) - 15; Total Titles in Print - 45. **Subjects:** Corporate governance, global investing, South Africa, Northern Ireland, energy and the environment, social issues. **Discounts:** Please inquire. **Percentage of Sales to:** Individuals - 8%; Libraries - 26%; Corporations - 66%. **Selected Titles:** *Can States Stop Corporate Takeovers; Junk Bonds and Tender Offer Financing; U.S. and Canadian Business in South Africa, 1987; Black South Africans' Views on Sanctions; U.S. Arms Exports: Policies and Contractors; The Nuclear Weapons Industry.*

★4161★
James H. Boykin
1260 NW 122nd St.
Miami, FL 33167   Ph: (305)681-7663

Description: Publishes on history. Reaches market through commission representatives, trade and telephone sales, and wholesalers. **Principal Officers and Managers** James H. Boykin, Author and Publisher. **Number of New Titles:** 1993 (est.) - 1; Total Titles in Print - 7. **Subjects:** History, political science. **Discounts:** Please inquire. **Percentage of Sales to:** Libraries - 5%; Individuals - 8%; Bookstores - 87%. **Selected Titles:** *Beta, Bene, and the Peripheral Diaspora; World Blacks: Self Help and Achievement; Black Jews; Thank God for Black Power; Imperialism Theory and Practice; Political Intrigue in the Establishment of the Nature of Jesus and Mary,* all by James H. Boykin.

★4162★
Joint Center for Political and Economic Studies
1090 Vermont Ave. NW, Ste. 1100   Ph: (202)789-3500
Washington, DC 20005-4961   Fax: (202)789-6390

Description: Conducts programs in research, training, technical assistance, and information, with the aim of increasing the effectiveness of Black elected officials specifically, and Black Americans generally, in all aspects of governance. Offers *Focus,* a monthly newsletter and the annual, *Black Elected Officials: A National Roster.* Reaches market through direct mail. Formerly known as M/Joint Center for Political Studies. **Principal Officers and Managers** Eddie N. Williams, President; John Gladney, Executive Vice-President; Eleanor Farrar, Senior Vice-President; Milton Morris, Vice-President, Research. **Number of New Titles:** 1991 - 6, 1992 - 8, 1993 (est.) - 9; Total Titles in Print - 20. **Discounts:** Universal Schedule - 20% (2). **Selected Titles:** *Black State Legislators, 1992: A Survey and Analysis of Black Leadership in the State Capitols* by David Bositis; *Keep Hope Alive! Super Tuesday and Jesse Jackson's 1988 Campaign for the Presidency* by Penn Kimball; *Major Studies of Minority Business: A Bibliographic Review* by Timothy Bates; *Minorities and Privatization* by Robert Suggs; *Poverty, Inequality, and the Crisis of Social Policy* edited by Katherine McFate; *Elected and Appointed Black Judges in the United States, 1991.*

★4163★
Just Us Books, Inc.
301 Main St., Ste. No. 22-24   Ph: (201)672-7701
Orange, NJ 07050   Fax: (201)677-7570

Description: Publishes books and learning materials for children that focus on the African-American experience. Offers audio cassettes and posters. Publishes a children's newspaper *Harambee.* Accepts unsolicited manuscripts with a query and self-addressed stamped envelope. Editorial phone number: (201) 676-4345. Reaches market through direct mail, trade sales, and distributors and wholesalers, including Baker & Taylor Books, Quality Books, Inc., Inland Book Co., and Red Sea Press. Free telephone number for orders: (800) 886-7701. **Principal Officers and Managers** Wade Hudson, President and CEO; Cheryl Willis-Hudson, Vice-President and Publisher; Willie Hudson, Sales. **Number of New Titles:** 1992 - 4, 1993 (est.) - 5; Total Titles in Print - 16. **Discounts:** Bookstores - 40-47%. **Percentage of Sales to:** Libraries - 10%; Bookstores - 55%; Non-Book Retail Outlets - 5%; Individuals - 15%; Schools - 15%.

Selected Titles: *Afro-Bets ABC Book, Bright Eyes Brown Skin,* both by Cheryl Willis Hudson; *Afro-Bets First Book About Africa* by Veronica Freeman Ellis; *Afro-Bets Book of Black Heroes from A to Z* by Wade Hudson and V. W. Wesley; *Jamal's Busy Day* by W. Hudson and G. Ford; *When I Was Little* by T. Igus and Higgins Bond.

★4164★
Kansas City Black Pages
1601 E. 18th St., Ste. 315   Ph: (816)421-0400
Kansas City, MO 64108   Fax: (816)472-0240

Description: Publishes directories for the minority community and corporations of Kansas City. Reaches market through commission representatives and telephone sales. **Principal Officers and Managers** Arnette D. French, Publisher; Kenneth Stone, Jr., Manager. **Selected Titles:** *Kansas City Black Pages; Chicago Black Pages; Dallas Black Pages; Fort Worth Black Pages.*

★4165★
Kitchen Table: Women of Color Press
PO Box 908
Latham, NY 12110

Description: "The first publisher in North America with a commitment to publishing and distributing the work of Third World women of all racial/cultural heritages, sexualities, and classes." **Principal Officers and Managers** Myrna Bain, Audre Lorde, Cherrie Moraga, Mariana Romo-Carmona, Barbara Smith, Collective Members.

★4166★
Lambeth Press
143 E. 37th St.
New York, NY 10016   Ph: (212)679-0163

Description: Publishes scholarly books with popular appeal. Reaches market through direct mail. **Subjects:** Religion, African-Americans. **Selected Titles:** *Separation of Church and State* by Robert L. Cord; *Cursillo: Anatomy of Movement* by Marcene Marcoux; *God Comes to America: Father Divine* by Kenneth Burnham; *Defender of the Race: Bishop Holly* by David Dean; *Lemuel Heynes: A Bio-Bibliography, Afro-American Education: A Bibliographic Index,* both by Richard Newman.

★4167★
Love Child Publishing
6565 Sunset Blvd., Ste. 318
North Hollywood, CA 91601   Ph: (213)960-5490

Description: Publishes career guides and reference guides on African-Americans in the entertainment industry. Offers the bimonthly *Black Talent News* and talent consulting and counseling services. Accepts unsolicited manuscripts. Reaches market through direct mail and advertising. **Principal Officers and Managers** Tanya Monique Kersey, Publisher. **Number of New Titles:** 1991 - 3, 1992 - 4, 1993 (est.) - 3; Total Titles in Print - 4. **Discounts:** Bookstores - 20% (2-4), 40% (5-99), 44% (100). **Percentage of Sales to:** Bookstores - 50%; Libraries - 25%; Individuals - 25%. **Selected Titles:** *Black State of the Arts* by Tanya Monique Kersey and Bruce Hawkins; *1992-93 Black Talent Resource Guide, The Performer's Plan,* both by Tanya Monique Kersey; *Original Monologues for African American Performers* by Sabrina Norman.

★4168★
M. L. Williams Publishing Co., Inc.
PO Box 53552
1315 Walnut St., Ste. 1624   Ph: (215)735-1121
Philadelphia, PA 19105   Fax: (215)471-9550

Description: Publishes titles on African-Americans in legal and related professions. Offers services and products to assist minority lawyers in marketing legal services. Also offers audio cassettes, informational pamphlets, a biannual mid-year supplement, and a quarterly newsletter. Accepts unsolicited manuscripts. Reaches market through direct mail and trade sales. **Principal Officers and Managers** Marshall L. Williams, Publisher, Editor, Chairor; Dennis Jemmerson, Subscription Director. **Discounts:** Bookstores - 35% (3-10), 50% (11); Libraries - 20% (2-5), 40% (6). **Percentage of Sales to:** Libraries - 70%; Bookstores - 10%; Corporations - 10%; Individuals - 10%. **Selected Titles:** *National Directory of Black Law Firms* by G. Ware; *1991-92 National Directory of Minority Law Firms, Directory of Black Lawyers in Pennsylvania, Delaware, and New*

York, Marketing Legal Services and Increasing Profitability, all by M. L. Williams.

★4169★
Majority Press
PO Box 538   Ph: (508)655-1631
Dover, MA 02030   Fax: (508)655-5636
Description: Specializes in college texts and adult nonfiction in African-American, Caribbean, and African studies. Reaches market through direct mail and trade sales. Telephone number for placing orders only: (617) 828-8450. **Principal Officers and Managers** E. L. Zabo. **Number of New Titles:** 1991 - 4, 1992 - 2; Total Titles in Print - 14. **Discounts:** Bookstores - 40%; School Bookstores - 20%; Distributors - Please inquire. **Selected Titles:** *Literary Garveyism: Garvey, Black Arts, and the Harlem Renaissance; Marcus Garvey: Hero; The Pan-African Connection; Race First* all by Tony Martin; *Philosophy and Opinions of Marcus Garvey* edited by Amy Jacques Garvey; *Brazil: Mixture or Massacre* by Abdias do Nascimento.

★4170★
Melvett Chambers, Author/Publisher
PO Box 8475
Denver, CO 80201   Ph: (303)371-8729
Description: Publishes books on the history of Black Americans, past and present. Also offers calendars and cookbooks. Reaches market through direct mail, trade sales, Ingram Book Co., ABA, and Baker & Taylor. **Principal Officers and Managers** Melvett G. Chambers, Author and Publisher. **Number of New Titles:** 1991 - 2, 1992 - 2, 1993 (est.) - 4; Total Titles in Print - 5. **Discounts:** Retailers - 20% (1-4), 40% (5-24), 42% (25-99), 44% (100-499), 46% (500-999), 47% (1000); Libraries - 20%. **Percentage of Sales to:** Libraries - 30%; Bookstores - 50%; Individuals - 10%; Non-Book Retail Outlets - 10%. **Selected Titles:** *The Black History Trivia Quiz Book, The Denver-Metro Child Care Preschool Directory, Soul Cookin' Southern Style,* all by Melvett G. Chambers; *Your Place or Mine* by Sue Browning; *Life Begins at the Golden Age* by Billie A. Grant; *African People's Contributions to World Civilizations* by Dr. Paul Hamilton.

★4171★
Michigan State University
African Studies Center
100 International Center   Ph: (517)353-1700
East Lansing, MI 48824-1035   Fax: (517)336-1209
Description: Promotes understanding of Africa and aids scholarly research. Also publishes *African Studies Center Newsletter* and three triennial journals: *African Urban Studies, Northeast African Studies,* and *Rural Africana.* Reaches market through direct mail. **Principal Officers and Managers** David Wiley, Director; Harold Marcus, Associate Director for Publications. **Number of New Titles:** 1992 - 1; Total Titles in Print - 51. **Discounts:** Bookstores - 15%. **Percentage of Sales to:** Libraries - 31%; Bookstores - 14%; Individuals - 18%; Organizations - 37%. **Selected Titles:** *Linguistic Bibliography of the Non-Semitic Languages of Ethiopia* by Peter Unseth; *Music, Ritual, and Falasha History* by Kay K. Shelemay; *African Dress* by Joanne Bubolz Eicher; *Africa on Film and Videotape, 1960-1981: A Compendium of Reviews* by David Wiley et al., *After the Millenium* by Lidwein Kapteijns and Jay Spaulding; *State Transformation and National Integration: Gedeo and the Ethiopian Empire, 1895-1935* by Charles W. McClellan.

★4172★
Montclair State College
Center for Economic Research on Africa (CERAF)
School of Business Administration
Dept. of Economics & Finance   Ph: (201)893-7299
Upper Montclair, NJ 07043   Fax: (201)893-5455
Description: Publishes research monographs on Africa's economic situation. Also offers a database. Accepts unsolicited manuscripts. Reaches market through direct mail and trade sales. **Principal Officers and Managers** Phillip LeBel, Executive Director. **Number of New Titles:** 1991 - 1, 1992 - 1; Total Titles in Print - 6. **Percentage of Sales to:** Individuals - 20%; Libraries - 80%. **Selected Titles:** *Policy Options for Ethiopias Coffee Exports* by Samia Z. Gutu; *Managing Africa's Economic Recovery; Economic Choices for Substainable Agriculture in Africa; New Initiatives for Africa's Debt; Europe 1992: Africa and the U.S.*

★4173★
Mphahlele K. Lukman, Inc.
9110 Ave. ''A''
Brooklyn, NY 11236   Ph: (212)485-7009
Description: Publishes on sociology, biology, African history, anthropology, and biochemistry as it relates to the origin of skin color. Reaches market through direct mail and telephone sales. **Principal Officers and Managers** Mphahlele K. Lukman, Author and Publisher. **Selected Titles:** *The Critical Issues of Skin Colour: A Treatise on the Sociological, Economic, and Political Reality of Blacks in a White Society* by Lukman.

★4174★
National Action Council for Minorities in Engineering
3 W. 35th St.
New York, NY 10001   Ph: (212)279-2626
Description: "Council seeks to increase the number of African American, Hispanic, and American Indian students enrolled in and graduating from engineering schools." Publishes career guidance and financial aid information, program development models, and data and statistics. Offers *NACME News* triannually; also offers posters. Reaches market through direct mail. **Principal Officers and Managers** George Campbell, Jr., President; Lea E. Williams, Executive Vice-President; Issac W. Saunders, Vice-President, Resource Development; Ron Denes, Vice-President, Communications and Public Relations. **Discounts:** Please inquire. **Selected Titles:** *The Sky's Not the Limit* (poster and brochure); *The Student's Guide to Engineering Schools; NACME Statistical Report 1988; MEPs/USA: The Directory of Precollege and University Minority Engineering Programs.*

★4175★
National Black Music Foundation
902 42nd Ave. N.
PO Box 90639
Nashville, TN 37209   Ph: (615)321-3319
Description: Promotes music "born out of the Black experience." Also publishes newsletters, a catalog of new publications and recordings, and a quarterly magazine. Accepts unsolicited manuscripts. Distributes for Theoda Records, Mester Music Publications, and Carrie Records. Reaches market through direct mail. Formerly listed as James Hendrix Enterprises. **Principal Officers and Managers** James Hendrix, Founder and Director. **Number of New Titles:** 1992 - 10, 1993 (est.) - 6; Total Titles in Print - 581. **Discounts:** Bookstores - 40%; Libraries - 50%; Sheet Music Dealers - 40%. **Percentage of Sales to:** Libraries - 25%; Bookstores - 40%; Sheet Music Dealers - 35%. **Selected Titles:** *I Remember Tom: Sports Documentary of the 1930's* (book), *Caravan: Tribute to Senior Citizens, To Be at Peace with God, Let God Take Over, All I Well, My Mother's Faith in God,* (all sheet music) all by James Hendrix.

★4176★
National Center for Urban Ethnic Affairs
PO Box 20
Washington, DC 20064   Ph: (202)232-3600
Description: Established to develop neighborhood programs and policies which are grounded in the appreciation of ethnic cultural diversity. **Principal Officers and Managers** John A. Kromkowski, President. **Number of New Titles:** 1991 - 4, 1992 - 2; Total Titles in Print - 15. **Selected Titles:** *Reclaiming the Inner City, Reversing Urban Decline,* both by Ed Marciniak; *A Guide to the Language of Neighborhoods* by William Watman; *The Self-Help Bridge: A Manual for Support Groups for the Jobless* by Ellie Wegener; *Non-Profits with Hard Hats: Building Affordable Housing* by Kelly, Kuehn, and Marciniak; *Pieces of A Dream* by Baroni, et al.

★4177★
Network Communications, Inc.
PO Box 26398
San Diego, CA 92196-0398   Ph: (619)792-9756
Description: Publishes on affirmative action and equal employment opportunity. Reaches market through direct mail. **Principal Officers and Managers** David J. Miramontes, President. **Discounts:** Bookstores - 40%; Libraries - 25%; Distributors - 40%. **Percentage of Sales to:** Libraries - 20%; Bookstores - 25%; Non-Book Retail

Outlets - 35%; Individuals - 20%. **Selected Titles:** *How to Deal with Sexual Harassment* by David J. Miramontes.

★4178★
New Day Press, Inc.
Karamu House
2355 E. 89th St.
Cleveland, OH 44106   Ph: (216)795-7070

Description: Publishes books on Black history and biography for children and young adults. Accepts unsolicited manuscripts. Reaches market through direct mail. **Principal Officers and Managers** Ebraska Ceasor, President; Charlotte Durant, Vice-President; Carl Boyd, Treasurer; Shirley Hayes, Secretary. **Discounts:** Universal - 20% (2-5), 30% (6-30). **Percentage of Sales to:** Libraries - 40%; Bookstores - 1%; Individuals - 19%; Schools - 40%. **Selected Titles:** *Blacks in Ohio* by Mary Shepard et al.; *Ouladah the African Boy* by Suzanne Hartman; *The First Freedom Ride* by Martha L. Smith; *Walk in My Footsteps* by Martha Grooms; *Henry Box Brown* by Pamela Pruitt and Brenda Johnston; *Black Image Makers* by Edith Gaines et al.

★4179★
Omenana
116 Howland St.
Roxbury, MA 02121   Ph: (617)445-0161

Description: A nonprofit organization that publishes material about Africa. **Principal Officers and Managers** Dibinga wa Said, Vice-President; Musau Misenga, Sales Manager. **Subjects:** Religion, humanities, social sciences. **Discounts:** Bookstores - 40% **Percentage of Sales to:** Libraries - 50%; Bookstores - 38%; Non-Book Retail Outlets - 10%; Individuals - 2%. **Selected Titles:** *African Religion* by Aloysius Lugira; *Class Struggles and National Liberation in Africa* by Nzonoola-Ntalaja; *Corporate Class Ethics and Apartheid; Ethico-Embryonic Theories of Abortion and Development* by Naolela wa Kabongo; *The Religion of the Yoruba* by J. Olumide Kayode.

★4180★
Open Hand Publishing Inc.
PO Box 22048
Seattle, WA 98122   Ph: (206)447-0597

Description: A literary/political press dedicated to the promotion of social change. Offers postcards. Distributes for Africa World Press. Reaches market through the Talman Co., Inc. **Principal Officers and Managers** P. Anna Johnson, President. **Number of New Titles:** 1991 - 1, 1992 - 4, 1993 (est.) - 4; Total Titles in Print - 21. **Subjects:** African-American studies, bilingual children's literature. **Discounts:** Please inquire. **Percentage of Sales to:** Libraries - 40%; Bookstores - 40%; Non-Book Retail Outlets - 5%; Individuals - 15%. **Selected Titles:** *Mississippi to Madrid: Memoir of a Black American in the Abraham Lincoln Brigade* by James Yates; *Self-Determination: An Examination of the Question and Its Application to the African-American People; The Making of Black Revolutionaries; Sammy Younge, Jr.: The First Black College Student to Die in the Black Liberation Movement,* all by James Forman; *The Black West* by William Loren Katz; *The Invisible Empire: Impact of the Klu Klux Klan on History* by William Loren Katz.

★4181★
Path Press, Inc.
53 W. Jackson Blvd., Ste. 724   Ph: (312)663-0167
Chicago, IL 60604   Fax: (312)663-5318
                                      Free: 800-669-9700

Description: Publishes books by and about Black Americans and Third World peoples. Accepts unsolicited manuscripts. Reaches market through commission representatives, direct mail, and catalog. **Principal Officers and Managers** Bennett J. Johnson, President; Herman C. Gilbert, Executive Vice-President; Ethelyn J. Baker, Secretary. **Number of New Titles:** 1991 - 3, 1992 - 3; Total Titles in Print - 7. **Subjects:** Fiction, nonfiction, poetry. **Discounts:** Bookstores & Libraries - 20-46%. **Percentage of Sales to:** Libraries - 50%; Bookstores - 35%; Non-Book Retail Outlets - 10%; Book Parties - 5%. **Selected Titles:** *To Benji with Love* by Mary Wilson; *Congo Crew* by William Goodlett; *Everyday in African-American History* by Al Boswell; *Up North Big City Street* by Zack Gilbert; *The Negotiations* by Herman C. Gilbert; *What Happens When Children Write* by Darlene Smith.

★4182★
Paul G. Partington
7320 S. Gretna Ave.
Whittier, CA 90606   Ph: (213)695-7960

Description: Self-publisher on Black studies. **Principal Officers and Managers** Paul G. Partington, President. **Discounts:** Please inquire. **Percentage of Sales to:** Libraries - 90%; Individuals - 10%. **Selected Titles:** *W. E. B. DuBois: A Bibliography of His Published Writings* by P. G. Partington.

★4183★
Place in the Woods
3900 Glenwood Ave.   Ph: (612)374-2120
Golden Valley, MN 55422   Fax: (612)593-5593

Description: Publishes biographical research and analysis of minority achievements, especially of leaders not covered in textbooks. Accepts unsolicited manuscripts; query first. Reaches market through direct mail, distribution in the Reading Is Fundamental, Head Start, and Migrant Education programs nationwide, and through wholesalers and jobbers. **Principal Officers and Managers** Roger A. Hammer, Editor and Publisher. **Number of New Titles:** 1992 - 2, 1993 (est.) - 3; Total Titles in Print - 7. **Subjects:** Humanities, minorities, affirmative action, equal employment opportunity, reading, education. **Discounts:** Bookstores & Libraries - 20%. **Percentage of Sales to:** Libraries - 30%; Schools - 30%; Distributors - 10%; Individuals - 30%. **Selected Titles:** *African America: Heralding a Heritage; The People: Native American–Thoughts and Feelings; American Woman: Hidden in History, Forging the Future; Hispanic America: Freeing the Free, Honoring Heroes; My Own Book; The PR (Public Relations) Handbook,* all by Hammer.

★4184★
Poets Pay Rent, Too
PO Box 75796, Sanford Sta.
Los Angeles, CA 90075   Ph: (213)462-6565

Description: Supports and sponsors authors and events relating to Black Americans. Publishes on theatre, film, television, poetry, and literature. Formerly known as Togetherness Productions/Poets Pay Rent, Too. **Principal Officers and Managers** Saundra Sharp, Publisher and Editor. **Discounts:** Bookstores - 40%; Libraries - 30%. **Selected Titles:** *Soft Song, In the Midst of Change, Black History Film List: 150 Films and Where to Find Them, The Sistuhs,* (play), all by Saundra Sharp; *Bloodlines* by Robert E. Price.

★4185★
Project BAIT Publishing
13217 Livernois
Detroit, MI 48238-3162   Ph: (313)931-3427

Description: Purpose is to produce limited editions of manuscripts by Black American writers (cartoons, novels, short stories, essays, plays, and poetry). Also publishes a Black arts magazine, *THEDAMU.* Accepts unsolicited nonfiction manuscripts for magazine. **Principal Officers and Managers** David Rambeau, Publisher; Titilaya Akanke, Managing Editor; Nehemiah Pitts, Associate Editor; Charles Allen, Illustrator. **Number of New Titles:** 1992 - 12. **Discounts:** Universal Schedule - 40%. **Selected Titles:** *A Brick for Mr. Jones* by Charles W. Moore; *Caught in the Act, Slide On, Out in the Street, The Great White Sale,* (play) all by Demon Smith; *ACE* (musical) by David Rambeau.

★4186★
R & M Publishing Co.
PO Box 1276
Holly Hill, SC 29059   Ph: (706)738-0360

Description: Publishes books for students and laypersons on U.S. history, politics, socio-psychology, curriculum development, art appreciation, and genealogy. Also offers a mailing list. Accepts unsolicited manuscripts. Reaches market through direct mail, trade sales, Baker & Taylor Books, Key Sea Press, and Quality Books, Inc. **Principal Officers and Managers** Mack B. Morant, Publisher; Charlotte Orange, Editor-in-Chief; Cassandra F. Williams, Secretary; William Harvey, Editor. **Number of New Titles:** 1992 - 2; Total Titles in Print - 11. **Discounts:** Bookstores - 10-55%. **Percentage of Sales to:** Libraries - 20%; Bookstores - 30%; Non-Book Retail Outlets - 20%; Individuals - 20%; Others - 10%. **Selected Titles:** *Seasons in Life* by Bonnie Gear; *Only Winning Counts: A Practical Guide to*

Winning Elections in Your Community by Nona Tevis; *The Insane Nigger* by Mack B. Morant; *Guyanese Seed of Soul: How to Prepare West Indian Food* by Yvonne John; *Prose and Poetic Expressions of a Black Woman* by Marie Ransom; *Sleepy Willie Talks About Life* by Horace Mungin.

★4187★
Raw Ink Press
Southwest Sta.
PO Box 70417
Washington, DC 20024-0417   Ph: (202)686-4686
Description: Publishes poetry dealing with Black affairs, women's issues, and single parenting. Reaches market through direct mail. Formerly known as Rashad Associates/Raw Ink Press. **Principal Officers and Managers** Johari M. Rashad, President. **Number of New Titles:** 1992 - 1; Total Titles in Print - 3. **Discounts:** Bookstores - 20%; Libraries - 25%. **Percentage of Sales to:** Libraries - 25%; Non-Book Retail Outlets - 25%; Individuals - 50%. **Selected Titles:** *(R)evolutions; Woman, Too; Steppin' Over the Glass: Life Journeys in Poetry and Prose,* all by Johari M. Rashad.

★4188★
Red Sea Press, Inc.
15 Industry Ct.   Ph: (609)771-1666
Trenton, NJ 08638   Fax: (609)771-1616
Description: The commercial affiliate of Africa World Press. Publishes and distributes books on the Third World in general, but in particular the Horn of Africa (Red Sea region). Offers a set of posters and plans to distribute cards and calendars. Reaches market through commission representatives, direct mail, trade sales, Baker & Taylor, Book House, Midwest Library Services, Inland Book Co., Blackwell North America, and Liberation Distributors. **Principal Officers and Managers** Kassahun Checole, Publisher and President; Pamela A. Sims, Administrative Assistant. **Number of New Titles:** 1992 - 15; Total Titles in Print - 33. **Discounts:** Bookstores - 20% (1-4), 40% (5); Jobbers - 20%. **Percentage of Sales to:** Libraries - 5%; Bookstores - 75%; Individuals - 20%. **Selected Titles:** *Scraps of Life: Chilean Arpilleras, Women of Smoke: Latin American Women in Literature and Life,* both by Marjorie Agosin; *Red Tears: War, Famine and Revolution in Ethiopia* by Dawit Wolde Giorgis; *Peasants and Nationalism in Eritrea: A Critique of Ethiopan Studies* by Jordan Gebre Medhin; *Eritrea and the United Nations and Other Essays* by Bereket Habte Selassie; *The Long Struggle of Eritrea* edited by Basil Davidson and Lionel Cliffe.

★4189★
Rev. Dr. Charles L. Hoskins
St. Matthew's Episcopal Church
1401 W. Broad St.
Savannah, GA 31401   Ph: (912)234-8126
Selected Titles: *Black Episcopalians in Georgia: Strife, Struggle and Salvation; Been in the Storm So Long: Black Savannahians in the 1930's,* both by Charles L. Hoskins.

★4190★
Richard Bailey Publishers
PO Box 1264
Montgomery, AL 36102-1264   Ph: (205)287-5138
Description: Publishes history books about the African-American experience in the South. Accepts unsolicited manuscripts. Reaches market through commission representatives, direct mail, telephone sales, trade sales, distributors, and wholesalers. **Principal Officers and Managers** Richard Bailey, Owner. **Number of New Titles:** 1991 - 1, 1992 - 1; Total Titles in Print - 1. **Discounts:** Bookstores - 40%; Libraries - Up to 25%; Distributors - 55%. **Percentage of Sales to:** Libraries - 10%; Bookstores - 50%; Non-Book Retail Outlets - 1%; Individuals - 25%; Distributors - 14%. **Selected Titles:** *Neither Carpetbaggers nor Scalawags: Black Officeholders during Reconstruction of Alabama, 1867-1878* by Richard Bailey.

★4191★
Rufus Shaw Publishing
PO Box 152432   Ph: (214)331-1925
Dallas, TX 75315   Fax: (214)691-2776
Description: Publishes personal financial manuals for Black Americans. Reaches market through direct mail, trade sales, and telephone sales. **Principal Officers and Managers** Rufus Shaw, Jr., President; Lynn M. Flint, Vice-President; Debra Dean, Operations Chief. **Discounts:** Bookstores - 40%; Libraries - 15%. **Percentage of Sales to:** Libraries - 10%; Bookstores - 50%; Individuals - 40%. **Selected Titles:** *How to Be a Rich Nigger, Hustling: The Art of Black Financial Survival, Street Economics,* all by Rufus Shaw, Jr.

★4192★
Rumble, Inc.
PO Box 22151
Sacramento, CA 95822   Ph: (916)427-8705
Description: Publishes on interpersonal relationships of the Black experience. Offers the newsletter *Rumble.* **Principal Officers and Managers** Grace Douglas, Publisher. **Discounts:** Bookstores - 40% (3). **Percentage of Sales to:** Libraries - 25%; Bookstores - 10%; Non-Book Retail Outlets - 2%; Individuals - 63%. **Selected Titles:** *The Griot: An Anthology of African Necromancers* by Grace Carter-Douglas.

★4193★
Russell Mootry, Jr. Associates
810 Grove Ave.
Holly Hill, FL 32117   Ph: (904)255-6871
Description: Publishes on Black Americans. Reaches market through direct mail. **Principal Officers and Managers** Russell Mootry, Jr., President. **Number of New Titles:** 1991 - 1. **Selected Titles:** *Black Diamonds: Profiles of Successful Blacks in a Small Southern Community* by Russell Mootry, Jr.

★4194★
Sabayt Publications, Inc.
PO Box 64898   Ph: (312)667-2227
Chicago, IL 60664-0898   Free: 800-735-2881
Description: Publishes bookstore sidelines (pocket-size books, note cards, etc.) on African-American history and culture. Reaches market through direct mail, telephone sales, Baker & Taylor, Ingram, and other wholesalers and distributors. **Principal Officers and Managers** Janet C. Bell, President. **Number of New Titles:** 1992 - 1, 1993 (est.) - 1; Total Titles in Print - 2. **Discounts:** Bookstores - 40%; Libraries - 20%; Wholesalers - 50%. **Percentage of Sales to:** Libraries - .5%; Bookstores - 90%; Non-Book Retail Outlets - 4%; Corporations - .5%; Individuals - 2%; Schools - 3%. **Selected Titles:** *Famous Black Quotations (And Some Not So Famous); Famous Black Quotations on Women, Love, and Other Topics,* both by Janet Cheatham Bell.

★4195★
Seymour-Smith Publishers
PO Box 381063
Germantown, TN 38138   Ph: (901)754-4418
Description: Publishes books for multicultural education and scientific developments in behavior, athletics, and nutrition. **Principal Officers and Managers** Kim G. Andrews, Vice-President, Editorial Development; Lionel A. Mosley, Vice-President, Business Operations. **Subjects:** Black American psychology, language. **Selected Titles:** *Black Language* by Malachi Andrews and Paul Owens; *Psychoblackology* by Malachi Andrews.

★4196★
Shamal Books, Inc.
GPO Box 16
New York, NY 10116
Description: Publishes new writers, mostly poets, of African-American/Caribbean descent. Also offers typesetting, book design, and layout. Reaches market through direct mail and book fairs. **Principal Officers and Managers** Louis Reyes Rivera, Publisher and Editor; Barbara Killens-Rivera, Managing Editor. **Subjects:** Poetry, history, novels, drama. **Discounts:** Bookstores - 40% (10). **Percentage of Sales to:** Libraries - 20%; Bookstores - 5%; Individuals - 40%; Wholesalers - 35%. **Selected Titles:** *Free!* by Sekou Sundiata; *This One for You, Who Pays the Cost* 2nd ed., both by Louis Reyes Rivera; *WomanRise* edited by Louis Reyes Rivera; *Nommo* by Zizweomowale-Wa-Ngafua; *Mississippi to Madrid* by James Yates.

★4197★
Southern Africa Project
1400 I St. NW, Ste. 400
Washington, DC 20005 Ph: (202)628-6700

Description: Private, nonprofit organization working to aid political prisoners in South Africa and to promote awareness in the U.S. of human rights violations in South Africa. **Principal Officers and Managers** Gay McDougall, Director. **Selected Titles:** *Southern Africa: A Special Report; Deaths in Detention and South Africa's Security Laws; South Africa 1985: Maritial Law in the Townships.*

★4198★
Spanish Main Press
Red Hook Plaza, Ste. 237 Ph: (809)775-9277
St. Thomas, VI 00802 Fax: (809)494-4775

Description: Publishes books on the histories and peoples of the Caribbean Islands. Offers a quarterly newsletter, *The Caribbean Connection,* and limited edition art prints and charts. **Principal Officers and Managers** Fritz Seyfarth, Managing Director; Inga Wilmerding, Marketing Manager. **Number of New Titles:** 1991 - 4, 1992 - 4; Total Titles in Print - 15. **Subjects:** Sailing, treasure hunting, adventure. **Selected Titles:** *Adventure! Under a Spread of Sail* by Fritz Seyfarth; *Tales of the Caribbean; Mavericks in Paradise; Pirates of the Virgin Islands; The Caribbean on Five Dollars a Day: A Sea Gypsy Handbook for Living in Paradise.*

★4199★
Steladon Press
PO Box 4732
Upper Marlboro, MD 20775 Ph: (301)350-3669

Description: Publishes adult fiction by and/or about African-Americans. Does not accept unsolicited manuscripts. Reaches market through direct mail and wholesalers and distributors, including Baker & Taylor, D & J Book Distributors, and The Highsmith Co. **Description:** Publishes adult fiction by and/or about African-Americans. Does not accept unsolicited manuscripts. Reaches market through direct mail and wholesalers and distributors, including Baker & Taylor, D & J Book Distributors, and The Highsmith Co. **Number of New Titles:** 1991 - 1, 1993 (est.) - 1; Total Titles in Print - 1. **Principal Officers and Managers** Stephen DeBrew, President; Valencia Strange, Assistant Director, Marketing. **Principal Officers and Managers** Stephen DeBrew, President; Valencia Strange, Assistant Director, Marketing. **Number of New Titles:** 1991 - 1, 1993 (est.) - 1; Total Titles in Print - 1. **Subjects:** African-American fiction. **Subjects:** African-American fiction. **Discounts:** Bookstores - 40%; Libraries - Please inquire. **Discounts:** Bookstores - 40%; Libraries - Please inquire. **Percentage of Sales to:** Bookstores - 40%; Individuals - 60%. **Percentage of Sales to:** Bookstores - 40%; Individuals - 60%. **Selected Titles:** *Death of a Native Alien* by Stephen DeBrew. **Selected Titles:** *Death of a Native Alien* by Stephen DeBrew.

★4200★
Studio Museum in Harlem Museum Shop
144 W. 125th St.
New York, NY 10027 Ph: (212)864-4500

Description: Publishes African and African-American fine arts exhibition catalogs. Reaches market through direct mail. **Principal Officers and Managers** Joan Deroko, Shop Manager; Claudette Brown, Assistant Manager. **Discounts:** Bookstores - 40% (5); Libraries - 15%. **Percentage of Sales to:** Libraries - 1%; Bookstores - 10%; Non-Book Retail Outlets - 10%; Individuals - 79%. **Selected Titles:** *Tradition and Conflict: Images of a Turbulent Decade 1963-1973* by Campbell; *Faith Ringgold: 20 Years of Painting, Sculpture, etc.* edited by M. Wallace; *Jack Whiten: Ten Years* by Henry Gelzahler; *Harlem Hey Day: The Photography of J. Vanderzee* by Dawson and Thomas; *Ritual and Myth: A Survey of African American Art* by Driskell and Hammond; *Howardena Pindell: Odyssey* by Terrie Rouse.

★4201★
Third World Press
7524 S. Cottage Grove Ave.
PO Box 730 Ph: (312)651-0700
Chicago, IL 60619 Fax: (312)651-7286

Description: Directed towards developing a complete understanding of African and African-American history and culture. Publishes on

history, sociology, political science, poetry, fiction, and children's literature. Accepts unsolicited manuscripts; reviewed from June to October only. Reaches market through direct mail, trade sales, Baker & Taylor, BookPeople, Lushera Books, and Liberation Distributors. **Principal Officers and Managers** Haki R. Madhubuti, Publisher and Editor; Bakari Kitwana, Donna Williams, Senior Editors; Lynn Wade, Sales Manager; Carolyn Dennis, Marketing Manager. **Number of New Titles:** 1991 - 12, 1992 - 35. **Discounts:** Bookstores - 30-44%; College Bookstores - 30%. **Percentage of Sales to:** Libraries - 15%; Bookstores - 70%; Individuals - 15%. **Selected Titles:** *I've Been a Women* by Sonia Sanchez; *To Disembark* by Gwendolyn Brooks; *The Destruction of Black Civilization* by Chancellor Williams; *Black Men: Obsolete, Single, Dangerous* by Haki R. Mandhubuti; *Wings Will Not Be Broken* by Daniel Holmes; *The Brass Bed and Other Stories* by Pearl Cleage.

★4202★
Tivoli Publishing Co.
2718 Brooklyn Ave.
PO Box 412164
Kansas City, MO 64141 Ph: (816)923-2546

Description: Publishes works by African-Americans. Accepts unsolicited manuscripts. Reaches market through direct mail and Baker & Taylor. **Principal Officers and Managers** Telester F. Powell, Owner. **Number of New Titles:** 1991 - 1, 1992 - 1; Total Titles in Print - 2. **Subjects:** Poetry, short stories, folktales. **Discounts:** Bookstores & Libraries - Please inquire. **Percentage of Sales to:** Libraries - 3%; Bookstores - 15%; Non-Book Retail Outlets - 10%; Individuals - 50%; Others - 22%. **Selected Titles:** *The Awakening, Awaiting Your Arrival, Trials and Tribulations: Looking for a Miracle,* all by Telester F. Kelly-Powell; *Modern Marriage: How They Keep It Together* by Rose S. Bell.

★4203★
Tom Paine Institute
3120 N. Romero Rd., No. 39 Ph: (602)887-3098
Tucson, AZ 85705 Fax: (602)887-3098

Description: Promotes discussion of "what constitutes humane and equitable political structures." Reaches market through direct mail and major small press distributors. **Principal Officers and Managers** Alfred F. Andersen, Dorothy N. Andersen, Directors. **Subjects:** Political philosophy, political science. **Discounts:** Please inquire. **Percentage of Sales to:** Libraries - 50%; Bookstores - 25%; Individuals - 25%. **Selected Titles:** *Liberating the Early American Dream* by Alfred F. Andersen.

★4204★
Tucker Publications, Inc.
PO Box 580 Ph: (708)969-3809
Lisle, IL 60532 Fax: (708)969-3895

Description: Publishes on health care issues concerning Black Americans, including *The Association of Black Nursing Faculty Journal.* Offers a mailing service and a database. Accepts unsolicited manuscripts. Reaches market through direct mail. **Principal Officers and Managers** Sallie Tucker-Allen, President; S. Monique Allen, Vice-President and Treasurer. **Number of New Titles:** 1991 - 5, 1992 - 5, 1993 (est.) - 3; Total Titles in Print - 5. **Discounts:** Bookstores - 20%. **Percentage of Sales to:** Libraries - 20%; Bookstores - 5%; Corporations - 5%; Individuals - 10%; Colleges - 60%. **Selected Titles:** *The Directory of Black Nursing Faculty* 2nd ed. by Sallie T. Allen; *Learning to Live with Hypertension: A Self-Care Guide for Black Elders* by Davis, McGadnen, and Kuziel-Perri.

★4205★
Unicorn/Fitzgerald
808 Charlotte St.
Fredericksburg, VA 22401 Ph: (703)371-3253

Principal Officers and Managers Ruth Coder Fitzgerald, General Manager. **Subjects:** Local history. **Discounts:** Bookstores - 40% (in lots of 10). **Percentage of Sales to:** Libraries - 25%; Bookstores - 10%; Non-Book Retail Outlets - 30%; Individuals - 25%; Mail Orders - 10%. **Selected Titles:** *A Different Story: A Black History of Fredericksburg, Stafford, and Spotsylvania, Virginia* by Ruth Coder Fitzgerald.

★4206★
Universal Black Writer Press
PO Box 5, Radio City Sta.
New York, NY 10101-0005

Description: Publishes historical and cultural information, books, audio tapes, and materials for Black writers and readers of Black literature. Also publishes the works of contemporary African-descended writers, Black history quizzes, and a Black travel newsletter. Conducts seminars and offers consultation on small press publishing. Reaches market through direct mail. **Principal Officers and Managers** Linda Cousins, Publisher and Editor; Richard Bartee, Marketing Director; Sonia Diaz, Associate Editor. **Discounts:** Bookstores - 40%; Libraries - 20%. **Percentage of Sales to:** Libraries - 35%; Bookstores - 15%; Individuals - 50%. **Selected Titles:** *Ancient Black Youth and Elders Reborn: Poetry, Short Stories, Oral Histories, and Deeper Thoughts of African American Youth and Elders* edited by Linda Cousins; *Ancestral Poetsong: Poetworks of Black History, Love, Laughter, and Life* (tape), *A Son Born from Jim-Lee and Me* (tape), *How to Start and Operate a Home Business,* all by Linda Cousins; *Caribbean Bound! Culture Roots, Places, and People.*

★4207★
University of California, Los Angeles
Center for Afro-American Studies
160 Haines Hall
405 Hilgard Ave.　　Ph: (310)825-3528
Los Angeles, CA 90024-1545　　Fax: (310)206-3421

Description: Publishes the work of scholars worldwide through its publications series, which focuses on significant issues affecting Black people. These include the *Afro-American Culture and Society Series, CAAS Special Publications, Community Classics,* and the *Minority Economic Development Series.* Also publishes the annual *CAAS Report.* **Principal Officers and Managers** J. Eugene Grigsby, Acting Director; Toyomi Igus, Managing Editor; Ross Steiner, Assistant Editor. **Number of New Titles:** 1991 - 2, 1992 - 2; Total Titles in Print - 21. **Discounts:** Bookstores - 20% (1-4), 30% (5-49), 35% (50); Textbook Sales - 20%. **Percentage of Sales to:** Libraries - 25%; Bookstores - 65%; Individuals - 10%. **Selected Titles:** *Castro, the Blacks, and Africa* by Carlos Moore; *Deep South* by Allison Davis, Burleigh and Mary Gardner; *Workers and Workplace Dynamics in Reconstruction Era Atlanta* by Jonathan W. Mcleod; *Black Folk Here and There, Vols. 1-2* by St. Clair Drake; *Black Character in the Brazilian Novel* by Giorgio Marotti; *Minority Economic Development Series.*

★4208★
University Place Book Shop
821 Broadway
New York, NY 10003　　Ph: (212)254-5998

Description: Publishes mostly reprints on Blacks, Africa, and chess. **Principal Officers and Managers** Walter Goldwater, Owner; William P. French, Manager. **Discounts:** Bookstores - 20% (single copies). **Selected Titles:** *All-Night Visitors* by Clarence Major; *Education in the British West Indies* by Eric Williams; *Radical Periodicals in America* by Walter Goldwater. *According to Hoyle* by John Rather and Walter Goldwater.

★4209★
Uraeus Publishing, Inc.
PO Box 50058
Washington, DC 20004-0058　　Ph: (202)726-0842

Description: Publishes history books and other types of publications from the perspective of Black Americans. Accepts unsolicited manuscripts; include a self-addressed, stamped envelope. Reaches market through direct mail, trade sales, and Baker & Taylor. **Principal Officers and Managers** Richard Morris, Publisher; Clifton West, Project Manager **Number of New Titles:** 1991 - 1, 1993 (est.) - 1; Total Titles in Print - 4. **Discounts:** Please inquire. **Percentage of Sales to:** Libraries - 5%; Bookstores - 90%; Non-Book Retail Outlets - 5%. **Selected Titles:** *Adam, the Altaic Ring and the Children of the Sun; Mo; Where Did Those Dudes Come From; A Black Man's Bible,* all by James R. Granger, Jr.

★4210★
Urban Research Press, Inc.
840 E. 87th St.　　Ph: (312)994-7200
Chicago, IL 60619　　Fax: (312)994-5191

Description: Publishes on history, education, and music history. Reaches market through trade sales, Krochs & Brentanos, and the distributors. Formerly listed as Urban Research Institute, Inc. **Principal Officers and Managers** Dempsey J. Travis, President; Eldrea Ware, Marketing Director; K. Kitti, Controller. **Number of New Titles:** 1991 - 1, 1992 - 3; Total Titles in Print - 10. **Subjects:** Education, African-Americans. **Discounts:** Bookstores - 40%; Libraries - 30%. **Percentage of Sales to:** Libraries - 50%; Bookstores - 50%. **Selected Titles:** *Real Estate Is the Gold in Your Future, Harold: The People's Mayor, An Autobiography of Black Chicago, An Autobiography of Black Jazz, An Autobiography of Black Politics,* all by Dempsey J. Travis; *I Like Me* by Blanche P. Gaston; *I Like Gym Shoe Soup* by Edye Deloch-Hughes.

★4211★
Vera Pigee
2234 Edison St.
Detroit, MI 48206　　Ph: (313)883-6618

Description: Self-publisher of books on the history of the civil rights movement. Reaches market through commission representatives, direct mail, and telephone sales. **Principal Officers and Managers** Vera Pigee, Author, Manager. **Discounts:** Bookstores & Libraries - 30%. **Selected Titles:** *The Struggle of Struggles, Pts. I-II* by Vera Pigee.

★4212★
Very Serious Business Enterprises
PO Box 356
Newark, NJ 07101　　Ph: (609)641-0776

Description: Publishes about money management and self-improvement for the Black community. Reaches market through direct mail and trade sales. **Principal Officers and Managers** George Trower-Subira, Owner. **Discounts:** Bookstores - 40%; Libraries - 20%. **Percentage of Sales to:** Bookstores - 40%; Non-Book Retail Outlets - 20%; Individuals - 35%. **Selected Titles:** *Black Folks Guide to Making Big Money in America, Black Folks Guide to Business Success,* both by George Trower-Subira.

★4213★
Wayne State University
Center for Black Studies
586 Student Center Bldg.
Detroit, MI 48202　　Ph: (313)577-3436

Principal Officers and Managers Alvin Aubert, Interim Director. **Selected Titles:** *Black English and the Education of Black Children and Youth* edited by Geneva Smitherman.

★4214★
White Sound Press
1615 W. Harrison Ave.
Decatur, IL 62526　　Ph: (217)423-0511

Description: Publishes on the history and culture of the Bahama Islands. Accepts unsolicited manuscripts; include a self-addressed, stamped envelope. Reaches market through direct mail. **Principal Officers and Managers** Steve Dodge, President. **Discounts:** Bookstores - 40%; Libraries - 10%. **Percentage of Sales to:** Libraries - 10%; Bookstores - 80%; Non-Book Retail Outlets - 5%; Corporations - 3%; Individuals - 2%. **Selected Titles:** *The Complete Guide to Nassau, Abaco: The History of an Out Island and Its Cays,* both by Steve Dodge; *A Guide and History of Hope Town* by Steve Dodge and Vernon Malone; *Political Leadership in the Bahamas* by Dean Collinwood and Steve Dodge; *The Bahamas Index: 1987* edited by Steve Dodge and Robert McInitire; *The Bahamas between Worlds* by Dean Collinwood.

★4215★
WREE (Women for Racial and Economic Equality)
198 Broadway, Rm. 606
New York, NY 10038　　Ph: (212)385-1103

Principal Officers and Managers Sally Chaffee Maron, Camille Cooper, National Chairors. **Number of New Titles:** 1992 - 4. **Subjects:** Women's issues, racism. **Discounts:** Bookstores &

Libraries - 40%. **Selected Titles:** *Seeds of Ourselves* by Bernadine; *Facts about U.S. Women 1991.*

★4216★
Wright-Armstead Associates
2410 Barker Ave., Ste. 14-G
Bronx, NY 10467   Ph: (212)654-9445

Description: Publishes on history, ethnic studies, and social sciences. Reaches market through direct mail, telephone sales, and major small press wholesalers and distributors. **Principal Officers and Managers** Madrue Chavers-Wright, Publisher; Sara E. Messmer, Editor; Benjamin Armstead, Sales Representative. **Number of New Titles:** 1991 - 1, 1992 - 1; Total Titles in Print - 1. **Subjects:** African American genealogy. **Discounts:** Bookstores - 20% (5-9 copies of the same title), 40% (10). **Percentage of Sales to:** Libraries - 50%; Bookstores - 5%; Non-Book Retail Outlets - 10%; Individuals - 35%. **Selected Titles:** *The Guarantee* by Madrue Chavers-Wright.

★4217★
Wyndham Hall Press
52857 C.R. 21   Ph: (219)848-4834
Bristol, IN 46507   Fax: (219)522-4271
                                         Free: 800-952-0185

Description: An academic/scholarly publisher of college and university monographs. Accepts unsolicited manuscripts that are typed. Reaches market through direct mail, distributors, and wholesalers. **Principal Officers and Managers** John H. Morgan, President. **Number of New Titles:** 1993 (est.) - 40; Total Titles in Print - 165. **Subjects:** Ethnic studies, social-behavioral-political sciences, history, religion, philosophy, education. **Discounts:** Bookstores - 20%; Libraries - None. **Percentage of Sales to:** Libraries - 50%; Bookstores - 40%; Individuals - 10%. **Selected Titles:** *The American School and the Melting Pot* by Isser and Schwartz; *Black Theatre* by Molette and Molette; *Single Parents in Black America* by Annie S. Barnes; *Enduring the Soviets* by Anthony T. Bouscaren; *From Here to There: Moving a Library* by Dennis C. Tucker; *Computers in Criminal Justice* by F. Schmalleger.

(17) Broadcast Media

Networks

★4218★
Black Entertainment Television (BET)
1899 9th St. NW
Washington, DC 20018   Ph: (202)636-2400
Robert L. Johnson, President

★4219★
National Black Network
10 Columbus Circle
New York, NY 10019   Ph: (212)586-0610
Sydney L. Small, Chairman

★4220★
Sheridan Broadcasting Network
1 Times Sq. Plaza, 18th Fl.
New York, NY 10036   Ph: (212)575-0099
E. J. "Jay" Williams Jr., President

Radio Stations

Alabama

★4221★
WAGG-AM
424 16th St. N.   Ph: (205)254-1820
Birmingham, AL 35203   Fax: (205)254-1833

Frequency: 1320. **Network Affiliation:** Independent. **Format:** Religious. **Key Personnel:** Kirkwood Balton, Gen. Mgr. **Operating Hours:** Sunrise-sunset. **Owner:** Booker T. Washington Broadcasting Service, Inc.

★4222★
WAPZ-AM
Rte. 6, Box 43
Wetumpka, AL 36092   Ph: (205)567-2251

Frequency: 1250. **Network Affiliation:** American Urban Radio. **Format:** Gospel. **Key Personnel:** Clarence E. Stewart, Gen. Mgr. **Operating Hours:** 5 a.m.-6:30 p.m. **Owner:** J&W Promotion.

★4223★
WATV-AM
3025 Ensley Ave.
Box 39054
Birmingham, AL 35208   Ph: (205)780-2014

Frequency: 900. **Network Affiliation:** ABC. **Format:** Full Service. **Key Personnel:** Erskine R. Faush, Pres./Gen. Mgr.; Shelley Stewart, V.P./Sales Mgr.; Ron January, Music Dir. **Operating Hours:** Continuous; 10% network, 90% local. **Owner:** Birmingham Ebony Broadcasting, Inc.

★4224★
WAYE-AM
1408 3rd Ave. W.   Ph: (205)786-9293
Birmingham, AL 35208   Fax: (205)786-9296

Frequency: 1220. **Network Affiliation:** Independent. **Format:** Black Gospel. **Key Personnel:** MelRose Fowler, Office Mgr. **Operating Hours:** Continuous. **Owner:** Willis Broadcasting.

★4225★
WBIL-FM
PO Box 666   Ph: (205)727-2100
Tuskegee, AL 36083   Fax: (205)727-2969

Frequency: 95.9. **Format:** Adult Contemporary; Blues; News; Urban Contemporary. **Key Personnel:** George Clay, Gen. Mgr.; Joanna Williams, Office Mgr.; Costee McNair, Program Dir. **Operating Hours:** Continuous. **Owner:** New World Communications.

★4226★
WBLX-AM
1204 Dauphin St.   Ph: (205)432-7609
Mobile, AL 36604   Fax: (205)432-2054

Frequency: 660. **Network Affiliation:** ABC; Satellite Music. **Format:** Adult Urban Contemporary. **Key Personnel:** David Clark, Gen. Mgr.; Morgan Sinclair, Operations Mgr.; James Simon, Gospel Music Dir. **Operating Hours:** Continuous. **Owner:** April Broadcasting.

★4227★
WBLX-FM
1204 Dauphin St.   Ph: (205)432-7609
Mobile, AL 36604   Fax: (205)432-2054

Frequency: 92.9. **Network Affiliation:** ABC. **Format:** Urban Contemporary. **Key Personnel:** David Clark, Gen. Mgr.; Skip Cheatham, Program Dir.; Jeff Hedgemon, Gen. Sales Mgr.; Marlene Chadwick, Business Mgr. **Operating Hours:** Continuous. **Owner:** April Broadcasting.

★4228★
WBTG-FM
1605 Gospel Rd.
PO Box 518
Sheffield, AL 35660   Ph: (205)381-6800
Frequency: 106.3. **Network Affiliation:** USA Radio. **Format:** Southern Gospel. **Key Personnel:** Paul Slatton, Gen. Mgr./National Sales Mgr.; Lincoln Hughes, News Dir.; Chad Payne, Program Dir.; Jacky Ward, Music Dir.; Gary Lovette, Local Sales Mgr.; Mike Simon, Promotions Mgr. **Operating Hours:** 5 a.m.-midnight; 10% network, 90% local. **Owner:** Slatton & Associates Broadcasters Inc.

★4229★
WCOX-FM
Box 820   Ph: (205)682-9048
Camden, AL 36726   Fax: (205)682-4726
Frequency: 102.3. **Format:** Black Gospel; Religious; Talk. **Key Personnel:** Leroy T. Griffith, Gen. Mgr.; William Pompey, Pres.; Paul Johnson, Producer. **Operating Hours:** 5 a.m.-midnight. **Owner:** Down Home Broadcasting, Inc.

★4230★
WENN-FM
424 16th St. N.   Ph: (205)254-1820
Birmingham, AL 35203   Fax: (205)254-1833
Frequency: 107.7. **Network Affiliation:** Independent. **Format:** Urban Contemporary. **Key Personnel:** Kirkwood Balton, Gen. Mgr. **Operating Hours:** Continuous. **Owner:** Booker T. Washington Broadcasting Service, Inc.

★4231★
WEUP-AM
PO Box 11398   Ph: (205)837-9387
Huntsville, AL 35814   Fax: (205)837-9404
Frequency: 1600. **Network Affiliation:** American Urban Radio. **Format:** Urban Contemporary. **Key Personnel:** Virginia Caples, Gen. Mgr./Owner; Hundley Batts, Sr., Sales Coordinator/Owner; Dee Handley, Station Mgr.; Shirley Pride, Traffic Mgr.; Steve Murry, Program and Music Dir. **Operating Hours:** Continuous. **Owner:** Dr. Virginia Caples and Hundley Batts, Sr.

★4232★
WGOK-AM
Box 1425   Ph: (205)432-8661
Mobile, AL 36633   Fax: (205)432-1921
Frequency: 900. **Network Affiliation:** Southern Broadcasting. **Format:** Urban Contemporary. **Key Personnel:** Irene Wehe, Gen. Mgr.; Charles Merritt, Jr., Program Dir.; Terry Roberds, Station Mgr.; Dickie Roberds, Pres. **Operating Hours:** Continuous.

★4233★
WJLD-AM
1449 Spaulding Ishkooda Rd.   Ph: (205)942-1776
Birmingham, AL 35211   Fax: (205)942-4814
Frequency: 1400. **Network Affiliation:** Satellite Music. **Format:** Adult Urban Contemporary. **Key Personnel:** Gary Richardson, Pres./Gen. Mgr.; Curtis Bell, Music Dir.; Bob Friedman, Sales Mgr. **Operating Hours:** Continuous; 25% network, 75% local. **Owner:** Richardson Broadcasting Corp.

★4234★
WMMV-FM
PO Box 901   Ph: (205)433-9577
Spanish Fort, AL 36527-0901   Fax: (205)433-9578
Frequency: 105.5. **Network Affiliation:** CBS; American Urban Radio. **Format:** Urban Contemporary. **Key Personnel:** W.H. Phillips, Gen. Mgr.; Sonny Love, Operations; Gwin Chesnutt, Sales Mgr. **Operating Hours:** Continuous. **Owner:** Faulkner-Phillips Media Inc.

★4235★
WNPT-FM
229 3rd St.   Ph: (205)758-3311
Northport, AL 35476   Fax: (205)349-4824
Frequency: 102.9. **Network Affiliation:** NBC. **Format:** Talk; News; Blues. **Key Personnel:** Ellis J. Parker, Gen. Mgr.; Ruth Harris,

Station Mgr.; Jim Lawson, Program Dir. **Operating Hours:** Continuous; 10% network, 90% local. **Owner:** W.A.N.R., Inc.

★4236★
WSLY-FM
11474 U.S. Hwy. 11
York, AL 36925   Ph: (205)392-5234
Frequency: 99.3. **Format:** Blues. **Key Personnel:** William B. Grant, Owner/Gen. Mgr./Chief Engineer; Tim Craddock, Program and News Dir., Sales; Pat Pasten, Sales. **Operating Hours:** Continuous. **Owner:** William B. Grant.

★4237★
WTQX-AM
1 Valley Creek Circle
Selma, AL 36701   Ph: (205)872-1570
Frequency: 1570. **Format:** Blues; Religious; Jazz. **Key Personnel:** Bob Bailey, Gen. Mgr.; Allen Taylor, Jr., Station Mgr. **Operating Hours:** Sunrise-sunset. **Owner:** WTQX Radio.

★4238★
WTSK-AM
142 Skyland Blvd.   Ph: (205)345-7200
Tuscaloosa, AL 35405   Fax: (205)349-1715
Frequency: 790. **Network Affiliation:** American Urban Radio. **Format:** Black traditional. **Key Personnel:** Houston Pearce, Gen. Mgr. **Operating Hours:** Continuous.

★4239★
WTUG-FM
142 Skyland Blvd.   Ph: (205)345-7200
Tuscaloosa, AL 35405   Fax: (205)349-1715
Frequency: 92.9. **Network Affiliation:** American Urban Radio. **Format:** Urban Contemporary. **Key Personnel:** Houston Pearce, Gen. Mgr. **Operating Hours:** Continuous. **Owner:** Radio South, Inc.

★4240★
WVAS-FM
915 S. Jackson St.
Montgomery, AL 36101-0271   Ph: (205)293-4287
Frequency: 90.7. **Network Affiliation:** ABC. **Format:** Jazz. **Key Personnel:** John F. Knight, Jr., Gen. Mgr.; Stephen B. Myers, Program Mgr.; Carol Y. Stephens, Music Dir. **Operating Hours:** 19 hrs. daily; 5% network, 95% local. **Owner:** Alabama State University.

★4241★
WXVI-AM
422 S. Court   Ph: (205)263-3459
Montgomery, AL 36104   Fax: (205)263-3483
Frequency: 1600. **Network Affiliation:** Southern Broadcasting. **Format:** Blues. **Key Personnel:** Robert F. Bell, Gen. Mgr. **Operating Hours:** Continuous. **Owner:** Robert F. Bell.

★4242★
WZMG-AM
915 Saugahatchee Lake Rd.
PC Box 2329   Ph: (205)745-4656
Opelika, AL 36803   Fax: (205)749-1520
Frequency: 1520. **Network Affiliation:** Independent. **Format:** Urban Contemporary; Gospel. **Key Personnel:** Gary Fuller, Pres./Gen. Mgr.; Clarence Van Cure, Gen. Sales Mgr. **Operating Hours:** Sunrise-sunset; 100% local. **Owner:** Fuller Broadcasting Co., Inc.

★4243★
WZZA-AM
1570 Woodmont Dr.
Tuscumbia, AL 35674   Ph: (205)381-1862
Frequency: 1410. **Format:** Urban Contemporary; Talk; News; Soul; Gospel. **Key Personnel:** Bob Carl Bailey, Pres./Gen. Mgr.; Music Dir.; Odessa Bailey, Mgr. **Operating Hours:** Continuous; 10% network, 90% local. **Owner:** Muscle Shoals Broadcasting.

Arizona

★4244★
KJZZ-FM
1435 S. Dobson Rd.
Mesa, AZ 85202

Ph: (602)834-5627
Fax: (602)835-5925

Frequency: 91.5. **Network Affiliation:** National Public Radio (NPR). **Format:** Public Radio; Jazz; News. **Key Personnel:** Carl Matthusen, Gen. Mgr.; Scott Williams, Program Dir.; Laura Carlson, News Dir.; Bill Shedd, Music Dir.; Bob Glazar, Development Dir. **Operating Hours:** Continuous; 30% network, 70% local. **Owner:** Maricopa Community College District.

Arkansas

★4245★
KAYZ-FM
2525 Northwest Ave.
El Dorado, AR 71730

Ph: (501)862-1031
Fax: (501)863-4555

Frequency: 103.1. **Network Affiliation:** Arkansas Radio. **Format:** Country. **Key Personnel:** Bob Parks, V.P./Gen. Mgr./Sports and Promotions Dir.; Jim Lewis, News and Program Dir. **Operating Hours:** Continuous. **Owner:** Noalmark Broadcasting Corp.

★4246★
KCAT-AM
PO Box 8808
Pine Bluff, AR 71611-8808

Ph: (501)534-5000

Frequency: 1340. **Network Affiliation:** American Urban Radio. **Format:** Urban Contemporary; Religious. **Key Personnel:** J.B. Scanlon, Owner/Gen. Mgr. **Operating Hours:** Continuous; 10% network, 90% local. **Owner:** J.B. Scanlon.

★4247★
KCLT-FM
307 Hwy 49B
Box 2870
West Helena, AR 72390

Ph: (501)572-9506
Fax: (501)572-1845

Frequency: 104.9. **Network Affiliation:** Southern Broadcasting; American Urban Radio. **Format:** Urban Contemporary. **Operating Hours:** Continuous. **Owner:** West Helena Broadcasters Inc.

★4248★
KELD-AM
2525 Northwest Ave.
El Dorado, AR 71730

Ph: (501)863-6162
Fax: (501)863-4555

Frequency: 1400. **Network Affiliation:** CNN Radio. **Format:** News; Talk. **Key Personnel:** Bob Parks, Gen. Mgr.; Jim Lewis, News Dir. **Operating Hours:** 5 a.m.-midnight. **Owner:** Noalmark Broadcasting Corp.

★4249★
KITA-AM
723 W. 14th St.
Little Rock, AR 72202

Ph: (501)375-1440

Frequency: 1440. **Network Affiliation:** International Broadcasting; Ambassador Inspirational Radio; Moody Broadcasting. **Format:** Talk; Ethnic; Religious. **Key Personnel:** Gary Vaile, Gen. Mgr.; Erin Marchese, Program Dir.; Ulysses Robinson, Music Dir.; Kenneth Robinson, Program Mgr. **Operating Hours:** Continuous. **Owner:** Kita Ltd. Partnership.

★4250★
KJWH-AM
214 Van Buren
Camden, AR 71701

Ph: (501)836-9393

Frequency: 1450. **Network Affiliation:** Arkansas Radio; ABC. **Format:** News; Religious; Urban Contemporary. **Key Personnel:** Gary Coates, Owner; Don Jackson, News Director; Carna Coates, Bookkeeper. **Operating Hours:** 10% network, 90% local.

★4251★
KLRC-FM
John Brown University
PO Box 3100
Siloam Springs, AR 72761

Ph: (501)524-3131
Fax: (501)524-9548

Frequency: 101.1. **Network Affiliation:** USA Radio. **Format:** Religious (Contemporary Christian). **Key Personnel:** Mike Flynn, Mgr.; Rick Sparks, Program Dir. **Operating Hours:** 6 a.m.-midnight; 8% network, 92% local. **Owner:** John Brown University.

★4252★
KMTL-AM
PO Box 6460
North Little Rock, AR 72116

Ph: (501)835-1554

Frequency: 760. **Format:** Gospel. **Operating Hours:** Sunrise-sunset.

★4253★
KMZX-FM
314 N. Main St., Ste. 106
North Little Rock, AR 72114

Ph: (501)376-1063

Frequency: 106.3. **Network Affiliation:** Mutual Broadcasting System. **Format:** Adult Urban Contemporary. **Key Personnel:** Kenn Flemmons, Gen. Mgr.; Neal Scoggins, Program Dir. **Operating Hours:** Continuous. **Owner:** Lonoke Broadcasting, Inc.

★4254★
KNEA-AM
603 W. Matthews
Jonesboro, AR 72401

Ph: (501)932-8381
Fax: (501)932-6397

Frequency: 970. **Network Affiliation:** Arkansas Radio; Ambassador Inspirational Radio. **Format:** Gospel; Top 40. **Key Personnel:** Paul R. Boden, Gen. Mgr.; Donna K. Rogers, Station Mgr.; Jerry Jay, Program Dir./Music Dir.; Patsy O'Brien, Sales Mgr. **Operating Hours:** 6 a.m.-10 p.m.; 20% network, 80% local. **Owner:** Paul R. Boden.

★4255★
KXAR-FM
Hwy. 29 at I-30
Hope, AR 71801

Ph: (501)777-3601
Fax: (501)777-3535

Frequency: 101.7. **Network Affiliation:** American Urban Radio. **Format:** Urban Contemporary. **Key Personnel:** Bill Hoglund, Pres.; Dorian Cox, News Dir.; W.A. "Big Daddy" Griffin, Program Dir. **Operating Hours:** Continuous; 5% network, 95% local. **Owner:** KdB, Inc.

California

★4256★
KACE-FM
161 N. LaBrea Ave.
Inglewood, CA 90301

Ph: (310)330-3100
Fax: (310)412-7803

Frequency: 103.9. **Network Affiliation:** Independent. **Format:** Urban Contemporary. **Key Personnel:** Willie Davis, Pres.; Anne Davis, Gen. Mgr. **Operating Hours:** Continuous. **Owner:** All Pro Broadcasting Inc.

★4257★
KBLX-FM
601 Ashby Ave.
Berkeley, CA 94710

Ph: (510)848-7713
Fax: (510)658-0894

Frequency: 102.9. **Network Affiliation:** Independent. **Format:** Jazz; Adult Contemporary; Alternative/Independent/Progressive. **Key Personnel:** Harvey Stone, Pres./Gen. Mgr. **Operating Hours:** Continuous. **Owner:** Inner City Broadcasting Corp.

★4258★
KDAY-AM
1700 N. Alvarado St.
Los Angeles, CA 90026-1777

Frequency: 1580. **Network Affiliation:** ABC. **Format:** Urban Contemporary. **Key Personnel:** Edward J. Kerby, Pres./Gen. Mgr.;

Rochelle Lucas, Sales Mgr.; Jack Patterson, Program Dir./Music Dir. **Owner:** Redi Media.

★4259★
KDIA-AM
100 Swan Way   Ph: (510)633-2548
Oakland, CA 94621   Fax: (510)633-0414

Frequency: 1310. **Network Affiliation:** ABC. **Format:** Urban Contemporary; Oldies. **Key Personnel:** Aleta Dwyer-Carpenter, V.P./Gen. Mgr.; Jeff Harrison, Program Dir.; Phil Hartman, Chief Engineer; Chauncey Bailey, Public Affairs Dir.; Robert Sherwood, News Dir.; Milton Shaw, Traffic Dir.; Michael Thomas, Controller. **Operating Hours:** Continuous; 2% network, 98% local. **Owner:** Ragan Henry.

★4260★
KEST-AM
185 Berry St., Ste. 6500, Bldg. 2   Ph: (415)978-5378
San Francisco, CA 94107   Fax: (415)978-5380

Frequency: 1450. **Network Affiliation:** Independent. **Format:** New Age; Talk; Ethnic. **Key Personnel:** Allan Schultz, Gen. Mgr.; Tom Johnson, Program Dir.; Jamie Arbona, Natonal Sales Mgr. **Operating Hours:** Continuous. **Owner:** Douglas Broadcasting.

★4261★
KFOX-FM
123 W. Torrance Blvd.   Ph: (310)374-9796
Redondo Beach, CA 90277   Fax: (301)318-2578

Frequency: 93.5. **Network Affiliation:** Independent. **Format:** Talk. **Key Personnel:** Tom McCulloch, Gen. Mgr. **Operating Hours:** Continuous. **Owner:** KFOX, Inc.

★4262★
KGFJ-AM
1100 S. LaBrea Ave.   Ph: (213)930-9090
Los Angeles, CA 90019   Fax: (213)930-9056

Frequency: 1230. **Network Affiliation:** Mutual Broadcasting System; ABC. **Format:** Urban Contemporary; Oldies. **Key Personnel:** Bill Shearer, V.P./Gen. Mgr.; Theresa Randle Price, Gen. Mgr. Sales Mgr.; Carol Lima, Retail Sales Mgr.; Shirley Jackson, Operations Mgr.; John Morris, Program Dir./Chief Engineer; Martha Jackson, Public Service Dir. **Operating Hours:** Continuous. **Owner:** East-West Broadcasting.

★4263★
KGGI-FM
2001 Iowa Ave., Ste. 200   Ph: (714)684-1991
Riverside, CA 92507   Fax: (714)274-4949

Frequency: 99.1. **Network Affiliation:** Independent. **Format:** Contemporary Hit Radio (CHR). **Key Personnel:** Steve Virissimo, Gen. Mgr.; Bob Lienhard, Gen. Sales Mgr. **Operating Hours:** Continuous; 100% local. **Owner:** American Media, Inc.

★4264★
KJAZ-FM
1131 Harbor Bay Pkwy., Ste. 200
Alameda, CA 94501   Ph: (510)769-4800

Frequency: 92.7. **Network Affiliation:** Independent. **Format:** Jazz. **Key Personnel:** Jerry Dean, Operations Mgr.; Tim Hodges, Gen. Mgr./PRD; Bob Parlocha, Music Dir.; Denise Culver-Nelson, Mktg. and Promotions Dir. **Operating Hours:** Continuous, 100% local. **Owner:** Ronald H. Cowan.

★4265★
KJLH-FM
3847 Crenshaw Blvd.   Ph: (213)299-5960
Los Angeles, CA 90008   Fax: (213)290-1284

Frequency: 102.3. **Network Affiliation:** ABC. **Format:** Urban Contemporary. **Key Personnel:** Karen Slade, Gen. Mgr.; Cheryl Womak, Local Sales Mgr.; Al Ward, National Sales Mgr. **Operating Hours:** Continuous. **Owner:** Stevland Morris.

★4266★
KJOP-AM
15279 Hanford Armona Rd.   Ph: (209)584-5242
Lemoore, CA 93245   Fax: (209)584-0310

Frequency: 1240. **Format:** Spanish Country. **Key Personnel:** Jesus Larios, Gen. Mgr.; Federico Gomez, Program Dir.; Juan Rodriguez, News Dir.; Joe Hernandez, Sales Mgr.; John Pembroke, Owner. **Operating Hours:** 4 a.m.-11 p.m. **Owner:** Radio Rey Inc.

★4267★
KKBT-FM
6735 Yucca St.   Ph: (213)466-9566
Hollywood, CA 90028   Fax: (213)466-2592

Frequency: 92.3. **Format:** Urban Contemporary. **Key Personnel:** Craig Wilbraham, V.P./Gen. Mgr.; Liz Kiley, V.P./Operations Mgr.; Mike Stradford, V.P./Program Dir.; John Monds, Music Dir./Asst. Program Dir.; Sharon Kramer, Controller. **Operating Hours:** Continuous. **Owner:** Evergreen Media Corp.

★4268★
KKGO-FM
PO Box 250028   Ph: (310)478-5540
Los Angeles, CA 90025   Fax: (310)478-4189

Frequency: 105.1. **Network Affiliation:** Independent. **Format:** Jazz; Classical. **Key Personnel:** Saul Levine, Gen. Mgr. **Operating Hours:** Continuous. **Owner:** Mount Wilson FM Broadcasters, Inc.

★4269★
KMAX-FM
3844 E. Foothill Blvd.   Ph: (213)681-2486
Pasadena, CA 91107   Fax: (818)351-6218

Frequency: 107.1. **Network Affiliation:** Independent. **Format:** Religious; Foreign Language. **Key Personnel:** Linda Johnson-Hayes, V.P./Gen. Mgr. **Operating Hours:** Continuous. **Owner:** Douglas Broadcasting.

★4270★
KMJC-AM
4875 N. Harbor Dr.
San Diego, CA 92106-2304   Ph: (619)224-1556

Frequency: 910. **Network Affiliation:** Independent. **Format:** Talk; Ethnic; Religious; Urban Contemporary. **Key Personnel:** Carl W. James, Station Mgr.; Dick Warren, Chief Engineer; David Manzi, Public Service and Music Dir.; Roger Good, Public Affairs Dir. **Operating Hours:** Continuous; 100% local. **Owner:** Bartell Hotels.

★4271★
KMYX-FM
333 Palmer Dr., Ste. 300   Ph: (805)834-4000
Bakersfield, CA 93309   Fax: (805)834-8842

Frequency: 103.9. **Format:** Mellow Album-Oriented Rock (AOR); Adult Contemporary. **Key Personnel:** Lydia Vernon, Gen. Sales Mgr.; Kendall Marshall, Program Dir. **Operating Hours:** Continuous. **Owner:** Bakersfield Radio Partners, L.P.

★4272★
KPOO-FM
PO Box 425000   Ph: (415)346-5373
San Francisco, CA 94142   Fax: (415)346-5173

Frequency: 89.5. **Network Affiliation:** Independent. **Format:** Full Service. **Key Personnel:** Jerome Parson, Program Dir.; Marylyn Fowler, Publicity; Joe Rudolph, Gen. Mgr. **Operating Hours:** Continuous.

★4273★
KRML-AM
PO Box 22440   Ph: (408)624-6431
Carmel, CA 93922   Fax: (408)625-5598

Frequency: 1410. **Network Affiliation:** Independent. **Format:** Jazz. Simulcasts KJAZ-FM. **Key Personnel:** Gilbert Wisdom, Gen. Mgr./Owner; Johnny Adams, Program and Music Dir.; David Kimball, Sales Mgr. **Operating Hours:** Continuous. **Owner:** Gilbert Wisdom.

★4274★
KSDS-FM
1313 12th Ave.
San Diego, CA 92101   Ph: (619)234-1062

Frequency: 88.3. **Network Affiliation:** Independent. **Format:** Jazz. **Key Personnel:** James Dark, Gen. Mgr.; Hope Shaw, Station Mgr.; Tony Sisti, Program Dir.; Phyllis Hegeman, Music and Promotions Dir.; Hope Shaw, News Dir.; Fred Lewis, Sports Dir. **Operating Hours:** 6 a.m.-midnight Sun.-Thur., 6 a.m.-2 a.m. Fri.-Sat.; 100% local. **Owner:** San Diego Community College District.

★4275★
KUOR-FM
1200 E. Colton Ave.   Ph: (909)792-0721
Redlands, CA 92374   Fax: (909)793-2021

Frequency: 89.1. **Network Affiliation:** Independent. **Format:** Jazz. **Key Personnel:** William Bruns, Gen. Mgr.; Scott Sterl, Bus. Dir. **Operating Hours:** Continuous. **Owner:** University of Redlands.

──────── **Connecticut** ────────

★4276★
WKHL-FM
100 Prospect St.
Stamford, CT 06901   Ph: (203)327-1400

Frequency: 96.7. **Format:** Oldies. **Key Personnel:** John Fullam, Gen. Mgr.; Al Tacia, Gen. Sales Mgr.; J.C. Haze, Program Dir. **Operating Hours:** Continuous. **Owner:** Chase Broadcasting.

★4277★
WKND-AM
544 Windsor Ave.
PO Box 1480   Ph: (203)688-6221
Windsor, CT 06095   Fax: (203)688-0711

Frequency: 1480. **Network Affiliation:** American Urban Radio. **Format:** Full Service; Urban Contemporary. **Key Personnel:** Melonae McLean, Program Dir.; Lloyd Wimbish, News Dir.; Thornton Anderson, Gen. Mgr. **Operating Hours:** 6 a.m.-6 p.m. during winter; 6 a.m.-8:30 p.m. during summer. **Owner:** Hartcom Inc.

★4278★
WNHC-AM
112 Washington Ave.   Ph: (203)234-1340
North Haven, CT 06473   Fax: (203)239-6712

Frequency: 1340. **Format:** Urban Contemporary; Adult Contemporary. **Key Personnel:** Edith Acabbo-Willis, Pres./Gen. Mgr.; Stan Boston, Program Dir.; Will Mebane, Sales Mgr. **Operating Hours:** Continuous; 100% local. **Owner:** Willis Communications, Inc.

★4279★
WTIC-AM
1 Financial Plaza   Ph: (203)522-1080
Hartford, CT 06103   Fax: (203)549-3431

Frequency: 1080. **Network Affiliation:** CBS. **Format:** Full Service. **Key Personnel:** Gary Zenabi, Pres./Gen. Mgr.; Greg Moceri, Program Dir. **Operating Hours:** Continuous. **Owner:** Ten Eighty Corp.

★4280★
WTIC-FM
1 Financial Plaza
Hartford, CT 06103   Ph: (203)522-1080

Frequency: 96.5. **Format:** Contemporary Hit Radio (CHR). **Key Personnel:** Gary Zenobi, Gen. Mgr.; Dana Lundon, Music Dir.; Tom Mitchell, Program Dir.; Steve Salhany, Promotions Dir.; Vin Turco, Sales Mgr. **Operating Hours:** Continuous. **Owner:** 1080 Corp.

★4281★
WYBC-FM
165 Elm St.
PO Box WYBC   Ph: (203)432-4118
New Haven, CT 06520   Fax: (203)432-9652

Frequency: 94.3. **Network Affiliation:** Independent. **Format:** Jazz; Urban Contemporary; Alternative/Independent/Progressive. **Key Personnel:** Antonious L. Porch, Gen. Mgr. **Operating Hours:** Continuous. **Owner:** Yale Broadcasting Co. Inc.

──────── **District of Columbia** ────────

★4282★
WDCU-FM
4200 Connecticut Ave. NW   Ph: (202)282-7588
Washington, DC 20008   Fax: (202)282-3671

Frequency: 90.1. **Network Affiliation:** Independent. **Format:** Jazz; Public Radio. **Key Personnel:** Edith Smith, Gen. Mgr.; Debbie Akwei, Membership and Promotions Dir.; Ernest White, Community and Public Affairs Dir.; Faunee, Asst. Program Dir. **Operating Hours:** Continuous. **Owner:** University of the District of Columbia.

★4283★
WHUR-FM
529 Bryant St. NW   Ph: (202)806-3500
Washington, DC 20059   Fax: (202)806-3522

Frequency: 96.3. **Format:** Urban Contemporary. **Key Personnel:** Millard J. Watkins, III, Gen. Mgr.; B.K Kirkland, Program Dir.; S. Jeannett Tyce, Gen. Sales Mgr.; Ellis Terry, Jr., Operations Dir.; Barbara Jacobs, Traffic Mgr.; Alaina Moss, Promotions Dir.; Bill Christian, News Dir.; John Thomas, Chief Engineer. **Operating Hours:** Continuous. **Owner:** Howard University.

★4284★
WJZE-FM
5321 1st Pl. NE   Ph: (202)722-1000
Washington, DC 20011   Fax: (202)722-9098

Frequency: 100.3. **Network Affiliation:** Independent. **Format:** Jazz. **Key Personnel:** John Columbus, Gen. Mgr.; Bob Linden, Program Dir.; John Turk, Operations Mgr.; Kathy Franseen, Sales Mgr. **Operating Hours:** Continuous. **Owner:** United Broadcasting Co.

★4285★
WKYS-FM
4001 Nebraska Ave. NW   Ph: (202)686-9300
Washington, DC 20015   Fax: (202)686-2028

Frequency: 93.9. **Network Affiliation:** Independent. **Format:** Adult Contemporary; Contemporary Hit Radio (CHR). **Key Personnel:** Skip Finley, Pres.; Barbara Prieto, Program Dir.; John Irving, News Dir.; Richard F. Boland, Dir. of Financial Administration; Rob Ferguson, Creative Services Dir. **Operating Hours:** Continuous; 100% local. **Owner:** Albimar Communications.

★4286★
WMMJ-FM
400 H St. NE
Washington, DC 20002   Ph: (202)675-4800

Frequency: 102.3. **Network Affiliation:** NBC; American Urban Radio. **Format:** Adult Urban Contemporary. **Key Personnel:** Catherine L. Hughes, CEO/Owner; Alfred Liggins, Pres.; Jack Malloy, CFO; Ed Turner, Station Mgr.; Hector Hannibal, Program Dir. **Operating Hours:** Continuous. **Owner:** Radio One, Inc.

★4287★
WOL-AM
400 H St. NE
Washington, DC 20002   Ph: (202)675-4800

Frequency: 1450. **Network Affiliation:** NBC; American Urban Radio. **Format:** Adult Urban Contemporary; Talk. **Key Personnel:** Alfred Liggins, Pres./Gen. Mgr.; Ray Bryd, Program Dir.; Anthony Washington, Nat'l Sales Mgr.; Ed Turner, Station Mgr.; Jack Malloy, Chief Finance Officer. **Operating Hours:** Continuous. **Owner:** Radio One, Inc.

★4288★
WPFW-FM
702 H St. NW   Ph: (202)783-3100
Washington, DC 20016   Fax: (202)783-3106
Frequency: 89.3. **Network Affiliation:** Pacifica. **Format:** Jazz; News; World Music. **Key Personnel:** Leon C. Collins, Gen. Mgr.; Donald J. Foster, Exec. Producer; Tom Porter, Program Dir.; Bob Daughtry, Assoc. Producer/Promotions Dir.; Dr. Diem Jones, Membership/Development Dir. **Operating Hours:** Continuous. **Owner:** Pacifica Foundation.

★4289★
WUST-AM
815 V St. NW   Ph: (202)462-0011
Washington, DC 20001   Fax: (202)667-5880
Frequency: 1120. **Network Affiliation:** American Urban Radio. **Format:** Gospel. **Key Personnel:** Lou Hankins, Gen. Mgr./Program Dir. **Operating Hours:** Sunrise-sunset.

★4290★
WYCB-AM
529 14th St. NW, Ste. 228   Ph: (202)737-6400
Washington, DC 20045   Fax: (202)638-3027
Frequency: 1340. **Network Affiliation:** Mutual Broadcasting System. **Format:** Gospel; Inspirational. **Key Personnel:** Karen Jackson, Gen. Mgr.; Don Miller, Program Dir. **Operating Hours:** Continuous. **Owner:** Broadcast Holdings, Inc.

─────────── **Florida** ───────────

★4291★
WAMF-FM
Florida A&M University
314 Tucker Hall
Tallahassee, FL 32307   Ph: (904)599-3083
Frequency: 90.5. **Network Affiliation:** Independent. **Format:** Jazz; Ethnic; Urban Contemporary. **Key Personnel:** Phillip Jeter, Gen. Mgr.; Phillip Keirstead, News Dir. **Operating Hours:** 7 a.m.-1 p.m. Sun.-Thur., 7 a.m.-4 p.m. Fri. and Sat.; 100% local. **Owner:** Florida A&M University.

★4292★
WANM-AM
300 W. Tennessee   Ph: (904)222-1070
Tallahassee, FL 32301   Fax: (904)561-3645
Frequency: 1070. **Network Affiliation:** CNN Radio. **Format:** News. **Operating Hours:** Sunrise-sunset.

★4293★
WAVS-AM
4124 SW 64th Ave.   Ph: (305)584-1170
Davie, FL 33314   Fax: (305)581-6441
Frequency: 1170. **Network Affiliation:** Independent. **Format:** Ethnic (Caribbean); Urban Contemporary. **Key Personnel:** Dr. Roy H. Bresky, Pres.; Winsome Charlton, Office and Traffic Mgr.; Winston Barnes, Program and News Dir.; Tony Blair, Sales Mgr.; Ray A. Hooper, Gen. Mgr. **Operating Hours:** Continuous; 100% local. **Owner:** Radio WAVS, Inc.

★4294★
WCGL-AM
4035 Atlantic Blvd.
Jacksonville, FL 32207   Ph: (904)399-0606
Frequency: 1360. **Network Affiliation:** Independent. **Format:** Gospel. **Key Personnel:** Rev. R.D. Jennings, Gen. Mgr. **Operating Hours:** Daytime. **Owner:** JBD Communication.

★4295★
WEDR-FM
Box 551748   Ph: (305)623-7711
Opa Locka, FL 33054   Fax: (305)624-2736
Frequency: 99.1. **Network Affiliation:** Independent. **Format:** Urban Contemporary. **Key Personnel:** Jerry Rushin, V.P./Gen. Mgr. **Operating Hours:** Continuous. **Owner:** WEDR Inc.

★4296★
WEXY-AM
412 W. Oakland Park Blvd.   Ph: (305)561-1520
Fort Lauderdale, FL 33311-1712   Fax: (305)561-9830
                                      Free: 800-648-8063
Frequency: 1520. **Format:** Religious; Urban Contemporary. **Key Personnel:** Henry Greene, Program Dir.; Rev. Elroy Barber, Advertising Dir. **Operating Hours:** Continuous. **Owner:** Ms. Juno M. Beattie.

★4297★
WFHT-FM
345 Office Plaza   Ph: (904)877-1014
Tallahassee, FL 32301   Fax: (904)877-1015
Frequency: 101.5. **Format:** Contemporary Hit Radio (CHR). **Key Personnel:** Jeff Piersol, Gen. Mgr./Gen. Sales Mgr.; Jeff Sammons, Gen. Sales Mgr. **Operating Hours:** Continuous. **Owner:** Broad Based Comm., Inc.

★4298★
WHJX-FM
10592 E. Balmoral Circle, Ste. 1   Ph: (904)696-1015
Jacksonville, FL 32218   Fax: (904)696-1011
Frequency: 101.5. **Network Affiliation:** ABC. **Format:** Urban Contemporary. **Key Personnel:** Jim Jerrels, V.P./Gen. Mgr.; Sandra Rockwell, Controller; Phil Tuck, Chief Engineer. **Operating Hours:** Continuous. **Owner:** Eagle Broadcasting Co.

★4299★
WHQT-FM
1401 N. Bay Causeway   Ph: (305)759-4311
Miami, FL 33141   Fax: (305)757-7516
Frequency: 105.1. **Network Affiliation:** Independent. **Format:** Contemporary Hit Radio (CHR)/Urban Contemporary. **Key Personnel:** Bob Green, V.P./Gen. Mgr. **Operating Hours:** Continuous. **Owner:** Cox Enterprises, Inc.

★4300★
WJHM-FM
37 Skyline Dr., Ste. 4200
Lake Mary, FL 32746   Ph: (407)333-0072
Frequency: 101.9. **Network Affiliation:** NBC. **Format:** Urban Contemporary. **Key Personnel:** David Donahue, Gen. Mgr.; Lee Cutler, Gen. Sales Mgr. **Operating Hours:** Continuous; 3% network, 97% local. **Owner:** Beasley Reed Broadcasting.

★4301★
WJST-FM
3101 W. Hwy. 98   Ph: (904)785-9594
Panama City, FL 32401   Fax: (904)785-9494
Frequency: 94.5. **Format:** Country. **Key Personnel:** Dick Moran, Station Mgr.; John J. Demeter, Operations Mgr. **Operating Hours:** Continuous; 10% network, 90% local. **Owner:** Asterisk Broadcasting, Inc.

★4302★
WLIT-AM
3033 Riviera Dr., No. 200
Naples, FL 33940-4134   Ph: (803)248-9040
Frequency: 1330. **Format:** Urban Contemporary. **Key Personnel:** Randall Ramsey, Station Mgr.; Michael Burgess, Program Dir.; Rahim Akram, Music Dir.; Cherly Hall, Promotions Dir. **Operating Hours:** 6 a.m.-midnight; 10% network, 90% local. **Owner:** Beasley Broadcast Group.

★4303★
WLOQ-FM
170 W. Fairbanks Ave.
PO Box 2085
Winter Park, FL 32789
Ph: (407)647-5557
Fax: (407)647-4495
Frequency: 103.1. **Network Affiliation:** Independent. **Format:** Jazz.
Key Personnel: Denise Gargailo, Business Mgr. **Operating Hours:**
Continuous; 5% network, 95% local. **Owner:** Herb Gross.

★4304★
WLQY-AM
11645 Biscayne Blvd., Ste. 102-B
Miami, FL 33181-3138
Ph: (305)891-1729
Fax: (305)891-1583
Frequency: 1320. **Format:** Religious; Hispanic; Ethnic (Haitian,
Jamaican). **Key Personnel:** Sandra B. Herzberg, Gen. Mgr.
Operating Hours: Continuous. **Owner:** Genesis Commmunications II
Inc.

★4305★
WLTG-AM
1821 N. East Ave., Ste. H
Panama City, FL 32405
Ph: (904)784-9873
Frequency: 1430. **Network Affiliation:** Independent; Unistar; EFM.
Format: Information; News; Talk; Sports. **Key Personnel:** John Gay,
Gen. Mgr.; Peggy Gay, Office Mgr.; Vincent Childs, PSA Dir.
Operating Hours: 6 a.m.-9 p.m.; 100% local. **Owner:** Hour Group
Broadcasting, Inc.

★4306★
WLVJ-AM
1601 Belvedere Rd., Ste. 204 E.
West Palm Beach, FL 33406-1543
Ph: (407)688-9585
Fax: (407)688-9601
Frequency: 640. **Network Affiliation:** Ambassador Inspirational
Radio; USA Radio; International Broadcasting. **Format:** Inspirational;
Talk; News. **Key Personnel:** Stanley W. Bowman, Gen. Mgr.; Ken
Vaughn, Operations Mgr. **Operating Hours:** 6 a.m-11 p.m.; 32%
network, 12% local. **Owner:** South Florida Radio.

★4307★
WMBM-AM
814 1st St.
Miami Beach, FL 33139
Ph: (305)672-1100
Frequency: 1490. **Network Affiliation:** American Urban Radio.
Format: Urban Contemporary. **Key Personnel:** Edward Margolis,
Gen. Mgr.; Michael Norman, Program Dir. **Operating Hours:**
Continuous. **Owner:** Margolis Broadcasting Co. Ltd.

★4308★
WPOM-AM
6667 42nd Terrace N.
West Palm Beach, FL 33407
Ph: (407)844-6200
Fax: (407)840-0061
Frequency: 1600. **Format:** Urban Contemporary. **Key Personnel:**
Ronald Leonard, Gen. Mgr. **Operating Hours:** Continuous; 100%
local. **Owner:** WPOM Partners, Inc.

★4309★
WPUL-AM
2598 S. Nova Rd.
Daytona Beach, FL 32119
Ph: (904)767-1131
Fax: (904)254-7510
Frequency: 1590. **Network Affiliation:** Independent. **Format:** Jazz;
Urban Contemporary; Oldies. **Key Personnel:** Charles W. Cherry,
Station Mgr. **Operating Hours:** 6 a.m-9 p.m. **Owner:** PSI
Communications Inc.

★4310★
WRBD-AM
4431 Rock Island Rd.
Fort Lauderdale, FL 33319
Ph: (305)731-4800
Fax: (305)739-7917
Frequency: 1470. **Network Affiliation:** American Urban Radio.
Format: Classic Rhythm & Blues; Urban Contemporary. **Key
Personnel:** John Ruffin, Pres./Gen. Mgr.; Greg Cooper, Program
Dir.; Hank Mosby, Sales Mgr. **Operating Hours:** Continuous. **Owner:**
John Ruffin.

★4311★
WRFA-AM
800 SE 8th Ave.
Largo, FL 34649
Ph: (813)581-7800
Fax: (813)584-4805
Frequency: 820. **Network Affiliation:** USA Radio. **Format:** Religious
(Christian Lifestyle). **Key Personnel:** Freeman E. Teuton, Gen. Mgr.;
Jack Fichter, Gen. Sales Mgr.; David Grachek, Music Dir.; Andy
Porter, Production Mgr. **Operating Hours:** 5 a.m.-midnight. **Owner:**
Norman Bie.

★4312★
WRXB-AM
1700 34th St. S.
St. Petersburg, FL 33711
Ph: (813)327-9792
Fax: (813)321-3025
Frequency: 1590. **Network Affiliation:** Independent. **Format:** Urban
Contemporary. **Key Personnel:** J. Eugene Danzey, Gen.
Mgr./Owner; Michael Danzey, V.P.; Valorie D. Garner, Station Mgr.;
Jay Johnson, Program Dir.; Robert Sanchez, Music Dir. **Operating
Hours:** Continuous. **Owner:** J. Eugene Danzey.

★4313★
WSVE-AM
4343 Spring Grove Rd.
Jacksonville, FL 32209-3629
Ph: (904)766-1211
Frequency: 1280. **Network Affiliation:** Southern Broadcasting.
Format: Religious. **Key Personnel:** Walter A. Brickhouse, V.P.; Sam
Nelson, Program Dir.; Steve Crumbley, Natl. Program Dir. **Operating
Hours:** Continuous; 10% network. **Owner:** Willis Broadcasting Corp.

★4314★
WSWN-AM
2001 State Road 715
PO Box 1505
Belle Glade, FL 33430
Ph: (407)996-2063
Fax: (407)996-1852
Frequency: 900. **Network Affiliation:** ABC; Florida Radio. **Format:**
Urban Contemporary. **Key Personnel:** Vern Thacker, Gen. Mgr.; Joe
Fisher, Program Dir. **Operating Hours:** 6 a.m.-midnight; 2% network,
98% local. **Owner:** Dee Rivers Group.

★4315★
WTMP-AM
5207 Washington Blvd.
Tampa, FL 33619
Ph: (813)626-4108
Fax: (813)621-0616
Frequency: 1150. **Network Affiliation:** American Urban Radio.
Format: Urban Contemporary. **Key Personnel:** Ronald M. Jordan,
Gen. Mgr.; Chris Turner, Program Dir. **Operating Hours:**
Continuous. **Owner:** Westervilee Communications.

★4316★
WTOT-AM
140 W. Lafayette St., Ste. A
PO Box 569
Marianna, FL 32446
Ph: (904)482-3046
Fax: (904)526-7702
Frequency: 980. **Network Affiliation:** NBC; Florida Radio. **Format:**
Urban Contemporary. **Key Personnel:** Lina M. Parish, Gen.
Mgr./Sports Dir.; Don Moore, News Dir. **Operating Hours:** 5 a.m.-
midnight; 10% network, 90% local.

★4317★
WTWB-AM
PO Box 7
Auburndale, FL 33823
Ph: (813)967-1570
Frequency: 1570. **Network Affiliation:** ABC. **Format:** Southern
Gospel. **Key Personnel:** Richard Boyce, Gen. Mgr. **Operating
Hours:** Sunrise-sunset. **Owner:** L.M. Hughey.

★4318★
WVIJ-FM
3279 Sherwood Rd.
Punta Gorda, FL 33980
Ph: (813)624-5000
Frequency: 91.7. **Network Affiliation:** USA Radio. **Format:** News;
Southern Gospel; Eclectic. **Key Personnel:** Dan Kolenda, Jr.,
Pres./Gen. Mgr.; John Kolenda, Program Dir.; James Kolenda,
Production Dir. **Operating Hours:** Continuous; 25% network, 75%

local. **Owner:** Port Charlotte Educational Broadcasting Foundation Inc.

★4319★
WYFX-AM
400 Gulfstream Blvd.   Ph: (407)737-1040
Delray Beach, FL 33444   Fax: (407)278-1040
Frequency: 1040. **Network Affiliation:** Southern Broadcasting. **Format:** Urban Contemporary. **Key Personnel:** Gary Lewis, Pres./Gen. Mgr.; Mike James, Program Dir. **Operating Hours:** Continuous. **Owner:** Beach Broadcasting Company, Inc.

★4320★
WZAZ-AM
2611 WERD Radio Dr.   Ph: (904)389-1111
Jacksonville, FL 32204   Fax: (904)389-5039
Frequency: 1400. **Network Affiliation:** CBS; ABC. **Format:** Urban Contemporary. **Key Personnel:** Glenn Bryant, Gen. Mgr./V.P.; Kelly Carson, Program Dir.; Peggy Austin, Gen. Sales Mgr. **Operating Hours:** Continuous.

────────── **Georgia** ──────────

★4321★
WAOK-AM
120 Ralph McGill Blvd., Ste. 1000
Atlanta, GA 30365   Ph: (404)898-8900
Frequency: 1380. **Network Affiliation:** ABC; Unistar; Mutual Broadcasting System. **Format:** Religious. **Key Personnel:** Rick Mack, Gen. Mgr./V.P. **Operating Hours:** Continuous. **Owner:** Summit Broadcasting Communications.

★4322★
WCLK-FM
111 James P. Brawley Dr. SW   Ph: (404)880-8273
Atlanta, GA 30314   Fax: (404)880-8869
Frequency: 91.9. **Network Affiliation:** National Public Radio (NPR). **Format:** Public Radio; Jazz. **Key Personnel:** Reggie Hicks, Gen. Mgr.; Tony Phillips, Public Affairs and News Dir.; Bobby Jackson, Program Dir.; Deborah Strahorn, Mktg. Dir.; Shelia Tenney, Membership Coord. **Operating Hours:** Continuous; 30% network, 70% local. **Owner:** Clark Atlanta University.

★4323★
WDCY-AM
8451 S. Cherokee Blvd., Ste. B
Douglasville, GA 30134   Ph: (404)920-1520
Frequency: 1520. **Network Affiliation:** Georgia Radio. **Format:** Southern Gospel. **Key Personnel:** Jim O'Neal, Program Dir.; Delores Barker, Office Mgr.; Fred Brewer, News Dir. **Operating Hours:** Sunrise-sunset; 100% local. **Owner:** William Dunn.

★4324★
WFAV-FM
PO Box 460   Ph: (912)273-1404
Cordele, GA 31015-0460   Fax: (912)273-1404
Frequency: 98.3. **Network Affiliation:** NBC; Georgia Radio. **Format:** Country. **Key Personnel:** Michael Knight, Program Dir.; Trae McClain, Asst. Program and Music Dir.; Lee Ann Rivers, Sales Mgr.; Stu Cooper, News and Public Affairs Dir. **Operating Hours:** 5% network, 95% local. **Owner:** Silverstar Communications, Inc.

★4325★
WFXM-FM
369 2nd St.
PO Box 4527
Macon, GA 31208   Ph: (912)742-2505
                                        Fax: (912)742-8299
Frequency: 100.1. **Network Affiliation:** American Urban Radio; Mutual Broadcasting System. **Format:** Urban Contemporary. **Key Personnel:** Albert E. Smith, Gen. Mgr.; George Threatt, Operations Mgr.; Sharon Wilson, Traffic Mgr.; Patricia Glass, Sales Mgr.; Wanda Harvey, Office Mgr. **Operating Hours:** Continuous. **Owner:** Ken Woodfin.

★4326★
WGML-AM
PO Box 615
Hinesville, GA 31313-3611   Ph: (912)368-3399
Frequency: 990. **Format:** Ethnic; Religious. **Key Personnel:** E.D. Steele, Mgr. **Operating Hours:** Daytime.

★4327★
WGOV-AM
Hwy. 84 W.
PO Box 1207   Ph: (912)242-4513
Valdosta, GA 31603   Fax: (912)247-7676
Frequency: 950. **Network Affiliation:** ABC. **Format:** Urban Contemporary. **Key Personnel:** Mike Mink, Music Dir. **Operating Hours:** Continuous; 100% local. **Owner:** Dee Rivers Group.

★4328★
WGUN-AM
2901 Mountain Industrial Blvd.   Ph: (404)491-1010
Tucker, GA 30084-3073   Fax: (404)491-3019
Frequency: 1010. **Network Affiliation:** Independent. **Format:** Southern Gospel. **Key Personnel:** Randy Adams, Sales Mgr.; Mark McKinnon, Program Dir.; Preston Mobley, Music Dir.; Jackie Wilkinson, Traffic Mgr.; Dick Schroeder, Gen. Mgr. **Operating Hours:** 6 a.m.-midnight; 100% local. **Owner:** Dee Rivers Group.

★4329★
WHCJ-FM
Box 31404
Savannah, GA 31402   Ph: (912)356-2399
Frequency: 88.5. **Format:** Jazz. **Key Personnel:** Carol Gordon, Gen. Mgr. **Operating Hours:** 8 a.m.-9 p.m. Mon. through Thur.; 8 a.m.-midnight Fri.

★4330★
WHGH-AM
PO Box 2218   Ph: (912)228-4124
Thomasville, GA 31799   Fax: (912)225-9508
Frequency: 840. **Network Affiliation:** American Urban Radio. **Format:** Urban Contemporary. **Key Personnel:** Curtis T. Thomas, Gen. Mgr.; Sheryl T. Cason, Office Mgr.; Adrian Guyton, Program/Music Dir. **Operating Hours:** Sunrise-sunset; 9% network, 91% local. **Owner:** Gross Broadcasting Co.

★4331★
WIBB-AM
369 2nd St.
PO Box 4527
Macon, GA 31208   Ph: (912)742-2505
Frequency: 1280. **Format:** Urban Contemporary/Gospel. **Key Personnel:** Albert E. Smith, Gen. Mgr.; Patricia Glass, Gen. Sales Mgr.; Jess Branson, Sales Mgr.; George Threatt, Operations Mgr. **Owner:** Davis Broadcasting Co., Inc.

★4332★
WIGO-AM
1532 Howell Mill Rd.
Atlanta, GA 30318   Ph: (404)352-3943
Frequency: 1340. **Network Affiliation:** American Urban Radio. **Format:** Urban Contemporary; Oldies. **Key Personnel:** Roger Amato, CEO; Al Parks, Gen. Mgr. **Operating Hours:** Continuous; 5% network, 95% local. **Owner:** Allied Media of Georgia.

★4333★
WJGA-FM
PO Box 3878   Ph: (404)775-3151
Jackson, GA 30233   Fax: (404)957-9915
Frequency: 92.1. **Network Affiliation:** Independent. **Format:** Adult Contemporary 6 a.m. to 6 p.m.; Urban Contemporary 6 p.m. to 1 a.m. **Key Personnel:** Don Earnhart, Gen. Mgr. **Operating Hours:** 6 a.m.-1 a.m. **Owner:** Tarkenton Broadcasting Inc.

★4334★
WKIG-AM
226 E. Bolton St.
Glennville, GA 30427   Ph: (912)654-3580
Frequency: 1580. **Network Affiliation:** NBC. **Format:** Gospel. **Key Personnel:** Judy W. Cobb, Mgr. **Operating Hours:** Sunrise-sunset; 98% network, 2% local. **Owner:** Tattnall County Broadcasting Co.

★4335★
WKXK-FM
Hwy. 341 N.
PO Box 1150   Ph: (912)825-5547
Fort Valley, GA 31030   Fax: (912)742-8299
Frequency: 97.9. **Network Affiliation:** American Urban Radio; Mutual Broadcasting System. **Format:** Country. **Key Personnel:** Albert E. Smith, Gen. Mgr.; George Threatt, Operations Mgr.; Patricia Glass, Sales Mgr.; Sharon Wilson, Traffic Dir.; Wanda Harvey, Office Mgr. **Operating Hours:** Continuous. **Owner:** Ken Woodfin.

★4336★
WKZK-AM
PO Box 1454   Ph: (706)738-9191
Augusta, GA 30903   Fax: (706)738-9191
Frequency: 1600. **Network Affiliation:** American Urban Radio. **Format:** Gospel. **Key Personnel:** Garfield Turner, Program Mgr.; Walter B. Robinson, Jr., Owner and Gen. Mgr.; Dora Clayton, Rep. **Operating Hours:** 6 a.m.-sunset. **Owner:** Gospel Radio Inc.

★4337★
WLOV-AM
823 Berkshire Dr.   Ph: (706)678-2125
Washington, GA 30673   Fax: (706)678-1925
Frequency: 1370. **Network Affiliation:** Satellite Music; Gannett News. **Format:** Oldies. **Key Personnel:** Rodney Holloway, Mgr.; Jan VanDiver, Program Dir./News Dir. **Operating Hours:** 18 hours daily; 60% network, 40% local. **Owner:** Ptak Broadcasting, Inc.

★4338★
WLOV-FM
823 Berkshire Dr.   Ph: (706)678-2125
Washington, GA 30673   Fax: (706)678-1925
Frequency: 100.1. **Network Affiliation:** Satellite Radio. **Format:** News; Sports; Pure Gold. **Key Personnel:** Rodney Holloway, Sales Mgr.; Jan VanDiver, Program Dir. **Operating Hours:** 6 a.m.-midnight; 60% network, 40% local. **Owner:** Ptak Broadcasting, Inc.

★4339★
WPGA-FM
PO Drawer 980   Ph: (912)987-2980
Perry, GA 31069   Fax: (912)987-7595
Frequency: 100.9. **Network Affiliation:** ABC. **Format:** Urban Contemporary. **Key Personnel:** Lowell Register, Gen. Mgr.; Janice Register, Bookkeeper; John Lynn, Station Mgr. **Operating Hours:** Continuous. **Owner:** Register Data Systems.

★4340★
WQVE-FM
Box 434   Ph: (912)294-0010
Camilla, GA 31730   Fax: (912)294-0010
Frequency: 105.5. **Network Affiliation:** Georgia Radio. **Format:** Urban Contemporary. **Key Personnel:** Ron Allen, Gen. Mgr.; Lee Sherman, Jr., Program Dir. **Operating Hours:** Continuous; 75% network, 25% local. **Owner:** W.H. Nesmith, Jr.

★4341★
WRDW-AM
1480 Eisenhower Dr.
Augusta, GA 30907   Ph: (706)667-8001
Frequency: 1480. **Network Affiliation:** American Urban Radio. **Format:** Urban Contemporary. **Key Personnel:** Betty Beard, Gen. Mgr. **Operating Hours:** Continuous. **Owner:** Advertisement Network System.

★4342★
WROM-AM
PO Box 5031   Ph: (706)234-7171
Rome, GA 30162-5031   Fax: (706)234-8043
Frequency: 710. **Network Affiliation:** Mutual Broadcasting System. **Format:** Gospel. **Key Personnel:** Parnick Jennings, Pres./Gen. Mgr.; Jim McRee, Sales Mgr. **Operating Hours:** Sunrise-sunset. **Owner:** Inspiration Radio, Inc.

★4343★
WSFT-AM
PO Box 689
Thomaston, GA 30286   Ph: (404)647-5421
Frequency: 1220. **Network Affiliation:** NBC; Georgia Radio. **Format:** Country. **Key Personnel:** Claude D. Thames, Gen. Mgr.; John W. Thames, Station Mgr./News Dir. **Operating Hours:** 6 a.m.-sunset; 20% network, 80% local. **Owner:** Upson Broadcasting Co.

★4344★
WSNT-AM
PO Box 150
Sandersville, GA 31082   Ph: (912)552-5182
Frequency: 1490. **Network Affiliation:** NBC. **Format:** Urban Contemporary; Country. Simulcasts WSNT-FM. **Key Personnel:** James C. Whaley, Mgr.; Curtis Parsons, Sports Dir.; Michael Howell, News Dir. **Operating Hours:** 6:00 a.m.-midnight; 10% network, 90% local. **Owner:** Cleatus Brazzell.

★4345★
WSNT-FM
PO Box 150
Sandersville, GA 31082   Ph: (912)552-5182
Frequency: 93.5. **Network Affiliation:** NBC. **Format:** Urban Contemporary; Country. Simulcasts WSNT-AM. **Key Personnel:** James C. Whaley, Mgr.; Curtis Parsons, Sports Dir.; Michael Howell, News Dir. **Operating Hours:** 6:00 a.m.-midnight; 10% network, 90% local. **Owner:** Cleatus Brazzell.

★4346★
WTHB-AM
Box 1584   Ph: (803)279-2330
Augusta, GA 30903   Fax: (803)279-8149
Frequency: 1550. **Network Affiliation:** ABC; CBS. **Format:** Gospel. **Key Personnel:** William S. Jaeger, Gen. Mgr.; Carl Conner, Jr., Natl. Program Dir.; Carroll Redd, Operations Mgr.; Bill Berry, Gen. Sales Mgr. **Operating Hours:** Sunrise-sunset. **Owner:** Davis Broadcasting Inc.

★4347★
WTJH-AM
2146 Dodson Dr.   Ph: (404)344-2235
East Point, GA 30344   Fax: (404)344-0647
Frequency: 1260. **Format:** Inspiration. **Key Personnel:** Rhodell Lewis, Program Dir.; Valencia Williams, Office Mgr.; Kevin Jones, Music Dir. **Operating Hours:** Continuous. **Owner:** Willis Broadcasting.

★4348★
WVEE-FM
120 Ralph McGill Blvd., Ste. 1000   Ph: (404)898-8900
Atlanta, GA 30365-6901   Fax: (404)898-8916
Frequency: 103.3. **Network Affiliation:** NBC. **Format:** Urban Contemporary. **Key Personnel:** Rick Mack, V.P./Gen. Mgr.; Glenn Way, Gen. Sales Mgr.; Anita Harris, Local Sales Mgr. **Operating Hours:** Continuous. **Owner:** Summit Broadcasting Corp.

★4349★
WXAG-AM
2145 S. Milledge Ave.
Athens, GA 30605   Ph: (404)549-1470
Frequency: 1470. **Network Affiliation:** American Urban Radio. **Format:** Gospel. **Key Personnel:** Julia A. Hunter, Gen. Mgr.; Lee King, Program and News Dir. **Operating Hours:** 6 a.m.-midnight. 15% network, 85% local. **Owner:** Classical Communications Ltd.

★4350★
WXRS-AM
Box 1590
Swainsboro, GA 30401

Ph: (912)237-1590
Fax: (912)237-3559

Frequency: 1580. **Format:** Urban Contemporary; Black Gospel. **Key Personnel:** Bobby Gardner, Music Dir.; Dean Morgan, News Dir.; Jeff Wiggins, Program Dir./Sports Dir. **Operating Hours:** Continuous; 50% network, 50% local. **Owner:** Lacom Communications, Inc.

★4351★
WYZE-AM
1111 Blvd. SE
Atlanta, GA 30312

Ph: (404)622-7802

Frequency: 1480. **Network Affiliation:** Georgia Radio. **Format:** Gospel. **Key Personnel:** C.T. Taylor, Gen. Mgr.; Regina A. Slaughter, Program Mgr.; Helen J. Humphries, Chief Financial Officer. **Operating Hours:** 6 a.m.-midnight. **Owner:** GHB Broadcasting Corp.

Illinois

★4352★
WBCP-AM
PO Box 1023
Champaign, IL 61820

Ph: (217)359-1580

Frequency: 1580. **Network Affiliation:** American Urban Radio. **Format:** Adult Urban Contemporary. **Key Personnel:** Lonnie Clark, Pres.; Greg Ludwig, Gen. Sales Mgr.; James Shepherd, Program Dir. **Operating Hours:** 6 a.m.-10 p.m. **Owner:** WBCP Inc.

★4353★
WBEE-AM
15700 Campbell Ave.
Harvey, IL 60426

Ph: (708)331-7840
Fax: (708)333-7840

Frequency: 1570. **Network Affiliation:** Independent. **Format:** Jazz. **Key Personnel:** Charles Sherrell, Pres.; Carl Farley, Gen. Mgr. **Operating Hours:** Continuous. **Owner:** Mariner Broadcasters, Inc.

★4354★
WCFJ-AM
1000 Lincoln Hwy.
Ford Heights, IL 60411

Ph: (708)758-8600
Fax: (708)758-8602

Frequency: 1470. **Network Affiliation:** Independent. **Format:** Gospel; Religious (Christian Contemporary). **Key Personnel:** Darryl Chavers, Gen. Mgr. **Operating Hours:** Continuous. **Owner:** Liberty Temple Full Gospel Church.

★4355★
WESL-AM
149 S. 8th St.
East St. Louis, IL 62201

Ph: (618)271-1490
Fax: (618)875-0600

Frequency: 1490. **Network Affiliation:** American Urban Radio; Unistar; Mutual Broadcasting System. **Format:** Gospel. **Key Personnel:** Frank Davis, Pres./Gen. Mgr.; Pastor Larry Brown, Program Dir.; Betty Robinson, Office Mgr. **Operating Hours:** Continuous. **Owner:** WESL Gateway Communications.

★4356★
WGCI-FM
332 S. Michigan Ave., Ste. 600
Chicago, IL 60604

Ph: (312)984-1400
Fax: (312)987-4483

Frequency: 107.5. **Network Affiliation:** Independent. **Format:** Urban Contemporary. **Key Personnel:** Marv Dyson, Gen. Mgr. **Operating Hours:** Continuous. **Owner:** Gannet Co.

★4357★
WJPC-AM
820 S. Michigan Ave.
Chicago, IL 60605

Ph: (312)322-9400
Fax: (312)322-0918

Frequency: 950. **Network Affiliation:** Independent. **Format:** Urban Adult Contemporary. Simulcasts WLNR-FM. **Key Personnel:** Lillian

Terrell, Operations Mgr.; Jay Alan, Program Dir. **Operating Hours:** Continuous. **Owner:** Johnson Communications.

★4358★
WKDC-AM
130 North York
Elmhurst, IL 60126

Ph: (708)530-1530

Frequency: 1530. **Format:** Jazz; Ethnic; Big Band/Nostalgia. **Key Personnel:** Frank Blotter, Pres.; Robert Merdian, Mgr. **Operating Hours:** 6 a.m.-sundown; 100% local.

★4359★
WKKC-FM
6800 S. Wentworth Ave.
Chicago, IL 60621

Ph: (312)846-8531
Fax: (312)962-0667

Frequency: 89.3. **Network Affiliation:** Independent. **Format:** Full Service. **Key Personnel:** Kevin Brown, Station Mgr.; Bill Lattin, News Dir.; James Kelly, Program and Music Dir.; Tracey Williams, Sales, Promotions, and Mktg. Dir.; Joyce Genus, Gen. Mgr. **Operating Hours:** 8 a.m.-midnight; 100% local. **Owner:** Kennedy-King College.

★4360★
WKRO-AM
Rte. 1, US-51
Box 311
Cairo, IL 62914

Ph: (618)734-1490
Fax: (618)734-0884

Frequency: 1490. **Network Affiliation:** ABC. **Format:** Country. **Operating Hours:** 6 a.m.-10 p.m.; 7% network, 93% local. **Owner:** William T. Crain.

★4361★
WLNR-FM
820 S. Michigan Ave.
Chicago, IL 60605

Ph: (312)322-9400

Frequency: 106.3. **Format:** Urban Adult Contemporary. Simulcasts WJPC-AM. **Key Personnel:** Lillian Terrell, Operations Mgr. **Operating Hours:** Continuous. **Owner:** Johnson Communications.

★4362★
WLUV-FM
2272 Elmwood
Rockford, IL 61103

Ph: (815)877-9588
Fax: (815)877-9649

Frequency: 96.7. **Network Affiliation:** ABC; Satellite Music. **Format:** Sports; Urban Contemporary (Soul); The Heat. **Key Personnel:** Angelo Joseph Salvi, Gen. Mgr.; Virgie Lameyer, Office Mgr. **Operating Hours:** Continuous. **Owner:** Angelo Joseph Salvi.

★4363★
WPNA-AM
408 S. Oak Park Ave.
Oak Park, IL 60302

Ph: (708)524-9762
Fax: (708)848-9220

Frequency: 1490. **Network Affiliation:** Independent. **Format:** Ethnic; News; Religious. **Key Personnel:** Margaret Sas, Gen. Mgr.; Jerry Obrecki, Sales Mgr.; Len Petrulis, Public Affairs Dir. **Operating Hours:** Continuous; 100% local. **Owner:** Alliance Communications, Inc.

★4364★
WSBC-AM
4949 W. Belmont Ave.
Chicago, IL 60641

Ph: (312)282-9722

Frequency: 1240. **Format:** Black Gospel; Ethnic. **Key Personnel:** Daniel R. Lee, Pres.; Roy J. Bellavia, Gen. and Program Mgr.; Mark Nielsen, Chief Engineer. **Operating Hours:** 6 a.m.-8:30 a.m., 10 a.m.-11 a.m., 2 p.m.-3:30 p.m., 8 p.m.-10 p.m., 11 p.m.-midnight. **Owner:** Diamond Broadcasting, Inc.

★4365★
WSIE-FM
Southern Illinois University
Box 1773
Edwardsville, IL 62026

Ph: (618)692-2228
Fax: (618)692-2233

Frequency: 88.7. **Network Affiliation:** National Public Radio (NPR); American Public Radio (APR). **Format:** Public Radio; Jazz; News.

Key Personnel: Roy Gerritsen, Gen. Mgr.; Jim Bafaro, News/Public Affairs Dir.; Mark Ellebracht, Music Dir.; David Caires, Chief Engineer. **Operating Hours:** Continuous; 10% network, 90% local. **Owner:** Southern Illinois University.

★4366★
WVAZ-FM
800 S. Wells, Ste. 250   Ph: (312)360-9000
Chicago, IL 60607   Fax: (312)360-9070
Frequency: 102.7. **Network Affiliation:** Unistar. **Format:** Adult Contemporary/Urban Contemporary mix. **Key Personnel:** Barry A. Mayo, Pres./Gen. Mgr.; Hal West, Natl. Sales Mgr.; Cris Wilson, Gen. Sales Mgr.; Kristen Hartman, Local Sales Manager. **Operating Hours:** Continuous. **Owner:** Broadcasting Partners, Inc.

★4367★
WVON-AM
3350 S. Kedzie Ave.   Ph: (312)247-6200
Chicago, IL 60623   Fax: (312)247-9067
Frequency: 1450. **Network Affiliation:** Mutual Broadcasting System; American Urban Radio. **Format:** Talk; Religious. **Key Personnel:** Keshia Chavers, Exec. Producer; Peggy Salmon, Exec. Producer. **Operating Hours:** 10 p.m.-1 p.m. **Owner:** Midway Broadcasting.

★4368★
WXKO-FM
PO Box 465   Ph: (217)562-3949
Pana, IL 62557   Fax: (217)562-3945
Frequency: 100.9. **Network Affiliation:** Satellite Music. **Format:** Country. **Key Personnel:** Cole Studstill, Station Mgr.; John Broux, News Dir.; DeeAnn Carroll, Sales Mgr. **Operating Hours:** Continuous; 90% network, 10% local. **Owner:** Southeastern Video, Inc.

─────────── Indiana ───────────

★4369★
WLTH-AM
3669 Broadway
Gary, IN 46409   Ph: (219)884-9409
Frequency: 1370. **Network Affiliation:** Independent. **Format:** News; Talk. **Key Personnel:** Greg Brown, Gen. Mgr./Pres. **Operating Hours:** 6 a.m.-2 a.m. **Owner:** Lorenza P. Butler.

★4370★
WPZZ-FM
645 Industrial Dr.   Ph: (317)736-4040
Franklin, IN 46131   Fax: (317)542-9690
Frequency: 95.9. **Network Affiliation:** Southern Broadcasting. **Format:** Urban Contemporary. **Key Personnel:** Eric Blakey, Program Dir.; John C. Asher, Operations Dir.; Kevin Simmons, Sales Mgr.; Pam Coomer, Business Mgr. **Operating Hours:** Continuous; 10% network, 90% local. **Owner:** Willis Broadcast Co.

★4371★
WSLM-FM
Radio Ridge
Hwy. 56 E.
PO Box 385   Ph: (812)883-5750
Salem, IN 47167   Fax: (812)883-2797
Frequency: 98.9. **Network Affiliation:** Independent. **Format:** Gospel; Sports; Talk. **Key Personnel:** Don H. Martin, Owner/Gen. Mgr.; Rick Martin, News Dir.; Becky Lynn Coomer, Program Dir.; John Wood, Sports Dir.; Elmo Brough, Advertising Mgr. **Operating Hours:** 6 a.m.-midnight; 100% local. **Owner:** Don H. Martin.

★4372★
WTLC-FM
2126 N. Meridan St.   Ph: (317)923-1456
Indianapolis, IN 46202   Fax: (317)924-9684
Frequency: 105.7. **Network Affiliation:** Independent. **Format:** Urban Contemporary. **Key Personnel:** Amos Brown, Gen. Mgr. **Operating Hours:** Continuous. **Owner:** Panache Broadcasting.

★4373★
WVPE-FM
2424 California Rd.   Ph: (219)262-5660
Elkhart, IN 46514   Fax: (719)262-5700
Frequency: 88.1. **Network Affiliation:** American Public Radio (APR); National Public Radio (NPR). **Format:** Jazz; News; Public Radio. **Key Personnel:** Tim Eby, Station Mgr.; Doug Cunningham, News Dir. **Operating Hours:** 5 a.m.-midnight; 30% network, 70% local. **Owner:** Elkhart Community School Corp.

★4374★
WWCA-AM
487 Broadway, Ste. 207   Ph: (219)886-9171
Gary, IN 46402   Fax: (219)886-3684
                             Free: 800-873-4600
Frequency: 1270. **Format:** Gospel. **Key Personnel:** Abe Rycraw, Operations Mgr.; K.L. Ford, Program Dir.; Karen Clark, Office Mgr. **Operating Hours:** Continuous. **Owner:** Willis Broadcasting.

★4375★
WYCA-FM
6336 Calumet Ave.
Hammond, IN 46324   Ph: (219)933-4455
Frequency: 92.3. **Format:** Religious. **Key Personnel:** Taft Harris, Station Mgr.; Joyce Topper, Office Mgr.; Tracie Reynolds, Program Dir. **Operating Hours:** Continuous. **Owner:** Donald Crawford.

─────────── Iowa ───────────

★4376★
KBBG-FM
527 1/2 Cottage St.
Waterloo, IA 50703   Ph: (319)234-1441
Frequency: 88.1. **Network Affiliation:** National Public Radio (NPR). **Format:** Blues; Gospel; Jazz. **Key Personnel:** William Jackson, Production Mgr. **Operating Hours:** 5:30 a.m.-midnight Mon.-Thur., Sat.; 5:30 a.m.-2 a.m. Fri.; 6 a.m.-midnight Sun. **Owner:** Afro American Community Broadcasting Inc.

★4377★
KCCK-FM
6301 Kirkwood Blvd. SW   Ph: (319)398-5446
Cedar Rapids, IA 52406   Fax: (319)398-5492
Frequency: 88.3. **Network Affiliation:** American Public Radio (APR). **Format:** Jazz. **Key Personnel:** Steve Carpenter, Mgr.; George Dorman, News Dir.; Diane Allender, Music Dir.; Ken Rinehart, Program Dir. **Operating Hours:** 5 a.m.-1 a.m. Mon.- Fri., Continuous Sat. and Sun.; 16% network, 84% local. **Owner:** Kirkwood Community College.

★4378★
KIGC-FM
William Penn College
N. Market & Trueblood Aves.
Oskaloosa, IA 52577   Ph: (515)673-1095
Frequency: 88.7. **Network Affiliation:** Independent. **Format:** Contemporary Hit Radio (CHR); Jazz; Urban Contemporary; Blues; Religious (Christian). **Key Personnel:** Don DeBoef, Gen. Mgr.; John Doerge, Faculty Adviser. **Operating Hours:** 7 a.m.-midnight; 100% local. **Owner:** William Penn College.

★4379★
KTFC-FM
Box 102-A, Rte. 2
Sioux City, IA 51106   Ph: (712)252-4621
Frequency: 103.3. **Network Affiliation:** Satellite Radio. **Format:** Gospel. **Key Personnel:** Don Swanson, Owner/Gen. Mgr. **Operating Hours:** Continuous.

─────────────── **Kansas** ───────────────

★4380★
KEYN-FM
2829 Salina Ave.   Ph: (316)838-7744
Wichita, KS 67204   Fax: (316)832-0061
Frequency: 103.7. **Format:** Adult Contemporary; Oldies. **Key Personnel:** Rick Parrish, Gen. Mgr./V.P.; Dan Hogan, Gen. Sales Mgr.; Dave Windsor, Regional Sales Mgr.; Dennis Kinkaid, Program Dir. **Operating Hours:** Continuous. **Owner:** Cleer Channel Communications.

★4381★
KQAM-AM
2829 Salina Ave.   Ph: (316)838-7744
Wichita, KS 67204   Fax: (316)832-0061
Frequency: 1410. **Network Affiliation:** ABC; Mutual Broadcasting System. **Format:** Big Band/Nostalgia; Sports. **Key Personnel:** Rick Parrish, Gen. Mgr./Gen. Sales Mgr.; Dan Hogan, Sales Mgr.; Dave Windsor, Regional Sales Mgr.; Jerry Vaughn, Operations Mgr./Program Dir.; April Pate, Traffic Dir. **Operating Hours:** Continuous. **Owner:** Clear Channel Communications.

─────────────── **Kentucky** ───────────────

★4382★
WCKU-FM
651 Perimeter Dr., Ste. 102   Ph: (606)269-9540
Lexington, KY 40517   Fax: (606)269-9241
Frequency: 102.5. **Network Affiliation:** ABC. **Format:** Urban Contemporary. **Key Personnel:** Bill Clary, Program and Music Dir.; Cindy Ware, Sales and Gen. Mgr. **Operating Hours:** Continuous. **Owner:** High Communications Partnership.

★4383★
WLLV-AM
515 S. 3rd St.
Louisville, KY 40202   Ph: (502)581-1240
Frequency: 1240. **Network Affiliation:** Independent. **Format:** Gospel. **Key Personnel:** Archie Dale, V.P./Gen. Mgr. **Operating Hours:** Continuous. **Owner:** Full Force, Inc.

★4384★
WLOU-AM
2549 S. 3rd St.
Louisville, KY 40208   Ph: (502)636-3535
Frequency: 1350. **Network Affiliation:** American Urban Radio. **Format:** Urban Contemporary. **Key Personnel:** Charles Mootry, V.P./GMR; Vanessa Gentry, Traffic Mgr./Office Mgr.; Neal O'Rea, Chief Engineer; Chuck Cain, Sales Mgr. **Operating Hours:** Continuous. **Owner:** Johnson Communications.

★4385★
WQKS-AM
905 S. Main St.   Ph: (502)886-1480
Hopkinsville, KY 42240   Fax: (502)886-6286
Frequency: 1480. **Network Affiliation:** ABC; American Urban Radio. **Format:** Urban Contemporary. **Key Personnel:** Glenn Buxton, Gen. Mgr. **Operating Hours:** Continuous; 5% network, 95% local. **Owner:** Regional Broadcasting, Inc.

★4386★
WRLV-AM
PO Box 550
Salyersville, KY 41465   Ph: (606)349-6125
Frequency: 1140. **Network Affiliation:** KyNet; ABC. **Format:** Gospel. **Key Personnel:** C.K. Belhasen, Pres./Sales and Promotion Gen. Mgr. **Operating Hours:** Sunrise-sunset; 10% network, 90% local. **Owner:** Licking Valley Radio Corp.

★4387★
WTCV-AM
PO Box 685
Greenup, KY 41144   Ph: (606)473-7377
Frequency: 1520. **Network Affiliation:** KyNet. **Format:** Southern Gospel. **Key Personnel:** Robert L. Scheibly, Exec. V.P.; Ronnie Bell, Station Mgr.; Tina Adams, Music Dir.; Tito LaFrond, News Dir. **Operating Hours:** Continuous; 5% network, 95% local. **Owner:** Greenup County Broadcasting.

★4388★
WWXL-AM
Rte. 5, Box 50
Manchester, KY 40962   Ph: (606)598-5102
Frequency: 1450. **Format:** Gospel. **Key Personnel:** Ermel Ison, Gen. Mgr./Gen. Sales Mgr.; Lonnie Marcum, Operations Mgr. **Operating Hours:** 5:30 a.m.-midnight. **Owner:** Wilderness Hills Broadcasting Inc.

─────────────── **Louisiana** ───────────────

★4389★
KBCE-FM
Box 69   Ph: (318)793-4003
Boyce, LA 71409   Fax: (318)793-8888
Frequency: 102.3. **Network Affiliation:** American Urban Radio. **Format:** Urban Contemporary. **Key Personnel:** Gus E. Lewis, Pres./Gen. Mgr. **Operating Hours:** Continuous. **Owner:** Gus E. Lewis.

★4390★
KFXZ-FM
3225 Ambassador Caffery Pkwy.   Ph: (318)898-1112
Lafayette, LA 70506-7214   Fax: (318)988-0443
Frequency: 106.3. **Network Affiliation:** ABC. **Format:** Urban Contemporary. **Key Personnel:** Al J. Wallace, V.P.; John Marver, Sales Mgr.; Carey Martin, Operations and Music Dir.; M. Patton, Chief Engineer; Bernie Morrison, Office Mgr.; J. Evans, News Dir. **Operating Hours:** Continuous; 2% network, 98% local. **Owner:** Citywide Broadcasting Company, Inc.

★4391★
KGRM-FM
Drawer K   Ph: (318)274-2734
Grambling, LA 71245   Fax: (318)274-3245
Frequency: 91.5. **Format:** Urban Contemporary. **Key Personnel:** Calvin Miles, Gen. Mgr.; David Dickinson, Operations Mgr. **Operating Hours:** 6:00 a.m.-midnight. **Owner:** Grambling State University.

★4392★
KJCB-AM
413 Jefferson St.
Lafayette, LA 70501   Ph: (318)233-4262
Frequency: 770. **Network Affiliation:** ABC. **Format:** Jazz; Religious; Urban Contemporary; Oldies. **Key Personnel:** Joshua Jackson, Sr., Pres.; Horatio Handy, Gen. Mgr. **Operating Hours:** Continuous. **Owner:** Joshua Jackson, Sr.

★4393★
KOKA-AM
PO Box 103   Ph: (318)222-3122
Shreveport, LA 71161   Fax: (318)221-9802
Frequency: 980. **Network Affiliation:** NBC; American Urban Radio.
Format: Religious (Black). **Key Personnel:** Cary D. Camp, Owner;
Diane Camp, Gen. Mgr.; Eddie Giles, Program Dir. **Operating Hours:**
5 a.m.-midnight. **Owner:** Cary D. Camp.

★4394★
KRUS-AM
Box 430
500 N. Monroe St.
Ruston, LA 71270   Ph: (318)255-2530
Frequency: 1490. **Network Affiliation:** AP. **Format:** Urban
Contemporary. **Key Personnel:** Dan Hollingsworth, Pres./Gen. and
Sales Mgr.; James Cooper, Music and Sports Dir.; Gene Haynes,
News Dir. **Operating Hours:** 20 hours daily; 1% network, 99% local.
Owner: Ruston Broadcasting Co., Inc.

★4395★
KSLU-FM
Box 783, University Sta.   Ph: (504)549-2330
Hammond, LA 70402   Fax: (504)549-5014
Frequency: 90.9. **Network Affiliation:** American Public Radio (APR).
Format: Public Radio; Jazz. **Key Personnel:** Ron Nethercutt, Gen.
Mgr.; Paul Varnado, Mktg. Mgr.; Ken Benitez, News Dir.; Larry
Ward, Chief Engineer; Craig Williams, Program Dir.; Joyce Savoie,
Bus. Mgr.; John Pisiotta, Music Dir. **Operating Hours:** Continuous;
35% network, 65% local. **Owner:** Southeastern Louisiana University.

★4396★
KTRY-AM
Box 1075
Bastrop, LA 71220
Frequency: 730. **Format:** Urban Contemporary. **Key Personnel:**
Henry Cotton, Pres./Gen. Mgr./Program Dir.; Lewis McDuff, Music
Dir.; Raife Smith, Chief Engineer. **Owner:** North Delta Broadcasting
Inc.

★4397★
KXLA-AM
Hwy. 80
Box 990
Rayville, LA 71269   Ph: (318)728-6990
Frequency: 990. **Network Affiliation:** Southern Broadcasting.
Format: Gospel. **Key Personnel:** Mathew Peace, Gen. Mgr.
Operating Hours: 6 a.m.-12 a.m.; 10% network, 90% local. **Owner:**
Ouachita Broadcasting Co.

★4398★
KXZZ-AM
311 Alamo St.   Ph: (318)436-7277
Lake Charles, LA 70601   Fax: (318)436-7278
Frequency: 1580. **Network Affiliation:** American Urban Radio.
Format: Urban Contemporary. **Key Personnel:** Albert Johnson,
Pres./Owner; Dixie Johnson, CEO/Owner; Gary Allen, Gen. Mgr.;
James Williams, Program Dir. **Operating Hours:** Continuous; 100%
local. **Owner:** Dixie Broadcasters, Inc.

★4399★
KYEA-FM
516 Martin St.   Ph: (318)322-1491
West Monroe, LA 71292   Fax: (318)325-7203
Frequency: 98.3. **Network Affiliation:** American Urban Radio; ABC;
NBC. **Format:** Urban Contemporary. **Key Personnel:** Vivian Ross,
Gen. Mgr.; Anthony Snearly, Financial Dir. **Operating Hours:**
Continuous; 100% local. **Owner:** Frank D. Stimley.

★4400★
WABL-AM
Bankston Rd.
PO Box 787   Ph: (504)748-8385
Amite, LA 70422   Fax: (504)748-3918
Frequency: 1570. **Network Affiliation:** ABC; Louisiana; Unistar.
Format: Full Service; Urban Contemporary. **Key Personnel:** Charles
Hart, Gen. Mgr. **Operating Hours:** Sunrise-sunset; 30% network,
70% local. **Owner:** Amite Broadcasting Co., Inc.

★4401★
WBOK-AM
1639 Gentilly Blvd.   Ph: (504)943-4600
New Orleans, LA 70119   Fax: (504)944-4662
Frequency: 1230. **Network Affiliation:** Independent. **Format:**
Religious. **Key Personnel:** Annette Pete, Gen. Mgr. **Operating
Hours:** Continuous. **Owner:** Willis Broadcasting Corporation.

★4402★
WQUE-AM
1440 Canal St., Ste. 800
New Orleans, LA 70112   Ph: (504)581-1280
Frequency: 1280. **Network Affiliation:** Independent. **Format:** Urban
Contemporary. **Key Personnel:** Derek Monette, Program Dir.; Karen
Cortello, Music Dir.; Monica Pierre, News Dir.; John S. Rockweiler,
Gen. Mgr. **Operating Hours:** Continuous; 100%. **Owner:** Clear
Channel Communications.

★4403★
WQUE-FM
1440 Canal St.   Ph: (504)581-1280
New Orleans, LA 70112   Fax: (504)561-8682
Frequency: 93.3. **Network Affiliation:** Independent. **Format:** Urban
Contemporary. **Key Personnel:** Karen Cortell, Music Dir.; Jay
Michaels, Program Dir.; Jeff White, News Dir.; Ken Wente, Gen. Mgr.
Operating Hours: Continuous; 100%. **Owner:** Clear Channel
Communications.

★4404★
WWOZ-FM
PO Box 51840
New Orleans, LA 70151   Ph: (504)568-1239
Frequency: 90.7. **Network Affiliation:** American Public Radio (APR).
Format: Jazz; Heritage. **Key Personnel:** David Freedman, Gen.
Mgr.; Emory White, Program Dir. **Operating Hours:** 6 a.m.-2 a.m.;
100% local. **Owner:** Friends of WWOZ Inc.

★4405★
WXOK-AM
7707 Waco Dr.
Baton Rouge, LA 70806   Ph: (504)927-7060
Frequency: 1460. **Network Affiliation:** Independent. **Format:** Urban
Contemporary. **Key Personnel:** Dennis Lee, Gen. Mgr. **Operating
Hours:** Continuous. **Owner:** Winnfield Life Broadcasting Inc.

★4406★
WYLD-AM
2228 Gravier   Ph: (504)822-1945
New Orleans, LA 70119   Fax: (504)826-7723
Frequency: 940. **Format:** Religious; Urban Contemporary. **Key
Personnel:** Alan H. Lee, Program Dir.; Carl Chargois, Promotions
Coord.; Mike Smith, Music Dir. **Operating Hours:** Continuous; 5%
network, 95% local. **Owner:** Inter Urban Broadcasting Co.

─────────────── **Maryland** ───────────────

★4407★
WANN-AM
PO Box 631
Annapolis, MD 21404   Ph: (410)269-0700
Frequency: 1190. **Network Affiliation:** Independent. **Format:**
Country. **Key Personnel:** M.H. Blum, Pres.; M.W. Pittman,

Engineering V.P.; R.Z. Goldberg, Sales V.P.; Jeff Blum, News Dir.; Robert M. White, Dir. of Promotion & Programming. **Operating Hours:** Sunrise-sunset. **Owner:** Annapolis Broadcasting Corp.

★4408★
WBGR-AM
3000 Druid Park Dr.
Baltimore, MD 21215
Ph: (410)367-7773
Fax: (410)367-4702

Frequency: 860. **Network Affiliation:** American Urban Radio. **Format:** Gospel. **Key Personnel:** Maurice Hulbert, Gen. Mgr.; Norven Goldsberry, Program Dir. **Operating Hours:** Continuous; 5% network, 95% local. **Owner:** Jack Mortenson.

★4409★
WBZE-AM
PO Box 1650
Waldorf, MD 20604-1650
Ph: (301)870-8700

Frequency: 1030. **Network Affiliation:** American Urban Radio. **Format:** Gospel. **Key Personnel:** Reggie Hales, Gen. Mgr. **Operating Hours:** Sunrise-sunset. **Owner:** Peter Gurickus.

★4410★
WEAA-FM
Hillen Rd. & Coldspring Ln.
Baltimore, MD 21239
Ph: (410)319-3564

Frequency: 88.9. **Network Affiliation:** National Public Radio (NPR); AP. **Format:** Public Radio; Gospel; Ethnic (Caribbean); Jazz. **Key Personnel:** Wendy Williams, Acting Gen. Mgr.; Joe Lee, Program Dir.; Paula Smith, Promotions Dir.; Gale Reed, News Dir.; Gary Ellerbe, Asst. Music Dir. **Operating Hours:** 18 (Continuous hours on weekends); 5% network, 95% local. **Owner:** Morgan State University.

★4411★
WEBB-AM
3000 Druid Park Dr.
Baltimore, MD 21215
Ph: (301)367-9322
Fax: (301)367-6780

Frequency: 1360. **Network Affiliation:** Independent. **Format:** Adult Contemporary. **Key Personnel:** Alex McCamey, Gen. Mgr. **Operating Hours:** Continuous. **Owner:** Allied Media.

★4412★
WESM-FM
University of Maryland, Eastern Shore
Backbone Rd.
Princess Anne, MD 21853
Ph: (301)651-2816
Fax: (301)651-2819

Frequency: 91.3. **Network Affiliation:** American Public Radio (APR); National Public Radio (NPR); American Urban Radio. **Format:** Eclectic. **Key Personnel:** Robert A. Franklin, Dir.; Milton Blackman, Program Dir.; Michael Jenkins, Music Dir.; Connie Williams, Public and Community Affairs Dir.; Dave Collins, Program Mgr. **Operating Hours:** 5 a.m.-2 a.m.; 30% network, 70% local. **Owner:** University of Maryland, Eastern Shore.

★4413★
WJDY-AM
1633 N. Division St.
Salisbury, MD 21801
Ph: (301)742-5191

Frequency: 1470. **Network Affiliation:** CBS. **Format:** Urban Contemporary. **Key Personnel:** J.P. Connor, Jr., Gen. Mgr.; Brad Connor, Sales Mgr. **Operating Hours:** Sunrise-sunset. **Owner:** Connor Broadcasting.

★4414★
WWIN-AM
200 S. President St., 6th Fl.
Baltimore, MD 21202
Ph: (410)332-8200
Fax: (410)752-2252

Frequency: 1400. **Network Affiliation:** Unistar. **Format:** Gospel/Inspirational. **Key Personnel:** Alfred Liggins, Gen. Mgr.; Debbie Edwards, Business Mgr.; Karl Goehring, Chief Engineer; Mike Roberts, Program Dir.; Pam Somers, Station Mgr./Sales Mgr. **Operating Hours:** Continuous. **Owner:** Ragan Henry.

★4415★
WWIN-FM
200 S. President St., 6th Fl.
Baltimore, MD 21202
Ph: (410)332-8200
Fax: (410)752-2252

Frequency: 95.9. **Network Affiliation:** Unistar. **Format:** Urban Contemporary. **Key Personnel:** Alfred Liggins, Gen. Mgr.; Debbie Edwards, Business Mgr.; Karl Goehring, Chief Engineer; Terri Avery, Program Dir.; Pam Somers, Station Mgr./Sales Mgr. **Operating Hours:** Continuous. **Owner:** Radio One of Maryland, Inc.

★4416★
WXTR-FM
5210 Auth Rd.
Marlow Heights, MD 20746
Ph: (301)899-3014
Fax: (301)505-0374

Frequency: 104.1. **Network Affiliation:** Independent. **Format:** Oldies. **Key Personnel:** Robert Longwell, Pres.; Bob Duckman, Program Dir. **Operating Hours:** Continuous. **Owner:** Four Seasons Communications.

─────────── **Massachusetts** ───────────

★4417★
WILD-AM
90 Warren St.
Boston, MA 02119
Ph: (617)427-2222
Fax: (617)427-2677

Frequency: 1090. **Network Affiliation:** American Urban Radio; ABC. **Format:** Urban Contemporary. **Key Personnel:** Bernadine Foster Nash, Pres./CEO; Monte Bowens, Gen. Mgr.; Neal Perlstein, Gen. Sales Mgr.; Stephen Hill, Program Dir.; Brian Higgins, News Dir.; Dana Hall, Music Dir. **Operating Hours:** Sunrise-sunset. **Owner:** Nash Communications Corp.

★4418★
WJJW-FM
N. Adams State College
Campus Center
North Adams, MA 01247
Ph: (413)663-9136

Frequency: 91.1. **Network Affiliation:** Independent. **Format:** Jazz; Ethnic; Religious; Urban Contemporary; Oldies; Alternative/Independent/Progressive. **Key Personnel:** Paul Lyons, Gen. Mgr.; Dawn Fraser, Program Dir.; Jason Lindholm, Music Dir. **Operating Hours:** 7 a.m.-3 a.m. **Owner:** N. Adams State College.

★4419★
WLVG-AM
670 Cummins Way
Boston, MA 02126-3243
Ph: (617)576-2895

Frequency: 740. **Network Affiliation:** Independent. **Format:** Religious; Urban Contemporary. **Key Personnel:** Rev. E.W. Jackson, Sr., Gen. Mgr.; Allen Redd, Asst. Gen. Mgr.; Don Long, Production Dir.; Theodora Jackson, Traffic Supervisor. **Operating Hours:** Sunrise-sunset; 100% local. **Owner:** Inspiration Communications.

★4420★
WMLN-FM
1071 Blue Hill Ave.
Milton, MA 02186
Ph: (617)333-0311
Fax: (617)333-6860

Frequency: 91.5. **Network Affiliation:** Mutual Broadcasting System. **Format:** Eclectic. **Key Personnel:** Alan Frank, Broadcast Dir.; Gavin Spittle, Station Mgr. **Operating Hours:** Continuous; 5% network, 95% local. **Owner:** Curry College.

★4421★
WWKX-FM
8 N. Main St.
Attleboro, MA 02703-2282
Ph: (508)222-1320
Fax: (508)761-9239

Frequency: 106.3. **Network Affiliation:** CBS. **Format:** Contemporary Hit Radio (CHR). **Key Personnel:** Gene Lombardi, Gen. Mgr.; Bill O'Brian, Program Dir.; Joseph Lembo, Gen. Sales Mgr. **Operating Hours:** Continuous. **Owner:** Ten Mile Communications.

Michigan

★4422★
WCHB-AM
32790 Henry Ruff Rd.
Inkster, MI 48141

Ph: (313)278-1440
Fax: (313)722-8495

Frequency: 1440. **Network Affiliation:** Independent. **Format:** Religious; Blues. **Key Personnel:** Mary Bell, Pres.; Wendell Cox, V.P./Gen. Mgr.; Eric Bass, Gen. Sales Mgr.; Terry Arnold, Program Dir.; Treva Bass, Chief Engineer. **Operating Hours:** Continuous; 2% network, 98% local. **Owner:** Bell Broadcasting Co.

★4423★
WCXT-FM
220 Polk
Hart, MI 49420

Ph: (616)873-7129
Fax: (616)873-7120

Frequency: 105.3. **Format:** Adult Contemporary. **Key Personnel:** Yvette Jernudd, Office Mgr.; Mark Waters, Program Dir. **Operating Hours:** Continuous. **Owner:** Waters Broadcasting.

★4424★
WDZZ-FM
1830 Genesee Tower
Flint, MI 48503

Ph: (313)767-0130
Fax: (313)238-7310

Frequency: 92.7. **Network Affiliation:** CBS. **Format:** Urban Contemporary. **Key Personnel:** Micheal Dach, Gen. Mgr.; Terry Chisolm, Program Dir.; Debi Collins, Sales Mgr. **Operating Hours:** Continuous. **Owner:** McVay Broadcasting of Flint, Inc.

★4425★
WFLT-AM
317 S. Averill
Flint, MI 48506

Ph: (313)239-5733

Frequency: 1420. **Network Affiliation:** Independent. **Format:** Religious (Christian); Gospel. **Key Personnel:** Rev. A.J. Pointer, Pres.; Rev. J.C. Curry, V.P.; Stephanie Davis, Traffic Dir.; Jeff Lavalley, Operations Mgr. **Operating Hours:** Continuous. **Owner:** Christian Broadcasting Assoc.

★4426★
WGPR-FM
3146 E. Jefferson Ave.
Detroit, MI 48207

Ph: (313)259-8862
Fax: (313)259-6662

Frequency: 107.5. **Network Affiliation:** Independent. **Format:** Urban Contemporary. **Key Personnel:** George Mathews, Pres. **Operating Hours:** Continuous. **Owner:** Intl. Masons, Inc.

★4427★
WGVU-FM
301 W. Fulton
Grand Rapids, MI 49504-6492

Ph: (616)771-6666
Fax: (616)771-6625
Free: 800-442-2771

Frequency: 88.5. **Network Affiliation:** National Public Radio (NPR); AP. **Format:** Public Radio; Jazz; News; Information. **Key Personnel:** Michael T. Walenta, Gen. Mgr.; Scott Hanley, Station Mgr.; Rob Willey, Program Mgr.; David Moore, News Dir.; Chris Barbee, Producer/Reporter/Sports Dir. **Operating Hours:** Continuous; 25% network, 75% local. **Owner:** Grand Valley State University.

★4428★
WILS-AM
PO Box 25008
Lansing, MI 48909-5008

Ph: (517)393-1320
Fax: (517)393-0882

Frequency: 1320. **Network Affiliation:** Satellite Music. **Format:** Classic Country. Simulcasts WILS-FM 5:30-9 a.m. **Key Personnel:** Bill Files, V.P./Gen. Mgr. **Operating Hours:** Continuous. **Owner:** MacDonald Broadcasting.

★4429★
WJLB-FM
645 Griswold St., Ste. 633
Detroit, MI 48226-4177

Ph: (313)965-2000
Fax: (313)965-1729

Frequency: 97.9. **Network Affiliation:** Westwood One Radio. **Format:** Urban Contemporary. **Key Personnel:** Verna S. Green, V.P./Gen. Mgr.; Shel Leshner, Gen. Sales Mgr.; Steve Hegwood, Program Dir.; Myrna Johnson, Business Mgr.; Maureen Barkume, Promotions Dir.; Mildred Gaddis, News Dir. **Operating Hours:** Continuous; 5% network, 95% local. **Owner:** Booth American.

★4430★
WJZZ-FM
2994 E. Grand Blvd.
Detroit, MI 48202

Ph: (313)871-0590
Fax: (313)871-8770

Frequency: 105.9. **Network Affiliation:** Independent. **Format:** Jazz. **Key Personnel:** Mary Bell, Pres.; Wendell Cox, V.P.; Eric B. Bass, Gen. Sales Mgr.; Robert Bass, Asst. to the Pres.; Terry Arnold, Program Dir.; Treva Bass, Chief Engineer; Deborah F. Copeland, Local Sales Mgr. **Operating Hours:** Continuous; 100% local. **Owner:** Bell Broadcasting Co.

★4431★
WKWM-AM
PO Box 828
Kentwood, MI 49518-0828

Ph: (616)676-1237
Fax: (616)676-2329

Frequency: 1140. **Network Affiliation:** American Urban Radio. **Format:** Urban Contemporary. **Key Personnel:** Richard Culpepper, Gen. Mgr.; Frank Grant, Station Mgr./Program Dir. **Operating Hours:** Sunrise-sunset; 100% local. **Owner:** Michelle Broadcasting.

★4432★
WLLJ-AM
Box 393
206 E. State
Cassopolis, MI 49031-0393

Ph: (616)445-2543

Frequency: 910. **Network Affiliation:** AP; American Urban Radio; Satellite Music. **Format:** Adult Contemporary; Urban Contemporary; Oldies. **Key Personnel:** Larry Langford, Jr., Owner and Pres.; Darlene Harris, Station Mgr. **Operating Hours:** Continuous; 90% network, 10% local. **Owner:** Larry Langford, Jr.

★4433★
WMTG-AM
PO Box 1310
Dearborn, MI 48121

Ph: (313)846-8500
Fax: (313)846-1068

Frequency: 1310. **Network Affiliation:** Independent. **Format:** Classic Soul. **Key Personnel:** Gary Fischer, V.P./Gen. Mgr. **Operating Hours:** 6 a.m.-midnight. **Owner:** Paramount Communications.

★4434★
WNMC-FM
1701 E. Front St.
Traverse City, MI 49684

Ph: (616)922-1091

Frequency: 90.9. **Network Affiliation:** IBS. **Format:** Jazz; Ethnic; Urban Contemporary; Alternative/Independent/Progressive; Blues; Talk; Folk. **Key Personnel:** Teresa O'Hara, Gen. Mgr.; Michael Lloyd, Music Dir. **Operating Hours:** 20 hours daily; 100% local. **Owner:** Northwestern Michigan College.

★4435★
WQBH-AM
Ste. Penobscot Bldg.
Detroit, MI 48226

Ph: (313)965-4500

Frequency: 1400. **Format:** Urban Contemporary; Blues; Jazz. **Operating Hours:** Continuous. **Owner:** TXZ, Inc. dba Detroit Broadcasting, Inc.

★4436★
WTLZ-FM
126 N. Franklin St., Ste. 514
Saginaw, MI 48607

Ph: (517)754-1071
Fax: (517)754-4292

Frequency: 107.1. **Network Affiliation:** ABC; Satellite Radio. **Format:** Jazz; Ethnic; Religious; Urban Contemporary. **Key Personnel:** Jack Lich, CEO/Gen. Mgr.; Kermit Crockett, Program Dir.; D'Ante Toussaint, News and Public Service Dir.; Rosa Chaffer, Traffic and Continuity Dir.; Chris Banks, Religious Programming Dir. **Operating Hours:** Continuous; 10% network, 90% local. **Owner:** WTL, Inc.

★4437★
WXLA-AM
101 Northcrest Rd., Ste. 4   Ph: (517)484-9600
Lansing, MI 48906-1262   Fax: (517)484-9699
Frequency: 1180. **Network Affiliation:** Independent. **Format:** Urban Adult Contemporary. **Key Personnel:** Helena Dubose, Gen. Mgr. **Operating Hours:** Sunrise-sunset. **Owner:** Mid Michigan Diamond Broadcasters.

★4438★
WYCE-FM
2820 Clyde Park Ave. SW
Wyoming, MI 49509-2995   Ph: (616)530-7506
Frequency: 88.1. **Format:** Full Service; Hispanic; Ethnic (African, British Isles). **Key Personnel:** Lee Ferraro, Station Mgr.; Thom Bland, Operation Coord. **Operating Hours:** 5:30 a.m.-3 a.m.; 100% local. **Owner:** Grand Rapids Cable Access, Inc.

Minnesota

★4439★
KBEM-FM
1555 James Ave.
Minneapolis, MN 55411   Ph: (612)627-2833
Frequency: 88.5. **Network Affiliation:** American Public Radio (APR); ABC. **Format:** Public Radio; Jazz. **Key Personnel:** Robert Montesano, Station Mgr.; J.D. Ball, Music Dir./Program Dir. **Operating Hours:** Continuous; 5% network, 95% local. **Owner:** Minneapolis Public Schools.

★4440★
KTCJ-AM
Butler Sq., Ste. 210C
100 N. 6th St.
Minneapolis, MN 55403
          Fax: (612)333-2997
Frequency: 690. **Network Affiliation:** Independent. **Format:** Album-Oriented Rock (AOR). Simulcasts KTCZ-FM. **Key Personnel:** Doug Brown, Gen. Mgr. **Operating Hours:** Sunrise-sunset: 100% local. **Owner:** American Media.

Mississippi

★4441★
WACR-FM
1910 14th Ave. N.
PO Box 1078   Ph: (601)328-1050
Columbus, MS 39703   Fax: (601)328-1054
Frequency: 103.9 & 95.7. **Format:** Urban Contemporary. **Key Personnel:** Danny Byrd, Gen. Mgr.; Sherwinn Prescott, Gen. Sales Mgr.; Jerold Jackson, Program Dir. **Operating Hours:** Continuous. **Owner:** T & W Communications, Inc.

★4442★
WALT-AM
3436 Hwy. 45 N.
Box 5797   Ph: (601)693-2661
Meridian, MS 39302   Fax: (601)483-0826
Frequency: 910. **Network Affiliation:** ABC. **Format:** Urban Contemporary. **Key Personnel:** Steve Poston, Program Dir.; Sheila McLain, News Dir.; Becky Harry, Sales Mgr. **Operating Hours:** Continuous. **Owner:** New South Communications, Inc.

★4443★
WAML-AM
318 W. 5th St.
PO Box 367
Laurel, MS 39440   Ph: (601)425-4285
Frequency: 1340. **Network Affiliation:** NBC Mississippi;. **Format:** Gospel. **Key Personnel:** Gerald Williams, Gen. Mgr.; Mike Golden,

Operations Mgr.; Kathy McDonniel, Station Mgr. **Operating Hours:** 6 a.m.-midnight. **Owner:** Pine Belt Broadcasting.

★4444★
WBAD-FM
PO Box 4426   Ph: (601)335-9265
Greenville, MS 38704-4426   Fax: (601)335-5538
Frequency: 94.3. **Network Affiliation:** American Urban Radio. **Format:** Urban Contemporary. **Key Personnel:** William D. Jackson, Owner/Mgr.; Stanley S. Sherman, Sec./Treas./Owner; Troop Williams, Program Dir. **Operating Hours:** 21 hrs. daily; 8% network, 92% local. **Owner:** Stanley S. Sherman.

★4445★
WESY-AM
7 Oaks Rd.
PO Box 5804   Ph: (601)378-9405
Greenville, MS 38704-5804   Fax: (601)335-5538
Frequency: 1580. **Network Affiliation:** American Urban Radio. **Format:** Religious; Urban Contemporary. **Key Personnel:** William D. Jackson, Mgr.; Truman Ford, Music Dir.; Stanley S. Sherman, Sec./Treas./Owner. **Operating Hours:** Sunrise-sunset; 8% network, 92% local. **Owner:** William D. Jackson.

★4446★
WJMG-FM
1204 Gravel Line St.
Hattiesburg, MS 39401   Ph: (601)544-1941
Frequency: 92.1. **Network Affiliation:** American Urban Radio. **Format:** Urban Contemporary; Adult Contemporary. **Owner:** Circuit Broadcasting Co.

★4447★
WKKY-FM
PO Box 1919
McComb, MS 39648-1919   Ph: (601)475-4108
Frequency: 104.9. **Network Affiliation:** ABC. **Format:** Urban Contemporary. **Key Personnel:** Michael Redd, Gen. Mgr.; Lee Crawford, News,Music and Program Dir.; Eric Suthoff, Production Mgr. **Operating Hours:** Continuous. **Owner:** Wayne Dowdy.

★4448★
WKRA-AM
1400-B E. Salem Ave.
PO Box 398
Holly Springs, MS 38635   Ph: (601)252-1110
Frequency: 1110. **Network Affiliation:** Mississippi. **Format:** Country; Black Contemporary Gospel. **Key Personnel:** Rick Williams, Program Dir./News Dir. **Operating Hours:** Sunrise-sunset. **Owner:** Ralph H. Doxey.

★4449★
WKXG-AM
Browning Rd.
PO Box 1686   Ph: (601)453-2174
Greenwood, MS 38930   Fax: (601)455-5733
Frequency: 1540. **Network Affiliation:** American Urban Radio. **Format:** Urban Contemporary; Blues; Gospel. **Key Personnel:** Wes Sterling, Gen. Mgr.; Milton Glass, Station Mgr.; Herman Anderson, Program Dir.; Rea Holmes, Office Mgr. **Operating Hours:** 6 a.m.-10 p.m.; 10% network, 90% local. **Owner:** Telesouth Communications, Inc.

★4450★
WKXI-AM
222 Beasley Rd.   Ph: (601)957-1300
Jackson, MS 39206   Fax: (601)956-0516
Frequency: 1300. **Network Affiliation:** ABC. **Format:** Adult-Oriented Soul. Simulcasts WKXI-FM. **Key Personnel:** Stan Branson, Program Dir.; Becky Elkin, Sales Mgr. **Operating Hours:** Continuous. **Owner:** Opus Media Group.

★4451★
WLTD-FM
224 Shiloh Dr.
Jackson, MS 39212-3048
Frequency: 106.3. **Network Affiliation:** Southern Broadcasting. **Format:** Urban Contemporary; Blues. **Key Personnel:** Philip Scott, V.P./Gen. Mgr.; James Williams, Sales Mgr.; Samual Brown, Program, Music, and News Dir. **Operating Hours:** 6 a.m.-1 a.m.; 8% network, 92% local. **Owner:** J. Scott Communications.

★4452★
WMIS-AM
20 E. Franklin
Natchez, MS 39120   Ph: (601)442-2522
Frequency: 1240. **Network Affiliation:** NBC; American Urban Radio. **Format:** Urban Contemporary. **Key Personnel:** Diana E. Nutter, Pres.; Jim Nutter, Sec./Treas.; Jim Dulaney, Gen. Mgr./V.P.; Donnie Staford, Operations Mgr.; Lee Nichols, Music Dir. **Operating Hours:** Continuous.

★4453★
WMLC-AM
PO Box 949
Monticello, MS 39654   Ph: (601)587-7997
Frequency: 1270. **Network Affiliation:** USA Radio. **Format:** Gospel. **Key Personnel:** Dave Nichols, II, Gen. Mgr./Owner; Donna Nichols, Program Dir.; Dave Henry, Sales Mgr. **Operating Hours:** Sunrise-sunset. **Owner:** Monticello Broadcasting.

★4454★
WNBN-AM
1290 Hawkins Crossing Rd.
Meridian, MS 39301   Ph: (601)483-7930
Frequency: 1290. **Network Affiliation:** American Urban Radio. **Format:** Religious (Gospel); Urban Contemporary; Blues. **Key Personnel:** Mac Carter, Sales Mgr.; Rev. Bobby Wallace, Program Dir. **Operating Hours:** 5 a.m.-10:35 p.m. **Owner:** Frank Rackley.

★4455★
WOAD-AM
1850 W. Lynch St.   Ph: (601)948-1515
Jackson, MS 39203   Fax: (601)354-1984
Frequency: 1400. **Network Affiliation:** NBC. **Format:** Black Gospel. **Key Personnel:** Carl Haynes, V.P./Gen. Mgr.; Jimmy Anthony, Program and Music Dir.; Gwen Cannon, Station Mgr.; Judi Patterson, Gen. Sales Mgr.; Michelle Walker, News Dir. **Operating Hours:** Continuous. **Owner:** Holt Communications Corp.

★4456★
WORV-AM
1204 Graveline
Hattiesburg, MS 39401   Ph: (601)544-1941
Frequency: 1580. **Network Affiliation:** American Urban Radio. **Format:** Urban Contemporary; Gospel; Blues. **Key Personnel:** Vernon Floyd, Gen. Mgr. **Operating Hours:** Sunrise-sunset.

★4457★
WQIS-AM
Rte. 2, Box 151   Ph: (601)425-1491
Laurel, MS 39441   Fax: (601)426-8255
Frequency: 890. **Network Affiliation:** ABC. **Format:** Urban Contemporary. **Key Personnel:** Jay Schneider, Gen. Mgr. **Operating Hours:** Sunrise-sunset. **Owner:** Design Media, Inc.

★4458★
WRDC-AM
114 T.M. Jones Hwy.
Boyle, MS 38730   Ph: (601)843-8225
Frequency: 1410. **Network Affiliation:** American Urban Radio. **Format:** Religious; Urban Contemporary. **Key Personnel:** Joseph Appiah, Owner/Gen. Mgr.; Louis Cotton, Music and Program Dir.; G. Brooke, Office Mgr.; Larry Scott, Sports Dir.; E. Fontaine, Promotions Dir.; E. Hemphill, News Dir. **Operating Hours:** Continuous; 5% network, 95% local. **Owner:** Joseph Appiah.

★4459★
WRJH-FM
PO Box 145
Brandon, MS 39043   Ph: (601)825-5045
Frequency: 97.7. **Network Affiliation:** Christian Broadcasting (CBN). **Format:** Gospel. Simulcasts WRKN-AM. **Key Personnel:** June Harris, Gen. Mgr.; Vickie Ferrer, Office Mgr.; Jeff Steele, Program Dir.; Stan Carter, Chief Engineer. **Operating Hours:** 6 a.m.-midnight.

★4460★
WRKN-AM
PO Box 145
Brandon, MS 39043   Ph: (601)825-5045
Frequency: 970. **Network Affiliation:** Christian Broadcasting (CBN). **Format:** Gospel. Simulcasts WRJH-FM. **Key Personnel:** June Harris, Gen. Mgr. **Operating Hours:** Sunrise-sunset.

★4461★
WTYJ-FM
20 E. Franklin   Ph: (601)442-2522
Natchez, MS 39120   Fax: (601)446-9918
Frequency: 97.7. **Network Affiliation:** NBC; American Urban Radio. **Format:** Urban Contemporary. **Key Personnel:** Diana E. Nutter, Pres.; Jim Nutter, Sec./Treas.; David Shaw, Station and Sales Mgr.; Donnie Staford, Operations Mgr. **Operating Hours:** Continuous. **Owner:** Natchez Communication, Inc.

Missouri

★4462★
KATZ-AM
1139 Olive St., Ste. 303   Ph: (314)241-6000
St. Louis, MO 63101   Fax: (314)241-7498
Frequency: 1600. **Network Affiliation:** Satellite Music; ABC; American Urban Radio. **Format:** Urban Contemporary. **Key Personnel:** Tracy Lewis, Gen. Mgr.; Rod King, Operations Mgr. **Operating Hours:** Continuous. **Owner:** Inter Urban Broadcasting of St. Louis.

★4463★
KATZ-FM
1139 Olive St., Ste. 303   Ph: (314)241-6000
St. Louis, MO 63101   Fax: (314)241-7498
Frequency: 100.3. **Network Affiliation:** Independent; ABC. **Format:** Jazz. **Key Personnel:** Tracy Lewis, Gen. Mgr. **Operating Hours:** Continuous. **Owner:** Inter Urban Broadcasting of St. Louis.

★4464★
KCXL-AM
2420 E. Linwood Blvd., Apt 110   Ph: (816)333-2583
Kansas City, MO 64109-2142   Fax: (816)523-4010
Frequency: 1140. **Network Affiliation:** American Urban Radio. **Format:** Adult Contemporary; Urban Contemporary. **Key Personnel:** Chuck Moore, Gen. Sales Mgr.; Dell Rice, Program Mgr./Music Dir.; Vera Boyd, PSA Dir. **Operating Hours:** Sunrise-sunset. **Owner:** Kansas City Communications.

★4465★
KIRL-AM
3713 Hwy. 94 N.   Ph: (314)946-6600
St. Charles, MO 63301   Fax: (314)946-6662
Frequency: 1460. **Format:** Jazz; Gospel; Urban Contemporary. **Key Personnel:** William E. White, Chrmn./Gen. Mgr./Music Dir.; Bernie Hayes, News Dir.; Columbus Gregory, Program Dir.; Sharon Walters, Office Mgr. **Operating Hours:** Continuous. **Owner:** Bronco Broadcasting Co., Inc.

★4466★
KMJM-FM
PO Box 4888   Ph: (314)361-1108
St. Louis, MO 63108   Fax: (314)361-2276
Frequency: 107.7. **Network Affiliation:** Independent. **Format:** Urban Contemporary. **Key Personnel:** Linda O'Connor, Gen. Mgr. **Operating Hours:** Continuous. **Owner:** Noble Broadcasting.

★4467★
KPRS-FM
11131 Colorado Ave.
Kansas City, MO 64137-2546 Ph: (816)763-2040
Frequency: 103.3. **Network Affiliation:** American Urban Radio; ABC. **Format:** Urban Contemporary; Blues; News. **Key Personnel:** Mildred Carter, Owner/Chairman of the Board; Michael Carter, Owner/President. **Operating Hours:** Continuous. **Owner:** KPRS Broadcasting Corp.

★4468★
KPRT-AM
11131 Colorado   Ph: (816)763-2040
Kansas City, MO 64137-2546 Fax: (816)966-1055
Frequency: 1590. **Network Affiliation:** American Urban Radio. **Format:** Gospel. **Key Personnel:** Michael Carter, Gen. Mgr./Pres.; Freddie Bell, Program Dir. **Operating Hours:** Continuous. **Owner:** Mildred Carter.

★4469★
KSTL-AM
814 N. 3rd. St.
St. Louis, MO 63102   Ph: (314)621-5785
Frequency: 690. **Network Affiliation:** Independent. **Format:** Ethnic; Religious; International Music. **Key Personnel:** C. F. Haverstick, Pres.; Doris Grebas, Gen. Mgr.; David Dale, Program Dir.; Mike Pyle, Sales Mgr. **Operating Hours:** Sunrise-sunset; 100% local. **Owner:** Radio St. Louis, Inc.

Nevada

★4470★
KCEP-FM
330 W. Washington St.   Ph: (702)648-4218
Las Vegas, NV 89106   Fax: (702)647-0803
Frequency: 88.1. **Network Affiliation:** American Urban Radio. **Format:** Blues; Urban Contemporary. **Key Personnel:** Louis Conner, Jr., Operations Supervisor. **Operating Hours:** Continuous; 15% network, 85% local. **Owner:** EOB/Clark County.

New Jersey

★4471★
WBJB-FM
Brookdale Community College
Lincroft, NJ 07738   Ph: (908)224-2252
Frequency: 90.5. **Network Affiliation:** National Public Radio (NPR); American Public Radio (APR); AP. **Format:** Jazz. **Key Personnel:** Stewart W. Edwards, Sales, Station and Promotions Mgr. **Operating Hours:** 6 a.m.-midnight; 100% local. **Owner:** Brookdale Community College.

★4472★
WNJR-AM
One Riverfront Plaza, Ste. 345 Ph: (201)642-8000
Newark, NJ 07102   Fax: (201)642-5208
Frequency: 1430. **Format:** Ethnic (Multicultural). **Key Personnel:** Herb Lefkowitz, V.P./Gen. Mgr.; Stevonne Wilson-Sampson, Gen. Sales Mgr.; Les Englehart, Chief Engineer. **Operating Hours:** Continuous. **Owner:** Douglas Broadcasting.

★4473★
WUSS-AM
1507 Atlantic Ave.   Ph: (609)345-7134
Atlantic City, NJ 08401 Fax: (609)345-4286
Frequency: 1490. **Network Affiliation:** American Urban Radio. **Format:** Urban Contemporary. **Key Personnel:** Dob Mehl, Gen. Mgr. **Operating Hours:** Continuous; 5% network, 95% local. **Owner:** James Cuffee.

★4474★
WZXL-FM
3010 New Jersey Ave.   Ph: (609)522-1416
Wildwood, NJ 08260   Fax: (609)729-9264
Frequency: 100.7. **Format:** Classic Rock (Adult). **Key Personnel:** Loryn Deane, Sales Mgr.; Art Camiolo, Gen. Mgr. **Operating Hours:** 24; 100% Local. **Owner:** Vinrah of New Jersey/Mediacomm National.

New York

★4475★
WAER-FM
215 University Pl.   Ph: (315)443-4021
Syracuse, NY 13244-2110 Fax: (315)443-2148
Frequency: 88.3. **Network Affiliation:** National Public Radio (NPR); Mutual Broadcasting System. **Format:** Public Radio; Jazz; News; Sports. **Key Personnel:** David Anderson, Gen. Mgr.; Joe Lee, Program Dir.; Jim Johnston, News Dir.; Bob Stein, Devel. Dir. **Operating Hours:** 5 a.m.-1 a.m.; 30% network, 70% local. **Owner:** Syracuse University.

★4476★
WBLK-FM
712 Main St., Ste. 112   Ph: (716)852-5955
Buffalo, NY 14202   Fax: (716)852-6605
Frequency: 93.7. **Network Affiliation:** CBS. **Format:** Urban Contemporary. **Key Personnel:** Mark Plimpton, Gen. Mgr./Gen. Sales Mgr.; Franklin W. Lorenz, Pres.; Eric Faison, Program Dir. **Operating Hours:** Continuous. **Owner:** WBLK Broadcasting Corp.

★4477★
WBLS-FM
801 2nd Ave.   Ph: (212)661-3344
New York, NY 10017   Fax: (212)808-5295
Frequency: 107.5. **Network Affiliation:** American Urban Radio; ABC. **Format:** Urban Contemporary. **Key Personnel:** David Lampel, Pres./Gen. Mgr.; Mike Love, Program Dir.; Bill Froelich, Gen. Sales Mgr.; Pierre M. Sutton, Chm. **Operating Hours:** Continuous. **Owner:** Inner City Broadcasting Corp.

★4478★
WDKX-FM
683 E. Main St.   Ph: (716)262-2050
Rochester, NY 14605   Fax: (716)262-2626
Frequency: 103.9. **Network Affiliation:** Independent. **Format:** Urban Contemporary; Jazz; News; Sports. **Key Personnel:** Andrew Langston, Gen. Mgr.; Gloria M. Langston, Station Mgr.; Andre Marcel, Program Dir. **Operating Hours:** Continuous; 100% local. **Owner:** Monroe County Broadcasting Co. Ltd.

★4479★
WGMC-FM
Box 300   Ph: (716)621-9233
North Greece, NY 14515   Fax: (716)621-8692
Frequency: 90.1. **Network Affiliation:** Mutual Broadcasting System. **Format:** Jazz; Ethnic; Bluegrass; Sports. **Key Personnel:** Eric Gruner, Operations Dir.; Charyll Monk, Underwriting Dir.; Eric Gruner, Program Dir. **Operating Hours:** 19 hours daily; 1% network, 99% local. **Owner:** Greece Central School District.

★4480★
WLIB-AM
801 2nd Ave.   Ph: (212)661-3344
New York, NY 10017   Fax: (212)808-5295
Frequency: 1190. **Network Affiliation:** Independent. **Owner:** Inner City Broadcasting Corp. **Key Personnel:** Pierre M. Sutton, Chairman; David Lampel, Pres.**. Mgr.; Claude Tait, Program Dir.; Adrian Council, Gen. Sales Mgr. **Format:** Talk; News; Ethnic (Haitian). **Operating Hours:** Sunrise-sunset.

★4481★
WLKA-FM
Box 155   Ph: (716)394-1550
Canandaigua, NY 14424   Fax: (716)394-2301
Frequency: 102.3. **Network Affiliation:** ABC. **Format:** Jazz. **Key Personnel:** Jim Heredeen, Gen. Mgr.; Kim Whitbeck, Office Mgr.; Connie Daly, Program Dir. **Operating Hours:** Continuous. **Owner:** Dell Broadcasting Co.

★4482★
WRKS-FM
1440 Broadway   Ph: (212)642-4300
New York, NY 10018   Fax: (212)642-4336
Frequency: 98.7. **Network Affiliation:** ABC. **Format:** Urban Contemporary. **Key Personnel:** Charles M. Warfield, Jr., V.P./Gen. Mgr. **Operating Hours:** Continuous. **Owner:** Summit Broadcasting Corp.

★4483★
WTHE-AM
260 E. 2nd St.   Ph: (516)742-1520
Mineola, NY 11501   Fax: (516)742-2878
Frequency: 1520. **Network Affiliation:** UPI. **Format:** Religious. **Key Personnel:** Paul W. Ploener, Gen. Mgr.; George Adee, Chief Engineer. **Operating Hours:** Sunrise-sunset. **Owner:** Universal Broadcasting.

★4484★
WUFO-AM
89 LaSalle Ave.   Ph: (716)834-1080
Buffalo, NY 14214   Fax: (716)837-1438
Frequency: 1080. **Network Affiliation:** American Urban Radio. **Format:** Urban Contemporary; Gospel. **Key Personnel:** Lenore Williams, Operations Mgr. **Operating Hours:** 6 a.m.-9 p.m. **Owner:** Sheridan Broadcasting Corp.

★4485★
WWRL-AM
41-30 58th St.   Ph: (718)335-1600
Woodside, NY 11377   Fax: (718)651-9749
Frequency: 1600. **Network Affiliation:** NBC; American Urban Radio; Mutual Broadcasting System. **Format:** Gospel; Talk. **Key Personnel:** Vince Sanders, V.P./Gen. Mgr. **Operating Hours:** Continuous. **Owner:** Unity Broadcasting Network New York, Inc.

───────────── **North Carolina** ─────────────

★4486★
WAAA-AM
4950 Indiana Ave.
Box 11197
Winston-Salem, NC 27106   Ph: (919)767-0430
Frequency: 980. **Network Affiliation:** American Urban Radio. **Format:** Urban Contemporary. **Key Personnel:** Ms. Mutter D. Evans, Pres./Gen. Mgr. **Operating Hours:** 5 a.m.-midnight. **Owner:** Media Broadcasting Corp.

★4487★
WBCG-FM
PO Box 38
Murfreesboro, NC 27855   Ph: (919)398-4111
Frequency: 98.3. **Network Affiliation:** North Carolina News. **Format:** Urban Contemporary. **Key Personnel:** Sammy Doughtie, Gen. Mgr.; Tony Doughtie, Program Mgr.; Dana Edwards, Sales Mgr.; Nita Futrell, Music Dir.; Bob Ward, Operations Mgr. **Operating Hours:** 6 a.m.-midnight; 65% network, 35% local. **Owner:** Dr. M. Scott Edwards.

★4488★
WBMS-AM
PO Box 718   Ph: (919)763-4633
Wilmington, NC 28402   Fax: (919)395-2723
Frequency: 1340. **Network Affiliation:** American Urban Radio. **Format:** Urban Contemporary. **Key Personnel:** Frank McNeil, Gen. Mgr.; Kenny Grady, Program Dir.; Gerald McKinnon, Sales Mgr. **Operating Hours:** 5 a.m.-1 a.m. **Owner:** Frank McNeil.

★4489★
WBTE-AM
Hwy. 175
Windsor, NC 27983   Ph: (919)794-3131
Frequency: 990. **Network Affiliation:** North Carolina News. **Format:** Contemporary Gospel. **Key Personnel:** Louise R. Hughes, Gen. Mgr. **Operating Hours:** Daylight; 5% network, 95% local. **Owner:** Jean M. Stevens.

★4490★
WBXB-FM
Box 0   Ph: (919)482-2224
Edenton, NC 27932   Fax: (919)482-5290
Frequency: 100.1. **Network Affiliation:** American Urban Radio. **Format:** Gospel. **Key Personnel:** William L. Bonner, Station Mgr. **Operating Hours:** Continuous. **Owner:** Edenton Christian Radio.

★4491★
WCKB-AM
PO Box 789
Hwy. 421 S.   Ph: (919)892-3133
Dunn, NC 28335   Fax: (919)892-3135
Frequency: 780. **Network Affiliation:** North Carolina News. **Format:** Gospel. **Key Personnel:** Charles L. Fowler, Pres.; Al Myatt, News and Sports Dir.; Lottie Hendrickson, Traffic Mgr.; Margie Taylor, Program Dir.; Ronald C. Tart, Sales and Gen. Mgr. **Operating Hours:** Sunrise-sunset; 100% local. **Owner:** North Carolina Central Broadcasters.

★4492★
WDRV-AM
212 Signal Hill Dr.
Statesville, NC 28677   Ph: (704)872-0956
Frequency: 550. **Network Affiliation:** CBS. **Format:** Gospel; News; Information; Sports. **Key Personnel:** David Wise, Program, Music, and Sports Dir.; Angela Henley, Traffic and Office Mgr.; Dave Arnold, Gen. Sales Mgr.; Thomas Gentry, Gen. Mgr. **Operating Hours:** 6 a.m.-10 p.m.; 10% network, 90% local. **Owner:** Statesville Family Radio, Inc.

★4493★
WDUR-AM
2515 Apex Hwy.
Durham, NC 27713   Ph: (919)596-2000
Frequency: 1490. **Network Affiliation:** Southern Broadcasting; Satellite Music. **Format:** Adult Urban Contemporary. **Key Personnel:** Gary Weiss, V.P./Gen. Mgr. **Operating Hours:** Continuous. **Owner:** Pinacle Broadcasting Company Inc.

★4494★
WEGG-AM
Rte. 2 Hwy. U.S. 117 N.
PO Box 608
Rose Hill, NC 28458   Ph: (919)289-2031
Frequency: 710. **Network Affiliation:** ABC; Southern Farm; Southern States. **Format:** Southern Gospel; Black Gospel; Agricultural. **Key Personnel:** Patricia Pratt, News Dir.; Jeff B. Wilson, Sales and Gen. Mgr.; Kay Garriss, Office Mgr./Program Dir.; Suzanne Wilson, Farm Dir.; Scott Saueraugh, Sports Dir. **Operating Hours:** Sunrise-sunset; 5% network, 95% local. **Owner:** Jeff B. Wilson.

★4495★
WFXC-FM
5400 S. Miami Blvd., No. 116   Ph: (919)941-0700
Morrisville, NC 27560   Fax: (919)941-1074
Frequency: 107.1. **Network Affiliation:** Satellite Music. **Format:** Adult Urban Contemporary. **Key Personnel:** Gary Weiss, V.P./Gen. Mgr. **Operating Hours:** Continuous. **Owner:** Pinnacle Broadcasting.

★4496★
WGCR-AM
PO Box 720   Ph: (704)884-9427
Pisgah Forest, NC 28768-0720   Fax: (704)883-9427
Frequency: 720. **Format:** Gospel; News; Talk. **Key Personnel:** Randy C. Barton, Gen. Mgr.; Robin Baker, Traffic Mgr.; Larry W. Spears, Program Dir.; Kristi H. Johnson, News Dir.; Suzanne M. Horton, Office Mgr. **Operating Hours:** Sunrise-sunset; 20% network, 80% local. **Owner:** Anchor Baptist Broadcasting Association, Inc.

★4497★
WGIV-AM
520 Hwy. 29 N.
PO Box 128   Ph: (704)342-2644
Concord, NC 28025   Fax: (704)343-9820
Frequency: 1600. **Network Affiliation:** American Urban Radio; Southern Broadcasting; North Carolina News. **Format:** Ethnic; Blues; Gospel. **Key Personnel:** Chester Williams, Gen. Mgr.; Pete Brown, Gen. Sales Mgr.; Fred Graham, Program Dir. **Operating Hours:** Continuous; 70% network, 30% local. **Owner:** Broadcasting Partners, Inc.

★4498★
WGSP-AM
4209 F. Stewart Andrew Blvd.   Ph: (704)527-9477
Charlotte, NC 28217   Fax: (704)527-9210
Frequency: 1310. **Network Affiliation:** Independent. **Format:** Gospel. **Key Personnel:** Laurence Means, Gen. Mgr.; Letricia Loftin, Program Dir. **Operating Hours:** Continuous. **Owner:** Willis Broadcasting.

★4499★
WGTM-AM
PO Box 3837
Wilson, NC 27895   Ph: (919)243-2188
Frequency: 590. **Format:** Gospel. **Key Personnel:** Mary Haddock, Program Dir.; Celestine Willis, Gen. Mgr. **Operating Hours:** 7 a.m.-8 p.m. **Owner:** Spirit Broadcasting Corp.

★4500★
WIDU-AM
145 Roman St.
Drawer 2247   Ph: (919)483-6111
Fayetteville, NC 28302   Fax: (919)483-6601
Frequency: 1600. **Network Affiliation:** Independent. **Format:** Gospel. **Key Personnel:** Wes Cookman, Owner/Pres.; Sandra Loften, Gen. Mgr.; Andre Deloach, Program Dir. **Operating Hours:** Continuous. **Owner:** Wes Cookman.

★4501★
WIKS-FM
207 Glenburnie Dr.
PO Box 12684   Ph: (919)633-1500
New Bern, NC 28561   Fax: (919)633-0718
Frequency: 101.9. **Network Affiliation:** Independent. **Format:** Urban Contemporary. **Key Personnel:** Steve Taylor, Pres.; Mike Binkley, V.P./Gen. Mgr.; B.K. Kirkland, Program Dir.; Jack Wygard, Promotions Dir.; Raecheal Pettigrew, Business Mgr. **Operating Hours:** Continuous; 99% local. **Owner:** Steve Taylor.

★4502★
WJMH-FM
4002 E. Spring Garden   Ph: (919)855-6500
Greensboro, NC 27407   Fax: (919)855-5899
Frequency: 102.1. **Network Affiliation:** Independent. **Format:** Ethnic; Contemporary Hit Radio (CHR); Urban Contemporary. **Key Personnel:** Brian Douglas, Program Dir.; J.D. Dunning, Music Dir.; Kent Dunn, Sales Mgr.; Brian Beasley, V.P./Gen. Mgr. **Operating Hours:** Continuous. **Owner:** Beasley Broadcast Group.

★4503★
WJOS-AM
1141 Elk Spur St.
PO Box 1038   Ph: (919)835-2511
Elkin, NC 28621   Fax: (919)835-5248
Frequency: 1540. **Network Affiliation:** ABC; North Carolina News. **Format:** Southern Gospel. **Key Personnel:** David Howard, News Dir.; John Wishon, Station, Music, and Promotion Mgr.; Chris Newman, Sports Dir.; Leon Reece, Gen. Mgr. **Operating Hours:** Sunrise-sunset. **Owner:** Tri-County Broadcasting Co. Inc.

★4504★
WLLE-AM
522 E. Martin St.
Raleigh, NC 27601   Ph: (919)833-3874
Frequency: 570. **Network Affiliation:** Southern Broadcasting; American Urban Radio. **Format:** Blues. **Key Personnel:** Henry Monroe, Gen. Mgr.; Prentice Monroe, Gen. Mgr. **Operating Hours:** Continuous; 100% local. **Owner:** Henry & Prentice Monroe.

★4505★
WNAA-FM
NC A&T State University
Price Hall, Ste. 200   Ph: (919)334-7936
Greensboro, NC 27411   Fax: (919)334-7960
Frequency: 90.1. **Network Affiliation:** American Urban Radio. **Format:** Jazz; Urban Contemporary; Eclectic; Gospel. **Key Personnel:** Tony Welborne, Gen. Mgr.; Yvonne Anderson, Music and Program Dir.; Judith Malik, Public Affairs Dir.; Larry Allen, Chief Engineer. **Operating Hours:** 6 a.m.-3 a.m.; 100% local. **Owner:** NC A & T State University.

★4506★
WOKN-FM
PO Box 804
Goldsboro, NC 27530
Frequency: 102.3. **Network Affiliation:** USA Radio. **Format:** Urban Contemporary. **Key Personnel:** Jimmy Swinson, Music Dir.; Avetta J. Swinson, Traffic Dir. **Operating Hours:** Continuous; 100% local. **Owner:** Jimmy Swinson.

★4507★
WOOW-AM
304 Evans St. Mall
Greenville, NC 27834   Ph: (919)757-0365
Frequency: 1340. **Network Affiliation:** American Urban Radio. **Format:** Talk; Jazz; Gospel; Blues. **Key Personnel:** Jim Rouse, Pres./Gen. Mgr.; Criss Morant, Office Mgr.; S. Alleyne, Music Dir. **Operating Hours:** 5 a.m.-midnight. **Owner:** The Minority Voice, Inc.

★4508★
WPEG-FM
520 Hwy. 29 N.
PO Box 128   Ph: (704)786-9111
Concord, NC 28025   Fax: (704)788-7628
Frequency: 97.9. **Network Affiliation:** Independent. **Format:** Urban Contemporary. **Key Personnel:** Matt Ross, Gen. Sales Mgr.; Wayne K. Brown, Mgr.; Michael Saunders, Program Dir. **Operating Hours:** Continuous. **Owner:** Broadcasting Partners, Inc.

★4509★
WQMG-AM
1060 Gatewood Ave.   Ph: (919)272-5121
Greensboro, NC 27405   Fax: (919)274-8897
Frequency: 1510. **Format:** Inspirational; Gospel. **Key Personnel:** Rees Poag, Owner/Pres.; Pete Brown, Gen. Mgr.; Sam Weaver, Program Dir. **Operating Hours:** Daylight hours. **Owner:** Rees Poag.

★4510★
WQOK-FM
8601 Six Forks Rd., Ste. 609 Ph: (919)848-9736
Raleigh, NC 27615   Fax: (919)848-4724
Frequency: 97.5. **Network Affiliation:** ABC. **Format:** Urban Contemporary. **Key Personnel:** Brenda Rand-Davis, Promotions Dir.; Cy Young, Program Dir.; Tre Tailor, News Dir.; Bill Pope, Gen. Sales Mgr. **Operating Hours:** Continuous. **Owner:** Four Chiefs, Inc.

★4511★
WRCS-AM
Rte. 1, Box 13B
Ahoskie, NC 27910   Ph: (919)332-3101
Frequency: 970. **Format:** Black Gospel. **Key Personnel:** Linda Futrell, Operations Dept.; James R. Wiggins, Management. **Operating Hours:** 6 a.m.-sunset.

★4512★
WRRZ-AM
701 Bus. S.
Clinton, NC 28328   Ph: (919)592-2165
Frequency: 880. **Network Affiliation:** North Carolina News. **Format:** Country; Ethnic (Spanish). **Key Personnel:** Dave Denton, Program and News Dir.; Andy Stewart, Music Dir. **Operating Hours:** Sunrise-sunset; 5% network, 95% local. **Owner:** D. Patrick Dixon and David Denton.

★4513★
WRSV-FM
600 N. Grace St.
PO Box 2666   Ph: (919)442-9776
Rocky Mount, NC 27802   Fax: (919)985-6818
Frequency: 92.1. **Network Affiliation:** Southern Broadcasting. **Format:** Blues; Religious; Urban Contemporary. **Key Personnel:** Charles O. Johnson, General Manager; Angela Smith, Administrative Assistant. **Operating Hours:** Continuous; 2% network, 98% local. **Owner:** Northstar Broadcasting Corp.

★4514★
WRVS-FM
1704 Weeksville Rd.
Box 800   Ph: (919)335-3517
Elizabeth City, NC 27909   Fax: (919)335-3731
Frequency: 89.9. **Format:** Urban Contemporary. **Key Personnel:** Edith J. Thorpe, Gen. Mgr.; Benjamin Fagan, Program Dir.; Kimberley Pierce, News Dir.; Dorothy Keith, Traffic Coord. **Operating Hours:** 6 a.m.-1 a.m. **Owner:** Elizabeth City State University Board of Trustees.

★4515★
WSMX-AM
PO Box 16056   Ph: (919)761-1545
Winston-Salem, NC 27115-6056 Free: 800-766-9769
Frequency: 1500. **Network Affiliation:** Southern Broadcasting. **Format:** Religious. **Key Personnel:** Sarah Bailey, Station Mgr.; Melissa Westfall, Music Dir. **Operating Hours:** Sunrise-sunset. **Owner:** Gospel Media, Inc. dba WSMX Radio Station.

★4516★
WSMY-AM
PO Box 910   Ph: (919)536-3115
Roanoke Rapids, NC 27870   Fax: (919)536-3045
Frequency: 1400. **Network Affiliation:** ABC. **Format:** Talk; News; Top 40; Religious; Urban Contemporary. **Key Personnel:** Gene Creasy, Regional Mgr.; Susan Jones, News Dir.; Amy Moran, Sales Mgr. **Operating Hours:** Continuous. **Owner:** Moran Communications Inc.

★4517★
WSNC-FM
Winston-Salem State University
601 MLK Junior Dr.   Ph: (919)750-2320
Winston-Salem, NC 27110   Fax: (919)750-2459
Frequency: 90.5. **Network Affiliation:** ABC; American Urban Radio. **Format:** Talk; Jazz; News; Eclectic; Sports; Urban Contemporary; Oldies. **Key Personnel:** Dr. Brian C. Blount, Faculty Advisor; Joe Watson, Operations Mgr.; Kimberly Harris, News Dir.; Ronald Vample, Sports Dir.; Rob McMauen, Production Mgr.; Kevin Harrell, Traffic Mgr.; Veleska Mathes, Music Dir.; Ronald Vample, Sports Dir. **Operating Hours:** 7 a.m.-1 a.m.; 5% network, 95% local. **Owner:** Winston-Salem State University.

★4518★
WSRC-AM
3202 Guess Rd.   Ph: (919)477-7999
Durham, NC 27705   Fax: (919)477-9811
                             Free: 800-873-4600
Frequency: 1410. **Network Affiliation:** American Urban Radio. **Format:** Sports; Religious; News. **Key Personnel:** Harold Jackson, Program, Music and Sports Dir.; Anthony Lee, Sales Mgr.; Joann Jones, Office Mgr.; Chester Davis, Mgr. **Operating Hours:** Continuous. **Owner:** Willis Broadcasting.

★4519★
WTNC-AM
726 Salem St.
PO Box 1920   Ph: (919)472-0790
Thomasville, NC 27360   Fax: (919)472-0388
Frequency: 790. **Network Affiliation:** Southern Broadcasting; American Urban Radio. **Format:** Religious. **Key Personnel:** Silvia Romaine, Gen. Mgr.; Arwyn Palmer, Program Dir. **Operating Hours:** Continuous. **Owner:** Alvin R. Rooks, Sr.

★4520★
WVCB-AM
PO Box 314
Shallotte, NC 28459   Ph: (919)754-4512
Frequency: 1410. **Network Affiliation:** North Carolina News. **Format:** Gospel. **Key Personnel:** John G. Worrell, Gen. Mgr. **Owner:** John G. Worrell.

★4521★
WWIL-AM
PO Box 701
Wilmington, NC 28402-0701   Ph: (919)763-3364
Frequency: 1490. **Network Affiliation:** American Urban Radio. **Format:** Jazz; Adult Contemporary; Gospel; Talk. **Key Personnel:** Henry Jacobs, Gen. Mgr. **Operating Hours:** Continuous. **Owner:** Foursome Communications.

★4522★
WYZD-AM
131 1/2 Atkin St.
PO Box 797   Ph: (919)386-8134
Dobson, NC 27017   Fax: (919)386-8298
Frequency: 1560. **Format:** Gospel. **Key Personnel:** John Comer, Pres./Owner. **Operating Hours:** Daylight hours. **Owner:** Dobson Broadcasting, Inc.

★4523★
WZFX-FM
225 Green St., Ste. 900
Fayetteville, NC 28302

Ph: (919)486-4991
Fax: (919)486-6720
Free: 800-768-3699

Frequency: 99.1. **Network Affiliation:** ABC. **Format:** Contemporary Hit Radio (CHR). **Key Personnel:** Derek Thompson, V.P./Gen. Mgr.; Frank Dawkins, Program Dir.; Sonny Pasan, Sales Mgr.; Simone Enolm, News Dir.; Cal Andrews, Sr. Account Exec.; Robin Gray, Office Mgr.; Lynn Carraway, Gen. Sales Mgr. **Operating Hours:** Continuous; 1% network, 99% local. **Owner:** Joyner Communications.

★4524★
WZOO-AM
Box 460
Asheboro, NC 27204-0460

Ph: (919)672-0985

Frequency: 710. **Network Affiliation:** Independent. **Format:** Southern Gospel. **Key Personnel:** Huey Turner, Sales Mgr./Promotions Dir.; D.W. Long, Pres./Owner; Max Parrish, Chief Engineer. **Operating Hours:** Sunrise-sunset. **Owner:** Faith Enterprise.

Ohio

★4525★
WABQ-AM
8000 Euclid Ave.
Cleveland, OH 44103

Ph: (216)231-8005

Frequency: 1540. **Network Affiliation:** Independent. **Format:** Gospel. **Key Personnel:** Denver Wilborn, Sales Mgr.; Dorothy Long, Bus. Mgr. **Operating Hours:** Sunrise-sunset. **Owner:** Jack Linn.

★4526★
WAKR-AM
1735 S. Hawkins Ave.
Akron, OH 44320

Ph: (216)869-9800
Fax: (216)864-6799

Frequency: 1590. **Network Affiliation:** Mutual Broadcasting System. **Format:** News; Talk. **Key Personnel:** Peter Acquaviva, Gen. Mgr.; Harve Alan, Operations Mgr.; Steve Stroup, Gen. Sales Mgr. **Operating Hours:** Continuous; 25% network, 75% local. **Owner:** US Radio LP.

★4527★
WBBY-FM
114 Dorchester Sq.
Box 14
Westerville, OH 43081

Ph: (614)891-1829
Fax: (614)891-9229

Frequency: 103.9. **Network Affiliation:** NBC. **Format:** Jazz. **Key Personnel:** Audith Frizzell, Gen. Mgr. **Operating Hours:** Continuous.

★4528★
WCIN-AM
106 Glenwood
Cincinnati, OH 45217

Ph: (513)281-7180
Fax: (513)281-6125

Frequency: 1480. **Format:** Classic Rock; Oldies. **Key Personnel:** John C. Thomas, Gen. Mgr.; Beryle Jackson, Office Mgr.; Sue Johnson, Traffic Mgr.; Lincoln Ware, Program Dir. **Operating Hours:** Continuous.

★4529★
WCKX-FM
510 E. Mound St.
Columbus, OH 43215-5539

Ph: (614)464-0020
Fax: (614)464-2960

Frequency: 106.3. **Network Affiliation:** ABC. **Format:** Urban Contemporary. **Key Personnel:** Vince Fruge, V.P./Gen. Mgr.; Frank Kelly, Program Dir.; John Tysen, Sales Mgr. **Operating Hours:** Continuous. **Owner:** Sunrise Broadcasting.

★4530★
WCPN-FM
The Joseph E. Cole Centre, Ste. 300
3100 Chester Ave.
Cleveland, OH 44114

Ph: (216)432-3700

Frequency: 90.3. **Network Affiliation:** National Public Radio (NPR); American Public Radio (APR). **Format:** Jazz; News; Public Radio. **Key Personnel:** Kathryn Jensen, Gen. Mgr. **Operating Hours:** 5 a.m.-12:30 a.m. **Owner:** Cleveland Public Radio, Inc.

★4531★
WIZF-FM
7030 Reading Rd., No. 316
Cincinnati, OH 45237

Ph: (513)351-5900
Fax: (513)351-0020

Frequency: 100.9. **Network Affiliation:** Independent. **Format:** Urban Contemporary. **Key Personnel:** Frederick L. Valentine, Gen. Mgr.; Tori Turner, Program Dir. **Operating Hours:** Continuous. **Owner:** Tom Lewis.

★4532★
WJMO-AM
11821 Euclid Ave.
Cleveland, OH 44106

Ph: (216)795-1212
Fax: (216)791-9035

Frequency: 1490. **Network Affiliation:** ABC. **Format:** Urban Contemporary. **Key Personnel:** Curtis E. Shaw, Gen. Mgr.; Jenese Simmons, Office Mgr. **Operating Hours:** Continuous. **Owner:** United Broadcasting Co.

★4533★
WJMO-FM
2156 Lee Rd.
Cleveland Heights, OH 44118

Ph: (216)371-3534
Fax: (216)371-0174

Frequency: 92.3. **Network Affiliation:** ABC. **Format:** Contemporary Hit Radio (CHR). **Key Personnel:** Curtis E. Shaw, V.P./Gen. Mgr.; Keith Clark, Program Dir.; John Zwisler, Sales Mgr.; Sandra Barnett, Office Mgr. **Operating Hours:** Continuous. **Owner:** United Broadcasting Co.

★4534★
WJTB-AM
105 Lake Ave.
Elyria, OH 44035

Ph: (216)327-1844

Frequency: 1040. **Network Affiliation:** Independent. **Format:** Urban Contemporary. **Key Personnel:** James Taylor, Gen. Mgr. **Operating Hours:** Sunrise-sunset. **Owner:** Taylor Broadcasting Co.

★4535★
WMMX-AM
Box 1110
Fairborn, OH 45324

Ph: (513)878-9000

Frequency: 1110. **Network Affiliation:** USA Radio. **Format:** Gospel. **Key Personnel:** Tim Livingston, Station Mgr.; Norman Livingston, Gen. Mgr. **Operating Hours:** Sunrise-sunset. **Owner:** L and D Broadcasters.

★4536★
WNOP-AM
1518 Dalton Ave.
Cincinnati, OH 45214

Ph: (513)241-9667

Frequency: 740. **Format:** Jazz. **Key Personnel:** Al Vontz, Gen. Mgr.; William Faulkner, Operations and Station Mgr.; Val Coleman, Sales Mgr.; Fred Williams, Engineer. **Operating Hours:** 12 hours daily; 95% local. **Owner:** Dayton Heidelberg Distributing Co.

★4537★
WNRB-AM
PO Box 625
Niles, OH 44446

Ph: (216)652-0106
Fax: (216)652-9354

Frequency: 1540. **Network Affiliation:** ABC. **Format:** Urban Contemporary; Contemporary Hit Radio (CHR). **Key Personnel:** Dominic Baragona, Gen. Mgr.; Robert Doane, Pres.; Gary Zocolo, V.P./Operations Mgr. **Operating Hours:** Sunrise-sunset. **Owner:** W.N. Broadcasting.

★4538★
WONE-FM
1735 S. Hawkins   Ph: (216)869-9800
Akron, OH 44320   Fax: (216)864-6799
Frequency: 97.5. **Network Affiliation:** ABC. **Format:** Classic Rock.
Key Personnel: Peter Acquaviva, V.P./Gen. Mgr.; Steve Stroup,
Gen. Sales Mgr.; Harve Allen, Operations Mgr.; Jeff Daniels, Music
Dir. **Operating Hours:** Continuous. **Owner:** US Radio LP.

★4539★
WVKO-AM
4401 Carriage Hill Ln.   Ph: (614)451-2191
Columbus, OH 43220   Fax: (614)451-1831
Frequency: 1580. **Network Affiliation:** Southern Broadcasting;
Unistar. **Format:** Urban Contemporary. **Key Personnel:** Al Fetch,
Gen. Mgr. **Operating Hours:** Continuous. **Owner:** Saga
Communications.

★4540★
WVOI-AM
PO Box 5408
Toledo, OH 43613   Ph: (419)243-7052
Frequency: 1520. **Network Affiliation:** American Urban Radio.
Format: Urban Contemporary. **Key Personnel:** Ken McDowell, Dr.,
Gen. Mgr./Owner; Linda Hennoy, Program Dir.; Terry Guy, Music
Dir. **Operating Hours:** Continuous. **Owner:** McDowell
Communications Co. of Ohio, Inc.

★4541★
WXTS-FM
2400 Collingwood
Toledo, OH 43620
                    Fax: (419)729-8425
Frequency: 88.3. **Network Affiliation:** Independent. **Format:** Jazz.
Key Personnel: John Kuschell, Station Mgr. **Operating Hours:**
Continuous; 100% local.

★4542★
WZAK-FM
1729 Superior Ave.   Ph: (216)621-9300
Cleveland, OH 44114   Fax: (216)771-4164
                                   Free: 800-543-1993
Frequency: 93.1. **Network Affiliation:** CBS. **Format:** Urban
Contemporary. **Key Personnel:** Xenophon Zaphis, Pres./Gen. Mgr.;
Michael J. Hibler, V.P./Sales; Lee Zapis, V.P./Operations; George
Cohn, Natl. Sales Mgr.; Lynn Tolliver, Program Dir.; Bobby Rush,
Music Dir.; Pam Halter, Controller; Christina Giannetti, Promotions
Dir.; Neil Curry, Traffic Dir.; Renee Zapis, Office Mgr. **Operating
Hours:** Continuous; 100% local. **Owner:** Xenophon Zapis.

Oklahoma

★4543★
KALU-FM
Box 837
Langston, OK 73050   Ph: (405)466-2314
Frequency: 90.7. **Format:** Eclectic. **Key Personnel:** Ernest
Holloway, Pres.; Lester V. LeSure, Gen. Mgr.; John Hernandez,
Chief Engineer.

★4544★
KPRW-AM
4045 NW 64th   Ph: (405)848-9870
Oklahoma City, OK 73116   Fax: (405)843-5288
Frequency: 1140. **Network Affiliation:** American Urban Radio;
Business Radio. **Format:** News; Talk. **Key Personnel:** Larry Bastida,
Gen. Mgr. **Operating Hours:** 6 a.m.-7 p.m. **Owner:** Surrey
Broadcasting.

★4545★
KTOW-FM
8886 W. 21st St.   Ph: (918)245-0254
Sand Springs, OK 74063   Fax: (918)245-0255
Frequency: 102.3. **Network Affiliation:** Independent. **Format:** Urban
Contemporary. **Key Personnel:** Tim Barraza, Gen. Mgr.; Tony
Barrow, Program Dir.; Gunnar Guinan, Operations Mgr. **Operating
Hours:** Continuous. **Owner:** Luther Grahm.

★4546★
KXOJ-AM
Box 1250   Ph: (918)224-2620
Sapulpa, OK 74067   Fax: (918)224-4984
Frequency: 1550. **Network Affiliation:** ABC; Oklahoma News.
Format: Urban Contemporary. **Key Personnel:** Mike Stevens, Gen.
Mgr./Owner. **Operating Hours:** Continuous. **Owner:** Mike Stevens.

Oregon

★4547★
KMHD-FM
26000 SE Stark   Ph: (503)661-8900
Gresham, OR 97030   Fax: (503)669-6999
Frequency: 89.1. **Format:** Jazz. **Key Personnel:** John Rice, Gen.
Mgr.; Tom Costello, Station Mgr. **Operating Hours:** 6 a.m.-2 a.m.
Owner: Mount Hood Community College.

Pennsylvania

★4548★
WADV-AM
720 E. Kercher Ave.
PO Box 940
Lebanon, PA 17042   Ph: (717)273-2611
Frequency: 940. **Network Affiliation:** Mutual Broadcasting System.
Format: Southern Gospel. **Key Personnel:** Fred W. Krug, V.P./Gen.
Mgr.; Luke G. Hess, Accounting Executive; Kristy Lee, Program Dir.
Operating Hours: 5 a.m.-midnight. **Owner:** F.W.K. Inc.

★4549★
WAMO-FM
411 7th Ave., Ste. 1500   Ph: (412)471-2181
Pittsburgh, PA 15219   Fax: (412)391-3559
Frequency: 105.9. **Network Affiliation:** American Urban Radio.
Format: Urban Contemporary. **Key Personnel:** Ronald R.
Davenport, Chairman; Dave Smith, Program Dir.; Art Goewey, Music
Dir.; Jerry Lopes, News Dir.; Alan Lincoln, Sales Mgr. **Operating
Hours:** Continuous; 5% network, 95% local. **Owner:** Sheridan
Broadcasting Corp.

★4550★
WCXJ-AM
7138 Kelly St.   Ph: (412)243-3050
Pittsburgh, PA 15208   Fax: (412)243-0644
Frequency: 1550. **Network Affiliation:** American Urban Radio.
Format: Urban Contemporary; Talk. **Key Personnel:** Del King, Gen.
Mgr./Program Dir.; Helen Hurst, Executive Dir. **Operating Hours:** 18
hrs. daily. **Owner:** Homewood Brushton Rev. & Dev. Corp.

★4551★
WDAS-AM
Belmont Ave. & Edgely Dr.   Ph: (215)878-2000
Philadelphia, PA 19131   Fax: (215)878-3478
Frequency: 1480. **Network Affiliation:** Independent. **Format:**
Religious; Talk. **Key Personnel:** Kernie L. Anderson, Gen. Mgr.;
Chris Squire, Station Mgr.; Clarence Blair, Operations Mgr.
Operating Hours: Continuous. **Owner:** Unity Broadcasting Network,
Inc.

★4552★
WDAS-FM
Belmont Ave. at Edgely Rd.   Ph: (215)878-2000
Philadelphia, PA 19131   Fax: (215)877-3931
Frequency: 105.3. **Network Affiliation:** Independent. **Format:** Urban Contemporary. **Key Personnel:** Kernie L. Anderson, Gen. Mgr.; Christopher Squire, Station Mgr. **Operating Hours:** Continuous. **Owner:** Unity Broadcasting Network, Inc,.

★4553★
WIBF-FM
Benjamin Fox Pavilion, Ste. A-104
PO Box 1188   Ph: (215)887-5400
Jenkintown, PA 19046   Fax: (215)886-4972
Frequency: 103.9. **Format:** Ethnic; Religious. **Key Personnel:** Douglas Henson, Gen. and Sales Mgr.; Matt McGuigan, News Dir.; Larry Molinaro, Music Dir. **Operating Hours:** Continuous; 60% network, 40% local. **Owner:** Fox Broadcasting Co.

★4554★
WJSM-AM
Rte. 2 Box 87
Martinsburg, PA 16662   Ph: (814)793-2188
Frequency: 1110. **Network Affiliation:** Standard Broadcast News. **Format:** Southern Gospel. Simulcasts WJSM-FM. **Key Personnel:** Larry Walters, Gen. Mgr. **Operating Hours:** Continuous. **Owner:** Martinsburg Broadcasting.

★4555★
WJSM-FM
Rte. 2, Box 87
Martinsburg, PA 16662   Ph: (814)793-2188
Frequency: 92.7. **Network Affiliation:** Standard Broadcast News. **Format:** Southern Gospel. Simulcasts WJSM-AM. **Key Personnel:** Larry Walters, Pres./Gen. Mgr.; Deborah J. Walters, Office Mgr.; Hap Ritchey, Music Dir. **Operating Hours:** Continuous. **Owner:** Martinsburg Broadcasting, Inc.

★4556★
WKDU-FM
3210 Chestnut St.   Ph: (215)895-5920
Philadelphia, PA 19104   Fax: (215)895-1414
Frequency: 91.7. **Network Affiliation:** Independent. **Format:** Jazz; Ethnic; Religious; Urban Contemporary; Alternative/Independent/Progressive; Public Affairs. **Operating Hours:** Continuous. **Owner:** Drexel University.

★4557★
WLIU-FM
Office of Student Activities   Ph: (215)932-8300
Lincoln University, PA 19352   Fax: (215)932-9105
Frequency: 88.7. **Format:** Public Radio; Adult Contemporary; Jazz; Blues; Urban Contemporary; New Age; Religious; News. **Key Personnel:** Terrence Johnson, Program Mgr.; David Sullivan, Station Mgr.; Earnest R. Smith, Program Dir. **Operating Hours:** Noon-3 a.m. **Owner:** Lincoln University.

★4558★
WPLW-AM
201 Ewing Rd.   Ph: (412)922-0550
Pittsburgh, PA 15205   Fax: (412)922-0553
Frequency: 1590. **Format:** Religious. **Key Personnel:** Robert Hickling, Gen. Mgr. **Operating Hours:** 6 a.m.-sunset. **Owner:** Hickling Broadcasting Corp.

★4559★
WRAW-AM
1265 Perkiomen Ave.   Ph: (215)376-7173
Reading, PA 19602   Fax: (215)376-1270
Frequency: 1340. **Network Affiliation:** Satellite Music. **Format:** Middle-of-the-Road (MOR). **Key Personnel:** Mike Shannon, Gen. Mgr.; Mike Rubright, Gen. Sales Mgr.; Bob Minnick, Program Dir.; David Stein, News Dir. **Operating Hours:** Continuous; 90% network, 10% local. **Owner:** Dr. Frank A. Franco.

★4560★
WRFY-FM
1265 Perikomen Ave.   Ph: (215)376-6671
Reading, PA 19602   Fax: (215)376-1270
Frequency: 102.5. **Network Affiliation:** Independent. **Format:** Contemporary Hit Radio (CHR). **Key Personnel:** Mike Shanon, Gen. Mgr./V.P.; Helene D. Franco, Business Mgr.; Mike Rubright, Gen. Sales Mgr.; Al Burke, Prog. Dir.; David Stein, News Dir.; Michael Browne, Music Dir. **Operating Hours:** Continuous; 100% local. **Owner:** US Radio. LP.

★4561★
WRTI-FM
Annenberg Hall
13th & Diamond St.   Ph: (215)787-8405
Philadelphia, PA 19122   Fax: (215)787-4870
Frequency: 90.1. **Network Affiliation:** American Public Radio (APR); AP; National Public Radio (NPR). **Format:** Public Radio; Jazz. **Key Personnel:** W. Theodore Eldredge, Gen. Mgr.; Clyde Robertson, News Dir. **Operating Hours:** Continuous. **Owner:** Temple University.

★4562★
WSAJ-AM
Grove City College
PO Box 1058
Grove City, PA 16127   Ph: (412)458-2185
Frequency: 1340. **Network Affiliation:** Independent. **Format:** Jazz; Classical. **Key Personnel:** Everett DeVelda, Gen. Mgr.; Deena Philage, Program Dir.; Matt Pitzer, Student Gen. Mgr. **Operating Hours:** 7:15-8:45 p.m. Tues.-Thurs.; 6:30-7:30 p.m. Sun. **Owner:** Grove City College.

★4563★
WSGD-FM
1 Montage Mountain Rd., Ste. B   Ph: (717)341-9494
Moosic, PA 18507   Fax: (717)344-3661
                                      Free: 800-283-9494
Frequency: 94.3. **Network Affiliation:** Independent. **Format:** Oldies. **Key Personnel:** Mike Raymond, Gen. Mgr.; Scotty Young, Program Dir.; Ann Montoro, News Dir. **Operating Hours:** Continuous; 100% local. **Owner:** S & P Broadcasting Co.

★4564★
WURD-AM
5301 Tacony St.
PO Box 233   Ph: (215)533-8900
Philadelphia, PA 19137   Fax: (215)533-5679
Frequency: 900. **Network Affiliation:** Mutual Broadcasting System. **Format:** Gospel. **Key Personnel:** L.E. Willis, Pres.; Charles Grundy, Gen. and Gen. Sales Mgr. **Owner:** Beasley Broadcasting of Eastern Pennsylvania, Inc.

★4565★
WUSL-FM
440 Domino Ln.   Ph: (215)483-8900
Philadelphia, PA 19128   Fax: (215)483-5930
Frequency: 98.9. **Format:** Urban Contemporary. **Key Personnel:** Bartley D. Walsh, Pres./Gen. Mgr.; Martin Conn, Gen. Sales Mgr.; Dave Allan, Program Dir.; Loraine Ballard Morrill, News Dir.; Jacqueline Allen, Promotions Dir.; Monica Lewis, Local Sales Mgr. **Operating Hours:** Continuous. 98% local, 2% other. **Owner:** Tak Communications, Inc.

★4566★
WVAM-AM
2727 W. Albert Dr.
Altoona, PA 16602   Ph: (814)944-9456
Frequency: 1430. **Network Affiliation:** ABC. **Format:** Country. **Key Personnel:** Eric Donaldson, V.P./Gen. Mgr.; Ray Hurner, Program Dir.; Dave Bithell, News Dir. **Operating Hours:** Continuous; 25% network, 75% local. **Owner:** Music Broadcasting, Inc.

Rhode Island

★4567★
WOTB-FM
140 Thames St.
Newport, RI 02840
Ph: (401)846-6900
Frequency: 100.3. **Network Affiliation:** ABC. **Format:** Jazz. **Key Personnel:** William Lancaster, Jr., Gen. Mgr./Sales Mgr. **Operating Hours:** Continuous. **Owner:** Bernard Perry.

★4568★
WRIB-AM
200 Water St.
East Providence, RI 02914
Ph: (401)434-0406
Frequency: 1220. **Network Affiliation:** Independent. **Format:** Religious; Ethnic. **Key Personnel:** John Pierce, Gen. Mgr. **Operating Hours:** 6 a.m.-10 p.m. **Owner:** Carter Broadcasting.

South Carolina

★4569★
WASC-AM
840 Wofford
Spartanburg, SC 29304
Ph: (803)585-1530
Frequency: 1530. **Network Affiliation:** ABC; American Urban Radio. **Format:** Urban Contemporary. **Key Personnel:** K. Joe Sessons, Gen. Mgr. **Operating Hours:** Daylight. **Owner:** New South Broadcasting.

★4570★
WCIG-FM
U.S. Hwy. 76
Mullins, SC 29574
Ph: (803)423-1140
Frequency: 107.1. **Network Affiliation:** South Carolina. **Format:** Urban Contemporary. **Key Personnel:** James F. Ramsey, Pres./Mgr.; Eugene Brantley, Operations Mgr. **Operating Hours:** 6 a.m.-midnight; 8% network (news only), 92% local. **Owner:** Mullins and Marion Broadcasting Co.

★4571★
WCOS-AM
2440 Millwood Ave.
Box 748
Columbia, SC 29202
Ph: (803)256-7348
Fax: (803)779-7572
Frequency: 1400. **Network Affiliation:** Independent. **Format:** Country. Simulcasts WCOS-FM. **Key Personnel:** Lisa Brabham, Bus. Mgr.; Glenn Garrett, Music and Program Dir.; Barry Smith, Gen. Mgr.; Dave Block, Operations Mgr. **Operating Hours:** Continuous. **Owner:** U.S. Radio, L.P.

★4572★
WCOS-FM
2440 Millwood Ave.
Box 748
Columbia, SC 29202
Ph: (803)256-7348
Fax: (803)779-7572
Frequency: 97.5. **Network Affiliation:** ABC. **Format:** Country. Simulcasts WCOS-AM. **Key Personnel:** Lisa Brabham, Bus. Mgr.; Glenn Garrett, Music and Program Dir.; Barry Smith, Gen. Mgr.; Dave Block, Operations Mgr. **Operating Hours:** Continuous. **Owner:** US Radio, L.P.

★4573★
WDOG-FM
PO Box 442
Allendale, SC 29810
Ph: (803)584-3500
Frequency: 93.5. **Network Affiliation:** ABC; South Carolina News. **Format:** Country; Urban Contemporary. **Key Personnel:** H. Carl Gooding, Pres./Gen. Mgr.; Charles R. "Rick" Gooding, Program, Sales Mgr., and Night Music Dir.; Lisa Gooding, Traffic Dir. **Operating Hours:** 6 a.m.-midnight. **Owner:** Good Radio Broadcasting.

★4574★
WFXA-FM
104 Bennett Ln.
North Augusta, SC 29841
Ph: (803)279-2330
Fax: (803)279-8149
Frequency: 103.1. **Network Affiliation:** ABC; CBS. **Format:** Urban Contemporary. **Key Personnel:** Pamela Harris, Accounting; Bill Berry, Sales Mgr.; Walter Brumbeloe, Chief Engineer; Carl Conner, Program and Music Dir.; Carroll Redd, News and Program Dir.; Eleanor Hodges, Traffic and Office Mgr.; Bill Jaeger, Gen. Mgr. **Operating Hours:** Continuous; 98% local. **Owner:** Davis Broadcasting Co., Inc.

★4575★
WHYZ-AM
PO Box 4309
Greenville, SC 29608
Ph: (803)246-1970
Fax: (803)246-8121
Frequency: 1070. **Network Affiliation:** CBS. **Format:** Urban Contemporary. **Key Personnel:** Steven Brisker, Station Mgr.; Pandura Bonner, Gen. and Sales Mgr. **Operating Hours:** Continuous. **Owner:** Greenville Family Brodcasting.

★4576★
WJKI-AM
Box 576
Woodruff, SC 29388
Ph: (803)476-2191
Frequency: 1510. **Network Affiliation:** ABC. **Format:** Gospel. **Key Personnel:** Furman Boyce, Pres./Gen. Mgr.; Carol Richards, Program Dir.; Vince Hayes, Account Exec. **Operating Hours:** 6:30 a.m.-8:30 p.m.; 10% network, 90% local. **Owner:** Jackie Cooper Media, Inc.

★4577★
WLBG-AM
Box 1289
Laurens, SC 29360
Ph: (803)984-3544
Fax: (803)984-3545
Frequency: 860. **Format:** Urban Contemporary. **Key Personnel:** Emil Finley, Pres.; Kevin St. John, Program Dir. **Operating Hours:** 6 a.m.-midnight.

★4578★
WLGI-FM
Rte. 2, PO Box 69
Hemingway, SC 29554
Ph: (803)558-2977
Fax: (803)558-2921
Frequency: 90.9. **Network Affiliation:** Independent. **Format:** Talk; Ethnic; Urban Contemporary; Gospel. **Key Personnel:** Bill Willis, Program Dir.; Gregory Kintz, Production and Technical Support Dir.; Ernest Hilton, Music Dir.; Laurie "CJ" Cohen, Community Relations Dir.; Steven Kozlow, Gen. Mgr. **Operating Hours:** 6 a.m.-9 p.m.; 100% local.

★4579★
WLWZ-FM
PO Box 19104
Greenville, SC 29602-9104
Ph: (803)235-4600
Fax: (803)370-3403
Frequency: 103.9. **Network Affiliation:** CBS; American Urban Radio. **Format:** Ethnic; Urban Contemporary. Simulcasts WELP-AM. **Key Personnel:** Wayne Walker, Program Dir.; Rocky Valentine, Music Dir.; Julia L. Thompson, Business Mgr.ness Mgr.; Curtis Downey, V.P./Gen. Mgr. **Operating Hours:** Continuous. **Owner:** Voyager Communications III.

★4580★
WMCJ-AM
314 Rembert Dennis Blvd.
PO Box 67
Moncks Corner, SC 29461
Ph: (803)761-6010
Fax: (803)761-6979
Frequency: 950. **Network Affiliation:** South Carolina News. **Format:** Gospel. **Key Personnel:** Dorothy Mitchum, V.P./Gen. Mgr.; Susanna Footmam, News Dir.; Clary Butler, Pres. **Operating Hours:** Continuous. **Owner:** Berkeley Broadcasting Corp.

★4581★
WMNY-AM
Rte. 1, Box 189
Santee, SC 29142-9718   Ph: (803)854-2671
Frequency: 1370. **Network Affiliation:** USA Radio. **Format:** Gospel. **Operating Hours:** 6 a.m.-9 p.m. **Owner:** Clarence Jones.

★4582★
WMTY-AM
PO Box 459   Ph: (803)223-4300
Greenwood, SC 29648   Fax: (803)223-4096
Frequency: 1090. **Network Affiliation:** ABC; South Carolina News. **Format:** Urban Contemporary. Simulcasts WMTY-FM. **Key Personnel:** Betty L. Black, Gen. Mgr.; Stan Lewis, Operations Mgr./News Dir. **Operating Hours:** 6 a.m.-two hours past sunset. **Owner:** United Community Enterprises.

★4583★
WMTY-FM
PO Box 459   Ph: (803)223-4300
Greenwood, SC 29648   Fax: (803)223-4096
Frequency: 103.5. **Network Affiliation:** ABC; South Carolina News. **Format:** Urban Contemporary. Simulcasts WMTY-AM. **Key Personnel:** Betty L. Black, Gen. Mgr.; Stan Lewis, Operations Mgr./News Dir. **Operating Hours:** 5 a.m.-12.30 a.m. **Owner:** United Community Enterprises.

★4584★
WPAL-AM
1717 Wappoo Rd.   Ph: (803)763-6330
Charleston, SC 29407   Fax: (803)769-4857
Frequency: 730. **Network Affiliation:** American Urban Radio. **Format:** Rhythm & Blues. **Key Personnel:** William Sanders, Pres./Gen. Mgr.; Juanita W. LaRoche, V.P./Asst. Gen. Mgr.; Don Kendricks, Operations Mgr.; Tony Robertson, News Dir. **Operating Hours:** Continuous; 5% network, 95% local.

★4585★
WQIZ-AM
Box 903   Ph: (803)566-1100
St. George, SC 29477   Fax: (803)529-1933
Frequency: 810. **Network Affiliation:** American Urban Radio. **Format:** Gospel. **Key Personnel:** C.A. Barton, Gen. Mgr. **Operating Hours:** Sunrise-sunset. **Owner:** Lowcountry Media Inc.

★4586★
WQKI-AM
Riley Road
St. Matthews, SC 29135   Ph: (803)874-2777
Frequency: 710. **Network Affiliation:** American Urban Radio. **Format:** Urban Contemporary. **Key Personnel:** Andy Henderson, Music Dir.; Ron Shuler, Sports; Robert Newsham, Mgr. **Operating Hours:** Sunrise-sunset; 10% network, 90% local. **Owner:** Robert Newsham.

★4587★
WSSB-FM
Box 7656
Orangeburg, SC 29117   Ph: (803)536-8938
Frequency: 90.3. **Network Affiliation:** American Urban Radio; UPI. **Format:** Education and Entertainment (African-American). **Key Personnel:** Gil Harris, Gen. Mgr./Sports Dir.; Dawna Diggs, Public Affairs, News and Program Dir. **Operating Hours:** Continuous. **Owner:** WSSB-FM.

★4588★
WTGH-AM
PO Box 620   Ph: (803)796-9533
Columbia, SC 29202   Fax: (803)796-7706
Frequency: 620. **Network Affiliation:** Independent. **Format:** Gospel. **Key Personnel:** Raleigh Williams, Gen. Mgr.; Josh Lorrick, Station Mgr.; Bobby Waitons, Program Dir.; Isaac Heyward, Sales Mgr. **Operating Hours:** Continuous. **Owner:** Midland Communications.

★4589★
WUJM-AM
PO Box 1165   Ph: (803)824-8943
Goose Creek, SC 29445-1165   Fax: (803)824-8940
Frequency: 1450. **Network Affiliation:** Mutual Broadcasting System. **Format:** Urban Contemporary. Simulcast of WUJM-FM. **Key Personnel:** C.J. Jones, Pres.; Bob Casey, Programming V.P.; Lyn Greene, Bus. Mgr. **Operating Hours:** Continuous. **Owner:** Jones-Eastern Radio.

★4590★
WUJM-FM
PO Box 1165   Ph: (803)824-8943
Goose Creek, SC 29445-1165   Fax: (803)824-8940
Frequency: 94.3. **Network Affiliation:** Mutual Broadcasting System. **Format:** Urban Contemporary. Simulcasts WUJM-AM. **Key Personnel:** Jim Gooden, News Dir. **Operating Hours:** Continuous; 98% local, 2% other. **Owner:** Jones-Eastern Radio, Inc.

★4591★
WVGB-AM
PO Box 1477   Ph: (803)524-4700
Beaufort, SC 29901   Fax: (803)525-6305
Frequency: 1490. **Network Affiliation:** American Urban Radio. **Format:** Religious; Oldies. **Key Personnel:** William A. Galloway, Pres.; Vivian M. Galloway, V.P.; Donzella Hendix, Gen. Mgr. **Operating Hours:** Continuous. **Owner:** William A. Galloway.

★4592★
WWDM-FM
PO Box 9127   Ph: (803)495-2558
Columbia, SC 29290   Fax: (803)695-8605
Frequency: 103.1. **Format:** Urban Contemporary. **Key Personnel:** John Marshall, Owner/Gen. Mgr.; Andre Carson, Program Dir. **Operating Hours:** Continuous. **Owner:** John Marshall.

★4593★
WWPD-FM
Box 1103
Marion, SC 29571
Frequency: 94.3. **Network Affiliation:** Satellite Network News. **Format:** Adult Contemporary. **Key Personnel:** Bishop L.E. Willis, Sr., Pres. **Operating Hours:** Continuous. **Owner:** Bishop L. E. Willis, Sr.

★4594★
WWWZ-FM
PO Box 30669   Ph: (803)556-9132
Charleston, SC 29417   Fax: (803)769-0876
Frequency: 93.5. **Network Affiliation:** American Urban Radio. **Format:** Urban Contemporary. **Key Personnel:** Clifford Fletcher, Pres.; Dean H. Mutter, Exec. V.P.; Bonnie Schwartz, Production and Traffic Dir. **Operating Hours:** Continuous; 100% local. **Owner:** Millennium Communications.

★4595★
WYNN-AM
170 E. Palmetto St.
PO Box 100531   Ph: (803)662-6364
Florence, SC 29501-0531   Fax: (803)669-2654
Frequency: 540. **Format:** Oldies (Black Classics). **Key Personnel:** James N. Maurer, Pres.; Pansy Morgan, Sales Mgr.; Olie Williams, Program Dir.; Paige Smith, Office Mgr. **Operating Hours:** Continuous; 1% network, 99% local. **Owner:** Forjay Broadcasting Corp.

★4596★
WYNN-FM
170 E. Palmetto St.
PO Box 100531   Ph: (803)662-6364
Florence, SC 29501-0531   Fax: (803)669-2654
Frequency: 106.3. **Format:** Urban Contemporary. **Key Personnel:** James N. Maurer, Pres.; Pansy Morgan, Sales Mgr.; Fred Brown, Program Dir.; Ernie Frierson, Public Affairs Dir.; Paige Smith, Office

Mgr. **Operating Hours:** Continuous; 1% network, 99% local. **Owner:** Forjay Broadcasting Corp.

★4597★
WZJY-AM
1233 Ben Sawyer Blvd.
Mount Pleasant, SC 29464   Ph: (803)881-2482
Frequency: 1480. **Network Affiliation:** CNN Radio. **Format:** Gospel. **Key Personnel:** Micah Fields, Gen. Mgr.; Clyde Jones, Gen. Sales Mgr.; Edwin Wright, Program Dir.; Sam Dennis, Public Affairs. **Operating Hours:** Continuous. **Owner:** Magdalene Williams.

——————— Tennessee ———————

★4598★
KWAM-AM
80 N. Tillman   Ph: (901)323-2679
Memphis, TN 38111   Fax: (901)324-8866
Frequency: 990. **Network Affiliation:** Independent. **Format:** Gospel. **Key Personnel:** Bill Squartino, Gen. Mgr. **Operating Hours:** 5 a.m.-midnight. **Owner:** Rivers Network.

★4599★
WABD-AM
150 Stateline Rd.   Ph: (615)431-5555
Clarksville, TN 37040   Fax: (615)431-4986
Frequency: 1370. **Network Affiliation:** Independent. **Format:** Urban Contemporary. **Key Personnel:** Tom Cassetty, Gen. Mgr.; Lee Erwin, Operations Mgr.; Jerry Silvers, Program and Music Dir.; Chris Baker, News Dir. **Operating Hours:** Continuous; 100% local. **Owner:** Southern Broadcasting Corp.

★4600★
WBCV-AM
26 1/2 6th St.
PO Box 68
Bristol, TN 37621   Ph: (615)968-5221
Frequency: 1550. **Network Affiliation:** Independent. **Format:** Gospel. **Key Personnel:** Jennings Dotson, Gen. Mgr. **Operating Hours:** Sunrise-sunset. **Owner:** Sunshine Broadcasters.

★4601★
WBOL-AM
PO Box 191
Bolivar, TN 38008   Ph: (901)658-3690
Frequency: 1560. **Network Affiliation:** American Urban Radio. **Format:** Talk; News; Southern Gospel; Urban Contemporary. **Key Personnel:** Opal J. Shaw, Program Mgr.; Johnny W. Shaw, News Dir.; Daniel Bufford, Music Dir. **Operating Hours:** Sunrise-sunset. **Owner:** Shaw's Broadcasting.

★4602★
WCOR-AM
3765 N. Chapel Rd.
Franklin, TN 37064-7823   Ph: (615)459-7777
Frequency: 710. **Network Affiliation:** Independent. **Format:** Southern Gospel. **Key Personnel:** Larry Garner, Gen. Mgr.; Chris Goodson, Program Dir. **Operating Hours:** 6 a.m.-8 p.m. **Owner:** Jack Barsack.

★4603★
WDIA-AM
112 Union Ave.   Ph: (901)529-4300
Memphis, TN 38103   Fax: (901)529-9557
Frequency: 1070. **Network Affiliation:** Independent. **Format:** Urban Adult Contemporary. **Key Personnel:** Rick Caffey, Gen. Mgr. **Operating Hours:** Continuous. **Owner:** Ragan Henry National Ltd. Partnership.

★4604★
WETB-AM
PO Box 4127
Johnson City, TN 37602   Ph: (615)928-7131
Frequency: 790. **Network Affiliation:** USA Radio. **Format:** Southern Gospel. **Key Personnel:** Steve Nelson, Office Mgr.; Scott Onks, Program Dir.; Gary Ward, Operations Mgr.; Loretta Gouge, Sales Mgr. **Operating Hours:** 6 a.m.-11 p.m. **Owner:** Paul Gobble, Jr. & Robert Morrison.

★4605★
WEVL-FM
518 S. Main St.
Memphis, TN 38103-4443   Ph: (901)528-0560
Frequency: 89.9. **Network Affiliation:** Independent. **Format:** Full Service. **Key Personnel:** Judy Dorsey, Station Mgr.; Brian Craig, Program Dir.; Les Edwards, Pres. **Operating Hours:** 6 a.m.-2 a.m.; 90% local, 10% other. **Owner:** Southern Communication Volunteers.

★4606★
WFKX-FM
425 E. Chester
Jackson, TN 38301   Ph: (901)427-9616
Frequency: 95.9. **Network Affiliation:** Independent. **Format:** Urban Contemporary. **Key Personnel:** James E. Wolfe, Jr., Pres./Gen. Mgr.; Betty Schreiber, Sales Mgr.; Dave Shaw, Program Dir. **Operating Hours:** Continuous; 100% local. **Owner:** Wolfe Communications, Inc.

★4607★
WHRK-FM
112 Union Ave.   Ph: (901)529-4397
Memphis, TN 38103   Fax: (901)529-9557
Frequency: 97.1. **Network Affiliation:** Independent. **Format:** Urban Contemporary. **Key Personnel:** Rick Coffey, Gen. Mgr. **Operating Hours:** Continuous. **Owner:** Ragan Henry National Ltd. Partnership.

★4608★
WJTT-FM
409 Chestnut St., Ste. A154   Ph: (615)265-9494
Chattanooga, TN 37402   Fax: (615)266-2335
Frequency: 94.3. **Format:** Urban Contemporary. **Key Personnel:** James Brewer, II, V.P./Gen. Mgr.; Jamie Naas, Bus. Mgr.; Micheal Long, Sales Mgr.; Keith Landecker, Program Dir. **Operating Hours:** Continuous. **Owner:** Jettcom, Inc.

★4609★
WKJQ-AM
Iron Hill Rd.
PO Box 576
Parsons, TN 38363   Ph: (901)847-3011
Frequency: 1550. **Network Affiliation:** Independent. **Format:** Gospel. **Key Personnel:** Ralph D. Clenney, Mgr.; Edna Maxwell, Traffic Dir.; Dwight Lancaster, News Dir.; Steve Clenney, Asst. Mgr. **Operating Hours:** Sunrise-sunset; 100% local. **Owner:** Ralph D. Clenney.

★4610★
WLOK-AM
363 S. 2nd St.   Ph: (901)527-9565
Memphis, TN 38103   Fax: (901)525-4322
Frequency: 1340. **Network Affiliation:** American Urban Radio; NBC. **Format:** Religious. **Key Personnel:** Art Gilliam, Gen. Mgr.; Sandra Hayesn, Program Dir.; Michael Anderson, Gen. Sales Mgr. **Operating Hours:** Continuous; 2% network, 98% local. **Owner:** Gilliam Communications, Inc.

★4611★
WMDB-AM
3051 Stokers Ln.   Ph: (615)255-2876
Nashville, TN 37218   Fax: (615)255-2876
Frequency: 880. **Network Affiliation:** Independent. **Format:** Top 40; Gospel. **Key Personnel:** Dr. Morgan Babb, Gen. Mgr./Program Dir. **Operating Hours:** Sunrise-sunset. **Owner:** Dr. Morgan Babb.

★4612★
WMOT-FM
Middle Tennessee State University
PO Box 3   Ph: (615)898-2800
Murfreesboro, TN 37132   Fax: (615)898-2774
Frequency: 89.5. **Network Affiliation:** National Public Radio (NPR). **Format:** Jazz; News. **Key Personnel:** John L. High, Dir. of Broadcasting; John Egly, Operations Dir.; Randy O'Brien, News Dir.; Gary Brown, Chief Engineer; Greg Lee, Program Dir.; Laura L. McComb, Development Coordinator; Shawn Jacobs, News Producer; Rhonda Wimberly, Traffic Dir. **Operating Hours:** 5 a.m.-midnight Sun.-Thur., 6 a.m.-2 a.m. Fri. & Sat.; 30% network, 70% local. **Owner:** Middle Tennessee State University.

★4613★
WNAH-AM
44 Music Sq. E.   Ph: (615)254-7611
Nashville, TN 37203   Fax: (615)254-4565
Frequency: 1360. **Network Affiliation:** Mutual Broadcasting System; American Urban Radio. **Format:** Gospel. **Key Personnel:** Hoyt Carter, Jr., Gen. Mgr./Program Dir. **Operating Hours:** Continuous. **Owner:** Hermitage Broadcasting Co.

★4614★
WNOO-AM
1200 Mountain Creek Rd.   Ph: (615)894-1023
Chattanooga, TN 37405   Fax: (615)875-3066
Frequency: 1260. **Network Affiliation:** American Urban Radio. **Format:** Blues; Gospel. **Key Personnel:** Fred Webb, Pres./Gen. Mgr.; Frank St. James, Program Dir.; Cherri McIntyre, Operations Mgr./Sales Mgr.; Diane Crane, Traffic Mgr. **Operating Hours:** Sunrise-sunset. **Owner:** Tennessee Communications L.P.

★4615★
WQQK-FM
1320 Brick Church Pike
PO Box 70085   Ph: (615)227-1470
Nashville, TN 37207   Fax: (615)227-2740
Frequency: 92.1. **Network Affiliation:** ABC. **Format:** Adult Contemporary; Jazz; Urban Contemporary; Oldies. **Key Personnel:** Scott Peters, Gen. Mgr.; Tony Jackson, Program Dir.; Lisa Godleyn, News Dir.; Jeff White, Traffic Dir.; Amy Porter, Promotions Dir.; Clinton Hooper, Chief Engineer; Debbie Keen, Accountant. **Operating Hours:** Continuous. **Owner:** Phoenix Communications Group, Inc.

★4616★
WRKM-AM
102 Z Country Ln.   Ph: (615)735-1350
Carthage, TN 37030   Fax: (615)735-0381
Frequency: 1350. **Network Affiliation:** Tennessee Radio. **Format:** Gospel. **Key Personnel:** Judith A. Wood, Owner/V.P.; John Wood, Sports Dir.; Kevin Chase, News Dir.; Dennis Banka, Music and Program Dir./Production Mgr.; Tracey Preston, Traffic Mgr. **Operating Hours:** 5 a.m.-7 p.m. 5% network, 95% local. **Owner:** John Wood.

★4617★
WSMS-FM
Memphis State University
Memphis, TN 38152   Ph: (901)678-3176
Frequency: 91.7. **Network Affiliation:** Independent. **Format:** Jazz. **Key Personnel:** Robert W. McDowell, Gen. Mgr. **Operating Hours:** 6 a.m.-midnight; 100% local. **Owner:** Memphis State University.

★4618★
WTBG-FM
Box 198
Brownsville, TN 38012   Ph: (901)772-3700
Frequency: 95.3. **Network Affiliation:** ABC; CNN Radio; Tennessee Radio. **Format:** Country. **Key Personnel:** Carlton Veirs, Pres.; Kim Howse, Traffic Dir.; Pam Joyner, Music Dir. **Operating Hours:** 6 a.m.-midnight; 2% network, 98% local. **Owner:** Brownsville Wireless Group.

★4619★
WVOL-AM
1320 Brick Church Pike
PO Box 70085   Ph: (615)227-1470
Nashville, TN 37207   Fax: (615)227-2740
Frequency: 1470. **Network Affiliation:** American Urban Radio. **Format:** Ethnic; Religious; Urban Contemporary. **Key Personnel:** Scott Peters, Gen. Mgr.; Jeff White, Traffic Dir.; Clarence Kilcrease, Community Affairs/Program Dir.; Amy Porter, Promotions Dir.; Debbie Keen, Accountant; Clinton Hooper, Chief Engineer. **Operating Hours:** Continuous. **Owner:** Phoenix Communications Group, Inc.

★4620★
WXSS-AM
2265 Central Ave.
Memphis, TN 38104-5516   Ph: (901)726-1030
Frequency: 1030. **Network Affiliation:** Independent. **Format:** Jazz; Blues; Gospel. **Key Personnel:** Pervis Spann, Gen. Mgr.; Cynthia Andrews, Office Mgr. **Operating Hours:** Continuous. **Owner:** Minority Broadcasting Midwest.

—————————— Texas ——————————

★4621★
KALO-AM
7700 Gulfway   Ph: (409)963-1276
Port Arthur, TX 77642   Fax: (409)963-1640
Frequency: 1250. **Network Affiliation:** American Urban Radio. **Format:** Urban Contemporary; Gospel. **Key Personnel:** Ron Mathis, V.P./Gen. Mgr. **Operating Hours:** Continuous Tues.-Sun., 5 a.m.-midnight Sun. **Owner:** Clear Channel Communications.

★4622★
KAZI-FM
4700 Loyola Ln., No. 104   Ph: (512)926-0275
Austin, TX 78723   Fax: (512)929-0115
Frequency: 88.7. **Format:** Urban Contemporary; Contemporary Jazz; Gospel; Rap; Reggae. **Key Personnel:** Marion Nickerson, Acting Gen. Mgr./Program Dir.; J. Hunt, Music Dir.; JoAnn Williams, Traffic Dir.; Sharon Jones, PSA Dir. **Operating Hours:** Continuous. **Owner:** Austin Community Radio, Inc.

★4623★
KBWC-FM
711 Wiley Ave.
Marshall, TX 75670   Ph: (903)938-8341
Frequency: 91.1. **Format:** Urban Contemporary. **Key Personnel:** Melvin C. Jones, Sr., Mgr.; Ruby Sibley, Asst. Mgr.; Marvette Washington, Music Dir. **Operating Hours:** 16 hours daily; 25% network, 75% local. **Owner:** Wiley College.

★4624★
KCHL-AM
Box 1067   Ph: (512)359-1067
San Antonio, TX 78294   Fax: (512)359-8832
Frequency: 1480. **Format:** Jazz; Gospel; Adult Contemporary. **Key Personnel:** John Hiatt, Pres./Gen. Mgr.; Mac McClennehan, Program Dir.; Steve Hahn, News Dir.; Joe McCormack, Promotions Dir. **Operating Hours:** Continuous. **Owner:** Hiatt Communications, Inc.

★4625★
KCOH-AM
5011 Almeda   Ph: (713)522-1001
Houston, TX 77004   Fax: (713)521-0769
Frequency: 1430. **Network Affiliation:** American Urban Radio. **Format:** Urban Contemporary; Talk. **Key Personnel:** Mike Petrizzo, Exec. V.P./Gen. Mgr.; Travis O. Gardner, V.P./Music, Program and Promotions Dir.; Michael Harris, News Dir./Talk Show Host; Ralph Cooper, Sports Dir. **Operating Hours:** Continuous; 10% network, 90% local. **Owner:** KCOH, Inc.

★4626★
KDLF-AM
3185 Merriman St.
Port Neches, TX 77651   Ph: (409)727-2177
Frequency: 1150. **Network Affiliation:** USA Radio. **Format:** Gospel.
Key Personnel: Michael Devillier, Mgr.; Lauri Grantham, Office Mgr.
Operating Hours: 6 a.m.-9 p.m. **Owner:** Christian Crusade Corp.

★4627★
KHRN-FM
Hwy. 6 S., Box 1075
Hearne, TX 77859   Ph: (409)279-9211
Frequency: 94.3. **Format:** Urban Contemporary; Hispanic; Gospel.
Key Personnel: Pamela J. Walker, Gen. Mgr.; Joe Lee Walker, Sales
Mgr.; A.J. Whiteside, Program Dir. **Operating Hours:** 6 a.m.-
midnight. **Owner:** Freckles Broadcasting, Inc.

★4628★
KHVN-AM
545 E. John Carpenter Fwy., Ste. 1700   Ph: (214)988-7525
Irving, TX 75062   Fax: (214)988-1003
Frequency: 970. **Network Affiliation:** ABC; Unistar. **Format:**
Gospel. **Key Personnel:** Howard Toole, V.P./Gen. Mgr.; Buddy
Howell, Gen. Sales Mgr.; Warren Brooks, Program Dir. **Operating
Hours:** Continuous. **Owner:** Summit Broadcasting Corp.

★4629★
KIIZ-AM
Box 2469
Harker Heights, TX 76543   Ph: (817)699-5000
                               Fax: (817)628-8840
Frequency: 1050. **Network Affiliation:** Independent. **Format:** Urban
Contemporary. **Key Personnel:** Ken Williams, Owner; Tim Thomas,
Gen. Mgr.; Jimi Carrow, Program Dir. **Operating Hours:** Sunrise-
sunset. **Owner:** Mid-Texas Communications.

★4630★
KJBX-AM
6602 Quirt   Ph: (806)745-5800
Lubbock, TX 79408   Fax: (806)745-8644
Frequency: 580. **Network Affiliation:** ABC. **Format:** Adult
Contemporary. Simulcasts KRLB-FM. **Key Personnel:** Chuck Heinz,
Gen. Mgr.; Kenny Dowe, Operations Mgr. **Operating Hours:**
Continuous; 100% local. **Owner:** Algonquinn Corp.

★4631★
KJMZ-FM
545 E. John Carpenter Fwy., 17th Fl.   Ph: (214)556-8100
Irving, TX 75062   Fax: (214)988-1003
Frequency: 100.3. **Format:** Urban Contemporary. **Key Personnel:**
Howard Toole, V.P./Gen. Mgr.; Stephen Giles, Sales and Station
Mgr.; Tom Casey, Program Dir.; Renie Hale, Promotions Dir.; Jay
Douglas, Production Dir. **Operating Hours:** Continuous. **Owner:**
Summit Broadcasting Corp.

★4632★
KKDA-FM
PO Box 530860
Grand Prairie, TX 75053   Ph: (214)263-9911
Frequency: 104.5. **Network Affiliation:** Independent. **Format:** Urban
Contemporary. **Key Personnel:** Hyman Childs, Owner/Gen. Mgr.;
Michael Spears, Gen. Mgr. **Operating Hours:** Continuous. **Owner:**
Hyman Childs.

★4633★
KMHT-FM
PO Box 330
Huntsville, TX 77342-0330   Ph: (214)938-6789
Frequency: 103.9. **Network Affiliation:** Satellite Music; AP. **Format:**
Blues; Urban Contemporary. **Key Personnel:** Paul Adcock, Gen.
Mgr.; Nora Adcock, Sales Mgr.; Brenda Watkins, Operations Mgr.
Operating Hours: Continuous, except midnight-6 a.m. Mon. **Owner:**
Bayou Broadcasting, Inc.

★4634★
KMJQ-FM
24 Greenway Plaza, No. 1508   Ph: (713)623-0102
Houston, TX 77046   Fax: (713)623-0106
Frequency: 102.1. **Network Affiliation:** Independent. **Format:** Urban
Contemporary. **Key Personnel:** Ernest Jackson, Sr. V.P./Gen. Mgr.;
Ron Atkins, Program Dir. **Operating Hours:** Continuous. **Owner:**
Noble Broadcast Group.

★4635★
KMXO-AM
221 N. Leggett
Abilene, TX 79603   Ph: (915)672-5700
Frequency: 1500. **Format:** Talk; Hispanic; News; Eclectic; Country;
Religious; Urban Contemporary; Classical. **Key Personnel:** Ray
Silva, Owner, Pres., and Mgr.; Cecar Cano, Music Dir.; Felicha Band,
Assistant Mgr. **Operating Hours:** Sunup-sundown. **Owner:** Ray
Silva.

★4636★
KNBO-AM
PO Box 848
New Boston, TX 75570   Ph: (214)628-2561
Frequency: 1530. **Network Affiliation:** USA Radio. **Format:**
Contemporary Christian; Southern Gospel; Inspirational. **Key
Personnel:** Richard E. Knox, Pres./Gen. Mgr. **Operating Hours:**
Sunrise-sunset; 33% network, 67% local. **Owner:** Bowie County
Broadcasting Co., Inc.

★4637★
KNTU-FM
University of North Texas
Box 13585
Denton, TX 76203   Ph: (817)565-3688
Frequency: 88.1. **Network Affiliation:** Texas State. **Format:** Jazz.
Key Personnel: Samuel J. Sauls, Station Mgr.; J. Russell Campbell,
News/PA and Station Development Mgr.; Frank Bonner, Chief
Engineer. **Operating Hours:** 6 a.m.-midnight. **Owner:** University of
North Texas.

★4638★
KPVU-FM
PO Box 156
Prairie View, TX 77446-0156   Ph: (409)857-4511
Frequency: 91.3. **Format:** Jazz; Top 40; Gospel. **Key Personnel:**
Dr. Lori Gray, Gen. Mgr.; Larry Coleman, Program Dir.; Carol Means,
News Dir.; Carol Campbell, Devel. and Promotions Coord.
Operating Hours: 20 hours daily. **Owner:** Prairie View A&M
University.

★4639★
KRBA-AM
121 Calder Sq.
PO Box 1345   Ph: (409)634-6661
Lufkin, TX 75901   Fax: (409)632-5722
Frequency: 1340. **Network Affiliation:** Texas State. **Format:** Ethnic;
Country; Religious. **Key Personnel:** Shirley Yates, Gen. Mgr.;
Melanie Quine, Office Mgr./Traffic Dir. **Operating Hours:**
Continuous. **Owner:** Darrell E. Yates.

★4640★
KRZI-AM
1018 N. Valley Mill Dr.
Waco, TX 76710   Ph: (817)772-0930
Frequency: 1580. **Network Affiliation:** Unistar. **Format:** Oldies;
Hispanic; Black Gospel. **Key Personnel:** Van D. Goodall, Jr.,
Pres./Gen. Mgr.; Roland Richter, News Dir.; Robert Lauck, Gen.
Mgr.; Jay Ehret, Sales Mgr.; Tyler Thorsen, Operations Mgr.
Operating Hours: 6 a.m.-midnight: 80% network, 20% local. **Owner:**
KRZI, Inc.

★4641★
KSAQ-FM
217 Alamo Plaza, Ste. 200
San Antonio, TX 78205
Ph: (210)271-9600
Fax: (210)271-0489
Frequency: 96.1. **Network Affiliation:** ABC; NBC. **Format:** Album-Oriented Rock (AOR). **Key Personnel:** Charles Andrews, Jr., Pres./Gen. Mgr.; Alec Drake, Operations V.P.; Jeannie Nelson, Exec. V.P.; Bill Thorman, Program Dir. **Operating Hours:** Continuous. **Owner:** Inner City Broadcasting.

★4642★
KSAU-FM
Dept. of Communications
Box 13048
Nacogdoches, TX 75962
Ph: (409)568-4000
Fax: (409)568-1117
Frequency: 90.1. **Network Affiliation:** ABC. **Format:** Jazz; Alternative/Independent/Progressive (modern rock). **Key Personnel:** Sherry Williford, Gen. Mgr.; Eric Wilson, Station Mgr. **Operating Hours:** 10 a.m.-2 a.m. 1% network, 99% local. **Owner:** Stephen F. Austin State University.

★4643★
KSGB-AM
No. A-2
3105 Arkansas Ln.
Arlington, TX 76016
Ph: (817)469-1540
Frequency: 1540. **Network Affiliation:** Independent. **Format:** Gospel. **Key Personnel:** Mary Gaines, Gen. Mgr.; Jack Stuart, Sales Mgr.; Jerome Thomas, Music Dir. **Operating Hours:** 6 a.m.-1 a.m. **Owner:** Stuart Gaines Broadcasting.

★4644★
KSJL-AM
217 Alamo Plaza, Ste. 200
San Antonio, TX 78205
Ph: (210)271-9600
Fax: (210)271-0489
Frequency: 760. **Network Affiliation:** NBC; ABC. **Format:** Urban Adult Contemporary. **Key Personnel:** Charles Andrews, Jr., Pres./Gen. Mgr.; Jeannie Nelson, Exec. V.P.; Alec Drake, Operations V.P.; Bill Thorman, Program Dir. **Operating Hours:** Continuous. **Owner:** Inner City Broadcasting.

★4645★
KSKY-AM
4144 N. Central Expy., No. 266
Dallas, TX 75204-2102
Ph: (214)352-3975
Free: 800-783-5759
Frequency: 660. **Network Affiliation:** Independent. **Format:** Gospel. **Key Personnel:** Bill Simmons, Gen. Mgr.; Freda Wells, Public Affairs and Program Dir.; Kathie Watson, Sales Mgr. **Operating Hours:** Continuous. **Owner:** Broadcasting Partners of Dallas, Inc.

★4646★
KTSU-FM
3100 Cleburne Ave.
Houston, TX 77004
Ph: (713)527-7905
Frequency: 90.9. **Network Affiliation:** Independent. **Format:** Jazz; Religious; Oldies. **Key Personnel:** Claude Roberts, Gen. Mgr./Devel. Dir.; Detria Ward, Operations Mgr.; Carliss Haley, Traffic Mgr. **Operating Hours:** Continuous; 100% local. **Owner:** Texas Southern University Board of Regents.

★4647★
KWWJ-AM
4638 Decker Dr.
Baytown, TX 77520
Ph: (713)424-7000
Fax: (713)424-7588
Frequency: 1360. **Network Affiliation:** American Urban Radio. **Format:** Religious. **Key Personnel:** Dewayne Cook, Program Dir.; Donovan Howard, Promotions Dir.; Sharon B. Rolon, Music Dir.; Corliss A. Rabb, Public Affairs Dir.; Darrell E. Martin, Gen. Mgr. **Operating Hours:** Continuous. **Owner:** Salt of the Earth Broadcasting Corp.

★4648★
KYOK-AM
24 Greenway, No. 1590
Houston, TX 77046
Ph: (713)621-1590
Fax: (713)623-0106
Frequency: 1590. **Network Affiliation:** Independent. **Format:** Urban Contemporary. **Key Personnel:** Ernest Jackson, Sr. V.P./Gen. Mgr.; Tony Richards, Program Dir. **Operating Hours:** Continuous. **Owner:** Noble Broadcast Group.

★4649★
KZEY-AM
PO Box 4248
Tyler, TX 75712
Ph: (903)593-1744
Fax: (903)593-2666
Frequency: 690. **Format:** Urban Contemporary. **Key Personnel:** Roger Whitehurst, Gen. Mgr./er; John Sims, News and Sports Dir.; Dwayne Williams, Program and Music Dir.; Becky Lusk, Traffic Dir. **Operating Hours:** Continuous. **Owner:** Rose Communications, Inc.

─────────────── **Utah** ───────────────

★4650★
KMXB-AM
5282 South 320 West, Ste. D-272
Salt Lake City, UT 84107
Ph: (801)264-1075
Fax: (801)269-8595
Frequency: 1230. **Network Affiliation:** Satellite Music. **Format:** News, Sports. **Key Personnel:** Ruk Adams, Gen. Mgr.; Steve Poulsen, Marketing/Natl. Sales. **Operating Hours:** Continuous. **Owner:** RVI A California L.P.

─────────────── **Virginia** ───────────────

★4651★
WANT-AM
PO Box 6747
Richmond, VA 23230
Ph: (804)353-9113
Frequency: 990. **Network Affiliation:** Independent. **Format:** Urban Contemporary. **Key Personnel:** John Galloway, Gen. Mgr.; Valerie Clayton, Office Mgr.; Lorenzo Thomas, Program Dir. **Operating Hours:** Continuous. **Owner:** Nancy Freeman.

★4652★
WARR-AM
553 Michigan Dr.
Hampton, VA 23669-3899
Ph: (919)257-2121
Frequency: 1520. **Network Affiliation:** American Urban Radio. **Format:** Religious; Blues; Jazz; Urban Contemporary. **Key Personnel:** J. L. Wright, Sales and Station Mgr. **Operating Hours:** 6 a.m.-8:15 p.m.

★4653★
WBSK-AM
645 Church St., Ste. 201
Norfolk, VA 23510
Ph: (804)627-5800
Fax: (804)627-4048
Frequency: 1350. **Network Affiliation:**; ABC American Urban Radio. **Format:** Urban Contemporary. **Key Personnel:** Carletta Harriell, Gen. Sales Mgr.; Debra Jones, Sales Asst.; Toni Bailey, Promotions Dir. **Operating Hours:** Continuous. **Owner:** US Radio.

★4654★
WBTX-AM
PO Box 337
Broadway, VA 22815
Ph: (703)896-8933
Fax: (703)896-1448
Frequency: 1470. **Network Affiliation:** Christian Broadcasting (CBN). **Format:** Gospel. **Key Personnel:** David M. Eshleman, Pres./Owner; Jim Snavely, Music and News Dir. **Operating Hours:** 6 a.m.-sunset; 5% network. **Owner:** Massanutten Broadcasting Co., Inc.

★4655★
WCDX-FM
2809 Emerywood Pkwy., Ste. 300   Ph: (804)672-9300
Richmond, VA 23294   Fax: (804)672-9314
Frequency: 92.7. **Network Affiliation:** Independent. **Format:** Urban Contemporary; Top 40. **Key Personnel:** Ben Miles, Gen. Mgr.; Aaron Maxwell, Program Dir.; Larry Jones, Gen. Sales Mgr. **Operating Hours:** Continuous. **Owner:** Sinclair Telecable.

★4656★
WCLM-AM
4719 9 Mile Rd.
Richmond, VA 23223   Ph: (804)236-0532
Frequency: 1450. **Network Affiliation:** Independent. **Format:** Jazz; Soft Rock. **Key Personnel:** Kheni White, Gen. Mgr. **Operating Hours:** Continuous; 100% local. **Owner:** Momentum Broadcasting Inc.

★4657★
WFTH-AM
5021 Brook Rd.
Richmond, VA 23227   Ph: (804)262-8624
Frequency: 1590. **Format:** Gospel. **Key Personnel:** Jack Johnson, Gen. Mgr./Gen. Sales Mgr./Program Mgr.; William Moore, Program Dir./Music Dir./News Dir.; M. Grainger, III, Chief Engineer. **Owner:** Tri-City Christian Radio Inc.

★4658★
WGCV-AM
10600 Jefferson Davis Hwy.
Richmond, VA 23237   Ph: (804)275-1234
Frequency: 1240. **Network Affiliation:** Independent. **Format:** Gospel. **Key Personnel:** Connie Balthrop, Gen. Mgr.; Cavell Phillips, Program Dir. **Operating Hours:** Continuous. **Owner:** Paco-John Broadcasting Corp.

★4659★
WHOV-FM
Hampton Institute   Ph: (804)727-5670
Hampton, VA 23668   Fax: (808)727-5084
Frequency: 88.1. **Format:** Alternative/Independent/Progressive; Eclectic. **Key Personnel:** Frank Sheffield, Gen. Mgr.; Brian Custer, Promotions Dir.; William Mills, News Dir.; Doug Foreman, Music Dir. **Operating Hours:** 17 hours daily; 95% local. **Owner:** Hampton Institute.

★4660★
WILA-AM
865 Industrial Ave.
PO Box 3444
Danville, VA 24543   Ph: (804)792-2133
Frequency: 1580. **Network Affiliation:** American Urban Radio. **Format:** Urban Contemporary (Heart & Soul). **Key Personnel:** Lawrence Toller, Program Dir.; Mary Crews, News Dir.; Frances McMillan, Pres. **Operating Hours:** Sunrise-sunset; 1% network, 99% local. **Owner:** Frances R. McMillan.

★4661★
WKBY-AM
Rte. 2, Box 105A   Ph: (804)432-8108
Chatham, VA 24531   Fax: (804)432-9529
Frequency: 1080. **Network Affiliation:** American Urban Radio. **Format:** Religious; Urban Contemporary. **Key Personnel:** Harold James, Station Mgr.; Vickie Prittchett, Music and News Dir.; Bonnie Hansen, Sales Mgr. **Operating Hours:** Sunrise-sunset. **Owner:** William L. Bonner.

★4662★
WMYK-FM
645 Church St., Ste. 400   Ph: (804)622-4600
Norfolk, VA 23510   Fax: (804)624-6515
                                    Free: 800-873-4600
Frequency: 92.1. **Format:** Urban Contemporary. **Key Personnel:** Paul Lucci, Gen. Mgr.; Lon Goldman, Local Sales Mgr. **Operating Hours:** Continuous. **Owner:** Edge Broadcasting Co.

★4663★
WOWI-FM
645 Church St., Ste. 201   Ph: (804)627-5800
Norfolk, VA 23510-2809   Fax: (804)624-6515
Frequency: 102.9. **Network Affiliation:** American Urban Radio. **Format:** Urban Contemporary. **Key Personnel:** Carletta Harriell, Gen. Sales Mgr.; Debra Jones, Sales Asst.; Toni Bailey, Promotions Dir. **Operating Hours:** Continuous; 5% network. **Owner:** US Radio.

★4664★
WPAK-AM
800 Old Plank Rd.
Farmville, VA 23901   Ph: (804)392-8114
Frequency: 1490. **Network Affiliation:** American Urban Radio. **Format:** Urban Contemporary. **Key Personnel:** Rick Darnell, Pres./Gen. Mgr./Gen. Sales Mgr.; Stan Williams, Program Mgr./Program Dir./Music Dir.; Reginald Foster, Chief Engineer. **Owner:** Rick R. Darnell.

★4665★
WPLZ-FM
2809 Emerywood Pkwy., No. 300
Richmond, VA 23294   Ph: (804)672-9300
Frequency: 99.3. **Network Affiliation:** Independent. **Format:** Urban Contemporary. **Key Personnel:** Ben Mills, Gen. Mgr.; Phil Daniel, Program Dir. **Operating Hours:** Continuous. **Owner:** Sinclair Communications.

★4666★
WREJ-AM
6001 Wilkinson Rd.   Ph: (804)264-1540
Richmond, VA 23227   Fax: (804)264-2809
Frequency: 1540. **Network Affiliation:** Business Radio. **Format:** Business News; Talk; Information. **Key Personnel:** Jon C. King, V.P./Gen. Mgr. **Operating Hours:** Sunrise-sunset; 80% network; 20% local. **Owner:** 1540 Broadcasting Corp.

★4667★
WTJZ-AM
553 Michigan Dr.
Hampton, VA 23669   Ph: (804)723-1270
Frequency: 1270. **Format:** Gospel; Religious. **Key Personnel:** Eric C. Reynolds, Pres./Gen. Mgr./Gen. Sales Mgr.; Natt Williams, Operations Mgr. **Owner:** Broadcasting Corp. of Virginia.

★4668★
WTOY-AM
2614 Cove Rd. NW   Ph: (703)362-9558
Roanoke, VA 24017   Fax: (703)362-9544
Frequency: 1480. **Network Affiliation:** American Urban Radio. **Format:** Urban Contemporary. **Key Personnel:** Andrea Hicks, Gen. Mgr. **Operating Hours:** 5:30 a.m.-midnight. **Owner:** Ward Broadcasting Corp.

★4669★
WVST-FM
Virginia State University
Box 9010   Ph: (804)524-5932
Petersburg, VA 23806   Fax: (804)524-5826
Frequency: 91.3. **Network Affiliation:** American Urban Radio. **Format:** Classical; Jazz; Blues; News; Sports; Religious. **Key Personnel:** Paul Alatorre, Station Mgr.; Will Harris, Program Dir.; Jerry Carter, Development Dir.; Denise Tyson, Traffic Dir. **Operating Hours:** 6 a.m.-1 a.m.; 5% network, 95% local. **Owner:** Virginia State University.

Washington

★4670★
KARI-AM
4840 Lincoln Rd.   Ph: (206)734-4221
Blaine, WA 98230   Fax: (206)371-5500
Frequency: 550. **Network Affiliation:** USA Radio; International Broadcasting. **Format:** Gospel. **Key Personnel:** Gary L. Nawman, Operations Mgr.; Jan Larsen, News Dir.; Jim Scott, Chief Engineer; Don Bevilacqua, Gen. Mgr. **Operating Hours:** Continuous. **Owner:** Birch Bay Broadcasting Co., Inc.

★4671★
KEWU-FM
KEWU-R T.V.
Dept. MS. 104   Ph: (509)359-2850
Cheney, WA 99004-2495   Fax: (509)359-7028
Frequency: 89.5. **Network Affiliation:** Independent. **Format:** Jazz. **Key Personnel:** Marvin E. Smith, II, Gen. Mgr.; N. J. Brown, Station Mgr. **Operating Hours:** 6 a.m.-midnight. 100% local. **Owner:** Eastern Washington University.

★4672★
KKFX-AM
101 Nickerson St., Ste. 260   Ph: (206)728-1250
Seattle, WA 98109-1620   Fax: (206)728-1949
Frequency: 1250. **Format:** Urban Contemporary. **Key Personnel:** Robert L. Wikstrom, Gen. Mgr.; Tom Reddick, Program Dir./Promotions Mgr. **Operating Hours:** Continuous.; 100% local. **Owner:** Bingham Communications Group, Inc.

★4673★
KRIZ-AM
2600 S. Jackson St.   Ph: (206)329-7880
Seattle, WA 98144   Fax: (206)322-6518
Frequency: 1420. **Network Affiliation:** Independent. **Format:** Urban Contemporary. Simulcasts KZIZ-AM Tacoma, WA. **Key Personnel:** Chris Bennett, CEO/Gen. Mgr.; Frank Barrow, Operations Mgr. **Operating Hours:** Continuous. **Owner:** Kris Broadcasting, Inc.

★4674★
KUJ-AM
Rte. 5, Box 513   Ph: (509)529-8000
Walla Walla, WA 99362   Fax: (509)525-3727
                          Free: 800-648-9099
Frequency: 1420. **Network Affiliation:** Unistar. **Format:** Oldies. **Key Personnel:** Trudy Hermanns, Gen. Mgr.; Betty Newkirk, Office and Traffic Mgr. **Operating Hours:** Continuous; 100% network. **Owner:** KUJ Ltd. Partnership.

West Virginia

★4675★
WVKV-AM
PO Box 1080
Hurricane, WV 25526   Ph: (304)562-9155
Frequency: 1080. **Format:** Gospel. **Key Personnel:** Teresa Milliken, Station Mgr.; Jim Milliken, Gen. Mgr. **Operating Hours:** Daytime. **Owner:** Milliken Investment Corp.

Wisconsin

★4676★
WLUM-FM
2500 N. Mayfair Rd., No. 390   Ph: (414)771-1021
Milwaukee, WI 53226-1409   Fax: (414)771-3036
Frequency: 102.1. **Network Affiliation:** Independent. **Format:** Contemporary Hit Radio (CHR). **Key Personnel:** Steve Sinicropi, V.P./Gen. Mgr. **Operating Hours:** Continuous. **Owner:** Willie D. Davis.

★4677★
WMVP-AM
4222 W. Capitol Dr., Ste. 1290   Ph: (414)444-1290
Milwaukee, WI 53216   Fax: (414)444-1409
Frequency: 1290. **Network Affiliation:** Satellite Radio. **Format:** Urban Contemporary. **Key Personnel:** Victor Singleton, Promotions Dir.; Don Rosette, Gen. Mgr.; Billy Young, Program Dir.; Roger Williams, Gen. Sales Mgr.; Ella Smith, Community Relations Dir.; Larry Bandy, News Dir. **Operating Hours:** Continuous. **Owner:** Suburbanaire, Inc.

★4678★
WNOV-AM
3815 N. Teutonia Ave.
Milwaukee, WI 53206   Ph: (414)449-9668
Frequency: 860. **Network Affiliation:** Independent. **Format:** Blues; Gospel. **Key Personnel:** Sandra Robinson, Station Mgr. **Operating Hours:** 5:30 p.m.-8:30 p.m. **Owner:** Gerald Jones.

★4679★
WYMS-FM
5225 W. Vliet St.   Ph: (414)475-8389
Milwaukee, WI 53208   Fax: (414)475-8413
Frequency: 88.9. **Network Affiliation:** American Public Radio (APR); AP. **Format:** New Age; Jazz; Ethnic; Blues. **Key Personnel:** Peter Zehren, News Dir.; Roger Dobrick, Station Mgr.; Bill Bruckner, Music Dir. **Operating Hours:** Continuous; 10% networrk, 90% local. **Owner:** Milwaukee Public Schools.

Television Stations

California

★4680★
KNTV-TV
645 Park Ave.
San Jose, CA 95110   Ph: (408)286-1111
Frequency: 11. **Network Affiliation:** ABC. **Format:** Commercial TV. **Key Personnel:** Stewart Park, Gen. Mgr./Program Dir.; Lisa Owen, Program Coord.; Terry McElhatton, News Dir.; Marty Edelman, Gen. Sales Mgr. **Operating Hours:** 6 a.m.-2 a.m. **Owner:** Granite Broadcasting, Inc.

District of Columbia

★4681★
WHMM-TV
2222 4th St. NW   Ph: (202)806-3200
Washington, DC 20059   Fax: (202)806-3300
Frequency: 32. **Network Affiliation:** Public Broadcasting Service (PBS). **Format:** Public TV. **Key Personnel:** Edward Jones, Jr., Gen. Mgr.; William Pratt, Production Mgr. **Operating Hours:** 8 a.m-12:30 a.m.; 60% network, 40% local. **Owner:** Howard University Board of Trustees.

Florida

★4682★
WTVT-TV
3213 W. Kennedy Blvd.   Ph: (813)876-1313
Tampa, FL 33609   Fax: (813)875-8329
Frequency: 13. **Network Affiliation:** CBS. **Format:** Commercial TV. **Key Personnel:** David Whitaker, Pres.; Bob Franklin, Operations and News Dir.; Artie Scheff, Promotions Mgr.; Mark Higgins, Gen. Sales Mgr. **Operating Hours:** Continuous. **Owner:** WTVT, Inc.

Georgia

★4683★
WFXL-TV
1211 N. Slappey Blvd.
Albany, GA 31708

Ph: (912)435-3100
Fax: (912)435-0485
Free: 800-999-1276

Frequency: 31. **Network Affiliation:** Fox; Independent. **Format:** Commercial TV. **Key Personnel:** Manny Cantu, Gen. Mgr.; Bettina Smith, Program Dir.; Jaxen Riley, Production Mgr.; Carol Ayres, Natl. Sales Mgr. **Operating Hours:** Continuous. **Owner:** Newsouth Broadcasting, Inc.

★4684★
WGXA-TV
PO Box 340
Macon, GA 31297

Ph: (912)745-2424
Fax: (912)750-4347

Frequency: 24. **Network Affiliation:** ABC. **Format:** Commercial TV. **Key Personnel:** Ken Gerdes, V.P./Gen. Mgr.; Frank Shurling, Gen. Sales Mgr.; Richard Blanton, Chief Engineer; Kim Bene, Operations Mgr. **Operating Hours:** 80% network, 20% local. **Owner:** WGXA-TV.

★4685★
WRDW-TV
PO Drawer 1212
Augusta, GA 30913-1212

Ph: (803)278-1212
Fax: (803)279-8316

Frequency: 12. **Network Affiliation:** CBS. **Format:** Commercial TV. **Key Personnel:** William G. Evans, V.P. and Gen. Mgr.; Robert E. French, Gen. Sales Mgr.; Steve Johnston, Local Sales Mgr.; Charles Moody, Broadcast Operations Mgr.; Brian Travring, V.P./News and Operations; Jim Myers, Chief Engineer. **Operating Hours:** Continuous weekdays; 6 a.m.-2 a.m. Sat.-Sun. **Owner:** Television Station Partners.

Illinois

★4686★
WEEK-TV
2907 Springfield Rd.
Peoria, IL 61611

Ph: (309)698-2525

Frequency: 25. **Network Affiliation:** NBC. **Format:** Commercial TV. **Key Personnel:** Dennis Upah, Gen. Mgr./Program Dir.; John C. Deushane, Dir. of Sales; Phil Supple, News Dir. **Operating Hours:** Continuous; 60% network, 40% local. **Owner:** Granite Broadcasting Corp.

Indiana

★4687★
WPTA-TV
3401 Butler Rd.
Box 2121
Fort Wayne, IN 46801

Ph: (219)483-0584

Frequency: 21. **Network Affiliation:** ABC. **Format:** Commercial TV. **Key Personnel:** Barbara Wigham, Pres./Gen. Mgr.; Jan D'italia, Program/Community Affairs Dir.; Greg Johans, Sports Dir.; Bill Schneider, Assignment Editor. **Operating Hours:** 5:30 a.m.-2 a.m.; 52% network, 48% local. 24 hrs. Mon.-Fri. **Owner:** Granite Broadcasting Corp.

★4688★
WRTV-TV
1330 N. Meridian St.
Indianapolis, IN 46206

Ph: (317)635-9788
Fax: (317)269-1400

Frequency: 6. **Network Affiliation:** ABC. **Format:** Commercial TV. **Key Personnel:** John C. Long, V.P./Gen. Mgr.; Sharon Chalfin, Gen. Sales Mgr.; Kenneth Ladage, Operations Mgr.; David Baer, News Dir.; Judith Waugh, Public Affairs Dir.; Richard Pratt, Engineering Dir.; Paul Montgomery, Advertising and Promotions Dir.; Martin L. Siddall, Dir. of Business Affairs. **Operating Hours:** 5:30 a.m.-2:30

a.m.; 56% network, 44% local. **Owner:** McGraw-Hill Broadcasting Co., Inc.

Kentucky

★4689★
WKYT-TV
Box 5037
Lexington, KY 40555

Ph: (606)299-0411
Fax: (606)299-2494

Frequency: 27. **Network Affiliation:** CBS. **Format:** Commercial TV. **Key Personnel:** Ralph Gabber, Gen. Mgr.; Barbara Carden, Program Dir.; Brenda Turley, Controller; Mike Kanarek, Operations Mgr. **Operating Hours:** 6 a.m.-1 a.m. **Owner:** Kentucky Life Insurance.

Louisiana

★4690★
WNOL-TV
1661 Canal St.
New Orleans, LA 70112

Ph: (504)525-3838
Fax: (504)569-0908

Frequency: 38. **Network Affiliation:** Fox. **Format:** Commercial TV. **Key Personnel:** Bob Lawrence, Chief Engineer. **Operating Hours:** Continuous except Mon. 1 a.m.-6 a.m. **Owner:** Quincy Jones Broadcasting, Inc.

Maine

★4691★
WVII-TV
371 Target Industrial Circle
Bangor, ME 04401

Ph: (207)945-6457
Fax: (207)942-0511

Frequency: 7. **Network Affiliation:** ABC. **Format:** Commercial TV. **Key Personnel:** Peter K. Orne, Pres./Gen. Mgr. **Operating Hours:** 5 or 5:30 a.m.-midnight or 2:30 a.m. **Owner:** Seaway Communications.

Michigan

★4692★
WGPR-TV
3146 E. Jefferson Ave.
Detroit, MI 48207

Ph: (313)259-8862
Fax: (313)259-6662

Frequency: 62. **Network Affiliation:** Independent. **Format:** Commercial TV. **Key Personnel:** George Mathews, Pres./Gen. Mgr.; D. Roger Williams, Admin. Asst.; Michelle DeSouza, Admin. Asst.; Joseph Spencer, Program Dir.; Patricia Watson, Sales Mgr.; Lucia Marvin, News Dir.; James O. Dogan, Station Mgr.; Celestine Harris, Promotions Dir. **Operating Hours:** Continuous. **Owner:** Intl. Masons, Inc.

Minnesota

★4693★
KBJR-TV
KBJR Bldg.
Duluth, MN 55802

Ph: (218)727-8484
Fax: (218)727-1737

Frequency: 6. **Network Affiliation:** NBC; Fox. **Format:** Commercial TV. **Key Personnel:** Maria A. Moore, Pres./Gen. Mgr.; John Leifheir, Gen. Sales Mgr. **Operating Hours:** Continuous (except 2-6 a.m. Sun.). **Owner:** Granite Broadcasting Corp.

----------- **Mississippi** -----------

★4694★
WLBM-TV
PO Box 1712
Jackson, MS 39215-1712
Frequency: 30. **Network Affiliation:** NBC. **Format:** Commercial TV.
Key Personnel: Pluria Marshall, V.P./Gen. Mgr.; Alfred Martin, Sales
Mgr.; Don Spann, Production/Operations Mgr.; Danny Johnson,
Chief Engineer. **Owner:** Pluria Marshall.

★4695★
WLBT-TV
715 S. Jefferson St.   Ph: (601)948-3333
Jackson, MS 39205   Fax: (601)960-4435
Frequency: 3. **Network Affiliation:** NBC. **Format:** Commercial TV.
Key Personnel: Dan Modisett, Pres./Gen. Mgr. **Operating Hours:**
Continuous; 70% network, 30% local. **Owner:** Civic
Communications.

----------- **New York** -----------

★4696★
WHEC-TV
191 East Ave.   Ph: (716)546-5670
Rochester, NY 14604   Fax: (716)454-7433
Frequency: 10. **Network Affiliation:** NBC. **Format:** Commercial TV.
Key Personnel: Arnold Klinisky, V.P./Gen. Mgr. **Operating Hours:**
Continuous Sun.-Thur.; sign-off at 3 a.m. Fri. and 2 a.m. Sat. **Owner:**
Viacom Broadcasting.

★4697★
WKBW-TV
7 Broadcast Plaza   Ph: (716)845-6100
Buffalo, NY 14202   Fax: (716)842-1855
                              Free: 800-234-9529
Frequency: 7. **Network Affiliation:** ABC. **Format:** Commercial TV.
Key Personnel: Paul Cassidy, Pres./Gen. Mgr.; Steve Van Vlist,
News Dir.; Tim Gilbert, Gen. Sales Mgr.; John DiScuillo, Promotions
Dir.; Don Holland, Engineering. **Operating Hours:** Continuous; 35%
network, 65% local. **Owner:** Queen City Broadcasting, Inc.

----------- **Ohio** -----------

★4698★
WGTE-TV
Box 30
136 Huron St.   Ph: (419)243-3091
Toledo, OH 43602   Fax: (419)243-9711
Frequency: 30. **Network Affiliation:** Public Broadcasting Service
(PBS). **Format:** Public TV. **Key Personnel:** Shirley Timonere,
Pres./Gen. Mgr. **Operating Hours:** 6:45 a.m.-midnight. **Owner:**
Public Broadcasting Foundation of Northwest Ohio.

----------- **Texas** -----------

★4699★
KTXS-TV
Box 2997   Ph: (915)677-2281
Abilene, TX 79604   Fax: (915)676-9231
Frequency: 12. **Network Affiliation:** ABC. **Format:** Commercial TV.
Key Personnel: Clay Milstead, Gen. Mgr. **Operating Hours:** 6 a.m.-
12:30 a.m. **Owner:** Lamco Communications, Inc.

----------- **Virginia** -----------

★4700★
WJCB-TV
3700 Washington Ave., 4th Fl.
Newport News, VA 23607-3947   Ph: (804)627-7500
Frequency: 49. **Format:** Commercial TV. **Key Personnel:** Dwight
Green, Gen. Mgr. **Operating Hours:** 7 a.m.-Midnight.

----------- **Wisconsin** -----------

★4701★
WJFW-TV
S. Oneida Ave.
PO Box 858   Ph: (715)369-4700
Rhinelander, WI 54501   Fax: (715)369-1910
Frequency: 12. **Network Affiliation:** NBC. **Format:** Commercial TV.
Key Personnel: Marie Platteter, Gen. Mgr. **Operating Hours:** 6 a.m.-
2 a.m. **Owner:** Seaway Communications.

(18) Videos

★4702★
The ABA Commission on Minorities and Judicial Administration Division
American Bar Association
Commission on Public Understanding
About the Law
750 N. Lakeshore Dr.
Chicago, IL 60611   Ph: (312)988-5000

1988. **Program Description:** Issues of prejudice in the courtroom. **Length:** 15 mins. **Format:** Beta, VHS, 3/4U. **Acquisition:** Purchase, Rent/Lease. **Use:** Institution, CCTV, Home, SURA.

★4703★
ABC News: Mandela—The Man and His Country
MPI Home Video
15825 Rob Roy Dr.   Ph: (708)687-7881
Oak Forest, IL 60452   Fax: (708)687-3797

1990. **Program Description:** Following his release from prison in 1990, ABC News prepared this comprehensive biography of Nelson Mandela, from his place of birth to the celebration that accompanied his freedom. **Length:** 50 mins. **Format:** Beta, VHS. **Acquisition:** Purchase. **Use:** Institution, Home.

★4704★
About the United Nations: Africa Recovery
Cinema Guild
1697 Broadway   Ph: (212)246-5522
New York, NY 10019   Fax: (212)246-5525

1990. **Program Description:** In this edition of the educational series produced for grades 5-12, a Zambian reporter comments on the major problems threatening Africa today and what might be done to solve them. Includes a 48 page guide book for teachers. **Length:** 15 mins. **Format:** VHS. **Acquisition:** Purchase. **Use:** Home.

★4705★
About the United Nations: Apartheid
Cinema Guild
1697 Broadway   Ph: (212)246-5522
New York, NY 10019   Fax: (212)246-5525

1990. **Program Description:** This volume of the series produced for students in grades 5-12 is hosted by a young South African girl who describes the various injustices of the apartheid system. Included is a 48 page teacher's guide. **Length:** 10 mins. **Format:** VHS. **Acquisition:** Rent/Lease. **Use:** Home.

★4706★
Abraham Lincoln and the Emancipation Proclamation
AEF/Capital Communications   Ph: (615)868-2040
3807 Dickerson Rd.   Fax: (615)868-5239
Nashville, TN 37207   Free: 800-822-5678

1973. **Program Description:** An examination of the dilemma confronting Lincoln over the troubling issue of Negro slavery. **Length:** 25 mins. **Format:** Beta, VHS, 3/4U. **Acquisition:** Purchase. **Use:** Institution, SURA.

★4707★
Acoustic Sounds from Africa
Island Video
182 Fairchild Ave.
Plainview, NY 11803   Ph: (516)349-0333

1990. **Program Description:** Music from Senegal by Baaba Maal and Sooliman Rogie. Includes "Laare" and "My Lovely Elizabeth." **Length:** 50 mins. **Format:** VHS. **Acquisition:** Purchase. **Use:** Home.

★4708★
Adam Clayton Powell
Phoenix/BFA Films
468 Park Ave., S.   Ph: (212)684-5910
New York, NY 10016   Free: 800-221-1274

1977. **Program Description:** The story of the controversial black congressman and his struggle against oppression and injustice to blacks in America. The program contains an interview with Powell, conducted shortly before his death by WABC-TV's Gil Noble. **Length:** 58 mins. **Format:** Beta, VHS, 3/4U. **Acquisition:** Purchase. **Use:** Institution, SURA.

★4709★
Affirmative Action: Is It the Answer to Discrimination
American Enterprise Institute for Public
  Policy Research
1150 17th St. NW
Washington, DC 20036   Free: 800-462-6420

197?. **Program Description:** A panel of lawyers, academicians, and journalists meet to discuss the legality of granting preference to people on the basis of sex, race, and national origin. **Length:** 60 mins. **Format:** 3/4U. **Acquisition:** Rent/Lease, Purchase. **Use:** Institution, BCTV.

★4710★
Africa
Public Media Video   Ph: (312)878-2600
5547 N. Ravenswood Ave.   Fax: (312)878-8406
Chicago, IL 60640-1199   Free: 800-826-3456
1986. **Program Description:** An eight-part documentary about the continent, its people and terrain. Two programs per tape. **Length:** 106 mins. **Format:** Beta, VHS. **Acquisition:** Purchase. **Use:** Home.

★4711★
Africa
Film Video Library
University of Michigan
919 S. University Ave., Rm. 207
Ann Arbor, MI 48109-1185   Ph: (313)764-5360
1977. **Program Description:** A look at the black against black conflicts in Africa, which are more critical than the black/white struggle that often overshadows them. **Length:** 29 mins. **Format:** 3/4U, Special order formats. **Acquisition:** Rent/Lease, Purchase. **Use:** Institution, CCTV, CATV, BCTV.

★4712★
Africa: A Continent of Many Nations
United Learning, Inc.
6633 W. Howard St.   Ph: (708)647-0600
PO Box 48718   Fax: (708)647-0918
Niles, IL 60714-0718   Free: 800-424-0362
1990. **Program Description:** The culture, history and geography of the African continent. **Length:** mins. **Format:** VHS. **Acquisition:** Purchase, Duplication. **Use:** Institution, CCTV, CATV, Home, SURA.

★4713★
Africa: A New Look
International Film Foundation
155 W. 72nd St.
New York, NY 10023   Ph: (212)580-1111
1981. **Program Description:** This program shows how urbanized Africa has become by focusing on the people who live and work on the continent today. **Length:** 27 mins. **Format:** 3/4U, Special order formats. **Acquisition:** Purchase. **Use:** Institution, SURA.

★4714★
Africa: A Voyage of Discovery
1988. **Program Description:** A four-part look at the history and cultures of the Dark Continent. Originally aired on the Arts & Entertainment channel. **Length:** 57 mins. **Format:** VHS. **Acquisition:** Purchase. **Use:** Home.

★4715★
Africa: An Introduction (Revised)
Phoenix/BFA Films
468 Park Ave., S.   Ph: (212)684-5910
New York, NY 10016   Free: 800-221-1274
1981. **Program Description:** This show is an overview of Africa and the many different people who make up the population. **Length:** 22 mins. **Format:** Beta, VHS, 3/4U. **Acquisition:** Purchase. **Use:** Institution, SURA.

★4716★
Africa Calls: Its Drums and Musical Instruments
Carousel Film & Video
260 5th Ave., Rm. 405   Ph: (212)683-1660
New York, NY 10001   Fax: (212)683-1662
1971. **Program Description:** An African lives, works, and communicates through his music. **Length:** 23 mins. **Format:** Beta, VHS, 3/4U. **Acquisition:** Purchase. **Use:** Institution, SURA.

★4717★
Africa Church Growth and Development
UMCom Video
810 12th Ave., S.   Ph: (615)242-6277
Nashville, TN 37203   Free: 800-251-4091
1980. **Program Description:** The program features a number of religious leaders discussing the state of the Church in Africa.

Length: 30 mins. **Format:** Beta, VHS, 3/4U. **Acquisition:** Rent/Lease, Purchase. **Use:** Institution.

★4718★
Africa in Focus
Journal Films, Inc.   Ph: (708)328-6700
930 Pitner Ave.   Fax: (708)328-6706
Evanston, IL 60202   Free: 800-323-5448
1990. **Program Description:** An overview of several African nations, examining geography, sociology, culture, economy and future outlook. **Length:** 20 mins. **Format:** Beta, VHS, 3/4U, Special order formats. **Acquisition:** Purchase, Rent/Lease. **Use:** Institution, SURA.

★4719★
African-American Art: Past and Present
Baker & Taylor Video
501 S. Gladiolus   Fax: 800-775-3500
Momence, IL 60954   Free: 800-775-2300

1992. **Program Description:** A three-volume comprehensive survey of African-American art with more than 400 visuals gathered from private collections. Covers decorative arts to 20th century artists, including Malvin Gray Johnson, Selma Burke, David Hammons, and Archibald Motey, Jr. **Length:** 90 mins. **Format:** VHS. **Acquisition:** Purchase. **Use:** Institution.

★4720★
African Art and Sculpture
Carousel Film & Video
260 5th Ave., Rm. 405   Ph: (212)683-1660
New York, NY 10001   Fax: (212)683-1662
1971. **Program Description:** Reveals the African's sense of beauty and curiosity as displayed in works of art. **Length:** 21 mins. **Format:** Beta, VHS, 3/4U. **Acquisition:** Purchase. **Use:** Institution, SURA.

★4721★
The African Continent: An Introduction
Coronet/MTI Film & Video   Ph: (708)940-1260
108 Wilmot Rd.   Fax: (708)940-3640
Deerfield, IL 60015   Free: 800-777-8100
1962. **Program Description:** A geographical, historical, and cultural overview of the world's second largest continental, stressing the emergence of peoples, of new independent countries, and of rapidly developing nations. **Length:** 16 mins. **Format:** Beta, VHS, 3/4U, Special order formats. **Acquisition:** Rent/Lease, Purchase, Duplication License. **Use:** Institution, CCTV, SURA.

★4722★
African Journey
Public Media Video   Ph: (312)878-2600
5547 N. Ravenswood Ave.   Fax: (312)878-8406
Chicago, IL 60640-1199   Free: 800-826-3456
1989. **Program Description:** A moving, cross-cultural drama of friendship. A young black American goes to Africa for the summer to be with his divorced father who is working in the diamond mines. There he meets a young black African like himself; they overcome cultural clashes and learn respect for one another. Beautiful scenery, filmed in Africa. Part of the "Wonderworks" series. **Length:** 174 mins. **Format:** VHS. **Acquisition:** Purchase. **Use:** Home.

★4723★
African Masks: Dance of the Spirit
University of Iowa
Audiovisual Center
C-215 Seashore Hall
Iowa City, IA 52242   Ph: (319)335-2539
1988. **Program Description:** The music, dance, costumes and masks of African tribes are displayed. **Length:** 30 mins. **Format:** VHS, 3/4U. **Acquisition:** Purchase. **Use:** Institution, CCTV, SURA.

★4724★
African Masks: Yaaba Soore, Path of the Ancestors
University of Iowa
Audiovisual Center
C-215 Seashore Hall
Iowa City, IA 52242   Ph: (319)335-2539
1987. **Program Description:** This film explains what the various African tribal masks represent. **Length:** 17 mins. **Format:** VHS, 3/4U. **Acquisition:** Purchase. **Use:** Institution, CCTV, SURA.

★4725★
African Origins
Afro-Am Distributing Company
407 E. 25th St., Ste. 600   Ph: (312)791-1611
Chicago, IL 60616   Fax: (312)791-0921
19??. **Program Description:** A look at African history from the time of the Egyptians on. **Length:** 60 mins. **Format:** VHS. **Acquisition:** Purchase. **Use:** Institution, Home, SURA.

★4726★
African Religions and Ritual Dances
Carousel Film & Video
260 5th Ave., Rm. 405   Ph: (212)683-1660
New York, NY 10001   Fax: (212)683-1662
1971. **Program Description:** Reenactment of a Yoruba ritual cult dance. **Length:** 19 mins. **Format:** Beta, VHS, 3/4U. **Acquisition:** Purchase. **Use:** Institution, SURA.

★4727★
African Soul: Music, Past and Present
Carousel Film & Video
260 5th Ave., Rm. 405   Ph: (212)683-1660
New York, NY 10001   Fax: (212)683-1662
1971. **Program Description:** A demonstration of early African music and song, including an original African jazz performance. **Length:** 17 mins. **Format:** Beta, VHS, 3/4U. **Acquisition:** Purchase. **Use:** Institution, SURA.

★4728★
African Story Journey
Churchill Films
12210 Nebraska Ave.   Ph: (310)207-6600
Los Angeles, CA 90025   Fax: (310)207-1330
1992. **Program Description:** Diane Ferlatte dramatically recounts classic African folktales set in Africa and the Caribbean, and more modern stories set in the American South and urban ghettos. Delightful blend of lush scenery and spirited music combine for a fine performance. **Length:** 20 mins. **Format:** VHS. **Acquisition:** Purchase. **Use:** Institution.

★4729★
African Story Magic
Live Home Video
15400 Sherman Way, Ste. 500
Van Nuys, CA 91410-0124   Ph: (818)988-5060
19??. **Program Description:** A young boy finds the roots of African folklore on a magical journey that takes him from his inner-city streets. **Length:** 27 mins. **Format:** VHS. **Acquisition:** Purchase. **Use:** Home.

★4730★
The African Village Life Series
International Film Foundation
155 W. 72nd St.
New York, NY 10023   Ph: (212)580-1111
197?. **Program Description:** This series of programs focuses on specific regions and records objectively the lives of African people. Each part is available individually. Non-narrative. **Length:** 12 mins. **Format:** 3/4U, Special order formats. **Acquisition:** Purchase. **Use:** Institution, SURA.

★4731★
The Africans
Annenberg/CPB Collection   Ph: (202)879-9600
901 E St. NW   Fax: (202)864-9846
Washington, DC 20004   Free: 800-LEA-RNER
1986. **Program Description:** This series of programs examines the history and culture of Africa, from the time of the pharaohs to the modern struggle against apartheid in South Africa. **Length:** 60 mins. **Format:** Beta, VHS, 3/4U. **Acquisition:** Rent/Lease, Purchase, Duplication, Free Loan. **Use:** Institution, CCTV, CATV, SURA.

★4732★
Afro-American Music, Its Heritage
Communications Group West
1640 5th St., Ste. 202   Ph: (310)451-2525
Santa Monica, CA 90401   Fax: (310)451-5020
1972. **Program Description:** Represents 250 years of Black music, from the talking drums of West Africa to contemporary rhythm and blues, and gospel. **Length:** 16 mins. **Format:** Beta, VHS, EJ, 3/4U. **Acquisition:** Rent/Lease, Purchase. **Use:** Institution, CCTV, SURA.

★4733★
Afro-American Perspectives
Maryland Public Television   Ph: (410)356-5600
11767 Owings Mills Blvd.   Fax: (410)581-4338
Owings Mills, MD 21117-1499   Free: 800-873-6154
1979. **Program Description:** ''Afro-American Perspectives'' presents a college credit course combining televised lessons, on-campus seminars, and related work assignments. Focuses on the black American: the heritage and the struggles as one component in a complex society. **Length:** 30 mins. **Format:** Beta, VHS, 3/4U. **Acquisition:** Rent/Lease, Purchase. **Use:** Institution, CCTV, CATV, BCTV.

★4734★
After the Hunger and the Drought
California Newsreel
149 Ninth St., Ste. 420   Ph: (415)621-6196
San Francisco, CA 94103   Fax: (415)621-6522
1988. **Program Description:** African writers and intellectuals discuss the issues important to the process of rebuilding their nations. Crucial is the debate over the role of traditionalism and use of Western methods to reach large numbers of people. **Length:** 54 mins. **Format:** VHS. **Acquisition:** Purchase, Rent/Lease. **Use:** Institution.

★4735★
Alberta Hunter: My Castle's Rockin'
V.I.E.W. Video   Ph: (212)674-5550
34 E. 23rd St.   Fax: (212)979-0266
New York, NY 10010   Free: 800-843-9843
1988. **Program Description:** Portrays the life of Hunter, a blues singer and songwriter in the 1920s and '30s, who later lapsed into obscurity. She left show business to become a nurse but made her triumphant comeback at age 82. Features many of her hit songs, including ''The Love I Have for You,'' ''Handy Man,'' ''Downhearted Blues,'' and ''Darktown Strutters Ball.'' **Length:** 60 mins. **Format:** VHS. **Acquisition:** Purchase. **Use:** Home.

★4736★
Allan Boesak: Choosing for Justice
California Newsreel
149 Ninth St., Ste. 420   Ph: (415)621-6196
San Francisco, CA 94103   Fax: (415)621-6522
1984. **Program Description:** Documentary of Allan Boesak, the black religious leader who was elected head of the World Alliance of Reformed Churches with its 70 million members. His election stunned South African white rulers, and paved the way for Boesak to found the United Demococratic Front (UDF), a multi-racial, anti-apartheid group. Narrated by James Earl Jones. **Length:** 28 mins. **Format:** VHS, Special order formats. **Acquisition:** Purchase, Rent/Lease. **Use:** Institution.

★4737★
Almos' a Man
Monterey Home Video
28038 Dorothy Dr., Ste. 1
Agoura Hills, CA 91301
Ph: (818)597-0047
Fax: (818)597-0105
Free: 800-424-2593
1978. **Program Description:** Richard Wright's story of a black teenage farm worker in the late 1930s who must endure the pains of growing up. From the "American Short Story" series. **Length:** 51 mins. **Format:** Beta, VHS. **Acquisition:** Purchase. **Use:** Home.

★4738★
Alvin Ailey: Ailey Dances
Music Video Distributors
O'Neill Industrial Center
1210 Standbridge St.
Norristown, PA 19403
Ph: (215)272-7771
Fax: (215)272-6074
Free: 800-888-0486
1987. **Program Description:** Four different performances of the Ailey troupe are shown. Taped in New York City, 1982. Includes "Night Creatures," "Revelations," "The Lark Ascending," and "Cry." **Length:** 85 mins. **Format:** Beta, VHS. **Acquisition:** Purchase. **Use:** Institution, Home.

★4739★
American Patchwork: Jazz Parades
PBS Video
11858 La Grange Ave.
Los Angeles, CA 90025
Ph: (213)820-0991
Fax: (213)826-4779
1990. **Program Description:** A history and exhibition of America's jazz musicians. **Length:** 60 mins. **Format:** VHS. **Acquisition:** Purchase. **Use:** Home.

★4740★
The American South: Black Political Development
Proud To Be. . .A Black Video Collection
1235-E East Blvd., Ste. 209
Charlotte, NC 28203
Ph: (704)523-2227
1989. **Program Description:** Focuses on the point of time where the civil rights movement turned into direct action to reach political and economic goals. **Length:** 30 mins. **Format:** VHS. **Acquisition:** Purchase. **Use:** Home.

★4741★
The American South: The Civil Rights Movement
Proud To Be. . .A Black Video Collection
1235-E East Blvd., Ste. 209
Charlotte, NC 28203
Ph: (704)523-2227
1989. **Program Description:** Highlights the evolution of the South's civil rights movement. Includes speeches by Martin Luther King, Jr., John F. Kennedy, and Lyndon Johnson and clips of sit-ins and freedom riders. **Length:** 30 mins. **Format:** VHS. **Acquisition:** Purchase. **Use:** Home.

★4742★
America's Music, Vol. 5: Rhythm and Blues 1
Century Home Video, Inc.
PO Box 34727
Los Angeles, CA 90034-0727
1987. **Program Description:** Footage of R&B greats includes Ruth Brown, Billy Preston, Gloria Lynne, Sheer Delight, Billy Eckstine and more. **Length:** 60 mins. **Format:** VHS. **Acquisition:** Purchase. **Use:** Home.

★4743★
America's Music, Vol. 6: Rhythm and Blues 2
Century Home Video, Inc.
PO Box 34727
Los Angeles, CA 90034-0727
1987. **Program Description:** The R&B greats featured here include, Brook Benton, Mary Wells, O.C. Smith and Scatman Crothers. **Length:** 60 mins. **Format:** VHS. **Acquisition:** Purchase. **Use:** Home.

★4744★
America's Music, Vol. 9: Jazz Then Dixieland 1
Music Video Distributors
O'Neill Industrial Center
1210 Standbridge St.
Norristown, PA 19403
Ph: (215)272-7771
Fax: (215)272-6074
Free: 800-888-0486
1987. **Program Description:** The masters of jazz include, Louis Armstrong, Al Hirt, Woody Herman and Della Reese. **Length:** 60 mins. **Format:** VHS. **Acquisition:** Purchase. **Use:** Home.

★4745★
America's Music, Vol. 11: Soul 1
Century Home Video, Inc.
PO Box 34727
Los Angeles, CA 90034-0727
1987. **Program Description:** Featured artists in this retrospective are, James Brown, Ben E. King, Tyrone Davis and Maxine Nightingale. **Length:** 60 mins. **Format:** VHS. **Acquisition:** Purchase. **Use:** Home.

★4746★
America's Music, Vol. 12: Soul 2
Century Home Video, Inc.
PO Box 34727
Los Angeles, CA 90034-0727
1987. **Program Description:** This volume contains clips of soul greats Gladys Knight, Rufus Thomas, Jerry Butler, Carla Thomas, Freda Payne, Percy Sledge and more. **Length:** 60 mins. **Format:** VHS. **Acquisition:** Purchase. **Use:** Home.

★4747★
America's Music, Vol. 13: Gospel 1
Music Video Distributors
O'Neill Industrial Center
1210 Standbridge St.
Norristown, PA 19403
Ph: (215)272-7771
Fax: (215)272-6074
Free: 800-888-0486
1987. **Program Description:** Featured artists in this retrospective are, Andre Crouch, The Winans, Marion Williams and Mahalia Jackson. **Length:** 60 mins. **Format:** VHS. **Acquisition:** Purchase. **Use:** Home.

★4748★
America's Music, Vol. 14: Gospel 2
Music Video Distributors
O'Neill Industrial Center
1210 Standbridge St.
Norristown, PA 19403
Ph: (215)272-7771
Fax: (215)272-6074
Free: 800-888-0486
1987. **Program Description:** The artists profiled in this edition include Linda Hopkins, Wentley Phipps and Sandra Crouch and Friends. **Length:** 60 mins. **Format:** VHS. **Acquisition:** Purchase. **Use:** Home.

★4749★
Among Brothers: Politics in New Orleans
PBS Video
11858 La Grange Ave.
Los Angeles, CA 90025
Ph: (213)820-0991
Fax: (213)826-4779
1987. **Program Description:** This program examines the new urban politics where blacks often run for elected office against other blacks. The tape also examines new coalition building. **Length:** 60 mins. **Format:** Beta, VHS, 3/4U. **Acquisition:** Rent/Lease, Purchase, Duplication, Off-Air Record. **Use:** Institution, CCTV, Home, SURA.

★4750★
Among Good Christian People
Third World Newsreel
335 W. 38th St., 5th Fl.
New York, NY 10018
Ph: (212)947-9277
Fax: (212)594-6417
1991. **Program Description:** Co-director Woodson documents her story as a Black lesbian raised as a Jehovah Witness as she comes to terms with her sexuality, lifestyle, and spiritual yearnings. **Length:** 30 mins. **Format:** VHS, 3/4U. **Acquisition:** Rent/Lease, Purchase. **Use:** Institution.

★4751★
Amos 'n' Andy: Anatomy of a Controversy
Nostalgia Family Video
PO Box 606
Baker City, OR 97814   Ph: (503)523-9034
1983. **Program Description:** A documentary examining both sides of the racial argument surrounding the old sitcom, including interviews with Jesse Jackson and Redd Foxx. A complete episode of the show is included. **Length:** 60 mins. **Format:** Beta, VHS. **Acquisition:** Purchase. **Use:** Home.

★4752★
Anansi
Rabbit Ears Home Video
131 Rowayton Ave.   Ph: (203)857-3760
Rowayton, CT 06853   Fax: (203)857-3777
1991. **Program Description:** Anansi is a spider who manages to outwit a prideful snake but then gets caught up in his own lies. Adaptation of a Jamaican folktale which features the reggae music of UB40. **Length:** 30 mins. **Format:** VHS. **Acquisition:** Purchase. **Use:** Home.

★4753★
Anasa Briggs: Apartheid
1983. **Program Description:** The details of apartheid in South Africa are examined - -divestiture, federal constraints, public protests and more. **Length:** 30 mins. **Format:** Beta, VHS, 3/4U. **Acquisition:** Rent/Lease, Purchase. **Use:** Institution, SURA.

★4754★
Anasa Briggs: Blacks in Agriculture
Format: Beta, VHS, 3/4U. **Acquisition:** Rent/Lease, Purchase. 1983. **Length:** 30 mins. **Program Description:** A Look at how corporate monopolies, socioeconomic influences and racial stereotypes have all but kept blacks from the agriculture industry. **Use:** Institutional, SURA.

★4755★
Anasa Briggs: Gospel Festival
1984. **Program Description:** A look at gospel music, with a performance by 40 singers from various churches in the San Diego area. **Length:** 30 mins. **Format:** Beta, VHS, 3/4U. **Acquisition:** Rent/Lease, Purchase. **Use:** Institution, SURA.

★4756★
Anasa Briggs: Martin Luther King Jr. Memorial Special
Format: Beta, VHS, 3/4U. **Acquisition:** Rent/Lease, Purchase. 1984. **Length:** 30 mins. **Program Description:** Briggs interviews the administrators of San Bernadino, California, regarding their involvement in the building of a King memorial in their town, in the form of a 11-foot bronze statue. **Use:** Institution, Home.

★4757★
Anasa Briggs: Water of Your Bath
1984. **Program Description:** Briggs looks at the work of modern black poets Langston Hughes, Margaret Walker, Don L. Lee, Notzake Shange, Sonia Sanchez and others. **Length:** 30 mins. **Format:** Beta, VHS, 3/4U. **Acquisition:** Rent/Lease, Purchase. **Use:** Institution, Home.

★4758★
Ancient Africans
International Film Foundation
155 W. 72nd St.
New York, NY 10023   Ph: (212)580-1111
197?. **Program Description:** This film traces the roots of African history from Stone Age ruins to the fabled Kingdoms of Kush and Zimbabwe in the east and Ghana, Mali, and Songhai in the west. **Length:** 27 mins. **Format:** 3/4U, Special order formats. **Acquisition:** Purchase. **Use:** Institution, SURA.

★4759★
And the Children Shall Lead
Public Media Video
5547 N. Ravenswood Ave.   Ph: (312)878-2600
Chicago, IL 60640-1199   Fax: (312)878-8406
          Free: 800-826-3456
1985. **Program Description:** From the PBS "Wonderworks" series. Glover and Burton host and narrate this program on civil rights from a child's point of view. **Length:** 60 mins. **Format:** VHS. **Acquisition:** Purchase. **Use:** Home.

★4760★
Any Child is My Child
Cinema Guild
1697 Broadway   Ph: (212)246-5522
New York, NY 10019   Fax: (212)246-5525
1989. **Program Description:** The oppression of children by the apartheid regime in South Africa is the focus of this film. **Length:** 54 mins. **Format:** Beta, VHS, 3/4U. **Acquisition:** Purchase. **Use:** Institution.

★4761★
Apartheid, Part 5
PBS Video
11858 La Grange Ave.   Ph: (213)820-0991
Los Angeles, CA 90025   Fax: (213)826-4779
1987. **Program Description:** A documentary with rare footage of the 1987 confrontations between dissident white Africaners and black leaders from the outlawed African National Congress (ANC) in racially torn South Africa. **Length:** 60 mins. **Format:** Beta, VHS, 3/4U. **Acquisition:** Purchase, Rent/Lease. **Use:** Institution, SURA.

★4762★
Archie Shepp: "I Am Jazz. . .It's My Life"
Music Video Distributors
O'Neill Industrial Center   Ph: (215)272-7771
1210 Standbridge St.   Fax: (215)272-6074
Norristown, PA 19403   Free: 800-888-0486
1984. **Program Description:** Jazz musician Archie Shepp has been playing music since the 1950's and throughout the years has developed political and social theories related to jazz music as a movement. In addition to performing in this film he speaks on the African origins of jazz, and on what he perceives as the revolutionary purpose of jazz. He also talks about the invisibility and isolation of Black people in society. **Length:** 52 mins. **Format:** VHS. **Acquisition:** Purchase. **Use:** Home.

★4763★
Are People All the Same
Pyramid Film & Video
Box 1048   Ph: (310)828-7577
2801 Colorado Ave.   Fax: (310)453-9083
Santa Monica, CA 90406   Free: 800-421-2304
1977. **Program Description:** This part of the "Who We Are" series features live action and animation showing children the meaning of race and the uniqueness of each and every person. **Length:** 9 mins. **Format:** Beta, VHS, 3/4U. **Acquisition:** Rent/Lease, Purchase, Duplication License. **Use:** Institution, Home, SURA.

★4764★
As I Remember It: A Portrait of Dorothy West
Women Make Movies
462 Broadway, Ste. 501   Ph: (212)925-0606
New York, NY 10013   Fax: (212)925-2052
1991. **Program Description:** A recollection of the life of African-American author Dorothy West who, although her father was born a slave, lived a middle class life in Boston during the early 1900s. The viewer learns not only about Ms. West but about other leaders of the Harlem Renaissance of the 1920s. **Length:** 56 mins. **Format:** VHS. **Acquisition:** Purchase. **Use:** Institution.

★4765★
The Autobiography of Miss Jane Pittman
1974. **Program Description:** The history of blacks in the South is seen through the eyes of a 110-year-old former slave. From the Civil War through the Civil Rights movement, Miss Pittman relates every

piece of black history, allowing the viewer to experience the injustices. Tyson is spectacular in moving, highly acclaimed television drama. Received nine Emmy awards; adapted by Tracy Keenan Wynn from the novel by Ernest J. Gaines. **Length:** 110 mins. **Format:** Beta, VHS. **Acquisition:** Purchase. **Use:** Home.

★4766★
Back Inside Herself
Women Make Movies
462 Broadway, Ste. 501   Ph: (212)925-0606
New York, NY 10013   Fax: (212)925-2052
1984. **Program Description:** This poetic film urges black women to reject imposed notions and create their own identities. **Length:** 5 mins. **Format:** Beta, VHS, 3/4U. **Acquisition:** Purchase, Rent/Lease. **Use:** Institution, SURA.

★4767★
Backyard
First Run/Icarus Films   Ph: (212)727-1711
153 Waverly Pl.   Fax: (212)989-7649
New York, NY 10014   Free: 800-876-1710
1983. **Program Description:** Ross McElwee turned his camera on his family and neighbors in their genteel Southern town, without embarrassment. The interdependencies and estrangement of Southern blacks and whites living together is explored. **Length:** 60 mins. **Format:** VHS. **Acquisition:** Purchase. **Use:** Home.

★4768★
The Barriers
Film Video Library
University of Michigan
919 S. University Ave., Rm. 207
Ann Arbor, MI 48109-1185   Ph: (313)764-5360
1970. **Program Description:** An exploration of the patterns of urban development unique to the U.S. , and the white attitudes that combine to create a black ghetto. **Length:** 29 mins. **Format:** 3/4U, Special order formats. **Acquisition:** Rent/Lease, Purchase. **Use:** Institution, CCTV, CATV, BCTV.

★4769★
Beauty Basics for the Contemporary Black Woman
Cambridge Career Products   Ph: (304)344-8550
PO Box 2153   Fax: (304)744-9351
Charleston, WV 25328-2153   Free: 800-468-4227
1987. **Program Description:** The Broadway star tells black women how to make themselves up so they'll look their best. **Length:** 30 mins. **Format:** VHS. **Acquisition:** Purchase. **Use:** Institution, Home.

★4770★
Beauty in the Bricks
Media Project, Inc.
PO Box 4093
Portland, OR 97208
1988. **Program Description:** Just because a 15-year-old black girl lives in a low income project, doesn't mean she can't lead a normal life, with dreams like most other privileged children. This program follows the routine of Karen Morgan and her friends. At the conclusion, Karen is accepted into a Dallas high school for gifted children. **Length:** 29 mins. **Format:** Beta, VHS. **Acquisition:** Rent/Lease, Purchase. **Use:** Institution.

★4771★
Bebe's Kids
Paramount Home Video
5555 Melrose Ave.
Los Angeles, CA 90038-3197   Ph: (213)956-5000
1992. **Program Description:** When ladies' man Robin falls for the lovely Jamika, he gets some unexpected surprises when he takes her out on a first date to an amusement park. It seems Jamika has a little boy and she is also babysitting for her neighbor Bebe's three trouble-making kids. What follows is a day of torment as the children try to sabotage Robin's romantic intentions. Film takes some funny pot-shots at black culture, white people, and Disneyland. The children are amusing, especially baby PeeWee, a tot with chronically dirty diapers and Tone Loc's gravelly voice. Based on characters created by comedian Robin Harris. The video includes the seven-

minute animated short "Itsy Bitsy Spider." **Length:** 74 mins. **Format:** Beta, VHS. **Acquisition:** Purchase. **Use:** Home.

★4772★
Becoming a Woman in Okrika
Filmakers Library, Inc.
124 E. 40th
New York, NY 10016   Ph: (212)808-4980
1991. **Program Description:** A Nigerian village is the site of this wonderful tale about a young girl's coming of age. Narrated by a woman, a society's tradition continues to be preserved. Includes non-gratuitous topless footage. **Length:** 27 mins. **Format:** VHS. **Acquisition:** Purchase, Rent/Lease. **Use:** Institution.

★4773★
Behind the Mask: A Fresh Approach to Fighting Prejudice
Anson Schloat   Ph: (914)747-0177
175 Tompkins Ave.   Fax: (914)747-1744
Pleasantville, NY 10570-9973   Free: 800-833-2004
19??. **Program Description:** In this animated short on prejudice, a "Red" meets two "Blues" and stereotypes them because they are unfamiliar. When the Blues react, all colors learn a lesson. **Length:** 8 mins. **Format:** VHS. **Acquisition:** Purchase. **Use:** Institution.

★4774★
Behind the Scenes
CAMERA THREE PRODUCTIONS, INC.
PO Box 994   Ph: (203)927-1964
Kent, CT 06757   Fax: (203)927-1965
197?. **Program Description:** Juanita Hall introduces and sings songs made famous by blues singers such as Bessie Smith and Billie Holliday in this program. **Length:** 30 mins. **Format:** Beta, VHS, EJ, 3/4U, Q. **Acquisition:** Duplication, Free Duplication. **Use:** Institution, SURA.

★4775★
Benedita Da Silva
Cinema Guild
1697 Broadway   Ph: (212)246-5522
New York, NY 10019   Fax: (212)246-5525
1990. **Program Description:** Chronicles the 1990 re-election campaign of the first black woman Senator in Brazil, who overcame her beginnings in a Brazilian slum. **Length:** 30 mins. **Format:** VHS, 3/4U. **Acquisition:** Rent/Lease, Purchase. **Use:** Institution.

★4776★
Bernard's Gang
New Dimension Media, Inc.   Ph: (503)484-7125
85803 Lorane Hwy.   Fax: (503)484-5267
Eugene, OR 97405   Free: 800-288-4456
1987. **Program Description:** A teenage boy becomes a leader of a gang in a South African shanty town. **Length:** 28 mins. **Format:** Beta, VHS. **Acquisition:** Purchase. **Use:** Institution.

★4777★
The Best of Black Journal
William Greaves Productions, Inc.   Ph: (212)265-6150
230 W. 55th St.   Fax: (212)315-0027
New York, NY 10019   Free: 800-874-8314
1970. **Program Description:** A series of programs that encompass various aspects of the black experience from the fine arts to politics. **Length:** 25 mins. **Format:** Beta, VHS. **Acquisition:** Rent/Lease, Purchase. **Use:** Institution, BCTV.

★4778★
Beyond Black and White
J. Miller Associates   Ph: (818)508-6553
13949 Ventura Blvd., Ste. 310 Fax: (818)508-6572
Sherman Oaks, CA 91423   Free: 800-331-8454
1984. **Program Description:** Dramatizes the psychological and sociological origins of prejudice against minorities and women. **Length:** 28 mins. **Format:** Beta, VHS, 3/4U. **Acquisition:** Purchase. **Use:** Institution, CCTV.

★4779★
Biko: Breaking the Silence
California Newsreel
149 Ninth St., Ste. 420
San Francisco, CA 94103   Ph: (415)621-6196
   Fax: (415)621-6522

1988. **Program Description:** This film traces Steve Biko's role in the Black Consciousness movement in South Africa. Biko, who was allegedly murdered by the government, played a unique and powerful role in opposing apartheid. **Length:** 52 mins. **Format:** VHS, Special order formats. **Acquisition:** Rent/Lease, Purchase, Duplication. **Use:** Institution, Home, SURA.

★4780★
Bill Moyers: Circle of Recovery
Mystic Fire Video
PO Box 1092
Cooper Sta.
New York, NY 10276   Ph: (212)941-0999
   Fax: (212)941-1443

1991. **Program Description:** The struggle of seven African-American men to beat their various addictions and become role models for others in their community. The program examines the societal assumption that blacks cannot shake chemical addiction and return to lives of fulfillment. A leaflet, "How to Find a Circle of Recovery," is included with the video. **Length:** 60 mins. **Format:** VHS. **Acquisition:** Purchase. **Use:** Home.

★4781★
Bird
Music Video Distributors
O'Neill Industrial Center
1210 Standbridge St.
Norristown, PA 19403   Ph: (215)272-7771
   Fax: (215)272-6074
   Free: 800-888-0486

1988. **Program Description:** The richly-textured, though sadly one-sided biography of jazz sax great Charlie Parker, from his rise to stardom to his premature death via extended heroin use. A remarkably assured, deeply imagined film from Eastwood that never really shows the Bird's genius of creation. The soundtrack features Parker's own solos re-mastered from original recordings. **Length:** 160 mins. **Format:** Beta, VHS, LV. **Acquisition:** Purchase. **Use:** Home.

★4782★
Black America Series
Centre Communications
1800 30th St., Ste. 207
Boulder, CO 80301   Ph: (303)444-1166
   Fax: (303)444-1168
   Free: 800-886-1166

1990. **Program Description:** Various black people who have made important contributions to their race are profiled. **Length:** 32 mins. **Format:** Beta, VHS, 3/4U. **Acquisition:** Purchase, Rent/Lease. **Use:** Institution, SURA.

★4783★
Black American Conservatives
PBS Video
11858 La Grange Ave.
Los Angeles, CA 90025   Ph: (213)820-0991
   Fax: (213)826-4779

1992. **Program Description:** Black conservative leaders support community-based entrepreneurship, proven through history to be highly effective, in place of less effective governmental aid. **Length:** 58 mins. **Format:** VHS. **Acquisition:** Purchase. **Use:** Home, Institution.

★4784★
Black Americans
Society for Visual Education, Inc. (SVE)
1345 Diversey Pkwy.
Chicago, IL 60614-1299   Ph: (312)525-1500
   Fax: (312)525-9474
   Free: 800-829-1900

1989. **Program Description:** Black Americans who have made notable achievements in their fields are given brief biographies in these two programs. **Length:** 20 mins. **Format:** VHS, 3/4U. **Acquisition:** Purchase, Duplication. **Use:** Institution, CCTV, Home.

★4785★
Black Americans: Artists, Entertainers and Athletes
Afro-Am Distributing Company
407 E. 25th St., Ste. 600
Chicago, IL 60616   Ph: (312)791-1611
   Fax: (312)791-0921

19??. **Program Description:** An inspirational overview of contributions by outstanding black Amreicans including Leontyne Price, Henry O. Tanner and Althea Gibson. **Length:** 20 mins. **Format:** VHS. **Acquisition:** Purchase. **Use:** Home.

★4786★
Black Americans of Achievement Series
Library Video Co.
PO Box 1110
Bala Cynwyd, PA 19004   Ph: (215)667-0200
   Fax: (215)667-3426
   Free: 800-843-3620

1992. **Program Description:** Companion to the Chelsea House "Black Americans of Achievement" book series, this set of twelve videos (five titles listed here) chronicles the lives and achievements of African-American men and women in many different professions and time eras. Combines interviews, historical and live action footage for comprehensive coverage. **Length:** 30 mins. **Format:** VHS. **Acquisition:** Purchase. **Use:** Institution.

★4787★
Black Americans, Part 1
Dallas County Community College District
Center for Educational Telecommunications
Dallas Telecourses
9596 Walnut St.
Mesquite, TX 75243   Ph: (214)952-0303
   Fax: (214)952-0329

1980. **Program Description:** This is the first of two programs that trace the history of black Americans from the Reconstruction period through World War II. **Length:** 28 mins. **Format:** 3/4U. **Acquisition:** Purchase. **Use:** Institution, CCTV.

★4788★
Black Americans, Part 2
Dallas County Community College District
Center for Educational Telecommunications
Dallas Telecourses
9596 Walnut St.
Mesquite, TX 75243   Ph: (214)952-0303
   Fax: (214)952-0329

1980. **Program Description:** In the second program the history of black Americans from the Civil Rights Movement of the 1950s to contemporary issues is discussed. **Length:** 28 mins. **Format:** 3/4U. **Acquisition:** Purchase. **Use:** Institution, CCTV.

★4789★
Black Americans: Political Leaders, Educators and Scientists
Afro-Am Distributing Company
407 E. 25th St., Ste. 600
Chicago, IL 60616   Ph: (312)791-1611
   Fax: (312)791-0921

19??. **Program Description:** An overview of the contributions made by several notable black Americans, including Thurgood Marshall and Shirley Chisholm. **Length:** 20 mins. **Format:** VHS. **Acquisition:** Purchase. **Use:** Institution, Home, SURA.

★4790★
Black and White: "Unless We. . .Live Together"
AEF/Capital Communications
3807 Dickerson Rd.
Nashville, TN 37207   Ph: (615)868-2040
   Fax: (615)868-5239
   Free: 800-822-5678

1973. **Program Description:** Martin Luther King's words set the tone for this examination of black-white relations over the years. **Length:** 16 mins. **Format:** Beta, VHS, 3/4U. **Acquisition:** Purchase. **Use:** Institution, SURA.

★4791★
Black and White: Uptight
Phoenix/BFA Films
468 Park Ave., S.
New York, NY 10016   Ph: (212)684-5910
   Free: 800-221-1274

1969. **Program Description:** Prejudice is the issue in this probing show. The social and economic differences that exist between blacks and whites are examined. Narration by Robert Culp. **Length:** 35 mins. **Format:** Beta, VHS, 3/4U. **Acquisition:** Purchase. **Use:** Institution, SURA.

★4792★
The Black Athlete
Pyramid Film & Video
Box 1048   Ph: (310)828-7577
2801 Colorado Ave.   Fax: (310)453-9083
Santa Monica, CA 90406   Free: 800-421-2304

1979. **Program Description:** The changing role of blacks in sports is reviewed. Footage of early black athletes such as Jack Johnson, Joe Louis, and Jackie Robinson is included with interviews of O. J. Simpson, Harry Edwards, Muhammed Ali, Arthur Ashe, and others. **Length:** 58 mins. **Format:** Beta, VHS, 3/4U. **Acquisition:** Rent/Lease, Purchase, Duplication License. **Use:** Institution, Home, SURA.

★4793★
Black Catholics: People of Hope
Franciscan Communications   Ph: (213)746-2916
1229 S. Santee St.   Fax: (213)747-9126
Los Angeles, CA 90015   Free: 800-421-8510

1987. **Program Description:** Black activity in the Catholic church is followed. **Length:** 28 mins. **Format:** Beta, VHS, 3/4U. **Acquisition:** Purchase, Rent/Lease. **Use:** Institution, SURA.

★4794★
Black Caucus
Film Video Library
University of Michigan
919 S. University Ave., Rm. 207
Ann Arbor, MI 48109-1185   Ph: (313)764-5360

1970. **Program Description:** A look at the movement of the black man, from the outskirts of political participation to the heart of politics. Part of the "Black Experience" series. **Length:** 29 mins. **Format:** 3/4U, Special order formats. **Acquisition:** Rent/Lease, Purchase. **Use:** Institution, CCTV, CATV, BCTV.

★4795★
Black Celebration: A Rebellion Against the Commodity
Video Data Bank
School of the Art Institute of Chicago   Ph: (312)899-5172
37 S. Wabash Ave.   Fax: (312)263-0141
Chicago, IL 60603   Free: 800-634-8544

1988. **Program Description:** Tony Cokes juxtaposes re-edited broadcast and archival footage with quotations in the form of text and voice-overs to provide a provocative look at the urban Black riots of the 1960s. **Length:** 17 mins. **Format:** VHS, 3/4U. **Acquisition:** Rent/Lease, Purchase. **Use:** Institution.

★4796★
Black Dimensions in American Art
AIMS Media   Ph: (818)773-4300
9710 DeSoto Ave.   Fax: (818)341-6700
Chatsworth, CA 91311-4409   Free: 800-367-2467

1970. **Program Description:** This program examines the important creations of America's most celebrated black artists, representing every major style in painting today. **Length:** 11 mins. **Format:** Beta, VHS, 3/4U. **Acquisition:** Purchase, Duplication License. **Use:** Institution, SURA.

★4797★
The Black Experience
Film Video Library
University of Michigan
919 S. University Ave., Rm. 207
Ann Arbor, MI 48109-1185   Ph: (313)764-5360

1970. **Program Description:** This program looks at the origins of black Americans: how history has shaped their attitudes, and crucial choices blacks have made to influence history's course. **Length:** 29 mins. **Format:** 3/4U, Special order formats. **Acquisition:** Rent/Lease, Purchase. **Use:** Institution, CCTV, CATV, BCTV.

★4798★
Black Experience and American Education
Film Video Library
University of Michigan
919 S. University Ave., Rm. 207
Ann Arbor, MI 48109-1185   Ph: (313)764-5360

1970. **Program Description:** A look at how the American education system has affected and has been affected by the black experience. Part of the "Black Experience" series. **Length:** 29 mins. **Format:** 3/4U, Special order formats. **Acquisition:** Rent/Lease, Purchase. **Use:** Institution, CCTV, CATV, BCTV.

★4799★
Black Girl
University of California - Berkeley
  Extension Media Center
2176 Shattuck Ave.
Berkeley, CA 94704   Ph: (510)642-0460

1982. **Program Description:** A black girl struggles against obstacles to become a ballet dancer. **Length:** 30 mins. **Format:** VHS, 3/4U. **Acquisition:** Purchase, Rent/Lease. **Use:** Institution, SURA.

★4800★
Black Heroes
Society for Visual Education, Inc. (SVE)   Ph: (312)525-1500
1345 Diversey Pkwy.   Fax: (312)525-9474
Chicago, IL 60614-1299   Free: 800-829-1900

1989. **Program Description:** Harriet Tubman, Nat Turner, Martin Luther King, Jr., and others who have advanced the cause of racial equality are profiled. **Length:** 20 mins. **Format:** VHS, 3/4U. **Acquisition:** Purchase, Duplication. **Use:** Institution, CCTV, Home.

★4801★
Black Heroes: Builders, Dreamers and More

19??. **Program Description:** The focus here is on educators and religious leaders including W.E.B. DuBois, Charlotte Hawkins Brown, Dr. King and more. **Length:** 20 mins. **Format:** VHS. **Acquisition:** Purchase. **Use:** Institution, Home, SURA.

★4802★
Black Heroes: Freedom Fighters, Cowboys and More

19??. **Program Description:** A look at characters such as Crispus Attucks, Harriet Tubman, Nat Turner, Buffalo Soldiers and black cowboys at the Chisholm Trail. **Length:** 20 mins. **Format:** VHS. **Acquisition:** Purchase. **Use:** Institution, Home, SURA.

★4803★
Black History: Lost, Stolen or Strayed
Phoenix/BFA Films
468 Park Ave., S.   Ph: (212)684-5910
New York, NY 10016   Free: 800-221-1274

1968. **Program Description:** Bill Cosby is narrator of this eye-opening show which reviews the black contribution to the development of the United States. **Length:** 54 mins. **Format:** Beta, VHS, 3/4U. **Acquisition:** Purchase. **Use:** Institution, SURA.

★4804★
Black Is My Color: The African American Experience
Rainbow Educational Video, Inc.   Ph: (516)589-6643
170 Keyland Ct.   Fax: (516)589-6131
Bohemia, NY 11716   Free: 800-331-4047

1992. **Program Description:** In an attempt to teach children to appreciate black culture and the cultural, scientific and political contributions of its people, a multi-cultural group of children discusses what it means to be black in America. Elaborated upon with film clips, photographs and commentary, topics discussed include slavery; the Abolitionists; the Civil War; Reconstruction and Segregation; and Civil Rights. Comes with teacher's guide. **Length:** 15 mins. **Format:** VHS. **Acquisition:** Purchase. **Use:** Institution.

★4805★
Black Jazz & Blues
Music Video Distributors
O'Neill Industrial Center Ph: (215)272-7771
1210 Standbridge St. Fax: (215)272-6074
Norristown, PA 19403 Free: 800-888-0486

19??. **Program Description:** Three classic jazz/blues shorts, "St. Louis Blues" (1929), "Symphony in Black" (1935), and "Caldonia" (1945). Features Bessie Smith, Duke Ellington, Lewis Jordan, and Billie Holiday. **Length:** 44 mins. **Format:** Beta, VHS. **Acquisition:** Purchase. **Use:** Home.

★4806★
Black Journal
WNET/Thirteen Non-Broadcast
356 W. 58th St.
New York, NY 10019 Ph: (212)560-3045

1977. **Program Description:** A series of current-interest interviews with the common theme of black presence in a white world. **Length:** 30 mins. **Format:** Beta, VHS, 3/4U. **Acquisition:** Rent/Lease, Purchase. **Use:** Institution, CCTV, Home.

★4807★
Black Like Me
Rhino Home Video Ph: (310)828-1980
2225 Colorado Ave. Fax: (310)453-5529
Santa Monica, CA 90404 Free: 800-843-3670

1964. **Program Description:** Based on John Howard Griffin's successful book about how Griffin turned his skin black with a drug and traveled the South to experience prejudice firsthand. Neither the production nor the direction enhance the material. **Length:** 107 mins. **Format:** Beta, VHS. **Acquisition:** Purchase. **Use:** Home.

★4808★
Black Literature
NETCHE (Nebraska ETV Council for
 Higher Education)
1800 N. 33rd St.
Box 83111
Lincoln, NE 68583 Ph: (402)472-3611

1971. **Program Description:** These programs illustrate the fact that black literature includes a dynamic and forceful body of work by writers with a wide variety of experiences and styles. **Length:** 30 mins. **Format:** EJ. **Acquisition:** Rent/Lease, Purchase, Subscription. **Use:** Institution, CCTV, BCTV, SURA.

★4809★
Black Men: Uncertain Futures
Maryland Public Television Ph: (410)356-5600
11767 Owings Mills Blvd. Fax: (410)581-4338
Owings Mills, MD 21117-1499 Free: 800-873-6154

19??. **Program Description:** Explores the plight and future of the black urban male in America. Includes discussions with young black men, the media's portrayals of black men, and an examination of problems and solutions offered by experts. **Length:** 60 mins. **Format:** Beta, VHS, 3/4U. **Acquisition:** Rent/Lease, Purchase. **Use:** Institution, CCTV.

★4810★
Black Music in America: From Then Till Now
Learning Corporation of America Ph: (708)940-1260
108 Wilmot Rd. Fax: (708)940-3600
Deerfield, IL 60015-9990 Free: 800-621-2131

1971. **Program Description:** The history of the black contribution to American music. Includes performances by Louis Armstrong, Mahalia Jackson, Duke Ellington, Count Basie, Nina Simone, and Bessie Smith. **Length:** 28 mins. **Format:** Beta, VHS. **Acquisition:** Rent/Lease, Purchase. **Use:** Institution, SURA.

★4811★
Black Music Now
NETCHE (Nebraska ETV Council for
 Higher Education)
1800 N. 33rd St.
Box 83111
Lincoln, NE 68583 Ph: (402)472-3611

1970. **Program Description:** Professor Baker discusses jazz as an art form and the role of black music in black culture. **Length:** 30 mins. **Format:** VHS, EJ. **Acquisition:** Rent/Lease, Purchase, Subscription. **Use:** Institution, CCTV, BCTV, SURA.

★4812★
Black Olympians 1904-1984: Athletics. . .in America
Churchill Films
12210 Nebraska Ave. Ph: (310)207-6600
Los Angeles, CA 90025 Fax: (310)207-1330

1986. **Program Description:** A mini-history of the role of the black athlete in the Olympic Games, including Jesse Owens, the Mexico City '68 salute and more. **Length:** 28 mins. **Format:** VHS, 3/4U. **Acquisition:** Purchase. **Use:** Institution, Home, SURA.

★4813★
Black Panthers: Huey Newton/Black Panther Newsreel
International Historic Films, Inc. (IHF)
PO Box 29035 Ph: (312)927-2900
Chicago, IL 60629 Fax: (312)927-9211

1968. **Program Description:** A film focusing on the "Free Huey Newton" rally in California; a separate video features an interview with Newton from Alameda County Jail, plus the Panther 10-point plan presented by Bobby Seale. **Length:** 53 mins. **Format:** Beta, VHS, 3/4U. **Acquisition:** Purchase. **Use:** Institution, Home.

★4814★
Black Paths of Leadership
Churchill Films
12210 Nebraska Ave. Ph: (310)207-6600
Los Angeles, CA 90025 Fax: (310)207-1330

1986. **Program Description:** Profiles of three important black leaders in American history: Booker T. Washington, W.E.B. DuBois and Marcus Garvey. **Length:** 28 mins. **Format:** VHS, 3/4U. **Acquisition:** Purchase. **Use:** Institution, Home, SURA.

★4815★
Black People Get AIDS Too
Churchill Films
12210 Nebraska Ave. Ph: (310)207-6600
Los Angeles, CA 90025 Fax: (310)207-1330

1988. **Program Description:** The myth that AIDS is a white male disease is explored in this video. Available in two different versions. **Length:** 20 mins. **Format:** Beta, VHS, 3/4U. **Acquisition:** Purchase, Rent/Lease, Duplication License. **Use:** Institution, Home, SURA.

★4816★
Black Plays in White Theater
CAMERA THREE PRODUCTIONS, INC.
PO Box 994 Ph: (203)927-1964
Kent, CT 06757 Fax: (203)927-1965

197?. **Program Description:** The attitude of white people towards plays written by black authors is discussed in this program. **Length:** 30 mins. **Format:** Beta, VHS, EJ, 3/4U, Q. **Acquisition:** Duplication, Free Duplication. **Use:** Institution, SURA.

★4817★
The Black Policeman: Writing. . .Black Exemplars
AEF/Capital Communications Ph: (615)868-2040
3807 Dickerson Rd. Fax: (615)868-5239
Nashville, TN 37207 Free: 800-822-5678

1973. **Program Description:** Profile of Bill Baldwin, a Washington D.C. policeman, a man who loves his job. During riots, Baldwin worked night and day to save the city, and was then the victim of prejudice. The honest way he dealt with his problem is the focus of this program. **Length:** 16 mins. **Format:** Beta, VHS, 3/4U. **Acquisition:** Purchase. **Use:** Institution, SURA.

★4818★
Black Power in America: Myth or Reality
Facets Multimedia, Inc.
1517 W. Fullerton Ave.
Chicago, IL 60614   Ph: (312)281-9075
1988. **Program Description:** Focuses on some of the changes in society since the 1960s Civil Rights movement by looking at contemporary education and successful individuals who have achieved power and influence. **Format:** VHS. **Acquisition:** Purchase. **Use:** Home, Institution.

★4819★
The Black Presence in the Caribbean
NETCHE (Nebraska ETV Council for
  Higher Education)
1800 N. 33rd St.
Box 83111
Lincoln, NE 68583   Ph: (402)472-3611
1970. **Program Description:** The history of blacks in the Caribbean is summarized. **Length:** 30 mins. **Format:** Beta, VHS, 3/4U. **Acquisition:** Purchase, Rent/Lease, Subscription. **Use:** Institution, CCTV, BCTV, SURA.

★4820★
Black Roots in Africa
Atlantis Productions
1252 La Granada Dr.   Ph: (805)495-2790
Thousand Oaks, CA 91360   Fax: (805)495-0717
197?. **Program Description:** Traces the historical and cultural roots of American Blacks in Africa. **Length:** 17 mins. **Format:** Beta, VHS, 3/4U. **Acquisition:** Purchase. **Use:** Institution, SURA.

★4821★
Black Shadows on a Silver Screen
Proud To Be. . .A Black Video Collection
1235-E East Blvd., Ste. 209
Charlotte, NC 28203   Ph: (704)523-2227
19??. **Program Description:** Highlights the contributions of African Americans to early films. Features many early film clips. **Length:** 57 mins. **Format:** VHS. **Acquisition:** Purchase. **Use:** Home.

★4822★
Black Studies
University of Arizona VideoCampus
Harvill Bldg., No. 76
Box 4   Ph: (602)621-1735
Tucson, AZ 85721   Fax: (602)621-8136
1980. **Program Description:** A series which discusses the native origins and roots of black Americans. Programs are available individually. **Length:** 60 mins. **Format:** Beta, VHS, EJ, 3/4U. **Acquisition:** Rent/Lease, Purchase. **Use:** Institution, CCTV, Home.

★4823★
Black Studies: Then and Now
Society for Visual Education, Inc. (SVE)   Ph: (312)525-1500
1345 Diversey Pkwy.   Fax: (312)525-9474
Chicago, IL 60614-1299   Free: 800-829-1900
1992. **Program Description:** A series of four videos which present an overview of African-American history. Subjects include role models, the history of African-Americans during slavery and the Civil War, and the origins and celebration of Kwanzaa and other holidays. Designed for grades 4-6. **Length:** 60 mins. **Format:** VHS. **Acquisition:** Purchase. **Use:** Institution.

★4824★
Black to the Promised Land
First Run/Icarus Films   Ph: (212)727-1711
153 Waverly Pl.   Fax: (212)989-7649
New York, NY 10014   Free: 800-876-1710
1992. **Program Description:** Takes a look at the lives of 11 African-American teenagers from Bedford-Stuyvesant, Brooklyn to Kibbutz Lehavot Habashan, Israel. The teenagers are taken by their Jewish teacher to work for three months on the Israeli kibbutz. Challenges to stereotypes are felt by both the Israelis and the African-American

teenagers. **Length:** 95 mins. **Format:** VHS, Special order formats. **Acquisition:** Purchase. **Use:** Institution.

★4825★
The Black West
All Media Productions
Educational Div.
1514 Wealthy SE, Ste. 260
Grand Rapids, MI 49506   Ph: (616)459-9703
1992. **Program Description:** Focuses on the contributions of African-Americans to the Westward expansion and settlement. Unbiased narrative features true stories about African-American fur traders, explorers, cowboys, outlaws, swindlers, a lawman, and a woman. Includes expressive artwork and upbeat music. **Length:** 24 mins. **Format:** VHS. **Acquisition:** Purchase. **Use:** Institution.

★4826★
The Black West
Beacon Films   Ph: (708)328-6700
930 Pitner Ave.   Fax: (708)328-6706
Evanston, IL 60202   Free: 800-323-5448
1982. **Program Description:** Cowboy George Ellison, rodeo star Frank Greenway, and frontiersperson Eunice Norris share the experience of being black in the Wild West in this program, part of the "Were You There" series. **Length:** 28 mins. **Format:** Beta, VHS, 3/4U. **Acquisition:** Purchase. **Use:** Institution, SURA.

★4827★
Black Wings
Proud To Be. . .A Black Video Collection
1235-E East Blvd., Ste. 209
Charlotte, NC 28203   Ph: (704)523-2227
19??. **Program Description:** Focuses on the first African American aviators and the obstacles they encountered. Filmed in color and black and white. **Length:** 18 mins. **Format:** VHS. **Acquisition:** Purchase. **Use:** Home.

★4828★
Black Women Writers
Films for the Humanities & Sciences   Ph: (609)452-1128
PO Box 2053   Fax: (609)275-3767
Princeton, NJ 08543   Free: 800-257-5126
1990. **Program Description:** Writers such as Angela Davis, Alice Walker, Michelle Wallace, Mtosake Shange and Maya Angelou explain critical judgements, stating that their success is due to the focus of their critism being placed on black males. **Length:** 28 mins. **Format:** Beta, VHS. **Acquisition:** Purchase. **Use:** Institution.

★4829★
Blacks and the Constitution
PBS Video
11858 La Grange Ave.   Ph: (213)820-0991
Los Angeles, CA 90025   Fax: (213)826-4779
1987. **Program Description:** A look at how the rights of blacks have changed in this country from slavery times to the present, with respect to the Constitution. **Length:** 60 mins. **Format:** VHS, 3/4U. **Acquisition:** Purchase, Rent/Lease. **Use:** Institution, CCTV, CATV.

★4830★
Blacks and the Movies
NETCHE (Nebraska ETV Council for
  Higher Education)
1800 N. 33rd St.
Box 83111
Lincoln, NE 68583   Ph: (402)472-3611
1977. **Program Description:** Presents an interview with film critic Donald Bogle. **Length:** 30 mins. **Format:** EJ, 3/4U. **Acquisition:** Rent/Lease, Purchase, Subscription. **Use:** Institution, CCTV, BCTV, SURA.

★4831★
Blacks, Blues, Black
PBS Video
11858 La Grange Ave.   Ph: (213)820-0991
Los Angeles, CA 90025   Fax: (213)826-4779
1967. **Program Description:** Angelou develops and demonstrates
history, heritage, and habits of blacks and how their mores and
values have been preserved and assimilated into society. **Length:** 57
mins. **Format:** Beta, VHS, 3/4U. **Acquisition:** Rent/Lease, Purchase,
Off-Air Record. **Use:** Institution, CCTV, CATV.

★4832★
Blacks Britannica
Facets Multimedia, Inc.
1517 W. Fullerton Ave.
Chicago, IL 60614   Ph: (312)281-9075
1978. **Program Description:** Provides an analysis of the racial and
economic oppression of blacks within modern British society using
the context of British history and economic post-war crises. Also
offers a look at the growing politicization of blacks in England.
Length: 58 mins. **Format:** VHS. **Acquisition:** Purchase. **Use:** Home.

★4833★
Blind Tom
Barr Films
3490 E. Foothill Blvd.
PO Box 5667
Pasadena, CA 91107   Free: 800-234-7878

1991. **Program Description:** Dramatizes the life of Thomas
Bethune, better known as "Blind Tom." Born into slavery in 1849,
he displayed a remarkable talent for music which was exploited by
his owner, even after slavery was abolished. **Length:** 30 mins.
Format: VHS. **Acquisition:** Purchase, Rent/Lease. **Use:** Institution.

★4834★
Bloodlines and Bridges: The African Connection
PBS Video
11858 La Grange Ave.   Ph: (213)820-0991
Los Angeles, CA 90025   Fax: (213)826-4779
1986. **Program Description:** This program follows Marian Crawford,
an American orphan, who travels to Africa in search of her family's
past. **Length:** 30 mins. **Format:** Beta, VHS, 3/4U. **Acquisition:**
Purchase, Rent/Lease, Duplication, Off-Air Record. **Use:** Institution,
CCTV, Home, SURA.

★4835★
The Bloods of 'Nam
PBS Video
11858 La Grange Ave.   Ph: (213)820-0991
Los Angeles, CA 90025   Fax: (213)826-4779
1987. **Program Description:** This documentary follows the lives of
black soldiers who fought against discrimination in the army and
disillusionment when they returned home. **Length:** 58 mins. **Format:**
Beta, VHS, 3/4U. **Acquisition:** Purchase, Rent/Lease. **Use:**
Institution, SURA.

★4836★
Blues 1
Video Gems
12228 Venice Blvd., No. 504
Los Angeles, CA 90066
1983. **Program Description:** Brock Peters is the host of this historic
journey to the roots of the Blues. **Length:** 58 mins. **Format:** Beta,
VHS. **Acquisition:** Purchase. **Use:** Home.

★4837★
Body and Soul: Body, Part 1
Phoenix/BFA Films
468 Park Ave., S.   Ph: (212)684-5910
New York, NY 10016   Free: 800-221-1274
1968. **Program Description:** Harry Reasoner examines the black
American's contribution to sports in America. He interviews key
athletes such as Harry Edwards, leader of those who threatened

Olympic Games boycott. **Length:** 24 mins. **Format:** Beta, VHS,
3/4U. **Acquisition:** Purchase. **Use:** Institution, SURA.

★4838★
Booker T. Washington: Life and the Legacy
William Greaves Productions, Inc.
230 W. 55th St.
New York, NY 10019   Ph: (212)246-7221
1982. **Program Description:** A docudrama about the life and times
and controversial ideas of Booker T. Washington. **Length:** 30 mins.
Format: Beta, VHS. **Acquisition:** Rent/Lease, Purchase. **Use:**
Institution, BCTV.

★4839★
Booker T. Washington's Tuskegee America
Afro-Am Distributing Company
407 E. 25th St., Ste. 600   Ph: (312)791-1611
Chicago, IL 60616   Fax: (312)791-0921
1981. **Program Description:** A biography of Washington-his life,
career and achievements. **Length:** 25 mins. **Format:** Beta, VHS,
3/4U. **Acquisition:** Rent/Lease, Purchase, Duplication License. **Use:**
Institution, SURA.

★4840★
Bound to Strike Back
California Newsreel
149 Ninth St., Ste. 420   Ph: (415)621-6196
San Francisco, CA 94103   Fax: (415)621-6522
1987. **Program Description:** The first documentary to infiltrate
South Africa's press restrictions and give Americans a taste of
events in the strife-torn country. **Length:** 35 mins. **Format:** VHS,
Special order formats. **Acquisition:** Purchase, Rent/Lease. **Use:**
Institution.

★4841★
The Boy King
Coronet/MTI Film & Video   Ph: (708)940-1260
108 Wilmot Rd.   Fax: (708)940-3640
Deerfield, IL 60015   Free: 800-777-8100
1988. **Program Description:** The early life of civil rights leader Martin
Luther King, Jr. is examined in this drama. **Length:** 48 mins. **Format:**
Beta, VHS, 3/4U. **Acquisition:** Purchase, Rent/Lease. **Use:**
Institution, SURA.

★4842★
The Boyhood of Martin Luther King
FilmFair Communications
1560 Sherman Ave., No. 100
Evanston, IL 60201-4817
1984. **Program Description:** A dramatization of events from Martin
Luther King's childhood which influenced his later years. **Length:** 14
mins. **Format:** Beta, VHS, 3/4U. **Acquisition:** Purchase, Duplication
License. **Use:** Institution, SURA.

★4843★
Boyz N the Hood
Columbia Tristar Home Video
3400 Riverside Dr.   Ph: (818)972-8193
Burbank, CA 91505-4627   Fax: (818)972-0937
1991. **Program Description:** Singleton's debut as a writer and
director is an astonishing picture of young black men, four high
school students with different backgrounds, aims, and abilities trying
to survive Los Angeles gangs and bigotry. Excellent acting
throughout, with special nods to Fishburne and Gooding, Jr. Violent
outbreaks outside theaters where this ran only proves the urgency
of its passionately nonviolent, pro-family message. Hopefully those
viewers scared off at the time will give this a chance in the safety of
their VCRs. Singleton appears on the cassette on behalf of the
United Negro College Fund; he received Oscar nominations for Best
Original Screenplay and Best Director, making him the youngest
director ever so honored. The laserdisc version includes two extra
scenes and an interview with Singleton. **Length:** 112 mins. **Format:**
Beta, VHS, 8mm, LV. **Acquisition:** Purchase. **Use:** Home.

★4844★
Brown v. Board of Education
Coronet/MTI Film & Video   Ph: (708)940-1260
108 Wilmot Rd.   Fax: (708)940-3640
Deerfield, IL 60015   Free: 800-777-8100
1991. **Program Description:** Dramatization of the landmark decision features excerpts of the legal arguments which changed American schools forever. **Length:** 18 mins. **Format:** VHS. **Acquisition:** Purchase. **Use:** Institution.

★4845★
Brown vs. the Board of Education
Afro-Am Distributing Company
407 E. 25th St., Ste. 600   Ph: (312)791-1611
Chicago, IL 60616   Fax: (312)791-0921
19??. **Program Description:** A look at the 1954 Supreme Court decision which over turned the practice of segregation in public schools. **Length:** 10 mins. **Format:** VHS. **Acquisition:** Purchase. **Use:** Institution, Home, SURA.

★4846★
Busted Dreams
New Jersey Network
1573 Parkside Ave.
Trenton, NJ 08625   Ph: (609)530-5252
1983. **Program Description:** A group of black people talk about the tough circumstances which have destroyed their dreams. **Length:** 30 mins. **Format:** VHS, 3/4U. **Acquisition:** Rent/Lease, Purchase. **Use:** Institution.

★4847★
Careers for the 21st Century: African-American Role Model Series
Takeoff Video Educational Excellence
8808 St. Charles Rock Rd.   Fax: (314)427-0163
St. Louis, MO 63114   Free: 800-462-5232

199?. **Program Description:** 31 African-American individuals in a variety of professions explain what they do in terms that the potential entrant into the field can understand. Two volumes, available separately. **Length:** mins. **Format:** VHS. **Acquisition:** Purchase. **Use:** Institution.

★4848★
Chain of Tears
California Newsreel
149 Ninth St., Ste. 420   Ph: (415)621-6196
San Francisco, CA 94103   Fax: (415)621-6522
1991. **Program Description:** A dramatic, heartwrenching documentary of the black children who are victims in the struggle to overcome apartheid. Features shocking accounts of detention and torture of young people by South African police and authroities. Filmed on location in Moazmbique, Angola and in the black townships of South Africa. **Length:** 52 mins. **Format:** VHS. **Acquisition:** Purchase, Rent/Lease. **Use:** Institution.

★4849★
Charlotte Forten's Mission: Experiment in Freedom
Facets Multimedia, Inc.
1517 W. Fullerton Ave.
Chicago, IL 60614   Ph: (312)281-9075
1985. **Program Description:** Fact-based story, set during the Civil War. A wealthy, educated black woman, determined to prove to President Lincoln that blacks are equal to whites, journeys to a remote island off the coast of Georgia. There she teaches freed slaves to read and write. Part of the "American Playhouse" series on PBS. Preceded by "Solomon Northrup's Odyssey." **Length:** 120 mins. **Format:** VHS. **Acquisition:** Purchase. **Use:** Home.

★4850★
Children of Apartheid
California Newsreel
149 Ninth St., Ste. 420   Ph: (415)621-6196
San Francisco, CA 94103   Fax: (415)621-6522
1987. **Program Description:** The contrast between the lives of the children of South African President P.W. Botha and African National Congress leader Nelson Mandela reveals the dramatic difference bewtween black and white South Africa. Hosted by Walter Cronkite. **Length:** 49 mins. **Format:** VHS. **Acquisition:** Purchase, Rent/Lease. **Use:** Institution, Home.

★4851★
Children of Pride
Praeses Productions
28 Greene St.
New York, NY 10013   Ph: (212)925-1599
1984. **Program Description:** A documentary about a black Harlem man who has adopted over a dozen handicapped black children, the family thus formed, and the tribulations he's confronted in the process. **Length:** 60 mins. **Format:** Beta, VHS, 3/4U. **Acquisition:** Purchase. **Use:** Institution, Home.

★4852★
Children of Wax: A Folktale from Zimbabwe
Churchill Films
12210 Nebraska Ave.   Ph: (310)207-6600
Los Angeles, CA 90025   Fax: (310)207-1330
1988. **Program Description:** One of a group of five African children runs into trouble when he decides to go outside during the day instead of waiting for the cooler night. **Length:** 6 mins. **Format:** Beta, VHS, 3/4U. **Acquisition:** Purchase, Rent/Lease, Duplication License. **Use:** Institution, Home, SURA.

★4853★
The Children Were Watching
Direct Cinema Limited   Ph: (213)652-8000
PO Box 69799   Fax: (213)652-2346
Los Angeles, CA 90069-9976   Free: 800-345-6748
1960. **Program Description:** A look at families facing integration as a six-year-old black girl enters school in New Orleans. **Length:** 58 mins. **Format:** Beta, VHS, 3/4U, Special order formats. **Acquisition:** Rent/Lease, Purchase. **Use:** Institution, Home, SURA.

★4854★
Choices
BNA Communications, Inc.   Ph: (301)948-0540
9439 Key West Ave.   Fax: (301)948-2085
Rockville, MD 20850   Free: 800-233-6067
1990. **Program Description:** A 12-part training course, designed to help train managers in EEO and affirmative action. Tapes are available as a set or individually. Trainer and participant manuals are included. **Length:** mins. **Format:** Beta, VHS, 3/4U. **Acquisition:** Rent/Lease. **Use:** Institution.

★4855★
The Civil War, Episode 1: The Cause—1861
PBS Video
11858 La Grange Ave.   Ph: (213)820-0991
Los Angeles, CA 90025   Fax: (213)826-4779
1990. **Program Description:** The blowout PBS hit mini-series, five years in the making by author and filmmaker Ken Burns, is a staggering historical achievement. Episode 1 focuses on the causes of the Civil War from the schism created by Lincoln's election, John Brown's assault on Harper's Ferry, and the firing on Fort Sumpter. Also available as a set for $179.95. **Length:** 99 mins. **Format:** VHS, 3/4U. **Acquisition:** Purchase, Rent/Lease, Duplication License, Off-Air Record. **Use:** Institution, CCTV, CATV, Home.

★4856★
The Civil War, Episode 2: A Very Bloody Affair—1862
PBS Video
11858 La Grange Ave.   Ph: (213)820-0991
Los Angeles, CA 90025   Fax: (213)826-4779

1990. **Program Description:** Second in the enormously popular PBS series looks at the unexpectedly extreme costs in human life of the War Between the States. **Length:** 69 mins. **Format:** VHS, 3/4U. **Acquisition:** Purchase, Rent/Lease, Duplication License, Off-Air Record. **Use:** Institution, CCTV, CATV, Home.

★4857★
The Civil War, Episode 3: Forever Free—1862
PBS Video
11858 La Grange Ave.   Ph: (213)820-0991
Los Angeles, CA 90025   Fax: (213)826-4779

1990. **Program Description:** Third volume in the PBS Emmy-nominated mini-series covers Antietam, Robert E. Lee and Stonewall Jackson planning Confederate strategy, and Lincoln's decision to free the slaves. **Length:** 76 mins. **Format:** VHS, 3/4U. **Acquisition:** Purchase, Rent/Lease, Duplication License, Off-Air Record. **Use:** Institution, CCTV, CATV, Home.

★4858★
The Civil War, Episode 4: Simply Murder—1863
PBS Video
11858 La Grange Ave.   Ph: (213)820-0991
Los Angeles, CA 90025   Fax: (213)826-4779

1990. **Program Description:** Union forces meet disaster at Fredericksburg, and Gen. Lee wins a victory but loses Stonewall Jackson in the fourth episode of the Emmy-nominated PBS min-series. **Length:** 62 mins. **Format:** VHS, 3/4U. **Acquisition:** Purchase, Rent/Lease, Duplication License, Off-Air Record. **Use:** Institution, CCTV, CATV, Home.

★4859★
The Civil War, Episode 5: The Universe of Battle—1863
PBS Video
11858 La Grange Ave.   Ph: (213)820-0991
Los Angeles, CA 90025   Fax: (213)826-4779

1990. **Program Description:** Gettysburg, the battleground which claimed 150,000 American lives, is examined in the 5th episode of the Emmy-nominated PBS mini-series. **Length:** 95 mins. **Format:** VHS, 3/4U. **Acquisition:** Purchase, Rent/Lease, Duplication License, Off-Air Record. **Use:** Institution, CCTV, CATV, Home.

★4860★
The Civil War, Episode 6: Valley of the Shadow of Death—1864
PBS Video
11858 La Grange Ave.   Ph: (213)820-0991
Los Angeles, CA 90025   Fax: (213)826-4779

1990. **Program Description:** Profiles of Grant and Lee are offered, plus Sherman's assault on Atlanta, in this volume from the Emmy-nominated PBS mini-series. **Length:** 70 mins. **Format:** VHS, 3/4U. **Acquisition:** Purchase, Rent/Lease, Duplication License, Off-Air Record. **Use:** Institution, CCTV, CATV, Home.

★4861★
The Civil War, Episode 7: Most Hallowed Ground—1864
PBS Video
11858 La Grange Ave.   Ph: (213)820-0991
Los Angeles, CA 90025   Fax: (213)826-4779

1990. **Program Description:** The nation re-elects Abraham Lincoln, and the North turns General Lee's mansion into Arlington National Cemetery in this episode of the Emmy-nominated PBS mini-series. **Length:** 72 mins. **Format:** VHS, 3/4U. **Acquisition:** Purchase, Rent/Lease, Duplication License, Off-Air Record. **Use:** Institution, CCTV, CATV, Home.

★4862★
The Civil War, Episode 8: War is All Hell—1865
PBS Video
11858 La Grange Ave.   Ph: (213)820-0991
Los Angeles, CA 90025   Fax: (213)826-4779

1990. **Program Description:** Sherman marches to the sea and Lee surrenders to Grant in this episode from the Emmy-nominated PBS mini-series. **Length:** 69 mins. **Format:** VHS, 3/4U. **Acquisition:** Purchase, Rent/Lease, Duplication License, Off-Air Record. **Use:** Institution, CCTV, CATV, Home.

★4863★
The Civil War, Episode 9: The Better Angels of Our Nature—1865
PBS Video
11858 La Grange Ave.   Ph: (213)820-0991
Los Angeles, CA 90025   Fax: (213)826-4779

1990. **Program Description:** In this final episode of the Emmy-nominated PBS mini-series, Lincoln's assasination is examined, and the central characters of the war are summarized. **Length:** 68 mins. **Format:** VHS, 3/4U. **Acquisition:** Purchase, Rent/Lease, Duplication License, Off-Air Record. **Use:** Institution, CCTV, CATV, Home.

★4864★
Clemente & Robinson
First Run Video
3620 Overland Ave.   Ph: (310)202-8990
Los Angeles, CA 90034   Fax: (310)838-5212

19??. **Program Description:** Biographies of baseball greats Roberto Clemente and Jackie Robinson. **Length:** 45 mins. **Format:** Beta, VHS. **Acquisition:** Purchase. **Use:** Home.

★4865★
Clinical Cerebrovascular Disease in Hypertensive Blacks
Emory Medical Television Network
Emory University
Emory Medical Television Network-
    Department C
1440 Clifton Rd., NE
Atlanta, GA 30322   Ph: (404)616-3556

1986. **Program Description:** A look at stroke in blacks and how it is caused by environmentally-caused hypertension. **Length:** 33 mins. **Format:** VHS, 3/4U. **Acquisition:** Rent/Lease, Purchase, Subscription. **Use:** Institution, CCTV, CATV, BCTV, SURA.

★4866★
Coffee Colored Children
Women Make Movies
462 Broadway, Ste. 501   Ph: (212)925-0606
New York, NY 10013   Fax: (212)925-2052

1988. **Program Description:** A semi-autobiographical film about the effects of racism on children. **Length:** 15 mins. **Format:** Beta, VHS, 3/4U. **Acquisition:** Purchase, Rent/Lease. **Use:** Institution, SURA.

★4867★
Color Adjustment
California Newsreel
149 Ninth St., Ste. 420   Ph: (415)621-6196
San Francisco, CA 94103   Fax: (415)621-6522

1991. **Program Description:** The modern history of race relations in the U.S. in the arena of television. Traces the progress of blacks from caricatures to victims to mainstream as portrayed by TV. On two cassettes. **Length:** 45 mins. **Format:** VHS. **Acquisition:** Rent/Lease, Purchase. **Use:** Institution.

★4868★
The Color of Friendship
Learning Corporation of America   Ph: (708)940-1260
108 Wilmot Rd.   Fax: (708)940-3600
Deerfield, IL 60015-9990   Free: 800-621-2131

1981. **Program Description:** A black student and a white boy strike up a friendship at a recently integrated junior high which is put to the test when racial strife breaks out (shown as an ABC Afterschool

Special). **Length:** 47 mins. **Format:** Beta, VHS, 3/4U. **Acquisition:** Rent/Lease, Purchase. **Use:** Institution, SURA.

★4869★
The Color Purple
Warner Home Video, Inc.
4000 Warner Blvd.
Burbank, CA 91522   Ph: (818)954-6000
1985. **Program Description:** Celie is a poor black girl who fights for her self-esteem when she is separated from her sister and forced into a brutal marriage. Spanning 1909 to 1947 in a small Georgia town, the movie chronicles the joys, pains, and people in her life. Adaptation of Alice Walker's acclaimed book features strong lead from Goldberg (her screen debut), Glover, Avery, and talk-show host Winfrey (also her film debut). It's hard to see director Spielberg as the most suited for this one, but he acquits himself nicely, avoiding the facileness that sometimes flaws his pics. Brilliant photography by Allen Davian and musical score by Quincy Jones (who co-produced) compliment this strong film. **Length:** 154 mins. **Format:** Beta, VHS, LV. **Acquisition:** Purchase. **Use:** Home.

★4870★
Color Schemes
Women Make Movies
462 Broadway, Ste. 501   Ph: (212)925-0606
New York, NY 10013   Fax: (212)925-2052
1989. **Program Description:** The misconceptions of racial assimilation is explored through the metaphor of "color wash." **Length:** 28 mins. **Format:** Beta, VHS, 3/4U. **Acquisition:** Purchase, Rent/Lease. **Use:** Institution, SURA.

★4871★
Color Us Black
1968. **Program Description:** A look at the black man's struggle for identity over and above the white norm, as explained by a student group from Howard University. **Length:** 60 mins. **Format:** 3/4U, Special order formats. **Acquisition:** Rent/Lease, Purchase. **Use:** Institution, CCTV, Home, SURA.

★4872★
Combating Racism
Chinese for Affirmative Action
17 Walter U. Lum Pl.   Ph: (415)274-6750
San Francisco, CA 94108   Fax: (415)397-8770
1973. **Program Description:** In this program various community representatives from San Francisco are interviewed as to what can be done to combat racism. Among those interviewed were Leaonard Carter, George Tamsak, Mack Hall, Shone Martinez, John Chinn, and Margaret Cruz. **Length:** 30 mins. **Format:** EJ. **Acquisition:** Loan. **Use:** Institution, CCTV.

★4873★
Corridors of Freedom
California Newsreel
149 Ninth St., Ste. 420   Ph: (415)621-6196
San Francisco, CA 94103   Fax: (415)621-6522
1987. **Program Description:** Documentary of the eight African nations who formed the Southern African Development Coordination Conference (SADACC) in 1981 in order to wrest themselves from the long arm of South African oppression. **Length:** 52 mins. **Format:** VHS. **Acquisition:** Purchase, Rent/Lease. **Use:** Institution.

★4874★
Country Lovers, City Lovers
MGM/UA Home Video, Inc.
10000 W. Washington Blvd.
Culver City, CA 90232   Ph: (310)280-6212
1972. **Program Description:** Two adaptations of short stories by South African novelist Nadine Gordimer about interracial love. **Length:** 121 mins. **Format:** Beta, VHS. **Acquisition:** Purchase. **Use:** Home.

★4875★
Cry Freedom
MCA/Universal Home Video
70 Universal City Plaza   Ph: (818)777-6419
Universal City, CA 91608-9955   Fax: (818)733-0226
1987. **Program Description:** A romantic look at the short life of South African activist Steven Biko, and his friendship with the white news editor, Donald Woods. The film focuses on Woods' escape from Africa while struggling to bring Biko's message to the world. Based on a true story. **Length:** 157 mins. **Format:** Beta, VHS, LV. **Acquisition:** Purchase. **Use:** Home.

★4876★
A Cry of Defiance
Film Video Library
University of Michigan
919 S. University Ave., Rm. 207
Ann Arbor, MI 48109-1185   Ph: (313)764-5360
1970. **Program Description:** A discussion of social movements created by the black community in opposition to white bigotry. Part of the "Black Experience" series. **Length:** 29 mins. **Format:** 3/4U, Special order formats. **Acquisition:** Rent/Lease, Purchase. **Use:** Institution, CCTV, CATV, BCTV.

★4877★
Cry, the Beloved Country
Monterey Home Video   Ph: (818)597-0047
28038 Dorothy Dr., Ste. 1   Fax: (818)597-0105
Agoura Hills, CA 91301   Free: 800-424-2593
1951. **Program Description:** A black country minister travels to Johannesberg to be with his son after the youth is accused of killing a white man. Through the events of the trial, the horror, oppression, and destruction of South Africa's apartheid system are exposed. Startling and moving, the first entertainment feature set against the backdrop of apartheid. Still trenchant; based on the novel by Alan Paton. **Length:** 111 mins. **Format:** VHS. **Acquisition:** Purchase. **Use:** Home.

★4878★
Cycles
Women Make Movies
462 Broadway, Ste. 501   Ph: (212)925-0606
New York, NY 10013   Fax: (212)925-2052
1988. **Program Description:** A lively experimental film that reflects on black womanhood. **Length:** 15 mins. **Format:** Beta, VHS, 3/4U. **Acquisition:** Purchase, Rent/Lease. **Use:** Institution, SURA.

★4879★
Dance Like a River: Odadaa! Drumming and Dancing in the U.S.
1985. **Program Description:** Odadaa!, a Ga dance troup from the African country of Ghana, is seen rehearsing and performing traditional dances, as well as at rest in their Washington, D.C. home. **Length:** 45 mins. **Format:** VHS, 3/4U. **Acquisition:** Purchase, Rent/Lease. **Use:** Institution, Home.

★4880★
Dance Theatre of Harlem
Corinth Video
34 Gansevoort St.   Ph: (212)463-0305
New York, NY 10014   Free: 800-221-4720
1990. **Program Description:** A wonderful look at the Harlem Dance Theater and it's performers. **Length:** 117 mins. **Format:** Beta, VHS. **Acquisition:** Purchase. **Use:** Home.

★4881★
The Dancing Lion: An African Folktale
FilmFair Communications
1560 Sherman Ave., No. 100
Evanston, IL 60201-4817
1978. **Program Description:** Differentiates African Music from Western Music by its rhythms. **Length:** 11 mins. **Format:** Beta, VHS, 3/4U. **Acquisition:** Purchase, Duplication License. **Use:** Institution, SURA.

★4882★
A Day to Remember: August 28, 1963
PBS Video
11858 La Grange Ave.   Ph: (213)820-0991
Los Angeles, CA 90025   Fax: (213)826-4779
1978. **Program Description:** Documentary about the 1963 civil
rights demonstration in Washington, DC, led by Dr. King. **Length:** 29
mins. **Format:** Beta, VHS, 3/4U. **Acquisition:** Purchase, Rent/Lease,
Off-Air Record. **Use:** Institution, CCTV, CATV, Home.

★4883★
Deep North
Facets Multimedia, Inc.
1517 W. Fullerton Ave.
Chicago, IL 60614   Ph: (312)281-9075
1988. **Program Description:** Looks at racial prejudice since the
findings of the '60s Kerner Commission Report. Groups of New
Yorkers try psychodrama and group therapy to see if misperceptions
and racist feelings can be altered. **Length:** mins. **Format:** VHS.
Acquisition: Purchase. **Use:** Home.

★4884★
The Different Drummer: Blacks in the Military
Films Inc. Video
5547 N. Ravenswood Ave.   Ph: (312)878-2600
Chicago, IL 60640-1199   Free: 800-323-4222
1983. **Program Description:** This series examines the history of
Black involvement in all American military conflicts from colonial
times to the present day. **Length:** 58 mins. **Format:** Beta, VHS,
3/4U. **Acquisition:** Rent/Lease, Purchase. **Use:** Institution, SURA.

★4885★
**Digging for Slaves: The Excavation of American Slave
Sites**
Films for the Humanities & Sciences   Ph: (609)452-1128
PO Box 2053   Fax: (609)275-3767
Princeton, NJ 08543   Free: 800-257-5126
1992. **Program Description:** Through recent finds, archaeologists
are able to reconstruct the daily lives of American slaves and the
culture they brought with them from Africa. **Length:** 50 mins.
Format: VHS. **Acquisition:** Purchase. **Use:** Institution.

★4886★
Discovering History
The Media Guild
11722 Sorrento Valley Rd., Ste. E   Ph: (619)755-9191
San Diego, CA 92121   Fax: (619)755-4931
1991. **Program Description:** Three videos relate experiences of
women, minorities, and immigrants in America, and stress the
importance of participating in the system through voting. **Length:** 12
mins. **Format:** VHS. **Acquisition:** Purchase. **Use:** Institution.

★4887★
Do the Right Thing
MCA/Universal Home Video
70 Universal City Plaza   Ph: (818)777-6419
Universal City, CA 91608-9955   Fax: (818)733-0226
1989. **Program Description:** An uncompromising, brutal comedy
about the racial tensions surrounding a white-owned pizzeria in the
Bed-Stuy section of Brooklyn on the hottest day of the summer, and
the violence that eventually erupts. Ambivalent and, for the most
part, hilarious; Lee's coming-of-age. **Length:** 120 mins. **Format:**
Beta, VHS, LV. **Acquisition:** Purchase. **Use:** Home.

★4888★
Dr. Martin Luther King
Afro-Am Distributing Company
407 E. 25th St., Ste. 600   Ph: (312)791-1611
Chicago, IL 60616   Fax: (312)791-0921
19??. **Program Description:** A general overview of Dr. King's work
plus an introduction to the Civil Rights movement. **Length:** 15 mins.
Format: VHS. **Acquisition:** Purchase. **Use:** Institution, Home, SURA.

★4889★
Dr. Martin Luther King, Jr.
Society for Visual Education, Inc. (SVE)   Ph: (312)525-1500
1345 Diversey Pkwy.   Fax: (312)525-9474
Chicago, IL 60614-1299   Free: 800-829-1900
1988. **Program Description:** From his childhood to his death in
1968, the life of Dr. King is revealed. **Length:** 15 mins. **Format:** VHS,
3/4U. **Acquisition:** Purchase, Duplication. **Use:** Institution, CCTV,
Home.

★4890★
Dr. Martin Luther King, Jr. . . .An Amazing Grace
CRM/McGraw-Hill Films
674 Via de la Valle
PO Box 641
Del Mar, CA 92014
1978. **Program Description:** This program takes several stirring
speeches by Dr. Martin Luther King, Jr. to give a first-hand account
of this man, known as the "peaceful warrior." Even though he felt
violence was not the answer, his leadership caused a civil rights
movement beginning in 1955 with the bus boycott to one of full-scale
international importance. Available as a whole or in two parts.
Length: 62 mins. **Format:** Beta, VHS, 3/4U. **Acquisition:** Purchase.
Use: Institution, SURA.

★4891★
Don't Leave Out the Cowboys
19??. **Program Description:** A look at black cowboys, from the days
of the Old West and modern times as well. **Length:** 22 mins. **Format:**
VHS. **Acquisition:** Purchase. **Use:** Institution, Home, SURA.

★4892★
Don't Look Back: The Story of Leroy "Satchel" Paige
ABC Distribution Company
Capital Cities/ABC Video Enterprises
825 7th Ave.
New York, NY 10019-6001   Ph: (212)887-1725
1981. **Program Description:** Drama of the legendary baseball
pitcher who helped break down racial barriers, based on his
autobiography. Made-for-TV fare. Gossett hits a home run in the
lead, but the overall effort is a ground-rule double. **Length:** 98 mins.
Format: VHS. **Acquisition:** Purchase. **Use:** Home.

★4893★
A Dream Deferred
Film Video Library
University of Michigan
919 S. University Ave., Rm. 207
Ann Arbor, MI 48109-1185   Ph: (313)764-5360
1970. **Program Description:** After the American Revolution, slavery
became unique to blacks and provided for the early economic
development of our nation. Part of the "Black Experience" series.
Length: 29 mins. **Format:** 3/4U, Special order formats. **Acquisition:**
Rent/Lease, Purchase. **Use:** Institution, CCTV, CATV, BCTV.

★4894★
The Dred Scott Decision
Afro-Am Distributing Company
407 E. 25th St., Ste. 600   Ph: (312)791-1611
Chicago, IL 60616   Fax: (312)791-0921
19??. **Program Description:** A video "filmstrip" covering the
historical court battle which saw an American slave sue the
government for his freedom. **Length:** 15 mins. **Format:** VHS.
Acquisition: Purchase. **Use:** Institution, Home, SURA.

★4895★
Ease 'Em Back
Education Development Center, Inc.
55 Chapel St., Ste. 901   Ph: (617)969-7100
Newton, MA 02160   Free: 800-225-4276
19??. **Program Description:** This video program documents the
development of the EDC "Ethnic Studies Project: African Art and
Culture." It shows students of all age levels enthusiastically involved
in the creation of different African arts and crafts: tie-dying, batiking
cloth, weaving, and making religious masks, to name a few. **Length:**

60 mins. **Format:** 3/4U, Special order formats. **Acquisition:** Rent/Lease, Purchase. **Use:** Institution, CCTV, CATV, BCTV.

★4896★
EAV History of Jazz
Educational Audio Visual (EAV)
6465 N. Avondale
Chicago, IL 60631　　　　　　　　　　Free: 800-431-2196

1988. **Program Description:** Pianist Taylor demonstrates the history of jazz from its gospel roots to the avant-garde. Archival footage includes performances by Billie Holiday, Charlie Parker, Dave Brubeck, and Dizzy Gillespie. **Length:** 48 mins. **Format:** VHS. **Acquisition:** Purchase. **Use:** Institution.

★4897★
Ebony/Jet Guide to Black Excellence: The Entertainers
Public Media Video　　　　　　　　　Ph: (312)878-2600
5547 N. Ravenswood Ave.　　　　　　Fax: (312)878-8406
Chicago, IL 60640-1199　　　　　　　Free: 800-826-3456

1992. **Program Description:** Three African-Americans explain how their persistence helped them become successful entertainers. Meet Bill Cosby, author and actress Maya Angelou, and film and TV star Charles Dutton. **Length:** 35 mins. **Format:** VHS. **Acquisition:** Purchase. **Use:** Home.

★4898★
Ebony/Jet Guide to Black Excellence: The Entrepreneurs
Public Media Video　　　　　　　　　Ph: (312)878-2600
5547 N. Ravenswood Ave.　　　　　　Fax: (312)878-8406
Chicago, IL 60640-1199　　　　　　　Free: 800-826-3456

1992. **Program Description:** A look at three African-Americans who have built their own businesses: John H. Johnson of Johnson Publishing Company, Joshua I. Smith of the Maxima Corporation, and Oprah Winfrey, talk show host and CEO of Harpo Productions. **Length:** 35 mins. **Format:** VHS. **Acquisition:** Purchase. **Use:** Home.

★4899★
Ebony/Jet Guide to Black Excellence: The Leaders
Public Media Video　　　　　　　　　Ph: (312)878-2600
5547 N. Ravenswood Ave.　　　　　　Fax: (312)878-8406
Chicago, IL 60640-1199　　　　　　　Free: 800-826-3456

1992. **Program Description:** Meet three African-Americans who have become leaders and have opened the doors for others: L. Douglas Wilder, governor of Virginia; Marian Wright Edelman, founder and president of the Children's Defense Fund; and Dr. James P. Comer, the director of the Child Study Center at Yale University. **Length:** 35 mins. **Format:** VHS. **Acquisition:** Purchase. **Use:** Home.

★4900★
Education: A Basic Human Right
Cinema Guild
1697 Broadway　　　　　　　　　　　Ph: (212)246-5522
New York, NY 10019　　　　　　　　　Fax: (212)246-5525

1992. **Program Description:** Examines the separate school system in South Africa which has miseducated generations of black youth due to the policy of apartheid. Interviews educators, parents, and students about the problems facing the black educational system as well as the social problems of South Africa. **Length:** 45 mins. **Format:** VHS. **Acquisition:** Purchase, Rent/Lease. **Use:** Institution.

★4901★
EEOC Story
William Greaves Productions, Inc.　　Ph: (212)265-6150
230 W. 55th St.　　　　　　　　　　　Fax: (212)315-0027
New York, NY 10019　　　　　　　　　Free: 800-874-8314

1972. **Program Description:** An informal look at how The Equal Employment Opportunity Commission helps out women, minorities and the business world. **Length:** 38 mins. **Format:** Beta, VHS. **Acquisition:** Rent/Lease, Purchase. **Use:** Institution, BCTV.

★4902★
1861-1877: Civil War Reconstruction
CRM/McGraw-Hill Films
674 Via de la Valle
PO Box 641
Del Mar, CA 92014

1965. **Program Description:** This program examines the political conflicts over the issue of slavery that led to the Civil War. It also illustrates how the Emancipation Proclamation and the Thirteenth, Fourteenth and Fifteenth Amendments sought to protect the Negro's newly won freedom. Part of the "History of the Negro in America" series. **Length:** 20 mins. **Format:** Beta, VHS, 3/4U. **Acquisition:** Purchase. **Use:** Institution, CCTV, SURA.

★4903★
El-Hajj Malik el-Shabazz (Malcolm X)
CRM/McGraw-Hill Films
674 Via de la Valle
PO Box 641
Del Mar, CA 92014

1978. **Program Description:** This program follows the rise of Malcolm X as a leader and outstanding spokesman for the Black American movement. Several unanswered questions are raised about his violent death. Available as a whole or in two parts. **Length:** 58 mins. **Format:** Beta, VHS, 3/4U. **Acquisition:** Purchase. **Use:** Institution, SURA.

★4904★
Epidemiology of Hypertension in Blacks: World
Emory Medical Television Network
Emory University
Emory Medical Television Network-
　Department C
1440 Clifton Rd., NE
Atlanta, GA 30322　　　　　　　　　Ph: (404)616-3556

1986. **Program Description:** A symposium-based discussion on the effects of modern living on the Negro physiology. **Length:** 30 mins. **Format:** VHS, 3/4U. **Acquisition:** Rent/Lease, Purchase, Subscription. **Use:** Institution, CCTV, CATV, BCTV, SURA.

★4905★
Equal Opportunity
Barr Films
3490 E. Foothill Blvd.
PO Box 5667
Passadena, CA 91107　　　　　　　　Free: 800-234-7878

1983. **Program Description:** This program explores the meaning of equal opportunity within the context of affirmative action, racial discrimination, past discrimination, union contracts, seniority, fairness and the Bill of Rights. **Length:** 22 mins. **Format:** Beta, VHS, 3/4U. **Acquisition:** Rent/Lease, Purchase. **Use:** Institution, SURA.

★4906★
Equal Treatment/Equal Opportunity
Gulf Publishing Company
PO Box 2608　　　　　　　　　　　　Ph: (713)529-4301
Houston, TX 77252-2608　　　　　　　Fax: (713)520-4438

1984. **Program Description:** This program is designed to help the workforce to understand what comprises discrimination. **Length:** 17 mins. **Format:** Beta, VHS, 3/4U. **Acquisition:** Purchase. **Use:** Institution, SURA.

★4907★
Equality
PBS Video
11858 La Grange Ave.　　　　　　　　Ph: (213)820-0991
Los Angeles, CA 90025　　　　　　　　Fax: (213)826-4779

1977. **Program Description:** Explores the meaning of equality from the vantage points of many Americans; attempts to determine if equality is a valid concept in terms of age, sex, race, and economic opportunity. **Length:** 60 mins. **Format:** Beta, VHS, 3/4U. **Acquisition:** Rent/Lease, Purchase, Off-Air Record. **Use:** Institution, CCTV, CATV.

★4908★
Ethnic Notions
California Newsreel
149 Ninth St., Ste. 420   Ph: (415)621-6196
San Francisco, CA 94103   Fax: (415)621-6522
1987. **Program Description:** Documentary which probes the stereotypical images white Americans have of blacks, that have contributed to racial prejudice in this country. Cartoons, songs, feature films, advertisments, folklore and children's rhymes that depict Negros as Uncle Toms, Sambos, Mammies, Coons, pickaninnies and uncontrollable brutes are examined in terms of white America's ever-changing desire to justify racism. **Length:** 56 mins. **Format:** VHS. **Acquisition:** Purchase, Rent/Lease, Duplication. **Use:** Institution.

★4909★
The Eye of the Storm
Center for Humanities, Inc.
Communications Park   Ph: (914)666-4100
Box 1000   Fax: (914)666-5319
Mount Kisco, NY 10549   Free: 800-431-1242
1984. **Program Description:** This program provides a valuable lesson in prejudice when a school teacher singles out blue eyed students as a minority group. **Length:** 25 mins. **Format:** Beta, VHS, 3/4U. **Acquisition:** Purchase. **Use:** Institution, SURA.

★4910★
Eyes on the Prize
PBS Video
11858 La Grange Ave.   Ph: (213)820-0991
Los Angeles, CA 90025   Fax: (213)826-4779
1986. **Program Description:** A comprehensive six-part series on the history of the American Civil Rights Movement from World War II to the present. Includes Rosa Parks and the bus boycott, the leadership of Martin Luther King, Jr., and the last great march in Selma, among other moments. Each tape is 60 minutes long. **Length:** 360 mins. **Format:** Beta, VHS, 3/4U. **Acquisition:** Purchase, Rent/Lease, Off-Air Record. **Use:** Institution, CCTV, CATV.

★4911★
Eyes on the Prize 2: America at the Racial Crossroads (1965-1985)
PBS Video
11858 La Grange Ave.   Ph: (213)820-0991
Los Angeles, CA 90025   Fax: (213)826-4779
1987. **Program Description:** The American civil rights movement, from the mid-sixties to mid-eighties, is traced. **Length:** 30 mins. **Format:** VHS, 3/4U. **Acquisition:** Purchase. **Use:** Institution, CCTV, Home, SURA.

★4912★
Fade to Black
Video Data Bank
School of the Art Institute of Chicago   Ph: (312)899-5172
37 S. Wabash Ave.   Fax: (312)263-0141
Chicago, IL 60603   Free: 800-634-8544
1990. **Program Description:** Filmmakers Tony Cokes and Don Trammel present a meditation on contemporary race relations as two black men discuss events in life and cinema. **Length:** 32 mins. **Format:** VHS, 3/4U. **Acquisition:** Rent/Lease, Purchase. **Use:** Institution.

★4913★
Famous Black Americans
Society for Visual Education, Inc. (SVE)   Ph: (312)525-1500
1345 Diversey Pkwy.   Fax: (312)525-9474
Chicago, IL 60614-1299   Free: 800-829-1900
1992. **Program Description:** A four-volume set designed to introduce youngsters to African-American role models in history, politics, and the arts from the time of the Civil War to the modern era. **Length:** 60 mins. **Format:** VHS. **Acquisition:** Purchase. **Use:** Institution.

★4914★
Farrakhan the Minister
WNET/Thirteen Non-Broadcast
356 W. 58th St.
New York, NY 10019   Ph: (212)560-3045
1972. **Program Description:** Black Muslim Minister Louis Farrakhan tells of his hopes and plans for the Black people of America in an interview with Ellis Haizlip. **Length:** 58 mins. **Format:** Beta, VHS, 3/4U. **Acquisition:** Rent/Lease, Purchase. **Use:** Institution, CCTV, Home.

★4915★
Fat Black Mack
Films Inc. Video
5547 N. Ravenswood Ave.   Ph: (312)878-2600
Chicago, IL 60640-1199   Free: 800-323-4222
1970. **Program Description:** A mix of animation, music and enchantment work to tell the story of Mack, a black feline upset with his appearance. When Mack ultimately accepts himself, he realized color is irrelevant to character. The film is designed to help develop self-identity and encourage pride in young black children. **Length:** 5 mins. **Format:** Beta, VHS, 3/4U. **Acquisition:** Purchase. **Use:** Institution.

★4916★
The FBI's War on Black America
MPI Home Video
15825 Rob Roy Dr.   Ph: (708)687-7881
Oak Forest, IL 60452   Fax: (708)687-3797
1990. **Program Description:** During the late '50s and early '60s, J. Edgar Hoover and the FBI felt threatened by what they saw as a militant black movement in America. They developed the Counter Intelligence Program, or COINTELPRO. This video examines how this organization may have been involved in subverting civil rights movements, and what role it may have played in the assassinations of Martin Luther King, Jr., Malcolm X and others. **Length:** 50 mins. **Format:** VHS. **Acquisition:** Purchase. **Use:** Home.

★4917★
Fields of Endless Day
National Film Board of Canada
1251 Avenue of the Americas, 16th Fl.
New York, NY 10020-1173   Ph: (212)586-5131
1987. **Program Description:** This film takes a look at the history of the black population in Canada. **Length:** 59 mins. **Format:** Beta, VHS, 3/4U. **Acquisition:** Purchase, Rent/Lease. **Use:** Institution, SURA.

★4918★
Fight Against Slavery
Time-Life Video and Television
1450 E. Parham Rd.   Ph: (804)266-6330
Richmond, VA 23280   Free: 800-621-7026
1977. **Program Description:** The history of slavery in a powerful, haunting six-part dramatization filmed on location in Africa. **Length:** 56 mins. **Format:** Beta, VHS, 3/4U, Special order formats. **Acquisition:** Rent/Lease, Purchase. **Use:** Institution, SURA.

★4919★
Fighter for Freedom-The Frederick Douglass Story
National AudioVisual Center
National Archives & Records
  Administration
8700 Edgeworth Dr.   Ph: (301)763-1896
Capitol Heights, MD 20743-3701   Free: 800-788-NAVC
1987. **Program Description:** This is a documentary on the life of the famous freed slave. **Length:** 17 mins. **Format:** Beta, VHS, 3/4U. **Acquisition:** Purchase. **Use:** Institution, SURA.

★4920★
Finally Got the News
Cinema Guild
1697 Broadway
New York, NY 10019

Ph: (212)246-5522
Fax: (212)246-5525

1970. **Program Description:** A look inside the automobile factories in Detroit through the eyes of black workers. Examines the Black Revolutionary Workers efforts to create a new union. **Length:** 55 mins. **Format:** Beta, VHS, 3/4U. **Acquisition:** Rent/Lease, Purchase, Duplication. **Use:** Institution, SURA.

★4921★
Flyers in Search of a Dream
PBS Video
11858 La Grange Ave.
Los Angeles, CA 90025

Ph: (213)820-0991
Fax: (213)826-4779

1986. **Program Description:** The intriguing story of America's pioneering black aviators during the golden age of aviation in the 1920s and 1930s. **Length:** 60 mins. **Format:** Beta, VHS, 3/4U. **Acquisition:** Purchase, Rent/Lease, Off-Air Record. **Use:** Institution, CCTV, CATV, Home.

★4922★
Follow the Drinking Gourd
Afro-Am Distributing Company
407 E. 25th St., Ste. 600
Chicago, IL 60616

Ph: (312)791-1611
Fax: (312)791-0921

1993. **Program Description:** The story of runaway slaves seeking freedom via the Underground Railroad. **Length:** 12 mins. **Format:** VHS. **Acquisition:** Purchase. **Use:** Institution, Home, SURA.

★4923★
Follow the North Star
Time-Life Video and Television
1450 E. Parham Rd.
Richmond, VA 23280

Ph: (804)266-6330
Free: 800-621-7026

1975. **Program Description:** A suspenseful adventure examining the issues of freedom, conscience and civil liberties during the time when the country was split over the slavery question. **Length:** 47 mins. **Format:** Beta, VHS, 3/4U, Special order formats. **Acquisition:** Rent/Lease, Purchase. **Use:** Institution, SURA.

★4924★
For Us, the Living
Media Home Entertainment
510 W. 6th St., Ste. 1032
Los Angeles, CA 90014

Ph: (213)236-1336
Fax: (213)236-1346

1988. **Program Description:** The life and assassination of civil rights activist Medgar Evers are dramatically presented in this production of "American Playhouse" for PBS. Insight into the man is given, not just a recording of the events surrounding his life. Adapted from the biography written by Evers' widow. **Length:** 84 mins. **Format:** Beta, VHS. **Acquisition:** Purchase. **Use:** Home.

★4925★
400 Years Without a Comb: The Inferior Seed
Aylmer Press
PO Box 2735
Madison, WI 53701

Ph: (608)251-0890

1989. **Program Description:** African heritage is the subject of this film. Topics discussed include cosmetic tips and grooming. **Length:** 72 mins. **Format:** VHS. **Acquisition:** Purchase. **Use:** Institution.

★4926★
Four Women
Third World Newsreel
335 W. 38th St., 5th Fl.
New York, NY 10018

Ph: (212)947-9277
Fax: (212)594-6417

1981. **Program Description:** The music of Nina Simone is used to create a dance piece that tackles four pejorative stereotypes about black women. **Length:** 7 mins. **Format:** VHS, 3/4U. **Acquisition:** Rent/Lease, Purchase. **Use:** Institution.

★4927★
Framing the Panthers in Black and White
Video Data Bank
School of the Art Institute of Chicago
37 S. Wabash Ave.
Chicago, IL 60603

Ph: (312)899-5172
Fax: (312)263-0141
Free: 800-634-8544

1990. **Program Description:** Covers the FBI's Counterintelligence Program against political activism in the 1960s and '70s, specifically the campaign against the Black Panther Party by focusing on one of its targets, Dhoruba Bin Wahad, a former Panther leader. **Length:** 30 mins. **Format:** VHS. **Acquisition:** Purchase. **Use:** Institution.

★4928★
Frederick Douglass
Library Video Co.
PO Box 40351
Philadelphia, PA 19106

Ph: (215)627-6667
Free: 800-843-3620

1992. **Program Description:** From the "Black Americans of Achievement Series," this segment focuses on the life and achievements of Frederick Douglass. His rise from slavery, his work in the abolitionist publishing business, and his contributions to the suffrage movement are all documented here. **Length:** 30 mins. **Format:** VHS. **Acquisition:** Purchase. **Use:** Institution.

★4929★
Frederick Douglass: An American Life
Harpers Ferry Historical Association, Inc.
PO Box 197
Harpers Ferry, WV 25425

Ph: (304)535-6881

1984. **Program Description:** A dramatized biography of the Negro leader and abolitionist. **Length:** 30 mins. **Format:** Beta, VHS. **Acquisition:** Purchase. **Use:** Home.

★4930★
Free at Last
Encyclopedia Britannica Educational
   Corporation
310 S. Michigan Ave.
Chicago, IL 60604

Ph: (312)347-7000

1990. **Program Description:** The life of Martin Luther King, Jr. is dramatized by school children and newsreel footage. **Length:** 19 mins. **Format:** VHS. **Acquisition:** Purchase. **Use:** Institution.

★4931★
Free Paper Come
Time-Life Video and Television
1450 E. Parham Rd.
Richmond, VA 23280

Ph: (804)266-6330
Free: 800-621-7026

1977. **Program Description:** This episode of "Fight Against Slavery" follows one of the most important rebellions in which slaves fought for their own freedom, led by Daddy Sharp, in Jamaica in 1832. **Length:** 53 mins. **Format:** Beta, VHS, 3/4U, Special order formats. **Acquisition:** Rent/Lease, Purchase. **Use:** Institution, SURA.

★4932★
Freedom Bags
Filmakers Library, Inc.
124 E. 40th
New York, NY 10016

Ph: (212)808-4980

1990. **Program Description:** Documents the migration of Black women from the South to the North in search of employment during the first part of the century. **Length:** 32 mins. **Format:** VHS. **Acquisition:** Purchase. **Use:** Institution.

★4933★
Freedom Frontier
Media Project, Inc.
PO Box 4093
Portland, OR 97208

1976. **Program Description:** This program documents the history of black people in the state of Oregon. **Length:** 55 mins. **Format:** Beta, VHS, EJ, 3/4U. **Acquisition:** Rent/Lease, Purchase. **Use:** Institution, CCTV, SURA.

★4934★
Freedom Man
Afro-Am Distributing Company
407 E. 25th St., Ste. 600   Ph: (312)791-1611
Chicago, IL 60616   Fax: (312)791-0921

19??. **Program Description:** Dramatization of Benjamin Banneker, the self-taught, black colonial farmer who became an expert at math and eventualy went on to survey the newly-constructed capitol. **Length:** 60 mins. **Format:** VHS. **Acquisition:** Purchase. **Use:** Institution, Home, SURA.

★4935★
The Freedom Station
PBS Video
11858 La Grange Ave.   Ph: (213)820-0991
Los Angeles, CA 90025   Fax: (213)826-4779

1988. **Program Description:** The story of a young black girl hiding in a farm family's root cellar along Harriet "Moses" Tubman's Underground Railroad in 1850. **Length:** 30 mins. **Format:** VHS, 3/4U. **Acquisition:** Purchase, Rent/Lease, Duplication License, Off-Air Record. **Use:** Institution, CCTV, CATV, Home, SURA.

★4936★
From Dreams To Reality - A Tribute to Minority Inventors
National AudioVisual Center
National Archives & Records
   Administration   Ph: (301)763-1896
8700 Edgeworth Dr.   Free: 800-788-
Capitol Heights, MD 20743-3701   NAVC

1986. **Program Description:** Ossie Davis narrates this tribute to minority inventors in an effort to motivate minority students to become scientists. **Length:** 28 mins. **Format:** Beta, VHS, 3/4U. **Acquisition:** Purchase. **Use:** Institution, SURA.

★4937★
From Sunup
Maryknoll World Productions   Ph: (914)941-7590
PO Box 308   Fax: (914)945-0670
Maryknoll, NY 10545   Free: 800-227-8523

1988. **Program Description:** The lives of African women who have to work constantly just to squeeze out a meager living are portrayed. **Length:** 28 mins. **Format:** VHS. **Acquisition:** Purchase, Rent/Lease. **Use:** Institution.

★4938★
From These Roots
William Greaves Productions, Inc.
230 W. 55th St.
New York, NY 10019   Ph: (212)246-7221

1974. **Program Description:** Narrated by Brock Peters, this view of the 1920's "Harlem Renaissance" features the work of Cab Calloway, Paul Robeson, Ethel Waters, Duke Ellington, Langston Hughes and Claude MacKay. Music by Eubie Blake. **Length:** 28 mins. **Format:** Beta, VHS, 3/4U. **Acquisition:** Purchase. **Use:** Institution, Home.

★4939★
Fundi: The Story of Ella Baker
First Run/Icarus Films   Ph: (212)727-1711
153 Waverly Pl.   Fax: (212)989-7649
New York, NY 10014   Free: 800-876-1710

1986. **Program Description:** Ella Baker's nickname "Fundi" comes from the Swahili word for a person who passes skills from one generation to another. This film documents Baker's work in the civil rights movement of the 1960s, and her friendship with Dr. Martin Luther King. **Length:** 45 mins. **Format:** 3/4U. **Acquisition:** Purchase. **Use:** Institution, SURA.

★4940★
Gathered into One
UMCom Video
810 12th Ave., S.   Ph: (615)242-6277
Nashville, TN 37203   Free: 800-251-4091

1982. **Program Description:** This tape looks at the growing needs of the Ethnic Minority Local Church. **Length:** 20 mins. **Format:** 3/4U. **Acquisition:** Rent/Lease, Purchase. **Use:** Institution, CATV, BCTV.

★4941★
Generations of Resistance
California Newsreel
149 Ninth St., Ste. 420   Ph: (415)621-6196
San Francisco, CA 94103   Fax: (415)621-6522

1980. **Program Description:** Documentary produced by the United Nations is the outstanding record of black opposition to white supremacy in South Africa. Featuring archival footage and interviews with early battle survivors, the film documents how each black protest has led to greater state violence. **Length:** 52 mins. **Format:** VHS, Special order formats. **Acquisition:** Purchase. **Use:** Institution.

★4942★
George Washington Carver: A Man of Vision
1988. **Program Description:** The life of the black scientist and inventor is recalled through his discoveries and writings. Includes one teacher's guide and one set of Blackline Masters. **Length:** 29 mins. **Format:** VHS. **Acquisition:** Purchase. **Use:** Institution, CCTV, CATV, Home, SURA.

★4943★
Gettin' to Know Me
Great Plains National (GPN)
1800 N. 33rd St.   Ph: (402)472-2007
Box 80669   Fax: (402)472-1785
Lincoln, NE 68501-0669   Free: 800-228-4630

1979. **Program Description:** The Jacksons, a contemporary Southern black family, maintain their family's character by remembering and exploring the black folklore that is their heritage. Programs are available individually. **Length:** 30 mins. **Format:** Beta, VHS, 3/4U. **Acquisition:** Purchase. **Use:** Institution, CCTV, CATV, BCTV.

★4944★
Glory
Columbia Tristar Home Video
3400 Riverside Dr.   Ph: (818)972-8193
Burbank, CA 91505-4627   Fax: (818)972-0937

1989. **Program Description:** A rich, historical spectacle chronicling the 54th Massachusetts, the first black volunteer infantry unit in the Civil War. The film manages to artfully focus on both the 54th and their white commander, Robert Gould Shaw. Based on Shaw's letters, the film uses thousands of accurately costumed "living historians" (re-enactors) as extras in this panoramic production that was Oscar-nominated for best picture of 1989. A haunting, bittersweet musical score pervades what finally becomes an anti-war statement. Stunning performances throughout, with exceptional work from Freeman and Washington. **Length:** 122 mins. **Format:** Beta, VHS, 8mm, LV. **Acquisition:** Purchase. **Use:** Home.

★4945★
Go Down Death
Nostalgia Family Video
PO Box 606
Baker City, OR 97814   Ph: (503)523-9034

1941. **Program Description:** In this early all-black film, a minister is caught in a moral dilemma literally between Heaven and Hell. Scenes of the afterlife are taken from early silent films. **Length:** 63 mins. **Format:** Beta, VHS. **Acquisition:** Rent/Lease, Purchase. **Use:** Home.

★4946★
Gotta Make This Journey: Sweet Honey in the Rock
Museum of Modern Art (MOMA)
Circulating Film & Video Library
11 W. 53rd St.
New York, NY 10019
1983. **Program Description:** A documentary about the radical Black women's singing group Sweet Honey in the Rock, centering on their ninth anniversary concert. Interspersed throughout the concert footage are interviews with the singers and with other Black women. **Length:** 58 mins. **Format:** Beta, VHS, 3/4U. **Acquisition:** Purchase, Rent/Lease. **Use:** Institution, Home.

★4947★
A Grateful Peasantry
Time-Life Video and Television
1450 E. Parham Rd.   Ph: (804)266-6330
Richmond, VA 23280   Free: 800-621-7026
1977. **Program Description:** This episode of "Fight Against Slavery" focuses on Parliament's great slavery debate in 1792 which concluded with the passage of an amendment to gradually abolish slavery. **Length:** 56 mins. **Format:** Beta, VHS, 3/4U, Special order formats. **Acquisition:** Rent/Lease, Purchase. **Use:** Institution, SURA.

★4948★
Great Americans: Martin Luther King, Jr.
Britannica Films
310 S. Michigan Ave.   Ph: (312)347-7958
Chicago, IL 60604   Fax: (312)347-7966
1982. **Program Description:** Three of Martin Luther King Jr's friends speak of him. Also, some remarks from his wife are included. **Length:** 24 mins. **Format:** Beta, VHS, 3/4U. **Acquisition:** Rent/Lease, Purchase, Trade-in. **Use:** Institution, SURA.

★4949★
The Greedy Child: Senegal
Films for the Humanities & Sciences   Ph: (609)452-1128
PO Box 2053   Fax: (609)275-3767
Princeton, NJ 08543   Free: 800-257-5126
1991. **Program Description:** African folktale relates the story of Joomay, a lazy boy whose greed gets him into trouble. Actors speak their native language, while the narration is in English. **Length:** 26 mins. **Format:** VHS. **Acquisition:** Purchase, Rent/Lease. **Use:** Institution.

★4950★
Green Pastures
MGM/UA Home Video, Inc.
10000 W. Washington Blvd.
Culver City, CA 90232   Ph: (310)280-6212
1936. **Program Description:** An adaptation of Marc Connelly's 1930 Pulitzer Prize-winning play which attempts to retell Biblical stories in Black English Vernacular of the '30s. Southern theater owners boycotted the controversial film which had an all-Black cast. **Length:** 93 mins. **Format:** Beta, VHS. **Acquisition:** Purchase. **Use:** Home.

★4951★
Guess Who's Coming to Dinner
Columbia Tristar Home Video
3400 Riverside Dr.   Ph: (818)972-8193
Burbank, CA 91505-4627   Fax: (818)972-0937
1967. **Program Description:** Controversial in its time. A young white woman brings her black fiance home to meet her parents. The situation truly tests their open-mindedness and understanding. Hepburn and Tracy (in his last film appearance) are wonderful and serve as the anchors in what would otherwise have been a rather sugary film (although the screenplay won an Academy Award). Houghton, who portrays the independent daughter, is the real-life niece of Hepburn who garnered an Oscar for her performance. Other Oscar nominations for Best Picture, Best Actor (Tracy), Supporting Actor (Kellaway), Supporting Actress (Richards), Director, Art Direction, Set Decoration, and Film Editing. **Length:** 108 mins. **Format:** Beta, VHS, LV. **Acquisition:** Purchase. **Use:** Home.

★4952★
Guts, Gumption and Go-Ahead: Annie Mae Hunt Remembers
Media Projects
5215 Homer St.
Dallas, TX 75206
1992. **Program Description:** Dramatization of the life of African-American feminist, Annie Mae Hunt. Archival footage and family photos illustrate her struggles and triumphs as she educated six children, purchased her own home, sold Avon, and became politically active. **Length:** 24 mins. **Format:** VHS. **Acquisition:** Purchase. **Use:** Institution.

★4953★
Half Slave, Half Free
Sony Video Software (SVS, Inc.)
1700 Broadway, 16th Fl.   Ph: (518)972-8870
New York, NY 10019   Fax: (518)972-0907
1985. **Program Description:** The true story of a free black man in the 1840s who is kidnapped and forced into slavery for 12 years. Made for television as part of the "American Playhouse" series on PBS. Followed by "Charlotte Forten's Mission: Experiment in Freedom." **Length:** 113 mins. **Format:** Beta, VHS. **Acquisition:** Purchase. **Use:** Home.

★4954★
Hallelujah!
MGM/UA Home Video, Inc.
10000 W. Washington Blvd.
Culver City, CA 90232   Ph: (310)280-6212
1929. **Program Description:** Haynes plays an innocent young man who turns to religion and becomes a charasmatic preacher after a family tragedy. He retains all his human weaknesses, however, including falling for the lovely but deceitful McKinney. Great music included traditional spirituals and songs by Berlin, such as "At the End of the Road" and "Swanee Shuffle." Shot on location in Tennessee. The first all-black feature film and the first talkie for director Vidor was given the go-ahead by MGM production chief Irving Thalberg, though he knew the film would be both controversial and get minimal release in the deep South. **Length:** 90 mins. **Format:** VHS. **Acquisition:** Purchase. **Use:** Home.

★4955★
Hands that Picked Cotton
PBS Video
11858 La Grange Ave.   Ph: (213)820-0991
Los Angeles, CA 90025   Fax: (213)826-4779
1985. **Program Description:** This program allows viewers to draw their own conclusion on the politics of the south, where blacks have gained political power but are still working for economic progress. **Length:** 60 mins. **Format:** Beta, VHS, 3/4U. **Acquisition:** Rent/Lease, Purchase, Duplication, Off-Air Record. **Use:** Institution, CCTV, Home, SURA.

★4956★
Hank Aaron
First Run Video
3620 Overland Ave.   Ph: (310)202-8990
Los Angeles, CA 90034   Fax: (310)838-5212
19??. **Program Description:** Highlights and interviews are used to profile baseball's all-time home run king. **Length:** 30 mins. **Format:** Beta, VHS. **Acquisition:** Purchase. **Use:** Home.

★4957★
A Hard Road to Glory: The Black Athlete in America
Eastman Kodak Company
c/o Wood Knapp
Knapp Press
5900 Wilshire Blvd.
Los Angeles, CA 90036   Ph: (213)937-5486
1987. **Program Description:** Tennis player Arthur Ashe and actor James Earl Jones narrate this documentary, which features footage of Jackie Robinson, Jesse Owens and Joe Louis. **Length:** 60 mins. **Format:** Beta, VHS, 8mm. **Acquisition:** Purchase. **Use:** Institution, Home.

★4958★
Harlem in the Twenties
Britannica Films
310 S. Michigan Ave.   Ph: (312)347-7958
Chicago, IL 60604   Fax: (312)347-7966
1987. **Program Description:** Harlem didn't become a predominantly black area until the twenties, and has remained so ever since. **Length:** 10 mins. **Format:** Beta, VHS, 3/4U. **Acquisition:** Purchase, Trade-in. **Use:** Institution, SURA.

★4959★
The Heart of Dixie
Orion Home Video
1888 Century Park E.
Los Angeles, CA 90067   Ph: (310)282-0550
1989. **Program Description:** Three college co-eds at a southern university in the 1950s see their lives and values change with the influence of the civil rights movement. College newspaper reporter Sheedy takes up the cause of a black man victimized by racial violence. **Length:** 96 mins. **Format:** Beta, VHS, LV. **Acquisition:** Purchase. **Use:** Home.

★4960★
Heat Wave
Turner Home Entertainment Company
1 CNN Center
N. Tower, 12th Fl.
Atlanta, GA 30348   Ph: (404)827-2000
1990. **Program Description:** The Watts ghetto uprising of 1965 is a proving ground for a young black journalist. Excellent cast and fine script portrays the anger and frustration of blacks in Los Angeles and the U.S. in the 1960s and the fear of change felt by blacks and whites when civil rights reform began. **Length:** 92 mins. **Format:** Beta, VHS. **Acquisition:** Purchase. **Use:** Home.

★4961★
Heritage in Black
Britannica Films
310 S. Michigan Ave.   Ph: (312)347-7958
Chicago, IL 60604   Fax: (312)347-7966
1969. **Program Description:** A 200-year panorama that stretches from the first struggles of black people to be free of chains to today's struggles to be free of invisible bonds. **Length:** 27 mins. **Format:** Beta, VHS, 3/4U. **Acquisition:** Rent/Lease, Purchase, Trade-in. **Use:** Institution, SURA.

★4962★
The Heritage of Slavery
Phoenix/BFA Films
468 Park Ave., S.   Ph: (212)684-5910
New York, NY 10016   Free: 800-221-1274
1968. **Program Description:** CBS News reporter George Foster interviews descendants of plantation owners and presentday black activists, demonstrating the parallels between attitudes under slavery and now. **Length:** 53 mins. **Format:** Beta, VHS, 3/4U. **Acquisition:** Purchase. **Use:** Institution, SURA.

★4963★
A Hero Ain't Nothin' But a Sandwich
Paramount Home Video
5555 Melrose Ave.
Los Angeles, CA 90038-3197   Ph: (213)956-5000
1978. **Program Description:** A young urban black teenager gets involved in drugs and is eventually saved from ruin. Slow-moving, over-directed and talky. However, Scott turns in a fine performance. Based on Alice Childress' novel. **Length:** 107 mins. **Format:** Beta, VHS. **Acquisition:** Purchase. **Use:** Home.

★4964★
Hey, Cab
Phoenix/BFA Films
468 Park Ave., S.   Ph: (212)684-5910
New York, NY 10016   Free: 800-221-1274
1970. **Program Description:** Dramatizes a true experience of a black journalist, Bob Teague. A cab deliberately bypasses the black man stranded on the rain swept curb. Based on "Letters to a Black Boy." **Length:** 11 mins. **Format:** Beta, VHS, 3/4U. **Acquisition:** Purchase. **Use:** Institution, SURA.

★4965★
High Five: Celebrating African-American Teens
HRM Video
175 Tompkins Ave.   Ph: (914)769-7496
No. V212   Fax: (914)747-1744
Pleasantville, NY 10570-9973   Free: 800-431-2050
1992. **Program Description:** Five minority teenagers who have made outstanding contributions to their fields despite personal hardships are profiled and serve as role models for youth of all races. **Length:** 30 mins. **Format:** VHS. **Acquisition:** Purchase. **Use:** Institution.

★4966★
The History of Great Black Baseball Players
Fries Home Video
6922 Hollywood Blvd., 12th Fl.   Ph: (213)466-2266
Hollywood, CA 90028   Fax: (213)466-2126
1989. **Program Description:** Career profiles of memorable black ballplayers, including Monte Irvin, Lou Brock, Ozzie Smith, Hank Aaron, and the pioneers of the 1920 Negro National League. **Length:** 45 mins. **Format:** Beta, VHS. **Acquisition:** Purchase. **Use:** Home.

★4967★
A History of Racist Animation
Whole Toon Access
PO Box 369   Ph: (206)391-8747
Issaquah, WA 98027-0369   Fax: (206)391-9064
19??. **Program Description:** Commentary provides a historical perspective for the stereotypes and changing tastes provided in these cartoons which feature Bugs Bunny, Popeye, and Superman, among others. **Length:** 90 mins. **Format:** VHS. **Acquisition:** Purchase. **Use:** Home.

★4968★
The House of Dies Drear
Home Vision Cinema   Ph: (312)878-2600
5547 N. Ravenswood Ave.   Fax: (312)878-8648
Chicago, IL 60640-1199   Free: 800-826-3456
1988. **Program Description:** A modern-day African American family moves into an old house that turns out to be haunted by the ghost of a long dead abolitionist. The family is transported back to the days of slavery as they interact with the ghost. Based on the story by Virginia Hamilton. Aired on PBS as part of the "Wonderworks" family movie series. **Length:** 107 mins. **Format:** VHS. **Acquisition:** Purchase. **Use:** Home.

★4969★
The Human Race Club: Unforgettable Pen Pal
Knowledge Unlimited, Inc.   Ph: (608)836-6660
Box 52   Fax: (608)831-1570
Madison, WI 53701-0052   Free: 800-356-2303
1987. **Program Description:** Kids get a lesson from A.J. and the Human Race Club on discrimination and prejudice in this episode of the cartoon series. **Length:** 30 mins. **Format:** VHS. **Acquisition:** Purchase. **Use:** Home.

★4970★
Humanity Defiled
Film Video Library
University of Michigan
919 S. University Ave., Rm. 207
Ann Arbor, MI 48109-1185   Ph: (313)764-5360
1970. **Program Description:** The emergence of slavery in the new world colonies and the alternatives open to whites are examined. **Length:** 29 mins. **Format:** 3/4U, Special order formats. **Acquisition:** Rent/Lease, Purchase. **Use:** Institution, CCTV, CATV, BCTV.

★4971★
An I for An I
Video Data Bank
School of the Art Institute of Chicago   Ph: (312)899-5172
37 S. Wabash Ave.   Fax: (312)263-0141
Chicago, IL 60603   Free: 800-634-8544
1988. **Program Description:** Lawrence Andrews' work confronts racist culture and its effects on the mind and the body as it pleads for an alternative to violence. **Length:** 18 mins. **Format:** VHS, 3/4U. **Acquisition:** Rent/Lease, Purchase. **Use:** Institution.

★4972★
"I Have a Dream" - Martin Luther King, Jr.
King Features Entertainment
235 E. 45th St.   Ph: (212)455-4000
New York, NY 10017   Free: 800-526-5464
1983. **Program Description:** This program chronicles the life of the great civil rights leader from his birth to the tragic assassination in 1968. **Length:** 14 mins. **Format:** Beta, VHS, 3/4U. **Acquisition:** Rent/Lease, Purchase. **Use:** Institution, SURA.

★4973★
"I Have a Dream. . ." - The Life of Martin Luther King
Phoenix/BFA Films
468 Park Ave., S.   Ph: (212)684-5910
New York, NY 10016   Free: 800-221-1274
1968. **Program Description:** Brings a better understanding of the philosophies and ideals that King exemplified. Actual news footage is used. **Length:** 35 mins. **Format:** Beta, VHS, 3/4U. **Acquisition:** Purchase. **Use:** Institution, SURA.

★4974★
I Know Why the Caged Bird Sings
Knowledge Unlimited, Inc.   Ph: (608)836-6660
Box 52   Fax: (608)831-1570
Madison, WI 53701-0052   Free: 800-356-2303
1979. **Program Description:** A black writer's memories of growing up in the rural South during the 1930s. Strong performances from Rolle and Good. Made-for-television film is based on the book by Maya Angelou. **Length:** 100 mins. **Format:** Beta, VHS. **Acquisition:** Purchase. **Use:** Home.

★4975★
I Know Why the Caged Bird Sings
Afro-Am Distributing Company
407 E. 25th St., Ste. 600   Ph: (312)791-1611
Chicago, IL 60616   Fax: (312)791-0921
197?. **Program Description:** A video supplement to be used when reading the Maya Angelou classic. Actually a filmstrip enhanced by computer to give a livelier, pseudo-animated appearance. **Length:** mins. **Format:** VHS. **Acquisition:** Purchase. **Use:** Institution, Home, SURA.

★4976★
I Talk about Me—I Am Africa
Facets Multimedia, Inc.
1517 W. Fullerton Ave.
Chicago, IL 60614   Ph: (312)281-9075
1980. **Program Description:** Looks at the system of South African apartheid through a variety of theatrical performances, including a women's theatre troupe performing in an illegal shantytown. **Length:** 54 mins. **Format:** VHS. **Acquisition:** Purchase. **Use:** Home.

★4977★
I Wonder Why
CRM/McGraw-Hill Films
674 Via de la Valle
PO Box 641
Del Mar, CA 92014
1964. **Program Description:** A young black girl wonders in a monolog of her thoughts, "Why don't people like me" **Length:** 6 mins. **Format:** Beta, VHS, 3/4U. **Acquisition:** Rent/Lease, Purchase. **Use:** Institution, SURA.

★4978★
Ida B. Wells: A Passion for Justice
William Greaves Productions, Inc.   Ph: (212)265-6150
230 W. 55th St.   Fax: (212)315-0027
New York, NY 10019   Free: 800-874-8314
19??. **Program Description:** A look at the pioneering journalist, activist, suffragette, and anti-lynching crusader of the late 19th and early 20th centuries. Includes photographs, lithographs, and interviews with historians and scholars. **Length:** 53 mins. **Format:** VHS. **Acquisition:** Purchase, Rent/Lease. **Use:** Institution.

★4979★
I'm Not Prejudiced But. . .Korean Merchants in Black Neighborhoods
Ethnovision, Inc.
2122 S. St.
Philadelphia, PA 19146   Ph: (215)735-2188
1988. **Program Description:** Discussions are held on racial stereotypes, developing new attitudes and behavior, intergroup relations and removing all misconceptions about race. **Length:** 26 mins. **Format:** VHS. **Acquisition:** Rent/Lease, Purchase. **Use:** Institution, Home.

★4980★
Images: Tribute to Harold Washington
Facets Multimedia, Inc.
1517 W. Fullerton Ave.
Chicago, IL 60614   Ph: (312)281-9075
1987. **Program Description:** The first black mayor of Chicago (in 1983) is profiled. Includes interviews and photographs. **Length:** 24 mins. **Format:** VHS. **Acquisition:** Purchase. **Use:** Home, Institution.

★4981★
Imani
Film Ideas, Inc.   Ph: (708)480-5760
3710 Commercial Ave., Ste. 13   Fax: (708)480-7496
Northbrook, IL 60062   Free: 800-475-3456
1991. **Program Description:** A number of topics in African-American culture are discussed, including the origin and meaning of Kwanzaa, the "Middle Passage," and African-American art and culture. **Length:** 15 mins. **Format:** VHS. **Acquisition:** Purchase. **Use:** Institution.

★4982★
Imitation of Life
MCA/Universal Home Video
70 Universal City Plaza   Ph: (818)777-6419
Universal City, CA 91608-9955   Fax: (818)733-0226
1959. **Program Description:** Remake of the successful 1939 Claudette Colbert outing of the same title, and based on Fanny Hurst's novel, with a few plot changes. Turner is a single mother, more determined to achieve acting fame and fortune than function as a parent. Her black maid, Moore, is devoted to her own daughter (Kohner), but loses her when the girl discovers she can pass for white. When Turner discovers that she and her daughter are in love with the same man, she realizes how little she knows her daughter, and how much the two of them have missed by not having a stronger relationship. Highly successful at the box office, with Oscar nominations for Kohner and Moore. **Length:** 124 mins. **Format:** Beta, VHS. **Acquisition:** Purchase. **Use:** Home.

★4983★
In a Jazz Way: A Portrait of Mura Dehn
Filmakers Library, Inc.
124 E. 40th
New York, NY 10016   Ph: (212)808-4980
1986. **Program Description:** Mura Dehn recalls her days as one of the nation's top jazz dancers, choreographers, and dance filmmakers. She reflects on the social conditions that created jazz dance, Be-Bop, and breakdancing. **Length:** 30 mins. **Format:** VHS, 3/4U. **Acquisition:** Rent/Lease, Purchase, Duplication. **Use:** Institution, Home, SURA.

★4984★
In Black and White: Civil Rights Organizations
New Jersey Network
1573 Parkside Ave.
Trenton, NJ 08625   Ph: (609)530-5252

1988. **Program Description:** This program explores the history and current programs of the National Urban League, the National Association for the Advancement of Colored People, and the National Council of Negro Women. **Length:** 30 mins. **Format:** VHS, 3/4U. **Acquisition:** Rent/Lease, Purchase. **Use:** Institution.

★4985★
In Motion: Amiri Baraka
Facets Multimedia, Inc.
1517 W. Fullerton Ave.
Chicago, IL 60614   Ph: (312)281-9075

1985. **Program Description:** Charts the life and career of political activist and writer Baraka and his commitment to social change. Includes excerpts from his play "The Dutchman," as well as other works. **Length:** 60 mins. **Format:** VHS. **Acquisition:** Purchase. **Use:** Home, Institution.

★4986★
In Remembrance of Martin
PBS Video
11858 La Grange Ave.   Ph: (213)820-0991
Los Angeles, CA 90025   Fax: (213)826-4779

1986. **Program Description:** This program documents the celebrations in Atlanta during the observance of the first federal holiday for Martin Luther King Day. Historical footage and interviews are combined with the festivities throughout the city. **Length:** 60 mins. **Format:** Beta, VHS, 3/4U. **Acquisition:** Purchase, Rent/Lease, Off-Air Record. **Use:** Institution, CCTV, CATV.

★4987★
In Search of the American Dream: A Story of the African-American Experience
Films for the Humanities & Sciences   Ph: (609)452-1128
PO Box 2053   Fax: (609)275-3767
Princeton, NJ 08543   Free: 800-257-5126

199?. **Program Description:** The African-American experience is documented through visits to historical sites and commentary in six programs (52 minutes each). **Length:** 52 mins. **Format:** VHS. **Acquisition:** Purchase. **Use:** Institution.

★4988★
In the Best of Times
Pennsylvania State University, Audio-Visual
   Services
Special Services Bldg.   Ph: (814)865-6314
1127 Fox Hill Rd.   Fax: (814)863-2574
State College, PA 16803-1824   Free: 800-826-0132

1980. **Program Description:** This part of the "U.S. Chronicle" series examines Seattle's economic boom, benefitting everyone except the unemployed blacks of Seattle. **Length:** 29 mins. **Format:** 3/4U, Special order formats. **Acquisition:** Rent/Lease, Purchase. **Use:** Institution, SURA.

★4989★
In the Land of Jim Crow: Growing Up Segregated
Coronet/MTI Film & Video   Ph: (708)940-1260
108 Wilmot Rd.   Fax: (708)940-3640
Deerfield, IL 60015   Free: 800-777-8100

1991. **Program Description:** African-Americans recount their childhood experiences of growing up with segregation in the days before the civil rights movement. **Length:** 26 mins. **Format:** VHS. **Acquisition:** Purchase. **Use:** Institution.

★4990★
In the Shadow of the Capitol
PBS Video
11858 La Grange Ave.   Ph: (213)820-0991
Los Angeles, CA 90025   Fax: (213)826-4779

1984. **Program Description:** This program investigates how several former black civil rights activists grapple with politics, power and hard times. **Length:** 60 mins. **Format:** Beta, VHS, 3/4U. **Acquisition:** Rent/Lease, Purchase, Off-Air Record. **Use:** Institution, CCTV, CATV.

★4991★
Inside Stories: In Service
Beacon Films   Ph: (708)328-6700
930 Pitner Ave.   Fax: (708)328-6706
Evanston, IL 60202   Free: 800-323-5448

1991. **Program Description:** A successful Black woman recalls the sacrifices her family and friends made as domestic servants while she was growing up so that she could become whatever she wanted. A valuable message on taking care of other people. Based on a story by Maxine Tynes. Comes with guide. **Length:** 26 mins. **Format:** VHS. **Acquisition:** Purchase, Rent/Lease. **Use:** Institution.

★4992★
Integration in Public Schools
New York State Education Department
Center for Learning Technologies
Media Distribution Network, Rm. C-7,
   Concourse Level
Albany, NY 12230   Ph: (518)474-3852

1974. **Program Description:** The problems that educators and administrators face with racial integration in schools is examined. **Length:** 30 mins. **Format:** Beta, VHS, EJ, 3/4U, Q. **Acquisition:** Duplication License, Free Duplication. **Use:** Institution, SURA.

★4993★
An Interview with Clarence Muse

1979. **Program Description:** A vital voice in the black theatre, Clarence Muse founded the famed Lafayette Theatre Players and performed in vaudeville, legitimate stage, films, radio and TV. A few months before his death, Clarence Muse taped this conversation. **Length:** 180 mins. **Format:** 3/4U. **Acquisition:** Rent/Lease, Duplication, Duplication License. **Use:** Institution, CCTV, Home, SURA.

★4994★
Is It OK to Be Me
Pyramid Film & Video
Box 1048   Ph: (310)828-7577
2801 Colorado Ave.   Fax: (310)453-9083
Santa Monica, CA 90406   Free: 800-421-2304

1977. **Program Description:** This part of the "Who We Are" series shows children how it feels to be a minority, what it means to be prejudiced, and two separate ways of treating people who are different. **Length:** 6 mins. **Format:** Beta, VHS, 3/4U. **Acquisition:** Rent/Lease, Purchase, Duplication License. **Use:** Institution, Home, SURA.

★4995★
"Isitwalandwe": The Story of the South African Freedom Charter
Cinema Guild
1697 Broadway   Ph: (212)246-5522
New York, NY 10019   Fax: (212)246-5525

1980. **Program Description:** Documents the adoption of the South African Freedom Charter, a blueprint for a future non-racial and democratic South Africa. **Length:** 51 mins. **Format:** Beta, VHS, 3/4U. **Acquisition:** Purchase. **Use:** Institution.

★4996★
It's Not a One Person Thing
Green Mountain Post Films
PO Box 229
Turners Falls, MA 01376   Ph: (413)863-4754

1978. **Program Description:** A look at the formation of the poverty-fighting Federation of Southern Cooperatives in the heat of the civil rights movement in 1967. **Length:** 30 mins. **Format:** Beta, VHS, 3/4U. **Acquisition:** Rent/Lease, Purchase. **Use:** Institution, CCTV, BCTV, SURA.

★4997★
The Jackie Robinson Story
Nostalgia Family Video
PO Box 606
Baker City, OR 97814   Ph: (503)523-9034

1950. **Program Description:** Chronicles Robinson's rise from UCLA to his breakthrough as the first black man to play baseball in the major league. Robinson plays himself; the film deals honestly with the racial issues of the time. **Length:** 76 mins. **Format:** VHS. **Acquisition:** Purchase. **Use:** Home.

★4998★
Jane Kennedy—To Be Free
PBS Video
11858 La Grange Ave.   Ph: (213)820-0991
Los Angeles, CA 90025   Fax: (213)826-4779

1971. **Program Description:** Jane Kennedy, a nurse turned civil rights/antiwar activist, who was jailed for erasing computer tapes used by a company manufacturing napalm, talks about her beliefs and her commitment to them. **Length:** 27 mins. **Format:** Beta, VHS, 3/4U. **Acquisition:** Rent/Lease, Purchase, Off-Air Record. **Use:** Institution, CCTV, CATV.

★4999★
Jazz in Exile
Music Video Distributors
O'Neill Industrial Center   Ph: (215)272-7771
1210 Standbridge St.   Fax: (215)272-6074
Norristown, PA 19403   Free: 800-888-0486

1982. **Program Description:** A profile of several well-known American jazz musicians, including Dexter Gordon and Phil Woods, who made their reputations and spent their careers in Europe. **Length:** 58 mins. **Format:** Beta, VHS. **Acquisition:** Purchase. **Use:** Home.

★5000★
Jesse Jackson: We Can Dream Again
MPI Home Video
15825 Rob Roy Dr.   Ph: (708)687-7881
Oak Forest, IL 60452   Fax: (708)687-3797

1988. **Program Description:** News coverage, from beginning to triumphant conclusion, of Jackson's speech at the 1988 Democratic convention on July 19, 1988, where Michael Dukakis was eventually chosen as the nominee. The video was released 5 days after the speech. **Length:** 60 mins. **Format:** Beta, VHS. **Acquisition:** Purchase. **Use:** Home.

★5001★
The Jesse Owens Story
Paramount Home Video
5555 Melrose Ave.
Los Angeles, CA 90038-3197   Ph: (213)956-5000

1984. **Program Description:** The moving story of the four-time Olympic Gold medal winner's triumphs and misfortunes. A made-for-television movie. **Length:** 174 mins. **Format:** Beta, VHS. **Acquisition:** Purchase. **Use:** Home.

★5002★
Joe Louis
Facets Multimedia, Inc.
1517 W. Fullerton Ave.
Chicago, IL 60614   Ph: (312)281-9075

19??. **Program Description:** A brief look at the boxer known as the "Brown Bomber" who became the youngest heavyweight champ at the age of 23. Includes footage of his knockout of Max Schmeling. **Length:** 24 mins. **Format:** VHS. **Acquisition:** Purchase. **Use:** Home, Institution.

★5003★
Joe Louis: For All Time
ESPN Home Video
PO Box 3390
Department B
Wallingford, CT 06494   Ph: (203)661-6040

1990. **Program Description:** Comprehensive video biography of the man who is arguably history's greatest heavyweight champion. In color with black and white footage. **Length:** 89 mins. **Format:** VHS. **Acquisition:** Purchase. **Use:** Home.

★5004★
John Coltrane: The Coltrane Legacy
Music Video Distributors
O'Neill Industrial Center   Ph: (215)272-7771
1210 Standbridge St.   Fax: (215)272-6074
Norristown, PA 19403   Free: 800-888-0486

1987. **Program Description:** A musical portrait of the legendary saxophonist, featuring rare performances from his few television appearances in the 50s and early 60s. Selections include "So What," "My Favorite Things," "Ev'ry Time We Say Goodbye," and "Afro Blue," from the collection of jazz film historian David Chertok. Some portions are in black and white. **Length:** 61 mins. **Format:** Beta, VHS, LV. **Acquisition:** Purchase. **Use:** Home.

★5005★
JUBA
PBS Video
11858 La Grange Ave.   Ph: (213)820-0991
Los Angeles, CA 90025   Fax: (213)826-4779

1978. **Program Description:** A series of four programs, designed to teach children an awareness of and appreciation for the cultural traditions of African-Americans. **Length:** 15 mins. **Format:** VHS, 3/4U. **Acquisition:** Purchase, Rent/Lease, Duplication License, Off-Air Record. **Use:** Institution, CCTV, CATV, Home, SURA.

★5006★
Juice
Paramount Home Video
5555 Melrose Ave.
Los Angeles, CA 90038-3197   Ph: (213)956-5000

1992. **Program Description:** Day-to-day street life of four Harlem youths as they try to earn respect ("juice") in their neighborhood. Q, an aspiring deejay, is talked into a robbery by his friends but everything takes a turn for the worse when one of the others, Bishop, gets hold of a gun. The gritty look and feel of the drama comes naturally to Dickerson in his directorial debut. Prior to his first film, Dickerson served as cinematographer for Spike Lee's "Do the Right Thing" and "Jungle Fever." **Length:** 95 mins. **Format:** VHS. **Acquisition:** Purchase. **Use:** Home.

★5007★
Jungle Fever
MCA/Universal Home Video
70 Universal City Plaza   Ph: (818)777-6419
Universal City, CA 91608-9955   Fax: (818)733-0226

1991. **Program Description:** A married black architect's affair with his white secretary provides the backdrop for a cold look at an interracial love affair. Lee focuses more on the discomfort of the friends and families involved than with the intense world created by the lovers for themselves. The movie provides the quota of humor and fresh insight we expect from Lee, but none of the joyous sexuality experienced by the black lovers in "She's Gotta Have It." In fact, Lee tells us that interracial love is unnatural, never more than skin deep. His lovers have "Jungle Fever," a blind obsession with the allure of the opposite race. A very fine cast but if you don't agree with Lee's viewpoint, a real disappointment as well. **Length:** 131 mins. **Format:** Beta, VHS, LV. **Acquisition:** Purchase. **Use:** Home.

★5008★
Kasa Twene: The Drum That Talks
Film Video Library
University of Michigan
919 S. University Ave., Rm. 207
Ann Arbor, MI 48109-1185   Ph: (313)764-5360

1974. **Program Description:** Ghanese drummer Kwasi Aduonum demonstrates the beauty and the powers of description and communication in the drum of Africa. **Length:** 29 mins. **Format:** 3/4U, Special order formats. **Acquisition:** Rent/Lease, Purchase. **Use:** Institution, CCTV, CATV, BCTV.

★5009★
Keeping the Faith
PBS Video
11858 La Grange Ave.   Ph: (213)820-0991
Los Angeles, CA 90025   Fax: (213)826-4779

1987. **Program Description:** A history of the Black church which played which played a key role in the 1960s Civil Rights Movement. **Length:** 58 mins. **Format:** Beta, VHS, 3/4U. **Acquisition:** Purchase, Rent/Lease. **Use:** Institution, SURA.

★5010★
King: Montgomery to Memphis
Pacific Arts Video   Ph: (310)820-0991
11858 La Grange   Fax: (310)826-4779
Los Angeles, CA 90025   Free: 800-538-5856

1988. **Program Description:** A documentary about the work of civil rights leader Dr. Martin Luther King, Jr. The film traces the movement King led from the Montgomery bus boycott to the peaceful Reverend's assassination in Memphis. **Length:** 103 mins. **Format:** Beta, VHS, LV. **Acquisition:** Purchase. **Use:** Home.

★5011★
Kwanzaa
Afro-Am Distributing Company
407 E. 25th St., Ste. 600   Ph: (312)791-1611
Chicago, IL 60616   Fax: (312)791-0921

19??. **Program Description:** An interview with Dr. Maulana Karanga in which he discusses the foundation for the seven day African holiday, celebrated from December 26 to January 1, which he developed. **Length:** 50 mins. **Format:** VHS. **Acquisition:** Purchase. **Use:** Institution, Home, SURA.

★5012★
Kwanzaa: A Cultural Celebration
Maryland Public Television   Ph: (410)356-5600
11767 Owings Mills Blvd.   Fax: (410)581-4338
Owings Mills, MD 21117-1499   Free: 800-873-6154

19??. **Program Description:** Provides a look at the African-American celebration through sharing the special foods and activities of the holiday. **Length:** 30 mins. **Format:** Beta, VHS, 3/4U. **Acquisition:** Rent/Lease, Purchase. **Use:** Institution, CCTV.

★5013★
Lady Day: The Many Faces of Billie Holiday
Kultur Video   Ph: (908)229-2343
121 Hwy. No. 36   Fax: (908)229-0066
West Long Branch, NJ 07764   Free: 800-458-5887

1991. **Program Description:** Splendid exploration of the woman behind the jazz legend. Special interviews with her peers, vintage footage, and extraordinary performance clips compose this look at Holiday's success and suffering. Also features narration from "Lady Sings the Blues," her autobiography. **Length:** 60 mins. **Format:** VHS. **Acquisition:** Purchase. **Use:** Home.

★5014★
Lady Sings the Blues
Paramount Home Video
5555 Melrose Ave.
Los Angeles, CA 90038-3197   Ph: (213)956-5000

1972. **Program Description:** Jazz artist Billie Holiday's life becomes a musical drama depicting her struggle against racism and drug addiction in her pursuit of fame and romance. What could be a typical price-of-fame story is saved by Ross' inspired performance as the tragic singer. Songs include "God Bless the Child" and "Lover Man." Oscar nominated for director. **Length:** 144 mins. **Format:** Beta, VHS, LV. **Acquisition:** Purchase. **Use:** Home.

★5015★
Land Where the Blues Began
Phoenix/BFA Films
468 Park Ave., S.   Ph: (212)684-5910
New York, NY 10016   Free: 800-221-1274

1982. **Program Description:** This documentary examines the life of poor blacks in rural Mississippi, and the style of music developed by them, known as the blues. **Length:** 60 mins. **Format:** Beta, VHS, 3/4U. **Acquisition:** Purchase. **Use:** Institution, SURA.

★5016★
The Larry P. Case

1978. **Program Description:** A look at the Larry P. case, a class-action suit brought by parents of black children in the San Francisco School District to end the use of culturally-biased I.Q. tests. **Length:** 30 mins. **Format:** 3/4U, Special order formats. **Acquisition:** Purchase. **Use:** Institution, CCTV, Home, SURA.

★5017★
Last Breeze of Summer
Carousel Film & Video
260 5th Ave., Rm. 405   Ph: (212)683-1660
New York, NY 10001   Fax: (212)683-1662

1992. **Program Description:** Touching story of black woman's memory of her pivotal stance as a student against segregated schools in the pre-civil rights South. **Length:** 30 mins. **Format:** VHS. **Acquisition:** Purchase. **Use:** Home.

★5018★
The Law and Handicapped Children in School:
  Assessment

1978. **Program Description:** A look at culturally biased I.Q. tests in assessing the educational abilities of minority groups. **Length:** 30 mins. **Format:** 3/4U, Special order formats. **Acquisition:** Purchase. **Use:** Institution, CCTV, Home, SURA.

★5019★
Lay My Burden Down

1966. **Program Description:** A look at the plight of the Negro tenant farmers of the South, and the hardships faced by his family. **Length:** 60 mins. **Format:** 3/4U, Special order formats. **Acquisition:** Rent/Lease, Purchase. **Use:** Institution, CCTV, Home, SURA.

★5020★
Liberators: Fighting on Two Fronts in World War II
Direct Cinema Limited   Ph: (213)652-8000
PO Box 69799   Fax: (213)652-2346
Los Angeles, CA 90069-9976   Free: 800-345-6748

1992. **Program Description:** Recounts the story of American black battalions fighting segregation and discrimination in the armed forces even as they fought for their country in WWII. The documentary highlights black troops who were among the first to liberate the Nazi concentration camps of Dachau and Buchenwald. Shown on PBS' "American Experience." **Length:** 90 mins. **Format:** VHS. **Acquisition:** Purchase. **Use:** Home.

★5021★
The Life and Death of Malcolm X
Simitar Entertainment
3850 Annapolis Ln.   Ph: (612)559-6660
Plymouth, MN 55447   Fax: (612)559-0210

19??. **Program Description:** Documents the life and death of Malcolm X through his speeches, interviews and never before seen footage. Also includes a confession from Talmadge Hayer, one of Malcolm's assassins. **Length:** 90 mins. **Format:** VHS. **Acquisition:** Purchase. **Use:** Home, Institution.

★5022★
Listen Up!: The Lives of Quincy Jones
Warner Home Video, Inc.
4000 Warner Blvd.
Burbank, CA 91522   Ph: (818)954-6000

1991. **Program Description:** A biography of the music legend responsible for various movie scores ("In the Heat of the Night," "In Cold Blood," "The Color Purple"), record productions (Michael Jackson's "Thriller") and arrangements for the industry's top stars (Sinatra, Streisand, etc.). Included is a behind-the-scenes look at the making of the Grammy winning "Back on the Block" album. **Length:** 116 mins. **Format:** VHS, LV. **Acquisition:** Purchase. **Use:** Home.

★5023★
A Little Joke
Churchill Films
12210 Nebraska Ave.   Ph: (310)207-6600
Los Angeles, CA 90025   Fax: (310)207-1330

1985. **Program Description:** An animated film about two schoolgirls whose friendship is strained because one repeats a racial joke she heard from the other. For kids. **Length:** 12 mins. **Format:** VHS, 3/4U. **Acquisition:** Purchase. **Use:** Institution, Home, SURA.

★5024★
Livin' the Blues
Raedon Entertainment
8707-D Lindley Ave., Ste. 173   Ph: (818)582-2550
Northridge, CA 91325   Fax: (818)773-9770

1989. **Program Description:** The pursuit of the American Dream as seen by youths from the ghetto. Blues music drives their survival in the urban jungle. **Length:** 90 mins. **Format:** Beta, VHS. **Acquisition:** Purchase. **Use:** Home.

★5025★
Long Shadows
James Agee Film Project
316 1/2 E. Main St.   Ph: (615)926-8637
Johnson City, TN 37601   Free: 800-352-5111

1986. **Program Description:** An analysis of how the resonating effects of the Civil War can still be felt on society, via interviews with a number of noted writers, historians, civil rights activists and politicians. **Length:** 88 mins. **Format:** Beta, VHS, 3/4U. **Acquisition:** Purchase. **Use:** Institution, SURA.

★5026★
The Long Walk Home
Live Home Video
15400 Sherman Way, Ste. 500
Van Nuys, CA 91410-0124   Ph: (818)988-5060

1989. **Program Description:** In Montgomery Alabama, in the mid 1950s, sometime after Rosa Parks refused to sit in the black-designated back of the bus, Martin Luther King Jr. led a bus boycott. Spacek is the affluent white wife of a narrow-minded businessman while Goldberg is their struggling black maid. When Spacek discovers that Goldberg is supporting the boycott by walking the nine-mile trek to work, she sympathizes with the woman's familial responsibilities and tries to help. Hubby becomes unhappy camper when given the news and the plot marches inevitably toward a white-on-white showdown on racism while more quietly exploring gender equality between the women. Outstanding performances by Spacek and Goldberg, and a great fifties feel. **Length:** 95 mins. **Format:** VHS, LV. **Acquisition:** Purchase. **Use:** Home.

★5027★
Look Out Sister
Nostalgia Family Video
PO Box 606
Baker City, OR 97814   Ph: (503)523-9034

1948. **Program Description:** Jordan and an all-black cast star in this musical satire of westerns. "Two Gun" Jordan saves a dude ranch from foreclosure and wins the girl. Lots of black culture, slang and music from the '40s. Broad but enjoyable humor. Songs include "Caldonia" and "Don't Burn the Candle at Both Ends" plus 9 more. **Length:** 64 mins. **Format:** VHS. **Acquisition:** Purchase. **Use:** Home.

★5028★
Looking for Langston
Third World Newsreel
335 W. 38th St., 5th Fl.   Ph: (212)947-9277
New York, NY 10018   Fax: (212)594-6417

1989. **Program Description:** A look at the Harlem Renaissance, Langston Hughes, and black gay sexuality featuring the poetry of Essex Hemphill mixed with a blues/jazz soundtrack. **Length:** 45 mins. **Format:** VHS, 3/4U. **Acquisition:** Rent/Lease, Purchase. **Use:** Institution, Home.

★5029★
Losing Just the Same

1966. **Program Description:** The hope and despair of the American black community is examined, as seen in the story of one urban family. **Length:** 60 mins. **Format:** 3/4U, Special order formats. **Acquisition:** Rent/Lease, Purchase. **Use:** Institution, CCTV, Home, SURA.

★5030★
Louie Bluie
Music Video Distributors
O'Neill Industrial Center   Ph: (215)272-7771
1210 Standbridge St.   Fax: (215)272-6074
Norristown, PA 19403   Free: 800-888-0486

1985. **Program Description:** A documentary about the life and times of Armstrong, the last original black string musician, with views on his other talents, such as painting. **Length:** 60 mins. **Format:** Beta, VHS. **Acquisition:** Purchase. **Use:** Home.

★5031★
Louis Armstrong
King Features Entertainment
235 E. 45th St.   Ph: (212)455-4000
New York, NY 10017   Free: 800-526-5464

1983. **Program Description:** The words and music of Louis "Satchmo" Armstrong are featured in the program along with interviews with Billy Taylor, Peggy Lee, Al Hibbler and Satchmo himself. **Length:** 13 mins. **Format:** Beta, VHS, 3/4U. **Acquisition:** Rent/Lease, Purchase. **Use:** Institution, SURA.

★5032★
Louis Armstrong
Direct Cinema Limited   Ph: (213)652-8000
PO Box 69799   Fax: (213)652-2346
Los Angeles, CA 90069-9976   Free: 800-345-6748

1968. **Program Description:** A look at the virtuoso jazzman's personality as expressed through his music. **Length:** 58 mins. **Format:** Beta, VHS, 3/4U, Special order formats. **Acquisition:** Rent/Lease, Purchase. **Use:** Institution, Home, SURA.

★5033★
Louis Armstrong: The Gentle Giant of Jazz
AIMS Media   Ph: (818)773-4300
9710 DeSoto Ave.   Fax: (818)341-6700
Chatsworth, CA 91311-4409   Free: 800-367-2467

1988. **Program Description:** A biography of the masterful trumpet genius, covering his life from poverty in New Orleans to worldwide acclaim. **Length:** 24 mins. **Format:** Beta, VHS, 3/4U. **Acquisition:** Purchase, Duplication License. **Use:** Institution, SURA.

★5034★
Louis Farrakhan at Madison Square Garden
Simon Wiesenthal Center
9760 W. Pico Blvd.   Ph: (310)553-9036
Los Angeles, CA 90035-4792   Fax: (310)553-8007

1985. **Program Description:** This program contains excerpts from Louis Farrakhan's 1985 appearance at Madison Square Garden. Intended for classroom and group discussions. **Length:** 40 mins. **Format:** Beta, VHS. **Acquisition:** Purchase. **Use:** Institution, SURA.

★5035★
Macumba
Filmakers Library, Inc.
124 E. 40th
New York, NY 10016   Ph: (212)808-4980
1984. **Program Description:** The roots and beliefs of African spirit religions practiced throughout the continent is explained. **Length:** 43 mins. **Format:** Beta, VHS, 3/4U. **Acquisition:** Purchase. **Use:** Institution.

★5036★
Mahalia Jackson and Elizabeth Cotten: Two Remarkable Ladies
1974. **Program Description:** A close-up look at a pair of successful black women performers: "Mahalia Jackson," a filmed biography of the legendary singer, and "Freight Train," the courageous story of pioneer folksinger Elizabeth Cotten. **Length:** 58 mins. **Format:** Beta, VHS. **Acquisition:** Purchase. **Use:** Home.

★5037★
Maids and Madams: Apartheid Begins in the Home
Filmakers Library, Inc.
124 E. 40th
New York, NY 10016   Ph: (212)808-4980
1986. **Program Description:** The relationship between maid and madam in South Africa is a microcosm of the apartheid system. Some white employers are kind, while others are brutal. This film examines this complex relationship, where the black women are trapped by racial injustice and the white women by fear. **Length:** 52 mins. **Format:** VHS, 3/4U. **Acquisition:** Rent/Lease, Purchase, Duplication. **Use:** Institution, Home, SURA.

★5038★
Makhalipile: The Dauntless One
Cinema Guild
1697 Broadway   Ph: (212)246-5522
New York, NY 10019   Fax: (212)246-5525
1989. **Program Description:** Profiles the life and work of Archbishop Trevor Huddleston, who has fought relentlessly against racial tyranny in South Africa. **Length:** 54 mins. **Format:** Beta, VHS, 3/4U. **Acquisition:** Purchase. **Use:** Institution.

★5039★
Malcolm X
Carousel Film & Video
260 5th Ave., Rm. 405   Ph: (212)683-1660
New York, NY 10001   Fax: (212)683-1662
1965. **Program Description:** A biography of black activist Malcolm X beginning with his eighth grade year in school as an honor student and class president, to his assassination because of his beliefs. **Length:** 23 mins. **Format:** Beta, VHS, 3/4U. **Acquisition:** Purchase. **Use:** Institution, SURA.

★5040★
Malcolm X: El Hajj Malik El Shabazz
Proud To Be. . .A Black Video Collection
1235-E East Blvd., Ste. 209
Charlotte, NC 28203   Ph: (704)523-2227
1991. **Program Description:** Probing look into the life and suspicious death of Malcolm X, one of the century's most intriguing leaders. **Length:** 60 mins. **Format:** VHS. **Acquisition:** Purchase. **Use:** Home.

★5041★
Man & Boy
Columbia Tristar Home Video
3400 Riverside Dr.   Ph: (818)972-8193
Burbank, CA 91505-4627   Fax: (818)972-0937
1971. **Program Description:** A black Civil War veteran, played by Bill Cosby, encounters bigotry and prejudice when he tries to set up a homestead in Arizona. Also known as "Ride a Dark Horse." **Length:** 98 mins. **Format:** Beta, VHS. **Acquisition:** Purchase. **Use:** Home.

★5042★
Man in Africa: Heritage and Transition
New York State Education Department
Center for Learning Technologies
Media Distribution Network, Rm. C-7,
  Concourse Level
Albany, NY 12230   Ph: (518)474-3852
196?. **Program Description:** This series examines the people and cultures of Africa. **Length:** 30 mins. **Format:** Beta, VHS, EJ, 3/4U, Q. **Acquisition:** Duplication, Free Duplication. **Use:** Institution, SURA.

★5043★
Manchild Revisited: A Commentary by Claude Brown
PBS Video
11858 La Grange Ave.   Ph: (213)820-0991
Los Angeles, CA 90025   Fax: (213)826-4779
1987. **Program Description:** This program graphically illustrates the problems being faced by young black men in this country. Claude Brown takes viewers into America's urban areas where violent crime, drug abuse, unemployment, and family abandonment are everyday occurrences. **Length:** 60 mins. **Format:** Beta, VHS, 3/4U. **Acquisition:** Purchase, Rent/Lease, Duplication, Off-Air Record. **Use:** Institution, CCTV, Home, SURA.

★5044★
Mandela-Free at Last
JCI Video
5312 Derry Ave., No. M
Agoura Hills, CA 91301-4524
1990. **Program Description:** A portrait of Nelson Mandela and South Africa painted on the occasion of his release from prison. Features clandestine footage smuggled out of the country, plus Mandela's complete first speech after his release. Produced by the Emmy Award-winning series "South Africa Now." **Length:** 79 mins. **Format:** Beta, VHS. **Acquisition:** Purchase. **Use:** Home.

★5045★
Mandela in America
Music Video Distributors
O'Neill Industrial Center   Ph: (215)272-7771
1210 Standbridge St.   Fax: (215)272-6074
Norristown, PA 19403   Free: 800-888-0486
1990. **Program Description:** An overview of the freed South African Marxist's United States tour. Features celebrity interviews with Spike Lee, Jane Fonda and Eddie Murphy, plus musical commentary from Ice-T, Tracy Chapman, Johnny Clegg, Aretha Franklin, Sweet Honey in the Rock, and many others. Included, for the first time on video, is Stevie Wonder's "Keep Our Love Alive," written especially for the Mandela visit. Portions of the video's profits are donated to the Nelson Madela Freedom Fund. **Length:** 90 mins. **Format:** VHS. **Acquisition:** Purchase. **Use:** Home.

★5046★
Mapandangare: The Great Baboon
FilmFair Communications
1560 Sherman Ave., No. 100
Evanston, IL 60201-4817
1978. **Program Description:** An evening of music and storytelling in an African village. **Length:** 10 mins. **Format:** Beta, VHS, 3/4U. **Acquisition:** Purchase, Duplication License. **Use:** Institution, SURA.

★5047★
The March on Washington Remembered
Encyclopedia Britannica Educational
  Corporation
310 S. Michigan Ave.
Chicago, IL 60604   Ph: (312)347-7000
1990. **Program Description:** Newsreel footage and folksongs describe the experience of the 1963 Civil Rights march on Washington D.C., while the movement is considered in light of the giant legislative leaps it spurred. **Length:** 19 mins. **Format:** VHS. **Acquisition:** Purchase. **Use:** Home, Institution.

★5048★
Marcus Garvey: Toward Black Nationhood
Films for the Humanities & Sciences   Ph: (609)452-1128
PO Box 2053   Fax: (609)275-3767
Princeton, NJ 08543   Free: 800-257-5126
198?. **Program Description:** This film exhibits how Marcus Garvey's call for an independent black nation in the 1920s influenced modern civil rights movements throughout the world. **Length:** 42 mins. **Format:** Beta, VHS, 3/4U. **Acquisition:** Purchase. **Use:** Institution, SURA.

★5049★
The Mark of the Hawk
American Video Corporation   Ph: (818)407-0590
8444 Reseda Blvd., Ste. M   Fax: (818)907-0598
Northridge, CA 91324   Free: 800-323-7979
1957. **Program Description:** A uniquely told story of African nations struggling to achieve racial equality after gaining independence. Songs include "This Man Is Mine," sung by Kitt. Also called "The Accused." **Length:** 83 mins. **Format:** VHS, Special order formats. **Acquisition:** Purchase. **Use:** Home.

★5050★
Marketing to Minorities
Quiet Advantage
1949 S. Manchester St., No. 34   Ph: (714)748-1840
Anaheim, CA 92802   Free: 800-794-4110
1991. **Program Description:** Methods for capturing the increasingly important market of minorities. **Length:** 30 mins. **Format:** VHS. **Acquisition:** Purchase. **Use:** Institution.

★5051★
Martin Luther King: An Amazing Grace
Facets Multimedia, Inc.
1517 W. Fullerton Ave.
Chicago, IL 60614   Ph: (312)281-9075
1991. **Program Description:** Documentary of Dr. King which remains the only one produced by African-Americans. Highlights the civil rights movement in the 1950s and 60s, and examines King's role in these revolutionary times. **Length:** 60 mins. **Format:** VHS. **Acquisition:** Purchase. **Use:** Institution, Home.

★5052★
Martin Luther King, Jr.: A Filmed Record, Montgomery to Memphis
Richard Kaplan Productions, Inc.
290 W. End Ave.   Ph: (212)787-0258
New York, NY 10023   Fax: (212)808-4983
1969. **Program Description:** A documentary look at the career of Dr. Martin Luther King, Jr., from the 1955 Montgomery, Alabama bus boycotts to his murder in 1968. **Length:** 26 mins. **Format:** 3/4U, Q. **Acquisition:** Rent/Lease, Purchase. **Use:** Institution, CCTV, CATV, BCTV, Home.

★5053★
Martin Luther King, Jr.: A Man of Peace
Journal Films, Inc.   Ph: (708)328-6700
930 Pitner Ave.   Fax: (708)328-6706
Evanston, IL 60202   Free: 800-323-5448
1968. **Program Description:** An intimate look at the man, the minister, the father, and the leader of the civil rights movement. King expresses his philosophy of non-violence, the future of the civil rights movement, and his personal feelings about death. **Length:** 29 mins. **Format:** Beta, VHS, 3/4U. **Acquisition:** Purchase. **Use:** Institution, SURA.

★5054★
Martin Luther King, Jr.: A Peaceful Warrior
Afro-Am Distributing Company
407 E. 25th St., Ste. 600   Ph: (312)791-1611
Chicago, IL 60616   Fax: (312)791-0921
19??. **Program Description:** Two children look into why they have no school on Dr. King's birthday, and discover some important lessons about American history. **Length:** 20 mins. **Format:** VHS. **Acquisition:** Purchase. **Use:** Institution, Home, SURA.

★5055★
Martin Luther King, Jr.: I Have a Dream
International Historic Films, Inc. (IHF)
PO Box 29035   Ph: (312)927-2900
Chicago, IL 60629   Fax: (312)927-9211
1986. **Program Description:** Complete presentation of Dr. King's most famous speech from August 28, 1963, plus original footage from the early days of the civil rights struggle. Watch closely as he finishes his prepared speech and, unsatisfied with it, begins the "I have a dream" segment. Included also is his "I have been to the mountaintop" speech, delivered just days before he was assassinated. **Length:** 25 mins. **Format:** Beta, VHS, 3/4U. **Acquisition:** Purchase. **Use:** Institution, Home.

★5056★
Martin Luther King, Jr.: Legacy of a Dream
Films Inc. Video
5547 N. Ravenswood Ave.   Ph: (312)878-2600
Chicago, IL 60640-1199   Free: 800-323-4222
1974. **Program Description:** A history of Dr. Martin Luther King's non-violence movement and its relevance today. (Some black and white footage). **Length:** 29 mins. **Format:** Beta, VHS, 3/4U, Special order formats. **Acquisition:** Purchase. **Use:** Institution.

★5057★
Martin Luther King, Jr.: Montgomery to Memphis
Films Inc. Video
5547 N. Ravenswood Ave.   Ph: (312)878-2600
Chicago, IL 60640-1199   Free: 800-323-4222
1970. **Program Description:** The life of Martin Luther King is explored, from his early days as a minister in Montgomery, to his assassination in 1968. (Also available in a 180-minute version which includes testimonials by outstanding Americans). **Length:** 103 mins. **Format:** Beta, VHS, 3/4U, LV, Special order formats. **Acquisition:** Purchase. **Use:** Institution, Home, SURA.

★5058★
Martin Luther King, Jr.: The Assassin Years
Centron Films
108 Wilmot Rd.   Ph: (708)940-1260
Deerfield, IL 60015-9990   Free: 800-621-2131
1978. **Program Description:** A look at Dr. King's early years, which also follows his great civil rights crusade throughout the South. He won the Nobel prize in 1964 and was killed four years later. **Length:** 26 mins. **Format:** Beta, VHS, 3/4U. **Acquisition:** Purchase. **Use:** Institution, SURA.

★5059★
Martin Luther King: The Legacy
The Media Guild
11722 Sorrento Valley Rd., Ste. E   Ph: (619)755-9191
San Diego, CA 92121   Fax: (619)755-4931
1989. **Program Description:** The importance and impact that the famous black right activist had is sadly remembered on the anniversary of his death. **Length:** 79 mins. **Format:** Beta, VHS, 3/4U. **Acquisition:** Purchase. **Use:** Institution, SURA.

★5060★
Mask
Video Out
1102 Homer St.
Vancouver, BC, Canada V6B 2X6   Ph: (604)688-4336
1963. **Program Description:** An image of the mask of a painted voice recurs throughout this story of a young black woman's search for identity. **Length:** 30 mins. **Format:** Beta, VHS, 3/4U. **Acquisition:** Rent/Lease. **Use:** Institution, SURA.

★5061★
Massachusetts 54th Colored Infantry
PBS Video
11858 La Grange Ave.   Ph: (310)820-0991
Los Angeles, CA 90025   Fax: (310)826-4779
1991. **Program Description:** The struggle of Blacks to prove themselves worthy in battle during the Civil War is explored through diary and journal accounts and oral history shared by descendents of

those who fought. **Length:** 60 mins. **Format:** VHS. **Acquisition:** Purchase. **Use:** Institution, Home.

★5062★
A Matter of Insurance
Time-Life Video and Television
1450 E. Parham Rd.   Ph: (804)266-6330
Richmond, VA 23280   Free: 800-621-7026
1977. **Program Description:** A dramatic change in public opinion occurs in this episode of the ''Fight Against Slavery'' series when a slave captain who has murdered more than 130 Africans is charged on an insurance claim, not murder. **Length:** 52 mins. **Format:** Beta, VHS, 3/4U, Special order formats. **Acquisition:** Rent/Lease, Purchase. **Use:** Institution, SURA.

★5063★
Mau Mau
Films Inc. Video
5547 N. Ravenswood Ave.   Ph: (312)878-2600
Chicago, IL 60640-1199   Free: 800-323-4222
1973. **Program Description:** This segment of ''Black Man's Land'' reveals that Mau Mau was an army set up to fight repression and aggression. Although they won their struggle against the British, the Mau Mau suffered the consequences. Also available in a 28-minute edited version. **Length:** 52 mins. **Format:** Beta, VHS, 3/4U. **Acquisition:** Purchase. **Use:** Institution, SURA.

★5064★
Maxine Sullivan: Love to Be in Love
Cinema Guild
1697 Broadway, Ste. 802   Ph: (212)246-5522
New York, NY 10019   Fax: (212)246-5525
1990. **Program Description:** A portrait of Maxine Sullivan (1911-1987), the legendary black vocalist who rose from obscurity to become one of the foremost black female vocalists in America. Traces her career through radio, TV and film with clips, photos and testimonials from other jazz stars. Footage in color and B&W. **Length:** 48 mins. **Format:** VHS. **Acquisition:** Purchase, Rent/Lease. **Use:** Institution, Home.

★5065★
The McMasters
Starmaker Entertainment, Inc.   Ph: (908)389-1020
151 Industrial Way, E.   Fax: (908)389-1021
Eatontown, NJ 07724   Free: 800-233-3738
1970. **Program Description:** Set shortly after the Civil War, the film tells the story of the prejudice faced by a black soldier who returns to the southern ranch on which he was raised. Once there, the rancher gives him half of the property, but the ex-soldier has difficulty finding men who will work for him. When a group of Native Americans assist him, a band of bigoted men do their best to stop it. The movie was released in two versions with different endings: in one, prejudice prevails; in the other, bigotry is defeated. Also called ''The Blood Crowd'' and ''The McMasters.Tougher Than the West Itself.'' **Length:** 89 mins. **Format:** VHS. **Acquisition:** Purchase. **Use:** Home.

★5066★
Men of Bronze
Pacific Arts Video   Ph: (310)820-0991
11858 La Grange   Fax: (310)826-4779
Los Angeles, CA 90025   Free: 800-538-5856
1977. **Program Description:** Valor and pride in the midst of prejudice is the theme of this film about the all-black 369th Infantry Regiment, which which spent 191 days under fire on the front lines during World War I. **Length:** 58 mins. **Format:** Beta, VHS, 3/4U. **Acquisition:** Purchase. **Use:** Institution, SURA.

★5067★
Mental Health Needs of Minority Children
Social Psychiatry Research Institute
150 E. 69th St.
New York, NY 10021   Ph: (212)628-4800
1981. **Program Description:** This program describes the special problems of minority groups, blacks, Hispanics and native Americans, with an emphasis on preventive work with children in school settings so as to avoid the continued high incidence of neurosis and psychoses in these populations. **Length:** 50 mins. **Format:** EJ, 3/4U. **Acquisition:** Rent/Lease, Purchase. **Use:** Institution, CCTV.

★5068★
Miles of Smiles, Years of Struggle
Benchmark Media   Ph: (914)762-3838
145 Scarborough Rd.   Fax: (914)762-3895
Briarcliff Manor, NY 10510   Free: 800-438-5564
1983. **Program Description:** The history of the Black Pullman Porters is told through a reunion of retired porters, archival films and stills, vintage Hollywood footage and a 100-year-old porter's widow. **Length:** 59 mins. **Format:** Beta, VHS, 3/4U. **Acquisition:** Purchase. **Use:** Institution, CCTV.

★5069★
Mini-Films on Prejudice
Anti-Defamation League of B'nai B'rith
Audio-Visual Dept.
823 United Nations Plaza
New York, NY 10017   Ph: (212)490-2525
1983. **Program Description:** A series of 30 and 60-second public service spots, mostly by celebrities, that serve as a motivating device to indicate what prejudice is all about. useful for students; also distributed free of charge to TV stations. Available together or separately. **Length:** 1 mins. **Format:** Beta, VHS, 3/4U. **Acquisition:** Purchase. **Use:** Institution, CCTV, CATV, BCTV, Home.

★5070★
Minister Malcolm X: Interview, 1963
Afro-Am Distributing Company
407 E. 25th St., Ste. 600   Ph: (312)791-1611
Chicago, IL 60616   Fax: (312)791-0921
196?. **Program Description:** A video complement to Malcolm X's autobiography, this film traces the origins of the black movement, and follows it beyond the leader's death. **Length:** 90 mins. **Format:** VHS. **Acquisition:** Purchase. **Use:** Institution, Home, SURA.

★5071★
A Minor Altercation
Cinema Guild
1697 Broadway, Ste. 802   Ph: (212)246-5522
New York, NY 10019   Fax: (212)246-5525
1976. **Program Description:** This video explores racial tensions in American public schools. **Length:** 30 mins. **Format:** Beta, VHS, 3/4U. **Acquisition:** Rent/Lease, Purchase, Duplication. **Use:** Institution, SURA.

★5072★
Minorities
CRM/McGraw-Hill Films
674 Via de la Valle
PO Box 641
Del Mar, CA 92014
1977. **Program Description:** This program from the ''American Condition'' series examines the economic status of black Americans today, with evidence of continued discrimination and its cost to all Americans. **Length:** 15 mins. **Format:** Beta, VHS, 3/4U. **Acquisition:** Rent/Lease, Purchase. **Use:** Institution, SURA.

★5073★
Minorities in Journalism: Making a Difference
PBS Video
11858 La Grange Ave.   Ph: (310)820-0991
Los Angeles, CA 90025   Fax: (310)826-4779
1989. **Program Description:** A look at how minority students can enter and get ahead in the various branches of journalism - print, radio, and TV. **Length:** 25 mins. **Format:** VHS, 3/4U. **Acquisition:** Purchase, Off-Air Record, Duplication License. **Use:** Institution, CCTV, CATV.

★5074★
Minority Youth: Felicia
Phoenix/BFA Films
468 Park Ave., S.   Ph: (212)684-5910
New York, NY 10016   Free: 800-221-1274

1971. **Program Description:** Discrimination and prejudice greatly affect young black people's goals. Felicia hopes to go to college to help improve the attitudes of the apathetic adults. **Length:** 12 mins. **Format:** Beta, VHS, 3/4U. **Acquisition:** Purchase. **Use:** Institution, SURA.

★5075★
The Miracle of Intervale Avenue
Ergo Media Inc.
668 Front St.   Ph: (201)692-0404
PO Box 2037   Fax: (201)692-0663
Teaneck, NJ 07666   Free: 800-695-3746

1979. **Program Description:** An intriguing documentary about a Jewish community in a decaying South Bronx area that continues to survive and the remarkable interacting of the Jews, Blacks and Puerto Ricans who help each other. **Length:** 65 mins. **Format:** Beta, VHS. **Acquisition:** Purchase. **Use:** Home.

★5076★
Mississippi Masala
Columbia Tristar Home Video
3400 Riverside Dr.   Ph: (818)972-8193
Burbank, CA 91505-4627   Fax: (818)972-0937

1992. **Program Description:** "Masala" is an Indian seasoning made of different-colored spices blended together, as this film is a blend of romance, comedy, and social conscience. An interracial romance sets off a cultural collision in a small Southern town. Mina is a young Indian woman whose family were exiled from Uganda in a purge of Asians by Idi Amin. They've settled, somewhat unwillingly, into running a motel in Greenwood, Mississippi. Demetrius is an ambitious black man with his own carpet-cleaning business. When Mina and Demetrius fall in love both families disapprove and it appears the lovers will be parted by the racial tensions. Washington and Choudhury are engaging as the lovers with Seth, as Mina's unhappy father, especially watchable. **Length:** 118 mins. **Format:** VHS, LV. **Acquisition:** Purchase. **Use:** Home.

★5077★
Mrs. Fannie Lou Hamer
William Greaves Productions, Inc.   Ph: (212)265-6150
230 W. 55th St.   Fax: (212)315-0027
New York, NY 10019   Free: 800-874-8314

19??. **Program Description:** Born in Mississippi in 1917, Mrs. Hamer became a dominant presence in the Civil Rights movement of the 1960s. In this interview, the founder of the Mississippi Freedom Democratic Party talks about her experiences growing up in the Deep South and her struggle for human rights. **Length:** 50 mins. **Format:** VHS. **Acquisition:** Purchase. **Use:** Institution.

★5078★
Mo' Better Blues
MCA/Universal Home Video
70 Universal City Plaza   Ph: (818)777-6419
Universal City, CA 91608-9955   Fax: (818)733-0226

1990. **Program Description:** Lee's fourth feature is on the surface a backstage jazz biopic. But there hasn't been a Lee feature that wasn't vitally concerned with complicated racial issues and though subtle and indirect, this is no exception. Bleek Gilliam is a handsome, accomplished jazz trumpeter who divides his limited extra-curricular time between Clarke (newcomer Williams), an aspiring jazz vocalist, and Indigo (junior Lee sibling Joie), a down-to-earth school teacher. What's interesting is not so much the story of self-interested musician and ladies' man Gilliam, but the subtle racial issues his life draws into focus. The Branford Marsalis Quartet provides the music for Bleek's group, scored by Lee's dad Bill (on whose life the script is loosely based). **Length:** 129 mins. **Format:** Beta, VHS, LV. **Acquisition:** Purchase. **Use:** Home.

★5079★
Motown 25: Yesterday, Today, Forever
Music Video Distributors
O'Neill Industrial Center   Ph: (215)272-7771
1210 Standbridge St.   Fax: (215)272-6074
Norristown, PA 19403   Free: 800-888-0486

1983. **Program Description:** The television all-star salute to Berry Gordy that features a musical duel between the Four Tops and The Temptations and the reunion of The Jackson Five. The show where Michael Jackson lip-synched "Billy Jean" and moonwalked to the big, big time. **Length:** 130 mins. **Format:** Beta, VHS, 8mm, LV. **Acquisition:** Purchase. **Use:** Home.

★5080★
MOVE: Confrontation in Philadelphia
Temple University
Dept. of Tadio-TV-Film
Annenberg Hall
Philadelphia, PA 19122   Ph: (215)204-8483

1980. **Program Description:** A look at the events leading up to the police arrest of MOVE, a radical black political commune. The video journalists reveal the complex relationship of media bias, police harrassment, and subtle economic motivation in the violent removal of MOVE. **Length:** 60 mins. **Format:** 3/4U. **Acquisition:** Rent/Lease, Purchase. **Use:** Institution, SURA.

★5081★
Music and Comedy Masters Series
Discount Video Tapes, Inc.
PO Box 7122   Ph: (818)843-3366
Burbank, CA 91510   Fax: (818)843-3821

1991. **Program Description:** This six volume series focuses on black show-business, including singing, dancing and comedy material. **Length:** mins. **Format:** VHS. **Acquisition:** Purchase. **Use:** Home.

★5082★
Music of the Spirits
Flower Films
10341 San Pablo Ave.   Ph: (510)525-0942
El Cerrito, CA 94530   Fax: (510)525-1204
                                     Free: 800-572-7618

1988. **Program Description:** Stella Madamombe, the mibra master of Zimbabwe, is profiled in this illuminating documentary probing the roots of African music. **Length:** 30 mins. **Format:** VHS. **Acquisition:** Purchase. **Use:** Home.

★5083★
My Past Is My Own
Pyramid Film & Video
Box 1048   Ph: (310)828-7577
2801 Colorado Ave.   Fax: (310)453-9083
Santa Monica, CA 90406   Free: 800-421-2304

1989. **Program Description:** Two black teenagers go back in time to the civil rights movement of the sixties. **Length:** 47 mins. **Format:** Beta, VHS, 3/4U. **Acquisition:** Purchase, Rent/Lease. **Use:** Institution, Home, SURA.

★5084★
The Nat "King" Cole Story
Karol Video
PO Box 7600
Wilkes Barre, PA 18773   Ph: (717)822-8899

1955. **Program Description:** Nat King Cole stars in this short documentary about his life from saloon pianist to recording artist. Songs include "Sweet Lorraine," "Pretend," and "Straighten Up and Fly Right." Narrated by Jeff Chandler. **Length:** 30 mins. **Format:** VHS. **Acquisition:** Purchase. **Use:** Home.

★5085★
Nationtime, Gary
William Greaves Productions, Inc.   Ph: (212)265-6150
230 W. 55th St.   Fax: (212)315-0027
New York, NY 10019   Free: 800-874-8314

1973. **Program Description:** This is a historical record of the First National Black Political Convention held in Gary, Indiana in 1972.

Length: 90 mins. **Format:** Beta, VHS. **Acquisition:** Rent/Lease, Purchase. **Use:** Institution, BCTV.

★5086★
Native Son
Nostalgia Family Video
PO Box 606
Baker City, OR 97814   Ph: (503)523-9034

1951. **Program Description:** A young black man from the ghettos of Chicago is hired as a chauffeur by an affluent white family. His job is to drive their head-strong daughter anywhere she wants to go. Unintentionally, he kills her, tries to hide, and is ultimately found guilty. Based on the classic novel by Richard Wright, who also stars. Remade in 1986. Unprofessional direction and low budget work against the strong story. **Length:** 91 mins. **Format:** VHS. **Acquisition:** Purchase. **Use:** Home.

★5087★
Native Son
Afro-Am Distributing Company
407 E. 25th St., Ste. 600   Ph: (312)791-1611
Chicago, IL 60616   Fax: (312)791-0921

197?. **Program Description:** A video supplement designed to be used when reading the Richard Wright novel. Originally a filmstrip, this video has been enhanced by computer to give an animated. **Length:** mins. **Format:** VHS. **Acquisition:** Purchase. **Use:** Institution, Home, SURA.

★5088★
Native Son
Live Home Video
15400 Sherman Way
PO Box 10124
Van Nuys, CA 91410-0124   Ph: (818)988-5060

1986. **Program Description:** This second film adaptation of the classic Richard Wright novel is chock full of stars and tells the story of a poor black man who accidentally kills a white woman and then hides the body. Changes in the script soft-soap some of the novel's disturbing truths and themes–so-so drama for those who have not read the book. **Length:** 111 mins. **Format:** Beta, VHS, LV. **Acquisition:** Purchase. **Use:** Home.

★5089★
The Negro Ensemble Company
Films for the Humanities & Sciences   Ph: (609)452-1128
PO Box 2053   Fax: (609)275-3767
Princeton, NJ 08543   Free: 800-257-5126

1987. **Program Description:** The goals and remarkable achievements of this black theater troupe are documented herein. **Length:** 58 mins. **Format:** Beta, VHS, 3/4U. **Acquisition:** Purchase. **Use:** Institution, SURA.

★5090★
The Negro Soldier
Republic Pictures Home Video
12636 Beatrice St.
Los Angeles, CA 90066-0930   Ph: (310)306-4040

1944. **Program Description:** A look at the participation of black soldiers in World War II. **Length:** 40 mins. **Format:** Beta, VHS, 3/4U. **Acquisition:** Purchase. **Use:** Institution, Home.

★5091★
New Jack City
Warner Home Video, Inc.
4000 Warner Blvd.
Burbank, CA 91522   Ph: (818)954-6000

1991. **Program Description:** Just say no ghetto-melodrama. Powerful performance by Snipes as wealthy Harlem drug lord sought by rebel cops Ice-T and Nelson. Music by Johnny Gill, 2 Live Crew, Ice-T and others. Available with Spanish subtitles. **Length:** 101 mins. **Format:** VHS, LV. **Acquisition:** Purchase. **Use:** Home.

★5092★
Nightline: Louis Farrakahn
Proud To Be. . .A Black Video Collection
1235-E East Blvd., Ste. 209
Charlotte, NC 28203   Ph: (704)523-2227

1984. **Program Description:** Farrakahn, the controversial leader of the Nation of Islam, discusses his relationship with Jesse Jackson during the 1984 presidential campaign. **Length:** 45 mins. **Format:** VHS. **Acquisition:** Purchase. **Use:** Home.

★5093★
No Middle Road to Freedom
California Newsreel
149 Ninth St., Ste. 420   Ph: (415)621-6196
San Francisco, CA 94103   Fax: (415)621-6522

1985. **Program Description:** Documentary that begins with a commemorative ceremony held to honor victims of apartheid, particularly the 42 persons killed in 1982 in the capitol of Lesotho. Chosen by the National Council of Churches as the main resource for its Mission Study on South Africa. **Length:** 40 mins. **Format:** VHS. **Acquisition:** Purchase, Rent/Lease. **Use:** Institution.

★5094★
No One Quite Like Me. . .Or You
Sunburst Communications, Inc.
39 Washington Ave.   Ph: (914)769-5030
Pleasantville, NY 10570   Free: 800-431-1934

1992. **Program Description:** The physical differences between people of various races are shown. Includes a segment on handicapped people. Comes with student worksheets, teacher's guide, and catalog kit. **Length:** 16 mins. **Format:** VHS. **Acquisition:** Purchase. **Use:** Institution.

★5095★
No Vietnamese Ever Called Me Nigger
Cinema Guild
1697 Broadway, Ste. 802   Ph: (212)246-5522
New York, NY 10019   Fax: (212)246-5525

1968. **Program Description:** A powerful documentary depicting through interviews with black Vietnam veterans the racism they confronted in the armed forces and at home. **Length:** 68 mins. **Format:** Beta, VHS, 3/4U. **Acquisition:** Rent/Lease, Purchase, Duplication. **Use:** Institution, SURA.

★5096★
Non-Apartheid Education Inside South Africa
Michigan State University
Instructional Media Center   Ph: (517)353-9229
East Lansing, MI 48826-0710   Fax: (517)336-2650

1988. **Program Description:** A look at racially mixed education opportunities in a country where such opportunities are not easy to find. **Length:** 32 mins. **Format:** Beta, VHS, 3/4U. **Acquisition:** Purchase, Rent/Lease. **Use:** Institution, CCTV.

★5097★
Notable Black Americans: Jackie Robinson
19??. **Program Description:** A profile of the man who broke the color barrier in Major League Baseball. **Length:** 20 mins. **Format:** VHS. **Acquisition:** Purchase. **Use:** Institution, Home, SURA.

★5098★
Notable Black Americans: Jesse Jackson
19??. **Program Description:** A profile of the Civil Rights activist, including his attempts to run for the U.S. presidency. **Length:** 20 mins. **Format:** VHS. **Acquisition:** Purchase. **Use:** Institution, Home, SURA.

★5099★
Notable Black Americans: Madame C.J. Walker
19??. **Program Description:** A profile of the woman who challenged racism and sexism to break into the world of business. **Length:** 20 mins. **Format:** VHS. **Acquisition:** Purchase. **Use:** Institution, Home, SURA.

★5100★
Notable Black Americans: Paul Robeson
19??. **Program Description:** A profile of the renaissance man who achieved international noteriety after attending Rutgers College. **Length:** 20 mins. **Format:** VHS. **Acquisition:** Purchase. **Use:** Institution, Home, SURA.

★5101★
Of Black America Series
Phoenix/BFA Films
468 Park Ave., S.   Ph: (212)684-5910
New York, NY 10016   Free: 800-221-1274
1968. **Program Description:** The Black heritage and history are presented in this five-part series. From the early days of slavery to the influence of soul music, narrator Bill Cosby and news reporters relate an examination of the Black struggle and plight. Programs are available individually. **Length:** 37 mins. **Format:** Beta, VHS, 3/4U. **Acquisition:** Purchase. **Use:** Institution, SURA.

★5102★
The Old African Blasphemer
Time-Life Video and Television
1450 E. Parham Rd.   Ph: (804)266-6330
Richmond, VA 23280   Free: 800-621-7026
1977. **Program Description:** This episode of the "Fight Against Slavery" series details the horrors of a typical slave ship's Atlantic crossing. At the helm is a captain who later became an abolitionist preacher. **Length:** 55 mins. **Format:** Beta, VHS, 3/4U, Special order formats. **Acquisition:** Rent/Lease, Purchase. **Use:** Institution, SURA.

★5103★
Old, Black and Alive!
The New Film Company, Inc.
7 Mystic St., Ste. 310   Ph: (617)641-2580
Arlington, MA 02174   Free: 800-462-2306
1979. **Program Description:** Seven elderly black people share their insight, faith and strength on the subject of aging. **Length:** 28 mins. **Format:** Beta, VHS, 3/4U. **Acquisition:** Rent/Lease, Purchase. **Use:** Institution, Home.

★5104★
On Black America
American Humanist Association
7 Harwood Dr.   Ph: (716)839-5080
PO Box 146   Fax: (716)839-5079
Amherst, NY 14226-0146   Free: 800-743-6646
1972. **Program Description:** The director of the Public Policy Training Institute and founder of the Congress of Racial Equality discusses the gains made in the struggle for equal rights and offers constructive guidelines for future action. Part of the "Humanist Alternative" series. **Length:** 30 mins. **Format:** 3/4U, Special order formats. **Acquisition:** Rent/Lease, Purchase. **Use:** Institution, CCTV, CATV.

★5105★
On My Own: The Traditions of Daisy Turner
Filmakers Library, Inc.
124 E. 40th
New York, NY 10016   Ph: (212)808-4980
1987. **Program Description:** Daisy Turner, a 102 year old black women, provides the viewer with an oral history of her family's history in rural Vermont. **Length:** 28 mins. **Format:** VHS, 3/4U. **Acquisition:** Rent/Lease, Purchase, Duplication. **Use:** Institution, Home, SURA.

★5106★
One in the Lord
UMCom Video
810 12th Ave., S.   Ph: (615)242-6277
Nashville, TN 37203   Free: 800-251-4091
1978. **Program Description:** This documentary studies the people and ministry of the ethnic minority local churches. **Length:** 30 mins. **Format:** 3/4U. **Acquisition:** Rent/Lease, Purchase. **Use:** Institution, CATV, BCTV.

★5107★
One Man's Property
Time-Life Video and Television
1450 E. Parham Rd.   Ph: (804)266-6330
Richmond, VA 23280   Free: 800-621-7026
1977. **Program Description:** This episode of the "Fight Against Slavery" series traces the events leading up to the Somerset Case in 1772, in which the judge declared that it was unlawful for one man to be the property of another on English soil. **Length:** 56 mins. **Format:** Beta, VHS, 3/4U, Special order formats. **Acquisition:** Rent/Lease, Purchase. **Use:** Institution, SURA.

★5108★
One More Hurdle
FilmFair Communications
1560 Sherman Ave., No. 100
Evanston, IL 60201-4817
1988. **Program Description:** The true story of a black girl who attempts to be a champion horse rider. **Length:** 47 mins. **Format:** Beta, VHS, 3/4U. **Acquisition:** Purchase, Duplication License. **Use:** Institution, SURA.

★5109★
Opportunities for the Disadvantaged
AEF/Capital Communications   Ph: (615)868-2040
3807 Dickerson Rd.   Fax: (615)868-5239
Nashville, TN 37207   Free: 800-822-5678
1977. **Program Description:** A look at the development of special strategies for the minority group, or the economically deprived. **Length:** 17 mins. **Format:** Beta, VHS, 3/4U. **Acquisition:** Purchase. **Use:** Institution, SURA.

★5110★
Other Faces of AIDS
PBS Video
11858 La Grange Ave.   Ph: (310)820-0991
Los Angeles, CA 90025   Fax: (310)826-4779
1989. **Program Description:** Jesse Jackson is interviewed about the much higher risk of AIDS in minority groups. **Length:** 60 mins. **Format:** VHS, 3/4U. **Acquisition:** Purchase. **Use:** Institution, CCTV, Home, SURA.

★5111★
Passin' It On
First Run/Icarus Films   Ph: (212)727-1711
153 Waverly Pl.   Fax: (212)989-7649
New York, NY 10014   Free: 800-876-1710
1992. **Program Description:** In 1971 Black Panther leader Dhorubha Bin Wahad (Richard Moore) was convicted of shooting two New York City policemen. In 1990 his conviction was overturned on a charge of prosecutorial misconduct, although the possiblity of a retrial exists. Utilizes archival footage and personal accounts to look at the Black Panthers and the political turmoil of the age. **Length:** 57 mins. **Format:** VHS, Special order formats. **Acquisition:** Purchase, Rent/Lease. **Use:** Institution.

★5112★
Paul Laurence Dunbar
Pyramid Film & Video
Box 1048   Ph: (310)828-7577
2801 Colorado Ave.   Fax: (310)453-9083
Santa Monica, CA 90406   Free: 800-421-2304
1973. **Program Description:** A tribute to the first black American to become a recognized poet. **Length:** 22 mins. **Format:** Beta, VHS, 3/4U, Special order formats. **Acquisition:** Rent/Lease, Purchase, Duplication License. **Use:** Institution, Home, SURA.

★5113★
Paul Robeson: The Tallest Tree in Our Forest
Phoenix/BFA Films
468 Park Ave., S.   Ph: (212)684-5910
New York, NY 10016   Free: 800-221-1274
1977. **Program Description:** A program which gives the viewer a rare opportunity to see, hear, and gain some insight into the scholar, actor, singer, and humanitarian Paul Robeson, who passed away in

1976. **Length:** 90 mins. **Format:** Beta, VHS, 3/4U. **Acquisition:** Purchase. **Use:** Institution, SURA.

★5114★
Picking Tribes
Women Make Movies
462 Broadway, Ste. 501
New York, NY 10013
Ph: (212)925-0606
Fax: (212)925-2052

1988. **Program Description:** A young woman's struggle to find an identity between her Black American and Native American heritages is examined through vintage photographs and watercolor animation. **Length:** 7 mins. **Format:** Beta, VHS, 3/4U. **Acquisition:** Purchase, Rent/Lease. **Use:** Institution, SURA.

★5115★
Plessy vs. Ferguson
Afro-Am Distributing Company
407 E. 25th St., Ste. 600
Chicago, IL 60616
Ph: (312)791-1611
Fax: (312)791-0921

19??. **Program Description:** A look at the 1896 Supreme Court decision legalizing segragation. **Length:** 11 mins. **Format:** VHS. **Acquisition:** Purchase. **Use:** Institution, Home, SURA.

★5116★
Poetry in Motion
Voyager Company
1351 Pacific Coast Hwy.
Santa Monica, CA 90401
Ph: (310)451-1383
Fax: (310)394-2156
Free: 800-446-2001

1982. **Program Description:** A performance anthology of 24 North American poets, including: Ntozake Shange, Amiri Baraka, Anne Waldman, William Burroughs, Ted Berrigan, John Cage, Tom Waits, and 17 others. **Length:** 90 mins. **Format:** LV. **Acquisition:** Purchase. **Use:** Home.

★5117★
The Politics of Resistance
Film Video Library
University of Michigan
919 S. University Ave., Rm. 207
Ann Arbor, MI 48109-1185
Ph: (313)764-5360

1970. **Program Description:** An examination of black insurrections of the 1700s and inner conflicts within the slave system. Part of the ''Black Experience'' series. **Length:** 29 mins. **Format:** 3/4U, Special order formats. **Acquisition:** Rent/Lease, Purchase. **Use:** Institution, CCTV, CATV, BCTV.

★5118★
Politics: The New Black Power
PBS Video
11858 La Grange Ave.
Los Angeles, CA 90025
Ph: (213)820-0991
Fax: (213)826-4779

1990. **Program Description:** The careers of nearly 20 black politicians, scholars, and other leaders are chronicled here. **Length:** 60 mins. **Format:** VHS, 3/4U. **Acquisition:** Purchase, Rent/Lease, Duplication License, Off-Air Record. **Use:** Institution, CCTV, CATV, Home, SURA.

★5119★
Portraits in Black
Videotakes
187 Parker Ave., Ste. 71
Manasquan, NJ 08736

1990. **Program Description:** An examination of the many and varied influences African-American culture has had on American society. **Format:** VHS. **Acquisition:** Purchase. **Use:** Home.

★5120★
Power Versus the People
William Greaves Productions, Inc.
230 W. 55th St.
New York, NY 10019
Ph: (212)265-6150
Fax: (212)315-0027
Free: 800-874-8314

1974. **Program Description:** A chronicle of the discriminators and discriminatees brought before the Equal Employment Opportunity Commission in Houston, Texas. **Length:** 36 mins. **Format:** Beta,

VHS, 3/4U. **Acquisition:** Rent/Lease, Purchase. **Use:** Institution, Home.

★5121★
Praise House
Third World Newsreel
335 W. 38th St., 5th Fl.
New York, NY 10018
Ph: (212)947-9277
Fax: (212)594-6417

1991. **Program Description:** The dance troupe Urban Bush Women use dance, chants, and field hollers to tell the story of a young black woman whose drive to express herself is limited by the working world. **Length:** 30 mins. **Format:** VHS, 3/4U. **Acquisition:** Rent/Lease, Purchase. **Use:** Institution.

★5122★
Prejudice: A Lesson to Forget
AEF/Capital Communications
3807 Dickerson Rd.
Nashville, TN 37207
Ph: (615)868-2040
Fax: (615)868-5239
Free: 800-822-5678

1973. **Program Description:** An interview with people who exhibit unconscious prejudices against minorities. **Length:** 17 mins. **Format:** Beta, VHS, 3/4U. **Acquisition:** Purchase. **Use:** Institution, SURA.

★5123★
Prejudice: Causes, Consequences, Cures
CRM/McGraw-Hill Films
674 Via de la Valle
PO Box 641
Del Mar, CA 92014

1974. **Program Description:** This program focuses on research findings and their implications for dealing with prejudice against women and racial, national, and ethnic groups. **Length:** 24 mins. **Format:** Beta, VHS, 3/4U. **Acquisition:** Purchase. **Use:** Institution, CCTV, SURA.

★5124★
The Prejudice Film
J. Miller Associates
13949 Ventura Blvd., Ste. 310
Sherman Oaks, CA 91423
Ph: (818)783-6018
Fax: (818)508-6572
Free: 800-331-8454

1984. **Program Description:** The historical background of contemporary forms of prejudice are examined in this program. **Length:** 28 mins. **Format:** Beta, VHS, 3/4U. **Acquisition:** Purchase. **Use:** Institution, CCTV.

★5125★
Prejudice: Perceiving and Believing
MTI Teleprograms, Inc.
108 Wilmot Rd.
Deerfield, IL 60015-9990
Ph: (708)940-1260
Free: 800-621-2131

1977. **Program Description:** How stereotyped classification by race, religion, and sex rather than by individual worth can prevent positive personal interactions. **Length:** 28 mins. **Format:** Beta, VHS, 3/4U. **Acquisition:** Rent/Lease, Purchase. **Use:** Institution, CCTV, SURA.

★5126★
Promised Land: Montgomery Two Decades after Martin Luther King, Jr.
Filmakers Library, Inc.
124 E. 40th
New York, NY 10016
Ph: (212)808-4980

1991. **Program Description:** Two decades after Martin Luther King Jr.'s assassination, the birthplace of the civil rights movement, Mobile, Alabama, still struggles with racism. **Length:** 50 mins. **Format:** VHS. **Acquisition:** Purchase. **Use:** Institution.

★5127★
Prophet of Peace: The Story of Dr. Martin Luther King, Jr.
University of California - Berkeley
  Extension Media Center
2176 Shattuck Ave.
Berkeley, CA 94704
Ph: (510)642-0460

1986. **Program Description:** Drawings by Morrie Turner highlight this biography of the famous civil rights activist. **Length:** 23 mins.

Format: VHS, 3/4U. **Acquisition:** Purchase, Rent/Lease. **Use:** Institution, SURA.

★5128★
Psychosocial and Environmental Factors in Hypertension in Blacks
Emory Medical Television Network
Emory University
Emory Medical Television Network-
Department C
1440 Clifton Rd., NE
Atlanta, GA 30322   Ph: (404)616-3556
1986. **Program Description:** A look at the epidemiologic evidence to surrounding the environmental affect on blacks' hypertension. **Length:** 24 mins. **Format:** VHS, 3/4U. **Acquisition:** Rent/Lease, Purchase, Subscription. **Use:** Institution, CCTV, CATV, BCTV, SURA.

★5129★
Pudd'nhead Wilson
MCA/Universal Home Video
70 Universal City Plaza   Ph: (818)777-6419
Universal City, CA 91608-9955   Fax: (818)733-0226
1987. **Program Description:** An adaptation of a Mark Twain story about a small-town lawyer who discovers the illicit exchange of a white infant for a light-skinned negro infant by a slave woman. Made for television as an "American Playhouse" presentation on PBS. **Length:** 87 mins. **Format:** Beta, VHS. **Acquisition:** Purchase. **Use:** Home.

★5130★
Quiet One
Nostalgia Family Video
PO Box 606
Baker City, OR 97814   Ph: (503)523-9034
1948. **Program Description:** Explores the ghetto's psychological effects on a ten-year old black child. **Length:** 68 mins. **Format:** Beta, VHS. **Acquisition:** Purchase. **Use:** Home.

★5131★
The Race for Mayor
Facets Multimedia, Inc.
1517 W. Fullerton Ave.
Chicago, IL 60614   Ph: (312)281-9075
1983. **Program Description:** Chicago's 1983 mayoral campaign is highlighted. U.S. Congressman Harold Washington became the first black elected to the position, overcoming the city's infamous Democratic "machine." **Length:** 29 mins. **Format:** VHS. **Acquisition:** Purchase. **Use:** Home, Institution.

★5132★
Race, Hatred, and Violence
HRM Video
175 Tompkins Ave.   Ph: (914)769-7496
No. V212   Fax: (914)747-1744
Pleasantville, NY 10570-0839   Free: 800-431-2050
19??. **Program Description:** Considers events in Bensonhurst and Howard Beach and explores motivations behind racial tension and violence. Includes interviews with community leaders, social activists, politicians, and legal and psychological experts. **Length:** 22 mins. **Format:** VHS. **Acquisition:** Purchase. **Use:** Institution.

★5133★
Race Movies: The Popular Art of the 1920s
National AudioVisual Center
National Archives & Records
Administration   Ph: (301)763-1896
8700 Edgeworth Dr.   Free: 800-788-
Capitol Heights, MD 20743-3701   NAVC
1985. **Program Description:** This video examines the works of early black filmmakers, from the very first movies to the heyday of the '20s. **Length:** 20 mins. **Format:** Beta, VHS, 3/4U. **Acquisition:** Purchase. **Use:** Institution, SURA.

★5134★
Racism and Minority Groups: Part 1
1973. **Program Description:** Each of the major racial minorities is presented in historic and current respective and members of each group respond to the series' presentations. Programs available individually. **Length:** 30 mins. **Format:** 3/4U. **Acquisition:** Rent/Lease. **Use:** Institution.

★5135★
Racism and Minority Groups: Part 2
1973. **Program Description:** These programs are a continuation of "Racism and Minority Groups I." Programs are available individually. **Length:** 30 mins. **Format:** 3/4U. **Acquisition:** Rent/Lease. **Use:** Institution.

★5136★
Racism 101
PBS Video
11858 La Grange Ave.   Ph: (310)820-0991
Los Angeles, CA 90025   Fax: (310)826-4779
1989. **Program Description:** Racism in such prestigious college campuses as Harvard, Smith and Columbia is examined in this program. **Length:** 58 mins. **Format:** Beta, VHS, 3/4U. **Acquisition:** Purchase, Rent/Lease. **Use:** Institution, SURA.

★5137★
A Raisin in the Sun
Fries Home Video
6922 Hollywood Blvd., 12th Fl.   Ph: (213)466-2266
Hollywood, CA 90028   Fax: (213)466-2126
1989. **Program Description:** An "American Playhouse," made for television presentation of the Lorraine Hansberry play about a black family threatened with dissolution by the outside forces of racism and greed when they move into an all-white neighborhood in the 1950s. **Length:** 171 mins. **Format:** Beta, VHS. **Acquisition:** Purchase. **Use:** Home.

★5138★
A Raisin in the Sun
Columbia Tristar Home Video
3400 Riverside Dr.   Ph: (818)972-8193
Burbank, CA 91505-4627   Fax: (818)972-0937
1961. **Program Description:** Outstanding story of a black family trying to make a better life for themselves in an all-white neighborhood in Chicago. The characters are played realistically and make for a moving story. Each person struggles with doing what he must while still maintaining his dignity and sense of self. Based on the Broadway play by Lorraine Hansberry. **Length:** 128 mins. **Format:** Beta, VHS, LV. **Acquisition:** Purchase. **Use:** Home.

★5139★
A Raisin in the Sun
Afro-Am Distributing Company
407 E. 25th St., Ste. 600   Ph: (312)791-1611
Chicago, IL 60616   Fax: (312)791-0921
197?. **Program Description:** A video supplement to be used when reading the Lorraine Hansberry classic. Originally a filmstrip, the video has been enhanced by computer to lend the appearance of animation. **Length:** mins. **Format:** VHS. **Acquisition:** Purchase. **Use:** Institution, Home, SURA.

★5140★
Ready to be a Wise Man
Direct Cinema Limited   Ph: (310)396-4774
PO Box 10003   Fax: (310)396-3233
Santa Monica, CA 90410   Free: 800-525-0000
1987. **Program Description:** Racial prejudice is explored in this film about a Southern minister's young son in the late 1950s. **Length:** 30 mins. **Format:** Beta, VHS, 3/4U. **Acquisition:** Purchase, Rent/Lease. **Use:** Institution, SURA.

★5141★
The Real Malcolm X: An Intimate Portrait of the Man
FoxVideo   Ph: (310)203-3900
2121 Avenue of the Stars, 25th Fl.   Fax: (310)774-5811
Los Angeles, CA 90067   Free: 800-800-2FOX

1992. **Program Description:** A look at the controversial and charismatic leader of the civil rights movement. Includes footage of Malcolm X, excerpts from his speeches, and interviews with his widow and contemporaries as well as younger artists who discuss his legacy. **Length:** 60 mins. **Format:** VHS. **Acquisition:** Purchase. **Use:** Home.

★5142★
Reflections: Three Black Women of Greensboro
Video Out
1102 Homer St.
Vancouver, BC, Canada V6B 2X6   Ph: (604)688-4336

1981. **Program Description:** Three women, the youngest of whom is 85 years old, discuss civil rights history, changes in race relations, present concerns, and their lifetime careers in Greensboro and North Carolina. **Length:** 17 mins. **Format:** Beta, VHS, 3/4U. **Acquisition:** Rent/Lease. **Use:** Institution, SURA.

★5143★
Remember Africville

1992. **Program Description:** Focuses on Africville, a black community near Halifax, Nova Scotia that was destroyed 20 years ago. Old movie footage, photos, and interviews show a tight-knit community that was integrated into Halifax by city planners and questions whether small segments of a community must pay the price of social progress. **Length:** 35 mins. **Format:** VHS, 3/4U. **Acquisition:** Purchase, Rent/Lease. **Use:** Institution.

★5144★
Renovascular Hypertension and Diabetic Nephropathy in Blacks
Emory Medical Television Network
Emory University
Emory Medical Television Network-
  Department C
1440 Clifton Rd., NE
Atlanta, GA 30322   Ph: (404)616-3556

1986. **Program Description:** A look for professionals on the clinical advantage of examining the paucity of renovascular hypertension in blacks. **Length:** 22 mins. **Format:** VHS, 3/4U. **Acquisition:** Rent/Lease, Purchase, Subscription. **Use:** Institution, CCTV, CATV, BCTV, SURA.

★5145★
Resurgence: The Movement for Equality vs. the Ku Klux Klan
First Run/Icarus Films   Ph: (212)727-1711
153 Waverly Pl.   Fax: (212)989-7649
New York, NY 10014   Free: 800-876-1710

1981. **Program Description:** A documentary about two opposing political forces: union and civil rights activists, and the ever present Ku Klux Klan and American Nazi Party. **Length:** 54 mins. **Format:** 3/4U. **Acquisition:** Purchase. **Use:** Institution, SURA.

★5146★
Revival

1989. **Program Description:** Various religious people talk about the growing role that blacks are playing in the Catholic Church. **Length:** 15 mins. **Format:** Beta, VHS. **Acquisition:** Purchase. **Use:** Institution, Home.

★5147★
Revolutionaries in Theology
NETCHE (Nebraska ETV Council for
  Higher Education)
1800 N. 33rd St.
Box 83111
Lincoln, NE 68583   Ph: (402)472-3611

1976. **Program Description:** The film shows that the rediscovery of the experience of the black church and the increased involvement of women in the life and leadership of the whole church are creating a revolution in the academic life of church. **Length:** 30 mins. **Format:** EJ, 3/4U. **Acquisition:** Rent/Lease, Purchase, Subscription. **Use:** Institution, CCTV, BCTV, SURA.

★5148★
Rhythm & Blues 1
Video Gems
12228 Venice Blvd., No. 504
Los Angeles, CA 90066

1983. **Program Description:** Gospel roots are joyously evident in this program documenting the Rhythm and Blues movement from the farms to the cities. **Length:** 57 mins. **Format:** Beta, VHS. **Acquisition:** Purchase. **Use:** Home.

★5149★
Rhythm & Blues Review
Glenn Video Vistas, Ltd.
6924 Canby Ave., Ste. 103   Ph: (818)881-8110
Reseda, CA 91335   Fax: (818)981-5506

1955. **Program Description:** A unique gathering of great musicians and singers. Selected from a series of musical shorts called Telescriptions. **Length:** 60 mins. **Format:** Beta, VHS. **Acquisition:** Purchase. **Use:** Home.

★5150★
Rhythm of Resistance: Black South African Music
Music Video Distributors
O'Neill Industrial Center   Ph: (215)272-7771
1210 Standbridge St.   Fax: (215)272-6074
Norristown, PA 19403   Free: 800-888-0486

1979. **Program Description:** Part of the PBS "Beats of the Heart" series, this video examines the role of music in Black South Africa's fight for freedom. **Length:** 60 mins. **Format:** VHS. **Acquisition:** Purchase. **Use:** Home.

★5151★
The Ribbon
First Run/Icarus Films   Ph: (212)727-1711
153 Waverly Pl.   Fax: (212)989-7649
New York, NY 10014   Free: 800-876-1710

1987. **Program Description:** A documentary about the "Peace Ribbon" which was made to protest the South African army's occupation of black townships. While the documentary was being made, a general state of emergency was declared, and the film follows the women who helped make the ribbon through this frightening and spiritually challenging time. **Length:** 50 mins. **Format:** 3/4U. **Acquisition:** Purchase. **Use:** Institution, SURA.

★5152★
Rich
AIMS Media   Ph: (818)773-4300
9710 DeSoto Ave.   Fax: (818)341-6700
Chatsworth, CA 91311-4409   Free: 800-367-2467

1988. **Program Description:** A black teenager fights to go on to college and become a success. **Length:** 21 mins. **Format:** Beta, VHS, 3/4U. **Acquisition:** Purchase, Rent/Lease. **Use:** Institution, SURA.

★5153★
Right On!: Poetry on Film
Facets Multimedia, Inc.
1517 W. Fullerton Ave.
Chicago, IL 60614   Ph: (312)281-9075

1971. **Program Description:** In 1968, in New York City, a trio of black performers created a combination of poetry, soul, jazz, blues, and gospel. The works of the "Original Last Poets"–Gylan Kain, Felipe Luciano, and David Nelson–are profiled. **Length:** 80 mins. **Format:** VHS. **Acquisition:** Purchase. **Use:** Home.

★5154★
The Road Home
AIMS Media
9710 DeSoto Ave.
Chatsworth, CA 91311-4409

Ph: (818)773-4300
Fax: (818)341-6700
Free: 800-367-2467

1989. **Program Description:** Charles Ratcliff, a black Vietnam vet, talks about war, violence, parenthood, and prejudice. **Length:** 9 mins. **Format:** Beta, VHS, 3/4U. **Acquisition:** Purchase, Rent/Lease. **Use:** Institution, SURA.

★5155★
The Rodney King Case: What the Jury Saw in California vs. Powell
MPI Home Video
15825 Rob Roy Dr.
Oak Forest, IL 60452

Ph: (708)687-7881
Fax: (708)687-3797

1992. **Program Description:** A condensed version of the Los Angeles police brutality trial involving Rodney King, the results of which caused the 1992 Los Angeles riots. Includes explanations of the law and a review of prosecution and defense tactics. Originally aired on cable's Courtroom Television Network. **Length:** 116 mins. **Format:** VHS. **Acquisition:** Purchase. **Use:** Home.

★5156★
Roll of Thunder
Knowledge Unlimited, Inc.
Box 52
Madison, WI 53701-0052

Ph: (608)836-6660
Fax: (608)831-1570
Free: 800-356-2303

19??. **Program Description:** A young girl and her family struggle to survive in the Deep South during the Great Depression in this story told with watercolors and pastels. **Length:** 46 mins. **Format:** VHS. **Acquisition:** Purchase. **Use:** Institution, Home, SURA.

★5157★
Roll of Thunder, Hear My Cry
Live Home Video
15400 Sherman Way, Ste. 500
Van Nuys, CA 91410-0124

Ph: (818)988-5060

1978. **Program Description:** A black family struggles to survive in Depression-era Mississippi in this inspiring, if somewhat predictable, television production. Look for the always impressive Freeman in a supporting role. Set in the South of 1933 and based on the novels of Mildred Taylor. **Length:** 110 mins. **Format:** Beta, VHS. **Acquisition:** Rent/Lease, Purchase. **Use:** Home.

★5158★
Roots: The Gift
Warner Home Video, Inc.
4000 Warner Blvd.
Burbank, CA 91522

Ph: (818)954-6000

1988. **Program Description:** It's Christmas, 1770, and Kunte Kinte (Burton) and Fiddler (Gossett) try to escape slavery via the Underground Railroad. In their attempt, they wind up giving the gift of freedom to several of their fellow slaves. A made for television movie based on the Alex Haley characters. **Length:** 94 mins. **Format:** VHS. **Acquisition:** Purchase. **Use:** Home.

★5159★
Roots, Vol. 1
Warner Home Video, Inc.
4000 Warner Blvd.
Burbank, CA 91522

Ph: (818)954-6000

1977. **Program Description:** The complete version of Alex Haley's made for television saga following a black man's search for his heritage, revealing an epic panorama of America's past. Available on six 90-minute tapes. **Length:** 90 mins. **Format:** Beta, VHS. **Acquisition:** Purchase. **Use:** Home.

★5160★
Roots, Vol. 2
Knowledge Unlimited, Inc.
Box 52
Madison, WI 53701-0052

Ph: (608)836-6660
Fax: (608)831-1570
Free: 800-356-2303

1977. **Program Description:** The history of the United States as seen by a black family, from their enslavement in Africa to the Civil Rights movement in the 1960's, based upon the true story of Alex Haley and his family. Received 37 Emmy nominations. Kunta Kinte is sold into plantation slavery and meets the old slave, Fiddler. **Length:** 90 mins. **Format:** Beta, VHS. **Acquisition:** Purchase. **Use:** Home.

★5161★
Roots, Vol. 3
Knowledge Unlimited, Inc.
Box 52
Madison, WI 53701-0052

Ph: (608)836-6660
Fax: (608)831-1570
Free: 800-356-2303

1977. **Program Description:** After repeated attempts at escape, Kunta Kinte is crippled by his captors. He then marries, has a daughter, and names her Kizzie. **Length:** 90 mins. **Format:** Beta, VHS. **Acquisition:** Purchase. **Use:** Home.

★5162★
Roots, Vol. 4
Knowledge Unlimited, Inc.
Box 52
Madison, WI 53701-0052

Ph: (608)836-6660
Fax: (608)831-1570
Free: 800-356-2303

1977. **Program Description:** The grown Kizzie is raped by her cruel owner. Her son becomes known as Chicken George for his handling of cockfights. **Length:** 90 mins. **Format:** Beta, VHS. **Acquisition:** Purchase. **Use:** Home.

★5163★
Roots, Vol. 5
Knowledge Unlimited, Inc.
Box 52
Madison, WI 53701-0052

Ph: (608)836-6660
Fax: (608)831-1570
Free: 800-356-2303

1977. **Program Description:** Now grown and trying to obtain his freedom, Chicken George and his family watch as the nation is plunged into civil war. **Length:** 90 mins. **Format:** Beta, VHS. **Acquisition:** Purchase. **Use:** Home.

★5164★
Roots, Vol. 6
Knowledge Unlimited, Inc.
Box 52
Madison, WI 53701-0052

Ph: (608)836-6660
Fax: (608)831-1570
Free: 800-356-2303

1977. **Program Description:** The Civil War over, Chicken George tries to make a new life for himself as a "freedman," yet encounters nothing but hostility. **Length:** 90 mins. **Format:** Beta, VHS. **Acquisition:** Purchase. **Use:** Home.

★5165★
Rosedale: The Way It Is

1976. **Program Description:** A look at racial tension in Rosedale, New York when the first black family moved into the white neighborhood. **Length:** 57 mins. **Format:** 3/4U, Special order formats. **Acquisition:** Rent/Lease, Purchase. **Use:** Institution, CCTV, Home.

★5166★
Round Midnight
Music Video Distributors
O'Neill Industrial Center
1210 Standbridge St.
Norristown, PA 19403

Ph: (215)272-7771
Fax: (215)272-6074
Free: 800-888-0486

1986. **Program Description:** An aging, alcoholic black American jazz saxophonist comes to Paris in the late 1950s seeking an escape from his self-destructive existence. A devoted young French fan spurs him to one last burst of creative brilliance. A moody, heartfelt homage to such expatriate bebop musicians as Bud Powell and Lester Young. In English and French with English subtitles. Available in a Spanish-subtitled version. **Length:** 132 mins. **Format:** Beta, VHS, LV. **Acquisition:** Purchase. **Use:** Home.

★5167★
Roy Wilkins: The Right to Dignity
National AudioVisual Center
National Archives & Records
Administration   Ph: (301)763-1896
8700 Edgeworth Dr.   Free: 800-788-
Capitol Heights, MD 20743-3701   NAVC
1978. **Program Description:** The story of Roy Wilkins' long career with the National Association for the Advancement of Colored People. His important role in the 1954 Brown v. Board of Education Supreme Court decision is highlighted, along with his activity in the Civil Rights legislation of the 1960s. **Length:** 20 mins. **Format:** Beta, VHS, 3/4U, Special order formats. **Acquisition:** Purchase. **Use:** Institution, SURA.

★5168★
Royal Federal Blues: The Black Civil War Soldiers
Peter Pan Industries
88 Saint Frances St.   Ph: (201)344-4214
Newark, NJ 07105   Fax: (201)344-0465
19??. **Program Description:** Greg McCampbell, an award-winning journalist, discusses black soldiers' roles during the Civil War. **Length:** mins. **Format:** VHS. **Acquisition:** Purchase. **Use:** Home, Institution.

★5169★
Running with Jesse
Facets Multimedia, Inc.
1517 W. Fullerton Ave.
Chicago, IL 60614   Ph: (312)281-9075
1986. **Program Description:** A profile of the political, social, and personal aspects of Jesse Jackson's 1984 campaign for the U.S. presidency and his Rainbow Coalition. **Length:** 57 mins. **Format:** Beta, VHS, 3/4U. **Acquisition:** Purchase, Rent/Lease. **Use:** Home, Institution, SURA.

★5170★
St. Louis Blues
Cinema Guild
1697 Broadway   Ph: (212)246-5522
New York, NY 10019   Fax: (212)246-5525
1929. **Program Description:** In her only filmed appearance, famed blues singer Bessie Smith sings "St. Louis Blues" in a lowdown cabaret after being betrayed and abused by her boyfriend. A Vitaphone two-reel short, with music by members of the Fletcher Henderson and vocal backup by the Hall Johnson Choir. **Length:** 17 mins. **Format:** VHS, 3/4U. **Acquisition:** Rent/Lease, Purchase, Duplication. **Use:** Institution, SURA.

★5171★
Sarafina!
Touchstone Home Video
500 S. Buena Vista St.
Burbank, CA 91521   Ph: (818)562-3883
1992. **Program Description:** Part coming-of-age saga, part political drama, part musical, and all emotionally powerful. Sarafina is a young girl in a township school in Soweto, South Africa in the mid-'70s, gradually coming into a political awakening amid the Soweto riots. Khumalo recreates her stage role as the glowing and defiant Sarafina with both Goldberg and Makeba good in their roles as, respectively, Sarafina's outspoken and inspirational teacher and her long-suffering mother. Adapted from Ngema's stage musical. **Length:** 98 mins. **Format:** Beta, VHS. **Acquisition:** Purchase. **Use:** Home.

★5172★
Scar of Shame
Facets Multimedia, Inc.
1517 W. Fullerton Ave.
Chicago, IL 60614   Ph: (312)281-9075
1927. **Program Description:** Explores the ill-fated romance between a successful black concert pianist and the lower-class woman he marries. Gives a look at the color caste system and divisions within the black community of the era. **Length:** 90 mins. **Format:** VHS. **Acquisition:** Purchase. **Use:** Home.

★5173★
School Daze
Columbia Tristar Home Video
3400 Riverside Dr.   Ph: (818)972-8193
Burbank, CA 91505-4627   Fax: (818)972-0937
1988. **Program Description:** Director/writer/star Lee's second outing is a rambunctious comedy (with a message, of course) set at an African-American college in the South. Skimpy plot revolves around the college's homecoming weekend and conflict among frats and sororities and African-Americans who would lose their racial identity and others who assert it. Entertaining and thought provoking. A glimpse at Lee's "promise," fulfilled in "Do the Right Thing." **Length:** 114 mins. **Format:** Beta, VHS, LV. **Acquisition:** Purchase. **Use:** Home.

★5174★
Scorpions
19??. **Program Description:** Young Jamal faces a world of problems growing up in the inner city, including his role in the street gang called the Scorpions. **Length:** 18 mins. **Format:** VHS. **Acquisition:** Purchase. **Use:** Institution, Home, SURA.

★5175★
Scott Joplin
Pyramid Film & Video
Box 1048   Ph: (310)828-7577
2801 Colorado Ave.   Fax: (310)453-9083
Santa Monica, CA 90406   Free: 800-421-2304
1977. **Program Description:** This is a biographical look at the life and work of ragtime composer Scott Joplin. **Length:** 15 mins. **Format:** Beta, VHS, 3/4U. **Acquisition:** Rent/Lease, Purchase, Duplication License. **Use:** Institution, Home, SURA.

★5176★
Search for a Black Christian Heritage
1989. **Program Description:** A series that was made with the intention of increasing the awareness of what blacks have contributed to Judeo-Christian heritage. **Length:** 120 mins. **Format:** Beta, VHS. **Acquisition:** Purchase. **Use:** Institution, Home.

★5177★
The Second American Revolution
PBS Video
11858 La Grange Ave.   Ph: (213)820-0991
Los Angeles, CA 90025   Fax: (213)826-4779
1982. **Program Description:** The revolution of Black America, from emancipation through Martin Luther King's historic march 100 years later. Ossie Davis and Ruby Dee join host Bill Moyers. Available on 2 tapes. **Length:** 120 mins. **Format:** Beta, VHS, 3/4U. **Acquisition:** Rent/Lease, Purchase, Off-Air Record. **Use:** Institution, CCTV, CATV.

★5178★
Separate But Equal
Republic Pictures Home Video
12636 Beatrice St.
Los Angeles, CA 90066-0930   Ph: (310)306-4040
1990. **Program Description:** One of TV's greatest history lessons, a powerful dramatization of the 1954 Brown vs. The Board of Education case that wrung a landmark civil rights decision from the Supreme Court. Great care is taken to humanize all the participants, from the humblest schoolchild to NAACP lawyer Thurgood Marshall (Poitier). On two cassettes. **Length:** 194 mins. **Format:** VHS, LV. **Acquisition:** Purchase. **Use:** Home.

★5179★
"Separate But Equal"
Britannica Films
310 S. Michigan Ave.   Ph: (312)347-7958
Chicago, IL 60604   Fax: (312)347-7966
1988. **Program Description:** In the 1890s, the Supreme Court ruled that though whites could keep blacks segregated, both groups had to have access to equal facilities. **Length:** 8 mins. **Format:** Beta, VHS, 3/4U. **Acquisition:** Purchase, Trade-in. **Use:** Institution, SURA.

★5180★
Shape of Darkness, An Exploration of African Art
Roland Collection
1344 S. 60th Ct.
Cicero, IL 60650-1007

1987. **Program Description:** An examination of the development of African art and civilization, focusing on art and ceremonial objects. Two untitled programs. **Length:** 26 mins. **Format:** VHS, 8mm, Special order formats. **Acquisition:** Purchase, Free Loan. **Use:** Institution, Home.

★5181★
She's Gotta Have It
CBS/Fox Video   Ph: (212)373-4800
1330 Avenue of the Americas, 5th Fl.   Fax: (212)373-4802
New York, NY 10019   Free: 800-800-2369

1986. **Program Description:** Lee wrote, directed, edited, produced and starred in this romantic comedy about an independent-minded black girl in Brooklyn and the three men and one woman who compete for her attention. Full of rough edges, but vigorous, confident, and hip. Filmed entirely in black and white except for one memorable scene. Put Lee on the film-making map. **Length:** 84 mins. **Format:** Beta, VHS. **Acquisition:** Purchase. **Use:** Home.

★5182★
Singing Stream: A Black Family Chronicle
Davenport Films
RR 1, Box 527   Ph: (703)592-3701
Delaplane, VA 22025   Fax: (703)592-3717

1987. **Program Description:** This film shows how the traditions of gospel music helped to promote family loyalty and purposefulness to a Southern black family from the 1930s to the present. **Length:** 57 mins. **Format:** Beta, VHS, Special order formats. **Acquisition:** Purchase. **Use:** Institution, Home, SURA.

★5183★
Sitting in Limbo
National Film Board of Canada
1251 Avenue of the Americas, 16th Fl.
New York, NY 10020-1173   Ph: (212)586-5131

1987. **Program Description:** Four black teenagers in Montreal cope with unemployment, pregnancy and relationships. **Length:** 96 mins. **Format:** Beta, VHS, 3/4U. **Acquisition:** Purchase, Rent/Lease. **Use:** Institution, SURA.

★5184★
1619-1860: Out of Slavery
CRM/McGraw-Hill Films
674 Via de la Valle
PO Box 641
Del Mar, CA 92014

1965. **Program Description:** This program first looks at slavery as it was practiced in Greece and Rome. It then moves to West Africa and shows civilization as it existed there before the beginning of the slave trade. Lastly, it depicts the Negro in America-as a freeman and slave, as patriot during the American Revolution, and as a participant in the abolitionist movement. Part of the "History of the Negro in America" series. **Length:** 20 mins. **Format:** Beta, VHS, 3/4U. **Acquisition:** Purchase. **Use:** Institution, CCTV, SURA.

★5185★
The Sky Is Gray
Monterey Home Video   Ph: (818)597-0047
28038 Dorothy Dr., Ste. 1   Fax: (818)597-0105
Agoura Hills, CA 91301   Free: 800-424-2593

1980. **Program Description:** A young black Louisiana boy journeys with his mother to the dentist, and on the way is confronted with prejudice and poverty. Set in the 1940s. Based on a story by Ernest Gaines. Made for television, with an introdution by Henry Fonda. **Length:** 46 mins. **Format:** Beta, VHS. **Acquisition:** Purchase. **Use:** Home.

★5186★
Slavery and Slave Resistance
Coronet/MTI Film & Video   Ph: (708)940-1260
108 Wilmot Rd.   Fax: (708)940-3640
Deerfield, IL 60015   Free: 800-777-8100

1978. **Program Description:** Story of slave oppression and resistance from the colonial period to the Civil War. **Length:** 25 mins. **Format:** Beta, VHS, 3/4U. **Acquisition:** Purchase. **Use:** Institution, CCTV, SURA.

★5187★
A Slave's Story
Learning Corporation of America   Ph: (708)940-1260
108 Wilmot Rd.   Fax: (708)940-3600
Deerfield, IL 60015-9990   Free: 800-621-2131

1972. **Program Description:** Dramatization of William and Ellen Craft's actual escape from slavery in 1848. **Length:** 29 mins. **Format:** Beta, VHS, 3/4U. **Acquisition:** Rent/Lease, Purchase. **Use:** Institution, SURA.

★5188★
A Soldier's Story
Columbia Tristar Home Video
3400 Riverside Dr.   Ph: (818)972-8193
Burbank, CA 91505-4627   Fax: (818)972-0937

1984. **Program Description:** A black army attorney is sent to a Southern base to investigate the murder of an unpopular sergeant. Features World War II, Louisiana, jazz and blues, and racism in and outside the corps. From the Pulitzer-prize winning play by Charles Fuller, with most of the Broadway cast. Fine performances from Washington and Caesar. **Length:** 101 mins. **Format:** Beta, VHS, LV. **Acquisition:** Purchase. **Use:** Home.

★5189★
Some are More Equal Than Others
Carousel Film & Video
260 5th Ave., Rm. 405   Ph: (212)683-1660
New York, NY 10001   Fax: (212)683-1662

1971. **Program Description:** Considers the legal treatment of ethnic minorities and shows how the system works mostly against the poor. **Length:** 40 mins. **Format:** Beta, VHS, 3/4U. **Acquisition:** Purchase. **Use:** Institution, SURA.

★5190★
Some People

1988. **Program Description:** The stories of seven black characters, living on the outside of society, are told through dance and vignette storytelling. **Length:** 19 mins. **Format:** 3/4U. **Acquisition:** Purchase, Rent/Lease. **Use:** Institution, SURA.

★5191★
Sometimes I'm Up, Sometimes I'm Down
New York State Education Department
Center for Learning Technologies
Media Distribution Network, Rm. C-7,
  Concourse Level
Albany, NY 12230   Ph: (518)474-3852

196?. **Program Description:** This film dramatizes what it was like to live in the slave colony of John's Island, South Carolina. **Length:** 30 mins. **Format:** Beta, VHS, EJ, 3/4U, Q. **Acquisition:** Duplication, Free Duplication. **Use:** Institution, SURA.

★5192★
Songololo: Voices of Change
Cinema Guild
1697 Broadway   Ph: (212)246-5522
New York, NY 10019   Fax: (212)246-5525

1990. **Program Description:** South Africa's black resistance movement is examined by looking at two cultural activists, poet Mzwakhe Mbuli and writer/performer Gcina Mhlophe. **Length:** 54 mins. **Format:** VHS, Special order formats. **Acquisition:** Purchase. **Use:** Institution.

★5193★
The Songs are Free
Music Video Distributors
O'Neill Industrial Center
1210 Standbridge St.
Norristown, PA 19403

Ph: (215)272-7771
Fax: (215)272-6074
Free: 800-888-0486

1991. **Program Description:** A PBS special on the music and songs of African-American culture, and the impact they have on the preservation of that culture. Bill Moyers' guest is Bernice Johnson Reagon, founder of the famed Sweet Honey in the Rock spiritual group. **Length:** 60 mins. **Format:** VHS, 3/4U. **Acquisition:** Purchase. **Use:** Institution, Home.

★5194★
Sophisticated Gents
Xenon
211 Arizona Ave.
Santa Monica, CA 90401

Free: 800-468-1913

1981. **Program Description:** Nine boyhood friends, members of a black athletic club, reunite after 25 years to honor their old coach and see how each of their lives has been affected by being black men in American society. Based on the novel "The Junior Bachelor Society" by John A. Williams. Originally made for television. **Length:** 200 mins. **Format:** VHS. **Acquisition:** Purchase. **Use:** Home.

★5195★
Sounder
Afro-Am Distributing Company
407 E. 25th St., Ste. 600
Chicago, IL 60616

Ph: (312)791-1611
Fax: (312)791-0921

197?. **Program Description:** A video supplement to the classic American novel by William Armstrong. Originally a filmstrip which has been enhanced via computer to give the appearance of animation. **Length:** mins. **Format:** VHS. **Acquisition:** Purchase. **Use:** Institution, Home, SURA.

★5196★
South Africa After Apartheid
National Geographic Educational Services
PO Box 98019
Washington, DC 20090

1992. **Program Description:** Examines the 40-year grip apartheid has held on South Africa, including its origins and its affect on the citizens and economy. Unbiased and factual presentation. **Length:** 25 mins. **Format:** VHS, Special order formats. **Acquisition:** Purchase. **Use:** Institution.

★5197★
South Africa Belongs to Us
California Newsreel
149 Ninth St., Ste. 420
San Francisco, CA 94103

Ph: (415)621-6196
Fax: (415)621-6522

1982. **Program Description:** With portraits of five ordinary women and four women leaders, the film depicts the struggle of the black women for human dignity in the face of apartheid: from the struggle of feeding her children to the total liberation of her people. **Length:** 35 mins. **Format:** VHS, Special order formats. **Acquisition:** Purchase, Rent/Lease. **Use:** Institution, SURA.

★5198★
South Africa: The Solution
Journal Films, Inc.
930 Pitner Ave.
Evanston, IL 60202

Ph: (708)328-6700
Fax: (708)328-6706
Free: 800-323-5448

1989. **Program Description:** Historical factors are given to show why South Africa is in the state it is today. A view is also given of how it might look in the future. **Length:** 38 mins. **Format:** Beta, VHS, 3/4U. **Acquisition:** Purchase, Rent/Lease. **Use:** Institution, SURA.

★5199★
South by Northwest
Great Plains National (GPN)
1800 N. 33rd St.
Box 80669
Lincoln, NE 68501-0669

Ph: (402)472-2007
Fax: (402)472-1785
Free: 800-228-4630

1975. **Program Description:** A series of docudramas exploring the role of black cowboys and pioneers in the development of the American Northwest from the late 1700's to the turn of the century. Programs available individually. **Length:** 29 mins. **Format:** Beta, VHS, 3/4U, Special order formats. **Acquisition:** Rent/Lease, Purchase, Duplication License, Off-Air Record. **Use:** Institution, CCTV, CATV, BCTV.

★5200★
Soweto to Berkeley
Cinema Guild
1697 Broadway
New York, NY 10019

Ph: (212)246-5522
Fax: (212)246-5525

1988. **Program Description:** This video traces the anti-apartheid movement at the University of California-Berkeley during the 1985-86 school year. **Length:** 50 mins. **Format:** Beta, VHS, 3/4U. **Acquisition:** Rent/Lease, Purchase, Duplication. **Use:** Institution, SURA.

★5201★
The Speeches of Martin Luther King, Jr.
MPI Home Video
15825 Rob Roy Dr.
Oak Forest, IL 60452

Ph: (708)687-7881
Fax: (708)687-3797

1991. **Program Description:** A compilation of the orations of the civil rights organizer tracing his beginnings as a minister, to his fateful last speech in Tennessee. **Length:** 60 mins. **Format:** VHS. **Acquisition:** Purchase. **Use:** Home.

★5202★
Spike Lee & Co.: Do It A Cappella
Music Video Distributors
O'Neill Industrial Center
1210 Standbridge St.
Norristown, PA 19403

Ph: (215)272-7771
Fax: (215)272-6074
Free: 800-888-0486

1990. **Program Description:** Join hosts Spike Lee and Debbie Allen as they visit a variety of talented a capella groups in this extended version of the PBS special. Groups include: True Image, Take 6, The Persuasions, Rockapella, The Mint Juleps and Ladysmith Black Mambazo. Songs include "Overture to the Barber of Seville," "Zombie Jamboree," "I Need You," "Don't Let Your Heart," "Looking for an Echo," "Get Away Jordan," "Something Within Me," "Flat Tire," "Under the Boardwalk," "Higher and Higher," "Phansi Em Godini," "The Lion Sleeps Tonight," "I'm Going Home on the Midnight Train," "Goldmine," "Trickle, Trickle," "Yes We Can Can," "I Want to Live Easy," "Set Me Free," "Ukhalanghami," "N'Kosi Sikeleli Africa," "Pretty Woman," "Up on the Roof," and "Pass on the Love." **Length:** 75 mins. **Format:** VHS, LV. **Acquisition:** Purchase. **Use:** Home.

★5203★
The Spirit of St. Elmo Village
Carousel Film & Video
260 5th Ave., Rm. 405
New York, NY 10001

Ph: (212)683-1660
Fax: (212)683-1662

1989. **Program Description:** Rozzell and Roderick Sykes, two black artists, were able to change a slum section of Los Angeles into a world of art and beauty. **Length:** 26 mins. **Format:** Beta, VHS, 3/4U. **Acquisition:** Purchase. **Use:** Institution, SURA.

★5204★
Spirit to Spirit: Nikki Giovanni
Direct Cinema Limited
PO Box 69799
Los Angeles, CA 90069-9976

Ph: (213)652-8000
Fax: (213)652-2346
Free: 800-345-6748

1987. **Program Description:** A visually arresting portrait of poet Nikki Giovanni against a background of some of her themes including the Civil Rights struggle and the Women's Movement. **Length:** 30 mins. **Format:** Beta, VHS, 3/4U. **Acquisition:** Purchase, Rent/Lease. **Use:** Institution, SURA.

★5205★
Stand and Be Counted: Reacting to Racism
HRM Video
175 Tompkins Ave.   Ph: (914)769-7496
No. V212   Fax: (914)747-1744
Pleasantville, NY 10570-9973   Free: 800-431-2050
19??. **Program Description:** Two stories illustrate families' and individual's reactions to racial violence in their neighborhoods and how they made a difference. **Length:** 15 mins. **Format:** VHS. **Acquisition:** Purchase. **Use:** Institution.

★5206★
Steps in Time: Scenes from 1840 Baltimore
PBS Video
11858 La Grange Ave.   Ph: (213)820-0991
Los Angeles, CA 90025   Fax: (213)826-4779
1988. **Program Description:** Take an inside look at a Baltimore household during the period before the Civil War. An excellent method for comparing race relations then and now. **Length:** 30 mins. **Format:** VHS, 3/4U. **Acquisition:** Purchase, Off-Air Record, Duplication License. **Use:** Institution, CCTV, CATV.

★5207★
Stories from the Black Tradition
Children's Circle   Ph: (203)222-0002
389 Newtown Tpke.   Fax: (203)226-3818
Weston, CT 06883   Free: 800-KIDS-VID
1992. **Program Description:** Five Caldecott award-winning classic children's books are featured: "A Story - A Story" by Gail E. Haley, "Mufaro's Beautiful Daughters" by John Steptoe, "Why Mosquitoes Buzz in People's Ears" retold by Verna Aardema, "The Village of Round and Square Houses" by Ann Grifalconi, and "Goggles!" by Ezra Jack Keats. **Length:** 52 mins. **Format:** VHS. **Acquisition:** Purchase. **Use:** Home.

★5208★
Storm of Strangers
Films Inc. Video
5547 N. Ravenswood Ave.   Ph: (312)878-2600
Chicago, IL 60640-1199   Free: 800-323-4222
1983. **Program Description:** This series introduces America's ethnic and racial minorities to each other. **Length:** 29 mins. **Format:** Beta, VHS, 3/4U. **Acquisition:** Purchase. **Use:** Institution, SURA.

★5209★
Straight Out of Brooklyn
HBO Home Video
1114 6th Ave.
New York, NY 10036   Ph: (212)512-7400
1991. **Program Description:** A bleak, nearly hopeless look at a struggling black family in a Brooklyn housing project. The son seeks escape through crime, his father in booze. An up-close and raw look at part of society seldom shown in mainstream film, its undeniable power is sapped by ragged production values and a loose narrative prone to melodrama. Rich (seen in a supporting role) was only 19 years old when he completed this, funded partly by PBS-TV's "American Playhouse." **Length:** 91 mins. **Format:** VHS. **Acquisition:** Purchase. **Use:** Home.

★5210★
Straight Up Rappin'
Filmakers Library, Inc.
124 E. 40th
New York, NY 10016   Ph: (212)808-4980
1992. **Program Description:** Explores rap music as a creative outlet for African-American youth and as a vehicle for educating children about drugs and other social dangers. **Length:** 28 mins. **Format:** VHS. **Acquisition:** Purchase, Rent/Lease. **Use:** Institution.

★5211★
Strange Fruit
Learning Corporation of America   Ph: (708)940-1260
108 Wilmot Rd.   Fax: (708)940-3600
Deerfield, IL 60015-9990   Free: 800-621-2131
1979. **Program Description:** Based on Lillian Smith's novel, this program tells the story of a black painter in Georgia, 1948, who faces racism. At first avoiding voter registration, he becomes involved and is killed. His death serves as an inspiration to his community. **Length:** 33 mins. **Format:** Beta, VHS. **Acquisition:** Rent/Lease, Purchase. **Use:** Institution, SURA.

★5212★
Strength
HRM Video
175 Tompkins Ave.   Ph: (914)769-7496
No. V212   Fax: (914)747-1744
Pleasantville, NY 10570-9973   Free: 800-431-2050
19??. **Program Description:** Dramatization centers around racial tension between groups of African-American and white youths. Prompts viewers to examine conflict resolution and alternatives to violence. **Length:** 10 mins. **Format:** VHS. **Acquisition:** Purchase. **Use:** Institution.

★5213★
Stubborn Hope
First Run/Icarus Films   Ph: (212)727-1711
153 Waverly Pl.   Fax: (212)989-7649
New York, NY 10014   Free: 800-876-1710
1985. **Program Description:** A chronicle of a few months in the life of South African exile, and well-known poet Dennis Brutus. **Length:** 28 mins. **Format:** 3/4U. **Acquisition:** Purchase. **Use:** Institution, SURA.

★5214★
The Sun Will Rise
1983. **Program Description:** A harrowing documentary about the members of the African National Congress who were sentenced to death for their anti-apartheid activities. **Length:** 35 mins. **Format:** 3/4U. **Acquisition:** Purchase. **Use:** Institution, SURA.

★5215★
A Sunday on Your Knees
Canyon Cinema
2325 3rd St., Ste. 338
San Francisco, CA 94107   Ph: (415)626-2255
1972. **Program Description:** A look at the "chalk-in" street art of Watts, L.A., a short lived creative expression in which all members of the community participated. **Length:** 6 mins. **Format:** 8mm. **Acquisition:** Rent/Lease. **Use:** Home.

★5216★
Survival Skills for Urban Youth
HRM Video
175 Tompkins Ave.   Ph: (914)769-7496
No. V212   Fax: (914)747-1744
Pleasantville, NY 10570-9973   Free: 800-431-2050
19??. **Program Description:** Series of three videos, each available individually, which address the three crucial factors contributing to a student's success or failure in high school: drugs, teen sexuality and early parenting, and self-esteem. Each video presents a scenario designed to encourage classroom discussion. **Length:** mins. **Format:** VHS. **Acquisition:** Purchase. **Use:** Institution.

★5217★
Television Linking Culture
New York State Education Department
Center for Learning Technologies
Media Distribution Network, Rm. C-7,
  Concourse Level
Albany, NY 12230   Ph: (518)474-3852
197?. **Program Description:** This tape shows how television programs produced under the Emergency School Aid Act can eliminate stereotyping and racial isolation. **Length:** 30 mins. **Format:**

Beta, VHS, EJ, 3/4U, Q. **Acquisition:** Duplication, Free Duplication. **Use:** Institution, SURA.

★5218★
The Thinnest Line
Women Make Movies
462 Broadway, Ste. 501
New York, NY 10013

Ph: (212)925-0606
Fax: (212)925-2052

1988. **Program Description:** An exploration of the friendship between two black women-one a filmmaker, the other a mother. **Length:** 10 mins. **Format:** Beta, VHS, 3/4U. **Acquisition:** Purchase, Rent/Lease. **Use:** Institution, SURA.

★5219★
This Far by Faith
California Working
5867 Oceanview Dr.
Oakland, CA 94618

1991. **Program Description:** Documents the coalition between labor and the civil rights leaders which helped secure better working conditions for the primarily Black female employees at a Mississippi catfish processing plant. **Length:** 29 mins. **Format:** VHS. **Acquisition:** Purchase. **Use:** Institution.

★5220★
This is the Home of Mrs. Levant Graham
Pyramid Film & Video
Box 1048
2801 Colorado Ave.
Santa Monica, CA 90406

Ph: (310)828-7577
Fax: (310)453-9083
Free: 800-421-2304

1971. **Program Description:** A portrait of an urban black mother. **Length:** 15 mins. **Format:** Beta, VHS, 3/4U. **Acquisition:** Rent/Lease, Purchase, Duplication License. **Use:** Institution, Home, SURA.

★5221★
Through Young People's Eyes
Cinema Guild
1697 Broadway
New York, NY 10019

Ph: (212)246-5522
Fax: (212)246-5525

1983. **Program Description:** This documentary examines the effects of poverty on black and Hispanic teenagers, especially girls. **Length:** 29 mins. **Format:** Beta, VHS, 3/4U. **Acquisition:** Rent/Lease, Purchase. **Use:** Institution, SURA.

★5222★
Thurgood Marshall: Portrait of an American Hero
PBS Video
11858 La Grange Ave.
Los Angeles, CA 90025

Ph: (213)820-0991
Fax: (213)826-4779

1985. **Program Description:** A look at the career of the late Supreme Court Justice, focusing on his involvement in the civil rights movement. **Length:** 30 mins. **Format:** VHS, 3/4U. **Acquisition:** Purchase, Off-Air Record, Duplication License. **Use:** Institution, CCTV, CATV, SURA.

★5223★
Tight Packers and Loose Packers
Time-Life Video and Television
1450 E. Parham Rd.
Richmond, VA 23280

Ph: (804)266-6330
Free: 800-621-7026

1977. **Program Description:** This episode of the "Fight Against Slavery" series examines the conflicts between the abolitionists and those with vested interests in the slave trade. **Length:** 57 mins. **Format:** Beta, VHS, 3/4U, Special order formats. **Acquisition:** Rent/Lease, Purchase. **Use:** Institution, SURA.

★5224★
Time and Dreams
Temple University Dept. of Radio-TV-Film
Philadelphia, PA 19122

Ph: (215)787-8483

1976. **Program Description:** A look at the changes that have come to Greene County since the coming of the civil rights movement. **Length:** 52 mins. **Format:** 3/4U. **Acquisition:** Rent/Lease, Purchase. **Use:** Institution, SURA.

★5225★
To Do Battle in the Land
Proud To Be. . .A Black Video Collection
1235-E East Blvd., Ste. 209
Charlotte, NC 28203

Ph: (704)523-2227

1984. **Program Description:** Focuses on the events that led up to the Civil War, particularly the invasion of Harper's Ferry. Filmed in black and white and color. **Length:** 27 mins. **Format:** VHS. **Acquisition:** Purchase. **Use:** Home.

★5226★
To Free Their Minds
William Greaves Productions, Inc.
230 W. 55th St.
New York, NY 10019

Ph: (212)265-6150
Fax: (212)315-0027
Free: 800-874-8314

1974. **Program Description:** A teacher learns how to deal with the demands of teaching an interracial class. **Length:** 24 mins. **Format:** Beta, VHS. **Acquisition:** Rent/Lease, Purchase. **Use:** Institution, BCTV.

★5227★
To Kill a Mockingbird
Knowledge Unlimited, Inc.
Box 52
Madison, WI 53701-0052

Ph: (608)836-6660
Fax: (608)831-1570
Free: 800-356-2303

1962. **Program Description:** Faithful adaptation of powerful Harper Lee novel, both an evocative portrayal of childhood innocence and a denunciation of bigotry. Peck's performance as southern lawyer defending a black man accused of raping a white woman is flawless. Lee based her characterization of "Dill" on Truman Capote, a childhood friend. With an Oscar-winning script by Horton Foote and a nominated score by Elmer Bernstein. Other Oscar nominations include supporting actress Badham, director, and Best Picture. **Length:** 129 mins. **Format:** Beta, VHS, LV. **Acquisition:** Purchase. **Use:** Home.

★5228★
Toni Morrison
Home Vision Cinema
5547 N. Ravenswood Ave.
Chicago, IL 60640-1199

Ph: (312)878-2600
Fax: (312)878-8648
Free: 800-826-3456

1988. **Program Description:** In this documentary, Pulitzer Prize winning author Toni Morrison discusses her novel "Beloved." **Length:** 30 mins. **Format:** Beta, VHS. **Acquisition:** Purchase. **Use:** Home.

★5229★
Toni Morrison
Facets Multimedia, Inc.
1517 W. Fullerton Ave.
Chicago, IL 60614

Ph: (312)281-9075

19??. **Program Description:** An interview with Pulitzer Prize-winning novelist Morrison as she discusses the black experience in America, writing about ordinary people, and dealing with painful material. **Length:** 55 mins. **Format:** VHS. **Acquisition:** Purchase. **Use:** Home, Institution.

★5230★
The Torture of Mothers
Essenay Entertainment
22D Hollywood Ave.
Ho-Ho-Kus, NJ 07423

Ph: (201)652-1989
Fax: (201)652-1973
Free: 800-343-5540

1980. **Program Description:** An account of events surrounding the actions of five black school children in Harlem in the 1960s. One afternoon the youths overturned a number of fruit stands, resulting in the harrassment of their families by police. This video includes excerpts from media reports of the incident and interviews with the mothers of the children, recorded at the time of the trouble. **Length:** 60 mins. **Format:** VHS. **Acquisition:** Purchase. **Use:** Home.

★5231★
A Tribute to Alvin Ailey
Home Vision Cinema   Ph: (312)878-2600
5547 N. Ravenswood Ave.   Fax: (312)878-8648
Chicago, IL 60640-1199   Free: 800-826-3456

1992. **Program Description:** Although he passed away in 1989, Ailey's spirit lives on. The Alvin Ailey American Dance Theater pays homage to its founder with colorful, stunning performances, including "For Bird with Love," a tribute to jazz great Charlie Parker and "Episodes." **Length:** 120 mins. **Format:** VHS. **Acquisition:** Purchase. **Use:** Home.

★5232★
A Tribute to Billie Holiday
Media Home Entertainment
510 W. 6th St., Ste. 1032   Ph: (213)236-1336
Los Angeles, CA 90014   Fax: (213)236-1346

1979. **Program Description:** This tribute to Billie Holiday features the talents of Nina Simone, Maxine Weldon, Morganna King, Carmen McRae, and Esther Phillips. The orchestra was arranged and conducted by Ray Ellis with additional arranging by Tommy Newsom. **Length:** 57 mins. **Format:** Beta, VHS. **Acquisition:** Purchase. **Use:** Home.

★5233★
Tribute to John Coltrane
Home Vision Cinema   Ph: (312)878-2600
5547 N. Ravenswood Ave.   Fax: (312)878-8648
Chicago, IL 60640-1199   Free: 800-826-3456

198?. **Program Description:** A once-in-a-lifetime session to pay homage to jazz great John Coltrane. **Length:** 57 mins. **Format:** VHS, LV. **Acquisition:** Purchase. **Use:** Home.

★5234★
Tribute to Malcolm X

1969. **Program Description:** A profile of Malcolm X and the influence he had on the black liberation movement, as told by his widow, Betty Shabazz. **Length:** 15 mins. **Format:** 3/4U, Special order formats. **Acquisition:** Rent/Lease, Purchase. **Use:** Institution, CCTV, Home, SURA.

★5235★
The Triumph of Charlie Parker: Celebrating Bird
Kultur Video   Ph: (908)229-2343
121 Hwy. No. 36   Fax: (908)229-0066
West Long Branch, NJ 07764   Free: 800-458-5887

1977. **Program Description:** Recounts the life and musical triumphs of Charlie "Bird" Parker, recognized as one of Jazz's most enduring and influential artists. **Length:** 60 mins. **Format:** Beta, VHS, LV. **Acquisition:** Purchase. **Use:** Home.

★5236★
Troublemakers
Cinema Guild
1697 Broadway   Ph: (212)246-5522
New York, NY 10019   Fax: (212)246-5525

1966. **Program Description:** The Newark Community Union Project, founded by Tom Hayden in 1965, is examined. The project encourages blacks to become involved in the community. **Length:** 54 mins. **Format:** Beta, VHS, 3/4U. **Acquisition:** Rent/Lease, Purchase, Duplication. **Use:** Institution, SURA.

★5237★
The True Story of "Glory" Continues
Columbia Tristar Home Video
3400 Riverside Dr.   Ph: (818)972-8193
Burbank, CA 91505-4627   Fax: (818)972-0937

1991. **Program Description:** The true story of the 54th Massachusetts, the all black unit which served in the Civil War and upon which the movie "Glory" was based. Included are contemporary photos and sketches. **Length:** 45 mins. **Format:** VHS. **Acquisition:** Purchase. **Use:** Home.

★5238★
Tuskegee Airmen
Carousel Film & Video
260 5th Ave., Rm. 405   Ph: (212)683-1660
New York, NY 10001   Fax: (212)683-1662

1992. **Program Description:** The Tuskegee Airmen were a valiant all-Black flying squadron in WWII who united against racism to bravely serve their country. Today they are successful in their careers and serve as role models to America's youth. **Length:** 23 mins. **Format:** VHS. **Acquisition:** Purchase. **Use:** Institution.

★5239★
Tuskegee Institute
King Features Entertainment
235 E. 45th St.   Ph: (212)455-4000
New York, NY 10017   Free: 800-526-5464

1983. **Program Description:** This program profiles the Tuskegee Institute and some of its famous alumni such as Booker T. Washington and George Washington Carver. **Length:** 15 mins. **Format:** Beta, VHS, 3/4U. **Acquisition:** Rent/Lease, Purchase. **Use:** Institution, SURA.

★5240★
Two Centuries of Black American Art
Pyramid Film & Video
Box 1048   Ph: (310)828-7577
2801 Colorado Ave.   Fax: (310)453-9083
Santa Monica, CA 90406   Free: 800-421-2304

1976. **Program Description:** A survey of the range of black American art, from the slave era to today's cosmopolitan black artists. **Length:** 26 mins. **Format:** Beta, VHS, 3/4U, Special order formats. **Acquisition:** Rent/Lease, Purchase, Duplication License. **Use:** Institution, Home, SURA.

★5241★
Two Dollars and a Dream
Filmakers Library, Inc.
124 E. 40th
New York, NY 10016   Ph: (212)808-4980

1988. **Program Description:** A vivid biography of Madame C.J. Walker, a child of slaves, who became America's first women millionaire by manufacturing skin and hair care products. **Length:** 56 mins. **Format:** VHS, 3/4U. **Acquisition:** Rent/Lease, Purchase, Duplication. **Use:** Institution, Home, SURA.

★5242★
220 Blues
Phoenix/BFA Films
468 Park Ave., S.   Ph: (212)684-5910
New York, NY 10016   Free: 800-221-1274

1970. **Program Description:** "220 Blues" is a sensitive study of awakening racial awareness. Sonny is a star high school track man and has the widespread admiration of his peers. **Length:** 18 mins. **Format:** Beta, VHS, 3/4U. **Acquisition:** Purchase. **Use:** Institution, SURA.

★5243★
Uncle Tom's Cabin
Grapevine Video
PO Box 46161
Phoenix, AZ 85063   Ph: (602)245-0210

1914. **Program Description:** Satisfying version of Harriet Beecher Stowe's tale from the view of a founder of the underground railroad. Lucas was the first black actor to garner a lead role. **Length:** 54 mins. **Format:** Beta, VHS. **Acquisition:** Purchase. **Use:** Home.

★5244★
Uncle Tom's Cabin
Worldvision Home Video, Inc.
1700 Broadwaay
New York, NY 10019-5905

1987. **Program Description:** The first American sound version of this film. Excellent cast and interestingly adapted script are perfect for a message that is still socially relevant today. Based on the novel by Harriet Beecher Stowe. Made for television. **Length:** 110 mins. **Format:** VHS. **Acquisition:** Purchase. **Use:** Home.

★5245★
Under Our Skin: Exploring Racial and Cultural Differences
HRM Video
175 Tompkins Ave.
No. V212
Pleasantville, NY 10570-9973

Ph: (914)769-7496
Fax: (914)747-1744
Free: 800-431-2050

19??. **Program Description:** Documents a diverse group of high school students staging a play, and their experiences and perceptions. Addresses stereotypes, discrimination, intervention techniques, classroom dynamics, cultural identity, and cross-racial friendships. **Length:** 32 mins. **Format:** VHS. **Acquisition:** Purchase. **Use:** Institution.

★5246★
Vanishing Family: The Crisis in Black America
Carousel Film & Video
260 5th Ave., Rm. 405
New York, NY 10001

Ph: (212)683-1660
Fax: (212)683-1662

1988. **Program Description:** This documentary examines the disintegration of the black family structure. The social structure erected by the state, welfare assistance, and the lack of male role models are focused on. **Length:** 64 mins. **Format:** VHS, 3/4U. **Acquisition:** Purchase. **Use:** Institution, SURA.

★5247★
Vegetable Soup
Maryland Public Television
11767 Owings Mills Blvd.
Owings Mills, MD 21117-1499

Ph: (410)356-5600
Fax: (410)581-4338
Free: 800-873-6154

1975. **Program Description:** This is a series of 39 programs designed to educate young people about the various different racial, ethnic and economic groups through the use of music, animation, puppetry and live action. **Length:** 30 mins. **Format:** Beta, VHS, 3/4U. **Acquisition:** Rent/Lease, Purchase. **Use:** Institution, CCTV, CATV, BCTV.

★5248★
Vidalia McCloud—A Family Story
Carousel Film & Video
260 5th Ave., Rm. 405
New York, NY 10001

Ph: (212)683-1660
Fax: (212)683-1662

1988. **Program Description:** A documentary focusing on one family of Black Americans in a migrant town in Central Florida over a three year period. During this time the mother, Vidalia, worked as a fruit picker, short order cook and at times collected welfare. **Length:** 28 mins. **Format:** VHS, 3/4U. **Acquisition:** Purchase. **Use:** Institution, SURA.

★5249★
Video Workshops: Countering the Conspiracy to Destroy Black Boys
Afro-Am Distributing Company
407 E. 25th St., Ste. 600
Chicago, IL 60616

Ph: (312)791-1611
Fax: (312)791-0921

197?. **Program Description:** Dr. Jawanza Kunjufu explains and clarifies the message from his book which theorizes that there is a conspiracy to retard the progress of young black men. **Length:** 60 mins. **Format:** VHS. **Acquisition:** Purchase. **Use:** Institution, SURA.

★5250★
Video Workshops: Developing Positive Self-Images and Disipline in Black Children
Afro-Am Distributing Company
407 E. 25th St., Ste. 600
Chicago, IL 60616

Ph: (312)791-1611
Fax: (312)791-0921

197?. **Program Description:** Dr. Jawnza Kunjufu offers this video supplement to his book which covers such wide ranging subjects as black identity in a white world, value comparisons, non-punitive discipline, parental involvement and more. **Length:** 60 mins. **Format:** VHS. **Acquisition:** Purchase. **Use:** Institution, SURA.

★5251★
Visions of the Spirit: A Portrait of Alice Walker
Women Make Movies
462 Broadway, Ste. 501
New York, NY 10013

Ph: (212)925-0606
Fax: (212)925-2052

1989. **Program Description:** Pulitzer Prize-winning author Alice Walker is profiled in this documentary which shows the writer as mother, daughter, philosopher and activist. **Length:** 58 mins. **Format:** Beta, VHS, 3/4U. **Acquisition:** Purchase, Rent/Lease. **Use:** Institution, SURA.

★5252★
Voice of the Fugitive
Films Inc. Video
5547 N. Ravenswood Ave.
Chicago, IL 60640-1199

Ph: (312)878-2600
Free: 800-323-4222

1978. **Program Description:** This is the story of the "underground railroad" where many slaves went in order to get their freedom in Canada. From the "Adventures in History" series. **Length:** 28 mins. **Format:** Beta, VHS, 3/4U. **Acquisition:** Rent/Lease, Purchase. **Use:** Institution, SURA.

★5253★
Voices of Sarafina
New Yorker Video
16 W. 61st St.
New York, NY 10023

Ph: (212)247-6110
Fax: (212)307-7855
Free: 800-447-0196

1988. **Program Description:** The cast of the Broadway hit musical "Sarafina" play and sing the music of South Africa. Exhilarating performances of anti-apartheid modern music as well as ancient folk music of the region. Unusual and exciting cast of mostly amateur young people. **Length:** 90 mins. **Format:** VHS. **Acquisition:** Purchase. **Use:** Home.

★5254★
Way Down South
Nostalgia Family Video
PO Box 606
Baker City, OR 97814

Ph: (503)523-9034

1939. **Program Description:** The orphan son of a plantation owner tries to take over his father's estate, only to find out that the place has been run into the ground by a corrupt lawyer and a cruel slave driver. Langston Hughes and Clarence Muse–both black–collaborated on the screenplay, but the film was released by a then-major distributor. German-born director Vorhaus was in his second year in Hollywood, after making his mark in Britain directing talkies. **Length:** 62 mins. **Format:** VHS. **Acquisition:** Purchase. **Use:** Home.

★5255★
We Learn About the World
Video Knowledge, Inc.
29 Bramble Ln.
Melville, NY 11747

Ph: (516)367-4250
Fax: (516)367-1006

1980. **Program Description:** This program portrays the adventures of a young black boy who lives in the city. **Length:** 30 mins. **Format:** Beta, VHS, 3/4U. **Acquisition:** Purchase. **Use:** Institution, Home.

★5256★
We Shall Overcome
PBS Video
11858 La Grange Ave.
Los Angeles, CA 90025

Ph: (213)820-0991
Fax: (213)826-4779

1989. **Program Description:** The story of the struggle that black Americans have faced in order to reach equality, as traced through the evolution of the song "We Shall Overcome." **Length:** 58 mins. **Format:** VHS, 3/4U, LV. **Acquisition:** Purchase. **Use:** Institution, Home.

★5257★

"We Shall Overcome": A History of the Civil Rights Movement

Knowledge Unlimited, Inc.
Box 52
Madison, WI 53701-0052
Ph: (608)836-6660
Fax: (608)831-1570
Free: 800-356-2303

1989. **Program Description:** The history of the civil rights movements is reviewed beginning with slavery, addressing reconstruction and "Jim Crow" segregation, and concluding with the turbulent events in the 50s and 60s. **Length:** 20 mins. **Format:** VHS. **Acquisition:** Purchase. **Use:** Institution.

★5258★

We Still Have a Dream

Maryland Public Television
11767 Owings Mills Blvd.
Owings Mills, MD 21117-1499
Ph: (410)356-5600
Fax: (410)581-4338
Free: 800-873-6154

1988. **Program Description:** Six people who marched on Washington in 1963 talk about how things have changed. **Length:** 30 mins. **Format:** Beta, VHS, 3/4U. **Acquisition:** Purchase. **Use:** Institution, CCTV, CATV, BCTV.

★5259★

What Color is Skin

Pyramid Film & Video
Box 1048
2801 Colorado Ave.
Santa Monica, CA 90406
Ph: (310)828-7577
Fax: (310)453-9083
Free: 800-421-2304

1977. **Program Description:** This part of the "Who We Are" series combines live action and animation to show that individual skin coloring is determined by the amount of melanin in the skin. **Length:** 9 mins. **Format:** Beta, VHS, 3/4U. **Acquisition:** Rent/Lease, Purchase, Duplication License. **Use:** Institution, Home, SURA.

★5260★

What Could You Do with a Nickel

First Run/Icarus Films
153 Waverly Pl.
New York, NY 10014
Ph: (212)727-1711
Fax: (212)989-7649
Free: 800-876-1710

1982. **Program Description:** A documentary about 200 black and hispanic women employed by the City of New York who joined together to form the first domestic workers union in the United States. **Length:** 26 mins. **Format:** 3/4U. **Acquisition:** Purchase. **Use:** Institution, SURA.

★5261★

What Makes Me Different

Pyramid Film & Video
Box 1048
2801 Colorado Ave.
Santa Monica, CA 90406
Ph: (310)828-7577
Fax: (310)453-9083
Free: 800-421-2304

1977. **Program Description:** This part of the "Who We Are" series combats prejudice by explaining and discussing some of the physical differences among people. **Length:** 9 mins. **Format:** Beta, VHS, 3/4U. **Acquisition:** Rent/Lease, Purchase, Duplication License. **Use:** Institution, Home, SURA.

★5262★

What's a Heaven For

National AudioVisual Center
National Archives & Records
Administration
8700 Edgeworth Dr.
Capitol Heights, MD 20743-3701
Ph: (301)763-1896
Free: 800-788-NAVC

1966. **Program Description:** A portrayal of Booker T. Washington in a collage of Cine-art to show his emerging philosophy and the impact he had as a freed slave upon his people and his country. **Length:** 17 mins. **Format:** Beta, VHS, 3/4U, Special order formats. **Acquisition:** Purchase. **Use:** Institution, SURA.

★5263★

Where Did You Get That Woman

Music Video Distributors
O'Neill Industrial Center
1210 Standbridge St.
Norristown, PA 19403
Ph: (215)272-7771
Fax: (215)272-6074
Free: 800-888-0486

1987. **Program Description:** A poignant profile of a black woman who works as a washroom attendant. Her telling insights of the affluent people she serves are especially ironic, given the circumstances of her meager existence. **Length:** 28 mins. **Format:** Beta, VHS. **Acquisition:** Purchase. **Use:** Institution.

★5264★

Where Dreams Come True

NASA Lyndon B. Johnson Space Center
Audiovisual Department
NASA Rd. 1
Houston, TX 77058
Ph: (713)483-4321

1979. **Program Description:** This video explores and explains the career opportunities in NASA for minorities and women. Jobs range from clerks, secretaries, and electricians all the way to astronauts, system analysts, and computer programmers. **Length:** 28 mins. **Format:** 3/4U, 1C, Q. **Acquisition:** Free Loan. **Use:** BCTV, SURA.

★5265★

Who Killed Martin Luther King

Kultur Video
121 Hwy. No. 36
West Long Branch, NJ 07764
Ph: (908)229-2343
Fax: (908)229-0066
Free: 800-458-5887

19??. **Program Description:** Program focuses in on the role played by James Earl Ray in the assassination of the civil rights leader. **Length:** 52 mins. **Format:** VHS. **Acquisition:** Purchase. **Use:** Home.

★5266★

Who's Different

Phoenix/BFA Films
468 Park Ave., S.
New York, NY 10016
Ph: (212)684-5910
Free: 800-221-1274

1986. **Program Description:** Two high schoolers learn about the evils of prejudice. **Length:** 26 mins. **Format:** Beta, VHS, 3/4U. **Acquisition:** Purchase. **Use:** Institution, SURA.

★5267★

William H. Johnson: Art and Life of an African American Artist

Knowledge Unlimited, Inc.
Box 52
Madison, WI 53701-0052
Ph: (608)836-6660
Fax: (608)831-1570
Free: 800-356-2303

19??. **Program Description:** The life and work of William H. Johnson, an African American artist, is the focus of this video. Politics in the era between 1920 and 1940, the social climate, and Johnson's contributions are presented through vintage photos, period music, and of course, his paintings. **Length:** 25 mins. **Format:** VHS. **Acquisition:** Purchase. **Use:** Institution.

★5268★

Wilma

Columbia Tristar Home Video
3400 Riverside Dr.
Burbank, CA 91505-4627
Ph: (818)972-8193
Fax: (818)972-0937

1977. **Program Description:** Based on the true story of Wilma Rudolph, a young black woman who overcame childhood illness to win three gold medals at the 1960 Olympics. **Length:** 100 mins. **Format:** Beta, VHS. **Acquisition:** Purchase. **Use:** Home.

★5269★

Winnie and Nelson Mandela

California Newsreel
149 Ninth St., Ste. 420
San Francisco, CA 94103
Ph: (415)621-6196
Fax: (415)621-6522

1986. **Program Description:** Documentary of the man and woman who most personify South Africa's freedom movement, and their unique love story. Told from Winnie's viewpoint, the film highlights her merciless harassment by authorities following Nelson's imprisonment. Also available in a 30-minute version. **Length:** 58

mins. **Format:** VHS, Special order formats. **Acquisition:** Purchase, Rent/Lease. **Use:** Institution.

★5270★
Winnie (Mandela)
Carousel Film & Video
260 5th Ave., Rm. 405   Ph: (212)683-1660
New York, NY 10001   Fax: (212)683-1662
1987. **Program Description:** This documentary concentrates on Winnie Mandela, the leading figure in South Africa's anti-apartheid. Also depicted are scenes of extreme violence in this struggling country. **Length:** 15 mins. **Format:** VHS, 3/4U. **Acquisition:** Purchase. **Use:** Institution, SURA.

★5271★
With These Hands
Filmakers Library, Inc.
124 E. 40th
New York, NY 10016   Ph: (212)808-4980
1988. **Program Description:** Three African women tell of their daily struggle to feed their families. Their efforts are often stifled by a male dominated culture that sees farming as demeaning and as a source of quick profits. **Length:** 55 mins. **Format:** VHS. **Acquisition:** Rent/Lease, Purchase, Duplication. **Use:** Institution, Home, SURA.

★5272★
A Woman Called Moses
Xenon
211 Arizona Ave.
Santa Monica, CA 90401
                Free: 800-468-1913
1978. **Program Description:** The story of Harriet Ross Tubman, who bought her freedom from slavery, founded the underground railroad, and helped lead hundreds of slaves to freedom before the Civil War. Based on the novel by Marcy Heldish. **Length:** 200 mins. **Format:** VHS. **Acquisition:** Purchase. **Use:** Home.

★5273★
The Women of Brewster Place
J2 Communications   Ph: (310)474-5252
10850 Wilshire Blvd., Ste. 1000   Fax: (310)474-1219
Los Angeles, CA 90024   Free: 800-521-8273
1989. **Program Description:** Seven black women living in a tenement fight to gain control of their lives. Based on the novel by Gloria Naylor. **Length:** 180 mins. **Format:** Beta, VHS. **Acquisition:** Purchase. **Use:** Home.

★5274★
Words by Heart
Public Media Video   Ph: (312)878-2600
5547 N. Ravenswood Ave.   Fax: (312)878-8406
Chicago, IL 60640-1199   Free: 800-826-3456
1984. **Program Description:** An African American family in turn of the century Missouri faces issues of discrimination and prejudice. Twelve-year-old Lena wins a speech contest and begins to question their place in the community and their aspirations for a better life. Based on a book by Ouida Sebestyen. Aired by PBS as part of the "Wonderworks" family movie series. **Length:** 116 mins. **Format:** VHS. **Acquisition:** Purchase. **Use:** Home.

★5275★
World Turned Upside Down
Films Inc. Video
5547 N. Ravenswood Ave.   Ph: (312)878-2600
Chicago, IL 60640-1199   Free: 800-323-4222
1976. **Program Description:** James Armistead, a black slave, is recruited by Lafayette to spy on Lord Cornwallis in the Revolutionary War. He learns the British strategy, warns Lafayette, and the Americans defeat Cornwallis in this segment of the "Ourstory" series. **Length:** 27 mins. **Format:** Beta, VHS, 3/4U. **Acquisition:** Purchase. **Use:** Institution, SURA.

★5276★
Yes, Ma'am
Filmakers Library, Inc.
124 E. 40th
New York, NY 10016   Ph: (212)808-4980
1981. **Program Description:** This program looks at black household workers of New Orleans who have spent their whole working lives employed by one wealthy white family, and the strong attachments that have developed on both sides. **Length:** 48 mins. **Format:** Beta, VHS, 3/4U. **Acquisition:** Purchase. **Use:** Institution.

★5277★
You Have Struck a Rock
California Newsreel
149 Ninth St., Ste. 420   Ph: (415)621-6196
San Francisco, CA 94103   Fax: (415)621-6522
1981. **Program Description:** The story of black South African women who led opposition to apartheid in the 1950s by refusing to accept the pass system imposed by the white government. Features interviews with women, now in their 70s and 80s, who were imprisoned for organizing campaigns defying the government. **Length:** 28 mins. **Format:** VHS, Special order formats. **Acquisition:** Purchase, Rent/Lease. **Use:** Institution, Home.

★5278★
You Must Remember This
Public Media Video   Ph: (312)878-2600
5547 N. Ravenswood Ave.   Fax: (312)878-8406
Chicago, IL 60640-1199   Free: 800-826-3456
199?. **Program Description:** When Uncle Buddy (Guillaume) receives a mysterious trunk, Ella's curiosity gets the best of her. She opens the trunk to discover a number of old movies made by W.B. Jackson–Uncle Buddy. Ella takes the films to a movie archive to find out about her uncle's past as an independent black filmmaker. After researching the history of black cinema, Ella convinces her uncle to be proud of his contribution to the film world. Includes a viewers' guide. Part of the "Wonderworks" series. **Length:** 110 mins. **Format:** VHS. **Acquisition:** Purchase. **Use:** Home.

★5279★
Your Move
University of California - Berkeley
  Extension Media Center
2176 Shattuck Ave.
Berkeley, CA 94704   Ph: (510)642-0460
1982. **Program Description:** A young black couple encounter many problems after they move to a different city. **Length:** 25 mins. **Format:** VHS, 3/4U. **Acquisition:** Purchase, Rent/Lease. **Use:** Institution, SURA.

★5280★
Zajota and the Boogie Spirit
Filmakers Library, Inc.
124 E. 40th
New York, NY 10016   Ph: (212)808-4980
1990. **Program Description:** African music and dance is surveyed from its beginnings to the present. Considers modern influences of music and movement on ancient traditions. **Length:** 20 mins. **Format:** VHS, Special order formats. **Acquisition:** Purchase. **Use:** Institution.

★5281★
Zora Is My Name!
PBS Video
11858 La Grange Ave.   Ph: (310)820-0991
Los Angeles, CA 90025   Fax: (310)826-4779
1990. **Program Description:** The funny, moving story of Zora Neal Hurston, a Black writer known for her stories and folklore of the rural South of the '30s and '40s. **Length:** 90 mins. **Format:** VHS, LV. **Acquisition:** Purchase. **Use:** Home.

ALPHABETICAL NAME AND SUBJECT INDEX

This is an alphabetical listing of all organizations, agencies, and publications included in BAID. Subject terms are bolded with the appropriate citations listed immediately below. Index references are to **entry numbers** rather than to page numbers. Consult the "User's Guide" for more detailed information about the index.

Affirmative Action (continued)

Connecticut Education Department - Affirmative Action **3186**

Connecticut Human Resources Department - Affirmative Action **3187**

EEO Resource Directory: Technical Assistance Guide for Southern California Personnel Practitioners **4002**

Equal Employment Advisory Council **171**

Equal Employment Opportunity Award **2855**

Equal Opportunity **4905**

Fair Employment Practices Summary of Latest Developments **3888**

Hawaii Health Department - Affirmative Action Office **3203**

Hawaii Office of the Governor - Affirmative Action Office **3206**

Houston Affirmative Action Office **3383**

Illinois Commerce and Community Affairs Department - Equal Employment Opportunity and Affirmative Action **3209**

Illinois Secretary of State - Affirmative Action Officer **3214**

Indiana Personnel Department - Affirmative Action Division **3219**

Iowa Human Services Department - Policy Coordination Division - Affirmative Action Bureau **3225**

King County Office of Human Resource Management Affirmative Action **3404**

Maine Human Services Department - Management, Budget, and Policy Office - Affirmative Action **3243**

Maine Transportation Department - Public Affairs and Human Resources Management - Equal Opportunity and Employee Relations **3244**

Maryland Higher Education Commission - Affirmative Action **3250**

Massachusetts Administration and Finance Executive Office
    Affirmative Action Central Regional Office **3258**
    Affirmative Action Office **3259**

Massachusetts Bay Transportation Authority - Affirmative Action and Equal Employment Opportunity Division **3262**

Massachusetts Human Services Executive Office - Corrections Department - Affirmative Action Office **3264**

Michigan Agriculture Department - Affirmative Action Office **3268**

Michigan Social Services Department - Affirmative Action and Equal Opportunity Office **3274**

Minnesota Education Department - Human Resources Department - Affirmative Action Office **3279**

Minnesota Human Services Department - Affirmative Action and Civil Rights Office **3284**

Minnesota Jobs and Training Department - Affirmative Action Office **3285**

Minorities in Business Insider **3905**

Minority Business Enterprises - Albuquerque Affirmative Action Office **3309**

Missouri Administration Office - Affirmative Action Office **3289**

National Equal Employment/Affirmative Action Exemplary Practices Award **2902**

Nebraska Personnel Department - Affirmative Action/Recruitment **3298**

Network Communications, Inc. **4177**

New Jersey Personnel Department - Equal Employment Opportunity Affirmative Action Division **3308**

New York Agriculture and Markets Department - Affirmative Action Program **3312**

New York Alcoholism and Substance Abuse Division - Affirmative Action Bureau **3313**

New York Housing and Community Renewal Division - Community Affairs and Affirmative Action Office **3323**

New York Insurance Department - New York City Office - Affirmative Action **3327**

Office of Personnel Management - Affirmative Action Program **3267**

Ohio Employment Services Bureau - Affirmative Action Office **3343**

Oklahoma Health Department - Affirmative Action Division **3352**

Oregon Human Resources Department - Affirmative Action Unit **3355**

Oregon Office of the Governor - Affirmative Action Director **3357**

Pennsylvania Corrections Department - Affirmative Action Office **3359**

Pennsylvania Office of the Governor - Administration Office - Affirmative Action Bureau **3368**

Pennsylvania Public Welfare Department - Civil Rights Compliance **3369**

Place in the Woods **4183**

State Personnel Board - Affirmative Action and Exam Services **3181**

Tennessee Personnel Department - Human Resources Development - Affirmative Action Division **3382**

Tennessee (State) Human Rights Commission - Resource Library **1959**

U.S. Department of Energy - Office of Administration and Management - Office of Equal Opportunity - Affirmative Action Programs Division **2968**

U.S. Department of Health and Human Services - Office for Civil Rights - Equal Employment Opportunity/Affirmative Action **2988**

U.S. Department of Housing and Urban Development - Assistant Secretary for Fair Housing and Equal Opportunity - Office of Operations and Management - Office of Affirmative Action and Equal Employment Opportunity **2999**

U.S. Department of Labor - Office of Administration and Management - Directorate of Civil Rights - Office of Equal Employment Opportunity and Affirmative Action **3017**

U.S. Department of State - Office of the Secretary - Equal Employment Opportunity and Civil Rights Office - Affirmative Action Outreach **3023**

U.S. Smithsonian Institution - Office of Equal Opportunity and Minority Affairs - Affirmative Action Program **3099**

Wisconsin Employment Relations Department - Affirmative Action Division **3415**

Wisconsin Health and Social Services Department - Affirmative Action/Civil Rights Office **3416**

Affirmative Action and Equal Employment Opportunity Award **2822**

Affirmative Action Compliance Manual for Federal Contractors **3841**

Affirmative Action Department - Minority Business Enterprise Program **3154**

Affirmative Action, Inc. **3952**

Affirmative Action: Is It the Answer to Discrimination **4709**

Affirmative Action Register **3952**

Afram Press **4076**

Africa

ACAS Bulletin **3839**

ACOA Action News **3840**

Africa **4710, 4711**

Africa: A Continent of Many Nations **4712**

Africa: A New Look **4713**

Africa: A Voyage of Discovery **4714**

Africa: An Introduction (Revised) **4715**

Africa Calls: Its Drums and Musical Instruments **4716**

Africa Church Growth and Development **4717**

Africa Faith and Justice Network **4**

Africa Fund **5**

Africa House **2005**

Africa in Focus **4718**

Africa Insider **3842**

Africa News **3843**

Africa News Service, Inc. **7**
    Library **1815**

Africa Today **3750**

Africa World Press **8, 4078**

African-American Institute **10, 4079**
    Africa Policy Information Center **1817**

African-American Labor Center **11**

African American Museum—Newsletter **3844**

African-American Traveler **3845**

African & Caribbean Imprint Library Services **4080**

The African Continent: An Introduction **4721**

African Journey **4722**

African Origins **4725**

African Religions and Ritual Dances **4726**

African Soul: Music, Past and Present **4727**

African Studies Association **19**

African Studies Association/Crossroads Press **4081**

African Studies Center—Newsletter **3847**

American Civil Liberties Union **39**   (continued)
    Wisconsin Affiliate **1685**
    Wyoming Affiliate **1701**
American Civil Liberties Union; District of Columbia **739**
American Civil Liberties Union Foundation (ACLU) **40**, **3871**
American Civil Liberties Union of the National Capital
  Area **2824**
American College of Healthcare Executives Foundation **2535**
American College Theatre Festival **2889**
American Colonization Society - Charity and Social Welfare
  Organization **41**
American Committee on Africa (ACOA) **42**, **3840**
American Constitutional and Civil Rights Union **43**
American Coordinating Committee for Equality in Sport and
  Society **44**
American Dental Hygienists' Association Institute - Institute for
  Oral Health **2529**
American Development Corp. **3483**
American Economic Association **2538**, **2539**
American Economic Association/Federal Reserve System
  Minority Graduate Fellowships in Economics **2538**
American Economic Association Summer Minority Program at
  Stanford University **2539**
American Enterprise Institute for Public Policy Research **4709**
American Film Institute Alumni Association **2898**
American Foundation for Negro Affairs **45**
American Foundation for Pharmaceutical Education **2526**
American Friends Service Committee (AFSC) **3930**
American Fund for Dental Health **2531**
American Geological Institute **2603**
American Health and Beauty Aids Institute **46**
American Heart Association **2533**
American Home Economics Association Foundation **2569**, **2573**
American Humanist Association **5104**
American Institute of Certified Public Accountants **2534**
American Institute of Islamic Studies **47**
American Jazz Masters Fellowship Awards **2827**
American League of Financial Institutions **48**
*American League of Financial Institutions—Directory of
Members and Associate Members* **3955**
American League of Financial Institutions—Membership
  Roste **3955**
American Library Association
    Library and Information Technology Association **2597**,
    2886
    Office for Library Personnel Resources **2598**
    Reference and Adult Services Division **2851**
    Social Responsibilities Round Table **2847**
American Library Association (ALA) **4028**
American Mohammedan Society **259**
American Museum of Negro History **263**
American Muslim Mission **1713**
American Muslims **1713**
The American News **3705**
American Nurses' Association **2893**
    Ethnic/Racial Minority Fellowships Programs **2559**, **2630**
American Patchwork: Jazz Parades **4739**
American Physical Society **2560**
American Physical Therapy Association **2842**, **2896**, **2897**
American Planning Association **2544**, **2545**
American Political Science Association **2546**, **2907**, **3980**
American Psychological Association **2540-2542**, **3984**
American Psychological Association Minority Fellowship in
  Neuroscience **2540**
American Psychological Association Minority Fellowships in
  Psychology-Clinical Training **2541**
American Psychological Association Minority Fellowships in
  Psychology-Research Training **2542**
American Publishing Co. **3699**
American Respiratory Care Foundation **2593**
American Savings and Loan League **48**
American Society for Microbiology **2543**, **2625**
American Society for Microbiology Predoctoral Fellowships in
  Microbiology for Minority Students **2543**
American Society for Public Administration **2902**
The American Society of Criminology **2547**
American Sociological Association - Minority Fellowship
  Program **2563**
The American South: Black Political Development **4740**
The American South: The Civil Rights Movement **4741**
American Urban Radio Networks **3503**

American Video Corporation **5049**
*American Visions: The Magazine of Afro-American
Culture* **3754**
American Women's Clergy Association **14**
Americans Concerned about Southern Africa **161**
Americans for Civic Participation **446**
America's Music, Vol. 5: Rhythm and Blues 1 **4742**
America's Music, Vol. 6: Rhythm and Blues 2 **4743**
America's Music, Vol. 9: Jazz Then Dixieland 1 **4744**
America's Music, Vol. 11: Soul 1 **4745**
America's Music, Vol. 12: Soul 2 **4746**
America's Music, Vol. 13: Gospel 1 **4747**
America's Music, Vol. 14: Gospel 2 **4748**
Amherst College - Department of Black Studies **2345**
Amherst; University of Massachusetts at - W.E.B. DuBois
  Department of Afro-American Studies **2469**
Amiri Baraka; In Motion: **4985**
Amistad Research Center **2657**
    Library/Archives **1827**
Amnesty International of the U.S.A. **49**
Among Brothers: Politics in New Orleans **4749**
Among Good Christian People **4750**
Amos 'n' Andy: Anatomy of a Controversy **4751**
AMSCO Wholesalers Inc. **3501**
Amsterdam News **3525**
Anacostia Museum **2025**
Anaheim Minority Business Development Center **558**
Anansi **4752**
Anasa Briggs: Apartheid **4753**
Anasa Briggs: Blacks in Agriculture **4754**
Anasa Briggs: Gospel Festival **4755**
Anasa Briggs: Martin Luther King Jr. Memorial Special **4756**
Anasa Briggs: Water of Your Bath **4757**
Ancestors; African Masks: Yaaba Soore, Path of the **4724**
Ancient Africans **4758**
Ancient Egyptian Museum **2053**
And the Children Shall Lead **4759**
Andersen Memorial Scholarships; Hugh J. **2587**, **2873**
The Anderson-Dubose Co. **3424**
Andre's and Co. **4088**
Andrew Cacho African Drummers and Dancers **2026**
Animation; A History of Racist **4967**
Anisfield - Wolf Book Awards/Exploring Human Diversity and
  Prejudice **2828**
Ankh Enterprises **4089**
Ann Arbor; University of Michigan -
    Center for Afro American and African Studies **2471**, **2792**
    Program for Research on Black Americans **2793**
Ann Tanneyhill Award **2829**
Annenberg/CPB Collection **4731**
*Annie Mae Hunt Remembers; Guts, Gumption and Go-
Ahead:* **4952**
Ansaaru Allah Community **1714**
Anson Schloat **4773**
Anthropologists; Association of Black **61**
Anti-Defamation League of B'nai B'rith **5069**
Anti-Repression Resource Team **50**
Antioch Association of Metaphysical Science **1715**
Antioch College - African-American Studies **2346**
Any Child is My Child **4760**
AOIP **51**
APA Planning Fellowships **2544**
APA Undergraduate Minority Scholarships **2545**
Apartheid
    ABC News: Mandela—The Man and His Country **4703**
    About the United Nations: Apartheid **4705**
    Africa Fund **4077**
    Africa Network **6**
    Allan Boesak: Choosing for Justice **4736**
    American Coordinating Committee for Equality in Sport and
     Society **44**
    Anasa Briggs: Apartheid **4753**
    Any Child is My Child **4760**
    Apartheid, Part 5 **4761**
    Artists and Athletes Against Apartheid **52**
    Artists United Against Apartheid **53**
    Biko: Breaking the Silence **4779**
    Bound to Strike Back **4840**
    Chain of Tears **4848**
    Corridors of Freedom **4873**
    Cry Freedom **4875**

Index

Business (continued)

Bakersfield Minority Business Development Center **563**
Baltimore Council for Equal Business Opportunity **1001**
Baton Rouge Minority Business Development Center **969**
Beaumont Minority Business Development Center **1585**
Birmingham Minority Business Development Center **512**
Black Business Alliance **87**
Black Business and Professional Association **573**
Black Business Association **1552**
BLACK CAREERS **3757**
Black Data Processing Associates **91**
Black Economic Research Team Inc. **4102**
Black Enterprise **3761**
Black Enterprise—Top Black Businesses Issue **3960**
Black Entrepreneurs Press **4103**
The Black Pages of New England **3961**
Booker T. Washington Business Association **1071**
Boston Minority Business Development Center **1038**
Bronx Minority Business Development Center **1269**
Brooklyn Minority Business Development Center **1271**
Buffalo Minority Business Development Center **1275**
Building Concerns **3861**
Bureau of Business and Economic Research **1124**
Business and Professional Association of Pittsburgh **1495**
Business Equity and Development Corporation **592**
Business League of Baltimore **1006**
Buyers' Guide to Minority Business **3968**
California State and Consumer Services Agency - Small and Minority Business Office **3179**
Caribbean Business Directory & Yellow Pages **3970**
Caribbean Exporters, Importers and Business Services Directory **3971**
Central Savannah River Area Business League **832**
Certified Minority Business Enterprises & Women Business Enterprises in Rhode Island **3972**
Chapter to Chapter **3867**
Charlotte Minority Business Development Center **1349**
Cincinnati Minority Business Development Center **1396**
Cleveland Business League **1398**
Cleveland Minority Business Development Center No. 1 **1401**
Cobblestone Communications **4125**
Columbia Minority Business Development Center **1539**
Columbus Minority Business Development Center **2684**
Community and Industrial Development - Minority and Small Business Development Agency **3412**
Conference of Minority Public Administrators **145**
Connecticut Minority Business Development Center **704**
CORPORATE HEADQUARTERS **3776**
Corporate Leadership Award **2849**
Corpus Christi Minority Business Development Center **1591**
Cultural Diversity at Work Newsletter **3880**
Dallas/Fort Worth Black Pages **3976**
Delaware Transportation Department - Disadvantaged Business Enterprise **3190**
Denver Minority Business Development Center **694**
Detroit Minority Business Development Center **1073**
Directory of African American Design Firms **3977**
Directory of Certified Minority and Women-Owned Business Enterprises **3981**
Directory of Certified Minority Business Enterprises **3982**
Directory of Certified Minority, Women, and Disadvantaged Business Enterprise **3983**
Directory of Minority- and Women-Owned Business Enterprises **3986**
Directory of Minority and Women Owned Businesses **3987**
Directory of Minority and Women-Owned Investment Bankers **3988**
Directory of Minority Business in Wisconsin **3990**
Directory of Minority Construction Contractors and Subcontractors **3991**
Directory of Minority Management Consulting Firms **3992**
Directory of Minority Public Relations Professionals **3994**
Directory of Minority Suppliers **3995**
Directory of Minority Truckers **3996**
Directory of Operating Small Business Investment Companies **3997**

District of Columbia Arts and Humanities Commission - Human Rights and Minority Business Opportunity Commission **3192**
District of Columbia Economic Development - Human Rights and Minority Business Development Department **3193**
Dollars & Sense Magazine **3780**
Durham Business and Professional Chain **1350**
El Paso Minority Business Development Center **1598**
Ethnic Employees of the Library of Congress **177**
Executive Leadership Council **179**
Fayetteville Business and Professional League **1351**
Fayetteville Business League **1352**
Fayetteville Minority Business Development Center **1353**
Federation of Southern Cooperatives and Land Assistance Fund **182**
Florida First Coast Chapter/National Business League **766**
Fresno Minority Business Development Center **607**
Gary Minority Business Development Center **918**
GE Foundation Minority Student Scholarships **2576**
Golden State Business League **608**
Minority Business Development Agency—Directory of Regional & District Offices and Funded Organizations **4031**
Greater New York Business League **1282**
Greenville/Spartanburg Minority Business Development Center **1541**
Harlem Institute of Fashion **4151**
Harlem Minority Business Development Center **1289**
Honolulu Minority Business Development Center **856**
Houston Minority Business Development Center **1609**
Illinois Minority and Female Business Enterprise Directory **4017**
Indiana Administration Department - Minority Business Development Division **3216**
Indianapolis Minority Business Development Center **922**
Inter-American Travel Agents Society **211**
International Association of African and American Black Business People **212**
International Association of Black Business Educators **213**
International Black Toy Manufacturers Association **217**
International Business in South Africa **4018**
Interracial Council for Business Opportunity **228**
Investor Responsibility Research Center, Inc. **4160**
Jackson Minority Business Development Center **1129**
Jacksonville Minority Business **3201**
Jacksonville Minority Business Development Center **773**
Kansas City Black Pages **4164**
Kansas City Minority Business Development Center **1148**
Kansas Commerce and Housing Department - Minority Business Office **3227**
Kansas Minority-Owned & Women-Owned Directory **4020**
Kentucky Economic Development Cabinet - Community Development Department - Small and Minority Business Division **3232**
King County Affirmative Action - Minority/Women's Business Enterprise **3401**
Laredo Minority Business Development Center **1611**
Las Vegas Minority Business Development Center **1174**
List of 8(a) Approved Contractors **4023**
List of Minority Firms in North & South Carolina **4024**
Little Rock Minority Business Development Center **545**
Los Angeles Minority Business Development Center **622**
Louisiana Economic Development Department - Minority and Women's Business Enterprise Division **3236**
Louisiana Office of the Governor - Minority Business Development Office **3238**
Louisville Minority Business Development Center **960**
Lubbock/Midland-Odessa Minority Business Development Center **1612**
Majestic Eagles **247**
Making Success Happen Newsletter **3903**
Manhattan Minority Business Development Center **1296**
Maryland/DC Minority Supplier Development Council Minority Business Directory **4026**
Maryland Transportation Department - Minority Business Enterprise and Equal Opportunity Office **3255**
Massachusetts Minority and Women's Business Assistance Office **3265**
Massachusetts State of Minority and Women Business Assistance **3266**

Equal Employment Opportunity Commission; U.S. **3043**
(continued)
Employment Discrimination - State and Local Fair
Employment Practices Agency Contracts (30.002) **3140**
Employment Discrimination - Title VII of the Civil Rights
Act of 1964 (30.001) **3141**
Houston District Office **3053**
Indianapolis District Office **3054**
Library **1968**
Los Angeles District Office **3055**
Memphis District Office **3056**
Miami District Office **3057**
Milwaukee District Office **3058**
New Orleans District Office **3059**
New York District Office **3060**
Office of Federal Operations - Federal Sector Programs -
Affirmative Employment Programs Division **3061**
Office of Program Operations - Federal Sector Programs -
Affirmative Employment Programs Division **3062**
Philadelphia District Office **3063**
Phoenix District Office **3064**
St. Louis District Office **3065**
San Antonio District Office **3066**
San Francisco District Office **3067**
Seattle District Office **3068**
Washington District Office **3069**
Equal Opportunity **4905**
Equal Opportunity Commission; Georgia **3100**
Equal Opportunity Commission; Nebraska **3297**
Equal Opportunity Day Award **2856**
Equal Opportunity Department; Phoenix - Community Relations
Committee - Fair Housing Services **3161**
Equal Opportunity Division; Indianapolis **3221**
Equal Opportunity Office; Hillsborough County **3200**
Equal Opportunity Publications Scholarship **2567**
Equal Rights Commission; Nevada **3299**
Equal Rights Congress **172**
Equal Rights Congress; Los Angeles **621**
Equal Rights; Police Officers for **1444**
Equal Treatment/Equal Opportunity **4906**
Equality **4907**
Equality; Black Police Officers United for Justice and **871**
Ergo Media Inc. **5075**
ERIC Clearinghouse for the Urban Disadvantaged **2682**
ERIC Clearinghouse on Urban Education **1872**
Columbia University **2682**
ESPN Home Video **5003**
Essai Seay Publications **4141**
Essenay Entertainment **5230**
Essence **3784**
Essence Communications, Inc. **3438**, **3784**
Essex County Education Association **1201**
Essex County; Urban League of **1229**
Eta Phi Beta **173**
Ethiopian Community Mutual Assistance Association **174**
Ethiopian Refugee Project of the Third Baptist Church **603**
Ethiopian Zion Coptic Church **1745**
Ethnic Affairs; National Center for Urban **362**, **4176**
*Ethnic-American Cultural Heritage; How and Where to Research
Your* **4015**
*Ethnic and Religious Genealogical and Historical Societies and
Archives; List of 96* **4025**
Ethnic and Special Studies; Society of **456**
Ethnic Anonymous **175**
Ethnic, Cultural, and Heritage Organization of New
Orleans **973**
Ethnic Cultural Preservation Council **176**
Ethnic Directory; Cleveland **3973**
Ethnic Employees of the Library of Congress **177**
Ethnic Genealogy: A Research Guide **4003**
*Ethnic Groups in California: A Guide to Organizations and
Information Resources* **4004**
Ethnic Heritage Center; Michigan **2088**
Ethnic Heritage Council **3816**
Ethnic Heritage Council of the Pacific Northwest **1669**
Ethnic Leadership Supplemental Grants; Presbyterian Church
Racial/ **2626**
Ethnic Materials and Information Exchange Round Table **178**
American Library Association (ALA) **3884**
Ethnic Minorities; ASC Fellowship for **2547**
Ethnic Minority Directory of Professionals in Psychology **3984**

Ethnic Minority Professionals in Psychology; Directory of **3984**
Ethnic Minority Psychology Award; Distinguished Contribution
to **2852**
Ethnic Minority Students; Leonard M. Perryman Communications
Scholarship for **2596**
Ethnic Notions **4908**
Ethnic Organizations Directory; Michigan **4027**
Ethnic People of Color; NSNA Breakthrough to Nursing
Scholarships for **2623**
*Ethnic Periodicals in Contemporary America: An Annotated
Guide* **4005**
Ethnic Publications and Cultural Institutions; Center for the
Study of - Kent State University **2719**
Ethnic Recruitment; Texas State Scholarship Program for **2648**
Ethnic Studies; Balch Institute for **2659**
Ethnic Studies; Journal of **3797**
Ethnic Studies; National Association for **277**
Ethnicity and Race in America; Center for Studies of -
University of Colorado at Boulder **2781**
Ethnicity in America; Center for the Study of Race and -
Brown University **2667**
Ethnicity; Research Center on the Psychobiology of - University
of California, Los Angeles **2776**
Ethnohistory Parting Ways; The Museum of Afro-
American **2077**
Ethnovision, Inc. **4979**
Ethridge Construction Inc.; J.E. **3497**
Eubie Blake National Museum **2066**
Evangelical Association; National Black **336**
Evangelical Church and Missionary Association;
International **1762**
Evangelical Life and Soul Saving Assembly of the U.S.A.;
National Baptist **1777**
Evangelical Lutheran Church in America - Division for Higher
Education and Schools **2568**
Evangelical Lutheran Church in America Scholarships **2568**
Evangelism and Counseling Association; Black **825**
Evangelist Association **4142**
Evangelistic Centers; Deliverance **1744**
Evans-Tibbs Collection **2030**
Evanston Black Police Association **880**
Evanston Brothers **881**
Evansville Black Coalition **914**
The Evening Whirl **3598**
Evers College; City University of New York - Medgar **2229**
Every Wednesday **3599**
Executive Leadership Council **179**
The Eye of the Storm **4909**
Eyes on the Prize **4910**
*Eyes on the Prize 2: America at the Racial Crossroads (1965-
1985)* **4911**
Facets Multimedia, Inc. **4818**, **4832**, **4849**, **4883**, **4976**, **4980**,
4985, **5002**, **5051**, **5131**, **5153**, **5169**, **5172**, **5229**
Facts Newspaper **3600**
Fade to Black **4912**
FAIR **1202**
Fair Employment Practice Service **3886**
Fair Employment Practices **3886**
Fair Employment Practices Guidelines **3887**
*Fair Employment Practices Summary of Latest
Developments* **3888**
Fair Employment Report **3889**
Fair Housing
Baltimore City Housing Authority - Fair Housing and Equal
Opportunity **3245**
Boston Fair Housing Commission **3256**
California Department of Fair Employment and
Housing **3171**
California State and Consumer Services Agency - Fair
Employment and Housing Commission **3178**
Citizens for Fair Housing **1007**
Dayton Human Relations Council **4133**
Fair Housing Center of Greater Grand Rapids **1076**
Fair Housing Center of Metropolitan Detroit **1077**
Fair Housing Council of Orange County **604**
Fair Housing Council of San Gabriel Valley **605**
Fund for an Open Society **190**
Guardians Association - New York City Housing **1285**
Hollywood-Mid L.A. Fair Housing Council **612**
Hope Fair Housing Center **883**
Housing Opportunities Made Equal **1648**

Nebraska; Urban League of **1170**
Negro Airmen International **424**
The Negro Almanac: A Reference Work on the African American **4054**
The Negro Educational Review **3811**
The Negro Educational Review, Inc. **3811**
The Negro Ensemble Company **5089**
Negro Ensemble Co., Inc. **2148**
Negro History Bulletin **3812**
Negro Musicians Association **264**
Negro National Bowling Association **355**
The Negro Soldier **5090**
Negro Trade Union Leadership Council **1509**
Neighborhood Fund **897**
Neighborhood Housing Development; Association of **1256**
Neighborhood Institute **898**
NETCHE (Nebraska ETV Council for Higher Education) **4808, 4811, 4819, 4830, 5147**
Network Communications, Inc. **4177**
Network International **138**
Network Solutions, Inc. **3462**
Neuroscience; American Psychological Association Minority Fellowship in **2540**
Nevada Black Chamber of Commerce **1177**
Nevada Black Police Association **1178**
Nevada Economic Development Commission **4032**
Nevada Equal Rights Commission **3299**
Nevada Human Resources Department **3300**
Nevada, Las Vegas; University of - Ethnic Studies Program **2476**
Nevada; Professional Black Fire Fighters of Clark County **1179**
New American **1311**
New Bayview **3667**
New Bethel Church of God in Christ (Pentecostal) **1780**
New Breed of Firefighters **790**
New Brunswick Minority Business Development Center **1217**
New Brunswick Minority Fire Fighters **1218**
New College of California - New College Library **1922**
New Community College of Baltimore **1831**
New Day Press, Inc. **4178**
New Day Publishing Enterprises **3656**
New Dimension Media, Inc. **4776**
New England; The Black Pages of **3961**
New England Minority Purchasing Council **1051, 4043**
The New Film Company, Inc. **5103**
New Freedom Theater **2184**
New Hampshire Human Rights Commission **3301**
New Haven; Firebird Society of **707**
New Haven Silver Shields **711**
New Haven; Urban League of Greater **718**
New Images **3921**
The New Iowa Bystander **3668**
New Jack City **5091**
New Jersey Afro-American **3669**
New Jersey Attorney General's Office (Law and Public Safety Department) - Civil Rights Division **3302**
New Jersey; Black United Fund of **1192**
New Jersey - Camden College of Arts and Sciences; Rutgers State University of - Africana-American Studies **2425**
New Jersey Commerce and Economic Development Department - Development for Small Business, Women and Minority Business Division **3303**
New Jersey - Douglas College; Rutgers State University of - Africana Studies **2426**
New Jersey Health Department - Minority Health Office **3304**
New Jersey Human Services Department - Family Development Division **3305**
New Jersey Law and Public Safety Department - Civil Rights Division **3306**
New Jersey Network **4846, 4984**
New Jersey - Newark College of Arts and Sciences; Rutgers State University of - Afro-American and African Studies Department **2427**
New Jersey Office of Legislative Services - Institutions, Health and Welfare Committee **3307**
New Jersey Personnel Department - Equal Employment Opportunity Affirmative Action Division **3308**
New Jersey Public Policy Research Institute **2741**
New Jersey; Vulcan Pioneers of **1234**
New Jersey; William Paterson College of - Department of African and Afro-American Studies **2504**

New Mexico Black Lawyers Association **1238**
New Mexico; Black Officers Association of **1237**
New Mexico Highway and Transportation Department - Equal Opportunity Program **3310**
New Mexico Labor Department - Human Rights Division **3311**
New Mexico Minority Suppliers Directory **4041**
New Mexico; University of - African-American Studies Department **2477**
New Muse Community Museum of Brooklyn **2149**
New Observer **3670**
New Orleans; Among Brothers: Politics in **4749**
New Orleans Association of Black School Educators **981**
New Orleans; BANOFF of **968**
New Orleans Black Media Coalition **982**
New Orleans Business League **983**
New Orleans Data News Weekly **3671**
New Orleans; Ethnic, Cultural, and Heritage Organization of **973**
New Orleans Human Resources - Policy and Planning - Administrative Unit - Human Rights **3240**
New Orleans Minority Business Development Center **984**
New Orleans; Southern University - **2297**
New Orleans; Urban League of Greater **993**
New Paltz; State University of New York at - Black Studies Department **2445**
New-Penn-Del Minority Business Resource Council **1510**
New Phoenix of Detroit **1094**
New Pittsburgh Courier **3672**
The New Research Traveler & Conventioneer **3813**
The New Times **3673**
The New Times Group, Inc. **3673**
New Visions **3814**
New York Action Committee; Black **1260**
New York African Studies Association **3922**
New York African Studies Association—Newsletter **3922**
New York Agriculture and Markets Department - Affirmative Action Program **3312**
New York Alcoholism and Substance Abuse Division - Affirmative Action Bureau **3313**
New York Association of Black Journalists **1312**
New York Association of Black School Educators **1313**
New York; Association of Minority Business Enterprises of **1255**
New York at Albany; State University of - Center for Women in Government **2764**
New York at Binghamton; State University of - Fernand Braudel Center for the Study of Economies, Historical Systems, and Civilizations **2765**
New York Attorney General's Office (Law Department) - New York City Office - Civil Rights Bureau **3314**
The New York Beacon **3674**
New York; Black United Fund of **1266**
New York; Bronx Community College of the City University of - Cultural Affairs - Blacks and Puerto Rician Study Options **2320**
New York; Bronze Shields of Suffolk County, **1270**
New York; Brooklyn College of City University of - Africana Research Center **2665**
New York Business League; Greater **1282**
New York; Catholic Interracial Council of **121, 1277**
New York; City College of City University of - Department of African and Afro-American Studies **2363**
New York City Corrections; Guardians Association - **1284**
New York City Housing; Guardians Association - **1285**
New York City Human Resources Administration - Library **1923**
New York City Office of Business Development **3986**
New York City Technical College of City University of New York - Library **1924**
New York; City University of - Center for Social Research **2676**
New York; College of Staten Island of City University of - Institute for African American Studies **2368, 2679**
New York; Concerned Black Film Makers of **1278**
New York Division of Human Rights
    Albany Regional Office **3315**
    Binghamton Regional Office **3316**
    Buffalo Regional Office **3317**
    Nassau County Regional Office **3318**
    New York City (Brooklyn - Staten Island) Regional Office **3319**

Pennsylvania Education Department - Postsecondary/Higher Education Office - Equal Employment Opportunity Office (EEO) **3360**

Pennsylvania General Services Department
    Minority Construction Information Center **3361**
    Minority Development Office **3362**

Pennsylvania; Historical Society of - Library **1881**

Pennsylvania Human Relations Commission **3363**
    Harrisburg Regional Office **3364**
    Philadelphia Regional Office **3365**
    Pittsburgh Regional Office **3366**

Pennsylvania; Lincoln University - **2265**

Pennsylvania Minority Business Enterprise Council **3367**

Pennsylvania Office of the Governor - Administration Office - Affirmative Action Bureau **3368**

Pennsylvania Public Welfare Department - Civil Rights Compliance **3369**

Pennsylvania State University, Audio-Visual Services **4988**

Pennsylvania Transportation Department - Administration - Equal Opportunity Bureau **3370**

Pennsylvania; University of
    Afro-American Studies Program **2483**
    Center for Cultural Studies **2798**
    Center for the Study of Black Literature and Culture **2799**
    Institute for Research on Higher Education **2800**

Pensacola Voice **3686**

Pentecostal Apostolic Church; Bible Way **1726**

Pentecostal Assemblies of the World **1786**

Pentecostal Church of God **1787**

Pentecostal Church of God of America, Inc.; Alpha and Omega **1711**

Pentecostal Church of God of America; True Fellowship **1799**

Pentecostal Churches of Apostolic Faith **1788**

Pentecostal); New Bethel Church of God in Christ (**1780**

Penumbra Theatre Company **2848**

People Against Racist Terror (PART) **3945**

Pepsi-Cola of Washington, DC, L.P. **3446**

Percy R. Johnson Memorial Fire Fighters Association **987**

Performing Arts
    African American Drama Company of California **2006**
    Afrikan American Studio Theater Co. **2079**
    Afrikan Poetry Theater **2118**
    Afro-One Dance, Drama, and Drum Theater **2109**
    Alliance for Community Theaters **2063**
    Andrew Cacho African Drummers and Dancers **2026**
    Artists Doing Business Worldwide **2120**
    ArtSourceBook Minority Artists and Organizations in Pennsylvania **3956**
    Audelco Recognition Award **2831**
    Audience Development Committee **75**
    Behind the Scenes **4774**
    The Best of Black Journal **4777**
    Billie Holiday Theater **2123**
    Black American **3538**
    Black Awareness in Television **86**
    Black Experience Ensemble **2125**
    Black Plays in White Theater **4816**
    Black Repertory Company **2101**
    Black Repertory Group **2010**
    Black Spectrum Theater Co. **2129**
    Black Theater Troupe **2004**
    Black Theatre Directory **3965**
    Brown University - Rites and Reason **2668**
    Chicago City Theater Company/Joel Hall Dancers **2055**
    Contemporary Black American Playwrights & Their Plays: A Biographical Directory & Dramatic Index **3974**
    Crossroads Theater Company **2111**
    Detroit Public Library - Music and Performing Arts Department **1866**
    Directory of Minority Arts Organizations **3989**
    EDEN Theatrical Workshop **2020**
    Emmy Gifford Children's Theater **2105**
    Frederick Douglass Creative Arts Center **2135**
    Harambee Arts Festival **2158**
    Harlem School of the Arts **2140**
    Harmonie Park Playhouse and Actors Lab **2084**
    Hatch-Billops Collection, Inc. **1878**
    Henry Street Settlement's Art Center **2142**
    Homowa Foundation for African Arts and Culture **202**
    Indiana University Bloomington - Afro-American Arts Institute **2704**
    Inner City Cultural Center - Langston Hughes Memorial Library **1890**
    An Interview with Clarence Muse **4993**
    Jomandi Productions **2047**
    Just Us Theater Company **2048**
    Karamu House **2173**
    Look Out Sister **5027**
    McCree Theater and Performing Arts Center **2087**
    Memphis Black Arts Alliance **2195**
    Music and Comedy Masters Series **5081**
    National Black Theater Institute **2146**
    National Black Touring Circuit **2147**
    National Center for Afro-American Artists **2076**
    The Negro Ensemble Company **5089**
    Negro Ensemble Co., Inc. **2148**
    New Freedom Theater **2184**
    North Carolina Black Repertory Company **2160**
    Oakland Ensemble Theater **2018**
    Pin Points Traveling Theater **2035**
    Rosetta LeNoire Award **2913**
    Sarafina! **5171**
    Sign of the Times Cultural Art Center **2036**
    TABS Center **2093**
    Theater North **2180**
    Wayne County Minority Performing Arts Series **2154**
    Wyndham Hall Press **4217**

Pergamon Press, Inc. **3790**

Periodicals in Contemporary America: An Annotated Guide; Ethnic **4005**

Perryman Communications Scholarship for Ethnic Minority Students; Leonard M. **2596**

Personnel Bureau; South Dakota - Equal Employment Opportunity **3377**

Personnel Department; Indiana - Affirmative Action Division **3219**

Personnel Department; Maryland - Equal Opportunity Officer **3254**

Personnel Department; Nebraska - Affirmative Action/Recruitment **3298**

Personnel Department; New Jersey - Equal Employment Opportunity Affirmative Action Division **3308**

Personnel Department; Tennessee - Human Resources Development - Affirmative Action Division **3382**

Personnel in City Government; Association of Black **560**

Personnel Management; Office of - Affirmative Action Program **3267**

Personnel Management; U.S. Office of
    Federal Employment for Disadvantaged Youth - Part-time (27.003) **3143**
    Federal Employment for Disadvantaged Youth - Summer (27.004) **3144**
    Office of Equal Employment Opportunity **3079**

Personnel Office; North Carolina State - Equal Opportunity Services Division **3332**

Personnel Practitioners; EEO Resource Directory: Technical Assistance Guide for Southern California **4002**

Peter Pan Industries **5168**

PFB Project **439**

Phelps-Stokes Fund **2823, 2845**

Phi Beta Sigma **440**

Phi Delta Kappa; National Sorority of **416**

Philadelphia and Vicinity; Black Clergy of **1492**

Philadelphia Association of Black Journalists **1512**

Philadelphia; Barristers Association of **1491**

Philadelphia Black Media Corporation - Temple University **1513**

Philadelphia Black Womens Health Project **1514**

Philadelphia Coca-Cola Bottling Co., Inc. **3422**

Philadelphia Federation of Black Business and Professional Organizations **1515**

Philadelphia; Library Company of **1898**

Philadelphia Minority Business Development Center **1516**

Philadelphia New Observer **3687**

The Philadelphia Tribune **3688**

Philadelphia Tribune Co. **3689**

The Philadelphia Tribune (Metro Edition) **3689**

Philadelphia Urban Coalition **1517**

Philadelphia; Urban League of **1524**

Philadelphia; Valiants of **1527**

Philander-Smith College **2283**

San Francisco/Oakland Minority Business Development Center **663**
San Francisco Post **3708**
San Francisco Redevelopment Agency **3977, 3988, 3991-3993, 3996, 4034, 4036, 4037**
San Francisco State University - School of Ethnic Studies - Black Studies Department **2518**
San Francisco; University of California, - Northern California Comprehensive Sickle Cell Center **2777**
San Gabriel Valley; Fair Housing Council of **605**
San Jose Minority Business Development Center **664**
San Jose State University - Afro-American Studies Department **2430**
San Juan Minority Business Development Center **1530**
Sanamu African Art Museum **2179**
Sanctified Church); Church of God (**1737**
Santa Barbara City College - Ethnic Studies Department **2339**
Santa Barbara Minority Business Development Center **665**
Santa Barbara; University of California,
    Black Studies Library Unit **1977**
    Center for Black Studies **2778**
    Department of Black Studies **2456**
Santa Clara Black Fire Fighters Association **666**
Santa Clara County Association of Black School Educators **667**
Santa Clara County; Black Peace Officers of **579**
Santa Clara Valley Urban League **668**
Santa Fe Pacific Achievement Scholarships for Outstanding African American Students **2635**
Santa Fe Pacific Foundation **2635**
Sara Lee Foundation **2636**
Sara Lee National Achievement Scholarships **2636**
Sarafina! **5171**
"Satchel" Paige; Don't Look Back: The Story of Leroy **4892**
Savannah Brotherhood Fire Fighters Association **849**
Savannah Minority Business Development Center **850**
Savannah River Area Business League; Central **832**
Savannah State College **2289**
The Savannah Tribune **3709**
Savannah Tribune, Inc. **3709**
Save Our Sons and Daughters—Newsletter **3937**
Save Our Sons and Daughters (SOSAD) **3937**
SBNA Scholarship **2637**
S.C. Black Media Group **3578**
Scar of Shame **5172**
Scholarship Award **2917**
Scholarship; Black Student's Guide to **3964**
Scholarship Fund; Inner-City **1291**
Scholarships, Fellowships, Loans See Chapter 8
Schomburg Center for Research in Black Culture **1321, 2150, 2759**
Schomburg Collection of Negro Literature and History **2759**
School Daze **5173**
School Educators; Abeny Association of Black **1239**
School Educators; Akron Association of Black **1369**
School Educators; Arkansas Association of Black **543**
School Educators; Atlanta Metropolitan Association of Black **823**
School Educators; Austin Association of Black **1582**
School Educators; Chicago Association of Black **873**
School Educators; Cleveland Heights Association of Black **1400**
School Educators; Colorado Association of Black **691**
School Educators; Dallas Association of Black **1592**
School Educators; Delaware Association of Black **721**
School Educators; Delaware Valley Association of Black **1496**
School Educators; District of Columbia Association of Black **1013**
School Educators; Fort Worth Association of Black **1599**
School Educators; Franklin County Association of Black **1408**
School Educators; Greater Cincinnati Association of Black **1410**
School Educators; Greater Pittsburgh Association of Black **1500**
School Educators; Houston Area Association of Black **1604**
School Educators; Indianapolis Association of Black **921**
School Educators; Inland Association of Black **614**
School Educators; Iowa Association of Black **942**
School Educators; Jacksonville Association of Black **770**
School Educators; Kalamazoo Association of Black **1084**
School Educators; Kansas Association of Black **947**

School Educators; Lake County Association of Black **887**
School Educators; Las Vegas Association of Black **1172**
School Educators; Long Island Association of Black **1293**
School Educators; Lorain County Association of Black **1414**
School Educators; Massachusetts Association of Black **1043**
School Educators; Memphis Association of Black **1557**
School Educators; Metro Baltimore Association of Black **1017**
School Educators; Metro Cleveland Association of Black **1418**
School Educators; Metro Detroit Association of Black **1087**
School Educators; Metro Milwaukee Association of Black **1689**
School Educators; Miami Association of Black **778**
School Educators; Minnesota Association of Black **1113**
School Educators; Montgomery County Association of Black **1019**
School Educators; National Alliance of Black **270**
School Educators; New Orleans Association of Black **981**
School Educators; New York Association of Black **1313**
School Educators; Newark Association of Black **1220**
School Educators; Niagra Association of Black **1316**
School Educators; Northwest Indiana Association of Black **932**
School Educators; Nothern Virginia Association of Black **1655**
School Educators; Ohio Association of Black **1435**
School Educators; Oklahoma City Metropolitan Association of Black **1470**
School Educators; Oregon Association of Black **1482**
School Educators; Pomona Association of Black **646**
School Educators; Sacramento Association of Black **649**
School Educators; San Francisco Association of Black **660**
School Educators; Santa Clara County Association of Black **667**
School Educators; South Carolina Association of Black **1547**
School Educators; Springfield Area Association of Black **1447**
School Educators; Texas Association of Black **1634**
School Educators; Tulsa Area Association of Black **1473**
School Educators; Utah Association of Black **1642**
School Educators; Westchester Association of Black **1336**
School Educators; Will County Association of Black **908**
School of the Arts; Harlem **2140**
Science
    AHA Minority Scientist Development Award **2533**
    American Society for Microbiology Predoctoral Fellowships in Microbiology for Minority Students **2543**
    Association of Muslim Scientists and Engineers **73**
    Association of Muslim Social Scientists **74**
    AT&T Bell Laboratories Cooperative Research Fellowships for Minorities **2548**
    Corporate Sponsored Scholarships for Minority Undergraduate Physics Majors **2560**
    GEM Ph.D. Science Fellowships **2579**
    HRSA-BHP MARC Honors Undergraduate Research Training Awards **2586**
    IBM Minority Fellowships **2588**
    Living Legacy Award **2887**
    Minority Student Scholarships in Earth, Space, and Marine Sciences **2603**
    NAACP Willems Scholarship **2606**
    National Association of Black Geologists and Geophysicists **288**
    National Consortium for Graduate Degrees for Minorities in Science and Engineering **377**
    National Network of Minority Women in Science **404**
    National Organization for the Professional Advancement of Black Chemists and Chemical Engineers **408**
    National Physical Science Consortium Fellowships **2616**
    National Society of Black Physicists **980**
    NIH Postdoctoral Fellowship Awards for Minority Students **2621**
    Ortho/McNeil Predoctoral Minority Fellowship in Antimicrobial Chemotherapy **2625**
    St. Louis Science Center **2103**
    U.S. Department of Education - Office of Assistant Secretary for Postsecondary Education - Minority Science Improvement (84.120) **3112**
Science of Living Institute; United Church and **1802**
Science Temple of America; Moorish **1766**
Scientific Analysis; Institute for **2709**
Scientists; Black Americans: Political Leaders, Educators and **4789**
Scorpions **5174**
Scott Decision; The Dred **4894**
Scott Joplin **5175**

U.S. Department of Housing and Urban Development
(continued)
Assistant Secretary for Fair Housing and Equal
Opportunity **2998**
Office of Operations and Management - Office of
Affirmative Action and Equal Employment
Opportunity **2999**
Office of Fair Housing and Equal Opportunity
Equal Opportunity in Housing (14.400) **3126**
Fair Housing Assistance Program - State and Local
(14.401) **3127**
Non-Discrimination in Federally Assisted Programs (On
the Basis of Race, Color, or National Origin)
(14.405) **3128**
Non-Discrimination in the Community Development
Block Grant Program (On the Basis of Race, Color,
National Origin, Sex, Handicap, or Age)
(14.406). **3129**
Region I, Boston **3000**
Region II, New York **3001**
Region III, Philadelphia **3002**
Region IV, Atlanta **3003**
Region V, Chicago **3004**
Region VI, Ft. Worth **3005**
Region VII, Kansas City **3006**
Region VIII, Denver **3007**
Region IX, San Francisco **3008**
Region X, Seattle **3009**
Office of Small and Disadvantaged Business Utilization -
Minority Business **3010**
Office of the General Counsel - Office of Equal
Opportunity and Administrative Law **3011**
Office of the Secretary - Martin Luther King, Jr. Federal
Holiday Commission **3012**
U.S. Department of Justice
Civil Rights Division **3013**
Civil Rights Prosecution (16.109) **3130**
Desegregation of Public Education (16.100) **3131**
Equal Employment Opportunity (16.101) **3132**
Fair Housing and Equal Credit Opportunity
(16.103) **3133**
Protection of Voting Rights (16.104) **3134**
Community Relations Service (16.200) **3135**
Justice Management Division - Office of Small and
Disadvantaged Business Utilization **3014**
Office of Justice Programs - Office for Civil Rights **3015**
U.S. Dept. of Labor **3765**
Employment Standards Administration - Non-discrimination
and Affirmative Action By Federal Contractors and
Assisted Construction Contractors (17.301) **3136**
Office of Administration and Management
Directorate of Civil Rights **3016**
Directorate of Civil Rights - Office of Equal
Employment Opportunity and Affirmative
Action **3017**
Office of Small Business and Minority Affairs **3018**
Office of the Solicitor - Civil Rights Division **3019**
United States Department of State **2855**
Bureau of Human Rights and Humanitarian Affairs **3020**
Office of Small and Disadvantaged Business
Utilization **3021**
Office of the Secretary
Equal Employment Opportunity and Civil Rights
Office **3022**
Equal Employment Opportunity and Civil Rights Office
- Affirmative Action Outreach **3023**
U.S. Department of the Interior
Policy, Management, and Budget
Office of Small and Disadvantaged Business
Utilization **3024**
Office of the Assistant Secretary - Office of Equal
Opportunity **3025**
Office of the Assistant Secretary - Office of
Historically Black College and University Programs
and Job Corps **3026**
U.S. Department of the Treasury **4060**
U.S. Department of Transportation
Coast Guard, United States
Office of Acquisition - Contract Support Division—
Small and Minority Business **3027**
Office of Civil Rights **3028**

Federal Aviation Administration
Assistant Administrator for Civil Rights **3029**
Office of Civil Rights - Historically Black Colleges and
Universities **3030**
Federal Highway Administration
Office of Civil Rights **3031**
Office of Civil Rights - Program Operations
Division **3032**
Federal Railroad Administration - Civil Rights Office **3033**
Federal Transit Administration
Human Resource Programs (20.511) **3137**
Office of Civil Rights **3034**
National Highway Traffic Safety Administration - Office of
Civil Rights **3035**
Office of Civil Rights **3036**
Minority Colleges and Universities **3037**
Office of Small and Disadvantaged Business Utilization -
Minority Business Resource Center **3038**
Research and Special Programs Administration - Office of
Civil Rights **3039**
U.S. Environmental Protection Agency
Office of Civil Rights **3040**
National Black Employment Programs **3041**
Office of Small and Disadvantaged Business
Utilization **3042**
U.S. Equal Employment Opportunity Commission **3043**
Atlanta District Office **3044**
Baltimore District Office **3045**
Birmingham District Office **3046**
Charlotte District Office **3047**
Chicago District Office **3048**
Cleveland District Office **3049**
Dallas District Office **3050**
Denver District Office **3051**
Detroit District Office **3052**
Employment Discrimination - Equal Pay Act (30.010) **3138**
Employment Discrimination - Private Bar Program
(30.005) **3139**
Employment Discrimination - State and Local Fair
Employment Practices Agency Contracts (30.002) **3140**
Employment Discrimination - Title VII of the Civil Rights
Act of 1964 (30.001) **3141**
Houston District Office **3053**
Indianapolis District Office **3054**
Library **1968**
Los Angeles District Office **3055**
Memphis District Office **3056**
Miami District Office **3057**
Milwaukee District Office **3058**
New Orleans District Office **3059**
New York District Office **3060**
Office of Federal Operations - Federal Sector Programs -
Affirmative Employment Programs Division **3061**
Office of Program Operations - Federal Sector Programs -
Affirmative Employment Programs Division **3062**
Philadelphia District Office **3063**
Phoenix District Office **3064**
St. Louis District Office **3065**
San Antonio District Office **3066**
San Francisco District Office **3067**
Seattle District Office **3068**
Washington District Office **3069**
U.S. General Accounting Office - Civil Rights Office **3070**
U.S. General Services Administration - Business Services
(39.001) **3142**
U.S. Information Agency - Bureau of Management - Office of
Equal Employment Opportunity and Civil Rights **3071**
U.S. League of Financial Institutions **3955**
U.S. Minority Business Development Agency **4031**
U.S. National Aeronautics and Space Administration
Office of Equal Opportunity Programs **3072**
Affirmative Action **3073**
Discrimination Complaints Division **3074**
Minority University Research and Education
Programs **3075**
Minority University Research and Education Programs
- Historically Black Colleges and Universities **3076**
Minority University Research and Education Programs
- Other Minority Universities **3077**
Office of Small and Disadvantaged Business Utilization -
Minority Business **3078**